RADICAL ENLIGHTENMENT

Philosophy and the Making of Modernity 1650–1750

JONATHAN I. ISRAEL

UNIVERSITY PRESS

OXFORD

UNIVERSITY PRESS

Great Clarendon Street, Oxford OX2 6DP

Oxford University Press is a department of the University of Oxford.
It furthers the University's objective of excellence in research, scholarship,
and education by publishing worldwide in

Oxford New York

Auckland Bangkok Buenos Aires Cape Town Chennai
Dar es Salaam Delhi Hong Kong Istanbul Karachi Kolkata
Kuala Lumpur Madrid Melbourne Mexico City Mumbai Nairobi
São Paulo Shanghai Taipei Tokyo Toronto

Oxford is a registered trade mark of Oxford University Press
in the UK and in certain other countries

Published in the United States
by Oxford University Press Inc., New York

British Library Cataloguing in Publication Data

Data available

Library of Congress Cataloging in Publication Data

Israel, Jonathan Irvine.
Radical enlightenment : philosophy and the making of modernity, 1650–1750 / Jonathan
I. Israel.
p. cm.
Includes bibliographical references and index.
1. Enlightenment—Europe. 2. Europe—Civilization—17th century.
3. Europe—Civilization—18th century.
4. Spinoza, Benedictus de, 1632–1677. I. Title.
B802 I.87 2001 940.2'5—dc21 00-044086

ISBN 0–19–820608–9 (hbk)
ISBN 0–19–925456–7 (pbk)

10 9 8 7 6

Typeset by Best-set Typesetter Ltd., Hong Kong
Printed in Great Britain
on acid-free paper by
Ashford Colour Press Ltd,
Gosport, Hants

Preface

There are various ways of interpreting the European Enlightenment, some long cultivated in the historiography, others of more recent provenance. One formidable tradition of study adopts a primarily 'French' perspective, seeing the wider European phenomenon as a projection of French ideas and intellectual concerns, especially those of Montesquieu, Voltaire, Diderot, D'Alembert, d'Holbach, and Rousseau. Another approach, which enjoys support not only among Anglophone but also some continental scholars, envisages the Enlightenment as an intellectual reorientation inspired chiefly by English ideas and science, especially the endeavours of Locke and Newton. In recent years, it has also become fashionable to claim there was not one Enlightenment but rather an entire constellation or family of 'Enlightenments', related but distinct, growing up in numerous different national contexts. Finally, there has also been an incipient tendency latterly to distinguish between a mainstream 'moderate' and a more radical underground Enlightenment, albeit usually with the latter being deemed essentially marginal to the wider phenomenon.

One of my two main purposes in this work is to argue for another and different way of approaching the subject. The French perspective, though it has much to offer, remains increasingly susceptible to the charge that it underestimates the extensive philosophical and scientific borrowing all major eighteenth-century French thinkers engaged in. The 'English' approach might seem initially more plausible, not least since Voltaire's original stance was based almost wholly on Locke and Newton. Yet given the slow and sporadic reception of Locke and Newton outside Britain, and still more the often penetrating criticism their ideas were subjected to, this perspective is, in reality, even more vulnerable not just to the charge that it overly inflates the role of a particular nation but also that it fails to grasp the wider play of forces involved. As for the idea that we are dealing with a whole family of Enlightenments, there are seemingly insuperable objections to this too. For this notion encourages the tendency to study the subject within the context of 'national history' which is decidedly the wrong framework for so international and pan-European a phenomenon. Worse still, it unacceptably ignores or overlooks the extent to which common impulses and concerns shaped the Enlightenment as a whole.

My first goal then is to try to convey, however imperfectly and tentatively, a sense of the European Enlightenment as a single highly integrated intellectual and cultural movement, displaying differences in timing, no doubt, but for the most part preoccupied not only with the same intellectual problems but often even the very same books and insights everywhere from Portugal to Russia and from Ireland to Sicily. Arguably, indeed, no major cultural transformation in Europe, since the fall of the Roman Empire, displayed anything comparable to the impressive cohesion of European intellectual culture in the late seventeenth and early eighteenth century. For it was then that western and central Europe first became, in the sphere of ideas, broadly a single arena integrated by mostly newly invented channels of communication, ranging from newspapers, magazines, and the salon to the coffee-shop and a whole array of fresh cultural devices of which the erudite journals (invented in the 1660s) and the 'universal' library were particularly crucial.

My second objective is to demonstrate that the Radical Enlightenment, far from being a peripheral development, is an integral and vital part of the wider picture and was seemingly even more internationally cohesive than the mainstream Enlightenment. Frequently, the moderate mainstream were consciously, even desperately, reacting to what was widely perceived as the massively dangerous threat posed by radical thought. Many scholars will, I assume, be rather surprised by the prominence given here to the role of Spinoza and Spinozism not only on the continent but even in the British context where, historiographically, there has been a persistent refusal to acknowledge that Spinoza had any influence at all. Yet a close reading of the primary materials strongly suggests, at least to me, that Spinoza and Spinozism were in fact the intellectual backbone of the European Radical Enlightenment everywhere, not only in the Netherlands, Germany, France, Italy, and Scandinavia but also Britain and Ireland.

Of course, neither the Enlightenment itself, and still less its consequences, were limited to Europe. There is indeed a further dimension to the problem of how to interpret the Enlightenment. For if the Enlightenment marks the most dramatic step towards secularization and rationalization in Europe's history, it does so no less in the wider history not just of western civilization but, arguably, of the entire world. From this, it plainly follows, it was one of the most important shifts in the history of man. Fittingly, there exists a vast and formidable literature on the topic. Yet there are comparatively few general surveys and large-scale interpretative works, and it is possible to question whether it really receives the emphasis it deserves in the study and teaching of modern history, in comparison, for example, with the Renaissance and the Reformation. These too, of course, were vast and fundamental changes, at any rate in western civilization. Nevertheless, these earlier great cultural movements, limited as they were to western and central Europe, are really only adjustments, modifications to what was essentially still a theologically conceived and ordered regional society, based on hierarchy and ecclesiastical authority, not universality and equality.

By contrast, the Enlightenment—European and global—not only attacked and severed the roots of traditional European culture in the sacred, magic, kingship, and hierarchy, secularizing all institutions and ideas, but (intellectually and to a degree in practice) effectively demolished all legitimation of monarchy, aristocracy, woman's subordination to man, ecclesiastical authority, and slavery, replacing these with the principles of universality, equality, and democracy. This implies the Enlightenment was of a different order of importance for understanding the rise of the modern world than the Reformation and Renaissance, and that there is something disproportionate and inadequate about its coverage in the existing historiography. But to assess its assuredly overriding global significance one must first gauge the Enlightenment as a whole, which means, in my view, giving due weight to the Radical Enlightenment and, equally, emancipating ourselves from the deadly compulsion to squeeze the Enlightenment, radical and mainstream, into the constricting strait-jacket of 'national history'.

Acknowledgements

One of the chief delights of studying intellectual history is the opportunity it affords for long and deep discussions with friends and colleagues. Certainly I have become convinced that one's views and perceptions in this area are more likely to be substantially influenced and moulded through conversation and dialogue than is the case in some or most other areas of historical enquiry. In particular, I owe an immense debt of gratitude, as well as vast intellectual stimulation, to my friends Richard H. Popkin, Patrick Chorley, Wim Klever, Yosef Kaplan, Anthony McKenna, Winfried Schröder, Malcolm de Mowbray, Wiep van Bunge, and Adam Sutcliffe. In addition, I am glad to have the opportunity to thank for their help with more specific points, texts, bibliographical guidance, as well as yet more stimulating discussion, Michiel Wielema, Sarah Hutton, Miguel Benítez, Marc Bedjaï, Manfred Walther, Piet Steenbakkers, Fokke Akkerman, Herman De Dijn, Stuart Brown, Rienk Vermij, Giuseppina Totaro, Silvia Berti, Mordechai Feingold, Wijnand Mijnhardt, Wyge Velema, David Katz, Andrew Fix, Nathan Wachtel, Charles Amiel, Theo Verbeek, Ed Curley, Steven Nadler, Nicholas Tyacke, David d'Avray, Enrico dal Lago, Henk van Nierop, and Justin Champion.

Since a work such as this necessarily involves extensive research in archives and libraries abroad, and it proved far from easy to obtain support for it, I am happy to record my gratitude to the Dutch Language Union and to University College London for meeting much of the cost. For his unstinting encouragement while he was at the Oxford University Press I am also much indebted to Tony Morris. Finally, I am immensely appreciative of the vast amount of expert help provided by numerous librarians and archivists in many parts of Europe and, most of all, the staff at the British Library.

Contents

FINLAND

S W E D E N

Åbo
+

Uppsala
+

St Petersburg

INGRIA
(to Russia
in 1721)

ESTONIA

Stockholm

(to Russia
in 1721)

LIVONIA

Baltic Sea

COURLAND

RUSSIAN

EMPIRE

⊕ Koenigsberg

LITHUANIA

Danzig

EAST
PRUSSIA

○ Warsaw

P O L A N D

SILESIA

AUSTRIA

A U S T R I A - H U N G A R Y

○ Vienna

HUNGARY

TRANSYLVANIA

Black Sea

O T T O M A N   EMPIRE

Constantinople

NAPLES

Sea

GREECE

PART I | THE RADICAL ENLIGHTENMENT

I | INTRODUCTION

i. Radical Thought in the Early Enlightenment

To many a courtier, official, teacher, lawyer, physician, and churchman, philosophy and philosophers seemed to have burst upon the European scene in the late seventeenth century with terrifying force. Countless books reflect the unprecedented and, for some, intoxicating, intellectual and spiritual upheaval of those decades, a vast turbulence in every sphere of knowledge and belief which shook European civilization to its foundations. A sense of shock and acute danger penetrated even the most remote and best defended fastnesses of the west. The Spanish physician Diego Matheo Zapata, writing in 1690—before his own conversion to Cartesianism— implored the cohorts of Cartesians and *Malebranchistas* besieging every citadel of traditional learning in Spain to desist, warning that it was not just received philosophy and science which was at stake but also, ultimately, the beliefs of the people, the authority of Church and Inquisition, the very foundations of Spanish society.[1] A Spanish professor of medicine claimed, in 1716, that Descartes' philosophy had thrown all Europe into the greatest intellectual and spiritual perplexity seen for centuries.[2] In less isolated regions the agitation was no less. A Zeeland preacher, writing in 1712, appalled by the impact of Descartes, Spinoza, and Bayle, despairingly compared the Netherlands of his time to the ancient Athens of the warring Hellenistic philosophy schools, a land racked by intellectual controversy where rival schools of thought battled ceaselessly, philosophy divided the ruling élite, and even the common people were proving susceptible to new ideas, letting themselves be 'led like children through the whirlwinds of thought', the helpless prey of philosophical seducers and, through new ideas, becoming entrapped in the 'Devil's snares'.[3] Parts of this tide of new concepts, moreover, were of a distinctly radical character, that is, totally incompatible with the fundamentals of traditional authority, thought, and belief.

During the later Middle Ages and the early modern age down to around 1650, western civilization was based on a largely shared core of faith, tradition, and authority. By contrast, after 1650, everything, no matter how fundamental or deeply rooted, was questioned in the light of philosophical reason and frequently challenged or replaced by startlingly different concepts generated by the New Philosophy and what may still

---

[1] Zapata, *Verdadera Apologia*, 40–5, 49, 64.   [2] Boix y Moliner, *Hippocrates aclarado*, prólogo x.
[3] Tuinman, *Johan Kalvijn's Onderrichting*, i, 3–4.

usefully be termed the Scientific Revolution. Admittedly the Reformation had earlier engendered a deep split in western Christendom. But throughout the sixteenth century and the first half of the seventeenth, there was still much, intellectually and spiritually, that the western segments of Christendom shared. Mid-seventeenth-century Europe was still, not just predominantly but overwhelmingly, a culture in which all debates about man, God, and the World which penetrated into the public sphere revolved around 'confessional'—that is Catholic, Lutheran, Reformed (Calvinist), or Anglican issues, and scholars fought above all to establish which confessional bloc possessed a monopoly of truth and a God-given title to authority. It was a civilization in which almost no one challenged the essentials of Christianity or the basic premises of what was taken to be a divinely ordained system of aristocracy, monarchy, land-ownership, and ecclesiastical authority.

By contrast, after 1650, a general process of rationalization and secularization set in which rapidly overthrew theology's age-old hegemony in the world of study, slowly but surely eradicated magic and belief in the supernatural from Europe's intellectual culture, and led a few openly to challenge everything inherited from the past—not just commonly received assumptions about mankind, society, politics, and the cosmos but also the veracity of the Bible and the Christian faith or indeed any faith. Of course, most people at all levels of society were profoundly disquieted by such sweeping intellectual and cultural change and frightened by the upsurge of radical thinking. Jeremiads were heard everywhere. In Germany, from the 1670s onwards, there was a powerful reaction to the sudden stream of 'godless' books appearing in both Latin and the vernacular and obviously designed to overthrow all conventionally accepted values and beliefs.[4] University students were assumed to be especially vulnerable. A treatise by a Leipzig theologian published in 1708 sought to equip German professors with ready-made, concise Latin answers and philosophical demonstrations with which to combat the tide of philosophical atheism, deism, Naturalism, fatalism, and Neo-Epicureanism, and especially the penetration of the kind of radical thought which 'calls God Nature' and equates 'His intelligence, energy, and capability, with *Natura Naturans*', that is, the most systematically philosophical form of atheism.[5]

Whereas before 1650 practically everyone disputed and wrote about confessional differences, subsequently, by the 1680s, it began to be noted by French, German, Dutch, and English writers that confessional conflict, previously at the centre, was increasingly receding to secondary status and that the main issue now was the escalating contest between faith and incredulity. Instead of theological controversy, 'now', exclaimed an English publicist abhorring Anthony Collins' *A Discourse of Freethinking* (1713), a work which rejects scriptural authority and provoked deep outrage, 'now religion in general is the question; religion is the thing stabb'd at; the controversie now is,

---

[4] Müller, *Atheismus devictus*, 28–39; Lassenius, *Besiegte Atheisterey*, preface, i–vi; Undereyck, *Närrische Atheist*, 609–11.

[5] Rechenberg, *Fundamenta*, preface and pp. 4, 21, 61.

whether there ought to be any form of religion on earth, or whether there be any God in Heaven.'[6]

Revealed religion and ecclesiastical authority long remained the chief targets of the new radical thinkers. But they were by no means the only ones. A prominent late seventeenth-century German court official, the Freiherr Veit Ludwig von Seckendorff (1626–92), observed in 1685 that what the radicals ultimately intended was to make 'life in this world' the basis of politics.[7] This, he explained, amounted to a revolution in outlook and expectations which potentially changed everything. Numerous theologians, he grants, strove valiantly to counter the disastrous impact of the new radical ideas, especially Spinozism, which he saw as the backbone of the radical challenge in the sphere of faith and Church authority. But what was insufficiently grasped in the Germany of his day and inadequately opposed, in his opinion, were the consequences of such ideas as Spinoza's for politics, the public sphere, and the individual's place in society. For in Spinoza, he avers, nothing is based on God's Word or commandment so that no institutions are God-ordained and no laws divinely sanctioned: hence the only legitimacy in politics is the self-interest of the individual.[8] Nor did the mounting strife over the nature and status of morality reverberate any less stridently. The Dutch preacher, Johannes Aalstius, held in his general introduction to Christian ethics, published at Dordrecht in 1705, that the new radicalism, and especially Spinozism, overturns the entire structure of divinely ordained morality.[9] Were such influences to gain wide acceptance, he predicted, mankind would in the future concern itself only with individual happiness in this life.[10] To many it appeared a frightful prospect.

It is, furthermore, a drama which profoundly involved the common people, even those who were unschooled and illiterate. What did they know of the Scientific Revolution or the new philosophical ideas, one might well ask? Surely, it is often supposed, there was turmoil on the surface but little change in the minds and outlook of the great majority. But while it is true that the intellectual revolution of the late seventeenth century was primarily a crisis of élites—courtiers, officials, scholars, patricians, and clergy, it was precisely these élites which moulded, supervised, and fixed the contours of popular culture. Consequently, an intellectual crisis of élites quickly made an impact on ordinary men's attitudes too and by no means only the minority of literate artisans and small bourgeoisie. Doubtless some officials, theologians, and academics toyed with trying to confine the more awesome shifts in ideas to the sphere of élite culture so as to preserve intact the existing structures of authority and belief among the common people. After 1650, as those pervaded by the new concepts increasingly doubted the existence of Hell and the reality of eternal torment for the damned, for example, some consideration was given to whether it might be possible to screen such

---

[6] *An Answer to the Discourse on Free-Thinking*, preface.
[7] Seckendorff, *Christen-Staat*, i, 12; on Seckendorff, see Pleticha, *Adel und Buch*, 82–3.
[8] Seckendorff, *Christen-Staat* ii, 139–41; Walther, 'Machina Civilis', 202; Funkenstein, *Theology*, 338–44.
[9] Aalstius, *Inleiding tot de Zeden-leer*, 512.
[10] Ibid., 512–14; similarly see Poiret, *Cogitationes rationales*, 592–602, 606, 629.

disbelief from the general population.[11] But attempting such wholesale deception would have involved restructuring the entire system of cultural relations between élites and common people on the basis of consciously, systematically, and universally propagated fraud and deceit, scarcely a feasible project.

In practice, ordinary folk could not be shielded from the philosophical revolution transforming the outlook and attitudes of Europe's élites.[12] To many the consequences of this seemed alarming in the extreme. Especially worrying, according to Seckendorff, was the growing trend among ordinary folk to mock Holy Scripture, reject Heaven and Hell, doubt the immortality of the soul, and question the existence of Satan, demons, and spirits.[13] If one demands proof that new ideas were rapidly transforming attitudes and beliefs throughout society, such proof was abundantly evident on every side and in every part of Europe. Indeed, surely no other period of European history displays such a profound and decisive shift towards rationalization and secularization at every level as the few decades before Voltaire. 'The triumph of the mechanical philosophy,' it has been rightly asserted, 'meant the end of the animistic conception of the universe which had constituted the basic rationale for magical thinking.'[14] In England a veritable sea-change had taken place by the early eighteenth century. In Holland medals were issued in the 1690s celebrating the slaying of Satan and the end of belief in magic and witchcraft. In Germany the key public campaign, based on new philosophical ideas, which brought the trying and burning of witches to an end, took place during the first decade of the eighteenth century. Similarly, as has been justly observed of society and culture in Venice, if one wants to know when the crucial shift took place which led to the end of cases of sorcery, the virtual end of ecclesiastical control over intellectual life, and the first emergence of women into the public sphere as putatively equal to men in intellect, artistic capabilities, and personal freedom, then that decisive moment occurred in the period between 1700 and 1750.[15]

If one accepts there is a direct and crucial connection between the intellectual revolution of the late seventeenth century and the wide-ranging social and cultural change in Europe in the period immediately preceding Voltaire, then the implications for the history of Enlightenment thought are far-reaching. There is indeed an urgent need for Enlightenment historians to put much more emphasis on what was happening before and down to the 1740s. Indeed, there is a case for arguing that the most crucial developments were already over by the middle of the eighteenth century. Certainly the Radical Enlightenment arose and matured in under a century, culminating in the materialistic and atheistic books of La Mettrie and Diderot in the 1740s. These men, dubbed by Diderot the 'Nouveaux

---

[11] Walker, *Decline of Hell*, 4–6.

[12] Ibid.; Thomas, *Religion and the Decline of Magic*, 643–7.

[13] Seckendorff, *Christen-Staat*, i, 1–2, 41–4, 74–5 and ii, 31, 174, 191.

[14] Thomas, *Religion and the Decline of Magic*, 664.

[15] Georgelin, *Venise*, 714–17, 720–2, 731–2, 1129.

Spinosistes',[16] wrote works which are in the main a summing up of the philosophical, scientific, and political radicalism of the previous three generations. Seen in this light they represent the extreme, most uncompromising fringe of the general trend in culture and ideas towards rationalization and secularization. But their less radical colleagues undoubtedly had a far greater impact on attitudes and popular culture. In fact, neither the Reformation of the sixteenth century nor the so-called 'High Enlightenment' of the post-1750 period—often little more than footnotes to the earlier shift—even begins to compete with the intellectual upheaval of the Early Enlightenment in terms of sheer impact, and the depth and extent of the intellectual and spiritual changes it brought about. It may be that the story of the High Enlightenment after 1750 is more familiar to readers and historians, but that does not alter the reality that the later movement was basically just one of consolidating, popularizing, and annotating revolutionary concepts introduced earlier. Consequently, even before Voltaire came to be widely known, in the 1740s, the real business was already over.

Most accounts of the European Enlightenment concentrate on developments in only one or two countries, particularly England and France. Although it is often taken for granted that this is where the most important philosophical and scientific developments in the century 1650–1750 took place, there are strong grounds for questioning the validity of such an approach. For the intellectual scenario of the age was extremely wide-ranging and was never confined to just one or two regions. It was, on the contrary, a drama played out from the depths of Spain to Russia and from Scandinavia to Sicily. Its complexity and awesome dynamic force sprang not only from the diversity and incompatibility of the new philosophical and scientific systems themselves but also from the tremendous power of the traditionalist counter-offensive, a veritable 'Counter-Enlightenment' which, as with the Counter-Reformation of the sixteenth century, generated a major reorganization and revitalization of traditional structures of authority, thought, and belief. For the age of confessional antagonism, broadly the period 1520–1650, had equipped Europe's governments, churches, courts, schools, and universities with newly devised or reinforced mechanisms of spiritual and intellectual control which proved extremely effective in tightening the cohesion of society and culture, and strengthening the State and ecclesiastical authority, and therefore represented an accumulation of power and influence which was not going to be lightly abandoned anywhere.

However, even the most assertive and intolerant of these instruments of doctrinal supervision, such as the Calvinist *consistoires* or the Spanish Inquisition, were primarily geared to eradicate theological dissent and were soon partly, if not largely, outflanked and neutralized by the advance of new philosophies and scientific ideas which posed a much tougher problem for ecclesiastical authority to deal with than had religious heresy, especially as it proved difficult to separate what was compatible from what was incompatible with established religious doctrine. Hence, before long, confusion, hesitation, and a rapid fragmentation of ideas prevailed everywhere, even in

---

[16] [Diderot], *Encyclopédie* XV, 474; Proust, *Diderot*, 121, 289.

7

Rome itself.[17] Furthermore, in the new context, in contrast to the past, none of Europe's rulers, not even the Papacy, could easily decide on, or consistently adopt, a coherent intellectual and spiritual strategy. Opinion was simply too divided for this to be feasible. Should rulers and the Churches try to suppress both the moderate Early Enlightenment and its radical offshoots by shoring up the structures of the past, or should they discard the old structures and ally with one or another strand of the moderate Enlightenment—Neo-Cartesianism as expounded by Malebranche, or Newtonianism perhaps, or the widely adopted system of the German philosopher Christian Wolff (1679–1754), to forge a new orthodoxy and a more cogent front against the radical wing? Although this or that ruler chose one or the other path, the overall result was one of collective disarray and bafflement. Historically, State and Church had worked closely together and since the mid-sixteenth century had met the challenge of confessionalizing the population with spectacular success. Whether Catholic, Lutheran, Calvinist, or Anglican, the people of western and central Europe had everywhere been grouped into cohesive doctrinal blocs formidably resistant to rival theologies. But once the main thrust of dissent ceased to be theological and became philosophical, there set in an inexorable slackening and loss of coordination in State–Church collaboration in the cultural, educational, and intellectual spheres.

Whatever strategies governments and Churches adopted, the European intellectual arena grew more complex, fragmented, and uncertain. Paolo Mattia Doria (1662–1746), the Genoese patrician and *érudit* who resided in Naples from the late 1680s, subsequently playing a key part in that city's spectacular intellectual life during the Early Enlightenment, a seasoned observer of the philosophical currents of the age,[18] in 1732 published a book deploring the sudden fervour for the ideas of Locke and Newton 'in Rome, in Naples, and in other parts of Italy' and the progress of English empiricism, since the late 1720s, in a land already rent from top to bottom by warring philosophies.[19] What he terms the 'furore Lockense' served, in his view, only to escalate and convolute further what was now a five-cornered contest in which scholastic Aristotelianism, though in full retreat, still fought on tenaciously against three competing cohorts of respectable *moderni*—*Lochisti*, the *Cartesiani-Malebranchisti*, and the devotees of the Leibnizian-Wolffian system. The *Lochisti* might be gaining ground rapidly, and many clergy had joined them, but all they would accomplish, admonished Doria, would be to further split the middle ground. By contributing to the pulverization of Italy's former cultural, intellectual and spiritual cohesion, they were simply opening the door, albeit inadvertently, to the awesome fifth column, the radicals or *Epicurei-Spinosisti* as he terms them—who reject all authority and established ideas and despise Revelation, the Church, and Christian morality.[20] Italy was in the grip of a gigantic and horrifying dilemma. Doria considered Locke dangerous, Cartesianism

---

[17] Ferrone, *Intellectual Roots*, 2, 4–8.   [18] Conti, *Paolo Mattia Doria*, 9, 53, 61, 71–2.

[19] Doria, *Difesa della metafisica*, 3–4, 31–3, 40, 49.

[20] Ibid., 31–3; see also Doria, *Discorsi critici filosofici*, 6, 24, 112; Doria, *Filosofia*, i, 146–7, 172, 184–5, 226–7.

'damaging to civil society',[21] and Pierre Bayle of Rotterdam *perniciosissimo*;[22] yet all these were innocence itself, he declares, compared with the threat to Church and society posed by the radicals.[23] For those 'who deny God the attributes of goodness, love, intelligence and providence', the *Spinosisti*, not only demolish all religion but are also 'destructive of civil society'.[24]

Advocates of the mainstream moderate Enlightenment in the early eighteenth century before Voltaire simultaneously promised that the new ideas, and the sweeping away of ignorance and superstition, would confer immense benefits on mankind while warning—often no less stridently than their conservative opponents—of the terrible dangers inherent in the proliferating intellectual turmoil. Christian Thomasius (1655–1728), for example, chief herald of the Early Enlightenment in Protestant Germany and Scandinavia, did not doubt that the war on 'superstition' in which he himself was a prominent participant, and the application of new ideas in society, what he termed *philosophia practica*, offered humanity great advantages whether in administration, government, medicine, education, technology, or reforming the legal system.[25] But with deep disquiet, he also acknowledged that the intellectual upheaval was stimulating a vast upsurge in incredulity and *Atheisterey*—like Bayle, he defines 'atheism' to mean denial of divine Providence and reward and punishment in the hereafter. Not the least disturbing aspect of this erosion of faith, he held, was the manner in which countless false and hypercritical champions of piety, mostly, he says, ignorant bigots and obscurantists, seize the opportunity to condemn and vilify upright well-meaning *philosophes* (such as himself) before the public.[26] The honestly enlightened, striving for the improvement of society, found themselves inextricably caught up, he maintains, in a vast conflict on two fronts, battling ignorance and superstition on one side, and the 'Atheisten' on the other.[27]

The most pressing priority in the new context, it was universally acknowledged, was to overcome the growing fragmentation of ideas and, by means of solid demonstrations and convincing arguments, restore stable and enduring structures of authority, legitimacy, knowledge, and faith. But if the need was obvious, how was it to be met? Without a consensus as to the criteria of truth and legitimacy, without an agreed methodology and principles, the task was impossible. Some progress towards the common goal might be made if leading intellects were less inclined to feud with each other and more unified in their attacks on the Radical Enlightenment; but even this limited goal appeared increasingly unattainable. In Italy, the gaps between the three main enlightened moderate camps proved unbridgeable. In Germany, the often virulent struggle between the eclectic Thomasians and the more systematic Wolffians

---

[21] Doria, *Difesa della metafisica*, 319; Doria, *Discorsi critici filosofici*, 24, 33–6, 48–9.

[22] Doria, *Difesa della metafisica*, 284.

[23] Ibid., 31, 170, 198, 272–3, 287; Doria, *Risposta* 4–5, 26, 31–2, 73–4.

[24] Doria, *Difesa della metafisica*, 283, 287; Doria, *Risposta*, 26, 74; Doria, *Filosofia*, i, 146–7, 237–8; Doria, *Lettere e ragionamenti*, 297–301; Doria, *Il Capitano filosofo*, i, 3.

[25] Thomasius, *Von der Kunst*, 8–11; Koch, *History of Prussia*, 70; Kuehn, 'German *Aufklärung*', 309–10.

[26] Thomasius, *Von der Kunst*, 144, 148, 152.   [27] Ibid., 152.

proved irresolvable.[28] Meanwhile, nothing caused more dismay than the ambivalence and corrosive scepticism of one of the most widely read and influential thinkers of the age, Pierre Bayle (1647–1706). Bayle, his critics complained, 'avoue, il prouve, il repète cent fois que la raison est incompatible avec la religion';[29] but when he infers from this that individuals must therefore be guided solely by faith and the dictates of divine Revelation, was he being serious or playing libertine games with his readership? No one seemed to know for sure. Was Bayle, who was to be the 'Patron Saint' of so many eighteenth-century thinkers including Voltaire, Diderot and d'Holbach, a sincere Christian, as he and his defenders claimed, or as his enemies insisted, an atheist, wreaking philosophico-theological havoc on all sides and duping the public.[30] And if Bayle was the prime enigma, there were also others, not least Locke and Vico.

Those who undertook to wrestle with the intellectual dilemmas of the age were labelled by Thomasius, using the French term *philosophes*. In the late seventeenth century it was a term just beginning to acquire a new and revolutionary resonance. If philosophy itself was as old as pre-classical Greece—or older—it had assuredly been marginal to the life of society since the advent of the Christian empire in late antiquity, from the time of Constantine the Great onwards. From then until around 1650, philosophy had remained the modest 'serving-maid', as some called it, of theology and in an essentially ancillary relationship to the other great vocational disciplines, law and medicine. It was only with the intellectual crisis of the late seventeenth century that the old hierarchy of studies, with theology supreme, and philosophy and science her handmaidens, suddenly disintegrated. With this philosophy was released from her previous subordination and became once again an independent force potentially at odds with theology and the Churches. No longer the ancillary of others, philosophers became a new breed, formidably different from the subservient, abstract theoreticians of former times. However unsettling in a society expressly based on authority, tradition, and faith, it was henceforth—at any rate down to the dawn of the nineteenth century—the exponents of philosophy (which then included both theoretical and experimental science), as much as, and eventually even more than, the still strongly entrenched theologians and lawyers, who dominated the intellectual agenda and determined the outcome of controversies. Presenting and popularizing the new findings, concepts, and theories, the *philosophes*—of whom Fontenelle and Boulainvilliers were the first in France to acquire European reputations—suddenly discovered that they too could exert a practical impact in the real world—in ideas in the first place but through ideas also on education, politics, religion, and general culture. Philosophy became not just emancipated but also powerful. This happened, as the French historian of thought Boureau-Deslandes noted in 1737, because *philosophes* had discovered how to influence debates about education, moral notions, the arts, economic policy, administration, and 'toute la

---

[28] Kuehn, 'German *Aufklärung*', 310–13.

[29] Jaquelot, *Conformité de la foi*, 238; [Jurieu], *Philosophe de Rotterdam*, 49.

[30] Ibid., 5, 49, 54; Spinelli, *De origine mali*, 1, 3, 36; Labrousse, *Pierre Bayle*, ii, 605; Knetsch, *Pierre Jurieu*, 344, 371–5, 397; on Bayle as the 'Patron Saint' of the *philosophes*, see Wokler, 'Multiculturalism', 75.

conduite de la vie'.[31] Even in lands remote from the forefront of intellectual innovation, the power of philosophy in the new context was undeniable. When the medical
revolution—based primarily on Dutch ideas—began in Spain in the 1680s, the Valencian physician Juan de Cabriada, a devotee in particular of the famous Professor Dele
Boe Sylvius, at Leiden, expressly identified *libertad filosófica* (liberty to philosophize),
and especially to study Cartesianism, and receive up-to-date information about philosophical debates from 'Germany, France and other provinces', as the prime engine of
change, the instrument with which to smash down Spain's outmoded, medical culture, based on Galen, with its age-old zeal for blood-letting and purging.[32]

Hence Europe's war of philosophies during the Early Enlightenment down to 1750
was never confined to the intellectual sphere and was never anywhere a straightforward two-way contest between traditionalists and *moderni*. Rather, the rivalry
between moderate mainstream and radical fringe was always as much an integral part
of the drama as that between the moderate Enlightenment and conservative opposition. In this triangular battle of ideas what was ultimately at stake was what kind of
belief-system should prevail in Europe's politics, social order, and institutions, as well
as in high culture and, no less, in popular attitudes.[33]

Of the two rival wings of the European Enlightenment, the moderate mainstream,
supported as it was by numerous governments and influential factions in the main
Churches, appeared, at least on the surface, much the more powerful tendency.
Among its primary spokesmen were Newton and Locke in England, Thomasius and
Wolff in Germany, the 'Newtonians' Nieuwentijt and 's-Gravesande in the Netherlands, and Feijóo and Piquer, in Spain. This was the Enlightenment which aspired
to conquer ignorance and superstition, establish toleration, and revolutionize ideas,
education, and attitudes by means of philosophy but in such a way as to preserve and
safeguard what were judged essential elements of the older structures, effecting a
viable synthesis of old and new, and of reason and faith. Although down to 1750, in
Europe as a whole, the struggle for the middle ground remained inconclusive, much
of the European mainstream had, by the 1730s and 1740s, firmly espoused the ideas
of Locke and Newton which indeed seemed uniquely attuned and suited to the
moderate Enlightenment purpose.

By contrast, the Radical Enlightenment, whether on an atheistic or deistic basis,
rejected all compromise with the past and sought to sweep away existing structures
entirely, rejecting the Creation as traditionally understood in Judaeo-Christian civilization, and the intervention of a providential God in human affairs, denying the possibility of miracles, and reward and punishment in an afterlife, scorning all forms of
ecclesiastical authority, and refusing to accept that there is any God-ordained social
hierarchy, concentration of privilege or land-ownership in noble hands, or religious

---

[31] Boureau-Deslandes, *Histoire critique*, i, preface, pp. ix–x; see also La Mettrie, *Preliminary Discourse*,
163–70.
[32] Cabriada, *Carta philosóphica médica-chymica*, 4–5; López Piñero, *Joan de Cabriada*, 58, 89; Israel,
'Counter-Reformation', 41, 52.
[33] Jacob, *Radical Enlightenment*, 20–3, 93.

sanction for monarchy.[34] From its origins in the 1650s and 1660s, the philosophical radicalism of the European Early Enlightenment characteristically combined immense reverence for science, and for mathematical logic, with some form of non-providential deism, if not outright materialism and atheism along with unmistakably republican, even democratic tendencies.

Down to the 1750s the principal luminaries of the moderate Enlightenment were uninterruptedly battling on several different fronts simultaneously. Divided among themselves into three main separate factions contending for the middle ground, they were at the same time engaged in fending off traditionalists on one flank and radicals on the other. Hence it became a typical feature of intellectual conflict that moderates endeavoured to shield themselves against conservatives by stressing, even exaggerating, the gulf dividing them from the universally reviled and abhorred radicals while, simultaneously, traditionalists sought a tactical advantage, in their public discourse, by minimizing the gap separating the latter from the moderates as much as possible. A classic instance of such manoeuvring was the controversy surrounding the publication of Montesquieu's *L'Esprit des Lois*, a landmark of moderate Enlightenment thought, in 1748. Scarcely had it appeared than it was vociferously decried, especially by the Jesuits in France, Italy, and Austria as 'Spinosiste et déiste' in inspiration, since it treats morals and laws as essentially natural, man-made contrivances bearing no relation to any God-given absolute standard.[35] At this point it was also retrospectively pointed out that Montesquieu's earlier work, the *Lettres Persanes* (1721) was similarly infused with Spinozist ideas about morality and law and that when discussing the Emperor Theodosius once again 'Spinoza est le modèle que l'auteur a voulu imiter'.[36] Forced to reply, Montesquieu published a brochure at Geneva, in February 1750, maintaining (not altogether convincingly) that the accusation was self-contradictory since Spinozism, properly understood, is incompatible with deism. In any case, he insisted on his own Christian allegiance, and belief in a providential God 'comme Créateur et comme conservateur' of the universe; he had always condemned, he claimed, those who assert that the world is governed by blind fate and scrupulously differentiated in his writing the material world from 'les intelligences spirituelles'.[37] Montesquieu's assurances that 'il n'y a donc point de Spinosisme dans *l'Esprit des Lois*'[38] were cautiously accepted by most governments, including, after a protracted controversy, the imperial court at Vienna, though the papal Inquisition at Rome, after considerable hesitation, rejected his defence and banned the book anyway in November 1751.

The question of Spinozism is indeed central and indispensable to any proper understanding of Early Enlightenment European thought. Its prominence in European intellectual debates of the late seventeenth and early eighteenth century is generally

---

[34] Doria, *Il Capitano Filosofo*, i, 3–4; Capasso, *Institutiones Theologicae*, i, 190–1.

[35] Montesquieu, *Oeuvres complètes*, 808; Vernière, *Spinoza*, 454–60; Rotondò, 'Censura ecclesiastica', 1490–1; Ferrone, *Intellectual Roots*, 27.

[36] [Gaultier], Lettres Persanes *convaincues*, 34–6, 101.

[37] Montesquieu, *Oeuvres complètes*, 808–9.   [38] Ibid., 809; Davidson, 'Toleration', 231.

far greater than anyone would suppose from the existing secondary literature; one of the chief aims of this present study is to demonstrate that there has been a persistent and unfortunate tendency in modern historiography to misconstrue and underestimate its significance. Admittedly, the term 'Spinosisme' as used in the French Enlightenment, or *Spinozisterey*, as it was called in Germany, was frequently employed, as in the campaign against Montesquieu, rather broadly to denote virtually the whole of the Radical Enlightenment, that is, all deistic, Naturalistic, and atheistic systems that exclude divine Providence, Revelation, and miracles, including reward and punishment in the hereafter, rather than strict adherence to Spinoza's system as such.[39] Yet this does not mean that it was a vague or meaningless usage. On the contrary, the extremely frequent and extensive use of the terms Spinozism and *Spinosistes* in Early Enlightenment discourse, not least in Bayle, who devoted the longest single article in his *Dictionnaire historique et critique* to the subject of Spinoza and *Spinosisme*, is precisely intended to connect—and with considerable justification, as we shall see—Spinoza's philosophy with a wide-ranging network of other radical thought. Thus, for example, the most voluminous eighteenth-century European encyclopaedia, Zedler's *Grosses Universal Lexicon* (see pp. 135, 655 below), published at Leipzig and completed in 1750, provides separate entries for 'Spinoza' and 'Spinozisterey' both of which are individually considerably longer than what is said about 'Locke'.[40] The pattern is the same in the later French *Encyclopédie* edited by Diderot and d'Alembert: for all the lavish praise heaped on Locke by d'Alembert in his preliminary discourse to the *Encyclopédie*—praise which, as we shall see, may have had a diversionary purpose—in the body of the *Encyclopédie* itself the coverage given to Locke is far less, scarcely one fifth, of the coverage accorded to Spinoza.[41]

The *Grosses Universal Lexicon* lists the leading 'Spinozists' apart from Spinoza himself as 'Leenhof, Kuyper, Lucas, Boulainvilliers, Cuffeler, the author of *Philopater*, Wyermars, Koerbagh, Lau, Lahontan, Moses Germanus, Stosch and Toland'.[42] In addition, a second list is given of those suspected of being strongly influenced by Spinoza, namely 'Geulincx, Bredenburg, Bekker, Deurhoff, Burman, Wachter and [Jacob] Wittichius'. Today most of these names, aside from those of Boulainvilliers and Toland, are largely or entirely forgotten. Yet there is little justification for ignoring or marginalizing these writers since even a cursory examination of their writings shows that their views are more radical and, in some cases, more innovative than those of numerous figures who, for one reason or another, are far more familiar to those who study and discuss the Enlightenment today. For this reason, another key objective of this present study is to redress the balance somewhat in their regard too.

---

[39] Hence Bayle's dictum 'on appelle Spinosistes tous ceux qui n'ont guère de religion, et qui ne s'en cachent pas beaucoup', quoted in Bohrmann, *Spinozas Stellung*, 76; Wolff defines *Spinosisterey* in his *Natürliche Gottesgelahrheit*, vi, pp. 36–113.

[40] Zedler, *Grosses Universal Lexicon*, xxxix, pp. 75–86 and for 'Spinozisterey' pp. 88–95; for 'Locke' see Ibid. xviii, pp. 107–13.

[41] For 'Locke', see [Diderot and d'Alembert], *Encyclopédie*, ix, 625–7; for 'Spinoza', see ibid., xv, 463–74.

[42] Zedler, *Grosses Universal Lexicon*, xxxix, 86.

ii. The 'Crisis of the European Mind'

As employed in this present work, the term 'Crisis of the European Mind' denotes the unprecedented intellectual turmoil which commenced in the mid-seventeenth century, with the rise of Cartesianism and the subsequent spread of 'mechanical philosophy' or the 'mechanistic world-view', an upheaval which heralded the onset of the Enlightenment proper in the closing years of the century.[43] Admittedly, new philosophical and scientific ideas such as Cartesianism cannot claim all the credit for engineering the resulting revolutionary transformation in European culture. New kinds of theological controversy often contributed both to weakening the internal cohesion of the main confessional blocs and, as has been shown in the case of the decline of belief in Hell and eternal torment for the damned, to driving some of the most characteristic changes of attitude regarding traditional beliefs during this most decisive of all periods of cultural change.[44] Yet it was unquestionably the rise of powerful new philosophical systems, rooted in the scientific advances of the early seventeenth century and especially the mechanistic views of Galileo, which chiefly generated that vast *Kulturkampf* between traditional, theologically sanctioned ideas about Man, God, and the universe and secular, mechanistic conceptions which stood independently of any theological sanction. What came to be called the 'New Philosophy', which in most cases meant Cartesianism, diverged fundamentally from the essentially magical, Aristotelian, 'pre-scientific' view of the world which had everywhere prevailed hitherto and worked to supplant it, projecting a rigorous mechanism which, in the eyes of adversaries, inevitably entailed the subordination of theology and Church authority to concepts rooted in a mathematically grounded philosophical reason—albeit most 'Cartesians' of the 1650s and 1660s never intended to undermine theology's hegemony or weaken the sway of the churches to anything like the extent which rapidly resulted.[45]

This transitional phase, or prelude to the Early Enlightenment, arguably corresponds to the larger part of the second half of the century, down to the 1680s. In these years, the sway of theology, ecclesiastical authority, and divine-right monarchy appeared broadly still intact but was perceptibly being weakened by the onset of alarming rifts and fissures. Sporadically, especially in France and Italy, various manifestations of clandestine atheistic and deistic traditions reaching back via such authors as Bodin, Bruno, and Giulio Cesare Vanini, the alleged 'atheist' burned at the stake in Toulouse in 1619, and then through earlier Italian thinkers, notably Machiavelli and Pomponazzi, to ancient Rome and Greece, appeared, albeit usually in the veiled, camouflaged manner of the sixteenth- and early seventeenth-century libertines. This form of intellectual dissent, termed *libertinisme érudit*, still an appreciable force in the

---

[43] Casini, *Introduzione*, i, pp. x–xi.
[44] Walker, *Decline of Hell*, 4, 8, 59–70.
[45] Yates, *Giordano Bruno*, 448–52; Verbeek, *Descartes and the Dutch*, 34–77; Schmidt-Biggemann, 'Spinoza dans le cartésianisme', 71–6.

late seventeenth century, sought to mask, but simultaneously to disseminate, views opposed to prevailing theological and metaphysical orthodoxies by presenting opinions and quotations culled mostly from classical authors in innovative and seditious ways, paying particular attention to sceptical, irreverent, and atheistic sources such as Lucian, Epicurus, and Sextus Empiricus, and historians of philosophy such as Diogenes Laertius.[46]

This was a potent intellectual undercurrent, especially in France and Italy, and one which played a notable role in preparing the ground for the rise of the Radical Enlightenment, especially by creating a sophisticated audience potentially receptive to its message and promoting the theory, insinuated particularly by Machiavelli and Vanini, of the political origin of organized religion.[47] However, such erudite *libertinismo* was never strictly part of the phenomenon of the Radical Enlightenment itself. For the perfecting of the erudite libertine techniques was chiefly a feature of the early seventeenth century—especially the work of Gabriel Naudé (1600–53) and François de la Mothe Le Vayer (1588–1672)—when there was still little or no possibility of producing or propagating a systematic philosophy explicitly at odds with the prevailing orthodoxies. The *libertins érudits*, however seditious, were essentially precursors of the Radical Enlightenment operating behind a dense layer of camouflage.

From the 1650s, particularly in the relatively freer atmosphere of the Netherlands and England, the opportunity to forge an explicit and systematic philosophical radicalism existed. Nevertheless, all new streams of thought which gained any broad support in Europe between 1650 and 1750, such as the philosophies of Descartes, Malebranche, Le Clerc, Locke, Newton, Thomasius, Leibniz, or Wolff, sought to substantiate and defend the truth of revealed religion and the principle of a divinely created and ordered universe. If the great thinkers of the late seventeenth and early eighteenth century uniformly reviled bigotry and 'superstition' and discarded, if not expressly rejected, belief in magic, divination, alchemy, and demonology, all except Spinoza and Bayle sought to accommodate the new advances in science and mathematics to Christian belief (if not always to that of one or other Church) and the authority of Scripture. They asserted as fundamental features of our cosmos the ceaseless working of divine Providence, the authenticity of Biblical prophecy, the reality of miracles, immortality of the soul, reward and punishment in the hereafter, and, in one way or another—sometimes highly unorthodox as with Le Clerc, Locke and Newton—Christ's mission as the Redeemer of Man.

Admittedly, fragmentation of ideas as such was not entirely a new phenomenon. For there had never been a single accepted corpus of philosophy and science, linked to theology, which was universally acknowledged and taught in the west. It is true that before 1650, as afterwards, Europe's philosophical heritage was ramified and diverse.

---

[46] Popkin, *History of Scepticism*, 87–109; Gregory, 'Libertinisme érudit', 325–7.

[47] Machiavelli's most notorious exposition of this doctrine comes in the *Discorsi* where he recounts the story of the Roman king Numa Pompilius who 'turned to religion as something entirely necessary for a ruler wishing to maintain an orderly society', Gregory, 'Libertinisme érudit', 325–7; Machiavelli, *The Prince* and *The Discourses*, 146.

Nor since the Reformation had there been a single dominant theology. Instead, four competing principal Churches—the Catholic, Lutheran, Calvinist, and Anglican—had each in its own manner secured a locally dominant position in spiritual life, education, and general culture. Each confessional bloc exhibited its own distinct theological tradition, exegetical methodology, ecclesiastical hierarchy, and network of institutions of higher learning.

Yet despite the profound disarray and distress generated by the Reformation and sporadic wars of religion, by the late sixteenth century a generally stable and imposing façade of spiritual and intellectual unity had been restored, each main confessional bloc succeeding in the territory it dominated in establishing a cultural hegemony which was both locally overwhelming and remarkably resilient. After around 1590, changes in Europe's confessional boundaries, even in the midst of the horrors of the Thirty Years' War (1618–48), became increasingly rare. Furthermore, while remaining irreconcilably antagonistic towards each other, these hegemonic Churches all successfully built, each in its own sphere, a confessional uniformity, not only within their own ranks but, in most cases (other than in the Dutch Republic and England) also in society as a whole. They were able to confine lesser Churches and fringe sects to a completely marginal status, or eliminate them altogether. Even in confessionally hybrid states such as the electorate of Brandenburg-Prussia which, in 1701, became a monarchy, there was a strong propensity before 1650 for the constituent territories to belong predominantly to one or another confession; thus in Brandenburg, Pomerania, and East Prussia the Lutheran and, in Cleves, Mark, and Ravensberg, the Reformed (Calvinist). Finally, all four main church blocs found they could agree, if not on questions of authority and numerous secondary points of theology, then broadly, on the core Christian doctrines to be upheld and protected.

The four principal confessions also largely agreed as to the metaphysical, logical, and scientific underpinning, namely scholastic Aristotelianism, best adapted to reinforcing and extending the sway of their ultimately convergent theologies.[48] Hence, while scholastic Aristotelianism in the seventeenth century was by no means either entirely uniform, nor as inflexible and unwilling to debate the new mechanistic theories as is sometimes implied,[49] it was nevertheless, in both Catholic and Protestant lands, throughout Europe until the 1650s overwhelmingly *philosophia recepta*, the officially and ecclesiastically sanctioned philosophy prevailing in universities and academies, and dominating philosophical and scientific discourse and textbooks.[50] Characteristic ingredients of this common Aristotelian legacy included the idea that all knowledge comes initially through the senses, and that the human mind—as Locke concurred later, in opposition to Descartes—is first a 'tabula rasa', and the key notion that all things are constituted of matter and form, the latter emanating from the soul or essence of things so that bodies and souls cannot be separate entities in

[48] Phillips, *Church and Culture*, 136–42; Schmitt, 'Rise', 801–3; Van Ruler, *Crisis of Causality*, 34, 38–42.
[49] Mercer, 'Vitality and Importance', 40–3.
[50] Lessaca, *Colyrio philosóphico*, 7–10; Schmitt, 'Rise', 799–801.

themselves, a concept resulting in the celebrated doctrine of 'substantial forms'.[51] This concept of innate propensities in turn shaped scientific procedure by giving priority to classifying things according to their 'qualities' and then explaining the specific responses and characteristics of individual things in terms of primary group properties. Behaviour and function consequently arise, and are determined by, the soul or essence of things rather than mechanistically. Hence there is a conceptual but no observable or measurable dividing line between the 'natural' and 'supernatural', a distinction which could only be clearly made following the rise of the mechanistic world-view.

If discrepancies, tensions, and contradictions abounded, it is nevertheless true that a broadly coherent culture took shape in most of Europe between the Reformation and the middle of the seventeenth century, favoured and supported by an elaborate apparatus of royal, ecclesiastical, and academic authority. Powerful instruments of religious and intellectual censorship had been forged to deal with the problem of religious heresy and these could in turn be put to use to tighten the linkage between theology and approved philosophy. From the mid-sixteenth century onwards, Europe was a civilization in which formal education, public debate, preaching, printing, bookselling, even tavern disputes about religion and the world, were closely supervised and controlled. Virtually nowhere, not even in England or Holland after 1688, was full toleration the rule, and hardly anyone subscribed to the idea that the individual should be free to think and believe as he or she thought fit.[52] Still at the end of the seventeenth century, 'le dogme de la tolérance', as a French correspondent urged Leibniz, in 1691, was widely considered exceedingly dangerous despite the rapidly growing support for it, indeed the worst of all errors, because it is the one which encourages acquiescence in all the others—and was perceived as being primarily promoted by Socinians and 'ceux qu'on nomme Déistes et Spinosistes'.[53]

Consequently, the cultural and intellectual system prevailing in mid-seventeenth-century Europe, with the partial exception only of England and the United Provinces was—deep confessional divisions notwithstanding—doctrinally coherent, geared to uniformity, authoritarian, and formidably resistant to intellectual innovation and change. As such, it harmonized admirably not only with the dominant ecclesiastical and aristocratic hierarchies presiding over Church and society but also the pervasive princely absolutism of the age. Yet, astonishingly, it was precisely when the monarchical principle was most dominant, in France, Germany, Scandinavia, and Italy alike, that this common European culture, based on the primacy of confessional theology and scholastic Aristotelianism over belief, thought, education, and scholarship, first faltered, then rapidly weakened, and finally disintegrated.[54] From the 1650s onwards, first in one land, then another, variants of the New Philosophy breached the defences of authority, tradition, and confessional theology,

[51] Phillips, *Church and Culture*, 137–8; Van Ruler, *Crisis of Causality*, 58–61; Mercer, 'Vitality and Importance', 64.
[52] Israel, 'Intellectual Debate', 21–36.   [53] Leibniz, *Otium Hanoveranum*, 262–3.
[54] Thomas, *Religion and the Decline of Magic*, 643–4.

fragmenting the old edifice of thought at every level from court to university and from pulpit to coffee-shop.[55]

In places, even entire countries, Cartesianism gained an imposing general preponderance which here and there lasted many decades. Yet despite its broad and vigorous impetus internationally from around 1650 down to the 1720s, there was never much likelihood that it could supplant *philosophia aristotelico-scholastica* as the new generally accepted consensus, welding philosophy, science, and theology coherently into a new unity receiving both official and ecclesiastical sanction. In the first place there were too many internal intellectual difficulties and tensions within Cartesianism, which, in the longer run, sapped its unity, cogency, and momentum. Secondly, there was little prospect that Europe's princely courts and Churches would uniformly espouse Descartes' system as formerly they had that of Aristotle. For leading voices within all Churches either hesitated or expressed strong opposition, some unsure whether Cartesianism was really as useful and effective a prop for the core doctrines of Christianity as Descartes and his followers claimed, others convinced that Cartesianism was, on the contrary, prejudicial to Christianity and the ecclesiastical interest. Then thirdly, Aristotelianism, though badly shaken and widely disparaged, was by no means eliminated but rather adapted and fought back, with considerable effect.[56] Even in the United Provinces and England, where the new mechanistic ideas gained an early primacy, Aristotelianism remained an appreciable factor in the equation.[57] Post-1650 Aristotelians in northern and southern Europe not only deplored the mechanistic systems of Descartes, Gassendi, and others as incompatible with traditional epistemology, metaphysics, and science but as a first step towards irreligion and atheism.[58] According to Giovanni Battista Benedetti (or De Benedictis; 1620–1706), rector of the Jesuit college in Naples at the end of the seventeenth century, chief advocate of scholastic Aristotelianism in Italy, and, after the publication of his *Philosophia perpatetica* (1687), a formidable presence also in Spain and Portugal, the *Cartesiani* and *Malebranchisti*, for all their disclaimers, were calling divine Providence into doubt and undermining belief in the core Christian 'mysteries'.[59]

The Cartesians failed, moreover, to maintain any real sense of unity among themselves. Rather, especially in France, they split into openly warring factions with the three leading figures—Antoine Arnauld (1632–94), Nicolas Malebranche (1638–1715), and Pierre-Sylvain Régis (1632–1707)—all at each other's throats.[60] Furthermore, Descartes' system proved unable to sway not only many clergy and academics, within all confessional camps, but also some of the most acute thinkers and scientists of the

[55] Benedetti, *Lettere Apologetiche*, 115–16, 121; Kors, *Atheism in France*, i, 374–8.

[56] Kors, *Atheism in France*, i, 270–85; Manzoni, Il 'Cattolicesimo Illuminato', 11–12; Mindán, 'Corrientes filosóficas', 473–7; Mercer, 'Vitality and Importance', 57–66.

[57] Krook, *John Sergeant*, 22–4; Van Ruler, *Crisis of Causality*, 316–19.

[58] Mercer, 'Vitality and Importance', 57.

[59] Benedetti, *Lettere Aplogetiche*, 116–20, 182–3, 293, 311; Benedetti, *Difesa della scolastica teologia*, 136–7, 172–4; Benedetti, *Difesa della terza Lettera*, 17, 58–9, 91, 137–40, 154; Ferrone, *Intellectual Roots*, 2–3.

[60] [Aubert de Versé], *L'Impie convaincu*, 156; Sleigh, *Leibniz and Arnauld*, 30–3, 153–6; Nadler, *Arnauld*, 79–90; Kors, 'Scepticism', 211–12.

age; and while some among the latter, like the renowned Dutch physicist, Christian Huygens, kept their reservations to themselves, others, including Locke in England, Leibniz in Germany, and Vico in Naples, not only formidably criticized their great precursor but presented imposing new philosophical systems of their own which sapped confidence in Cartesianism much as Descartes had discredited Aristotelianism.

A further factor which greatly contributed to the depth and intensity of the general crisis of the European mind was the susceptibility of all major Churches, and many minor ones, made brittle by internecine wrangling both theological and philosophical, to experience major new and enduring rifts within their own ranks. In effect, practically every Church itself became deeply divided, in part over matters connected with current philosophical and scientific debates, while simultaneously beset by fresh forms of internal theological dissension. Hence philosophy served both to complicate and intensify conflicts between rival theological factions, though in Italy and France it also frequently happened that even priest-professors belonging to the same religious orders took opposite sides in the struggle for and against the 'New Philosophy'.[61] Thus Jansenists and anti-Jansenists (especially the Jesuits) engaged, from the 1640s onwards, in vociferous strife within the Catholic Church in France and both parts of the Netherlands, as well as less noisily in Italy, even while both sides had in addition to cope with splits between Cartesians and anti-Cartesians within their own ranks. No less acrimonious was the rivalry erupting within the Dutch Reformed Church between the liberal (Cocceian) and orthodox Calvinist (Voetian) wings, antagonism exacerbated by the tendency of the former to champion Cartesianism and the latter scholastic Aristotelianism.[62] Similarly, the Anglican Church in Britain and Ireland divided theologically and intellectually (as well as politically) in the late seventeenth century between the traditionalists or 'high-flyers' and the liberal 'Latitudinarian' wing which proved receptive to Newtonianism if, at first, not to Locke. Even the clergy of Spain and Portugal, hitherto rock solid in their unity and commitment to scholasticism, fell into disarray towards the close of the seventeenth century as the Aristotelians strove (unsuccessfully, on the whole) to mobilize the Inquisition against the 'innovatores' while the Cartesians and *Malebranchistas* pointed out that John Wycliffe and many another 'appalling heretic' had wallowed in Aristotle.[63] Intellectually, the Iberian Peninsula may have struck other Europeans as remote and backward. Juan de Cabriada warned his compatriots in 1686 that due to their insufficient awareness of current philosophical and scientific developments elsewhere, they were disdained in other European lands like the 'Indians of America'.[64] Yet for all that, by the 1680s Spain too was becoming deeply fragmented by the New Philosophy and, despite the time lag, the bitter struggles over philosophy and science that erupted there in the early eighteenth century were in essence not greatly different from those convulsing the rest of Europe.

[61] Mindán, 'Corrientes filosóficas', 473–4; Kors, *Atheism in France*, i, 277–9.
[62] Israel, *Dutch Republic*, 889–99.
[63] Nájera, *Maignanus redivus*, 304; Mindán, 'Corrientes filosóficas', 473–9.
[64] Cabriada, *Carta philosóphica*, 230–1.

The concept of a 'crisis of the European mind' in the late seventeenth century as a transitional phase sandwiched between the confessional era and the Enlightenment was introduced into modern historiography by the Belgian historian of thought Paul Hazard (1878–1944) in his seminal work *La Crise de la conscience européenne* (Paris, 1935) though, with his eye chiefly on developments in France, he tended to date the onset of the crisis unacceptably late, to around 1680.[65] More convincingly, Hazard described the intellectual upheaval as 'all-embracing, imperious, profound', a turmoil which 'though born of the seventeenth century was destined to leave its impress on virtually the whole of the eighteenth'.[66] His claim that the 'daring utterances of the *Aufklärung* . . . pale into insignificance before the aggressive audacities of [Spinoza's] *Tractatus Theologico-Politicus* [and] the amazing declarations of the *Ethics*' while 'neither Voltaire nor Frederick II ever came near the ungovernable anti-clerical, anti-religious frenzy of Toland and his like' remains valid, as does his thesis that the decisive break-through of modern rationalism and secularization to predominance in western civilization occurred during the final decades of the seventeenth century and the opening years of the eighteenth.[67]

Indeed, some such notion as that introduced by Hazard is essential—as long as we modify his dates—since there has to be some sort of label to describe the prelude before the Enlightenment, that is, roughly the decades 1650–80, when the cohesion and unity of the confessional outlook, the ascendancy of theological orthodoxy and scholastic Aristotelianism, frayed under the impact of the New Philosophy.[68] In this present study, the period 1650–80 is designated the phase of transition or 'crisis of the European mind' preceding the onset of the Enlightenment, and the period 1680–1750 the more dramatic and decisive period of rethinking when the mental world of the west was revolutionized along rationalistic and secular lines. By the 1750s, all major intellectual innovations and accomplishments of the European Enlightenment were well advanced if not largely complete.

The 'crisis of the European mind' was a collective, but also a deeply unsettling and traumatic individual experience, not least for the scientists themselves, of whom Blaise Pascal (1623–62)was probably the most eloquent in expressing the mental and emotional agonies such profound soul-searching could involve. Pascal painstakingly rescues and reaffirms his Christian faith by dividing reality into totally separate compartments. As for Descartes, Pascal maintains in his posthumously published *Pensées* (1670) that he finds his offence unforgivable: for instead of by-passing the whole question of God, as he ought to have done, he has Him merely press a button 'pour mettre

---

[65] See, for instance, Jacob, 'Crisis of the European Mind', 251–6; Phillips, *Church and Culture*, 100–70; Vermij, *Secularisering*, 58.

[66] Hazard, *European Mind*, 502.

[67] See Jacob, 'Crisis of the European Mind', 251–2; Heyd, *'Be Sober and Reasonable'*, 1–10; Craven, *Jonathan Swift*, 3–7, 185–6; Hazard's dating of the onset of the 'Crisis' to the 1680s can no longer be justified, since the general fragmentation of the intellectual scene under the impact of the New Philosophy begins, especially in England and the Dutch Republic, but also elsewhere, much earlier than this.

[68] Casini, *Introduzione*, i, pp. x–xi; Casini, *L'universo-macchina*, 33–8.

le monde en mouvement; après cela, il n'a plus que faire de Dieu'.[69] Another eminent scientist of the period, the Danish anatomist and geologist Nicholas Steno (1638–87), with no less passion than Pascal, eventually concluded that faith and science cannot be easily or satisfactorily reconciled and abandoned the latter completely to champion the former. Lorenzo Magalotti (1636–1712), secretary of the first of the European scientific academies of the later seventeenth century, in Florence, and a man in touch with all the latest scientific developments internationally, was no less tormented. During his years in Vienna (1674–8) he lapsed into a deep and irreversible personal intellectual crisis, even admitting, in January 1676, to his morbidly devout sovereign, Cosimo III, Grand Duke of Tuscany, that despite every effort to keep up his Catholic allegiance, deep down the new ideas had stifled his faith,[70] an admission almost certainly connected with his falling into disgrace at the Tuscan court on his return there in 1678.

The European crisis had far-reaching intellectual and religious and also, at least potentially, political implications. Hazard has been criticized for giving insufficient emphasis to the political aspects of the 'crisis', that is the reaction against divine-right monarchy and absolutist ideology and the onset of republican political theories linked expressly, or tacitly, to radical philosophy. It has also been suggested that Hazard failed to grasp the extent to which the intellectual legacy of the English Revolution of the 1640s, and especially the social and religious ideas of the Levellers and Diggers with their democratic, and sometimes communistic, inclinations, may have served not just as a source of radical ideas for the Radical Enlightenment as a whole, but conceivably, even constituted the ideological driving force of the entire European phenomenon, especially its political and social radicalism.[71]

Although it cannot be said that its political thought was one of its most prominent or developed features, undeniably the Radical Enlightenment was republican, did reject divine-right monarchy, and did evince anti-aristocratic and democratic tendencies. Democratic republicanism was a particularly marked feature of the writings of the Dutch, English, and Italian radicals though it is also encountered, albeit much more faintly, in French and German contexts. However, there is little of a concrete nature to suggest that the continental Radical Enlightenment did in fact principally derive from English influence and example. On the whole, it seems more likely that the phenomenon derives from a broader, international context. After all, there were other quasi-revolutionary upheavals in mid-seventeenth-century Europe, notably the Frondes and the Massaniello rising (and the brief establishment of a republic) in Naples in 1647–8, which made a scarcely less profound impression on the European consciousness in general and radical minds in particular than the revolutionary upheaval in England. Then, judging by the intense interest it aroused, one might well insist that the Glorious Revolution of 1688–91 was actually more important as

---

[69] Pascal, *Pensées*, 94.   [70] Casini, *Introduzione*, i, 233–4; Cochrane, *Florence*, 275–313.
[71] Hill, *World Turned Upside Down*, 179, 219, 268; Jacob, *The Radical Enlightenment*, 22–49; Jacob, 'Crisis of the European Mind', 254–60.

a political exemplum to the radical minds of the early Enlightenment than anything that happened earlier, and this was not in essence a national achievement of the English—nor was it then regarded as such—but essentially a consequence of Dutch *raison d'état* and a large-scale invasion from the continent.[72] Furthermore, it seems that in Britain itself the social libertarianism of the mid-seventeenth century faded away in the late seventeenth century and did not reappear until the end of the eighteenth.[73]

Finally, while it is clear that a highly developed republican tradition of political thought evolved in England from the 1650s onwards, and its characteristics have been studied in great detail by scholars, it is far from evident that this corpus of ideas was the prime inspiration for the radical republican tradition with which we are concerned in this present study. What has been termed the 'Anglicization of the republic'[74] produced certain specific features—an emphasis on land as the basis of political influence and an orientation towards the outlook and needs of the English gentry—which render this corpus of thought appreciably different from the alternative republican tradition, essentially urban and commercial, originating in the work of such writers as Johan and Pieter de la Court, and Spinoza's Latin master, Franciscus van den Enden, with its uncompromising anti-monarchism and egalitarian tendency, a tradition which sprang up on the continent and leads in direct line of descent to the revolutionary rhetoric of Robespierre and the French Jacobins.

In any case, focusing on national contexts is assuredly the wrong approach to an essentially European phenomenon such as the Radical Enlightenment. The movement or current was an international network bent on far-reaching reform philosophically, socially, ethically, in matters of gender and sexuality, and also politically, drawing inspiration from a wide range of sources and traditions, albeit from the 1660s onwards it evinced a high degree of intellectual cohesion, revolving in particular around Spinoza and Spinozism. Given the range of its sources and its widespread impact, as well as an immense anti-radical reaction extending to every corner of Europe, the most essential prerequisite for a balanced view of its origins, development, structure, and reception is to adopt a very broad European view. However difficult it may be to achieve a balanced coverage across a region as culturally diverse as Europe, it is essential to work in that direction if so crucial a manifestation of European history and culture is not to be largely overlooked and marginalized simply because it is too far-ranging and pervasive to be coped with in terms of traditional notions of 'national' history.

[72] Israel, *Anglo-Dutch Moment*, 1–43, 105–62.   [73] Pocock, *Virtue, Commerce and History*, 51–5.
[74] Pocock, *Machiavellian Moment*, 383–95.

2 | GOVERNMENT AND PHILOSOPHY

i. The Advent of Cartesianism

By 1648 Europe's rulers had been engulfed for over a century in inter-confessional conflict. Most of this incessant strife had been ideological and political rather than physical but, in France and the Low Countries, between the 1560s and the 1590s, and in Germany and Bohemia during the Thirty Years' War (1618–48), there had also been unprecedented slaughter, savagery, and destruction. Rarely had this war of confessions been a straightforward conflict between Catholics and Protestants. More often, the religious battle was triangular or even quadrilateral, as in Lutheran Germany where the new State Church simultaneously fought Catholicism, Calvinism, and radical Protestant fringe movements, such as Anabaptism, Spiritualism, and Socinianism. Between the mid-sixteenth and mid-seventeenth century, confessionalization and the resulting war of the Churches constituted Europe's prime engine of cultural and educational change. So powerful indeed was the ideological, intellectual, and general cultural impulse of confessionalization that monarchs, patricians, and republics had little choice but to take sides, selecting one main bloc or another, and imposing their own local confessional agenda. Education, social welfare, the arts, scholarship, no sphere of activity remained free from the unrelenting demands of confessional and theological rivalry.

Some rulers, plainly, were more zealous for confessional uniformity, and given to campaigns to stamp out dissent, than others. Some permitted an informal toleration of selected dissenters for one reason or another, often because they valued their economic contribution or lacked the means to eliminate them militarily. A few states, such as the Dutch Republic, Brandenburg-Prussia, and, until the mid-seventeenth century, also Poland, embraced a broader, more formal toleration of confessions. There were also cases, such as Brandenburg-Prussia after 1613, where the prince chose a different confessional allegiance to that prevailing among his subjects. Yet everywhere organized Churches of one theological complexion or other were deemed indispensable pillars of the social order, arbiters of belief, morality, education, and censorship, and the ultimate guardians of authority, by élites and populace alike. So great indeed was the cultural ascendancy of the dominant or State Churches in their respective zones of hegemony that confessional theology long remained the principal and overriding criterion in assessing all intellectual debate and innovation.

Before 1650, science and philosophy accordingly were of little immediate concern to rulers and ruling élites. Because these activities were subjected to the claims of confessional theology, and practised in institutional contexts directly or indirectly under ecclesiastical supervision, princes and parliaments could safely ignore philosophy and science as something largely peripheral to the business of government. If, in the early seventeenth century, various European rulers were renowned connoisseurs of art and architecture, few saw any need to concern themselves with philosophy or science. From the 1640s, however, beginning on the continent with the onset of the Cartesian controversies in the United Provinces and, in England, with the intellectual ferment and proliferation of religious sects resulting from the Civil War (1642–7), this hitherto prevailing pattern of confessionally regulated cultural cohesion progressively disintegrated, initiating one of the most decisive intellectual and cultural shifts in western history. As the supremacy of theology waned, non-theological accounts of man, God, and the world, that is, the New Philosophy, especially Cartesianism, penetrated with such novel and unsettling consequences that rulers, however unaccustomed to such a role, found themselves compelled to intervene. After around 1650 governments had no alternative but to endeavour to cope with the vast issues, cultural, intellectual, theological, and political, raised by the New Philosophy and science, rendering philosophical matters an integral and essential part of their statecraft. Government intervention often provided some semblance of intellectual stability in a particular country or region for a time, but overall it simply added to the growing fragmentation of thought, since there was little scope for co-ordinating cultural, educational, or censorship policy between states. Moreover, even where vigorous intervention effectively ensured a particular intellectual stance, the respite was mostly temporary, not just because monarchs' successors often preferred a different philosophical stance from their predecessors, but because the intellectual controversies of the age stirred such profound anxieties and dissension that even the greatest potentates, such as Louis XIV or the Swedish kings, and, in Italy, the Pope, proved powerless altogether to quell the commotion.

In continental Europe, major intellectual turmoil developed first in the Dutch Republic and the Calvinist states of Germany. In order to avail himself of the relative intellectual freedom reigning there, Descartes had chosen to live and work from the 1620s onwards mainly in the United Provinces, and it was there he wrote his chief works of philosophy, established his fame, and launched his philosophical enterprise, a project which Bayle and most of the *philosophes* of the eighteenth century, for all their criticism, continued to venerate as marking the true beginning of 'modernity' and 'enlightenment' in men's ideas.[1] By the late 1640s his influence in the Dutch

---

[1] On the *philosophes'* awareness that Descartes' was the first to seek to 'change the general way of thinking', starting an intellectual revolution which culminated in the mid eighteenth-century Enlightenment, see Schouls, *Descartes*, 66–71; Wessell, *G. E. Lessing's Theology*, 47–62; and Anderson, *Treatise*, 129–52; on the early break-through of Cartesianism in the Netherlands, see Scholder, *Birth*, 114–15, Verbeek, *Descartes and*

universities, and Dutch scholarship, medicine, and science, at a time when it was still almost unnoticed in his native land, was already far-reaching. Except for Groningen, where the academic senate managed to damp down the agitation, all the Dutch universities, especially Utrecht and Leiden, lapsed into a philosophical struggle unprecedented in European history since ancient times for acrimony, duration, and divisiveness.[2] The result was a deep and abiding split between philosophical conservatives, broadly the scholastic Aristotelians, whose chief spokesman was the famous Utrecht professor Gijsbertus Voetius (1589–1676), and innovators, primarily Cartesians, intent on revolutionizing not just philosophy but also physics, astronomy, medicine, and in some respects even Bible criticism and theology, along the lines of Descartes' mechanistic world-view.

But the resistance to the New Philosophy proved as fervent and tenacious as its support. As was later the case everywhere, champions of *philosophia aristotelio-scholastica* in the Netherlands claimed to be defending faith and ecclesiastical as well as intellectual authority, adhering, like Voetius, to a fundamentalist, hard-line confessional orthodoxy. Yet the continent-wide contest which began in the Dutch Republic was not straightforwardly one between *novatores* and the presiding public Churches. On the contrary, before long the Dutch and German Reformed Churches were no less plunged in internecine strife and acrimony than the universities.[3] In northern Calvinist lands, Reformed orthodoxy had been increasingly challenged since the 1640s by a new, liberal theological tendency inspired especially by Johannes Cocceius (1603–69), originally from the Calvinist city of Bremen, but since 1650 professor of theology at Leiden.[4] The ensuing theological struggle between liberal and conservative wings within the Dutch public Church then became entwined with the issue of Cartesianism in such a way that the theological split paralleled and became linked to the growing rift over philosophy and science.

Originally mostly matter for learned wrangling in Latin, very soon the hugely divisive issues at stake also began to be debated in taverns, passenger barges, and popular pamphlets in the vernacular.[5] One of the most fiercely contested issues was the status of philosophical reason itself, the Cartesio-Cocceians, as their opponents expressed it, maintaining that 'philosophy is a divine truth as sure as Holy Scripture, a Letter of God, and infallible, a measuring-rod of Scripture, so that whatever contradicts it is false' while the Aristotelio-Voetians insisted that philosophy should not be free in the way that Descartes envisaged, indeed has no independent status or absolute validity but is merely ancillary to theology.[6] A leading Cartesio-Cocceian and champion of philosophical reason, Christopher Wittichius (1625–87), whose career spanned both

---

the Dutch, 81–90; Van Ruler, *Crisis of Causality*, 2–37; Van der Wall, 'Orthodoxy and Scepticism', 121–31; Israel, *Dutch Republic*, 889–903.

[2] Mowbray, 'Libertas', 33; Verbeek, 'Tradition and Novelty', 167–8, 174–5, 182.
[3] Wittichius, *Consensus Veritatis*, 1–2, 6.   [4] Israel, *Dutch Republic*, 667–8, 889–99.
[5] Verbeek, 'Philosophie cartésienne', 234–40; Van der Wall, 'Orthodoxy and Scepticism', 124–6.
[6] Ryssenius, *Oude rechtsinnige waerheyt*, 11; Mastricht, *Novitatum Cartesianarum Gangraena*, 34–5, 61; Schouls, *Descartes*, 13–19.

the Lower Rhine and the Dutch Republic, held that 'what we know from within, by means of pure reason, we must deem to be revealed to us by God.'[7] Another Cartesio-Cocceian, Louis Wolzogen, averred that the origin and 'cause of the use of right reason' is God Himself. Like Wittichius, Wolzogen judged it impossible that God's Revelation should conflict with the natural light—that is, our, or rather Descartes', 'clear and distinct ideas'.[8]

Such sweeping reverence for philosophical reason, as well as the Cocceians' proneness to query traditional renderings of Hebrew and Greek in the authorized States Bible,[9] and construe passages of Scripture as allegories or figurative usages, not intended to be understood literally, provoked the Voetian charge that their adversaries were systematically subordinating the Bible to philosophical reason. For the Cartesians, they charged, 'philosophy and philosophers are the interpreters of Scripture in matters of nature'[10] for whom, on many points, Holy Writ 'speaks according to the erroneous notions of the common people of the time'.[11] Wittichius and other Cartesio-Cocceians did indeed argue that 'philosophical knowledge of natural things can not be had from the sacred books'[12] but nevertheless indignantly denied they were reducing theology to philosophy or encroaching on the authority of Scripture.[13] For decades, the exalted status the Cartesio-Cocceians accorded 'philosophy' continually aroused their opponents' condemnation and wrath. Later, in a vitriolic attack on Wittichius entitled *Novitatum Cartesianarum Gangraena* (1677) by Petrus van Mastricht—who (from 1678) was Voetius' successor at Utrecht—the *novatores'* veneration of 'philosophy' was exploited to buttress the accusation that, for all their denying it, at bottom the Cartesians embrace Spinoza's doctrine that God and Nature are one.[14] After 1670, Cartesians were continually obliged to counter the smear that their proofs for the existence, and their concept, of God were suspect and that they were somehow responsible for Spinozism,[15] while Voetians, eager to make the most of such hard-hitting rhetoric, lost no opportunity to tar their opponents as 'Spinosistische Cartesianen'.

A related issue was the respective positions of philosophy and theology in the hierarchy of scholarly disciplines. Voetius' theological defence of Aristotelian 'substantial forms' on the grounds that Genesis and Proverbs specify 'permanent natures' and 'distinct species of things', in a manner which validates the scholastic concept, is closely

---

[7] Ryssenius, *Oude rechtsinnige waerheyt*, 11.

[8] Ibid.; Foerthsius, *Selectorum theologeorum breviarium*, i, 32; Benedetti, *Difesa della terza lettera*, 244, 278.

[9] Brink, *Toet-steen der Waerheyt*, 25.

[10] Mastricht, *Novitatum Cartesianarum Gangraena*, 34–49; Allinga, *Cartesianismi Gangraena*, 12–13; Masius, *Dissertationes*, 14; Thijssen-Schoute, *Nederlands Cartesianisme*, 35–7; Verbeek, 'From "learned ignorance",' 38.

[11] Mastricht, *Novitatum Cartesianarum Gangraena*, 62–73, 96–105; Ryssenius, *Oude rechtsinnige waerheyt*, 17.

[12] Wittichius, *Consensus Veritatis*, 3, 14, 238; Verbeek, *Descartes and the Dutch*, 74; Scholder, *Birth*, 124–5.

[13] Wittichius, *Consensus Veritatis*, 3, 11, 53; Verbeek, 'Tradition and Novelty', 187, 196.

[14] Allinga, *Cartesianismi Gangraena*, 43–4; Burman, *Burmannorum Pietas*, 158–9.

[15] Helvetius, *Adams oud graft*, 200–16; Burman, *Burmannorum Pietas*, 60, 68–77; Van Bunge, *Johannes Bredenburg*, 147–8; Hubert, 'Premières réfutations', 22–8; Verbeek, *Descartes and the Dutch*, 72, 77; Goudriaan, *Philosophische Gotteserkenntnis*, 173–87.

related to his insistence on the primacy of theology over all learning, including philosophy.[16] By rejecting 'substantial forms' and, in their antagonists' view, contradicting Scripture, the Cartesians seemed to be supplanting theology's God-given supremacy and enthroning reason, that is, making reason all-powerful, as a leading Italian Aristotelian later expressed it, and theology 'powerless',[17] and in this way also usurping the rightful authority of the Church. The consequences of such a revolution in ideas, and in the hierarchy of intellectual disciplines, according to conservatives, Protestant and Catholic alike, would be socially, morally, religiously, and also politically catastrophic.

No less fraught with tension, from the 1650s, was the Copernican thesis revived by Galileo and espoused by the Cartesio-Cocceians, of the earth's motion around the sun. Copernicus and Galileo may have potentially revolutionized astronomy and cosmography, but until the 1650s the Copernican controversy had barely ruffled the surface of intellectual consciousness in most of Europe. Only around the middle of the century, when it came to be adopted as a key element of the New Philosophy, and Descartes' mechanistic conception of the universe simultaneously became a prime target of the scholastic Aristotelians, did there arise a wider appreciation of what was involved.[18] Voetius and the Calvinist orthodox were primarily concerned, in this controversy, with upholding the authority of Scripture and the unity of truth, including the Aristotelian conception of 'substantial forms', rather than assessing the astronomical evidence as such. By the late 1650s, heliocentrism and its implications for 'philosophy' and religion were being vehemently disputed in popular as well as learned publications in the Netherlands,[19] a phenomenon which materialized only somewhat later in most other parts of Europe. Wittichius, Frans Burmannus (1628–79), and other leading Cartesio-Cocceians held that 'philosophy', both theoretical and experimental, corroborates the truth of the Copernican thesis that the earth moves around the sun, and that its verification in turn confirms that 'Scripture,' as Wittichius puts it, 'speaks according to the outward appearance of things as they seem to our senses.'[20] This, protested orthodox Calvinists, was tantamount to claiming 'God says things to us He knows are not true, in other words lies to us; since, in the story of Joshua and elsewhere [Ecclesiastes 1: 4–7; Psalms 19: 5–7], Holy Scripture plainly affirms the sun circles the earth, this must be so.'[21] Wittichius indignantly denied that his view that Scripture explains natural things 'according to the opinion of the vulgar' implies that God deliberately lies to us or that he was subordinating theology to reason.[22] But this point proved as irresolvable as it was fundamental, given that there was so much, philosophically and theologically, at stake. The Voetian campaign

---

[16] Van Ruler, *Crisis of Causality*, 34; Garber, *Descartes' Metaphysical Physics*, 105.

[17] Benedetti, *Difesa della scolastica teologia*, 136–7, 172–4.

[18] Vermij, 'Het Copernicanisme', 357–62; Van Ruler, *Crisis of Causality*, 19–34.

[19] Goeree, *Kerklyke en Weereldlyke*, 639.

[20] Wittichius, *Consensus Veritatis*, 14, 19–34. 136–52; Brink, *Toet-steen der Waerheid*, 84.

[21] Mastricht, *Novitatum Cartesianarum Gangraena*, 62, 392–5; Ryssenius, *Oude Rechtsinnige* Waerheyt, 39–41; Verbeek, *Descartes and the Dutch*, 74, 89.

[22] Wittichius, *Consensus Veritatis*, 357–8.

against Copernican heliocentrism, vigorously resumed by Petrus van Mastricht and Melchior Leydekker (1642–1721) in the 1670s and 1680s, persisted down to the end of the century.[23]

The 'God' of the Cartesians, objected their opponents, was no longer the true God who governs and conserves the universe, and intervenes in human affairs, but some abstract 'principle', essentially just Professor Wittichius' 'Deus primaria est motus causa' (God is the first cause of motion). The commotion in the universities became so intense that by the mid-1650s it was impossible for the States of Holland any longer to stand aside. Guided by their Pensionary, Johan de Witt (1625–72), a gifted mathematician and something of a Cartesian himself, who in this matter was advised by a leading Cartesio-Cocceian, the Leiden theologian Abraham Heidanus (1597–1678), the States promulgated an edict on philosophy designed to 'prevent abuse of freedom to philosophize to the detriment of true theology and Holy Scripture'.[24] This carefully crafted enactment, passed in October 1656, over the objections of the Aristotelio-Voetians and Leiden burgomasters, conceded enough to the orthodox to reduce friction and quell the student unrest recently witnessed at Leiden, while simultaneously—despite banning mention of Descartes' name and the titles of his books from lectures and disputations—conserving the core of 'freedom to philosophize'. To accomplish this, De Witt, Heidanus, and the States of Holland sought to separate theology and philosophy as much as possible, declaring them different spheres of activity. Where an overlap was unavoidable, the philosophers, stipulated the decree, must defer to theology and eschew contentious interpretation of Scripture 'according to their principles'.[25] All six of Leiden's professors of theology and philosophy—three for each discipline—were required to endorse the edict before the academic curators, swearing on oath to uphold its terms, including the ban on mentioning Descartes' name in lectures. Though basically a victory for the Cartesians, and an endorsement of 'freedom to philosophize', the decree nevertheless also deftly echoed, at least superficially, the Leiden academic senate's original ban on teaching Cartesianism.

Comparative calm followed, though tension remained acute, until the Dutch 'disaster year' of 1672 when Louis XIV invaded in overwhelming force, the populace rioted, and the De Witt régime was overthrown. With the ensuing restoration of the stadholderate, and elimination of the regent faction which favoured the Cartesio-Cocceian faction, the Voetians had their opportunity to engineer a counter-offensive, first in Holland and Zeeland and, after the French retreat in 1673, also in Utrecht. The new orthodox Calvinist head of the Leiden theology faculty, Friedrich Spanheim (1632–1701), presided over this vigorous but ultimately futile attempt to extirpate Cartesianism from Dutch academic culture, an initiative which had little lasting impact other than further embittering the atmosphere and provoking renewed student unrest.[26] It proved impossible, in the circumstances of the late seventeenth century, to wean a large part of the professorate and student body, or for that matter of

---

[23] Brink, *Toet-steen der Waerheid*, 84; Vermij, *Secularisering*, 65; Vermij, 'Het Copernicanisme', 364–5.

[24] Verbeek, 'From "learned ignorance" ', 36; Israel, *Dutch Republic*, 892–4.

[25] Ibid.; Rowen, *John de Witt*, 402–7.   [26] Bontekoe, *Apologie*, 36, 365.

the Reformed Church's preachers, away from their Cartesian allegiance or to nullify the newly-won status of philosophy and science.

In 1676, spurred by Spanheim, the recently purged Leiden curators drew up a list of twenty Cartesio-Cocceian propositions deemed especially reprehensible by Voetians, including the methodological requirement to begin by doubting everything 'even the existence of God' besides Wittichius' maxim that 'Scripture speaks according to the prejudices of the common people' and the radical Cartesian doctrine (which none of the Cartesio-Cocceian professors would admit to accepting) that 'philosophy is the interpreter of Scripture,'[27] concepts that those directing the anti-Cartesian drive wished to see banned from teaching. The young Stadholder, William III, approved the list of condemned tenets and the ban was duly posted up around Leiden in Latin and Dutch, in the name of both curators and burgomasters. The authors responsible for these forbidden doctrines were named and, besides Descartes himself, predictably included, Wittichius, Wolzogen, and Cocceius.[28] But the Cartesio-Cocceian party was sufficiently strongly entrenched to resist with an appreciable effect. At Leiden Heidanus, Wittichius, and the scientist Burchardus de Volder, the first professor to introduce practical experiments in physics at a Dutch university, joined forces to devise, and anonymously publish, a devastating critique of the curators' intervention which became a best-seller.[29] For their defiance, Heidanus was dismissed from his chair, and Wittichius and De Volder severely reprimanded, but to little avail. By the early 1680s it was obvious that Wittichius and De Volder were the real victors. The attempt to enforce the revived hegemony of scholastic Aristotelianism collapsed. From the 1680s down to around 1720 Cartesianism enjoyed an incomplete, and still fiercely challenged, but nevertheless fairly general ascendancy in all the universities and civic high schools, from Franeker to 's-Hertogenbosch, and broadly over Dutch intellectual life as a whole.

ii. Cartesianism in Central Europe

Consequently, the Netherlands became the chief source of a powerful intellectual current, basically a modified, academic Cartesianism, which spread rapidly across Germany and the rest of northern Europe. Descartes' native land, meanwhile, where both Church and universities were, as we shall see, predominantly hostile to the New Philosophy, played a much less prominent role as an engine of mechanistic ideas in pre-Enlightenment Europe, a circumstance insufficiently stressed by historians. The primacy of the Netherlands as an exporter of Cartesian ideas and mechanistic thinking within Europe was due firstly to Cartesianism's early breakthrough in the Dutch scholarly world and secondly to Holland's pre-eminence in publishing and exporting Descartes' works, as well as the major commentaries on his philosophy. But it was also

[27] Cramer, *Abraham Heidanus*, 102–3; Thijssen-Schoute, *Nederlands Cartesianisme*, 49–52; Goudriaan, *Philosophische Gotteserkenntnis*, 181, 240; Israel, *Dutch Republic*, 897.

[28] Cramer, *Abraham Heidanus*, 103–5, 152; Thijssen-Schoute, *Nederlands Cartesianisme*, 49.

[29] Israel, *Dutch Republic*, 897.

due to the high prestige of the Dutch universities internationally and especially their unmatched capacity in this period to attract large numbers of foreign students, particularly from Germany, Scandinavia, and Hungary but also Scotland, England, and France.

In Germany, the penetration of Cartesian philosophy and science in the 1650s, began, predictably, in the north-west German Calvinist states which maintained close cultural links with the Dutch Reformed Church.[30] Here too the penetration of Cartesian ideas was fiercely contested.[31] In 1651, at the university of Nassau-Dillenburg, at Herborn,[32] where Wittichius (who was then teaching there) and a young professor, Johannes Clauberg (1622–65), originally from Solingen but trained at Leiden and destined to become one of the foremost Cartesian expositors in Europe, had been quietly infiltrating Cartesian ideas into their teaching for several years, uproar ensued when the two professors openly espoused Cartesianism in the lecture-room. Protests from the theology faculty obliged the prince, Count Ludwig Heinrich, to intervene. But how was he to decide which was the philosophy best suited to the smooth functioning of higher education in his state and the stability of society? Requiring guidance, he sent a circular to all five Dutch universities enquiring about their policies on philosophy. All five senates replied that they had banned Cartesianism as disruptive and 'harmful', though Groningen somewhat spoilt the effect by adding that, in contrast to Leiden and Utrecht, there the prohibition was also enforced in practice.[33] Swayed by the Aristotelio-Voetian case, Ludwig Heinrich prohibited Cartesianism in Nassau-Dillenburg and expelled both Clauberg and Wittichius from his lands. Herborn thenceforth remained for decades a bastion of Reformed orthodoxy and scholastic Aristotelianism.

Other German Calvinist princes, however, reacted very differently.[34] The pre-eminent ruler in northern Germany, the Great Elector Friedrich Wilhelm (ruled 1640–88) of Brandenburg-Prussia had spent part of his youth at the Stadholder's court in The Hague and studied briefly at Leiden. Subsequently, the Dutch context remained fundamental to his statecraft and, as has often been remarked, in every field from military and economic organization to architecture. Furthermore, he not only married the eldest daughter of the Dutch Stadholder, Frederick Henry, but shared his father-in-law's tolerant outlook in theological and intellectual matters. A Calvinist ruler over a predominantly Lutheran land, he was compelled furthermore to devise policies apt to ease, rather than exacerbate, the ceaseless and disruptive antagonism between the Lutheran and Calvinist confessional blocs. Thus, for both personal and political reasons, the court at Berlin consistently inclined towards the Cartesio-Cocceians rather than Voetian-style Calvinist orthodoxy.[35]

[30] Schneppen, *Niederländische Universitäten*, 76; Von Roden, *Universität Duisburg*, 159, Mennonöh, *Duisburg*, 156, 174, 228.

[31] De Boys, *Schadelickheyt*, 3; Von Roden, *Universität Duisburg*, 160.

[32] Wittichius, *Consensus Veritatis*, 1–2.

[33] Tepelius, *Historia Philosophiae Cartesianae*, 70–9, Mowbray, 'Libertas', 33, 46.

[34] Ring, *Geschichte*, 108–9; Von Roden, *Universität Duisburg*, 160–3; Hautz, *Geschichte* ii, 179–99.

[35] Landwehr, *Kirchenpolitik*, 173, 190–2, 203–6, 209, 353.

Until the founding of Halle, in 1694, there were three universities in the electorate—Frankfurt an der Oder, Königsberg, and the most recent, constituted in 1654, the predominantly Calvinist academy of Duisburg, in Cleves. Frankfurt and Königsberg, though long Lutheran by tradition, were increasingly required, after 1650, not just to cease polemical attacks on Calvinism but to learn to accommodate both confessions. Hence, while initially, in the 1650s, Cartesianism chiefly flourished on the Lower Rhine while elsewhere in Brandenburg-Prussia it was robustly opposed by Lutheran and Calvinist orthodox alike, the Elector refused to intercede anywhere to support scholastic Aristotelianism. When the synods condemned the advance of mechanistic ideas in the universities and civic high schools, Friedrich Wilhelm ruled that university professors were accountable only to him and not to the ecclesiastical authorities.[36] On one occasion, he answered complaints about the spread of Cartesianism, by remarking that he saw no reason why students should not be taught both the old and new philosophies and thereby learn to argue *pro et contra*.[37]

Despite rumours that the Cartesians predominated at Frankfurt an der Oder as early as 1656, there is no firm evidence of Cartesian hegemony in Frankfurt until the 1680s.[38] At Duisburg, on the other hand, Cartesianism became dominant as early as 1651 when the future university, then still a civic high school, received both Clauberg and Wittichius, who were welcomed and assigned chairs there by the elector's 'Stadholder', the former governor of Dutch Brazil, Count Johan Maurits van Nassau-Siegen.[39] While Duisburg later lost its brief prominence in German intellectual life after the French devastation of Cleves, in 1672–8, during the 1650s and 1660s it was one of the chief breeding-grounds of the New Philosophy in the Empire. Besides Clauberg and Wittichius, a third leading exponent of Cartesianism at Duisburg, in the years 1657–61, was the widely influential medical professor Theodore Craanen, originally from Cologne but trained in Holland, a theorist who reduced all bodily processes to mechanistic cause and effect and so admired Descartes that Bayle later styled him 'un grand zélateur de ce philosophe'.[40]

The next most important German Calvinist prince—until a Catholic line succeeded to the electorate in 1685—was the ruler of the Palatinate. The Elector Karl Ludwig (ruled 1649–80) had lived longer in Holland than Friedrich Wilhelm and was even fonder of the Dutch model, especially as regards toleration and intellectual matters. A great-grandson of William the Silent, through his paternal grandmother (a half-sister of the Stadholder Frederick Henry) brought up chiefly at The Hague, Karl Ludwig championed toleration against the wishes of most of his subjects, as well as the Calvinist clergy, permitting freedom of worship not only to Lutherans and Catholics but also Jews, Spiritualists, and even Socinians. This prince's aversion to rigid confessional thinking, and his taste for Cartesianism, persuaded his more

---

[36] Ring, *Geschichte*, 108.   [37] Varrentrapp, *Grosse Kurfürst*, 13–14.
[38] Ibid., 202, 229; Mühlpfordt, 'Die Oder-Universität', 56.
[39] Varrentrapp, *Grosse Kurfürst*, 13; Verbeek, *Descartes and the Dutch*, 84.
[40] Thijssen-Schoute, *Nederlands Cartesianime*, 271; Mennonöh, *Duisburg*, 218.

conservative subjects that he was practically a freethinker himself.[41] Especially unpalatable to the Reformed orthodox were his academic statutes of 1672 which, apart from chairs in theology, abolished the requirement for professors to belong to the Reformed Church and hence threatened what over the last century had been Heidelberg's solidly Calvinist identity.[42]

In a curious irony of history, one of the first non-Calvinists offered a chair at Heidelberg was none other than Spinoza himself, who received a fulsome invitation from the elector in February 1673. With equal courtesy the philosopher declined, preferring not to put Karl Ludwig's guarantee of 'freedom to philosophize'—provided he did not 'disturb the established religion of the state'[43]—to the test.[44] The elector's court *philosophe*, Urbain Chevreu (1613–1701), who spent the years 1671–8 in the Palatinate, later recounted how Spinoza's name came to the elector's attention.[45] Originally, after the publication in 1663 of his 'geometric' exposition of Descartes' system, Spinoza enjoyed an entirely respectable reputation in Germany as one of the chief expositors of Cartesianism alongside Clauberg, Wittichius, Heereboord, Andreae, Geulincx, and Mansvelt. Moreover, while such leading scholars as Leibniz and Jacob Thomasius knew soon after its appearance that Spinoza was also the author of the universally deplored *Tractatus Theologico-Politicus* (1670), Karl Ludwig and Chevreu were seemingly still unaware of this in 1673. Hearing Chevreu speak 'fort avantageusement de Spinosa', the elector, who was also *rector magnificentissimus* of his university and an accomplished Latinist, asked for extracts from the book on Descartes to be read to him. Greatly impressed, he at once ordered the famous invitation to be sent, ignoring the protests of his sub-rector, a Calvinist theologian, who did know about the *Tractatus* and tried to point out the danger. In later years, the Palatine elector's prestigious offer to Europe's most reviled philosopher was publicly explained as a lamentable error arising from Spinoza's 'deception' in originally posing as a 'Cartesian'.[46]

On Karl Ludwig's death the Palatinate's philosophical stance changed abruptly. The last Calvinist elector, Karl der Fromme (ruled 1680–85), desired to restore the primacy of Calvinist theology and confessional criteria, and, guided by his orthodox court preacher, tried to suppress Cartesianism and reinstate Aristotelianism.[47] Policy then shifted again after his death, when the electorate devolved upon the Catholic house of Neuburg, rulers of Jülich-Berg, who chiefly resided at Düsseldorf. Heidelberg, moreover, was again devastated by the French during the Nine Years' War (1688–97), and the university temporarily closed. On being reopened in 1700 the then ruler, Wilhelm von Neuburg (ruled 1690–1716), a noted champion of toleration and ally of the Dutch against Louis XIV, wished to revive the university as a multi-confessional, intellectually liberal, pro-Cartesian establishment. A step which particularly bolstered Cartesian influence was the elector's purchase, in 1706, of the 4,973 books of the recently deceased Utrecht professor of German background, Johannes Georg Graevius

---

[41] Mayer, 'Spinoza's Berufung', 40.   [42] Hautz, *Geschichte*, ii, 199.
[43] Colerus, *Vie de B. de Spinosa*, 87; Mayer, 'Spinoza's Berufung', 35.
[44] Spinoza, *Letters*, 249–51.   [45] Chevreu, *Chevraeana*, ii, 99–100.
[46] Halma, *Aanmerkingen*, 81–2.   [47] Hautz, *Geschichte*, ii, 206.

(1632–1705?),[48] a life-long adherent of Descartes, as well as a correspondent of Leibniz and a member of the Cartesian coterie at Utrecht, styled the 'college of sçavants' who had participated prominently in the Dutch comets controversy of 1664–5. This renewed ascendancy of Cartesianism, however, also proved temporary. After the end of the War of the Spanish Succession, in 1713, when the Dutch alliance was no longer needed, especially under Karl Philipp von Neuburg (ruled 1716–42), who espoused a much more traditional Catholic approach to educational matters than his predecessor, intellectual policy in Jülich-Berg and the Palatinate underwent another volte-face.[49] A rigidly Catholic confessional stance was imposed, the sway of the anti-Cartesian Jesuit academy of Düsseldorf (where the library contained not a single book by Descartes, Leibniz, or Spinoza)[50] asserted, and the university at Heidelberg entrusted to the Jesuits. With this, the status of philosophy in the Palatinate had turned full circle since 1650 and, for a time, *philosophia aristotelio-scholastica* again reigned supreme as the official philosophy of the Neuburg territories, universities, and court.

For the same reasons Cartesianism penetrated the Calvinist territories of Germany before reaching Lutheran and Catholic states, it also appeared relatively early in the German-speaking Swiss Reformed cantons. The Reformed Church in German-speaking Switzerland traditionally maintained close ties with both the Palatinate and the United Provinces and hence the New Philosophy also made early and rapid progress there. Dutch cultural influence in Reformed Switzerland flowed especially strongly via academic links, some 250 Swiss students studying at Leiden alone during the half century 1650–1700.[51] At Zürich, Cartesianism was introduced into university teaching in the late 1650s by Johannes Lavater (1624–95) and his colleague Caspar Waser,[52] adherents of a Swiss Cartesianism derived mainly from the works of Clauberg and the Leiden professor Adriaen Heereboord (1614–61) rather than directly from Descartes.[53] Before long, though, the impact of Cartesianism here too proved unsettling, with vehement protests from the preachers soon obliging the city government to curtail freedom to philosophize.[54] A still more abrupt volte-face, occurred at Bern where Cartesianism was introduced by one of the professors, David Wyss, in 1662. By 1668 antagonism between Cartesians and Aristotelians at Bern and Lausanne was so intense that the cantonal government felt obliged to adopt the Church's advice and ban all teaching of Cartesian philosophy and science as 'gefährlich und schädlich' (dangerous and damaging).[55] The prohibition was extended by decrees of March and April 1669, when the sale and distribution in the canton of Cartesian handbooks and commentaries, besides Descartes' own works, was forbidden, and students returning from the Netherlands were required henceforth to sign a formula formally

---

[48] Ibid., ii, 232.   [49] Ibid., ii, 230, 255–7; Whaley, 'A Tolerant Society?', 181.
[50] Enderle, 'Jesuitenbibliothek', 163.   [51] Hoiningen-Hune, *Beiträge*, 32.
[52] Rother, 'Teaching of Philosophy', 62 3, 65.   [53] Ibid., 65.
[54] Hoiningen-Huene, *Beiträge*, 32–4; Geiger, *Basler Kirche*, 142–4.
[55] Hoiningen-Huene, *Beiträge*, 34–5; Guggisberg, *Bernische Kirchengeschichte*, 457; Santschi, *Censure à Genève*, 44.

repudiating Cartesianism. The ban was further tightened in March 1671, with stiffer penalties, threatening professors with loss of their chairs and students their study stipends if they disobeyed.

Yet despite the hopes of the doyen of the Dutch anti-Cartesian counter-offensive, Spanheim, who wrote to a Swiss colleague in 1676, wishing 'your Switzerland luck [in the fight to resist Cartesianism] and that Basel should stick firmly to the old orthodoxy',[56] the hard line adopted at Bern and, to a lesser extent, Zürich was not replicated in the other Reformed cantons. On the contrary, from the 1660s first Basel and later Geneva gradually became havens of the New Philosophy. At Basel the presiding figure in cultural and intellectual affairs during the third quarter of the century was Lukas Gernler (1625–75), a theology professor and an admirer of Cocceius, who corresponded with several Cartesio-Cocceians in the Netherlands, including Burmannus at Utrecht.[57] Gernler supported the advent of Cartesianism, urging the Basel authorities to grant 'freedom to philosophize' provided nothing which was taught impugned Scripture's account of natural things.[58] The Cartesianism taught at Basel from around 1660 was evidently again based primarily on Heereboord. At Geneva, meanwhile, Cartesianism penetrated noticeably later than elsewhere in Switzerland and when it did, in the late 1660s, it percolated, not as in German-speaking Reformed Switzerland from the Netherlands, but France, being introduced into lectures at the university by Jean-Robert Chouet, a Genevan who previously worked in France, where he had established Descartes' philosophy a few years earlier at the Huguenot academy at Saumur.

The Swiss cantons, then, were and remained divided, partly for and partly against mechanistic philosophy. Moreover, not only did it prove impossible to achieve a coordinated Swiss Reformed stance on philosophy, medicine, and science, but even within cantons dissension proved unavoidable. There was a continual tension between the New Philosophy and Reformed orthodoxy and, as part of this, between heliocentrism and the old astronomy. Not only were the universities and consistories divided, but even key individuals such as Gernler were to no small degree split within themselves. Like his friend Maresius at Groningen, Gernler's disquiet mounted with the passage of time. He and his colleagues at Basel disliked Voetius, but were also perturbed by the acrimony and divisiveness which seemed everywhere to mark the progress of Cartesianism, and especially its undeniable tendency to produce radical offshoots. In particular, Gernler became deeply alarmed on hearing of the *Tractatus Theologico-Politicus*. Writing to Switzerland's pre-eminent Bible scholar at the time, his friend Johann Heinrich Heidegger (1633–98) at Zürich, soon to emerge as the foremost adversary of Spinozism in Switzerland, he passed on news obtained from Groningen, that the author of that execrable work was a Dutch Jew called 'Spinosa', information which almost simultaneously reached the learned Heidegger from Heidelberg and Marburg.[59]

[56] Hoiningen-Huene, *Beiträge*, 37.   [57] Geiger, *Basler Kirche*, 142–4.   [58] Ibid., 143.

[59] *Nova Literaria Helvetica*, ii, 9–10; Jöcher, *Allgemeines Gelehrten Lexicon*, ii, 1440–1.

iii. The New Philosophy conquers Scandinavia and the Baltic

The outbreak of the Cartesian controversies in the Baltic followed directly on the Cartesian penetration of Central Europe. At the principal Swedish university, Uppsala, Cartesian ideas in philosophy, science, and medicine were introduced into lectures by the leading medical professor Petrus Hoffvenius (1630–82) backed by the university rector Olaus Rudbeck (1630–1702) early in the 1660s. As a student, Hoffvenius had met Descartes in person during the latter's four-month residence in Stockholm at the end of his life.[60] But the French philosopher's stay in Sweden had almost no direct impact on the Baltic intellectual scene.[61] Only later did the New Philosophy enter mainstream Swedish intellectual life, after the study trip undertaken by Hoffvenius and Rudbeck to Leiden and Utrecht in the late 1650s.[62] It was there that the two scholars became fervent converts. When he openly introduced Cartesian ideas into his lectures back in Sweden, Hoffvenius precipitated a major rift within the academic faculties at Uppsala, with the consequence that, in 1664, the ecclesiastical estate of the Swedish parliament, or Riksdag, petitioned the regency government, ruling since the demise of Charles X in 1660, for a general ban on Cartesianism in the kingdom.[63]

In the Swedish monarchy, as in Denmark-Norway-Holstein, the Lutheran Church was an immensely powerful institution and the only truly cohesive cultural force binding the constituent parts of the empire together. The opposition of the Church automatically placed the innovators in a difficult position. According to the clergy's submission to the Riksdag, Cartesianism is a doctrine which acknowledges the truth of Scripture in *res fidei* (matters of faith) but not in chronology, cosmology, or natural science, and claims that the Bible speaks 'in accordance with the ignorant notions of the common people'.[64] Rudbeck fought back with some success, owing to the support of the university's chancellor, Magnus Gabriel de la Gardie, the country's wealthiest nobleman, a grandee who had himself studied philosophy and was a noted bibliophile, possessing the largest library in Sweden after that of the Crown, and who sat on the ruling regency council. Even so, a highly fraught compromise was the best that could be attained, leaving Hoffvenius if not silenced then obliged to refrain from lecturing on the broad principles of Cartesianism.[65] Henceforth he confined his teaching to purely technical topics, avoiding sensitive philosophical and scientific questions.

Nevertheless, during the 1670s a suffused, unobtrusive Cartesianism slowly penetrated in Sweden, as in Denmark-Norway. In 1678 Hoffvenius published a batch of scientific treatises, under the title *Synopsis physica*, a compendium based chiefly on Clauberg and De Raey, which remained the standard physics handbook in Sweden

---

[60] Åkerman, *Queen Christina*, 49.
[61] Ibid., 45–9, 59; Sandblad, 'Reception', 255.
[62] Lindborg, *Descartes i Uppsala*, 344.
[63] Ibid., 345; Annerstedt, *Uppsala universitets historia*, ii, 91–8.
[64] Lindborg, *Descartes i Uppsala*, 345.
[65] Ibid., 346.

until the end of the century.[66] Behind the scenes Hoffvenius spread Cartesian ideas and heliocentric astronomy without mentioning Descartes' name or stating openly what he was doing. Others, though, were less discreet. In 1679 Niels Celsius (1658–1724), one of Hoffvenius' ablest students and a ardent Cartesian, provoked uproar at Uppsala during a public disputation by reiterating Descartes' maxim that scientific observation is the only basis of authority in astronomy and openly criticizing those who insist on a literal reading of Scripture—often, he suggested, under a false cloak of piety—to obstruct progress in science.[67]

Finally, in the mid-1680s erupted a full-scale theologico-philosophico-scientific battle between the defenders of the old and the partisans of the new philosophy. In this contest, the Swedish Church, backed by part of the divided Uppsala philosophy school, faced the medical, and the rest of the philosophy, faculty. In the Riksdag, the ecclesiastical estate urged the king, Charles XI (ruled 1660–97), to proclaim Aristotelianism the official philosophy of the monarchy and ban Cartesianism, recommending that instruction in physics at Uppsala be transferred from the (now strongly Cartesian) medical faculty to the philosophy faculty, where it should be entrusted to a reliable Aristotelian and opponent of heliocentrism.[68] In some perplexity, the king sent copies of the petition to all faculties at Uppsala, requiring responses in writing.

In Denmark at this time, leading theologians, such as Hector Gottfried Masius, at Copenhagen, buttressed their charge that Cartesianism imperils Lutheran orthodoxy by citing Descartes' systematic use of doubt in metaphysics, even to the point of doubting the existence of God, at any rate as a philosophical procedure, and deploring the pernicious influence of Cartesio-Cocceian methods of Bible exegesis.[69] The Uppsala theology faculty argued likewise, echoing the protests of the Dutch anti-Cartesians, especially Petrus van Mastricht who, in his *Novitatum Cartesianarum Gangraena*, charged that Cartesianism subordinates Scripture to a philosophy based on mechanistic principles, deeming Scripture to be adjusted to the 'ignorant notions' of the common people.[70] The latter principle the Uppsala theologians expressly attributed to Wittichius but also, ominously for the Cartesians, to the *Tractatus Theologico-Politicus*, cited here as an anonymous work.[71]

The philosophy faculty granted that an unrestricted *philosophandi licentia* (freedom to philosophize) would harm society, but insisted that a carefully limited, responsible freedom of disputation is essential for teaching philosophy and for scientific research. Denmark, it was pointed out, was no less staunchly Lutheran than Sweden, and there discussion of Cartesian doctrines was permitted, as was shown by recent academic disputations at Copenhagen and Kiel in Holstein-Gottorp.[72] Sweden's standing in the world, and Swedish scholarship, would assuredly suffer, it was held, if teaching and disputing Cartesianism were banned in the monarchy: for wherever freedom to

---

[66] Lindborg, *Descartes i Uppsala*; Lindroth, *Svensk lärdomshistoria*, ii, 454.
[67] Sandblad, 'Reception', 258–9.
[68] Lindborg, *Descartes i Uppsala*, 347; Lindroth, *History of Uppsala*, 73.
[69] Masius, *Dissertationes academicae*, 14–16.
[70] Lindroth, *Svensk lärdomshistoria*, ii, 461–2; Lindborg, *Descartes i Uppsala*, 347.
[71] Annerstedt, *Uppsala universitetshistoria*, ii, 322.   [72] *Schwedische Bibliothec*, ii, 77.

philosophize 'is not tolerated not only *physica* but also moral philosophy, philology, and the general humanities are ruined as is universally known'.[73] Circumventing the delicate issues of heliocentrism and Descartes' use of doubt, the medical professors stressed the scientific and humanistic value of Cartesian concepts for scientific research and methodology, basing their arguments on Heereboord, De Raey, and Wittichius. This text was largely compiled by Johan Bilberg (1646–1717), professor of mathematics since 1679, and now the leading Swedish Cartesian. A warm admirer of Dutch learning, Bilberg also sought to impart new momentum to Copernican astronomy in Sweden though, as it was still not possible anywhere in the Baltic openly to espouse heliocentrism in publications and the lecture-room, he did so mostly in manuscript texts and private classes at his home.[74]

Deeply disquieted, the Swedish Court sought a balanced approach to the dilemmas of the New Philosophy, setting up a commission comprising not only officials and churchmen but also declared Cartesians, including Bilberg himself.[75] Aiming at compromise, this body sought a *modesta philosophandi libertas* while preventing an unrestricted *philosophandi licentia*.[76] But it took time to devise a suitable formula which would satisfy the needs of both religion and scholarship; and, in the meantime, the vexed situation served only to inflame the quarrel at Uppsala and foment strife in the other universities. Controversy flared at Lund, a new institution founded in 1666 as an instrument to 'Swedify' the provinces recently conquered from Denmark, and also at the Finnish university, at Åbo, founded by Gustavus Adolphus in 1640. At the time it was set up, around half the professors teaching there had received at least part of their academic training in Holland,[77] and down to the early eighteenth century Dutch influences remained conspicuously strong. As at Uppsala, it was the medical professors trained in Holland, such as Elias Tillandz, who introduced Cartesian doctrines, and again, it was the orthodox Lutheran theologians who resisted.[78] The anti-Cartesian camp in Finland was headed by Johan Gezelius (1615–90), former *Generalsuperintendens* of the Lutheran Church in Livonia, and latterly Bishop of Åbo, author of a handbook of Aristotelian philosophy.

Only in March 1689 did the commission conclude, advising the king that while *philosophia cartesiana* unquestionably assists the progress of natural science, medicine, and mathematics, inadequate regulation of freedom to philosophize undermines religion, morality, and society. Accordingly, neither the old nor the new philosophy should be banned in Sweden-Finland. Rather the king should impose a carefully regulated *libertas philosophandi* designed to prevent encroachment by philosophy on theology and especially any 'philosophisk critique' of the Bible.[79] The ensuing royal decree on philosophy, adopting this solution, was promulgated at Stockholm on 17 April 1689. In striving to separate philosophy from theology as much as possible, the edict bears distinct affinities with Holland's decree on philosophy of 1656.

---

[73] Ibid.   [74] Sandblad, 'Reception', 260–3.   [75] Bring, *Samling*, ii, 133.
[76] *Schwedische Bibliothec*, ii, 115.   [77] Wansink, *Politieke wetenschappen*, 10.
[78] Rein, *Åbo universitets lärdomshistoria*, x, 106–49; Wrangel, *Betrekkingen*, 305–6.
[79] Bring, *Samling*, ii, 128–33; Lindroth, *Svensk lärdomshistoria*, ii, 464.

Yet the anti-Cartesians had been partially vindicated and, in the 1690s, continued to oppose Cartesianism with great tenacity both in Sweden and, still more, in Finland. It was only around 1700 that the Swedish Cartesians gained that broad hegemony over the academic and intellectual life of the country which in the early eighteenth century was characteristic of Uppsala, Lund, and Åbo alike, as well as the medical and scientific establishment in Stockholm.[80] At Lund, the supremacy of a Neo-Cartesianism inspired principally by Wittichius, De Volder, Andala, and Malebranche was confirmed in 1710 with the appointment of a pupil of Bilberg, Andreas Rydelius (1671–1738), who remained for several decades the pre-eminent exponent of Cartesian philosophy and theology in the Baltic.[81]

The impressive flowering of Swedish science during the first half of the eighteenth century thus unfolded within a matrix which during its formative period, until the 1730s, was predominantly Cartesian. In medicine, Lars Roberg, who studied for many years in Holland and was a pupil in particular of De Volder, did much to change medical thought and teaching in Sweden and established the first academic hospital (on the Leiden model). Similarly, the astronomers Olof Hiorter and Anders Celsius, after whom the centigrade thermometer is named, emerged from a Cartesian background, as did the great naturalist Carl Linnaeus (1707–78) who began his academic career in a Lund dominated by Rydelius, in 1727, and, at least as regards his early formation, also Emanuel Swedenborg (1688–1772) first a scientist but later, after his revolt against rationalist philosophy, perhaps the greatest mystic of the eighteenth century.

iv. France: Philosophy and Royal Absolutism

In France the main impact of the Cartesian controversies was felt appreciably later than in the Netherlands, Germany, Switzerland, and Scandinavia, but earlier than in Italy and the rest of Catholic Europe.[82] The implications of the New Philosophy were clear enough by 1650, but through the 1650s and 1660s all sections of the Church in France and nearly the entire academic establishment firmly opposed the advance of Cartesianism. This is true indeed even of the Jansenists, habituated though they were to dissent, and the Huguenots. Thus, in 1656, the governors of the comparatively liberal Huguenot academy of Saumur—Sedan was reputedly more conservative—considered whether to permit the teaching of Cartesian ideas but at that stage resolved against precisely because this philosophy had proved so disruptive in the Dutch and German universities.[83] Among Jansenists meanwhile, Pascal's disparagement of Descartes as 'inutile et incertain', a philosopher who reduces God to the status of a divine mechanic who exists 'pour mettre le monde en mouvement',[84] was not in itself untypical. Admittedly, one leading Jansenist spokesman, Antoine Arnauld (1612–94), was also a leading advocate of Cartesianism. But he was an isolated figure in this respect and by ardently espousing Cartesianism aroused no small anxiety among

---

[80] Lindroth, *Svensk lärdomshistoria*, ii, 465–570; Lindroth, *History of Uppsala*, 126.

[81] Rosén, *Lunds universitets historia*, ii, 206–10.   [82] Brockliss, 'Curricula', 584–5.

[83] Heyd, *Between Orthodoxy and Enlightenment*, 4.   [84] Pascal, *Pensées*, 94.

friends and allies within Jansenism, who had some reason to fear his philosophical proclivities would render them even more suspect in the eyes of the Crown and episcopal hierarchy than they were already.[85]

Meanwhile, official disapproval of Cartesian philosophy, encouraged by the papal ban on Descartes' works of 1663, became slowly more resolute and emphatic. When Descartes' remains were transferred to the imposing church of Sainte Geneviève-du-Mont, in Paris, in 1667, it was forbidden for any funeral oration to be delivered.[86] In 1670–1, prompted by the Sorbonne and the Jesuits, the *Parlement* of Paris discussed whether to impose a general prohibition on the publication and distribution of Descartes' works in France.[87] Opinion was divided and nothing followed, but this served only to increase the pressure on the Crown to give a clearer lead. The Sorbonne repeatedly reaffirmed its condemnation of Descartes' doctrines, as was widely noted in Spain and Italy as well as France.[88] The largest teaching order, the Jesuits, increasingly stifled those voices within their own ranks sympathetic to Cartesianism.[89] The second largest, the Oratorians, lapsed into deep divisions over philosophy. A teaching ban was vigorously urged in the highest circles and gradually the Court edged towards this. Louis XIV finally intervened, in August 1671, forbidding the teaching of Cartesian philosophy in the colleges and universities of France by royal decree, but stopping short of prohibiting the publication, sale, and distribution of Cartesian books. Henceforth instruction in Cartesianism took place mainly through private lectures of the sort Pierre Régis gave in Toulouse and other provincial towns during the 1670s, or private tuition.[90]

Louis' decision to throw the weight of royal authority behind the cause of *philosophia aristotelio-scholastica* pleased the Sorbonne, the Jesuits, and most bishops but created a harsh quandary for the Oratorians.[91] A teaching and preaching order founded in 1611, they were within France—though they mostly lacked comparable influence elsewhere—the chief rivals of the Jesuits in providing secondary education for young men and preparing novices for the priesthood. By the mid-1670s there was unmistakable evidence that the Oratorians were not observing the ban seriously and that the order generally, and its most eminent philosopher, Father Nicolas Malebranche (1638–1715) specifically, were tilting towards the New Philosophy. Malebranche at this juncture was working on his first great book, the *De la Recherche de la Vérité* (1674–5). The ban was also disconcerting for many others. The young Pierre Bayle, for instance, having fled to Geneva after abjuring his conversion to Catholicism and returning to the Protestant faith of his family, abandoned the Aristotelianism he had imbibed from his Jesuit teachers in Toulouse and embraced Cartesianism; yet, on returning to France, he could no longer teach Cartesianism openly. Hence, on

---

[85] Nadler, *Arnauld*, 19–20.   [86] Phillips, *Church and Culture*, 293.
[87] Allard, 'Angriffe', 1; Nadler, *Arnauld*, 20.
[88] Palanco, *Dialogus Physico-Theologicus*, praefatio, p. ii; Benedetti, *Lettere Apologetiche*, 120.
[89] Kors, *Atheism in France*, i, 272.
[90] Formey, *Histoire abrégée*, 274; Allard, 'Angriffe', 1; Brockliss, 'Scientific Revolution in France', 69, 76.
[91] Phillips, *Church and Culture*, 100–1, 171–2, 185–7; Briggs, *Communities of Belief*, 353–4.

assuming his chair at the Huguenot academy at Sedan, Bayle found himself obliged to lead a philosophical double life, professing Cartesianism (for the time being) privately and scholastic Aristotelianism in lectures.[92]

The king's objective was to prevent in France the kind of intellectual turmoil which had engulfed other lands. The scientists recruited into the new royal Académie des Sciences, in Paris, were not pressured to identify with one philosophy or another; but neither were they permitted to engage in philosophical polemics for or against Cartesianism, or any other philosophy, the king being entirely unwilling to relegate the judgement of philosophical truth. Meanwhile, the Oratorians' persistence in teaching Cartesianism in defiance of the king's wishes angered many and aggravated the traditional rivalry between the two main teaching orders. The Jesuits accused the Oratorians of endangering Church and society, though Bayle suggests they did so chiefly out of pique at seeing the best students desert their colleges for those of their competitors. But however that may be, the Jesuits, backed by much of the hierarchy, eventually persuaded the king to make an example of their rivals. Intervening through the Archbishop of Paris, he compelled them to acknowledge their 'errors' and sign an abject formula of submission, which was duly ratified by the sixth general assembly of the order, in Paris, in September 1678.[93]

The rules to which the Oratorians submitted represented what was effectively now the official policy of the French monarchy on philosophy. The key points were a general requirement to keep philosophy subordinate to theology and the authority of the Church, that freedom of the will be taught in the 'manner of Aristotle', and that there be no departure from the 'principes de physique d'Aristote communément reçus dans les collèges'. There was to be no teaching of the 'doctrine nouvelle de Monsieur Descartes, que le Roy a défendu qu'on enseignât pour de bonnes raisons'.[94] Moreover, henceforth professors of philosophy had to teach seven fundamental doctrines of metaphysics directly contrary to those of Descartes, in particular affirming that extension is not the essence of matter, and that in every body there is a 'forme substancielle réellement distinguée de la matière' and that the soul is really present in, and united with, the whole human body.[95] Also obligatory was the doctrine that a void is not impossible. Finally, it was forbidden to teach any kind of political theory, or anything concerning the principles of monarchy.

Louis desired uniformity, order, and hierarchy, intellectual as well as political, social, and ecclesiastical. But nothing is harder than to control men's minds and, as an astute observer noted at the time, Louis was bound to weaken his monarchy, and the sway of authority in France, by introducing new tensions rooted in matters 'purement philosophiques', causing numerous loyal Catholics, clergy among them, to resent this 'new yoke' at a time when society and the Church were already convulsed by the Jansenist controversies. To require teachers and scholars to articulate concepts contrary to what they inwardly judged to be truth was to drive them 'insensiblement

---

[92] Labrousse, *Pierre Bayle*, ii, 39, 41.
[93] [Bayle], *Recueil de documents*, 4–13, 24–5; Phillips, *Church and Culture*, 296.
[94] [Bayle], *Recueil de documents*, 9–12.   [95] Ibid.

à la révolte', creating intellectual antagonism ultimately bound to find expression in 'entreprises téméraires contre l'autorité légitime'.[96] The king, furthermore, was endangering the authority of the Church and reverence for its teaching: for by insisting the 'mysteries' of the Christian faith 'dépende des principes de la philosophie, et que notre religion et Aristote sont tellement liez qu'on ne puisse renverser l'un sans ébranler l'autre', Louis was linking what the people believe to disputed philosophical tenets which experience showed were crumbling daily under the assaults of the 'nouveaux philosophes'.[97] By thus encumbering the French Church with outmoded philosophical and scientific doctrines, Louis, some of his subjects alleged, was needlessly giving the Protestants a huge and unwarranted advantage.

But the king had made up his mind. The 'principes de Descartes' were 'formally banned in the schools of the kingdom' as a leading early eighteenth-century French scientist later put it, and there were orders that one should teach only the 'philosophie d'Aristote'.[98] In subsequent decades the ban on teaching Cartesianism, and the obligation to teach only *philosophia aristotelio-scholastica*, was continually reaffirmed through a long series of edicts of the Sorbonne.[99] Scholars who refused to acquiesce, especially if they openly opposed royal policy, were firmly dealt with. Pierre Valtentin Faydit had been expelled from the Oratorians in 1671 for his excessively zealous espousal of Cartesianism. Father Malebranche, whose books, published in the Netherlands, were banned in France,[100] was forbidden to teach and driven into semi-isolation. Antoine Arnauld, albeit more for Jansenism than publicly supporting Cartesianism, felt obliged to flee to Holland in 1679.

But in France as in the rest of Europe, monarchical and ecclesiastical authority were insufficiently strong to hold the line against the New Philosophy. While there was no formal instruction in Cartesianism in the colleges and universities, and members of the Académie des Sciences were barred from debating philosophical questions, Cartesianism percolated slowly but inexorably into all segments of French intellectual life.[101] By the 1680s it was obvious that royal policy on philosophy was becoming distinctly frayed at the edges and Church and universities intellectually increasingly divided. Nevertheless, adversaries of the new ideas, especially the Jesuits, showed little willingness to relent even during the closing years of Louis' reign, so that until 1715 there was no sign of the policy being abandoned.[102] As late as 1705, the University of Paris reissued its ban on the teaching of Cartesianism.[103]

A principal factor affecting the lines of combat was the rapid growth, from the 1680s onwards, of radical thought. It was doubtless inevitable in France as elsewhere that

[96] Ibid., 43.   [97] Ibid., 44.   [98] Dortous de Mairan, *Éloge*, 3.
[99] Kors, *Atheism in France*, i, 294; Briggs, *Communities of Belief*, 353–4.
[100] Sauvy, *Livres saisis*, 85, 136–8.   [101] Allard, *Angriffe*, 2–3; Phillips, *Church and Culture*, 294–5.
[102] From 1706 the French Jesuits renewed their campaign against Cartesianism on a nation-wide basis. Three of their own professors who resisted, being sympathetic to Malebranche and Cartesianism—François de la Pillonière, Rodolphe du Tertre, and Yves-Marie André were subjected to heavy pressure resulting in the first being silenced and the second performing a sensational volte-face, and publicly attacking Malebranche in 1713; see Vernière, *Spinoza*, 423–4; Kors, *Atheism in France*, i, 277–9.
[103] Brockliss, 'Scientific Revolution in France', 73.

traditionalists should take to labelling their opponents accomplices of the *Spinosistes* while, in reply, the Cartesians should bend every effort to show that their teaching, far from threatening, provided the best protection for, the core Christian 'mysteries'. Without doubt radicalism imparted added plausibility to Jesuit accusations against Descartes and Malebranche. The accusation that Malebranche's system which, according to the Jesuit *Journal de Trévoux* in 1708, effectively 'annihilates the Divinity by reducing it to the totality of the world', was a form of back-door Spinozism was publicized in particular by the famous Jesuit controversialist, Father René-Josèphe Tournemine (1661–1739), chief editor of the *Journal de Trévoux* for many years, who did not hesitate to label *Malebranchisme* a 'spinosisme spirituel'.[104] His influential *Réflexions sur l'athéisme* (1713), published originally as a preface to Fénelon's *Démonstration de l'existence de Dieu* (Paris, 1713), features a robust refutation of Spinoza considered by some the most effective advanced on the Catholic side of the confessional divide.[105]

According to Tournemine, Spinoza (like Malebranche) roots his philosophy in Cartesianism except that it superadds the reduction of matter and spirit into one substance, an inference, he insists, as confused and illogical as anything can be. 'Ce système, que son obscurité seule rend célèbre' at once collapses, asserts Tournemine, under the impact of the 'argument from design'.[106] Any discerning person who ponders the marvels of nature, including the bodily structures of the tiniest creatures, understands that all this cannot be the result of blind fatality: 'toute la nature montre l'existence de son auteur'.[107] Equally inconceivable, he held, is Spinoza's doctrine of 'one substance' for 'rien n'est plus clairement démontré que l'impossibilité d'une matière pensante'.[108] 'Ce rare génie', as Tournemine sarcastically styles the philosopher who, armed with obscure terminology, seeks to make the incompatible compatible, unifying matter and spirit, had indeed conjured up the greatest intellectual threat of the age but one which, under analysis, proves to be philosophical nonsense.[109] Malebranche, granted Tournemine, was no atheist but a loyal Catholic. In fact, in Tournemine's opinion there are no true atheists, since no one can really believe the universe was not created by an intelligent Creator: 's'il y a eu des hypocrites d'athéisme, il n'y a jamais eu de véritables athées.'[110] Hence there are no genuine Spinozists, despite the sinister claims of 'Monsieur Bayle' to the contrary. But if all deism, atheism, and Spinozism, according to Tournemine, is ultimately hypocrisy, falsehood, and affectation, this did not alter the fact that France was now teeming with *Spinosistes* and 'de prétendus athées Cartesiens et Malebranchistes', adept at employing Malebranche to undermine belief in divine Providence, striving to unify matter and spirit and reduce everything to general laws of nature.[111]

---

[104] D'Argens, *Philosophie du Bons-Sens*, ii, 363–6; Northeast, *Parisian Jesuits*, 64.

[105] [Tournemine], 'Préface', 7–37; this text of Tournemine reappeared with the 1715 Amsterdam edition of Fénelon's book and again, as an annex to Fénelon's *Oeuvres philosophiques*, in 1718.

[106] [Tournemine], 'Préface', 18–20, 27. [107] Ibid., 7. [108] Ibid., 35. [109] Ibid., 36–7.

[110] Northeast, *Parisian Jesuits*, 80–1; Phillips, *Church and Culture*, 259–60.

[111] [Tournemine], 'Préface', 12–13.

v. Reaction in the Italian States

Although the question of the New Philosophy did not become a major public issue in Italy until the 1670s, from that point on government and Church were compelled to wrestle with the dilemmas created by the New Philosophy in the Italian states no less strenuously than in lands north of the Alps. Indeed, there was such an intensity of intellectual debate, much of it of high quality, that Italy rapidly emerged as one of the most heavily contested philosophical and scientific arenas of the Early Enlightenment. The appreciable differences in government policy regarding new ideas, as between states, resulted primarily from the divergent preferences of individual rulers, the two dominant models being, on the one hand, the Tuscany of Cosimo III—and, after 1730, the kingdom of Savoy—where, over many decades, a stringently conservative policy was pursued, opposed to both wings of the Enlightenment, and, on the other hand, a more flexible and liberal, or at least more hesitant, posture such as prevailed in Venice and, most dramatically, until the 1720s in Naples.

The reactionary stance adopted in Florence was almost entirely due to princely whim. In the past the Medici grand dukes of Tuscany had generally been at the forefront of patronage of learning and science as well as the arts. The grand-ducal court protected Galileo as far as was possible, after the papal condemnation of Copernican astronomy in 1633, down to the great scientist's death in 1642, and would have preferred to give him a grander, more public, funeral than the Church was willing to countenance. Nevertheless, while the patronage of science continued subsequently, and Leopoldo de' Medici (1617–75), younger brother of Grand Duke Ferdinand II (ruled 1621–70), founded Europe's first true academy of science, the Accademia del Cimento (1657–67), in Florence, providing his scientists with laboratories, apparatus, and research funds, as well as premises for them in the Palazzo Pitti, great care was taken to fence off the wider questions of science and philosophy, including further discussion of Galileo's heliocentric system, from the purely empirical research the Medicean academy sponsored. The Florentine model of scientific enquiry after Galileo's retraction, so far as published and public debate was concerned, was pure experimental work eschewing all broader intellectual issues. Even the very fact that Galileo championed Copernican heliocentricism was publicly suppressed.

In private, especially at Court in Florence and in the declining, but not moribund, University of Pisa, Galilean principles and Cartesian philosophy were nevertheless avidly explored and discussed. That Florence was still a focus of scientific work, and also, behind a discreet veil, of wider intellectual endeavour was reflected in the spiritual odyssey of Magalotti and, in 1666, by the entry into the grand duke's service of the Danish biologist and geologist Nicholas Steno (1638–86), at the time a fervent Cartesian and one of the ablest scientific minds in Europe. In fact, while studying at Leiden (1660–3), Steno had embraced not just Cartesianism but also, albeit briefly, radical tendencies and become a friend of Spinoza.[112] On settling in Florence, though, Steno converted from Lutheranism to Catholicism and soon also discarded his Cartesianism. But he still closely followed philosophical developments and initially forged ahead with his scientific work, producing, among other things, a pioneering theory of geological evolution. A few years later he underwent a second conversion, and abandoned philosophy and science completely, resolving to devote his formidable energies henceforth to furthering the cause of the Counter-Reformation. Becoming a priest in 1675, Steno rose to become one of the most influential ecclesiastics in the intellectual sphere in Catholic Europe.[113]

A new stringency regarding Cartesianism, Galilean astronomy, and intellectual freedom generally, followed the accession of the immensely devout Grand Duke Cosimo III (ruled 1670–1723).[114] Cosimo had already shown signs of hostility to the New Philosophy during his tour of Holland in 1667 when, accompanied among others by Magalotti, he encountered several of Steno's Dutch scientist friends. Hearing that Cosimo viewed his book on Descartes negatively, Spinoza also wanted an interview, but was told that the prince preferred not to receive 'such a man'.[115] On becoming grand duke in 1670, Cosimo vigorously championed the clergy's claims to supremacy over Tuscany's intellectual and cultural life, collaborated with the Inquisition in censoring books and controlling the book-trade, and leaned heavily on the university at Pisa, which he considered a dangerous nest of 'innovators'.[116] This once flourishing academy still boasted some eminent professors, but the rigid conservatism, and prohibition on Cartesianism imposed by Cosimo accelerated the steady shrinkage in student numbers noticeable there since the mid-seventeenth century, the university continuing to contract until, by the 1730s, a mere 200 students remained.[117]

The suffused, discreet character of Florentine participation in the early Enlightenment was exemplified by such figures as Magalotti, Alessandro Marchetti (c.1632–1714), a philosophy professor at Pisa, immersed in Galileo and Descartes but debarred from teaching the ideas he was preoccupied with, who eased his frustration by translating Lucretius' great Epicurean poem, *De Rerum Natura*, into Italian during the years 1664–8 but was then forbidden to publish it,[118] and the grand duke's famous librarian, Antonio Magliabechi (1633–1714), the most celebrated librarian of the age.[119] Magliabechi's correspondents, Bayle and Leibniz among them, were to be found every-

---

[112] Scherz, *Pionier der Wissenschaft*, 20–1; Totaro, 'Niels Stensen', 148.

[113] Van de Plas, *Niels Stensen*, 34–7.   [114] Totaro, 'Antonio Magliabecchi', 555.

[115] Casini, *Introduzione*, i, 232; Totaro, 'Niels Stensen', 161.

[116] Ibid., 162; Carranza, *Monsignor Gaspare Cerati*, 8, 18; Davidson, 'Unbelief and Atheism', 84.

[117] Carranza, *Monsignor Gaspare Cerati*, 209; Ferrone, *Intellectual Roots*, 4; Di Simone, 'Admission', 307–8.

[118] Marchetti tried again to publish his translation after Cosimo's accession, offering to dedicate his translation to the new Grand Duke himself, but again he was forbidden to publish it; nevertheless, his translation became well-known in Tuscany, Rome, and beyond, circulating widely in manuscript until finally it appeared in November 1718, three years after his death, as a clandestine publication with 'London' falsely given on the title-page, probably at Naples; Saccenti, *Lucrezio*, 19–20; Stone, *Vico's Cultural History*, 222.

[119] Holberg, *Memoirs*, 63.

where and even the most recondite bibliographical news reached him from every land.[120] His phenomenal memory, keen intelligence, and huge personal library, as well as his grasp of what was in the books he perused, made him a veritable oracle of contemporary learning and the international Republic of Letters. When visiting Italy, eminent *érudits* from abroad, including Leibniz, who visited Florence late in 1689, judged it essential not just call on Magliabechi but also, at least in part, to base their wider intellectual strategy in Italy on his advice.[121] Through Magliabechi, information about—and for the favoured few—access to prohibited ideas, books, and manuscripts was readily available even in the heart of Cosimo III's Tuscany.

For half a century scarcely any new philosophical and scientific ideas received official encouragement in the grand duchy with the exception, during the closing years of Cosimo's rule, of English philosophical concepts judged directly useful to the strengthening of belief in revealed religion, especially the 'argument from design' in the version propounded by such writers as John Ray and William Derham. This indubitably involved some concession to modernity, for this kind of physico-theology was ultimately inseparable from Copernican heliocentrism, and closely associated with Boyle and Newtonianism. But despite the qualms of the Inquisition, which nearly blocked the project, the Tuscan Court eventually concluded that the advantages of espousing such reasoning outweighed the drawbacks. A friend of Newton and a scientist skilled at wielding the microscope, as well as a vicar, William Derham (1657–1735) had delivered the London Boyle Lectures in 1711–12, adhering closely to Ray in affirming that the intricacy and complexity of the bodily structures revealed by science proves the world 'a work too grand for anything less than a God to make'.[122] When publication of the Italian translation of Derham's *Physico-theology* (1713), was finally authorized in Florence, in July 1719, it was stressed that his and Ray's physico-theology was not just acceptable from the Catholic standpoint but positively 'useful'.[123]

The death of Cosimo ushered in a period of partial liberalization in the grand duchy and a noticeable lessening of the Church's sway, under the last of the Medici grand dukes, Gian Gastone (ruled 1723–37).[124] Fond of boys and drinking to excess, Gian Gastone, who had lived for some years in central Europe, had a taste for new and foreign philosophy, especially Leibniz and Wolff. Discarding his father's policies, he showed distinctly less reverence for the Church, reduced the disabilities affecting the Jews, and eased Cosimo's draconian restrictions on the book trade. He also permitted the professors of Pisa, after half a century of repression, freedom to discuss the new philosophies and scientific concepts though, much to the resentment of some professors, he also appointed the crypto-deist Giovanni Alberto de Soria (1707–67), who was

---

[120] Fardella, *Animae humanae incorporea*, preface, p. v; Mastellone, *Pensiero politico*, 100; Totaro, 'Antonio Magliabechi', 549–51.

[121] Robinet, *G. W. Leibniz. Iter Italicum*, 28–30, 215; Waquet, *Modèle français*, 397–9

[122] Quoted in Willey, *Eighteenth-Century Background*, 44.

[123] Derham, *Dimostrazione*, 381; Ferrone, *Intellectual Roots*, 78–9.

[124] Casini, *Introduzione*, i, 227; Carranza, *Monsignor Gaspare Cerati*, 21; Burr Litchfield, *Emergence*, 276.

to emerge in the 1730s and 1740s as one of the leading philosophical minds in Italy, to a lectureship in philosophy there, in 1727, at the startlingly young age of 20. De Soria was seen as belonging to the intellectual following of Marchetti and widely suspected of being a modern 'adherent' of Epicurus, a member of the philosophical underground, steeped in libertine ideas, reaching back to Vanini, Bruno, Pomponazzi, and Machiavelli, and allegedly receptive to the new deistic ideas infiltrating from beyond the Alps.[125] Certainly De Soria revered the memory of his gifted predecessor, boldly praising his Italian rendering of Lucretius as 'nobilissima'. De Soria classified him significantly as a disciple of Democritus, implying that Marchetti had adhered to an uncompromisingly mechanistic view of causation and (like the Spinozists) the innateness of motion in matter as well as the oneness of body and soul.[126]

Gian Gastone's liberalizing attitude quickly led to friction with the ecclesiastical authorities, in no way lessened by his decision in 1731 to permit a notorious deist, the Baron von Stosch—latterly driven from Rome as an undesirable influence and a suspected spy for the British government (in particular, regarding the Court of James, the Old Pretender to the British thrones)[127]—to settle in Florence, bringing his splendid collection of art and antiquities, and a library reportedly teeming with every sort of heterodox and freethinking literature.[128] Even more irritating to the Papacy was Gian Gastone's decision in 1734 to erect a handsome monument to Galileo, capped by a portrait bust of the great scientist, in one of the main churches of Florence, Santa Croce, whither, a century after his condemnation in Rome, Galileo's remains were duly transferred amid the pomp of a public commemoration.

Despite several interventions by the Inquisition to try to reverse the erosion of its authority, including an ultimately unsuccessful attempt to get Stosch expelled from the grand duchy, the trial and imprisonment of a friend of De Soria, the deist poet, Tommaso Crudeli, an admirer of Marchetti and Sarpi accused of denigrating theology as 'superfluous and useless', and, finally, in 1745, a crack-down on De Soria himself, an incident cited by the ecclesiastical authorities as a 'great example for teaching [scholars] to be very moderate and circumspect in their speech',[129] intellectual censorship in Tuscany continued to ease, and official encouragement of moderate Enlightenment trends to increase from the late 1720s onwards. Curiously, at that very moment, as Italy's formerly most reactionary state shifted to a more flexible stance, its place as the chief opponent of the Enlightenment in Italy was taken by a principality which had previously kept to a liberal intellectual policy linked to political and administrative reform—Piedmont, or the kingdom of Savoy.

Administrative reform in Savoy culminated in the early 1720s when the king, Vittore Amadeo II (ruled 1675–1730), reorganized secondary education in the kingdom, reducing the teaching functions of the clergy and refounding the University of Turin under a new constitution, effectively transferring it from ecclesiastical to royal control.[130]

---

[125] Fardella, *Animae humanae incorporea*, 276–7.   [126] De Soria, *Raccolta*, ii, 36–8.
[127] Montesquieu, *Oeuvres complètes*, 262.   [128] Borroni Salvadori, 'Tra la fine', 566, 571.
[129] Ferrone, *Intellectual Roots*, 272–3; see also Cochrane, *Florence*, 356, 362; Davidson, 'Toleration', 231–2.
[130] Symcox, *Victor Amadeus II*, 222–5; Carpanetto and Ricuperati, *Italy*, 144–6; Di Simone, 'Admission', 314.

Briefly, this process was accompanied by an official espousal of moderate Enlightenment thought. Indeed, after the War of the Spanish Succession (1702–13) something approaching a Neo-Cartesian and *Malebranchiste* ascendancy set in.[131] When the revived university reopened its doors, in November 1720, the inaugural oration delivered by Bernardo Andrea Lama (d.1760), a Neapolitan disciple of Malebranche who had spent some years in Paris and was later, during the 1730s, one of the chief disseminators of Newtonianism in Italy,[132] included a scathing attack on the scholastic Aristotelianism still widely favoured in southern Europe. Thus, even though the friction between the Court at Turin and the Papacy during this reign was essentially jurisdictional rather than doctrinal, it nevertheless to some extent encouraged innovative scientific and philosophical debates and trends.

What was widely discerned at the time as a crucial change in intellectual policy ensued, following the Concordat of 1727 between Vittore Amadeo and the Pope, heralding a marked shift in the attitude of the Court to philosophy and related issues. From 1727 the Pope, 'charmé de la devotion du roi', as Montesquieu puts it,[133] made substantial concessions over ecclesiastical jurisdiction and privilege in return for Savoy's support for the doctrinal and ideological goals of the Church. The Inquisition was restored and, in the late 1720s, especially after the accession of Carlo Emmanuele III (ruled 1730–73), philosophical debate came to be frowned upon and prominent adherents of the new systems were regarded as a readily expendable asset.

In 1730 a joint royal and papal investigation began into what were deemed suspicious and undesirable tendencies at the university. Several professors were purged. Lama departed for the friendlier atmosphere of Vienna.[134] The officials secular and ecclesiastical who purged the university attributed the blight to the allegedly excessive intellectual freedom which results from theology being dominated by philosophy, instead of philosophy by theology, as in any properly ordered society. Even so, they reported, matters had not lapsed to the point that Creation by a providential God was denied, or anyone held the 'world is eternal', or other pernicious concepts 'through which one arrives finally at the impious doctrine of Benedetto Spinosa which has caused a villainous atheism in many regions of Europe'.[135] After 1730 Savoy gained the reputation of being virtually the most unenlightened land in Europe. In the late 1730s, the marquis d'Argens derided the Savoyards as a benighted people virtually impervious to modern thought. When one mentions the names of the *savants* of Europe to them, he sneered, they ask only whether they are 'good Catholics'; there, he added, Le Clerc passes for a simpleton, Bayle 'pour un sot', and Arnauld for a liar.[136]

The readiest point of entry in northern Italy for first Cartesianism, then radical and Leibnizian ideas, and, after 1730, for Newtonianism and finally Wolffianism, was the Venetian Republic, including Padua, then still probably the liveliest university town in the peninsula. Casanova, who studied there in the early 1740s, stresses the

---

[131] Venturi, 'Gli anni '30', 92.
[132] Galiani and Grandi, *Carteggio*, 82–3; Symcox, *Victor Amadeus II*, 219; Ferrone, *Intellectual Roots*, 32, 97.
[133] Montesquieu, *Oeuvres complètes*, 235.   [134] Rotondò, 'Censura ecclesiastica', 1485.
[135] Ibid.   [136] D'Argens, *Lettres juives*, i, 331 and ii, 74–5.

extraordinary vitality and lack of discipline among the students. Book censorship in the Venetian Republic was patently weaker, and the powers of the Inquisition more limited, than probably anywhere else in Italy.[137] There were also numerous learned men familiar with intellectual life abroad among the patricians as well as the academic fraternity. When Leibniz visited Venice, in March 1689 and again early in 1690, he became friendly with Michelangelo Fardella (1650–1718), a Sicilian friar who had become a leading luminary in both Padua and Venice, 'because I saw he combined meditation on intellectual things with understanding of mathematics, and because he pursued truth with great ardour'.[138] Fardella was already known as the foremost Italian Cartesian advocate of his generation, and a fervent champion of Descartes' two-substance doctrine, which he judged the best shield for Christian belief against the modern *Epicurei*. Insisting on the human soul's entire separateness from the body,[139] in his *Filosofia Cartesiana Impugnata* (1698) Fardella accounts Cartesianism, if only cardinals and bishops would see it, their surest and best defence against the atheism of 'Democrito, Obbes e Spinosa'.[140] Yet, despite initial reservations, Fardella's growing admiration for Leibniz also prompted him, like other Venetian intellectuals later, to promote Leibnizian influence, especially among Padua's mathematicians and scientists.

But if Venice was the gateway to Italy for Cartesianism, Leibnizianism, and much else from the 1680s onwards, it was equally a focus of determined traditionalist resistance. Suspected (with some reason) of Protestant inclinations, casting doubt on transubstantiation, and implying that vows of chastity are contrary to the Law of Nature, Fardella himself was investigated by the Inquisition, in 1689.[141] Despite memories of Sarpi and the republic's former resistance to papal pretensions, ecclesiastical power and old-style piety both loomed large. Montesquieu concluded during his visit to the city in 1728, that 'les Jésuites ont rendu les sénateurs dévots de façon qu'ils font tout ce qu'ils veulent à Venise. O tempora ! O mores!'.[142] Historically, there had long been an undercurrent of Naturalism, and free thought and libertine tendencies may have been more rife than ever under the surface, but outwardly Venice was still a culture steeped in conventional religiosity. Indeed, it was also in Venice that Montesquieu commented sardonically: 'jamais on n'a vu tant de dévots, et si peu de dévotion qu'en Italie'.[143] But if, as events later proved, ecclesiastical power seemed more imposing than it was in reality, intermittently the Papacy, the Inquisition, and the Jesuits could mobilize the Venetian government against new intellectual trends, and not without considerable local support. For many onlookers, including Fardella, were deeply apprehensive of the new *Epicurei* and their 'atheistic' ideas. Nor was anyone in the slightest doubt as to who, ultimately, was the chief inspirer of the modern *Epicurei*. If Casanova mentions only one modern philosopher in the preface to his memoirs where he explains his philosophy of life, nothing was more apt than that that one should be Spinoza.

---

[137] Georgelin, *Venise*, 714–17, 1128; Waquet, *Modèle français*, 230.

[138] Leibniz, *Philosophical Essays*, 101; Robinet, *G. W. Leibniz Iter*, 43.

[139] Fardella, *Utraque Dialectica*, i, 105–6, 114; Fardella, *Animae Humanae Incorporea*, 81–2, 123, 251–77, 380–8.

[140] Fardella, *Filosofia Cartesiana*, 1st lettera, 18.   [141] Robinet, *G. W. Leibniz Iter*, 405–6.

[142] Ibid., 220.   [143] Montesquieu, *Oeuvres complètes*, 216.

From the 1670s down to the 1720s, however, by far the most important intellectual ferment in Italy was that which welled up in Naples. By 1680 a philosophical coterie inspired by an ardent Cartesianism had taken shape there which was unique in Italy in extent, vigour, and creativity. Earlier, a libertine underground had flourished since the Renaissance, feeding on the usual stock writers of Franco-Italian libertine culture— Epicurus, Lucretius, Lucian, Machiavelli, Pomponazzi, Cardano, Bodin, and Montaigne—and, judging from the scope and character of subsequent debates, seems to have moulded a philosophically aware coterie familiar with Naturalistic and republican ideas and mentally already attuned to deploying philosophy against prevailing structures of authority, tradition, and faith. Yet without the rise of the New Philosophy, the Neapolitan *novatores* would in all probability never have emerged into the open or become an effective vehicle for the propagation of new philosophical and scientific ideas in Italian culture more widely.

Cartesianism provided a matrix capable not just of accommodating, but also inseparably blending, both a moderate stream, eager to overthrow the hegemony of scholastic Aristotelianism while remaining loyal to the Church, and the libertine Naturalistic undercurrent. Known as the Accademia degli Investiganti, these *érudits* publicly declared themselves admirers of Descartes and devotees of philosophy, science, and mathematics. They also invoked, if to a lesser extent, Gassendi, Marchetti, the physicist Borrelli, Emanuel Maignan, and Robert Boyle.[144] While they insisted with growing boldness on the necessity and usefulness of 'freedom to philosophize',[145] the régime, unlike that in Tuscany, discreetly encouraged their activities. In particular, the Neapolitan *moderni* enjoyed the favour of the marqués del Carpio (viceroy, 1683–7) and the Andalusian grandee Don Luis de la Cerda, duke of Medinaceli (viceroy, 1696–1702), who had known Queen Christina in Rome and, on arriving in Naples, showed a keen interest in philosophy as well as art, opera, and bordellos.

Among early leaders of the Neapolitan Cartesians were physicians such as Tommaso Cornelio (1614–84) who, as early as 1661, styled Descartes a glittering new light to the age, outshining by far Bacon, Gassendi, and all other moderns,[146] and Leonardo di Capoa (1617–95), an implacable foe of Galenist medicine. Other luminaries included Francesco d'Andrea (1625–98), a legal official, and the legendary philologist and teacher, Gregorio Caloprese (1650–1714), a 'great Cartesian', Vico called him, who spent much of his time south of Paestum in the coastal town of Scalea, where he established his philosophical school.[147] No less fervent a Cartesian was the merchant philosopher Giuseppe Valletta (d. 1714), Leibniz's host when he reached Naples in 1689, and owner of the most impressive private library—of some 16,000 volumes—in the city.[148] His library, which was visited by the viceroy in 1688 and liberally served all

---

[144] Quondam, *Cultura e ideologia*, 55–61; Mastellone, *Francesco d'Andrea*, 108–9; Mastellone, *Pensiero Politico*, 86–90, 185; Suppa, *l'Accademia*, 11–13.

[145] Cornelio, *Progymnasmata Physica*, 93–4; Capoa, *Del Parere*, i, 60–2, and ii, 140–1.

[146] Cornelio, *Progymnasmata Physica*, 93–4; Mastellone, *Pensiero politico*, 119.

[147] Quondam, *Cultura e ideologia*, 17–18, 42, 48–9; Suppa, *L'Accademia*, 11–13.

[148] Robinet, *G. W. Leibniz Iter*, 28–30, 38–9.

the Cartesian fraternity, who also often held their meetings there, was effectively the headquarters of the Investiganti.[149] A younger but no less dedicated Cartesian, who came to the fore in the 1690s, initially an admirer of Fardella, was the lawyer, Costatino Grimaldi (1667–1750).

Cartesianism created a new context in Naples in that henceforth an organized intellectual opposition, openly aspiring to supplant traditional academic culture in the viceroyalty,[150] and comprising both moderate and radical impulses, rapidly penetrated all public and private intellectual discourse. The interplay of moderate and radical tendencies was perceptible from the outset, moreover, being inherent, for instance, in Caloprese's teaching method, which first solidly grounded his followers in Cartesianism and then required the deployment of Descartes' arguments to refute Lucretius and the modern atheists, especially Spinoza.[151] As early as 1671 the Congregation of the Holy Office, in Rome, warned the Archbishop of Naples about the spread of the 'ideas of Descartes which some apply in the theological field with exceedingly dangerous consequences'.[152] It was not until the mid-1680s, though, that there occurred a direct clash between ecclesiastical and academic authority and the spreading New Philosophy which, in Naples, additionally assumed an anti-Jesuit and pro-Jansenist tinge.[153] In 1685–6 there was a flurry of sermons in the city, publicly decrying 'Renato' and Gassendi as 'atheists' and 'very dangerous'. In March 1688, a lawyer who had attended gatherings in Valletta's house denounced the group to the Inquisition as mockers of Christ and 'atheists'. Little more happened, however, until after the arrival of the new hard-line Archbishop of Naples, Cardinal Giacomo Cantelmo (1645–1702), who remained in office from 1691 until his death. Orchestrated by this prelate and his ally, Benedetti, rector of the Jesuit college, a general campaign was unleashed against Cartesianism, *filosofi moderni*, and 'atheism', the Jesuits, here as elsewhere, being especially eager to safeguard their hold over secondary education in the viceroyalty.[154]

In 1691 the Inquisition arrested two of the more junior Investiganti, Basilio Gianelli and Giacinto de Cristoforo, accusing them of denying miracles, Heaven and Hell, and the divinity of Christ, as well as claiming Christ was an 'impostor', that there are no saints, the Pope has no legitimate authority, there were men before Adam—a clear echo of La Peyrère—that men are composed of atoms like animals, and 'all things are ruled by Nature'.[155] This episode, dubbed the 'trial of the atheists', caused a considerable stir throughout Italy and as far afield as Madrid. In the end, the efforts of the archbishop, the Jesuits, and the Inquisition were thwarted by the Spanish viceroy and his officials, who refused to accept that Cartesianism and the New Philosophy should be generally condemned.[156] Furthermore, the viceroy objected to the Inquisition's pro-

[149] Robinet, *G. W. Leibniz Iter*; Comparato, *Giuseppe Valletta*, 88–9; Waquet, *Modèle français*, 92.
[150] Quondam, *Cultura e ideologica*, 55–6, 215–18.   [151] Ibid., 49–50; Spinelli, *Riflessioni*, 2.
[152] Grimaldi, *Memorie*, 9; Davidson, 'Unbelief and Atheism', 83–4.
[153] Quondam, *Cultura e ideologia*, 48, 61, 218.   [154] Grimaldi, *Memorie*, 3–6.
[155] Osbat, *L'Inquisizione a Napoli*, 255–6, 265–6, 271; Gregory,' Libertinisme érudit', 334.
[156] Stone, *Vico's Cultural History*, 34–5.

cedure, and even expelled the senior inquisitor for exceeding his powers, provoking a commotion over the scope of Inquisition jurisdiction in the viceroyalty, which transferred responsibility for resolving the imbroglio to Madrid and Rome. Hence, the lack of co-operation between government and ecclesiastical authorities precluded any clear-cut conclusion. Even so, the campaign did not entirely founder. Cristoforo languished in the archbishop's dungeon until 1697, the Investiganti were firmly pinned on the defensive and henceforth obliged constantly to affirm their Catholic orthodoxy, while the dangers of Cartesianism, atomism, Naturalism, and texts such as Marchetti's Lucretius were abundantly advertised.[157]

By the 1690s, in Rome as in Naples, the ecclesiastical hierarchy was in arms against the *Cartesiani* and other new-fangled *fisico-matematici*, and still more their radical offshoots. The papal authorities in Rome formally banned Spinoza *in toto* by a decree of August 1690.[158] But neither the offensive against Cartesianism, nor that against Spinoza, could succeed simply by asserting, however impressively, the power and authority of the Papacy, the episcopacy, the religious orders, and the Inquisition. The princely and viceregal courts of Italy had to be persuaded of the need to impose, or more accurately re-impose, stringent intellectual and academic discipline. The whole enterprise depended on launching a successful publicity campaign, demonstrating the dangers forcefully enough to produce firm and co-ordinated peninsula-wide action. But this, in turn, obliged the Church's spokesmen to enter the intellectual arena themselves, and engage directly in philosophical polemics with Cartesians and *Malebranchistes*, and it was precisely here that supporters of reaction proved unable to muster enough authority and cogency to overwhelm their adversaries.

Nevertheless, powerful anti-Cartesian and anti-Gassendist polemics poured forth in Latin and Italian alike. In 1694 Bernardo de Rojas published his *De formarum generatione contra Atomistas* at Naples, championing Aristotle's doctrine of 'substantial forms', lambasting Gassendi as a disciple of the ancient atheistic Greek thinkers Democritus and Epicurus,[159] and styling Descartes' doctrine of motion as external to and separate from matter deeply flawed and apt to generate vast confusion and danger.[160] Meanwhile, the foremost publicist against the *Cartesiani* in the vernacular was the indefatigable Benedetti, who followed up his *Philosophia peripatetica* (four volumes, Naples, 1687), with the widely read *Lettere apologetiche in difesa della teologia scolastica* (Naples, 1694), published under the pseudonym Benedetto Aletino, and maintaining the New Philosophy leads inevitably to spiritual catastrophe and weakening of Catholic belief.[161]

Compelled to defend themselves and their friends, without hope of obtaining ecclesiastical permission to publish, d'Andrea and Valletta penned vigorous defences of Cartesianism which then circulated in manuscript from the mid-1690s.[162] Valletta

[157] Comparato, *Giuseppe Valletta*, 143–8; Ferrone, *Intellectual Roots*, 3–4, 17–18.
[158] Totaro, 'L'Index', 362.   [159] Rojas, *De formarum generatione*, 116–19.   [160] Ibid., 153–8.
[161] Bendedetti, *Lettere apologetiche*, 182–3, 293, 312; Galiani and Grandi, *Carteggio*, 259–60; Casini, *Introduzione*, i, 246–7.
[162] Comparato, *Giuseppe Valletta*, 219–24.

stressed Descartes' philosophical and scientific cogency and, no less adamantly his Catholic zeal, claiming Aristotelian anti-Cartesianism is basically a 'Protestant' tendency, ascribing the vitriolic encounters among the 'Calvinists' of Holland, Germany, and Switzerland to an international Calvinist conspiracy designed to vitiate a philosophy which is modern, true, and supportive of the Catholic Church.[163] Descartes' 'fondamento principale', according to Valletta, is divine Providence and his other key point the 'immortality of the soul'.[164] Extolling the achievements of the French philosophers, Malebranche, Nicole, and Arnauld, he insisted (rather dubiously) that outside Italy Cartesianism was now widely accepted in Catholic countries and warmly espoused in the 'best universities of Europe'.[165]

No more than Caloprese could Valletta circumvent the thorny issue of Spinoza, since the crux of Benedetti's Aristotelian offensive was the accusation that Descartes' ideas tend inherently to Naturalism and atheism. If Jesuits, the Inquisition, and adherents of Aristotle's 'substantial forms' claimed atheistic philosophy and Naturalism were now the paramount danger in Italy, and that the threat was rooted in Cartesianism, Valletta stressed the differences between Descartes and Spinoza, considering this vital if he was to vindicate modern philosophy and repel the Jesuit onslaught. His critics' prime error, he insisted, was their failure to realize that it was Spinoza, not Descartes, who forms the chief root of modern Naturalism and unbelief,[166] Valletta held that, unless swiftly rectified, this colossal error would destroy everything, including the Church. By failing to grasp the true nature of Italy's philosophical predicament, and attacking the wise Descartes, scholastics and traditionalists were in effect serving as the unwitting tools of the Spinozists. In a later work, the *Istoria filosofica* (1704), Valletta styles Spinoza a 'monster of Aristotelian impiety' whose denial of divine Providence, Revelation, and the immortality of the soul, as well as of Biblical prophecy, the Devil, Heaven and Hell, shows that 'in fact he was never a *Renatista*'.[167] Far from manifesting affinities with Descartes, Spinoza's true kinship is with the atheistic pagan Aristotle, the ruinous consequences of whose system, he alleged, were daily becoming clearer.

Backed by the ecclesiastical authorities, only Aristotelians could publish polemical works of philosophy in Italy until the late 1690s, at any rate outside the Venetian Republic. But from 1699 pro-Cartesian works began to appear also in Naples, albeit semi-clandestinely. In that year, Costatino Grimaldi completed his *Risposta* to Benedetti and, knowing ecclesiastical permission to publish in Naples or anywhere in Italy was out of the question, sent the manuscript to be discreetly printed in Geneva (or Cologne) in 500 copies, and then smuggled back into the viceroyalty, stoking a fresh uproar.[168] Benedetti's aim, held Grimaldi, was to discredit the Naples *letterati* by linking them as a group to the 'heretics' of northern Europe. But this, he contended, following Valletta, was an outrageous calumny, since in reality it is Aristotelianism

---

[163] Valletta, *Lettera*, 55, 57, 70–1.   [164] Ibid.   [165] Ibid., 61–9.   [166] Ibid., 71.

[167] Valletta, *Opera filosofiche*, 325–6; see also [Grimaldi], *Risposta alla terza lettera*, 240–3; Mastellone, *Pensiero politico*, 192.

[168] Mastellone, *Pensiero politico*, 157–8.

which nourishes, and the New Philosophy which undermines, Protestantism.[169] When Benedetti then published a second *Lettera*, turning his guns on Grimaldi, the latter answered with a second *Risposta* again printed abroad, and smuggled back in 1702, with the connivance of the viceroy's officials, this time in 600 copies. In 1703, again with the clandestine backing of the secular authorities, Grimaldi's reply to Benedetti's third *Lettera* was published this time in 750 copies, and in Naples itself, albeit with 'Cologne' falsely declared on the title-page.[170]

In these publications unlicensed by ecclesiastical authority, Grimaldi adopts a more abrasive style than had his hero Fardella in Venice. Where Benedetti repeatedly cites the condemnation of Cartesianism by various northern European universities, urging this as proof that Cartesianism harms religion and is intellectually pernicious, Grimaldi mocks the Sorbonne[171] and asks why Neapolitans should defer to judgements about philosophy reached in Dutch, Swiss, and German universities.[172] The principal antagonists of Descartes in northern Europe, he mentions in particular Voetius and Petrus van Mastricht, were indubitably heretics, while the foremost French philosophical commentators, Arnauld, Clerisier, Malebranche, and Régis, were committed Cartesians and good Catholics.[173] As Fardella insisted, Descartes' doctrine of two substances safeguards the immortality of the soul and the realm of spiritual forces, providing the key to successfully combining the New Philosophy with Catholic teaching and ecclesiastical authority.

Benedetti could not allow such pretensions to go unchallenged.[174] Backed by influential friends in Rome, he struck back with his *Difesa della Terza Lettera* (Rome, 1705), again emphasizing Louis XIV's implacable hostility to Cartesianism and that French royal policy on philosophy was being urged and supported by the foremost ecclesiastics in France. Nor by any means was it simply the Sorbonne but also Louvain, the prime seat of learning in the Catholic Netherlands and, by decree of the senate of May 1667, Caen university which had denounced Descartes as intellectually subversive, harmful to faith, and fatal to authority.[175] Catholics, furthermore, ought not to disdain the judgments of Voetius and Mastricht, or the prohibition of Cartesianism in Protestant universities,[176] for however deplorable their theology they correctly diagnose the intellectual perils inherent in the New Philosophy. Hence both Catholic and Protestant universities agree that Cartesianism is damaging and 'this is not good for you, believe me, Signore Grimaldi!' The precise implications of Descartes' two substances might be debatable but Cartesianism, argues Benedetti, plainly generates radical offshoots which, as everyone sees, destroy faith, tradition, and morality. Noting that the anonymous writer (Lodewijk Meyer) of the *Philosophia S. Scripturae Interpres*, a work which had caused great scandal in the north, expressly invokes Descartes and derives his venomous principles from the latter's philosophy,[177] Benedetti adduced as the

---

[169] [Grimaldi], *Risposta alla lettera apologetica*, 29, 62; Grimaldi, *Discussioni*, i, 103, 128–9.
[170] Giannone, *Opere*, 64; Stone, *Vico's Cultural History*, 65–71; Mastellone, *Pensiero politico*, 157–9.
[171] Grimaldi, *Risposta alla terza lettera*, 35, 51.   [172] Ibid., 62, 66, 68.   [173] Ibid., 60–1, 66, 82.
[174] Mastellone, *Pensiero politico*, 158–9.   [175] Benedetti, *Difesa della terza lettera*, 5–6, 12, 16–19, 22.
[176] Ibid., 45–9, 90.   [177] Ibid., 60, 244; Totaro, 'L'Index', 361.

clearest proof that Cartesianism produces atheistic and Naturalistic ideas the intellectual genesis of Spinoza himself: does not the anonymous author (Jarig Jelles) of the preface to Spinoza's *Opera Posthuma* insist that in his youth Spinoza steeped himself in Descartes? Benedetti also cites Bayle's article on Spinoza to prove that Spinoza's doctrine that God is equivalent to the unalterable laws of nature derives directly from the mechanistic categories introduced by Descartes. If Spinozism demolishes Christian faith, Cartesianism, maintains Benedetti, corrodes true belief by rendering incomprehensible the Church's teaching on the Trinity, the Incarnation, and the Eucharist as well as making it hard to conceive of angels.[178]

The viceroys' discreet support for the Neapolitan *Cartesiani*, a group which at the end of the 1690s and opening years of the new century, included Vico and Paolo Mattia Doria, assumed more concrete form during the viceroyalty of Medinaceli who encouraged the *letterati* to set up a literary academy which held its inaugural meeting in the viceregal palace in March 1698. Over the next years, Doria participated extensively in its proceedings and Vico on its fringes, but the surviving evidence shows the formal debates of the Accademia de Medina Coeli were confined to exclusively neutral humanistic, historical, and philological topics, deliberately eschewing contentious philosophical, theological, and scientific issues.[179] The policy of the viceregal régime, evidently, was to shield the *Cartesiani* from their opponents and encourage their activity, while simultaneously avoiding giving public support to the New Philosophy.

Medinaceli lost his enthusiasm for the academy which bore his name, however, following the Bourbon succession to the Spanish throne in 1700, and the onset of a period of acute political instability in Spanish Italy, with part of the nobility supporting the new Bourbon monarchy and part plotting with Vienna to drive the Spaniards out and bring Naples and the other territories back under Habsburg sway. The atmosphere of political intrigue was further intensified by the Neapolitans' lively recollection of the Masaniello revolution of 1647–8, when the common people rose in revolt against both the Spanish régime and the nobility, and, briefly, a Neapolitan republic was established.

A plot to assassinate Medinaceli while he was out late at night visiting his favourite soprano foundered, as did the attempt by the mainly aristocratic conspirators to capture the principal citadel in Naples. Efforts to incite the common people, invoking Masaniello, were equally unsuccessful, and finally the viceroy's troops overpowered the hard core anti-Bourbon faction in fighting in the heart of the city. The conspirators, headed by the Prince of Macchia, were executed and their heads displayed on pikes. Shaken, Medinaceli evidently decided that philosophy might indeed be subversive; at any rate, he dissolved his academy and withdrew his support for Cartesianism. Vico, Doria, and the rest appear, nevertheless, to have reacted with shock and horror to the factionalism and selfish motives of the noble insurgents and were largely unsympathetic to what they considered the irrationality and violence of the

---

[178] Benedetti, *Difesa della terza lettera.*, 139–40, 154.
[179] Levine, 'Giambattista Vico', 61–3; Stone, *Vico's Cultural History*, 58.

Massaniello insurgency.[180] Their political ideal was to curb both baronial and popular lawlessness through enlightened government based on the rule of law and, in the case of Doria, an admirer of the Dutch Republic, promoting republican values and consciousness.[181]

Six years later, in 1707, Spanish Bourbon rule in Naples did collapse and an invading Austrian army drove the Spaniards out. Doria, Vico, Grimaldi, and others, deeply affected by the political instability and intrigues of 1700–2, now had to adjust to the new Austrian Habsburg régime, directed from Vienna, which, for some years, remained in a somewhat precarious position, being opposed by the Papacy as well as the Spanish and French kings. Furthermore, the new Austrian viceroy quickly became embroiled in dispute with Rome over ecclesiastical privilege and benefices, which in turn prompted the new administration, like its predecessor, to trim back the Church's social and political influence and, linked to this, to encourage criticism of the jurisdictional claims of the Papacy, the episcopacy, the Inquisition, and religious orders.

This institutional friction between the new Austrian Habsburg régime and the papal government in Rome subtly influenced the changing intellectual atmosphere by inducing the authorities to adopt the same comparatively permissive attitude as their Spanish predecessors to the publication of books censured by the Church. Grimaldi, for instance, was commissioned to write and publish tracts affirming the right of the Neapolitan state to tax ecclesiastical lands, which were promptly banned by the Papacy. At the same time, with ecclesiastical book censorship being deliberately subverted by the new régime, the philosophical coterie could publish semi-clandestinely at Naples a variety of philosophical works acceptable to officialdom, which the ecclesiastical authorities opposed. These included a new edition of Galileo's writings in 1710, an Italian translation of Adrien Baillet's biography of Descartes in 1713, with 'Basel' given on the title-page, and in 1722, with 'Turin' falsely declared the place of publication, the first Italian translation of Descartes' *Principia* under the title *I principi della filosofia*, together with a remarkable preface defending the right of women to participate in philosophical debate, penned by Giuseppa Leonora Barbapiccola, a follower of Doria and translator of the text.[182]

By the opening years of the Austrian Habsburg régime, it was clear that Cartesianism had become powerfully entrenched in Naples and Sicily and was, in practice, being condoned by the secular authorities. However, here as elsewhere, Cartesianism could not supplant Aristotelianism in academic life or secondary education, and was strenuously resisted by much of the clergy. Consequently philosophy, and with it high culture and higher education, was progressively fragmented in Naples, creating an unprecedented intellectual disarray which, in turn, impelled philosophical enquiry onward into new and uncharted waters. Giambattista Vico (1668–1744), for instance, had in the 1690s been a more ardent Cartesian than he later cared to admit.[183] By

---

[180] Mastellone, *Pensiero politico*, 198–207.
[181] Ibid., 215–16; Zambelli, 'Il rogo postumo', 162, 183; Mastellone, 'Holland as a political model', 581–2.
[182] On this publication, see Barbapiccola, 'Traduttrice', 5–8; Stone, *Vico's Cultural History*, 214–15.
[183] Levine, 'Giambattista Vico', 61, 65–6.

1707–8, however, he had experienced a change of heart, concluding that neither Cartesianism nor *Malebranchisme* could resolve the new spiritual impasse. In a public oration at the university, delivered before the new Austrian viceroy in 1708, Vico publicly denounced Cartesianism while, still more, deploring the now growing confusion in higher studies in which 'students' education is so warped and perverted' that a student may well be taught logic by an Aristotelian, physics by an Epicurean, general philosophy by a Cartesian, medicine by a Galenist so that while university graduates 'may become extremely learned in some respects, their culture as a whole (and the whole is really the flower of wisdom) is incoherent'.[184]

Eventually, this quandary was to discredit philosophy itself. After two leading figures of the Neapolitan Enlightenment, Giannone and Grimaldi, fell out of favour and were banned by the secular authorities in the 1720s, the government in Naples began to turn against the new spirit of philosophical enquiry and criticism. Indeed, it became increasingly suspicious of 'philosophy', and Naples eventually lost its former centrality in Italian intellectual life. But until the 1740s the effect was intellectually creative rather than deadening. After Vico and Doria a third major thinker of the Neapolitan Enlightenment arose in the shape of Antonio Genovesi (1712–69) who later, in the 1750s, was to repudiate philosophical enquiry as a seductive but hopeless quest, insisting that the Christian Enlightenment must now concentrate exclusively on practical objectives, eschewing theoretical issues. But as a young scholar, in the 1730s and 1740s, Genovesi emulated Caloprese, Vico, and Doria in seeking overarching metaphysical solutions to the awesome intellectual dilemmas of the age. One of the most comprehensively learned and acute observers of the Italian scene, where subsequently he focused on plans for the improvement of commerce, agriculture, administration, transportation, and law, in the 1740s he tried to identify which philosophical stream of the moderate Enlightenment provided the best bulwark against radical ideas. His two major philosophical works, his *Elementa metaphysicae* (1743) and *Elementorum artis logicocriticae libri V* (1745), are grand surveys in which Genovesi examines all five chief philosophical traditions fighting for mastery of Italy's intellectual life—the scholastic Aristotelianism of the schools and four classes of *moderni*. He finds all the modern trends formidable, acknowledging that all had made vast inroads in Italian culture. Cartesianism deserves considerable respect. Genovesi praised Descartes for demolishing scholasticism, using 'doubt' as an instrument of enquiry to overcome scepticism, and introducing 'freedom to philosophize'; and agrees that the human soul is *substantia incorporea*, totally distinct from matter.[185] But, like Vico and Doria, he also finds Cartesianism seriously flawed, solid insights fatally laced with error, leading ultimately to 'fanaticism' and the overthrow of Christian truth:[186] after all, out of Cartesianism, he concluded scathingly, emerged 'Bekkerianismus et Spinozismus'.[187] Secondly, there were the *Leibnitiani*, or adherents of the Leibnizian-Wolffian system,

---

[184] Vico, *On the Study Methods*, 77, Lilla, *G. B. Vico*, 47–52.
[185] Genovesi, *Elementorum artis*, 22–6, 512–14.   [186] Ibid., 27, 514.
[187] Ibid., 530; Genovesi, *Elementa metaphysicae*, ii, 9.

since the 1690s likewise a powerful force first in Venice and then in all Italy. But here too Genovesi detected weaknesses which led him to infer that the Leibnizian-Wolffian system could not conquer the Italian philosophical arena.[188] Next came the empiricism of Newton and Locke, which again Genovesi approves of in part but then ultimately rejects as incapable of providing an adequate basis for the stable coexistence of reason and faith.[189]

The fourth main category of moderns, and by far the worst, were the radical deists, who deny Christ's Gospel and miracles and reject the absoluteness of 'good' and 'evil' as well as the immortality of the soul—which Locke's empiricism, he notes, disconcertingly fails to rescue.[190] While Genovesi himself was criticized by traditionalists for not attacking the *fatalisti* strenuously enough,[191] he entirely agrees with them that radical ideas pose a grave threat to morality, civil society, and all mankind. Moreover, while he briefly mentions other figures, he is emphatic that the 'head of the modern deists is Spinoza',[192] insisting that the whole thrust of the first part of his *Elementa* is directed principally against the *Democritici* and *Spinozisti*.[193] Striving to overturn Spinoza's Bible criticism, Genovesi lauds Huet's 'most splendid' *Demonstratio* and invokes Houtteville. Attempting to break Spinoza's system, he assails the *Ethics* as well as the *Tractatus Theologico-Politicus* and also such Spinozistic writers as Cuffeler and Boulainvilliers.[194] But ultimately, he found that both he himself and the high culture of his time were trapped in an irresolvable intellectual quandary. He trusts in his faith, repudiating not only radical thought but the supposedly rational Christianity of Le Clerc, insisting that only the 'Church is the legitimate interpreter of Holy Scripture'.[195] But his quest for philosophical truth lapsed into an inconclusive and deeply frustrating deadlock and while he warned of the dangers of turning theology completely away from and against philosophy,[196] he finally became convinced there is simply no fully viable, philosophically coherent basis for enlightened government, education, and high culture.

Caught in this insoluble metaphysical impasse, Genovesi concluded that none of the modern philosophical systems adequately make sense of the world, or are altogether safe for society or individuals to trust in. Ultimately, the *Cartesiani*, *Newtoniani*, and *Leibniziani* are all unreliable and unsatisfactory, just as the Aristotelians are and still more the deism and atheism of the new *Epicurei*: 'nam ex Cartesianismo profluxit Bekkerianismus et Spinozismus, ex Gassenistarum secta materialismus, Leibnitiana philosophia vergit ad idealismum, Neutoniana ad purum mechanismum' (For from Cartesianism flowed Bekkerianism and Spinozism; from the Gassendist sect issued materialism, Leibnizian thought leads to idealism, and Newtonianism to pure

---

[188] Genovesi, *Elementorum artis*, 463–79, 517–18.

[189] Genovesi, *Elementa metaphysicae*, i, 26–33 and ii, 63, 98; Venturi, *Illuminati*, v, 7–8.

[190] Genovesi, *Elementa metaphysicae*, i, 25–6, 41–56, 98–105, 188–9 and ii, 11-38, 137–66, 235–85; Genovesi, *Elementorum artis*, 27, 274–5, 514–30; Ferrone, *Intellectual Roots*, 252.

[191] Genovesi, *Lettere filosofiche*, i, 30–2.   [192] Genovesi, *Elementa metaphysicae*, ii, 11.

[193] Genovesi, *Lettere filosofiche*, i, 32.   [194] Genovesi, *Elementa metaphysicae*, i, 41, 50 6, 98 100.

[195] Genovesi, *Elementorum artis*, 343.   [196] Genovesi, *Lettere filosofiche*, i, 40.

mechanism).[197] Pantheistic atheism, avers Genovesi, reaches back to the Pythagoreans and Eleatics of ancient Greece[198] and is now the chief threat to the well-being of Italy. But how can the *Spinozisti* be defeated philosophically? Genovesi admits that he simply does not know.[199] Perhaps, in the end, only faith, the human heart, and determined government action can repel the threat.

Thus pure philosophy came to appear bankrupt, more apt to mislead than help man towards his salvation. In his discourse of 1753 on the true goals of the arts and sciences, his manifesto proclaiming the future direction of the Neapolitan Enlightenment, and the cultural stance an enlightened Neapolitan government should embrace, Genovesi publicly rebukes—and turns his back on—the world of abstract philosophy, extolling instead the practical and technical potential of the Enlightenment, a posture henceforth the hallmark of his work. In this text, written in Italian and intended for a broad audience, Genovesi again broaches Spinoza but now no longer pronounces his name, merely alluding darkly but with evident apprehension to the 'most impious and cold-hearted of the philosophers of the last century'.[200]

[197] Quoted in Venturi, *Illuminati*, v, 13–14; see also Genovesi, *Elementa metaphysicae*, ii, 9; Genovesi, *Lettere filosofiche*, i, 37–9.

[198] Genovesi, *Elementa metaphysicae*, ii, 9.

[199] Venturi, *Illuminati*, v, 12; Carpanetto and Ricuperati, *Italy*, 253–5.

[200] Genovesi, *Discorso*, 96.

3 | SOCIETY, INSTITUTIONS, REVOLUTION

i. Philosophy and the Social Hierarchy

Is there a social dimension that helps explain the timing and psychological origins of the rise of radical thought? That the chief breeding-grounds of radical ideas during the century 1650–1750 were large, internationally orientated, dynamic cities with exceptionally high levels of immigration from a wide area, commercial and manufacturing, as well as governmental centres, such as Amsterdam, The Hague, London, Paris, Venice, Naples, Berlin, Vienna, Copenhagen, and Hamburg, where traditional, sharply delineated social hierarchies and forms of deference were perceptibly eroding, suggests that there may be. Radical ideas, seemingly, were nurtured within an urban milieu characterized by exceptional fluidity of social relations and movement between social strata, features which correspond directly to the freer, more flexible intellectual framework which emerged.

Historians in recent decades have become conscious of the evolution in western and central Europe during the century and a half before the French Revolution of a wholly new kind of public sphere for debate, exchange of ideas, and opinion-forming, located outside the formal consultative procedures and assemblies of the past, a public sphere which emerged only where a high degree of social and cultural interchange existed outside the deliberations of formal political, judicial, and ecclesiastical bodies and institutions.[1] Among the novelties in European life generating this forum of public opinion formation beyond the sway of princely courts, the judiciary, the Church, and parliaments were the new erudite journals, 'universal' libraries, literary clubs, lexicons, and encyclopaedias, culminating in the great *Encyclopédie* (seventeen volumes, Paris, 1751–65) of Diderot and D'Alembert, and generally the new post-1648 Republic of Letters,[2] as well as, more mundanely, newspapers, gentlemen's magazines, tea- and coffee-houses and, after around 1730, also Masonic lodges.[3]

Except the last, all these new cultural institutions and forms of sociability were products of the last part of the seventeenth century and conclusively demonstrate the

[1] Habermas, *Structural Transformation*, 27–38; Chartier, *Cultural Origins*, 20–30; Goodman, *Republic of Letters*, 11–22.
[2] Habermas, *Structural Transformation*, 25.   [3] Van Dülmen, *Society*, 10.

decisive impact of the period 1680–1750, or the early Enlightenment, as distinct from the post-1750 High Enlightenment, in the transformation of European society and culture. Equally, they confirm the crucially formative role in generating the new outlook of the major commercial and courtly cities of especially north-western Europe. The style and flavour of the Early Enlightenment 'public sphere' might fairly be described as a cross between the aristocratic and the commercial with, as its overriding feature, the de-emphasizing of social grades and status, breaking with the hierarchical values of traditional society. Its concern with polite sociability between men (and to a much lesser extent women) of contrasting backgrounds, and a predilection for conversation urbane, cosmopolitan, and unencumbered with pedantic erudition, arose naturally and automatically from the advent of new associations and locations with no fixed rules of access, which—as in the case of the tea and coffee shops which began to proliferate in Holland, London, and Hamburg from the 1660s and 1670s—provided a social space not specific to any one class.[4] The result was the emergence of a new type—the polished gentleman and knowledgeable 'man of the world' who is unclassifiable under the old social criteria. Noting that this new sphere of polite conversation was the preserve of no one social class, Doria calls it a forum of 'complete liberty', prominently featuring noblemen and women, but to which men of middling and even humble birth could readily gain admittance once furnished with the necessary veneer of *buon gusto*, a mixture of social graces and reading which, in principle, was available to anyone.[5] Casanova, the ultimate pseudo-gentleman as well as libertine, was highly educated, highly polished, and regularly mixed with aristocrats and fine ladies, as well as lesser mortals, but he was the son of an obscure actor in a big city (Venice) and, in his later years, he was employed as a nobleman's librarian.

The quasi-aristocratic tone of the developing 'public sphere' could not, therefore, preclude its being a levelling force generating new space for social mingling. Among French writers who significantly contributed to the burgeoning corpus of radical thought were several nobles, but the foremost figures, apart from Boulainvilliers and d'Argens, came from a wide spectrum of middling backgrounds: Bayle was the son of a Huguenot pastor, Fontenelle stemmed from a Rouennais legal family, the latter's atheistic disciple Du Marsais was a private tutor,[6] La Mettrie was the son of a Saint Malo textile merchant, while Diderot was the illegitimate son of a master cutler. The Dutch radicals from the brothers Koerbagh, sons of a manufacturer, to Mandeville, a city physician, were predominantly, like Spinoza himself, a merchant's son, from an urban, often Amsterdam or Rotterdam middle-class background. Among German radicals, Tschirnhaus was an aristocrat while Knutzen and Edelmann were sons of organists, Stosch and Wachter the offspring of Protestant pastors, and Lau of an official. Among the Italians, Radicati and Conti were nobles, albeit the first was disowned by his family, rejected by his class, and died in destitution, while Giannone was of obscure parentage and Vico an underpaid, undervalued, junior professor.

---

[4] Chartier, *Cultural Origins*, 20–3, 154–7; Jacob, *Living the Enlightenment*, 8–9; Goodman, *Republic of Letters*, 24–9.

[5] Doria, *Lettere e ragionamenti*, ii, 338.   [6] Saint-Simon, *Mémoires*, xxvii, 163; Proust, *Diderot*, 32, 520.

Aristocrats who became *philosophes*, regularly rubbing shoulders with non-noble scholars, writers, and publishers, as well as professionals, pseudo-gentry, and *bourgeois gentilhommes*, were apt to be detached in some significant way from the traditional culture and outlook of the nobility. Mostly, they had been disowned or belonged to a highly fluid, cosmopolitan fringe found in large capital cities. The prolific marquis d'Argens sprang from the judicial *noblesse de robe* in Aix-en-Provence but was estranged from his family and lived from his writing in Holland, deprived of his former affluent status and lifestyle, until he began a new career as a German courtier in the 1740s. By contrast, the typically provincial aristocracy and gentry of Europe, rural and small-town élites residing in localities over which their families had presided for generations, were profoundly conservative in their reading and, whether Protestant or Catholic, highly resistant to new intellectual trends. Research into the libraries of the nobility of rural Franconia, for instance, reveals a lack of interest in modern philosophy or science, as complete as that of the provincial aristocracies of Brittany and Normandy.[7] As in the past, the cultural world of the rural nobility was thoroughly traditional, steeped in law, juridical politics, and theology. Those libraries of aristocrats and high officials which do reveal affinities with the intellectual world of the *philosophes* were usually encountered in dynamic cultural centres in which traditional social barriers had become increasingly blurred.

The public sphere of the pre-1750 Enlightenment, then, generated a new reading culture, conversational style, and intellectual framework. One unmistakable sign of change was the receding of Latin from its age-old hegemony over intellectual activity, and the emergence of the vernacular in its place, a shift which itself entailed a cultural revolution, for the first time firmly separating the world of polite conversation from that of academic disputation and theological and legal scholarship. If French became the language of non-academic intellectual discourse among Europe's higher social echelons,[8] by 1700 a remarkable crop of popular philosophical writers had appeared further down the social scale who conversed, read, and wrote primarily in their own vernacular languages. But the widening gulf between old and new was far more than just a matter of language; it was also one of style. Especially esteemed in the new arena were clear, concise, readily grasped proofs, stripped of the pedantry and academic terminology and jargon of traditional scholarly discourse.[9]

That men are unlikely to acquire radical habits of thought from a sedentary existence in a traditionally hierarchical milieu was asserted by several contemporary writers. As the Hamburg pastor Johannes Müller observed in 1672, country folk were the social segment least affected by new philosophical ideas, while ordinary artisans and merchants were, if not entirely, then mostly immune. The real menace, he believed, was the open outlook of persons—courtiers, diplomats, soldiers, and 'men of the world'—who travel widely, continually mixing in different cultural and religious contexts, particularly if they frequent lands such as France, England, and Holland

---

[7] Roche, *Republicains des lettres*, 96–9, 102. [8] Doria, *Lettere e ragionamenti*, ii, 338.
[9] Lassenius, *Besiegte Atheisterey*, preface, pp. iii–vi; Breithaupt, *Zufällige Gedancken*, 13–14, 26.

where, according to him, libertine thinking was rife.[10] Immanuel Weber (1659–1726), a connoisseur of the Lutheran German small courts who, in 1684, became chamberlain of the principality of Schwarzburg-Sonderhausen, dedicated his philosophical dialogue on atheism, published in 1696, to Count Christoph Ludwig of Stolberg-Königstein since, according to him, this prince was one of the few remaining paragons of old-fashioned princely piety, a ruler genuinely opposed to foreign fashion and the extravagant styles rampant in most late seventeenth-century courts, and hostile to the new philosophical ideas which Weber was attacking.[11] The craze for opera, ballet, theatre, masquerades, and other such pleasure-seeking, declares Weber, instils irresistibly precisely those most addicted to foreign novelties with a yearning for philosophy with which to stifle qualms of conscience and fear of divine retribution. Hence the fad for philosophy now sweeping the German courts, far from being designed to edify and uplift, he insists, has an essentially irreligious and immoral purpose.

Habitués of the German Protestant princely courts, according to Weber, read Hobbes and debated Bayle's appalling proposition that atheists can lead a virtuous life.[12] One routinely distinguished between 'practical' and 'theoretical' atheists, acknowledging the latter to be, if much less numerous, the more pernicious of the two varieties, being impervious to pious admonition and prone to try to sway others.[13] Every German courtier, he says, knows Spinoza is the chief, most infamous, and most dangerous of 'theoretical' atheists, and consequently, he places more emphasis on him than other morally and religiously subversive writers. Alas, many had been corrupted, he avers, by Spinoza's denying the divine authorship of Scripture, and claiming the prophets were not divinely inspired but just ordinary men in the grip of exceptional 'fantasies', as well as his designating the Biblical miracles 'purely natural happenings which only seem supernatural to us because we are ignorant of their natural causes'.[14] German courtiers, he adds, also commonly knew the doctrine of one substance and Bayle's argument that Spinoza represents the culmination and systematization of ancient strains of philosophical atheism stretching back to the pre-Socratic Greeks.

But if Spinoza is the unmatched arch-atheist of modern times, there were plenty of lesser figures infiltrating and morally debilitating the German courtly world of the 1690s. In particular, he mentions—evidently following Müller here—the Sephardic Jewish deist Uriel da Costa,[15] the Amsterdam writer and associate of Spinoza 'Frederik Warmond' [i.e. Adriaen Koerbagh][16] whose *Bloemhof*, he remarks, rejects the Trinity and Christ's divinity and divine mission, and claims Moses was not the author of the

---

[10] Müller, *Atheismus Devictus*, 32; Otto, *Studien*, 20.

[11] Weber, *Beurtheilung*, dedication and preface, pp. 4–4v.   [12] Ibid., 22–6.

[13] Ibid., 26, 140–1; see also Undereyck, *Närrische Atheist*, 14, 38–40; Masius, *Dissertationes*, 28; Breithaupt, *Zufällige Gedancken*, 9–14; Schröder, *Ursprünge*, 67.

[14] Weber, *Beurtheilung*, 83–4; Otto, *Studien*, 39, 41–2, 115.

[15] Uriel da Costa (c.1583–1640) had been a crypto-Jew in Portugal but became a deist in Holland; he committed suicide in Amsterdam in 1640.

[16] Graesse, *Trésor des livres* iv, 39; see below, pp. 185–96.

Pentateuch,[17] and two more Dutchmen—Adriaen Beverland,[18] whose *De Peccato naturali* he calls a 'frivolous little book' which mocks the concept of Original Sin, and the famous Balthasar Bekker,[19] who had done more than anyone to sap German courtiers' belief in Satan, magic, possession, spirits, and witchcraft.[20] But the philosophical basis is Spinozism; what is principally needed to defeat this contagion, he urges, is a good supply of cogent refutations of Spinoza. Warning against the Socinian Frans Kuyper, he chiefly recommends Henry More, Mansvelt, Velthuysen, Huet, Blyenbergh, Poiret, Abbadie, Wittichius, and Pierre Yvon.[21]

In France, it was the celebrated court preacher Father Jean-Baptiste Massillon who first sounded the alarm regarding the progress among the aristocracy of philosophy, in a series of sermons against 'incredulity' beginning in 1699.[22] In a later sermon, delivered in 1704, also in the royal chapel at Versailles, with some of those he was criticizing sitting before him, he interprets this sudden aristocratic thirst for philosophy, much like Weber, as a form of rebellion against religion and the Church. He denounces it as an arrogant bid for personal independence, a device for quietening uneasy consciences with a veneer of high-sounding verbiage to camouflage profligacy and lust. He refuses to believe anyone deep in his heart genuinely doubts the existence of a 'souverain Créateur de l'Univers' who rewards the deserving and punishes the wicked.[23] Only to gratify carnal appetites while warding off disapproval and the risk of disgrace had some nobles donned philosophical arguments as their new armour. The true origin of the spreading enthusiasm for philosophy, held Massillon, was thus moral depravity, concupiscence, and pride, the philosophical unbeliever flaunting a wicked 'singularité qui le flatte et fait qu'il suppose en lui plus de force et plus de lumières, que dans le reste des hommes'.[24] Such *incrédules* use philosophy to tranquillize themselves and coax others, thereby creating more and more *incrédules*.[25] Yet not everyone is ready prey for the new philosophical seducers. There are still many devout men and women who heed the admonitions of the clergy. Massillon vows a war on philosophies total and unremitting which would end in the triumph of Christ and the Church. In classical antiquity, he recalls, religion, authority, and morality had then too almost been overwhelmed by a similar mania for philosophy. The entire known world resounded to the clamour of philosophers and philosophies; yet in the end, all the philosophy schools of the Hellenistic and Roman world were humbled, vanquished, and ground to dust, compelled to admit that in Christ there is a 'philosophie plus sublime' than that of any philosopher.[26]

Massillon distinguishes two distinct strains of New Philosophy invading the courtly world of Paris and Versailles. Both are corrupting and based on 'raison orgueilleuse'. But the philosophy of the Cartesians and providential deists who postulate 'un Dieu oisif, retiré en lui-même . . . ne daignant pas à s'abaisser à regarder ce qui passe sur la

---

[17] Weber, *Beurtheilung*, 128–9.   [18] See below, pp. 87–8.   [19] See below, pp. 378–92.

[20] Weber, *Beurtheilung*, 131–4.   [21] Ibid., 140–1.   [22] Pauthe, *Massillon*, 17–18, 184, 221.

[23] Massillon, *Pensées*, 119, 267–8; Pauthe, *Massillon*, 184, 221.

[24] Massillon, *Pensées*, 155–6; see also [Mauduit], *Traité de religion*, 280, 284.

[25] Massillon, *Pensées*, 248–50, 264; Assoun, 'Spinoza, les libertins', 187.   [26] Massillon, *Pensées*, 37.

terre', and virtually indifferent to the men he has created,[27] while harmful, is yet not so fatal as the more radical tendency, championed by hardened *esprits forts*, defined, according to Massillon, by advocacy of an 'enchaînement fatal d'événements', a God lacking both freedom and power. It is these new philosophical *incrédules* who deny divine Providence and believe in nothing except what is demonstrated by mathematical reason, in other words, Spinoza's followers, who threaten mankind with moral, religious, and social annihilation.[28]

Avoiding direct engagement with the Cartesians, Massillon alludes to them, and all other modern mechanists except Spinoza, only indirectly, citing ancient Greek thinkers as surrogates for those he says are again disseminating the 'vains préceptes de la philosophie'. By identifying Spinoza alone among modern philosophers spreading dangerous ideas by name, Massillon emphasizes his unparalleled centrality in the rise of French incredulity. What an amazing phenomenon it is, he stresses, that Spinoza a foreigner of obscure and low birth, should be apotheosized in France into a modern philosophical 'saint' in the imaginations of libertine courtiers and aristocrats, ladies as well as men, a model upon which to base not just their thoughts but their very lives. Spinoza has indeed, he laments, become the universal 'saint' of the *esprits forts*.[29] His explanation for this strange phenomenon is partly psychological and partly moral. Despite their arrogant airs, French noblemen who profess unbelief are not wholly swayed in their hearts by the philosophical verbiage they spout, not really firm in their impiety. Driven by apprehension and anxiety to try to drown the gnawing self-reproach within them, they feel impelled to find philosophers capable of stiffening their courage and resolution—'des impies véritables, fermes et intrépides dans l'impi-eté'.[30] So strong is this impulse that some 'madmen' even went to search out the infamous Spinoza in his homeland—an allusion to Saint-Evremond as well as Condé, who had had Spinoza summoned to his presence at Utrecht in 1673, and according to at least one professed former friend of the philosopher, Henri Morelli (if not to most modern scholars), did actually confer with him at length.[31]

By venerating their 'saint' of impiety, claims Massillon, the new heretics had lapsed into a credulity far more irrational and despicable than any they reproach loyal Christians with. 'Ce monstre', as he calls Spinoza, had built his own philosophical system, needing no one to help him cultivate atheism and iniquity. But he had built it upon the most preposterous and tedious paradoxes and contradictions. His system is nonsensical. 'Hors d'impiété, tout est inintelligible,' he affirms, so that were it not for his denying a providential God and miracles, his work would long since have sunk without trace into oblivion. It is not then his intellectual cogency but matchless impiety which had conferred on Spinoza his unrivalled status.

---

[27] Ibid., 292–3.   [28] Ibid., 293.   [29] Ibid.; Vernière, *Spinoza*, 286–7.

[30] Massillon, *Pensées*, 258; Vernière, *Spinoza*, 214.

[31] Assoun, 'Spinoza, les libertins', 183–90, 202–7; this remains one of the vexed points of Spinoza scholarship and has been ever since Bayle kept changing his mind about whether Condé and Spinoza did in fact confer at Utrecht or not; see also Charles-Daubert and Moreau, *Pierre Bayle. Écrits*, 23, 49, 165–6; Popkin, *The Third Force*, 146–7, 330.

If, in Paris and London, the Radical Enlightenment flourished amid a fluid, mixed world of nobles and non-nobles, bourgeois and sons of artisans, at Vienna it had less prolific and few indigenous roots and was mainly based among the coterie around Prince Eugene of Savoy (1663–1736) and his intimates, again a mixture of nobles and non-noble *érudits*. This group largely consisted of foreigners, such as his favourite aide-de camp, Baron Georg Wilhelm von Hohendorf (d.1719), a Prussian Junker by origin who had, however, served many years in the Ottoman army as a mercenary, learnt excellent Greek in Constantinople, and was an expert in the religion, customs, and erotic life of the Levant, and the French *savant*, deist, and dealer in rare books Nicolas Lenglet Dufresnoy, a man who had intrigued against the French regent and seen the inside of the Bastille in 1719, and who was the prince's guest in Vienna in the years 1721–3.[32] Other participants included (briefly) the English deist John Toland, and, for much longer, the Neapolitan refugee *savant* of radical inclinations, Pietro Giannone. As has been emphasized, the influence of this libertine philosophical coterie on the local élites of Austria and Bohemia was extremely slight;[33] but in a wider, international context with their contacts in Germany, Holland, Flanders, France, and Italy, it was undoubtedly of much greater significance. Eugene supported Leibniz's proposals for an academy of sciences in Vienna and was known as a patron of philosophy and science, while the fame of his 'magnifica biblioteca', as Giannone called it, with its many rarities, reverberated across Europe.[34] Eugene's library was Giannone's laboratory and it was there, among its unrivalled profusion of forbidden books and manuscripts, that he was able to steep himself, as he could not in Italy, in the works of Spinoza, Toland, and other radical writers.[35]

A leading personality of the age, as well as a famous military commander, diplomat, and courtier, Eugene of Savoy had entered the Emperor's service at the time of the Turkish siege of Vienna in 1683, and later played a leading role, alongside Marlborough, among the generals of the anti-Louis XIV coalition during the War of the Spanish Succession (1702–13). Afterwards, among other posts, he served as governor-general of the Austrian Netherlands (1716–25) with one of his residences in Brussels, though he was frequently absent during those years in Vienna and elsewhere. Publicly renowned as a collector of art and a sponsor of Jansenism, privately he was a noted connoisseur of courtesans and the erotic, and a frenetic bibliophile with a special liking for suspect philosophical and erotic literature.[36] His closest associate in philosophical, as well as military and convivial matters, was Hohendorf, who probably first introduced both Toland and Lenglet Dufresnoy to him and who certainly procured for him many of his choicest rare books and manuscripts.[37]

Among the extreme rarities in his library was an original annotated manuscript of *La Religion Chrétien conduit par la raison éternelle'* (1704), a Spinozistic text by the

---

[32] Ricuperati, 'Giannone', 62–3; Sheridan, *Nicolas Lenglet Dufresnoy*, 38–40, 46–7, 85.

[33] Evans, 'Über die Urspriinge', 14.

[34] De Soria, *Raccolta*, i, 143; Giannone, *Opere*, III; Van Dülmen, *Society*, 27.

[35] Giannone, *Vita*, 112–13, 139; Marini, 'Documenti', 705–7; Ricuperati, 'Libertinismo', 630, 637, 654.

[36] Schröder, *Ursprünge*, 412, 414, 427.   [37] Sheridan, *Nicolas Lenglet Dufresnoy*, 49.

lapsed Catholic monk, and later Calvinist preacher, Yves de Vallone (c.1666–1705) which the prince probably acquired, together with other *libri prohibiti*, while visiting Holland in 1707,[38] and, in a copy discovered by Toland in Amsterdam in 1709, the *Gospel of Barnabas*, a rarity prized by Muslims and Jews but reviled by the Churches, since it recounts Jesus' life and passion expressly denying his divinity and Resurrection. Toland had become interested in the topic of the Nazarenes, or Jewish Christians, the alleged source of this 'gospel', while studying at Leiden years before—the text figures prominently in his *Nazarenus*—and it was presumably through him that it found its way into Eugene's library.[39] Hohendorf too amassed a famous collection scarcely less prolific in *clandestina* philosophical and erotic than that of his master.[40] Besides everything by Spinoza, Lodwijk Meyer's *Philosophia*, and many other key published radical writings of the late seventeenth century, he possessed numerous 'forbidden' manuscripts including Boulainvilliers' *Essay de métaphysique*, De Vallone's *Religion du Chrétien*, and, still more impious, the foremost of the German examples of the genre—the *Symbolum Sapientiae* (or *Cymbalum Mundi*),[41] and the most notorious of all the clandestine manuscripts—*La Vie et l'Esprit de Mr Benoît de Spinosa*.[42]

The psychological roots of radical thought, according to Massillon, Weber, and other hostile observers, lay in pride, the desire to be independent of the Church and of others, and the need for a philsophical screen of justification for sexual profligacy.[43] Eugene and Hohendorf vividly personify the link between what was a veritable cult of the erotic, an almost open flouting of conventional morality and religion, and a fascination for 'forbidden' philosophy. But the pride entailed was not necessarily aristocratic, or that of any class, but rather of those who chose to disdain and place themselves outside the norms and traditional attitudes of the society in which they lived.[44] But if the independent-minded defied religion, ecclesiastical authority, and society, thereby, in the opinion of most, fatally imperilling their souls, it must indeed have seemed advisable and reassuring to seek out philosophical arguments demonstrating the soul is not immortal, that there is no supernatural governance of the lives of men, nor reward or punishment in the hereafter.[45] Why live in dread of divine retribution for profligacy, adultery, and debauchery if one can live entirely free of remorse and dread of the Day of Judgement? And precisely in this field—with his 'geometric' demonstrations that the impious and dissolute need not fear divine retribution—Spinoza was invaluable, furnishing more, better, and pithier arguments and proofs against revealed religion, divine Providence, and supernatural forces than any other philosopher of the age, even Hobbes.[46]

[38] O'Higgins, *Yves de Vallone*, 68.
[39] Champion, *Pillars of Priestcraft*, 125; Champion, 'Introduction', 8, 11, 58.
[40] Ricuperati, *L'Esperanza civile*, 407.
[41] Marchand, *Dictionnaire*, ii, 319; Schröder, *Ursprünge*, 408–16.
[42] [Hohendorf]. *Bibliotheca Hohendorfiana*, ii, 7, 66 and iii, 261–2; Schröder, *Ursprünge*, 412, 417, 480.
[43] Massillon, *Pensées*, 155; Veyssière de la Croze, *Dissertation sur l'athéisme*, 267.
[44] Turner, 'Properties of Libertinism', 80–1.
[45] Veyssière de la Croze, *Dissertation sur l'athéisme*, 455.   [46] Doria, *Lettere e ragionamenti*, ii, 319–36.

ii. Shaftesbury, Radicati, Vauvenargues

Many nobles figure among the ranks of the radical writers and thinkers of the early Enlightenment—Lahontan, Boulainvilliers, d'Argens, Vauvenargues, the third Earl of Shaftesbury, Conti, Radicati, and, of course, Spinoza's friend Ehrenfried Walter von Tschirnhaus—among others that spring to mind. Yet each of these men of privileged birth became in some way estranged or detached from his particular family or noble group, and doubtless partly in consequence of becoming isolated or remote from his class, was drawn into forging, through philosophy, a new kind of meritocracy of mind and attitude, reflecting the extreme social fluidity postulated by deistic and libertarian premises. An obvious instance is Anthony Ashley Cooper, third Earl of Shaftesbury (1671–1713), originator of the 'moral sense' theory, a deist who passionately believed there is an objective basis for morality and the 'public good' separate from that decreed by revealed religion, arguing however against Hobbes and Spinoza that the private 'good' of the individual is not the only motivation for human action and that there is a way to balance self-interest against the individual's benevolent or moral sense, and allegiance to the 'public good'.[47]

Shaftesbury sought to place morality, 'politeness', and sociablity on a new intellectual basis, and did so inspired by a vision of a novel type of society ruled not by any traditional landed élite but a new kind of élite of affairs and ideas—an élite of the cultured, well-meaning, and gentlemanly. Moreover, his social and moral conception was closely linked to his role as a radical ideologue of the 'Glorious Revolution'.[48] In his post-aristocratic philosophy, 'liberty' is the basis for a new and more enlightened culture—'liberty' not just in the constitutional sense defined by the Glorious Revolution, but liberty as a political and social condition, liberty defined by debate, criticism, and cultural exchange, what has been called 'a condition of unlimited interpersonal interaction'.[49] The Revolution ended England's age-old domination by Court and Church and created every likelihood that the country would now be politically and culturally dominated (as indeed it was) by the landed gentry. But Shaftesbury, whose extreme sensibility and delicate health, as well as aversion to the mainstream politics of his own class, led him to retire from active politics, undertook in his intense and lonely intellectual odyssey to show how his new ideal of 'politeness'—which was fiercely derided by Jonathan Swift—could help create a wider, more accessible space in which elements from the commercial and professional classes of London and the other cities could participate alongside the gentry and the rising pseudo-gentry.[50]

Other radical thinkers of noble extraction were similarly removed from the normal context of aristocratic life and activity. Henri de Boulainvilliers, comte de Saint Saire (1658–1722) was another deist of impeccable noble pedigree and perhaps comes

---

[47] Mortensen, 'Shaftesbury', 648–9; Hundert, *Enlightenment's Fable*, 122–3; McNaughton, 'British Moralists', 205–6.

[48] Klein, *Shaftesbury*, 1–2, 8–9.   [49] Ibid, 198.   [50] Ibid., 182–5; Craven, *Jonathan Swift*, 87–92.

closest to being a *philosophe* who believed in the reality of noble status and its structural importance for society and politics. Yet Saint-Simon was not alone in considering him a personage somehow detached from his class by his profound intellectual engagement. Like Shaftesbury, Boulainvilliers became deeply addicted to the pleasures of reading and the mind and, as Lenglet Dufresnoy remarked, it was surprising, even disconcerting 'de voir un homme de sa naissance joindre des réflexions si profondes à une érudition aussi grand et aussi variée que la sienne'.[51] Where Shaftesbury argues against, but also parallels, Spinoza's ethical project, detaching morality from any connection with theology and revealed religion, elevating intellectual love of the universe above physical pleasure, and deeming virtue the highest pleasure of the mind, a 'virtue' that unites the private and the public good, Boulainvilliers, for his part, emerged as the profoundest and most influential of all the exponents of Spinozism in early eighteenth-century France.

But others were still more drastically alienated from the claims and pretensions of aristocracy than Shaftesbury or Boulainvilliers. The most uncompromising radical of aristocratic background, and one of the few to declare the impossibility of reforming society on enlightened lines without redistribution of land and property, was also arguably the most thoroughly estranged from his family and class.[52] Count Alberto Radicati di Passerano (1698–1737), scion of an ancient Piedmontese lineage, had arrived at the Court of Turin at the age of 9 as a page. Not the least of the many misfortunes which marred his short and tragic life was a disastrous marriage to a Piedmontese noble lady, contracted when he was 17, which led to bitter strife with her family, culminating in nine months of imprisonment on allegations which turned out to be false. This experience doubtless contributed not just to his subsequent feelings of estrangement but also his highly unconventional views on marriage and sex. After spending the years 1719–21 in Regency France, about which nothing is known but where, presumably, he deepened his acquaintance with freethinking and radical thought,[53] he returned to Savoy, where he participated in the tentative reformist initiatives of the early 1720s. But what, even then, struck the king's ministers in Turin as a disquietingly radical tendency left him dangerously exposed after the *rapprochement* between the Savoyard Court and the Papacy, in 1726–7, and the re-establishment of the Inquisition in the kingdom.[54] Increasingly at odds with his own as well as his wife's family, and intensely fearful of the Inquisition, which he regarded as his mortal enemy, Radicati fled into exile in northern Europe, from which he was never to return, and which led to his gradual impoverishment and social marginalization.[55]

Steeped in Machiavelli, Sarpi, and Bayle, Radicati also at some point discovered Spinoza, who became the prime influence on the further elaboration and growing radicalism of his ideas on society and politics, as well as in philosophy and religion.[56] He was entirely at one with Spinoza in regarding 'democratical' government 'the

---

[51] Quoted in Sheridan, *Nicolas Lenglet Dufresnoy*, 134.   [52] Carpanetto and Ricuperati, *Italy*, 115.
[53] Venturi, *Saggi*, 25–6   [54] Symcox, *Victor Amadeus II*, 215–16; Davidson, 'Toleration', 236–7, 247.
[55] Jacob, *Radical Enlightenment*, 172–3; Berti, 'Radicati in Olanda', 510–15.
[56] Ferrone, *Intellectual Roots*, 118, 274; Berti, 'At the Roots', 564.

most ancient and agreeable to the natural and free condition of men'.[57] An early draft of his *Discours moraux, historiques et politiques*, which he presented to the Savoyard king before his exile, in 1729, and which scandalized the Court with its remarks about the Church, probably already savoured of the republicanism fully evident in the final version. In England, Radicati became a militant deist and connoisseur of radical literature, exploring, besides much else, the writings of Blount, Toland, Collins, and Tindal, and styling the latter 'un savant auteur de notre parti'.[58] His most famous work, the 94-page *Philosophical Dissertation upon Death* was translated by Thomas Morgan and published in London in 1732. Here Radicati rejects Newtonianism, insisting motion is inherent in, not external to, matter, denies divine Providence, affirming the laws of nature to be unalterable, and rejects the notions of absolute 'good' and 'evil', including the Christian teaching on death and suicide. He argues, like Spinoza and Shaftesbury, that 'good' can be determined only by what benefits society and the individual.[59] Thus where pain and misery outweigh what is worthwhile in life, suicide is both a perfectly natural and also a 'good' solution.[60]

Publication of this treatise, which he designated a 'consolation for the Unhappy', provoked an immediate outcry.[61] The Attorney-General accounted the *Dissertation* 'the most impious and immoral book I have ever read'.[62] George II's consort, Queen Caroline, a well-read lady and admirer of Samuel Clarke, Newton's chief philosophical spokesman, perusing the book a few weeks after its appearance, recorded her shock at being confronted with such a work 'wherein the author embraces the atheism of Spinoza and afterwards draws conclusions from his doctrine that destroy all society and virtue'.[63] In November 1732, the author, translator, and publisher were all arrested. Radicati was briefly imprisoned and then released on bail but found the atmosphere confronting him in London so intimidating he soon went into his second exile, settling this time at The Hague.[64] He died at Rotterdam, completely destitute, in 1737.

A French nobleman who died at a still earlier age, a *philosophe* born into the *noblesse de robe* but eventually socially marginalized, was Luc de Clapiers, marquis de Vauvenargues (1715–47). Like d'Argens, a native of Aix-en-Provence, Vauvenargues chose a military career, and served in a crack royal regiment for ten years (1733–43) until obliged to retire without prospects owing to his physical collapse during a campaign against the Austrians in Bohemia. Disfigured, sick, immersing himself in solitary study in the dreary lodgings he rented in Paris, Vauvenargues brooded and read, developing a sombre philosophy of life expressed in a concise aphoristic style in a series of essays and fragments all written during the decade 1737–47.[65]

---

[57] Radicati, *Twelve Discourses*, 203. [58] Venturi, *Saggi*, 249–51; Ferrone, *Intellectual Roots*, 143, 274.

[59] [Radicati], *A Philosophical Dissertation*, 5–6, 8, 11, 29, 60; Alberti, *Alberto Radicati*, 28, 151; Carpanetto and Ricuperati, *Italy*, 118.

[60] [Radicati], *A Philosophical Dissertation*, 88–90; Hazard, *European Thought*, 131–2.

[61] Ibid., 131; Jacob, *Radical Enlightenment*, 172–3; Carpanetto and Ricuperati, *Italy*, 118.

[62] Jacob, *Radical Enlightenment*, 172–3. [63] Ibid.

[64] Wielema, *Filosofen*, 96–8; Jacob, *Living the Enlightenment*, 83.

[65] Hazard, *European Thought*, 35, 366.

Like Radicati—and indeed all radical thinkers of the Early Enlightenment—Vauvenargues expressly rejects the 'cause occulte de M. Newton', maintaining that motion is innate in matter and affirming the 'ordre immuable et nécessaire' of all that happens.[66] He too rejects 'freedom of the will' and asserts the relativity of 'good' and 'evil'.[67] 'On n'a point de volonté,' he contends, 'qui ne soit un effet de quelque passion ou de quelque réflexion,' adding 'donc l'homme ne peut agir que par les lois de son Dieu'.[68] As with Spinoza, 'God' in Vauvenargues is not the Creator of the universe, the source of good and evil, the guardian and judge of man, or the divine legislator who lays down the rules of morality. He is simply the totality of nature and its unalterable laws. Accordingly, for Vauvenargues, morality is constructed by man and 'l'humanité est la première des vertus.'[69] The primary influences shaping his philosophy were Bayle and especially Spinoza, whom he could hardly avoid discovering through reading Boulainvilliers, a virtually inevitable source for such a figure at the time.[70] But the Spinozism of Vauvenargues is an intensely moralistic, individual philosophy, if also a political stance in the service of the liberated individual. Preoccupied with the implications of Spinoza's system for lifestyle and morality, he seems utterly remote from the polemics and Biblical criticism of the *Tractatus* and the carefully crafted system-building of the *Ethics*. Typically *vauvenarguien* is his wrestling with the paradox lodged at the heart of Spinoza's system, that all human decisions and actions are determined necessarily, and there is no free will, but that yet this fatalism 'n'exclut point la liberté', that is, a liberty including security of life, buttressed by political and social conditions and laws.[71]

Vauvenargues' politics reflects the uninhibitedly secular, individualistic character of his thought. Adopting the Hobbesian-Spinozist principle that neither natural law nor natural morality exist, and that 'good' and 'bad' begin with the legislation and moral rules established by men in the context of the State, justice for Vauvenargues exists only under a sovereign. But since justice is really nothing other than the power of institutions and the legal process established and maintained by rulers and legislators, its quality will vary greatly from State to State and from time to time. Since men are naturally, and inevitably, determined to self-preservation and self-aggrandisement, absolute justice is unattainable, and the real purpose of the legal machinery in any State is to minimize friction and limit the disruptive effects on society and other individuals of each person's natural drives. 'Les hommes sont ennemis-nés les uns des autres', he asserts, 'non à cause qu'ils se haïssent, mais parce qu'ils ne peuvent s'agrandir sans se traverser.'[72] Unlike Hobbes and Locke, however, Vauvenargues does not contrast the state of nature where men are at war with one another with life under the State, separating the two by postulating a basic contract. Rather, like Spinoza, he

---

[66] Bove, 'Puissance', 186–8.   [67] Vauvenargues, *Oeuvres*, i, 62–3.
[68] Ibid., ii, 98–9, 103; Gay, *The Enlightenment*, ii, 191; Bove, 'Puissance', 188.
[69] Vauvenargues, *Oeuvres*, ii, 215; Mercier, *Réhabilitation*, 421–2.
[70] Bove, 'Politique', 333; Bove, 'Puissance', 185.
[71] Vauvenargues, *Oeuvres*, ii, 106, 117; Bove, 'Puissance', 187.
[72] Bove, 'Politique', 336.

sees no real distinction between the state of nature, where men always have some mutual interests and collaborate for purposes of common defence and safety, and civil society where the State, to a greater or lesser extent, serves the needs of all.[73] In particular, Vauvenargues, like all the radicals, dislikes and rejects Hobbes' notion that with the forming of the State, the individual surrenders his natural right, including his natural right to criticize and judge.

Unavoidably, some groups and individuals will always be more powerful and richer than others. Inequality being inherent in society, the laws made by the State always have a provisional and relative, rather than an absolute or permanent character, being in effect a way of stabilizing and minimizing the harmful effects of a hierarchy and inequality which has no intrinsic legitimacy—God-ordained or otherwise. Vauvenargues did not emulate Radicati, or the German plebeians Knutzen and Edelmann, in suggesting that this illegitimate inequality should be erased through redistribution of property. However, as in Diderot later, whatever tends to level hierarchy and inequality also tends towards the good of the community as a whole. Like Boulainvilliers, Vauvenargues is a firm opponent of royal absolutism. But he also warns, following Spinoza, that it serves no useful purpose to engage in revolution, or throw out a tyrant, if the people do nothing to change such systems of law and authority as pave the way for despotism. If the people want no more tyranny then they must learn to change their laws and create a well-ordered republic or constitutional monarchy. Vauvenargues does not share Spinoza's distaste for Cromwell, though; rather, he sees him not as a king under another name but an enemy of monarchy, illustrating the rise in the eighteenth century of the new myth of Cromwell, a feature of the radicalism of the age, as an enemy of tyranny and man of the people.[74]

Vauvenargues, Radicati, and Doria, like Shaftesbury, were nobles but, unlike Boulainvilliers and d'Holbach, adhered to a political republicanism characterized by levelling and anti-aristocratic as well as anticlerical tendencies. Accordingly, they may be bracketed together with Spinoza, Van den Enden, Koerbagh, Leenhof, and Mandeville among the Dutch, Knutzen and Edelmann among the Germans, Radicati among the Italians, and Toland in England, as radical thinkers postulating, and to some extent actively envisaging, the destruction of the institutional and monarchical structure of the *ancien régime* and, in part, its hierarchical social system, as well as its theological and philosophical underpinning.

iii. The Revolutionary Impulse

During the early Enlightenment era, the prevailing European political legacy against which defenders of 'liberty' chiefly reacted was the near universal expansion of the monarchical State in the direction of absolutism, that is, the new forms of monarchical and bureaucratic power, what Boulainvilliers calls *l'autorité arbitraire*, associated above all with the rule of Louis XIV (1643–1715). France under Louis XIV was indeed

---

[73] Ibid., 338–40.   [74] Ibid., 346; Jacob, *Living the Enlightenment*, 23–5.

conceived by ideological opponents, such as Shaftesbury, as a malign power threatening the entire world with 'universal monarchy, a new abyss of ignorance and superstition'.[75] Smaller absolutist states had evolved, meanwhile, since the middle of the seventeenth century, parallel to that of France, in Brandenburg-Prussia, other German states, Sweden, pre-1688 England, Naples, and Savoy, which were no less inclined to suppress representative institutions, and established privileges and liberties, in the name of unrestricted monarchical authority. These too sought to debar the free expression of ideas, sometimes, as in the case of the absolutism of Vittore Amadeo II of Savoy, driving abroad and engendering a fierce reaction in opponents, such as Radicati, who passionately denounced every ideological strand of the new monarchical absolutism.[76]

The reaction was psychological, philosophical, and also political and ideological. Since the royal absolutism against which radical thinkers reacted could not easily be reformed or corrected piecemeal this, in turn, and for the first time in European history, engendered an implicit and incipient, but nevertheless real and enduring, preoccupation with revolution. The social radicalism of the English Revolution of the 1640s, and the violence of the French Frondes (1648–53), and the Masaniello insurrection and Neapolitan republic of 1647–8, had lent revolution a generally unsavoury image, so that open advocacy of insurrection and revolutionary violence in order to achieve fundamental political and social change, though it did occur, was heard only very rarely in the Early Enlightenment period. There were certainly passionate advocates of equality and redistribution of property, such as Spinoza's Latin master, Van den Enden, Knutzen, the Baron Lahontan, and Radicati, men who clearly envisaged or dreamt of a dramatically new social and economic order, but even these did not call for the mobilization of the masses—though Van den Enden at least did urge revolutionary conspiracy—in order to achieve it.

Yet the radical thinkers of the Early Enlightenment aspired to sweep monarchical absolutism away and remodel human society, politics, and culture on the basis of 'liberty', and this had to mean, in some sense, envisaging and condoning revolution. If, moreover the mid-seventeenth-century revolutions were largely or completely discredited, this still left the more alluring model of revolution—a seemingly civilized, gentle revolution which almost bloodlessly (at least in England, if not in Scotland and Ireland) toppled divine-right despotism and arbitrary power—namely the Glorious Revolution of 1688–91. Political ferment in Britain had triggered massive intervention by the States General and, following a seaborne invasion from the Netherlands of unprecedented magnitude, the Dutch Stadholder, William III, together with the Dutch States General and the English Whig opposition, had successfully removed James II, establishing a parliamentary State in which real power increasingly accrued to Parliament or, in effect, the English landed gentry. For continental Europe, no less than Britain, Ireland, and North America, the Glorious Revolution proved of crucial

---

[75] Klein, *Shaftesbury*, 189.   [76] Symcox, *Victor Amadeus II*, 223–5.

significance not just by rolling back the tide of divine-right monarchy and weakening Louis XIV internationally, but by generating a new political culture of representation, rights, and 'freedom'.[77] Its achievements and principles, moreover, even if they interpreted these quite differently from the vast majority of more conservative observers, were warmly espoused by such publicists and ideologues as Blount, Shaftesbury, Toland, Walten, Leenhof, Radicati, Mandeville, Vauvenargues, and (more covertly) Diderot.

The Revolution of 1688 fundamentally transformed British institutions. But in their diverse ways of explaining or justifying what had happened most English political commentators, pamphleteers, and spokesmen, Tory and Whig, tended to negate, minimize, or at least refuse fully to acknowledge the kind of republican, pro-revolution, libertarian implications which radical ideologues of the Revolution insisted on proclaiming as its message.[78] Thus the Dutch radical and apologist of the Revolution, Ericus Walten, contemptuously rebuts the divine-right doctrine of the Anglican clergy, insisting that such teaching will quickly reduce the subjects of kings to 'slavery' and that subjects always have the right of armed opposition to monarchs and their representatives 'if they act illegally and attack them in their religion, freedoms, and property'.[79] Walten argues that the sovereign power originates in the people, that all men are born free by nature, and that 'this natural freedom always remains in its entirety' until and unless adjusted by formal contract.[80]

Similarly, in his *Anglia Libera* (1701), Toland accounts Parliament, or any legislature, 'only a fiduciary power to make laws for the good of the society, and since no people can be suppos'd to intend their liberty and property shou'd be destroy'd by the authority they delegate to their representatives, 'tis plain that whenever these neglect to fulfil their trust, or that they use it to contrary ends from those design'd by their principals', then the people may 'not only defend themselves against their legislators (as well as from others attempting to enslave or destroy them) but may likewise place this power afresh in such persons, and after what manner or form they shall think most conducing to their security, welfare, and felicity'.[81] According to Toland, James II forfeited his right to rule in England, Scotland, and Ireland not only by violating his coronation oath but, more fundamentally, by 'an open breach . . . of the natural relation or original compact between all kings and their subjects'.[82] Because James sought to 'subvert our laws and liberties', the 'free people of this kingdom invited over the Prince of Orange, under whom they put themselves in a posture of defence and successfully recover'd the just rights of themselves and their posterity'.[83] And on this basis, he adds,

---

[77] Speck, *Reluctant Revolutionaries*, 242–51; Israel, *Anglo-Dutch Moment*, 31–43.

[78] Ashcraft, *Revolutionary Politics*, 561–77; Speck, *Reluctant Revolutionaries*, 247.

[79] Walten, *Regtsinnige Policey*, 6; Israel, *Dutch Republic*, 856.

[80] Walten, *Regtsinnige Policey*, 4, 24–5, 27; Van Bunge, 'Eric Walten', 43.

[81] Toland, *Anglia Libera*, 26; it is possible to disagree with the view that 'Toland's opinions on free speech, civil liberty and religious toleration' were 'ordinary Whig principles'; see Stromberg, *Religious Liberalism*, 159.

[82] Toland, *Anglia Libera*, 22–3.   [83] Ibid.

the people 'may safely conclude that no king can ever be so good as one of their own making; as there is no title equal to their approbation, which is the only divine right of all magistracy, for the voice of the people is the voice of God'.[84]

Such ideas were enthusiastically endorsed by Count Radicati. Indeed, in Radicati the revolutionary impulse went further than in almost any other Early Enlightenment *philosophe*. For not only does he affirm unequivocally that if the prince or magistrates alter or change the laws 'the people have a right to depose and punish them, according to their deserts seeing that the conditional obedience promised to them, ceases as soon as they cease to do their duty,'[85] but Radicati also insists that republics are intrinsically better than other kinds of government, and especially monarchies, which are 'the worst of all', but that, in order to succeed they have to be placed on a democratic basis. The 'republics of Geneva, Switzerland, and others,' he says, 'notwithstanding they designed to settle a perfect democracy, were not able to succeed in it, because they did not establish it upon a proper foundation.'[86] What this 'proper foundation' entails, holds Radicati, is a fundamental social and economic reorganization so that 'men are equal in nobility, power and riches'. To this end, he asserts, 'all possessions must belong to the republic, which like a good mother, must distribute them to every man, according to his necessities; so that no man must be reduced to beggary, and no man must enjoy superfluities.'[87] Influenced perhaps by reading the Baron Lahontan's eulogy of equality in his *Nouveaux voyages* of 1703, Radicati goes so far as to condemn private property itself as 'inconsistent with the nature of a democratical government, and destroying it in its very infancy'.[88]

Meanwhile, the 'despotism of Louis XIV', as Tom Paine later expressed it, 'so humbled and at the same time fascinated the mind of France' that the people sank into a 'sort of lethargy . . . from which it showed no disposition to rise'; according to him, 'the only signs which appeared of the spirit of Liberty during those periods are to be found in the writings of the French philosophers.'[89] Apart from a few of the libertine nobles who imbibed republican ideas abroad, this is indeed true, and the first *philosophe* who rejected the whole ideological apparatus of Louis' absolutism was unquestionably Boulainvilliers, who was thoroughly averse to the style and pretensions of his government, which he calls despotic and 'odieux'.[90] Especially he abhors divine-right rhetoric and the use of ecclesiastical sanction and theological arguments to buttress Louis' rule. The learned count's political ideas evidently developed between the mid-1690s and 1720, precisely the period in which his Spinozist system more generally evolved, so it is not surprising to find unmistakable links between his philosophy and political ideology. He regarded Bossuet as one of those most responsible for foisting divine-right ideology on France and, consequently, one of those chiefly responsible for the political corruption of the country. Any observer who is 'suffisament éclairé', he holds, 'regardera le système politique de l'Illustre Bossuet,

[84] Toland, *Anglia Libera*, 26.   [85] Radicati, *Twelve Discourses*, 202; Giannone, *Opere*, p. xxiv.
[86] Radicati, *Twelve Discourses*, 205.   [87] Ibid., 204; Ferrone, *Intellectual Roots*, 275.
[88] Radicati, *Twelve Discourses*, 204.   [89] Paine, *Rights of Man*, 93.
[90] Boulainvilliers, *Mémoires*, 1; Ellis, *Boulainvilliers*, 77; Venturino, *Ragioni*, 252.

évêque de Meaux, comme un des plus honteux témoignages de l'indignité de notre siècle et de la corruption des coeurs'.[91] Bossuet had forcefully given expression to the divine-right concept and, in Boulainvilliers' view, 'il n'y a rien en effet de si mauvaise foi que l'abus perpétuel qu'il a fait des textes de la Sainte Écriture pour former de nouvelles chaînes à la liberté naturelle des hommes, et pour augmenter le faste et la dureté des rois.'[92]

The vitriolic anticlericalism in Boulainvilliers, as in that of all representatives of philosophical radicalism in the Early Enlightenment, was rooted in the conviction that the clergy were colluding with absolutist rulers, buttressing divine-right monarchy, and proclaiming the royal will a magical sacral power out of self-interest, to extend thereby their own authority and sway. But the hub of Boulainvilliers' critique of Louis' monarchy is not his repudiation of its pseudo-sacred divine-right status, buttressed by the Church, but his view of absolutism as a form of violence which methodically usurps rights and powers historically vested in a network of lesser institutions and bodies, thereby amassing an illicit and arbitrary power which unjustly heaps all manner of new fiscal, bureaucratic, and war-related burdens on the common people.[93] Yet Boulainvilliers laments and deplores monarchical despotism without offering any real strategy for remedying the setback. Like Spinoza himself, he seemed immobilized between his detestation of tyranny, on one side, and fear of undermining the authority of the State on the other. Boulainvilliers passionately believes in the natural liberty of men but not in the people's right to participate in politics. Indeed, he was very far from being a democrat, desiring rather a kind of quasi-republic of the nobility, such as had lately emerged in England, where nobles share power with the monarch and balance his authority. He believed that such a thing had once existed in France but been gradually undermined by kings assisted by the negligence of the nobility themselves.

After Louis' death, Boulainvilliers was one of those who hoped there would be a revival of the French States General, and the *parlements,* with the nobility taking the lead, and that this would suffice not just to limit royal power in the future but produce a more equitable distribution of taxation and, in a republican sense, 'ranimer l'idée du bien public'.[94] Clearly Boulainvilliers had considerable sympathy for the post-1688 settlement in England, foreshadowing Montesquieu in his conviction that the balance between Crown and Parliament achieved in Britain represented the most successful instance in the Europe of his day of an arrangement of political institutions designed to secure liberty and the 'public good'.

Yet Boulainvilliers could not approve the manner in which the 'crowned republic' devised in England had come into being. For it was the fruit of a revolution which

---

[91] Boulainvilliers, *Lettres*, iii, 68; Assoun, 'Spinoza, les libertins', 192; Venturino, *Ragione*, 271.

[92] Boulainvilliers, *Lettres*, ii, 68; Venturino, *Ragione*, 271; see also Keohane, *Philosophy*, 251–6; Phillips, *Church and Culture*, 302–8.

[93] Venturino, *Ragione*, 274–93.

[94] Boulainvilliers, *Mémoires*, 12–13; Vernière, *Spinoza*, 395–8; Ellis, *Boulainvilliers*, 110, 145; Pocock, *Machiavellian Moment*, 476; Brogi, *Cerchio*, 18–19.

dethroned the legitimate monarch and expelled his most loyal supporters, and had, moreover, only come about owing to conspiracy, treason, and a huge foreign invasion. The French nobility and people had unfortunately not been as 'attentive à ses privileges et libertés' as they should have been but, by 1719, once his hopes that the new regency government would abandon the oppressive practices of the past and revive the States General had been dashed, Boulainvilliers could see no way to rectify the situation. However constituted, sovereignty, in his eyes, could not justifiably be challenged and opposed with conspiracy and violence. Hence there was simply no way to remodel politics and society from below.[95] This left him without any solution to his problem other than philosophical resignation, and recommending the people to be likewise resigned, in the face of a corrupt, deformed, and sporadically despotic Bourbon monarchical state.

Boulainvilliers' predicament was precisely that of Spinoza earlier and Diderot later.[96] According to Spinoza, the purpose of the State is to secure the freedom and common good, of all, and if the State becomes malign, or despotic, revolution may well be the consequence. His system means no form of government can claim a God-given sanction or any inherent legitimacy based on authority or tradition. There is no other sanction or legitimacy for the sovereign than the acquiescence and approval of the people. This means the path to self-liberation is always available and legitimate (if not always advisable) and that violent resistance to the sovereign, and revolution, consequently is sometimes inevitable, sometimes to be recommended, and, in itself, beyond blame.[97] If any government acts contrary to the interests of the people, it will automatically lose their acquiescence and its power to enforce its will, authority, and legislation.

Yet, at the same time, Spinoza maintains that revolutionary violence against a tyrant will generally have no useful result, stressing the danger involved 'in removing a monarch even if his tyranny is apparent to all'.[98] He does not have a high opinion of the common people and believes their veneration of their institutions is so ingrained that once they are 'accustomed to royal rule . . . they will despise and mock a lesser authority'. Thus, when removing a despotic king, the people generally appoint another in his place who, he argues, if he does not wish to reign on sufferance, 'must deter the people from daring to repeat such action' and will, therefore, almost certainly seek to intimidate 'the people rejoicing in regicide as in a glorious deed' and refuse to acknowledge 'the people as judge of kings and master over him'.[99] Thus, he argues, 'a people has often succeeded in changing tyrants but never in abolishing tyranny or substituting another form of government for monarchy', claiming that English experience offers a sad example of this truth, Cromwell being merely a king

---

[95] Venturino, *Ragione*, 306.

[96] Giancotti Boscherini, 'Réalisme et utopie', 37–41; Balibar, *Spinoza and Politics*, 31–9. Payne, *Philosophes and the People*, 31, 149–53, 161–5.

[97] Blom, *Rise of Naturalism*, 199, 215, 238; Bove, *Stratégie du* conatus, 252–64, 284–90, 296.

[98] Spinoza, *TTP*, 277.

[99] Ibid.; Balibar, *Spinoza and Politics*, 39.

under another name. In his opinion, nothing was done in the English commonwealth of the late 1640s and 1650s to establish a genuine republic. Nor, in his view, did the Romans really succeed in progressing from monarchy to a viable republic. When the Roman Empire reverted to being a monarchy, under Augustus, he says, this was 'merely a change of name as in England'.[100]

Hence the best thing for any people, even when being tyrannized over, is simply to acquiesce in whatever form of government they are accustomed to. The Dutch Revolt against Spain, he argues, was a successful revolution and entirely justified, not owing to any general right, or advisability, of resistance to tyrants but simply because Holland was not a monarchy and had never been subject to a sovereign monarch, sovereignty there having always been vested in the States. When Philip II of Spain, as Count of Holland, tried to usurp that sovereign power, he was violently and justifiably overthrown, at least in the northern Netherlands. But, insists Spinoza, 'it is by no means true that the States revolted against him since, in fact, they recovered their original sovereignty which had almost been lost.'[101] Not a very convincing argument, the reader may well judge, but convenient for Spinoza in his dilemma of claiming, on the one hand, that the State exists for the common good and benefit of all, while arguing, on the other, that the forcible removal of despots is mostly inadvisable and the revolutionary impulse of the Dutch Revolt, except where the people are accustomed to republican ideas, mostly not to be emulated.[102]

Diderot's political thought arose not from any deep preoccupation with earlier political thinkers but through his being led to explore the social and political implications of his general philosophy, based as it was, by the late 1740s, on an atheistic Naturalism and *fatalisme*.[103] Doubtless he became more politically conscious also as a result of his personal experiences and imprisonment at the hands of arbitrary, royal government in the late 1740s. Early in his career as a *philosophe*, Diderot translated and was deeply impressed with the work of Shaftesbury, whose influence on his first major work, the *Pensées philosophiques* (1746), is marked.[104] But it was then mainly the philosophical and ethical ideas of Shaftesbury, rather than his social and political concerns, which interested him, albeit with one notable exception—the idea of 'natural sociability'. During the 1740s, Diderot also read and absorbed other radical predecessors, notably Spinoza,[105] Bayle, Lahontan,[106] Fontenelle,[107] Saint-Hyacinthe, Lévesque de Burigny, and La Mettrie;[108] and through perusing these authors, Diderot refined and elaborated his own philosophical system which, he came to realize only later, had wide-ranging political implications. These he was prompted to think through in the late 1740s, while commencing work on the *Encyclopédie*, and especially during intense discussions with his then comrade Rousseau in the years around 1750.

Indeed, it is remarkable how little Diderot's political thought owes to his great

[100] Spinoza, *TTP*, 278.   [101] Ibid., 279.   [102] Curley, 'Kissinger, Spinoza', 330–5.

[103] Proust, *Diderot*, 255–321; Jimack, 'French Enlightenment', i, 244–8.

[104] Diderot, *Pensées philosophiques*, 10–11, 13, 23, 34–6; Venturi, *Jeunesse de Diderot*, 48–9.

[105] Vernière, *Spinoza*, 559–60.   [106] Diderot, *Pensées philosophiques*, 65.

[107] Proust, *Diderot*, 312–13.   [108] Diderot, *Lettre*, 96–8.

predecessors Locke and Montesquieu, or any notion of separation of powers by constitutional means, the political hub, one might say, of the mainstream moderate Enlightenment; he rules out all notion of a binding contract or constitutional checks designed to limit the sovereign power.[109] Scarcely less striking, despite claims to the contrary, is how little it owes to Hobbes. Until the early 1750s, Diderot had not in fact read Hobbes, or at least not referred to him, and in his main political articles in the *Encyclopédie* he only invokes him to deplore his failure to make any real distinction between 'subject' and 'citizen'.[110] For Diderot the 'citizen' is not obliged to obey the sovereign unconditionally, but retains his right to judge and criticize, and by implication something more.[111] For the State exists not just to maintain order and security, as Hobbes argues, but also for what Diderot calls 'conservation de la liberté'.[112] Since the *Encyclopédie* had to pass the censors, and did so only with difficulty, one could hardly expect to find Diderot using its pages for the purpose of openly rejecting the principle of monarchy or criticizing the traditions of French royal government. Nowhere in his political articles, as was remarked at the time, did he, or indeed could he have written disparagingly of monarchy or accorded the people any right to oppose despotic monarchical rule.

Nevertheless, discerning eyes noticed a subversive undercurrent which went far beyond merely encouraging the public to exercise critical judgement, based on reason, about everything; indeed, it had revolutionary implications integrally linked to his Naturalism and *fatalisme*. In the first place, as an ecclesiastical critic remarked in March 1752, a period when the project of the *Encyclopédie* was under particular pressure,[113] there was Diderot's principle that all political authority comes from the hands of the people from whom it is assigned to the monarch, a concept which removes all trace of divine-right justification. If the will of God and the Christian religion provide the foundations of a Christian society, then a monarch owes his crown to God, and not to the people, and is answerable only to Him.[114] If the king receives his authority from the people, then the implication is that he is answerable to the people and is no longer in the first place God's lieutenant on earth and the guardian of Christ's Church.

Then, in the second place, precisely by rejecting Hobbes' conception of man under the State as a 'subject' and insisting that he is a 'citizen', Diderot advances a conception of the public good which he (not Rousseau) was the first to dub the 'general will'. This obliges the sovereign to provide individuals and society collectively not just with the security, stability, and order in exchange for which they departed from the 'state of nature' but also to ensure the laws accord with the moral standards and aspirations of society, that is, they embody the 'general will'.[115] Furthermore, his political articles strongly imply that there is a crucial difference between the legitimate monarch who rules in accordance with the 'volonté générale' of his people and the tyrant who rules

---

[109] Proust, *Diderot*, 347–50, 432, 586.   [110] Ibid., 428–9; Glaziou, *Hobbes en France*, 142, 149.

[111] Article 'Citoyen', *Encyclopédie*, iii, 488–9; Glaziou, *Hobbes en France*, 147.

[112] Hazard, *European Thought*, 406; Proust, *Diderot*, 589.   [113] Chartier, *Cultural Origins*, 41–3.

[114] Proust, *Diderot*, 352–3.   [115] Ibid., 426–9; Talmon, *Origins*, 41.

in his own interest, disregarding the public good. In his article 'Citoyen', Diderot asserts that the more the ruler renders everyone equal under the law the better the 'general will' is served, adding that maximizing equality and minimizing hierarchy are basic functions of a just monarchy. 'Plus les citoyens approcheront de l'égalité de prétensions et de fortune,' he says, 'plus l'état sera tranquille.'[116] Equality, he says, might theoretically seem a characteristic of democracy rather than monarchy, but even in the most perfect democracy 'l'entière égalité entre les membres est une chose chimérique,' and stability is in practice best ensured by monarchy.[117]

According to Diderot, then, sovereignty cannot be divided, and the crucial distinction between governments is not whether they are monarchical or democratic but whether they are just or unjust, 'free' or despotic, in the sense of upholding the 'general will'. It is perfectly true that Diderot never defines the 'liberty' the State exists to uphold, and rules out all possibility of justified popular resistance against the despot who tramples the *volonté générale* under foot.[118] Already as a young writer, he expressly rebuked Shaftesbury for praising those who assassinate tyrants.[119] But in Diderot's political writing the questions of *liberté* and revolution are nevertheless left hanging in the air, an unsolved paradox, a *non sequitur* bringing political theory full circle back to the quandary embedded in Spinoza and Boulainvilliers. Though coherent, Diderot's political philosophy is inherently unstable, indeed explosive: if legitimate government is rooted in the principle of the 'general will', then just and justifiable government is practically realizable only under an enlightened philosopher-king.

The essence of the radical intellectual tradition from Spinoza to Diderot is the philosophical rejection of revealed religion, miracles, and divine Providence, replacing the idea of salvation in the hereafter with a highest good in the here and now. In this tradition human happiness is envisaged partly as possessive individualism but partly as a shared sociability which places the highest good in the laws devised by society to permit the maximum amount of 'liberty' to each individual, in other words, laws which embody the common good. Diderot, like Spinoza, emphasizes the need to inculcate obedience to society's laws, defining true 'religion' as veneration for those laws and society's best interest and true piety as 'obedience' to the common good. This new form of quasi-religious reverence was eloquently expressed by Diderot's predecessor and older colleague working on the *Encyclopédie*, César Chesneau du Marsais (1676–1756?), a disciple of Fontenelle, in a text clandestinely printed allegedly at 'Amsterdam' in 1743, entitled *Le Philosophe*,[120] where he argues that despite the 'fables' which the people believe about the Flood, fire from on high, and lively imagery of eternal torment in Hell (as well as that of reward in Heaven), experience shows that religion provides only a feeble brake on crime, dishonesty, and wrongdoing: 'la superstition ne fait sentir que foiblement combien il importe aux hommes par rapport à leur intérêt présent de suivre les loix de la societé';[121] indeed, Du Marsais goes so far

---

[116] Article 'Citoyen', *Encyclopédie*, iii, 489.   [117] Ibid.; Payne, *Philosophes and the People*, 168–9.
[118] Proust, *Diderot*, 431, 438.   [119] Ibid., 590.
[120] On Du Marsais' authorship of *Le Philosophe*, see Mori, 'Du Marsais', 176–7, 191.
[121] [Du Marsais], *Le Philosophe*, 191–3.

as to call 'la société civile . . . pour ainsi dire, la seule divinité' that the true philosopher acknowledges on earth—he reveres it, he honours it with his probity, by his scrupulous attention to his duties and by a sincere desire not to be a useless member of it.[122]

If the concept of the secular 'common good' intrinsic to radical thought and Spinozism is allowed to spread, then inevitably political and social revolution based on notions of the 'general will', and the call for equality, seemingly becomes inevitable. The political instability the progress of these ideas must entail can thus only be precluded by rolling back the advance of radical thought as such. But to repel and overcome radical thought it was not necessary to attack the entire corpus of radical writers. Reviewing the situation in 1757, the Abbé François Pluquet, in his three-volume *Examen du fatalisme*, confirmed, as had so many before him, that there had indeed been a vast sea-change in French culture and intellectual life since the late seventeenth century, and that philosophical incredulity had unquestionably penetrated on a massive scale. What was at stake were two opposed visions of the world, one based on Revelation, religion, and miracles, the other rejecting these in favour of a philosophical determinism and materialism rooted in the idea that there is no divine governance of the world and no hereafter. The intellectual war now in progress is a war for humanity and for the world. But if the enemy is to be defeated then it is important to grasp how, strategically, the enemy can most effectively be attacked. There is, he insists, a high degree of intellectual interdependence connecting the recent writings of La Mettrie and (the unmentioned) Diderot, first to the earlier wave of clandestine and anonymous printed polemics against prevailing structures of authority of which the collection (edited probably by Du Marsais) entitled the *Nouvelles libertés de penser* ('Amsterdam', 1743)[123] was foremost, and then, further back, to the collaborators and interpreters of Spinoza, of whom he cites Cuffeler, Bredenburg, Leenhof, and Wachter in particular. But ultimately, he insisted, the entire edifice of modern incredulity, with all its social and cultural implications, derives from Spinoza. All philosophical systems which are *fataliste*, and postulate that there is only one substance in the world, he argues, rest on and in the final analysis derive from, 'le Spinosisme'.[124]

Hence the only way to check and defeat the fatalistic atheism of the militant *philosophes* now pervading French life is to demolish the foundations of Spinoza's system. Many writers had taken up their pens against Spinoza, yet still his philosophy remained unconquered. Early opponents such as Wittichius had completely failed. The celebrated Bayle 'lui-même, ce destructeur infatigable de toute doctrine systématique' who had destroyed so many, had nevertheless dismally failed to overwhelm

---

[122] [Du Marsais], *Le Philosophe*, 188; Beales, 'Christians and *Philosophes*', 71.

[123] In fact published illegally in Paris in 1742, edited probably by Du Marsais; it contained, besides Du Marsais' own *Le Philosophe*, several other pieces including Fontenelle's fatalistic *Traité de la liberté*; [Pluquet], *Examen*, i, 387–97; Mori, 'Du Marsais', 177–8, 189.

[124] [Pluquet], *Examen*, ii, preface, p. i.

Spinoza or even correctly understand his system.[125] Fénelon had failed no less obviously. Others, such as the great English philosopher Samuel Clarke and the formidable Isaac Jaquelot, had tried to overthrow his system by targeting a few key propositions which they considered fundamental, failing to realize that 'pour réfuter le fatalisme qui ne suppose qu'une substance' it is insufficient to overthrow parts, or even the whole of the upper edifice: one must demolish the foundations and this, alas, had not been done.[126] Nor had any recent controversialists done much better. It seemed an impossible situation and yet the truth had to be faced: 'on a souvent écrit contre ce philosophe, mais, à ce que beaucoup de personnes pensent, avec assez peu de succès.'[127]

---

[125] Ibid., ii, preface, p. ii and p. 95; Vernière, *Spinoza*, 443.   [126] [Pluquet], *Examen*, ii, preface, p. iv.

[127] Ibid., ii, preface, p. ii.

4 | WOMEN, PHILOSOPHY, AND SEXUALITY

i. The Emancipation of Women

The revolutionary implications of radical thought for Europe's institutions, monarchical governments, and aristocratic social order could, at most, be only faintly glimpsed in the decades down to the mid-eighteenth century. Politically, the ultimate significance of the new radical ideas was not to become fully evident until the 1790s. Very different was the case with issues of sexuality, eroticism, and the place of women in society. Here the unsettling ramifications of philosophical naturalism and Spinozism, as well as Bayle's radical separation of morality from religion, became apparent at an early stage and were elaborated by such radical writers as Beverland, Leenhof, Radicati, Mandeville, Doria, and d'Argens.

The shift of intellectual debate in Europe from Latin to French, and from the academic sphere to courts, coffee-houses, clubs, and salons, enabled some women, especially noble ladies supplemented with a sprinkling of escaped nuns, actresses, female singers, courtesans, and others who were relatively well-educated, to discover the new philosophy and science and by means of intellectual 'enlightenment' transform their outlook and lives. Such was the impetus of philosophy in these decades that it could not only shatter authority, tradition, and the belief system of the past but also, for the first time, challenge and indeed fundamentally alter existing patterns of social and cultural relations between men and women.

Intellectually, women for the first time became an audience and an active presence. Thus Fontenelle remarks, in the preface to his *Entretiens sur la pluralité des mondes* (1686), that he writes primarily 'pour les femmes' and those men who know little Latin, explaining that he esteems native insight and judgement, what he calls 'esprit', male or female, far higher than mere erudition, however great, which indeed, he notes, can sometimes be entirely devoid of true understanding.[1] But he seeks not just to educate women about science but also to 'enlighten' them and by so doing activate them in society. His aim, as he puts it, is to win over his fictional 'Madame la marquise' for the 'party of philosophy'.[2] Other *philosophes* similarly envisaged themselves as

---

[1] Fontenelle, *Entretiens*, preface, pp. Aiv–v; Niderst, *Fontenelle*, 284; Brockliss, 'Scientific Revolution', 70.
[2] Fontenelle, *Entretiens*, 1–3.

popularizers of the new philosophy and science outside the world of professional scholarship and the Republic of Letters. The marquis d'Argens saw his philiosophical writing as primarily intended 'à l'usage des cavaliers et du beau sexe'.[3]

Admittedly, most contemporaries, male and female, viewed such infiltration of philosophical and scientific ideas among women, and still more the involvement of women in intellectual debate—let alone their entry into Fontenelle's 'partie de la philosophie'—with unease bordering on alarm. There was much resistance to, and condemnation of, such developments. Nor was this reaction groundless from a conservative viewpoint. For the intellectual shift undoubtedly did erode traditional notions of virtue, family, and social roles, crucially challenging woman's existing subordinate status. Furthermore, it raised issues of sexuality, male and female, in a way which disturbed not only traditionalists but also those committed to a moderate form of Enlightenment. For, in general, the more radical the philosophical standpoint, the more emphatic the levelling and egalitarian tendencies implicit in ideas which, in turn, generated a growing impulse not just towards the emancipation of woman but of the human libido itself.

Should men and women think the same thoughts and on the same basis? Fontenelle, championing a relentlessly mechanistic world-view, professed to want to free literate, educated, spirited ladies from the 'obscurité' of imagining the physical world around us to be moved by an unseen chaos of supernatural and magical forces and spirits.[4] But this meant persuading women to discard the fantasies of the past and think mathematically and mechanistically. One might suppose women naturally more suited to 'imagination' than precise thinking, mused Montesquieu, but it seemed to him undeniable that Descartes and the Cartesians had powerfully demystified the feminine mind, propelling it from the sphere of 'poetry' towards philosophy, no less than that of men.[5] If modern philosophy overturns previous ideas about nature and the universe, 'réduisant tout à la communication des mouvements', it did so for women no less than men, at least potentially, creating a common intellectual 'monde' where one speaks only 'd'entendement pur, d'idées claires, de raison, de principes, de conséquences'.[6] If, for the time being, something nevertheless remained of tradition and woman's subordination, it was perhaps fortunate, Montesquieu added, that it was Cartesianism and its variants which had dominated the philosophical scene hitherto, for if matters went any further, 'si quelque peuple allait s'infatuer du système de Spinoza', nothing at all would remain of imagination, tradition, and 'poetry' or, he implied, of womanly deference to man.[7] As it was, the new philosophical ladies of the salons perceived that 'la tyrannie des hommes', as the marquise de Lambert expressed it, exists 'par la force plutôt que par le droit naturelle'.[8]

The first and most obvious result of woman's arrival in the arena of philosophy was the advent of the high-born patroness of new ideas. Of these none was more widely

---

[3] Johnston, *Marquis d'Argens*, 47.   [4] Fontenelle, *Entretiens*, 14, 59.
[5] Montesquieu, *Oeuvres complètes*, 902.   [6] Ibid.   [7] Ibid.
[8] Lambert, *Reflexions nouvelles*, 7, 9.

celebrated than the Duchess, later Electress, Sophie von der Pfalz (1630–1714), wife of Ernst August (ruled 1679–98) of Braunschweig-Lüneburg, a principality known from the 1690s as the electorate of Hanover. Wife of one elector and sister to another (the philosophically inclined Karl Ludwig of the Palatinate), her eldest son became—shortly after her death, in 1715—George I of England, Scotland, and Ireland. Originally a keen devotee of Cartesianism, Sophie had an acute, enquiring mind and always placed great emphasis on the importance of 'philosophy'. Having been brought up in a liberal Calvinist milieu in Holland by her Stuart mother—Descartes' friend, Princess Elizabeth—but married to a Lutheran prince, she never entirely suppressed her early aversion to Lutheran pastors.[9] Her horizons broadened by travel in Italy as well as Germany and the Netherlands, she liked to show her independent-mindedness, and early on in her married life caused rumours that she was given to perusing profane literature during sermons. Writing to her brother after receiving from the great Danish scientist-priest Nicholas Steno, then embarking on his drive to win high-born recruits for the Catholic Counter-Reformation in northern Germany, a letter full of devout sentiments in 1678, she irreverently mocked his piety.[10] Indeed, she went so far as to confide to Karl Ludwig that, in her view, there is much in the Christian religion which conflicts with the dictates of sound reason.[11]

Descartes, moreover, was just a start. In March 1679 she informed her brother she was reading the recently published French edition of the *Tractatus Theologico-Politicus*—presumably she would not had it remained available only in Latin—and found it 'admirable'.[12] A week later, reading on, she was still more enthusiastic: '[Spinoza's] livre est effectivement bien rare et tout à fait selon la raison.'[13] Still more irreverently, she remarked that if it was true, as she had heard, that Spinoza had recently died, then surely some churchman must have poisoned him 'car la plupart du genre humain vit du mensonge'.[14] At Osnabrück, where she and her husband held court from 1661 to 1679 while he was the episcopal administrator of the principality, she learned more about Spinoza's life from various courtiers, including the marquis de Rébenac, son of one of Louis XIII's generals. Furthermore, Sophie encouraged interest in Spinoza among others there as well as at Hanover after her husband succeeded his elder brother as duke in 1679. Delighting in the intellectual progress of her younger son, Friedrich August—she considered George a frustratingly dull fellow by comparison—she reported to Heidelberg, in July 1679, that the young prince 'sait Descartes et Spinoza casi par coeur'.[15]

Meanwhile, Leibniz had become councillor and librarian at Hanover where, as he assured Tschirnhaus, he was delighted by the prevailing atmosphere of intellectual freedom. Before long he had won Sophie's confidence, gently steering her towards an attitude of antipathy towards both Cartesianism and Spinozism and a growing appreciation of Leibnizianism. But if Leibniz advised, he always respected her as a

---

[9] Bodemann, 'Herzogin Sophie', 55.   [10] Ibid., 81.   [11] Ibid., 82.
[12] *Briefwechsel der Herzogin Sophie*, 350.   [13] Ibid., 353.
[14] Ibid., 368.   [15] Ibid., 368.

philosophical force in her own right, and in later years the two frequently discussed the further evolution of the European philosophical scene, as well as his own system and, after 1700, such new thinkers as Toland, with whom both conversed at length and to whom both rapidly conceived a dislike.

But women not only emerged as patronesses of philosophy, influencing matters behind the scenes, as hostesses as it were of philosophical debate, but also as direct public participants in the escalating European war of philosophies. A woman with a formidable philosophical reputation for a time was Voltaire's mistress, Gabrielle-Émilie, marquise du Châtelet, whom he celebrated in print in 1738, as a paragon of female intellectual power, and a true disciple of Newton and of 'truth'.[16] Furthermore, this 'Minerve de la France', as he calls her, not only shared his conversation, scientific experiments, and bed but soon rebelled against his uncompromising Newtonianism, demonstrating a spirited independence of mind.[17] When Voltaire insisted she read Locke, she urged him to read Leibniz. Engaging a young Swiss savant, Samuel König, a devotee of Wolff, to tutor her in mathematics, she systematically explored Wolffianism, and by 1739 was in contact with Wolff himself. For a while, indeed, Wolff placed such importance on her intervention that he believed he would, through her—his 'Apostle to the French'—check the progress of what he called Voltaire's 'Newtonianischen Philosophie' and the 'not very useful principles of the present-day English' in France, hastening that of Wolffianism.[18]

Wolff's Huguenot ally in Berlin, Jean Henri Samuel Formey (1711–97), modelled the heroine of his philosophical novel, *La Belle Wolfienne*, on Voltaire's marquise. A key work of philosophical popularization of the Early Enlightenment, it appeared in Frankfurt in six volumes in 1741–2, and was plainly directed at women as much as, or more than, men. Its object is to persuade readers that the Leibnizian-Wolffian philosophy is the best and only way to rescue 'la vertu, la société, [et] l'église' from the radicals and 'fatalistes' and, in particular, Spinoza, the forces posing the greatest threat to religion, authority, and civilization.[19] Initially, its heroine learns, Spinoza won 'quelques partisans' eager to throw off the yoke of religion which had become burdensome to them.[20] But eventually the philosophical tide turned and now the Leibnizian-Wolffian system had triumphed: Spinoza's 'ordre éternel, immuable, indépendent où Dieu n'y entre par rien' was everywhere collapsing before Wolff's proofs that another set of general laws would have been possible had God so chosen.[21] But if Spinoza's *nécessité* now lay crushed under Wolff's *raison suffisante*, according to the Wolffians, Gabrielle-Émilie's prestige as a high-level broker in the international power-game of philosophy was soon impaired by doubts as to whether she was really 'une dame solidement savante'. Some mocked her pretensions, dismissing her as a superficial female, vain and coquettish, 'aiant l'esprit vif, inquiet, curieux et bisarre', a

---

[16] Voltaire, *Éléments*, preface and poem dedicated to Madame du Châtelet.
[17] Hazard, *European Thought*, 279.
[18] Wolff to Manteuffel, 7 June 1739, in Ostertag, *Philosophische Gehalt*, 8.
[19] Formey, *La Belle Wolfienne*, i, 57–9.   [20] Ibid., ii, 30–2.
[21] Ibid., ii, 58–61, iv, 41, 115, and vi, xiii, 34, 110–11.

woman merely affecting to cultivate philosophy for the purpose of 'couvrant l'irregularité de sa conduite'.[22]

That at least a few high-born ladies amassed whole collections of radical philosophical literature for their private use is demonstrated by such examples as that of Caroline von Hessen (1721–74), wife of the Landgrave of Hesse-Darmstadt. By the 1740s this lady was in regular contact with a Frankfurt bookseller who had been in difficulties with the authorities on more than one occasion for selling forbidden philosophical books.[23] Daughter of a pious mother, her father, Duke Christian III of Pfalz-Zweibrücken-Birkenfeld, was widely reputed a libertine and freethinker. Her personal cabinet of books, remarkably, included not only Bayle, Locke, and Montesquieu but Mandeville's *Free Thoughts on Religion* (1720) in its French edition of 1722, Collins—again in French, La Mettrie, and several works of the marquis d'Argens.[24]

But could woman's intellectual emancipation be detached from a wider emancipation social, legal, political, theological, and sexual? There was no reason to think so. Admittedly, Spinoza himself argues that women are naturally too weak to assert themselves and stand up to men, and invariably let themselves be dominated. This indeed is his reason for excluding them from participation in his democratic republic: because they are weak and dependent they are not equal to men.[25] He evidently considered it impossible for women to free themselves from subjection to men. But his argument also implies, indeed requires, that if woman can somehow free herself from masculine domination and rival man in power and assertiveness, then there would no longer be any reason for refusing her equal access to the political process. As regards sexuality, Spinoza holds that in one's own interest one ought avoid scandalizing the moral notions of the community among which one lives. But equally, in his naturalistic philosophy, sexual pleasure, the libido, in so far as it is life-enhancing is a good thing and, in principle, in no way different outside marriage than within it.[26] Consequently, there is no justifiable basis for restricting woman's sexual pleasure any more than there is for curtailing that of men.

Spinoza himself showed little interest in sexual issues and yet, paradoxically, his naturalistic system became the intellectual basis of by far the most important advance towards emancipation of the libido, including that of women, to emerge in the Early Enlightenment period. Several writers took up the point that if woman's subjection to man within marriage, the family, and law, is not after all ordained by a providential God and has no basis in Revelation, then the entire system of relations between the sexes prevailing in Christian, Jewish, Muslim, and other societies lacks justification or basis, as does the one-sided repression of female sexuality. Woman should be in a position of equality to man, but had in fact been rendered shamefully subordinate: 'is not every woman that is married,' exclaims Mandeville, 'a slave to her husband?'[27]

---

[22] Ostertag, *Philosophische Gehalt*, 39.   [23] Bräuning-Oktavio, 'Bibliothek', 682–3.
[24] Ibid., 744–59, 834.   [25] Spinoza, *Opera*, ii, 359–60; Matheron, 'Femmes et serviteurs', 376–80.
[26] Matheron, 'Spinoza et la sexualité', 439–40, 457.   [27] [Mandeville], *Virgin Unmask'd*, 127–8.

Adriaan Beverland (1650–1716) was the first to develop a radical standpoint in this sphere and, like his successors, proceeds from a specifically Spinozist position. A Zeelander and a veteran student who, from July 1669, spent a whole decade studying at Franeker, Oxford, Utrecht, and Leiden, becoming an accomplished classicist and a devotee of Ovid, Catullus, and Petronius, he was also noted for his libertine lifestyle.[28] The surviving portrait of him by Arie de Vois (see Plate 9) fully conveys the irreverence, affluence, and pursuit of the erotic which inspired his student years and linked him to his loyal ally Jacob de Goyer (d.1706), in Utrecht.[29] A tireless researcher into the sexual history of ancient Greece and Rome, Beverland combined his expertise in this area with radical ideas to produce a philosophy of life centring around the liberation of the sexual impulse and glorification of the sexual act.[30] Particularly striking is his conclusion that desire for sexual pleasure is fundamental in everyone and that, whatever form it may take and however it may be repressed, this longing is a universal human trait. One consequence is that Beverland thinks puritanical attitudes and ascetism, whatever pious justifications may be adduced, always derive from ignorance, affectation, and hypocrisy.[31] A second is his conclusion that womanly modesty and chastity are invariably an imposed or self-imposed imprisonment and form of deception, and that underneath all women are pleasure-seekers and sensualists no less than men. According to his scheme, there is no such thing as a woman who is 'pure' and chaste in mind.[32] 'The feminine sex has the same passions as does ours,' insisted Beverland, but is forced to stifle it to a greater extent, sexual desire in women being generally condemned as contrary to womanly modesty.[33] Thus only within the restrictions of marriage can women satisfy their desires.

Beverland gained immediate notoriety in 1678, with the publication of his *De Peccato Originali*, a work which caused a public scandal, was banned, and, for many years, available only with difficulty and in Latin, despite being reprinted several times in 1678–9, but which later gained wider currency after appearing in 1714 in a clandestine edition in French; in 1746 a German translation, from the French, was published at Frankfurt.[34] In this erudite if irreverent tract, Beverland insists that Moses did not write the Five Books and comments on the corrupt state of the Biblical text;[35] and claims, invoking Hobbes, La Peyrère, Koerbagh, and Richard Simon, as well as Spinoza, that Scripture employs terms and expressions adapted to the primitive and ignorant minds of the ancient Hebrews, which can only be properly understood in the

---

[28] De Smet, 'Realm', 48–9.   [29] De Smet, *Hadrianus Beverlandus*, 22, 66.

[30] De Smet. 'Realm', 57; Elias, 'Spinozistisch Erotisme', 300–2.

[31] Elias, 'Spinozistisch Erotisme', 308.   [32] Ibid., 310.

[33] 'Le sexe féminin a les mêmes passions que notre sexe, cependant il se trouve condamné à étoufer tout sentiment de convoitise, comme contraire à la pudeur et à la modestie des femmes. Il n'a donc que la voie du marriage pour se satisfaire ouvertement'; [Beverland], *L'État de l'homme*, 107, 109–10.

[34] [Beverland], *L'État de l'homme*, preface; Van Bunge, 'Einleitung', 30; De Smet, *Hadrianus Beverlandus*, 78–9, 86.

[35] [Beverland], *De peccato Originali*, 110–11, 122–4; Ryssenius, *Justa defensio*, 3, 16; De Smet, *Hadrianus Beverlandus*, 118–19, 127–8.

light of philosophy.[36] The story of the Fall, he maintains, is a poetic allegory referring to nothing more than the discovery of sexual intercourse by Adam and Eve and the transmission of the sexual urge from generation to generation.[37] Already in 1679, some observers correctly realized that Spinoza had also inspired in Beverland a form of philosophical pantheism which had now become linked to a general theory of eroticism.[38]

Shortly after its publication, the South Holland Synod condemned the book as a 'foul and blasphemous tractate'. Delegates were sent to protest to the Pensionary of the States of Holland, Caspar Fagel, complaining that Beverland had abused Scripture and was insinuating lascivious thoughts into the minds of the young, reading out the most offensive passages in his presence.[39] Fagel agreed the book should be suppressed. The university curators, summoned to 'clip his wings', had Beverland arrested in October 1679 and imprisoned in the Leiden town hall. He was tried by an academic court a few weeks later, found guilty as charged, and sentenced to the formal retraction of his blasphemous propositions, a heavy fine, and confiscation of a second treatise entitled *De Prostibulis Veterum* (On the Brothels of the Ancients) as well as expulsion from the university and long-term banishment from the provinces of Holland and Zeeland.[40] He was also obliged to undertake never to write such 'obscenities' again.

Briefly he sought refuge in Utrecht, but was soon expelled from there too. In March 1680 he fled to England, according to rumour, threatening to produce fresh 'impieties' and send these to Holland 'as revenge' for the humiliation and punishment to which he had been subjected. In London he was befriended by the libertine savant Isaac Vossius, friend and ally of the deists Saint-Evremond and Temple. Fragments of Beverland's *De Prostibulis Veterum* were reportedly incorporated by Vossius into the preface of his edition of Catallus of 1684.[41] After Vossius' death, in 1689, Beverland, as the latter's executor, tried to engineer his rehabilitation in his homeland by gratifying the new king of England, the Dutch Stadholder, William III, in particular by helping to procure Vossius' large and valuable library for Leiden, frustrating the efforts of Richard Bentley and others to obtain it for Oxford's Bodleian. These manoeuvres failed to restore his standing in Holland, however, and he stayed in England, where he died, forgotten and completely destitute, in 1716.

Similar ideas soon also surfaced in other writers suspected of radical tendencies and were obviously spreading in society. According to Bayle, female sexual modesty and chastity has nothing to do with love of God or morality, and the chief reason why women abstain far more than men from sexual promiscuity is that 'les hommes ont établi la gloire des femmes dans la chasteté.'[42] Were women able to satisfy the desires

---

[36] Beverland, *De Peccato Originali*, 4–6, 17, 105, 110; Beverland, *Hadrianus Beverlandus*, 128–9.

[37] De Smet, 'Realm', 47, 57; Elias, 'Spinozistisch Erotisme', 287.

[38] De Smet, *Hadrianus Beverlandus*, 129, 147.

[39] ARH OSA North Holland Synod, acta Edam, Aug. 1679, p. 6 and acta Alkmaar, Aug. 1680, p. 3; De Smet, *Hadrianus Beverlandus*, 35.

[40] Knuttel, *Acta*, v, 321; De Smet, 'Realm', 49.   [41] Katz, 'Isaac Vossius', 179–81.

[42] Bayle, *Pensées diverses*, ii, 81.

of nature without compromising their reputations, he suggests, 'elles porteroient la débauche plus loin que ne font les hommes.'[43] In his *Dictionnaire*, Bayle devotes several articles to ancient philosopher-courtesans, such as Hipparchia and Laïs, whom he describes as clever, beautiful, and extraordinarily dissolute, and whose sexual exploits he by no means seems to condemn.[44] According to Lahontan, whose *Voyages* were widely read and scandalized many, not only did the Canadian Indians adhere to naturalistic principles about God and Nature which bore an uncanny resemblance to Spinozism, they also left their daughters free, outside marriage, to enjoy the use of men for sex just as they pleased.[45]

Traditionalists, by contrast, drew reassurance from the universally agreed fact that women were less attracted to philosophy, less inclined to atheism, and generally more devout than men.[46] Radical thinkers such as Toland might claim that this piety, and disinclination for philosophy, was due to lack of exposure to enlightened ideas: 'women are equally capable of all improvements with the men, had they but equally the same advantages of education, travel, company, and the management of affairs.'[47] Similarly, in 1709 Mandeville has one of his female interlocutors complain that women are always at a grave disadvantage in conversation since men receive all the education at schools and universities, asking 'why should we venture then (their head-pieces being so much better furnished than ours) to hold arguments, or parley with them?'[48] But among the great majority, male and female, who abhorred radical ideas most people, while loath to permit women such opportunities of reading, contact, and travel, preferred to believe there is an innate gender difference which renders woman naturally more devout and resistant to the corrosive effects of concupiscence and radical ideas than men. One of Toland's innumerable critics, William Wotton, in his *Letter to Eusebia* (1704) assured his fictional lady correspondent that 'if indeed your sex should enter into the irreligious notions which now prevail too much amongst the men, the next generation would be irrecoverably lost'; but 'God be thanked,' he added, 'religion keeps up its authority, in a great measure with your sex still, and God grant it may ever do so.'[49]

There were diverse ways of explaining this alleged innate gender difference and some were prepared to devote much ink to elucidating the point. It was a hallowed tradition to claim that women innately have less intellectual capacity than men, but such a view, in the new context, had certain obvious tactical disadvantages. Theodore Undereyck (1635–93), a prominent German Calvinist pastor, based at Bremen, worried lest 'Naturalists' and libertines should exploit the common prejudice that women possess less judgement, as well as intellect, than men, to suggest the undeniable fact that the 'female sex is more opposed to atheism and dedicated to God . . . than the male sex' proves piety is in some way feminine and therefore foolish.[50] To counter this

---

[42] Ibid.   [44] Bayle, *Historical and Critical*, 95–103, 440–1; Wootton, 'Pierre Bayle', 208–12.
[45] Lahontan, *Nouveaux Voyages*, ii, 143.   [46] Bayle, *Pensées diverses*, ii, 25–6.
[47] Quoted in Wotton, *Letter to Eusebia*, 74.
[48] [Mandeville], *The Mysteries of Virginity*, 27–8.   [49] Wotton, *Letter to Eusebia*, 73.
[50] Undereyck, *Närrische Atheist*, 279–80; as, for instance, Bayle seems to do; Bayle, *Pensées diverses*, ii, 25–6.

threat, he observes that women are naturally more moderate in their passions, and less inclined to study than men. Thus, he concludes that women's disinclination to read and 'limited understanding' should not be regarded as foolishness but rather a gift from God, a wondrous treasure, enabling women to end up, spiritually, both wiser and more sensible than men.[51] Where numerous men imagine they possess more intellect than others and think that to impress their fellows 'one must believe not what others believe but rather what others do not believe,'[52] and distance oneself from the opinions of the 'common man', a form of arrogance which infuses the *esprits forts*, women are mercifully free of such pride and consequently more devout, God-fearing, and submissive to authority. Admittedly, Undereyck grants, there are also dissolute women. But even the most debauched, he says, have usually been made so by men, are less inclined to blasphemy, profanity, and sacrilege than men, and can be more readily persuaded to revert to a God-fearing way of life.[53]

Undereyck also tries to turn to advantage the conflation of body and soul so characteristic of the Naturalists and Spinozists he strives to combat. The 'atheists', he affirms, contend that mind and body are one and that the bodily impulses and needs of men and women also infuse their minds and outlook. This, he says, can only reinforce the implication that devotion to Christ is an unthinking, female characteristic. But in reality, he insists, following Descartes, body and spirit are totally distinct principles and can not interact. Consequently, if women are less given to impiety than men, as they are, it is a fallacy to attribute this crucial difference to inherent physical differences. Rather, the innate difference is spiritual in quality, 'after the Fall' greater obstacles having been put in the path of the male sex in attaining salvation than in that of women.[54] Furthermore, holds Undereyck, God so created men that in their attitude to women they aspire always to be lord and master while imparting a quite different nature to woman, filling her with longing to accept man as her lord and master.[55] That man dominates and woman obeys is therefore an innate but not a bodily difference bestowed by God in the Creation. It is this spiritual disparity which accounts for women being inherently readier than men to submit to Christ the Lord.[56] However, this same fundamental difference means that if, for whatever reason, woman is not as dependent as she should be on father, brother, or husband—as may happen with youthful widows and unmarried women—then woman's vanity, more unthinking, impulsive, and animal-like than that of men, is more apt to be corrupted and seduced.[57] Woman's frivolity and passion for beautiful clothes and jewellery shows what great perils her irrationality poses for society. The only answer is for society and the State to strengthen authority, marriage, and the family.

In certain select social contexts, however, it was difficult to be sure that woman was more immune to radical thought than man. Appalled by the penetration of philosophy among the French courtly aristocracy by around 1700, Father Massillon took the

---

[51] Undereyck, *Närrische Atheist*, 281; see also Rambach, *Christliche Sitten-Lehre*, 701–2.
[52] Undereyck, *Närrische Atheist*, 281–2.   [53] Ibid., 282–3.   [54] Ibid., 286–7, 297.
[55] Ibid., 298–302.   [56] Ibid., 305–6.   [57] Ibid., 310–14.

view that French noble ladies were barely less prone to follow the lead of the *esprits forts* than the aristocratic male. Are not the high-born ladies of Versailles and the great châteaux of France, he asks, nowadays more gorgeously coiffured and attired than ever while at the same time prattling incessantly about the 'eternal truths of geometry' and subtleties of metaphysics?[58] But if it was obvious to him that women in fact can take to reading philosophy and cultivating the intellect, this new phenomenon, he believed, stemmed from aristocratic pride and a rebellious desire to gratify the lusts of the body in defiance of morality and the Church.

In the fraught intellectual atmosphere of the times, skirmishes over key *exempla* drawn from history, variously interpreted to show that women could, or could not, justifiably or actually vie with men in mattters philosophical abounded. A female intellectual martyr gleefully lionized by Toland was the lovely Hypatia of fifth-century Alexandria, the 'glory of her own sex and the disgrace of ours', a young woman celebrated alike for her beauty and wisdom. She surpassed everyone as a teacher of philosophy, Toland assured readers, and was 'daily surrounded by a circle of young gentlemen'.[59] Unfortunately, this paragon ventured to express anticlerical opinions during a jurisdictional dispute between the civic governor and Bishop Cyril of Alexandria. For speaking against priestly power, says Toland, she was assailed in the year AD 415 by an indignant mob incited by the clergy. The people 'stripped her stark naked', killed her, and 'tore her to pieces'. Cyril, later made a saint by the Church, is accounted by Toland the 'contriver' of this murder 'and his clergy the executioners of his implacable fury'.[60] Needless to say, this effort to 'blast the reputation of the venerable Saint Cyril' outraged opponents, prompting one to retort that Hypatia, on the contrary, was a 'most impudent school-mistress', a shameless 'She-philosopher' who in order to repel one unwanted suitor employed a strategem—throwing her menstruating towel in his face—which the 'most common prostitute in Venice would blush at'.[61]

ii. Conversational Freedom; Sexual Freedom

As attitudes associated in particular with Parisian high society during the Regency period, following the death of Louis XIV in 1715, spread, albeit often in diluted form, across Europe, it was increasingly felt that the fashion for freer interaction between men and women posed severe practical problems by eroding traditional social and moral values. The transformed, intellectually and sexually freer, Parisian milieu generated a new type of 'gentleman', for which the freethinker Saint-Evremond was often seen as the prototype—the elegant talker who disdains war, politics, and religion and seeks distinction among his fellow men through a combination of philosophical grasp, wit, irreverent writing, and refined pleasure-seeking.[62] But it was not the *Evremondisti*, as such men were dubbed in Neapolitan high society, who posed the main

---

[58] Massillon, *Pensées*, 119, 267–8.   [59] Toland, *Tetradymus*, 103, 108–9, 122.
[60] Ibid., 126, 130-1, 135; Jöcher, *Allgemeines Gelehrten Lexicon*, ii, 1798.
[61] Lewis, *History of Hypatia*, 5, 9.   [62] Hazard, *European Mind*, 149–54.

challenge. For such masculine pretensions and hedonism were not in themselves either particularly novel or disturbing. Rather it was the new concept of 'free conversation' between men and women who were not in close family proximity which was unsettling. It is true this 'free conversation' between gentlemen and ladies, while encompassing philosophy, religion, and science, mostly excluded politics and legal issues.[63] But the crucial point was that it generated a new kind of social space for women, underpinned by philosophy, characterized by liberty of speech outside the family framework.

A remarkable discussion of the impact of the new attitudes on women, and relations between the sexes, was that of the veteran Neapolitan philosopher—something of an *Evremondiste* and crypto-Spinozist himself—Paolo Mattia Doria. Indeed, little known though it is, his 454-page *Ragionamenti*, published at 'Francfort' (Naples?) in 1726, 'in which it is shown that woman, in almost all the chief virtues, is not inferior to man', a work dedicated to Duchess Aurelia d'Este of Limatola, is a classic of the Early Enlightenment. The essential problem, he makes clear, is that the new fashion for 'liberty of conversation between men and women', now part of the cult of refinement and 'buon gusto' emanating from the Parisian salons, necessarily entails a weakening of traditional forms of supervision of women by masculine relatives. For in the new context, not only is there more intermingling of men and women on a freer basis, but also, and scarcely less disturbing, women now hear much more of what men say to each other—that is, they have more opportunity to learn about politics, social realities, religion, and even sex.[64] This ineluctably means some erosion of traditional standards of purity, chastity, authority, and family honour.[65]

Philosophy, he shows, is having immense practical consequences for society. For however much women may have been excluded from intellectual discourse in the past, the reality is that women are just as capable of grasping the truths of philosophy, and discussing philosophical propositions, as men. They also have an equal right to participate in the progress of philosophy.[66] The evidence for this he draws from the history of ancient Greek philosophy. Epicurus in particular, he remarks, had sought female philosophical disciples whose intellectual attainments are beyond dispute. He makes much of the most clebrated of the Greek hetaerae, Aspasia, friend of the great statesman Pericles and famous for her wisdom and profound knowledge of philosophy.[67] Her house was one of the prime venues for philosophical discourse in late fifth-century Athens, he points out, and among others, was frequented by Socrates. Of course, he admits, one must condemn Aspasia and other such Greek philosophical ladies despite their intellectual brilliance and wisdom, for they were, as he puts it, as lustful and lascivious as they were beautiful and wise.

Precisely this, according to Doria, is the problem. For since the late seventeenth century, a new 'Epicureanism' (i.e. Spinozism) backed by scepticism was again

---

[63] Doria, *Lettere e ragionamenti*, ii, 332–8; De Soria, *Racccolta di opuscoli*, ii, 83–4.
[64] Doria, *Lettere e ragionamenti*, ii, 336–8; Doria, *Ragionamenti ne' quali*, 364–5.
[65] Doria, *Lettere e Ragionamenti*, ii, 339–42; Doria, *Ragionamenti ne' quali*, 364–5.
[66] Doria, *Ragionamenti ne' quali*, 216–17.   [67] Ibid., 228–9.

pervading society, and the inevitable consequence of permitting 'libertà di conver-sare' is that women will again become philosophically aware and therefore 'infected' by Epicureanism and scepticism and consequently more vulnerable than before to sinful and lascivious thoughts. 'Libertà di conversare' for women inevitably means more opportunity for intimacy and amorous dalliance outside marriage.[68] How can the undesirable and harmful consequences of this be avoided or at least minimized? Many men, notes Doria, endeavour to resist the advance of 'libertà di conversare' and revert to old-fashioned propriety, debarring women from intellectual discourse and contacts. Yet such a conservative strategy, he argues, can not possibly work unless we are to go to the extremes of the 'barbarous Turks' and literally lock up our womenfolk at home, precluding all contact with the outside world.[69] A régime of restrictions short of virtual imprisonment of women by men would serve merely to keep women ignorant of philosophy—and here his argument takes a radical twist—and therefore highly vulnerable to seductive words and apt to resort to deceit and subterfuge to meet their lovers.[70] Only philosophy then can inculcate true virtue, even if, at the same time, it transforms traditional relations between the sexes.

The solution, held Doria, is to recognize that it is essential in the new context to 'bene educare le donne' (educate women well).[71] Girls must be taught from an early age to love virtue for its own sake, rather than having chastity imposed on them, and must learn proper, safe and uplifting ideas.[72] Human nature being what it is, he admits, sexual attraction will sometimes overwhelm reason, but this is just as much a problem with men as women. In the end, he concludes, and here he reveals his crypto-Spinozist colours, the level of virtue among women will reflect the general level of virtue in society, that is, the worthiness or unworthiness of the attitudes of the men alongside whom women live and who determine their education, the laws to which they are subject, and their religion.[73] If corrupt conduct, adultery, and seduction go unchecked among men, then so they will, in corresponding degree, among women. Thus the deplorably promiscuous ladies of Imperial Rome, with Messalina and Agrippina fore-most among them, simply reflected the execrable corruption of manners which, according to Doria, arose after the fall of the republic.[74] Doria's final conclusion is that women are equally suited to intellectual endeavour as men, equally prone to vice and virtue, and equally in need of mind and body being kept in a healthy, harmonious balance.[75]

One of those who imbibed such views from Doria in Naples, and set herself to cul-tivate philosophy was Giuseppa-Eleonora Barbapiccola, the translator—from French,

---

[68] Ibid., 372–90; Doria, *Lettere e ragionamenti*, ii, 346.

[69] Doria, *Ragionamenti ne' quali*, 393–4.   [70] Ibid., 390–1.

[71] Ibid., 395, 407; the argument is similar to that advanced in 1673 by Poulain de la Barre and later in a work entitled M.N.C., *Les Femmes savantes* (Amsterdam, 1718), the latter insisting that 'l'ignorance est la mère de tous les vices' while condemning the 'sentimens injustes et désavantageux' which men in general, and espe-cially 'le peuple ignorant' have of woman's intellectual capability, 'avant décidé que l'étude ni les sciences ne conviennent point au beaux sexe'; see *L'Europe Savante*, vi (1718), 195–7.

[72] Doria, *Ragionamenti ne' quali*, 405–8.   [73] Ibid., 408, 426–8.

[74] Ibid., 451.   [75] Ibid., 422–3, 426, 451–2.

not Latin—of Descartes' *Principia* into Italian.[76] An acquaintance of Vico, Giuseppa-Eleonora also drew inspiration from Valletta, Spinelli, and Grimaldi.[77] She was, moreover, as she reveals in her preface, a woman with a mission. Her aim in translating Descartes was not just to propagate Cartesian ideas among those who knew no Latin, but to spread awareness of Cartesianism among women in particular and draw fellow women into philosophical debate.[78] She too extols the women philosophers of classical Greece, lauding Aspasia as 'teacher' and later wife of Pericles, though she demurely passes over in silence the issues of sexuality raised by Doria. She admits that most ladies of position waste their time on frivolous pursuits such as discussing the latest fashions and choosing ribbons, but insists that such deplorable inadequacy is due not to 'nature but wretched education'.[79] Like Doria, she appeals for a fundamental reform of schooling for girls.[80]

A woman of the Early Enlightenment participating in philosophical debate among men had either, like Barbapiccola, to evade the subject of sex or, like the Parisian *salonnière*, Madame de Lambert, insist that women in the Republic of Letters must have a reputation for 'virtue'.[81] Consequently, the sexual issues involved could only be explored in print by male writers, and the plea for emancipation of the libido, male and female, could only be widely urged by masculine radical thinkers. The result predictably horrified contemporary opinion. Beverland, Leenhof, and Radicati went furthest, broaching the question of sexuality from their Spinozist premise that good and bad are purely relative concepts and that ethics must be built on the principle that no absolute morality exists. Rather than innate or inherited concepts, the criterion for a sound ethics can only be what does, or does not, benefit the community and the individual.[82] Thus neither religion nor social customs can provide genuine guidance, as indeed is obvious, claims Radicati, from the bewildering variety of attitudes and norms they prescribe. Thus while 'primitive Christians highly praised such women and virgins as killed themselves when they were in manifest danger of having their chastity violated', among other religions female abstinence is not held in remotely comparable esteem.[83] On the contrary, the 'husbands of the city of Calicut, East India', he contends, 'very lovingly interchange their wives' while those of other East Indian regions 'send their daughters to the temples that they may be deflowered by the priests and believe that, in so doing, they make a most holy sacrifice to their gods'.[84] Similarly, he held, there is no absolute standard of decency and indecency. 'In Sicily, Spain, Portugal, etc.,' he points out, 'a virtuous woman or maiden would blush extremely to be saluted or kissed by a man, or if he should see her naked breasts,

---

[76] She apparently read the *Ragionamenti* before its publication; see Barbapiccola, 'Traduttrice', 2, 5; Stone, *Vico's Cultural History*, 214, 271.

[77] Barbapiccola, 'Traduttrice', 11–12, 15.   [78] Ibid., 8.

[79] Ibid., 7; see also Poulain de la Barre, *Equality*, 121–4.

[80] Her ideal of the virtuous woman philosopher she saw realized in Descartes' friend and protectress, Princess Elizabeth of Bohemia, and also the Dutch paragon of learning, Anna Maria von Schurman (1607–78); Barbapiccola, 'Traduttrice', 5–7.

[81] Lambert, *Réflexions nouvelles*, 8.   [82] [Radicati], *A Philosophical Dissertation*, 29–30.

[83] Ibid., 33.   [84] Ibid., 34, 39.

whereas, at the same time, a French or English damsel alike virtuous, suffers it without the least disturbance or emotion; and this because the first have been taught that these things are indecent and the second that they are allowable.'[85]

Applying his principle (not unlike Mandeville's) that 'those things which contribute to the public quiet and happiness' are good and such as 'conduce towards its disquiet and ruin' bad, Radicati avers complete sexual freedom, including that of women, to be good.[86] He deplores the repressive effect of convents, which merely obliges every young woman unfortunate enough to be so confined to masturbate 'in some measure to mitigate the boilings of her concupiscence'.[87] The more sexually repressive a society, or as he expresses it, the more the 'foolish and unjust separation of the different sexes which is practised in many places', the more homosexuality in all its forms flourishes, claiming there was less homosexuality in England and Holland than in southern Europe precisely because in those northern climes women enjoy more sexual freedom.[88] The cult of virginity, and prohibition on intercourse before marriage for girls, he condemns as a generally harmful thing. One appalling consequence, according to Radicati, is that unmarried girls who, overcome by desire, have intercourse and become pregnant so dread the disapproval and condemnation of society that they frequently abandon or even kill their illegitimate offspring.[89]

The new notion of self-discovery as well as discovering the world, through philosophy and 'libertà di conversare' between the sexes, explains that remarkably close linkage between philosophy and sex so pervasive in the European Enlightenment. Moreover, it was especially women, or so it seemed to the philosophical liberators of the Early Enlightenment, who were in need of advice about how to free themselves from the subjection and repression of the past, advice that could not be otherwise than simultaneously philosophical and sexual. The chief significance of *Thérèse Philosophe* (1748), the best and most serious of the Early Enlightenment erotic philosophical works—according to the marquis de Sade, *Thérèse* is the only one 'qui ait agréablement lié la luxure et l'impieté, et qui . . . donnera enfin l'idée d'un livre immoral'[90]—most certainly does not lie, as has been claimed, in having been published 'precisely at the moment when the first great barrage of Enlightenment works burst into print'.[91] Rather, its importance lies in its being a reworking of much earlier Enlightenment ideas, especially Spinozism, in the erotic sphere, having been written, almost certainly in view of the numerous echoes between it and known works of the marquis—by d'Argens, either during his years in Holland in the 1730s or soon after in Germany.[92]

---

[85] Ibid., 58.   [86] Ibid., 59–60; Ferrone, *Intellectual Roots*, 275.
[87] [Radicati], *A Philosophical Dissertation*, 60.   [88] Ibid., 67–8.   [89] Ibid., 71–3.
[90] Pigeard de Gurbert, 'Thérèse', 151; Heumakers, 'De Sade', 114.
[91] Darnton, *Forbidden Best-Sellers*, 90.
[92] Pigeard de Gurbert, 'Thérèse', 151, 168; Berkvens-Stevelinck and Vercruysse, *Métier*, 77; if it is indeed the work of d'Argens, as 18th-century connoisseurs such as De Sade and most modern commentators have surmised, then it almost certainly reflects the intellectual world of the 1730s and early 1740s, rather than the later phase to which Darnton refers.

The crucial point is that the author expresses what has been termed his 'naturalisme à la Spinoza'[93] through the perceptions and words of a young woman who undergoes a long and eventful process of sex education.[94] According to the author's hedonistic philosophy, there is no difference between physical and spiritual salvation which are one and the same, and to be found exclusively in this world. Since intellectual and sensual striving for the supreme good are, in reality, inextricably entwined, philosophy becomes literally the bed-fellow of pleasurable sex. As in Beverland, Leenhof, and Radicati, all notions of absolute good and evil are abolished in favour of an ethics of relativity and, again following Spinoza, the only overriding moral restraint which survives is the imperative to respect and defer to the human laws of the society in which one dwells 'qui sont comme les liens des besoins mutuels de la société'.[95] One suffers unhappiness or worse if one rebels against the laws of one's country, not because rebellion is innately wrong but, as Thérèse expresses it, because one is then persecuted by the rigour of the law, remorse, and the hatred and contempt of one's fellow citizens which is, she thinks, as it should be, for in seeking one's own fulfilment and pleasure 'chacun doit être attentif à ne rien faire qui blesse la félicité de son voisin'.[96]

It is a text in which conventional glorification of virginity is replaced by the open eulogizing of sexual pleasure for women no less than men—but only such forms of sensual gratification as do no injury to others. Cultivation of piety gives way to extolling the ethic of the worldly 'honnête homme' and his female equivalent, exaltation of God's commandments to veneration of the human law. During her period as a young nun, Thérèse had led a pinched, truncated, wretched life under the guidance of her Catholic confessors. Step by step she had emancipated herself from such slavery through voyeurism, masturbation, learning from more enlightened men and also from erotic books. Thérèse eulogizes masturbation as what gave her back joy in life and her psychological and bodily health.[97] Finally, Thérèse discovers love and extra-marital intercourse and, pondering it all with the seriousnesss life deserves, becomes a *philosophe*, finding happiness and worldly salvation. As for religion: 'il n'y a point de culte, Dieu se suffit à lui-même.'[98]

---

[93] Heumakers, 'De Sade', 114.

[94] Ibid.; Maréchal, *Dictionnaire*, 300; a typical formula expressed in several erotic novels of the period, including notably one of the earliest of the genre, *Venus dans le cloître* (c.1682), in which a young nun, Agnes, learns to become 'éclairée' through masturbation, lesbian love, and discussion with an 'enlightened' older nun, and discovers that society's emphasis on female chastity is part of the system of fear and repression rooted in superstition from which women in particular need to be liberated, and also, much later, John Cleland's *Fanny Hill*, which was influenced by the French genre and originally drafted, it seems, in the 1730s, though not published until 1749; Marchand notes that an *Anti-Thérèse* by M. de T. . . . was published at The Hague in 1750 which claimed to be a 'réfutation de *Thérèse Philosophe*' but was in reality even more 'corrupt' than the original; see Marchand, *Dictionnaire*, ii, 319.

[95] [D'Argens], *Thérèse Philosophe*, 135.   [96] Ibid.

[97] Ibid., 53–6; Pigeard de Gurbert, 'Thérèse', 159–60; Darnton, *Forbidden Books*, 96.

[98] [D'Argens], *Thérèse Philosophe*, 147.

5 | CENSORSHIP AND CULTURE

i. French Royal Censorship

A crucial factor shaping the rise of radical thought in Europe—as well in a different way, the moderate Enlightenment—was the impact of censorship, secular and ecclesiastical. While it is true that Europe's intellectual censorship in early modern times was unsystematic and frequently inefficient, providing minimal scope for co-ordination across political and jurisdictional borders and exhibiting all the chaotic, bewildering, institutional, and procedural variety characteristic of the *ancien régime*, one must not underestimate either its broad impact or the degree of ideological convergence all varieties of institutionalized censorship manifested in fighting radical ideas. All across the continent, albeit with varying degrees of intensity, unacceptable views were suppressed and publishers, printers, and booksellers, as well as authors of books embodying illicit ideas punished.

Even in Europe's two freest societies—the Dutch Republic and England—lands where urban culture was most prevalent, and the rigid social hierarchies of the past had become most fluid, radical writers were more profoundly influenced by censorship than is often realized. In Britain there was a marked easing of censorship after the Glorious Revolution, and especially the expiry of the Licensing Act in 1695, a phenomenon linked to a more general receding of the Church of England's influence in cultural life.[1] Nevertheless, appreciable constraints remained. Deistic writers who denied miracles and the divine authorship of Scripture, decried the established Church, or the constitutional outcome of the Glorious Revolution, could not ignore restrictions imposed by parliamentary authority. Especially, the Blasphemy Act of 1698, which expressly outlawed denial of Christ's divinity, and rejection of the Trinity (except for Jews, who were exempt from its provisions), was not to be treated lightly. Toland's first book, *Christianity not Mysterious* (1696), may have been timed to exploit the demise of the Licensing Act, but that did not prevent its being denounced, and publicly burnt, by both the English and Irish Parliaments, while Toland himself was obliged to flee Ireland, where he had returned in expectation of appointment to a government post, orders being issued for his prosecution as a 'public and inveterate enemy to all reveal'd religion . . . one who openly affected to be

---

[1] Goldie, 'Theory', 331–3; Bossy, 'English Catholics'. 375; Israel, 'William III and Toleration', 161–2; Casini, *Introduzione*, I, 49.

head of a sect'.[2] In 1710 the House of Commons condemned Matthew Tindal's *Rights of the Christian Church Asserted* (1706) and a second work of 1709, defending that text, works denying the ecclesiastical power all independent authority, as well as an English translation of Jean Le Clerc's long review of the former, all three being publicly burned by the common hangman, because Tindal, according to William Carroll, endeavours to establish the 'state of nature' and 'fundamentally subverts all natural and reveal'd religion, and overthrows our Constitution both in Church and state'.[3]

Soon after Anthony Collins, shaken by the outcry against his *Discourse of Free-Thinking* (1713), took refuge for a time in the Netherlands. On returning, he took charge himself of the delicate task of distributing his anonymously published discourse, enjoining his Huguenot friend, Pierre des Maizeaux. when, through him, entrusting 120 copies to a London bookseller, to 'caution Mr Robinson never to have above 3 or 4 of my books of *Freethinking* to lye in his shop at a time, and not to publish [i.e. advertise] them in any publick manner'.[4] Less prudent Thomas Woolston who, unlike Collins and others, unwisely put his name to his publications, even when denying Christ's miracles and Resurrection, claiming 'liberty of thinking, writing and judging for ourselves in religion is a natural, a Christian and a Protestant right,'[5] was tried by the Lord Chief Justice in person, at the Guildhall in March 1729, and sentenced to a year's imprisonment and a 100-pound fine. Unable to pay, moreover, the luckless Woolston remained in prison after serving his year, and there he died in 1733. Out of caution, David Hume decided to omit his strictures about miracles from his *A Treatise of Human Nature* (1739–40), publishing these only some years later, and he continued to exercise a degree of self-censorship down to the 1750s and beyond.[6]

No doubt, as the eighteenth century dawned and progressed, society gradually edged towards a greater appreciation of religious toleration and intellectual freedom. Champions of the moderate Enlightenment mostly denounced unrelenting adherence to past attitudes as apt to play straight into the hands of the radicals, though few would go as far as the Newtonian William Whiston, who styled traditional intolerance a dreadful thing, providing a 'fatal handle to the Deists, Atheists and Libertines to abhor the offerings of the Lord and blaspheme the name of Christ'; indeed, 'suspect all religion to be a cheat.'[7] In France, the *Malebranchiste* Abbé Houtteville insisted in 1722 that the new practical toleration and freedom of opinion in France had progressed too far and was actively assisting the disastrous advance of Naturalism, fatalism, materialism, and 'Spinosisme'.[8] But increasing secularization also generated a mounting tension between ecclesiastical mechanisms of control—the role of the Churches having been paramount in the past—and the expanding administrative

---

[2] Toland, *A Collection*, i, pp. xi, xix; Craven, *Jonathan Swift*, 17–21; Berman, 'Enlightenment', 151–2.
[3] Carroll, *Spinoza Reviv'd, Part the Second*, 6–7; Brown, 'Theological Politics', 196.
[4] BL Add. MS 4282, fo. 130, Collins to Des Maizeaux, 26 Apr. 1717.
[5] Woolston, *A Fourth Discourse*, 70; see also Fitzpatrick, 'Toleration', 45.
[6] Gaskin, *Hume's Philosophy of Religion*, 145; Gay, *The Enlightenment*, i, 72–3.
[7] Whiston, *Reflexions*, 50.
[8] Houtteville, *Religion chrétienne*, i, p. viii; Israel, 'Locke, Spinoza and the Philosophical Debate', 6.

apparatus and ambitions of the State. In France in 1702, there was a sensational dispute between the ecclesiastical and secular arms when Bossuet himself, to his evident distress, was required, but refused, to submit a publication of his own against Richard Simon to the royal censorship: the bishops found themselves ceasing to be the agents, and themselves becoming the objects of royal book supervision.[9]

In the France of Louis XIV there were frequent book-burnings by the regional *parlements*, numerous edicts suppressing particular books, and regular inspections of bookshops by the police, as well as stringent checks of travellers' baggage at the frontiers. Certainly, there were illicit editions within France, and censorship was not sufficiently rigorous to stop an incessant stream of forbidden books percolating from outside into the libraries of nobles, savants, officials, and clergy. But it was incisive enough to render the French market for libertine and dissident books largely dependent on external sources of supply and surreptitious methods of distribution. One consequence was that highly placed persons needed foreign contacts, especially with Holland where most clandestine book production and export was concentrated, to procure illicit reading matter, and even then success was far from guaranteed. In October 1682, the former editor of the *Journal des Sçavants*, the Abbé Gallois, having vainly sought copies of Spinoza and Simon's *Histoire critique du Nouveau Testament* in Paris, requested the celebrated scientist Christian Huygens, at The Hague, to help. Huygens made no mention of the Richard Simon but agreed to send Spinoza's works from Holland if he could devise a suitable strategem, such as concealing the volumes in the bags of the Dutch ambassador about to depart for Paris: 'car vous n'ignorez pas les deffences et les exactes recherches que l'on fait sur vos frontières en matière de livres jusqu'à fouiller dans les valises des voyageurs.'[10] The following year Bayle, virtually all of whose writings were to be banned in France,[11] wrote from Rotterdam, advising his brother that it was almost impossible to find anyone willing to accept forbidden books on Dutch ships bound for France as there was considerable risk involved and the skippers feared confiscation of their cargoes along with the books.[12]

Among the most celebrated episodes of Louis XIV's book censorship were the banning of the great exegetical works of Richard Simon, the refusal of the lieutenant-general of police in Paris in 1681 to authorize Pierre Bayle's first major work, the *Pensées diverses* (despite his having written in the guise of a Catholic apologist), the latter's subsequent flight to Holland with the manuscript hidden in his baggage, and the banning of Bayle's *Dictionnaire* of 1697.[13] The suppression of Simon's *Histoire critique du Vieux Testament* in 1678 is especially remarkable, since the book had already been licensed by the chief *censeur des livres* at the Sorbonne, and the *supérieur général* of the Oratoire, and 1,300 copies printed and bound when Bossuet intervened at the highest level—with Chancellor Le Tellier. A prohibition order, issued by the *Conseil*

---

[9] Hazard, *European Mind*, 239–40; Phillips, *Church and Culture*, 272–5.

[10] Huygens, *Oeuvres complètes*, viii, 402, 406.   [11] Mellot, 'Relations ambiguës', 215.

[12] Sauvy, *Livres saisis*, 9.

[13] Prat, 'Introduction', pp. xiv–xv; nevertheless, Bayle remained curiously silent on the subject of the liberty of the press; Labrousse, *Pierre Bayle*, ii, 549–50.

d'en haut, was signed by Colbert on 15 June 1678, upon which the lieutenant-general of police in Paris seized and burnt the entire stock.[14] This reverse, and his expulsion from the Oratoire the same year, isolated Simon within French cultural life, and obliged him henceforth to rely on publishers in Holland, as well as entailing the permanent exclusion of his publications from France, at least officially. This did curiously little, though, to mitigate his strong distaste for Dutch liberty. Rather, he continued to disparage Dutch freedom of expression as corrupt and unprincipled, inspired 'par une raison d'intérêt et d'avarice'.[15] Meanwhile Bossuet, while helping extend French intellectual censorship, had to obtain forbidden books for his own use circuitously from abroad. Having been instrumental in suppressing Simon, and then Le Clerc's reply to Simon, a book he judged 'encore plus injurieux à Sainte Écriture' than Simon's, he had to go to considerable lengths to procure copies for his own use via Geneva.[16]

The censorship system prevailing in France until Louis XIV's death in 1715 was unwieldy and, involving as it did compromises between competing jurisdictions, entailed considerable overlap and lack of clarity. Illicit literature from Holland seeped in by sea, in particular via Rouen, and also by various land routes.[17] Numerous sources attest to this extensive penetration, even of France's most closely guarded spiritual strongholds. In 1690 the worried abbess of the famous convent of Fontevrault, near Tours, alerted Bishop Huet to the growing spirit of rebellion in Northern French nunneries and monasteries, ascribing this frightening development explicitly to the flow of forbidden books from Holland, which, she says, was teaching even the most mediocre inmates of the cloisters to discard all authority and prefer to examine and judge every intellectual issue in a critical light for themselves.[18]

Nevertheless, pressure of censorship meant that forbidden books entered France only with difficulty and at considerable cost, which, in turn, resulted in their availability being largely retricted to aristocratic and high official or ecclesiastical circles, or else a few large cities, notably Paris and Rouen. It has been suggested that we should not take an 'overly highbrow, overly metaphysical view of intellectual life in the eighteenth century' and remember that 'a lot of trash somehow got mixed up in the eighteenth-century idea of philosophy.'[19] But while erotic material was undoubtedly more integral to what was regarded as *philosophique* in the eighteenth century than is the case today, what the evidence for the more crucially formative early eighteenth century proves is, in fact, precisely the opposite—the strikingly high proportion of genuinely philosophical works featuring in the illicit trade.

A notable success for the Paris police was the arrest in 1705 of Joseph Huchet, librarian and secretary to a royal official, Antoine de Courtin, resident in the Place Royale, then, as now, among the more select quarters of Paris. Huchet had been caught when

---

[14] Hazard, *European Mind*, 227; Steinmann, *Richard Simon*, 124–9.   [15] Simon, *Lettres choisies*, 47, 59.
[16] Steinmann, *Richard Simon*, 229, 257.   [17] Mellot, 'Relations ambiguës', 211–13.
[18] She referred to 'ces livres de Hollande qui ont inondé le monde depuis quelques années' causing monks and nuns to regard submission to authority 'comme un effet de la foiblesse et de l'ignorance où ils vivaient avant ces belles découvertes'; quoted in Gaiffe, *L'Envers du Grand Siècle*, 87–8.
[19] Darnton, *Literary Underground*, 2.

the authorities learnt from an informer that he kept a depot for 'all the books of Holland' in Courtin's town house.[20] With his seized books and correspondence, he was sent to the Bastille. Until the outbreak of war in 1702, Huchet had been receiving his illicit supplies of books from a *libraire* in Rouen named Dedun, who had imported them by sea, hidden among other cargo, from Rotterdam.[21] Since the outbreak of war, Huchet had obtained his books overland via a *libraire* in Liège named Jean-François Bronckhart, who concealed them in coaches.

Interrogated by the lieutenant-general of police, the marquis d'Argenson, in person on 6 July 1705, Huchet admitted receiving crates of forbidden books from Holland and Liège, which he stored in rooms belonging to the duchesse de Choiseul and other noblemen and ladies.[22] Originally from Alençon, he had arrived in Paris, where he had since lived for over twenty years, at the age of 18 to study philosophy at the Jesuit college of Clairmont under 'Father Martineau'. Further enquiries implied additional *magasins de livres* concealed in the Hôtel de Sully and the Hôtel de Condé, and he was asked what he did in those aristocratic establishments which he had been seen entering frequently.[23] He admitted being on friendly terms with the staff at the former, where the duchesse de Verneuil had kindly provided him with a room for his books; at the Hôtel de Condé he had no store-room, though he was on excellent terms with the secretaries and especially the 'superintendant des bastimens' of Monseigneur the Prince. Parcels of books consigned to him from Liège had apparently been arriving directly at the door of the Hôtel de Sully, where they were taken care of by Monsieur de la Forêt, *officier* of the duchesse de Verneuil. Everything suggested that Huchet's clientele was aristocratic and bureaucratic, his own employer, he admitted, being an avid connoisseur of 'mauvais livres de Hollande'.

Huchet's supplies came from Holland and the term 'livres de Hollande' was used in the interrogations as a generic term for forbidden literature in general. His storerooms contained an abundance of Catholic theology, especially Janseniana, and also erotica, two favourite bawdy novels being *Venus dans le cloître* and *Le Moine secularisé*, as well as scandalous chronicles, though these were not necessarily 'trash', the most sought after being Bussy-Rabutin's *Histoire amoureuse des Gaules*, a prose classic eagerly read by the French aristocracy of the day but at the time available only from Holland.[24] Another main component, Huchet's lists reveal, were runs of learned periodicals in French, particularly Le Clerc's *Bibliothèque Universelle*, the *Nouvelles de la République des Lettres*, and the *Histoire des Ouvrages des Savants*. Finally there were philosophical books proper, especially the *Dictionnaire* of Bayle which, for decades, was published exclusively in Holland and—almost as frequent—that of Moréri, beside works of Fontenelle, Saint Evremond, and Pascal, particularly the *Lettres provinciales*, a text on the papal Index since 1657 and banned and publicly burnt in Paris in 1660. Additional key items were Simon's *Histoire critique du Vieux Testament* and its companion on the

---

[20] Bib. Arsenal MS 10561/4, De Witte to Huchet, Paris, 10 July 1705.
[21] Ibid., 10561/2, Dedun to Huchet, Rouen, 8 Dec. 1699 and 8 June 1701.
[22] Ibid., 10561/1 interrogatoire, The Bastille, 6 July 1705.
[23] Ibid., 10561/5 interrogatoire, The Bastille, 31 Aug. 1705. [24] Weil, 'Rôle des libraires', 283.

New Testament,[25] Bayle's *Pensées diverses* and *Commentaire philosophique*, again works available only from Holland, and works of Le Clerc, Jaquelot, and Abbadie, as well as the notorious *Voyages* of Lahontain. There were also a few banned items in Latin, notably the clandestine Amsterdam Socinian compilation, *Bibliotheca Fratrum Polonorum* by Frans Kuyper, and, though much less common than Bayle or Le Clerc, a solitary English work—Locke's *Essay* in French translation.

Uncovering a network of depots in high society town houses was a triumph for d'Argenson. Accustomed to surveillance, the *libraires* avoided keeping *clandestina* in their shops, which meant d'Argenson and his *commissaires* needed accurate tip-offs, or uncommon luck, to catch them out. A Paris police document of January 1702 mentions a pedlar caught selling forbidden literature who agreed to talk but, it transpired, knew nothing useful. He implicated the Paris *libraires* Guilan, Rémy, Bellay, and Langlois as traffickers. But this in itself, the *commissaire* reported to d'Argenson, 'c'est nous donner avis que la Seine passe à Paris.' For these same men had been raided by the police many a time and were entirely suspect 'mais l'on ne trouve jamais de magasin chez eux, ils l'ont ailleurs, et c'est ce qu'il faut découvrir.'[26] The shops mentioned were raided again all the same and more scraps of incriminating evidence gleaned— letters in code about the forbidden book trade between Rouen and Paris and, at the shop of the incorrigible Rémy, who had already twice seen the inside of the Bastille, a few *clandestina*.[27]

Two brothers brought to the Bastille for selling forbidden books in September 1712, Charles and Jacques Cocquaire, had, like Huchet, studied philosophy under the Jesuits, in their case at Rennes. Settling in Paris, Jacques had been a *domestique* in aristocratic town houses for many years, and later earned his bread teaching Latin and mathematics. He knew philosophy and he knew forbidden books. His brother served in the dragoons during the Nine Years' War (1688–97) and, after temporary service in aristocratic households, had been a minor official commandeering forage for the cavalry in Flanders during the new war. In this capacity he was well-placed to engage in the illicit book traffic but had been caught consigning boxes of 'livres de Hollande' to his brother in Paris.[28]

One of the most notable coups of the Paris police in this field was the uncovering in 1739 of the illegal traffic conducted by the *maître d'hôtel* of the Venetian ambassador, a certain Charles Stella. His correspondence revealed that he dealt in the usual prohibited varieties—Janseniana, erotica, satirical chronicles,[29] and appreciable quantities of 'philosophical' books, and that his chief supplier was Pieter de Hondt (1696–1764), a well-known publisher since 1726 at The Hague.[30] His hidden depot was seized and several collaborators uncovered, including a printer who had worked in Holland and was also sent to the Bastille, and the Abbé Nicolas Lenglet Dufresnoy (1674–1755),

---

[25] Bib. Arsenal MS 10562, lists of books in sections 9, 11, and 16.   [26] *Archives de la Bastille*, x, 407–8.
[27] Ibid., x, 408–9.   [28] Bib. Arsenal MS 10604: dossier Charles and Jacques Cocquaire.
[29] Fénélon's *Télémaque*, widely interpreted as a satire on Louis and his Court and a major item in Huchet's business, had evidently lost none of its popularity since Louis' death.
[30] Bib. Arsenal MS 11447, pp. 135–7; on De Hondt, see Kossmann, *Boekhandel te's Gravenhage*, 56.

a disreputable but clever intriguer, one of the foremost connoisseurs of clandestine books of the age.[31] Stella's lists reveal the centrality in the traffic of the late 1730s of d'Argens' works, his depot containing numerous copies of the latter's *Lettres cabalistiques* and *Lettres juives*. Other principal items were Beverland's *Peché originel*, the Spinozistic novel the *Voyages de Jacques Massé*, Arpe's *Apologia* for Vanini, and, most significant in terms of radical philosophical content, *La Vie et l'esprit de Mr Benoît de Spinosa* and Spinoza's *Opera Posthuma*.[32]

In France there was, over time, a growing trend for the secular rather than ecclesiastical arm to preside, and the royal administration rather than the *parlements*. The stringency of the censorship, moreover, was considerably relaxed by stages after the end of the War of the Spanish Succession in 1713. During the last months of Louis' reign, in 1714–15, there was a post-war influx of foreign visitors and a flurry of printing activity in Paris,[33] stimulated by some easing of supervision under the direction of the Abbé Bignon. He, however, retired from the directorship of the *censure des livres* early in 1715, affording the Jesuits, the visiting librarian of Wolfenbüttel observed, what could later be seen as their last ray of hope of gaining control.[34] In 1714 there was even an attempt to bring out an edition of Bayle's *Letters* in Paris, though permission for this was finally refused.[35] After 1715 there was unquestionably more scope for publishing philosophically, scientifically, and even theologically controversial books. It was doubtless for this reason, and especially in the hope of ending the ban in France on Bayle's *Dictionnaire* that, in 1720, Marchand dedicated the third edition, his new four-volume Rotterdam version of that great work, to the French regent, the duc d'Orléans.[36] The new regency government, headed by the freethinking duke, did indeed wish to render it easier—partly for intellectual and political, but also for plain economic reasons—for less than entirely orthodox works to be sold in France and reduce the censorship functions of the Church. This was gradually contrived in part by instituting a new middle category of books which were neither licensed by the ecclesiastical or secular authorities nor expressly forbidden. But this development placed French writers in an often perplexing dilemma; for there was still a crucial, if not always clear, borderline between what was permissible and what was not, and appreciably more freedom to publish in the United Provinces than France.[37] However, as d'Argens remarked in 1738, if one tried to smuggle books by French authors published in Holland into France, these were still subject to searches and likely to be seized at the frontiers: 's'il en pénètre plusieurs, c'est par ruse et par finesse.'[38]

The system of tacit exemptions was used with growing frequency towards the middle of the eighteenth century. In high official circles a desire to increase the number of permissions for works the Crown had no particular wish to admit that it tolerated

[31] Bib. Arsenal MS 11447, pp. 64, 73; Sheridan, *Nicolas Lenglet Dufresnoy*, 46–8, 50, 58, 76 7.
[32] Bib. Arsenal MS 11447, pp. 155, 159, 161, 163, 168; Weil, 'Rôle des libraires', 282, 286.
[33] BL MS 4284, fo. 13. Ganeau to Des Maizeaux, Paris, 23 Mai. 1/14 (?).
[34] Ibid. fos. 80–80v. Hasperg to Des Maizeaux, Paris, 9 May 1715.   [35] Ibid., fo. 12.
[36] Berkvens-Stevelinck, *Prosper Marchand*, 66–7, 147.
[37] Chartier, *Cultural Origins*, 38–50; Weil, 'Role des libraires', 281.   [38] D'Argens, *Lettres juives*, i, 24.

became widespread.[39] By 1732 it had even become possible to prepare a Parisian edition of Bayle's *Dictionnaire*.[40] Interference with Jansenist, Quietist, and Protestant theological works noticeably diminished. Yet lack of clarity about what was allowed and what was not served to aggravate as much as ease friction. For not only was the system readily abused, with booksellers claiming particular books had been tacitly permitted when they had not, but it encouraged jurisdictional clashes between royal officials and the Parlement of Paris, the most spectacular of which concerned the disputed permission and privileges of the *Encyclopédie* during almost a decade and a half from 1745 to 1759, a predicament worsened by an extraordinary amount of official wavering and lack of consensus over whether to permit that great undertaking or not.[41]

In France, then, the largest and most important book market in Europe, a degree of liberalization set in from 1715, albeit to a markedly lesser extent than in England after 1695. Although something of the sort also happened elsewhere, as in Venice, it is arguable that in most cases where initiative in censorship and intellectual supervision passed from ecclesiastical into secular hands, as in several Italian states, Austria, and, eventually, Spain and Portugal, the transition brought no real widening of freedom of thought. Indeed, if anything, the result was more rigour, since the new mechanisms of control, upholding existing structures of authority, was more efficient than the old. As for the United Provinces, a country which, before 1688, had been the freest in Europe and where censorship had from the outset been operated by the secular arm—the provincial assemblies and city governments, albeit often at the prompting of the public Church—there was little indication during the early eighteenth century of significant relaxation of the laws of 1653, 1656, 1674, and 1678 enacted to suppress Socinian, other anti-Trinitarian, and Spinozistic publications.[42]

ii. Philosophy and Censorship in Central Europe

The most striking feature of the general evolution of censorship in Europe between 1650 and 1750, leaving aside political censorship, which was and remained stringent everywhere, is the marked shift, accompanying the secularization of procedures, away from a theological focus to suppression of proscribed secular, 'philosophical' ideas. In this respect, arguably, Dutch censorship strategy in the late seventeenth and early eighteenth century, which primarily targeted radical philosophical authors, pointed the way for the subsequent development of European censorship as a whole. Whether in Protestant or Catholic lands, the chief objective ceased to be the imposition of one or other confessional stance and instead now became the suppression of Naturalism, fatalism, materialism, and Spinozism, along with works harmful to 'good morals'.

In Switzerland, disarray among the cantons over Cartesianism, and subsequently

[39] Chartier, *Cultural Origins*, 50. [40] BL Add. MS 4284, fo. 14.
[41] Chartier, *Cultural Origins*, 41–2. [42] Israel, *Dutch Republic*, 684, 788–90, 816–17, 920–1, 1047–9.

Newtonianism, by no means precluded convergence of aims and tightening of procedures, from the 1670s onwards, with regard to radical and deistic ideas. In 1674 the *consistoire* at Geneva sounded the alarm after copies of the *Tractatus Theologico-Politicus* were discovered in the hands of local students.[43] Subsequently there were frequent references to 'mauvais livres' entering from abroad, that is, Socinian works, erotic books, attacks on the divine authorship of Scripture, and—most reprehensible of all—'Spinosa, Hobbesius et de semblables . . . ceux qu'on appelle déistes'.[44] Little or none of this material was published in Switzerland. Most emanated from the Netherlands, booksellers in Geneva and Lausanne handling such *clandestina* obtaining supplies both from source and via the Frankfurt book fairs.[45] Energetic efforts were made to stop the traffic. In June 1683 the Geneva city government initiated an enquiry, trying to unmask the *libraires* who were importing such forbidden books.[46] A new and stricter system of *Zensur* started at Zurich in 1698 introduced unprecedentedly strict procedures for inspecting bookshops, printers, and bookbinders.[47]

In Germany, censorship rested chiefly in the hands of the individual princely and city governments which, in Catholic areas, were often themselves ecclesiastical régimes. In addition, it was considered useful particularly among the mass of smaller states to maintain the system of censorship headed by the Imperial *Bücherkommission* based in Frankfurt, which monitored the book fairs, traditionally the main entry gate for foreign publications sold in Germany. Admittedly, interference from Vienna and accusations of anti-Protestant bias produced a degree of friction between the commission and the book trade which may have contributed to the decline of the Frankfurt book fairs from the 1670s.[48] But the Imperial Book Commission nevertheless continued to play a notable role in German cultural life, particularly in suppressing such notorious deistic compilations as the 'Wertheim Bible' which, as we shall see, created a considerable stir throughout central Europe in the mid-1730s.

After 1670, German publishing, and the book trade were increasingly dominated by Leipzig. Whereas in 1650 Frankfurt still handled twice as many books as the Saxon city, in the 1670s Leipzig overtook and, by 1700, handled twice as many books as Frankfurt. The shift arose chiefly from the disruptive impact of war in the Rhineland and also changes in methods of advertising and distributing books internationally. In particular, the advent of the erudite journals provided a new method of advertising books, which reduced the incentive for publishers to travel long distances to display their wares.[49] This disadvantaged Frankfurt, where the book trade traditionally involved the physical presence of booksellers visiting the fairs, and worked in favour of Leipzig, which became the foremost publishing centre not just of Protestant Germany but all central Europe. To supervise the Leipzig book trade, the electors of Saxony relied on the electoral *Bücherkommission*, set up after the Reformation in 1569, a joint board of representatives of the university, the Lutheran consistory, and city

---

[43] Santschi, *Censure à Genève*, 44.   [44] Ibid.   [45] Ibid., 78.   [46] Ibid., 46.
[47] Hilgers, *Index der verbotenen Bücher*, 276.
[48] Laeven, 'Frankfurt and Leipzig', 187; Stein, 'Leibniz', 80–1.
[49] Laeven, 'Frankfurt and Leipzig', 188–91; Stein-Karnbach, 'G. W. Leibniz'. 1212, 1278.

government, charged with identifying harmful publications and inspecting the bookshops.[50]

Yet the decline of the fairs, and the rise of Leipzig, did not mean imports of foreign-produced books became less important. Stimulated by the journals, imports from abroad, while entering increasingly via the seaports, especially Hamburg, held steady or increased. It is true that very few books were imported from England or France, but this is because in the first case book prices were much higher than on the continent, and in the second, because of the severe restrictions on publishing. It is also true that consignments from Italy and Antwerp never recovered after the Thirty Years' War. But exports of Dutch publications in Latin, French, Dutch, and German to Germany expanded and fundamentally influenced German cultural life, especially in those areas—erotica, philosophy, science, and unorthodox theology—most likely, in the Early Enlightenment context, to attract the attention of the censorship authorities.[51]

During the second half of the seventeenth century German book censorship was, to a large extent, still confessionally orientated. Censorship strategy was determined by churchmen whether Lutheran, Calvinist, or Catholic and its prime purpose was to exclude works deemed dangerous from a theological standpoint. Indeed, before 1700 few philosophically, scientifically, or politically radical works appeared in Germany, and the few that did, such as Knutzen's manifestos of 1674 and Friedrich Wilhelm Stosch's Spinozistic *Concordia Rationis et Fidei* (1692), were relentlessly suppressed.[52] After 1700, the appearance of radical works (published and in manuscript) became more frequent while, at the same time, the confessional emphasis in censorship receded albeit more rapidly in Protestant than Catholic lands.

In Saxony, censorship was thoroughly overhauled in the late 1690s, with the discarding by August the Strong (Elector of Saxony, 1694–1733; king of Poland as 'August II', 1697–1704 and 1709–33) of his family's former Lutheran allegiance as a result of his conversion to Catholicism in order to secure the Polish throne.[53] The public Church in the electorate remained Lutheran, but the Court in Dresden ceased its former active promotion of the Lutheran cause. All three major confessions recognized in the Empire under the articles of the Peace of Westphalia were now free to publish and bring in books from outside, provided they eschewed inflammatory polemicizing against each other. Theologians eventually disappeared completely from the censorship commission in Leipzig.[54] Henceforth, electoral censorship aimed to eradicate only politically undesirable texts, erotica, unorthodox fringe theology, and radical philosophy advocating Naturalism, fatalism, and Spinozism.

A still more startling step away from traditional censorship criteria followed the accession of Frederick the Great in 1740. The advent of a would-be *roi philosophe* and

[50] Kobuch, *Zensur und Aufklärung*, 34–6.

[51] Laeven, 'Frankfurt and Leipzig', 191; Goldfriedrich, *Geschichte*, 220–1; Stein, 'Leibniz', 84; Mennenöh, *Duisburg*, 176–8.

[52] Schröder, 'Einleitung', 10–11.

[53] Goldfriedrich, *Geschichte*, 463–5; Whaley, 'A tolerant Society?', 182.

[54] Kobuch, *Zensur und Aufklärung*, 39.

admirer of Voltaire, on the throne of the most powerful state in northern Germany, a ruler who personally loathed and despised traditional confessional thinking and priorities, inevitably had a profound impact on cultural life, and by no means only within the confines of Prussia itself. In Frederick's kingdom theological censorship all but ceased and, while political censorship remained exceedingly tight, a measure of intellectual freedom was introduced.[55] This, however, applied more to debate and publications held in Latin or French than the vernacular language of the country. Frederick drew the line at the propagation of radical and irreligious philosophy in the language of the common people.

Meanwhile, the relative effectiveness of book censorship in Saxony, Prussia, and other large German principalities owed much to the heavy concentration of book production and the book trade in only a few cities—especially Leipzig, Frankfurt, Hamburg, and Nuremberg—and a tiny number of university towns, mainly Halle and Jena. Leipzig in 1700, a city of 28,000, housed eighteen publishers and booksellers, and a whole community of printers, bookbinders, and illustrators.[56] By contrast, most central and east-central European cities, including Vienna and Prague, then had remarkably few bookshops by the standards of Amsterdam, The Hague, London, Paris, or Venice. Munich and Hanover were simply not places to buy books; Berlin reputedly had but a single bookshop and Koenigsberg, a university town, only three.

Broadly then, intellectual censorship in Protestant Europe was still a formidable force in 1750 but was now firmly under State control and chiefly aimed at suppressing non-providential deism, Naturalism, materialism, and other radical strains in the local vernacular, whether German, Dutch, French or English, as well as works expressing political or social ideas regarded as seditious and notions about sexuality deemed incompatible with 'good morals'. By contrast, secularization of the censorship machinery occurred appreciably later in Catholic central Europe. In Catholic states the censorship authorities were inevitably preoccupied chiefly with book imports from abroad, or from German Protestant lands, since book production was remarkably meagre compared with the output in Leipzig and other Lutheran cities. This was primarily because confessionalization in Catholic Germany, Austria, and Bohemia-Moravia had created a culture much less orientated to books and the printed word than was the case in Lutheran and Calvinist areas. One result of this difference was that control of the book trade itself tended to gravitate into Protestant hands. Even in Vienna, centre of a burgeoning Catholic Habsburg empire where papal and Italian influence was strong, and a rigorous Jesuit-controlled censorship in force, at least eight of the twelve booksellers in the city in 1730 were Protestants.[57]

---

[55] Blanning, 'Frederick the Great', 273–6; Blanning, 'Frederick the Great and German Culture', 543–6; Whaley, 'A tolerant Society?', 184–5.

[56] Goldfriedrich, *Geschichte*, 83; Stein, 'Leibniz', 84; during the decade 1730–9, Leipzig produced a total of 2,719 publications while Nuremberg, which dominated book production in southern Germany, produced 766, as against 725 for Halle and 653 for Jena; see Goldfriedrich, *Geschichte*, 83.

[57] Ibid., 385.

The Jesuits, entrusted with academic and book censorship in Austria since the onset of the Thirty Years' War, when Ferdinand II had charged them with the eradication of Protestant intellectual influence from his lands, had no wish to relinquish their grip over this powerful cultural device.[58] However, by the 1740s, favoured though they were by the devout Empress Maria Theresa, this surviving stronghold of clerical power was coming increasingly under siege from secularizing forces of the moderate Enlightenment at Court, led by Count Kaunitz. The turning-point was the Jesuits' decision in 1750 to follow Rome, Turin, and other conservative Catholic capitals in banning the import and sale of Montesquieu's *Esprit des Lois*. Montesquieu, backed by French diplomacy and elements at the Austrian court, protested. The empress was embarrassed by the adverse publicity the affair provoked and eventually, in 1753, agreed to transfer the responsibility for book and academic censorship to a new State censorship commission chaired by Gerard van Swieten, the Dutch Catholic disciple of Boerhaave, brought in earlier to reform Vienna University.

This body, no less than the Leipzig book commission, eloquently illustrates the tendency of the moderate Enlightenment in most of Europe to reform censorship in a manner calculated to ease confessional rigidities and end the sway of theology, but without effectively widening the scope of intellectual freedom. It was never indeed the intention of leaders of the moderate Enlightenment in central Europe that their cultural and educational reforms should entail less, or no, intellectual censorship. Leibniz, for instance, had no doubt the escalation in publishing needed careful watching and regulation. He considered publishers and booksellers little more than unscrupulous businessmen keen to profit from whatever would sell, no matter how insidious or worthless. Forceful censorship was essential, in his opinion, if society was to be plied chiefly with 'useful' books, that is, works apt to contribute positively to the physical and spiritual well-being of mankind, a criterion designed to exclude a great deal, including radical philosophy.[59] Leibniz was indeed fascinated by the possibilities of positive censorship, and during the 1660s he toyed with plans to publish a twice-yearly guide to new publications, listing the 'good' books and condemning the 'bad'. He remained a firm supporter of empire-wide censorship, and of the Imperial Book Commission which, indeed, he desired to see strengthened, and provided with catalogues of approved works, in the compiling of which he wished to participate.[60]

In choosing Van Swieten, a protégé of Kaunitz, to direct the Austrian state censorship, Maria Theresa was committing her territories to a particular type of enlightened cultural policy. For Van Swieten was equally committed to far-reaching reform along moderate lines and preserving Austria from radical influences. Obstruction of the entry into Austria of Montesquieu, Leibniz, Wolff, Thomasius, Newton, and Locke ceased, these being the safe writers. But openly deistic, Naturalistic, and erotic works

---

[58] Brechka, *Gerard van Swieten*, 123–4; Klingenstein, 'Van Swieten und die Zensur', 94–5.

[59] Stein, 'Leibniz', 78–9; on Thomasius, see Pott, 'Einleitung', 33.

[60] Ibid., 80–1; censorship also figured prominently in his famous plans for the Berlin Academy of Sciences drafted in 1700, one of its projected functions being to serve as a new kind of censorship commission which would impose positive as well as negative guidance.

were rigorously banned.[61] During the years of his chairmanship, Van Swieten personally listed hundreds of books as 'damnatur' in his register of prohibited titles. Moreover, in his eyes, Voltaire fell on the wrong side of the borderline between 'Christian' and deist Enlightenment and joined Hume, Diderot, and Spinoza in the banned category. Voltaire paid him back in his usual fashion with some scathing remarks in print.

iii. Philosophy and Censorship in Southern Europe

In Italy, meanwhile, one of the fiercest battles of the Early Enlightenment was in progress. So pervasive was the power and influence of the Church in Italian cultural and intellectual life in 1650 that an observer might well have judged its dominance all but impregnable. Yet appearances proved deceptive. By the early eighteenth century it became obvious that the Enlightenment was in reality a force too pervasive and ubiquitous for the Papacy and the Inquisition to curb. So rapidly did ecclesiastical power weaken that by 1750 the Church authorities had effectively lost their age-old control of the machinery of censorship in such key states as Venice, Naples, and Tuscany, and intellectual censorship itself functioned in new ways and directions.

The trial of the 'atheists' in Naples, in the 1680s, signalled the start not just of a conflict over Cartesianism and the status of philosophy in relation to theology, but a general attempt to intimidate the new Neapolitan philosophical coterie and curb intellectual freedom itself.[62] The Inquisition ban on Leonardo di Capoa's controversial *Del Parere*, in 1693, for example, was certainly an attack on Neapolitan Cartesianism but, equally, a resounding rejection of Di Capoa's call for 'liberty to philosophize' and daring praise of the 'philosophers of Holland' who defend that freedom.[63] The expulsion of the Spaniards, and the establishment of a rival Austrian Habsburg regime in the viceroyalty in 1707, introduced new political and dynastic tension in Naples and also renewed existing disagreements between the secular authorities and the Papacy. But while these proved enduring and hard to resolve, as far as the Austrian authorities were concerned, the quarrel had no deep cultural or intellectual ramifications. It had nothing to do with ideas, religion, or attitudes to life and was purely a contest about ecclesiastical revenues and jurisdiction. Yet to rebuff papal claims, the new régime required appropriate arguments justifying limits on ecclesiastical power, and this inevitably encouraged the expression of political theories, philosophical concepts, and concepts of history inimical to papal, Inquisition, and ecclesiastical, pretensions in more than a purely jurisdictional sense.[64]

---

[61] Brechka, *Gerard van Swieten*, 124–6.

[62] Rotondò, 'Censura ecclesiastica', 1481; Mastellone, *Pensiero politico*, 107, 142; Davidson, "Toleration', 235.

[63] Capoa, *Del Parere*, i, 61–2 and ii, 140–2; Mastellone, 'Holland as a Political Model', 581; the 1714 edition cited here was clandestinely printed in Naples by the celebrated printer Lorenzo Cicarelli, declaring 'Cologne' the place of publication; see Stone, *Vico's Cultural History*, 16–17, 28.

[64] Carpanetto and Ricuperati, *Italy*, 106–7.

The new viceroy tacitly allowed publication of Cartesian books and employed the services of philosophically minded jurists such as Costatino Grimaldi. This, in turn, inevitably injected an element of ideological and philosophical conflict which was no part of the Austrian government's agenda but proved inherent in the situation. Thus when Grimaldi published a two-volume work, sponsored by the Austrian authorities, on ecclesiastical taxation in Naples, and this was banned by the Papacy in 1709, the whole issue of ecclesiastical censorship itself became the focus of 'philosophical' scrutiny. In 1710 Grimaldi penned a critique of the Roman Inquisition, asking by what right the ecclesiastical authorities exercised censorship over political and jurisdictional matters, which then circulated in manuscript. This was the question about which the Austrian authorities encouraged discussion. But Grimaldi and his friends had wider concerns and his manuscript, entitled 'Aviso critico', not only accuses the Roman Inquisition of infringing the legitimate powers of the new Neapolitan regime,[65] but insists that ecclesiastical censorship can be justified only with respect to matters of faith and morals and, even then, should be supervised by the secular authority, as in the Venetian Republic. Lambasting the papal Inquisitors for their bigotry and ignorance—and praising the French Crown for operating a secular system of censorship—Grimaldi holds that determining the truth or falsity of propositions other than those expressly embodied in the Church's doctrines resides entirely outside the Church's jurisdiction.[66] Indeed, judging the truth or falsity of propositions which are not strictly theological, he concludes, is solely the responsibility of philosophy and science.

Hence Austrian protection for those at the head of the philosophical ferment in Naples rested on a contradiction which was eventually bound to become clear and generate a head-on collision between political authority and intellectual liberty. The episode which definitively revealed this underlying contradiction started with the publication at Naples in 1723 of one of the outstanding works of the age—Giannone's *Historia civile del regno di Napoli*, a work often styled the first of the great Enlightenment histories, which were to culminate in those of Voltaire, Hume, and Gibbon.[67] Readers did not have to look far to discover the 'philosophical' message in Giannone's history. He describes Naples as a prosperous and vigorous society in the Middle Ages, attributing its subsequent slide into ruin and impoverishment to a combination of Spanish misrule and ecclesiastical manipulation and exploitation. The, in his view, excessive and highly damaging donations of money, land, and other property to monasteries and ecclesiastical foundations, Giannone ascribes to the 'ignoranza e la superstizione' of the people who, in their anxiety to rescue their souls from Purgatory, were easily induced by the clergy to give unstintingly to the Church.[68]

---

[65] NBN MS XV E 23 Grimaldi, 'Avviso critico', pp. 30, 35, 184–5; Stone, *Vico's Cultural History*, 150–2.

[66] NBN MS XV E 23 Grimaldi 'Avviso critico', pp. 11–12, 44.

[67] Gay, *The Enlightenment*, ii, 372–3; Carpanetto and Ricuperati, *Italy*, 107–8; Stone, *Vico's Cultural History*, 210–11.

[68] Giannone, *Historia civile*, 466–71.

Both Giannone's name and that of his publisher appeared on the title-page. The work was published in 1,100 copies. Though it lacked the usually requisite ecclesiastical approbations, Giannone expected the Austrian authorities to shield him from the inevitable clerical backlash. But here, he quickly discovered, he was mistaken. After a brief lull while the book's significance sank in, there was uproar in the city. The friars and the papal nuncio, incensed by the implication that the Church had deliberately fomented belief in false miracles in order to increase its hold over the credulous, orchestrated a general outcry. There were disturbances in the streets. From the pulpit the people were told that Giannone had denied the 'miracles' of Naples' patron saint, San Gennaro.[69] The saint was consequently angry and liable not to perform his annual 'miracle' of liquefying his congealed blood behind the glass of the reliquary containing his hands in Naples cathedral, an annual event without which, Montesquieu noted,[70] the populace of Naples was apt to be plunged in consternation and despair. The viceroy, Cardinal Althann, had instructions to defend the interests of the Austrian Court but also to seek improved relations with the Papacy. Consequently he attempted neither to quell the commotion nor protect Giannone. The most he would do was provide a pass enabling the embattled *philosophe* to flee the viceroyalty by boat. From Trieste Giannone proceeded to Vienna, where he was given a sympathetic reception and lived in exile for many years.[71]

Giannone's history was placed on the papal Index in April 1723, and both author and publisher were excommunicated.[72] Through his nuncio in Vienna, the Pope also demanded Giannone's arrest by the Emperor but was refused. Charles VI (ruled 1711–40) and his ministers chose instead to provide Giannone with a small pension, enabling him to subsist on the fringes of the Austrian Court.[73] Nevertheless, the whole episode, and especially the emotional reaction of the Neapolitans, appreciably strengthened the Pope's hand in his battle with the Austrian authorities over Church revenues and jurisdiction in the viceroyalty. This was reflected, among other things, in Grimaldi's ill-fated attempt to repeat his earlier success in publishing intellectually daring works in Naples without Inquisition approval and in defiance of the Church. His first three volumes against Benedetti having sold out by 1710, and the fourth and fifth volumes remaining unpublished, circulating only in manuscript, Grimaldi had obtained permission from the secular authorities to bring out his entire five-volume defence of the New Philosophy and 'freedom to philosophize'. But there was no prospect of obtaining the normally requisite ecclesiastical approval. Accordingly, Grimaldi decided to print the work clandestinely in his own home, again citing a false place of publication, this time 'Lucca', but now placing his real name on the title-page.[74] Despite the Giannone affair, Grimaldi remained confident that his extensive propaganda services on behalf of successive viceroys ensured protection against ecclesiastical retaliation. He was deeply shocked therefore, when, in

---

[69] Giannone, *Vita*, 80–5; Marini, 'Documenti', 696.   [70] Montesquieu, *Oeuvres complètes*, 279–80.
[71] Giannone, *Vita*, 85–90.   [72] Rotondò, 'Censura ecclesiastica', 1420.
[73] Marini, 'Documenti', 696–7, 705–6.   [74] Grimaldi, *Memorie*, 44–5.

September 1726, after the Jesuits succeeded in getting his work banned in Rome, the viceroy decided to prohibit his text in Naples too.[75] His entire stock of copies was seized and destroyed.

Little changed to improve the prospects for the Neapolitan philosophical coterie over the next years. The defeat of the Austrians in southern Italy, and the reimposition of a Bourbon regime closely linked to Spain in 1734, revived the quarrels over ecclesiastical jurisdiction in Naples but did nothing to ease the position of the enlightened intellectual avant-garde.[76] Indeed, their prospects worsened. Giannone, whose *Historia civile* was banned by the new ruler, the future Charles III of Spain, as by the old, was refused permission to return.[77] Grimaldi, having thus far had only his books banned by Althann, was now himself expelled from Naples in the wake of Giannone. Moreover, the jurisdictional quarrels between Rome and the régime in Naples were largely settled by the Concordat of 1741. In exchange for improved relations and a resumption of co-operation, the Papacy agreed to accept curtailment of ecclesiastical jurisdiction and fiscal privileges, as well as relinquishing control over censorship, the book trade, and the university. Secularization of censorship in Naples was largely completed in 1746 when the Bourbon régime, the first government in Italy to do so, abolished the local tribunal of the Roman Inquisition. This was certainly a step towards modernization, but a great many 'philosophical' books, including those of Giannone and Grimaldi, remained as firmly banned as before.

But if ecclesiastical censorship ended in Naples and Tuscany as well as Savoy and Venice, it was still a significant factor in the 1750s in several smaller states, such as Parma and Modena, as well as the sizeable territory making up the Papal States themselves. If it was beyond the power of the Pope to keep modern science and philosophy out of Rome, it was certainly not beyond his capability to curb discussion and propagation of new ideas in his own state. When Leibniz arrived in Rome in 1689, he campaigned discreetly behind the scenes, trying to persuade the cardinals and the Holy Office to lift their prohibitions on Cartesianism and heliocentrism and embrace the safer elements of the New Philosophy and science. He received quiet encouragement from a distinguished scholarly circle, mostly linked to the Accademia Fisico-Matematica, a scholarly coterie founded in 1677 by Cardinal Giovanni Giustino Ciampini (d.1698), an ally of the ageing Queen Christina of Sweden, who donated some of the group's scientific instruments and in whose palazzo the academy met,[78] Ciampini together with other eminent *savants* in Rome, such as the scientist Alfonso Borelli, the classicist Gianvicenzo Gravina (1664–1718)—a disciple of the Cartesian hermit of Scalea, Caloprese—and the historian of religion, Bianchini, had carved out an inner space for regular philosophical and scientific debate, albeit secluded behind a thick veil of discretion and conventional theology.[79] But neither Leibniz's endeavours nor the Accademia's support could significantly alter the wider Roman context.

[75] Galiani and Grandi, *Carteggio*, 258–9; Rotondò, 'Censura ecclesiastica', 1417, 1485.
[76] Venturi,'Gli anni '30', 115.   [77] Giannone, *Vita*, 260–5.
[78] Åkerman, *Queen Christina*, 254–5.
[79] Ferrone, *Intellectual Roots*, 5–6; Gardair, *Le 'Giornale'*, 145–51; Davidson, 'Toleration', 230–2.

The group in Rome could thus quietly discuss but not publish or propagate new philosophical and scientific ideas. In 1700 Gravina wrote an oration on the stages in the evolution of human knowledge, entitled *Oratio de sapientia universa*, in which he triumphantly affirms the liberation of 'philosophy from Aristotelian slavery' by Bacon, Gassendi, Galileo, and Descartes.[80] But he could not publish it in Rome and, like numerous other Italian philosophical writings of the period, it circulated in manuscript until it was eventually published in Naples. The same constraints applied to a new scholarly and scientific private academy which evolved in Rome around Celestino Galiani (1681–1753) in the years 1708–20. Galiani was an erudite monk converted from Aristotelianism to Cartesianism in 1703, who then, in around 1713, discarded the Cartesian-Malebranchiste legacy in favour of Newton and Locke, whose *Essay* he read shortly before 1710.[81] Subsequently, as Bishop of Taranto from 1731, he was a leader of the Catholic Enlightenment in Naples where, since early in the century, he had had links with Valletta, Grimaldi, and Vico.

Carefully secluding themselves from watchful eyes, the new academy, like its predecessor, inwardly promoted a moderate Enlightenment of ideas to replace the intellectual structures of the past, which would simultaneously serve as a reliable buttress for the Church in its war against non-providential deism and atheism. A living bridge between the two academies was Francesco Bianchini (1662–1729) whose *Storia universale provata* (1697), inspired by Bossuet and Huet, seeks to overthrow the new Bible criticism of La Peyrère, Spinoza, and their followers. He was especially drawn to Huet's idea that not only the ancient Jews and Christians, but all the peoples and religions of antiquity—the Chinese, Peruvians, and most of the Greeks included—believed in divine Providence and the Creation of the universe from nothing.[82] Even the Flood, he insists, is recorded not only in Scripture 'but in the traditions of every civilized nation'.[83] Later, in 1713, Bianchini visited England and met Newton, whose philosophy he enthusiastically embraced, believing it the best antidote to the radical ideas undermining belief in the divine authorship of Scripture, miracles, and the God-ordained role of the Church.[84]

From the second decade of the new century Galiani, Bianchini, and their allies in Rome sought, above all, to propagate the new English ideas. But there were substantial obstacles to doing so. After a brush with the Inquisition in 1711, Galiani vowed to remain quiet and refrain from ever publishing his own work. The only way for a philosopher to succeed in Rome, he assured friends, was to share one's thoughts merely with a few trusted allies, 'taking care not to expose them to the masses'.[85] He was to stick to this strategy all his life, being content to play an inconspicuous role behind the scenes, convening small-group discussions, circulating manuscripts, and

---

[80] Gravina, *Orationes*, 137.

[81] Galiani and Grandi, *Carteggio*, 11–15; Rotondò, 'Censura ecclesiastica', 1486; Ferrone, *Intellectual Roots*, 18–39, 122–82.

[82] Bianchini, *Istoria universale provata*, 65, 71.   [83] Ibid., 187, 201.

[84] Ibid., 22–4; Stone, *Vico's Cultural History*, 188.

[85] Galiani and Grandi, *Carteggio*, 15; Ferrone, *Intellectual Roots*, 124.

corresponding privately in Italy and abroad. A key ally was his Maltese friend and teacher, Abbot Domenico Bencini, a pupil of Gravina and lecturer in polemical theology at the College De Propaganda Fidei, an expert on the history of religion and the Bible, one of whose tasks was to train young ecclesiastics to fight the new breed of philosophical heresies challenging the authority and doctrines of the Church. Bencini's views are notable for his constant stress on the danger posed by Hobbes, Spinoza, and other 'atheists'. In his chief work, the *Tractatio Historico-Polemica* (Turin, [1720]), Bencini strives, above all, to overturn the Spinozist theory of the fraudulence and purely political character of organized religion.[86] Although Spinoza's *Tractatus* had been on the Index since 1679,[87] Bencini has no doubt that Spinoza and the *Spinosisti* who deny revelation and miracles, and claim 'that everything narrated in Scripture which is true happened according to the laws of nature and that all things happen necessarily', constitute the chief threat to religion, morality, and civil society in his time.[88] If the deists claim Moses, Christ, and Mohammed are the three great Impostors, the three real deceivers of mankind, counters Bencini, are Herbert of Cherbury, Hobbes, and Spinoza.[89] Following Huet, Bencini affirms on linguistic grounds that Moses, not Ezra, as Spinoza holds, wrote the Five Books and that all the apparent discrepancies identified by Hobbes and Spinoza can in fact be adequately explained without prejudicing Scripture's status as divine Revelation and that, whatever the *Spinosisti* say, the Decalogue is not a political device invented by Moses and was truly given to man by God.[90] The expression 'Spinosisti', as used by Bencini, denotes a large cohort of philosophical radicals whose intellectual base derives from, or is fundamentally linked to, or has broad affinities with Spinoza's system. This broader matrix includes the *Philosophia S. Scripturae Interpres* (of Lodewijk Meyer),[91] and what he terms the '*Mundus Fascinatus*' meaning Bekker's *Betoverde Weereld* which, he says, supplements Spinoza by denying that Satan, demons, angels, spirits, and witches can influence the minds and bodies of men.[92]

Except only the Papal States among larger territories, ecclesiastical control of intellectual life and book censorship crumbled last in the Iberian Peninsula. But here too, beginning in the 1740s and ending in the 1760s, enlightened ideas—and perhaps even more the increasingly obvious impotence of the traditional machinery to respond effectively to new intellectual challenges—powered the rapid dismemberment of the old system. But again, this by no means involved a shift towards intellectual freedom. Nor was this even the intention. A plan to institute a Spanish royal academy of sciences, drawn up in 1750, envisaged vesting strong censorship powers in the new body—in a style reminiscent of Leibniz—to prevent the publication of books deemed 'pernicious, useless, puerile, unworthy of public attention, contrary to good morals, against good ideas, or contrary to the rules of the sciences and arts'.[93] While in both

---

[86] Ferrone, *Intellectual Roots*, 145–50.
[87] Hilgers, *Index*, 93–4; Reusch, *Index der verbotenen Bücher*, 866–73; Totaro,. 'La Congrégation', 360–1.
[88] Bencini, *Tractatio*, 25–6.   [89] Ibid., 25; Ferrone, *Intellectual Roots*, 148.
[90] Bencini, *Tractatio*, 145, 151, 188, 197–8, 258–9, 367; Gotti, *Veritas*, ii, 1–2, 86.
[91] Bencini, *Tractatio*, 27.   [92] Ibid., 28.   [93] Ozanam, 'L'idéale académique', 198, 203–4.

Spain and Portugal the Inquisition remained outwardly in place, if not intact, and as a cultural and spiritual symbol continued to be defended by many, arrests and executions became increasingly rare from the 1740s onwards, and the Holy Office was progressively stripped by the two Iberian Crowns of effective power to censure books, intellectuals, and academic curricula. In effect, control of censorship was transferred to the governmental sphere.

In Portugal where, by the late 1740s, a full-scale public controversy over philosophy, science, and education had erupted, the inadequacy and bafflement of the Inquisition in the face of this new phenomenon of philosophical debate was manifest. Those who urged reform were moved as much by its ineffectiveness as any desire to curb its power to persecute, though at least a few enlightened nobles, most notably D. Luis da Cunha (d.1749) who drafted wide-ranging plans for the reform of Portugal's institutions in 1748, were genuinely revolted by the Inquisition's arbitrary and secretive procedures, use of torture, obscurantism, and continuing obsession with the alleged threat of 'Judaism'.[94] Among those urging change, the Oratorian Luis António Verney (1713–92), chief spokesman of the moderate Enlightenment in Portugal, and an ardent advocate of Locke and Newton, insisted, like Leibniz, Thomasius, and Van Swieten, on the need for vigorous censorship to ward off dangerous ideas but, equally, that Portugal's censorship must acquire a new and secular basis.[95] From 1750, Portugal's powerful chief minister under King José I (reigned 1750–77), Sebastião José de Carvalho e Melo (1699–1782), later marquês de Pombal, endeavoured to reform Portugal and its overseas empire. Having served as Portuguese envoy in London and then, for five years (1744–9) in Vienna, where he witnessed the advent of the Austrian Enlightenment and knew Van Swieten, he undoubtedly had some grasp of the wider European context.[96]

Such was the prestige of the Inquisition, though, among bishops, clergy, and much of the general population, that 'enlightened' Portuguese aristocrats, such as Luis da Cunha and Pombal, saw little prospect of simply abolishing it;[97] indeed, as regards formal procedures, it was not until 1768 that there was a real break with the past. In that year Pombal set up a new state censorship commission, the Real Mesa Censória, consisting of a *presidente* and seven commissioners of whom only one was an Inquisitor.[98] Controlled and funded directly by the Crown, the commission consisted partly of secular officials and partly of ecclesiastics with instructions to pursue the traditional censorship goals of the Inquisition—namely eradicating heretical, Jewish, and Muslim books, as well as books apt to corrupt morals—but also to shoulder the new task of suppressing the 'perverse philosophers of recent times', especially deistic and atheistic authors.[99] In the first two years of its existence, the Real Mesa drew up a comprehensive catalogue of the books it thought fit to prohibit. The works of Spinoza,

---

[94] Da Cunha, *Testamento político*, 75–7, 82–7.   [95] Marques, *A Real Mesa Censória*, 8.
[96] Ribeiro Correia, *Sebastião José de Carvalho e Melo*, 82–3, 94.
[97] Da Cunha, *Testamento político*, 77; Maxwell, 'Pombal', 103–4, 107.
[98] Marques, *A Real Mesa Censória*, 12, 31, 35–6; Maxwell, 'Pombal'. 103.
[99] Marques, *A Real Mesa Censória*, 47–50.

Rousseau, Diderot, d'Argens, La Mettrie, Blount, Collins, Toland, Tindal, Shaftesbury, Mandeville, Beverland—indeed, virtually the entire radical Enlightenment—were expressly prohibited.[100] Other anti-Christian writers, notably Voltaire and Hume, were, of course, also banned, as were Locke's *Essay* and *Reasonableness of Christianity*.

In Iberia, the restructuring of the machinery of censorship and intellectual control under the impact of the Enlightenment produced a context only marginally less stifling intellectually than the one replaced. The new science and medicine had gained official approval and were being encouraged. But the spirit of philosophical enquiry was still being discouraged, only now in new terminology and with new mechanisms of control. The Inquisition had become redundant for all practical purposes, but it was still important to State and Church in both Iberian kingdoms that the aura surrounding the Inquisition, and with it the culture of censorship and strict intellectual control, should be respected. The final bitter irony for Portugal's *esprits forts*, as well as foreign champions of the Enlightenment, was Pombal's forthright decree of December 1769, banning all books which criticize the Inquisition, a tribunal reviled and vilified throughout Europe by men of the Enlightenment, moderate and radical, but in Spain and Portugal still for reasons of State, and to protect the prestige of the Church, designated 'util e necessaria'.[101]

The decree sought to justify forbidding criticism of the Inquisition on the basis of the official new enlightenment philosophy of the two crowns. 'Natural Religion', proclaims the edict, is insufficient to uphold that most essential and necessary bond and unifying force in society—belief in an omnipotent God, the 'Supreme Creator' of heaven and earth, who reveals His truth and 'mysteries' only partly through the 'light of natural reason'. Hence revealed religion remains 'absolutely and indispensably necessary for being able to think and feel fittingly about God'.[102] Accordingly, the calumnies about the Portuguese Inquisition circulating abroad, accounting it 'cruel e sanguinaria' when in fact it acts benignly and is authorized by Pope and Crown, are 'abominable', harmful, and must be curbed. The decree required all copies of such works as Bayle's *Dictionnaire*, Van Limborch's history of the Inquisition, and Basnage's histories, containing 'biased and scandalous' stories about the Holy Office, to be surrendered on pain of severe punishment to the Real Mesa within thirty days.[103]

iv. Freedom of Thought, Expression, and of the Press

The history of European censorship between 1650 and 1750 thus clearly demonstrates that the moderate Enlightenment, however far-reaching institutionally and intellectually the changes it brought about, largely rejected freedom of thought, the principle of 'libertas philosophandi' (freedom to philosophize) which Spinoza, in contrast to

---

[100] Marques, *A Real Mesa Censória*, 50, 123–203; Machado de Abreu, 'Recepción de Spinoza', 109.
[101] Lúcio de Azevedo, *História*, 347–8; Freitas, *Pombal e o Santo Ofício*, 57, 60–1.
[102] Freitas, *Pombal e o Santo Ofício*, 58. [103] Ibid., 62–5; Lúcio de Azevedo, *História*, 348.

Hobbes, Locke, and the official stance of the *Encyclopédie*, proclaimed as one of his chief objectives. To most scholars and academics of the age rigorous censorship had to be not just maintained, but upgraded and modernized, because belief in a providential God appeared indispensable as a binding and unifying force in society and consequently 'atheistic' ideas had to be forcefully suppressed. As the Swedish Wolffian, Samuel Klingenstierna, declared in an oration at Uppsala in 1743, the State must suppress three classes of damaging books—those that damage 'good morals', those that harm the State, and, above all, those that attack 'religion', because denial of God means destroying all obligation, duties, and civil pacts, the very underpinning of society itself.[104]

Klingenstierna's argument espouses Locke's principle denying 'atheism (which takes away all religion) to have any right of toleration at all'[105] and it is indeed striking how little inclination one finds among the founding fathers of the moderate Enlightenment to promote the case for unrestricted intellectual freedom and a free press. For freedom of conscience and of religious practice, the pivot of Le Clerc's, van Limborch's, and Locke's toleration, no matter how liberally defined, by no means leads to, or necesssarily implies, unrestricted access to ideas and arguments, and, still less, to the unimpeded right to express ideas freely.[106] Even Bayle, whose doctrine of toleration is, in general, broader than Locke's, is extremely reticent when it comes to freedom of the press which, indeed, he nowhere seriously urges.[107]

It is thus invariably the case that arguing for full freedom of expression of ideas, access to ideas, and liberty of the press during the Enlightenment is a radical and not a moderate position.[108] Koerbagh, Blount, Toland, Leenhof, Tindal, Mandeville, d'Argens, and others are plainly in favour, though they only make isolated remarks on the subject. The one sustained philosophical basis for such a position is that of Spinoza, so that, here again, there is sufficient reason to classify such a stance as essentially 'Spinozist' in tendency if not always in inspiration.[109] It is owing to the radical philosophical positions he has already adopted on man, nature, and society that Spinoza can insist that the 'state can pursue no safer course than to regard piety and religion as consisting solely in the exercise of charity and just dealing and that the right of the sovereign, in both the religious and secular spheres, should be restricted to men's actions, with everyone being allowed to think what he will and say what he thinks'.[110]

Consequently, despite the end of ecclesiastical control over censorship, mid-eighteenth-century Europe still presented, in the eyes of radical thinkers, a thoroughly dismal prospect. D'Argens, speaking through his fictitious Chinese observer of the European scene in the late 1730s, remarks that were the great philosophers of

---

[104] Klingenstierna, *Dissertatio academica*, 21–2.   [105] Locke, *A Third Letter*, 236.
[106] Sina, *L'Avvento della ragione*, 344–7; Wootton, 'Introduction', 109–10; Israel, 'Locke, Spinoza and the Philosophical Debate', 17.
[107] Labrousse, *Pierre Bayle*, ii, 549–51; Israel, 'Locke, Spinoza and the Philosophical Debate', 16–17.
[108] Redwood, *Reason, Ridicule and Religion*, 81.
[109] Israel, 'Spinoza, Locke and the Enlightenment', 109–11; Israel, 'Intellectual Debate', 28–32.
[110] Spinoza, *TTP*, 299.

ancient Greece and Rome so often discussed in his day to return to life, they would all be pounced upon and suppressed by authority and the people—burnt in Spain and Italy, he suggests, and incarcerated in Paris and Vienna: 'Thales, Anaximander, Anaximenes, Pherecydes, Anaxagoras, Empedocles and Epicurus', he observes, would all meet an unenviable fate.[111] Furthermore, held d'Argens, while it was the clergy who opposed Descartes, tried to render Locke odious, and persecuted Malebranche, it was assuredly the common people who make all this possible and who chiefly obstruct the advance of 'philosophy' by gullibly and uncritically adopting the views of those they consider the guardians of religion while simultaneously despising the greatest philosophers without knowing anything of their work.[112]

Only with the further progress of toleration and freedom of thought, and the progress of 'philosophy', would it eventually prove possible to disarm the clergy and strip them of their influence over the people. Thankfully, declares d'Argens, a start had been made in Holland, and it is to that land Europe is principally indebted for the publication 'des ouvrages des plus grands hommes'. Indeed, he adds elsewhere, without the liberty afforded by the Dutch, half the works of Bayle could never have seen the light of day. Had he lived elsewhere than in Holland, this great *philosophe* would either never have dared write them or else would have been suppressed by a crowd of monks.[113]

---

[111] D'Argens, *Lettres Chinoises*, i, 123.   [112] Ibid., i, 127.
[113] D'Argens, *Mémoires de Monsieur*, 308–9.

6 | Libraries and Enlightenment

i. The 'Universal Library'

Libraries, especially large libraries, esteemed for rare books and manuscripts, may be described as the workshop of the early Enlightenment both moderate and radical. It was assuredly in Europe's libraries—princely, academic, aristocratic, and private—that the opening up of fresh horizons and many revolutionary new insights of the period originated. Furthermore, while the Radical Enlightenment, when propagating ideas and distributing forbidden books, remained a clandestine, forbidden movement, in the refined ambience of Europe's great libraries it could unmask bibliographically, gaining an allotted work-space and a fortified base. But this was a base which evolved only after the middle of the seventeenth century with the advent of the newly burgeoning collections on philosophy and science. For such a development required a totally new perception of books and libraries. Only after the Thirty Years' War, and the onset of the intellectual crisis, did a changed and dramatically widened culture of reading, publishing, and bibliophilia develop, which then, in turn, helped drive the revolution in ideas.

Until the mid-seventeenth century, marking the end, broadly speaking, of Europe's confessional era, European libraries and librarianship were shaped by the two great cultural impulses of the sixteenth century—the Renaissance and the Reformation. It sufficed for any prince, patrician, ecclesiastic, or nobleman eager to impress contemporaries with his magnificence, status, or love of learning, to display some of the Greek and Roman classics in fine bindings, a few humanistic works, and a selection of theological and pious texts expounding whichever confession he professed. Court, civic, university, and aristocratic, as well as ecclesiastical libraries were invariably small and usually doctrinally narrow. To have amassed large quantities of literature describing different faiths and contrary theological traditions, or heresies of one's own Church, or philosophies other than those taught in the colleges, would have seemed superfluous if not positively suspect. Furthermore, accounts of distant parts of the world and non-European peoples and cultures were scarce and seldom sought after. Science and philosophy beyond what was in the classics were found mainly in the personal libraries of university professors, who, however, acquired little that was not in Latin and narrowly academic. Even the grandest libraries of the confessional era, such as the Biblioteca Marciana in Venice, built and adorned in the 1550s, were designed to hold only very restricted numbers of books, most of the Marciana's wall-space being covered with large murals, including several by Tintoretto and Veronese.

Dramatically different was the 'universal' library, institutional and private, of the post-confessional era. An entirely new phenonemon, it evolved rapidly into a potent cultural force which, in the case of libraries owned by individuals, whether nobles, professionals, academics, or clergy, culminated during the first half of the eighteenth century before beginning to decline from around 1750.[1] After that, so great was the output of books and periodicals, it was no longer feasible for any but rulers, large institutions, and the wealthiest nobles to seek true comprehensiveness in the ordering of their libraries.[2] Thus the classic age of the 'universal library' lasted from around 1670 to 1750. Its advent was often fairly rapid in the case of leading princely, aristocratic, and the best private scholarly libraries, but noticeably slower in civic and university collections, and slowest of all in ecclesiastical libraries.

The first prominent *érudit* fully to express the ideal of the post-confessional, Early Enlightenment library was Gabriel Naudé (1600–53), one of the century's most renowned intellectual 'libertines'.[3] Having organized several large libraries in France and, for cardinals, in Rome, Naudé's ideas on bibliography and librarianship were largely shaped by his own experience. While briefly, late in life, he also tended Queen Christina's books in Stockholm, the real summit of his career was as keeper of Mazarin's library, which, in the 1640s under his care, became the largest and most impressive in France. The Bibliothèque Mazarine, open to *érudits* for research from 1643, was indeed the first of the *grandes bibliothèques* of the new era. The guiding conception behind the Mazarine, however, was rooted in Naudé's libertine philosophical vision. Steeped in the Italian philosophical heretics of the Renaissance—Pomponazzi, Campanella, Cardano, and Vanini—and a confirmed Pyrrhonist as well as an admirer of Montaigne and a friend of Gassendi, Naudé was unrivalled for his breadth of erudition and bibliographical grasp.

Naudé's treatise on libraries and librarianship, the *Advis pour dresser une bibliothèque*, first published in 1644 (and published in an English translation by John Evelyn in 1661), advocates, in line with his libertine principles, the ideal of the non-polemical, non-confessional, 'universal' library. He insists on 'universality' rather than theological specificity as the true guiding principle for a library of stature.[4] Moreover, the 'universality' he invokes encompassed not just all religions and philosophies but also science and all knowledge. Authority and tradition need to be balanced against innovation and new research. True bibliophiles must acquire the output of all the best modern, as well as ancient, authors, invariably selecting the best editions both in the original language and, where appropriate, French or Latin translation to facilitate the perusal of works in less familiar languages, such as Greek and Arabic. Libraries of any

---

[1] Raabe, 'Gelehrtenbibliotheken', 107, 114, 119.   [2] Ibid., 119.

[3] Popkin, *History of Scepticism*, 87–90; Åkerman, *Queen Christina*, 80, 82, 259; Hessel, *Leibniz*, 6.

[4] Naudé, *Advis*, 22, 28: 'une bibliothèque dressée pour l'usage du public doit estre universelle'; Hessel, *Leibniz*, 6.

standing should acquire the writings of 'all those who have innovated or changed things in the sciences' for to ignore innovation is to leave our minds weak and enslaved to outmoded notions.[5] In astronomy, he recommends Copernicus, Kepler, and Galileo because these are the men who had transformed that science. In theology, it is no extravagance, he insists, to include heretical writers because Protestant texts have to be refuted and Catholics have always been permitted to own the Talmud and Koran, works which 'vomit a thousand blasphemies against Jesus Christ and our faith and are more dangerous than those of the Protestants'.[6] If the inevitable consequence is the proliferation of much larger libraries than in the past, Naudé urges collectors and librarians to ensure cohesion by shelving books by discipline, starting with the oldest authorities and commentaries on their writings, and proceeding by stages to the most recent, thereby conveying a coherent sense of the development of each branch of learning.[7] He reproaches the Biblioteca Ambrosiana, the great library instituted by Cardinal Borromeo in Milan, one of the few regularly open to the public in his day, for shelving books 'indifféremment', that is, without regard to intellectual order.

Neither the contents nor the use of a *grande bibliothèque* can be adequate or orderly unless the head librarian is a genuine scholar with the requisite erudition to assemble, classify, and order books systematically. A great library must be accessible to readers. But this is impossible without crucial facilities, especially a well-planned and conscientiously maintained catalogue and sufficient supervision by salaried assistants to keep regular opening hours, which should be announced. Naudé judged that there were then only three libraries in all Europe affording the kind of regular access he recommends, namely the Ambrosiana, the Angelica in Rome, and the Bodleian in Oxford. These, however, were not necessarily the best and most comprehensive European libraries. Hitherto, the foremost—Naudé ranks highest the Vatican, the Medici library in Florence, Venice's Marciana, the Antoniana in Padua, and the Bibliothèque du Roy, founded by Francis I in Paris—lacked regular opening hours and were closed to most readers. By the time his treatise was published, however, the great collection he had created, the Mazarine, outstripped all the rest, though it was soon temporarily dispersed during the French civil conflict of the Frondes (1648–53).

Needless to say, there was no sudden comprehensive change across the board. The disruptive impact of the Thirty Years' War and the Frondes exerted an inhibiting effect which lasted some years. Furthermore, many rulers and nobles with long-established libraries, as well as ecclesiastics, universities, and municipalities, showed little inclination down to, and even beyond, the early eighteenth century to discard the old pattern of the small, confessionally based library anchored in authority and tradition. In 1750 there were still many libraries of the old type. As late as 1770 middle-sized German Jesuit libraries, such as those of Düsseldorf and Münster, typically boasted only 4,000 to 6,000 volumes, mostly by Jesuit authors, and they still wholly lacked Descartes, Spinoza, Leibniz, and Locke, let alone Voltaire, Diderot, D'Alem-

---

[5] Naudé, *Advis*, 33.   [6] Ibid., 38.   [7] Ibid., 89–90, 92.

bert, and Rousseau.[8] Yet during the early eighteenth century many hitherto traditional, confessionally orientated libraries seemingly felt compelled to break with the past and conspicuously to step up spending on acquisitions and facilities. The libraries of the great Benedictine and Augustinian abbeys of Bavaria and Austria, bastions of confessional thinking though they were, in the 1720s began buying furiously in science, philosophy, and other new disciplines, several of their libraries rising above 15,000 volumes by the 1740s.[9]

If the great libraries of Italy presided down to the early seventeenth century, it was the *grandes bibliothèques* of France and Germany which predominated during the Early Enlightenment. Mazarin reconstituted his collection of 40,000 books after the Frondes and, on his death, left it to his new foundation, the Collège Mazarin, or Collège des Quatre Nations, the site of his huge Baroque tomb as well as his 'spiritual' and educational legacy, situated opposite the Louvre on the banks of the Seine. Accommodated from the late 1660s in what, under Colbert's direction and designed by the royal architect, Louis Le Vau, was reckoned among the finest buildings in Paris, the Bibliothèque Mazarine remained one of the foremost Parisian collections, open to readers from all over Europe throughout the age of the Early Enlightenment and beyond.

It was rivalled—but in comprehensiveness, if not rarities, scarcely surpassed—only by the Bibliothèque du Roy. Having acquired many of Mazarin's manuscripts and Fouquet's 'superbe bibliothèque', the French royal library, by the time Louis XIV's personal rule began in 1661, overflowed with duplicates, unidentified items, and uncatalogued rarities. All this, and the library's accelerating growth, prompted the king, on Colbert's recommendation, to introduce major stuctural changes. Systematic shelving and cataloguing began, under Colbert's direction, in January 1668.[10] Naudé's chief precondition, a scholarly, full-time, professional librarian capable of conceiving and ordering a 'universal' library, was satisfied in the person of Nicolas Clément (*c.*1647–1712), a Lorrainer, previously Colbert's librarian, whom even Richard Simon acknowledged exhibited a 'merveilleuse connoissance des livres . . . de cette magnifique bibliothèque'.[11] But being of undistinguished birth, Clément, however superbly qualified, had to remain content with the lesser title of 'sous-bibliothécaire'.

By 1683 Clément had finished his catalogue of the royal manuscripts and begun his seven-volume folio index of the king's printed books ordered by subject. The library meanwhile grew steadily and strengthened its 'universal' character, helped by the issuing of instructions to French envoys abroad to keep an eye on the book trade and acquire novel, special, and rare items for the king. By 1688, reportedly, the royal collection comprised 10,000 manuscripts and over 43,000 printed books. At this point Clément embarked on a new and more sophisticated catalogue, featuring a double classification system, with eventually thirteen volumes listing books by

[8] Enderle, 'Jesuitenbibliothek', 157, 163, 184–5.   [9] Heilingsetzer, 'Wissenschaftspflege', 66, 96–8.
[10] *Mémoire historique sur la Bibliothèque du Roy*, 28.   [11] Simon, *Lettres choisies*, 143.

subject and nineteen by author.[12] After Louis' death, the regent, Philippe, duc d'Orléans, resolved to move the royal library to the present site of the Bibliothèque
Nationale, in the rue de Richelieu. Supervised by the then librarian, the pleasure-
loving but erudite Abbé Jean-Paul de Bignon (1662–1743), the mighty collection was
transferred to its spacious new quarters in 1724. But while the French royal library
possessed dazzling strengths, especially in rarities and oriental manuscripts, its great
weakness (which Bignon did little to rectify), was its acquiring modern works almost
exclusively in French, Latin, and Italian, eschewing English, German, Dutch, and
other non-Latin tongues.

Learned readers of the Early Enlightenment, French or foreign, researching in
France invariably concentrated chiefly on Paris. 'It has been truly said,' remarked the
Danish *savant*, Ludvig Holberg, who spent fourteen months exploring the Parisian
libraries in 1714–15, and subsequently returned several times, 'that there are more
libraries in Paris than are to be found in the whole of the rest of the kingdom,' noting
that besides such 'public' libraries as the Mazarine and Saint Victor, there were several
ample monastic libraries 'access to which may be easily obtained'.[13] Holberg also
regularly frequented the 'excellent library' of the Abbé de Bignon, the royal librarian
and a court preacher of exceptional eloquence, who rose to become *président* of the
Académie des Sciences. In the early eighteenth century his personal library was
reckoned one of the best in France until, to the dismay of many, it was closed, packed
away, and shipped off to Holland, where it was sold in 1725. Comprising nearly 30,000
books, this collection took The Hague booksellers Pierre de Hondt and Jean Swart
(who were allowed to use part of the Binnenhof for the purpose), eight weeks to
auction.[14]

A few fine libraries evolved in French provincial cities, but even these often ended
up in Paris. Among these was the late seventeenth-century collection of over 15,600
printed volumes and 450 manuscripts assembled by Louis Emery Bigot (1626–89), a
leader of the *noblesse de robe* of Rouen, which was then inherited by heirs in Paris. This
library was catalogued by the young Prosper Marchand in 1706, for the Parisian booksellers who auctioned it.[15] The choicest private libraries in Paris often belonged to
key officials and members of the *noblesse de robe*, among them that of Bertrand de
Chauvelin, the royal keeper of the seals, consulted sometimes by Saint-Hyacinthe
and other early eighteenth-century *philosophes*,[16] and that of Bernard de Rieux, *président* of the Parlement of Paris, who, despite helping to direct the royal censorship,
assembled an outstanding collection of forbidden manuscripts and clandestine
printed literature, including everything by Spinoza.[17] Yet the court nobility—unlike the often deeply conservative mass of the provincial nobility—also produced
some of the great bibliophiles of the age. The famously astute Marc-René, marquis

[12] *Mémoire historique sur la Bibliothèque du Roy*, 38, 41.
[13] Holberg, *Memoirs*, 123–4; Marion, *Recherches*, 37.
[14] Lankhorst, 'Ventes aux enchères', 207.
[15] Berkvens-Stevelinck, *Prosper Marchand*, 13, 17–18.
[16] Carayol, *Thémiseul de Saint-Hyacinthe*, 72.
[17] Ibid., 133; Vernière, *Spinoza*, 613.

d'Argenson (1652–1721), appointed *lieutenant-général* of police in Paris in 1697, may have enforced book censorship in Paris for over twenty years but was also an avid collector of rare books, censored or not. His younger relative, René-Louis de Voyer, marquis d'Argenson (1694–1757) was a close friend of the radical *philosophe* Boulainvilliers and acquired many of his manuscripts; his splendid library, inherited by his son the marquis de Paulmy, was transferred in 1755 into the building later known as the Bibliothèque de l'Arsenal, which remains today one of the principal historic libraries of Paris.[18]

Initially, even the Bibliothèque du Roy and the Mazarine, as well as Europe's other foremost libraries such as the Bibliotheca Augustiana at Wolfenbüttel, the imperial library in Vienna, and the electoral library in Berlin (from 1701 the Prussian Royal Library), relied on bequests, gifts, and sporadic purchases rather than planned acquisitions based on a regular income. Only from the late seventeenth century onwards, commencing with Wolfenbüttel and the Bibliothèque du Roy, did planned acquisitions and an assigned income become the rule for Europe's *grandes bibliothèques*.[19] As both the size and the use of libraries increased, not only was there pressure to spend more on books and library staff, but also to provide seating and desks, extend opening hours, and even install heating and lighting.[20] Moreover, as the concept of the universal library developed and great collections became less rare, the impulse to transfer the books into grander, more impressive buildings, which began with the relocation of the Mazarine, inexorably gathered momentum. The famous Rotunda (see Plate 10) built to accommodate the books at Wolfenbüttel was inaugurated in 1704, while the imposing new quarters for the Bibliothèque du Roy were completed in 1724, just ahead of the magnificent new Hofbibliothek in Vienna, reconstructed between 1722 and 1729 to designs by Fischer von Erlach, where the Neapolitan radical *philosophe* Giannone was one of the first and most avid readers.[21] In 1738, by which date the imperial library had been swollen by the acquisition of the famous collections, acquired after their deaths, of Prince Eugene of Savoy and Baron Hohendorf, the latter's 7,000 books acquired at auction in The Hague in 1720, the emperor's collection had reportedly grown to nearly 200,000 titles.[22]

First-rank 'universal' libraries, even by the middle of the eighteenth century, were inevitably few and far between. Paris was the only place they were to be encountered in France, the Bodleian was the nearest thing in Britain, while in the entire Holy Roman Empire scarcely more than four could be specified, namely Wolfenbüttel, Vienna, Berlin, and Dresden. The first of these, the Augustiniana, probably the largest in Europe, from the mid-seventeenth century to the early eighteenth, was founded by Duke August of Brunswick-Wolfenbüttel (d.1666), a bibliomaniac prepared to spend much of his state revenue on books. As early as the mid-1660s, his library reportedly comprised 130,000 volumes, many purchased in Holland by the duke's resident, the

---

[18] Sheridan, *Nicolas Lenglet Dufresnoy*, 135; Sheridan, 'Lenglet Dufresnoy', 426–7.
[19] Bléchet, 'Quelques acquisitions', 15.   [20] Bowden, *Leibniz as a Librarian*, 15.
[21] Lemmerich, 'Künstlerische Ausstattung', 323, 334–5. Giannone, *Opere*, 205.
[22] Ibid.; Wangermann, *Austrian Achievement*, 29–31.

libertine historian Lieuwe van Aitzema.[23] After Leibniz became director at Wolfen-büttel, as well as the smaller Court library at Hanover, in 1676, the great library was open to all respectable readers irrespective of confessional background. Montesquieu, who visited Wolfenbüttel in 1729, declared the 'bibliothèque . . . une véritable belle chose'.[24] Vienna and Berlin, meanwhile, though lagging somewhat behind until the early years of the new century, were also impressive. The Berlin Hofbibliothek grew by 1694, reportedly, to around 90,000 printed items in over 20,000 bound volumes.[25]

Leibniz emerged as the leading advocate of the 'universal' library concept in Germany, and later, through his links with Czar Peter the Great, also in Russia.[26] He proudly styled the Augustiniana, in 1695, an 'assemblée des plus grands hommes de tous les siècles et de toutes les nations qui nous disent leurs pensées les plus choisies'.[27] Keen to enhance the library as an instrument of research and intellectual exploration, he emulated Clément in stressing the need for comprehensive subject catalogues, as well as those of authors and titles.[28] A reorganized general catalogue, compiled under his direction, was installed in 1699. It was likewise he who secured an assigned regular income for the library, though his plea for heating and lighting in winter in at least one room, as in Berlin, 'car le froid et le soir servent de prétexte en hyver pour ne rien faire', was rejected on grounds of the increased fire risk.

The magnificent court library at Dresden was largely the creation of Elector Augustus II of Saxony (ruled 1694–1733) who, from 1697, was also King of Poland. This famous collection, supplemented in 1718 with the books of the recently deceased Duke Moritz Wilhelm of Sachsen-Zeitz, featured numerous rarities and Near Eastern manuscripts acquired in Poland and at Constantinople, besides a comprehensive run of western publications. In 1728, in prompt emulation of Paris and Vienna, this collection was also transferred to grander surroundings, being installed in three pavilions of the famous Dresden Zwinger.[29] The library's European standing was further enhanced in 1743, with the publication of a three-volume catalogue of its treasures compiled by its erudite librarian, Johann Christian Götze (1692–1749).

Increasingly, it was expected that *grandes bibliothèques* should demonstrate their pre-eminence by publishing their catalogues, a process culminating in the 1740s with the appearance of the catalogue of the Bibliothèque du Roy.[30] The resulting volumes were themselves scholarly research tools of the first order. The three covering the royal holdings in theology, brought out in 1742, for example, disclose that the king possessed not just virtually all Catholic theological literature but much of the output of the Lutherans, Calvinists, Anglicans, Greek Orthodox, and fringe Protestants as well, besides rich holdings of Islamic and Jewish books and a choice assortment of 'Athées,

[23] Goldfriedrich, *Geschichte*, 66; Raabe, 'Niederländische Büchererwerbungen', 224.
[24] Montesquieu, *Oeuvres complètes*, 324–5.   [25] Paunel, *Staatsbibliothek*, 23, 44
[26] Bowden, 'Leibniz as a Librarian', 4, 8; Kopanev, 'Nederlandse uitgevers', 95.
[27] Bowden, 'Leibniz as a Librarian', 3.   [28] Ibid., 6; Hessel, *Leibniz*, 8.
[29] [Götze], *Merckwürdigkeiten*, preface; Ebert, *Geschichte*, 45–60.
[30] *Mémoire historique sur la Bibliothèque du Roy*, 57.

Impies et Libertins', including an entire section of 'Spinosistes' under which category appeared, among others, the writings of Charles Blount.[31] Strikingly, the French king's bookshelves featured no fewer than five copies of Spinoza's *Tractatus Theologico-Politicus*, two in Latin and three in French.

A 'great library', insisted Leibniz, is characterized above all by universality and comprehensiveness. Consequently, it must be up-to-date, reflecting not just past progress in each branch of learning but the current state of knowledge and debate. Since few collections could measure up to such a standard, even the most assiduous researchers often encountered greater problems in finding the materials they required than Leibniz deemed acceptable.[32] In part the difficulty was met, for the affluent at least, by a growing fashion for leisurely European library tours, such as that which Denmark's foremost man of letters, Ludvig Holberg (1684–1754), undertook at the age of 20, in 1714–15, in particular to Paris and Rome. In Paris, Holberg read especially in the Mazarine where, he later recalled, Bayle's *Dictionnaire* was the work in greatest demand, being seized each day at opening time with 'extraordinary avidity' by whichever eager researcher could reach the prized volumes first.[33]

To supplement the *grandes bibliothèques* readers, even in Paris, had to rely also on the major private libraries. Mindful that there were very few of these which were truly comprehensive, Leibniz also encouraged the formation of small, select libraries which, if thoughtfully planned, could still in some degree be 'universal'. That wealthy bibliophiles should be capable of assembling a selection of books accurately reflecting the current state of ideas without the advice of an *érudit* such as himself was hardly to be expected. Accordingly, to show what such a small 'universal' library would be like, Leibniz penned a select bibliography for the enlightened reader comprising just 2,500 titles.[34] Later, in Berlin, the learned Huguenot pastor, Jean-Henri Samuel Formey, following his example, in 1746 published his recommendations on how to form a 'bibliothèque peu nombreuse mais choisie'. Any reader wishing to appraise contemporary philosophical debate, judged Formey, needs the works of Wolff, Leibniz, Locke, Malebranche, Fontenelle, and Jean Le Clerc in particular.[35] Furthermore, given that Christianity was now under relentless attack from deistic and Naturalistic *philosophes*, the small 'universal' library must include what he deemed the three most effective defences of revealed religion against Naturalism, fatalism, and materialism, which, he says, were Abbadie's *Traité*, Houtteville's *Religion Chrétienne*, and Burnet's *Défence de la religion*.

In Italy, meanwhile, libraries which had led Europe in the sixteenth century fell conspicuously behind during the later seventeenth, though Montesquieu, visiting the Marciana and the Ambrosiana in 1728, praised the facilities at the former and was struck by how well the latter was maintained, its rich store of manuscripts, accessibility to the public, and provision of paper, ink, and pens for readers.[36] Yet both had entered a stagnant phase with scant buying of foreign books. While few libraries any-

---

[31] *Catalogue . . . de la Bibliothèque du Roy. Théologie*, iii, 248–50.   [32] Hessel, *Leibniz*, 6, 9.
[33] Holberg, *Memoirs*, 60.   [34] Bowden, 'Leibniz as a Librarian', 4.
[35] Formey, *Conseils*, 7–8, 15, 31.   [36] Montesquieu, *Oeuvres complètes*, 224, 232.

where could match the priceless holdings of the Medici at Florence, and acquisitions continued under Cosimo III after 1670, the new ruler's zeal to purge heterodox, libertine, and Protestant works from the library, and to preclude further procurement of 'forbidden books', deprived the collections of their 'universal' character. Some of the great Italian libraries did create reserved stores of 'prohibited works' but practised a rigorous censorship, refusing access to readers lacking dispensations from the Inquisition. Holberg spent four months in Rome early in 1716, exploring the public libraries, where he found the staff exceptionally obliging, not only responding promptly to every request but even furnishing pens, ink, and paper without charge. 'No-one was permitted, however, to read forbidden works without the permission of the Inquisitors,' he records, and since 'almost every book I asked for belonged to the prohibited category', he obtained little that he wanted.[37] Once, he recalls, he received Bayle's *Dictionnaire* from an attendant, a simple, unlettered monk who was afterwards 'severely reprimanded for his negligence by the librarian, a Dominican father and member of the College of Inquisitors'.[38]

The United Provinces were similarly a land lacking a great 'universal' library, despite being the country most visited by European bibliophiles and *érudits* buying for themselves and others, and the best place to locate bibliographical rarities. The books on sale included not only the published output of the Republic but the contents of numerous libraries transported from France, Germany, and the Habsburg southern Netherlands. Effectively, Holland was the headquarters of the European book trade. Between 1700 and 1750 no less than 1,037 book auctions took place in The Hague alone.[39] Much of what was sold remained in the Republic but was dispersed among innumerable medium-sized and small libraries owned by the country's large élite of officials, regents, lawyers, physicians, academics, publishers, and preachers. What was comprehensively lacking were federal, provincial, or civic collections of real size and distinction.

ii. The Crisis of the Universities

The library of the University of Leiden, perhaps the nearest approximation to a major public collection in the Netherlands, had impressed visitors in the early seventeenth century mainly on account of its unrivalled stock of Near Eastern and other oriental manuscripts. But in common with academic authorities throughout Europe, the curators were remarkably slow to embrace the new 'universal' library concept, preferring until the late 1680s to keep to the old pattern of buying only in Latin and sticking to time-honoured authorities. The transformation of the Leiden library into a comprehensive, Early Enlightenment resource began only in 1689 with the purchase, in London, of the library of the libertine scholar Isaac Vossius, whose 4,000 books included numerous rarities and modern philosophical, theological, and scientific

---

[37] Holberg, *Memoirs*, 88.   [38] Ibid.
[39] Lankhorst, 'Ventes aux enchères', 207.

works.[40] It was, in fact, only in 1689 that the library acquired even such essential 'moderns' as Galileo, Descartes, and Newton.

The slow and difficult transition of the European university library to the new model stemmed partly from intellectual and confessional inertia but probably still more from the wider social and cultural crisis of the universities evident in England from the 1660s for over a century and virtually throughout the continent during the late seventeenth and most of the eighteenth century. Since the Reformation and Counter-Reformation until the early seventeenth century, Europe's universities and university life had expanded dramatically almost everywhere, driven by the two great cultural and social impulses of the age—confessionalization and the bureaucratization of the monarchical State. Much larger numbers of young men trained in theology and law were needed than had been the case previously, to staff the expanding apparatus of Church and State.[41] Many new universities were founded while older ones grew,[42] albeit confined academically within a narrow range of disciplines overwhelmingly dominated by theology and law.[43] But then, after 1650, a combination of social and especially cultural factors plunged Europe's universities into the deepest and most prolonged crisis in their history. The confessionalization process was over and the hegemony of theology in academic life was beginning to recede.[44] Furthermore, while the monarchical State inexorably expanded, needing ever more officials, officers, and diplomats, the universities proved unable, despite a further growth in legal studies, and an incipient revolution in academic medicine, beginning in the 1660s, to offer teaching and facilities in most of the new subjects gaining ground in society and general culture. At most universities one simply could not study history, geography, chemistry, physics, biology, the new medicine, or modern languages systematically, and in many no modern philosophy either. To fill the gap there was a growing shift both to private tutoring for young noblemen and sons of officials, especially in modern languages, literature, Latin, mathematics, and science, and the establishment of specialized colleges, often mainly for nobles, training future army and naval officers, as well as special schools teaching medicine, surgery, mining, engineering, and architecture.

Hence the essence of the deep crisis in Europe's universities was lack of curricular flexibility and the funds with which to restructure and diversify teaching. There was no great secret about the causes of the crisis, which indeed were obvious enough. As a report to the senate of Heidelberg university stressed in March 1680, student numbers were falling, and would continue to do so, because of the paucity of professors and the inadequacy of teaching in older and especially new fields of study.[45] The prob-

[40] Hulshoff Pol, 'The Library', 435–8.

[41] Porter, 'University and Society', 33, 44, 93; Di Simone, 'Admission', 302.

[42] Schmidt-Biggemann,'New Structures', 500–9; Pedersen,'Tradition', 474–9; Frijhoff, 'Graduation', 386–8; Frijhoff, 'Patterns', 70–3.

[43] 'Theologie is the only thing that flourishes there,' remarked one disgruntled physician of Oxford, in 1667; see Porter, 'University and Society', 96.

[44] Schmidt-Biggemann, 'New Structures', 517–29; Frijhoff, 'Graduation', 384–5.

[45] Hautz, *Geschichte*, ii, 186–9.

lem was not to grasp what was undermining Europe's universities but to find the resources with which to transform them into larger, more diversified, and better funded institutions reflecting the changing requirements and expanding horizons of Early Enlightenment society.

In the circumstances, it was simply impossible for such an immense restructuring to be tackled, given the large number of universities,[46] in more than a handful of specially favoured, élite institutions. Consequently, after 1680 most universities not only ceased growing but steadily contracted. Nothing could have been less typical than the remarkably successful inauguration of the new Brandenburg-Prussian university of Halle, in July 1694, amid fanfares and in the presence of the Elector, 700 students, and academic celebrities such as Christian Thomasius and Franz Buddeus.[47] For except for Halle, Jena, Leipzig, and later the new Hanoverian university of Göttingen, the German universities overall were inexorably declining. Total student numbers at the now thirty-four German universities fell uninterruptedly from the 1680s throughout the eighteenth century, often, as at Greifswald and Erfurt, quite steeply.[48] Dwindling prestige and student numbers induced even the most inert to try desperately to upgrade their libraries. The collection at Greifswald, in Swedish Pomerania, was typical in this respect: small, confessionally rigid, restricted to old authors, and comprising a mere 1,100 volumes in 1713; it nearly quintupled in size to 5,286 volumes by 1748, and markedly expanded its range. Yet still the university continued to decline.[49]

Lack of adequate libraries were one of the most glaring deficiencies. But the formation of a modern 'universal' library was logistically complex and extremely costly, and apart from rare exceptions, notably Oxford, where endowed funding proved decisive, the resources were simply unavailable. Even at Oxford, where there was an alarming lack of books in modern languages, ensuring planned, balanced growth proved to be no simple matter. Having begun in 1602 with 2,000 volumes the Bodleian by 1674, when the first catalogue was compiled, had reached the not unimpressive size of 20,000 books and manuscripts.[50] A report of 1697 extolled the Bodleian as the 'glory of our university and kingdom in its kind', an attraction which draws 'hither strangers even from countries beyond the seas to their benefit and to the honour and profit of the nation' but also warned of the dangers of failing to maintain purchasing momentum.[51] The reputation not just of Oxford but of the kingdom was at stake. Besides spending on 'new accessions which are new helps and encouragements to learning',

---

[46] Owing to its political fragmentation, the Holy Roman Empire had an exceptionally large number of universities, around thirty in 1648 as compared with about twenty in France, five in the Dutch Republic, and two in England; McClelland, *State, Society and University*, 28; Frijhoff, 'Patterns', 90–4; reviewing the position in 1728, Capasso calculated there were then twenty-seven universities in Germany, a similar number in France, and no less than twenty in Spain; see Capasso, *Historiae philosophiae synopsis*, 450.

[47] [Tentzel], *Monatliche Unterredungen 1694*, 513–51.

[48] Chartier, 'Espace social', 391, 396; Di Simone, 'Admission', 303; McClelland, *State, Society, and University*, 28–33; Märker, *Geschichte*, 71; Seth, *Universitetet i Greifswald*, 73–4, 161–9.

[49] Goldfriedrich, *Geschichte*, 66.   [50] Philip and Morgan, 'Libraries', 664–5.

[51] BL MS Harl. 7055, fos. 42–3. 'Some Thoughts concerning the Bodleian Library' (dated 7 June 1697).

particular priorities were to complete the 'great catalogue', put the Bodleian's estimated 2,995 manuscripts in proper order, and ensure 'every book, shelf, etc. be well brushed and dusted once a year'.[52]

When Halle was inaugurated in 1694 it was not yet considered essential to concentrate bibliographical resources in the university library.[53] The elector's advisers expected Halle's advantageous location, and the numerous eminent professors attracted from elsewhere, would suffice to ensure success. It was then still regarded as normal for a leading academy to rely chiefly, for its bibliographical resources, on its professors, who would bring their own books with them. Thus, in its early years Halle's luminaries included Jakob Thomasius who, at his death, in 1684, owned 8,441 books, his son Christian Thomasius (1655–1728) who amassed more, the theologian Friedrich Benedikt Carpzow (d.1699) who boasted 15,512 volumes and the theologian Siegmund Jakob Baumgarten (1706–57), a famous bibliophile who possessed 17,500 titles.[54] But attitudes changed noticeably in the early eighteenth century. It came to be recognized that a university required library strength beyond that of its professors if it was to attain the intellectual universality upon which its standing was now seen to rest. It was the vision and energy of Burchard Gotthelf Struve (1671–1738), during the years he was librarian (1697–1704) there, and the local prince's support, which made possible the ambitious restructuring and expansion which transformed Jena's library into a renowned public collection drawing scholars from across Protestant Europe, the factor which in turn enabled Jena to remain at the forefront of German universities.[55]

However, it was at Göttingen that the ideal of the 'universal' library was most impressively realized in the academic context. An entirely new university founded in 1734 by George II, king of England, Scotland, and Ireland and Elector of Hanover, in part as a mercantilist measure to draw prestige, students, and the trade they brought with them away from the three great east-central German universities—Leipzig, Jena, and Halle. It was planned from the outset that Göttingen's library should eclipse all other academic libraries in Germany, and announced in the Hamburg press, as early as 1732, that the new foundation would boast a large, well-furnished reading-room designed as an integral part of the main university building.[56] The concept, scope, and facilities of the library, predictably, were strongly influenced by the legacy of Leibniz.[57] On opening, in 1734, it already contained 12,000 volumes purchased by the State from private collections, including that of the renowned bibliophile Von Uffenbach, in Frankfurt. Boosted by its assigned annual income, as well as gifts, Göttingen's holdings rose to 16,000 volumes by 1746 and around 30,000 by the late 1750s.[58]

In Sweden–Finland the issue of university libraries was a pressing one, in view of

[52] BL MS Harl. 7055, fo. 43.   [53] Frühsorge, 'Zur Rolle', 64–5, 73.

[54] Raabe, 'Gelehrtenbibliotheken', 112–13.

[55] Knoche, 'Universitätsbibliotheken', 428–9; Struve also started a fashion for publishing historical and descriptive accounts of university libraries.

[56] Hessel, *Leibniz*, 9–12; Fabian, 'Göttingen', 210–18.   [57] Hessel, *Leibniz*, 9.

[58] Ibid., 16–17; Fabian, 'Göttingen', 219–30.

the comparative rarity of noble and other major private libraries, especially after the royal library in Stockholm was devastated by fire in 1697. In the late seventeenth century the only major aristocratic library in Sweden belonged to the chancellor of Uppsala university, the richest nobleman in the land, Magnus Gabriel de la Gardie (1622–86) who amassed some 8,000 books. Apart from the royal library, no other collections could aspire to 'universal' status. Even the rich and famous general Carl Gustaf Wrangel (1613–76), a noted bibliophile by Swedish standards, left a mere 2,400 volumes at his castle at Skokloster.[59] Gradually, Uppsala university library came to be viewed as the major Swedish collection for scholars and researchers. In 1669, La Gardie donated a collection of medieval Icelandic and other rare manuscripts and subsequently transferred more of his books to the university library. But it was only around 1700, when it began to be systematically reorganized and expanded as a modern 'universal' library, that it emerged as the foremost library of the Swedish monarchy. Rehoused in the Gustavianum, the principal building of the university. the library grew under the competent care of its librarian, Eric Benzelius the Younger (1675–1743), a scholar with wide European connections, who subscribed to the new learned periodicals, instituted planned regular acquisitions, bought at Dutch book auctions and even in Paris, and compiled a new catalogue, rendering Uppsala by 1720 one of the largest and best academic libraries in Europe.[60]

iii. Shelving the Two Enlightenments

In an age in which the *grandes bibliothèques* were few and far between and even those that existed might suddenly be annihilated—the great Lisbon earthquake of 1755 eliminated most of the royal library there, the flames reportedly consuming 70,000 books[61]—the private 'universal' library was of crucial importance. After around 1750, the diversification of knowledge and the proliferation of publications outstripped what even the most zealous individual bibliophile could acquire, and the ideal of the 'universal' library fell into desuetude except for large institutional collections. But until around 1750 the large private library covering all fields was one of the prime motors of the Enlightenment. Some of the choicest were found in places where there was no Court, no university, and no great aristocrats. At Hamburg, for example, were the famous collections of Johann Albert Fabricius (1668–1736), a professor at the civic gymnasium who amassed 32,000 volumes, most said to be enhanced with 'good annotations' in his own hand, Michael Richeys (d.1761), who likewise possessed over 30,000 books, the noted Hebraist, Johan Christian Wolf (1683–1739) with 25,000, and Johann Friedrich Mayer (1650–1712), over many years the chief spokesman of Lutheran orthodoxy in the city, who had 18,000 books.[62] Most of these Hamburg collections included radical works, though few could compete in this respect with the highly expert anti-Epicurean and anti-Spinozist deist Hermann Samuel Reimarus

---

[59] Losman, 'Skokloster', 95.   [60] Lindroth, *History of Uppsala*, 60–5.

[61] Maxwell, 'Pombal', 81.

[62] Jöcher, *Allgemeines Gelehrten-Lexicon*, ii, 488–9; Raabe, 'Gelehrtenbibliotheken', 107, 113.

(1694–1768) who possessed Spinoza, Beverland, Bredenburg, and Cuffeler in Latin, Dirk Santvoort and Wyermars in Dutch, and—most unusually—Toland, Collins, and Mandeville in English.[63]

In Dresden the Court library may have been the chief attraction for the erudite, but only slightly less imposing, bibliographically speaking, was the library of 30,000 titles amassed by the Lutheran superintendant, Valentin Ernst Loescher (1673–1749), who owned copies of practically every impious work of the age. Smaller but more specialized in 'prohibited books' on which he was an acknowledged expert, was the library of Johann Christian Gottfried Jahn who possessed, besides the complete works of Vanini, Spinoza, and Leenhof, Meyer's *Philosophia*, Koerbagh's *Bloemhof*, Cuffeler's *Specimen*, Wyermars' *Den Ingebeelde Chaos*, Boulainvilliers' *Vie de Mahomed*, Lenglet Dufresnoy's *Refutation*, and a remarkable collection of clandestine philosophical texts in manuscript.[64]

The very fact that such private libraries as those of Loescher and Jahn in Dresden contained extensive collections of radical philosophical literature, printed and manuscript, which were the objects of careful research, illustrates the ambiguous role of the 'universal' library as an instrument of the incipient Enlightenment. Such libraries were centres of study but also meeting-places for groups of *érudits* who discussed the books they found there and the ideas they contained, and stimulated in each other an involvement with radical, as well as mainstream, Enlightenment thought. The notorious connoisseur and collector of clandestine philosophical literature, Peter Friedrich Arpe, author of the *Apologia pro Vanino* (Apology for Vanini), published at 'Cosmopolis' (i.e. Rotterdam) in 1712, who originated from Kiel, seemingly acquired his taste for such material while studying at Copenhagen and mixing in the prestigious intellectual circles attached to the Danish capital's main private libraries.[65] Among those whose books he regularly perused was Christian Reitzer (1665–1736), a jurist possessing most of the republican works of Johan and Pieter de la Court, and hundreds of other volumes in Dutch.[66] a champion of Cartesianism and freedom of thought with a large library, including numerous 'forbidden' works, and Frederik Rostgaard (1671–1745), professor of classical philology at the university, whose 8,187 books, auctioned in 1726, included two manuscript copies of Bodin's *Colloque Heptoplomères*, the 1534 edition of Pomponazzi's *De Immortalitate Animae*, Beverland's works, Cuffeler's *Specimen*, Wachter's *Spinozismus*, and several other Spinozistic works.[67]

Copenhagen was indeed a major focus of early Enlightenment bibliophilia, although the university library, one of the most extensive in Europe, with over 10,000 volumes as early as 1662, was decimated by a fire which swept through the university

---

[63] *Catalogus bibliothecae beati Herm. Sam. Reimari*, i, 71–80, 157, 164, 166, 176–82; Schröder, *Ursprünge*, 82, 284, 318.

[64] [Jahn], *Verzeichnis der Bücher*, 1634, 1713, 1803, 1958, 1977, 2074, 2194–8; Schröder, *Ursprünge*, 416, 458, 469, 512.

[65] Mulsow, 'Freethinking', 204–5.　　　[66] Reitzer, *Appendix Librorum*, pp. A4–5, B3v.

[67] [Rostgaard], *Bibliotheca Rostgardiana* (1726), 225, 227, 292, 472, 520, 749; Ellehøj and Grane, *Københavns universitet*, iv, 374.

in October 1728.[68] Denmark's foremost bibliomaniac was assuredly Count Otto Thott (1703–85) who, as a student in 1725, accompanied Holberg on forays into the Parisian libraries. Thott purchased books everywhere and on every subject, his library eventually totalling an estimated 120,000 volumes, the posthumously published catalogue of which ran to twelve volumes.[69] It included one of the most extensive collections of forbidden philosophical books and manuscripts to be found anywhere in eighteenth-century Europe.[70]

Perhaps nowhere else, though, was the contribution of the private 'universal' library to the progress of the early Enlightenment, moderate and radical, more crucial than in Italy, where the impact of censorship, the unavailability of foreign books, and the decay of the great libraries all conspired to create a situation in which a few medium and large private libraries containing rare foreign works and 'libri prohibiti' provided the indispensable channel through which flowed the philosophical ferment of the late seventeenth century, and later. In Naples in the 1680s and 1690s, the library of Giuseppe Valletta served as the headquarters and discussion forum of the philosophical *novatores*.[71] More impressive still, and vital to the nurturing of the Early Enlightenment in Florence, were the 25,000 books and 2,873 manuscripts belonging to Magliabechi, a bibliomaniac who sought, read, wrote about, and discussed books to the point of neglecting everything else, even his personal appearance.[72] A bibliographical titan, who influenced many without ever having published a book himself, and in whose honour a celebratory medal was cast, portraying him seated, holding a book, Magliabechi, like Naudé and Leibniz, considered universality—the encompassing of the whole of human thought and knowledge—the test of a *libreria grande*. Even a small, select library, he urged Cardinal Francesco Maria de' Medici when, in 1695, the latter was planning such a collection for the Villa di Lampeggio, must have a 'universal core' if it is to be of any standing. He advised the cardinal to shelve all the Greek, Roman, and Arabic philosophers one would find in a great library plus Bacon, Gassendi, Descartes, and Bayle besides such (officially banned) works as Campanella's *Opera philosophica*, Hobbes' *Opera omnia*, and the works of Malebranche.[73]

A key toehold for the Radical Enlightenment in Italy from the 1720s until the middle of the century, located originally in Rome and then in Florence, was the library of the legendary deist, freemason, and open homosexual, the Baron Philip von Stosch (1691–1751). Son of a Brandenburg burgomaster, he spent the years 1706–15 studying at Frankfurt an der Oder, Wittenberg, Leipzig, Jena, Leiden, Oxford, Cambridge (where he spent some months studying with Richard Bentley), and Paris, where he became friendly with Bignon. Subsequently, Stosch cultivated his antiquarian, artistic, and

---

[68] Ellehøj en Grane, *Københavns universitet*, iv, 363.   [69] Holberg, *Memoirs*, 125.

[70] Benítez, *Face cachée*, 26–7, 30–1, 41, 51.

[71] Carpanetto and Ricuperati, *Italy*, 81; Stone, *Vico's Cultural History*, 2–4.

[72] Totaro, 'Antonio Magliabechi', 549–50; Laeven, De 'Acta Eruditorum', 157; Goldgar, *Impolite Learning*, 152–3.

[73] Totaro, 'Antonio Magliabechi', 556.

bibliographical interests mainly in Rome. A paid agent of the English Crown who, among other activities, spied on the Stuart Court in exile, he was obliged to leave Rome as an undesirable influence, following the election of Pope Clement XII in 1730 but, as we have seen, he was permitted to settle in a Florence just emerging from the stagnation of the age of Cosimo III. While residing in Italy, Stosch, defying the Inquisition, imported forbidden books by sea, via Livorno, from the Dutch Republic, obtaining at least some from Charles Levier at The Hague, whom he evidently knew. The importance of his library lay not in its overall size of some 7,000 books, but his collection, unrivalled in Italy, of 'libri prohibiti': he possessed everything by Spinoza, most of Toland, Collins, and Mandeville, besides Fontenelle, Lahontan, La Mettrie, Bekker's *Betoverde weereld* in French, and several key radical works in Dutch, including Koerbagh's *Bloemhof* and Leenhof's *Hemel op Aarde*.[74] After his death, his library was catalogued and auctioned in Florence in 1759. The library accrued to the Bibliotheca Marucelliana, a recently opened public institution in Florence, still in use today; but, of course, only the books which were not banned were shelved for public use, the forbidden material being inconspicuously tucked away in the librarian's home.[75] Early eighteenth-century Italy was a land where much was veiled, forbidden books concealed, and great public libraries seemed, as Le Clerc put it, describing the Ambrosiana, 'more set off with statues, pictures and other ornaments . . . than by any great number of its books'.[76] Yet for connoisseurs, initiates, and those sufficiently resolute, furnished with Inquisition dispensations or not, everything was discreetly available near at hand—behind closed doors.

iv. Lexicons and *Dictionnaires*

An appreciable factor enhancing the comprehensiveness, philosophical, theological, and scientific, of Early Enlightenment libraries, especially those of smaller and medium sizes, even those comprising a mere few hundred books, were the multi-volume encyclopaedias, *dictionnaires*, and lexicons which were one of the most striking manifestations of the intellectual revolution of the period. Encyclopaedic works yielding expert summaries of wide swathes of new and older knowledge provided an invaluable guide to the present state of research and thought within reach of all with the money to procure such relatively costly items. The vogue began in 1674 with the publication of Louis Moréri's *Grand Dictionnaire*, gained momentum with Bayle's *Dictionnaire* of 1697, continued with Ephraim Chambers' two-volume *Encyclopaedia* of 1728, and culminated finally in the celebrated *Grande Encyclopédie* of Diderot and d'Alembert. Constantly revised and expanded, chiefly at Amsterdam, Moréri's compilation, among the foremost of these works, went through no fewer than twenty editions down to 1759.[77] A triumph of the genre, visually as well as intellectually, and a major contribution to the advancement of toleration, was the thirteen-

---

[74] [Stosch], *Bibliotheca Stoschiana*, i, 159 and ii, 130, 161, 217–19; Ferrone, *Intellectual Roots*, 73, 305.
[75] Totaro, 'Nota', 111–12. [76] *Monsieur Le Clerc's Observations*, 5.
[77] Raabe, 'Gelehrte Nachschlagewerke', 101.

volume *Ceremonies et coûtumes religieuses de tous les peuples du monde,* published at Amsterdam in 1723. Compiled by Jean-Frédéric Bernard (*c.*1683–1744) and magnificently illustrated by the engravings of Bernard Picart (1673–1733), the work embodied an immense effort to record the religious rituals and beliefs of the world in all their diversity as objectively and authentically as possible.

The first Dutch-language encyclopaedia, aimed at *savants* and the relatively uneducated alike, appeared at Amsterdam between 1733 and 1737.[78] In Germany Early Enlightenment enthusiasm for lexicons and encyclopaedias developed into a veritable mania. 'Lexicons are now so much in vogue' remarked a German periodical, in 1714, 'that soon one will be buying and selling them as one does snuff.'[79] Esteemed for their lively and stimulating, if far from always systematic or concise mix of theology, philosophy, history, geography, and science, the dictionaries of Moréri and Bayle showed publishers what the public thirsted for. In 1709 a Leipzig consortium brought out an amended (and unattributed) German version of the sixth edition of Moréri, revised at Amsterdam by Le Clerc, under the title *Allgemeines Historisches Lexicon,* with a preface by Buddeus. By 1750 this Leipzig version had itself gone through six editions.[80] Its initial success was followed by that of a dictionary of *savants*, the *Compendiöse Gelehrten-Lexicon* (1715), and an encyclopaedia of arts and sciences—Johann Theodor Jablonski's *Allgemeines Lexicon der Künste und Wissenschaften*, published by Thomas Fritsch of Leipzig in 1721, besides Johann Georg Walch's *Philosophischen Lexicon* of 1726.[81] Dwarfing all these, however, was the stupendous project of Johann Heinrich Zedler (1706–63), the *Grosses vollständiges Universal-Lexicon aller Wissenschaften und Künste*, a gigantic encyclopaedia in sixty-four volumes, published at Leipzig, which began to appear in 1731 but, owing to logistical difficulties and cost, was completed only in 1750.[82]

The depth and extent of the impact of the early Enlightenment on European society and culture is powerfully revealed by the content of these massive works which were expressly produced for a broad market, an audience of scholars and philosophers certainly, but also the new élites of officials, diplomats, patricians, professionals, and courtiers, and even their wives and daughters. They demonstrate that in fifty or sixty years 'philosophy', or what we today would call philosophy, science, and technology, were widely acknowledged to have fundamentally changed the world. At the same time, the lexicons were, in themselves, an effective weapon in the further battle against superstition and ignorance, being strongly pervaded by the views on toleration, and the condemnation of bigotry and fanaticism, typical of Bayle, Le Clerc, Bernard, Marchand, Buddeus, and other key compilers of the lexicalogical literature.[83] No less prevalent in the lexicons, and consequently soon in society generally, was an uncompromising reverence for new philosophy, science, and research, and the suffused, ubiquitous disparagement of older ideas and scholarship.

The lexicons and *dictionnaires* enabled anyone with access to them to acquire a

---

[78] This is the *Woordenboek* compiled by David Frans van Hoogstraten and L. J. Schuer.
[79] Quoted in Raabe, 'Gelehrte Nachschlagewerke', 98.   [80] Ibid., 102.   [81] Ibid., 106–8.
[82] Ibid., 110.   [83] Bots and Van de Schoor, 'Tolerance', 143–4.

knowledge of any dimension of the Early Enlightenment, including radical thought, which was summarized and discussed in varying levels of detail in all these compendia. Still worse, some thought, was the way in which one of the most influential and sought-after of the *dictionnaires*, that of Bayle, went out of its way to point out the pervasive presence of atheistic, deistic, and materialistic philosophies throughout the whole history of human thought, seemingly almost with the deliberate intention of coaxing readers to focus their minds on radical arguments. Equally impossible to ignore was Bayle's contention that 'Spinozism', in one form or another, has always infiltrated human minds. 'Il n'y a presque point de siècle où le sentiment de Spinoza n'ait été enseigné,' he maintained, adding that 'cet impie n'a que le malheureux avantage d'être le premier qui l'ait reduit en système selon la méthode géométrique.'[84] Thus Bayle highlights and not infrequently makes positive comments about such thinkers as Zeno of Elea, Xenophanes, Melissus, Parmenides, Anaxagoras, and Democritus among the ancients, while at the same time unfailingly pointing to the links with Spinoza. Hence Democritus, though his views on motion in matter are declared almost as absurd as Spinoza's, is nevertheless styled by Bayle 'l'un des plus grands philosophes de l'antiquité'.[85] Similarly, Xenophanes' view of God is judged an 'impiété abominable, c'est un Spinozisme plus dangereux que celui que je refute dans l'article de Spinoza'.[86] Nor was Bayle any less insistent regarding the pervasive role of 'Spinozism' in Renaissance thought. It was Bayle, for example, who transformed the image of Giordano Bruno in European culture from that of a heretical mystic into that of a precursor of radical deism, a philosopher whose thought 'est au fond toute semblable au Spinosisme',[87] a notion amplified subsequently, following Bayle, in the dissertation on atheism of 1711, by Veyssière de la Croze, librarian of the Hofbibliothek in Berlin.[88]

Whether or not the 'philosopher' of Rotterdam was deliberately unsettling readers, stimulating interest in atheistic philosophy, and reminding people about Spinoza at every turn, a fraught question about which there was considerable disagreement, it was generally agreed that Bayle's *Dictionnaire* was extremely problematic and in some ways damaging from a Christian standpoint. Relentless in demonstrating the incoherence and irrationality of every point of view, all systems were seemingly demolished by his corrosive rational criticism. Bayle relentlessly uncovers the inconsistencies of others, 'mais de principes,' objected Formey, 'vous en chercheriez vainement chez lui, s'il en a un, c'est celui de n'en point avoir.'[89]

Their capacity to serve as potential vehicles of radical thought, and Bayle's special brand of critical rationalism, were often perceived as negative aspects of the lexicons from which readers should be shielded. These were doubtless among the reasons for the banning of the *dictionnaires* of Moréri and Bayle in France under Louis XIV. With

---

[84] Bayle, *Dictionnaire*, iii, 2455.
[85] Cantelli, *Teologia e ateismo*, 231–4; Paganini, *Analisi della fede*, 348–53.
[86] Bayle, *Dictionnaire*, iii, 3043.
[87] Charles-Daubert and Moreau, *Pierre Bayle. Écrits*, 119; Ricci, 'Bruno "Spinozista" ', 42, 46–7.
[88] Veyssière, *Dissertation sur l'athéisme*, 284–6, 317.   [89] [Formey], *Pensées raisonnables*, 44, 67.

the passage of time though, such objections came to be outweighed in most people's minds by the perceived benefits of spreading awareness of new knowledge and science. But however one weighed good and bad in the lexicons, undeniably they turned into a philosophical engine of war which massively invaded the libraries, public and private, of the whole continent. Their influence was ubiquitous and could not be reversed.

v. The Early Enlightenment in National Context

With regard to key themes, and the timing and intensity of debates, the Early Enlightenment was an impressively unified process across Europe, indeed a remarkable demonstration of the essential cohesion of European history. Nothing could be more mistaken than to suppose that national arenas evolved in relative isolation from each other or that national contexts were decisive in shaping the broad pattern of intellectual development. But, somewhat paradoxically, even while Europe's intellectual and social élites were to some extent culturally cosmopolitan, they were nevertheless in some ways also remarkably parochial. This conjunction of universal intellectual concerns and tendencies with, in particular, an extremely limited exposure to most foreign languages and books, created a highly peculiar combination of cultural universality and narrowness which suffused every part of the Early Enlightenment and frequently obtrudes even in the greatest figures. Vico, for instance, a universal thinker of impressive range, though steeped in Latin, professed (not altogether accurately) never to read anything in modern languages other than his native Italian.[90]

The prevailing pattern in reading, intellectual debate, and library acquisitions was to embrace Latin and French in addition to the local tongue (where the latter served as a significant vehicle of book culture) but not anything else. Latin remained fundamental to European culture throughout the period, though it was occasionally noticed by the early eighteenth century that its use was declining gradually everywhere in favour of French.[91] Hence British libraries of any stature would be plentifully stocked with books and manuscripts in Latin and French as well as English, but astoundingly lacking, except to a small degree Greek, Hebrew, and Italian, in anything else. In this respect (if no other) Locke's personal library of over 3,000 volumes was entirely typical. Over a third of his books were in English and another third in Latin, with a further 18 per cent in French.[92] The rest, amounting to under 5 per cent, mostly comprised works in Greek and Italian, leaving Dutch, German, and Spanish almost totally excluded, despite his having lived and worked for six years in the Netherlands and knowing some Dutch. Indeed English, Scottish, Irish, and English-speaking

---

[90] Levine, 'Giambattista Vico', 68.

[91] See, for instance, [Le Clerc], *Bibliothèque Universelle*, xxvi (1718), 5.

[92] Harrison and Laslett, *Library of John Locke*, 19; Locke, significantly, had two sets of Spinoza's *Opera Posthuma*, besides the *TTP* and other works connected with Spinoza, including Meyer's *Philosophia*, Aubert de Versé's *L'Impie convaincu*, and Lamy's *Nouvel Athéisme renversé*; ibid. 223, 238.

American intellectual culture was virtually completely devoid of acquaintance with books and periodicals in other Germanic languages. The early eighteenth-century catalogues of Saint Andrews University Library, to give a Scottish example, contain almost nothing in modern languages other than English and French.[93]

France, even at the height of the Enlightenment, was equally parochial and selective regarding books, periodicals, and library acquisitions. Overwhelmingly, French libraries featured books and periodicals in French and Latin with practically nothing even in Italian, Spanish, and Portuguese, related languages readily understood, let alone English, Dutch, or German, languages little taught or known, though a fashion for studying English arose around 1720 and gained some momentum in the wake of the *anglomanie* of the 1730s and 1740s. Typical was the library of Jean-Jacques Dorthous de Mairan (1678–1771), a high-society *érudit* reputed to expound science in fashionable circles with the ease and grace of a Fontenelle and who, in 1740, succeeded him as secretary to the Académie des Sciences in Paris. Mairan, in the course of his successful career, amassed 3,400 books which were auctioned after his death in 1771. Over one third were in Latin and the rest mainly French; despite his (post-1720) Newtonianism and interest in Italian science, he owned scarcely a handful of publications in English and Italian and practically nothing in German, Dutch, or Spanish.[94]

Similarly, in Italy almost all private libraries and even the great collections, including that of a bustling trading republic such as Venice, the Biblioteca Marciana, procured books predominantly in Italian and Latin with a sprinkling in French. The consequences of this exclusion of books in other major languages were then compounded by the fact the Italian erudite journals usually reviewed only foreign works which appeared in Latin.[95] Yet the wide prestige the Italian language had formerly enjoyed north of the Alps had, by this date, largely dissolved. Italy was a force in the Early Enlightenment, or as Le Clerc put it in 1718, still produced 'plusieurs livres utiles' in the context of contemporary intellectual debate, but there was little appreciation of this in most of northern Europe, since hardly anyone any longer read Italian or bothered to obtain Italian books.[96] Nevertheless, it is important to bear in mind that there was still a zone of Italian cultural influence where Early Enlightenment books and ideas emanating from Italy played the leading role before 1750, extending from Vienna in the north and to the Levant, Spain, and Portugal in the Mediterranean.

By contrast Scandinavia, the Baltic, and northern Germany presented a completely different scenario. The only country in Europe outside the British Isles, the library catalogues suggest, where English functioned as a major cultural language down to 1750 was Denmark-Norway, where many libraries contained scientific and philosophical works in English, that of the erudite Christian Worm (d.1738), Bishop of Sjaelland, for example, including English editions of Boyle, Locke, Thomas Burnett, John

---

[93] See St AUL MS LY 105/5 and MS 105/7.
[94] Roche, 'Un savant', 48, 64, 70; Guerlac, *Newton on the Continent*, 65–7, 113–14.
[95] Gardair, *Le 'Giornali de' Letterati*, 313–15.   [96] [Le Clerc], *Bibliothèque Universelle*, xxvi (1718), 5–6.

Edwards, Richard Bentley, and John Tillotson.[97] But in the rest of Scandinavia and the Baltic, where there was also no local tongue which functioned as a regular vehicle of intellectual discourse, neither French nor English was particularly strongly represented before the 1730s. Here, besides Latin, it was incontrovertibly German and Dutch which served as the two preponderant modern languages of cultural exchange. The fact that Dutch generally outweighed English as a medium of cultural exchange in the north may be deeply perplexing to the modern reader accustomed to a world in which English overwhelmingly predominates. But over the centuries the Hanseatic cities had been culturally as well as commercially dominant in the north, and the Low German of the Hanseatics, which was closer to Dutch than what is now termed 'German', had been the lingua franca over a vast area. This meant that, certainly down to the mid-eighteenth century, Dutch books were more frequently bought and sold, and more widely understood in Scandinavia and the Baltic than books in English, among nobles as well as merchants, academics, and professionals. This pattern was more marked in Sweden-Finland than Denmark–Norway but nevertheless applied in the latter too. Not untypically, the Danish Count of Daneschiold in Samsoe, whose library of 8,000 books was auctioned in Copenhagen in 1732, and who had a taste for political thought, had his Hobbes in Latin and Locke in French but the brothers de la Court, among others, in Dutch.[98]

Northern Germany was similarly more receptive to Dutch than English or French and for the same reason—the continuing prevalence of Low German. At this time the Dutch still called their own language *Nederduitsch* (or Low 'Deutsch'), as distinct from High German, but made little distinction between Dutch and Low German, a tendency replicated in German and also English usage, seventeenth-century Englishmen distinguishing between 'High Dutch' (i.e. German) and 'Low Dutch' (i.e. Dutch plus Low German) rather than between Dutch and German as we do now. Consequently, throughout the area from the Rhineland to East Prussia, the Dutch language and its books tended to circulate more and be more readily available than publications in English or French. Admittedly, French was very widely used in Court and diplomatic circles and, by the early eighteenth century, was becoming more familiar in scholarly and mercantile circles. Yet, not infrequently, even the largest libraries were remarkably thin in French as well as English editions, though few collections were quite as extreme in this respect as the huge library of 42,000 titles built up in the late seventeenth and early eighteenth century by the chancellor of the Court of Gottorp, near Kiel, Johann Adolph Kielmann von Kielmannsegg, and his son, the Baron Friedrich Christian. The Bibliotheca Kielmanseggiana, auctioned at Hamburg in April 1718, almost entirely comprised works in Latin, German, and Dutch, with practically nothing in French or English.[99] Typically, the Kiel professor Andreas Ludwig

---

[97] See *Catalogus Librorum Beati D. Christiani Wormii*; the library was auctioned in Copenhagen, soon after his death, on 3 Feb. 1738.

[98] [Daneschiold], *Bibliotheca*, 232, 242, 245, 285, 332.

[99] [Kielmanns-Egge], *Bibliotheca* (3 vols, Hamburg, 1718).

Koenigsmann, a figure immersed in the philosophical wars of the period, whose library was auctioned in Copenhagen in October 1729, owned Locke's *Essay* and Toland in Latin, Collins in French, and generally few books in English, but possessed the *Nagelate Schriften,* Spinoza's posthumous works in their Dutch version, as well as Pieter Balling's *Licht op den Kandelaar,* and other radical as well as moderate works in Dutch.[100]

Dutch libraries, despite the primacy of the Netherlands in Europe's book and periodical trade, were scarcely any less parochial. Libraries belonging to those with claims to erudition consisted principally of works in Latin and Dutch, increasingly also with an admixture of French but rarely anything else. The hundreds of libraries belonging to Dutch professionals, academics, preachers, and regents auctioned at The Hague, Amsterdam, and Rotterdam between 1650 and 1750 contained very little in English, German, or southern European languages. The Dutch situation was complicated, though, from the early 1680s, by the Huguenot influx from France, bringing in numerous *savants* and preachers bibliographically limited in a different way, being mostly unwilling, even after decades of residence in the United Provinces, to read anything except French or Latin.

Geographically, the European Early Enlightenment was an impressively widespread phenomenon. But if significant developments can be seen everywhere on the continent, even well before 1700, from Portugal to Russia and from Ireland to Naples, it is undoubtedly true that certain key national contexts, actually five—France, Britain, Germany, Italy, and the Netherlands—generated nearly all the major impulses and intellectual innovations driving this great cultural transformation. This raises the issue of whether and, if so, how, to rank the various countries generating the Enlightenment. For, taking Europe as a whole, the pace and intensity of change varied appreciably from country to country and period to period, so that even though the five principal givers and receivers all contributed to this vast reworking of fundamental ideas and values, and learnt from each other, there were nevertheless striking imbalances at different times in the tally of giving and receiving.

It used often to be held that 'the Enlightenment' was essentially French and centred on Paris. Nowadays, it is not infrequently claimed that 'continental Europe looked to England as the source of the Enlightenment,'[101] a view sometimes expressed not only by Anglophone but also German and Italian—if rarely by French—scholars.[102] Another notion which has recently become influential is that there was not one Enlightenment but many different national Enlightenments, that the Enlightenment 'occurred in too many forms to be comprised within a single definition and history, and that we do better to think of a family of Enlightenments, displaying both family resemblances and family quarrels'.[103] But all considered, it seems best to discard all these perceptions and return to the idea of a single European Enlightenment,

---

[100] Koenigsmann, *Catalogus,* 8, 21, 94–5, 98, 109.

[101] Harrison, *'Religion' and the Religions,* 176; Hampson, *The Enlightenment,* 36–9; see also Jacob, *Living the Enlightenment,* 15, 21, 26.

[102] Cassirer, *Philosophy,* 7–18; Ferrone, *Intellectual Roots,* 8–22.   [103] Pocock, *Barbarism,* i, 9.

except now it should be seen as a European Enlightenment that most emphatically was not inspired by any single nation, be it France, England, or the Netherlands, but rather had its centre of gravity in north-western Europe and particularly in the inner circuit linking Amsterdam, the other main Dutch cities, Paris, London, Hamburg, and Berlin, albeit with a subsidiary southern base in Naples, Venice, and Florence. Consequently, what chiefly needs to be stressed is that Britain and France were far from being the only major sources of 'enlightened' ideas and that it is indispensable, if one is to avoid serious distortion, to analyse the ebb and flow of ideas within a much broader European context than has been usual in the past.

7 | THE LEARNED JOURNALS

i. Changing Europe's Intellectual Culture

The dictionaries and lexicons were a ubiquitous and irreversible engine of enlightenment. But from the 1680s, it became clear that there had arisen an even more powerful machine undermining traditional structures of authority, knowledge, and doctrine—namely the erudite periodicals. Possibly no other cultural innovation, observed Scipio Maffei (1675–1755), one of the chief heralds of the Venetian Enlightenment, in 1710, had exerted so immense an impact on Europe, over the previous four decades, as these journals.[1] Everywhere, awareness of new ideas and knowledge, new books and debates, had been enhanced and enriched. It was, indeed, no exaggeration to maintain that, through the journals, Europe had, for the first time, amalgamated into a single intellectual arena. Henceforth, debates, controversies, the reception of new books and theories and their evaluation, were not just facilitated and accelerated but also projected beyond the national contexts hitherto determining the reception of new publications and research and thereby transformed into an international process of interaction and exchange.

Contemplating the rise of this powerful new cultural device in 1718, the inaugural preface of a leading learned periodical, *L'Europe Savante* of The Hague, observed that the journals' success had come neither quickly nor easily.[2] Rather, for many years progress had been hampered by appreciable obstacles. While the first example of the genre, the Parisian *Journal des Scavants*, established in 1665, had rudimentarily performed the functions of the later journals—publicizing and evaluating new books, reporting scientific advances and scholarly debates, and providing obituaries of recently deceased *savants*—it also encountered formidable official and ecclesiastical obstruction and had been obliged to steer conspicuously clear of the more contentious theological and philosophical issues.[3] Moreover, apart from the London *Philosophical Transactions* (also founded in 1665), designed to publicize the scientific work of the Royal Society, a journal similarly silent on the wider philosophical questions, no new erudite review subsequently appeared anywhere in Europe for nearly two decades until the founding, in 1682, of the *Acta Eruditorum* of Leipzig. The *Acta*,

---

[1] *Giornale de' Letterati* (Venice) i, 13; Berengo, *Giornali veneziani*, pp. xii–xiv; Carpanetto and Ricuperati, *Italy*, 127; Waquet, *Modèle français*, 355.

[2] *L'Europe Savante*, i, preface, pp. i–vii.   [3] Dann, 'Vom *Journal des Scavants*', 63–4.

edited by Otto Mencke (1644–1707), backed by an annual subsidy from the Elector of Saxony, and published in Latin to boost its international appeal, proved highly successful, and despite appearing on the papal Index in 1702 was widely admired in Catholic as well as Protestant lands. It was openly adopted as their model by the three founders—Maffei, the crypto-radical Antonio Vallisnieri, and Apostolo Zeno—of the Venetian *Giornale de'Letterati*, launched in 1710.[4] The *Acta*'s enduringly high prestige, throughout the half-century it was operative until 1731, was primarily due to the excellent quality of its regular reviewers, especially Mencke himself, Wilhelm Ernst Tentzel (1659–1707), von Seckendorf, and the venerable Buddeus who, between 1694 and 1707 contributed over 100 reviews, as well as Leibniz.[5]

After 1682, fresh learned periodicals appeared in brisk succession.[6] The first of the Dutch-based ones, and also the first of the genuinely 'critical' journals, the *Nouvelles de la République des Lettres*, edited by Pierre Bayle, appeared in March 1684, followed in 1686 by the *Bibliothèque Universelle* (1686–93) of Jean Le Clerc, a venture financed by four leading Amsterdam publishers. Soon after appeared the *Histoire des Ouvrages des Sçavans* (1687–1709). As general periodicals proliferated, a new variant emerged in the late 1690s with the advent of the review serving a particular region, the original model for which was the *Nova Literaria Maris Balthici*, founded at Lübeck in 1698, its style of linking local scholarly developments with the wider arena then being expressly adopted by the *Nova Literaria Helvetica* founded at Zürich in 1703.[7]

While French and Latin predominated, there was also soon a demand for book news and reviews in German and Dutch. In 1688, at Leipzig, Christian Thomasius, much impressed by the recently founded reviews in French, especially Bayle's,[8] brought out the first issue of his ground-breaking *Monatgespräche*. According to Thomasius, the journals, by giving books greater publicity than in the past, were encouraging people to read and debate them.[9] That a journal devoted to reviewing the latest scholarly books and controversies could not just appear, but flourish, in German, sufficiently illustrates that the intellectual revolution had by this date penetrated well beyond the restricted circles of professional academics, lawyers, physicians, and clergymen who had monopolized erudite discussion in the past and confined it to Latin.[10] Other German-language journals appeared subsequently and again with success. A new Latin periodical, at Rostock, declared in 1721 that, while the French and Dutch had established the learned periodical as such, it was the Germans who established the vernacular review addressing a wider, essentially 'national' audience.[11]

Periodicals of regional character led a more precarious existence, and proved less durable, than those more European in scope. In France, Germany, Switzerland, and the Netherlands, publishers of reviews in the vernacular could at least count on a

---

[4] *Giornale de' Letterati* (Venice) i, 20; Goldfriedrich, *Geschichte*, 55–6.

[5] Laeven, *De Acta Eruditorum*, 43, 166.

[6] *L'Europe Savante*, i, preface, pp. iv–vi; Habermas, *Structural Transformation*, 25.

[7] *Nova Literaria Helvetica*, i, 6; Berengo, *Giornali veneziani*, 7.

[8] [Thomasius], *Monats-Gespräche*, i, 226–7, 234.   [9] Ibid., i, 234.

[10] Jaumann, *Critica*, 276–81.   [11] *Annales Literarii Mecklenburgenses*, i, 2.

substantial pool of educated, urban dwellers to swell their readership. Elsewhere, where urban culture was less developed, or where, as in Spain, Portugal, and to some extent Italy, intellectual debate in the vernacular had traditionally been discouraged by the ecclesiastical authorities, and the cultural context was therefore less favourable, learned periodicals faced continual difficulties in finding sufficient readers, as well as sometimes painful dilemmas of language and cultural perspective. The first issue of the *Dänische Bibliothec*, published at Copenhagen in 1738, lamented the lack of publicity given to Danish–Norwegian erudition in the wider world over many years, since the demise of the Lübeck *Nova Literaria*, and wished to correct this, while at the same time aspiring to spread awareness of wider intellectual developments in Denmark-Norway and, for this purpose, would have liked to review foreign books and debates in Danish.[12] But publication in Danish would hamper broadcasting Danish erudite news abroad, while Latin would obstruct the creation of a non-professional 'national' readership at home. The only solution, seemingly, was to publish in German.[13]

So numerous were the periodicals needed to service a cultural impulse as wide-ranging as the Early Enlightenment that, by 1718, according to *L'Europe Savante*, around fifty had come into existence in German, Italian, Dutch, and English, as well as French and Latin; and while some proved ephemeral many became firmly established.[14] Successful, durable journals, however, did not spread evenly across the continent. On the contrary, they became heavily bunched together, a circumstance which clearly demonstrates the formidable nature of the obstacles impeding the erudite press and the difficulty of creating conditions conducive to the flourishing of such vehicles of critical thinking. France, for example, proved generally unwelcoming. Even after the ecclesiastical authorities were reconciled, and the *Journal des Scavants* was relaunched in 1666, under the editorship of Abbé Jean Gallois, an *érudit* admirably qualified, being diligent, keenly interested in new scientific research and theories,[15] assured of Colbert's support,[16] and expert in English, German, Spanish, and diverse oriental languages as well as Latin, the publication faced continual difficulties throughout his editorship, until 1674;[17] and while subsequently Gallois' mediocre successor, the Abbé de la Roque, editor from 1675 to 1687, did little to improve matters with his prolix reviews, anti-Protestant bias, and incompetence in philosophy,[18] the basic reason for the French review's failure to win much prestige at home or abroad, which remained obvious under La Roque's successor, Louis Cousin, editor from 1687 to 1701, was the sheer difficulty of obtaining new books for review from abroad, even from Catholic capitals such as Rome, Venice, or Vienna, let alone Protestant centres such as Amsterdam, The Hague, Leipzig, or London. Royal and ecclesiastical

---

[12] *Dänische Bibliothec*, i, 2.   [13] Ibid., i, 3–4.

[14] *L'Europe Savante*, i, preface, p. v.   [15] Brockliss, 'Scientific Revolution', 70.

[16] Camusat describes Colbert as 'son ami plûtôt que son protecteur'; see [Camusat], *Histoire critique*, i, 215, 219, 231–2.

[17] [Camusat], *Histoire critique*, i, 218, 233.

[18] Camusat praised La Roque's exemplary diligence but accounts this 'la seule chose que l'on puisse louer en lui'; Ibid., ii, 2, 5–6.

censorship combined with stringent border searches proved an insurmountable impediment.[19] In 1684, while praising the newly established Leipzig and Amsterdam journals for their achievement in spreading awareness of new books all over Europe, including France, La Roque openly despaired of competing effectively with them. German books were all but unobtainable in France. Books from Holland 'qui est le lieu du monde où il s'en imprime le plus', could be procured only with extreme difficulty, owing to the authorities' wish to debar 'livres qui viennent d'un pays où l'on a la liberté de tout dire et de tout écrire'.[20] Furthermore, distribution to the rest of Europe from France, as from England, was slow and erratic.[21]

During the early eighteenth century there were barely two or three regular reviews of international standing appearing in France, one of which was the Jesuit *Mémoires de Trévoux*. Yet Britain too was completely marginalized as far as the European erudite periodical press was concerned. Nowhere was freer as regards censorship laws and procedures, but even after the *anglomanie* took hold in the 1730s and 1740s, knowledge of the English language on the continent was sparse and there was scant demand for English publications as such;[22] moreover, with a rapidly expanding book market of their own to service, English publishers showed little inclination to emulate their Dutch counterparts' habit of publishing great quantities of material in French. Efforts were made to establish French-language reviews elsewhere, notably Hamburg, where several issues of the *Journal de Hambourg* edited by Gabriel d'Artis (*c.*1660–*c.*1732) appeared in the mid-1690s, containing among other things, lively discussions of the Bekker controversy. and also, at a later stage, in Berlin.[23] But no other country came near competing with the impressive output of French-language journals in the Netherlands.

Meanwhile, more reviews in Latin appeared in Germany, building on the success of the *Acta*, notably at Halle, Jena, and Bremen. A Latin journal, the *Bibliotheca Librorum Novorum*, also appeared in the Netherlands, at Utrecht in 1697, but the Dutch review in Latin proved as unsuccessful as the French journal in Britain and Germany. After only five issues, the Utrecht *Bibliotheca* ceased publication in 1699. Hence, a virtually fixed division of labour had set in by the end of the seventeenth century, with Holland the headquarters of the French-language periodicals and northern Germany for those in Latin and German. But with Latin receding and French gaining as Europe's chief medium of intellectual discourse, this left the United Provinces in an unrivalled position.

From 1684 onwards down to the mid-eighteenth century, the United Provinces always produced more and more important journals than any other European country and its advantages as the base of this vital sector of the Early Enlightenment were indisputable. On launching his *Bibliothèque Universelle* in 1686, Le Clerc acknowledged

---

[19] Reesinck, *L'Angleterre*, 65, 68 9; Dann, 'Vom *Journal des Scavants*', 64; Bots, 'Role des périodiques', 49.

[20] Quoted in Reesinck, *L'Angleterre*, 69.

[21] *Nouvelles de République des Lettres*, i, preface; Reesinck, *L'Angleterre*, 65.

[22] Ibid., 53–5, 65.   [23] *Journal de Hambourg*, i, 133–5, 273–5.

that many readers would question the wisdom of initiating yet another review when those already established at Paris, Leipzig, and Rotterdam were deemed by many 'admirable'. But there had also been widespread criticism, he urged, especially as regards inadequate coverage of new books and controversial issues—no doubt he had Paris and Leipzig chiefly in mind—as well as complaints of bias.[24] Le Clerc planned to avoid these shortcomings and not only review comprehensively but also supply extensive excerpts. He expected to surpass his rivals, he indicated, in part simply because he was working in Amsterdam where 'all books' were to be found, the booksellers backing the venture being the 'mieux fournis et les plus fameux de l'Europe'.[25] Another advantage, he noted, was that one could more easily ventilate intellectually or theologically sensitive issues in the Dutch Republic than elsewhere 'comme on se trouve en un pais de liberté'.[26] The Dutch regents permitted a general religious toleration and he vowed faithfully to emulate the 'justice et l'equité de ces sages magistrats, en rapportant sans préjugé les sentimens de toutes les sociétés chrétiennes'.[27]

Bayle had deliberately eschewed such rhetoric, promising merely to criticize no ruler and to speak 'avec respect des Catholiques', hoping thereby to avoid proscription of his journal in France and other Catholic lands, but in vain.[28] His journal was forbidden in those countries, as was Le Clerc's. Nevertheless both authors were eventually highly esteemed by *savants* in France and Italy, some of whom had dispensations to read books denied to most of the laity, as well as northern Europe, and gained an authentically pan-European status. Moreover, where Bayle retired from editing in 1687, after just four volumes, his rival, Le Clerc, soldiered on for decades his unflagging output of long, penetrating, and balanced reviews in a tone reckoned less judgemental than Bayle's,[29] winning him respect and considerable influence everywhere, including Naples and Rome,[30] despite near universal hostility to his theological views. In 1693, the *Bibliothèque Universelle* ceased after twenty-five volumes, but he subsequently resumed reviewing, embarking on his *Bibliothèque Choisie* (1703–13) and later his *Bibliothèque Ancienne et Moderne* (1714–26). All together, during his career with the three titles spanning nearly forty years, Le Clerc produced no less than eighty-three volumes.[31] Visiting him in 1726, the year of his retirement from editing, aged 79, Holberg found him 'notwithstanding his advanced years, in full possession of both bodily and mental vigour'.[32]

The *Nouvelles de la République des Lettres*, having created an entirely new style of incisive 'critical' reviews,[33] lapsed for a decade following Bayle's departure. It was subsequently revived by Jaques Bernard, a Huguenot and, before emigrating from France,

---

[24] [Le Clerc] preface to *Bibliothèque Universelle*, i, pp. 3v–7v.   [25] Ibid., 8.

[26] Ibid., 8–8v; he affirmed that the regents 'permettent à tous les Chrétiens de servir Dieu, selon les mouvemens de leur conscience' without any coercion of anyone.

[27] Ibid., fo. 8v.   [28] Reesinck, *L'Angleterre*, 67; Bots, 'Refuge et le Nouvelles', 85–6.

[29] [Le Clerc], *Bibliothèque Universelle*, iii, 'avertissement'; Le Clerc, *Parrhasiana*, 269.

[30] Sina, *Vico e Le Clerc*, 10–11; Ferrone, *Intellectual Roots*, 66.

[31] Formey, *Conseils*, 31.   [32] Holberg, *Memoirs*, 140.

[33] [Thomasius], *Monats-Gespräche*, i, 226–7; Berkvens-Stevelinck, *Prosper Marchand*, 115, 123.

a pastor, who excelled in philosophy and studied, among others, under the young Le Clerc at Geneva. The revived *Nouvelles* was again a success, remaining under Bernard's competent editorship from 1699 to 1710 and then again from 1716 to 1718.[34] Also highly reputed, the *Histoire des Ouvrages des Savants*, based in Rotterdam and launched following Bayle's retirement, was edited by Henri Basnage de Beauval, a former lawyer of Rouen who produced it for twenty-two years (1687–1709). Like Bernard, Basnage emulated Bayle and Le Clerc in writing most of the reviews himself.[35] A protégé of Bayle, Basnage, though far less erudite, was an equally tireless champion of toleration and 'enlightened' intellectual impartiality. In his eyes, intolerance and bigotry were the pure fruit of ignorance and superstition: 'l'ignorance,' he held, 'est la cause de la plus part des maux qui affligent le genre humain.'[36] Venerating the high-mindedness and impartiality of Bayle and Le Clerc, he too promised to eschew all bias towards Catholic and other theological standpoints with which he disagreed.[37]

By contrast, the major early eighteenth-century French-language journals published in Holland, such as the *Journal Littéraire* (1713–37) of The Hague and the *Bibliothèque Raisonée* (1728–53) based at Amsterdam, shared out the burden of writing reviews and notices among whole panels of *savants*.[38] The *Journal Littéraire* became the internationally acknowledged model of a respected, erudite periodical of a consistently high standard, employing multiple authors. This publication, wrote Veyssière de la Croze, librarian to the Prussian king, to Marchand in 1731, 'est à mon avis le meilleur de tous les journaux'.[39] By the 1720s, the one-author method perfected by Bayle, Le Clerc, and Basnage de Beauval had become simply too onerous and inflexible. But regular team-work of consistent quality was a requirement which, in turn, posed a host of personal, logistical, and organizational difficulties. The short-lived *Journal Historique de la République des Lettres*, though originally conceived as a team effort, was soon effectively left to Marchand alone to produce but, for precisely this reason, lapsed after a mere three volumes (1722–3).[40]

Another important review in the Netherlands, and for many years the only one published in Dutch, was the *Boekzaal van Europe*, founded and edited in Rotterdam by Pieter Rabus (1660–1702).[41] Commencing in 1692, this periodical followed much the same procedure as the French-language journals, appearing every two months and offering long book reviews and erudite news. Bayle, who continued to watch the periodicals' progress with interest, noted in 1694 that this publication 'a beaucoup de débit'.[42] A total of fifty-seven volumes were produced by Rabus, a lawyer and teacher from a liberal Anabaptist background, whose model was Bayle's *Nouvelles* and who, until his death in 1702, strove indefatigably to provide high-quality intellectual debate

[34] *L'Europe Savante*, iv (1718), 154–6; Nicéron, *Mémoires*, i, 135.

[35] Ibid., ii, 207–8; Berkvens-Stevelinck, *Prosper Marchand*, 123–4.

[36] Basnage de Beauval, *Tolérance des religions*, 67–8.

[37] [Basnage de Beauval], *Histoire des Ouvrages*, i (Sept, 1687), preface, p. v.

[38] Berkvens-Stevelinck, *Prosper Marchand*, 110–13; Goldgar, *Impolite Learning*, 72.

[39] Quoted in Berkvens-Stevelinck, *Prosper Marchand*, 113.

[40] Ibid., 115–16.   [41] De Vet, *Pieter Rabus*, 102, 178.   [42] Bayle, *Lettres*, i, 545.

and judgement in the vernacular for the learned and less learned alike.[43] The journal resumed after his death under a new editor, renamed the *Boekzaal der Geleerde Weereld*.

Eventually, mused Bayle, proliferation 'de cette sorte d'écrits fera qu'on ne les voudra plus lire' since readers would find the same reviews and debates uselessly replicated everywhere.[44] But as the years passed and more journals appeared, there was little sign that such apprehensions were well-grounded. Nor was there any tendency for Dutch predominance in the field to slacken. In 1746 the Berlin *savant*, Jean-Henri Samuel Formey, observed that of nearly thirty erudite journals current in Europe enjoying an international reputation, only two were based in France, several in Germany and Italy, one in England, and no less than eighteen in the United Provinces.[45]

In Italy the obstacles hampering erudite periodicals remained formidable throughout the Early Enlightenment period. If Italians produced fewer books of philosophical and scientific interest than the English, Le Clerc noted in 1718, this was not due to intellectual deficiencies 'mais à cause du peu de liberté qu'il y a de publier ce qu l'on veut'.[46] Neither the first *Giornale de' Letterati* published at Rome between 1668 and 1683, nor its mediocre successor, the *Giornale Veneto de' Letterati* of Venice (1671–89), nor the several short-lived attempts after that, exerted much impact.[47] All were fatally enfeebled by the proximity of the Inquisition and difficulties in procuring foreign books.[48] Bolder, more successful, and more important, was the mildly anti-Jesuit and initially pro-Cartesian second *Giornale* (1710–40) established by Maffei, Vallisnieri, and Zeno at Venice.[49] Maffei's preface to the first issue in 1710 declared the thirteen-year gap since the last *Giornale* lapsed in 1697 a calamitous and also 'shameful' one, since there was then no other Italian periodical devoted to reviewing new scholarly writings and debates.[50] The renewed venture was widely welcomed, though Leibniz and other connoisseurs abroad were not overly impressed, and its success was mainly due to its shifting the focus away from international currents and debates to books published in Italy.[51]

The new review lasted thirty years, albeit becoming increasingly sporadic. If it studiously avoided the more troublesome intellectual issues and practiced much self-censorship, as was unavoidable in Italy at the time, it was nevertheless a potent factor in the progress of the Italian Enlightenment. Backed by its network of collaborators in Florence, Bologna, and Padua, the journal expressed the new 'enlightened' ideals of the age, not least by assuring readers it was permissible in Catholic lands to learn from northern, in particular, the Dutch erudite journals, including the *Bibliothèque Choisie*

---

[43] De Vet, *Pieter Rabus*, 1–10; Wielema, *Filosofen*, 79–83.
[44] Bayle, *Lettres*, ii, 649.   [45] Reesinck, *L'Angleterre*, 80.
[46] *Bibliothèque Ancienne et Moderne*, xxvi (1718), 5–6; Waquet, *Modèle français*, 36–8.
[47] Dooley, *Science, Politics*, 38–40.   [48] Ibid., 40–1; Gardair, *Le 'Giornale de' Letterati'*, 12–13.
[49] Berengo, *Giornali veneziani*, xi–xii; Generali, 'Il 'Giornale', 243, 252–3.
[50] *Giornale de' Letterati* (Venice), i, 51.
[51] Dooley, *Science, Politics*, 63; Waquet, *Modèle français*, 67.

edited by the 'eruditissimo Giovanni Clerico [i.e. Jean Le Clerc]', provided readers, mindful these periodicals were written by Protestants, were continually on their guard against 'dangerous' notions.[52] Starting in a discreetly Cartesian-*Malebranchiste* vein, the *eruditi* producing the journal edged towards a Leibnizian-Wolffian stance during the early years of its existence.[53] This reflected a wider tendency in the Venetian Republic during the second decade of the century, a time when Leibniz intensified his efforts to advance his philosophy there, with the help, among others, of Fardella and successive Leibnizian mathematicians, Jakob Herman (1707–13) and Niccolò Bernouilli (1716–19), at the University of Padua.

The Dutch French-language journals fulfilled a European role. Even so, their coverage was always weighted somewhat in favour of Dutch publications and, in some respects, debates.[54] Not surprisingly, the publishers who backed the journals, such as Leers, the Wetsteins, who financed the *Bibliothèque Raisonée*, and others, were concerned not only to publicize the views of their editors,[55] but also to promote sales of books they published or distributed. Thus Leers, for example, did not forget to append a note to the inaugural preface of the *Histoire des Ouvrages des Savants*, reminding readers that his shop was plentifully stocked with all titles reviewed in the journal.[56] While large quantities of books were imported to the United Provinces from France and these were also extensively reviewed, the proportion of books reviewed produced in France was usually less than that published in the United Provinces (whether in French, Latin, or Dutch) while, for the rest, only English and German books received even a modicum of regular coverage. Barely any attention was given to publications from Italy, Spain, Portugal, or Scandinavia. While data for the main Dutch journals shows that approaching 50 per cent of the books discussed were published in the United Provinces, with another 20 or 25 per cent produced in France, English books accounted for scarcely more than 10 per cent and German titles still less.[57]

Consequently, until around 1720, British and German books and disputes enjoyed only a very modest, subordinate profile internationally, notwithstanding the debates surrounding Newton and Locke, which eventually had a crucially important impact on the continent. That there was a pressing need—noted by Leibniz as early as 1702[58]—for a specialized French-language review providing comprehensive coverage of developments in British philosophy and science gradually became generally apparent. But it was not until 1717 that such a vehicle, the *Bibliothèque Angloise* of Amsterdam (1717–28), was launched. 'On peut dire en général,' remarked the journal's editor, Michel de La Roche, in his inaugural preface, 'que les livres anglois ne sont guères connus hors de cette isle' and that those issuing in French translation were simply too few to convey an adequate picture of the current state of ideas and science in Britain. Reviewing La Roche's inaugural volume, *L'Europe Savante* entirely agreed, lamenting

---

[52] *Giornale de' Letterati* (Venice), i, 23–4; Carpanetto and Ricuperati, *Italy*, 91.
[53] Generali, 'Il 'Giornale', 244, 252–3.   [54] Bots, 'Rôle', 54–7.
[55] Goldgar, *Impolite Learning*, 92–5.
[56] [Basnage de Beauval], *Histoire des Ouvrages*, i (Sept. 1687), p. v.
[57] Bots, 'Rôle', 53–4; Bots, 'Le Refuge', 91–2.   [58] Klopp, *Correspondance de Leibniz*, ii, 271–2.

the scarcity of knowledge of English, despite the recent advent of a fad for learning that language, and the even greater rarity of knowledge of English books in France and throughout continental Europe.[59] Both the *Bibliothèque Angloise* and its successor, the *Bibliothèque Britannique* (1733–47) with which Prosper Marchand was closely connected in its later years, assigned around 90 per cent of their space to reviewing English publications,[60] thereby contributing appreciably to the onset of the *anglomanie* which swept Europe in the 1730s and 1740s. Meanwhile a not dissimilar realization of the need to publicize German and Swiss book news led, in 1720, to the launching of a parallel organ, the *Bibliothèque Germanique* (1720–59), a review edited by Huguenot *érudits* mainly in Berlin but with the extensive participation of Dutch-based Huguenots, again notably Marchand.[61] This journal came to be somewhat dominated in the 1740s and 1750s by the leading Wolffian writing in French, Formey. A shorter-lived but potentially comparable, and by no means unsuccessful, specialized publication was the Neo-Cartesian *Bibliothèque Italique*, produced at Geneva in the years 1728–34, with which the liberal Calvinist theologian Jacques Vernet was associated, and which was linked to the Early Enlightenment movement in Venice, especially Maffei and Vallisnieri.[62]

The erudite journals were incontestably one of the most potent agents driving the Enlightenment in its vital formative phase down to 1750. Overwhelmingly orientated towards recent developments in the world of thought, scholarship, and science, they did much to shift the focus of the cultivated public's attention away from established authorities and the classics to what was new, innovative, or challenging, even when such innnovation arose in distant lands and unfamiliar languages. In an age when barriers of language and the vagaries of the book trade frequently impeded the circulation of books internationally, it was especially the journals which spread awareness of new discoveries, ideas, and controversies around Europe. As the Abbé de la Roque noted in 1684, where previously it took years for French readers to learn about new books appearing in Germany, since the advent of the Leipzig *Acta* and Bayle's *Nouvelles*, *savants* knew about what mattered within weeks.[63]

A second aspect of the journals' cultural sway was their unceasing advocacy of the new 'enlightened' ideals of toleration and intellectual objectivity. Bayle, Le Clerc, Basnage de Beauval, Bernard, Rabus, Marchand, and numerous lesser figures were all tireless champions of religious and intellectual freedom—albeit usually within definite limits—toleration for them being not just a guiding principle in confessional and political matters but inherent in their craft of erudite journalism and their wider vision of the unbiased intellectual life. Their quintessential task they saw as the propagation of a new ideal of impartial judgement, balanced presentation of views, polite debate eschewing all bigotry and invective. So powerful was this impulse it led at times to an excessive proneness to detachment, almost a fear of taking sides or embracing a

[59] *L'Europe Savante*, i, 319.   [60] Bots, 'Rôle', 55.
[61] Berkvens-Stevelinck, *Prosper Marchand*, 117–18, 207; Goldgar, *Impolite Learning*, 74–9.
[62] Ferrone, *Intellectual Roots*, 97; Carpanetto and Ricuperati, *Italy*, 109; Goldgar, *Impolite Learning*, 71.
[63] Bots, 'Rôle', 49.

clear position. It is assuredly no accident that precisely when the journals exerted their maximum influence on Europe, that is, between 1680 and 1750, the decisive shift in western and central European (as well as North American) civilization occurred, away from confessional culture to denigration of dogmatism, intolerance, superstition, bigotry, and ignorance. Doubtless such a fundamental change sprang from a complex interplay of social, cultural, and intellectual factors. But within this wider context, the cumulative impact of the journals on the fashionable attitudes of the age was unquestionably a factor of the first order.

A third major effect was the contribution of the journals to fragmenting the deeply rooted notion, championed by kings, parliaments, and Churches alike, that there existed a universally known, accepted, and venerated consensus of truth. The only point the periodicals collectively conveyed with absolute clarity was that knowledge of truth, theological, philosophical, and scientific, was in a complete state of flux and had become a swirling vortex of rival views and theories struggling to explain a burgeoning and increasingly bewildering mass of data. Whatever one's personal faith, the informed reader could only conclude that all semblance of consensus in Europe had collapsed, and a relentless pan-European war of philosophical and scientific systems had begun, the outcome of which no one could predict. The journals with their simultaneously confident, but yet hesitant, culture of impartiality, balance, and toleration, and frequently non-committal, inconclusive reviews, were totally destructive of the Baroque impulse—contracting but still residually prevalent in most of Europe around 1700—to insist that unity and cohesion could be restored through a more rigorous assertion of authority and confessional doctrine. The new ideal of unbiased detachment and deferring judgement, propagated by the periodicals, could always readily be justified by pointing to the need for more research and data, and the lack of 'certain evidence'.

Fourthly, and no less fundamentally, the journals proved to be one of the most powerful agents shaping and propagating the 'moderate, Christian Enlightenment', and simultaneously, defining and banishing to the margins the rival Radical Enlightenment. For their perennial summons, one might almost say their *raison d'être*, was to seek a middle course—however perplexing and strewn with rocks the disconcertingly wide, poorly charted, and far from readily navigable channel between—on the one hand, assailing superstition and ignorance, and on the other, upholding the essentials of faith and the legitimacy of God-ordained authority. If prejudice and obscurantism were the declared enemy, on one side, no less contrary to the professed values of the journals, and harmful to society in their view, was the challenge of philosophical Naturalism, fatalism, atheism, materialism, and Spinozism which, almost without exception, every review unwaveringly condemned. 'L'athéisme et la superstition,' insisted Basnage de Beauval in February 1696, 'sont deux extremitez également éloignées de la vraye religion.'[64]

---

[64] [Basnage de Beauval], *Histoire des Ouvrages*, xii (Feb. 1696), 246; the sentiment exactly matches Berkeley's definition of enlightened religion as the 'virtuous mean between incredulity and superstition'; see Berkeley, *Alciphron*, i, 277.

ii. The Journals and the Radical Enlightenment

That the journals invariably pledged to fight radical ideas was inevitable in the context of the age. For no dynasty, government, parliament, or municipality would tolerate anything less than overt and implacable hostility to trends universally deemed godless, pernicious, and destructive of the social and moral order. One can state with some certainty, however, that not all the editors, much less the contributors, privately conformed to such views. If the number of open adherents of radical ideas was always minuscule, owing to stringent condemnation and the heavy price to be paid for being associated with such views, there was also a constant likelihood the ranks of those professing to fight radical ideas included *érudits* who inwardly renounced what society insisted on. Such men themselves might easily come under a question mark. Bayle, in particular, was regarded as suspect by some.

However, while in general the dividing line between the Christian Enlightenment of the moderates and the proscribed tenets of the radicals seemed clear enough, there were nevertheless over the years more than a few extremely troublesome borderline cases which blurred the picture, lending radical writers room for manoeuvre and gravely embarrassing the journals' editors. One obvious dilemma resulting from the editors' vows to combat 'superstition' and radicalism with equal determination was the problem of how to react to Bayle's *Dictionnaire* of 1697, with its countless paradoxes, 'obscenities', and discussions of 'atheistic' thinkers.[65] Beyond its relentless critical rationalism (interpreted by some as scepticism), no one seemed entirely sure what the message of that immensely fascinating and widely read work was. But neither could one fail to notice that it was to some extent a powerful vehicle for radical ideas, owing to Bayle's penchant for discussing the opinions of numerous ancient and modern fatalistic and Naturalistic thinkers in a frequently circuitous and disconcerting manner. In the words of one of his critics, Jaques Saurin, a prominent Huguenot preacher at The Hague, Bayle was a genius who lived a sober, austere life, but used his pen 'à attaquer la chasteté, la modestie, toutes les vertus chrétiennes' and, while adamantly professing his allegiance to the Reformed faith, repeated the objections to Christianity of all the world's greatest heretics 'leur prêtant des armes nouvelles, et réunissant dans nôtre siècle toutes les erreurs des siècles passez'.[66]

Another unavoidably prickly batch of issues concerned the Devil, demons, angels, and spirits. The historical research of Van Dale, seconded by Fontenelle, revealing systematic priestly manipulation of the credulous and supposedly gullible common people in classical times may have posed no great difficulty.[67] Bayle, Le Clerc, and Basnage de Beauval, among others, firmly took the side of these writers against their Jesuit, Lutheran orthodox, and other opponents, who insisted that the Devil and lesser

---

[65] Mijnhardt, 'Dutch Enlightenment', 205; Bots, *Henri Basnage de Beauval*, ii, 140–2.
[66] *L'Europe Savante*, iv (July 1718), 62.   [67] [Camusat], *Histoire critique*, ii, 234–5.

demons had operated the ancient oracles. The learned periodicals pronounced the sanctuaries of the ancient world to have been (by and large) fraudulent.[68] But what guidance should they offer in the case of the Bekker controversies, where the issue was whether Satan and demons influence the affairs of men at all? In the Netherlands and northern Germany, where the Bekker controversies chiefly raged, there was plainly some support for his sweeping attack on traditional notions about Satan and spirits, yet most churchmen, and most of the public, indignantly denounced Bekker's claims as back-door Spinozism. This placed the journal editors in a thorny dilemma. While it was impossible, on the one hand, to side with fanatics and obscurantists championing crassly superstitious views about evil, magic, and witchcraft—Bekker, after all, had some eminently reasonable arguments and was also plainly being victimized by bigots—neither could one responsibly condone the total denial of diabolical power and magic, added to which his cause had incontrovertibly been espoused by freethinkers and crypto-Spinozists. Moreover, it was impossible to criticize the vehemence of the ecclesiastical authorities in such an important matter without gravely offending the civic and provincial authorities.

Among the city governments most hostile to Bekker was that of Rotterdam, where a pro-Voetian faction for the time being dominated the city hall, and where Rabus' journal, the *Boekzaal*, was published. Rabus' editorial policy was to support Bekker, albeit in the most judicious, indeed rather veiled, terms.[69] The city's Reformed consistory were nevertheless outraged and initiated a vigorous campaign against the journal, exerting sufficient pressure on the burgomasters, over the winter of 1693–4, to bring its very existence into question. In the event the periodical survived. But one can hardly say that it survived intact. Subsequently, Rabus was obliged to practice stiffer self-censorship, as well as showing the Reformed authorities greater deference. Even in more liberal Amsterdam, Le Clerc saw the need for an uncommon degree of discretion. Having delayed many months before making any pronouncement at all, he dedicated a thirty-page review to the first two volumes of Bekker's *Betoverde Weereld* (The World Bewitched) in September 1691, informing readers abroad that the uproar 'fait beaucoup de bruit dans ces provinces' and that many people unfamiliar with the Dutch language had been asking what it was all about. 'C'est ce qu'on n'a pas cru devoir refuser,' he explained apologetically, 'à leur curiosité.'[70] Obliged to explain Bekker's views 'le plus fidèlement qu'il sera possible', Le Clerc assured readers that while agreeing in part 'on ne prétend pas en aprouver par tout la doctrine.' Basnage de Beauval, who published his initial review earlier, in May 1691, was even readier to mince words. Like Le Clerc, and any journal editor of the time, Basnage was bound to judge Bekker's case, denying the existence of magic and demonic forces, partially

---

[68] [Le Clerc], *Bibliothèque Universelle*, vii (1687), 387–455; [Basnage de Beauval], *Histoire des Ouvrages*, xiii (1696), 246–58; Labrousse, *Pierre Bayle*, ii, 14.

[69] De Vet, *Pieter Rabus*, 270–3; Wielema, *Filosofen*, 80–1; Israel, *Dutch Republic*, 924, 928.

[70] [Le Clerc], *Bibliothèque Universelle*, xxi (1691), 122–51; Bots, *De 'Bibliothèque Universelle'*, 90.

valid, but equally compelled to insist that he goes too far; 'nier que le Diable puisse avoir aucune part à tout ce qui se passe dans le monde, c'est à l'égard de bien des gens presque autant que si l'on arrachoit Dieu de son ciel.'[71]

The journals appeared on the scene too late to be faced by the dilemma of having to review the works of Spinoza, Meyer, Koerbagh, Van den Enden, and Beverland. Other illicit works, such as the more radical texts of Fontenelle and much of the *oeuvre* of Boulainvilliers, circulated before 1750 mostly in manuscript, or in other cases were all but entirely suppressed and failed to circulate at all, as with the Biblical criticism of Yves de Vallone and Giannone. But there were also works, published from the 1680s onwards, which had an unmistakably radical content and which journal editors might have ignored but which, not infrequently, they discussed, explaining their contents, somewhat frigidly to be sure, but nevertheless more or less objectively. In such cases the occasional word of disapproval was doubtless usually genuine. However, in cases where editors are known to have been themselves deists and adherents of the Radical Enlightenment, it is possible to suspect that the journals were being deliberately used as a forum for airing radical views.

One of the more noteworthy of the short-lived journals, for example, *L'Europe Savante* (1718–20) was a Franco-Dutch production, produced by a group of deistic Catholic savants—Thémiseul de Saint-Hyacinthe (1684–1746), and his friends, the three brothers Jean Lévesque de Burigny, Gérard Lévesque de Champeaux, and Louis-Jean Lévesque de Pouilly, and the librarian of the Bibliothèque Sainte-Geneviève, Pierre François Le Couroyer—eager to profit from the freer atmosphere prevailing in Paris since the death of Louis XIV in 1715, to promote deistic ideas both in France and the Netherlands, albeit discreetly, with the encouragement, it is thought of the Baron Hohendorf, then in the Austrian Netherlands and in contact with Saint-Hyacinthe, as well as Marchand and other journal editors.[72] The journal was published by a Huguenot firm in The Hague, but some of the editorial work was carried out in Paris, where the three brothers were, though it seems that Saint-Hyacinthe, in Holland, was the principal editor. Among the books reviewed by *L'Europe Savante* in its first year was Collins' *A Philosophical Inquiry, concerning Human Liberty* (1717), published by R. Robinson of Saint Paul's Church Yard in London. The journal provided an unbiased account of Collins' Spinozistic rejection of free will and argument that all human action is necessarily determined, including his assertion that in the ancient world it was the Epicureans who believed in free will and were the largest group among the 'atheists' who 'étoient partisans de la liberté' while the Stoics, 'qui formoient la secte la plus nombreuse des Déistes, soutenoient la nécessité'. Among the Jews of antiquity it was the allegedly irreligious Sadduceans who claimed that man is free while 'les Esséniens et les Pharisiens, à qui Jésus-Christ ne reprochoit que leur hypocrisie, croioient que l'homme étoit nécessité.'[73] The review explains how Collins builds a system of

---

[71] [Basnage de Beauval], *Histoire des Ouvrages*, viii (1691), 410.

[72] Carayol, *Thémiseul de Saint-Hyacinthe*, 72, 79; Bots, 'Role', 53.

[73] *L'Europe Savante*, iv (July, 1718), 121–2; [Collins], *A Philosophical Inquiry*, 44, 58–60; Berman, 'Determinism' 252; Berman, *A History of Atheism*, 82.

morality on his doctrine of necessity, claiming that if man is not necessarily driven to act as he does 'par l'esperance du plaisir, et par crainte des peines, il n'a plus les idées de morale, il n'a plus de motifs pour se soumettre aux Loix'.[74] The reviewer's objections to Collins' exposition of a Spinozistic moral system are remarkably mild. At the crucial juncture he simply comments that the 'author' circumvents the difficulty of explaining how such a system could be compatible with reward and punishment in the hereafter.[75]

The journals, then, were one of the most powerful agents of cultural and intellectual change during the Early Enlightenment era. In the main they served as a pillar of the Christian moderate Enlightenment and an engine of war against both traditionalist notions and radical views. However, beyond setting broad perimeters and extolling toleration and objectivity, they never forged a coherent consensus of what, in philosophical, theological, and scientific terms, the essentials of the moderate mainstream Enlightenment actually were. At the same time, they helped define the clandestine Radical Enlightenment, which was beyond the pale of respectable opinion, but nevertheless failed to segregate it with absolute clarity from the moderate, mainstream Enlightenment, leaving residual but crucial unclassified areas of vagueness. Furthermore, adamant professions of impartiality made it impossible altogether to ignore highly contentious and radical works, the content of which then had to be explained without too obvious a show of disapproval. This in turn left room for insinuating judgements and reviews which leave an ambivalent impression or may not have been intended to undermine radical positions at all. Thus it is possible to argue that the journals in some degree also served to propagate the Radical Enlightenment.

[74] *L'Europe Savante*, iv (July, 1718), 127.   [75] Ibid.

PART II | THE RISE OF
PHILOSOPHICAL
RADICALISM

8 | SPINOZA

Spinoza, then, emerged as the supreme philosophical bogeyman of Early Enlightenment Europe. Admittedly, historians have rarely emphasized this. It has been much
more common, and still is, to claim that Spinoza was rarely understood and had
very little influence, a typical example of an abiding historiographical refrain
which appears to be totally untrue but nevertheless, since the nineteenth century,
has exerted an enduring appeal for all manner of scholars. In fact, no one else during
the century 1650–1750 remotely rivalled Spinoza's notoriety as the chief challenger of
the fundamentals of revealed religion, received ideas, tradition, morality, and what
was everywhere regarded, in absolutist and non-absolutist states alike, as divinely constituted political authority.

Admittedly, in Britain many (but by no means all) writers deemed Hobbes more
widely pervasive than Spinoza as a promotor of freethinking, irreligion, and
incredulity. But given Hobbes' politics, and his attitude to ecclesiastical power and
censorship, as well as his being (by his own admission) philosophically less bold
and comprehensive, he simply was not, and could not have been, the source and inspiration for a systematic redefinition of man, cosmology, politics, social hierarchy, sexuality, and ethics in the radical sense Spinoza was. When placed in a full historical
context, Spinoza evidently had no real rival even in England as the chief progenitor
and author of 'that hideous hypothesis', as Hume (ironically?) called it, the 'doctrine
of the simplicity of the universe, and the unity of that substance, in which [Spinoza]
supposes both thought and matter to inhere',[1] eliminating divine Providence and governance of the world, in other words, the Naturalistic, materialist, one-substance
undercurrent culminating in La Mettrie and Diderot.

But is it likely, one might well object, or even conceivable, that any single seventeenth-century author, let alone an aloof, solitary figure raised among a despised
religious minority who lacked formal academic training and status, can have fundamentally and decisively shaped a tradition of radical thinking which eventually
spanned the whole continent, exerted an immense influence over successive generations, and shook western civilization to its foundations? Can one thinker meaningfully
be said to have forged a line of thought which furnished the philosophical matrix,
including the idea of evolution, of the entire radical wing of the European Enlightenment, an ideological stance subscribed to by dozens of writers and thinkers right

---

[1] Hume, *Treatise of Human Nature*, 240–1.

across the continent from Ireland to Russia and from Sweden to Iberia? The answer, arguably, is yes. For even the last, the mid-eighteenth-century, phase in the formation of the Radical Enlightenment, the probing towards the concept of evolution from inert matter, and of higher from lower forms of life, was derived, as its foremost champion, Diderot, stressed, directly from the doctrine that motion is inherent in matter, a concept generally regarded with horror and universally acknowledged in Enlightenment Europe as quintessentially Spinozist. The claim that Nature is self-moving, and creates itself, became indeed the very trademark of the *Spinosistes*. Thus the origins of the evolutionary thesis seemingly reinforce Einstein's proposition that the modern scientist who rejects divine Providence and a God that governs the destinies of man, while accepting 'the orderly harmony of what exists', the intelligibility of an imminent universe based on principles of mathematical rationality, in effect believes 'in Spinoza's God'.[2]

Fundamental shifts in the mental world of western civilization no doubt originate in vast social forces and a multitude of cultural influences. But the examples of Erasmus and Calvin remind us how a few wholly outstanding individual minds may, at crucial moments, through their thoughts and writings, lend decisively formative expression to rising impulses across an entire continent. Spinoza, furthermore, appeared on the scene just as the implications of the New Philosophy and the rise of the mechanistic world-view were first becoming widely evident, providing new, exhilarating perspectives inconceivable just a few years before. Of course, the Naturalist and materialist philosophies of ancient Greece and Rome had persisted in the consciousness of western man in a widely suffused if strongly repressed, furtively cultivated, fashion, perceptible but heavily camouflaged, in the writings and conversation of the *libertins érudits*. But it was only in the 1650s and 1660s that prospects for reviving and reformulating such notions in conjunction with the mechanistic reasoning of Galileo and Descartes arose. Before then there was little opportunity to promulgate a bold, comprehensive, modern Naturalism, albeit less owing to official repression, such as the burning of Bruno and Vanini and the condemnation of Galileo, than because until Galileo's insights had been universalized by Descartes to produce the new rigorously mechanistic world-view, the indispensable conceptual apparatus—mathematical rationality as the sole and exclusive criterion of truth—remained lacking.

Bayle, then, showed consummate judgement in commencing his seminal article on Spinoza in his *Dictionnaire*, by stressing that the building-blocks of Spinoza's system were not new, but that he considered Spinoza the first 'qui ait réduit en système l'athéisme, et qui en ait fait un corps de doctrine lié et tissu selon les manières des geomètres'.[3] By joining up, and integrating in a powerfully coherent system, recent insights with concepts which had reverberated disparately and incoherently for millennia, Spinoza imparted order, cohesion, and formal logic to what in effect was a fun-

---

[2] Clark, *Einstein*, 502–3.　　[3] Charles-Daubert and Moreau, *Pierre Bayle. Écrits*, 29.

damentally new view of man, God, and the universe rooted in philosophy, nurtured by scientific thought, and capable of producing a revolutionary ideology. Hence, as we shall see, it was Spinoza more than any other thinker who provided the *esprits forts* of the early and mid-eighteenth century with most of their intellectual heavy guns.

By 1750 innumerable authors, French, German, Italian, Scandinavian, Iberian, Swiss, and English, as well as Dutch, had indignantly denounced Spinoza as the most pernicious and dangerous thinker of the era. Typically, Buddeus styled him, in 1717, the 'chief atheist of our age' (atheorum notstra aetate princeps).[4] But by that time Spinoza had been universally decried as the prince of atheists, Christendom's chief foe, the 'new Mahomet' for almost half a century. Nor was his infamous reputation confined to the world of learned and purely academic publications. Hence Thomasius could assert in 1688, in his *Monats-Gespräche*, a periodical addressed to a broad reading public, that in Germany it was commonly known in society who Spinoza was and that this had been the case ever since the publication of the *Tractatus* in 1670.[5] Exactly like Machiavelli and Hobbes, but unlike almost every other writer, Spinoza was usually referred to by the hundreds of Early Enlightenment authors who cite him by his surname alone.

But while Spinoza's notoriety mainly dates from after 1670, he was already acknowledged well before this among a small network of northern European *érudits* as ranking among the leading philosophical minds of the time. Indeed, there are hints that the later Spinoza legend began to evolve even before publication of his first book, his geometrical exposition of Descartes, in 1663. Thus, in the summer of 1661 while travelling through the Netherlands, Henry Oldenburg,[6] whose appointment as secretary of the London Royal Society was then pending, thought fit (despite a pressing schedule of high-level scholarly and scientific business) to go out of his way to visit, and spend many hours with, an aspiring young philosopher who had thus far published nothing and was devoid of academic links and international recognition. That he should seek him out in his modest house at Rijnsburg (near Leiden) suggests that Oldenburg was following the advice of persons who, even then, judged Spinoza one of the key thinkers of the age.[7]

It is indeed astounding that most of Spinoza's mature system should already have been clearly worked out and formulated by the time of Oldenburg's visit. Spinoza had set out his core ideas, a stance to which subsequently he unwaveringly adhered, in

---

[4] Buddeus, *Lehr-Sätze*, 144; 'Benoit de Spinoza . . . est estimé avec raison le chef et le maître des athées de notre siècle, n'ayant point reconnu d'autre Dieu que la Nature, ce qui est la même chose que s'il avoit nié l'existence de Dieu'; Buddeus, *Traité*, 78–9.

[5] [Thomasius], *Monats-Gespräche*, i, 338.

[6] Henry Oldenburg (c.1617–77) was born and raised in Bremen but studied from 1641 in the Netherlands; in 1653 he was sent as the agent of Bremen to London, where he settled permanently; closely linked to both Milton and Boyle, he was appointed secretary to the Royal Society in 1662; Hutton, 'Henry Oldenburg', 106–7.

[7] Popkin, 'Spinoza's Earliest Philosophical years', 49; Hutton, 'Henry Oldenburg', 107–8.

particular in his *Korte Verhandeling* (1660–1).[8] In this text he states his famous doctrine that every substance must be infinite, that one substance cannot produce another, and that therefore there is only one substance. Consequently, whatever exists belongs to that one substance which is God, while Extended and Thinking Nature are hence merely two attributes of the same thing. Accordingly, 'God is, in relation to his effects or creatures no other than an immanent cause,' that is, the totality of everything, while causality and creation are inherent in, and not external to, that one substance.[9] God's Providence is redefined as 'nothing but the striving we find both in Nature as a whole and in particular things, tending to maintain and preserve their being'.[10]

Natura naturans, the active or creative power of Nature which is God is distinguished from the actuality and creatures of nature, or *Natura naturata*.[11] Motion is declared inherent in matter and 'has been from all eternity and will remain to all eternity, immutable', the differences between one body and another arising naturally from the different proportions of motion and rest in each body.[12] Everything which happens occurs necessarily; there 'are no contingent things'; and nothing can be otherwise than it is.[13] Hence there are no miracles and no divinely given commandments. 'Good' and 'evil', accordingly, are not moral absolutes and do not exist in Nature, being purely relative notions concerning man. Spinoza promulgates his 'geometric' theory of the passions and expounds his theory of knowledge as grounded in sensation and built from our perceiving what is true and what is false through mathematical proportions and relationships so that while we make mistakes, and frequently believe things which are not true, we cannot believe erroneously such that truth can not be demonstrated to us 'through truth itself, as falsity is also [made] clear through truth'.[14] The eternal, unbreakable link between ideas and reality is such that all our notions are in some sense true, so that they are adequate or inadequate rather than strictly true or false. The seeming paradox that man is determined necessarily but nevertheless possesses liberty, through reason which is intrinsic to his *conatus*, or striving to conserve his being, is introduced. Finally, the existence of disembodied spirits and apparitions, including Satan and demons, is categorically ruled out.[15] Effectively, little is missing, apart from Spinoza's political philosophy and theory of the origin of religion.

Not only had Spinoza arrived at the essentials of his system by 1660, he was also perfectly aware of the radical implications of his ideas and the violent reaction they were likely to provoke. Since his philosophy stood in total contradiction to the tenets of Judaism and all forms of Christianity, as well as Cartesianism and the mainstream of

---

[8] Mignini, 'Spinoza's Theory', 28, 31; Mignini, 'Inleiding', 239; Klever, 'Spinoza's Life', 25; Mignini, *Etica*, 35; Nadler, *Spinoza*, 186.

[9] *Collected Works of Spinoza*, i, 66–73; Curley, *Behind the Geometrical Method*, 140, Donagan, 'Spinoza's Theology', 349–50.

[10] *Collected Works of Spinoza*, i, 84; Bove, *Stratégie du* Conatus, 26, 34, 51, 87–8.

[11] *Collected Works of Spinoza*, i, 91.   [12] Ibid., 91–2, 95; Klever, 'Moles in motu', 169.

[13] *Collected Works of Spinoza*, i, 85.   [14] Ibid., 120.   [15] Ibid., 145.

the western philosophical tradition since the end of antiquity, it was obvious that his philosophy could only be propagated clandestinely. Already in the *Korte Verhandeling*, Spinoza urges his friends in Amsterdam for whom he had written this outline not to be shocked by the novelty of his system 'for you know only too well that it is no objection to the truth of a thing that it is not accepted by many,'[16] and to judge his system on its intellectual merits and not any other basis: 'and since you are also aware of the character of the age in which we live, I would ask you urgently to be very careful about communicating these things to others.'[17] His admonition was not meant to dissuade his disciples from propagating his ideas but to urge them to proceed with great caution, choose only promising ground, and when expounding his system 'have no other aim or motive than the salvation of your fellow man and make as sure as possible you do not work in vain'.[18]

Even before he left Amsterdam in 1661, Spinoza had emerged as a leader, perhaps the leader, of the 'atheistic' circle which by then had taken shape in the city. A visiting Danish savant, Olaus Borch, who kept a travel diary of his 1661–2 visit to Holland, where he had come to research, meet scholars, and hear lectures by the Leiden professors Heereboord, Heidanus, and Dele Boe Sylvius, noted in May 1661 that 'here are some atheists in Amsterdam several of whom are Cartesians, among them a Jew who is an impudent atheist.'[19] In September 1661, after Spinoza had left Amsterdam and settled in Rijnsburg in quest of the tranquillity he needed to develop his philosophy, and shortly after Oldenburg's visit, Borch jotted in his diary that 'at Rijnsburg there is a Christian who is an apostate Jew, in fact practically an atheist who does not respect the Old Testament and considers the New Testament to be of no more weight than the *Koran* and Aesop's *Fables* and that, for the rest, this man lives in an exemplary and irreproachable fashion, his only occupation being the manufacture of telescopes and microscopes.'[20] Apparently it was already by this date part of the legend surrounding Spinoza that in his home he kept his Bible shelved next to the 'Koran and the Talmud'.[21] Later that month Borch gathered some additional snippets in learned conversation, notably that the near atheist of Rijnsburg was called 'Spinoza', that he was extremely redoubtable in philosophical debate, and that he 'excelled in Cartesian philosophy, indeed in many things surpasses Descartes himself with his distinct and cogent concepts'.[22] That Spinoza by 1661 could not only persuasively pick holes in Descartes in the presence of leading scholars but deploy his own system effectively, if in veiled terms, in conversation, is eloquently confirmed by Oldenburg's response. Spinoza had been characteristically cautious in their conversations and Oldenburg failed to perceive the essentials of his system. But he grasped enough to realize that Spinoza had somehow

---

[16] Ibid., 150.   [17] Ibid.   [18] Ibid.

[19] Klever, 'Spinoza and Van den Enden', 314; Bedjaï, 'Circonstances', 40.

[20] Klever, 'Spinoza and Van den Enden', 314.

[21] Sturm. *De Cartesianis*, 14; Bedjaï, 'Circonstances', 40.

[22] 'In philosophia Cartesiana excellere, imo ipsum in multis superare Cartesium distinctis sc. et probabilis conceptibus'; Borch, *Journal*, i, 228.

invalidated Descartes' doctrine of two substances, redefining the relationship of 'extension' and 'thought', and that he harboured fundamental criticisms of Bacon's empiricism as well as of Descartes.[23]

But if Spinoza was already by 1660 a mature and formidable philosopher deploying a complete new system, had disciples of his own, and could convince Oldenburg he had outflanked Cartesianism, crucial questions arise regarding Spinoza's intellectual development prior to 1660. First, if one assumes, as most scholars do, that he started his philosophical odyssey after or around the time of his expulsion from the Amsterdam Portuguese Jewish community at the age of 23, just four years before, in 1656, without previously having had any conventional higher education or even much Latin, how could he conceivably have reached such impressive heights so swiftly? The answer is undoubtedly that he did not embark on his philosophical project in 1656 but long before then, as is clearly indicated by a variety of evidence. Thus, his Collegiant friend, Jarig Jelles,[24] who knew him for most of his adult life from at least as early as 1654–5,[25] affirms in his preface to Spinoza's *Opera Posthuma* (1677), that long before Spinoza freed himself from the 'worldly obstacles and hindrances which generally obstruct the quest for truth', a reference to his abandoning commerce and Judaism in 1656, he had immersed himself in philosophy, and especially Cartesianism, rebelling inwardly against what his teachers in the synagogue schools had taught him.[26] Jelles stresses his 'burning desire to know', generating an indefatigable intellectual quest while he was still outwardly an observant Jew 'in which the writings of the famous Renatus Descartes, which came into his hands at that time, proved of great assistance'.[27] Similarly, the eighteenth-century historian of Amsterdam Sephardic Jewry, David Franco Mendes, who was undoubtedly relying here on folklore within the com-

---

[23] Spinoza, *Letters*, 59.

[24] Jarig Jelles (*c.*1620–1683), a former merchant in figs, raisins, and other Mediterranean fruit, is thought to have known Spinoza from the time the latter and his father were importing such products from Portugal; withdrawing from business in 1653 he devoted himself subsequently to full-time study; Jelles, like Simon Joosten de Vries (*c.*1633–1667) assisted Spinoza financially and is thought to have subsidized the publication of his *Principia Philosophiae Cartesianae* in 1663; the chief priority for Jelles, however was to integrate the new philosophy with his strongly rationalist Socinian Christian theology and, under pressure from fellow Collegiants who considered his zeal for philosophy incompatible with Christian truth, he wrote a short book in 1673, in the form of a letter to a friend (in fact Spinoza) and sent it to Spinoza, requesting his reactions. This text, entitled *Belydenisse des algemeenen en Christelyken geloofs*, remained in manuscript until 1684 when it was published, after his death, by his friend Rieuwertsz who appended a brief account of his life; the work is extremely rare, the copy in the Amsterdam University Library being the only known surviving exemplar. It starts by saying that the friend to whom it is addressed had asked him to formulate the principles of his faith because critics contend that the 'Cartesian philosophers' were expounding views incompatible with the essentials of Christianity; he asks his friend to ponder his arguments carefully, hoping to convince him that Cartesian principles do accord with Christianity; see Jelles, *Belydenisse*, 1–3; Spinoza, *Briefwisseling*, 306; Gebhardt, 'Religion Spinozas', 331; Kolakowski, *Chrétiens sans église*, 222–5.

[25] Vaz Dias and Van der Tak, 'Spinoza Merchant', 158, 166.

[26] Jelles, *Voorreeden*, 110–11; Kortholt, *De Tribus Impostoribus*, 140.

[27] Ibid.; Proietti, 'Le "Philedonius" ', 47–8; Klever, 'Spinoza's Life', 17–18.

munity, stresses that even as a boy—that is, many years before his expulsion—Spinoza vacillated in his Jewish belief, owing to philosophical influences among which was Cartesianism.[28]

But the clearest proof that Spinoza grappled with philosophy, as distinct from theological questions, for many years before his sensational break with the rabbis, elders, and congregation in 1656, is that he tells us so himself in his earliest surviving work,[29] the *Improvement of the Understanding* (c.1658). Here he dwells on the protracted gestation period between the effective commencement of his career as a philosopher and his (much later) break with Judaism and the Jewish community. He explains that in his youth he exhaustively considered what the 'highest good' in human life is. But for a long time, despite inferring that 'everything that usually arises in everyday life is vain and futile', he was nevertheless deterred from devoting himself whole-heartedly to philosophy by the practical consequences of discarding the lifestyle in which he had been raised, judging it 'inadvisable . . . to abandon something certain for something uncertain'.[30] In the Amsterdam Sephardic circles in which his father, Michael d'Espinosa (c.1588–1654), a moderately affluent merchant trading chiefly with Portugal who had been a member of the governing board of elders (*par-nasim*) of the synagogue, and he himself, mixed, the 'advantages which are acquired through honour and riches and which I would be compelled to do without were I to devote myself seriously to something different and new' were abundantly evident. Also he saw that 'if the highest happiness does lie in those things' and he irrevocably renounced them, he would have no way of recovering the 'highest good': 'equally, if it does not reside in such things and I devoted myself to them, then again I would not attain the highest happiness.'[31] Consequently, he long pondered 'whether it might be possible to achieve my new way of life, or at least certainty about it, without changing the order and form of my ordinary existence'. 'Often I tried this,' he says, 'but in vain.'[32] Philosophy and the requirements of business, religion, and status, he discovered, simply do not mix.

Nevertheless, a great deal more time elapsed before Spinoza finally abandoned his efforts to lead a double existence, combining outward conformity to faith, family, and status with a private immersion in philosophy. If he discarded the former, he had concluded, he would be sacrificing a lifestyle which is intrinsically shallow and uncertain for a higher good, uncertain not in nature 'but only with regard to achieving it'.[33] Yet despite being convinced of this now, still he wavered, finding, he admits, that rank, honour, money, and comfort are not so easily dispensed with. It is not enough to grasp the futility of what most men seek: 'for although I saw all this sufficiently clearly in my

---

[28] Franco Mendes, *Memorias*, 60–1; Méchoulan, '*Herem* à Amsterdam', 126–7.

[29] Mignini, 'Spinoza's Theory', 28, 31, 54; Proietti, 'Le "Philedonius"', 73–8; Curley, 'General Preface', p. xiii; Klever, 'Spinoza's Life', 21, 23, 25; Nadler, *Spinoza*, 175–6; De Dijn, however, argues against this new near consensus; see de Dijn, *Spinoza. The Way to Wisdom*, 5.

[30] Spinoza, *Opera*, ii, 5; *Collected Works of Spinoza*, i, 7; Nadler, *Spinoza*, 101.

[31] Spinoza, *Opera*, ii, 5.   [32] Ibid., 5.   [33] Ibid., 6.

mind, I could not, on that account lay aside all desire for money, pleasure, and esteem.'[34]

Spinoza was finally helped to the irredeemable break which fundamentally transformed his own life and eventually, through philosophy, the whole of western thought and culture, by a sequence of shattering blows to the family business.[35] In the early 1650s, his father's firm was virtually also his, since he was the eldest son after the death of his elder brother, Isaac, in 1649, and his father was frequently bedridden and, early in 1654, died.[36] The surviving data for his father's payments of community tax (*finta*), and his own subsequent payments between 1654 and his expulsion in 1656, contributions assessed on the basis of merchants' turnover, plainly illustrate the progressive decay of the business during his father's last years and the two years (1654–6) Spinoza himself presided over the firm now styled 'Bento y Gabriel d'Espinosa'.[37] The reasons for this commercial disintegration are not hard to discover. During the First Anglo-Dutch War (1652–4)—and during the eighteen months beforehand when over a hundred Dutch ships were seized by the English on the high seas[38]—numerous Amsterdam businesses were bankrupted and the firm of Spinoza was evidently among these.

A veritable catalogue of disaster beset the family firm, beginning in 1650 when a ship called *Den Prince*, homeward bound from the Canaries, carrying wine for Michael among others, was confiscated on the high seas by the English.[39] A cargo of sugar from Dutch Brazil, on an Enkhuizen vessel, the *Nachtegael*, consigned by Michael to his correspondents in Rouen, was taken by the English in the early summer of 1651.[40] Two Dutch vessels homeward bound from Portugal, with cargoes of olive oil for his account, the *Fortune* and the *Pieter and Jan*, one from Aveiro, the other from Lisbon, were seized by English warships later in 1651 and escorted into London. Michael sought restitution of his goods through his London agent, but owing to the severe tension between England and the Dutch Republic, followed by the outbreak of war, presumably without any positive result.[41] Next, in September 1651, the ship *'t Witte Valck* was intercepted by Barbary corsairs off Cape Saint Vincent, the pirates plundering 'diverse merchandise belonging to Michael Spinoza, Jewish merchant at Amsterdam', his losses this time being estimated by the Dutch consul at Salé at 3,000 guilders.[42] After the formal outbreak of war with England, the Spinozas, like all Amsterdam merchants, curtailed their overseas dealings drastically. Nevertheless risks were taken and more cargoes lost both to the English and to Barbary corsairs. An Amsterdam ship, *'t Vat*, having successfully eluded the English on its outward voyage in June 1652, calling

---

[34] Spinoza, *Opera*, 7; De Dijn, *Spinoza. The Way to Wisdom*, 24–5.
[35] Israel, 'Philosophy, Commerce, and the Synagogue', (forthcoming).
[36] Nadler, *Spinoza*, 79–81.   [37] Vaz Dias and Van der Tak, 'The Firm', 184–5.
[38] Groenveld, 'English Civil Wars', 561; Israel, *Dutch Republic*, 713–26.
[39] GAA NA 964 unpaginated deed of notary B. Baddel, 27 Nov. 1651.
[40] PRO HCA 30/495. Petition of 'Nicholas Joris' (J. Nunes da Costa), 14 Aug. 1651.
[41] GAA NA 967, pp. 300–1, deed 20 July 1651; Vaz Dias and Van der Tak, 'Spinoza Merchant', 146.
[42] De Castries, *Les sources inédites*, ser. 1, v, 311–13, 431, and vi, 99.

at Nantes and then Oporto, reached the Algarve, where it was to load olive oil, figs, and almonds for the Spinozas, but was caught and pillaged by Moorish corsairs in full view of the port of Faro, Michael again losing his whole cargo.[43] By 1655 the business was ruined, and Spinoza saddled with sizeable debts to his, and his father's, correspondents in Rouen, two powerful figures in the Portuguese crypto-Jewish community there, Duarte Rodrigues Lamego and Antonio Rodrigues de Morais.[44]

That the mature Spinoza, despite his republicanism, was no friend of the English Comonwealth which replaced early Stuart absolutism is plain enough. No doubt he had intellectual grounds for his undisguised disdain for the Cromwellian regime: if a people is 'accustomed to royal rule and constrained by that alone', he declares, in reference to the English monarchy, it is extremely difficult to remove a king, however tyrannical, without appointing another in his place.[45] 'A sad example of this truth,' he affirms, 'is provided by the English people' who removed their king 'but with his disappearance found it quite impossible to change their form of government' and 'after much bloodshed resorted to hailing a new monarch by a different name—as if the whole question at issue was a name.' Cromwell, insists Spinoza, maintained himself in power 'by extirpating the royal line, killing the king's friends, or those thought to be so', going to war against neighbours and 'destroying the peace lest tranquillity encourage murmuring and so that the people should divert their thoughts away from the king's execution to fresh matters that would engage their full attention'.[46] Too late Englishmen realized that, instead of saving their country, they had changed 'everything for the worse'. But while all this fits with the rest of his political thought, one can hardly believe, given the circumstances, that such fierce disparagement of Cromwell and the English Revolution is not also prompted by a measure of personal animus stemming from the disastrous losses Spinoza and his family had suffered at English hands.

The indications that Spinoza's philosophical odyssey, including his intellectual rebellion against revealed religion, began not in 1656 but a considerable time before undoubtedly has important implications for our understanding of the historical origins of Early Enlightenment radical thought. In the first place, the evidence implies that Spinoza's expulsion from the synagogue had little or nothing to do with any change in his ideas as such and was therefore only in an outward, superficial sense caused by theological heresy. It also means Spinoza's philosophical rebellion can not have been inspired, as has been repeatedly claimed in recent years, either by the most prominent other Jewish heretic in Amsterdam in the later 1650s, Juan de Prado (*c*.1612–*c*.1670), previously a crypto-Jew in Spain who had encountered deistic influences among crypto-Jewish friends in Andalusia,[47] but who did not arrive in Holland,

---

[43] Ibid., v, 348–50.   [44] Van der Tak, 'Spinoza Merchant', 163; Israel, *European Jewry*, 96.

[45] Spinoza, *TTP*, 277.   [46] Ibid., 278; Smith, *Spinoza, Liberalism*, 158–9.

[47] Orobio de Castro recalled in the 1660s that, on resuming his friendship with Prado in Andalusia in 1643, he found that the latter had now become a deist and had learnt his deism from a certain Marrano physician, called Juan Pinheiro, who died in Seville around 1662; Gebhardt, 'Juan de Prado', 285–90; Kaplan, *From Christianity*, 126.

where he continued his career as a deist, until 1655, or by the eccentric, Millenarian Bible critic of probable Marrano descent, Isaac La Peyrère,[48] who likewise arrived in Amsterdam only in 1655.[49] If we accept that for several years, probably as many as five or six before 1655, Spinoza was simultaneously a resolute philosophical rebel and outwardly an observant Jew, neither Prado nor La Peyrère can have precipitated his intellectual rebellion. While Jelles may have contributed to his early formation by encouraging his preoccupation with philosophy, and with Cartesianism especially, the only personage who seems likely to have guided him powerfully in a specifically radical direction at this early stage, as two early biographies of Spinoza both affirm, was his ex-Jesuit Latin master, Franciscus van den Enden (1602–74).

While Spinoza himself never mentions Van den Enden anywhere in his books or letters, other evidence proves conclusively that there was a close link between the two at this juncture in Spinoza's life, and that Van den Enden in some way helped direct Spinoza's early philosophical development. According to his principal biographer, Colerus, the budding thinker 'had the famous Francis vanden Ende for his master, who instructed him in the Latin tongue and first instill'd in him those principles which were the foundation of his future greatness', a claim frequently echoed in the early eighteenth century.[50] Maximilien Lucas, author of the earliest account of Spinoza's life, likewise notes that, besides Latin, Van den Enden taught Spinoza mathematics, Cartesian philosophy, and a little Greek.[51] Willem Goeree, a radical writer in his own right, later commented that, as a young man, he had known Van den Enden, frequented the same company as he, and 'more than once eaten and drunk with him' but learnt little that was edifying, so that he could readily imagine 'Spinoza too picked up few good principles from this master who was very generous in peddling his godless convictions to young and old alike and boasting he was rid of the fable of faith.'[52] Adriaen Koerbagh, he adds, 'through contact with this man did not absorb anything good . . . as is plain from all those offensive entries in his Dictionary, or stinking *Bloemhof*'.[53] The early eighteenth-century Amsterdam Anabaptist physician, Johannes Monnikhoff, whose brief account of Spinoza's life is based on Colerus and other early published sources but also incorporates some oral lore about Spinoza still current in Amsterdam in his day, claims it was Spinoza's parents who originally sent

---

[48] Isaac La Peyrère (1596–1676) was born of Huguenot parents in Bordeaux, his father possibly being of Portuguese New Christian extraction. A lawyer by training, in 1640 he became secretary to the Prince de Condé, who was not only a great soldier and political figure but also took a keen interest in philosophy, theology, and heterodox literature. In 1643 he published a Messianic work entitled *Du Rappel des juifs*. His most notorious work, the *Prae-Adamitae*, denying Adam was the first man and that Moses wrote the Five Books, was anonymously published in 1655 in five editions, mostly in Amsterdam, and immediately prohibited by the States of Holland. Arrested and imprisoned in Brussels in June 1656, he converted to Catholicism under duress. On Condé's return to Paris in 1659, La Peyrère became his librarian; see Popkin, *Isaac La Peyrère*, 5–25.

[49] Révah, *Marranes à Spinoza*, 186–218, 244–5; Popkin, 'Spinoza's Earliest Philosophical Years', 27–9; Kaplan, *From Christianity*, 132–51; Popkin, *Isaac la Peyrère*, 84–7; Yovel, *Spinoza*, 64–71.

[50] [Colerus], *Account of the Life*, 2; Colerus, *Vie de B. de Spinosa*, 6; Mencke, *Compendiöses Gelehrten Lexicon*, ii, 2160; Buddeus, *Lehr-Sätze*, 148; Walch, *Philosophisches Lexicon*, 155–7; Nadler, *Spinoza*, 104.

[51] Lucas, *La Vie*, 22–4; Franco Mendes, *Memorias*, 61.

[52] Goeree, *Kerklyke en Weereldlyke*, 665.   [53] Ibid.; Meinsma, *Spinoza*, 192.

him to the ex-Jesuit to learn Latin as a youth, and that, unknown to his father, Van den Enden also 'inculcated into him such ideas as afterwards provided the basis of his philosophy'.[54]

It would seem, then, that neither La Peyrère's Bible criticism nor Prado's deism nor any internal heretical tendencies within Amsterdam Sephardic Judaism of the mid-1650s guided Spinoza's early philosophical formation or planted the seeds of his spiritual rebellion. Rather, we may infer that Spinoza was caught up in the general intellectual turbulence in Holland precipitated by Cartesianism, and it was specifically Van den Enden who first pointed him in a radical direction, either at the beginning of the 1650s or, as seems far more likely, in the late 1640s, when Spinoza was in his late teens. But this, in turn, raises the question of what Monnikhoff's 'provided the basis' really signifies. Did Van den Enden merely encourage the youth in a rebellious and irreligious direction while teaching him Latin and the rudiments of Cartesianism, or was Van den Enden himself a cogently innovative thinker who preceded Spinoza in outlining the rudiments of what became the backbone of the European radical tradition? Unquestionably, there are affinities between Spinoza's and Van den Enden's ideas in the 1660s, when the radical philosophical coterie which later formed the Spinozist 'sect' or movement in the city first arose, and these have prompted at least two modern scholars to argue that Van den Enden was a kind of 'proto-Spinoza', the mastermind behind the Spinozist movement, and the first to formulate the fundamentals of Spinoza's system. The evidence of Van den Enden's own writings show these affinities are indeed extensive and striking and, it seems certain, as the poet Pieter Rixtel, a former student of Van den Enden, indicates in a poem dated March 1666, that by then Van den Enden understood 'God' as a philosophical category identical to Nature.[55]

Yet there is no evidence that in the 1640s or 1650s, as a consequence of involvement with Cartesianism, Van den Enden did formulate a systematic, mechanistic, atheistic philosophy; and it seems rather implausible when all the circumstances are carefully weighed that he was really much more than a lively stimulus to Spinoza's early intellectual formation. Certainly there is no reference to any coterie of philosophical 'atheists' in Amsterdam before around 1660–1 and not the slightest indication of anyone being 'converted' to atheistic views by Van den Enden prior to Spinoza. Still more significant, none of Van den Enden's surviving writings containing recognizably radical ideas with notable affinities with Spinoza's thought antedates 1661, by which time Spinoza was a mature philosopher whose system had already been complete probably for several years. Van den Enden himself affirms that he wrote no political theory, the field in which he chiefly excelled, before 1661 and by then he had at his disposal not just Spinoza's ideas and Machiavelli's, but several published writings of Johan and Pieter de la Court, laying the basis for a vigorous, unprecedentedly radical, Dutch republicanism.

---

[54] Monnikhoff, *Beschrijving*, 201–2; see also Franco Mendes, *Memorias*, 61.
[55] Meinsma, *Spinoza*, 193–4; Bedjaï, 'Éternité', 8–9; see also Van Til, *Voor-Hof der Heydenen*, 18; Klever, 'Spinoza's Life', 18.

Furthermore, as we shall see, except for Machiavelli, Van den Enden's main sources were all of recent provenance, published or in circulation at the end of the 1650s and the beginning of the 1660s.[56] Judging from his earlier interest in alchemy and Van Helmont's mystical speculations, it seems likely that Van den Enden had himself only recently discovered Descartes when the young Spinoza first came to him for Latin lessons, and that it was only subsequently that he developed his rigorous 'geometric' Naturalism. This would imply that Van den Enden's radicalism only slightly preceded Spinoza's in its inception and subsequently developed *pari passu*, or even in the wake of Spinoza. In any case, by 1660 at the latest he had clearly been far outstripped in his command of the intricacies of the New Philosophy by his young protégé.

Even so, Van den Enden was probably in an outward sense the leader of the 'atheistic', 'Cartesian' circle active in Amsterdam before Spinoza's departure in 1661, being the oldest, best known, and most forceful, as well as authoritative, person among the group. In April 1662, Borch noted, 'there are atheists here and especially Cartesians such as Van den Enden, Glasemaker, etc.', adding that while these 'atheists' speak a lot about 'God' what they mean by God is 'nothing other than the whole universe as lately became clear from a certain text in Dutch composed with much artifice, the name of the author of which has been suppressed'.[57] Borch is not referring here to any of Van den Enden's writings, which he does mention further on, but, scholars agree, he is almost certainly referring to the *Korte Verhandeling*, which is known to have been circulating in manuscript in Amsterdam in the months following Spinoza's departure from the city.[58]

According to the son of his publisher, Jan Rieuwertsz, in conversation with two young German savants sent from Halle to glean more information about Spinoza's life by Christian Thomasius in 1704, the persons with whom Spinoza chiefly associated in Amsterdam following his expulsion from the synagogue, from 1656 until 1661, were the older Rieuwertsz—later Spinoza's publisher in whose bookshop he would often have browsed—Van den Enden, Jan Hendrik Glazemaker,[59] the skilful translator of Descartes (and later Spinoza) into Dutch, Jarig Jelles, Pieter Balling,[60] and

---

[56] Mertens, 'Franciscus van den Enden', 720, 723, 725.

[57] Klever, 'Spinoza's Life', 24; Klever, 'Spinoza and van den Enden', 318.

[58] Bedjaï, 'Éternité', 11; Bedjaï, 'Docteur Franciscus van den Enden', 31.

[59] Jan Hendrik Glazemaker (*c.*1620–82) was born in Amsterdam of Mennonite parentage; a professional translator, he is known to have rendered over sixty works into Dutch, including the Koran, Montaigne, and Marcus Aurelius; he translated both more accurately and more soberly than was usual at the time; Akkerman, 'J. H. Glazemaker', 27–8.

[60] Pieter Balling (d.1664) was a Collegiant enthusiast for the New Philosophy who had been a factor working for Amsterdam merchants in Spain and probably knew Spinoza while the latter was still a merchant before 1656. They were close friends and collaborators and it was Balling, an accomplished Latinist and an exceptionally skilful translator, who rendered the *Principia Philosophiae Cartesianae* into Dutch. He is chiefly known for his short but fascinating pamphlet *Het Licht op den Kandelaar* (The Light on the Candlestick) originally published anonymously in Amsterdam in 1662 and widely mistaken for a Quaker tract. It was reissued in 1683, this time under Balling's name, by his friend Rieuwertz. It deplores the confusion and doubt generated on all sides by theological dispute and inter-confessional strife, insisting that mankind's sole guide in the face of this crisis of faith is the 'inner light', a concept apparently used

Lodewijk Meyer. From these men Spinoza learnt much. Yet as early as 1656, not only would he obviously have known considerably more Bible criticism, as well as far more Hebrew than any of the others, but in other respects too he was apparently disinclined to show the deference of a beginner. Indeed, Rieuwertsz remarked that Spinoza, after his departure from the Jewish community, was already sufficiently confident of his intellectual powers and philosophical skill to attempt to persuade not just Collegiant acquaintances but also Van den Enden to adopt his views.[61]

Consequently, it would seem that Spinoza's expulsion from the synagogue in 1656, however decisive as an event in his life and as a factor shaping his future, has nothing to do with his intellectual formation as such. In 1654–5, the synagogue records show, Spinoza continued as before as regards Jewish observance and synagogue attendance, conducting himself as a regular member of the community.[62] Only from late 1655 did he cease paying his dues and conducting himself as an observant Jew. Almost certainly, the crucial confrontation between Spinoza, backed by Juan de Prado, on one side, and on the other, Rabbi Saul Levi Morteira, and doubtless nearly everybody else present, over the fundamentals of Jewish belief, in a communal evening study class which the Amsterdam Sephardic poet Daniel Levi de Barrios later described in 1683 as an epic encounter in which the 'wise' Morteira championed religion 'against the thorns [in Spanish: *espinos*] in the meadows [in Spanish: *prados*] of impiety', an event which can not have occurred prior to Prado's arrival in 1655, in fact took place late that year.[63]

Ruined financially, Spinoza had now definitively made up his mind to cross the Rubicon—discarding respectability, social standing, and commerce and devoting himself wholeheartedly to philosophy. By publicly repudiating the fundamentals of rabbinic tradition and authority in so formal and provocative a manner, the young thinker virtually demanded to be expelled, indeed made it impossible for the synagogue authorities not to expel him. By severing his ties with the congregation in such a dramatic fashion, openly challenging the rabbis and the synagogue elders over the essentials of Jewish belief while shortly afterwards abandoning the family business, together with its remaining asssets and debts, to his younger brother Gabriel, he emancipated himself spiritually and philosophically, not just by breaking with organized religion and social status but also extricating himself from a

---

by Balling with deliberate ambiguity to denote either the light of pure reason or a Spiritualist inner guidance ensuing from mystical union with God. Elsewhere though, he urges the total submergence of theology in philosophy, claiming that the only solution to the religious predicament is to inculcate a 'clear and distinct knowledge of truth in a person's mind, revealing principles so evident and convincing that it is impossible to doubt them'; [Balling], *Het Licht*, 4; Meinsma, *Spinoza*, 172–4, 260–6; Lindeboom, *Stiefkinderen*, 351; Gebhardt, 'Pieter Balling's *Het Licht*', 189–90; Fix, *Prophecy and Reason*, 200–1; Klever, *Mannen rond Spinoza*, 27–9.

[61] Stolle, 'Notes', 514.   [62] Révah, *Marranes à Spinoza*, 367–9; Nadler, *Spinoza*, 118–20.

[63] Levi de Barrios, *Triumpho*: 'La Corona de la ley', 2; Vaz Dias and Van der Tak, 'Spinoza Merchant', 155–6; Révah, *Marranes à Spinoza*, 224–5; Kaplan, *From Christianity*, 265.

deepening morass of legal difficulties and debts relating to his failed business and family predicament.[64]

The precise reasons adduced by the community elders for his excommunication remain unknown. But it is plain from the form of excommunication used in July 1656, one of altogether exceptional vehemence and severity only very occasionally deployed in early modern times,[65] that he was proscribed for no ordinary deviance, sacrilege, financial irregularity, or heresy but open, systematic, premeditated, and blatant doctrinal rebellion of a fundamental kind that simply could not be ignored or smoothed over. Levi de Barrios later noted in 1683, as subsequently did Franco Mendes, that Spinoza was excommunicated due to his 'evil opinions'.[66] As the text of the ban itself indicates, nothing could have been easier for Spinoza, had he so wished, than to avoid excommunication. The door was left wide open for him to compromise, retract, and resume his seat in the synagogue. As far as the community elders (*parnasim*) and rabbis were concerned, he could with the greatest ease in the world, had he been willing to make some gesture of submission and repentence, revert to being a philosopher only inwardly. The *parnasim*, declares the text of his excommunication, had long known of the 'evil opinions and acts of Baruch de Spinoza' and 'endeavoured by various means and promises to turn him from his evil ways' but had only received 'daily more and more reports of the abominable heresies he practised and taught and his monstrous deeds, and, having many trustworthy witnesses who have confirmed all this in the presence of the said Spinoza', the elders ruled, 'with the rabbis' agreement, that the said Spinoza should be excommunicated and cast out from among the people of Israel'.[67]

The 'monstrous deeds' were presumably violation of the sabbath and other offences against Jewish observance and dietary laws; but what were the 'abominable heresies'? These can perhaps be reconstructed from several clues, including the precious testimony submitted to the Inquisition in Madrid in August 1659 by a Spanish-American friar, Fray Tomas Solano y Robles, captured by the English on a Spanish vessel sailing from South America to Seville, who, after leaving London, had spent eight months, from August 1658, in Amsterdam prior to embarking for Madrid. In Amsterdam Friar Tomas stayed in a hostelry much frequented by Spaniards and Portuguese where he had several conversations about religion with a 'certain Espinosa', a native of Holland 'who had studied at Leiden and is a good philosopher', and the latter's associate, Dr Juan de Prado, a physician.[68] This is the only contemporary reference to Spinoza having studied for a time at the University of Leiden, but it may well be accurate, as there is very little evidence about this particular phase of his life and later numerous hints suggest that he knew personally various key figures in the Dutch

---

[64] Israel, 'Philosophy, Commerce, and the Synagogue', (forthcoming).

[65] Méchoulan, '*Herem* à Amsterdam', 128; Kasher and Biderman, 'Why was Spinoza Excommunicated?', 100–1; Nadler, *Spinoza*, 127–9.

[66] Levi de Barrios, *Triumpho*, 85; Franco Mendes, *Memorias*, 60–1; Kaplan, *From Christianity*, 265.

[67] Révah, *Marranes à Spinoza*, 231; Kasher and Biderman, 'Why was Spinoza Excommunicated?', 100–1.

[68] Révah, *Marranes à Spinoza*, 198, 232; Yovel, *Spinoza*, 74; Klever, 'Spinoza's Life', 22.

academic world of the day.[69] Assuming this report is correct, his Leiden studies would most likely have taken place in the period from late 1656 to early 1658. More important though, the friar also commented on Spinoza's and Prado's opinions. He informed the Inquisitors that both men, of whom Spinoza, though the younger, was plainly the more formidable philosophically, 'had professed the Law of Moses' but been expelled from the synagogue because they had forsaken Judaism for 'atheism'. They had admitted to the friar that they were circumcised and had 'observed the law of the Jews' but subsequently changed their views because it seemed to them 'the said law is not true, that the soul dies with the body, and that there is no God except philosophically,' that is, no providential God.[70] Henceforth, since they believed the soul dies with the body 'they had no need of religion.' The synagogue records independently confirm that Prado denied, or was held to deny, the Creation, Revelation, and divine Providence, as well as immortality of the soul.[71]

Almost certainly these were not only already Spinoza's views in 1656 but for some years before. That his inner philosophical quest encompassed denial of the soul's immortality, divine Providence, and a God who rewards and punishes seems to be confirmed by the unquestionable fact that in 1656 Spinoza wrote a long and incisive treatise (now lost) in Spanish, defending his views against rabbinic authority which, according to Levi de Barrios, 'seemed at first like a vase of gold but, on closer scrutiny, turned out to be flowing with poison', a work in which he argued the Jews were no longer obliged to observe the Mosaic Law. Unless one supposes that he worked out the ideas in this treatise and elaborated this text wholly within the short space of time between the autumn of 1655 and his expulsion, an unconvincing assumption given his public clash with Morteira, it seems safe to conclude Spinoza inwardly denied that the Jewish Scriptures were divine Revelation, and therefore repudiated the essence of Judaism, long before 1656.[72] For his part, Prado was unquestionably Spinoza's ally and comrade in unfurling the banner of deistic revolt against the rabbis in the years 1655–8, besides being a source of interesting information about crypto-Judaism and crypto-deism in Spain. Having spent many years in Spanish universities, he may well have added something to the formulation of Spinoza's insights.[73] But knowing as he did far less about modern philosophy than Spinoza, and lacking knowledge of the Hebrew Bible and commentaries, it seems highly unlikely that he could have influenced the post-1656 development of Spinoza's thought in any significant way.

In the autobiographical passage of the *Improvement of the Understanding*, Spinoza stresses the great difficulty he experienced in sacrificing status, money, and honour for the sake of his career in philosophy. It took many years to complete this step, and when

---

[69] Nadler, *Spinoza*, 113, 163–5.

[70] Révah, 'Des Marranes à Spinoza', 198–9; Nadler, *Spinoza*. 130–1, 135.

[71] Gebhardt, 'Juan de Prado', 286–8; Kaplan, *From Christianity*, 140–3, 165–6; Yovel, *Spinoza*, 75–6.

[72] Levi de Barrios, *Triumpho*, 85; Van Til, *Voor-Hof der Heydenen*, 5; *La Vie et l'Esprit*, 60; Kaplan, *From Christianity*, 265; Klever, 'Spinoza's Life', 18.

[73] Kaplan, *From Christianity*, 135, 150, 160; Klever, 'Spinoza and Van den Enden', 317; Sutcliffe, 'Sephardi Amsterdam', 404.

he did, he was in part pushed to do so by the bankruptcy of his business. Yet there is also a crucial sense in which he never did so. Clearly, Spinoza was far from believing the true philosopher, a person such as himself, by temperament lacks the acumen to amass power, wealth, and status. Writing to Jelles in February 1671, Spinoza recounts the story of the ancient Greek philosopher Thales of Miletus, who grew so exasperated at being constantly chided for his poverty by friends that he decided to demonstrate that it was through choice, not necessity, that he lacked possessions. To prove he knew how to acquire what he judged unworthy of his effort, he engaged all the olive presses in Greece, having ascertained that the olive crop that year would be excellent; and when the olives were gathered he hired out dearly presses he had rented cheaply, thereby accumulating great wealth within a year, which he then distributed with a generosity equal to the shrewdness with which he gained it.[74]

Spinoza undoubtedly considered himself both worldly and shrewd, and while, from 1656, he invariably displayed a lofty lack of interest in money and property, one can scarcely say the same regarding position and reputation. On the contary, having dedicated himself fully to philosophy, he endeavoured not just to find the 'highest good' for himself but also, he intimates at the end of the *Korte Verhandeling*, to teach the path to 'salvation' to others, his object being, to paraphrase Marx, not just to meditate but to change the world, a goal in which eventually—and in a most extraordinary manner—he succeeded. Bayle remarks that Spinoza's friends claimed after his death that 'par modestie il souhaita de ne pas donner son nom à une secte.'[75] But whether or not he believed this to be true, Bayle notes that Spinoza unquestionably aspired, as Toland and others also remarked later, to found a (necessarily) clandestine philosophical 'sect' through the endeavours of which his philosophy, like that of his adolescent hero Descartes, would ultimately transform the world.

[74] Spinoza, *Letters*, 243–4.   [75] Charles-Daubert and Moreau, *Pierre Bayle, Écrits*, 24.

9 | VAN DEN ENDEN: PHILOSOPHY, DEMOCRACY, AND EGALITARIANISM

i. Democratic Republicanism

Van den Enden, Borch noted in his journal in April 1662, was a Cartesian and 'atheist' who denied the sacred mysteries and whose 'religion, indeed, is nothing other than sound reason, nor does he believe Christ to be God'; he added that Van den Enden had been forbidden by the city government to dispute any longer publicly in Amsterdam, since his discourse smacked of 'atheismum'.[1] Borch's jottings also reveal that, by the early 1660s, Van den Enden was accustomed to propagate his doctrines clandestinely, circulating his manuscript writings among trusted followers and sympathizers. His subsequent contribution to the growth of the radical tradition, moreover, was altogether remarkable.

His chief work, the *Free Political Institutions* (*Vrye Politijke Stellingen*), published in 1665, was mostly written between 1662 and 1664.[2] This uncompromising, muscular book is noteworthy for its egalitarianism, emphatic democratic tendency, and vitriolic anticlericalism. It is less a work of original thought, though, than an adept *mélange* of ingredients borrowed from Machiavelli, Johan and Pieter de la Court, Aitzema, Pieter Cornelisz Plockhoy, Spinoza, whose *Korte Verhandeling* he certainly knew and used, and possibly Van Velthuysen, but strikingly not Hobbes.[3] All his material, except Machiavelli, had only very recently been published or circulated in manuscript. He himself remarks that in championing democratic republicanism, the quest for a true and just commonwealth based on equality, he had been preceded, to his knowledge, by two writers in the Dutch language, an allusion doubtless to Johan de la Court,[4] in

---

[1] Klever, 'Spinoza and Van den Enden', 318–19.

[2] Bedjaï, 'Métaphysique', 296; Bedjaï, 'Franciscus . . . maître spirituel', 300.

[3] Mertens, 'Franciscus van den Enden', 720–1.

[4] Johan de la Court (1622–60), brother of the more famous Pieter de la Court (1618–85), a businessman active as a supplier of raw materials to the Leiden cloth industry, was an important source for the rise of the Dutch radical tradition, having developed a vigorous republican theory (much influenced by Machiavelli) in the 1650s and being the first Dutch writer to advocate a popular commonwealth, or democratic republic, as the best form of state. His democratic ideas were publicized in the *Consideratien van staat* which first

the first place, and secondly either the latter's brother, Pieter, or the Collegiant Plockhoy.[5] Van den Enden, evidently, was a man who mulled over what he read and knew how to select and weld his materials into a cohesive and impressive whole.[6] Nor was he wholly devoid of originality. For assuredly he struck a new note of militancy, scorning the 'foul self-seeking and vainglory' of those who praise monarchy as a godly form of government and insisting that a true republicanism can only be cogently conceived and advocated as part of a wider set of principles relating to religion, philosophy, and education, as well as government.

Unlike the brothers De la Court who expound their impassioned anti-monarchism at great length, insisting on the innate inferiority and baseness of monarchy, a system based on hierarchy, flattery, and oppression, Van den Enden takes the perversity and arbitrariness of kings and princes for granted and concentrates rather on developing his ideas for reforming education, advancing equality, and enlightening the people. For only in this way, he urges, can the superstition, greed, and obsequiousness which form the preconditions for monarchy be assailed and overcome.[7] Like the brothers De la Court and Spinoza, Van den Enden too is steeped in Machiavelli, whose *Discorsi* influenced him profoundly. But he is nevertheless noticeably more critical of the great Florentine than they, condemning in particular his statecraft of artifice, manipulating the apprehensions and credulity of the common people to secure power, but precluding thereby the very process of enlightenment which alone, in his view, can open the way to a just and free commonwealth.[8] If equality and enlightenment, in the sense of understanding the truth of things, are essential prerequisites for an enduring, well-ordered commonwealth, then a viable republic is inconceivable without, in particular, the drastic curtailment of organized religion which, according to Van den Enden—like Machiavelli, Vanini, and Spinoza—is nothing but a political device contrived to discipline and control the people through utilizing their ignorance and credulity.[9]

Basic to Van den Enden's revolutionary philosophy of education is his insistence on removing key areas of knowledge such as medicine, jurisprudence, science, philosophy, and theology from the hands of closed élites of supposed (but in fact bogus) experts who use arcane terminology and Latin to erect impenetrable walls to shut others out of their specialities and thereby control the business of law, medicine, religion, and so forth for their own profit and power. Van den Enden aims to render this knowledge accessible by projecting it in the public sphere, in everyday language and straightforward terms, readily understood by the common people. Moreover, the

---

appeared at Amsterdam in 1660, with further editions appearing in 1661–2, but they were progressively diluted in the subsequent publications of his brother; Wildenberg, *Johan en Pieter de la Court*, 9–11, 82–5; Haitsma Mulier, *Myth of Venice*, 124–9; Mertens, 'Franciscus van den Enden', 721, 725.

[5] Van den Enden, *Vrije Politieke Stellingen*, 160–1; Mertens, 'Franciscus van den Enden', 725.
[6] Van Gelder, *Getemperde vrijheid*, 254–5; Mertens, 'Franciscus van den Enden', 720–4, 731–2.
[7] Van den Enden, *Vrye Politijke Stellingen*, 139, 141–2, 150, 161.
[8] Ibid., 161, 175, 229; Mertens, 'Franciscus van den Enden', 722.
[9] Van den Enden, *Vrye Politijke Stellingen*, 153–7, 178–81.

'people' here clearly means women and girls as well as men and boys, even though women and servants, in Van den Enden's democratic vision, as in Spinoza's, are excluded from participation in decision-making and voting.[10] As in the brothers Koerbagh and Meyer, advocacy of popular enlightenment as the foundation of republican freedom here entails a markedly more optimistic view of human nature and capabilities than one finds in Spinoza.[11] Van den Enden, in effect, assumes the automatic onset of a harmonious coexistence of private interest and the common good in the people's commonwealth, closely related, as has been pointed out, to the concept of 'general will' developed later by Diderot and Rousseau.[12]

Essential components of Van den Enden's radical egalitarianism are the ideas of Plockhoy, who was closely associated with his first foray into the domain of political thought, the *Short Account* (1662) of 'New Netherland's situation, virtues, natural advantages and suitability for colonization',[13] a text which reflects the fervent commitment to settlement in North America prevalent among some fringe religious groups in Dutch society before the conquest of the colony by the English in 1664. A Zeelander from Zierikzee, who first made his mark among the Amsterdam Collegiants in the late 1640s, Plockhoy had long been an ardent advocate of equality and unrestricted religious toleration.[14] Attracted to the social radicalism which flourished briefly in England during and after the Civil War, he migrated there and, in 1659, published a pamphlet, *The Way to Peace and Settlement of these Nations*, imploring the now tottering Cromwellian régime to enact a fuller, more comprehensive religious freedom than it had yet been willing to countenance. A second tract, published in May 1659, entitled *A Way Propounded to Make the Poor in these and other Nations Happy*, unveils plans for forming a new kind of co-operative society on the outskirts of London, with eventually a daughter community 'about Bristoll, and another in Ireland where we can have a great deal of land for little money'.[15]

A pious Collegiant, Plockhoy taught Van den Enden no religion, philosophy, or political thought. But he undoubtedly contributed to his fervent egalitarianism and transmitted to him elements of his ideas on co-operative labour and lifestyle, concepts not without some significance in the history of socialism. Thus, nearly three centuries later, the Manchester Co-operative Union in 1934 acknowledged that if 'our co-operative movement must have a father or a founder Peter Cornelius Plockhoy has an excellent claim to that distinction'.[16] Plockhoy's aim was to create a 'little commonwealth' separate from the rest of society, an élite of work and spiritual values based on co-operative principles in order that 'we may the better eschue the yoke of the temporall and spirituall pharaohs, who have long enough domineered over our bodies and souls and set up again (as in former times) righteousness, love and brotherly sociableness, which are scarce any where to be found'.[17] The co-operative was to share

---

[10] Ibid., 154–6; Klever, *Mannen rond Spinoza*, 43.   [11] Mertens, 'Franciscus van den Enden', 722–3.
[12] Ibid., 723; Klever, *Mannen rond Spinoza* 29–31.   [13] Mertens, 'Franciscus van den Enden', 721.
[14] Lindeboom, *Stiefkinderen*, 378–81; Smith, *Religion and Trade*, 231–2; Séguy, *Utopie cooperative*, 25–33, 223.
[15] Plockhoy, *A Way Propounded*, 19.   [16] Downie, *Peter Cornelius Plockhoy*, 27.
[17] Plockhoy, *A Way Propounded*, 3; Hill, *World Turned Upside Down*, 346.

ownership, risk, capital, and work, and no form of hierarchy or leadership of any kind would be allowed. Profits would be shared among the members equitably and because only a quarter of the women were required for cleaning and cooking when groups of families live together in communal complexes or settlements, over three-quarters of the women and girls, he urges, would be free to engage in the same manual labour as the men. It remained unclear, though, a feature exploited by Plockhoy's enemies, how concomitant erosion of the family unit and strict monogamy would be prevented.[18]

In Plockhoy, the principle of equality plainly applies to women as much as men, though he does not stress this particularly, and derives from his fervent Collegiant, anti-Church convictions, his insistence on Christ's 'abolishing amongst his disciples all preheminency or domineering of one over another', so that the 'gifts and meanes of subsistence in the world (for necessity and delight) should be common'.[19] Van den Enden doubtless endorsed his requirement that clergy of whatever kind must be debarred from their ideal American commonwealth and that in its religious assembly there should be 'no preheminency, or sole privilege . . . of offering anything or of speaking first'.[20] Consequently, such a co-operative would need to vet prospective new members to ensure only 'honest, rationall, impartiall persons', that is, personalities free from rigid confessional allegiances as well as vice, were admitted. Those too mired in ordinary confessional thinking to be suitable as full members were to receive wages, and find their own accommodation, 'till they are fitted and prepared to be members of our society'.[21] The best kind of people, according to Plockhoy, were 'husbandmen', 'mariners', 'masters of arts and sciences', and 'useful handy craft-men', especially 'smiths of all sortes', carpenters, bricklayers, 'weavers of all sortes', bakers, brewers, shoe-makers, hat-makers, soap-boilers, rope-makers, sail-makers, net-makers, physicians, and so on.

Plockhoy's utopian vision is predicated on the rejection of all social hierarchy. 'Every one in the world which by his office or title is differenced from others,' he insists, 'conceives he is quite another thing and in himself better than others and must be reputed for one that is set together and composed of some finer substance, and designed to a sweeter life, yea to an higher place in heaven than others'.[22] Deference to noble status, for Van den Enden and Plockhoy alike, is sheer ignorance and superstition. Doubtless noble lineage 'puffeth up', contends Plockhoy, but 'what else is it but a meer name, the vanity whereof who sees it not? The very foundation of it is nothing else but the noyse of the tongue and the report of others'.[23] 'For princes are not born on purpose,' he held, 'to reare up stately palaces, the learned are not born for the writing of many unprofitable and for the most part frivolous books; the rich are not born to boast of their gold, silver and christal vessels; the rest of the people are not born for so many various unprofitable handy-crafts,' labouring so that the rich and powerful might enjoy a sweet life off their labour.[24] Honest, well-meaning, and unprejudiced

---

[18] Lindeboom, *Stiefkinderen*, 378.   [19] Plockhoy, *A Way Propounded*, 24.
[20] Ibid., 17.   [21] Ibid., 18.   [22] Ibid., 25; Lindeboom, *Stiefkinderen*, 379.
[23] Plockhoy, *A Way Propounded*, 26, 31.   [24] Ibid., 31.

men and women were to work in Plockhoy's utopia, sharing the fruits of their toil untroubled by rulers, nobles, lawyers, or clergy, an 'honest' week's work for members being fixed by him at thirty-six hours.[25]

With the Restoration of monarchy in England in 1660, Plockhoy despaired of realizing his utopian dreams there and returned to Amsterdam, where he and his followers, the 'Plockhoyisten', approached Van den Enden late in 1661, for his assistance as their spokesman and advocate in negotiations with the city government over a charter for establishing a Plockhoyist colony at Zwanendael, on the Delaware estuary, in New Netherland.[26] Van den Enden obliged with his customary fervour, bombarding the regent committee delegated by the city government to administer the Delaware settlements with memoranda proclaiming the advantages of Plockhoy's scheme, and proposing a detailed political constitution for the new society Plockhoy and his adherents aspired to found. The resulting text, in 117 articles, provided the basis of his subsequently published *Short Account.*[27] Echoing Plockhoy's call for complete toleration in the new society, Van den Enden fervently, if paradoxically, stipulates that conserving such spiritual and intellectual freedom necessarily entails exclusion from the colony of all Reformed preachers, devout Catholics, 'parasitic Jews', Quakers, Puritans, and 'rash and stupid believers in the Millenium besides all obstinate present-day pretenders to Revelation'.[28] More coherently, he also uncompromisingly denounced slavery and exploitation, extolling political and legal equality of status.[29]

Though less than enthusiastic about these ideas, the regents wished to accelerate New Netherland's colonization and a charter was agreed, funds advanced, and preparations made for the voyage. In July 1663, a group of forty-one Plockhoyisten disembarked at their new home on the Delaware. The co-operative had little time to consolidate, though, as all New Netherland, including New Amsterdam (New York), was overrun by the English the following year. It would seem though, that the prophet of co-operative labour never returned to Europe, but remained in North America with most of the others. Old, destitute and blind, he settled in 1694 among the Dutch and German Mennonites of Germantown, Philadelphia, where he died, presumably not long after.[30]

That Van den Enden also influenced Plockhoy emerges from the latter's *Short and Clear Project* (1662), written to advertise the attractions of the new society, a text echoing much of Van den Enden's pamphlet. The foundation of Plockhoy's new commonwealth was to be 'equality for all' firmly anchored in democratic decision-making based on voting, with major decisions requiring a two-thirds majority of free male citizens.[31] Furthermore, this was an equality which dissolved not only confessional but also racial barriers, for Van den Enden and Plockhoy held decidedly radical views regarding the Indians of New Netherland, a noble people, they insisted, without

---

[25] Downie, *Peter Cornelius Plockhoy*, 25.
[26] Van den Enden, *Vrye Politijke Stellingen*, preface; Smith, *Religion and Trade*, 233.
[27] Séguy, *Utopie coopérative*, 57, 60; Klever, 'Inleiding', 28–32.
[28] Smith, *Religion and Trade*, 234. [29] Klever, 'Inleiding', 37–8.
[30] Séguy, *Utopie coopérative*, 33–4. [31] Plockhoy, *Kort ende Klaer Ontwerp*, 210, 213.

affectation, who eschew utterly 'telling lies, swearing, slandering and other such like unrestrained passions' and are thoroughly worthy of emulation by Europeans.[32] Here again, Van den Enden foreshadows Lahontan and Rousseau.[33] Indeed, there can be no clearer instance of the revolutionary resonance of the cult of the 'noble savage' which, from Van den Enden on, was to be one of the *leitmotivs* of Europe's radical philosophical tradition. In his *Free Political Institutions*, Van den Enden weaves this into a general theory of the rationality and equality of all peoples—except only for the Hottentots of South Africa, should it prove true as alleged, he says, that they lack human reason.[34] As for the Indians of North America, Van den Enden, undeterred by his never having laid eyes on them, confidently attributes to them an indomitable and exemplary love of naturalness, freedom, and equality.

ii. Revolutionary Conspiracy

A notable feature of Van den Enden's thought is his deep preoccupation with France. If, as he maintains, education is the key to enlightenment, and enlightenment the key to creating a republic which serves the common good and provides freedom for all, then language is strategically crucial: 'as a general language, in any given part of the world', asserted Van den Enden, the most widely current—as, for example, the French language in Europe—'must be promoted and thoroughly inculcated and taught to young and old alike, in the cheapest and most convenient manner, and to women as well as men, girls as well as boys'.[35] But besides spreading their message in the language best suited to the purpose, Van den Enden, like Spinoza, was acutely conscious of the need for French connections and for avenues of access to French culture.

It had in fact been Van den Enden's practice, possibly ever since the Frondes (1648–53) to cultivate links with French noblemen opposed to the growth of royal absolutism. That massive insurgency involved many segments of the population and while it was mostly no more than a venting of anger and resentment against Mazarin, and his allies at the French Court and in the provinces, nevertheless sporadically, as in Bordeaux, also produced expressions of republican sentiment. Moreover, the upheaval bequeathed an emotional and psychological legacy which not only helped inspire later bouts of rebellion such as the Révolte des Gentilshommes of 1657–9 in several parts of the north, including Normandy, and such peasant insurrections as that of May 1658 known as the *guerre des Sabotiers*, and of 1662 in the Boulonnais, of which, the king's ministers suspected, disaffected nobles were the real instigators, but seemed also to afford a basis for a wider, more ideological campaign against royal absolutism.

Holland was the favourite place of refuge for French noble, religious, and intellectual dissidents, fleeing the ire of Louis XIV (as well as of English and Scottish malcontents plotting against the Stuart monarchy in Britain) and consequently it was also the

---

[32] Klever, 'Inleiding', 34–5.   [33] Mertens, 'Franciscus van den Enden', 723.
[34] Van den Enden, *Vrye Politijke Stellingen*, 169.   [35] Ibid., 155–6.

best place to forge links between political disaffection on the one hand, and the great new destabilizing force of the early Enlightenment—radical philosophy—on the other. One might object that malcontent French nobles, however enthralled by the anti-authoritarian, libertine tendencies of the new philosophical radicalism, were hardly likely to endorse its egalitarian, social levelling and democratic rhetoric. But, in fact, Van den Enden found that there were French dissident nobles eager not just to conspire against Louis XIV but also to cultivate his particular brand of radical philosophy and democratic republicanism.

Van den Enden, a brilliant teacher of Latin and other subjects, who spoke French, Spanish, and other tongues fluently, tutored and became friendly in Amsterdam with several French nobles. His closest French ally over many years was Gilles du Hamel, sieur de la Tréaumont (d.1674), who had fought in the Frondes, partly for and partly against the Crown, and later been implicated in the Révolte des Gentils-hommes. A political fugitive, he resided in Amsterdam during the years 1665–9.[36] In the years 1653–9 he also seems to have backed Condé and worked for the Spanish governor-general in Brussels. Besides La Tréaumont, Van den Enden established ties with several other French nobles, notably Guy-Armand de Gramont, comte de Guiche (1637–74), a libertine intriguer disgraced at the French Court in 1665, who left Paris in April that year 'pour aller en Hollande'.[37] Guiche, Van den Enden later confessed to the French authorities, was often present at the meetings in which he and La Tréaumont discussed republican political theory, and schemes for reforming the Dutch Republic, but not when they plotted how to foment sedition in France.[38] The conspiratorial object of Van den Enden's and La Tréaumont's conferences was to liberate Normandy from the French Crown and convert it into a Van den Enden-style republic.

Van den Enden's fervent espousal of the French dissident cause cost him his life. Increasingly at odds with the Amsterdam city government, and doubtless feeling less welcome after the trial of Adriaen Koerbagh by the Amsterdam magistracy in 1668, in which both he and Spinoza were cited as malign influences in the city, Van den Enden may well have considered emigration for some time before he actually left in 1671. Official pressure, it seems, helped precipitate his departure. According to a later radical source, Van den Enden 'fut tellement decrié à Amsterdam, à cause de son athéisme, qu'il fut obligé d'en sortir et de chercher fortune en France'.[39] But Van den Enden himself, later claimed, under interrogation in the Bastille, that he was summoned to Paris by 'plusieurs personnes de qualité' who had frequented his company in Amsterdam 'qui lui disoient que son beau talent ne devoit être enseveli en un si petit espace que la Hollande, et qu'il devait venir en France'.[40] He was referring here to La Tréaumont and Guiche, both of whom had returned to France and with whom Van den Enden now resumed contact.

---

[36] Bedjaï, 'Libertins et politiques', 29.   [37] Ibid., 30.   [38] *Archives de la Bastille*, vii, 420.
[39] *Recontre de Bayle et de Spinoza*, 17–18; See also the *Lettres Critiques sur divers écrits* i, 154–5.
[40] Quoted in Bedjaï, 'Libertins et politiques', 32.

His zest for education, philosophy, and political intrigue all undiminished, the aged schoolmaster settled in the Parisian quarter of Picpus, where he reopened his Latin school, calling it apparently the 'Temple des Muses'. A noted *savant*, he became acquainted with various French *érudits*, including Arnauld, and was visited, among others, by Leibniz.[41] Meanwhile, La Tréaumont was urging the feasibility of accomplishing 'en France l'exécution de cette république libre dont ils avoient discouru en Hollande' by stirring up revolt in Normandy, commencing with Quilleboeuf, a small port to which men, arms, and munitions could readily be shipped in from the Spanish Netherlands and which he knew intimately, having twice helped to capture it, in 1649 and 1657.[42] Several nobles joined the conspiracy, including Louis, the Chevalier de Rohan (1635–74), a veteran of the Frondes, who agreed to put himself at the head of the dissident group. Guiche too may have been implicated, but having gone off to participate, under Condé, in the French invasion of the Dutch Republic in 1672, and been one of the heroes of the 'passage of the Rhine', died of fever in the Palatinate later in the war.

Following the Spanish entry into the conflict on the Dutch side in 1673, Rohan and La Tréaumont solicited the help of the Spanish governor in Brussels with Van den Enden acting as go-between. The governor, the Conde de Monterrey, received a secret missive from the conspirators, revealing that they were planning a major insurrection against the French Crown, commencing in Quilleboeuf, and requesting a substantial subsidy and his promise that, once the port was secured, he would immediately dispatch 6,000 Spanish troops bringing arms for 20,000 Norman insurgents.[43] As part of the proposed collusion, Spain would permanently occupy Quilleboeuf and be declared protector of the 'république libre' the insurgents designed to establish in Normandy.

Early in September 1674 Van den Enden, now aged 72 but apparently not yet too old for cloak-and-dagger intrigue, travelled to Brussels to confer with Monterrey. Barely had he returned to Paris, on the evening of 17 September 1674, than he heard, on sitting down to dine, that Rohan had been arrested at Versailles, on the king's orders, after Mass on 11 September. Abandoning his dinner, he rose and fled but was caught the following day on the city's outskirts and conveyed, like Rohan, to the Bastille. Meanwhile, royal commissioners of police, accompanied by troops, had burst into La Tréaumont's lodgings in Rouen. Resisting arrest, the latter fired two shots at his assailants before being mortally wounded in the affray. As he lay dying, his rooms were searched and all his papers seized. Among the latter were found French translations of Van den Enden's published and unpublished works. During the next days several other aristocratic conspirators, including the Chevalier de Préaux and his mistress, Madame de Villars, taken from her château eight leagues from Rouen, were arrested in Normandy and brought to the Bastille.

[41] Leibniz, *Theodicy*, 351; Orcibal, 'Jansénistes face à Spinoza', 445.
[42] *Archives de la Bastille*, vii, 420; *Allgemeines Historisches Lexicon*, ii, 195; Meinsma, *Spinoza*, 460–1; Klever, 'Inleiding', 81.
[43] *Archives de la Bastille*, vii, 421.

The elderly ex-Jesuit was alternately interrogated and tortured several times between mid September and late November 1674. Louis himself was informed by Louvois of the Dutch schoolmaster who had plotted to overthrow his monarchy with philosophy. The conspiracy had evidently been revealed to the authorities by a young nobleman lodging and studying Latin with Van den Enden, who had observed the 'grande liaison' between him, La Tréaumont, and the Chevalier and, having 'reconnu Van den Enden pour un homme qui n'avoit point de religion, et qui parloit avec trop de liberté de la personne du roi', reported all this to the police. During his interrogation on 21 November, Van den Enden was asked to explain his republican ideas, which he did at some length, claiming that hitherto the literature of political thought had produced three different categories of republic, namely that of Plato ruled by a philosopher-king, that of Grotius, by which he presumably meant oligarchical systems such as those of Venice and the Dutch Republic, and the utopia of Thomas More.[44] In contrast to these concepts, Van den Enden claimed to have introduced a novel type of republic into political theory 'qu'il avoit proposée aux États de Hollande pour l'établir dans la Nouvelle-Hollande, dans l'Amérique', that is, the people's 'free republic' or democratic republic, a commonwealth based on the common good and the freedom of all the citizenry, and it was this new political concept he had taught La Tréaumont among others. The Norman nobleman had been greatly taken with his democratic republic and 'en a voulu faire une semblable pour la Normandie'.[45]

La Tréaumont may indeed have been a genuine convert to Van den Enden's revolutionary democratic republicanism, or at least have seen the seditious potential of his republican theories, since the police found at his several lodgings 'quelques projets de la manière de cette république et des placards qui devoient estre envoyez proprement en Normandie et ensuite dans toutes les autres provinces du royaume'.[46] For modern scholars, a particularly tantalizing item among the papers seized by the police was a French translation, presumably prepared by Van den Enden himself, of the complete text of the *Vrye Politijke Stellingen*, only the first part of which had been published in 1665, and the rest of which is now lost; the police, once their investigations were complete, burned all the material they had seized.

The plans to foment insurrection and establish a 'free republic' in Normandy, Van den Enden confessed, not without pride, were inspired by his own ideas and writings. He had little to lose by admitting this as there was no prospect of his escaping execution. The dénouement followed swiftly. A few days later, the conspirators were led down, at four in the afternoon, into the inner courtyard of the Bastille, which was packed with people lined with royal musketeers. The crowd reportedly was totally silent before this 'grand spectacle' framed by a scaffold and gallows. One by one, Rohan and the others, including Madame de Villars, were brought, in descending order of seniority, to the scaffold and beheaded. Only Van den Enden, as the sole

---

[44] Ibid., vii, 447. interrogation of 21 Nov. 1674.   [45] Ibid., 467.
[46] Quoted in Bedjaï, 'Franciscus . . . maître spirituel', 293–4.

commoner among the condemned, was denied the more elevated form of execution reserved for those of noble blood.[47] With his fellow conspirators all divided in two, the prophet of the 'free republic' was escorted to the gallows and unceremoniously hanged.

[47] *Archives de la Bastille*, vii, 486.

| RADICALISM AND THE PEOPLE: THE BROTHERS KOERBAGH

i. The Theologian Philosopher, Johannes Koerbagh (1634–1672)

Van den Enden's chief contribution to the formation of radical thought and the Amsterdam 'atheistic' circle was undoubtedly his impassioned and revolutionary summons to 'enlighten' the common people, instilling the lessons of philosophy by novel, carefully devised methods of popular education. The tragic story of the brothers Koerbagh vividly illustrates the appeal of this new impulse and even more the strength of governmental and ecclesiastical reaction against it. Their trial may well have been the very first example in Europe of official suppression of the philosophical 'enlightenment' of the people, as distinct from traditional suppression of theological heterodoxy, blasphemy, and so forth, and, as such, was the first act of a drama soon to reverberate across all Europe.

Adriaen Koerbagh (1632–69), born in the same year as Spinoza, and his younger brother, Johannes, were sons of a ceramics manufacturer, originally from Bergen-op-Zoom, who settled, married, and prospered in Amsterdam. Their father died young in 1644, leaving his family in circumstances of sufficient affluence to free them in adulthood from the need to work for their bread. In these comfortable circumstances, both youths had the opportunity to study in depth and explore the world philosophically. Enrolling first in the philosophy faculty at Utrecht in 1653, they read the standard philosophical literature of the day and doubtless witnessed something of the strife raging in the university over Cartesianism. Accustomed to the scholarly life—in all, Johannes spent more than ten years at university and his brother nine—both transferred to Leiden in 1656, Adriaen switching first to medicine and then law, and Johannes to theology.[1] The brothers probably first became acquainted with the circle around Van den Enden and Spinoza, including Lodewijk Meyer, Johannes Bouwmeester, and Abraham van Berckel[2] (1639–89), who were then all studying at Leiden, in the late 1650s. On completing his theological studies in 1660, Johannes passed his candidate's

---

[1] Vandenbossche, 'Adriaan Koerbagh', 1–3; Meinsma, *Spinoza*, 213; Klever, *Mannen rond Spinoza*, 87.

[2] Abraham van Berckel (or Berkel) (1639–89), originally from Leiden, was a doctor of medicine and the translator of the Dutch edition of Hobbes' *Leviathan* published at Amsterdam in 1667. A precocious youth, and a forceful personality with a quick wit, he enrolled in the university at Leiden at the age of 15 in 1654, later becoming particularly close to Adriaen Koerbagh. Although his identity in his Hobbes edition is

examination before the Reformed *classis* of Amsterdam and was enrolled as a trainee preacher of the public Church, signing the usual formula of credence in the articles of belief of the Reformed confession.[3]

Both brothers participated in Van den Enden's circle in Amsterdam during the early 1660s, two later radical writers, Adriaen Beverland and Willem Goeree, attesting that Adriaen Koerbagh learnt his atheistic ideas from Van den Enden.[4] Other evidence shows the brothers were intimates of Bouwmeester and Van Berckel.[5] It is not clear when and how they became friendly with Spinoza, but it is certain they knew him, Adriaen later disclosing, under questioning, that he had conferred with him about philosophical issues several times in the years 1661–3.[6] An additional link with radical circles was the marriage of their sister, Lucia Koerbagh, in 1662 to Johannes van Ravensteyn (1618–81), an Amsterdam bookseller specializing in republican, Cartesian, and Cocceian literature, who knew Van den Enden and was the father-in-law, by his first marriage, to Jacobus Wagenaar, another friend of Adriaen Koerbagh's and publisher of Van Berckel's translation of Hobbes' *Leviathan*, issued in Amsterdam in 1667.[7]

Johannes Koerbagh's familiarity with Spinoza's thought, at a time it was known only to a tiny circle, probably dates from around 1662, when he returned for a period to complete his studies at Leiden and when Spinoza was living in nearby Rijnsburg. Among other theology students there then were the later notorious Pontiaan van Hattem[8] and Johannes Casearius (*c*.1641–77) who, while studying at the university, lodged at Rijnsburg in Spinoza's house.[9] By the mid-1660s both brothers were living mainly in Amsterdam and both had become ardent advocates of Van den Enden's (and

hidden under the mysterious initials A.T.A.B., he became known to the magistrates as the culprit and fled Amsterdam, taking refuge in the autonomous jurisdiction of Culemborg; see Meinsma, *Spinoza*, 231, 242, 361–2; Gelderblom, 'The Publisher', 162–4.

[3] Meinsma, *Spinoza*, 198.

[4] Beverland, *De Peccato Originali*, 110; Goeree, *Kerklyke en Weereldlyke*, 665.

[5] Vandenbossche, 'Adriaan Koerbagh', 3, 17; Van Suchtelen, 'Nil Volentibus Arduum', 393; Gelderblom, 'Publisher', 164; Freudenthal, *Lebensgeschichte*, 119–20.

[6] Hubbeling, 'Zur frühen Spinozarezeption', 153; Jongeneelen, 'Philosophie politique', 252; Nadler, *Spinoza*, 113, 170.

[7] Gelderblom, 'Publisher', 165.

[8] Pontiaan van Hattem (1641–1706), originally from Bergen-op-Zoom, after becoming a Reformed preacher in Zeeland was unfrocked and expelled from the Church in 1683, when his teachings were formally condemned as heretical by the Synod of Zeeland and the Leiden and Utrecht theology faculties. Only from 1700 onwards, however, was he expressly denounced as a 'Spinozist'. Continuing to preach in private houses, he built up a not inconsiderable following in Zeeland and States Brabant. From 1714 Hattemism was officially banned in the United Provinces as pernicious, partly on the grounds that it was 'Spinozist'. Although recent scholars argue that his theology shows few real affinities with Spinoza's philosophy, his rejection of all forms of ecclesiastical authority and discipline, his plea for unrestricted toleration, and highly unorthodox views on 'good' and 'evil' and the nature of sin, regularly led to his teachings being denounced as 'at bottom the same as the philosophy of Spinoza' even in official documents. On 29 March 1714 all the Hattemist texts in manuscript the authorities had been able to seize were publicly burnt in front of Middelburg town hall; see Van Manen, 'Procedure', 273–38; Wielema, 'Spinoza in Zeeland', 104–8; Rothaan, 'Pontiaan van Hattem', 213–27.

[9] Meinsma, *Spinoza*, 230–1; Meijer, 'De Ioanne Caseario', 232–4; Wielema, 'Spinoza in Zeeland'. 104–5.

Meyer's) ideology of popular enlightenment. Adriaen Koerbagh's first publication, a dictionary of legal terms published in 1664, was a lexicon of lawyers' terminology and phrases, designed to explain legal usage in plain vernacular language.[10] His fierce attack on lawyers recalls Gerard Winstanley's earlier styling of the legal profession across the Channel as 'England's jailors', implying that the law was the people's prison.[11] Lawyers, observed Koerbagh, charge exorbitant fees for piling up heaps of turgid documents couched in arcane terminology purposely incomprehensible to non-lawyers, rendering the public helpless victims of their wiles, a conceited, grasping clique, who, instead of serving the common good, cunningly exploit their supposed expertise to generate wealth and bogus status for themselves. But where Winstanley, in utopian fashion, aspires to abolish lawyers and legal procedure,[12] Adriaen Koerbagh, like Van den Enden and Meyer, seeks to enlighten the people by showing how lawyers dupe them, and how to free themselves from thraldom to 'legalese', helping them master the workings of the law. The legal profession, they believed, can ultimately be marginalized and the people released from its tentacles. At the same time Koerbagh summons lawyers to acknowledge the errors of their corrupt and arrogant ways and abandon abstruseness, adopting instead plain, everyday language.

If lawyers are contemptible, profiting shamelessly from the public's gullibility, still worse and more addicted to the abstruse are the clergy. Adriaen Koerbagh's second work, also of 1664, appearing under his pseudonym 'Vrederyck Waarmond', was a political pamphlet published at Middelburg, roundly denouncing the evils of ecclesiastical interference in politics, a tendency fatal, he declares, to the common good. Just as the people were mercilessly abused before the Reformation, he asserts, by clergy practising such refined artifice, imposture, and pretence that men scarcely dared question the piety and sincerity of even the most debauched prelates and monks, so during the Dutch political crisis of 1617–18, Counter-Remonstrant preachers, hypocritically pretending religion was at risk, discredited the 'loyal patriots' headed by Oldenbarnevelt with a vile campaign of calumny and theological mystification, undermining legitimate political authority at ruinous cost to the public.[13] Praising the States of Holland for their robust stance during the 'public prayers controversy' of 1663–4,[14] Koerbagh denounces De Witt's Voetian opponents as 'machinateurs' and 'perturbateurs' who, to advance their own influence and standing, think nothing of subverting public order, the community, and the state.[15]

Much suggests the brothers worked closely together and held parallel views on philosophy, religion, and politics, as well as public enlightenment. By early 1666 Johannes Koerbagh's involvement with Socinian circles in Amsterdam and abrasive comments about the public Church made, among other places, at Collegiant meet-

---

[10] Entitled *'t Nieuw Woorden-Boek der Reghten* (Amsterdam, 1664), see Meinsma, *Spinoza*, 290; Thijssen-Schoute, *Nederlands Cartesianisme*, 362–3; Vandenbossche, 'Adriaan Koerbagh', 1, 17.

[11] Winstanley, *Law of Freedom*, 170–1, 377–8.   [12] Ibid., 378.

[13] [Koerbagh], *'t Samen-Spraeck*, preface, pp. i–iii.   [14] On this, see Israel, *Dutch Republic*, 760–6.

[15] [Koerbagh], *'t Samen-Spraeck*, 2, 31, 34–5; Jongeneelen, 'Unknown Pamphlet', 405–6.

ings, increasingly came to the notice of Amsterdam's Reformed consistory. Both brothers were cited disapprovingly at a meeting on 10 June 1666, Adriaen for his disorderly lifestyle—he was then cohabiting with a girl out of wedlock by whom he had an illegitimate child—and Johannes for spreading godless opinions.[16] A preacher sent to their house to investigate reported that Johannes Koerbagh held 'highly unsound and heretical opinions' about religion and was extremely obstinate in defending them. Both men eventually complied with summonses to appear before the consistory, where Adriaen was rebuked for keeping a girl in 'whoredom' and Johannes asked to justify his theological views. This he did at greater length, and raising more difficult issues than the assembly felt able to cope with at the time, it was decided to send one of their number, the preacher Petrus Leupenius, a specialist in combating Socinianism, to interview him at home.[17] Requiring Koerbagh to explain himself in writing on five key points, Leupenius received in response a text entitled 'Jan Keurbach's Short but Upright Answer to five Questions put to him by Pieter Leupenius, minister of the Word of God in this city' which was then discussed by the full consistory and copied verbatim into its records.[18]

This outline is of some significance, revealing as it does the core Spinozistic tenets the brothers later expounded more fully in their most radical works. Asked first what he understood by the concept 'God', Koerbagh replied that 'God' is the 'only, single, eternal, unending, omnipotent, omniscient and ubiquitous, independent, unchanging and supreme Being'. Asked next for his opinion of the doctrine of the Holy Trinity, Koerbagh replied he could not find the term 'Trinity' (*Drieeenigheid*) or any equivalent in Scripture and concluded therefore that no such doctrine can be inferred from the Bible. The notion 'there should be three distinct divine *personae* in the one Being of God' (in het eenvoudige weesen Godts), he added, 'can also not be demonstrated through clear and distinct reasoning'.[19] Consequently, veneration of the man Jesus as if he were divine is mere 'superstition'.[20] Commenting, thirdly, on the status of Scripture, Koerbagh held the Biblical books had been composed by God-fearing men at different times to the best of their abilities.[21] Asked what that meant, he refused to expand. Asked fourthly for his views on the resurrection of the dead, Koerbagh answered, again using Cartesian language, that he could derive no 'clear and distinct idea' about the matter. The last demand was for his views on Heaven and Hell. The concept of 'Heaven' in Scripture, he held, means nothing more than the blessed state of the chosen, while 'Hell' denotes the miserable condition of those not thus blessed.[22]

Investigation of Johannes Koerbagh's views resumed on 27 July, at the house of another *predikant*, Dr Langelius. The preachers wanted to know what Koerbagh

---

[16] GA Amsterdam MS 376/11, p. 225. Acta Kerkeraad, res. 10 June 1666.

[17] Ibid., p. 220. Acta Kerkeraad, res. 1 July 1666.   [18] Ibid., p. 235, res. 13 July 1666.

[19] Johannes Koerbagh, 'Korte doch Oprechten Antwoord', GA Amsterdam MS 376/11, p. 235.

[20] Ibid.; see also Adriaen Koerbagh, *Een Ligt schynende*, 167.

[21] See Johannes Koerbagh, 'Korte doch Oprechten Antwoord', p. 235.

[22] Ibid.; Meinsma, *Spinoza*, 341.

meant by calling God a 'single being' (*eenich weesen*). Since God is an infinite being, answered Johannes, there could not be any being, or any thing, apart from God, so that 'all created things are not beings but modifications or modes of being, limited or extended by rest and motion.'[23] Asked next to explain his views on Creation, Koerbagh answered that 'nothing was created out of nothing and can not be so created,' adding that any true notion of God shows He is identical to His Creation. Appalled, Langelius rebuked the young man severely for his blasphemous words, which resulted in a dramatic change in his demeanour. He became contrite and submissive when harangued, and was eventually persuaded, or so the minister supposed, that after all, God is distinct from His Creation and did 'create the universe from nothing'. Finally, he even acknowledged that the teaching of the Reformed Church is the truth and that God is really 'three in one' (Deum esse triunum).[24]

Summoned again before the consistory on 5 August, Johannes heard of the assembly's deep dismay at his earlier heretical utterances and, even more, his offence of propagating such views among 'ordinary and common folk'.[25] He was warned to desist completely from such activity and that, if he defied the consistory, he would be brought before the civic magistrates and severely punished. Both brothers were indeed somewhat more cautious for a while. Nevertheless, fresh reports reached the consistory the following summer that Johannes Koerbagh was 'once again beginning to speak of the Holy Scriptures and catechism in a very blasphemous manner'.[26] Two members were sent to reprimand him afresh. Though he flatly denied having spoken of Scripture or the Church's doctrines disparagingly and again undertook not to do so, six months later the consistory learnt from two young theology students, who had infiltrated a recent Collegiant meeting on the Rokin, that Johannes Koerbagh had been present, seated among the principal personalities, and had addressed the gathering, praising the Collegiants and affirming (in open violation of the law) that Christ is not the 'true God' but 'only an eminent teacher or prophet'.[27]

Summoned anew, Koerbagh, technically still a 'candidate' for the Reformed ministry, was again sternly reprimanded, at which he flew into a rage, began berating the consistory 'not like a doctor of theology . . . but a raving or possessed person', and was ordered outside until he had recovered his composure.[28] On his return, he was asked whether attending Collegiant meetings, and denigrating the Reformed confession and catechism, fitted with his having accepted and signed these formulations five years before. He had known no better then, he replied, but was wiser now. Exasperated by the pressure exerted on him, Johannes Koerbagh was becoming increasingly unwilling to veil his true feelings. Finally, the proceedings lapsed into a complete impasse when he was asked his opinion of the articles of the Netherlands Confession.

---

[23] GA Amsterdam MS 376/11, p. 236 'Naerder onderhandelingen', 27 July 1666; Weekhout, *Boekencensuur*, 103.

[24] GA Amsterdam MS 376/11, p. 236; Meinsma, *Spinoza*, 341.

[25] GA Amsterdam 376/11, p. 234. res. 5 Aug. 1666.   [26] Ibid. pp. 303, 307, res. 9 and 23 June 1667.

[27] Ibid. 351. res. 29 Dec. 1667.   [28] Ibid., p. 353. res. 5 Jan. 1668.

Again becoming agitated, he remained adamant that he would not be drawn on such matters 'even if he were to be torn to pieces'.

ii. The *Bloemhof*

In January 1668 the younger Koerbagh appeared twice more before the Amsterdam Reformed consistory, each time again becoming recalcitrant and abrasive.[29] In late February the Church authorities learnt that either his older brother alone, or both Koerbaghs, had brought out, under the pseudonym 'Vrederick Waarmond', a book entitled *Een Bloemhof van allerley Lieflijkheyd sonder verdriet (A Garden of All Kinds of Loveliness without Sorrow)*[30] reportedly crammed with 'blasphemous remarks about God, our Saviour Jesus Christ, the Son of God, and the divine and perfect Word of the Lord'.[31] Since the publication was plainly illegal under Holland's anti-Socinian legislation of 1653, spokesmen were promptly dispatched to the city hall, where the most offensive passages were read to the burgomasters, who were suitably appalled and immediately ordered the book's suppression. The stocks of copies were seized from the bookshops.[32] Some surfaced elsewhere later in April, however, notably in Utrecht, and there too the book was judged 'blasphemous' and confiscated.[33]

Amid a general outcry, with the book being universally condemned—except, naturally, in radical circles—as a 'scriptum pessimum, blasphemum, atheisticum',[34] Adriaen was quickly identified as its author and warned by the city's chief police officer, the *schout* (sheriff), that he must on no account leave Amsterdam. Nevertheless, the atmosphere confronting him became so forbidding that he decided to try to evade trial and suddenly fled into hiding in the judicially autonomous county of Culemborg, taking refuge under the assumed name 'Pieter Wilte' with his ally Van Berckel who was already in hiding there, following the suppression of his Dutch edition of Hobbes.

Meanwhile in Amsterdam, Johannes appeared again before the consistory on 1 March, but now less than ever mindful of Spinoza's motto *caute* (with caution), he lambasted the dogma of the Trinity as a *contradictio in terminis*, a meaningless formula nowhere found in Scripture, and reaffirmed that the world can not have been created *ex nihilo*.[35] Growing increasingly caustic and insubordinate, he added, to the stupefaction of all present, that there 'is only one infinite Spirit and one infinite Body which are

[29] GA Amsterdam 376/11. pp. 361, 364–5. res. 19 and 26 June 1668.

[30] *Een Bloemhof van allerley Lieflijckheid sonder verdriet geplant door Vrederick Waarmond ondersoecker der waarheyd. Tot nut en dienst van al die geen die der nut en dienst uyt trekken wil. Of Een vertaaling en uytlegging van al de Hebreusche, Griecksche, Latinjnse, Franse en andere vreemde bastaartwoorden en wijsen van spreken die ('t welk te beklagen is) soo inde Godsgeleertheyd, regtsgeleertheyd, geneeskonst als in andere konsten en weetenschappen en ook in het dagelijks gebruyk van spreeken inde Nederduytse taal gebruyckt worden, gedaen door Mr. Adr. Koerbagh regtsgel. en geneesmr.* (Amsterdam, 1668).

[31] GA Amsterdam Ms. 376/11,p. 372. res. 23 Feb. 1668.

[32] GA Amsterdam MS 376/11, p. 379. res. 15 Mar. 1668.

[33] GA Utrecht Kerkeraad viii, res. 13, 20 and 27 Apr. 1668.

[34] Vogt, *Catalogvs historico-criticus*, i, 484–5.

[35] GA Amsterdam MS 376/11, pp. 374, 377. res. 1 and 8 Mar. 1668.

distinguished solely in their respective modifications'.[36] When asked whether he had collaborated with his brother in writing the *Bloemhof*, he admitted having 'corrected some passages when it was in press', making it clear, though, that he saw nothing wrong with its contents.[37]

The *Bloemhof*, a work on which the brothers had been working since 1666, was, by any reckoning, an unprecedentedly provocative book. It is true that not only Spinoza, Van den Enden, and the brothers Koerbagh, but also diverse Socinian leaders known to Johannes and Adriaen, such as Jan Knol, equally rejected the divinity of Christ and the Trinity. But none of these had done so in print as outspokenly as the brothers Koerbagh, rejecting the Trinity not just as meaningless obfuscation but one deliberately used by churchmen to tighten their grip on theology and their authority and prestige in society.[38] A 672-page dictionary of terms, especially foreign words and technical terms, current in contemporary Dutch usage, the book explains the allegedly 'real' meanings in accessible everyday language and also how these terms were routinely abused to dupe, mislead, and mystify the ordinary man in the street.[39] Fired with zeal to enlighten the populace, they charged all the ecclesiastical, legal, medical, and academic élites with contriving heaps of obfuscating terms and expressions to veil truth and reserve zones of specialized knowledge exclusively for the charmed circle of those equipped with the requisite professional training.[40] In his preface Adriaen calls on all 'lovers of the Dutch language' to help strip away this vast barrier of pernicious jargon and false expertise and replace it with plain Dutch equivalents, thereby making vital and useful knowledge available to all.

A comparatively small number of entries dealing with issues of theology, ecclesiastical power, and politics, as Leibniz notes in his *New Essays*,[41] caused particular offence. The article on heresy and heretics, for instance, totally rejects the reality of any such concepts, claiming that these words are just another example of theological mystification.[42] The idea of 'heresy' is, he urges, intrinsically an 'abuse of power' whereby churchmen appropriate jurisdiction to which they are not entitled, authority which properly belongs to the secular power. In fact, by manipulating the ignorance of kings and princes who, historically, have been lamentably lacking, Koerbagh insists, in the very knowledge rulers require if they are to rule responsibly, namely 'true' or real theology—that is, 'worldly wisdom' (i.e. philosophy)—ecclesiastics have always cunningly arrogated influence to themselves. The term 'angel', he says, which merely denotes 'messenger' in 'bastard Greek', instead of being rendered into ordinary language with this meaning, in the States Bible had been deliberately left in its foreign form so that 'ordinary folk should not understand it and therefore not come to realize its real meaning'.[43]

---

[36] Ibid., p. 374. res. 1 March 1688.   [37] Ibid.

[38] Koerbagh, *Bloemhof*, 499, 632–3.   [39] Ibid., preface; Leibniz, *New Essays*, 277.

[40] Koerbagh, *Bloemhof*, preface; Vandenbossche, *Spinozisme en kritiek*, 3–4; Klever, *Mannen rond Spinoza*, 88.

[41] Leibniz, *New Essays*, 277.   [42] Koerbagh, *Bloemhof*, 337–9; Meinsma, *Spinoza*, 336–9.

[43] Koerbagh, *Bloemhof*, 268; Vandenbossche, *Spinozisme en kritiek*, 24.

Still more abrasively, in his article on 'Reformed Religion', Koerbagh judges the term a misnomer as applied to the public Church, since in fact it had never been 'reformed' but rather retained many of the deplorable defects characteristic of the Catholic religion. We would know if the 'Reformed' faith were really 'reformed', he affirms, for then it would be an entirely 'rational religion based on wisdom, truth, and reason' rather than meaningless obfuscation. Furthermore, a true religion would not need to be upheld by coercion and political authority 'like all other religions of the world that are known to me which need to be backed by the might of the sword, fire, flames, gallows, and the rack'.[44] The great defect of the religions of the world, he maintains, is that each and every one seeks to impose its 'incomprehensible confession with ignorance and violence'. Moses, according to Koerbagh, was both power-hungry and ruthless.

The divinity of Christ is flatly rejected, Jesus being accounted nothing more than a remarkable man conceived normally, albeit illegitimately, and without our knowing who his father was, 1,167 years ago.[45] In line with the ideas of Spinoza—but not Hobbes, whose *Leviathan* plainly also influenced the Koerbaghs' thought, if less so than that of their ally Van Berckel[46]—miracles are declared totally impossible, since 'nothing can happen against or above Nature'.[47] Moreover, not only 'angels', but also Satan, demons, sorcery, witchcraft, possession, exorcism, and divination are all dismissed as fabrications utterly devoid of truth or reality, devised solely to scare and manipulate the ignorant.[48]

iii. The Trial of the Brothers Koerbagh

In mid-April the Amsterdam magistrates learnt that the fugitive, Adriaen Koerbagh, was living under an assumed name in Culemborg. Apparently in a manic mood, he was reportedly engaging all kinds of people in conversation and 'disseminating his obscenities also there'.[49] Meanwhile, since finishing the *Bloemhof* late in 1667, he had been writing a new book, *A Light Shining in Dark Places*, and, on fleeing Amsterdam, had brought the incomplete manuscript with him. This he managed to finish during the hectic weeks after his flight, in Culemborg and nearby Utrecht.[50] On 1 March when Johannes again appeared before the Amsterdam consistory and again spoke in 'hard and discourteous terms', insisting the 'world was not created out of nothing', there was as yet no mention of any new text. But at some point during the next ten weeks advance copies of the first part of the new book began circulating in Amsterdam and Utrecht.

---

[44] Koerbagh, *Bloemhof*, 327–8; Klever, *Mannen rond Spinoza*, 101–2.
[45] Koerbagh, *Bloemhof*, 354; Meinsma, *Spinoza*, 366.
[46] Hubbeling, 'Zur frühen Spinozarezeption', 152–3; Jongeneelen, 'Philosophie politique', 254–6.
[47] Koerbagh, *Bloemhof*, 447; Vandenbossche, 'Adriaan Koerbagh', 12–13.
[48] Koelman, *Wederlegging*, 137; Edelmann, *Abgenöthigtes Glaubens-Bekentniss*, 288.
[49] GA Amsterdam MS 376/11, p. 383. res. 19 April 1668. [50] Meinsma, *Spinoza*, 366.

On 17 May the Amsterdam consistory heard that Johannes was now in prison, having been arrested by the magistrates on suspicion of involvement in the printing of 'a certain blasphemous book called *Een Ligt schijnende in duystere plaatsen*'. The consistory duly received one of the seized copies and extracts were read out to the assembly, which had certainly heard nothing comparable before. They reportedly listened 'with great consternation of the spirit'.[51] The printed copies of the first part of the work had been clandestinely produced in Utrecht and then sent to Amsterdam in packets and stored. These were seized by the magistracy after the printer in Utrecht had become afraid at what he was printing and refused to heed Johannes' and Van Berckel's exhortations that he should continue. He had surrendered everything to the Utrecht magistrates, who passed the material on to Amsterdam, and Johannes had been arrested. The reading out of extracts to the Amsterdam consistory was probably the only hearing *Een Ligt* ever received until the twentieth century. Thanks to the action of the printer, the Dutch magistracies succeeded in completely suppressing the text. But it is nevertheless historically significant, representing as it does the thinking of the Koerbaghs in its most developed form. Indeed, it reveals the full measure of the revolution in popular culture and education the Koerbaghs and their allies aspired to engineer. *Een Ligt*, in short, was one of the first and, by any reckoning, one of the most far-reaching texts of the European Radical Enlightenment.

Although the Amsterdam consistory was primarily shocked by the vehemence of the attack on the Christian religion and 'mysteries', *Een Ligt* is essentially a political and educational rather than a theological work.[52] It is a book about how and why organized religions are adopted by societies and the doctrinal and organizational forms the institutionalization of religion takes. The more powerful the clergy in any society, argue the Koerbaghs, the more they distort the original teachings of the founder of their faith in order to refine and extend their power. Hence the Catholic Church they designate the most magnificent and imposing of all Churches, and yet simultaneously, and for that very reason, the one with the most perverse and irrational doctrines.[53] The brothers define God as an eternal Being, consisting of infinite attributes, each of which is infinite in its kind, the truth about which, contrary to the dogmas of all revealed religion, has never been hidden or unrevealed but, on the contrary, has always been manifestly evident to all people in the world without exception 'through reason' by which alone the Word of God can be known.[54] Creation occurs only via the interaction and motion inherent in matter.[55] Here again Spinoza, and presumably the manuscript *Korte Verhandeling*, was their prime source of inspiration, though the work also shows obvious traces of Van den Enden, Lodewijk Meyer, Hobbes, and doubtless, in a lesser way, Van Berckel, Bouwmester, and others among their close intimates as well.[56] But while all the important concepts are derived from Spinoza, Van den Enden, Meyer, and Hobbes, the Koerbaghs unfailingly reformulate their

[51] GA Amsterdam, MS 376, p. 385. res. 17 May 1668; Meinsma, *Spinoza*, 363.
[52] Klever, *Mannen rond Spinoza*, 91.   [53] Koerbagh, *Een Ligt schijnende*, 5–6.
[54] Ibid., 25–6; Klever, *Mannen rond Spinoza*, 92–4.   [55] Klever, *Mannen rond Spinoza*, 95.
[56] Thijssen-Schoute, *Nederlands Cartesianisme*, 364–5; Vandenbossche, 'Adriaen Koerbagh', 7, 9–11.

ideas in ways which render them more easily and effectively expressed in everyday language.[57]

Enlightenment and knowledge of the kind the brothers Koerbagh wanted the people to imbibe they see as the key to human well-being, happiness, and freedom, in other words, the path to 'salvation'. By contrast, 'he who neglects to use his reason', they contend, 'lapses into every sort of ignorance and superstition from which all evil stems'.[58] A typically Spinozist feature of the Koerbaghs' thought is their insistence that whatever is true in theology is, *ipso facto*, identical to philosophical truth so that, by definition, there is no independent theological truth: 'everything that is true according to the world's wisdom is and must also be true in theology and everything that is true in theology must also be comprised within worldly wisdom, and is part of it, because in worldly wisdom is comprised the perfect knowledge of God'.[59]

The rejection of Christianity in *Een Ligt* thus derives from a purely philosophical framework which denies, *a priori*, that any revealed religion can convey truths which lie outside or beyond the realm of philosophy. Jesus, holds Adriaen, was a man, not God, and it is utterly false and untenable to say he died 'for us'.[60] Admittedly Jesus died a fearful death on the cross, but this is because his teaching conflicted with that of the ruling clergy and scholars of the Jews, 'who fearing to lose their authority and credibility among the common people' persuaded the Roman authorities to crucify him. 'Can his dying bring us any happiness or salvation? That I can not see with any reason in the world.'[61] Unlike the *Bloemhof*, *Een Ligt* includes a long refutation of the doctrine of the Trinity,[62] in which the Koerbaghs insist on its irrationality, repeating that the only theology which carries weight with them is the sort based on such mathematical reasoning as says that two and two make four.[63] As in Spinoza and Van den Enden, authority in spiritual, intellectual, and educational matters is assigned to the secular power alone. The Bible is declared confused and self-contradictory in many passages and the authors of the Old Testament books unknown, though Ezra (following Spinoza) is identified as the likeliest compiler.[64] As in the *Bloemhof*, the existence of Heaven, Hell, Satan, demons, angels, magic, divination, and witchcraft is altogether denied and miracles proclaimed completely impossible.

The arrest of Johannes and Van Berckel, and the seizure of the secret store of printed parts of *Een Ligt*, led to an intensified search for Adriaen, who by now had found a fresh hiding-place in Leiden. A price of 1,500 guilders was put on his head and, before long, his hideout was revealed to the magistrates by a 'friend' of the fugitive and Van Berckel in exchange for the money.[65] Two months after Johannes' imprisonment, his older brother was apprehended from his bed in Leiden, with his remaining books and papers, and handed over to the authorities in Amsterdam. Adriaen's first interrogation by the city's seven magistrates assembled with copies of the *Bloemhof* and *Een Ligt* arrayed before them, together with papers seized from both brothers'

---

[57] Klever, *Mannen rond Spinoza*, 92–3.   [58] Koerbagh, *Een Ligt schynende*, 29.
[59] Ibid., 37.   [60] Ibid., 125.   [61] Ibid., 126.   [62] Ibid., 63–104.
[63] Jongeneelen, 'Unknown Pamphlet', 410–11.   [64] Vandenbossche, 'Adriaan Koerbagh', 8–9.
[65] Meinsma, *Spinoza*, 364; Vandenbossche, 'Adriaan Koerbagh', 2–3.

rooms, and with the Utrecht printer present, took place on 20 July. Koerbagh readily confessed to having written the *Bloemhof* and *Een Ligt*. When asked who else had participated in writing them, and with whom he had discussed their contents, he insisted that he had written both books himself without the assistance of his brother or Van Berckel.[66] He admitted knowing Van den Enden and, when asked about Spinoza, owned to visiting him a few times some years before, but denied having discussed the intellectual content of his books with either. As regards collaboration with others, the most he would admit, when pressed, was that Van Berckel had corrected a few passages of *Een Ligt* and helped him find and deal with the printer. It was true that in Amsterdam since May 1667, he and his brother resided in the same house, belonging to their mother, and ate their meals together. But he claimed they had worked in different rooms and neither discussed nor collaborated in writing either book.[67] Further interrogations followed but nothing more was admitted or came to light.

Johannes too was questioned several times. He confessed to having discussed a few minor points with his brother but categorically denied being the joint author of either text.[68] Since it had previously been the younger more than the older brother who was known to be propagating forbidden doctrines in Amsterdam, and a Spinozist, neither the magistrates nor the consistory believed these disavowals, which do indeed seem incredible, given Johannes' obvious zeal for the same ideas as his brother professed and greater expertise in theology, Hebrew, and other relevant subjects. But both brothers stuck to this story and the only evidence against Johannes was circumstantial. The consistory's minutes recording his verbal denial of Christ's divinity and the Trinity was adduced, but here too, under Holland's anti-Socinian legislation of 1653, heavy punishment could be meted out only where there was clear evidence of writing, printing, or distributing anti-Trinitarian literature or indoctrinating others with anti-Trinitarian views, and this was lacking.[69] The magistrates were divided and discussed the matter for some time. Indeed, they came close to sentencing Johannes as well as Adriaen to prison but, since he had been in gaol for several months already, in the end they decided to release him.

There was never any doubt, though, that Adriaen would receive a heavy sentence. The undisguised, systematic denial in print of the truth of the Christian religion, and open disparagement of theology, was an unprecedented crime and one which, in the circumstances of the time, could not be dealt with lightly. Debating the sentence, several magistrates urged a large fine and twelve or fifteen years in prison, after which, should he survive, twelve years' subsequent banishment from Holland. Finally it was agreed to moderate this to a 4,000 guilder fine plus 2,000 guilders costs, ten years' imprisonment in the Amsterdam *Rasphuis*, and, in case of survival, ten years' subsequent banishment from Holland.[70] It was decided, though, not to make a public

---

[66] GA Amsterdam MS 5061/318 Confessie-Boeck, fo. 115; Meinsma, *Spinoza*, 365–7.
[67] GA Amsterdam 5061/318 Confessie-Boeck, fo. 118.
[68] GA Amsterdam 5061/318 Confessie-Boeck, fos. 119v, 121–2.
[69] GA Amsterdam 5059/39 no. 9 'Aantekeningen Hans Bontemantel', 469–71.
[70] Ibid., 463–6; Leibniz, *New Essays*, 277; Van Gelder, *Getemperde vrijheid*, 181.

spectacle of him or publish his sentence. A high proportion of the copies of the Koerbaghs' books had been successfully gathered in, including virtually all copies of *Een Ligt*, and all this material was now burnt. Taken away to his place of imprisonment, within months Adriaen was reportedly broken in both body and spirit. Johannes too, though he was the lucky one who was released, wrote nothing more and died young, outliving Adriaen by just three years.

11 | PHILOSOPHY, THE INTERPRETER OF SCRIPTURE

i. Lodewijk Meyer (1629–1681)

The first of the great public intellectual controversies generated by the rise of radical thought erupted in 1666 with the appearance of a short anonymous book entitled *Philosophia S. Scripturae Interpres*. The author of this sensational and inflammatory work—though his identity remained unknown during the furore and subsequently for many decades—was a prominent member of the philosophical coterie gathered around Spinoza and Van den Enden—the Amsterdam physician, Latinist, lexicographer, and man of the theatre, Lodewijk (Louis) Meyer (1629–81). From a Lutheran background, Meyer in temperament resembled Van den Enden more than Spinoza, being combative in debate and fond of conviviality, jesting, and women. A talented man with a strong sense of mission, he was erudite, in some respects a fervent Cartesian, and one of Spinoza's principal collaborators.[1]

Meyer enrolled at Leiden in 1654, studying first philosophy and, from 1658, medicine at a time when Adriaen Koerbagh, whom he presumably saw regularly, also belonged to that faculty.[2] Probably he already knew Spinoza in the late 1650s, especially if we accept that the latter did sit in on lectures for a time between July 1656 and the summer of 1658.[3] The principal Cartesians teaching philosophy at Leiden in 1657–8, at which point Meyer, Koerbagh, and Spinoza were seemingly all present, were Heereboord, De Raey, and from 1658, the forceful and innovative Arnold Geulincx.[4] All three young

---

[1] Monnikhoff, *Beschrijving*, 213; Klever, *Mannen rond Spinoza*, 61–4; Steenbakkers, *Spinoza's* Ethica, 17–18, 21, 27.

[2] Meinsma, *Spinoza*, 194–7; Nadler, *Spinoza*, 171–2.

[3] Révah, *Marranes à Spinoza*, 198; Proietti, 'Le "Philedonius"', 54.

[4] Arnold Geulincx (1623–69), originally from Antwerp, was a fervent Cartesian and Jansenist who, obliged to flee Louvain, took refuge in Leiden in 1658. He was officially allowed to give private classes and preside over disputations in philosophy from 1659 and promoted to professor in 1665. A firm champion of Descartes' two-substance theory, he is particularly noted for his work on the mind–body relationship, an area where he developed a form of 'occasionalism' not unlike that that of Malebranche later. He was one of five Leiden professors carried off in the plague epidemic of 1669. In his lifetime he published only the first part of his *Ethics* (1665). The full version of the latter, edited by his friend and pupil, the reformist doctor Cornelis Bontekoe, appeared in 1675, his works on physics and metaphysics only between 1688 and 1691. It was only in the early eighteenth century that a strong suspicion of a link between Geulincx and Spinoza arose; see Audi, *Cambridge Dictionary*, 296; Thijssen-Schoute, *Nederlands Cartesianisme*, 149–54.

radicals presumably became acquainted with these prominent academics.[5] Gaining Leiden doctorates in both philosophy and medicine in 1660, Meyer returned to Amsterdam, where he stayed for the rest of his life.

There his closest associate was a fellow physician, theatre connoisseur, and Latinist, Johannes Bouwmeester (1630–80), who had similarly read philosophy and medicine at Leiden during the 1650s and become friendly with Koerbagh. He too was close to Spinoza, who calls him 'learned' and his 'very special friend' in the sole surviving letter from an originally substantial correspondence between them, of June 1665. When visiting Amsterdam, Spinoza was evidently in the habit of discussing his philosophy at Bouwmeester's lodgings. Though excessively diffident and lethargic—Spinoza urges him to 'apply yourself with real energy to serious work, and prevail on yourself to devote the better part of your life to the cultivation of your intellect and your mind . . . while there is yet time, and before you complain time, and indeed you yourself, have slipped by'[6]—Bouwmeester was undoubtedly an erudite and perspicacious critic. Spinoza, the letter shows, accounted him an expert Latinist, esteemed his judgements in philosophical matters, and wanted more of them. Bouwmeester, as Spinoza feared, never achieved much, however, other than supplying some entries for Koerbagh's *Bloemhof* and rendering into Dutch, from Edward Pocock's Latin—doubtless with Meyer's and Spinoza's encouragement—the Arabic pantheistic novel, the *Life of Hai Ebn Yokhdan*, published by Rieuwertsz in 1672. In 1677, the year of Spinoza's death, Bouwmeester was one of the team, together with Meyer, Pieter van Gent, and Georg Hermann Schuller, which prepared his posthumous works for publication.[7]

Initially, Meyer manifested his radical zeal chiefly through literary and lexico-graphical work. As early as 1654 he edited a new edition of a lexicon called Hofman's *Nederlantsche Woordenschat*, a dictionary of foreign terms in current usage, giving their meaning in plain Dutch. He subsequently expanded it several times until, reaching its fifth edition in 1669, and now renamed *L. Meijer's Woordenschat*, it had assumed an imposing bulk. Divided into three sections—'bastard' terms, technical terms, and out-moded words no longer in everyday speech—its purpose was to elucidate foreign, Latin, and technical terms in current usage as variously applied in 'philosophy, mathematics, classics, botany, medicine, law or theology'.[8] His aim, he states, is to make the sciences and technical subjects 'known to his countrymen in their mother tongue', purging Dutch of superfluous jargon and foreign interpolations to produce a medium suitable for conveying the loftiest, most complex matters comprehensibly to the common man.[9] He rebukes professional scholars for hindering the acquisition of the vast amount of useful knowledge yielded by science by veiling everything in Latin, technical terminology, and pedantry in order to keep knowledge from the common people and monopolize it themselves.

---

[5] Thijssen-Schoute, *Nederlands Cartesianisme*, 104, 120, 126–7, 152; Nadler, *Spinoza*, 164–5.

[6] Spinoza, *Letters*, 179–80; Meinsma, *Spinoza*, 197.   [7] Steenbakkers, *Spinoza's* Ethica, 16.

[8] *L. Meijers Woordenschat*, 275, 288.

[9] Ibid., 17; Thijssen-Schoute, *Nederlands Cartesianisme*, 360–1; Lagrée and Moreau, 'Introduction', 3.

Though an accomplished if slightly eccentric Latinist,[10] Meyer regrets the fact that Latin was still so predominant in intellectual life since, he says, men must study nine or ten years to master that tongue sufficiently to digest academic works. Still more deplorable, he urges, was the burgeoning growth of a legal terminology incomprehensible to anyone lacking lengthy training in legal studies and Latin, thereby effectively debarring laymen from understanding the law and rendering them the defenceless pawns of grasping lawyers. Only by explaining technical, imported, and 'bastard' phraseology in everyday language, and supplying better lexicons to promote familiarity with specialized usage, could law, medicine, and other essential topics be rendered accessible, and the contemptible tyranny of money-grabbing professionals who fleece the people by controlling key specialities be overthrown.

Meyer, like Spinoza, Van den Enden, and the brothers Koerbagh, positively gloried in the power of philosophy and science to transform the world.[11] Though often called an ardent Cartesian, his total discarding of Descartes' two-substance doctrine shows that he is not in any meaningful sense a Cartesian.[12] Nevertheless, he considered Cartesianism a potent tool not just for demolishing outmoded intellectual structures but for helping to create a new universal outlook, shaped by science and scholarship, which would fundamentally change daily life and society. All that survives of a much wider correspondence between him and Spinoza are three letters dated 1663, concerning the forthcoming publication of the latter's geometric exposition of Descartes. But these suffice to prove Meyer was then the chief intermediary between Spinoza in Rijnsburg, and the radical philosophical circle in Amsterdam, as well as between the philosopher and his publisher, Rieuwertsz. They also show that Spinoza was in the habit of consulting Meyer, as well as Bouwmeester, about the formulation and presentation of his ideas.[13]

Meyer wrote the preface to this the only book his friend ever brought out under his own name, evidently to Spinoza's satisfaction, though he requested him to delete a polemical passage out of keeping with the general impression he wished to convey. 'I want everyone readily to accept that this book is meant for the benefit of all men,' he urged, 'and that in publishing it you are motivated only by a wish to spread the truth and that you . . . invite men, in a spirit of good will, to take up the study of the true philosophy and that your aim is the good of all'.[14] Meyer says in his preface that it was he who had urged the project on Spinoza while offering 'my help in publishing it should he require it'.[15] He fervently extols Descartes' mathematical method as the key to philosophical truth, and praises Spinoza's skill in setting out his system in 'geometric order', but also points out that there were parts of Descartes that Spinoza 'rejects as false and concerning which he holds a different opinion', apparently agreeing that Descartes' principles 'do not suffice to solve all the very difficult problems that occur

---

[10] Akkerman, *Studies*, 208–10, 214; Steenbakkers, *Spinoza's Ethica*, 17–35.
[11] Thijssen-Schoute, 'Lodewijk Meyer', 5–12; Klever, *Mannen rond Spinoza*, 63–85.
[12] Sassen, *Wijsgerig onderwijs*, 49; Thijssen-Schoute, *Nederlands Cartesianisme*, 389
[13] Spinoza, *Letters*, 101–9; Monnikhoff, *Beschrijving*, 215.   [14] Spinoza, *Letters*, 121–2.
[15] *Collected Works of Spinoza*, i, 224–30.

in metaphysics' and that 'different foundations are required, if we wish our intellect to rise to the pinnacle of knowledge.'[16] Rather daringly, he illustrates the difference between Descartes and Spinoza by remarking that, in the latter, the 'will is not distinct from the intellect, much less endowed with that liberty which Descartes ascribes to it', even hinting that Spinoza does not consider the mind a separate substance from the body.[17]

ii. The *Philosophia*

The clandestine printing and distribution of Meyer's most challenging text, the 115-page *Philosophia S. Scripturae Interpres*, subtitled *Exercitatio paradoxa*, in 1666 was plainly the work of Rieuwertsz.[18] Unsurprisingly, given the book's sensational content, there was an immediate outcry throughout the United Provinces, precipitating a major commotion of great importance in Dutch culture, which reverberated also in Germany, the Baltic, and to a lesser extent, Italy and England. Reaction to this 'rationalistischer *anti-Scriptuarius*' as the East Prussian librarian Michael Lilienthal later dubbed the unknown author,[19] was vehemently hostile but transcended mere rejection of the anonymous writer's arguments. Critics grasped that the book raised, in a new and daring manner, issues of overriding importance, and that it could not simply be brushed aside or decried, but had to be answered.[20] Meyer himself appreciated the novelty of his project and genuinely believed that by seeking to overthrow the entire edifice of theology as traditionally conceived, he was affording mankind a vast benefit.[21]

Anxious to spread the debate to the vernacular and 'enlighten' the people, Meyer followed up the Latin version the following year with a slightly expanded 137-page Dutch translation he prepared himself, and which was again published clandestinely by Rieuwertsz. Vigorously suppressed by the city governments, this vernacular edition seems never to have been subsequently reissued. The Latin version, by contrast, reappeared in 1674, frequently distributed bound together with Spinoza's *Tractatus*.[22] Later, during the High Enlightenment in 1776, a remarkable third, Latin edition appeared at Halle, with extensive critical notes and a new preface (but again without any attribution to an author) by Johannes Salomo Semler, one of the founders of modern Protestant Bible criticism.[23]

Meyer's basic thesis is that Scripture is frequently 'obscure and doubtful' in meaning and that there is no way to interpret it correctly except by means of 'philosophy' which he defines, praising Descartes while disparaging Aristotelianism,[24] as the 'true and certain knowledge of things' and the only valid instrument for resolving perplex-

---

[16] *Collected Works of Spinoza*, 229.   [17] Spinoza, *Opera*, i, 132–3; Nadler, *Spinoza*, 207.
[18] Klever, *Mannen rond Spinoza*, 62.   [19] Lilienthal, *Theologische Bibliothec*, 214.
[20] Ibid.; Leydekker, *Verder Vervolg*, 6–7; Mastricht, *Novitatum Cartesianarum Gangraena*, 104–48; Scholder, *Birth*, 132–3; Lagrée and Moreau, 'Introduction', 16; Van der Wall, 'Orthodoxy and Scepticism', 128–9.
[21] [Meyer], *Philosophia*, epilogue.   [22] Bamberger, 'Early Editions', 18–20.
[23] Altmann, *Moses Mendelssohn*, 566, 609; Otto, *Studien*, 347–8.
[24] [Meyer], *Philosophie d'Uytleghster*, 50–1.

ities in theology.[25] Thus, since philosophy teaches 'nothing can be made from nothing,' there can have been no Creation of the sort recounted in Scripture.[26] Where theologians dispute bitterly over the doctrine of the Trinity, some considering it a sacred 'mystery' and others a 'monster, a vast jumble of accumulated contradiction', philosophy settles the matter by showing the dispute to be both meaningless and superfluous.[27] From Wittichius and the Cartesio-Cocceians, he appropriates and gives a new twist to the maxim 'Nulla verae philosophiae dogmata theoligicis esse contraria', that no conclusions of 'the true philosophy' can be contrary to theology,[28] in effect completely merging theology into philosophy. From this, he claims, all mankind will immeasurably benefit; for the enthronement of philosophy will render redundant and eventually end the previously interminable wrangling of theologians which, over the centuries, has everywhere caused incalculable strife, instability, and misery.[29]

While his argument clearly tallies with that of a hard-hitting, radical tract entitled *De Jure Ecclesiasticorum*, anonymously published at Amsterdam in 1665, claiming all spiritual and worldly authority, as well as property claimed by ecclesiastics, or attributed to them by others, is appropriated 'unjustly and in an impious manner', since only the secular power can legitimately exercise public authority and as there is not the slightest basis in either the Old or the New Testament for any ecclesiastical authority, a text later ascribed, almost certainly correctly,[30] by Colerus and others to Meyer, hardly any one seemingly perceived the connection between the *Philsophia* and *De Jure* at the time.[31] However, the probability that *De Jure* is from Meyer's pen strengthens the likelihood that one of his prime objectives also in his *Philosophia* was to discredit and weaken as much as possible, and in all fields, the sway of the public Church.

Meyer's thesis that 'philosophy' is the only and 'infallible rule' by which to interpret Scripture[32] yielded a hermeneutics differing appreciably from Spinoza's, but also exhibiting striking affinities with it.[33] Theology, Meyer and Spinoza broadly agree, is not an independent source of truth, and only philosophy can teach what is true. Both writers consider the Bible a purely human and secular text, meaningful judgements about which can only be made by philosophers. Yet the two thinkers apply reason to Bible hermeneutics differently, leading Spinoza into an undeclared debate with his ally, in the *Tractatus Theologico-Politicus*, without anywhere mentioning him by

[25] Ibid., 37, 52–3, 126; Lagrée and Moreau, 'Introduction', 3.

[26] [Meyer], *Philosophia*, 59; Andala, *Cartesius verus*, 10.   [27] [Meyer], *Philosophie d'Uytleghster*, 56–7.

[28] [Meyer], *Philosophia*, 57.   [29] Ibid., epilogue; Moreau, 'Principes', 120; Lagrée, 'Sens et verité', 84.

[30] Bordoli, *Ragione e scrittura*, 5, 29–34.

[31] Published under the pseudonym 'Lucius Antistius Constans', with the place of publication given as 'Alethopolis'; see Goeree, *Kerklyke en Weereldlyke*, 666–7; Colerus, *Vie de B. de Spinoza*, 97; Basnage, *Histoire des Juifs*, ix, 1038; Wolf, *Bibliotheca Hebraea*, i, 241; Barbier, *Dictionnaire*, iii, 433; further on the *De Jure Ecclesiasticorum*, see below pp. 620–1; Meinsma, *Spinoza*, 291, 311; Blom, *Morality and Causality*, 105.

[32] [Meyer], *Philosophie d'Uytleghster*, 52–3, 126; Beeldthouwer, *Antwoordt*, 11–13; Gebhardt, *Supplementa*, 44–5; Lagrée, 'Sens et verité', 88–9; Klever, 'In defence of Spinoza', 217–18; Iofrida, 'Linguaggio', 33–4; Walther, 'Biblische Hermeneutiik', 227–31.

[33] Lagrée, 'Sens et verité', 85; Walther, 'Biblische Hermeneutik', 238.

name.[34] Where Spinoza offers an elaborate theory of what religion is, and how and why religion construes the world as it does, creating a new science of contextual Bible criticism, analysing usage and intended meanings, and extrapolating from context, using reason as an analytical tool but not expecting to find philosophical truth embedded in Scriptural concepts, Meyer is less concerned with what religion is than showing how Scripture's picturesque allegories and, in his view, hesitant stumbling towards truth point to, or can be aligned with, philosophical truth.[35] Thus where the Bible, for Spinoza, is not a guide to reality, for Meyer it has an inner core of meaning approximating to philosophical truth.[36]

Publication of the *Philosophia* at 'Eleutheropolis' (i.e. Amsterdam) deeply disquieted the Dutch Reformed Church, universities, and most dissident and fringe Churches, demonstrating the profound impact of radical ideas on the late seventeenth-century consciousness and their capacity to inflame existing tension between traditionalist and reforming impulses in mainstream culture. What began as an outcry against the *Philosophia* rapidly became an internecine quarrel among vying theological factions over exegetical methodologies, the function of reason in Bible interpretation, and the status of philosophy. Inevitably, the uproar generated a strong pressure to unmask the author of so impious and provocative a text and reveal the sources of such 'godless' ideas.[37] The favourite suspect, initially, was Lambert van Velthuysen, a Utrecht regent steeped in Cartesian philosophy and much reviled by orthodox Calvinists, but he was cleared, transferring the beam of suspicion to others, including Spinoza. But to the exasperation of almost everyone, nothing definite about the perpetrator could be discovered. Only after Meyer's death in 1681 did his circle of friends divulge the identity of the man who ignited one of the greatest, and most convoluted, intellectual battles of the age, though the question was still being used to tease the public in 1697, the Spinozistic novel, the *Life of Philopater*, alluding to the author of the *Philosophia* mysteriously as 'L. M.'[38]

Even after Colerus definitely concluded that Spinoza had not written it, reporting that those who knew affirmed Meyer to be the author, confusion persisted, especially outside the Netherlands, and during the eighteenth century the text was still often ascribed to Spinoza, although several key *savants* such as Leibniz, Loescher, Wolf, and Trinius all correctly attribute it to Meyer.[39] The discerning Leibniz knew considerably more, and earlier, than most foreign *érudits* about both the *Philosophia* and the clandestine intellectual milieu from which it emerged. During his visit to Amsterdam in 1676, he made a point of getting to know Meyer. Decades later, in his *Théodicée* (1710), the great German thinker recalled that 'in 1666 Lodewijk Meyer, a physician of Amsterdam, published anonymously the book entitled *Philosophia Scripturae Interpres*, by

---

[34] Lagrée. 'Sens et verité', 84–7; Walther, 'Biblische Hermeneutik', 274–5.

[35] Walther, 'Biblische Hermeneutik', 244–5; Macherey, *Avec Spinoza*, 169–70.

[36] Wolzogen, *De Scripturarum Interprete*, 274; Van der Wall, *Mystieke Chiliast*, 468.

[37] Ibid., 470–4.   [38] *Philopater*, 126.

[39] Loescher, *Praenotiones*, 153–5; Wolf, *Bibliotheca Hebraea*, iv, 796; Trinius, *Freydenker-Lexicon*, 360–2, 421; Hartmann, *Anleitung*, 150.

many wrongly ascribed to Spinoza, his friend; the theologians of Holland bestirred themselves and their written attacks on this book gave rise to great disputes among them.'[40]

The book indeed provoked general revulsion, especially among the Reformed consistories and preachers' district assemblies, or *classes*. On 24 July 1666 the *classis* Haarlem debated the problem of 'licentious books', specifying the *Philosophia* as the single most offensive and pernicious then circulating. Extracts were read out to the assembly by its *visitatores librorum*. It was agreed to raise the matter urgently at the forthcoming gathering of the North Holland Synod so that it should be apparent there how completely this book was filled with 'godlessness and blasphemy'.[41] At Leiden the book was formally condemned by both Cocceius and Wittichius in the name of the theology faculty.[42] In Friesland there was a considerable outcry led by Johannes van der Waeyen (1639–1701), later a prominent Cocceian but then still Voetian. The theologians of Friesland complained to the standing committee of the provincial States with the result that, late in 1666, Friesland became the first Dutch province formally to suppress a text produced by the Amsterdam Spinozist coterie.[43]

In Utrecht the response was no less agitated, the Reformed consistory urging the city burgomasters and, through them, in December 1666, the States of Utrecht, to follow the 'praiseworthy' example of Friesland and prohibit so despicable a work in their province too.[44] The burgomasters asked for the most 'atrocious' passages to be collected in files, which were circulated among the city regents and the provincial States. In this way, virtually the entire regent and the noble élite of Utrecht studied the more offensive of Meyer's formulations.[45] Nor did they disagree with the preachers that the work was subversive and intolerable. The States of Utrecht, the consistory heard on 18 March 1667, had duly instructed the magistracies throughout the province to seize all copies from bookshops and prevent its further sale, since the book 'violates the placards of the States General, and this province, against all Socinian and similar writings'.[46] As yet there was no province-wide ban in Holland, but the book was certainly seized from the bookshops in individual towns, and a general pressure was kept up by the consistories for a formal provincial prohibition. Thus, at the time of the French invasion, in June 1672, the consistory and *classis* of Haarlem identified four books as being especially appalling, 'soul-destroying', and apt for vigorous suppression, namely Spinoza's *Tractatus*, Hobbes' *Leviathan*, the *Bibliotheca Fratrum Polonorum*, and the 'fameus boeck *Philosophia Scripturae Interpres*'.[47]

At Amsterdam, meanwhile, some of the liveliest reaction was among the Collegiants, Rieuwertsz' own milieu, where Meyer himself, like Spinoza and the brothers Koerbagh, had numerous acquaintances. In the Dutch version Meyer speaks con-

---

[40] Leibniz, *Theodicy*, 82; Lagrée and Moreau, 'Introduction', 4.

[41] RNH Classis Haarlem VII, acta classis res. 24 July 1666.   [42] Leydekker, *Verder vervolg*, 6–7.

[43] Knuttel, *Verboden boeken*, 117.   [44] GA Utrecht Acta Kerkeraad vii. res. 24 dec. 1666.

[45] Ibid., res. 31 Dec. 1666 and 4 Feb. 1667.   [46] Ibid., res. 18 Mar. 1667.

[47] RNH classis Haarlem vii. acta classis, res. 14 June 1672; RNH classis Alkmaar, acta classis res. 19 July 1672.

temptuously of the public Church whose 'fortresses' his arguments had, like a conquering army, 'stormed and devastated',[48] but more respectfully of the Socinian and anti-Trinitarian fringe whom he—albeit carefully differentiating his philosophical from their theological stance[49]—summons to join him as friends in an unbreakable alliance against the common foe. None the less, Meyer chides them for their unwillingness to interpret Scripture wholly in accordance with 'reason', their invoking the Holy Ghost to assist and enlighten them, so that they too languish in confusion and theological strife of their own making. What Socinians and such Remonstrants as truly revere the memory of Episcopius should do, he urges, is follow him in making philosophy the sole and 'infallible measure' of Scripture.[50] Meyer adamantly denies there is any divine inspiration, or 'inner light', distinct from the 'natural light of reason', to aid man in this quest.[51]

For years the Collegiants had been subject to growing friction within their own ranks between their rationalizing, avowedly Socinian, and more conservative, Trinitarian wings, and while the latter reacted to Meyer's call indignantly, and the former more sympathetically, his intervention could only exacerbate their dissension.[52] Meyer declares philosophy the sole criterion of truth, proclaiming whatever contradicts the judgements of 'the true philosophy' misleading and false. To some extent Collegiants of all hues were bound to protest. The Anabaptist Messianist Jan Pietersz Beelthouwer (c.1603–c.1669), who in discussion had learnt to admire Spinoza's as yet generally still unknown exegetical principles, nevertheless emphatically rejected Meyer's contention that the Biblical prophecies are unclear and ambiguous, and his insinuation that the divine spirit does not infuse Scripture.[53] Ironically, Beelthouwer even invokes 'the most learned Spinoza' against the *Philosophia*, suggesting, as does other evidence, that Spinoza had been and remained extremely discreet and cautious in discussions and in his dealings with the Collegiants.

Meyer was assailed much more vehemently by another Collegiant acquaintance of Spinoza, the Millenarian Spiritualist Petrus Serrarius (1600–69), who presumably knew the identity of his antagonist. Being a firm anti-Socinian, Serrarius was profoundly disconcerted by a book which he nevertheless recognized to be of immense signficance.[54] In January 1667 he wrote to his close ally in spiritual matters, the Scots Millenarian and anti-Cartesian, John Dury, then in Basel, informing him of the uproar in the Netherlands over the *Philosophia*. Dury took the matter with due seriousness, losing no time in communicating this dramatic news to other friends, notably Switzerland's foremost Bible exegete at the time, Johann Heinrich Heidegger, at Zürich. No sooner had his impassioned tract against the *Philosophia* appeared than Serrarius dispatched copies to Basel, several of which Dury posted on to Zürich.

---

[48] [Meyer], *Philosophie d'Uytleghster*, 113.
[49] Ibid., Scholder, *Birth*, 135–6; Bordoli, *Ragione e scrittura*, 411.
[50] [Meyer], *Philosophie d'Uytleghster*, 119–26; Thijssen-Schoute, *Nederlands Cartesianisme*, 398.
[51] [Meyer], *Philosophie d'Uytleghster*, 122–3; Klever, *Mannen rond Spinoza*, 78.
[52] Zilverberg, 'Jan Pietersz Beelthouwer', 163–5; Van Bunge, *Johannes Bredenburg*, 106–7.
[53] Beelthouwer, *Antwoordt*, 21–3, 127; Bordoli, *Ragione e scrittura*, 246–56.
[54] Van der Wall, *Mystieke Chiliast*, 468–72.

Serrarius expends all his spiritual fervour against the bid to enthrone philosophy in place of divine inspiration and the Holy Ghost. Clothing his admonitions in impressive Biblical and Millenarian imagery, he proclaimed the limitations of any philosophy, and Cartesianism in particular. Granting Descartes' excellence in mathematics, he flatly denied that his mechanistic conception of the world is the key to truth physical and spiritual.[55] Whatever the *Philosophia* claims, the true meaning of Scripture, he insists, is grasped only through the 'inner light' and the guidance of the Holy Ghost.[56] To mistake philosophy for divine wisdom, 'natural light for the divine light, what is innate in man for what is received from God', he urges, is idolatry; for whoever takes that path prefers philosophy to Christ. He likens Cartesianism to the adulterous woman in Proverbs 7 who dares not show herself in broad daylight, which he interprets as the blessed age of the early Church. Only now, as dusk falls, in our corrupt era, does philosophy reveal herself and go out, like a harlot, to tempt men. Superficially, she is alluring. For who does not love philosophy, the love of wisdom? But underneath, she is a brazen whore. Has she not seduced the writer of the *Philosophia*, who runs after her like an ox to the slaughter-house? Has she not lured him from the family of the Lamb of God to bow before the new Golden Calf of reason?[57]

iii. The Wolzogen Disputes

The commotion entered a new phase with the publication in 1668 of a 274-page critique of Meyer's *Philosophia*, entitled *De Scripturarum Interprete*, by the liberal Calvinist professor Louis Wolzogen (1633–90). This work, accounted by Leibniz the principal 'Cartesian' reply to Meyer,[58] a copy of which graced Spinoza's own tiny library,[59] provoked extraordinary acrimony on all sides, markedly aggravating the antagonism between the vying ideological blocs within the Reformed Church by further pitting the Cartesio-Cocceians against the Voetians over the true method of interpreting Scripture and the relationship of philosophy to theology.[60] If virtually all Dutch theologians considered the *Philosophia*, noted Bayle later in his *Dictionnaire*, 'pernicieux et pis que Socinien', such was the outcry against Wolzogen 'que l'on cria contre sa réfutation autant ou plus que contre le livre même qu'il réfutoit'.[61]

Born to a family of Austrian Calvinist refugees in the same year as Spinoza, Wolzogen acquired excellent French studying at the Reformed academies of Saumur and Geneva. Subsequently he became a preacher with the French-speaking Reformed Church, first at Groningen, then Middelburg and, from 1664, Utrecht, where he doubled as a university professor. A veteran of the 'collège des sçavants', a noted Cartesian discussion group in Utrecht, headed by Frans Burman and including Velthuysen,

---

[55] Serrarius, *Responsio*, 14; Van der Wall, *Mystieke Chiliast*, 475.

[56] Fix, *Prophecy and Reason*, 173; Bordoli, *Ragione e scrittura*, 265.

[57] Serrarius, *Responsio*, 55.   [58] Leibniz, *Theodicy*, 82.   [59] Servaas van Rooijen, *Inventaire*, 191.

[60] Mastricht, *Novitatum Cartesianarum Gangraena*, 104–7, 116–24; Leydekker, *Verder vervolg*, 9–10; Hartmann, *Anleitung*, 150–1.

[61] Bayle, *Dictionnaire*, iii, 2582; Weekhout, *Boekencensuur*, 157–8, 311–16.

Graevius, and Mansvelt, Wolzogen, who apparently knew Meyer well,[62] was judged by his detractors altogether too worldly for a preacher, sporting as he did a powdered wig and indulging in profane amusements such as playing cards.[63] He avidly followed the latest intellectual debates. Moreover his library, auctioned in Amsterdam after his death, included numerous heterodox theological and philosophical works, such as La Peyrère's *Praeadamitae* and Spinoza's *Opera Posthuma*, as well as De la Court, Beverland, Van Dale, Bekker, and Aubert de Versé.[64]

The furore into which Wolzogen plunged in 1668 profoundly affected the whole of the rest of his life. The aim of his *De Scripturarum Interprete*, which appeared with approbations from the university curators and Utrecht city government, is clearly to segregate the legitimate use of reason in Bible hermeneutics from the illicit subordination of Holy Writ to philosophy advocated by the *Philosophia*.[65] Above all, his goal is to rescue Cartesio-Coccceian exegetical methods from the disastrous association with the *Philosophia* which the Voetians were doing their utmost to affirm. If the *Philosophia*'s arguments were to prevail, he agrees, then theology and ecclesiastical authority would collapse.[66] But his efforts to demonstrate a wide gulf between the respective positions of the *Philosophia* and the Cartesio-Cocceians landed him in a morass of difficulties, not least with regard to the troublesome issue of Socinianism. Although he denounces Socinianism, as anyone in his position had to do, he nevertheless held that the Socinians were right to eschew Biblical interpretations which conflict with reason, claiming that Socinian views resembled those of the *Philosophia* far less than the latter claimed.[67] 'Reason', he contends, cannot conflict with God's Word as revealed in Scripture and is essential to construing Scripture correctly.[68] His problem was that, while purporting to repudiate the *Philosophia*, he actually approximates to Meyer in several respects, in particular, entirely agreeing with his cardinal principle that philosophical truth cannot be contrary to theological truth.[69]

Wolzogen argued that reason should prevail in theology and Bible exegesis, but subject always to two indispensable provisos: first, one must only admit as 'natural truths' in theology propositions demonstrated by philosophy and science beyond all doubt, and secondly, one must exclude from truths identical in theology and philosophy the central 'mysteries' of the Christian religion which, by definition, transcend our reason.[70] Both the *Philosophia* and the Socinians violate these fundamental rules, he held, and are therefore greatly at fault. None the less the Socinians, he argued, err less reprehensibly than the *Philosophia*; for there remains a vast gulf between advocat-

---

[62] Bordoli, *Ragione e scrittura*, 289.

[63] Thijssen-Schoute, *Nederlands Cartesianisme*, 444–7; Kolakowski, *Chrétiens sans église*, 750.

[64] [Wolzogen], *Catalogus*, 11–12, 19–20, 30.

[65] Wolzogen, *De Scripturarum Interprete*, 221–6; Foersthius, *Selectorum Theologicorum Breviarium*, 32; Bayle, *Dictionnaire*, iii, 2582.

[66] Wolzogen, *De Scriptuarum Interprete*, 225–6.   [67] *Lettres sur la vie . . . de Louis de Wolzogue*, 44–5.

[68] Ibid.; Ryssenius, *Oude rechtsinnige Waerheyt*, 13, 20; Mastricht, *Novitatum Cartesianarum Gangraena*, 56, 61, 75; Benedetti, *Difesa della terza lettera*, 244, 278.

[69] [Meyer], *Philosophia*, 57.

[70] Thijssen-Schoute, *Nederlands Cartesianisme*, 448; Bordoli, *Ragione e scrittura*, 304–6.

ing the total subordination of Scripture to 'philosophy', like the *Philosophia*, and eschewing interpretation which contradicts reason, while otherwise explaining Scripture from Scripture, showing considerable reverence for the sacred text, as the Socinians do.[71]

While Wolzogen sincerely attacked the *Philosophia* for subordinating the Christian mysteries to philosophical criteria, his book nevertheless antagonized innumerable theologians for conceding too much ground to 'reason' and virtually vindicating the Socinians.[72] Wolzogen faced a hail of criticism from every part of the United Provinces for propounding errors not far removed from those he purported to refute, some of his assailants even suggesting he was in secret league with the writer of the *Philosophia*.[73] At Utrecht his assailants included Voetius and Essenius, in Zeeland Georgius de Raed, in States Brabant the most eminent professor of the high school at 's-Hertogenbosch, Reinier Vogelsang (*c*.1610–79), and in Friesland Van der Waeyen.[74] Furthermore, he was fiercely attacked within his own Walloon community by two strictly orthodox Calvinist preachers, Jean de Labadie and Pierre Yvon, at Middelburg.[75] A judgement produced by hostile colleagues at Deventer and published by his foes at Middelburg in 1669 accused Wolzogen of barely disguised Socinian tendencies.[76]

Wolzogen fought back tenaciously, and if his adversaries were many, and drawn from a broad theological spectrum, he also had formidable friends, who stood to lose much themselves should he be crushed and therefore came to his aid, selectively supporting his arguments and vouching for his orthodoxy. The exegetical methods and basic premises of the Cartesio-Cocceians, an entire intellectual current within the public Church and universities, were in the dock.[77] Hence Cocceius himself, Wittichius, Heidanus, Burman, and, in Friesland, the redoubtable Balthasar Bekker, all rallied to Wolzogen's side. Bekker wrote from Franeker in March 1669, responding to Wolzogen's pleas for help, assuring him he had read his treatise through twice, thoroughly approved his views and, furthermore, was convinced 'God will aid you in the future in persevering with as much courage and steadfastness as you have hitherto.'[78] It was a display of resolve under theological fire that Bekker himself would have occasion to recall in still more embattled circumstances over twenty years later.

Among other consequences, the Wolzogen furore provoked a major split within the Walloon Church, as became painfully clear at its synod at Naarden in 1669.[79] Fortunately for Wolzogen, Labadie's ultra-orthodox rigour and bullying tactics alienated much of the middle ground, enabling the Cartesio-Cocceians to snatch victory from the jaws of defeat. Wolzogen's orthdoxy as a Reformed minister was narrowly upheld, an outcome Labadie and his adherents strove to overturn at the next annual

---

[71] Wolzogen, *De Scripturarum Interprete*, 221, 225–6.   [72] Leibniz, *Theodicy*, 82.

[73] Vogelsang, *Contra libellum*, 186–9; Leydekker, *Verder Vervolg*, 9; Van Bunge, *Johannes Bredenburg*, 108.

[74] *Advisen van sommige theologanten van Utrecht*, 3–6; Sassen, *Wijsgerig onderwijs*, 49–56.

[75] *Lettres sur la vie . . . de Louis de Wolzogue*, 11; Leibniz, *Theodicy*, 82.

[76] *Oordeel van eenige theologanten tot Deventer*, 10–11, 24.   [77] Hartmann, *Anleitung*, 150–1.

[78] *Lettres sur la vie . . . de Louis de Wolzogue*, 132–7.

[79] *Récit véritable*, 18; Sassen, *Wijsgerig onderwijs*, 56.

gathering of the synod, at Dordrecht in March 1670. According to Labadie, Wolzogen's exegetical principles had been condemned by the universities of Utrecht, Franeker, and Harderwijk, and the high school at 's-Hertogenbosch, and should be forbidden by the Walloon Church. Wolzogen's adherents argued that only certain professors at those institutions had denounced his views, not those academies as such.[80] It was put to the vote. Again Wolzogen narrowly survived.

iv. The 'New Religion' of Philosophy

Where Wolzogen and his critics agreed was in classifying the *Philosophia* as something fundamentally new and revolutionary in the world of ideas and religion. With unprecedented boldness, it advocated nothing less than the total dissolution of theology and the hegemony in human affairs of the 'new system of philosophy'. In the Dutch text, Meyer says slightly more about this 'new system' than in the original Latin, explaining that it had been introduced first by Descartes but had now been modified, improved, and broadened 'by others who wish to follow in his footsteps and bring into the light the issues of God, the rational soul, man's highest happiness, and other such things'.[81] Most readers doubtless found this sweeping but vague contention thoroughly exasperating, but to the handful of initiates it was plain that Meyer was alluding to himself, Van den Enden, the brothers Koerbagh, Bouwmeester, and especially Spinoza.[82] In the thought-world of the *Philosophia*, philosophical principles as developed by these—to the public still largely unknown—men, and not the doctrines of the Churches and universities constituted ultimate and supreme truth.

Assuredly, few readers at the time grasped Meyer's meaning, or the full scope of his intellectual, educational, social, and political agenda. Nevertheless, there was a widespread feeling that the *Philosophia* represented more than just an outrageous assault on authority and religion, a realization that it was part of something wider and, if largely submerged for the moment, ultimately still more menacing, a suspicion strengthened, with the publication in January 1670 of the *Tractatus Theologico-Politicus*. Here, Spinoza claims that only those who fail to see the basic distinction between theology and philosophy dispute which prevails over the other.[83] Where the *Philosophia* insists that theology must be reduced to philosophy, Spinoza professes to assert —complying with the States of Holland edict of 1656—the complete separation of theology and philosophy: 'neither is theology dependent on reason, nor reason on theology.'[84] But few contemporaries were deceived by what was really just a tactical ploy. In Spinoza, theology is assigned a social function but no part in revealing the truth about Man, God, and the world.[85] Only philosophy can do that. By asserting, like

---

[80] *Récit véritable*, 11, 19, 42.

[81] [Meyer], *Philosophie d'Uytleghster*, 136; Beeldthouwer, *Antwoordt*, 10–13.

[82] Thijssen-Schoute, 'Lodewijk Meyer', 15–16; Van Bunge, *Johannes Bredenburg*, 108–9.

[83] Spinoza, *TTP*, 228.

[84] Ibid., 228–36; Yvon, *L'Impiété convaincue*, 362; however, some modern commentators take Spinoza at face value here; see Hubbeling, *Leven en werk*, 44; Thijssen-Schoute, 'Lodewijk Meyer', 16.

[85] Yvon, *L'Impiété convaincue*, 212, 400.

Meyer, that Scripture is full of obscurity, that the Hebrew wording is uncertain, and its vowels and accents were added later, that Biblical prophecy is nothing but the result of an overactive imagination,[86] that the prophets held contradictory beliefs and prejudices and agree only in the sphere of moral ideas, and finally, that the language of Scripture 'was adapted to the understanding and preconceived beliefs of the common people', Spinoza subverted theology, merging it with philosophy just as comprehensively as Meyer.

When, therefore, Spinoza concludes his chapter on the separation of theology and philosophy by deploring the 'absurdities, disruption and harm that have resulted from the fact men have thoroughly confused these two branches, failing to distinguish correctly between them, separating one from the other',[87] he is not in fact upholding the separation of spheres introduced by De Witt and the Cartesio-Cocceian camp. Rather he totally subverts theology's autonomy, eliminating its role in teaching men truth and the path to salvation. Hence, for both Spinoza and the *Philosophia*, 'the true method of interpreting Scripture,' as he expresses it in his famous maxim, 'does not differ at all from the method of interpreting nature but rather precisely accords with it.'[88] In other words, true theology is philosophy and, despite significant differences in method and argumentation, the final conclusions of Spinoza and Meyer, equating true theology with the sound conclusions of philosophy and science, are broadly the same. Both writers agree that Scripture is a man-made, not a God-given, text, that truth lies in philosophy alone, and that theological acrimony damages society, is pointless, and should be avoided.

A further effect of the strife over the *Philosophia* was that a key middle group of Reformed theologians, led by the Huguenot professor Samuel Maresius (Des Marets) (1599–1673) at Groningen, who, mindful of the threat to the unity of the public Church, had previously steered a middle course between the Cartesio-Cocceian and traditionalist camps, were now so disconcerted that they repudiated their earlier provisionally favourable view of Cartesianism.[89] Appalled by the *Philosophia*, in 1667 Maresius staged a series of disputations among his students, designed to demolish its arguments. Convinced that Cartesianism itself was the source of the venom, by 1669 he was fully committed to the anti-Cartesian drive in the Netherlands and was using his appreciable influence in Switzerland to stiffen the anti-Cartesian campaign also in progress there.[90] He then published his critique in 1670, under the title *De Abusu Philosophiae Cartesianae* (Concerning the Abuse of the Cartesian Philosophy), a book which did much to shift the emphasis in the European debate about Cartesianism away from Descartes' system to its radical offshoots which, according to Maresius, were from the outset inherent in it.

---

[86] Spinoza, *TTP*, 71–2, 233; Heidegger, *Exercitationes*, 304–6.   [87] Spinoza, *TTP*, 236.

[88] 'Dico methodum interpretandi Scripturam haud differre a methodo interpretandi naturam, sed cum ea prorsus convenire', Spinoza, *Opera*, iii, 98; Lagrée, 'Thème des deux livres', 9–10, 36–7; Klever, *Mannen rond Spinoza*, 79–80.

[89] Van der Wall, 'The *Tractatus*', 208–9; De Mowbray, 'Libertas', 45.

[90] Hoiningen-Huene, *Beiträge*, 35–6.

Fiercely critical of Wittichius, Heidanus, Burman, and Mansvelt, as well as Wolzogen, Maresius roundly blamed the Cartesians and their Cocceian allies for the mounting turmoil engulfing theological studies and the entire Reformed Church in Germany, Switzerland, and elsewhere, as well as the Netherlands, though he claimed that the Swiss Reformed Church was proving more successful than its counterpart in the Netherlands in checking the ferment.[91] The writer of the *Philosophia*, he grants, by wholly subordinating theology and Scripture to philosophy, had ventured far beyond Descartes and the academic Cartesians.[92] This clandestine author and his like were *pseudo-Cartesiani*, 'abusing' the New Philosophy, whom any reasonable observer should differentiate from *genuini Cartesiani*.[93] Yet it was too easy for the Cartesians simply to disown those perverting their master's system as dangerous delinquents for whom they were not responsible. For the insidious seeds, he alleged, lie deep in Cartesianism itself, the beginnings of the tendency to erode Scripture's authority and theology's supremacy being clearly discernible in the writings of Wittichius, Burman, Wolzogen, and their following, and not least in the corrosive effect of Cartesian philosophy on belief in angels and demons.[94]

The Cartesio-Cocceians had to reply, their chosen spokesmen being Wittichius and especially the author of a series of pamphlets lambasting Maresius and his supporters under the pseudonym 'Petrus van Andlo', a polemicist later identified by Bayle, among others, as the Utrecht professor, admirer of Wittichius, and writer of a long refutation of Spinoza, Regnerus van Mansvelt (1639–71).[95] 'Van Andlo' ridiculed Maresius' new stance, and public *rapprochement* with his old enemy Voetius, claiming the Cartesianism taught in the Dutch academies, so irresponsibly disparaged by Maresius at Groningen, was in fact the only means to overcome the atheistic threat and shore up the authority of Holy Writ and the Reformed Church, including belief in angels and demons.

Shaken by Van Andlo's counterblast, Maresius dashed off a 67-page 'vindication of his dissertation', claiming that he was not trying to discredit all Cartesians as Van Andlo charged, but simply to curb the abuse of Cartesian principles in theology.[96] This tract, appearing at Groningen late in 1670, reveals that Maresius had been making enquiries to uncover the intellectual background of the *Philosophia* and the *Tractatus Theologico-Politicus*. The latter, he had discovered, was penned by 'Spinoza, ex-Jew, blasphemer and formal atheist', whose atrocious views, Van Andlo notwithstanding, stem from Cartesianism and constitute as dire a threat to the Christian faith as had ever been known.[97] That Maresius closely followed the intricacies of the controversy over the *Philosophia* was also reflected in his own library which, when auctioned after his death, included almost everything published concerning the *Philosophia*, Wolzo-

---

[91] Maresius, *De Abusu*, praefatio, 25–7, 40.   [92] Ibid., 77.   [93] Sturm, *De Cartesianis*, 13–15.

[94] Maresius, *De Abusu*, 62–3, 77; Thijssen-Schoute, *Nederlands Cartesianisme*, 481; Van Bunge, *Johannes Bredenburg*, 103–4.

[95] Jöcher, *Allgemeines Gelehrten Lexicon*, ii, 378–9; Nauta, *Samuel Maresius*, 363–4; Scholder, *Birth*, 174.

[96] Otto, *Studien*, 17.   [97] Maresius, *Vindiciae Dissertationis suae*, 4.

gen, and the *Tractatus*.[98] Nothing is more pernicious than Spinoza's Bible criticism, held Maresius, insisting that its principles are derived directly from Cartesianism, albeit spiced with Machiavelli and Hobbes.[99] Van Andlo and his friends disclaim responsibility; but was it not they who first began the campaign for 'freedom to philosophize', arrogantly disregarding the strictures of the academic senates and guidelines fixed by the provincial States, with the consequence that there was now such excessive 'freedom to philosophize' that the very foundations of authority and orthodoxy were daily crumbling?[100] Van Andlo purports to defend Cartesianism, but he seems, suggested Maresius, with his unyielding advocacy of philosophy, 'rather a disciple of Spinoza than an adherent of Descartes'.[101]

Mansvelt retorted angrily with his 72-page 'observations' on Maresius' 'vindication', published at Leiden early in 1671. Contesting Maresius' charge that Cartesianism undermines belief in angels, demonstrating the soundness of Cartesianism regarding all Biblical categories of spirits and demons, he assured readers that, far from being a crypto-Spinozist mascarading as a 'Cartesian', he had never spoken to Spinoza, or even seen him, and utterly detested his 'absurd doctrines'.[102] Maresius replied again in a pamphlet entitled *Clypeus Orthodoxiae*, where he alludes to new enquiries intended to unmask this mysterious 'Petrus van Andlo' who, without provocation, had so shamefully attacked him. He had failed to identify the culprit but assured readers that 'he is no member of the Reformed Church but belongs to the same circle as the anonymous writer of the *Philosophia* . . . if indeed he and the latter are not one and the same.'[103] Van Andlo's purpose, he surmised, in thus widening the furore over the *Philosophia*, was to inflame passions sufficiently to precipitate a schism among the well-intentioned and thereby advance the cause of his 'Socinianism or Libertinism'.[104]

Maresius depicts the intellectual predicament of the Reformed Church and universities in the direst terms. Academic life in the Netherlands, he held, was seething with detestable 'doctrines unheard of hitherto until today', and saturated with libertinism and 'indifferentism', which had surged up with unprecedented force since the advent of Cartesianism in the middle of the century. These evil impulses had then gained fresh momentum from the *Philosophia*, which Marsius did not believe was by Spinoza but someone else, and still more, from the *Tractatus Theologico-Politicus*. Spinoza was openly challenging Christ's Church, promoting libertinism and undermining all authority, and doing so by building on the pernicious principles of Descartes and Hobbes.[105] Spinoza was leading the attack. But it was, held Maresius, Cartesianism which had sapped the Church's defences and opened the gates, enabling Spinoza to mount so appalling a threat. Moreover, even now, with the danger clearly manifest, the Cartesians continued to erode the authority of Holy Writ instead of springing to its defence. God, affirms the sacred text, commanded the sun and the moon to stand still in the sky so that Joshua could finish his battle, 'You maintain', he admonished his

---

[98] [Maresius], *Catalogus librorum*, 10–15, 20–1, 24, 27. [99] Maresius, *Vindiciae Dissertationis suae*, 4.
[100] Ibid., 6. [101] Ibid., 7.
[102] [Mansvelt], 'Van Andlo', *Animadversiones*, 7; Van Bunge, *Johannes Bredenburg*, 148–9.
[103] Maresius, *Clypeus Orthodoxiae*, preface. [104] Ibid. [105] Ibid., 10.

opponents, that this passage of Scripture conflicts with 'your clear and distinct philosophical concepts' and is not to be believed literally. But how will your 'philosophy' save you when the writer of the *Philosophia* resumes his wicked campaign, invoking Descartes' principles against the core mysteries of the Christian faith?[106]

A notable feature of the Maresius–Mansvelt exchange is the awareness it shows that the *Philosophia* and *Tractatus* were penned by different authors, but writers connected and part of the same philosophical underground.[107] This was also grasped by others, including observers abroad who, like Leibniz, realized that the controversies surrounding the *Philosophia* were something new and of profound significance for all Europe, some of whom, indeed, had personal knowledge of the clandestine philosophical coterie in the Netherlands which was beginning to exert so powerful an influence on the wider European scene. Among these was the Danish ex-scientist, Nicholas Steno, who probably knew Meyer as well as Spinoza and, in a pamphlet published at Florence in 1675, claimed that the turmoil in Protestant lands generated by the *Philosophia*, and the Wolzogen disputes, proved that Protestantism, with its misconceived summons to base theology on Scripture alone, ultimately produces nothing but the gravest confusion and perplexity. Only the Church of Rome, he held, can provide veritable spiritual guidance and reveal the true path to salvation.[108]

v. The *Philosophia* in England

In England too there were reverberations from the furore over the *Philosophia*. At Oxford, and especially among the so-called Cambridge Platonists, elements of the academic community were in touch, often via Locke's future friend, Limborch, with developments in the Netherlands. Other dons, and also the occasional erudite parish clergyman, simply pieced together what was happening by perusing recent foreign theological literature published in Latin. Unquestionably, the foremost English response to the *Philosophia* was that of a Puritan clergyman deprived of his living by the Crown in 1662, the Cambridge-educated John Wilson,[109] in his *The Scriptures Genuine Interpreter*, published in London in 1678. Appalled by the arguments of Wolzogen, who, 'having', as he put it, 'undertaken the patronage of the Protestant cause against this adversary [i.e. the *Philosophia*] doth so shamefully throw down his arms and run out of the field,'[110] Wilson had decided to enter the fray himself. He took up his pen, he explains in his preface, aware from the 'publisht writings of some reverend divines abroad what mischief this discourse, and some others, whose publication it occasioned, have already done in the Netherlands; so I am not without just fears, that those unfounded notions and corrupt principles that are, by this means, scattered abroad, may be quickly (if they be not already) propagated amongst our selves'.[111]

From his reading, Wilson perceived that the 'whole design of the [*Philosophia*], and

---

[106] Maresius, *Clypeus Orthodoxiae*, 11, 13.   [107] Van der Wall, 'The *Tractatus*', 209.
[108] Steno, *Ad virum Eruditum*, 3, 6, 12.
[109] According to Venn, John Wilson studied at Saint Catharine's College, Cambridge, for most of the 1630s and was Vicar of Kimpton, Hertfordshire, during the years 1657–62; see Venn, *Alumni*, iv, 429.
[110] Wilson, *Scriptures Genuine Interpreter*, 134.   [111] Ibid.

of that other tract that is prefixed to its latter edition (written, as is supposed, by the same author) is utterly to undermine and overthrow the credit of the Scriptures'.[112] It is plain, he adds, the *Philosophia* deems the Bible 'of no use to instruct us in any thing we know not, nor yet to confirm us in what we know', since 'all the use he allows it is only this, that by reading therein we may be occasion'd and excited to consider of the things there treated of, and examine the truth of them by philosophy: and as much as this might be said of the Jews' *Talmud*, or the Turks' *Alcoran*.'[113] The *Philosophia* professes to offer the means to solve all the difficulties of theology. But whence comes this strange notion, demands Wilson, that such questions can be resolved by philosophy? 'I have indeed oft wonder'd what should betray any to this fond and irrational conceit of resolving the agonies of distress'd consciences,' he remarks, 'till I met with a piece of new divinity in a late Belgick tractator'—referring here expressly to the *Tractatus Theologico-Politicus*—'and then I began to suspect out of what chimney came all this smoke.'[114] The central contention of the *Tractatus*, he says, is the idea that the prophetic revelations issue from the 'imagination', that the 'Prophets in their narrations, and in all matters of speculation (that is whatsoever was not matter of moral duty) did disagree among themselves; and consequently that what is said by one, is not to be explained by the words of another,' an assertion 'which (with other passages of like import) does at once call in question the whole truth and consequently the divine authority of the Scriptures.'[115]

This was an exceedingly worrying new development. 'The Belgick Exercitator,' asserts Wilson, 'rises higher in denying the Scriptures perspicuity, than any that I have ever met with: and with confidence affirms the Scripture to be universally obscure, and that no part of it is, of itself, clear and plain; and therefore denies, that one part of Scripture can be expounded by another.'[116] But what lies behind such abominable blasphemy? 'Whose design it is that the author of that Theologico-Political Tractat drives, except that of the great enemy of mankind, I know not: but he sufficiently manifests a vile esteem of the Holy Scriptures, and a desire to beget the like in others: for he takes very earnest pains with the utmost of his art and skill, to rake up and exagitate their seeming disagreements, as real contradictions, casting a great deal of scorn upon all expositors, as fools or madmen, that attempt to reconcile them.'[117] It is not easy, remarks Wilson, to classify this new menace. The 'Belgick tractator', he thought, discourses 'in this and sundry other odious passages, which I abhor to mention', in a way which 'doth apparently tend to promote the cause of the Antiscripturalists, besides the help it affords (which is not a little) to the Romish interest'; admittedly, grants Wilson, he 'would seem, by some expressions here and there, to intimate his dislike of the Pontifician party', but 'we know it is consistent enough with the politick principles of men of that way, to speak much more than he hath done, against that very cause that they are studiously projecting.'[118]

But while the 'Belgick tractator' was indeed, as Wilson supposed, the 'chimney'

---

[112] Ibid., 256.   [113] Ibid.   [114] Wilson, *An Appendix*, 52.
[115] Wilson, *Scriptures Genuine Interpreter*, 245.   [116] Ibid., 178.   [117] Ibid., 246.
[118] Ibid., 246–7.

from which the *Philosophia*'s smoke emanated, there were still vital parts of the puzzle missing. In particular, demands Wilson, 'where is that philosophy that the Exercitator [of the *Philosophia*] cryes up for so certain and infallible? Where is it? In the clouds? Sure it never was extant among men, save in the crazy conceits of some self-admirers.'[119] It may be the *Philosophia*'s 'grand design . . . utterly to cashier the Scripture as useless and unprofitable' and put in its place philosophy and the principles of reason, claiming these are 'undoubtedly true, free from danger of error, and therefore cannot deceive, being grounded upon unmoveable foundations' but 'as I said before, where is this philosophy to be found?'[120]

Aside from the system of Descartes which the Exercitator says has been superceded, Wilson detects few real indications other than the *Philosophia*'s rebuttal of the doctrine of Creation out of nothing, affirming the principle *ex nihilo nihil fit* (nothing is made from nothing).[121] Arguing thus, avers Wilson, 'he must necessarily maintain the eternity of preexistent matter.'[122] Yet, plainly, the Exercitator contemptuously rejects Aristotle's philosophy.[123] In all likelihood, infers Wilson, the underlying principles are nothing but intellectual confusion and chaos dressed up to appear rational by dint of sheer effrontery. The Exercitator pretends the new philosophical method of Bible interpretation 'being sure and infallible, will, if it be taken, forthwith banish all disputes about the sense of the Scriptures, and thereby restore peace to the Christian world. But I wonder how this should be effected by philosophy, which is itself so full of disputes, and the professors whereof are at such variance among themselves. Let them first reconcile their own differences before they undertake so great an enterprise elsewhere.'[124]

Ultimately, concludes Wilson, the author of the *Philosophia* offers no help at all to mankind. His arguments are so feeble that 'I cannot but wonder at his confidence. But he who hath no better weapons, must fight with a bull-rush. And it is now become the mode of polemick writers that have prurient wits, to sharpen their dull arguments with high confidence in themselves, and a proud contempt of their antagonists: in both which this author excels; but it is such an excellency, for which no wise or sober man will envy him.'[125] The danger was a real one, but one that could be readily defeated by means of solid, careful argument. Wilson ends with the pious hope that theological tracts such as his own would 'effectually vindicate the Scriptures, this Blessed Book, from the scorns and reproaches of atheists and Antiscripturalists'.[126]

vi. German and Scandinavian Reverberations

If in Italy and England the furore surrounding the *Philosophia* did not go unnoticed, in Germany and the Baltic it was regularly cited, over many decades, by anti-Cartesian

---

[119] Ibid., 96: Wilson notes in the margin, citing Van Velthuysen's *De usu rationis in theologia* 'and which another author of like principles does with profane boldness, magnifie as equal to the Holy Scripture for its compleat perfection and infallible certainty'.
[120] Wilson, *Scriptures Genuine Interpreter*, 104, 256.   [121] Ibid., 147–9; [Meyer], *Philosophia*, 59.
[122] Wilson, *Scriptures Genuine Interpreter*, 149.   [123] Ibid.; [Meyer], *Philosophie d'Uytleghster*, 48, 51.
[124] Wilson, *Scriptures Genuine Interpreter*, 254.   [125] Ibid., 252.   [126] Ibid., 263.

traditionalists as the culmination of a process by which the hidden but innate dangers of Cartesianism became manifest. For not only had the *Philosophia* invoked Descartes while claiming to supersede him but, as Leibniz puts it, many opponents 'held the opinion that the Cartesians, in confuting the anonymous philosopher, had conceded too much to philosophy'.[127] Thus, for example, a leading Lutheran authority, August Pfeiffer[128] at Lübeck, in his treatise on Bible hermeneutics, designates the *Philosophia* as the culmination of Cartesian arrogance and crassness, the point at which a total and irresolvable clash of theology and philosophy was revealed.[129]

The most influential of all late seventeenth-century academic attacks on Cartesianism in Germany and Scandinavia, the *Novitatum Cartesianarum Gangraena* (1677), written by Petrus van Mastricht whilst teaching at Duisburg in Cleves—albeit dedicated to William III and published in Amsterdam—reserves some of its most vehement passages for the *Philosophia* and the Wolzogen affair.[130] Its chief aim—ironically also one of Spinoza's objectives, advancing from the other side—is to ruin the project of Wittichius and his followers to reconcile theology and philosophy (including Galilean science) by means of Cartesianism. Unlike Maresius, but like Voetius, Mastricht judges Descartes' entire system, beginning with his procedural principle of 'universal doubt'—the 'primum Cartesianismi fundamentum'—a castrophe for mankind and the Reformed Church, which had destroyed the traditional role of philosophy as a handmaiden to theology and foisted the godless and arrogant 'magistracy' of philosophy on theology.[131] Everywhere one encountered furious disapproval of the *Philosophia*. But had not Wittichius, Velthuysen, Burman, and Wolzogen—Van Mastricht's four particular *bêtes noirs*—while not going as far as the author of that execrable text, or expressing themselves as impudently, nevertheless also, like him, proclaimed 'reason and philosophy' instead of Holy Writ the true and divine Revelation, the only source of absolute certainty?[132]

Mastricht considers the *Philosophia* and the writings of Spinoza, 'atheus quidem, sed Cartesianus' (an atheist certainly, but a Cartesian) the most dangerous and pernicious of all intellectual threats to mankind. By any reckoning Spinoza is the chief enemy.[133] But it is no use simply decrying Spinoza and the *Exercitator Paradoxus*, as he calls the writer of the *Philosophia*. For in reality there is no great gulf between Wittichius' and Wolzogen's methods of Bible exegesis and Spinoza's principle that Scripture speaks 'secundum erroneam vulgi opinionem' (according to the erroneous opinions of ordinary folk) or the Exercitator's contending 'philosophiam infallibilem esse Scripturae Interpretem' (philosophy to be the infallible interpreter of Scripture). In Mastricht the *Exercitator Paradoxus* is systematically deployed to flay the Cartesio-Cocceians. In his view, Wittichius, Velthuysen, Burman, and Wolzogen were pushing

---

[127] Leibniz, *Theodicy*, 82.

[128] August Pfeiffer (1640–98) was a noted expert in oriental languages and Bible exegesis. He was appointed to a chair at Wittenberg in 1659, but later became a senior ecclesiastic, rising to be Archdeacon of Saint Thomas' Church in Leipzig in 1681, and *Superintendens* at Lübeck from 1689.

[129] Pfeiffer, *Thesaurus Hermeneuticus*, 25.　　　[130] Scholder, *Birth*, 114, 120–5.

[131] Mastricht, *Novitatum Cartesianarum Gangraena*, 34.　　　[132] Ibid., 61.

[133] Ibid., 35, 38, 42–3, 48–9, 63, 70–3, 97.

the common people, indeed all of society, down the path to ruin, just like the *Exercitator paradoxus* and Spinoza, by devaluing belief in divine Providence and the divine inspiration of Scripture and, like them, undermining the people's faith in demons, angels, and other spirits, teaching the world that 'clear and distinct ideas' are the 'unica omnis veritatis norma' (the only criterion of all truth).[134] This is the same, he insists, as enslaving theology to philosophy.

Petrus van Mastricht was a Calvinist theologian. But in his capacity as a foremost critic of Cartesianism, neither Lutheran divines nor Catholic polemicists hesitated to adopt his arguments or quote his telling phrases. Thus the theology faculty at Uppsala adduced him as their principal authority in their efforts to persuade the Swedish Crown to condemn Cartesianism in 1687,[135] while the Neapolitan Jesuit, Benedetti, fulsomely approved of Mastricht's views, at least in this domain.[136] Michael Foertschius (1654–1724), dean of the Jena theology faculty, in his survey of the principal theological disputes of the age in 1708, identifies Mastricht as the most powerful reply to the 'abominable' *Philosophia*, Wolzogen, and Wittichius alike.[137]

Numerous collections of publications concerning the affair of the *Philosophia* were assembled in Germany and the Baltic. In Bremen, Gerhard van Mastricht, Petrus' brother and the town syndic, had copies of the *Philosophia*, Serrarius' *Responsio*, and nearly everything of Maresius, besides Spinoza's *Tractatus*.[138] The Lutheran *Generalsuperintendent* of the Swedish-administered former bishoprics of Bremen and Verden, Johannes Dieckmann (1647–1720), whose library was auctioned at Bremen in 1721, owned copies of the *Philosophia* and Spinoza's *Tractatus*, grouping these together with Wolzogen's works and those of Wittichius and Maresius.[139] The library of Gustav Schroedter, 'Adsessor' of the Lutheran Church at the Holstein court of Gottorp, auctioned at Altona in 1724, contained the *Philosophia*, Serrarius' *Responsio*, and Wolzogen's treatise, together with a variety of tracts 'contra Wolzogen'.[140] Few such collections, however, matched that of the Wolfenbüttel town and court physician—as well as botanist, numismatist, and general *savant*—Johann Heinrich Burckhard (1676–1738) whose library was auctioned there in 1738 and who had assiduously accumulated practically everything relevant to the disputes surrounding Wolzogen and the *Philosophia*.[141]

But the clearest proof that the *Philosophia* functioned as a regular focal point of intellectual debate in the Lutheran world, from the 1670s until well into the eighteenth century, is that it became established, like Spinoza, as a stock fixture of academic disputations on Bible hermeneutics. Refuting the 'new atheists' in this period became basic to theological training in the German and Baltic universities and, when profes-

---

[134] Mastricht, *Novitatum Cartesianarum Gangraena*, 403–90.

[135] Annerstedt, *Uppsala universitets historia*, annexes to vol. ii, p. 322; Lindroth, *Svensk lärdomshistoria*, ii, 461.

[136] Benedetti, *Difesa della terza lettera*, 45–6.

[137] Foertschius, *Selectorum Theologicorum Breviarium*, 32.

[138] Mastricht, *Catalogus*, 44, 54, 103, 111, 127.   [139] [Dieckmann], *Catalogus*, 409–12.

[140] Schroedter, *Catalogus bibliothecae*, 225, 494, 676.

[141] [Burckhard], *Bibliotheca Bvrckhardiana*, iii, 9–11.

sors exercised students in defending the integrity of Scripture, the writer of the *Philosophia* regularly joined Spinoza, Hobbes, and La Peyrère as one of the four standard antagonists to be overthrown. Thus, in a series of three set-piece public disputations 'contra atheos et naturalistas' staged at Rostock in May 1702, though Hobbes and Herbert of Cherbury also featured in the proceedings, the two chief targets were predictably Spinoza and the 'author of the *Philosophia Scripturae Interpres*'.[142] Four principal propositions were defended during this three-day display of Baltic erudition: first, the Five Books of Moses were upheld as 'truly and authentically the work of Moses' against 'Spinozam, Hobbesium et Peyrerium'; secondly, the claim that Scripture 'approves' the erroneous notions of the ignorant common people was disproved against 'Wittichiam et Spinozam'; thirdly, the contention 'philosophy is the interpreter of Scripture' was proven fallacious, against the 'author of the *Philosophia*', with the addendum that Wolzogen's refutation of the latter is totally inadequate; while, finally, it was shown that only the literal meaning of the Bible is valid, against the 'Cocceians' and especially the 'author of the *Philosophia*'. The event was pronounced a triumph for the Aristotelian anti-Cartesians then still predominant at Rostock, the final upshot being that reason is not the 'universal law' and 'philosophy must acknowledge the supremacy of theology' (philosophia imperium theologiae agnoscere debet).[143]

Yet, of course, discerning minds were not so sure. As so often, Leibniz showed particular skill in summing up and placing it all in context. He noted that the commotion surrounding the *Philosophia* was never actually resolved: there is, he concluded, 'no indication that any precise rules have yet been defined which the rival parties accept or reject regarding the use of reason in the interpretation of Scripture'.[144] Rather, the disputes over Bible exegesis, he remarked, became merged in the wider conflict about the relationship between faith and reason: 'afterwards in Holland people spoke of "rational" and "non-rational" theologians, a party distinction often mentioned by M. Bayle, who finally declared himself against the former.'[145]

[142] *Nova Literaria Maris Balthici* 1702, 155–8.
[143] Ibid., 158; see also Schmidt-Biggemann, 'Spinoza dans le cartésianisme', 74–81.
[144] Ibid.   [145] Leibniz, *Theodicy*, 83.

12 | MIRACLES DENIED

No other element of Spinoza's philosophy provoked as much consternation and outrage in his own time as his sweeping denial of miracles and the supernatural. In fact, Spinoza stands completely alone among the major European thinkers before the mid-eighteenth century in ruling out miracles. Hobbes had ventured to cast doubt on them, stressing that 'ignorant and superstitious men make great wonders of those works, which other men, knowing to proceed from nature . . . admire not at all,' underlining the 'aptitude of mankind, to give too hasty beleefe to pretended miracles'.[1] But equally, Hobbes grants there have been, and may be, miracles, that 'a miracle, is a work of God (besides his operation by way of nature, ordained in the Creation) done, for the making manifest to his elect, the mission of an extraordinary minister for their salvation,' and that only the public Church can rightly judge what is, and what is not, a miracle.[2] It is worth noting in passing that Hobbes does not rule out magic either, acknowledging the likelihood, affirmed by the account of Pharoah's magicians in the Book of Exodus, that wondrous events can also occur through the operations of magic.[3]

Between the rise of Christianity and the mid-eighteenth century then, only Spinoza categorically denies the possibility of miracles and supernatural occurrences wrought by magic. Equally, he was by far the best-known denier of miracles. Thus, the Lutheran professor Johann Heinrich Müller, in his inaugural lecture on the subject of miracles in the university of Altdorf (Nuremberg) in 1714, declared among those who bring miracles into question 'Benedictus Spinoza, the most renowned restorer and propagator of the myth that God is not distinct from the universe, is by far the most prominent.'[4] According to Spinoza, he notes, neither the Incarnation nor the Resurrection, nor any miracle attributed to Christ, ever occurred, and nor did any other miracles recounted in Scripture: indeed, according to him there have never been any 'miracles'. The Wolffian Wittenberg professor, Friedrich Christian Baumeister (1709–85), writing in 1738, speaks of 'Spinoza Atheorum pessimus' (Spinoza the worst of atheists), in the first place because he

---

[1] Hobbes, *Leviathan*, ch. xxxvii.   [2] Ibid.; Martinich, *Two Gods*, 236–44.

[3] Hobbes. *Leviathan*, ch. xxxvii; Martinich, *Two Gods*, 237, 244.

[4] 'inter quos facile eminet Benedictus Spinoza, celeberrimus ille mysterii, de Deo ab hoc universo non distincto, restaurator et propaguator'; Müller, *Dissertatio*, 13; see also Hulsius, *Spinozismi Depulsio*, 3.

explains Biblical miracles as natural effects 'concerning the causes of which we are ignorant'.[5]

Since miracles were seen as the 'first pillar' of faith, authority, and tradition by theologians at the time, Spinoza's rejection of the possibility of miracles seemed to bring all accepted beliefs, the very basis of contemporary culture, into question.[6] As with much else in Spinoza, broad hints, virtually a sketch of his teaching, are found in his *Cogitata Metaphysica*, published in 1663 as a supplement to his exposition of Descartes. Here, as in the earlier *Korte Verhandeling*, Spinoza maintains there is nothing which is contingent, that 'possibility and contingency' are mere defects of our understanding, and that 'as nothing happens except by the divine power alone, it is easy to see that whatever happens, happens by the power of God's decree and His will.'[7] Since there can be no change of mind, or inconsistency, in God, it follows that 'He must have decreed from eternity that He would produce those things which He now produces' and as what God decrees is necessary 'a necessity of existing has been in all created things from eternity.'[8] Again, several pages later, rather daringly, Spinoza reiterates that there can be no change 'in God' or 'God's decrees': 'for every change which depends on the will occurs in order that its subject may change into a better state' and since 'this can not take place in a perfect Being, there being no change except for the sake of avoiding some inadequacy, or acquiring something good which is lacking, neither of which can take place in God, we conclude that God is an immutable Being.'[9] 'For if men understood clearly the whole order of Nature,' asserts Spinoza, 'they would find all things just as necessary as are all those handled in mathematics.'[10] In this early work, published under his own name, Spinoza could not make his denial of miracles too obvious, so he deliberately muddies the water by acknowledging that 'there is the *ordinary* power of God, and his *extraordinary* power' and that the '*extraordinary* is exercised when He does something beyond the order of Nature e.g. all miracles, such as the speaking of an ass, the appearance of angels, and the like'. But he then immediately qualifies this, saying 'however, concerning this last it is possible, not without reason, for it to be greatly doubted; for it seems a greater miracle if God always governs the world with one and the same fixed and immutable order.'[11]

Very different in tone and style, if not content, is Spinoza's treatment of miracles in his *Tractatus Theologico-Politicus* of 1670. The uncompromising formulations of the soon notorious chapter VI 'On Miracles', or 'impious sophistries' as Henry More called them,[12] were to reverberate for decades through every land in Europe, echoed by the numerous attempts to refute them, echoes amplified among other publications by Müller's oration at Altdorf, which includes lengthy verbatim quotations from Spinoza's text.[13] The chapter begins with a clear hint that Spinoza, one of whose

[5] Baumeister, *Institutiones*, 314–15; Wolff, *Cosmologia generalis*, 399–410.
[6] Heidegger, *Exercitationes*, 304–32; Jäger, *Spinocismus*, 9–11; Concina, *Della religione rivelata*, i, 62–3; Gotti, *Veritas religionis Christianae*, v, 213–15.
[7] *Collected Works of Spinoza*, i, 308–9.   [8] Ibid., i, 309.
[9] Spinoza, *Opera*, i, 256–7; *Collected Works of Spinoza*, i, 322.   [10] *Collected Works of Spinoza*, i, 332.
[11] Spinoza, *Opera*, i, 267.   [12] More, *Ad V. C. Epistola*, 572–3.   [13] Müller, *Dissertatio*, 13–15.

purposes in publishing the *Tractatus* was to weaken the authority and prestige of the public Church with a view to making it easier for his allies and himself to publish their books, aspires not just to interpret the world but change it.[14] Spinoza openly derides the credulity of the multitude and the nonsensical nature of what most people believe. Indeed, in the entire history of modern thought, only Marx and Nietzsche have so openly and provocatively repudiated almost the entire belief-system of the society around them, as Spinoza does here. Most people, he insists, 'have no sound conception either of God or Nature, confuse God's decisions with human decisions, and imagine Nature to be so limited they suppose man to be its chief part'.[15]

Since 'the universal laws of Nature are God's decrees,' he argues, it follows from the necessity and perfection of the divine Nature that 'if anything were to happen in Nature contrary to her universal laws, it would also be necessarily contrary to the decree, intellect and Nature of God or, if anyone were to assert that God performs an act contrary to the laws of Nature, he would at the same time have to maintain that God acts contrary to His own Nature' which is absurd.[16] From this it follows, argues Spinoza, that the notion of 'miracle' can only be understood with respect to men's beliefs 'and means simply an event whose natural cause we—or at any rate the writer or narrator of the miracle—cannot explain in terms of any other normal happening'. Hence, a 'miracle' is simply something the cause of which cannot be explained according to philosophical 'principles known to us by the natural light of reason'.[17] Consequently, none of the 'miracles' or other supernatural happenings recounted in the Bible were, in fact, miracles or supernaturally caused.

Since 'miracles' are purely mental constructions in men's minds, with no objective reality, it follows that neither Biblical 'miracles', nor any other 'miracles' that might be claimed, 'afford us any understanding of God's essence or His existence, or His Providence, and that, on the contrary, these are far better understood from the fixed and immutable order of Nature'.[18] There may be much that we do not understand. But it is what we do understand 'clearly and distinctly' which provides the opportunity to attain a 'higher knowledge of God and shows with great clarity God's will and decrees so that those who have recourse to the will of God when there is something they do not understand are merely trifling; this being no more than a ridiculous way of acknowledging one's ignorance'.[19]

Crucial here is Spinoza's insistence that there is no difference between an 'event contrary to Nature' and a supernatural event. He grants that some authors claim there are events which do not contravene Nature but which nevertheless cannot be produced, or brought about, by Nature, and hence claim the supernatural is not

---

[14] Curley, 'Notes', iii, 113; Israel, *Dutch Republic*, 787–90; Israel, 'Spinoza, Locke', 109–10.

[15] Spinoza, *TTP*, 124–5.

[16] Ibid., 126; Concina, *Della religione rivelata*, i, 63; Mason, *God of Spinoza*, 127.

[17] Spinoza, *TTP*, 127; see also Musaeus, *Tractatus Theologico-Politicus . . . examinatus*, 3, 55, 65; Rechenberg, *Fundamenta*, 166–8; Grapius, *Systema*, ii, 56–63; Reusch, *Systema*, 433–5; Bilfinger, *Dilucidationes*, 202–20.

[18] Spinoza, *TTP*, 129; More, *Ad V. C. Epistola*, 574.

[19] Spinoza *TTP*, 129.; Batalier, *Vindiciae Miraculorum*, 40.

necessarily contrary to Nature. Later, for the Newtonians and others, the distinction between 'above Nature' and 'contrary to Nature' was to be fundamental. But 'if there were to occur in Nature anything that did not follow from her laws,' replies Spinoza, 'this would necessarily be opposed to the order which God maintains eternally in Nature through her universal laws.' This would be contrary to Nature and Nature's laws and, consequently, 'such a belief would cast doubt on everything and lead to atheism.'[20]

Accordingly, for Spinoza, miracles 'above nature', no less than 'miracles' contrary to Nature, are an absurdity, and when Scripture speaks of a 'miracle' this can 'mean nothing else, as we have said, but a natural event which surpasses, or is believed to surpass, human understanding'.[21] Significantly, he employs his conceptions of 'miracle' and 'Nature' to redefine what 'philosophy' and 'philosophers' are. Stressing the difficulties Biblical prophets encountered in reconciling the order of Nature 'with the idea they had formed of God's Providence', he holds that it is only 'philosophers who seek to understand things not from miracles but from clear conceptions' and hence only philosophers who locate salvation, or 'true happiness solely in virtue and peace of mind' and strive to 'conform with Nature, not make Nature conform to them'.[22] For philosophers know that God directs Nature in accordance with universal laws and not in accordance with human nature. The clear implication is that those who acknowledge miracles, refusing to base their conception of the universe on the unalterable laws of Nature, are merely deluded visionaries and not 'philosophers'.

By negating God's Will and Intelligence, Spinoza leaves no room for traditional notions of divine Providence. But he adroitly retains the phrase, redefining 'Providence' to signify something altogether different, that 'God's decrees and commandments, and consequently God's Providence are, in truth, nothing but Nature's order, that is to say when Scripture tells us this or that was done by God or God's Will, nothing more is meant than that it happened in accordance with Nature's law and order, and not, as the common people believe, that Nature temporarily suspended her action, or that her order was suspended.'[23] This is plain, given that men are driven by superstition, not the quest for truth, and consequently, holds Spinoza, appropriating Wittichius' maxim, incensing liberal and conservative Protestants alike in the process, Scripture explains things in accordance with the ignorant beliefs of the common people without attempting to 'teach things through their natural causes or engage in pure philosophy.'[24] Thus when in Genesis 9: 13 God tells Noah He will set a rainbow in the clouds, this action is definitely nothing other, contends Spinoza, than the reflection and refraction of the sun's rays in droplets of water in the sky. Similarly, when

---

[20] Spinoza, *TTP*, 130; Curley, 'Notes', 122–3.
[21] Spinoza, *TTP*, 131; Musaeus, Tractatus Theologico-Politicus . . . *examinatus*, 65–6; Heidegger, *Exercitationes*, 332, 343.
[22] Spinoza, *TTP*, 131.   [23] Ibid., 132; More, *Ad V. C. Epistola*, 573.
[24] Spinoza, *TTP*, 132; Batalier, *Vindiciae Miraculorum*, 40; Koelman, *Wederlegging*, 130–6; Hulsius, *Spinozismi Depulsio*, 33.

wind and fire are called messengers and ministers of God, in Psalm 104: 4, and other similar passages, clearly 'God's decree, command, edict and word,' he maintains, 'are nothing other than the action and order of Nature.'[25]

The Bible thus employs poetic language, according to Spinoza, to explain things which ultimately, but only very distantly, correspond to the truths which philosophers expound. In doing so, Scripture is concerned not with proximity to the truth but using 'such method and style as best serves to excite wonder and consequently to instil piety in the minds of the multitude'.[26] Hence, whenever we encounter something in the Bible which appears to have happened supernaturally, or contrary to Nature's order, this should not perplex us in any way: rather 'we may absolutely conclude everything narrated in Scripture which truly happened, happened according to the laws of Nature by which all things happen necessarily.'[27] Regarding the Hebrews crossing the Red Sea to escape Pharoah's army, recounted in Exodus 10: 14–19, he infers that an easterly wind blew with great vigour all night long and that when we are told, after the crossing, that the sea returned to its former depth at Moses' bidding (Exodus 15: 10), Scripture itself indicates, he points out, that this came about 'because God blew with his wind, that is a very strong wind'.[28] This crucial circumstance is, however, omitted from the main narrative, in order, says Spinoza, to heighten the wondrous effect of the 'miracle' on the multitude.

From this it follows, he continues, that if we are to interpret the accounts of marvellous events and miracles in the Bible correctly, one must first acquire the right kind of philological and historical expertise, 'one must know the beliefs of those who originally related, and left us written records of them' and learn to distinguish between what the people believed and what actually impressed itself on their perceptions. For if we do not, then we shall ourselves inevitably confuse the beliefs of the time with the people's understanding of what impressed itself on their senses and be unable to distinguish between what really happened and what were 'imaginary things and nothing but prophetic representations'.[29] For many things are related in the Bible as real, and were believed to be real, but which were nevertheless merely imaginary, or understood through poetic imagery such as that God, the 'Supreme Being, came down from Heaven and that Mount Sinai smoked because God descended upon it surrounded by fire'. Precisely because the wondrous events related in Scripture were believed to be real, and were couched in terms adjusted to the ignorant and superstitious minds of the multitude 'proiende non debent ut reales a philosophis accipi' (they should not therefore be accepted as real by philosophers). Spinoza rounds off the chapter with a further point concerning the metaphors and figures of speech habitual in Biblical Hebrew. 'He who does not pay sufficient attention to this', he warns, 'will ascribe to Scripture many miracles which the Biblical writers never intended as such, thus completely failing to grasp not only happenings

---

[25] Spinoza, *TTP*, 132; Heidegger, *Exercitationes*, 343.   [26] Spinoza, *TTP*, 133.
[27] Ibid.; Spinoza, *Opera*, iii, 91.   [28] Spinoza, *TTP*, 133.
[29] Ibid., 135; 'ne etiam confundamus res, quae revera contigerunt, cum rebus imaginariis, et quae non nisi representationes propheticae fuerunt', Spinoza, *Opera*, iii, 92.

and miracles as they really occurred but also the meaning of the writers of the Sacred Books.'[30]

In his chapter on miracles, as Spinoza remarks himself, he proceeds differently than in most of the *Tractatus Theologico-Politicus*, principally using philosophical and only secondarily philological and historical arguments, rather than vice versa, as elsewhere.[31] Consequently, he reveals here more of the metaphysical system which underpins his assault on revealed religion and which, to his mind, finally precludes all possibility that miracles can occur. He returned one last time to this life-long theme, now fully revealing his philosophy, in the appendix to Part I of his masterpiece, the *Ethics*. In general, Spinoza's style here is more austere and detached than in the *Tractatus*, but when he reverts to the theme of miracles something of the rebelliousness and emotion which fired his youth surge up once again. He has shown, he claims, that 'things could not have been produced by God in any other way, or in any other order, than how they have been produced' (Ethics I, Prop. XXXIII) and that therefore there never have been, and never could be, any wondrous happenings or miracles.[32] However, most people refuse to accept this and persecute whoever points it out: 'one who seeks the true causes of miracles and is eager, like a scholar, to understand natural things and not wonder at them like a fool, is generally denounced as an impious heretic by those the people revere as interpreters of Nature and the gods.' This they do because they 'know that if ignorance, or rather stupidity, is removed, then foolish wonder, the only means they have of justifying and sustaining their authority, goes with it'.[33] Here, in embryo, is the concept of priestcraft as a system of organized imposture and deception, rooted in credulousness and superstition, which loomed so large in the subsequent history of the Enlightenment and was to receive massive amplification in the books on ancient oracles and priestcraft published by Blount, Van Dale, and Fontenelle in the 1680s.

Spinoza's attack on miracles made an immediate and profound impression everywhere, in England and Italy no less than in Germany and France. In his powerful and moving reply, written in Florence in 1671 (though not published until September 1675),[34] the great Danish scientist-prelate, Nicolas Steno, implored the unnamed 'Reformer of the New Philosophy' to heed the insuperable risks and dangers he was creating for the whole of humanity, including himself, and consider 'how you throw everything into confusion' (omnia turbes).[35] Spinoza's aim was to reform the 'New Philosophy' and introduce an entirely new criterion of truth and conception of human salvation and happiness. But what of those who lack the intellectual grasp to

---

[30] Spinoza, *TTP*, 136–8; More, *Ad V. C. Epistola*, 577.

[31] Spinoza, *TTP*, 137–8; Mason, *God of Spinoza*, 127.

[32] Spinoza, *Opera*, ii, 73; *Collected Works of Spinoza*, i, 436; see also [Carroll], *A Letter to the Reverend*, 14; Concina, *Della religione revelata*, ii, 226.

[33] Spinoza, *Opera*, ii, 81; *Collected Works of Spinoza*, i, 443–4.

[34] Scherz, *Pionier der Wissenschaft*, 278; Totaro, 'Niels Stensen', 147–8.

[35] Steno, *Ad Novae Philosophiae Reformatorem*, 33; Spinoza, *Letters*, 313; presumably Steno sent the letter to Spinoza some years before it was published, but it is not known whether he ever reacted to it.

understand his concepts? Was he not consigning those 'unfit for your philosophy to a way of life like that of automata destitute of soul, born with a body only'?[36] Spinoza, 'a man who was once my good friend and even now, I hope, not unfriendly towards me (for I am persuaded the memory of our former close relationship still preserves a mutual love)', should on proper reflection yield to the entreaties of those who, like Steno himself, desire with all their hearts that he will reconsider while there is yet time and draw back from the fatal brink. It was of the highest importance, he urged, that Spinoza should open his eyes before it is too late and see that one 'finds only in Christianity a true philosophy, teaching of God what is worthy of God and of man what is proper to man, guiding its adherents to true perfection in all their actions'.[37]

Steno, an accomplished scientist skilled in Cartesian and Spinozist terminology, knew the supposedly scientific basis of Spinoza's objections to miracles and why he refused to acknowledge them, and tries to show that experience daily contradicts his philosophy. It is a true and continuing miracle, he insists, one we see every day around us, that sinners who have spent thirty or forty years, or more, in the gratification of their appetites 'should, in a moment, abandon all such wickedness and become the most holy examples of virtue'.[38] This collective miracle is subsumed and culminates in the spiritual glory of the Catholic Church. If he will but lay aside all prejudice and think objectively as his own philosophy 'will readily persuade you to do' and explore the teaching and promises of the Church, he will, urges Steno, assuredly find a higher and better truth. Steno's open letter was reviewed the year after its publication in Florence, in the *Giornale de' Letterati*, at Rome in 1676. The editors wished to publicize this powerful retort to the New Philosophy, and assertion of the Church's spiritual power, without, however, drawing attention to Spinoza's philosophy. Consequently, in the *Giornale*'s review there is no mention of Spinoza, the person to whom Steno so movingly appeals being designated merely as 'someone' who believes everyone is free to think what he wishes in matters of faith.[39]

Among those who joined in Steno's entreaties in Italy, writing to Spinoza from Florence in September 1675, was Albert Burgh (1650–1708), an Amsterdam regent's son whom the philosopher knew well personally. Burgh had studied at Van den Enden's school and, as a student at Leiden in the late 1660s, emerged as an impressively erudite young scholar, skilled in classics and philosophy who, as he says in the letter, admired Spinoza 'for the penetration and acuteness of your mind' and as a 'lover of truth, and indeed a most eager one'.[40] A declared disciple of Van den Enden, Spinoza, and their circle, he travelled to Italy in 1673, promising Spinoza 'to write to you should anything worthy of note occur during my journey'.[41] Keen to practise his philosophical

---

[36] Steno, *Ad Novae Philosophiae Reformatorem*, 33; Dunin Borkowski, *Spinoza*, iii, 165–7.

[37] Steno, *Ad Novae Philosophiae Reformatorem*, 35.

[38] Ibid., 36; Scherz, *Pionier der Wissenschaft*, 280–2.

[39] *Giornale de' Letterati* (Rome) 1676, 145; Totaro, 'Niels Stensen', 154.

[40] Spinoza, *Letters*, 303; Meinsma, *Spinoza*, 187, 205, 430–1; Hubbeling, 'Spinoza's correspondenten', 45; Nadler, *Spinoza*, 158, 336–7.

[41] Spinoza, *Letters*, 303; Kortholt, *De tribus Impostoribus*, 184; Totaro, 'Niels Stensen', 157.

debating skills, he encountered a priest in Venice who, however, answered his libertine arguments with such effect that there, and in Padua, he underwent a conversion and discarded his Spinozist convictions. Soon afterwards, with the encouragement of Steno (but to the distress of his Protestant family), he embraced the Catholic faith while in Rome. The news caused a sensation in Amsterdam and reached Spinoza, who 'could scarcely believe it when it was told me', well before the arrival of the promised letter.[42] Subsequently, Burgh became a Franciscan friar.

Burgh's epistle is one of the longest and most significant subsequently published in the *Opera Posthuma*. Though more emotional in tone than Steno's missive, it uses similar arguments and, indeed, may well have been written in concert with Steno. Burgh begins by mentioning his having recently sent a detailed account of his conversion, from Florence to Professor Craanen at Leiden, and expects Spinoza would learn more of what happened from him, an interesting sidelight on the philosopher's personal proximity to certain leading 'Cartesian' professors. For Burgh the overriding issue is the nature and criterion of truth. 'What does all your philosophy amount to,' he demands, 'except sheer illusion and chimaera? . . . Do you dare consider yourself greater than all those who have ever arisen in the . . . Church of God, the patriarchs, prophets, apostles, martyrs, doctors, confessors and virgins, the countless saints and even, blasphemously, our Lord Jesus Christ himself? Will you . . . mere ashes and food for worms, in your unspeakable blasphemy claim pre-eminence over the incarnate and infinite wisdom of the Eternal Father?'.[43] A philosophy claiming our universe is determined necessarily by geometric relationships is proven to be false by our everyday experience. Our reality is infused by the supernatural. Reason cannot explain the 'things done in witchcraft and in spells cast simply by the utterance of certain words, or by merely carrying on one's person those words or inscriptions marked out on some material, or the amazing behaviour of those possessed by demons'.[44]

But miracles are the central issue. Burgh replies to Spinoza's denial of the miraculous much as Bossuet, Huet, Denyse, and Houtteville did later, and essentially on the same lines as Limborch, Le Clerc, and subsequently, Locke. The proof lies in the eyewitness testimonies and the tradition of the Church. The Christian miracles are their own confirmation and cannot be doubted. Whatever philosophical arguments Spinoza may adduce, he cannot negate the 'countless miracles and portents which, after Christ, his Apostles and Disciples, and later many thousands of saints performed, through the omnipotent power of God, witnessing and confirming the truth of the Catholic faith and which, through that same omnipotent mercy and goodness of God, are performed even nowadays throughout the world. And if you cannot contradict these, as most certainly you cannot, why go on clamouring? Submit, see your errors and sins, embrace humility and be born again.'[45] If only he would consider the matter properly, how can Spinoza dare deny the significance of the consensus of countless numbers of men, 'thousands of whom greatly surpassed you, and still do, in doctrine,

---

[42] Spinoza, *Letters*, 340; Steno, *Epistolae*, i, 44.   [43] Spinoza, *Letters*, 305.
[44] Ibid., 305–6.   [45] Spinoza, *Opera*, iv, 285.

erudition, and true solidity of understanding, as in the perfection of their lives, who all unanimously, and with one voice, affirm that Christ, son of the living God Incarnate, suffered, was crucified, and died for the sins of mankind, rose again, was transfigured and reigns in Heaven with the eternal Father in unity with the Holy Spirit, as God' and that through Christ and 'subsequently the Apostles in his name, and the rest of the saints, through divine and omnipotent virtue, countless miracles were performed in the Church of God, and are still, which not only surpass human understanding but run counter to ordinary perceptions.'[46]

Spinoza, contends Burgh, attempts to argue against a prodigious accumulation of evidence transmitted across the centuries. His enterprise against miracles and the truth of Christianity is as futile as denying there was an ancient Roman civilization in the world when innumerable remnants of it remain and countless histories have been written about the Romans.[47] The glorious founding of the Christian religion is a matter of 'factual truth'.[48] The Roman Church is an uninterrupted sequence of testimony and authority stretching from the time of Christ, through every generation, until today. This is proof in itself but, besides this, Christ's Church spread throughout the world in an astoundingly short time, despite the endeavours of Roman emperors to prevent it, and their cruelly torturing and putting to death innumerable Christians. Consider, he urges, the durability of the Church, which has outlasted not only pagan religions and dynasties 'but the opinions of all philosophers'.[49] He admonishes Spinoza to consider the Apostles and their disciples and successors. 'These were men regarded by the world as unlettered who yet confounded all philosophers, although the Christian doctrine they taught conflicts with ordinary sense, exceeding and transcending all human reason.'[50] Although the Apostles and disciples were deemed 'abject, vile and ignoble men', in time even the Roman emperors became Christian and the Church grew until the 'ecclesiastical hierarchy attained that vastness of power such as may be admired today'.[51] Furthermore, all this was achieved through charity, gentleness, patience, and trust in God, not through arms or the clash of mighty armies.

These, 'the greatest miracles', are also facts; and if Spinoza requires yet more proof, he should ponder the Church's 'antiquity', its 'immutability whereby its teaching, and the administering of the sacraments just as ordained by Christ himself and the Apostles, is preserved intact' and its 'infallibility whereby it determines and decides all things pertaining to the Faith with supreme authority, sureness and truth, in accordance with the power bestowed on it to this end by Christ himself'. He should contemplate also its 'unity' and the fact that no soul can, on any pretext, be separate from the Church 'without its immediately incurring eternal damnation, unless it be reunited to the Church before death by repentence' as well as the Catholic religion's 'vast extension, whereby it is spread throughout the world which cannot be said of any other faith or philosophical doctrine'.[52] Final confirmation may be found, he adds,

---

[46] Spinoza, *Opera*, iv, 286; Spinoza, *Letters*, 307. [47] Spinoza, *Letters*, 307–8. [48] Ibid.
[49] Ibid., 308. [50] Spinoza, *Opera*, iv, 287. [51] Ibid. [52] Spinoza, *Letters*, 309–10.

echoing Steno, in the countless Catholics of both sexes who have 'lived admirable and holy lives, and through the omnipotent power of God wrought many miracles in the adored name of Jesus Christ' and also in that daily there are more conversions 'of very many people from a wicked life to a better, truly Christian, and holy life'. Such a combination of humility and submission with good works and holiness proves the 'most perfect heretic or philosopher that ever was can scarcely deserve to rank with the least perfect Catholics.' All this demonstrates beyond doubt that 'Catholic doctrine is the wisest and . . . superior to all other teachings of this world.'[53]

Burgh concludes by admonishing Spinoza to reflect 'on the miserable and restless lives of atheists, though they may sometimes put on a very cheerful appearance and try to present themselves as living a joyful life, completely at peace in their hearts'. If Spinoza were to persist in his 'abominable errors . . . what else do you expect but eternal damnation?' He begs him to reflect on how horrifying this is before it is too late. 'Think what little reason you have to mock the whole world except your wretched admirers; how foolishly proud and inflated you have become thinking of the excellence of your talent and by men's admiration of your utterly vain, indeed completely false and impious, doctrine.'[54] Summoning him to come to his senses and 'acknowledge the stupidity of your wisdom and that your wisdom is madness', Burgh explains that part of his 'Christian purpose' is 'to ask you not to persist in ruining others as well as yourself' and that he should consider that 'the Lord who, having called you so many times through others, is now calling you, perhaps for the last time, through me.'[55]

Spinoza's reply is incisive but also tense with barely controlled passion. Burgh asks how he knows his philosophy is the best of philosophies. Spinoza reverses this, demanding how Burgh knows he has found the best of religions.[56] As for the common consent of thousands of men and the unbroken tradition of the Church, Spinoza dismisses this as the 'same old song as that of the Pharisees'.[57] The Jews, he counters, can 'just as confidently as the Roman Church produce their innumerable witnesses who with no less perseverance report what they have merely heard from others as if they had experienced it themselves' and 'with equal arrogance boast that their church, continuing to this day, endures unchanged and unshaken despite the bitter hatred of pagans and Christians: of all religions they are best defended by [the argument] of antiquity.'[58] Moreover, the 'miracles they recount are enough to wear out a thousand narrators'and they have more martyrs by far than any other nation.[59] As for the glory and magnificence of the Catholic Church, Spinoza readily grants that it is singularly well-organized for power and profit, and he would believe it 'more suited to deceiving the people, and coercing the minds of men, than any other were it not for the Mohammedan Church which surpasses it by far', not only in its extent, and control over its faithful, but in its unity.[60] 'Nor since that superstition began, have there been any schisms in their church.'[61] He ends by exhorting Burgh to return to his senses, and

---

[53] Ibid., 311.   [54] Spinoza, *Opera*, 290.   [55] Spinoza, *Letters*, 312.
[56] Akkerman, *Studies*, 10.   [57] Spinoza, *Letters*, 342–3.   [58] Spinoza, *Opera*, iv, 321.
[59] Ibid.   [60] Ibid.   [61] Ibid.

discard 'destructive superstition' in favour of 'reason', reminding him he should peruse some Church histories and 'see how falsely they relate much about the Pope and by what events, and with what artifice, the Roman pontiff finally gained supremacy over the Church six hundred years after the birth of Christ.'[62]

Both Burgh's missive and Spinoza's reply were published in 1677, in the *Opera Posthuma*, and became a famous, and for many infamous, encounter in the Republic of Letters, pored over by cardinals, Protestant pastors, Cambridge dons, and courtiers alike. At Utrecht the Vicar Apostolic of the Dutch Catholic Church, Jan van Neercassel, remarked in September 1678, in a letter to the papal nuncio in Brussels, that there is 'scarcely anything more pernicious against the Christian and Catholic religion than the letter Spinoza sent that most noble young man, Albert Burgh, in Italy'.[63] At Hanover Leibniz, who learnt of Steno's letter shortly after Spinoza's death, commented in detail on both Steno's and Burgh's missives for his prince, the Duke of Brunswick.[64] At Cambridge, Henry More, who loathed Spinoza's philosophy above all for its rejection of miracles and the supernatural, including the demonic, identified the letter to Burgh as perhaps the most loathsome of all his writings, abominating his mockery of 'a divine justice which permits the Devil to deceive men with impunity but does not allow men, deceived and ensnared by the Devil, to go unpunished'.[65] On the contrary, answers More, Satan will be brought to account and it is 'a beautiful part of divine justice and Providence that human souls be tested and tried'.[66] Moreover, whereas Leibniz was in part sympathetic to Spinoza's championing of philosophic reason, More utterly scorns his preferring his contemptible philosophy, and the 'inane glory of quibbling' to the 'peace and salvation of the human race'. 'Oh Philosopher totally without shame and intellect,' he calls him, 'or rather most impudent impostor and hypocrite!'[67]

But it was perhaps especially in Italy, where Burgh and Steno acquired splendid reputations, that the clash reverberated most strongly in Venice, Florence, Rome, and Naples alike. The most explicit of all Spinoza's texts attacking organized religion, directed against the Catholic Church specifically, the reply to Burgh made an indelible impression, consummating Spinoza's status as the foremost denier of the miraculous and, as Genovesi expresses it, 'head of the most pernicious modern Deists'.[68] Taking the name 'Brother Franciscus de Hollandia' Burgh became a *consultore* of the Roman Inquisition, advising on the problem of Jansenism in the Low Countries and doubtless also on the spread of Spinozism.[69] Very likely, together with Steno, he was one of those who advised Cardinal Barberini and the Inquisition in 1677, on the need to pre-

---

[62] Spinoza, *Opera*, iv, 324; Nadler, *Spinoza*, 339–40; Gullan-Whur, *Within Reason*, 278–9.

[63] 'Letters to and from Neercassel', 336; Totaro, 'L'Index', 367; Totaro, 'Niels Stensen', 158.

[64] Steno, *Epistolae*, ii, 929; see pp. 507–9 below.

[65] Spinoza, *Letters*, 341; Colie, 'Spinoza in England', 185–7.

[66] More, *Confutio*, 102–3.

[67] 'o pudore omni et ingenuitate destitute philosophe, vel potius o impudentissime Impostor et Hypocrita!'; ibid., 102–3.

[68] Genovesi, *Elementa metaphysicae*, ii, 11, 235–7, 284–5.   [69] Totaro, 'Niels Stensen', 158.

vent the publication of Spinoza's *Ethics* and the subsequent banning of the *Tractatus Theologico-Politicus* by the Holy Office in March 1679.[70] Above all the denial of the Resurrection ('Resurrectio Christi allegorice est intelligenda'), stated also in Spinoza's letters to Oldenburg, continued subsequently to draw appalled attention. Cardinal Gotti, among others, reiterated the stock reply: the truth of the testimony of the Evangelists cannot be doubted, for good measure echoing Henry More's designation of Spinoza—'You, the most impudent of mortals'.[71]

[70] See below, p. 289.   [71] Gotti, *Veritas religionis Christianae*, v, 213–15.

13 | Spinoza's System

Spinoza's prime contribution to the evolution of early modern Naturalism, fatalism, and irreligion, as Bayle—and many who followed Bayle in this—stressed, was his ability to integrate within a single coherent or ostensibly coherent system, the chief elements of ancient, modern, and oriental 'atheism'.[1] No one else in early modern times did this, or anything comparable, and it is primarily the unity, cohesion, and compelling power of his system, his ability to connect major elements of previous 'atheistic' thought into an unbroken chain of reasoning, rather than the novelty or force of any of his constituent concepts which explains his centrality in the evolution of the whole Radical Enlightenment. It should not be overlooked, though, that some of his other contributions, notably his Bible criticism and revolutionary doctrine of substance, were highly innovative and, in themselves, exerted a vast international impact.

With his system Spinoza imparted shape, order, and unity to the entire tradition of radical thought, both retrospectively and in its subsequent development, qualities it had lacked previously and were henceforth perhaps its strongest weapons in challenging prevailing structures of authority and received learning and combating the advancing moderate Enlightenment. It was a system which reached its fullest and most mature expression only with the completion of his *Ethics* in 1675, but which, as we have seen, was in essentials extant as early as 1660.

Spinoza's starting-point in the *Ethics* is a set of propositions about the nature of reality or substance, including the contention that 'every substance is necessarily infinite' (I Prop. VIII) which proceed in seemingly logical progression to his famous tenet, the 'foundation of his whole impious doctrine', as Spinelli calls it,[2] that 'Except God, no substance can exist or be conceived' (I Prop. XIV). Where Descartes' unassailable first step is his 'cogito, ergo sum', Spinoza's is his assertion that our idea of the totality of what is, of an infinite and eternal being—God (or Nature)—is clear, consistent, self-contained, and undeniable.[3] Since everything that exists, he contends, exists in God (or

[1] Charles-Daubert and Moreau, *Pierre Bayle, Écrits*, 29; Spinoza, says Capasso, 'omnium primus atheismum nova methodo et systemate docuit'; Capasso, *Historiae Philosophiae Synopsis*, 394; see also Wagner, *Johan Christian Edelmanns verblendete Anblicke*, ii, 408.

[2] 'Praeter Deum nulla dari, neque concipi potest substantia', Spinoza, *Opera*, ii, 56; see also Spinelli, *Riflessioni*, 446; Wolff, *De Differentia nexus*, 53–4.

[3] *Collected Works of Spinoza*, i, 408–28; Hubbeling, *Spinoza*, 58–62; Harris, *Spinoza's Philosophy*, 19–24; Curley, *Behind the Geometrical Method*, 12–38.

Nature), and substance, as he defines it,[4] is what is absolutely independent in itself, there can be only one substance and therefore only one set of rules governing the whole of the reality which surrounds us and of which we are part. Whatever has been 'determined by God to produce an effect', he argues, 'cannot render itself undetermined' (I, Prop. XXVII). From this he infers that every individual thing which is finite 'can neither exist, nor be determined, to produce an effect unless it is determined by another cause' which, also being finite and determined, must in turn be determined by another cause similarly finite and determined, and so on to infinity. Hence, it follows logically that 'in nature there is nothing contingent, but all things have been determined from the necessity of the divine nature to exist and produce an effect in a certain way' (I Prop. XXIX). Hence also the chain of necessity is infinite, and infinitely complex, and only partially knowable through human science, not because elements of the chain are conceptually beyond the reach of human reason but because science cannot empirically take account of the whole of such a sequence.[5]

It is at this point that Spinoza introduces his distinction between *Natura Naturans* and *Natura Naturata*, the first designating what exists independently in itself and conceived through itself, namely 'God, insofar as he is considered to be a free cause', that is, nature understood as the creative power or potential of Nature,[6] the rules governing the working of the universe, the latter denoting, by contrast, the actuality or determinate state of nature: 'by *Natura Naturata* I understand whatever follows from the necessity of God's nature, or from any of God's attributes.' From this, Spinoza deduces that 'actual intellect, whether finite or infinite, like will, desire, love etc. pertain to *Natura Naturata*, not to *Natura Naturans*' (I Prop. XXXI), meaning that all manifestations of mind or minded-substance are part of Spinoza's single thinking-extended substance and therefore governed by the same set of rules—the laws of nature—as any other part of *Natura Naturata*. Hence it follows that 'will cannot be called a free cause, but only a necessary one' (I Prop. XXXII) and similarly that 'will and intellect are related to God's nature as motion and rest are, and as are absolutely all natural things which by Proposition XXIX must be determined by God to exist and produce an effect in a certain way.' This yields Spinoza's proposition that God does not produce any effect by freedom of the will and that 'will does not pertain to God's nature any more than do the other natural things but is related to him in the same way as motion and rest, and all other things which, as we have shown, follow from the necessity of the divine nature and are determined by it to exist and produce an effect in a certain way.'[7]

From here Spinoza proceeds to one of his most celebrated propositions: 'things could have been produced by God in no other way, and in no other order, than they have been produced' (Res nullo alio modo, neque alio ordine a Deo produci

---

[4] Descartes and Leibniz too accepted that, strictly speaking, 'substance' means that which is causally self-sufficient and indestructible; Bennett, *A Study*, 56.

[5] Mason, *God of Spinoza*, 62–4.

[6] Woolhouse, *Concept of Substance*, 49–50; Bennett, *A Study*, 118–19; Mason, *God of Spinoza*, 29–30.

[7] *Collected Works of Spinoza*, i, 435.

potuerunt, quam productae sunt)[8] (I, Prop. XXXIII). In his appendix to Part I of the *Ethics*, Spinoza claims to have demonstrated that while God is the 'free cause of all things', and the only free cause, all things have been predetermined by God, not through the freedom of his will 'but from God's absolute nature, or infinite power'.[9] It should be noticed that, contrary to what is often asserted, this is not in any meaningful sense 'pantheism'.[10] Since nothing is contingent, men too are determined in their conduct. That men suppose themselves to be free Spinoza ascribes to their consciousness of their desires and appetites while failing to perceive 'those causes by which they are disposed to wanting and willing, being ignorant of those causes'.[11] In reality, he contends, men always act, and are determined to do so, towards an end or goal, that is, they seek what they perceive to be to their benefit. Furthermore, seeing as they do 'both in themselves and outside themselves—many means that are very helpful in seeking their own advantage such as that eyes are for seeing, teeth for chewing, plants and animals for food, the sun for light, the sea for supporting fish', they are psychologically disposed to imagine that all natural things exist and were created 'as means to their own advantage'. This makes men believe there is some agency at work that created all these things for their use: 'for after they considered things as means, they could not believe that the things had made themselves.'[12] Hence men inferred 'there was a ruler, or a number of rulers of nature' and concluded that the 'gods direct all things for the use of men in order to bind men to them and be held by men in the highest honour.'[13]

It is easy to see from this, he argues, why men then develop different accounts of God, or the gods, and their desires and intentions, and also why men seek 'different ways of worshipping so that God might love them above the rest and direct the whole of nature according to the needs of their blind desire and insatiable greed'.[14] Religion is hence at bottom a psychological procedure, natural in origin and thought-processes, which became transformed into 'superstition' and set down deep roots in men's minds. Destructive and disturbing occurrences such as storms, earthquakes, diseases, and so forth were then explained as effects of divine wrath and resentment at men's supposed wrongdoing, disrespect towards the gods, and inadequacies in their worship and beliefs. Despite the fact, holds Spinoza, that the evidence of everyday life proves this false and that fortunate and unfortunate occurrences affect pious and impious alike without any distinction, the superstitious prejudice that what happens is directed by divine will in reference to men's thoughts, actions, and conduct became too deeply rooted to be erased. It is far easier to maintain that the ways and judgements of the gods far surpass men's understanding. Nor indeed would there have ever been any change in man's propensity to cloud his mind with 'superstition' and 'inadequate ideas' had not 'mathematics which is concerned not with ends, but only with the essences and properties of figures, shown men another standard of truth'.[15]

---

[8] Spinoza, *Opera*, ii, 73.   [9] *Collected Works of Spinoza*, i, 439; Wolff, *De Differentia nexus*, 13–14, 17, 23.
[10] Mason, *God of Spinoza*, 31–2.   [11] *Collected Works of Spinoza*, i, 440.   [12] Ibid., i, 441.
[13] Ibid.   [14] Ibid.   [15] Ibid.

In reality, 'Nature has no end set before it, and all final causes are nothing but human fictions.'[16]

However, most people do not grasp these fundamental truths and so 'when they see the structure of the human body they are struck by foolish wonder and because they do not know the causes of so great an art, they infer that it is constructed not by mechanical, but by divine, or supernatural art and constituted in such a way that one part does not injure another.'[17] Thus anyone who seeks the natural causes of what most men consider to be supernaturally devised, and to 'understand natural things and not to wonder at them, like a fool', is generally condemned as a heretic.[18] A further consequence of man's superstitious and ignorant disposition to imagine that everything that happens, happens on his account, is to judge that what is most valuable or significant in each thing, or happening, is what is most useful or advantageous to him and rate as most excellent those things by which he is most pleased. Hence men derived their abstract notions of 'good' and 'evil', as well as ideas such as warm, cold, beautiful, ugly, and so forth in terms of what seemed good, warm, or beautiful to them and, at the same time, believing themselves free and answerable for their conduct to the gods, likewise propounded the concepts of 'good' and 'evil', praise and blame, sin and merit, in relation to their attitudes and deeds. But because the things men imagine vary and conflict, it is by no means surprising, Spinoza notes in passing, 'that we find so many controversies to have arisen among men, and that they have finally given rise to scepticism'.[19] 'We see, therefore, that all the notions by which ordinary people are accustomed to explain nature are only modes of imagining and do not indicate the nature of anything, only the constitution of the imagination.'[20]

The second part of the *Ethics*, and the second stage of Spinoza's system, concerns the relationship of body and mind and the workings of the mind. It begins with definitions of 'extension' and 'mind' and the propositions that 'Thought is an attribute of God, or God is a thinking thing' (II, Prop. I) and equally that 'Extension is an attribute of God, or God is an extended thing' (II, Prop. II). The connecting link with the reasoning set out in Part I is the proposition (II, Prop. VII) that 'the order and connection of ideas is the same as the order and connection of things.' This is a difficult and challenging assertion which the modern reader is hardly likely to accept without serious question.[21] But Spinoza's rigid and dogmatic parallelism of mind and body does have a certain cogency if one takes him as meaning that his doctrine of one substance necessarily entails a parallel manifestation of extension for every mental manifestation, whether or not the latter is expressed in the form of an adequate or inadequate idea, or is even merely a whim, sensation, or primitive form of sensibility.[22] The two chains of phenomenona are conceptually but not actually separate, being distinct aspects of

---

[16] Ibid., i, 442.

[17] Ibid., i, 443; Spinoza here reiterates, but also gives a new twist to an argument which reaches back through Maimonides at least to Cicero; Wolfson, *Philosophy of Spinoza*, i, 434–8.

[18] *Collected Works of Spinoza*, i, 444.   [19] Ibid., i, 445.   [20] Ibid., i, 445–6.

[21] Bennett, *A Study*, 127–8; Curley, *Behind the Geometrical Method*, 62–70.

[22] Della Rocca, *Representation*, 18–29.

one and the same reality, and therefore they cannot interact or influence each other. But they are inherently linked in terms of cause and effect.

If all bodies belong to the same substance, as Spinoza contends, then the individuation of bodies has to be explained, and this he does by arguing that all bodies 'are distinguished from one another by reason of motion and rest, speed and slowness, and not by reason of substance'.[23] His view that all motion is inherent in matter and that there is no such thing as static 'extension', as Descartes thought, does indeed provide a conceptual tool with which he can explain the vast differences in texture, penetrability, weight, etc. between different kinds of solids, liquids, and gases. The fact, moreover, that a body which moves or is at rest must be determined to motion or rest by another body which has likewise been determined to motion or rest by another, and so on to infinity,[24] means that under the attribute 'extension' the entire universe consists of an interaction of mechanically related bodies. All modes by which a body is affected by another, holds Spinoza, follow partly from the nature of the body affected and partly from the affecting body.[25]

The human mind as the sensibility of the body, and therefore part of the individual body, 'does not know the human body itself, nor does it know that it exists, except through ideas of affection by which the body is affected' (II, Prop. XIX), that is, our mind, and indeed any mind, is in essence awareness of the impact of other bodies on the body, in other words, feelings, impressions, and emotions. Because the human mind, he argues, is the idea itself, or awareness of the human body, it cannot know itself 'except in so far as it perceives the ideas of the affections of the body'. Nor indeed can the human mind perceive any external body as it actually exists, except through its ideas of the impressions of its own body. This leads to the key doctrine that the 'ideas of the affections of the human body, in so far as they are related only to the human mind, are not clear and distinct, but confused' (II, Prop. XXVIII). Incorrect or false ideas, consequently, are no less based on reality than correct ideas but flow from the inadequate, mutilated and confused nature of our sense perceptions. With this Spinoza believed he had explained why most men's ideas are muddled or false and why mankind only slowly gropes its way to reason and, ultimately, philosophy.

Sense perception is thus the basis of all ideas, but in itself leads only to false ideas. Men suppose themselves to be free because they are conscious of their desires and actions but ignorant of the causes by which they are determined to desire and act as they do. Similarly, even when we know the real distance of the sun from the earth, we still imagine it to be closer to us than it is, says Spinoza, because the effect on our bodies is what determines our perception of the sun. True and false ideas, therefore, are equally 'real' and can only be differentiated from each other by introducing the criterion of mathematical measurements, proportions, and logic. Only reason can provide us with 'adequate' ideas and a demonstration based on reason, according to Spinoza, is one that uses mathematically verifiable measurements and calculation to differentiate what is true from what is false. Truth is thus the criterion both of itself

---

[23] *Collected Works of Spinoza*, i, 458.   [24] Ibid., i, 459.   [25] Ibid., i, 460.

and what is incorrect; 'he who has a true idea at the same time knows he has a true idea, and cannot doubt the truth of the thing' (II, Prop. XLIII). Given that mathematical proportion is Spinoza's sole criterion of truth, the difference between truth and falsehood must be exact and absolute. From this, the precise logic of mathematical rationality, it follows, holds Spinoza, that 'it is of the nature of reason to regard things as necessary, not as contingent' (II, Prop. XLIV) and that this necessity of rational demonstration is the same as the necessity of things and corresponds to the necessity of God's eternal nature. Since the mind is the sensibility of the body, it follows that 'there is no absolute, or free will and that the mind is determined to will this or that by a cause which is also determined by another, and this again by another, and so on to infinity' (II, Prop. XLVIII). Thus nature determines the mind in the same way it does physical things.

Since false ideas consist of real impressions involving incomplete or truncated ideas, they may well be followed by more men, and more adamantly, than true ideas. However, because they are inadequate, false ideas must always in every human mind be 'uncertain' in Spinoza's special technical sense, precisely because they are 'inadequate' and can be disproved by reasoning that those who hold false ideas, however obstinately, could in certain circumstances be brought to understand. False ideas are 'uncertain' even in the most dogmatic mind in the sense that no viable proofs can be adduced to defend them: 'for by certainty we understand something positive, not the absence of doubt.'[26] An idea in so far as it is an idea, according to Spinoza, must involve an affirmation or negation about something real which is either true or false in the sense of being a demonstrably adequate or inadequate interpretation of real facts.

Spinoza concludes Part II of the *Ethics* with a crucial further step, his doctrine that 'in the mind there is no volition, or affirmation or negation, except that which the idea, in so far as it is an idea, involves' (II, Prop. XLIX), that is, that there is no volition which is not an idea, leading to the corollary that 'will and the intellect are one and the same.'[27] This doctrine of ideas and the will, he says, teaches us that we act only from God's command and that we do this the more, the more perfect our actions are, and the more we understand God (or Nature). 'This doctrine, then, in addition to giving us complete peace of mind, also teaches us wherein our greatest happiness, or blessedness consists: viz. in the knowledge of God alone by which we are led to do only those things which love and morality advise.' From this, he says, we can see clearly how far men stray from a true valuation of virtue who expect to be rewarded by God for their good deeds. The doctrine, in his view, also teaches us to be calm and steadfast in the face of fortune and be prepared for both beneficial and adverse experiences. 'For all things follow from God's eternal decree with the same necessity as from the essence of a triangle it follows that its three angles are equal to two right angles.'[28] Such a doctrine also contributes to social life, he maintains, in that it teaches us to hate, despise, or mock no one, and envy no one, and also that we should be content with

---

[26] Ibid., i, 485.   [27] Ibid., i, 484–5; Klever, *Ethicom*, 250.   [28] *Collected Works of Spinoza*, i, 490.

what we have and be helpful to our neighbour 'not from unmanly compassion, partiality or superstition, but from the guidance of reason, as the time and occasion demand'.[29]

The third part of the *Ethics* concerns man's emotions and conduct. He begins by saying that reason can grasp the irrationality, inadequacy, and absurdity of what men do, and why they do it, since nothing in nature happens owing to any defect in it, for nature is always the same, and its virtue and power of acting are everywhere one and the same. 'So the way of understanding the nature of anything, of whatever kind, must also be the same, viz. through the universal laws and rules of nature.'[30] Hence human emotions such as hate, anger, envy, love, and so forth, considered in themselves, follow from the same necessity and force of nature as other particular things. Spinoza's technical term for emotion is 'affect' and in accordance with his stated principles he understands by 'affect' (*affectus*) 'affections of the body by which the body's power of acting is increased or diminished, aided or restrained, and, at the same time, the ideas of these affections.'[31]

In explaining his theory of the emotions, Spinoza reminds us that mind and body are not an interaction but a single identity. Hence the 'body cannot determine the mind to thinking, and the mind cannot determine the body to motion, rest or anything else (if there is anything else)' (III, Prop. II). The central doctrine around which he organizes this part of his system is the concept of *conatus*, that is, natural effort or inclination, the driving tendency as it were of every existing body. According to Spinoza 'no thing can be destroyed except through an external cause' (III, Prop. IV) and 'each thing, as far as it can, strives to persevere in its being' (Unaquaeque res, quantum in se est, in suo esse persevare conatur) (III, Prop. VI). This is more than just a natural instinct for self-preservation. Rather, what is meant is the striving to persist in one's own essence or nature: 'the striving by which each thing strives to preserve its being is nothing but the actual essence of the thing' (III, Prop. VII). This means beings and things are able to do nothing other than what follows necessarily from their determinate nature. Hence appetite or desire in man is simply a manifestation of the *conatus*, the endeavour of the human mind to persevere in its being.[32]

Man's nature is such that 'the mind, as far as it can, strives to imagine those things that increase or aid the body's power of acting' (III, Prop. XII). When, on the contrary, the 'mind imagines things that diminish or restrain its or the body's power of acting, it strives, as far as it can, to recollect things that exclude their existence' (III, Prop. XIII). These propositions, holds Spinoza, are the key to understanding what love and hate are.[33] Love is nothing but joy (or pleasure = *laetitia*) with the accompanying idea of an external cause, and hate is nothing but sadness (or pain = *tristitia*) with the accompanying idea of an external cause.[34] Hence one who loves necessarily strives to have present and preserve the thing he loves; while one who hates strives to remove and

---

[29] Collected Works of Spinoza. [30] Ibid., i, 492. [31] Ibid., i, 493; Hampshire, *Spinoza*, 135–6.
[32] Harris, *Spinoza's Philosophy*, 58–9; Hampshire, *Spinoza*, 122–7; Klever, *Ethicom*, 294–301; Bennett, *A Study*, 240–51; Garrett, 'Spinoza's Ethical Theory', 271.
[33] Klever, *Ethicom*, 311. [34] Harris, *Spinoza's Philosophy*, 59; Hampshire, *Spinoza*, 124–5.

destroy the thing he hates. He who imagines that what he loves is destroyed will be saddened, while he who imagines it is preserved will rejoice; and conversely, he who imagines that what he hates is destroyed will rejoice. This leads to the conclusion that 'we strive to further the occurrence of whatever we imagine will lead to joy [pleasure] and to avert or destroy what we imagine is contrary to it, or will lead to sadness [pain]' (III, Prop. XXVIII). Because *laetitia* (joy-pleasure) and *tristitia* (sadness-pain) are the primary emotions relating to the *conatus*, the individual's drive to conserve himself, 'among all the affects that are related to the mind in so far as it acts, there are none that are not related to *laetitia* or desire' (III, Prop. LIX).

Desire, maintains Spinoza, is appetite together with consciousness of it and appetite he deems the very essence of man in so far as he is predetermined to do what preserves and promotes his being. 'Joy [pleasure] is a person's passage from a lesser to a greater perfection' while 'sadness [pain] is a person's passing from a greater to a lesser perfection.'[35] In the fourth and penultimate part of the *Ethics* Spinoza focuses on the consequences of the inadequacy, or 'slavery', which results from man's inability to moderate or restrain his emotions. It is a form of bondage, he says, to be under the sway of emotion because the 'man who is subject to affects is under the control not of himself but of fortune in whose power he so entirely is that often, though he sees what is better for himself, still he is forced to follow what is worse.'[36] It is here that Spinoza introduces his celebrated doctrine of the relativity of good and evil. Since, as Spinoza believes he has proved in Part I, God (or Nature) exists for the sake of no end, having neither freedom nor intelligence (or goodness), the terms 'good' and 'evil' signify nothing of an intrinsic or absolute character 'nor are they anything other than modes of thinking, or notions we form because we compare things to one another.'[37] Indeed, he argues, the same thing can be alternately good, bad, or neutral, depending on circumstances, as cheerful music is respectively to the melancholy, mourners, and the deaf. Relatively, though, in relation to man these terms do assume meaning: 'by good I shall understand what we certainly know to be useful to us . . . by evil, however, I shall understand what we certainly know prevents our acquiring some good.'[38] From this Spinoza deduces that 'knowlege of good and evil is nothing but an effect of joy [pleasure], or sadness [pain], in so far as we are conscious of it' (IV, Prop, VIII) which in turn yields his key doctrine: 'from the laws of his own nature, everyone necessarily wants, or is repelled by, what he judges to be good or evil' (IV, Prop. XIX).

From this stems Spinoza's novel and seemingly paradoxical concept that 'virtue is human power itself, which is defined by man's essence alone, that is, solely by the striving by which man seeks to preserve his being. So the more each one strives and can preserve his being, the more he is endowed with virtue.'[39] One cannot, however, be said to be acting truly from virtue when one is determined to act on the basis of inadequate ideas. True virtue in man necessarily entails seeking to understand what really

---

[35] *Collected Works of Spinoza*, i, 531.   [36] Ibid., i, 543.

[37] Ibid., i, 545; Garrett, 'Spinoza's Ethical Theory', 272–3; Deleuze here draws a parallel with Nietzsche's *Beyond Good and Evil*, see Deleuze, *Spinoza*, 22.

[38] *Collected Works of Spinoza*, i, 543.   [39] Ibid., i, 557.

promotes the individual's self-conservation and advantage. This then leads directly to Spinoza's central ethical doctrine: 'acting absolutely from virtue is nothing else in us but acting, living and preserving our being (these three signifying the same thing) by the guidance of reason, from the foundation of seeking one's own advantage' (IV, Prop. XXIV).

Since no one strives to preserve his being for the sake of anything else, there can be no rational or meaningful system of morality except what is based on the striving to preserve one's being. But since we know nothing is certainly good or evil, except what helps or hinders our exercising our reason, only through reason can true virtue be pursued, and only by reason can men truly promote their own advantage. This leads to the proposition that 'knowledge of God is the mind's greatest good; its greatest virtue is to know God' (IV, Prop. XXVIII). When enslaved to, and torn by, their passions, men naturally oppose one another and lapse into conflict. But 'in so far as men live according to the guidance of reason, to that extent they must by nature always be in agreement' (Quatenus homines ex ductu rationis vivunt, eatenus tantum natura semper necessario conveniunt) (IV, Prop. XXXV).[40] It is when each man seeks his own advantage according to reason that men are most useful to one another and that social life flourishes most. For the more each person seeks his own advantage, and strives to preserve himself, the more he is endowed with virtue, or what is the same, the greater is his power of acting according to the laws of his own nature, that is, of living under the guidance of reason.

Admittedly, men rarely do live 'according to the guidance of reason'. Instead they are so constituted that they are usually envious of, and burdensome to, one another. Nevertheless, everyday experience shows that by helping one another, men can more easily provide themselves with the things they need and by joining forces repel the dangers that threaten them. 'The greatest good of those who seek virtue is common to all, and can be enjoyed by all equally' (IV, Prop. XXXVI). If men lived according to the guidance of reason, everyone would possess this 'highest good' without injury to anyone else. But because men are, on the contrary, mostly ruled by their passions, they are drawn in contrary directions and into strife. In order that men may be able to live harmoniously, and be of assistance to one another, it is necessary for each person to give up his or her individual natural right and thereby make one another confident that each will not attack or harm the next. Moreover, there is a mechanism in human nature by which this goal can be achieved. Because no 'affect' can be checked except by an emotion stronger than, and contrary to, the first, everyone can be made to refrain from doing harm only out of fear of suffering some greater injury than that harm.

Accordingly, society can be maintained provided it appropriates to itself the right everyone has by nature of avenging himself and of judging concerning 'good and evil'. In those circumstances, society acquires the power to impose a common framework of permitted and proscribed conduct, to make laws and to uphold them, main-

---

[40] Spinoza, *Opera*, ii, 232; Klever, *Ethicom*, 519–20; Garrett, 'Spinoza's Ethical Theory', 277.

taining those laws not by force of reason, which cannot restrain the passions, but by warnings, deterrents and penalties. Such a society, maintained by laws and the power it has of preserving itself, is called a state and those that live under, and are defended by its laws, citizens. Only in the context of the state, can it be and is it 'decided by common agreement what is good or what is evil'.[41] Sin, consequently, is nothing but disobedience to the norms of society, and the laws of the state, and can be punished only by the agencies of the state. 'Since those things are good which assist the parts of the body to perform their function, and joy [pleasure] consists in the fact that Man's power, in that he consists of mind and body, is aided and enhanced, all things that bring joy [pleasure] are good.'[42] However, unless tempered by reason and prudence, most forms of desire for joy (pleasure) are excessive and soon incur a contrary effect since things do not exist in order to affect us with joy, and their *conatus* is not determined for our advantage, and because most joy (pleasure) is connected only to one part of the body; and also because when we follow our emotions we esteem most the pleasures of the moment and cannot appraise future consequences 'with an equal affect of the mind'.[43]

The fifth and final part of the *Ethics* is concerned to show what 'freedom of the mind, or blessedness, is'.[44] It opens with some critical remarks dismissing Descartes' conception of the union of body and mind and 'all those things he claimed about the will and its freedom'.[45] Here Spinoza's key concept is that 'if we detach an emotion, or affect, of the mind from the thought of an external cause, and join them to other thoughts, then the love or hate toward the external cause and the fluctuations of the mind arising from these emotions are removed' (V, Prop. II). Consequently, the more we know and understand an emotion better, the more it is under our control and the less does the mind suffer from it. This leads to the famous doctrine: 'in so far as the mind understands all things to be necessary, it has a greater power over the affects, or is less acted on by them' (V, Prop. VI). Thus, for example, to lay aside fear 'we must recount and frequently imagine the common dangers of life, and how they can be best avoided and overcome by presence of mind and strength of character.'[46]

'It is common to everyone whose luck is bad and whose mind is weak', argues Spinoza, to brood on and express resentment towards those who have what they lack. Thus the poor man who is greedy does not stop talking about the vices of the rich and their misuse of money. The ambitious who are thwarted dwell on the emptiness and misuse of power and status. A man rejected by his lover might well think of nothing but the inconstancy and deceptiveness of women. But with such thoughts one only distresses oneself and shows others one cannot live calmly with one's own lack of success. Against this tendency in our nature, Spinoza insists that man can cultivate his reason and learn to 'moderate his affects and appetites from the love of freedom'.[47] This produces Spinoza's argument that 'the mind can bring it about that all the body's

---

[41] *Collected Works of Spinoza*, i, 567.   [42] Ibid., i, 593.   [43] Ibid.
[44] Ibid., i, 594.   [45] Ibid., i, 596–7.   [46] Ibid., i, 602.
[47] Ibid., i, 603; Garrett, 'Spinoza's Ethical Theory', 275–81.

affections, or images of things, are related to the idea of God' (V, Prop. XIV). The advantage in so doing is that love in one's affections is generalized to the maximum and hate minimized, for 'No one can hate God' (V, Prop. XVIII).

Spinoza having now 'completed everything which concerns this present life',[48] the final sections of the *Ethics* have an enigmatic, inscrutable quality, which many feel lacks the air of inevitablity and logical cogency prevailing hitherto. Already in the *Korte Verhandeling* Spinoza enunciates his doctrine of the human soul as being in one sense mortal, that is, in so far as it is united with the body something that perishes with the body, but in another sense having a kind of immortality, that is, in so far as it is part of the cause of the soul's existence, that is, God (or Nature), it must, like the totality of everything, remain immutable and immortal.[49] This then reappears in the *Ethics* as the celebrated teaching that 'the human mind cannot be absolutely destroyed with the body, but something of it remains which is eternal' (V, Prop. XXIII). In explaining this, Spinoza stresses that we do not attribute duration to the mind 'except while the body endures', nevertheless 'since what is conceived with a certain eternal necessity through God's essence itself is still something, this something which pertains to the essence of the mind will necessarily be eternal.'[50] This element of immortality, however one explains it, clearly has to do with the mind's ability to grasp eternally true ideas and the notion that by dwelling on eternal things, as everyone must in some degree, one shares, as it were, in eternity.

Closely connected with this element of immortality of the human soul, contends Spinoza, is the highest form of human knowledge. Our knowledge, he explains in Part II of the *Ethics*, consists of three kinds and is reached in three different ways. 'Knowledge of the first kind, opinion or imagination' is based on representation 'to us through the senses in a way that is mutilated, confused and without order for the intellect', that is, knowledge from sense perception or what Spinoza also terms 'knowledge from random experience'.[51] Reason, or 'the second kind of knowledge', is correct inference from 'common notions and adequate ideas of the properties of things', that is, logical deduction in terms of geometrically related proportions. The 'third kind, which we shall call intuitive knowledge,' says Spinoza, 'proceeds from an adequate idea of the formal essence of certain attributes of God to the adequate knowledge of the formal essence of things.'[52] The difference, seemingly, between the second and third kinds of knowledge is that the second requires formal steps of reasoning, as distinct from a direct intellectual grasp of properties characteristic of the latter, and also in that the second kind fails to reach the inmost essence and wider scheme of things.[53] The link between this third kind of knowledge and the element of immortality in human existence is his contention that 'the greatest striving of the mind, and its greatest virtue, is understanding things by the third kind of knowledge' (V, Prop. XXV) and that the 'greatest satisfaction of the mind there can be arises from

---

[48] *Collected Works of Spinoza*, i, 606.   [49] Ibid., i, 140–1.   [50] Ibid., i, 607.
[51] Ibid., i, 477; Wilson,'Spinoza's Theory', 116–17; Mason, *God of Spinoza*, 240–2.
[52] *Collected Works of Spinoza*, i, 478.
[53] Wilson, 'Spinoza's Theory', 118; Harris, *Spinoza's Philosophy*, 42–8; Klever, *Ethicom*, 219–25.

this third kind of knowledge' (V, Prop. XXVII). Desire to know things according to the third kind of knowledge cannot arise in man, asserts Spinoza, on the basis of sense perception or the first kind of knowledge, but only as a consequence of reason. Moreover, 'the third kind of knowledge depends on the mind, as on a formal cause, in so far as the mind itself is eternal' (V, Prop. XXXI), hence the more each of us is able to attain to 'this kind of knowledge, the more he is conscious of himself and God, that is, the more perfect and blessed he is.'[54] Consequently, Spinoza claims, 'the intellectual love of God, which arises from the third kind of knowledge, is eternal' (V, Prop. XXXIII) and 'there is nothing in nature which is contrary to this intellectual love, or which can take it away' (V, Prop. XXXVII). This yields the final proposition in Spinoza's universal philosophical quasi-religion: 'blessedness is not the reward of virtue, but virtue itself; nor do we enjoy it because we restrain our lusts; on the contrary, because we enjoy it, we are able to restrain them.'[55]

[54] *Collected Works of Spinoza*, i, 610.   [55] Ibid., 616–17.

14 | SPINOZA, SCIENCE, AND THE SCIENTISTS

i. Radical Thought and the Scientific Revolution

In August 1663 Henry Oldenburg, secretary of the Royal Society, and one of the closest observers of British and European science of the age, wrote to Spinoza, urging that he and Robert Boyle (1627–91), then the leading figure in English science, should join forces: 'unite your abilities in striving to advance a genuine and firmly based philosophy'—that is, an account of the universe: 'may I urge you especially, by the acuteness of your mathematical mind, to continue to establish basic principles, just as I ceaselessly try to coax my noble friend Boyle to confirm and illustrate them by experiments and observations frequently and accurately made.'[1] Spinoza's notable absence, or marginality, in most histories and lexicons of science might make this seem a bizarre proposal on Oldenburg's part. Far more usual is the claim that 'as far as the natural sciences and mathematics are concerned . . . though Spinoza was thoroughly competent and acquainted with some of the best work of his time, he contributed little of importance to research and theory.'[2] Yet there are grounds for arguing, as Oldenburg implied, that Spinoza does in fact have a special place in the history of scientific thought.

An accomplished practitioner of science himself, being a leading contributor to the development of the microscope before Leeuwenhoek, Spinoza's general philosophy was profoundly influenced by his conception of science and scientific method. Indeed, he would undoubtedly have been horrified by any suggestion that he and his philosophy are remote from modern science, not just because he spent much time experimenting, studying experiments, and discussing experimental results with scientists, as well as assembling microscopes and telescopes, but still more, because it was basic to his conception of his philosophy that his thought should be firmly anchored

---

[1] Spinoza, *Letters*, 124; Spinoza, *Opera*, iv, 75.

[2] Savan, 'Spinoza: Scientist and Theorist', 97; indeed, it is not uncommon to find still more negative judgements of Spinoza's role in science; thus Maull affirms that while 'Spinoza's interest in experimental science is well-documented . . . it was carefully bracketed from his larger metaphysical concerns' and that 'philosophically, as opposed to biographically, he was as remote from elementary "doing" of science, and especially from the idea of learning by experience, as Plato was'; Maull, 'Spinoza in the Century of Science', 3; Gabbey, 'Spinoza's Natural Science', 146.

in the rules and procedures of mathematics and science.[3] For Spinoza, as a thinker, claims to be seeking 'true ideas' about nature and how nature operates, conceived in terms of mathematically verifiable cause and effect. This led him to adopt a uniquely exacting and comprehensive notion of scientific rationality, driving him to reject, unremittingly and often scornfully, arguments, beliefs, and traditions which conflict with the laws of nature expressed in mechanistic, mathematically verifiable terms. Being more extreme, more of a maximalist, in this respect than any other scientific thinker before La Mettrie and Diderot—and considerably more so than Boyle or Newton—this in itself makes him an exceptional and noteworthy figure in the history of modernity and scientific thought.

Cartesians postulated a dichotomy of substance, conceiving reality to operate within two totally separate spheres or sets of rules governing reality, only one of which was mechanistic and subject to the laws of physical cause and effect. Boyle, Newton, and other English empiricists insisted that only what is proven to operate mechanistically, by experiment, is definitely known to be subject to cause and effect, leaving much else beyond what is humanly knowable. Hence, only Spinoza and his adherents claim that the mechanistic concepts yielded by the scientific advances of the seventeenth century are universally applicable, so that everything which exists obeys the same set of rules with no other reality, or mode of being, possible beyond or out-side the laws of motion governing Nature. 'Nothing, then,' concludes Spinoza, 'can happen in Nature to contravene her own universal laws, nor anything that is not in agreement with these laws or that does not follow from them.'[4] This, of course, is inherent in his 'one-substance' doctrine.

The discussion of 'miracles' in the *Tractatus Theologico-Politicus* vividly illustrates the centrality of scientific criteria and modes of explanation in the overall structure of Spinoza's system. He rebukes critics of 'those who cultivate the natural sciences', who prefer to remain ignorant of natural causes, because to close one's mind to science is to shut oneself off from the only certain and reliable criterion of truth we possess.[5] Nothing happens or exists beyond Nature's laws and hence there can be no miracles; and those that are believed, or alleged, to have occurred, in fact had natural causes which at the time men were unable to grasp. Characteristically, he seeks natural causes for every phenomenon which has impressed or frightened men, including humanity's love of miracles itself. The appeal of 'miracles' is so great, he observes, that men have not ceased to this day to invent miracles with a view to convincing peo-ple they are more beloved of God than others, and are the final cause of God's creation and continuous direction of the world.[6] Contriving and invoking 'miracles' and per-suading others to believe in them, is thus itself a natural phenomenon, as is the habit of those who proclaim and elaborate 'miracles' to denounce as 'impious' those who seek to explain them as natural events.[7]

---

[3] Klever, 'Anti-falsificationism', 124–7, 131.

[4] Spinoza, *TTP*, 126, Spinoza adds a footnote here explaining that 'by Nature, I do not mean simply matter and its modifications, but infinite other things besides matter.'

[5] Ibid., 124.   [6] Ibid., 125.   [7] Ibid., 140; *Collected Works of Spinoza*, i, 443–4.

At the core of Spinoza's philosphy, then, stands the contention that 'nothing happens in Nature that does not follow from her laws, that her laws cover everything that is conceived even by the divine intellect, and that Nature observes a fixed and immutable order,' that is, that the same laws of motion, and laws of cause and effect, apply in all contexts and everywhere.[8] Certainly, this is a metaphysical system which cannot be proved or disproved scientifically. But it is nevertheless also a 'scientific' theory conceivable only since the rise of the seventeenth-century 'mechanistic world-view', claiming as it does that the laws science demonstrates through experiment and mathematical calculation are universally valid and the sole criterion of truth. At a stroke Spinoza excludes 'miracles', the supernatural, magic, and divine Providence. At the core of the general appraisal of Spinoza as an 'atheist' in late seventeenth-century Europe is thus the evidently correct perception of writers such as Boyle, Henry More, Musaeus, Huet, and Loescher that Spinoza's denial of miracles, Providence, Satan, demons, angels, ghosts, and the immortal soul in man stems from his contention that everything in the universe that happens, or ever could happen, follows *ex fixo et immutabili Naturae ordine*, out of the fixed and immutable order of Nature.[9] One vehement late seventeenth-century antagonist denounced Spinoza as the founder of a new idolatry: worship of the 'spectre' of 'mathematical certitude'.[10] Hence Spinoza's conception of truth, and the criterion for judging what is true, is 'mathematical logic', and mathematical rationality universally applied provides, from Spinoza to Marx, the essential link between the Scientific Revolution and the tradition of radical thought.[11]

Not only was Spinoza's view of miracles, Providence, and Bible criticism based on what he and his scientific contemporaries called the 'principles of natural things', but so was every branch of his system. Admittedly his philosophy does not look 'scientific' to us today; but this stems from the—to us—strange terminology and format in which it is expressed. In his own eyes, his philosophy was based on modern science both experimental and deductive. In his treatise on the 'Improvement of the Understanding', Spinoza formulates criteria for judging the validity, or invalidity, of all reasoning in a way which makes no distinction between scientific method and philosophical procedure. Spinoza bases his case on the proposition that the sole criteria of truth are the 'principles of nature' expressed as mathematically verifiable equations. 'Spinoza's epistemological dogmatism,' it has been aptly observed, 'is probably the furthest removed from scepticism of any of the new philosophies of the seventeenth century. It is a genuine anti-sceptical theory trying to eradicate the possibility, or meaningfulness, of doubting or suspending judgement.'[12] Spinoza's reply to the sceptics is simply

---

[8] Spinoza, *TTP*, 126–7; Paty, 'Einstein et Spinoza', 196–7.

[9] Musaeus, *Tractatus . . . examinatus*, 54, 65–6; Hulsius, *Spinozismi Depulsio*, 33; Masius, *Dissertationes academicae*, 65–6; Popkin, *History of Scepticism*, 229–32; Geismann, 'Spinoza—beyond Hobbes and Rousseau', 42.

[10] Poiret, *Cogitationes rationales*, 74–5, 80.

[11] Paty, 'Einstein et Spinoza', 186–8; Yakira, 'What is a Mathematical Truth?', 74–5, 98.

[12] Popkin, *History of Scepticism*, 245.

that 'there is no speaking of the sciences with them; for if someone proves something to them, they do not know whether the argument is a proof or not.'[13] His point is that mathematical and scientific—that is, all—truths are those which are logically demonstrable from correctly adduced proofs. Data can be correctly or incorrectly explained, but not so that we are unable to judge whether the explanation is correct or not. If the validity of mathematical demonstrations is called in question, then nothing at all can be known and no investigative philosophy or science is possible. But such a sceptical position, he claims, is tenable only if one can 'see no impossibility and no necessity' in defiance of mathematical logic and mechanical laws which, in his view, is simply not possible in good faith. One cannot honestly deny the logical force of the proposition that two and two make four. He gives the example of the earth's rotundity.[14] Only science can prove the earth is round. One may well not believe it is round until shown the proofs. But it is impossible for someone who grasps the proofs to doubt or oppose them sincerely.

Science, consequently, is essential to acquiring meaningful knowledge about reality and therefore for human self-knowledge, happiness, and salvation. But science not only helps us grasp reality, and remove irrational fears and anxieties, it also improves human life in other ways by emancipating man from the anxieties and pressures arising from his basic bodily needs. 'Because health is no small means to achieving this end,' he asserts, as one who long suffered from chronic ill-health himself, 'the whole of medicine must be worked out and since, by ingenuity, many laborious things are made easy, and because we can gain time and convenience in life by it, technology is by no means to be despised.'[15] 'Everyone will now see,' he wrote, 'that I wish to direct all the sciences towards one end and goal, namely that we should be brought to the highest human perfection and, thus, whatever in the sciences does nothing to bring us to our aim, should be rejected as useless.'[16]

The rise of the 'mechanistic world-view' commencing with Galileo and Descartes, and especially, the formulation and refinement of the laws of motion, itself intensified the growing conceptual antithesis in European culture and thought between the 'natural' and 'supernatural'. The sharpening of this antithesis, in other words, is a typical and general seventeenth-century phenomenon. Descartes, Hobbes, Leibniz, Malebranche, and innumerable lesser figures all contributed in various ways to heightening awareness, and stimulating debate about, this growing dichotomy of reality. Yet, as the Lutheran professor Johannes Heinrich Müller averred in his inaugural lecture on miracles, at Altdorf in 1714, only Spinoza creates an absolute and irreconcilable antithesis between these increasingly distinct spheres, or ways of comprehending reality, dismissing the 'supernatural' as a total figment of our imagination. Re-embodying the principles of classical Greek atheism, according to Müller, Spinoza is the prime 'propagator' and 'restorer' of ideas which set the 'natural' in fundamental conflict with the 'miraculous', thereby threatening the whole basis of

[13] *Collected Works of Spinoza*, i, 22.   [14] Ibid., 25.
[15] 'mechanica nullo modo est contemnenda', ibid., 11.   [16] Ibid.

Christian (and, he might have added, also Jewish and Islamic) civilization—ideas, faith, authority, morality, and the political and social order.[17] In case anyone in the lecture-hall was unfamiliar with Spinoza's *Tractatus*, Müller declaimed verbatim several key passages, asserting the absolute validity of the laws of nature demonstrated by science, and that nothing can occur contrary to Nature, which adheres to an eternal, fixed, and immutable order. This, in Müller's view, represented the overriding philosophico-theologico-scientific challenge of the age. After briefly pondering Henry More's and Frans Kuyper's critiques of Spinoza's 'one-substance' system, he judges the Cartesian response, and above all, that of Regnerus van Mansvelt, the most effective way to rescue a two-sphere universe, separating body and spirit and accommodating the supernatural.[18]

The most important and exceptional element in Spinoza's scientific thought, then, is simply that natural philosophy, or science, is of universal applicability and that there is no reserved area beyond it. This implied a stark contrast between Spinoza's scientific rationality and that of every other leading philosopher and scientist of the age, not least Descartes. 'I recall,' noted Oldenburg in October 1665, unconsciously echoing Meyer's remarks in his preface to Spinoza's volume on Descartes,[19] 'that you some-where indicated that many of those matters which Descartes himself affirmed surpass human comprehension—indeed even matters more sublime and subtle—can be plainly understood by men and clearly explained.'[20] Everything that Descartes had said surpasses human understanding, Meyer had stated, can, according to Spinoza 'not only be conceived clearly and distinctly, but also explained very satisfac-torily—provided only Man's intellect is guided in the search for truth and knowledge of things along a different path from that which Descartes opened up'.[21] In effect, Descartes' mechanistic world-view was being radically extended to encompass the whole of reality.

ii. Spinoza and Huygens

Various contemporaries attested to Spinoza's skill in preparing lenses and building microscopes and telescopes, including Leibniz, who initiated his correspondence with Spinoza, writing from Frankfurt in October 1671, with the intimation that 'among your other achievements which fame has spread abroad I understand is your remark-able skill in optics.'[22] According to his first biographer, Lucas, Spinoza worked at his lenses and microscopes daily for several hours 'en quoi il excelloit de sort que si la mort ne l'eut point prévenu, il est à croire qu'il eut découvert les plus beaux secrets de l'op-tique'.[23] Problems in optics were clearly an abiding interest, and typically he chose the rainbow, a phenomenon for which men have felt awe, and attributed supernatural causes reaching back over the millennia, as a striking phenomenon for which he

[17] Müller, *Dissertatio*, 13–14; Hulsius, *Spinozismi Depulsio*, 34.   [18] Müller, *Dissertatio*, 15–17.
[19] *Collected Works of Spinoza*, i, 230.   [20] Spinoza, *Letters*, 190.
[21] *Collected Works of Spinoza*, i, 230.   [22] Spinoza, *Letters*, 245.   [23] *La Vie et l'esprit*, 34.

would try to demonstrate wholly natural causes. He is known to have laboured hard on this topic, probably in the mid-1660s, and penned a treatise about it but, dissatisfied with the result, had himself, according to Jelles, destroyed the manuscript shortly before his death. In his catalogue of Spinoza's works of 1719, Charles Levier, the Spinozist publisher active at The Hague, styles this treatise the 'traité de l'iris, ou de l'arc-en-ciel, qu'il a jetté au feu'.[24] Yet, even now, it is not certain that the text is irretrievably lost.

Among those most aware of Spinoza's work with microscopes was the pre-eminent scientist of the Dutch Golden Age, Christian Huygens. In the 1660s the Dutch microscope, in the later seventeenth century the most advanced in the west, was still at a rudimentary stage, magnifying by at most thirty to forty times, but its potential significance as an instrument of scientific research was evident, and Huygens considered himself, Spinoza, and the Amsterdam regent-scientist, Johannes Hudde, the three leading specialists labouring to improve and extend its capabilities. Huygens got to know Spinoza personally in the early 1660s and conferred with him about scientific matters on numerous occasions, particularly in the mid-1660s.[25] It emerges from letters sent by Huygens from Paris to his brother in Voorburg during 1667-8, in which he generally refers to Spinoza with a pinch of social disdain, as 'nostre Juif', 'nostre Israelite', 'le Juif de Voorburg', or simply 'l'Israélite', that Huygens and Spinoza disagreed about microscope lense sizes and curvatures. In deliberating with his brother, Huygens did not hide the fact that Spinoza was in some respects even more proficient with microscopes than he was himself.[26] On one occasion, in April 1668, he granted that 'il est vray que l'expérience confirme ce que dit Spinosa que les petits objectifs au microscope représentent plus distinctement les objets que les grands, avec des ouvertures proportionelles,' adding that the reason for this would be discovered 'quoyque le sieur Spinosa ni moy ne le sachions pas encore'.[27] On another point of optical research, where Huygens believed he had hit on something new, he urges his brother to say nothing about it to 'l'Israélite', with whom he evidently remained in touch from Paris, through his brother, lest Hudde and others 'ne pénétrassent dans cette spéculation qui a encore d'autres utilitez'.[28]

Below the surface, the barely suppressed rivalry between Huygens and Spinoza extended far beyond lenses and microscopes. For both men, the central issue in science at the time was to revise and refine Descartes' laws of motion and mechanics. That Spinoza participated prominently in Dutch scientific debate at the highest level, conferring with Hudde, De Volder, and other key scientific minds as well as Huygens, is proved, among other evidence, by a letter to Huygens, sent from Dunkirk in 1676 by

[24] [Levier], 'Catalogue', 60; Petry, 'Inleiding', 498; Gabbey, 'Spinoza's Natural Science', 152-4; Nadler, *Spinoza*, 264.

[25] Klever, 'Insignis Opticus', 50; Klever, 'Spinoza en Huygens', 14; Nadler, *Spinoza*, 203-4, 221-2.

[26] Klever, 'Insignis Opticus', 50-2.

[27] Huygens to Constantijn Huygens, Paris, 6 Apr. 1668 in Huygens, *Oeuvres complètes*, vi, 213; Klever, 'Insignis Opticus', 50-2.

[28] Huygens, *Oeuvres complètes*, vi, 215.

a Dutch hydraulics engineer then working for the French, who recalled that when he was in Amsterdam, eleven years before, thus in 1665, he had learnt much about Huygens' admirable feats in science 'in many marvellous gatherings and conversations in the company of Johannes Hudde, Benedictus de Spinoza and [Burchardus] de Volder [now] professor at the university of Leiden'.[29] Though always on superficially affable terms, especially between 1663 and 1665, when Spinoza on various occasions visited the brothers at their lordly residence of 'Hofwijck' at Voorburg,[30] Spinoza's relationship with the touchy Huygens developed into an inextricable mix of mutual regard and underlying antagonism. Sons of Constantijn Huygens, secretary to two Princes of Orange, and accustomed to courtly life, the brothers deemed themselves of incomparably higher social status than their Jewish friend. Yet while the hint of irritation in Huygens' attitude to the philosopher stemmed mainly from his obsessive need for seclusion and a sense of rivalry regarding Spinoza's formidable intellect, their relationship was further complicated by Spinoza's humble self-sufficiency and independence, which contrasted starkly with Christian's dependence first on his father and, from 1665, on Louis XIV's patronage, for the support and resources needed for his research and keeping up his social status.[31]

Spinoza respected Huygens and his scientific achievement but also became increasingly critical of him, an attitude again marked by clear signs of irritation. Of course, both men were uncommonly ambitious but in different ways. Huygens, vain and imperious, more openly thirsted for international renown and glory: he wanted, quite simply, to be the greatest scientist of his age, filling the kind of niche modern western culture generally accords to Newton, a greater scientist without doubt and one with whom Huygens became offended in 1673 and ceased to communicate.[32] Thus Huygens and Spinoza were both geniuses, each nurturing grandiose plans which subtly grated on the sensibilities of the other. Unlike Boyle, it is unlikely that Huygens was repelled by Spinoza's system as such. For, in contrast to his devout Calvinist father, Constantijn, Christian was only nominally loyal to the faith of his upbringing, privately adhering to a rationalistic deism which rendered him largely amenable to the sweeping vision of 'science' advocated by Spinoza.[33] Huygens was a master of scientific experiments and instruments but no pure empiricist, believing, not unlike Spinoza, that a mathematically anchored mechanistic world-view is an essential prerequisite and framework for the pursuit of purposeful scientific research.[34] That his deism ran deep is shown by his refusal, when desperately ill, to permit a clergyman to be brought to him, prompting his brother to rebuke him, after his recovery, for

---

[29] Huygens, *Oeuvres complètes*, viii, 3–4; Klever, 'Burchard de Volder', 193, 234.

[30] Parrochia, 'Physique et politique', 70–1; Keesing, 'Frères Huygens et Spinoza', 112, 121; Nadler, *Spinoza*, 203–4, 221–2.

[31] Keesing, 'Frères Huygens et Spinoza', 113–15.

[32] Ibid., 115–17; Andriesse, 'Melancholic Genius', 4.

[33] De Vries, 'Christiaan Huygens', 6–11; Keesing, 'Frères Huygens et Spinoza', 114, 127.

[34] De Vries, 'Christiaan Huygens', 6–9; Dijksterhuis, *Mechanisation*, 457–8.

showing insufficient concern for the salvation of his soul.[35] Huygens had foresaken miracles, theology, and faith. But this afforded no close bond with Spinoza, since the great physicist disliked discussing theological topics and was impeccably discreet in public, whereas Spinoza was already known as an 'atheist' in the 1660s and after publication of his *Tractatus* was universally considered an antagonist of Christianity. If Huygens ever responded to Leibniz's letter of December 1679, asking what he thought of Spinoza's *Ethics* and 'démonstrations prétendues'—no answer has survived—he is most unlikely to have revealed his innermost thoughts on the matter.[36]

At the root of the differences between Huygens and Spinoza was a latent friction—albeit one of which both were in some degree aware—about how to practise science and over methodology.[37] It was a tension not without affinities with the parallel encounter between Spinoza and Boyle. Huygens, nurtured on Descartes, came to reject not only Descartes' proofs of God's existence and the soul's immortality, but also most of his formulations in physics and mechanics, attributing his mistakes to an excessive addiction to abstract reasoning divorced from observation and experiment.[38] In this connection, Spinoza presumably struck Huygens as a more or less unreformed 'Cartesian', participating in scientific enquiry without engaging systematically in experimental work. Spinoza, for his part, though he liked experiments, invariably subordinated experiment and its results to what, to him, was a broadly correct, wider, theoretical and philosophical framework.

The chief points of discussion and disagreement concerned the laws of motion. In the summer and autumn of 1666, during the Second Anglo-Dutch War, there was a marked cooling in relations between Huygens and the Royal Society in London, for personal as well as war-related reasons, and at that point Oldenburg wrote several times to Spinoza, enquiring about Huygens' research, including his revision of Descartes' laws of motion.[39] Spinoza responded with two letters betraying distinctly mixed feelings about Huygens and his work. 'It is quite a long time,' he wrote, expressing doubt as to whether Huygens' promised treatise on dynamics would ever appear, 'since he began to boast his calculations had shown that the rules of motion, and laws of nature, are very different from those given by Descartes, and that those of Descartes are almost all wrong.'[40] Huygens had indeed been much preoccupied with the laws of motion since the late 1650s and had already penned in draft his treatise on centrifugal force, *De vi centrifuga*, by 1659.[41] But his conclusions had not been disclosed to other Dutch scientists, among them Spinoza. 'Yet up to now,' Spinoza assured Oldenburg, mistakenly assuming that Huygens' silence meant he had failed to achieve a

---

[35] De Vries, 'Christiaan Huygens', 17; Keesing, 'Frères Huygens et Spinoza', 117–18.

[36] Huygens, *Oeuvres complètes*, viii, 253.   [37] Andriesse, 'Melancholic Genius', 3, 5.

[38] De Vries, 'Christiaan Huygens', 9–10.

[39] Spinoza, *Letters*, 184, 189–90, 198; Feingold, 'Huygens', 26.

[40] Spinoza, *Letters*, 188; Feingold, 'Huygens', 24; Klever, 'Spinoza en Huygens', 19–20.

[41] Andriesse, 'Melancholic Genius', 4–5.

fundamental reformulation of the laws of motion, 'he has produced no evidence on this subject,' although 'a year ago he told me all his discoveries made by calculation regarding motion he had since found verified by experiment in England' which, he added, 'I can hardly believe.'[42]

Oldenburg took Spinoza to mean that Descartes' laws of motion were indeed invalid. But in his next letter Spinoza—who, especially at that juncture, had scarcely more reason than Huygens to be open and candid towards Oldenburg—sought to dispel this impression: 'if I remember rightly I said Mr Huygens thinks so while I did not assert that any of the rules were wrong except the sixth, regarding which I said I thought Mr Huygens also was in error.'[43] Descartes' Sixth Law of Motion holds that 'if a body A is at rest and exactly equal in size to a body B which moves towards it, then it must in part be pushed by B and in part cause B to rebound, so that if B approaches A with four degrees of velocity, it must transfer one degree to it and return in the direction from which it had come through the other three degrees.'[44] This is indeed invalid, but no less so than most of the rest of Descartes' laws.

Spinoza evidently wished to tell Oldenburg as little as possible, since we know he disagreed, regarding the laws of motion, with both Descartes and what he took Huygens' position to be. Descartes had laid the foundations, certainly being the first to envisage what a fully mechanistic system of physics would be like.[45] Spinoza agrees with him that matter is a single substance embracing the whole of physical reality and, consequently, that there is no vacuum and change in anything must proceed from superior force (*variatio in aliqua re procedit a vi fortiori*).[46] But, as emerges especially (but not only) from his correspondence with Tschirnhaus, for the rest Spinoza had long rejected Descartes' laws of nature. Writing to Tschirnhaus in May 1676, Spinoza affirms that 'from extension as conceived by Descartes, that is as an inert mass, it is not only difficult, as you say, but entirely impossible to demonstrate the existence of bodies, for matter at rest will not be set in motion except by a more powerful external cause,' adding 'and for this reason, I did not hesitate long ago to affirm that the Cartesian principles of natural things are useless not to say absurd.'[47] In stressing the impossibility of explaining the existence of individual bodies in the context of Descartes' concept of 'extension', Spinoza had indeed put his finger on one of the major logical flaws, or elements of incoherence, in Descartes' philosophy.[48]

For Descartes, motion is external to matter and introduced into the material world by God; more ambiguously, in his published book expounding Descartes' principles, Spinoza asserts that 'God is the principal cause of motion' and that 'since God is the

---

[42] Spinoza, *Letters*, 188.   [43] Ibid., 195; Gabbey, 'Spinoza's Natural Science', 165.

[44] *Collected Works of Spinoza*, i, 288–9; Klever, 'Spinoza en Huygens', 19.

[45] Williams, *Descartes*, 275–6.

[46] Klever, 'Moles in motu', 172–3; Gabbey. 'Spinoza's Natural Science', 164–7, 188.

[47] 'Et hac de causa non dubitavi olim affirmare, rerum naturalium principia cartesiana inutilia esse,ne dicam absurda'; Spinoza, *Opera*, iv, 332; Matheron, 'Physique', 107–8; Lécrivain, 'Spinoza et la physique cartésienne', 241; Klever, 'Moles in motu', 107–8.

[48] Cottingham, *A Descartes Dictionary*, 132; Klever, 'Spinoza en Huygens', 23.

cause of motion and rest . . . he still preserves them by the same power by which he created them . . . and, indeed, in the same quantity in which he first created them.'[49] In fact, already in the *Korte Verhandeling*, of 1661, it is plain that Spinoza conceived motion to be entirely inherent in matter and inseparable from 'extension'.[50] Furthermore, his attempt to solve Descartes' difficulty and explain the existence of individual bodies within an infinite continuum of 'extension', rests precisely on his concept of motion as inherent in matter, perceiving the differentiation of bodies, and of different kinds of matter, as stemming from the effects of motion, so that differences between objects, and different states of the same object, 'arise only from the different proportions of motion and rest'.[51] From this nothing is exempted: hence our own bodies possess a different proportion of motion and rest as unborn babies than they have during life outside the womb, or later when we are dead.[52]

Consequently, there is in Spinoza, in contrast to Descartes, Malebranche, Leibniz, or Locke, no such thing as motion, or any motive force, external to matter which, to the late seventeenth-century mind, was a deeply shocking and revolutionary idea.[53] Neither is there any such thing as inertia, rest being merely a balance of opposing pressures. Against such arguments, the Cartesians, down to the early eighteenth century, tenaciously persisted in defending their doctrine that since 'aucun corps ne se peut mouvoir luy-même,' as Régis expresses it, 'il n'y a que Dieu qui soit la cause première et totale de tout le mouvement qui est dans le monde.'[54]

That motion is inherent in matter, that bodies 'are distinguished from one another by reason of motion and rest',[55] and the connected idea that the cohesion, or solidity, of bodies derives from the air pressure around them, a form of pressure of bodies on bodies, together comprise a revolutionary 'scientific' insight which pervades the whole of Spinoza's system.[56] In some ways, it implies a strikingly 'modern' conception of both physics and biology, albeit, as he himself remarked to Tschirnhaus, he had not been given the time to develop it.[57] By defining motion as integral, rather than external to substance, and the factor which gives individuality to bodies, Spinoza not only challenges the Cartesian axiom that the 'force mouvante n'est autre chose que la volonté que Dieu a de mouvoir la matière'[58] but provides the first germ of the idea that the creation and evolution of living and inanimate bodies is a natural process inherent in the properties of nature itself. This 'principle of intrinsic mutation' (principium

---

[49] Garber, *Descartes' Metaphysical Physics*, 280–300; *Collected Works of Spinoza*, i, 276.

[50] Ibid., 91, 95–6; Lachterman, 'Laying down the Law', 128; Klever, 'Moles in motu', 168–70.

[51] *Collected Works of Spinoza*, i, 152; Bennett, *A Study*, 106–10; Klever, 'Spinoza en Huygens', 21.

[52] Klever, 'Motion of the Projectile', 338–9; Klever, 'Moles in motu', 178–87.

[53] Jelles, *Voorreeden*, 146–7; Wyermars, *De ingebeelde Chaos*, x, 81; Moniglia, *Dissertazione contra i Materialisti*, 155, 223, 228–31, 239–40.

[54] Régis, *Système de philosophie*, i, 305; see also Le Vassor, *De la véritable Religion*, 13; Rydelius, *Sententiae philosophicae*, 24; Geulincx, *Compendium physicae*, 106–7, 111.

[55] *Collected Works of Spinoza*, i, 459.

[56] Ibid., 458–62; Gabbey, 'Spinoza's Natural Science', 168–9, Klever, 'Spinoza en Huygens', 22–4.

[57] Spinoza, *Letters*, 352, 355; Jelles, *Voorreeden*, 44; Matheron, 'Physique', 108–9.

[58] Régis, *Système de philosophie*, i, 306; Geulincx, *Compendium physicae*, iii, 115.

mutationis intrinsicae), which was later defended by De Volder, and which, as Leibniz pointed out, leads irresistibly to a Spinozistic conception of the world,[59] became a characteristic feature of the radical tradition of thought, marking it off from Newtonianism as well as Cartesianism and Leibnizianism. Thus Adriaen Verwer, in his anti-Spinozist tract of 1683, identifies the thesis that motion is integral to matter, and the denial of the Cartesian concept of absolute rest, as one of the chief defining features of the popular Spinozism he encountered in Amsterdam at that time. Spinoza was to be followed in adopting this position by De Volder, Overcamp, Cuffeler, Tschirnhaus, Toland, and Wyermars, and later by La Mettrie, Diderot, and all those the latter styled 'nouveaux Spinosistes', meaning scientists and thinkers who envisage the creation of life, and mutation of life forms, as a process of natural evolution.[60]

iii. Spinoza versus Boyle

Another central strand of Spinoza's scientific thought is his critique of Boyle. Spinoza was by no means hostile to experiments and practical research. Though he lacked the resources to undertake elaborate experiments himself, he loved to study insects and other objects under his microscopes and, during the 1660s, was intermittently present at intricate experiments in Amsterdam and at the Huygens' residence. He believed, though, that, on their own, observation, experiment, and recording of data are neutral, inconclusive, and misleading. Observed data are only the raw material of scientific discourse and tell us little in themselves. Empiricism as a scientific theory made little sense to his mind because scientific experiment can only prove or disprove propositions once a coherent theoretical framework has been set up. For otherwise there are no benchmarks or criteria against which to set one's empirical findings. Hence, inferred Spinoza, experimental philosophy on its own can not demonstrate the fixed and immutable laws of nature nor determine the general contours and extent of scientific knowledge. In this sense, Spinoza did relegate observation and experiment to the secondary role of confirming or contradicting hypotheses, and it was on this ground that he was drawn into criticizing Boyle and the empiricism of the Royal Society.

Spinoza and Boyle, accordingly, nurtured antithetically different conceptions of the character and procedures of science.[61] Boyle considered the 'experimental way of philosophizing' the only secure basis for reliable knowledge, stressing the 'dimness and imperfections of our human understanding'.[62] Because 'knowledge of abstracted reason is so narrow and deceitful', he judged that the thinker 'who seeks for knowl-

[59] Klever, 'Burchard de Volder', 230–1.

[60] Verwer, *'t Mom-Aensicht*, xv–xvi; Jaquelot, *Dissertations*, 319; D'Holbach, *Système de la nature*, i, 18, 31, 50–1; Lachterman, 'Laying down the Law', 128–9; Vermij, 'Matter and motion', 280, 284; Klever, 'Einige von Spinozas naturwissenschaftlichen Prinzipien', 71–4; hence Nietzsche's notion that Darwinism is a 'Spinozistic dogma' was by no means devoid of logic, see Nietzsche, *The Gay Science*, fragment 349.

[61] Macherey, 'Spinoza lecteur', 746–8; Gabbey, 'Spinoza's Natural Science', 177–9.

[62] Boyle, *Theological Works*, ii, 6; Boyle, *Works*, iv, 75.

edge only in himself, will be ignorant of the greatest part of things, and hardly escape being mistaken in a great part of those things he knows'.[63] Boyle indeed despised such 'atheistical philosophers' as gave primacy to reason, 'those prevaricating pretenders to philosophy as little understanding the mysteries of Nature, as they believe those of Christianity'.[64] It is by 'reason unrestrained', he argued, that some philosophers 'have so grossly erred, as to deny all immaterial substances, and chose rather so far to degrade the Deity itself, as to impute to it a corporeal nature, than to allow any thing to have a being, that is not comprehensible by their imagination, which themselves acknowledge to be but a corporeal faculty'.[65] His aim was to construct, on the basis of purely experimental work, a systematically mechanistic universe, but one lacking inherent creative drive and accommodating, or at least relegating to the sphere of the unknowable, what is above, beyond, or 'thwarts' the natural order of things, in other words, that which is supernatural, or what he calls 'preternatural'.[66]

The chief inspirer of the 'argument from design', Boyle believed that the only way we can 'conceive how so great a fabric as the world can be preserved in order and kept from running again to a chaos' is to 'sufficiently consider the unsearchable wisdom of the divine architect'.[67] He held that a strict empiricism, following Bacon, provides the only valid basis for a genuinely scientific attitude, and that a solidly empirical stance leads, of itself, not just to a pious but a scientifically grounded reverence for revealed religion and a providential divine Creator: 'experimental philosophy gives so clear a discovery of the divine excellence apparent in the fabrick and conduct of the universe, and the creatures it contains, as may prevent the mind from ascribing such admirable effects to so incompetent and pitiful a cause, as blind chance, or the tumultuous jostling of the atomical particles of senseless matter, and consequently disposes us to the acknowledgement and adoration of a most intelligent power and benign author of things, to whom such excellent productions may most reasonably be ascribed.'[68]

As a mature scientist and thinker, Boyle devoted much time and energy to confronting philosophies and ideas of nature opposed to his mechanistic empiricism, conceptual constructs which, to his mind, blight faith in divine Providence and miracles. In particular, he fought scholastic Aristotelianism, still a potent force in England, as elsewhere during the later seventeenth century, and the kind of atheistic materialism he associated with Epicurus, Hobbes, and Spinoza.[69] Boyle, however, preferred to allude to, rather than directly combat the Dutch thinker, so that mostly, as during the curious exchange between the two over Boyle's experiments on nitre, they reacted to each other only indirectly, through their common friend, Oldenburg. Where

---

[63] Boyle, *Theological Works*, ii, 46.   [64] Ibid., 4.   [65] Boyle, *Works*, iv, 65.

[66] Boyle, *A Free Enquiry*, 40; Colie, *Spinoza in England*, 195–8; Wojcik, 'This due degree', 371–2.

[67] Boyle, *A Free Enquiry*, 60.

[68] Boyle, *Theological Works*, ii, 4.; Davis and Hunter, 'Introduction', pp. xiv–xvii; Wojcik, 'This due degree', 368.

[69] Colie, 'Spinoza in England', 196–7; Davis and Hunter, 'Introduction', pp. xvi–xx; Wojcik, 'This due degree', 368–72.

Oldenburg is not involved, Boyle's observations about the new materialists and Epicureans are too vague for us to be certain to whom he is referring. Thus, in his *Free Enquiry* of 1682, he warns that 'even in these times there is lately sprung up a sect of men, as well professing Christianity as pretending to philosophy, who (if I be not misinformed of their doctrine) do very much symbolise with the ancient heathens, and talk much indeed of God, but mean such a one as is not really distinct from the animated and intelligent universe, but is on that account very differing from the true God that we Christians believe in and worship.'[70] Despite the reference to 'Christianity', this may be an allusion to Spinoza and his circle, since Boyle adds: 'I find the leaders of this sect to be looked upon by some more witty than knowing men as the discoverers of unheard of mysteries in physics and natural theology, yet their hypothesis does not at all appear to me to be new,' whereupon he cites the atheistic philosophers of antiquity and, in particular, a passage of Lucan broadly equating God with nature.[71]

While insisting on the separation of experimental philosophy from metaphysical concerns,[72] Boyle, like Newton and Locke, nevertheless confidently deploys empiricism as the pivot of a wider philosophico-theologico-scientific system, based on what Boyle judged the incontrovertible backing experimental science lends 'the argument from design', and credence in divine Providence and the immortality of the soul.[73] Spinoza, for his part, disliked Boyle's approach and the whole policy of the Royal Society. His critique of English empiricism began at least as early as his meeting with Oldenburg in 1661. At Rijnsburg, Oldenburg afterwards recalled, he and Spinoza discussed 'God, infinite extension and thought, the difference and agreement of these attributes, the way the human soul is united with the body, and the principles of the Cartesian philosophy and the Baconian'.[74] Spinoza had evidently criticized both the latter, for Oldenburg presses him to explain again what defects he discerns 'in the philosophy of Descartes and of Bacon'. Spinoza, in his reply, brusquely dismisses Bacon's principles as being of little use, claiming that he speaks 'quite confusedly'.[75] From Oldenburg's mention, at the close of the letter, of Boyle's pending publication of his *Certain Physiological Essays* (1661) and his promise to send a copy, it seems that they had also already been discussing Boyle.

On forwarding a copy of Boyle's *Essays* to Spinoza later that year, Oldenburg asks him to comment, in particular, on Boyle's account of his experiments with nitre (saltpetre = potassium nitrate) and the nature of solidity and fluidity. Spinoza complied in April 1662, with a letter detailing various objections to Boyle's assumptions and methods. He expresses surprise that Boyle should undertake such an elaborate experiment to prove that the tangible qualities of matter such as heat, colour, and taste, depend only on mechanical circumstances such as motion, since, he says, this 'had already been more than adequately demonstrated by Bacon and later Descartes'; 'nor,' he added, 'do I see that this experiment offers more illuminating evidence than

---

[70] Boyle, *A Free Enquiry*, 47.   [71] Ibid.; Colie, 'Spinoza in England', 214.

[72] McGuire, 'Boyle's Conception of Nature', 525–6; Heyd, *'Be Sober and Reasonable'*, 242–3.

[73] Wojcik, 'This due degree', 368.   [74] Spinoza, *Letters*, 59; Hutton, 'Henry Oldenburg', 112.

[75] Spinoza, *Letters* 62–3; Gabbey, 'Spinoza's Natural Science', 170.

others that are readily enough available.'[76] He then turns to Boyle's demonstration that reuniting the parts of saltpetre causes an agitation of parts generating heat and a hissing sound. 'As far as heat is concerned,' he remarks sardonically, is not the same result 'equally clear from the fact that if two pieces of wood, however cold they are, are rubbed against each other, they yield a flame simply as a consequence of that motion?'[77] 'As for sound, I do not see that anything more remarkable is to be found in this experiment than in boiling ordinary water.'

In the same letter Spinoza similarly dismisses Boyle's experiments on fluidity. His demonstration that the invisible parts of a liquid are apparently in a state of agitation which, under varying conditions, might be visible or invisible to us, draws from Spinoza the wry comment that the point 'is sufficiently obvious without this experiment, and without expense, from the fact that in winter we see clearly enough that our breath moves whereas in summer, or a heated room, we cannot see that it moves'.[78] What is significant here is Spinoza's denial that Boyle can prove by means of 'chemical or any other experiments' any general point regarding the fluidity and solidity of bodies: 'for it is by reason and calculation that we divide bodies to infinity, and consequently also the forces required to move them; we can never confirm this by experiments.'[79] Here indeed is the crux of the controversy between Boyle and Spinoza. In the latter's eyes experiments can illustrate but never conclusively prove general propositions which we can espouse with certainty, by extrapolating 'in geometrical order' from what we know already.[80] Hence no experiment can prove there are no miracles, no angels, and no ghosts, that nothing supernatural can ever happen, or that, as Spinoza asserts in chapter xxv of the *Korte Verhandeling* on the basis of his premises, that 'devils . . . cannot possibly exist.'[81] For that matter, what experiment could ever finally establish that something cannot be created from nothing? Yet in Spinoza's view, all these 'truths' can be demonstrated by means of philosophical reason and must be acknowledged if we wish to attain truth and the highest degree of human perfection.

Boyle eventually responded to some of Spinoza's criticisms, in conversation with Oldenburg, who passed his reactions back to Spinoza in April 1663. Boyle, not without a hint of exasperation, claims a great difference between such everyday occurrences as Spinoza adduces and experiments, where we know what nature contributes and what things intervene. Wood, he observes, is much more composite than saltpetre, while an external flame is needed for boiling water, which was not the case in his experiment.[82] Through Oldenburg, Spinoza thanked Boyle, 'for being so good as to reply to my observations, in however cursory and preoccupied a way; I do indeed admit they are not of such importance that the learned gentleman, in replying to them, should spend time which he can devote to reflections of a higher kind.'[83] 'I do

---

[76] Spinoza, *Letters*, 76; Klever, 'Anti-falsificationism', 131.   [77] Spinoza, *Letters*, 76.

[78] Ibid., 81.   [79] Ibid., 78–9.

[80] Klever, 'Anti-falsificationism', 130–1; Gabbey, 'Spinoza's Natural Science', 177–80.

[81] *Collected Works of Spinoza*, i, 145.   [82] Spinoza, *Letters*, 98–9; Macherey, 'Spinoza lecteur', 747–8.

[83] Spinoza, *Letters*, 111.

not know,' he observed, though, 'why the distinguished gentleman boldly maintains he knows what nature contributes in the matter we are speaking of . . . I think I can infer that movement of air is the cause of sound more easily from the boiling of water . . . than I can from his experiment where the nature of things that meet is completely unknown and where heat is observed without our knowing how or from what causes it has arisen.'[84]

Spinoza's subordination, or better, his integration of empirical research into the operations of philosophical reason based on 'geometric' proportionality runs like a thread through the entire corpus of his work and is a central theme of his *Principia Philosophiae Cartesianae* of 1663. It is not a rejection of experiments, or a denial of experience, but does reject Bacon's and Boyle's empiricism as inherently limited and incapable, on its own, of grounding a meaningful science. For Spinoza, in contrast to Boyle, believed it is the senses, not the intellect, which are deceptive and weak. For the senses can not show those who seek the truth anything except the phenomena of nature, the causes of which they seek to investigate. Consequently, it is reason and intellect which do the real work, albeit proceeding on the basis of experience.[85]

Boyle, meanwhile, however unsympathetic to Spinoza, continued pondering his objections while offering no direct response. 'Mr Boyle and I often talk about you, your learning and your profound reflections,' Oldenburg advised Spinoza in April 1665, adding: 'we should like to see the offspring of your talent brought to birth and entrusted to the warm embrace of the learned, and we are confident that you will not disappoint us in this.'[86] Only in the mid-1670s, as realization of the implications of the *Tractatus Theologico-Politicus* sank in, did Oldenburg's apprehensions and Boyle's antipathy develop into a deeper sense of shock and hostility. The earlier harmonious relationship between Spinoza and the Royal Society of London was effectively at an end.[87] But Boyle was still troubled by Spinoza's ideas and, particularly in and around 1675, penned several papers on the subject of miracles, the Resurrection, and divine Providence, seeking thereby to render waverers and doubters 'less forward to condemn all those for deserters of reason, that submit to Revelation', consciously, as one of his secretaries notes, in 'answer to Spinosa'.[88]

Though Boyle the empiricist was profoundly critical of Cartesianism on various counts, he nevertheless also adhered to a strictly dichotomous conception of the universe, dividing reality between those things made by God proper to be known by man and the unknowable essence of God, the divine mysteries and the supernatural, and likewise regarded motion as introduced into the world from outside by God. He was equally an upholder of a mechanistic conception of reality, claiming that while miracles entail suspension of the normal laws of nature, the miraculous power of God is sparingly used and, as far as possible, operates alongside and through the mechanical

[84] Spinoza, *Letters*, 114–15; Klever, 'Anti-falsificationism', 133.
[85] Lécrivain, ' Spinoza et la physique cartésianisme', 249–50; Klever, 'Anti-falsificationism', 124–5; Gabbey, 'Spinoza's Natural Science', 180.
[86] Spinoza, *Letters*, 173.   [87] Colie, 'Spinoza in England', 199–200.
[88] Ibid., 199, 201, 213; Boyle, *Works*, iii, 537; Simonutti, 'Premières réactions', 126.

laws of nature. For Boyle, as for Descartes, since God 'is the Creator of matter and the sole introducer of local motion into it, so all the laws of that motion were at first arbitrary to Him; and depended upon His free will'.[89] On this ground, contends Boyle, the possibility of miracles is clear. He deems it certain the 'arbitrary laws'—in opposition to Spinoza's necessary laws—God has 'establish'd, in that little portion of his workmanship that we men inhabit, should now and then (though very rarely) be control'd or receded from'.[90]

Consequently, urged Boyle, we should 'interpret the passages of the holy Scripture, wherein these wonders are recorded', God being the author of the laws of Nature as well as of those supernatural phenomena, 'as to make the natural order of things no more overrul'd, surpass'd, or receded from, then is absolutely necessary to make out the truth of the relations, as they are delivered by the inspir'd historians'.[91] Hence, when God removed the frogs, one of the Ten Plagues with which he punished the Egyptians, 'he caus'd them to dye in the houses and the fields, and left it to the Egyptians to rid themselves of their carcasses, which they could not so do, but that, as the text relates, the land stank.'[92] That the 'mechanical laws of nature' can be superseded, or avoided, is proved for us every moment of the day, adds Boyle with an 'empirical' flourish, by what he calls the 'arbitrarious notions in the human body that cannot be truly accounted for by meer natural philosophy'.[93] Notably, the 'proof' our senses provide of man's 'arbitrary' will, Boyle argues, demonstrates that things can occur 'by some other power than meerely mechanical'.[94] In this way Boyle propounded a mainstream, broadly acceptable vision of science which, by demonstrating that the laws of science do not govern all reality, and the possibility of incorporeal powers infusing and transcending the 'regular operations of Nature', overturns and nullifies Spinoza's 'atheistic' universality and the invariability of the 'regular operations of nature'.

[89] Boyle. *Letters*, 213.   [90] Ibid., 214; Boyle, *Works*, iv, 65.

[91] Boyle, *Letters*, 214; Simonutti, 'Premières réactions', 127.

[92] Boyle, *Letters*, 214–15.   [93] Ibid., 215.

[94] Ibid., 215–16; Colie, 'Spinoza in England', 199–202; Shapin, *Scientific Revolution*, 43, 106.

15 | PHILOSOPHY, POLITICS, AND THE LIBERATION OF MAN

i. In Search of 'Freedom'

Many commentators on the history of political thought have pointed to the affinities between Hobbes and Spinoza.[1] But appreciably more important from a historical, and perhaps even a theoretical, perspective are the differences. The key distinction between Hobbes and Spinoza as political thinkers lies in their sharply contrasting conceptions of 'freedom'. Hobbes advances what Quentin Skinner termed 'a classic statement' of the 'negative' view of political liberty, by maintaining that 'liberty or freedom signifieth (properly) the absence of opposition; (by opposition, I mean externall impediments of motion;) and may be applyed no lesse to irrationall, and inanimate creatures, than to rationall.'[2] In Hobbes, liberty of the individual is reduced to that sphere which the sovereign, and laws of the State, do not seek to control: 'the liberty of a subject, lyeth therefore only in those things, which in regulating their actions, the sovereign hath praetermitted' which include 'liberty to buy and sell, and otherwise contract with one another; to choose their own aboad, their own diet, their own trade of life, and institute their children as they themselves think fitt; and the like'.[3]

All participation in the political process, the making of law, and forming of opinion, is hence excluded. Hobbes indeed disparages the republican, or positive, concept of freedom with which, he notes, seventeenth-century readers were by no means unfamiliar from reading classical texts.[4] Such liberty he deems antithetical not only to monarchy but to political continuity and stability, accusing those addicted to such ideas of 'favouring tumults' and 'licentious controlling the actions of their sovereigns'. The political liberty republicans extol he considers a ruinous illusion, a mythology manipulated by agitators and factions for their own ends, to undermine and weaken the sovereign. As regards personal freedom of the sort he acknowledges, he maintains it is the same in quality and extent whether one lives under a monarch or republic.[5]

---

[1] Petry, 'Hobbes', 150.
[2] Hobbes, *Leviathan*, ch. xxi; Skinner, 'Idea of Negative Liberty', 194–5; Skinner, 'Republican Ideal', 294; Balibar, *Spinoza and Politics*, 55–6.
[3] Hobbes, *Leviathan*, ch. xxi.   [4] Ibid.   [5] Ibid.

Strikingly different is Spinoza's conception of freedom, which is integrally linked to his advocacy of democracy and radical theory of toleration, as well as to his general philosophical system. When his friend Jelles enquired, in 1674, what was the basic difference between his political philosophy and that of Hobbes, Spinoza answered that it 'consists in this, that I always preserve the natural right in its entirety, and hold that the sovereign power in a state has a right over a subject only in proportion to the excess of its power over that subject; this is always the case in the state of nature.'[6] Thus, in place of Hobbes' assigning a contracted overriding power to the sovereign, Spinoza leaves the citizen with his natural right intact, according an automatic and inevitable 'right of resistance' (and power of resistance) wherever the State proves unable to assert its authority over its subjects, an incapacity the more likely the further one departs from democracy.[7] Effectively, Spinoza was the first major European thinker in modern times—though he is preceded here by Johan de la Court and Van den Enden—to embrace democratic republicanism as the highest and most fully rational form of political organization, and the one best suited to the needs of men. Monarchy, conversely, is deemed altogether less perfect, rational, and fitted to the genuine concerns of human society.

Political freedom Spinoza conceives not in the 'negative' sense affirmed by Hobbes, and later adapted in a liberal direction by Locke, but as a tendency or condition of man linked to securing forms of political organization which serve the needs of the community, and the common interest or common good, and are best calculated to preclude corruption and despotism. Consequently, liberty in Spinoza is not negatively defined as an absence of obstacles, or confined to the private sphere, but envisaged, as in Machiavelli and later Rousseau, as a positive good or inalienable potential, more apt to flourish in certain kinds of State than others. It involves specific kinds of interaction between the State and the individual and depends on successfully inculcating certain attitudes, and discouraging others, both in individuals and society.[8]

Particularly emphasized in Spinoza is the connection, crucial to his philosophy, between 'reason' and 'virtue'. The philosophical ground-plan for Spinoza's political thought is expounded most fully in Part IV of the *Ethics*, where he characterizes 'slavery' as being as much an internal condition of mind, or mental bondage, as the outcome of harsh external conditions.[9] 'Slavery' is in essence lack of power or capability to seek one's own advantage, thus potentially no less the consequence of unrestrained impulse and passions, the urge to act according to 'inadequate' ideas, as of external shackles. 'The more each individual strives, and is able, to seek his own advantage,' holds Spinoza, in *Ethics* IV Proposition XX, 'that is, conserve his being, the more he is endowed with virtue; conversely, in so far as each neglects his own advantage, that is, fails to conserve his being, he lacks power.'[10] While Spinoza identifies 'virtue' with

---

[6] Spinoza, *Letters*, 258; Petry, 'Hobbes', 151.

[7] Yvon, *L'impiété convaincue*, 411–12; Matheron, 'Fonction théorique', 268–9; Matheron, 'Problème de l'évolution', 264; Balibar, *Spinoza and Politics*, 34–6, 38–9, 104.

[8] Skinner, 'Idea of Negative Liberty', 195, 204.   [9] *Collected Works of Spinoza*, i, 543, 556.

[10] Ibid., i, 557.

'power', which is decidedly not how others conceive of virtue, his strange usage becomes closer to what is generally signified with his insistence on human 'virtue' being anchored in 'reason'. Since the mind's greatest 'good', its greatest 'virtue', is to know God, that is, to grasp the reality of things rationally,[11] man's essence, his striving or power, best conserves his existence when adjusted to the inevitable laws of Nature, resulting in a rational ordering of one's life, which, by definition, will be 'virtuous'. Irrational man, being guided by impulse and ruled by 'inadequate' ideas, is inconstant, unreliable, and apt to live in conflict and disharmony with others. It follows (Proposition XXXIV) that 'in so far as men are torn by affects which are passions, they tend to oppose one another.'[12] Social cohesion and political stability become possible only where men learn to live according to the guidance of 'reason'. The more reason advances, the more political stability and less conflict there is, and hence the more the State promotes the interests of all, which is its essential justification and purpose.

A 'free man', maintains Spinoza, is 'one who lives according to the dictates of reason alone' and 'is not led by fear but desires good directly, that is, acts, lives and conserves his being, from the foundation of seeking his own advantage'. This leads, at first glance, to the astounding result, that 'a free man always acts honestly, not duplicitously.'[13] It seems especially paradoxical since Spinoza has already noted that one can sometimes best preserve one's being by acting dishonestly rather than honestly.[14] But the difficulty is seemingly removed if one takes Spinoza's meaning to be that the ideal, entirely free man in the abstract would never act duplicitously, but that in practice one has to survive in a world filled with injustice, abuse, and violence.[15] In the actual world we inhabit there is no such thing as the completely honest or completely 'free' individual, so that reason and one's virtue may, on occasion, lead one to speak or act deceptively.

This conception of liberty as rooted in reason and the notion of reason's governance of man's self-love, or virtue, resulting in honest dealing and the quest for peace and harmony among men, is further elaborated in Spinoza's last work, the *Tractatus Politicus*. Earlier, in the *Tractatus Theologico-Politicus*, Spinoza, in line with the political thought of Johan and Pieter de la Court (of whose modifications of Hobbes' ideas he much approved)[16] and Van den Enden, ranks the democratic republic above monarchy and aristocracy, as the best type of governance, because it is the 'most natural form of state' and approaches most closely that freedom which Nature grants to every man.[17] In a democracy, liberty is enhanced in that one is consulted, and can participate in decision-making in some degree, whatever one's social status and educational background, through debate, the expression of opinion, and the mechanism of voting. 'In this way,' urges Spinoza, 'all men remain equal, as they were before in the state of nature.'[18]

---

[11] By Proposition XXVIII; see ibid., 559.

[12] Ibid., 562; Spinoza, *Opera*, ii, 231; Matheron, 'Problème de l'évolution', 262.

[13] *Collected Works of Spinoza*, i, 586; Garrett, 'A Free Man', 221.

[14] Garrett, 'A Free Man', 221–2, 224, 233, 236.   [15] Ibid., 230–2.   [16] Petry, 'Hobbes', 154–5.

[17] Spinoza, *TTP*, 243; Matheron, *Individu et communauté*, 303–12.   [18] Spinoza, *TTP*, 243.

Of course, such freedom can also be nurtured in the other types of State. Not all monarchies and aristocracies are so despotic as to reduce the mass of mankind to near slavery. Yet any State, monarchy or aristocracy, which is undemocratic but nevertheless seeks the welfare of the whole people and not just of the ruler, or oligarchy, as its supreme law, that is, any State in which freedom is encouraged must inevitably approximate to a democracy, because in such a State identifying and promoting the common good amid free expression of opinion must infuse and dominate its political life.[19] Unlike the slave who does not serve his own interest but that of others, the free man dwelling in a society where the common good is pursued is, by definition, acting rationally and freely in showing scrupulous respect and deference for the laws of his country. Consequently, 'that commonwealth whose laws are based on sound reason is the most free, for there everybody can be free as he wills, that is, can live unreservedly under the guidance of reason.'[20] In the later treatise, Spinoza asserts, with equal emphasis, that the 'more free we conceive a man to be, the less we can say he can fail to use reason and choose wrong in preference to good'; even though (as implied in Part IV of the *Ethics*) 'it is not in a man's power invariably to use reason and be always at the peak of freedom.'[21]

Because 'good' and 'evil', just and unjust, honest and dishonest, can exist, according to Spinoza, only in civil society within a context of law and law-making, penalties and law enforcement, and has no prior existence in the state of Nature, he insists—as do all writers in the radical tradition of the late seventeenth and early eighteenth century—in the interests of all, on the paramount and overriding need for general obedience to the law, equality before the law, and fair and consistent enforcement of society's principles of justice. Nevertheless, the free man acts rationally and freely also when he obeys laws which he does not believe serve the common good. Whatever the circumstances, the 'more a man is guided by reason, the more free he is', the more will he steadfastly submit to the laws of his country and the commands of his sovereign.[22] Nor does this entail any contradiction, says Spinoza, since the 'political order is naturally established to remove general fear and dispel general suffering, and thus its chief object is one which every rational man would try to promote in the state of Nature.'[23]

Spinoza loathes faction, instability, rebellions, wars, and 'contemptuous disregard for the law', seeing lawlessness as utterly destructive of the common good and the interests of society. Even so, one can not say that he was opposed to political revolution.[24] For according to his system, the State can be strong and stable only if it approximates to democracy, and the 'commonwealth does its best to achieve those conditions which sound reason declares to be for the good of all men'.[25] Only then can

---

[19] Ibid.; Walther, 'Transformation des Naturrechts', 87–8; Balibar, 'Spinoza: from Individuality', 34.
[20] Spinoza, *TTP*, 243.   [21] Spinoza, *Tractatus Politicus*, 270–1.   [22] Ibid., 283, 289.
[23] Ibid., 289.
[24] Undoubtedly, there is an element of contradiction in Spinoza's thought here; but the revolutionary implications of what he is saying are beyond doubt; Giancotti Boscherini, 'Réalisme', 38; Curley, 'Kissinger, Spinoza', 333–4.
[25] Spinoza, *Tractatus Politicus*, 289; Balibar, *Spinoza and Politics*, 68–70.

it command the assent of the majority without which the State will inevitably be prey to internal factions and discord. For genuine peace, order, and harmony in society can only subsist on the basis of such common consent. If rulers govern in contempt of the common good, essentially in their own interests, then there can be no political stability, however brutal its methods of suppression. 'Peace is not the mere absence of war, but a virtue based on strength of mind,' that is, involving men's participation. 'A state whose peace depends on the apathy of its subjects,' he asserts, 'who are led like sheep so that they learn nothing but servility, may more properly be called a desert than a commonwealth.'[26] Hence, while a free and rational man never disobeys the law, or opposes the government, sedition and disorder leading sometimes to revolution is nevertheless the unavoidable consequence of failure to respect the common good. Having the right, as he does, to oppose laws and policies in thought and expression of opinion, the free and rational man can contribute to changing the form of government, and presumably should in situations of chronic repression and instability.

ii. Monarchy Overturned

'The best type of state is easily identified,' holds Spinoza, 'from the purpose of the political order—which is simply peace and security of life.'[27] Hence the best State is 'one in which men live in harmony and the laws are kept unbroken'.[28] The measure of a State is the degree of order, peace, and respect for the law that it maintains. For human nature, contends Spinoza, is always the same, so that if crime and disorder prevail more in one society than another, this can only be because the first 'has not done enough to promote harmony, has not framed its laws with sufficient foresight, and so has failed to obtain its absolute right as a state'.[29] A defective State prone to internal strife, where fighting is a constant threat and laws are frequently violated, 'differs little from the state of Nature itself, where everyone lives according to his own whim with great danger to life'.[30]

Spinoza died before completing the *Tractatus Politicus*, leaving off just when he was starting the extended treatment of democracy to which the written sections on monarchy and aristocracy were leading up. In this work he grants there is a general mechanism in human societies tending towards the creation of monarchies from aristocracy and democracy.[31] Nevertheless his democratic republicanism powerfully infuses the whole of the surviving text.[32] Indeed, his treatment of monarchy can fairly be called a philosophical caricature in which the monarchical principle is consistently demeaned and made to look inadequate and corrupt besides a democratic republic. To render monarchy conducive to the harmony, peace, and common good of its subjects, Spinoza makes recommendations which effectively emasculate it, depriving it of all genuinely monarchical features, turning it, in effect, into a 'crowned republic',

---

[26] Spinoza, *Tractatus Politicus*, 311.   [27] Ibid., 308.   [28] Ibid.   [29] Ibid.
[30] Ibid.   [31] Matheron, *Individu et communauté*, 400–4, 411.
[32] Tosel, 'Théorie de la pratique', 200.

or a quasi-republic with a royal figurehead adapted to the will of the majority. Typically, Spinoza holds that the more the power (and the right) of the State is transferred to one man, the 'more wretched is the condition of his subjects'.[33] Therefore, to establish a stable monarchy it is crucial to ground it on foundations which ensure both security for the king and peace for the people, contriving that the king enjoys most power (and right) 'when he pays most attention to the people's welfare'.[34] In fact, he says, reducing a monarch's power to the absolute minimum is the only plausible way to ensure the people's welfare, since the arrangement of power in a monarchy means the 'man in whom the whole right of the state has been vested will always be more afraid of his citizens than of external enemies'.[35] Thus he will 'seek to protect himself from them and, instead of furthering their interests, plot against them and especially against those who have a reputation for wisdom or are too powerful because of their wealth'.[36] Kings then are creatures of fear and naturally prone to oppress their subjects.

To prevent their sons serving as foci for opposition, monarchical rulers who, according to Spinoza, usually fear rather than love their sons, educate them so that they should be as little skilled in the arts of statecraft, war, and peace, and as unlikely to be popular on account of their virtues, as possible: 'in this matter, ministers are very ready to comply with the king's wishes and make every effort to acquire a novice whom they can hoodwink as their next king.'[37] The constant seepage of power into the hands of ministers and favourites in monarchical states moves Spinoza to rule that, strictly speaking, monarchy is impossible: 'those who believe one man can hold the supreme right of a commonwealth are greatly mistaken.'[38] For the power of a single man is far too small to cope with the burdens of such a position, so that inevitably he seeks advisers, commanders, and favourites to assist him, entrusting his own security and interests to them: 'so that the state which is believed to be a pure monarchy is really an aristocracy in practice, but a concealed and not an open one, and therefore of the very worst type'.[39] This is obviously all the more so when the king is a child, invalid, unintelligent, unbalanced, or excessively aged, when the real conduct of affairs and therefore the real sovereignty lies in the hands of those closest to the monarch.

Absolutely essential is the need for the people to prevent their king possessing effective control of the army, or matters of war and peace.[40] It is best for the army to be recruited only from among the citizen body, a rota system involving all the men without their receiving pay for defending their State, which should be viewed as a public duty. For if mercenaries are hired, or some citizens recruited, for long-term paid service, 'the king will inevitably favour them more than the rest . . . though they are men who, having no profession but arms, and having too little to do, ruin

[33] Spinoza, *Tractatus Politicus*, 319.   [34] Ibid.

[35] Ibid., 317; Matheron, *Individu et communauté*, 409–11.   [36] Spinoza, *Tractatus Politicus*, 317.

[37] Ibid., 317–19.   [38] Ibid., 317; Blom, *Morality and Causality*, 235.

[39] Spinoza, *Tractatus Politicus*, 317; Balibar, *Spinoza and Politics*, 71–2.

[40] Spinoza, *Tractatus Politicus*, 319, 339, 341, 345.

themselves by extravagance in peace, and finally are led by their poverty to think of nothing but looting, sedition, and war'; such a monarchy. holds Spinoza, 'is really a state of war' in which 'soldiers alone enjoy freedom and the rest are slaves.'[41] Spinoza here may have toned down the passionate anti-monarchism of the brothers De la Court whom he praises, and frequently refers to,[42] but there are no grounds for supposing he is any less disdainful than they, or Van den Enden, of the fawning over princes and eulogizing of monarchs prevalent in Europe at the time. At one point he pushes his caricature of monarchy to the point of claiming that 'because the welfare of the people is the supreme law, or the king's highest right', a monarch must not be permitted to enact any decree or pass any judgement contrary to the views of the council of state, which Spinoza recommends should not only make all significant decisions but be composed of a large number of councillors who should be chosen, not by the king, but consist of elected candidates chosen by the various localities of the realm. If it is natural for monarchy to foment strife and war, and one of the chief virtues of democratic republics to prefer peace,[43] kings can be compelled to conform to society's need for peace and harmony if rendered powerless in relation to the council of state. Furthermore, provided the council is truly representative and large, Spinoza confidently predicts that the majority will never want militarism and war since these always menace security, and freedom and entail higher taxes.[44]

Also essential is that the members of the council of state should not be elected for life 'but for three, four, or five years at the most' so as to encourage political involvement and offer as many citizens as possible hope of one day entering the council.[45] Thus, in striving to safeguard political liberty and freedom of expression in limited monarchies, Spinoza stresses the vital role of the citizenry's public duties, advisory and military, and the need for popular involvement in the political process. He concludes his discussion of monarchy with the sardonic remark that, while there are no states which incorporate all the safeguards he recommends to ensure the 'best' kind of monarchy, we can nevertheless be certain from the evidence of history that such a heavily circumscribed monarchy 'is the best'. He then (no doubt tongue in cheek) cites the example of Aragon as an admirable monarchy, the exemplary loyalty of the Aragonese towards their rulers being 'combined with an equal steadfastness in defending their free institutions'.[46] However, even they eventually lost their grip on their constitutions, being deprived of their freedom by Philip II, 'who oppressed them with more success, but no less severity, than the United Provinces' so that subsequently they 'retained nothing but the fine titles and empty forms of freedom'. He closes with the observation that 'a people can preserve a considerable measure of freedom under a king as long as they ensure the king's power is regulated by the people's power and safeguarded by the people's armed might.'[47]

---

[41] Spinoza, *Tractatus Politicus*, 353.   [42] See Wernham, 'Introduction and Notes', 317, 319, 341, 353.
[43] Spinoza, *Tractatus Politicus*, 339.   [44] Ibid., 341.   [45] Ibid., 342–7.
[46] Ibid., 364–5; Blom, *Morality and Causality*, 236.   [47] Spinoza, *Tractatus Politicus*, 305.

iii. Spinoza, Locke, and the Enlightenment Struggle for Toleration

Precisely as the warring moderate and radical wings of the Enlightenment produced rival and antagonistic theories of religion, science, morality, law, and politics—the former extolling monarchical power, the latter democratic republicanism—so the two Enlightenments forged powerfully contrasting notions of toleration.[48] On the one side was what came to be widely acknowledged as the acceptable face of toleration, a toleration rooted in the Dutch Arminians—Episcopius, Limborch, Le Clerc—and, following them, John Locke. This was aptly characterized by the great Venetian theologian, Concina, in 1754, as essentially a '*tollerantismo* between the Christian Churches'.[49] Its core was freedom of worship and the peaceful coexistence of dissenting Churches alongside each national, or public, Church. What in their great majority eighteenth-century writers were entirely unwilling to endorse was the other kind of toleration—the radicals' demand for freedom of thought and expression, including the expression of ideas incompatible with the core tenets of revealed religion upheld by the Churches.[50]

Although William Carroll, as part of his effort to tar Locke by linking him to Spinoza, claims the two philosophers share the same 'principles of universal toleration in matters of religion',[51] in reality their respective conceptions are strikingly different. For Locke's theory is essentially a theological conception, asserting that it is for every individual not just to assume responsibility for seeking the salvation of his or her soul but, as Episcopius and Limborch urged, to perform openly that form of worship by which he or she seeks salvation.[52] Locke's toleration then revolves primarily around freedom of worship and theological discussion, placing little emphasis on freedom of thought, speech, and persuasion beyond what relates to freedom of conscience which, in principle might be Jewish or Mohammedan as well as Christian.[53] By contrast, the toleration of Spinoza (and Van den Enden) subsequently espoused by Walten, Leenhof, Wyermars, Toland, Collins, d'Argens, and Mandeville, among others, is essentially philosophical, republican, and explicitly anti-theological.[54] Freedom of thought and speech, designated *libertas philosophandi* by Spinoza, is the primary goal, while saving souls plays no part either in their advocacy of toleration or setting limits to toleration which, Spinoza concedes, may in a given society be advisable.

Precisely because it is a theological conception, Locke's toleration is grudging, on doctrinal grounds, in according toleration to some groups and emphatic in denying toleration to others.[55] In Locke three limitations on toleration are especially evident.

---

[48] Israel, 'Spinoza, Locke', 102–5; Israel, *Locke, Spinoza*, 11–14.
[49] Concina, *Della religione rivelata*, ii, 362.   [50] Israel, 'Spinoza, Locke', 102.
[51] [Carroll], *A Letter to the Reverend*, 16.
[52] Dunn, 'Claim to Freedom', 174–8; Harris, *Mind of John Locke*, 185–6; Israel, 'Toleration', 20–1.
[53] Dunn, 'Claim to Freedom', 174; Sina, *L'Avvento della Ragione*, 344–7.
[54] Israel, 'Toleration', 24–8; Israel, 'Intellectual Debate', 28–36; Israel, 'Spinoza, Locke', 107–11.
[55] Wootton, 'Introduction', 104–5.

First, his tolerance being what has been called a 'privilege' or 'immunity' from the form of worship otherwise generally prescribed, in England by Crown and Parliament or *mutatis mutandis* by sovereign authority in other lands, it can only unequivocally pertain to those who adhere to an organized, permitted congregation for which exemption can be claimed, such as, in the English case, Protestant dissenters, Quakers, Catholics, Jews, and potentially Muslims.[56] Those who subscribe to no precise form of worship, be they agnostics, deists, or *indifferenti*, while not expressly excluded, languish in a vague limbo, lacking any defined status or recognized freedom. If an individual's spiritual allegiance or status is such that no particular congregation or confession can be specified, it becomes unclear in that case what exactly the justification for toleration is.

Secondly, there is Locke's well-known equivocation (unlike Episcopius and Limborch, who are more accommodating on this point) regarding Catholics. The question whether they should be tolerated is left in doubt in Locke, because the secular authority is not obliged to permit Churches which claim an authority, such as that of the Pope, deemed by adherents to transcend that of the territorial sovereign and even be capable of nullifying it. A third major curtailment in Locke is the categorical exclusion of 'atheists', a broad and flexible category in contemporary parlance, which embraced non-providential deists and pantheists. Since they reject divine Providence, participate in no acknowledged form of worship, and do not seek to save their souls, by definition they are not entitled to toleration.[57] 'Those are not at all to be tolerated,' insists Locke, 'who deny the being of a God,' not least because 'promises, covenants, and oaths, which are bonds of human society, can have no hold upon an atheist.' According to Locke, the 'taking away of God but even in thought, dissolves all'.[58]

By contrast, in Spinoza, freedom of worship, far from constituting the core of toleration, is very much a secondary question, a topic which he discusses only briefly and peripherally. For in Spinoza toleration has primarily to do with individual freedom, not a coexistence of Churches, and still less the freedom of ecclesiastical structures to increase their followings, expand their resources, and build up their educational establishments. While everyone, he argues, should possess freedom to express religious beliefs in whatever way they choose, large congregations should be forbidden unless they belong to the State religion which, in Spinoza (like Rousseau) would ideally be a philosophical religion, not Christianity, what he calls a 'very simple universal faith' in which, he stresses, 'worship of God and obedience to Him consist solely in justice and charity towards one's neighbour.'[59] Doubtless, his excluding large dissenting congregations (among them that of his own upbringing in Amsterdam) was because this then creates an autonomous mechanism of control over the individual, independent of the law and the sovereign. While dissenters should be permitted as many churches

---

[56] Dunn, 'Claim to Freedom', 180–2; Marshall, *John Locke*, 367–9.

[57] Dunn, 'Claim to Freedom', 180–2; Harris, *Mind of John Locke*, 189.

[58] Locke, *Political Writings*, 421; later Locke again denied 'atheism (which takes away all religion) to have any right to toleration at all'; Locke, *A Third Letter for Toleration*, 236.

[59] Spinoza, *TTP*, 224; Matheron, *Individu et communauté*, 108–9.

as they wish, these should invariably be small and situated well apart. 'On the other hand,' he argues, 'it is most important that churches proclaiming the state religion should be large and magnificent and only patricians or senators be allowed to perform its principal rites' or be its 'guardians and interpreters'.[60] This again reflects Spinoza's view that it fatally damages the State to permit a largely autonomous clergy, or ecclesiastical hierarchy, which most people then consider divinely sanctioned, and a higher form of authority than the sovereign.[61]

The gulf separating Locke's and Spinoza's conceptions of toleration, originating in Locke's concern for saving souls and Spinoza's for ensuring individual freedom, is thus widened further by Spinoza's anxiety to whittle down ecclesiastical power.[62] It was indeed always characteristic of Radical Enlightenment toleration theory to try to erode and discredit ecclesiastical authority and as far as possible merge it into the political sovereign. This tendency, already conspicuous in the brothers De la Court and Van den Enden, as well as in *De Jure Ecclesiasticorum*, later powerfully re-emerges in Toland, Radicati, Tindal, and Mandeville.[63] Thus Radicati refuses to accept that any of the pretensions and privileges, including acquisition of property, by popes, bishops, and clergy, are justified by Scripture or anything else, and scorns the 'tricks of the secular and regular clergy to keep the vulgar in subjection and obedience'.[64] In marked contrast, in Locke toleration necessarily entails retreat by the State from the ecclesiastical sphere once the rights, exemptions, and prerogatives of acknowledged Churches are conceded.

It is essential to Spinoza's purpose that those who manage the affairs of the State should be prevented from splitting into sects and factions supporting rival creeds and clergies. For, if they do, not only is the power and capacity of the State irreparably impaired but, as the influence of competing ecclesiastical hierarchies grows, the ruling patricians, or elected office-holders, will themselves increasingly become prey to 'superstition', Spinoza's shorthand for subservience to ecclesiastical authority and theological tenets, since the rival political factions are bound to encourage churchmen on either side to extend their influence over the common people so as to mobilize them against each other, and thereby 'deprive their subjects of freedom to express their beliefs'.[65] In other words, one sees an inverse relationship in Spinoza between the degree of influence ecclesiastical hierarchies acquire where these are distinct from the ruling élite, and the measure of liberty individuals enjoy to express their views. Hence, the individual is freer the less he or she is under the sway of an organized Church.

In the democratic republic of the radicals it is not therefore the aspiration of individuals for spiritual redemption which drives the push for toleration, as in Locke and the mainstream Enlightenment, but rather the quest for individual liberty, freedom of thought, and freedom to publish ideas which may be 'philosophical' in the new sense

---

[60] Spinoza, *Tractatus Politicus*, 411.   [61] Israel, 'Locke, Spinoza', 12–13.
[62] Moreau, 'Spinoza et le *Jus circa Sacra*', 336.   [63] Israel, 'Intellectual Debate', 27–8.
[64] Radicati, *Twelve Discourses*, 75, 125, 160, 171.   [65] Spinoza, *Tractatus Politicus*, 411.

coined by Spinoza and his followers, and later embraced by the English deists and the French *philosophes*, meaning rooted in systems of thought based on 'natural reason' and, consequently, incompatible with, and opposed to, the Churches' theological conception of God, man, and the universe. Since, in the thought-world of Spinoza and his adherents, an individual's beliefs and ideas have a higher status, and are more beneficial to society, when they are 'philosophical' and based on natural reason rather than theological doctrines, the toleration of the Radical Enlightenment usually implies and sometimes explicitly asserts—as, for example, Spinoza does by refusing to allow large dissenting congregations—the right of the State to use its power to lessen the sway of theology in society and education. For to radical minds, toleration and individual liberty are depleted as and when ecclesiastical influence grows and maximized where ecclesiastical influence in culture, education, and politics is minimized.

Since, for Spinoza, the right of the State is the power of the State, it is essentially because it is impossible to control men's minds that the State should not attempt to do so: 'if no man, then, can give up his freedom to judge and think as he pleases, and everyone is by absolute natural right master of his own thoughts, it follows that utter failure will attend any attempt in a state to force men to speak only as prescribed by the sovereign despite their different and opposing opinions.'[66] Furthermore, the ultimate purpose of the State, insists Spinoza, whatever abuses actually occur, 'is, in reality, freedom' (finis ergo reipublicae revera libertas est).[67] When the State comes into being, each subject surrenders his right to act as he pleases but not his right to reason and judge for himself and, since everyone has this right, it follows, contends Spinoza, that everyone also retains the right (and power) to speak freely and express personal views without this damaging the State. Sedition arises, he maintains, only when citizens express political views directly hostile to the constitution of the State or in open defiance (as distinct from inactive disapproval) of the laws and decrees of the State.

A properly regulated commonwealth, then, holds Spinoza, 'grants every man the same freedom to philosophize which I have shown to be permitted to religious faith'.[68] Here Spinoza is referring back to the astounding passage where he expounds the seven basic articles of his ideal philosophical—or, for those who prefer, theological—State religion, claiming it makes no difference whether an individual embraces these tenets philosophically or theologically, or indeed what conclusions individuals draw as to their meaning: 'nor does it matter whether one believes God to be omnipresent actually or potentially, to govern things freely or by the necessity of his nature, whether he issues laws as a ruler or teaches them as eternal truths; whether man obeys God from free will or the necessity of the divine decree; or, finally, whether the rewarding of the good and punishment of wrongdoers is natural or supernatural.'[69] In short, Spinoza denies that theological doctrines, and the teachings of Churches, contain any truths at all. In his view, and following him, subsequently the radical tradition as a whole, the origin and purpose of theological tenets is to promote obedience to the State and its

[66] Spinoza, *TTP*, 292.   [67] Spinoza, *Opera*, ii, 241.   [68] Spinoza, *TTP*, 295.
[69] Ibid., 225–6; Spinoza, *Opera*, iii, 178; Israel, 'Spinoza, Locke', 107; Smith, *Spinoza, Liberalism*, 112–13.

laws or, as Radicati expresses it, 'religion was instituted by legislators in order to give strength and credit to their laws.'[70] Since the sole purpose of theological doctrines is to instil good conduct and obedience, and obedience and charity are the measures of genuine piety, 'everyone must adapt these dogmas of faith to his own understanding,' says Spinoza, 'and interpret them for himself in whatever way he thinks will best enable him to adopt them unreservedly.'[71] Nothing more plainly demonstrates Rousseau's hybrid status as a political thinker who combined elements of radicalism with the moderate Enlightenment, or rather Spinoza with Locke, than his insistence, in the last chapter of the *Contrat social*, on the State upholding a simple universal civil religion, distinct from Christianity, consisting of a few core tenets, an idea which he presumably borrowed from Spinoza, and then stipulating that these core tenets must include belief in a 'powerful, intelligent, benevolent, providential deity and reward and punishment in the hereafter'.[72]

Truth then, according to Spinoza and his followers, can only be grasped through natural reason and philosophically, and cannot be embodied in theological doctrines. It is for this reason that freedom of thought and speech, and not liberty of conscience and worship, constitute the core of toleration in Spinoza's thought. Impossible or not, efforts were and are constantly made to prescribe by law what should and should not be thought, read, and believed. The reason why, according to Spinoza, some men try to mobilize the law behind certain beliefs, and to suppress others, is in order to overcome rivals, win influence and the applause of the multitude, and so obtain high office. Such decrees are introduced for personal advantage but also, he argues, at great cost to the public. For by censuring this or that view, the State encourages and exacerbates doctrinal disputes. Such laws, he insists, 'have often been instituted to pander, or rather surrender to, the indignation of those who cannot endure enlightened minds by men who, by exercising an austere authority, easily turn the credulity of the seditious common people into rage, inciting them against whomsoever they wish'.[73] 'Therefore,' he contends, 'if honesty is to be esteemed above servility and sovereigns are to retain effective control, and not be forced to surrender to agitators, it is imperative to permit freedom of judgement and rule so that the divergent and conflicting views men express do not prevent them living together in peace. . . . This system of government,' he urges, 'is unquestionably the best, and its disadvantages least, because it is in closest accord with human nature.'[74]

By insisting that 'the less freedom of judgement is granted to men the further are they removed from the most natural state, and consequently the more repressive the régime,' Spinoza clears a much wider space for freedom of speech and the press than is allocated by Locke's or Rousseau's toleration, and simultaneously provides a method whereby the degree of freedom, or lack of freedom, in society can be measured.[75] For even at its widest, freedom of conscience and worship does not and can

---

[70] Radicati, *Twelve Discourses*, 224–5.   [71] Spinoza, *TTP*, 225.

[72] Rousseau, *Social Contract*, 307–8; Vernière, *Spinoza*, 484; Rosenblatt, *Rousseau and Geneva*, 265–6.

[73] Spinoza, *Opera*, iii, 244.   [74] Spinoza, *TTP*, 297; Balibar, *Spinoza and Politics*, 25–31.

[75] Israel, 'Spinoza, Locke', 110–11; Israel, *Locke, Spinoza*, 18–19.

not provide unrestricted access to all points of view, and especially not philosophical arguments conflicting with the *fundamenta* of revealed religion; nor indeed did Locke or Rousseau believe they should. Towards the end of the *Tractatus Theologico-Politicus*, Spinoza broaches what for him personally was the most urgent priority in the toleration debate—the question of freedom to publish views no matter how unpalatable to some, or most, segments of society. Undoubtedly, no other Early Enlightenment theory of toleration does in fact embrace full freedom to publish, neither that of Le Clerc, Locke, nor Bayle. Here too we find a wide gulf separating Spinoza from Hobbes. For Hobbes deems it 'annexed to the soveraignty, to be judge of what opinions and doctrines are averse, and what conducing to peace; and consequently, on what occasions, how farre, and what men are to be trusted withall, in speaking to multitudes of people; and who shall examine the doctrines of all bookes before they be published'.[76] But where Hobbes holds 'in the well governing of opinions, consisteth the well governing of mens actions, in order to their peace and concord,' Spinoza teaches that while the individual must submit to the sovereign regarding his actions, he is free in his thoughts, judgements, and in expressing his views, both verbally and in writing.

All attempts, admonishes Spinoza, to curb expression of views, and censure books, not only curtails legitimate freedom but endangers the State. The antagonism between the Remonstrants and Counter-Remonstrants, which brought the Dutch Republic to the verge of civil war in 1618, makes it 'clearer than the sun at noon', he avers, 'that the real schismatics are those who condemn the writings of others and seditiously incite the quarrelsome mob against authors rather than the authors themselves who usually write only for scholars and appeal to reason alone'.[77] Recapitulating at the close of the *Tractatus Theologico-Politicus*, Spinoza concludes 'that the state can pursue no safer course than regard piety and religion as consisting solely in charity and just dealing and that the right of the sovereign, both in the religious and secular spheres, should be restricted to men's actions, with everyone being allowed to think what he wishes and say what he thinks'.[78]

iv. Equality and the Quest for 'Natural Man'

The concept of 'equality' rooted in 'natural right' features prominently in Spinoza's political thought. His divergence from Hobbes regarding the retention of 'natural right' under the State and refusal to 'acknowledge any distinction between men and other individuals of Nature' as regards motives and whatever living creatures do according to the laws of their own nature,[79] induced him, and then in his wake the entire radical tradition of thought, to reappraise 'natural man', evaluating the state of nature very differently from Hobbes. Where the state of nature, in Hobbes, is a dark and fearsome realm, to which no one inhabiting the securer milieu of civil society under a sovereign wishes to glance back, for the radicals, 'natural man'

---

[76] Hobbes, *Leviathan*, ch. XVIII, sixth right of the sovereign; Curley, 'Kissinger, Spinoza', 318.
[77] Spinoza, *TTP*, 298.   [78] Ibid., 299.   [79] Ibid., 237.

remains crucially relevant to life in civil society and became a favourite tool of social and political analysis, helping to differentiate between what is superfluous, or contrary to nature, in man's political and social environment and what is inherent in his nature.

It is greatly to men's advantage, stresses Spinoza, 'to live in accordance with the laws and sure dictates of our reason' and 'in safety from fear as far as possible'.[80] Incontestably, to 'achieve a secure and good life, men had to unite in one body' and form a commonwealth.[81] Nevertheless, in both political treatises, Spinoza continually adduces the 'state of nature' as a measuring-rod for assessing political and moral phenomena, and identifying what is best and most essential in human existence. Hence, democracy is declared better than monarchy and aristocracy because it is the 'most natural form of state, approaching most closely to that freedom which Nature grants to every man'.[82] Transferring one's individual sovereign right (power) to act, as it was in the state of nature, to the majority rather than to one or a few, means no one is set above others: 'in this way all men remain equal, as they were before in the state of Nature.'[83] In the case of the ancient Hebrews whose State, holds Spinoza, was originally a democracy close to the state of nature, all men participated in politics, public offices were not restricted to a closed élite, 'laws remained uncorrupted' and were scrupulously observed, and there was only one civil war. Hence men were both restrained and helped on an equal basis. When, however, the Israelites ill-advisedly instituted a monarchy instead, the people were excluded from decision-making, 'there was practically no end to civil strife' and, as will always happen in such circumstances, the newly installed king sought to change the laws to his own advantage, reducing the people in such a way that it would 'not be found as easy to abolish monarchy as establish it'.[84]

In the *Tractatus Politicus* Spinoza reaffirms his view that democracy 'in which absolutely everyone who is bound only by the laws of his *patria*, and is otherwise independent, and who leads a decent life, has the right to vote in the supreme council and take up offices of state' is the best form of State; and that monarchy can only be stable and beneficial if the monarch's power is heavily restricted and the supreme law is the 'common good' and not that of the ruler.[85] Hence monarchy too, if it is to be viable, must incorporate the principle of equality to a great extent, providing unrestricted access to advisory offices, instituting universal military service among the male citizenry, and tending towards equality before the law. Where some writers of the time disdained the common people as more unruly, inconstant, irrational, and inclined to vice than their social superiors, Spinoza maintains 'all men have one and the same nature; it is power and culture which misleads us.'[86] If the common people know nothing of affairs of state, this is because those who rule in modern monarchies see to it that they are kept in ignorance.

---

[80] Ibid., 239.   [81] Ibid., 241.   [82] Ibid., 243; Balibar, 'Le Politique', 205.

[83] Spinoza, *TTP*, 243.   [84] Ibid., 277; Spinoza, *Opera*, iii, 226; Smith, *Spinoza, Liberalism*, 147–51.

[85] Spinoza, *Tractatus Politicus*, 443; Matheron, 'Fonction théorique', 270–1.

[86] Spinoza, *Tractatus Politicus*, 359; Balibar, 'Le Politique', 208–9; Walther, 'Philosophy and Politics', 54.

If equality was basic to the 'state of nature', so also was absence of landed property. 'If there is one thing an individual in the condition of nature cannot appropriate and make his own,' contends Spinoza, 'it is the land and the things pertaining to it.'[87] Consequently, when civil society and the State are created, the 'land and other assets belonging to it, are effectively the public property of the commonwealth, that is, they belong by right to all who have united and are therefore able to protect it, or to the man who they have all empowered to protect it for them.' Therefore the land is essential to the people 'as the basis for their defending their collective power, and freedom' and they must take care to regulate its use and disposal.[88] This remarkable linkage of equality, democracy and freedom, and the issue of the original ownership of the land, with the 'state of nature' and man's 'natural right', initiated a preoccupation with 'natural man' which runs like a thread through the Radical Enlightenment from Spinoza and Van den Enden, via Lahontan, Tyssot de Patot, and Radicati, to Rousseau, and ultimately the militant, revolutionary egalitarianism of Robespierre and the Jacobins. Spinoza himself, assuredly, abhors popular tumult and fears political revolution. But at the same time, while acknowledging that vast benefits accrue from the transition from the 'state of nature' to civil society under the State, he also demonstrates that monarchy and aristocracy, in other words, the institutionalized inequality which dominated European society in his time, are nothing else than forms of corruption and degeneration from the equality and democratic republicanism which represent the normative condition most 'natural' to man. The inequality and hierarchy dominant in European society and culture in his day is thus devoid of all legitimacy.

Images of primitive societies which evolved into earthly utopias based on 'natural religion', often strongly redolent of Spinozism and characterized by a high degree of social equality, became a familiar theme of Early Enlightenment intellectual culture, not least owing to the widespread impact of the *Voyages* of Lahontan who portrays the Canadian Iroquois Indians as wise and noble savages, steeped in a Spinozistic view of man and the universe, and to the Spinozistic novel, the *Voyages et aventures de Jacques Massé* (c.1714). It is a tradition which explicitly opposes Hobbes' harsh and allegedly distorted portrayal of 'natural man', culminating in Radicati, who scornfully dismisses Hobbes' account of the state of nature, claiming that 'savages and brutes of the same species, that follow the laws of nature only, are more sociable among themselves than men that are civilized, since they live together with great kindness and cordiality, and observe the laws of equity in everything, each enjoying the fruits of the earth, and'— a typically Radicatian touch—'their females; and suffering the rest to do so without envy or ambition, being all equal, and having everything in common'.[89] Writers such as Lahontan, Tyssot de Patot, and Radicati also foreshadow Rousseau in advancing the notion of moral degeneration with the advance of civil society: 'for where there is no inequality, there is neither emulation nor envy, and where there is no envy there is no ambition.'[90] As part of his case against Hobbes, Radicati offers the exemplum

---

[87] Spinoza, *Tractatus Politicus*, 350–1.   [88] Ibid.
[89] Radicati, *Twelve Discourses*, 32.   [90] Ibid., 33.

of the 'ancient inhabitants of the Canary Islands who, before they were discovered by Christians, had always lived in the blessed state of nature'. In his opinion, these good folk 'fed upon herbs and fruits, lay upon leaves in the forests, went naked, and their women, and all other things, were in common amongst them'.[91]

Radicati fervently reaffirms Spinoza's proposition that democracy is the political form closest to the state of nature. Claiming the 'religion of Christ differs not from the religion of nature' but had subsequently been perverted by the Churches and clergy, he maintains Christ's laws 'bearing an exact resemblence to those of nature . . . he proposed to settle a perfect democracy amongst men, the only method he could take to make them happy.'[92] For this purpose, he asserts, Christ 'introduced a community of goods, banished luxury and riches, and ordained that no man should be distinguished from another, well knowing that in a government really democratical, men ought to have all things in common, and be all equal'.[93] The inevitable tendency for oligarchies to develop, and for the most astute and powerful families to increase in wealth at the expense of the rest, and keep 'all the rest in dependence', apparent in Europe's existing republics, can only be countered, contends Radicati, by establishing a 'perfect democratical government' which means abolishing all social hierarchy and inequality of wealth for, he contends, this 'distinction of families far from being the bond of society is a perpetual occasion of division'.[94]

Radicati was an extremist who in various respects went further than other early eighteenth-century radicals. But he nevertheless powerfully reflects the wider tendency. Not a few agreed that 'every nation has a right to shake off a tyrant's yoke by all sorts of means,'[95] and that genuine 'democratical government is that where the whole authority is in the hands of the people indistinctly, and where men are equal in nobility, power and riches'.[96] He was an isolated voice only in his insistence that to achieve the true equality, which alone makes a democratic society viable, there must be community of property,[97] and in claiming that genuine democracy requires abolition of marriage and the family, and having women in common, since 'no father must know his children, nor the child his father, as such a superiority and knowledge could not suit with that community of goods, and that equality, which are the basis of a commonwealth.'[98]

A paragon of moderation compared to Radicati, Rousseau in his *Discours sur l'Inegalité* (1755) similarly deplores Hobbes for asserting that since man in the 'state of nature . . . has no idea of goodness he must naturally be wicked; that he is vicious because he does not know virtue'. On the contrary, holds Rousseau, uncorrupted morals prevail in the 'state of nature' and especially the admirable moderation of savages in expressing the sexual urge.[99] He praises the 'Caribbeans who have, as yet, least of all deviated from the state of nature, being in fact the most peaceable of people in their amours, and the least subject to jealousy, though they live in a hot climate which

---

[91] Ibid., 39.   [92] Ibid., 45.   [93] Ibid., 46.   [94] Ibid., 49–51.   [95] Ibid., 292–3.
[96] Ibid., 204.   [97] Ibid.   [98] Ibid., 46; Carpanetto and Ricuperati, *Italy*, 113–14.
[99] Rousseau, *Discourse*, 72–3.

seems always to inflame the passions'.[100] In general, Rousseau extols the moderation and lack of aggression of 'natural man' and the absence of slavery in his midst: for in the state of nature everyone is his own master.[101] According to Rousseau, 'the first man who, having enclosed a piece of ground, thought of saying "this is mine", and found people simple enough to believe him, was the real founder of civil society.'[102] Ever since, wars and terrible disorders were the rule. By contrast, the 'inequality of mankind is hardly felt and its influence is next to nothing in a state of nature'.[103]

While Rousseau's notion of the progressive moral degeneration of mankind from the moment civil society established itself diverges markedly from Spinoza's claim that human nature is always the same and that there is no virtue before civil society, there remains a strong unifying thread in that, for both philosophers, the pristine equality of the state of nature is our ultimate guide and criterion, not just in determining the character and legitimacy of any society's political arrangments but also in shaping the common good, 'volonté générale', or Spinoza's *mens una*, which alone can ensure stability and political salvation.[104] Without the supreme criterion of equality, the general will would indeed be meaningless. For both men the point of the State is the very antithesis of hierarchy and domination, being the establishment and preservation of liberty on the basis of equality. When in the depths of the French Revolution the Jacobin clubs all over France regularly deployed Rousseau when demanding radical reforms, and especially anything—such as land redistribution—designed to enhance equality, they were at the same time, albeit mostly unconsciously, invoking a radical tradition which reached back to the late seventeenth century.[105]

[100] Rousseau, *Discourse*, 78.   [101] Ibid., 81–2.   [102] Ibid., 84.   [103] Ibid., 82; Lemay, 'Part d'*Émile*', 378–9.

[104] Perrot, 'Spinoza, Rousseau', 408–9; Smith, *Spinoza, Liberalism*, 134–7; Viroli, *Jean-Jacques Rousseau*, 108–11.

[105] Kennedy, *Jacobin Clubs*, 91, 93, 104, 209, 224, 242; Lemay, 'Part d'*Émile*', 379–82.

16 | PUBLISHING A BANNED PHILOSOPHY

i. *The Tractatus Theologico-Politicus*

It is often claimed Spinoza's *Tractatus Theologico-Politicus* circulated in the Dutch Republic, despite the general hostility it encountered, more or less unhindered until the formal prohibition of 1674, and that in the early period after publication Holland's Pensionary, De Witt, personally intervened to prevent prohibition.[1] De Witt was undoubtedly involved in the high-level deliberations about this unprecedentedly unsettling book. He certainly read it as part of his official responsibilities and several times discussed the problem of Spinoza with delegates from the North and South Holland synods. Reformed Church records show that delegates from both synods translated, filed, and submitted what were considered particularly offensive passages from the book to the city governments and States of Holland, and that this material was given personally to the Pensionary.[2] Although there is no unequivocal proof, De Witt does indeed seem to have preferred not to proceed to a formal provincial ban on the *Tractatus*. It is a mistake, though, to deduce from this that he viewed the work in any way favourably or that it circulated freely until after his downfall in 1672. In fact, it is incorrect to suppose that it was not until the formal prohibition of July 1674 that the printing, sale, and circulation of the *Tractatus* was suppressed.[3]

Under the terms of Holland's anti-Socinian legislation of 1653, the city governments had ample powers to inspect bookshops and sequestrate stocks of copies of works such as Meyer's *Philosophia* and Spinoza's *Tractatus* and, intermittently at least, plainly did so. Meyer's book was not expressly banned by decree in Holland (as distinct from Friesland and Utrecht) either until 1674, but was none the less prohibited in towns where stocks of copies went on sale.[4] A clearly documented instance of early action

---

[1] See, for instance, H. E. Allison, *Benedict de Spinoza*, 18; Rowan, *John de Witt*, 410; Gregory, 'Introduction', 27; Japikse, 'Spinoza and De Witt', 13; Enno van Gelder, *Getemperde vrijheid*, 165–6, 176–85; Scruton, *Spinoza*, 12.

[2] ARH OSA 183 Acta North Holland Synod, Hoorn, 4 Aug. 1671 art. 40, p. 46 and ibid. vol. 184 Acta North Holland Synod, Enkhuizen, Aug. 1672, art. 38, p. 37.

[3] *Groot Placaat-Boeck*, iii, 523–4: 'Placaet tegens de Sociniaensche Boecken Leviathan en andere', The Hague, 19 July 1674; Israel, 'Banning of Spinoza's Works', 3–4.

[4] Israel, 'Banning of Spinoza's Works', 7–8.

against the *Tractatus* was the raiding of the bookshops in Leiden in May 1670. Barely a week after the local Reformed consistory first reacted to the *Tractatus'* 'contents and enormities, or rather obscenities, earnestly requesting that the same be seized and suppressed',[5] the burgomasters resolved 'to have a certain tractate entitled *Theologico Politicq* confiscated [from the bookshops] by the sheriff owing to its godless passages'.[6] In Utrecht the work was banned on a province-wide basis, following the provincial synod's petition to the States, in September 1671, which, however, was many months after the book's suppression in the city.[7]

Accordingly, it was no misapprehension which prompted the Utrecht professor, Graevius, writing to Leibniz in April 1671, to designate the *Tractatus* a '*liber pestilentissimus*' which, since it opens the window to atheism 'as widely as possible . . . is prohibited by the authorities'.[8] Nor, as this letter from a fervent Cartesian illustrates, was it by any means only the traditionalist Calvinist orthodox who abhorred Spinoza and his influence enough to support outright suppression of his work. Most, if not all, liberal Cartesio-Cocceian professors and theologians reacted similarly, including Frans Burman at Utrecht, who, on reading the book in April 1670, was deeply shocked, made extracts, noted the reports that Spinoza had written it, and subsequently urged allies at home and abroad, including his friend Jacobus Alting, at Groningen, to join forces with him to 'attack and destroy this utterly pestilential book'.[9]

The notion that Spinoza's *Tractatus* ever circulated freely is thus a myth lacking all basis in fact. What De Witt's involvement in deliberations about Spinoza does signify is the wholly exceptional and, in the perception of the authorities ecclesiastical and civic, incomparably seditious, character of his text. At a meeting in June 1670, the Amsterdam consistory, preparing proposals for the North Holland synod, urged more effective action against the 'printing of licentious books and, in particular, the appalling work entitled *Tractatus Theologico-Politicus*'.[10] Meeting at Schiedam in July 1670, the South Holland synod discussed 'all kinds of foul and godless books', identifying the *Tractatus* as a work 'as vile and blasphemous as any that are known of, or that the world has ever seen, and about which the Synod must complain to the utmost'.[11] Passages were read out, by the Amsterdam delegates, to the North Holland synod in August 1670,[12] and by May 1671 warnings about that 'abominable book' had reached Groningen.[13] In their conferences with De Witt on

[5] GA Leiden Acta Kerkeraad v, res. 9 May 1670, art. 4.

[6] Ibid. res. 16 May 1670 art. 2; GA Leiden St. arch. 191, p. 60 Notulenboek Burgemeesteren, res. 16 May 1670.

[7] Rijksarchief Utrecht, Provinciale kerkvergadering iii. Acta Synodi Provincialis, Sept. 1670 sessio 6, art. 4 and Acta 1671, sessio 6, art. 30; Freudenthal, *Lebensgeschichte Spinozas*, 130; Israel, 'Banning of Spinoza's Works', 9.

[8] Freudenthal, *Lebensgeschichte Spinozas*, 193.

[9] Burmannus, *Burmannorum Pietas*, 211, 228.

[10] GA Amsterdam Protocolboek Kerkeraad xii, p. 110. res. 30 June 1670; RNH classis Edam v, acta 28 July 1670.

[11] Knuttel, *Acta*, iv, 531.

[12] ARH OSA 183 Acta North Holland Synod, Amsterdam, 5 Aug. 1670, pp. 3, 16.

[13] Rijksarchief Groningen, *Acta*, provincial synod iii, res. 5 May 1671.

the question of seditious books in the years 1670–2, the delegates of the Holland synods repeatedly demanded a special edict of the States suppressing the four, in their view, most pernicious works of recent times—the *Tractatus Theologico-Politicus*, the *Philosophia*, Hobbes' *Leviathan*, and Frans Kuyper's Socinian compilation, the *Bibliotheca Fratrum Polonorum*.[14]

However, the deliberations dragged on inconclusively. The issue, though, was not whether these books should be banned. As De Witt himself observed in the States of Holland, in April 1671, and as the provincial high court confirmed, all these titles were unquestionably illegal under the edict of September 1653 and automatically subject to suppression and confiscation by the city governments.[15] The question was whether a higher level of public condemnation, focusing attention on these works specifically and possibly some others, and therefore lending them even greater notoriety than they had already, was advisable. Some regents were more sympathetic to the public Church's efforts to tighten book censorship in the Republic than others. A committee of the States, chaired by De Witt, was set up to deliberate and was still deliberating when the French invaded in June 1672.[16] Buoyed by the frenzy, anger, and fear which gripped the Reformed population in the summer of 1672, the preachers summoned the populace to purge themselves of their sins and the city governments to close the theatres, brothels, and dance-halls, as well as curb swearing, adultery, and the 'daily increasing boldness of the Papists'. Nor did they forget to renew their pressure on the States to stop the 'licentious printing and distribution of many pernicious books such as the *Bibliotheca Fratrum Polonorum*, the godless work called the *Leviathan*, the infamous *Philosophia Scripturae Interpres* and the incomparably impious *Tractatus Theologico-Politicus*'.[17]

Although it is not known whether he ever met Spinoza, De Witt indubitably knew a certain amount about him. But what was his attitude towards the philosopher? While the Pensionary was at odds with the orthodox Calvinist faction, did not hesitate to back the Cartesio-Cocceians within the Church and academic life, and was strongly opposed to any strengthening of the Church's role in matters of intellectual censorship, there is no reason to think he was privately any less inclined to condemn Spinoza than he was bound to officially whenever the latter's name and writings came up, as they frequently did, in meetings with synodal delegates and among the States. Quite possibly, he regarded Spinoza and his adherents as a genuine threat not just to religion, and the Cartesian philosophy with which he personally sympathized, but also the stability of society and the regent régime. A surviving fragment from a diary of the classicist Jacob Gronovius, who was then in contact with the Pensionary about various matters, reveals that in Dutch governing circles 'Spinosa' was then deemed much the most dangerous of the Dutch 'atheists' and considered by De Witt a

---

[14] ARH OSA 183 Acta Synod North Holland, Hoorn, 4 Aug. 1671, art. 7, pp. 7, 10 and art 40, p. 46; ARH OSA 184 Acta North Holland Synod, Enkhuizen, 2 Aug. 1672 art. 4, p. 6 and art. 38, 37.

[15] Freudenthal, *Lebensgeschichte Spinozas*, 125–6; Nadler, *Spinoza*, 296–7.

[16] Res. Holl. 24 Apr. 1671; Freudenthal, *Lebensgeschichte Spinozas*, 127.

[17] GA Haarlem Acta Kerkeraad ix, res. 10 June 1672.

miscreant deserving imprisonment.[18] According to Gronovius, De Witt was particularly alarmed lest the common people cease to believe in 'reward and punishment after this life'. When Spinoza heard that the Pensionary disapproved of his *Tractatus*, he sent someone to request an interview. De Witt, however, reportedly answered that 'he did not wish to see such a man cross his threshold.'[19]

Spinoza's *Tractatus* was always deemed an illegal publication and his adherents, from the outset, a clandestine 'sect'. Colonel Jean-Baptiste Stouppe, the Swiss officer commanding the French garrison in Utrecht in 1672–3, who wrote the anti-Dutch *Religion des Hollandois* (1674), described the situation accurately in the main—a description later echoed verbatim by Bayle in his *Dictionnaire*—when he observed that Spinoza's followers 'n'osent pas se découvrir, parce que son livre renverse absolument les fondemens de toutes les religions et qu'il a esté condamné par un décret public des États et qu'on a déffendu de le vendre, bien qu'on ne laisse pas de le vendre publiquement'.[20] In his published reply to Stouppe's insinuation that the Dutch authorities were excessively tolerant and far too inactive in curbing Spinoza, the Walloon pastor, Jean Brun, reminded readers that the regents had sought to suppress the *Tractatus* 'en sa naissance, et l'ont condamné, et en ont défendu le débit par un décrit public' as Stouppe himself admits. He knew for a fact, added the pastor, that the book was circulating 'en Angleterre, en Allemagne, en France, et même en Suisse [i.e. Stouppe's country], aussi bien qu'en Hollande'.[21]

Spinoza had stuck his neck out and now needed to be exceedingly careful. He had one or two friends among the regents, notably Hudde, but this hardly sufficed to protect him. Given the vehemence of the outcry, it is not surprising he became apprehensive on receiving a visit from an unnamed sympathizer among the Dutch professorate—presumably De Volder, or possibly Craanen[22]—from whom he learnt that a Dutch translation of his *Tractatus* which had been prepared was now about to be published. Deeply worried, since publication in the vernacular would inevitably intensify the commotion, and render him even more of a public enemy than he was already, he contacted the faithful Jelles, asking his help to locate the translation and 'if possible stop the printing'.[23] He implored Jelles to do this for him and 'for the cause', explaining it was the request also of 'many of his good acquaintances' who did not wish to see the book forbidden (by special decree of the States) as would assuredly happen should it appear in Dutch. It seems strange that Spinoza should have been unaware of Rieuwertsz' and Glazemaker's plans to bring out a Dutch version. But, however that may be, the necessary steps were taken and the vernacular edition aborted. As a consequence,

---

[18] Klever, 'A New Document', 385–6.   [19] Ibid.; Nadler, *Spinoza*, 256.

[20] Stouppe, *Religion des Hollandois*, 66; Charles-Daubert and Moreau, *Pierre Bayle. Écrits*, 43–4; Cohen, *Séjour de Saint-Évremond*, 72.

[21] Brun, *Véritable religion*, i, 159–60; Charles-Daubert and Moreau, *Pierre Bayle. Écrits*, 45; Israel, 'Banning of Spinoza's Works', 6.

[22] Meinsma assumes Graevius but this seems improbable; Craanen is a possibility, but the likeliest candidate surely is De Volder, professor at Leiden since 1670; Spinoza, *Letters*, 243; Meinsma, *Spinoza*, 392; Spinoza, *Briefwisseling*, 292.

[23] Spinoza, *Letters*, 243.

no Dutch version appeared until 1693, sixteen years after Spinoza's death and fifteen after the publication of the French translation.

Although, as this incident implies, Spinoza himself may have been only indirectly involved, a highly complex strategy lay behind the continuing and impressive diffusion of the *Tractatus* in Latin. Indeed, the early publication history of the work is both intriguing and historically significant, being a key factor in the early diffusion of Spinozism in Europe outside the Netherlands. It also illustrates the extraordinary adroitness of Spinoza's publisher, Jan Rieuwertsz the elder (*c.*1616–87), and the early role of the radical philosophical underground as a mechanism of clandestine book distribution. No one dared republish or pirate the 1670 quarto edition of so infamous a work as Spinoza's *Tractatus*, or so it seems, though there was a subsequent clandestine octavo edition. To all outward appearances there existed only these two early editions. Yet somehow, as Brun rightly observed, during the mid-1670s the book was selling right across Europe, penetrating far more extensively than would normally be possible under such circumstances.

The remarkable profusion of copies of the early editions of Spinoza's *Tractatus*, compared with the relative paucity of other illicit books of the period and even most legal ones, indeed constitutes a fascinating historico-bibliographical puzzle. Where other clandestine works of the period are today extremely rare, many major public libraries around the world are surprisingly well stocked with copies of the first Latin and French editions of the *Tractatus*. The research library of the University of California, at Los Angeles, for example, has five copies of the Latin text, while the former Bourbon royal library at Naples boasts no fewer than six, as does the Cambridge University Library. Library catalogues of the late seventeenth and early eighteenth century confirm that the book massively penetrated all parts of western and central Europe as well as the Netherlands, a geographical spread remarkable for the period.

One twentieth-century scholar, checking the catalogues of 113 libraries assembled in France between 1670 and 1780, found that nearly half had a copy of the *Tractatus* in one or other language, and sometimes both, boasting between them no fewer than thirty-three copies of the Latin first edition and twenty-nine in French.[24] Equally, libraries of academics and theologians in Protestant Germany and Scandinavia frequently featured copies of the *Tractatus*, and the Kiel professor Andreas Ludwig Koenigsmann, whose library was auctioned at Copenhagen in 1729, possessed two.[25] Innumerable nobles acquired copies, ranging from the great Condé in Paris, the Electress Sophia at Hanover, and Prince Eugene of Savoy, to the Baron von Stosch in Florence, and owners of such comparatively small libraries as the 4,000 volumes of the Danish diplomat Gerard Ernst Franck von Frankenau, auctioned in Copenhagen in 1714, and the small collection, catalogued in 1693, belonging to George Savile, Marquis of Halifax (1633–95) housed at Rufford.[26] Eventually even university libraries acquired

---

[24] Vernière, *Spinoza*, 386–7, 696. [25] [Koenigsmann], *Catalogus Bibliothecae*, 8.
[26] For the latter, see CUL MS Dd-9-51 'A Catalogue of the books at Rufford', 6–7, 10, 21.

1ª ed. 2)

TRACTATUS
THEOLOGICO-
POLITICUS

Continens

Diſſertationes aliquot,

Quibus oſtenditur Libertatem Philoſophandi non tantum
ſalva Pietate, & Reipublicæ Pace poſſe concedi: ſed
eandem niſi cum Pace Reipublicæ, ipſaque
Pietate tolli non poſſe.

Johann: Epiſt: I. Cap: IV. verſ: XIII.

*Per hoc cognoſcimus quod in Deo manemus, & Deus manet
in nobis, quod de Spiritu ſuo dedit nobis.*

HAMBURGI,
Apud *Henricum Künraht.* cIɔIɔ cLxx

FIGURE I. The title-page of Spinoza's *Tractatus Theologico-Politicus* clandestinely published at Amsterdam in 1670.

TABLE I. The Early Latin Editions of the *Tractatus Theologico-Politicus*.

Edition	Format	'Publisher'	Title-page date	Pagination misprints	Likely real date
1 Edition princeps	quarto	Künraht	1670	304 for 104	1669/1670
2 Bamberger ii	quarto	Künraht	1672	24 for 42	1672
				213 for 207	
3 Bamberger iii	quarto	Künraht	1670	(as for	1672/3
				Bamberger ii)	
4 octavo	octavo	(three different false titles and authors)			1673
5 'The English Edition'	octavo	(none)	1673		1674
6 'The English Edition'	octavo	(none)	1670		1674
7 Bamberger iv	quarto	Künrath	1670	830 for 130	1677/8
8 Bamberger v	quarto	Künrath	1670	92 for 192	1678

Sources: Gebhardt, 'Textgestaltung', iii, 363–72; Bamberger, 'Early Editions', 9–33; Kingma and Offenberg, *Bibliography*, 6–15.

copies, that belonging to the Uppsala University Library being inscribed 'Bibliotheca Uppsaliensis 1734'. In 1735 a copy featured in one of the exceedingly infrequent book auctions held in Oslo.[27]

This impressive and, for a clandestine work, unmatched diffusion was made possible, the evidence shows, by a complex operation designed to mask the launching of successive new editions and facilitate international distribution. Given the general outcry against the work, and the avid interest in it of *esprits forts* across the continent, one might expect pirated versions. But there is no evidence that any of the successive secret editions identified by bibliographers were produced outside Amsterdam, or by anyone other than Rieuwertsz.[28] The technique of bringing out multiple editions, each time in an almost identical format, utilizing virtually the same title-page, complete with the original date and publication details, had obviously been tried before.[29] But it was highly unusual for anything so elaborate to be attempted as the publishing schedule propelling the *Tractatus Theologico-Politicus*. Rieuwertsz brought out the original version in January 1670. A second edition, undetected by all but the most discerning, appeared in 1672, a version which corrected many of the misprints in the first edition, including the pagination error giving page 104 as '304' (see Table 1), but simultaneously introducing new typographical errors, including two new wrong page numbers.[30] Neither the first, second, nor subsequent editions mentions 'Amsterdam'

---

[27] Spidberg, *Catalogus librorum*, fo. 4v.

[28] Bamberger, 'Early Editions', 9–10, 15, 20; Van Eeghen, *Amsterdamse boekhandel*, iv, 63–5.

[29] Including in the case of Koerbagh's *Bloemhof* of which there are two or three slightly differing Editions; see Vandenbossche, *Spinozisme en kritiek*, 3–4.

[30] Bamberger, 'Early Editions', 17.

as the place of publication; the quarto versions all fictitiously declare 'Hamburg' while the octavo of 1674 specifies no place at all. All the quarto versions declare the same fictitious publisher 'Künrath' but the earlier editions misspell the name 'Künraht'. Finally, minute differences of spacing on title-pages and elsewhere are detectable only by meticulous comparison of copies.

Differentiating between the early editions of the *Tractatus* provides evidence of more than purely bibliographical interest. It also reveals something of Rieuwertsz'— and, in so far as he was involved, Spinoza's—strategy of clandestine distribution. Given the promptness and frequency of response to the *Tractatus* in Protestant Germany during 1670–1, it seems clear that Rieuwertsz' declaring 'Hamburg' the place of publication on the title-page was part of a wider ploy to market much of the early output in German lands, presumably in part to divert attention from Amsterdam.[31] The fact the first published refutation of the *Tractatus*, that of Jakob Thomasius, appeared in Leipzig, under the tile *Adversus anonymum, de libertate philosophandi*, as early as May 1670,[32] suggests that Thomasius had been pondering the book and formulating his reply for weeks, if not months, before that. Most leading German scholars read the book over the next year or so. Leibniz procured his from his regular bookseller in Frankfurt in October 1671, three months before Spinoza offered to send him a copy from The Hague 'if the *Tractatus Theologico-Politicus* has not yet reached you'.[33] Most surviving copies of the initial two editions are found in, or derive from, German and Dutch libraries. The variant with '1672' on the title-page is extremely rare and presumably a printer's error subsequently corrected in the next print-run to '1670'. One of these 'Hamburg, 1672' copies, belonging to a deceased official, was auctioned in June 1710 in the Danish-held town of Schleswig.[34]

Rieuwertsz' and Spinoza's experiment with using completely bogus title-pages as a method of smuggling additional stock into the book trade, 'sous différents titres bizarres et chimériques', as Bayle later put it, 'afin de tromper le public, et d'éluder les défenses des magistrats',[35] dates from 1673, when the eastern part of the Netherlands was under French occupation and communications with Germany, as well as France and England, disrupted by the war. This venture was directed, accordingly, mainly to the home market, and the neighbouring Spanish Netherlands, as indeed the choice of false titles suggests. Three spurious title-pages were used, one purporting to be the *Opera Chirurgica Omnia* by the Spanish physician Francisco Henríquez de Villacorta, a hint that these copies were earmarked for Antwerp and the Spanish Low Countries, and perhaps ultimately even Spain, lands then in alliance with the Dutch and relatively open to Dutch trade. The other two—the *Operum Historicum collectio* of 'Daniel Heinsius' and the *Opera omnia* of the highly influential Leiden medical professor Franciscus Dele Boe Sylvius—bore titles apt to appeal especially in the United Provinces. No doubt this ploy was also a sardonic snub to Leiden, both bogus attributions being to

---

[31] Bamberger, 'Early Editions', 30.   [32] Walther, 'Machina civilis', 187.
[33] Spinoza, *Letters*, 248; Vernière, *Spinoza*, 100.   [34] [Breyer], *Exquissitissima Bibliotheca*, 53.
[35] Charle-Daubert and Moreau, *Pierre Bayle. Écrits*, 56.

luminaries among the most illustrious of that university. At the university's indignant request, the Leiden burgomasters promptly raised the matter in the States of Holland, procuring a resolution for the immediate seizure throughout Holland of these 'forbidden and profane books under false titles'.[36]

Most of the 1674 octavo edition, by contrast, was provided with a so-called 'English' title-page, that is, one with a typically English typographical appearance, designed to give the impression that the volume had been printed in England.[37] This version was plainly intended for the English market, and it is assuredly no accident that the initial reception of Spinoza in Britain can be dated, from a wide variety of evidence, specifically to the years 1674–6. Writing to Henry Jenkes at Cambrige, Limborch recorded his pleasure, in December 1674, at the news of the furious outcry against the *Tractatus* in England, and not least Boyle's adamant condemnation of it.[38] He had heard, he assured Jenkes, that Spinoza himself was shaken by the strength of British outrage. In his reply, Jenkes reported that Cambridge dons and scholars were indeed engrossed in the *Tractatus* and filled with the profoundest repugnance.[39] Even Henry Oldenburg, who had closer links with Spinoza than anyone else in England, likewise only read the *Tractatus* at this time, as emerges from his letter of June 1675, regretting having been too negative in his (lost) previous letter of a few weeks before, and too swiftly swayed by the shallow notions 'of the common run of theologians and conventional formulae of the confessions'.[40] Having read the book a second time, he now saw that 'far from wishing to harm true religion and sound philosophy, on the contrary you are striving to establish and promote the true goal of the Christian religion, as well as the divine sublimity and excellence of a fruitful philosophy.'

Spinoza is most unlikely to have been persuaded by this volte-face to resume his earlier confidence in the secretary of the Royal Society. But he did put Oldenburg's offer of renewed friendship to the test by asking him to receive a batch of copies of the *Tractatus* for passing on to other prominent scholars in England. This placed Oldenburg in an embarrassing position. After his effusive apology, he could hardly decline outright; but neither did he relish being an accomplice in the illicit distribution of the *Tractatus*. 'I shall not refuse to receive some copies of the said treatise,' he answered 'but I would only ask this of you that . . . they should be addressed to a certain Dutch merchant staying in London who will have them sent to me,' adding that there was no need for any mention that the copies were for forwarding to himself. On this basis, he agreed to 'distribute them among my various friends and obtain a fair price for them'.[41]

Nevertheless, Oldenburg, like Boyle, Jenkes, and numerous others, was deeply

---

[36] Freudenthal, *Lebensgeschichte Spinozas*, 138; Israel, 'Banning of Spinoza's Works', 11.

[37] Bamberger, 'Early Editions', 20, 24.

[38] Van Limborch to Jenkes, Amsterdam, 20 Dec. 1674 printed in De Boer, 'Spinoza en Engeland', 334; Simonutti, 'Premières réactions anglaises', 130.

[39] Colie, *Light and Enlightenment*, 96; Simonutti, 'Premières réactions anglaises', 130.

[40] Spinoza, *Opera*, iv, 272.   [41] Ibid., iv, 273; Spinoza, *Letters*, 294; Hutton, 'Henry Oldenburg', 111.

shocked by the content of Spinoza's book. It was at this time, primarily in reaction to Spinoza, that Boyle wrote several papers justifying the fact that 'almost all mankind agrees in believing in general, that there have been true miracles,'[42] including his *Some Physico-Theological Considerations about the Possibility of the Resurrection*, intended, as he put it, to demonstrate that the 'philosophical difficulties, urged against the possibility of the Resurrection, were nothing near so insuperable, as they are by some pretended, and by others granted to be.'[43] Bishop Stillingfleet's shocked reaction to Spinoza's *Tractatus* was part of the same mid-1670s wave of revulsion, his *A Letter to a Deist*, alluding to Spinoza as 'mightily in vogue among many' and the prime source of the renewed challenge to revealed religion in England, being dated 11 June 1675. Meanwhile, in the fastnesses of Christ's College, Cambridge, the venerable Henry More read the *Tractatus* during 1676, and his friend and colleague Cudworth started the critique of it which infuses his *True Intellectual System of the Universe* (1678), either around the same time or shortly after.[44]

The shifts and pulses of intellectual history are sometimes significantly affected by political and military pressures, and the history of the diffusion of the *Tractatus* provides a remarkable illustration of this. The first three editions seemingly sold briskly in Germany and Holland, leaving few copies for other markets. The Third Anglo-Dutch War (1672–4) heavily disrupted communication between Britain and the Netherlands, so that at the time of the Anglo-Dutch peace, in April 1674, there had as yet been no significant impact in England. Hence Rieuwertsz' decision to invade with an 'English' edition and Spinoza's sudden interest in finding openings for his influence in London. Meanwhile, the war between the Dutch Republic and France continued and there was scant importing of Dutch products, including books, into that realm.[45] Only after Spinoza's death in early 1677, and the peace with France in 1678, was the path cleared for the initial diffusion of the *Tractatus* in France.

The French rendering appeared, under three different fictitious titles, in 1678 and sold widely, as numerous surviving copies indicate, in the Netherlands and Germany as well as France. At the same time, the two new Latin quarto editions of 1677–8 (see Table 1) seem to have been earmarked specially for the French market. Copies of early editions of Spinoza's *Tractatus* surviving in French public collections today mostly belong to these later editions produced after the Peace of Nijmegen (1678), the two copies in the municipal library of Toulouse, for example, being respectively of editions seven (bound together with Spinoza's book on Descartes) and eight and that in the civic library at Montpellier likewise of eight.

Hence, the equivalent French *frisson* of shock to that felt in Germany in 1670–1, and England in 1674–6, was delayed until 1678–81. It is true that several prominent *érudits* in

---

[42] Boyle, *Works*, iv, 65.

[43] Simonutti, 'Premières réactions anglaises', 128; see also Colie, 'Spinoza in England', 199–200.

[44] Boyle, *Works*, v, 514; Colie, *Light and Enlightenment*, 73–4; Colie, 'Spinoza in England', 185–7; De Vet, 'Learned Periodicals', 28–30; Cristofolini, *Cartesiani*, 118–19; see Hutton, 'Introduction', p. xiv.

[45] Israel, *Dutch Primacy*, 339–46.

Paris, notably Henri Justel[46] and Pierre-Daniel Huet, whose *Demonstratio* (1678) was aimed chiefly against Spinoza, and on which he had laboured for some years, encountered the text earlier. But the main diffusion of the Latin as well as the French version in France began only from 1678. Arnauld received his copy of the *Tractatus* in May 1678 from Holland, read it that summer, pronounced it 'un des plus méchans livres du monde' and, deeply shaken, resorted to Bossuet 'afin d'empêcher par son crédit qu'il ne se debitast en France'; he then proceeded to draft a strong refutation which, however, he unfortunately mislaid during his Dutch exile in Delft, and which was consequently never published.[47] It was in May 1679, at Sedan, that Pierre Bayle first read the *Tractatus* (in French) having previously known of the book only by hearsay. Le Clerc, writing to his friend Limborch from Grenoble, towards the end of a long stay in France, noted the depth and intensity of the impact in the provinces as well as Paris, in December 1681, declaring the *Tractatus* a book which dangerously mixes a good deal of poison with valuable insights and 'remedies' and which had estranged numerous ecclesiastics 'right across France' not just from the confession which they profess but from Christianity itself.[48] He added that while the position was not quite so dire among the Protestants the book might well inflict comparable damage among them too unless its poisonous parts were 'solidly refuted', a job which, if he was not mistaken, had as yet nowhere been tackled successfully.

ii. The Battle of the *Ethics*

By the mid-1670s Spinoza stood at the head of an underground radical philosophical movement rooted in the Netherlands but decidedly European in scope. His books were illegal but yet, paradoxically, excepting only Descartes, no other contemporary thinker had enjoyed, over the previous quarter of a century so wide a European reception, even if in his case that reception was overwhelmingly (even if far from exclusively) hostile. During the last years of his life, the chief focus of Spinoza's own endeavours to advance his philosophy, and widen his following were his attempts to arrange the clandestine publication and distribution of his chief work, the *Ethics*. In some ways this was an even more difficult undertaking than preparing the ground for the *Tractatus* in 1669. For while he was already known and feared in Holland then, he did not yet possess the kind of national and international notoriety which had dogged him since 1670, rendering him irreparably a focus of general indignation, anxiety, and surveillance. His every move was monitored by the secular and especially

---

[46] Henri Justel (1620–93), Huguenot royal secretary and *habitué* of the Bibliothèque du Roi, a man of wide erudition favoured by Colbert, who maintained scholarly contacts in various parts of Europe, including with Leibniz in Germany, and whose lodgings in Paris served a key rendezvous for *érudits*. The seminars held there ranged across the full spectrum of scholarly concerns, including scientific matters; see Vernière, *Spinoza*, 105–7; Phillips, *Church and Culture*, 177–8.

[47] Arnauld, *Oeuvres* x, pp. xv–xvi; 'Letters to and from Neercassel', 334; Vernière, *Spinoza*, 114.

[48] Le Clerc to Limborch, Grenoble, 6 Dec. 1681 in Meinsma, *Spinoza*, pp. 523–4; see also Simonutti, *Arminianesimo*, 51.

the ecclesiastical authorities. Furthermore, the relatively tolerant De Witt *régime* had been overthrown in 1672 and since the ensuing restoration of the stadholderate, and the purge of De Witt's supporters from the States of Holland, Zeeland, and Utrecht, the influence of the hard-line Calvinist orthodox, in both Church and higher education, had increased. Even the Cartesio-Cocceian faction in the universities, let alone radical thinkers, now found themselves under mounting pressure.[49]

Signs that Spinoza was being watched were especially evident in and around The Hague, where he lived and worked. What principally worried the secular and ecclesiastical authorities were indications that his ideas were beginning to penetrate society more widely. Hence it was noted at a meeting of the consistory of The Hague, in June 1675, that '[Spinoza's] utterly godless doctrines . . . begin to creep in more and more both here and elsewhere'; members of the assembly were urged to show the utmost vigilance and try to discover whatever they could about the renegade's activities, and especially whether 'there might be another book by him in the press.'[50] Similarly, in September 1675, the *predikant* responsible for the quarter where Spinoza dwelt was urged to redouble his efforts to glean information about Spinoza's activities, and the entire consistory was again admonished to 'work to discover, as exactly as possible, the state of affairs regarding the man, his teaching, and its propagation'.[51] Several members of Spinoza's coterie in The Hague, including the probable translator of the *Tractatus* into French, Saint-Glain, were native French-speakers and it is striking that at this juncture the French-speaking Reformed community became especially apprehensive. Meeting in their synod at Kampen in September 1675, the entire body of Walloon preachers in the Netherlands was admonished to collaborate with their colleagues in the Dutch Reformed Church 'pour chercher ensemble les moyens les plus convenables afin d'empêcher le nommé Spinoza de continuer de semer son impiété et son athéisme dans ces provinces'.[52]

Spinoza at the end of his life thus faced an extremely sombre and oppressive environment. Hitherto he had jealously guarded the manuscript of his *Ethics*, allowing it to circulate only in a handful of copies among a tiny number of particular friends and allies. He made his most determined effort to publish his masterpiece, travelling to Amsterdam for this purpose late in July 1675, a fortnight before the imposing newly completed Portuguese Jewish synagogue and community centre (including classrooms) were inaugurated amid much pomp and circumstance before a large part of the city's Christian as well as Jewish population, a concourse among which, out of curiosity, Spinoza and some of his friends may well have been present. But hardly had he begun conferring with Rieuwersz and preparing the text—there is no indication that printing actually began—than the Reformed authorities discovered what was afoot and a rumour, as Spinoza puts it, 'was spread everywhere that a certain book of

[49] Israel, *Dutch Republic*, 896–8.
[50] GA The Hague Hervormde Gemeente, iv, p. 47, res. kerkeraad 21 June 1675; Freudenthal, *Lebensgeschichte Spinozas*, 147–8; Nadler, *Spinoza*, 335.
[51] GA The Hague Hervormde Gemeente, iv, pp. 56–7. res. kerkeraad 16 Sept. 1675.
[52] Freudenthal, *Lebensgeschichte Spinozas*, 150–2; Vernière, *Spinoza*, 42.

mine about God was in the press in which I seek to show there is no God [nullum dari Deum], a rumour which was believed by many'.[53]

Spinoza, reporting to Oldenburg, described how the Reformed theologians denounced 'me to the Prince [of Orange] and the magistrates' and 'moreover, the stupid Cartesians because they are believed [by the orthodox and the populace] to favour me, in order to remove this imputation from themselves, did not cease everywhere to abominate my opinions and writings and still do.'[54] Learning, furthermore, that the Reformed synods 'are working everywhere against me, I decided to put off the edition I was preparing until I saw how the situation would unfold'. But Spinoza was simply too much in the public eye, and circumstances were too forbidding for him to proceed. For the moment he had no choice but to desist: 'in truth the position seems to get worse every day and I am uncertain what I should do.'[55] It was probably during this fraught visit to Amsterdam, during July and August 1675, that Limborch unexpectedly met his foremost spiritual antagonist at a dinner where both were guests, during which, or so he later assured Le Clerc, Spinoza could not restrain his impiety during the reciting of grace but ironically rolled up his eyes 'as if to convince us of our stupidity in praying to God'.[56]

At their next synod, at Middelburg, the French-speaking Reformed preachers reaffirmed their detestation of the 'blasphèmes et les impiétés du malheureux Spinosa', and again declared the urgent need for 'remèdes capables d'arrêter et d'extirper cette rongeante gangrène'.[57] The ecclesiastical authorities in the Netherlands were now fully geared for war against the man, his books, and a movement they perceived as a major and immediate threat. Spinoza spent the last eighteen months of his life in virtual seclusion at his lodgings, writing his *Tractatus Politicus*, and resigned, as his sickness of the lungs increasingly took hold, to making no further attempt to steer his *Ethics* through the press.

With his death at The Hague, on 21 February 1677, the remarkable drama surrounding this text entered a wholly new stage. As instructed by the dying Spinoza, his landlord, the artist Hendrik van der Spyck, secretly dispatched the chest containing his manuscripts by barge to Amsterdam, where Spinoza's friends and allies closeted them away and began planning the complex business of saving and deploying his philosophical legacy. Whatever strategy they decided on, the executors faced formidable difficulties and needed to take crucial editorial decisions.[58] They had to confer, concert strategy, and pool their efforts, while all the time avoiding detection by the authorities. They needed to decide whether to attempt to publish the *Ethics* or let it circulate in manuscript, and if to publish it, whether to bring out the *Ethics* alone or together with the rest of Spinoza's unpublished work, and whether in Latin only or also the vernacular.

---

[53] Spinoza, *Opera*, iv, 299; Meinsma, *Spinoza*, 440; Steenbakkers, *Spinoza's* Ethica, 7; Nadler, *Spinoza*, 333–5.

[54] Spinoza, *Opera*, iv, 299.   [55] Ibid.   [56] Meinsma, *Spinoza*, 526.

[57] Vernière, *Spinoza*, 42.

[58] Akkerman, *Studies*, 67, 77–8; Steenbakkers, *Spinoza's* Ethica, 57, 64–7.

Spinoza's manuscripts were carefully examined. Copying in manuscript began at once before any overall strategy had been agreed. No doubt there were several conferences between Rieuwertsz and the team of editors who participated in the project and are thought to have comprised six other former friends of the philosopher—Jelles, Meyer, Glazemaker, Bouwmeester, Schuller,[59] and Van Gent.[60] After a few weeks' deliberation, their minds were made up. The boldest and riskiest strategy was decided on: everything publishable, the letters included, would be brought out together as fast as possible simultaneously in Latin and Dutch.[61] Editing the Latin version was presumably entrusted to the skilled Latinists, Meyer, Bouwmeester, and Van Gent, while Jelles, Rieuwertsz, and Glazemaker took charge of the Dutch, with Schuller acting in a secondary capacity.

The decision to publish everything, and in two languages, considerably complicated and prolonged the clandestine procedure. Not only had everything to be prepared in fair copies for the printers—the printers worked from new, revised copies, not Spinoza's originals[62]—a great deal of translation had to be carried out swiftly but accurately, chiefly from Latin into Dutch, work undertaken by the skilled Glazemaker, but in the case of some letters and Jelles' preface, from Dutch into Latin. Although Glazemaker had at his disposal the earlier Dutch translation of Parts I and II of the *Ethics*, which Spinoza had had prepared in 1664–5, with the help of Pieter Balling, it was a remarkable feat to render the rest as fast and accurately as he did.[63] Besides overseeing the copying and translating, the editors discussed the letters, which often contained personal or, in their view, irrelevant matter which they preferred to delete, or matter deemed best withheld, and the problem of how to edit the three unfinished works—the *Tractatus Politicus*, *Tractatus de Intellectus Emendatione*, and the Hebrew Grammar. Finally, and here Meyer, Bouwmeester, and Van Gent carried the burden, much effort was expended in revising and polishing Spinoza's Latin.[64]

Meanwhile, the Reformed authorities at The Hague and in Amsterdam, and other adversaries were doing their best to prevent publication. The existence of the *Ethics* was an open secret. The question was, who had the manuscript and were there plans to publish, and, if so, where and when? A sizeable group, including copiers and printers, knew of the undertaking organized by Rieuwertsz in Amsterdam, and that in itself posed a security risk. Furthermore, various prominent personages abroad knew

---

[59] Georg Hermann Schuller (1651–79), came from Wesel, in Cleves, and studied medicine in Leiden before becoming a practising physician in Amsterdam. Besides being conceited, foolish, and a mediocre Latinist, he was a compulsive alchemist, who ran up huge debts by spending heavily on 'false processes' trying to make gold; nevertheless, he was a convinced, if indiscreet, 'Spinozist' and played some part in editing Spinoza's *Opera Posthuma*. Leibniz recruited him as his correspondent and agent in Amsterdam, to provide information about the radical circle and procure rare books and manuscripts; see Steenbakkers, *Spinoza's Ethica*, 50–63.

[60] Akkerman, *Studies*, 45–6; Steenbakkers, *Spinoza's Ethica*, 16.

[61] Schuller to Leibniz, Amsterdam 29 Mar. 1677 in Stein, *Leibniz und Spinoza*, 287–8.

[62] Steenbakkers, *Spinoza's Ethica*, 33, 45.

[63] Akkerman, 'J. H. Glazemaker', 26; Akkerman, *Studies*, 127–8.   [64] Akkerman, *Studies*, 46.

about the *Ethics* and Spinoza's frustrated efforts to publish it, and had a fair idea of its contents, notably Leibniz at Hanover, Justel and his friends in Paris, Oldenburg in London (though he died soon after Spinoza), and Steno and Burgh in Italy. Hence for many months Rieuwertsz' publishing house, and the manuscripts and transla-tions, effectively the core of Spinoza's philosophical legacy, lay in a precarious and highly vulnerable state.

Besides the Dutch Reformed, and its ally, the Walloon Church, others were also waiting to spring into action, to eliminate that philosophical armoury as soon as the requisite information could be obtained. In Italy, one or both of Spinoza's former allies, Steno and Burgh, alerted the Inquisition authorities to the pending danger to the Church. At Rome, a meeting was convened by the Pope's nephew, Cardinal Francesco Barberini, to discuss the threat and, on 18 September, Barberini wrote advising the Vicar Apostolic of the Dutch Catholic Church, Johannes van Neercassel (d.1686), that the Holy Office had learned that an atheistic work 'by Spinoza' existed in manuscript in Holland and that if this work were propagated it could seriously harm the 'purity of our Holy Catholic Faith'.[65] Neercassel was instructed to organize a campaign to prevent publication. Besides finding out whether the book was in the press, or likely to be, and all he could about Spinoza for the Inqui-sition, he was told to forward copies of his published works to Rome, as well as, if at all possible, a copy of the now notorious manuscript.

Neercassel chose to head his task force a Catholic priest in Amsterdam, Father Martin de Swaen, who had many contacts in the city and was the brother of a well-known merchant. De Swaen recruited an admirably ecumenical team, including an unnamed rabbi and a trainee Remonstrant preacher.[66] It was appar-ently the rabbi who informed the Catholic authorities that Spinoza's manu-scripts were in Rieuwertsz' keeping, information he presumably obtained from the philosopher's estranged relatives, Rebecca d'Espinosa, his half-sister, and his nephew Daniel de Casseres, who had gone to The Hague in May 1677 to investigate the circumstances of Spinoza's death with a view to claiming his property, but then, suspecting his meagre estate was encumbered with debts outstripping its value, waived their rights.[67] De Casseres was doubtless hostile to Spinoza and his legacy, being the son of his firmly orthodox rabbinic brother-in-law, Samuel de Casseres (d.1660).

Reporting to Rome on 25 December 1677, Neercassel advised Barberini that Spinoza's manuscripts had now been located in Amsterdam, in the keeping of a Mennonite bookseller named 'Jan Rieuwertsz'. But when asked whether he had in his possession an unpublished work by Spinoza, 'this bookseller assured me there are no manuscripts among Spinoza's legacy apart from that of *De Principiis Philosophiae Cartesianae* and that no other work of Spinoza's has been published

---

[65] Barberini to Neercassel, Rome, 18 Sept. 1677 in Orcibal, 'Jansénistes face à Spinoza', 460; 'Letters to and from Neercassel'. 330–1.

[66] Neercassel to de Swaen, Utrecht, 31 Oct. 1677 in Orcibal, 'Jansénistes face à Spinoza', 461.

[67] Vaz Dias and Van der Tak, 'Spinoza Merchant', 171; Nadler, *Spinoza*, 351.

B. D. S.

OPERA

POSTHUMA,

*Quorum series post Præfationem
exhibetur.*

cIↃ IↃ c LXXVII.

FIGURE 2. The title-page of Spinoza's *Opera Posthuma* clandestinely
published at Amsterdam in 1677–8.

apart from the *Tractatus Theologico-Politicus.*[68] All other enquiries 'amongst both
Christians and Jews' had uncovered no sign of any pending new book by Spinoza. It
was true, though, commented the Vicar General, that Spinoza's pernicious influence
in the Netherlands was growing and that Stouppe's *Religion des Hollandois* had
enhanced his reputation as the foremost enemy of revealed religion. Happily,
Catholics were less susceptible to Spinoza's venom than Protestants and heartily

---

[68] Neercassel to Barberini, Utrecht, 25 Nov, 1677 in Orcibal, 'Jansénistes face à Spinoza', 461; 'Letters to
and from Neercassel', 332.

detested his abominable ideas, which are, he added, as obscure as they are offensive. Three days later he posted off a copy of the (banned) *Tractatus Theologico-Politicus* to the papal nuncio in Brussels for forwarding to Rome.

Neercassel soon discovered Rieuwertsz had brazenly lied to throw him off the scent at a crucial moment.[69] Reporting to Leibniz early in November, Schuller advised that printing of the Latin version of Spinoza's posthumous works was now finished except for the index—the latter, expertly compiled by one of the Latinists in the team, possibly Van Gent, being not the least helpful of the editors' contributions.[70] At the end of December Schuller wrote to Hanover, assuring Leibniz that production was now complete, and distribution about to begin with the new year, albeit unaccountably neglecting to forewarn him that his name was given in full as the author of one of the printed letters to Spinoza.[71] Leibniz was extremely annoyed when he discovered that Schuller had failed to ensure that his name was deleted. Schuller apologized in March 1678, assuring the great German thinker that he had severely rebuked the publisher 'although I believe there is no danger [to yourself] as your letter contains nothing but mathematics'.[72]

It was indeed in January 1678 that Rieuwertsz started the risky business of infiltrating batches of both the Latin and Dutch versions—both giving only Spinoza's now legendary initials, 'B.D.S.', not his name, on the title-page—into the bookshops.[73] When the news broke, Neercassel was shaken and appalled but nevertheless promptly acquired copies for his own use and dispatch to Brussels and Rome. On perusing the volume, he was baffled to find, contrary to expectation, that Spinoza does not in fact propound atheism as normally understood 'but avowedly teaches Deism'.[74]

Something of the shock which pulsated through the Dutch public sphere with the appearance of Spinoza's *Opera Posthuma* can be gathered from the appalled reactions of the ecclesiastical authorities. If Arnauld at this time expressed profound foreboding at the possibility of Spinoza's influence spreading in France,[75] the Leiden Reformed consistory, when it discussed the *Opera Posthuma* at its meeting on 4 February 1678, accounted it 'a book which, perhaps since the beginning of the world until the present day . . . surpasses all others in godlessness and endeavours to do away with all religion and set impiety on the throne'.[76] Passages were read out so that the whole assembly should grasp the gravity of what they were up against. A delegation sent to the burgomasters declaimed more passages to them. Outraged, the burgomasters ordered the work's immediate seizure from the city's bookshops and agreed to 'seek prohibition of the book by decree of the States of Holland'.[77] At The Hague, the consistory

---

[69] 'Letters to and from Neercassel', 337.   [70] Steenbakkers, *Spinoza's Ethica*, 27.

[71] Schuller to Leibniz, Amsterdam, 31 Dec, 1677 in Stein, *Leibniz und Spinoza*, 291.

[72] Steenbakkers, *Spinoza's Ethica*, 62–3.

[73] GA The Hague, Hervormde Gemeente, Kerkeraad iv, 131. res. 11 Feb. 1678; Steenbakkers, *Spinoza's Ethica*, 7.

[74] 'Letters to and from Neercassel', 336–7.   [75] Ibid., 334.

[76] GA Leiden, Acta Kerkeraad vi, res. 4 Feb. 1678; Freudenthal, *Lebensgeschichte Spinozas*, 173–4.

[77] GA Leiden, Acta Kerkeraad vi, res. 11 Feb. 1678; Freudenthal, *Lebensgeschichte Spinozas*, 175.

applied to the provincial high court of Holland, where 'several frightful passages from the said book of Spinoza were read out aloud'; deeply indignant, the Hof ordered 'all copies of the said book to be seized from every bookshop in The Hague that very day'.[78]

Pressed by the North and South Holland synods to push through a general ban on Spinoza's works, Holland's Pensionary, Gaspar Fagel, was plied with Dutch-language extracts for himself and his regent colleagues. Addressing the States on the subject of Spinoza on 17 March, Fagel spoke of the dire threat to society his philosophy represented. He noted that the synods were greatly perturbed by three new publications— Spinoza's *Opera Posthuma*, the *Arcana atheismi*, supposedly refuting Spinoza but quite inadequately, according to the theologians, by the Socinian Kuyper, and a tract entitled *Dissertatio de Spiritu Sancto*. These texts, reported Fagel, were selling widely in Holland and since they, 'and especially that of the said Spinoza, contain very many profane, blasphemous, and atheistic propositions', the States had to take the matter earnestly in hand. The Hof was asked to advise and a special regent committee set up. Both concluded that Spinoza was in a class of his own as a pernicious influence and that a special decree was required, which mentioned no other writers or books, prohibiting his work *in toto*. A draft ban was prepared. On 25 June one of the regents most closely involved, Leiden's pensionary, Burgersdijk, advised the States that the committee had agreed that Spinoza's *Opera Posthuma* 'contain very many profane, blasphemous and atheistic propositions whereby not only the unlettered might be deflected from the only and true path to salvation' and that Spinoza's philosophy undermines belief in the 'Incarnation and Resurrection of Christ and other wholly fundamental articles of the universal Christian faith' and consequently must be generally condemned and suppressed.[79]

Dated the same day, the resulting edict in part adopted the wording used in this advice to the States to justify the exceptional and sweeping character of the measure. But it also added that Spinoza 'takes away' the authority of miracles 'whereby God Almighty manifested his divine power and omnipotence for the strengthening of the Christian faith', teaching that one should not believe in miracles and that, even when 'natural causes' can not be discerned, one should suspend judgement 'presupposing that men are not able to penetrate deeply enough in their knowledge of nature'.[80] Spinoza's denial of miracles and the miraculous, significantly, receives greater attention in the wording of the edict than any other feature of his thought. The placard is indeed a landmark in the Early Enlightenment encounter between revealed religion and philosophical reason, but also a symptom of a still wider phenomenon—the growing antagonism between the new mechanistic conception of reality when applied unreservedly, and the magical, mysterious,

---

[78] Knuttel, *Acta*, v, 236.

[79] 'de Mensch-werdinghe en Opstandinghe Christi, ende sulcks verscheyde seer essentiele Articulen van het algemeene Christelijcke Geloof', *Res. Holl.* 25 June 1678.

[80] *Groot Placaat-Boeck*, iv, 525–6: 'Placaet van de Heeren Staten van Hollandt ende West-Vrieslandt tegens het Boeck geintituleert B. D. Spinosa, Opera Posthuma', dated 25 June 1678.

'preternatural' universe mankind had always inhabited in the past. The States of Holland banned not just the *Opera Posthuma* but Spinoza's philosophy as such, because, in their own words, he considers everything supernatural and miraculous in Christianity and the Bible to be 'ignorance and a fountain of deception'.[81]

The edict banned Spinoza's philosophy, including all reprints, summaries, or extracts from his texts, or anything restating or reworking his fundamental ideas, laying down draconian penalties for authors, editors, printers, publishers, and booksellers who defied the law in this matter.[82] It was a prohibition of Spinoza and Spinozism by the provincial States backed by the city governments and, equally if not more, by the public Church which saw it as its task to assist with enforcing the terms of the prohibition. The *classes* of the South Holland synod agreed to institute regular checks on printers and bookshops in their districts to ensure that the edict was being rigorously enforced. The ban on Spinoza thus became a basic feature of Dutch political, cultural, and religious life. The Utrecht city council, on 24 October 1678, declared it their solemn duty to follow the 'laudable example of neighbouring States and authorities' and forbid anyone, especially 'all printers and booksellers', to print, obtain, distribute, or sell 'any Socinian or Arian books, these being blasphemous and wholly pernicious, and especially the *Bibliotheca Fratrum Polonorum*, the *Leviathan* of Hobbes, the *Philosophia Scripturae Interpres*, and the *Tractatus Theologico-Politicus* of Spinoza together with *B.D.S. Opera Posthuma*, and all other similar material in whatever language'.[83] Utrecht's printers and booksellers were required to appear before the civic magistrates within three days to surrender 'all printed or manuscript copies of such books'. Booksellers suspected of withholding copies were to be required to take an oath swearing they had not hidden any, on pain of a 100-guilder fine for a first refusal and, for a second, no longer being permitted to conduct business in Utrecht.

Inevitably, Holland's decree of June 1678 forbidding the sale of Spinoza's writings was far from watertight. Rieuwertsz and his associates had laid their plans well and, under the counter, dissemination of Spinozism in the Netherlands, as abroad, continued. Reporting to Rome, three months after the enactment of Holland's prohibition, Neercassel complained that the States' edict had produced 'scarcely any other fruit . . . than to increase the renown and prices of Spinoza's books'.[84] The illegal sale of Spinoza's texts could not be stopped and the reason, he stressed, was a deep-seated cultural and intellectual shift in Dutch society itself. There was a ready market for such books and much profit to be made from selling them. Mercifully, he added, 'our Catholics' who, he assured Barberini, 'detest all profane novelties', were entirely impervious to Spinoza's vile teaching; but among non-Catholics men were increasingly being 'seduced', as he puts it, into 'proudly judging questions of faith and religion' in terms of 'philosophy and the insane fallacy of the geometric method'

---

[81] Ibid.   [82] *Groot Placaat-Boeck*, iv, 525–6; Klever, 'Spinoza's Life', 53.

[83] Van de Water, *Groot Placaetboek . . . Utrecht*, iii, 432–3; Freudenthal, *Lebensgeschichte Spinozas*, 186 7.

[84] Orcibal, 'Jansénistes face à Spinoza', 466–7; 'Letters to and from Neercassel', 337; see also Leydekker, *Dr Bekkers Philosophise Duyvel*, 118–19.

instead of vesting their hopes of salvation in 'Christ omnipotent'.[85] The vast challenge posed by Spinoza, he affirmed, sprang from the growing prestige and force of mathematical reason and philosophy itself, and it was against this that the Church must now throw its whole weight, authority, and influence.

Yet widespread evasion of the prohibition does not mean that the banning of Spinoza's writings and philosophy, by the States of Holland, Utrecht, and subsequently the States General, for the whole of the United Provinces, was without effect. On the contrary, even though it was comparatively easy for buyers to procure copies in certain bookshops in Amsterdam and other cities, the Dutch secular authorities had now laid down a clear dividing line, promulgated by public decree, between a prohibited class of thought which abolishes the supernatural and the miraculous and acceptable philosophy compatible with Christian teaching and belief. Spinozism had been resoundingly proclaimed the core of a radical corpus of thought now condemned and outlawed by public authority. No one, whether publishers, booksellers, university teachers, or ordinary laymen, could henceforth publicly promote, display, exhibit, recommend, or favourably quote Spinoza and his writings. Printers and booksellers who infringed the public decree did so furtively, incurring a real risk of disgrace and punishment. The edict accordingly had an appreciable significance in shaping attitudes and fixing the status of ideas, laying down legally the separation between radical and moderate Enlightenment which, within a few years, was to extend across the whole of Europe.

---

[85] 'Letters to and from Neercassel', 338.

17 | THE SPREAD OF A FORBIDDEN MOVEMENT

i. The Death of a Philosopher

After suffering for many years his sickness of the lungs, a form of tuberculosis or phthisis, Spinoza passed away quietly on a Sunday afternoon when much of the neighbourhood, in the centre of The Hague, was at church, aged 44 years and three months, on 21 February 1677. He died, leaving no written will, apparently not yet expecting to die, in the house of the artist Van der Spyck, a member of the Lutheran consistory of The Hague, the congregation which Spinoza's second biographer, Johannes Colerus, later served as preacher.[1] The physician present at the end, according to Colerus, was Meyer, though other evidence suggests it was Schuller. Four days later his funeral procession, comprising six carriages and a substantial crowd, including friends from Amsterdam and not a few 'considerable persons', wound its way to the most handsome of the city's churches, the Nieuwe Kerk, where he was interred, the costs being paid by Rieuwertsz.[2] In accordance with Dutch custom, friends and neighbours then returned to the house to talk about the deceased over some bottles of wine. Spinoza's life was over. But as some present that afternoon must have remarked, or at least reflected, his philosophy, for the time being at least, survived in the conversation and minds of others.

Surely already then began a debate concerning the circumstances of his demise which, remarkably, was to reverberate for decades not only within the 'Republic of Letters' but, in the Netherlands at least, also among elements of the common people. For despite the reputed obscurity of his philosophy, it soon emerged, and increasingly so over the next decades, that his image, and a kernel of his thought, also endured in the minds and hearts of some ordinary folk, a development regarded by most contemporaries with profound unease. According to Johannes Aalstius, writing in 1705, despite the austere, forbidding façade of Spinoza's geometrical method, his essential

---

[1] The house had been built in 1646 and was originally owned by the great landscape painter Jan van Goyen, who had not lived there himself but hired it out from 1657 to a son of Jan Steen, who married Van Goyen's daughter Margaretha; Blase, *Johannes Colerus*, 183; Suchtelen, *Spinoza's sterfhuis*, 7; Steenbakkers, *Spinoza's Ethica*, 53, 55, 58; Nadler, *Spinoza*, 350.

[2] Colerus, *Vie de B. de Spinosa*, 173‒8; Monikhoff, *Beschrijving*, 213; Suchtelen, *Spinoza's sterfhuis*, 11; Nadler, *Spinoza*, 349‒50.

ideas are, in fact, quite easily grasped even by the unlettered and, ominously enough, were proving widely seductive.[3] Aalstius lists these fundamentals as the identification of God with the universe, the rejection of organized religion, the abolition of Heaven and Hell, together with reward and punishment in the hereafter, a morality of individual happiness in the here and now, and the doctrine that there is no reality beyond the unalterable laws of Nature and, consequently, no Revelation, miracles, or prophecy. These were notions readily understood by the unsophisticated and, if widely disseminated, would inevitably generate not just a seditious undercurrent within what was already then generally considered a new and 'enlightened' age, but a revolutionary resonance in culture, politics, and society.

Spinoza lived much of his life in seclusion, cherishing the tranquillity he needed to develop and refine his philosophy. Yet, via an amazing process of transmogrification, no sooner was he dead than he became a cult figure, a secular 'saint' and an object of hagiography in the eyes of disciples and followers, some of whom initiated a deliberate campaign to heroicize his image, deeming this an effectual means of advancing the radical intellectual programme to which they were committed. The editors of his posthumous works contributed by drawing attention admiringly, notably in Jelles' preface, to Spinoza's soon legendary austerity and single-minded pursuit of truth, and his maxim that one who aspires to teach others how to 'enjoy the highest good' should not desire that those he enlightens should name such knowledge after himself, a lofty stance which allegedly prompted him 'shortly before his death to ask that his name not be placed over his *Ethics* which, he directed, should be printed'. This is why, affirms Jelles, the 'name of our author on the title-page and elsewhere is indicated only with his initials'—B.D.S.[4]

More extravagantly hagiographic in tone was the biography of Jean-Maximilien Lucas, the foremost of Spinoza's French acolytes in The Hague, written seemingly soon after his death. Accusing Spinoza's enemies of ceaselessly hounding him during his life merely because he sought to teach the people to distinguish 'true piety' from hypocrisy, and fight 'superstition', Lucas claims that Spinoza approached death in a serene, indomitable spirit, as he knows, he says, from those who were present, almost as if elated to sacrifice himself for those who had scorned and persecuted him. As for his admirers, 'ceux que ses écrits ont rectifiez, et à qui sa présence étoit encore d'un grand secours dans le chemin de la verité', Lucas summons them to follow Spinoza's example, or at least glorify his name 'par l'admiration et la louange, si nous ne pouvons l'imiter' and thereby enhance his greatness and lasting fame: 'ce que nous reverons dans les grands hommes, est toujours vivant et vivera dans tous les siècles'.[5]

The battle was on to fix the image of the dying Spinoza in the perceptions and imagination of posterity. Much was at stake. For the final hours of a thinker who seeks to transform the spiritual foundations of the society around him, and is widely perceived as trying to do so, become heavily charged with symbolic significance in the eyes of

---

[3] Aalstius, *Inleiding*, 512–14; Kortholt, *De Tribus Impostoribus*, preface.   [4] [Jelles], 'Voorreeden', 112.
[5] *La Vie et L'Esprit*, 58–9.

both disciples and adversaries. The posthumous reputations of all noted freethinkers of the age were greatly affected by the fiercely contested reports of what did or did not happen on their deathbeds. Adriaen Koerbagh, in life tireless in assailing the accepted beliefs of society, was not only tried and imprisoned but figuratively stifled, reportedly having ended his days in utter despair, broken in body and spirit. Koerbagh, according to the preacher who visited him in prison, with a deacon of the consistory, five days before his expiry on 10 October 1669, had finally abjured, repudiating his former abominable views, wishing he had never written his 'blasphemous' books, and vowing, should he ever recover, 'never again to cultivate, or teach others, such opinions' as had ruined his life.[6] Similarly, Bekker allegedly died powerfully gripped by remorse, denying everything he had previously professed about the Devil's power, reports so insistent his son, Johannes Henricus Bekker, felt obliged to publish a pamphlet recording virtually everything his father said on his deathbed in an attempt to prove this was untrue.[7]

During the early eighteenth century comparable cases provided vast scope for controversy. The disputed circumstances surrounding the death of Radicati who, following his flight from England, spent his last years in Holland (1733–7), became a polemical arena in itself. Falling seriously ill in Rotterdam in October 1737, he was attended by the Huguenot preacher Daniel de Superville, who afterwards recounted in print that shortly before his death, on 24 October, the count was filled with dread and, finally, deeply penitent, was reconciled to Christ, renouncing all he had written against religion and unreservedly embracing the Reformed faith, though unfortunately he expired before a notary could record these details.[8] His conversion to piety at the last was widely celebrated and there was even an imaginary dialogue printed in which he predicts that his uplifting demise would finally deprive libertines and freethinkers of the feeble 'ressource de dire qu'il y a des gens qui sont fermement persuadés de l'inutilité de la religion'.[9] Such notions about Radicati were not believed by everyone, however, and were publicly contested by d'Argens, who insisted there was not a shred of evidence it was a 'bonne et véritable conversion'.[10]

There may have been firmer evidence that Fontenelle's atheistic disciple, Du Marsais, panicked on his deathbed and implored the Almighty to have mercy on his soul, summoning a priest, solemnly abjuring his previous views, and receiving the last rites.[11] But the stories about the death of the Oxford freethinker, Matthew Tindal (c.1657–1733), left everything uncertain. His physician had predicted he 'would certainly recant before he died', and that a severe bout of illness was all that was needed to 'furnish him with a new set of principles'.[12] And sure enough, or so some alleged, no sooner did he lie dying than he fell into the 'utmost terror to think he must soon

[6] Meinsma, *Spinoza*, 370–1; Evenhuis, *Ook dat was Amsterdam*, iii, 359.
[7] Knuttel, *Balthasar Bekker*, 357–8; Zedler, *Grosses Universal Lexicon*, iii, 873–4.
[8] Trinius, *Freydenker-Lexicon*, 401; Berti, 'Radicati in Olanda', 517–18; Wielema, *Filosofen*, 93–4.
[9] Berti, 'Radicati in Olanda', 515.   [10] Ibid., 517–18.
[11] Krauss, 'L'Énigme de Dumarsais', 521–2.
[12] *The Religious, Rational and Moral Conduct of Matthew Tindal*, 28–9.

appear before that God whom he had so outrageously offended'. However, some alleged, he was deflected from piety at the last by the antics of his deist disciple, Sedgewick Harrison, whose 'principles and morals' were reputedly 'as bad, if not worse, than Dr Tindal's' and whose scoffing so mortified Tindal that he changed his mind, reverting finally to desperate bravado.[13] Others, however, denied this, so that it was impossible to establish 'anything certain about his behaviour' at the end.[14]

Freethinkers' deathbed scenes, accordingly, were of great significance and generally bitterly contested. Even so, Koerbagh, Bekker, Radicati, Du Marsais, and Tindal were one thing, Spinoza quite another. For he was almost everywhere acknowledged as the *princeps*, the chief of atheists, deists, and *esprits forts*, or as an early eighteenth-century German theologian put it, 'der Chef der heutigen Atheisten' (the 'chief of modern Atheists'),[15] so that should it emerge that in his last hours he too, as so many others reputedly had, resorted to his knees, imploring the Almighty for forgiveness, embracing faith and piety, such a volte-face would be bound to have a sensational effect and help immeasurably in reducing the appeal of his philosophy, deflating his reputation, and disillusioning admirers. Indeed, it was no less crucial for opponents to unearth evidence detrimental to his image as a 'saint' of the unbelievers, as for followers to affirm his intrepid adherence to his principles until his last breath. This was a contest, moreover, which, by its nature, could perhaps never be resolved.

In this fight, conservatives enjoyed an initial advantage in that it was widely held that strict atheism is inherently implausible, if not impossible. As Montaigne put it, ascribing the insight to Plato, 'few men are so firm in their atheism that a pressing danger does not bring them to acknowledge divine power'.[16] But there was a vital difference between 'few' and none, and if radical philosophy was to be crushed and Europe's *esprits forts* stripped of their 'saint', radical claims regarding the dying Spinoza's constancy and serenity had to be disproved and discredited.[17] Furthermore, the *esprits forts* were powerfully bolstered by the account of Spinoza's life and death presented in the immensely influential writings of Pierre Bayle. For, inexplicably according to many, while Bayle polemicized against Spinoza's ideas, he simultaneously projected a highly positive picture of his personality and conduct.[18] During the course of his researches, Bayle contacted several of those who had known Spinoza and, in particular, the son of Spinoza's publisher, the younger Jan Rieuwertsz (c.1651–1723),[19] who made available to him, among other resources, the still unpublished manuscript of Lucas' biography.[20] Already in his first major work, the *Pensées diverses sur la comète* (1682), Bayle stresses Spinoza's great fortitude and steadfastness during his final illness and, in the astounding chapter where he maintains men do not generally live by their principles so that it is neither surprising that believing Christians often fail to lead

---

[13] *The Religious, Rational and Moral Conduct of Matthew Tindal*, 27.   [14] Ibid., 28.
[15] Breithaupt, *Zufällige Gedancken*, 24.   [16] Montaigne, *Complete Essays*, 497.
[17] La Mettrie, *Machine Man*, 24.
[18] Labrousse, *Pierre Bayle*, ii, 198–204; Cantelli, *Teologia e ateismo*, 231.
[19] On the latter, see Van Eeghen, *Amsterdamse boekhandel*, iv, 65.
[20] Labrousse, *Pierre Bayle*, ii, 204; Vernière, *Spinoza*, 27.

Christian lives, nor that professed atheists should live virtuous lives, he cites Spinoza as his chief exemplum of the latter.[21]

Clearly relishing the effect of this paradox on his readers, Bayle depicts Spinoza on his deathbed, professing to know the exact circumstances—even though these were not generally known—from 'un grand homme, qui le sait de bonne part', a typically tantalizing Baylean touch. Affirming that Spinoza 'étoit le plus grand Athée qui ait jamais été',[22] he reports that as he lay dying he summoned his landlady, instructing her that no clergyman of any description should be allowed to approach him during his final hours. His motive for issuing this instruction, Bayle claimed to know through testimony of the philosopher's friends—presumably he had discussed this with Rieuwertsz—was Spinoza's desire to die without dispute and without fear of lapsing into a delirium in which he might inadvertently say things which could subsequently be used to damage his reputation and philosophy. 'C'est à dire,' asserts Bayle, 'qu'il craygnoit que l'on ne debitast dans le monde, qu'à la veüe de la mort, sa conscience s'étant réveillée, l'avoit fait démentir de sa bravoure, et renoncer à ses sentimens'.[23] Bayle covers himself against accusations of eulogizing Spinoza by styling such behaviour 'une vanité . . . ridicule' and a 'folle passion'. But more than a few, perceiving the ambivalence of his words, must have wondered as to his real intentions.

Lucas and Bayle claimed inside knowledge, from impeccable sources, concerning what transpired on Spinoza's deathbed. But who were these irreproachable witnesses close to Spinoza and attending him when he died, and could they be trusted? The question vitally concerned not just Spinoza's posthumous standing, but also the wider, connected, controversy as to whether strict philosophical atheism is in fact possible. Are there men who sincerely believe there is no God? Many theologians and philosophers of the period, such as the French Oratorian Le Vassor, and the Jesuit Tournemine, held that acknowledging a providential God is innate in man, inherent in his consciousness, and can be categorically denied by no one.[24] Many men lead dissolute lives, perpetrating all manner of wrongdoing while nevertheless believing in God, and these, accordingly, were styled 'practical atheists'. Incontrovertibly, there were also 'speculative atheists' who assert there is no God. But these, so the theory went, abjure God only provisionally or fitfully and, when in dire need, or on the point of death, irresistibly falter, renounce atheism, and adore the divine majesty. Hence, strictly speaking, contends Tournemine, there are no true 'Spinosistes'.[25]

Le Vassor flatly contradicts Bayle's account of Spinoza's final days, insisting that Spinoza cannot genuinely have believed in his own philosophy, any more than other ostensible 'athées de spéculation'. If he refused to submit at the last, he resembled other crazed minds who fatally work themselves into a state of 'fausse bravoure' so as to perish unrepentant in the eyes of the world, 'pour s'aquérir la gloire d'avoir pensé

---

[21] Bayle, *Pensées diverses*, ii, 134.   [22] Ibid.   [23] Ibid., 135; Tournemine, 'Préface', 5–6, 12–13.
[24] Le Vassor, *De la véritable religion*, 3; Tournemine, 'Préface', 12–13; Levasseur, *Défense*, 9–10, 15; Kors, *Atheism in France*, i, 38–9.
[25] Tournemine, 'Préface', 3, 12.

autrement que les autres'. If Spinoza really refused to admit a pastor as he lay dying, then he did so out of a proud and perverse defiance, not philosophical conviction: 'ainsi Spinoza avoit peur de n'avoir pas autant de fermeté que Vanini'.[26] Parallel ideas also surfaced among contemporary Protestant theologians. In an oration at Copenhagen in January 1687, Hector Gottfried Masius (1653–1709), German Court preacher there since 1686, poured scorn on Bayle's account of Spinoza's death, maintaining that there are no true 'theoretical atheists', men who are categorically convinced there is no God.[27] But if there are no authentic 'athei speculativi perfecti et consummati', there are undoubtedly, affirms Masius, dangerous men, professed speculative doubters and mockers, 'athei speculativi indirecti et imperfecti', he calls them, at the head of whom stands Spinoza, the chief 'atheist' of Europe, he says, since Machiavelli and Pomponazzi.[28] Spinoza's philosophy, then, is senseless bravado, a form of imposture in which he himself did not believe, desperation and pride alone preventing his acknowledging God's truth as he lay dying. Masius sums up with his maxim 'athei practici multi, theoretici indirecti non pauci, directi et consummati nulli' (there are many practical atheists and not a few indirect theoretical atheists, but no direct and complete atheists).[29]

Others countered Bayle's account of Spinoza's last days by contradicting the story altogether and substituting another in its place. The Bremen Reformed preacher, Theodor Undereyck, in his 974-page polemic against atheism, *Der Närrische Atheist* (Bremen, 1689), was more hesitant than Masius regarding the impossibility of pure theoretical atheism but, like Le Vassor and Tournemine, no less adamant that 'all atheists in general', that is, *practicale Atheisten*, tentative *speculative Atheisten*, and, if there are any, pure *speculative Atheisten*, always falter when in dire distress and 'especially at the end of their lives, renounce their atheistic notions and recognize that very God who revealed Himself to us in Scripture, affirming there is no other God'.[30] Undereyck claimed to have reliable information that when on his deathbed Spinoza, far from remaining steadfast, became desperate, admitted his teaching was false, and not only acknowledged a providential God but also the truth of the Holy Trinity, vowing, should he recover, to write new books reversing all he had said previously.[31] This typified the last hours, holds Undereyck, of all such intellectually corrupt men. He also cites the case of a formidable scholar he had known, who studied at Leiden and became deeply engrossed in the writings of Hobbes and Spinoza, eventually confiding to friends that he had become a 'complete atheist'. On falling gravely ill, however, this *savant* became contrite, abandoned impiety, abjured Spinozism, and, finally, embraced Christian truth.[32]

Neither the passage of time nor the elusiveness of 'reliable' information about what really transpired during Spinoza's final days lessened the virulence of this debate. In his treatise on how to convert atheists to Christianity, published at Helmstedt in 1732, Christian Breithaupt, an adherent of the view that pure theoretical

---

[26] Le Vassor, *De la véritable religion*, 3. [27] Masius, *Dissertationes*, 9. [28] Ibid., 10–11.
[29] Ibid., 28–9. [30] Undereyck, *Närrische Atheist*, i, 379. [31] Ibid., 385. [32] Ibid., 386.

atheism is impossible, renewed the polemic against Bayle's account of Spinoza's last days.[33] Bayle contends that Spinoza refused to admit any clergyman to the house. But what, demands Breithaupt, does this really indicate? What it shows, he averred, is that contradictory impulses fought to master his proud and confused mind, and while he could suppress his true sentiments while healthy, on approaching death he lacked the inner wherewithal to keep up this pretence any longer. But yet, even more fearful of being exposed to the world as an impostor than he was of the Almighty, he had fatally refused to see a minister of God.[34]

It was precisely because the topic had assumed such significance that Colerus, finding himself lodged in the same room in The Hague, where Spinoza had lived in 1670–1, before moving to his last address, reading where the philosopher had read, written, and meditated, decided to investigate the story of his last days as thoroughly as he could.[35] Indeed, he devotes a considerable portion of his biography to recounting Spinoza's final hours. Detesting his ideas but fascinated by his personality, Colerus remarks that he was motivated to write about Spinoza's life partly by the incessant speculation regarding his death and reports that, at the last, he lapsed into terror, renounced his philosophy, and implored God to have mercy on his soul.[36] Colerus settled in The Hague in 1693 and may have begun his enquiries then, or soon after, that is, over sixteen years after Spinoza's death but not too late to interview some of those who had known him.[37] Having discussed Spinoza's end with relevant neighbours, in particular with Van der Spyck, Colerus concluded that the philosopher unquestionably did die serenely, not in deep dread, and that there was no last-minute change of heart. He also confirms that Spinoza resorted to no desperate measures to stiffen his courage, being able to attest, having examined the apothecary's bills himself, that he took no powerful drugs. Finally, Colerus expressly asserts that Spinoza did not implore God to have mercy on his soul.[38]

No one else investigated so thoroughly and his corroborating Spinoza's constancy on his deathbed, and his sober and blameless lifestyle, had an appreciable effect. Even before his biography appeared in 1705, Colerus was reputed the leading specialist on Spinoza's life in the Republic of Letters.[39] The Dutch version of Colerus' widely read biography was followed by French and English editions in 1706. But while, as a result, Bayle's account of Spinoza's end largely won the day, and Spinoza's reputation as the unwavering 'virtuous atheist' was henceforth impregnable, there remained a few last-ditch opponents, such as Father Concina at Venice, who continued until the mid-century and beyond, adamantly denying that Bayle's version of Spinoza's death could possibly be true.[40]

---

[33] Breithaupt, *Zufällige Gedancken*, 12.   [34] Ibid., 12–13.

[35] Blase, *Johannes Colerus*, 183; Suchtelen, *Spinoza's sterfhuis*, 8–9; Nadler, *Spinoza*, 288.

[36] Blase, *Johannes Colerus*, 185.   [37] Suchtelen, *Spinoza's sterfhuis*, 8.

[38] Blase, *Johannes Colerus*, 188; Suchtelen, *Spinoza's sterfhuis*, 10; Monikhoff, *Beschrijving*, 212–13; Meinsma, *Spinoza*, 470, 480; Colerus' claim that the physician who came from Amsterdam to tend Spinoza during his last days was Meyer is questioned by some scholars, who argue that this was Schuller; see Thijssen-Schoute, 'Lodewijk Meyer', 16–17; Steenbakkers, *Spinoza's Ethica*, 55–60; Nadler, *Spinoza*, 350.

[39] Blase, *Johannes Colerus*, 185, 197.   [40] Concina, *Della religione revelata*, ii, 213.

ii. Lucas, Saint-Glain, and the Hague Coterie

A crucial development in the evolution of Spinozism was the rendering and dissemination of Spinoza's philosophy and some at least of his texts in French. Spinoza's initial impact in France, as we have seen, occurred rather later than in the Netherlands, Germany, and England, commencing only after the end of the Franco-Dutch War (1672–8) and publication of the *Tractatus Theologico-Politicus* in French in 1678. But once the process began, it rapidly gained impetus, continuing down to the middle of the eighteenth century and beyond, a broad reception deriving primarily from favourable social and intellectual circumstances in France itself, but also partly from the prior preparation and transmission of the new radical outlook, and Spinoza's system, within a French-speaking and reading milieu in the Netherlands.

The French rendering of the *Tractatus* had a particularly wide impact, in France as elsewhere, and is a remarkably competent piece of work. It is thought to have been translated at The Hague and may well have been carried out with the knowledge, and under the supervision, of Spinoza himself.[41] Although it is not inconceivable that the whole work of translation was executed after his death, it seems more likely, since it appeared in 1678, that it was at least begun before Spinoza died. Much remains mysterious about this crucial translation. But there is some hard evidence to go on, thanks especially to the remarks of The Hague publisher Charles Levier (d.1735), who appended some notes about Spinoza's writings to his notorious 1719 edition of the clandestine manuscript *La Vie et l'Esprit de Mr Benoît de Spinosa*. Though mocked by Prosper Marchand, a former friend and collaborator, who ridiculed Levier's pretensions to be a 'Spinozist', styling 'Richer la Selve'—modifying his pseudonym into a pure anagram—as an 'homme extrêmement infatué du système de Spinosa, quoiqu'il ne fût nullement en état de le lire en original',[42] he was nevertheless a figure of some significance in the propagation of intellectual libertinism and Spinozism, and an active disseminator of clandestine philosophical manuscripts in French. He corresponded with numerous writers and members of the Republic of Letters of a radical turn of mind, including Saint Hyacinthe, Anthony Collins, and the Baron von Stosch, and shipped forbidden philosophical literature to France, Italy, and other parts of Europe.[43] The cornerstone of his 'Spinozism' was his fierce anticlericalism and hatred of 'superstition', as is evident from his turgid, posthumously published, two-volume didactic novel, the *Histoire de l'Admirable Dom Inigo de Guipuscoa, Chevalier de la Vierge* (The Hague, 1736), a work lambasting the Jesuits, or 'monarchie des Inighistes', as 'une secte ambitieuse et hypocrite', vowed to pay blind obedience to their General, and continually fascinating 'l'esprit du peuple crédule par les nouvelles superstitions' which they introduce.[44]

---

[41] Meinsma, *Spinoza*, 429; Vernière, *Spinoza*, 25–6; Popkin, *Third Force*, 145.

[42] Marchand, *Dictionnaire*, i, 325; Berti, 'L'Esprit de Spinosa', 10; Charles-Daubert, *Le 'Traité'*, 68.

[43] Carayol, *Thémiseul de Saint-Hyacinthe*, 52, 56, 64; Berti, 'Introduzione', pp xxii–iii; Charles-Daubert, *Le 'Traité'*, 72–4, 79, 82.

[44] [Levier], *Histoire de l'Admirable Dom Inigo*, i, 18–19; Charles-Daubert, *Le 'Traité'*, 68, 155.

According to Levier, the 1678 French version of the *Tractatus* appeared in successive print-runs, with three different false title-pages though, in fact, contrary to what others claimed, they were all the same edition.[45] This was done, he says, by the publisher 'pour tromper les Inquisiteurs'.[46] This tallies with Bayle's remark in his article on Spinoza in the *Dictionnaire*, that the *Reflexions Curieuses* was the original title and that the other two titles were used later as a device to evade the censorship.[47] Among recorded copies seized by the police in Paris during the 1680s and 1690s all three titles occur.[48] The order in which the bogus titles appeared, claims Levier,[49] was as follows:

(i.)   *Reflexions Curieuses d'un esprit des-interessé sur les matières les plus importantes au salut, tant public que particulier.* À Cologne, Chez Claude Emmanuel, 1678.

(ii.) *La Clef du sanctuaire par un sçavant homme de notre siècle.* À Leyde. Chez Pierre Warnaer, MDC LXXVIII.

(iii.) *Traité des cérémonies superstitieuses des juifs tant anciens que modernes.* À Amsterdam, Chez Jacob Smith, MDC LXXVIII.

Levier provides no information about who published the French translation, or where it was published. Modern bibliographers assume that it was brought out at Amsterdam by Rieuwertsz.[50] Nor does Levier mention that, not long after 1678, there was a second edition of the French version, imitating the first and scarcely distinguishable from it, and again employing all three bogus titles.[51] Regarding the identity of the translator, Levier reports that opinion was divided, some believing it to have been the work of Gabriel de Saint-Glain, others of Jean-Maximilien Lucas (1646–97) whom he describes as a journalist famous for his *invectives* against Louis XIV.[52] 'Ce qu'il y a de certain,' comments Levier, 'c'est que ce dernier étoit ami et disciple de Mr de Spinosa' and was the author both of the first biography of the philosopher and—or so Levier claimed, and it remains the most convincing attribution—of *L'Esprit de Spinosa*.[53]

Though Levier calls Lucas 'célèbre', both candidates remain decidedly obscure. All that is known of the Chevalier de Saint-Glain (*c*.1620–84) is that he was a minor Huguenot nobleman from Limoges who, after settling in Holland in the 1660s, served

---

[45] It is claimed in de Sauzay's *Nouvelles Littéraires* for 1719 that the three titles in fact correspond to three separate editions; but on this point, bibliographical research has proved Levier correct; see Kingma and Offenberg, 'Bibliography', 16.

[46] See Levier's footnote, *La Vie et l'Esprit*, 36.

[47] Charles-Daubert and Moreau, *Pierre Bayle. Écrits*, 56.   [48] Sauvy, *Livres saisis*, 31, 34, 42, 150.

[49] *La Vie et l'Esprit*, 36; according to an earlier note of Pierre des Maizeaux, however, the second of these titles was the first 'mais ce titre ayant fait beaucoup de bruit, on craignit qu'il ne préjudiciât au débit du livre', consequently the title was changed to *Traité des Cérémonies superstitieuses des Juifs* and only finally to the title which Levier gives as the first; Charles-Daubert and Moreau, *Pierre Bayle. Écrits*, 152; Gebhardt, 'Textgestaltung', iii, 388.

[50] Trinius, *Freydenker-Lexicon*, 420; Vernière, *Spinoza*, 25.

[51] Gebhardt, 'Textgestaltung', 388; Kingma and Offenberg, 'Bibliography', 16.

[52] *La Vie et L'Esprit*, 36; Meinsma, *Spinoza*, 6; see also Zedler, *Grosses Universal Lexicon*, xxxix, 81; Dunin Borkowski, *Spinoza*, i, 488–9.

[53] *La Vie et l'Esprit*, 36, Van Eeghen, *Amsterdamse boekhandel*, iii, 228–30; Charles-Daubert, 'Le "Traité"', 5, 67, 121, 125–6.

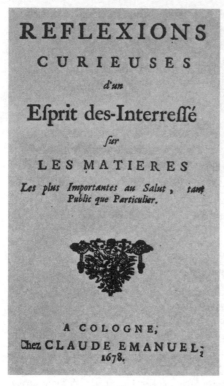

FIGURE 3. The false titles of two of the French printings of the *Tractatus Theologico-Politicus*.

in the Dutch army and later, it seems, as an aide or 'domestic' in the entourage of William III. Very likely, it was with the Prince's encouragement that he concentrated, after retiring from military service, on writing anti-Louis XIV propaganda.[54] In 1714 Pierre des Maizeaux,[55] in London, claimed to be reliably informed that it was indeed Saint-Glain who translated the *Tractatus*, testimony obtained from his friend Dr Morelli,[56] a Jewish physician who had practised at The Hague before moving to

[54] According to Pierre des Maizeaux, he was one of the editors of the *Gazette d'Amsterdam*, Francès, 'Gazetier français', 411; Vernière, *Spinoza*, 24–5.

[55] Pierre des Maizeaux (1673–1745) editor of Bayle's letters, was an only son of a Huguenot minister in the Puy-de-Dôme. He spent most of the 1690s studying theology in Switzerland, at Berne and Geneva, with a view to a career as a pastor. Meeting Bayle at Rotterdam in 1699 proved a turning-point in his life and he became a professional *savant*. After settling permanently in London, where he earned his keep as a tutor in aristocratic households, he remained one of Bayle's most stalwart correspondents and fervent admirers down to his death and became one of Anthony Collins' closest friends; he quarrelled bitterly with Marchand from 1713 onwards, largely over Bayle's legacy; see Goldgar, *Impolite Learning*, 131–9;.

[56] Henri Morelli (Henriques Morales) was a Sephardic Jew, originally from Cairo, who, according to Saint-Evremond and Des Maizeaux, had studied medicine in Italy and Holland before settling in The Hague, where, he subsequently claimed, 'J'ai connu très particulièrement M. Spinoza.' After settling later in England, he came into contact with Des Maizeaux around 1710. Morelli was the source of Bayle's infor-

England and professed to have been friendly with both Spinoza and Saint-Glain.[57] According to Morelli, Saint-Glain, originally a zealous Calvinist, after meeting Spinoza (around 1669) became, 'un de ses disciples et de ses plus grands admirateurs'.[58] That it was indeed the Sieur de Saint-Glain who rendered the *Tractatus* into French for Spinoza was in the eighteenth century often categorically asserted.[59] Marchand, however, doubted Morelli's trustworthiness, and everything claimed by Des Maizeaux—his rival for recognition as Europe's leading Bayle connoisseur—based on his testimony, so that, as Levier states, the Republic of Letters remained divided and many continued to regard Lucas as the translator.

What is incontrovertible is that the translator, whether Lucas or Saint-Glain, was intimate with Spinoza or key members of his circle. The evidence of the 1678 edition itself proves not just that the translator went to appreciable lengths in rendering the Latin faithfully but also consulted the (as yet unpublished) Dutch translation of the text prepared by Glazemaker who, indeed, being a highly skilled translator from both Latin and French into Dutch, may well have assisted in the project.[60] Still more remarkable, the 1678 French edition includes thirty pages of supplementary notes, rendered into French from Spinoza's own manuscript notes to the *Tractatus*, clarifications of the main text which he accumulated, annotating his own printed copy of the *Tractatus* after 1670, and which remained unpublished in either Latin or Dutch at the time of his death. This implies that either Spinoza or Rieuwertsz, who took charge of this, as of the rest of his manuscripts after the philosopher's death, made this unpublished material available to Lucas or Saint-Glain, and that, therefore, both translator and translation had the official imprimatur, as it were, of either the philosopher himself or at least the inner 'Spinozist' coterie of the late 1670s.[61]

Spinoza's supplementary notes to the *Tractatus* thus first appeared in the 1678 French edition. They were separately paginated under the title *Remarques curieuses, et nécessaires pour l'Intelligence de ce Livre* which, moreover, long remained the only printed version of this particular text, since none of the other early vernacular (i.e. English or Dutch) or Latin editions of the *Tractatus* include them. Moreover, two notes, numbers XX and XXVII—the latter elaborating on Spinoza's claim that the 'whole of Christ's doctrine' consists of moral as opposed to theological (or philosophical) teachings, citing the Sermon on the Mount—do not appear in the surviving Latin and Dutch manuscript versions of Spinoza's notes.[62] This last intriguing feature

---

mation (which he could not finally decide whether to believe or not) that Condé did in fact meet Spinoza in Utrecht in 1673; see Charles-Daubert and Moreau, *Pierre Bayle. Écrits*, 165–6; Popkin, *Third Force*, 145–6, 165, 169; Nadler, *Spinoza*, 318.

[57] Bayle, *Oeuvres diverses*, iv, 574; Vogt, *Catalogus historico-criticus*, ii, 687; Kingma and Offenberg, 'Bibliography', 16.

[58] Bayle, *Oeuvres diverses*, iv, 574; Charles-Daubert and Moreau, *Pierre Bayle. Écrits*, 152; Van Eeghen, *Amsterdamse boekhandel*, iii, 62–3.

[59] *Journal Littéraire* 1722, p. 459; Moréri, *Grand Dictionnaire* ix, 541.

[60] Francès, 'Gazetier français', 407.

[61] Gebhardt, 'Textgestaltung', iii, 389; Vernière, *Spinoza*, 25–6; Totaro, 'Nota', 108–9.

[62] Gebhardt, 'Textgestaltung', iii, 389; Klever, 'Omtrent Spinoza', 15.

means not only that the French version of the *Tractatus* is the most complete, but also strengthens the probability that the translator communicated, and discussed the translation, with Spinoza himself.

The *Tractatus Theologico-Politicus*, forbidden in France as in the Netherlands, was alone among Spinoza's writings in being clandestinely published in French during the age of the Enlightenment. Yet it was not an isolated undertaking on the part of Spinoza's French-speaking acolytes, being, as we have noted, closely connected in particular with the first biography of Spinoza, ascribed by Levier to Lucas, and the most widely known of all the clandestine philosophical manuscripts circulating in early Enlightenment Europe, the aggressively anti-religious *Traité des Trois Imposteurs* alternatively entitled *L'Esprit de Mr Benoît de Spinosa* also attributed, by Levier, to Lucas.[63] Marchand agrees with Levier that Lucas was 'sufficiently depraved and immoral' to conceive of such an impious undertaking but doubted, witheringly, whether someone of his mediocre talent and 'pitiable style' was capable of executing it.[64] But if Lucas was really as mediocre intellectually as Marchand suggests, this would equally be an objection to his being the highly skilled translator of the *Tractatus*. In any case, while there persists much uncertainty among scholars as to precisely when, and by whom, *L'Esprit* was written, it is widely accepted that it was produced by a coterie of radical-minded Huguenots in the Netherlands and that Levier, who published the first clandestine edition in 1719, was among those involved.

L'Esprit played a pivotal role, from the late seventeenth century onwards, in shaping a new kind of ideological militancy, rooted in Spinozism and expressed in French, in which 'philosophy' becomes a veritable engine of war, a battering-ram with which to smash down the theological foundations of *ancien régime* culture and society.[65] *L'Esprit*, moreover, like the French version of the *Tractatus* and Lucas' biography, and like Levier's activities and those of other Huguenots sympathetic to Spinozism, undeniably served as a cultural bridge linking developments in the Netherlands with the rapid growth, from the 1680s onwards, of Spinozism in France itself. It is especially this which lends the French-speaking Spinozist coterie in The Hague its enduring historical signficance. Even Lucas' not particularly impressive biography of Spinoza, unreliable in detail and excessively adulatory in tone, does not lack ideological force, urging those in quest of personal salvation to embrace 'tellement ses maximes et ses lumières' that their thoughts are guided entirely by Spinoza.[66] It extols Spinoza and his philosophy as being of incomparable brilliance and power, providing a light to humanity, or at least the wiser part of humanity, 'pas moins utile que la lumière de la soleil'. Mediocre as a piece of scholarship, it is a work which could not fail to bolster the image of Spinoza in French culture, and hence eighteenth-century Europe more generally, as the almost superhuman 'virtuous atheist' and 'saint' of the *esprits forts*,

---

[63] See Levier's remarks in *La Vie et l'Esprit*, 36; Meinsma, *Spinoza*, 6; Popkin, *Third Force*, 136, 145; Steenbakkkers, *Spinoza's Ethica*, 10.

[64] Marchand, *Dictionnaire*, i, 325; Charles-Daubert, *Le 'Traité'*, 119.

[65] Berti, 'Introduzione', pp. xv–xvi; Charles-Daubert, *Le 'Traité'*, 252–71.   [66] *La Vie et l'Esprit*, 58.

the intellectual hero who offers mankind a new path to personal and collective redemption in the shape of a revolutionary philosophy.

iii. The Rise of Dutch Spinozism

If the first signs of anxiety about the spread of Spinozist ideas in Dutch, and Dutch Huguenot, culture date, as we have seen, from the mid-1670s and concern mainly The Hague, from the 1680s there are many reports in Dutch and French sources affirming the rapid spread of Spinozist influence in different localities and at various levels of society. Three years after Spinoza's death, in 1680, his former adversary, Lambert van Velthuysen at Utrecht, noted that 'many men who are neither wicked nor stupid have become estranged from worship of the true God by Spinoza's arguments'.[67] Four years later the leading Dutch Sephardic controversialist, Isaac Orobio de Castro, who had long supposed Spinoza's philosophy would pose no great threat to society, deeming his writings too abstruse for the unlettered and toofallacious for the learned, admitted that experience had proved him wrong and that not only were some of the common people becoming contaminated by Spinoza's 'pestilential dogmata', and even glorying in them, but that even some of the erudite now professed his 'wretched doctrines'.[68] In 1686 Balthasar Bekker, in Amsterdam, noted that Spinoza's ideas were penetrating deeply, 'seducing' many of the best minds.[69] In 1687 the heterodox theologian Willem Deurhoff remarked that even some very simple folk had been drawn to Spinozism, as had no small number of sophisticated libertines.[70] An anonymous text of the early 1690s, decrying the rise of scepticism about miracles, identifies as a key element in the problem that 'support for the Atheist Spinoza in Holland', already evident for some years, was now patently growing.[71]

During the early eighteenth century it was frequently noted in the Dutch Republic, as in France, that the *Spinosistes* were a widespread and active force in society. An underground movement with no formal organization or institutions, it was no easy matter to assess its extent and influence. The Zeeland preacher Willem Spandaw claimed in 1700 that if godless philosophical impiety stretched back millennia, via Vanini to Zeno and the ancient Stoics, 'no one has brought godlessness to greater fruition than the acute Spinoza: France, England—the cadet school of monstrous opinions—the Netherlands and other lands besides, produce a whole crowd who venerate him as something marvellous' so that many embrace his views and 'fearlessly and openly proclaim themselves unbelievers'.[72] Jacques Basnage remarked of the Spinozist 'sect' in 1716 that 'on ne peut dire si elle est nombreuse, puisque ce sont des personnes dispersées en divers lieux, qui ne sont ni corps, ni

---

[67] Van Velthuysen, *Tractatus de Cultu Naturali*, dedication.
[68] Orobio de Castro, *Certamen philosophicum*, 389.
[69] Bekker, *Kort Begryp*, 39; Israel, *Dutch Republic*, 921.   [70] Deurhoff, *Voorleeringen*, 5.
[71] *Verhandeling van de Mirakelen*, 14.   [72] Spandaw, *Bedekte Spinosist*, dedication.

société'; but he, like others, noted that Spinozism had the strange characteristic of drawing converts from among both the artisan class and the highly educated.[73]

The Middelburg preacher Cornelis Tuinman (1659–1728) observed in 1719 that the 'number of Spinozists, unfortunately, is growing in the whole of our Fatherland'.[74] Not only were there Spinozists, there was even a class of declared ex-Spinozists ready to join in the war against Spinozism. The veteran explorer Jacob Roggeveen (1659–1729), the discoverer of Easter Island and Samoa, noted in 1719, in his preface to the third volume of the works of Van Hattem, that it was the latter's eloquence and cogency which had rescued him from unbelief, converting him from a 'Spinozist to a Christian'.[75] Only from the 1720s onwards did the Spinozist surge in the Netherlands lose its early momentum, and anxiety about the spread of radical ideas gradually waned. Looking back from the perspective of the 1790s, a later writer accurately noted that while 'formerly there had been very many, especially in the Netherlands, who cultivated Spinozism in secret', later the menace receded and the Spinozist movement lost impetus and declined.[76] English radical deism likewise receded after the first third of the eighteenth century, so that by 1790 Edmund Burke could rightly exclaim 'who born within the last forty years has read one word of Collins, and Toland, and Tindal, and Chubb, and Morgan, and that whole race that call themselves freethinkers?'[77] Thus, by the 1730s a noticeable shift had taken place on the European philosophical stage: the dynamic thrust of the Radical Enlightenment had shifted decisively from the Netherlands and England to France and Germany.

In the shaping of the European Radical Enlightenment, then, the Dutch Republic can fairly be said to have led the way, not only in terms of philosophical contributions but in a wider cultural sense, being the forum of crucial new mechanisms of cultural change, such as the Huguenot intellectual diaspora, the French-language journals, and a burgeoning book trade exporting to the whole of Europe, creating the conditions in which radical ideas could be effectively and rapidly transmitted. Consequently, not only were Spinozists undoubtedly more numerous in the Netherlands than elsewhere but, as we shall see, Dutch Spinozism performed a crucially formative role on the wider European intellectual stage.

Those swayed by Spinoza's arguments who became part of the radical philosophical underground, whether at a popular or more sophisticated level, inevitably found themselves driven into a psychological ghetto by the growing pressure exerted on them by the secular and ecclesiastical authorities and the force of mainstream public opinion. Where clandestine study groups formed, individuals could be encouraged and—what was sometimes even more important—any excess of zeal apt to endanger others could be curbed. Schuller in particular seems to have been impulsive and hotheaded and on one occasion when Spinoza was still alive, around 1675, caused a scandal among the radical underground. As Van Gent later recounted to Tschirnhaus, Schuller had unrestrainedly harangued a fellow alchemist, assuring him the world

---

[73] Basnage, *Histoire des Juifs*, ix, 1035.   [74] Tuinman, *Korte Afschetzing*, 13.
[75] Van Hattem, *Den Val van 's Werelts Af-God*, iii, voor-reden.   [76] Nieuhoff, *Over Spinozisme*, 40.
[77] Quoted in Brown, *British Philosophy*, 10, 18.

exists eternally and was not created, that there is no Last Judgement or eternal damnation, that the Devil does not exist, that Christ was not the son of God but of Joseph, and that there are no divinely inspired prophets or apostles.[78] Such behaviour was considered not just grotesquely indiscreet but liable to 'deliver us into the hatred of all'.[79] At Van Gent's request, Spinoza reportedly wrote a stern letter to Schuller, warning him to show more prudence.

A frequent mechanism of self-defence was to claim that they, and their hero, were being misconstrued and that they were not in fact 'atheists'. Deurhoff and Poiret considered it a typical tactic of the Spinozists of the 1680s and 1690's to complain incessantly that Spinoza was being misrepresented and that he was not propagating godlessness but a particular view of God.[80] The same point was made by Adriaen Pietersz Verwer, a Collegiant businessman of some erudition, and an enthusiastic participant in vernacular philosophical debate, who moved from Rotterdam to Amsterdam in 1680.[81] Verwer published a book against the Spinozists in 1683, which provides an intriguing glimpse into the fraught world of amateur philosophical debate in Amsterdam in the early 1680s, an arena where Spinozists and anti-Spinozists grappled unremittingly for the upper hand. The main hindrance, avers Verwer, to overcoming the Spinozist 'sect' in philosophical debate, and what makes them so insidious, was their cunning use of veiled expressions, coded language which seemingly speaks of 'God' and 'Christ' but is actually a device to deceive the unwary, circumvent the law and norms of common decency, and surreptitiously disseminate their venom.[82]

Describing encounters with seasoned Spinozists in Amsterdam, Verwer admits that their skill in debate had obliged him to reread Spinoza meticulously. His remark that at the time of writing in 1683, most of his antagonists had recently died, suggests he meant the now ageing membership of Spinoza's own Amsterdam circle, and especially Meyer (d.1681), Bouwmeester (d.1680), and Jelles (d.1683).[83] That Bouwmeester, however lethargic, still adhered doggedly to the radicalism of his youth emerges from some hostile comments about him in a pamphlet produced shortly after Spinoza's death, depicting him as a hardened unbeliever, who had not only given Adriaen Koerbagh lessons in 'atheism' and 'agrees with Spinoza and . . . the *Theological-Political Treatise*' but possesses 'all the secret writings of Doctor van den Enden, who died in France high in the air'.[84]

The way to defeat the Spinozist 'sect', holds Verwer, is to thwart their deceitful talk of 'God' by laying down a clear dividing line between those who believe in a deity distinct from His Creation, on whom man and all other creatures are 'dependent', and those who conceive man and all created things to be 'independent' of a Creator.[85] Only persons who assert the 'dependence' of man on a providential

---

[78] Steenbakkers, *Spinoza's* Ethica, 5.   [79] Ibid.

[80] Deurhoff, *Voorleeringen*, 20, 54; Poiret, *De Eruditione Solida*, 278–9, 293–7.

[81] [Verwer], *'t Mom Aensicht* pp. xii xiii; Melles, *Joachim Oudaen*, 124.   [82] Ibid., p. xviii.

[83] Ibid., pp. xii–xiv; Jongeneelen, 'Disguised Spinozism', 17.   [84] Bordoli, 'Account', 176–7.

[85] [Verwer], *'t Mom-Aensicht*, xvi, 11, 15, 29, 50.

God can attribute an absolute, objective status to 'good' and 'evil' and the entire existing edifice of theology, organized religion, morality, and law. If 'dependence' is denied, holds Verwer, then not only do organized religion, morality, and law as commonly understood disintegrate, but so do nearly all treatises written about political theory over the ages.[86] Those who oppose the Christian viewpoint, whom we ought term *Independenten* rather than 'atheists', Verwer suggests, since Spinoza's followers all insist on speaking of 'God' and rejecting the charge of atheism, belong, he says, to an ancient tradition of philosophy stretching back through Hobbes, Vanini, and Machiavelli, through the ages to the thinkers of classical Greece. Yet, affirms Verwer, expressing an idea which was to be taken much further by Bayle, in modern times it is above all Spinoza who revived, reworked, and systematized this ancient tradition.[87]

Most of those personally linked to Spinoza in Amsterdam died in the early 1680s. The philosophical discussion circle they established, however, survived after their deaths, down to at least the opening years of the new century, and undoubtedly remained consciously and overtly Spinozist in character.[88] One active member was the mathematician and physician Petrus van Gent (1640–95), who had known Spinoza and been one of the Latin editors of the *Opera Posthuma*, and had a detailed knowledge of Spinoza's thought and texts, as is shown by his surviving letters to Tschirnhaus, written after the latter returned to Saxony and with whom he remained in close contact.[89] During several visits to Amsterdam in the 1680s and subsequently, Tschirnhaus evidently stayed, and spent much of his time, with Van Gent and also Ameldonk Block (*c*.1651–1702), a Mennonite silk-merchant and amateur philosopher who joined the coterie, and whose chief contribution was to translate into Dutch Tschirnhaus' *Medicina Mentis*, published in Amsterdam in 1687.[90] Other participants, Van Gent's letters show, included the younger Jan Rieuwertsz, the Danish mathematician Georg Mohr, and the reformist physician Heydenryk Overcamp (1651–94), whose doctorate on gangrene had been quashed by the university senate at Leiden in 1677, apparently owing to objections to his philosophical terminology and suspected Spinozist tendencies.[91] In 1683 Overcamp published a robust critique of Descartes' concept of motion in which he firmly contends that motion must be conceived as inherent in matter.[92]

But the most distinguished member of the Amsterdam coterie and its principal link with university life was Mandeville's teacher and one of the most renowned scientists in the Republic, Burchardus de Volder. The involvement of such a widely known and eminent professor is indeed significant. Furthermore, there seems little doubt that De Volder, in his discreet way, went to some pains both to defend Spinoza's legacy and to disseminate it. When the young German scholar, Gottlieb Stolle, sent to Holland by Thomasius, among other things to collect data about Spinoza, came to interview him

---

[86] [Verwer], *'t Mom-Aensicht*, 15–16; [Cuffeler], *Specimen*, i, 230–5.
[87] [Verwer], *'t Mom-Aensicht*, 6–9.
[88] Klever, 'Clé d'un nom', 189–94; Vermij, 'Spinozisme en Hollande', 155–8.
[89] Klever, 'Clé d'un nom', 190–2.   [90] Vermij, 'Spinozisme en Hollande', 164–5.
[91] Thijssen-Schoute, *Nederlands Cartesianisme*, 286–7.   [92] Ibid., 312–13.

in July 1703, De Volder, who had known Spinoza at least since the mid-1660s, ventured a number of extraordinary if inscrutable remarks. He told Stolle that not only were there 'Spinozists' in Holland but even people who wished to be known as 'Spinozists'.[93] Nevertheless, very few readers really grasped Spinoza's thought, he assured the young *savant*, not without making it clear, though, that he, De Volder, was one who did. Bayle, by contrast, was clearly not, De Volder intimating that he had no high opinion of Bayle's long article on Spinoza in the *Dictionnaire*.[94] The fact that this highly unconventional, ex-Mennonite professor was in some way defending Spinoza did not escape the young man's attention.[95]

De Volder was one of the most influential figures in Dutch science and philosophy of the last third of the seventeenth century and the opening years of the eighteenth, and he had many contacts abroad, including former students, especially in Germany and the Baltic. His personal library of nearly 2,000 volumes was not large but was certainly rich in *Spinozana* and other radical thought. Besides Spinoza's *Opera Posthuma*, work on Descartes, and *Tractatus Theologico-Politicus*, he possessed, for example, Meyer's *Philosophia*, Cuffeler's *Specimen*, and numerous works of Johan and Pieter de la Court, besides Beverland's *De Peccato originali*, Van Dale's *De Oraculis*, Bekker's *Betoverde Weereld*, Wittichius' *Anti-Spinoza*, Bayle's *Dictionnaire*, and a Dutch account of the Neapolitan revolution of 1647–8—the *Napelse Beroerten van Mas Aniello* (1653).[96] An area in which it is perhaps possible to identify a clear convergence between De Volder and Spinoza is in their common critique of Boyle and the English empirical tradition in science. Thus, for example, in his oration delivered at Leiden in 1698 as *rector magnificus*, on the use of reason in science, De Volder roundly rejects the empiricist doctrine that experience and experiments are the exclusive basis of scientific knowledge. He argued that our ideas about the physical world are drawn from our minds and constructed from the store of ideas which we possess already. But at the same time that he dismissed the empiricists' notion that our minds are nothing but the conduit for sense-impressions, he was equally disparaging about Descartes' strict dichotomy of mind and extension. Experiments are essential, he grants, but are only meaningful when conceived within a framework based on philosophical reason.[97] Nor, in his estimation, as we may infer from his taste in reading matter, was the critical philosophical reason which directs us in science any different from that which should guide us in religion and politics.

Meanwhile, the Spinozist coterie at The Hague proved more productive in publications than that in Amsterdam. Leaving aside Morelli, three other figures are reputed to have been close to Spinoza—Lucas, Saint-Glain, and the remarkable Abraham Johannes Cuffeler (*c.*1637–94), a jurist attached to the Hof van Holland who had studied at Utrecht and Leiden universities in the late 1650s, and may well have met the brothers Koerbagh, Meyer, Bouwmeester, and Spinoza himself at that time. Cuffeler was accounted by Bayle a 'disciple de Spinoza' and by Van Gent, in a letter to

---

[93] Klever, 'Burchard de Volder', 195.   [94] Ibid., 197–8; Klever, 'Omtrent Spinoza', 3.
[95] Klever, 'Burchard de Volder', 197; Klever, *Mannen rond Spinoza*, 209.
[96] *Bibliotheca Volderina*, 3–7, 41, 84, 88.   [97] Klever, 'Burchard de Volder'. 216–18.

Tschirnhaus of May 1683, as 'summus amicus'.[98] Cuffeler's noteworthy 627-page work on logic, as Levier observes, is rooted in Spinoza's system, and was published in Amsterdam, by Rieuwertsz in 1684, omitting the author's name and using the same falsifications on the title-page—'Hamburgi, apud Henricum Kunraht'—as feature on the title-page of the *Tractatus Theologico-Politicus*, echoes intended doubtless both as a note of defiance and a clarion call to the faithful.

It was a work, as library catalogues of the period show, quite widely disseminated in Germany, Scandinavia, and France, as well as the Netherlands. After categorically reaffirming Spinoza's doctrine of one substance: 'in rerum natura non dari neque dari posse plures substantiae quam una',[99] it goes on to assert that God is perfect since all eternity, that no Creation in time is possible, and that the world was not created out of nothing but existed eternally (mundum non esse ex nihilo et fuisse ab aeterno).[100] The distinction between 'Natura Naturans' and 'Natura Naturata' is restated and, again following Spinoza, the essential motivation of creatures, including humans, is held to 'consist in the conservation of our life' (consistere in conservatione nostrae vitae).[101] Bearing out Verwer's remarks about Dutch Spinozist debating strategy in the 1680s, Cuffeler accounts Spinoza, 'noster philosophus', an incomparable thinker who has immensely benefited mankind, in return for which he has received only vitriolic abuse and calumny, having allegedly confused God with Nature, in outpourings by opponents who mostly fail to understand his philosophy correctly.[102] Cuffeler, as Bayle observes, singles out two refutations of Spinoza for special treatment: Verwer's polemic of the previous year and Willem van Blyenbergh's treatise published at Dordrecht in 1682, charging Spinoza with stripping God of all 'understanding' and 'will' and reducing Him to the laws of nature, deceptively claiming to establish an ethical system proclaiming virtue and charity while in reality annihilating the authentic foundations of morality which are rooted in Christianity.[103] Further, Cuffeler reaffirms the principles of Spinoza's Bible hermeneutics, accounting the ancient Hebrews both ignorant and superstitious so that Scripture had to be 'accommodated' to their limited grasp, and repeating Spinoza's strictures about the Hebrew language.[104]

Of particular importance, it has been argued, is Cuffeler's excursion, in the last part of the work, into physics and astronomy, and especially the laws of motion and gravity. Here Cuffeler emphatically contrasts Descartes' conception of motion as external to matter, which is in itself absolutely static, a doctrine he decries, with Spinoza's conception of motion as inherent in all being and the creative factor shaping the individuality of particular bodies.[105] A notable feature of this section is Cuffeler's elaboration

---

[98] [Bayle], *Nouvelles*, i, 320; Meinsma, *Spinoza*, 429; Schröder, *Spinoza*, 133; Siebrand, *Spinoza*, 49–64; Klever, *Mannen rond Spinoza*, 143.

[99] [Cuffeler], *Specimen* i, 14–15; Charles-Daubert and Moreau, *Pierre Bayle. Écrits*, 79.

[100] [Cuffeler], *Specimen*, i, 65–6, 106–7.   [101] Ibid., 90; Lange, *Caussa Dei*, 122–3.

[102] Charles-Daubert and Moreau, *Pierre Bayle. Écrits*, 78, 107; Schröder, 'Spinozam tota', 159.

[103] [Cuffeler], *Specimen*, i, 119–26; Blyenbergh, *Wederlegging*, 128, 352–4; [Pluquet], *Examen*, ii, 32–3; Charles-Daubert and Moreau, *Pierre Bayle. Écrits*, 107.

[104] [Cuffeler], *Specimen*, i, 253–65.   [105] Klever, *Mannen rond Spinoza*, 157–9.

of Spinoza's concept of the 'relativity of inertia', the idea that a body at rest is one subject to an equivalence of pressures from all sides.[106]

Another noteworthy Spinozist writer active in The Hague for some years was Petrus van Balen (1643–90).[107] Born to a well-connected family in Utrecht, Van Balen originally studied theology and entered on a fitful career in the Reformed Church, spending several years in The Hague during the early 1670s when he might have met Spinoza. Later he took up a preaching post in Breda but, following an accident, around the time of Spinoza's death in 1677, became subject to fits of depression, suffering a particularly bad bout in March of that year which (whether or not it had any connection with Spinoza's death) was certainly linked to a crisis of faith.[108] In 1678–81, after a prolonged scandal which he provoked by abandoning his duties in Breda without permission and then long rejecting, before finally again seeking, reconciliation with the Church,[109] he studied law and embarked on a new career. He later obtained a post as an advocate at the Hof van Holland in The Hague, where he became a colleague of Cuffeler who, presumably, stimulated both his Spinozism in general and his awakening interest in philosophical logic in particular. Like Cuffeler's *magnum opus*, the first part of Van Balen's chief work, entitled *On the Improvement of Thinking, or True Logic*, appeared in 1684, the same year in which he settled in Rotterdam, where he was to spend the rest of his short life. There, intriguingly, he not only lived in proximity to other Spinozists—and near-Spinozists, including Johannes Bredenburg—but also to Bayle and John Locke, who resided in Rotterdam in the years 1687–8, though it is not known what contacts, if any, he may have had with such eminent fellow philosophical writers.[110]

Where Cuffeler wrote in Latin, is abrasive in tone, and published clandestinely, omitting his name from the title-page, Van Balen wrote in a pure, carefully crafted but popular Dutch, making only subtle allusions to Spinoza, and putting his name on the title-page. Teasingly, the only accomplishment for which he overtly praises his hero is for the excellence of his Hebrew grammar.[111] What is significant in Van Balen's contribution is that he does not see philosophy as something only for specialists, reserved for those who know Latin and the requisite technical terms. On the contrary, he insists it is vital for everyone, since one's identity, outlook, and chances of salvation depend on one's personal ideas.[112] Taking his cue from the fifth part of Spinoza's *Ethics*, where human melancholy, distress, and lack of fulfilment are considered the consequences of individual inability to master unruly passions and drives, and therefore to pursue the 'highest good', Van Balen identifies the ignorance and mental obscurity gripping the common people as a calamity, depriving men of what is best in life. The individual, contends Van Balen, must learn to think critically for himself or herself, and thereby

---

[106] Ibid., 160.

[107] Van den Hoven, 'Inleiding', 14–17; Wielema, *Filosofen*, 84–6; Klever, *Mannen rond Spinoza*, 187–9.

[108] Van den Hoven, 'Inleiding', 16.

[109] GA The Hague, Hervormde Gemeente iv, pp. 150, 167, 177. res. Kerkeraad, 25 June 1679, 10 Oct. 1680, and 3 Oct. 1681.

[110] Wielema, *Filosofen*, 60–1.   [111] Van den Hoven, 'Inleiding', 17, 41–2.

[112] [Goeree], *Philalethes Brieven*, 253.

achieve a happier, more 'enlightened' existence, a goal attainable only by adopting what is best in recent philosophy.

Van Balen repeatedly compares teaching philosophical logic to curing bodily ailments by means of medical science.[113] Mankind is shrouded in a prevailing intellectual darkness which is literally also spiritual gloom and needs to 'be enlightened' by means, as he puts it—alluding to the title of Pieter Balling's *Het Licht op den Kandelaar* (1662)— of 'light from the candlestick' of pure reason.[114] Unlike most writers on the subject, Van Balen provides no technical analysis of thinking and rarely any special terminology. His unwavering purpose is, without saying so, to highlight, paraphrase in easier terms, and thereby elucidate key steps in Spinoza's system, revealing his underlying stance only when broaching the subject of Bible criticism, where he echoes Meyer and Spinoza in claiming there is much which is obscure in Scripture, which can be resolved only with the tools philosophy provides, beginning with the fact that Moses is not the author of the Five Books and the 'books of Joshua, Judges, Ruth, Samuel and Kings were composed in later times than those in which the narrative is set'.[115]

Spinoza wrote his major works in Latin and, in 1670, took steps to prevent the publication of the *Tractatus* in Dutch. Yet from the outset, in the mid and late 1660s, when the writings of Van den Enden, Meyer, and Koerbagh appeared in the vernacular, the unwavering objective of the radical philosophical movement in the Netherlands was to 'enlighten' the common people about religion, philosophy, science, and also politics. The twin editions of Spinoza's posthumous works in 1678, making available his *Ethics* in Dutch as well as Latin, likewise reflect the double strategy of trying simultaneously to infiltrate the world of learning and popular culture. The further elaboration of Spinozist thought in the 1680s, as the works of writers such as Cuffeler, Tschirnhaus, and Van Balen show, continued this philosophical 'war on two fronts', albeit for the moment more cautiously in the vernacular than in Latin.

In the 1690s, by contrast, there was a more forceful attempt to overwhelm the bastions of authority with an undisguised, full-frontal, philosophical assault mounted in the vernacular. It was in 1693, in the midst of the Bekker controversies, that the *Tractatus Theologico-Politicus* finally appeared in Glazemaker's Dutch version, carefully corrected, it seems, by Bouwmeester,[116] and which, according to a Spinozist source, had for twenty years lain quiescent but safe in the keeping of Lodewijk Meyer.[117] Published at Amsterdam under the ironic title the *Orthodox Theologian* (*De Rechtzinnige Theologant*) furnished with the time-honoured falsifications 'at Hamburg . . . by Henricus Koenraad', it is assumed to have been brought out and distributed by the younger Jan Rieuwertsz.[118] Another translation, a corrupt, inferior version of

---

[113] Van Balen, *Verbetering*, 54–7.   [114] Ibid., 51, 133, 137.

[115] Ibid., 125–7; Klever, *Mannen rond Spinoza*, 191–2.   [116] Akkerman, 'Inleiding', 26.

[117] *Philopater*, 195; *Lettres critiques*, 165.

[118] Thijssen-Schoute, *Uit de Republiek*, 259–60; Kingma and Offenberg, 'Bibliography', 23–4; Akkerman, 'Inleiding', 26.

Glazemaker's rendering, according to *Philopater* (1697), appeared the following year, ostensibly 'at Bremen'.[119] But by far the greatest scandal resulting from the publication of openly Spinozistic books in the vernacular, in the Netherlands, during the 1690s was provoked by the novel *Philopater* itself.

iv. *Philopater*

During the 1680s and 1690s Spinozists in the Dutch Republic became fairly practised at slipping inconspicuous allusions to Spinoza, and paraphrases of his ideas, into unlikely places in texts which superficially seemed to have little to do with philosophy. Most of such instances went unnoticed, or barely noticed, at the time, though often such infringements attracted retrospective attention later. Thus the work of popular theology and morality entitled *Schole van Christus*, by the Zwolle publisher and schoolmaster Barent Hakvoord, which by the time it reached its sixth edition in 1706 had grown to 448 pages, circulated widely for a long time without eliciting any hostile reaction, even though by the time it was reissued in its third edition in 1692, it already contained passages, buried among much else, denying that angels, devils, and other 'spirits' exist, deeming the notion that comets are supernatural signs a 'heathenish belief', and discussing Creation and the human soul in a style readily susceptible to a Spinozist reading. Yet it was not until 1707 that it was suddenly generally realized that it contained, as the Synod of Overijssel expressed it, many 'false and slanderous propositions taken from the writings of Spinoza'.[120] Hakvoord's friend in Zwolle, Frederik van Leenhof, employed the same surreptitious technique more systematically when he infused his Spinozistic ideology into his two books published in 1700 (by Hakvoord) on the subject of the Biblical King Solomon. Again there was little reaction until later.

A further example of such camouflage involved the Amsterdam publisher Aert Wolsgryn, who had collaborated in bringing out and distributing the 1693 edition of Hakvoord's book. A colleague of Hakvoord, Wolsgryn seems to have been both a convinced Spinozist and a regular vendor under the counter of Spinoza's books. In May 1695, police spies having gathered evidence about their illegal bookselling, Wolsgryn was summoned together with the younger Jan Rieuwertsz and another bookseller, severely reprimanded by the Amsterdam magistrates, and warned to stop selling Spinozistic books.[121] Undeterred, Wolsgryn promptly interpolated an epilogue comprising passages taken from Spinoza's *Ethics* into his 1695 Dutch edition of the celebrated Italian pastoral play, *Il Pastor Fido*, by Guarini.[122] Seemingly, nobody noticed. Indeed, ironically in view of that journal's professed hostility to Spinozism, the Rotterdam *Boekzaal van Europe* greeted this publication enthusiastically.[123] The ease with

---

[119] Akkerman, 'Inlciding', 26.   [120] ARH OSA 216, Acta Synod of Overijssel, 28 June 1707, art. 43.

[121] Van Eeghen, *Amsterdamse boekhandel*, iii, 162–4 and iv, 65.

[122] Thijssen-Schoute, *Uit de Republiek*, 198; Maréchal, 'Inleiding', 17.

[123] *Boekzaal van Europe*, July–Dec. 1695, p. 157.

which Wolsgryn slipped this through and his unconcern at the magistrates' reprimands, apparently contributed, both psychologically and materially, to the events which subsequently led to his humiliation and ruin.

Besides the unprecedented scale of the Bekker furore of 1691–3, another factor encouraging the radical invasion of vernacular reading culture in the 1690s was precisely the growing tendency at that time for the war against Spinoza to spill over from the erudite world of Latin into the vernacular.[124] A spiral effect of publicity set in. It was in reply to the *Rechtzinnige Theologant* that a Dutch-language version of Wittichius' *Anti-Spinoza*, prepared by the Amsterdam physician Abraham van Poot, was published in 1695, despite the obvious drawback that such a translation could not avoid offering renderings into Dutch of the numerous propositions of Spinoza's *Ethics*, which Wittichius analyses in his critique. The sense of frustration felt by those sworn to fight the menace of Spinozism among the wider population is palpable in Van Poot's preface: 'who Spinoza was and what heresy he propagated can not, I believe, be unknown to anybody.' What was especially worrying, in his view, was the widespread flouting of the law regarding dissemination of Spinozistic literature, and especially Spinoza's own works: 'his writings are to be found everywhere and, in this inconstant age, owing to their novelty, are in almost all book-shops'.[125]

The first part of the *Life of Philopater*, gaining 'more praise than it deserved' according to a hostile critic, had been published amid great acclaim in 1691.[126] Neither author nor publisher was declared on the title-page, though in this first half there was no illicit philosophy. A satirical attack on the struggle between the Voetians and Cocceians, even this part nevertheless caused unease in some quarters because of its subtle denigration of theological strife and passion, and an obvious appeal to those more secular-minded elements in society concerned to lessen the intellectual prestige of theology and theological debate. 'For under the jibes and taunts against one side and then the other,' noted one critic, the vehemently anti-Spinozist publisher François Halma, 'religion and truth itself were not a little jeered at and subjected to unremitting mockery'.[127] The author later turned out to be an Amsterdam schoolmaster and failed theology proponent by the name of Johannes Duijkerius (*c.*1662–1702), who was unable to secure a post in the public Church, owing to his stammer. Duijkerius was a man of blemished character, later reported by the city's Reformed consistory to be a drunkard and wife-beater, and rumoured by some to be a molester of the young girls in his charge.[128] When the main scandal broke in 1698, the Amsterdam consistory showed itself eager to link the unprepossessing Duijkerius also to the second half of the novel and indeed Spinozism more generally.

If publication of the first part of *Philopater* caused a stir, publication of the second, late in 1697, provoked general outrage. Indeed, there had been nothing comparable to the commotion it caused since Spinoza's *Opera Posthuma* appeared twenty years

---

[124] Israel, *Dutch Republic*, 924.   [125] Wittichius, *Ondersoek*, preface by Poot.

[126] Halma, *Aanmerkingen*, 1–2; Maréchal, 'Inleiding', 5–6.

[127] Halma, *Aanmerkingen*, 1; Buddeus, *Theses Theologicae*, 131.

[128] Maréchal, 'Inleiding', 13.

before. In Leiden, apparently the first city in which the book circulated, the Reformed consistory condemned it on 13 December, urging the burgomasters to seize it from the bookshops, as was promptly done, and press the Hof van Holland for a province-wide ban.[129] The Rotterdam consistory likewise denounced 'various foul and blasphemous extracts' from *Philopater* and sent delegates to the city hall, though there the burgomasters preferred to wait before actively suppressing the book, to gauge reaction elsewhere.[130] Appalled, The Hague consistory condemned the new *Philopater* on 4 January 1698 for its 'blasphemous mockery of the Almighty and His sacred Word and open advocacy of the godless views of Spinoza', noting that it had already been suppressed in other cities and submitting a selection of the worst passages to both the civic magistracy and the Hof.[131] The States of Friesland banned the book later in January as a work in which belief in God and the Holy Trinity, and the 'divine authority of the Holy Scripture are destroyed'.[132]

The novel tells the story of the experiences of a university student who, having gradually discarded Voetian for Cocceian theology in the first part, now discards the views of the Cartesio-Cocceians and becomes a budding Spinozist thinker.[133] Set in the early 1690s, when the uproar over Bekker was at its height, Philopater and his friends praise the Frisian pastor for his courage and back him against his opponents, but also mock his paradoxical claim that the Devil exists but cannot influence the lives of men, as feeble equivocation motivated by nothing more than anxiety to evade the charge of Spinozism.[134] *Philopater* more than compensates for Bekker's moderation, roundly denying not just the reality of witchcraft, sorcery, and magic, but of demons and Satan himself. In their discussions, Philopater and his comrades restate Spinoza's principal doctrines in clear and vigorous vernacular terms: miracles are declared impossible, while the 'order of nature is eternally fixed and immutable so that nothing happens except what necessarily follows therefrom'.[135] There is no divine Providence or immortality of the soul;[136] free will is proclaimed a chimaera and Descartes' teaching on body and mind 'absurd en frivool'.[137]

At the same time Spinoza's antagonists are vigorously rebutted. 'All the Cartesian theological philosophers,' remarks Philopator's closest ally, 'will never achieve their aim of killing off Spinoza and his followers, for his principles are unbreakable, too natural and pure to be destroyed'.[138] Wittichius, then the most familiar and topical of Spinoza's adversaries in the Dutch bookshops, it is claimed, only ostensibly attacked him in his *Anti-Spinoza*, being in reality an 'admirer' and 'great friend of the Heer Spinoza'. Those who knew the secret history of modern philosophy were allegedly aware that Wittichius wrote his *Anti-Spinoza* for no other reason than to mislead his enemies and deflect the growing suspicion that he himself was a concealed 'Spinosist'.[139]

---

[129] GA Leiden Acta Kerkeraad viii. res. 13 Dec. 1697.
[130] GA Rotterdam Acta Kerkeraad vii, pp. 599, 601. res. 18 Dec. 1697 and 1 and 8 Jan. 1698.
[131] GA The Hague, Acta Kerkeraad iv, 406. res. 4 Jan. 1698.   [132] Knuttel, *Verboden boeken*, 123.
[133] Thijssen-Schoute, *Nederlands Cartesianisme*, 547.   [134] *Philopater*, 152.   [135] Ibid., 153 4.
[136] Ibid., 156–7, 162–4.   [137] Ibid., 187.   [138] Ibid., 153.
[139] Ibid., 149–50; Buddeus, *Theses Theologicae*, 127; Hubbeling, 'Philopater', 500.

Generally, in Germany, as in the Netherlands, this was deplored as an appalling travesty and calumny.

In Amsterdam an 'extraordinary meeting' of the consistory was held on 9 January, to concert measures against the 'vile and blasphemous' second part of *Philopater*. Files of particularly outrageous passages were brought to the burgomasters.[140] Both civic and ecclesiastical authorities launched enquiries to unmask author and publisher. After a few weeks, the consistory concluded from hearsay evidence that the 'publisher of the offending book was Wolsgryn' and the author Duijkerius. Their findings were conveyed to the magistrates who, however, considered it insufficient for prompt action but did finally arrest Wolsgryn in March. Under interrogation, the latter confessed to having published the book and falsely declared 'Groningen' the place of publication and the imaginary 'Siewert van der Brug' the publisher on the title-page.[141] He had had 1,500 copies printed and started distribution only days before the initial outcry at Leiden. From then until his arrest in March, he had sold around 150 copies from his shop, besides those sent to booksellers in other towns. However, he insisted he was not the author and did not know who had written it, claiming that the manuscript had been posted to him anonymously.[142]

Duijkerius was also arrested and interrogated. But having admitted writing the first part of *Philopater,* he flatly denied responsibility for the second. Although he has been considered the main author in recent secondary literature,[143] the Amsterdam magistrates seem to have believed him since, soon afterwards, he was released, much to the disgruntlement of the consistory, which persisted in considering him guilty and promptly summoned him for their own interrogation. However, here again he adamantly denied writing the second part while confessing to having written the first and, among other shortcomings, to heavy drinking.[144]

Having completed their enquiries, the magistrates passed judgement on Wolsgryn in May. They seem to have concluded, probably correctly, that *Philopater*'s second part was concocted by a coterie rather than an individual and that, while Duijkerius participated, he was not the principal author. Wolsgryn, on the other hand, was held responsible not just as the publisher but the principal inspirer, organizer, and author of the text. In this connection, it is relevant to note a minor but revealing satirical piece entitled *Paterphilo*, which appeared anonymously at Harderwijk in 1697, a few weeks before the publication of *Philopater*, and which was clearly written by someone familiar with the method of *Philopater's* composition and its pending appearance, someone who surely belonged to the group of friends which together compiled it. According to this account, the Amsterdam Spinozistic circle which devised *Philopater* had much fun

---

[140] GA Amsterdam Acta Kerkeraad xvi, pp. 316–17. res. 2, 9 and 16 Jan. 1698.

[141] GA Amsterdam arch 5061/345. Confessie-Boeck, fos. 227v–8. hearing 7 Mar. 1698; Thijssen-Schoute, *Uit de Republiek*, 180, 197.

[142] GA Amsterdam arch 5061/345 Confessie-Boeck., fo. 229.

[143] Van Gelder, *Getemperde vrijheid*, 180; Thijssen-Schoute, *Nederlands Cartesianisme*, 296; Maréchal, 'Inleiding', 11–13.

[144] GA Amsterdam Acta Kerkeraad xvii, p. 6. res. 10 Apr. 1698.

putting their ideas together, consuming many a tankard of wine and pipe of tobacco in the process.[145]

But it was no fun for Wolsgryn to be the one who was made an example of, nor anything amusing about his punishment.[146] He incurred eight years imprisonment in the Rasphuis, followed, should he survive, by twenty-five years banishment from Holland, besides fines of 3,000 guilders 'according to the placard against printing Spinozistic books', and a further 1,000 guilders for selling illegal publications in Amsterdam.[147] Meanwhile, the Hof of Holland followed the Delegated States of Friesland and banned the novel in Holland and Zeeland, while the Rotterdam burgomasters belatedly seized the stock of copies there and had them publicly burned at the city hall.[148] News of the trial, and details of Wolsgryn's sentence under the laws suppressing 'Spinosistische boeken', were reported in numerous consistories, *classes*, and synods over the next months.[149] The prevailing view was that Wolsgryn received his just deserts, since the second part of *Philopater*, as the Rotterdam *Boekzaal van Europe* expressed it, was a work in which 'Spinoza's cause is taken up undiluted and undisguised'.[150]

Much of the 1697 edition of *Philopater* was destroyed by the authorities, while Wolsgryn's unenviable fate clearly had an inhibiting effect on those with radical sympathies. Until the late twentieth century, no one ever ventured to publish the book again. Nevertheless, the few hundred copies sold before Wolsgryn's arrest seem to have had some impact in the Republic and beyond, which emerges from the efforts of commentators and journal editors to counter its perceived influence. Halma, denouncing *Philopater* in a long preface to his Dutch translation of Bayle's article on Spinoza in 1698, was especially worried by the novel's summons to the common man to discard conventional theology and spurn the authority of Scripture, acknowledging only the Spinozists as genuine philosopher-theologians.[151] Another writer, using the pseudonym 'J.Roodenpoort', published two attacks on *Philopater*, including a 230-page parody of the novel in 1700. Here a Leiden student called Kakotegnus, unmistakably resembling Philopater, converts to Spinozism and becomes a hardened freethinker who goes about attempting to 'seduce' other students into regarding revealed religion as nothing more than a political device for the manipulation of society.[152] Kakotegnus, however, meets a pillar of Calvinist rectitude named Kakoethes who is more than a match for his sophistries against Revelation, miracles, and Providence.[153] Finally, Kakotegnus—rather like Duijkerius, who died miserably in impoverished disgrace two years later—expires alone and abandoned in wretched circumstances, bitterly

---

[145] Maréchal, 'Inleiding', 18–19.   [146] GA Amsterdam Acta Kerkeraad xvii, p. 9. res. 15 May 1698.

[147] Ibid.; Van Gelder, *Getemperde vrijheid*, 180; Thijssen-Scoute, *Uit de Republiek*, 197; Maréchal, 'Inleiding', 33.

[148] GA Rotterdam Acta Kerkeraad vii, p. 612. res. 13 May 1698.

[149] See, for instance, ARH OSA Synod of Gelderland Acta Harderwijk, 17 Aug. 1698; Rijksarchief Groningen Acta Synodi, Appingedam, 1 Mar. 1699.

[150] *Boekzaal van Europe* 1698, p. 292; De Vet, *Pieter Rabus*, 273.

[151] Halma, *Aanmerkingen*, 6; *Boekzaal van Europe* 1698, 294.

[152] [Roodenpoort], *Verleidend Levens-bedrijf*, 26–8, 33.   [153] Ibid., 6, 23, 54–5, 143.

repenting at the last, when it is too late, the Spinozistic blindness and arrogance which ruined his life. 'Spinozists' are depicted in this work as heartless scoundrels who, hiding their chicanery behind a fog of philosophical bombast, prey on the intellectually unwary, especially students who imagine themselves cleverer than other folk, leading their victims directly to damnation. Kakotegnus was warmly welcomed in the Dutch periodical press as an effective antidote, not just to the despicable *Philopater*, but the spread of Spinozism in society generally.[154]

Outside the Netherlands, *Philopater* also had some resonance, at least in the parts of Europe where Dutch functioned as a major cultural medium. Most copies surviving in libraries outside the Netherlands today are located in northern Germany, including two at Göttingen and another at Wolfenbüttel.[155] Early eighteenth-century German academic luminaries tended to know the book, Buddeus calls *Philopater* 'notissimus'.[156] The early eighteenth-century Koenigsberg librarian, Michael Lilienthal, refers to *Philopater* in terms implying that it counted in the Baltic area as one of the foremost freethinking texts of the early Enlightenment.[157] At Frankfurt am Main, Burgomaster von Uffenbach not only possessed copies of both parts of *Philopater* but also *Paterphilo*.[158] The spectacularly rich collection of radical literature, including *Philopater*, assembled in the Swedish enclave of Verden, belonging to a high government official, Samuel Triewald, was auctioned after being shipped to Sweden, in Stockholm in 1746.[159]

v. Dutch Radicalism at the Beginning of the Eighteenth Century

Philopater's suppression effectively curbed the open promotion of Spinozism through the medium of the novel. But this still left the option of insinuating radical concepts by means of veiled fictional devices, producing texts harder to target than *Philopater*. Such a vehicle, clearly radical if less concretely Spinozistic than *Philopater*, was a 286-page travel romance entitled *Description of the Mighty Kingdom of Krinke Kesmes*, published in 1708 at Zwolle, one of the prime centres of Spinozist influence in the Republic at the time, albeit with 'Amsterdam' declared on the title-page. Its author was Hendrik Smeeks (d.1721), a surgeon dwelling in that small provincial city and a member of the Reformed congregation there, who presumably knew both Hakvoord and Leenhof.

In this utopian story the hero, a Dutch merchant born of a Spanish father who spoke both Dutch and Spanish, is shipwrecked by a storm in the South Sea. Surviving, he finds himself at length in the mighty kingdom of Krinke Kesmes, part of the legendary 'South Land' of Australis. To his amazement he discovers that its inhabitants, despite having no contact with Europe or Asia, know all the languages of those continents and everything concerning their religions and philosophy. This was because following an earlier shipwreck, in the year AD 1030, a Persian vessel bound for

---

[154] *Twee-Maandelijke Uyttreksels* 1701, 686–92.   [155] Maréchal, 'Inleiding', 36–7.

[156] Buddeus, *Theses Theologicae*, 127.   [157] Lilienthal, *Theologische Bibliothec*, 377–9.

[158] *Bibliotheca Uffenbachiana*, i, 768.   [159] [Triewald], *Bibliotheca*, iv, 305.

Mecca, conveying 300 Muslim pilgrims of many nationalities, together with some Christian and Jewish slaves, had foundered on their shores, and the wise king then reigning had had all the Arabic texts, Latin and Greek testaments, and Hebrew books salvaged from the wreck and thus assembled a universal library of western and eastern theology and philosophy.[160] He then divided the survivors according to creed and language, attaching to each group a team of six young men of his own people, instructed to learn their tongue, customs, and ideas.[161]

Later, advised by Krinke Kesmes' chief philosopher, Sarabasa, their equivalent of Confucius, an immense cathedral was constructed with enough pulpits to accommodate simultaneous preaching of all the theologies of Europe and Asia. It was expected that by encouraging every confession freely to expound its tenets and dispute with the rest, it would rapidly emerge, through a selective process driven by cogent debate, which sect was the most persuasive and best. But to the horror of the inhabitants, instead of progressive edification, there was nothing but strident yelling and abuse, each clergyman claiming he had received his books of the law from God and denouncing the rest as heretics destined for eternal damnation.[162] To put a stop to this, the king decided to allow religious freedom to all but threatened with death anyone who engaged further in any form of religious dispute. Consequently, the people of Krinke Kesmes, including even the women, quickly lost interest in theology and turned instead with growing enthusiasm to philosophy.[163]

Choice of 'outward religion' in any given society, Smeeks repeatedly suggests, is made on the basis of political considerations: 'religion derives from the political regime and not the political regime from religion'.[164] Philosophy, not theology, is the only path which can guide us to truth. The Churches affirm the immortality of the soul; but philosophy shows no confidence can be placed in such a concept. The clergy maintain the existence of 'Heaven' and 'Hell' but philosophy teaches there is no reason to believe any such notions: 'theologians provide awesome, terrifying accounts of Hell yet neither they, nor we, know what, or where, Hell is, or how the godless will be punished there'.[165]

There was not enough explicit Spinozism in Smeeks' novel to cause the sort of reaction provoked by *Philopater*. Even so, the text was clearly sacrilegious and seditious, eulogizing 'philosophy' and deriding 'theology', and therefore, in the eyes of many, should be suppressed. At the gathering of the South Holland Synod at Dordrecht in July 1709, *Krinke Kesmes* was cited among various pernicious works currently in circulation which 'needed to be forbidden', though the gathering was noticeably more worried by Hakvoord's *Schole van Christus*, which it pronounced 'stuffed with many pernicious Spinozistic and atrocious propositions'.[166] The Synod of Gelderland, meeting at Nijmegen soon afterwards, welcomed the news that the Zwolle magistrates had now seized all copies of *Krinke Kesmes*, that 'foul and offensive book' written by 'a

---

[160] Smeeks, *Beschryvinge*, 75.   [161] Ibid., 76–8.   [162] Ibid., 79–82.   [163] Ibid., 95–112.
[164] Ibid., 115.   [165] Ibid., 112.
[166] 'als van vele pernicieuse Spinosistische ende grouwelike stellingen opgepropt', ARH OSA 97 South Holland Synod, Acta Dordrecht 9–19 July 1709, art. 14.

certain Hendrik Smeeks'.[167] Smeeks indeed faced personal disgrace and considerable social and psychological pressure. In July 1714 the South Holland Synod heard that the 'author of Crinkeh Kesmes' was still publicly under the 'censure' of the Zwolle consistory.[168] Not until 1717 was he deemed sufficiently penitent to merit readmission to the Lord's Supper. Yet as the decades passed, and the Enlightenment increasingly took hold, *Krinke Kesmes* gradually came to seem less threatening. Indeed, eventually the novel enjoyed a relatively wide reception in Dutch, German, and Scandinavian lands. A new Dutch edition appeared in 1721, followed by two more at Amsterdam, in 1732, a fourth at Deventer around 1740, and a fifth and sixth in 1755, while a German translation appeared at Leipzig in 1721 and was later reissued at Delitsch in 1748 and again in 1751.[169]

If the penetration of Spinozist ideas into Dutch vernacular culture became more obvious in the 1690s, it was from the first decade of the eighteenth century, according to the German scholar Jakob Friedrich Reimann, in his universal history of atheism of 1725, that the 'venom' of philosophical unbelief in Europe first began to be generated also outside traditional intellectual circles among the common people and in merchants' places of business.[170] A notable example of this new trend, according to Reimann, was Dirk Sandvoort, the son of a merchant who had no academic training but in 1703 published a treatise on motion and solid bodies (Latin translation, 1704), following this up in 1709 with a work on manners and lifestyle which effectively removes the foundations of Christian morality. In the latter, Sandvoort expounds a proto-Mandevillean theory of the social benefits of indulgence in fine clothes, pleasure, and possessions, pointing out that unemployment, homelessness, and penury in the world would greatly increase were people to heed the admonitions of preachers and adopt modesty and austerity as their rules of conduct.[171] His praise of ease, luxury, and encouragement to seek every comfort, and his explicit rejection of Christian 'humility', seemed also to convey undertones of sexual libertinism.

Under the guise of expounding a new philosophy, held Reimann, Sandvoort was really reviving ancient atheistic ideas, in particular Epicurean materialism, and unfortunately finding more than a few readers. While simultaneously in business as an iron dealer, he became a celebrity of the new urban middle-class coffee-shop deism, the popular philosophical discussion circles which in these years arose in Amsterdam, Rotterdam, The Hague, Middelburg, Zwolle, and also Utrecht, where Sandvoort published his books and spent much of his time. He liked to advertise himself as someone 'who was free from all superstition and did not believe anything except what could be mathematically proven to be true'.[172] Like Willem Goeree and Wyermars, Sandvoort exemplifies a new kind of vernacular, non-academic, philosophical materi-

---

[167] ARH OSA Synod of Gelderland, Acta Nijmegen, 14 Aug. 1709, art. 13 and Acta Zutphen, 20 Aug. 1710, art. 8.

[168] ARH OSA 98 South Holland Synod, Acta Gorcum, 3–13 July 1714, art. 13.

[169] Graesse, *Trésor de livres rares*, v, 421; Fausett, 'Introduction', p. xlvi.   [170] Reimann, *Historia*, 491.

[171] [Sandvoort], *Zedig Ondersoek*, 101–11.

[172] Wyermars, *Ingebeelde Chaos*, 2; Vermij, *Secularisering*, 74.

alism which was derived almost entirely from reading philosophical, scientific, and theological works in Dutch, and which found expression chiefly in conversation and group discussion. Sandvoort seems, in fact, to have known no language other than Dutch.[173]

Of course, scope for a non-academic, popular radicalism existed in the Netherlands from as far back as the 1660s, when the writings of Van den Enden, Meyer, Koerbagh, and Johan and Pieter de la Court had appeared. Since 1678, and the appearance of the *Opera Posthuma* in the vernacular, there was also, for the first time, an opportunity for readers without Latin to explore the intricacies of Spinoza's thought. Yet it took time to form a generation of men lacking formal higher education but intellectually and emotionally attuned to renounce traditional attitudes and values, and remodel their personal culture exclusively on the basis of philosophical rather than theological concepts. This new outlook presumably first took shape among popular debaters, who did little more than repeat what they found in philosophical books rather than making significant contributions as writers in their own right. A striking instance of such an intermediary type was Anthony van Dalen—not to be confused with the erudite Anthonie van Dale of Haarlem—who clashed with the Reformed consistory in The Hague in 1681. Denounced and reprimanded as a 'Spinozist' and 'Naturalist', this Van Dalen moved to Amsterdam in 1685, and was later described in 1689 as someone who held private 'collegien' on Sundays at which he strove to inculcate his godless opinions into others.[174]

Constantly seeking debate with local shopkeepers and tradesmen, Van Dalen was a classic philosophical zealot who went about compulsively lauding Spinoza, provoking arguments about Scripture, and dogmatically denying the existence of Satan, demons, and angels, as well as the miracles believed in by almost everyone around him.[175] He claimed that Scripture was tailored to the superstitious notions of the common people of the time and had no other purpose than to keep the ancient Israelites in 'peace, tranquillity, and discipline'. Likewise, he insisted that the world could not be created out of nothing, and on the absurdity of the doctrine of the Trinity.[176] Van Dalen angered the consistories of the Hague and Amsterdam by constantly haranguing people and pointing to passages in Spinoza or Scripture, supporting his arguments. It was quite another matter though to disseminate radical philosophical ideas in published texts, and here Sandvoort apparently did initiate a new trend. His work on manners and morality, published in 1709, provoked vehement protests from the local Reformed consistory, which in turn goaded the Utrecht burgomasters into banning the book and seizing the stocks of copies from the bookshops.[177]

A tragic case of an amateur popular philosopher who paid a terrible price for emulating Sandvoort was that of a lively young rival by the name of Hendrik Wyermars. Born around 1685, Wyermars was a self-taught merchant's clerk, entirely devoid of

---

[173] Ibid., 75. [174] Wielema, 'Onbekende aanhanger', 32.
[175] GA The Hague Acta Kerkeraad iv, p. 178 res. 11 Oct. 1681
[176] Ibid., 179; Wielema, 'Onbekende aanhanger', 34–6.
[177] ARH OSA 97 South Holland Synod, Acta Delft 8–10 July 1710 art. 14.

higher education and Latin.[178] The not unimpressive range of philosophical, scientific, and theological knowledge he mastered, he garnered exclusively from books and periodicals in Dutch. He was an incisive, challenging thinker, and an exclusive product of the early eighteenth-century Dutch intellectual scene. His was an uncompromising 'enlightened' radicalism of a popular variety, rooted entirely in a Neo-Cartesian and Spinozist matrix. Nowhere in his thought, as has been pointed out, is there any trace of the influence of Locke, Newton, or English deism.[179]

Wyermars published just one work, *De Ingebeelde Chaos* (The Imagined Chaos), a book produced in around 450 copies which went on sale in Amsterdam in June 1710. There was clearly a market for such a text: over 300 copies sold in under ten days. But the work also promptly came to the attention of the Amsterdam Reformed consistory, which condemned it on 26 June, as packed with 'all the dreadful and blasphemous views of Spinoza expounded in the clearest and most shameless way'.[180] When questioned, the publisher claimed not to have realized how 'harmful' the book was but readily complied with the consistory's admonition to withdraw it from sale. A consistorial delegation repaired to the burgomasters, armed with files of extracts, 'to complain about so bold and shameless an eruption of atheism in the sternest terms'. The burgomasters duly perused the extracts, consulted the rest of the city government, and eventually three months later, on 1 October 1710, Wyermars and his publisher were arrested and the unsold copies confiscated.[181]

According to Reimann, who Latinizes his name to 'Wirmarsius' and calls his book 'librum pestilentissimum', this young Amsterdammer, while pretending to refute Spinoza, Sandvoort, Leenhof, and Deurhoff, in reality opposes 'Moses and Christ . . . undermining the universal foundations of religion'.[182] His radical system, as Wyermars himself indicates by his references to his reading, was rooted chiefly in Spinoza, but also drew on an impressive canon of other radical sources, especially Lucretius, Hobbes, Bekker, Leenhof, Sandvoort, Deurhoff, and Fontenelle, whose work, by this time, had appeared in Dutch. Among Leenhof's works, Wyermars refers to the banned *Ophelderinge* and presumably also knew the *Hemel op Aarde*. The immediate stimulus to his writing, Wyermars states, was his disagreement with Sandvoort's argumentation in his 1703 treatise on motion and solid bodies.[183] Where Sandvoort held, or professed to hold, that the world had at some point come into existence and would end,[184] Wyermars declares the world eternal. In 1709 he had sent a long text about this to Sandvoort in Utrecht, he explains in his preface, but received no answer, which astounded not only him but also 'all those here with knowledge', meaning the participants in Wyermars' philosophical discussion group in Amsterdam. Only after holding on to the text for over six months and repeated reminders did

[178] Vandenbossche, 'Hendrik Wyermars', 321.   [179] Ibid., 322.
[180] GA Amsterdam Acta Kerkeraad xviii, p. 107. res. 26 June 1710.
[181] Ibid., 109. res. 3 July 1710; ARH OSA 216 Synod of Overijssel, Acta Zwolle, 9 June 1711, art. 8; ARH OSA 97, South Holland Synod, Acta Leiden, July 1711, art. 14.
[182] Reimann, *Historia*, 491–2.   [183] Wyermars, *Den Ingebeelde Chaos*, preface, p. i.
[184] [Sandvoort], *Vervolg* (1707), 'Na-reden', 1–2.

Sandvoort finally deign, in December 1709, to contact Wyermars through a mutual friend alluded to mysteriously as 'Monsieur G.R.' But to his intense disappointment, Sandvoort declined to enter into a full-scale debate in Amsterdam with Wyermars.

Wyermars opens his 187-page treatise by asserting the failure of 'Cartesius and his followers' to establish the laws of mechanics, rooted, he maintains, in their failure to grasp the true nature of 'motion' and their inadmissible resort to a supernatural first cause—'that is God'.[185] As in Sandvoort, it is axiomatic in Wyermars' philosophy that no appeal to any supernatural or divine power, or cause outside nature, is permissible. Philosophical explanation for both these popular thinkers must derive exclusively from mathematically proven laws of nature. Descartes, holds Wyermars, reduces motion to a deep and inexplicable 'mystery', appealing to the divinity to explain it, thereby totally obscuring not just the issue of 'motion' but that of the relationship of bodies to each other.[186] He then observes, citing the letter to Tschirnhaus of May 1676, that Spinoza 'who considered Descartes' principles in this area incorrect, was nevertheless unable to bring any of this into proper order'.[187] Spinoza had died before he could lay down the essentials of physics. Wyermars' aim was to go beyond Spinoza in this respect, sweeping away the 'imagined chaos and supposed world-formation of the ancient and modern philosophers . . . and especially the [mistaken] views about the formation of the world of Lucretius and Dirk Sandvoort', and to demonstrate that the universe exists and evolves eternally.[188]

'All specific things happen through the unalterable laws of nature,' asserts Wyermars, echoing Spinoza, and nothing occurs above, beyond, or against the inevitable order of nature.[189] The main element of artifice in his argumentation is his curious pretence that Spinoza, like Deurhoff, had argued against the immutability of the laws of nature.[190] Wyermars' central proposition is that the process of Creation, and the continuance of the universe, are in fact the same thing, so that everything continually evolves according to the same set of laws.[191] It is axiomatic for Wyermars that, in their disagreement about experiments and the nature of scientific knowledge, Spinoza was right and Boyle wrong and, indeed, he expressly reproaches Boyle (who had been published in Dutch) for insisting that things in the visible world were providentially 'created' by God. Since nothing happens except according to the unalterable laws of nature, it follows that the 'Creation' as described in Genesis is a piece of 'imagination' and indeed, he urges, everything in the Bible should be perceived as 'written according to the imagination and notions of the Hebrews'.[192] Only by treating Scripture as 'imaginative' allegory 'will we be able to render Holy Scripture not into transitory and fleeting but into eternal truths'.[193]

The investigation and trial of Wyermars and his publisher by the Amsterdam magistrates lasted a month. At the heart of the case stood the charge that the young

---

[185] Wyermars, *Den Ingebeelde Chaos.*, preface, pp. ii-iii; Vandenbossche, 'Hendrik Wyermars', 334.
[186] Wyermars, *Den Ingebeelde Chaos*, preface, p. x. [187] Ibid., pp. x, 81; Spinoza, *Letters*, 352, 355.
[188] Wyermars, *Den Ingebeelde Chaos*, preface, pp. x–xii; Vandenbossche, 'Hendrik Wyermars', 325.
[189] Wyermars, *Den Ingebeelde Chaos*, pp. xvii, 132–4, 141–2. [190] Ibid., p. xviii. [191] Ibid., 154–9.
[192] Ibid., 120–1; Vermij, *Secularisering*, 72. [193] Ibid., Vandenbossche, 'Hendrik Wyermars', 337–9.

author had restated Spinoza's system in a particularly impudent and 'bold' manner. His unrepentant attitude under interrogation counted further against him. Not only did he profess not to belong to any organized Church but, when charged with denying free will and adhering to a radical determinism, called his accusers hypocrites who, in their hearts, thought the same as himself. This was ill received. Whereas the abjectly contrite publisher got off with a mere two years' banishment (and Wolsgryn received eight years, and Adriaen Koerbagh ten), the Amsterdam magistracy, more alarmed than ever by the advance of Spinozism, sentenced Wyermars to no less than fifteen years' close imprisonment 'without pen, ink or paper' besides his 3,000 guilder fine in accordance with the 1678 edict against Spinozist books.[194] Should he survive—evidently he did—he would in addition be banished from the province for twenty-five years. There was no appeal and, as was subsequently announced to the South Holland Synod, 'Wyermars, the author of the *Ingebeelde Chaos*, has been locked up in the Rasphuis'.[195]

Most copies of Wyermars' book were impounded or handed in, and few of those sold before his arrest seem to have percolated outside Amsterdam. Wyermars himself survived his prison sentence and, while evading his banishment, in Amsterdam, subsequently kept a very low profile, while his 'fanatisch-atheistische' book, as a mid-eighteenth-century German bibliographer observed, was never reprinted and became 'very rare'.[196] Nevertheless, though almost completely forgotten today, this 'martyr' of radical thought did have some impact, not only in Amsterdam and among the Dutch clandestine Spinozist fraternity more generally, but throughout the Early Enlightenment era also in Germany and the Baltic. A few copies of his book found their way to German lands and at least one, in the library of Samuel Triewald, had by 1744 reached Stockholm.[197] More important, accounts of Wyermars and his ideas circulated and became an established feature of the German Enlightenment debate about the onset of philosophical atheism and freethinking, and Wyermars became one of the stock figures among the 'modern *Spinozisten*' deemed to be contaminating German culture.[198]

It was primarily the Lutheran theologian Christoph August Heumann (1681–1764), later a professor at Göttingen, who ensured Wyermars' reputation as a leading 'Spinozist' in Lutheran lands by publishing a 30-page review of his book in the *Acta philosophorum* in 1716, supplying key passages translated into German.[199] Heumann characterizes Wyermars as someone who, under pretence of refuting Spinoza, in fact expounds and clarifies his 'damned' doctrine in popular terms. Thanks chiefly to Heumann, Wyermars was regularly cited in eighteenth-century Germany,

---

[194] GA Amsterdam Acta Kerkeraad xviii, p.120. res. 9 Oct. 1710; Vandenboscche, 'Hendrik Wyermars', 324, 351.

[195] ARH OSA South Holland Synod, Acta Schoonhoven, July 1712, art. 13.

[196] [Jahn], *Verzeichnis*, 2192; for the information regarding Wyermars' subsequent fate, I am indebted to Michiel Wielema.

[197] [Triewald,] *Bibliotheca*, iv, 237.   [198] Schröder, 'Reception', 158, 161.

[199] Vandenbossche, 'Hendrik Wyermars', 325, 352; Schröder,' Reception', 158.

among others by Loescher, Reimann, Walch, Lilienthal, Ludovici, Trinius, Jahn, Brucker, and Baumgarten, and appears in Zedler's *Grosses Universal Lexicon* of 1744 as one of the fourteen core 'Spinozists' constituting the backbone of *Spinozisterey* in early eighteenth-century European thought.[200] But, apart from Baumgarten, few if any of these seem to have actually read Wyermars. Often the sole source of knowledge about his life and his ideas was, in fact, Heumann, supplemented by reports from Holland.[201] The Koenigsberg librarian, Michael Lilienthal, was himself studying in Holland in 1710–11, at the time of Wyermars' arrest and trial, and recalls the rigour with which the book was suppressed. He describes Wyermars as a merchant 'thoroughly acquainted with Spinoza's principles' who, while pretending to combat Spinoza, 'tries to give his hypotheses more form under the pretence of revealing the holy secrets within them'.[202] Siegmund Jakob Baumgarten, who did read the book, merely observes it was a 'scriptum maxime rarum', confirming Heumann's judgement that Wyermars denies the Creation and that his thought is basically Spinozist.[203]

There was a decided feeling in late seventeenth- and early eighteenth-century Germany and the Baltic until around 1720, if not longer, that Holland, the land Buddeus dubbed the 'libertorum Africa' (the Africa [i.e. jungle] of freethinkers),[204] was Europe's prime source of deistic and radical ideas. Equally it was, as we have seen, the view in late seventeenth- and early eighteenth-century France that the Netherlands was the prime fount of irreligious and democratic republican ideas. But to appreciate the full historical significance of this it is essential to note that it was not only, or perhaps even mainly, the texts themselves or translations which exerted this effect, but often German and French reports and summaries of intellectual controversies raging in the Netherlands, including accounts of the relatively numerous ecclesiastical and political investigations and trials in progress in the United Provinces since the 1660s. A major strand of such reportage, were the accounts, written and verbal, of the great public controversies over philosophy, unique at the time in scale and intensity, which erupted in the Dutch Republic in the wake of the furore over Meyer's *Philosophia* in 1666, down to the uproar over the younger Wittichius in 1720. The post-1666 Dutch philosophical controversies were indeed a European phenomenon of the very first importance.

---

[200] Zedler, *Grosses Universal Lexicon*, xxxix, 86.   [201] Vandenbossche, 'Hendrik Wyermars', 325.
[202] Lilienthal, *Theologische Bibliothec*, 268–9.
[203] Baumgarten, *Nachrichten*, v, 388–93; Graesse, *Trésor de livres rares*, vii, 480.
[204] Schröder, 'Reception', 161–2.

PART III | EUROPE AND THE 'NEW' INTELLECTUAL CONTROVERSIES (1680–1720)

18 | BAYLE AND THE 'VIRTUOUS ATHEIST'

The great series of public 'philosophical' controversies in the Netherlands included several, such as the ones over Meyer's *Philosophia* (1666–8) and the furore over Bekker (1691–4), which were short, sharp outbursts, over in a few years. Others, such as the controversy over Bayle's religious convictions and true philosophical intentions, had a more sporadic character and dragged on for decades. All, however, reverberated in significant ways beyond the immediate Dutch cultural world and had major implications for the wider European scene. Indeed, collectively, these controversies, stretching from the 1660s to the 1720s, contributed in a decisive fashion to the conceptualization and formulation of the European Radical Enlightenment as a whole and, scarcely less, to the moderate mainstream counter-offensive.

Assuredly, the most enigmatic and controversial, as well as probably the single most widely read and influential thinker of the Early Enlightenment, was the 'philosopher of Rotterdam'—Pierre Bayle (1647–1706). His pivotal role in the onset of the European Enlightenment has never been doubted. Though banned in France and the rest of Catholic Europe, his works were read everywhere and by everyone who claimed any sort of acquaintance with contemporary European intellectual life. But what precisely was his philosophical and confessional stance, what was the aim of his writing, and how were contemporaries to construe his fascinating and impressive but often profoundly bewildering *oeuvre*?

The son of a Reformed pastor, born in southern France, near the Spanish border, south of Toulouse, Bayle abandoned the faith of his upbringing at the age of 21, much to the distress of his family, in 1669, and, for a time, professed Catholicism.[1] During this period he studied with the Jesuits at Toulouse, imbibing their Aristotelian scholasticism. After a short time he became disillusioned with Catholicism and the Jesuits, however, and since relapse from Catholicism to Protestantism was strictly forbidden in France, fled to Geneva, where he reverted to the Reformed faith and spent the period 1670–4. There he was also converted to Cartesianism and when, after returning to France, he was appointed to a professorship at the Huguenot academy of Sedan, he had to expound Aristotelianism to his students while adhering inwardly to

---

[1] Labrousse, *Pierre Bayle*, ii, 627; Popkin, 'Introduction', p. xi.

Cartesianism and *Malebranchisme* although, after a time, he also grew sceptical about both the latter.

The suppression of the Huguenot academy of Sedan by decree of Louis XIV, in July 1681, led the already renowned 34-year-old scholar to emigrate to the United Provinces, together with the theologian Pierre Jurieu (1637–1713), the other of the two most noted Protestant professors then teaching in France. At this juncture, following an initiative of Adriaen Paets, a leading anti-Orangist regent and champion of religious toleration, the Rotterdam city government invited the two refugee celebrities to their city to teach in the newly founded civic academy, or *Illustre School*. Both were offered permanent professorships and both accepted, Rotterdam becoming Bayle's permanent home and the scene, over more than a quarter of a century, of the rest of his spectacular philosophical career.

His duties at the Rotterdam *Illustre School*, where he taught for twelve years (1681–93), were not especially onerous—three two-hour classes weekly, one in philosophy and two in history, and in addition a few informal classes at home.[2] The students at this not especially flourishing academy were youths preparing for university, older professional men eager to keep up their scholarly skills, and the occasional foreign visitor. Bayle accordingly found himself with ample time to pursue his historical and philosophical researches and develop his ground-breaking ideas. In Holland, moreover, he could research and write in an appreciably freer atmosphere than was then possible in France or elsewhere in continental Europe. He could openly disparage scholastic Aristotelianism and investigate every aspect of Descartes, Malebranche, and the 'New Philosophy'. None the less, he still taught in an educational foundation linked to the Reformed Church and, as at Sedan, had to teach, write, and act in a manner consonant with the demands of Reformed theology and practice. Indeed, throughout his Rotterdam years, Bayle participated in the life of the Reformed community, and always evinced a clear preference for the Reformed in his writings, as against, in particular, the Catholic faith, which he showed every sign of holding in low esteem. During the first five years of his career in Holland, he also remained on fairly close terms with the stringently orthodox Jurieu, whom initially he considered his patron and friend, as he had previously, at Sedan.

Outwardly, then, Bayle remained a loyal member of the French-speaking Reformed Church of the Netherlands, and one who argued—against Le Clerc, Limborch, and Jaquelot, but superficially like Jurieu—that reason cannot buttress faith and that the only plausible way to defend the Church's teaching and doctrines is to adopt a strictly 'fideist' stance.[3] However, there was at the time—as indeed there still is today—a remarkable measure of disagreement and perplexity about how seriously to take Bayle's alleged 'fideism' and what the underlying implications of his arguments and analyses actually were.[4] It is undoubtedly true that he had defenders at the

---

[2] Knetsch, *Pierre Jurieu*, 137–8; Wielema, *Filosofen*, 64.

[3] See Labrousse, *Pierre Bayle*, ii, 595–609; Labrousse, 'Reading Pierre Bayle', 8, 11, 15; Sandberg, *At the Crossroads*, 100, 104, 106; Kilcullen, *Sincerity and Truth*, 59–60, 102.

[4] Popkin, 'Introduction', pp. xxii–xxvi; Whelan, 'Wisdom', 231.

time—just as there are historians today—who upheld, and still uphold, the genuineness of his Christian faith, though even these mostly regard him as an elusive and heterodox believer, possibly holding to only a residual Christian stance.[5] But equally, there were critics then, just as there are historians today, who insisted that his real purpose was to undermine authority, theology, and ecclesiastical power through his peculiarly corrosive form of critical philosophical reason—in other words, that he was (except in his absolutist politics) a crypto-radical thinker and precursor of the anti-religious movement among French *philosophes* of the mid-eighteenth century.[6] Finally, there was also a middle group who defended Bayle against the charge of 'atheism' while admitting his thought was inadvertently dangerous, men such as the early eighteenth-century French Oratorian and *Malebranchiste*, the Abbé Claude-François Houtteville (1688–1742), who, while refusing 'de confondre M. Bayle avec ceux qui nous ont déclaré la guerre' nevertheless thought Bayle had planted many ideas in the minds of contemporaries 'dont il seroit facile d'abuser'.[7]

This triangular disagreement, which began in the early 1680s, in effect continues still today. Admittedly, it is sometimes argued that it was only later, among French readers of the age of Voltaire, that Bayle gained his reputation for freethinking and unbelief, and that those who view him as an *incrédule* fail to appreciate his specifically Calvinist context.[8] But in fact many Protestant as well as Catholic contemporaries considered him a highly suspect and 'atheistic' writer during, as well as immediately after, his own lifetime. In short, he was always a suspect writer.

The principal theme of Bayle's first major work, the *Pensées diverses sur la comète* (1682), is the prevalence throughout history of 'superstition' and 'idolatry' and the need to combat 'superstition' with philosophical reason. Arguably, this is also the central theme of his philosophical *oeuvre* as a whole. The occasion for writing the *Pensées diverses* was the unsettling stir throughout western Europe caused by several comets observed over the winter of 1680–1, a wave of anxiety fed by the ancient and deeply ingrained popular notion that comets are ill omens.[9] But while the question whether comets are supernatural portents was the pretext for writing, it is impossible to read the book without realizing that Bayle continually extrapolates from belief in comets as supernatural signs to build a comprehensive argument about commonly held beliefs and superstition in general. A deeply rooted and almost universally held view may originate, he argues, in a variety of factors, none of which, however, need have much to do with solid evidence and argument. A 'tradition' or 'superstition' can easily prevail, he maintains, in any society even if it has no rational foundation at all, owing

---

[5] Labrousse, *Pierre Bayle*, ii, 599–602; Popkin, 'Introduction', p. xxvi; Lennon, 'Bayle, Locke', 186–8; Wootton, 'Pierre Bayle', 199.

[6] Cantelli, *Teologia e ateismo*, 67–8, 234, 370; Paganini, *Analisi della fede*, 44, 359–60; Whelan, 'Wisdom', 231; Wootton, 'Pierre Bayle', 203–6; McKenna, 'Pierre Bayle at la superstition', 64–5.

[7] Houtteville, *Religion Chrétienne*, i, preface, pp. cxiii–cxiv; Rétat, *Dictionnaire de Bayle*, 182.

[8] Notably Mme Elisabeth Labrousse, see Labrousse, 'Reading Pierre Bayle', 8–11, 15; *Pierre Bayle*, ii, 609; Whelan, 'Wisdom', 231.

[9] Knuttel, *Balthasar Bekker*, 149–50.

to the compelling psychological force of what is commonly believed and because most men like to be relieved of the burdensome responsibility of examining opinions which are widely held: 'et enfin on s'est veu réduit à la necessité de croire ce que tout le monde croyoit, de peur de passer pour un factieux qui veut lui seul en savoir plus que tous les autres et contredire la vénérable antiquité.'[10]

Basic to Bayle's critique of 'superstition' is the proposition that simply because something has long been believed, or because everyone believes it, by no means signifies that there are adequate grounds for believing it to be true. No scholar, he maintains, can claim the truth, legitimacy, or force of a belief simply because it is buttressed 'par la tradition générale, et par le consentement unanime des hommes'.[11] For if this sufficed, one would have to grant that Roman superstition and trust in portents and omens, were 'de veritez incontestables, puis que tout le monde en étoit aussi preveu que des présages de comètes'.[12] As exempla of other 'opinions générales' which are in fact false and where philosophical reason, the only secure criterion, is 'tout à fait contre le sentiment commun', he cites the near universal belief that rain, drought, and exceptional heat or cold are governed by the conjunction of the moon. In reality, insists Bayle, 'à la réserve de quelques esprits philosophes', people do not question, or examine, the truth of what they believe; consequently, 'l'antiquité et la géneralité d'une opinion n'est pas une marque de vérité'.[13]

No philosophical observer reading the work at the time could fail to notice that with this Bayle blew a gap right through the arguments of the leading Catholic 'fideists' of the day, Bossuet and Huet, and completely undermined their endeavours to block the Spinozist and deist challenge. For they held that precisely the unbroken chain of tradition, and the incomparable sway of the Church, constitute incontestable proof of the truth of Christian teaching. Nor, indeed, were the generality of Protestant, any more than Catholic, theologians prepared to agree with Bayle that the 'consentement général des peuples' is not a proof of a providential God or the verity of Christian teaching. In the second part of his book Bayle demonstrates that things which men generally consider false, in reality are, or may be, true, such as that atheists can live virtuously and that a society of atheists could be well-regulated.[14] It is here that he raises the spectre of Spinoza, the 'virtuous atheist', who remained constant to his principles to the last, and all but eulogizes Vanini, maintaining that 'l'athéisme a eu des martyrs' just like revealed religions.[15]

Not surprisingly, the book was published anonymously.[16] Bayle was always aware his views were apt to arouse misgivings and possibly provoke recrimination from among his own community. Since arriving in Rotterdam he had formed links with the publisher Reinier Leers (1654–1714), who had amassed a substantial business publishing in French and smuggling much of his output into France, and henceforth published all Bayle's work. The first edition of the *Pensées diverses*, of 1682, bore the name

---

[10] Bayle, *Pensées diverses*, i, 37.   [11] Ibid., 127.   [12] Ibid., 128.
[13] Ibid., 271.   [14] Ibid., ii, 102–38; Poiret, *De Eruditione solida*, 309; Labrousse, *Pierre Bayle*, ii, 107–12.
[15] Bayle, *Pensées diverses*, ii, 135; [Crousaz], *Examen du Pyrrhonisme*, 666.
[16] Prat, 'Introduction', p. xviii; Wielema, *Filosofen*, 65.

of neither author nor publisher, however, and falsely declares 'Cologne' the place of publication. The same procedure was followed with the second edition of 1683. Moreover, the work is deliberately written as if by a Catholic, though this did nothing to prevent its being, and long remaining, banned in France. In short, as Bayle's biographer, Des Maizeaux, later noted, he 'prit toute sorte de précautions pour n'être pas reconnu auteur de cet ouvrage'.[17]

His protective screen was quickly penetrated, after Leers showed the manuscript to Paets, who then revealed its authorship to others. At first, though, despite some unease, especially in Jurieu's mind, there were no major repercussions. For the moment Bayle's position remained secure. Indeed, it was Jurieu who encouraged Bayle to assume the editorship of the *Nouvelles de la République des Lettres* in 1684, expecting to employ his formidable editorial talents to the advantage of the Reformed, and the disadvantage of the Catholic cause. With this aim Bayle was happy to concur. But equally, he used his journal to resume his relentless attack on 'superstition' and 'idolatry'. Indeed, the very first article in the *Nouvelles* was his review of Van Dale's *De Oraculis* in which he largely approves Van Dale's thesis that the ancient oracles had been operated not by demons, or any supernatural beings, but the cunning and impostures of ancient priests deftly exploiting the credulity of the people. He complimented Van Dale on going completely against what had been universally believed. 'L'entreprise,' he wrote, 'est assurément des plus hardies: c'est attaquer presque seul et tout à la fois non seulement les anciens payans qui attribuoient les oracles à leurs faux Dieux; mais aussi les Chrétiens de tous les siècles, qui les ont attribuez aux démons.'[18] Bayle qualifies his support for Van Dale, as he had to do, by saying he does not necessarily share Van Dale's views in full, but at the same time makes clear his principle that 'c'est rendre plus de service que l'on ne pense à la religion, que de refuter les faussetez qui semblent la favoriser.'[19] What Bayle really meant by 'religion', however, remained then, as it remains today, utterly elusive.[20]

If Jurieu was uneasy about the *Pensées diverses*, he was incensed by Bayle's next major work, the *Commentaire philosophique* (1686). Here again, Bayle concealed his authorship, the original edition affecting to have been 'traduit de l'anglais' of a certain 'Jean Fox de Bruggs' and published at 'Cantorbery'.[21] In this work, Bayle propounds a theory of toleration more sweeping even than that of his new patron, Paets. Jurieu was horrified. He too claimed that Louis XIV had behaved tyrannically and unjustifiably towards the Huguenots but held this view because, in the first place, he believed the Reformed Church to be the true church of God and, secondly, because the Huguenots had been conceded specific rights by the French Crown under the Edict of Nantes in 1598. He was not interested in general theories of toleration, leaving the Huguenots in the same position regarding rights and status as everyone else.[22] By contrast, Bayle defends religious toleration in a manner diverging dramatically from that

---

[17] Prat, 'Introduction', p. xv.   [18] [Bayle], *Nouvelles*, i (1684), 2.

[19] Ibid., 3; Mckenna, 'Pierre Bayle et la superstition', 52.

[20] Paganini, *Analisi della fede*, 44; Popkin, 'Introduction', pp. xxv–xxvi.

[21] Bayle, *Commentaire*, 45.   [22] Knetsch, *Pierre Jurieu*, 274–7.

of any previous theorist, postulating a much broader religious toleration than other intellectual spokesmen of his community, indeed one from which no group, however heretical, can be excluded in principle.

According to Bayle, those who adhere to heretical doctrines sincerely, and according to their conscience, are just as much worthy servants of the Lord as those who adhere to true Christian teaching. Insisting (once again) that reason is the only effective tool for determining such matters, he categorically affirms the hegemony of the 'solide raisonnement et . . . pures lumières de la véritable philosophie' in deciding questions of conscience, morality, and toleration. Indeed, Bayle completely divorces morality, and the right to tolerance, which he bases on respect for the conscience and the sense of duty of others, from any justification in, or by, faith.[23] Hence, in theory, even atheists, *indifferenti*, and infidels have to be tolerated. It was not owing to any moral, metaphysical, or theological justification but exclusively owing to his subservient attitude to the secular sovereign that Bayle finally leaves freedom of expression, and of the press, far more limited and vulnerable than do Spinoza and the professed radicals and concedes a mechanism for excluding atheists.[24]

In the opening chapter 'natural reason' is proclaimed the only instrument which can guide us. Indeed, so emphatic is Bayle's assertion of the 'jurisdiction de la lumière naturelle' that one can even read his aside about the Socinians stretching reason too far as subtly sarcastic and insinuating. In any case, no amount of miracles, he insists, and no amount of Biblical admonition, could make us believe things contrary to the basic axioms of our reason such as that the 'whole is larger than its part', or that if from two equal quantities one subtracts equal amounts, the residues must be equal, or make us suppose the essence of a thing can truly survive its destruction.[25] Remarkably, Bayle even asserts—whatever theologians may claim—that their own arguments and conduct prove that they too accept that 'le tribunal suprême et qui juge en dernier ressort et sans appel de tout ce qui nous est proposé, est la raison parlant par les axiomes de la lumière naturelle, ou de la métaphysique'.[26] Hence one can not claim, he says, that 'la théologie est une reine dont la philosophie n'est que la servante' since the theologians themselves confess by their conduct that they consider ' la philosophie comme la reine et la théologie comme la servante'.[27] This is why, he says, theologians always take such pains 'pour éviter qu'on ne les accuse d'être contraires à la bonne philosophie'.[28]

The personal break between Jurieu and Bayle, the first aligning with the Orangist faction in Dutch politics and the latter with Paets and the States party, became irreparable in 1690, after Bayle—this time employing a more elaborate subterfuge to conceal his authorship—published (or colluded with the publication of) the *Avis*

---

[23] Bayle, *Commentaire*, 356–7; Labrousse, *Pierre Bayle*, ii, 555, 581–2; Wielema, *Filosofen*, 66; McKenna, 'L'Éclaircissement', 313.

[24] Labrousse, *Pierre Bayle*, ii, 549–51; Lennon, 'Bayle, Locke', 186–7; Israel 'Spinoza, Locke,' 109.

[25] Bayle, *Commentaire*, 87; McKenna, 'Pierre Bayle et la superstition', 58.

[26] Bayle, *Commentaire*, 88.   [27] Ibid.

[28] Ibid.; McKenna, 'Pierre Bayle et la superstition', 58–9.

important, a key political tract urging the Huguenots of the diaspora not to support William III's invasion of Britain or take up arms against their rightful and legitimate king, Louis XIV, which is precisely what Jurieu was urging them to do.[29] Open strife erupted between Bayle and Jurieu in 1691, when the latter published a fierce reply to the *Avis important* in which Bayle is denounced as an 'impie', a man without religion and a political subversive and traitor. Bayle replied by ridiculing Jurieu's accusations in his *Cabale chimérique*, published in Rotterdam by Leers, moving Jurieu to protest to the Rotterdam burgomasters, demanding that Bayle be punished for libel. Bayle remained relatively secure for the moment, though, the States party regents being then still uppermost in the city. The burgomasters, anxious to calm the quarrel, forbade either party to publish anything further, against the other, without first clearing the text with the town pensionary.[30]

Only after the intervention of the Prince himself, following the Rotterdam riots of 1691, and the purging of seven anti-Orangist regents from the city government in 1692, did the Orangists and Voetians gain the upper hand in the city government, giving Bayle's enemies the opportunity to bring heavier guns to bear.[31] As the controversy escalated, Bayle persisted in affirming his Calvinist orthodoxy and, aided by opposition to Jurieu in the Walloon consistory, retained some support among the Huguenot leadership. Altogether during 1691–2, around twenty pamphlets for and against Bayle and Jurieu appeared, in Amsterdam and Leiden as well as The Hague and Rotterdam. But as the months passed, and the uproar intensified, Bayle's position slowly deteriorated. In November 1692, a joint committee of the Dutch and French consistories was set up 'in order to examine the writings of Mr Beil [i.e. Bayle]'.[32] In fact, the committee focused its attention almost entirely on the *Pensées diverses*, which several of the city's preachers confirmed 'he acknowledges to be his own.'[33] Various passages were read out to the Dutch consistory at its meeting on 28 January 1693 and condemned as 'appalling and intolerable in the Reformed Church'. In March this body passed a resolution to submit extracts documenting fifteen 'highly offensive and dangerous positions' of Professor Bayle to the burgomasters, requesting the city government to act against him as they thought fit.[34]

The consistory's indictment cites in particular Bayle's assertion that 'atheism is not a greater evil than idolatry,' that 'everything being uncertain in nature, the best thing is to keep to the faith of one's parents and profess the religion which is bequeathed to us from them,' that atheism does not necessarily encourage immoral conduct, that a society of atheists could be well regulated, that it is not necessary to acknowledge God to lead an upright life, and his styling Epicurus a 'most glorious promotor of religion'.[35] Also deplored was the extraordinary remark, deemed scandalous by Jurieu,

---

[29] Knetsch, *Pierre Jurieu*, 285–8, 315–16; Israel, *Anglo-Dutch Moment*, 34, 36.

[30] Labrousse, *Pierre Bayle*, ii, 549; Prat, 'Introduction', pp. xxi–xxiii; Knetsch, *Pierre Jurieu*, 317–18.

[31] Knetsch, *Pierre Jurieu*, 316, 322–4; Israel, *Dutch Republic*, 858.

[32] GA Rotterdam Acta des Kerckenraedts vii, p. 403. res. 26 Nov. 1692.

[33] Ibid., p. 408. res. 28 Jan. 1693.   [34] Ibid., p. 413. res. 11 Mar. 1693; Wielema, *Filosofen*, 65–6.

[35] GA Rotterdam Acta des Kerckenraedts vii, pp. 413, 423; Grapius, *Systema*, i, 26–37.

that 'il n'y a jamais eu de malheur moins à croindre que l'athéisme; et par conséquent Dieu n'a point produit de miracles pour l'empêcher.'[36] It was hard to believe that the insinuating ambiguity here was inadvertent. In any case, the outcome of the city government's deliberations was no longer in doubt. On 30 October 1693 the burgomasters stripped Bayle of his professorship with immediate effect, as well as his pension, and withdrew permission for him to give private classes at home.[37]

Contrary to what is often said, Bayle is strictly speaking neither a sceptic nor a 'fideist'. His position is that philosophical reason is the only tool we have to separate truth from falsehood, the only secure criterion, and that, consequently, by its nature religious faith can never be based on reason. The latter position was in the highest degree exasperating not only to true fideists such as Huet and Jurieu on one side, but even more to Le Clerc and an entire generation of rationalist theologians, striving to reconcile faith with reason, on the other: 'voilà donc,' exclaimed Isaac Jaquelot, 'la religion déclarée incompatible avec la raison par arrêt de Mr Bayle,' a judgement repeated so often in his works, he adds, one might almost say it is the chief reason for his writing.[38] But the ultimate paradox in Bayle is not that faith can never be explained or justified by reason, but that what is chiefly opposed to reason in his philosophy, namely 'superstition', is indistinguishable from faith. His principles irreducibly render one man's faith another's 'superstition' with no rational grounds or criteria being provided for differentiating one from the other.[39] Occasionally Bayle concedes that when Scripture asserts something categorically which contradicts an apparently self evident inference from natural reason, then we must follow Scripture and reject the maxim as false, at least as regards practical consequences.[40] The problem was to know whether he intended this seriously or, as so often, is merely teasing his readers. In any case, it was infinitely baffling that a philosopher who makes philosophy queen, and proclaims reason our only tool to know truth, recommends we should act contrary to reason whenever it conflicts with Scripture while offering no reason why we should.

With publication of the *Dictionnaire* in 1697, the question of whether Bayle had effectively combated Spinoza in the article dedicated to him, the longest in the entire work, became integral to the controversy.[41] Jaques Bernard, in particular, publicly complained that the pretended demolition of Spinoza's system was invalid, because Bayle had not properly understood (or deliberately misconstrued?) Spinoza's concept of God and substance. It was frequently claimed, from at least as early as 1700, as Bayle himself expressed it, 'que je n'ai pas entendu les sentimens de Spinoza'.[42] Bayle firmly rejected Bernard's disparaging remarks in the *Nouvelles de la République des Lettres*, in

---

[36] Bayle, *Pensées diverses*, i, 288–9.   [37] Prat, 'Introduction', p. xxv.

[38] Jaquelot, *Conformité de la foi*, 238; Cantelli, *Teologia e ateismo*, 342.

[39] McKenna, 'Pierre Bayle et la superstition', 64–5; Wootton, 'Pierre Bayle', 224–6.

[40] [Jurieu], *Philosophe de Rotterdam*, 54; Law, *Remarks*, 53; Kilcullen, *Sincerity and Truth*, 102–3.

[41] Poiret, *Cogitationum Rationalism*, 14–15; [Crousaz], *Examen du Pyrrhonisme* 81–2, 353–6; Naigeon, *Encyclopédie méthodique*, iii, 573; Cantelli, *Teologia e ateismo*, 232–8; Paganini, *Analisi della fede*, 359–66.

[42] Bayle, *Lettres*, iii, 839, 906–11.

June 1702, but this did little to resolve the nagging conundrum.[43] Was the article 'Spinoza' in the *Dictionnaire* a viable weapon against Spinoza, as Halma believed, or at best a bungled and useless attack, as Bernard maintained; or, as Poiret, Tournemine and many others concluded, was it a deliberate piece of mystification and deception designed to hide his real purpose from most readers? According to the Abbé Pluquet, writing in 1757, all those who had hitherto attempted to refute Spinoza had failed, but Bayle, the sharpest of philosophical critics, had, he says, failed more resoundingly than any adversary of Spinoza, having neither interpreted Spinoza correctly nor fought him effectively: 'le célèbre Bayle lui-même, ce destructeur indefatigable de toute doctrine systématique paroît avoir échoué à l'égard de celui-ci [i.e. Spinoza], et porté ses coups en l'air.'[44]

Whichever answer one gave, no one could deny, in any case, that Bayle places Spinoza not only at the heart of contemporary philosophical debate but at the heart of all ancient, medieval, and modern intellectual debate. After telling us, for example, that Xenophanes asserts 'l'unité de toutes choses', much like Parmenides and Melissus, and that his view of God is an abominable form of 'Spinozisme', he commences his long article on Zeno of Elea by affirming that this disciple of Parmenides, one of the major philosophers of antiquity, held views almost the same as those of Xenophanes and Parmenides concerning the unity, the incomprehensibility, and the immutability of all things, the clear implication being that the philosophy of the Eleatics too is akin to Spinozism.[45] Bayle takes the opportunity presented by what was known of Zeno's opinions to rehearse a mass of objections to the belief that motion exists outside matter and shows that all the proofs that motion is external to matter fail to stand up to reason. He then asserts, giving an excellent illustration of his general method, that he nevertheless shares the universal view that motion resides outside matter.[46] The usefulness of the exercise, he assures readers, lies in its showing the limitations of reason.[47] But if reason is truly our guide, then the reader can only infer that there is no way of maintaining that motion is external to matter rationally and that reason inexorably proves motion is inherent in matter. This is just one of innumerable examples of how Bayle deploys Pyrrhonism as a tactical device to push readers towards a conclusion opposed to the fideist position he pretends to adopt.[48]

The suspicion that Bayle, despite his professions of loyalty to the Reformed Church, was really a secret abetter of Spinozism and philosophical atheism, a patron of the 'deists', as most of Spinoza's disciples liked to call themselves, became so widespread as to become itself a weapon in the war of philosophies.[49] Radicati, for one, did not doubt that Bayle belonged to 'notre partie', that is, those who identify God with Nature, meaning non-providential 'deists', pantheists, and atheists, a club whom he

---

[43] Charles-Daubert and Moreau, *Pierre Bayle. Écrits*, II.   [44] [Pluquet], *Examen*, ii, pp. ii, 95.

[45] Bayle, *Dictionnaire*, iii, 3043; Bayle, *Historical and Critical Dictionary*, 350; Paganini, *Analisi della fede*, 348–53

[46] Bayle, *Historical and Critical Dictionary*, 366–72.   [47] Ibid., 372.

[48] McKenna, 'L'Éclaircissement', 313–16; Anderson, *Treatise*, 141, 159–60.

[49] Crousaz, *Examen du Pyrrhonisme*, 353–5, 710, 954; Cantelli, *Teologia e ateismo*, 56, 343.

lists as Democritus, Epicurus, Diagoras, Lucian, Socrates, Anaxagoras, Seneca, Hobbes, Blount, Spinoza, Vanini, Saint Evremond, Bayle 'et généralement tous ceux qu'on appelle athées speculatifs'.[50] An imagined dialogue between Bayle and Spinoza, published clandestinely at 'Cologne' in 1711, and reissued in 1713, written by an anonymous radical, sought to reinforce the association between the two in the reading public's consciousness by having its fictitious 'Bayle' confide to 'Spinoza' that 'nous convenions tellement dans nos principes qu'on m'accuse de Spinocisme' and that it was for that reason he had felt obliged to take up his pen and ostensibly attack (albeit with feeble arguments) 'votre système'.[51]

In England, it was perhaps especially Collins' praise of 'the acute and penetrating Mr Bayle', and the obvious link between Mandeville and Bayle, which intensified doubts as to the latter's real purpose.[52] The rise of English deism alarmed many and inevitably precipitated a search for the roots of this disturbing tendency which, in turn, brought Bayle increasingly under suspicion. In his *Free Thoughts On Religion*, Mandeville restates Bayle's paradox of the 'virtuous atheist', evidently, many inferred, for the same seditious purpose.[53] One of Mandeville's chief critics, William Law, tutor to Edward Gibbon's father, and an admirer of Whiston though no Newtonian, put a particular stress on the link between Mandeville and Bayle, insisting that the latter had greatly 'increased the numbers of infidels and libertines' and was the 'principal author amongst those, whose parts have been employ'd to arraign and expose virtue and religion as being only the blind effects of complexion, natural temper and custom'.[54] The freethinkers 'adore Mr Bayle's contradictions', insisted Law, and uphold his claim that a 'society of atheists, might be as virtuous men, as a society of other people professing religion' because it helps Mandeville's, and their, subversive idea that man is an entirely 'natural' being, a 'compound of various passions' and their 'ascribing all human actions to complexion, natural temper, etc.'[55]

Given Bayle's remarks on Spinoza's last hours, and the rising doubt about Bayle's own religious beliefs, it is not surprising that there was widespread interest among the Republic of Letters in the circumstances of his own demise. Here again many wished to hear of an exemplary Christian death. Des Maizeaux, his former protégé and his biographer, saw that he needed to investigate the matter with some care. He learnt from Bayle's publisher, in January 1707, that the 'philosopher of Rotterdam' died entirely alone, with no one present, leaving his theological books to Basnage, his other books to the younger Paets, and manuscripts to Leers. Years later, Des Maizeaux heard from David Durand, the Reformed minister closest to Bayle in his last years, and an exceptionally tolerant pastor, indeed a friend who supplied him with many a Latin quotation, that he had written to him 'quelques jours avant sa mort la lettre du monde

[50] Radicati, *Recueil*, 24–5; the English version, translated by Thomas Morgan, adds 'Collins'; see Radicati, *Twelve Discourses*, 11; Jacob, *Radical Enlightenment*, 216.

[51] *Rencontre de Bayle et de Spinosa*, 29; see also Struve, *Biblioteca philosophica*, 204; Dunin Borkowski, *Spinoza*, i, 68–9 and ii, 71.

[52] Collins, *A Philosophical Inquiry*, 27; Hundert, *Enlightenment's Fable*, 29–31.

[53] Mandeville, *Free Thoughts*, 4.   [54] Law, *Remarks*, 54, 99.   [55] Ibid., 2–4, 53, 99, 106.

la plus tendre pour l'obliger à lever tout espèce de scandale, par une confession édifi-ante des vérités chrétiennes, ou du moins des veritez de la religion naturelle'.[56] Unfor-tunately, all he received from Bayle by way of reply was a note replete with witticisms drawn from Horace and Martial without a single word about Christian truth. Basnage also reportedly 'alla voir M. Bayle dans les mêmes vuës', but 'n'y gagna rien'; at the end, evidently, 'le philosophe ne voulut plus voir personne', leaving only a cryptic note devoid of Christian sentiments.[57]

[56] BL Add. MS 4283, fo. 181. Durand to des Maizeaux, London, 13 July 1717.
[57] Ibid.; Popkin, 'Introduction', 26; Labrousse, *Pierre Bayle*, i, 268–70.

19 | THE BREDENBURG DISPUTES

Among the most protracted of the Dutch controversies was the bitter quarrel which erupted around the well-meaning figure of Johannes Bredenburg (1643–91), a dispute which reached such a pitch of intensity that it eventually generated a formal schism in the Dutch Collegiant movement. A fringe Church in numbers, the Collegiants, from their origins in the second quarter of the seventeenth century down to the early eighteenth, were disproportionately prominent in Dutch intellectual debate owing, above all, to the special emphasis they placed on the intellectual and spiritual freedom of the individual.[1] As such they were both a new and highly innovative phenomenon in the wider European, as well as Dutch, context, reflecting in a theological mode the wider psychological and spiritual reaction against the pressures of confessionalization gripping western culture in the late seventeenth century.[2]

The Collegiants might almost be described as an anti-Church, avowedly shedding all traditional accoutrements of ecclesiastical authority and power, as well as traditional notions of doctrinal orthodoxy. Joining the Collegiants, in contrast to other Churches, entailed no particular confessional allegiance or forms of outward observance or discipline, beyond a doctrinally vague, albeit usually fervent, commitment to Christian ideals. No one, whatever their views, was excluded from their midst, provided they accepted their manner of meeting and conducting their services. The Collegiants, observed Locke, 'admit to their communion all Christians and hold it our duty to join in love and charity with those who differ in opinion'.[3] But they also exhibited a strong commitment to debate and study, and were intensely dedicated to the advancement of Christian commitment by these means.

Furthermore, the dialectic of internal debate generated a gradual shift away from the mystical spiritualism and Millenarianism, which predominated among them in the 1640s and 1650s, towards an increasingly rationalist and 'enlightened' attitude, which prevailed later. For several decades these deliberations among the Collegiants, including the early stages of the Bredenburg controversies, took place in an edifying atmosphere of good will admirably free from intolerance and bigotry. Their 'colleges' could rightly claim to surpass any other Christian community known in Europe in their ability to accommodate a wide spectrum of theological and philosophical opinion. Nevertheless, so fraught was the general intellectual atmosphere by the last

---

[1] Lindeboom, *Stiefkinderen*, 345–52; Fix, *Prophecy and Reason*, 3–22.
[2] Israel, *Dutch Republic*, 587–90, 911–14.   [3] Locke, *Passages*, 307.

quarter of the century, and so acute their own internal *crise de conscience*, that finally it proved impossible any longer to sustain their traditional forbearance and unity in diversity. Such was the dissension gripping the movement, in the wake of the New Philosophy, that they increasingly succumbed to bitter internecine strife and finally, in the 1680s, to the open schism which took many years to heal. This deepening spiritual malaise, like that in society more generally, was in essence a quarrel about how to adapt new philosophical and scientific concepts to theology and traditional religious values.[4] For the Collegiants, the climax of the Bredenburg disputes in the 1680s also marked the culmination and resolution of this intensifying encounter with philosophy and the end of their epic debate as to the nature of Christian truth.[5] For the splintering of the movement into warring factions, and the difficulty of repairing the rift, drove them eventually into a deliberate and explicit boycott of philosophy and a halt to the efforts to find intellectual solutions to the issues disrupting their unity. After 1700 the movement effectively abandoned the attempt to reconcile theology with philosophy and science.[6]

The Bredenburg disputes were the climax of a long process reaching back to the 1650s when a fringe of Socinian, rationalist Collegiants, including Jelles and Pieter Balling, became immersed in Cartesianism and formed links with the radical philosophical clique around Van den Enden, Meyer, and Spinoza. So powerful was the impact of Cartesianism among the Collegiants, that the mystical Spiritualism and stress on the 'inner light' championed by figures such as Galenus Abrahamsz (1622–1706) and Serrarius coexisted more and more uneasily with the burgeoning rationalist tendency.[7] While all Collegiants agreed in rejecting the Quakers' radical strain of 'inner-light' inspiration, Cartesian Socinians, such as Jelles and Balling, differed from their traditionalist colleagues in identifying the 'inner light' which guides man and is the source of inner certainty, with a confident, ultimately philosophical, conception of human reason. Pieter Balling's much-discussed pamphlet *The Light on the Candlestick* (*Het Licht op den Kandelaer*) of 1662, seemed to many deftly to bridge the gap between the 'inner light' of the Spiritualists, a mystical emanation from God, and the philosophical reason of the Cartesians, while simultaneously emphasizing the urgent need to resolve this question.[8] According to Balling, at the time one of Spinoza's closest friends, mankind is adrift on a sea of confusion, scepticism, and perplexity and in dire need of rescue. Our hopes of salvation, he asserts, lie in finding the 'light of truth, the true light which enlightens every person who comes into the world',[9] for only this guide provides a 'principle which is certain and infallible and whereby growing and progressing one can ultimately reach a blessed state of salvation'.[10] Nevertheless, unlike the 'inner light' of Serrarius and the Quakers—the

---

[4] Fix, *Prophecy and Reason*, 252–6.   [5] Ibid., 243–6; Kühler, *Het Socinianisme*, 241–2, 246.

[6] Van Slee, *Rijnsburger Collegianten*, 257–66.

[7] Meihuizen, *Galenus Abrahamsz*, 59–60; Fix, *Prophecy and Reason*, 118, 146–61; Van Bunge, *Johannes Bredenburg*, 103–5.

[8] Van der Wall, *Mystieke Chiliast*, 227; Popkin, *Third Force*, 132–3; Nadler, *Spinoza*, 169.

[9] [Balling], *Het Licht*, 4.   [10] Ibid.; Klever, *Mannen rond Spinoza*, 18–21.

guidance of the Holy Spirit—Balling's 'true light', however well clothed in spiritual terms, turns out, on examination, to be essentially the 'clear and distinct knowledge of truth in the intellect of every person by which he is so entirely convinced as to the nature and essence of things that it becomes impossible to doubt it', in other words, the mathematical rationality of the Cartesians.[11]

Already perceptible by 1662, the incipient rift among the Collegiants or Rijnsburg-ers, as they were also known, became more obvious in the wake of the controversy over Meyer's *Philosophia* which, as we have seen, was vehemently denounced by Serrarius. Then, in the early 1670s, a prominent member of the Rotterdam college, Johannes Bredenburg (1643–91), a wine and brandy merchant married to a sister of the Collegiant poet and controversialist Joachim Oudaen, a man of some learning who retired from business during the slump of 1672–3 to dedicate himself fully henceforth to resolving the spiritual dilemmas troubling his community, began urging the radical Cartesian arguments championed earlier by Balling and Jelles with new emphasis and fervour.[12] Bredenburg's earliest pamphlets, profoundly influenced by Episcopius and Grotius, were pleas for a pure toleration among the Collegiants, to serve those outside as a model as perfect, complete, and uncontested as mankind can devise.[13]

He started his project to reconcile philosophy and religion with his *Treatise on the Origin of the Knowledge of God* (*Verhandeling van de oorsprong van de kennisse Gods*) which circulated among his discussion circle by 1673, though it remained unpublished until 1684. Here Bredenburg argues that neither Revelation nor miracles on their own can provide certain knowledge about God, or the truth of Christianity, and that those who rely exclusively on Revelation resemble the atheists, since both fail to perceive the hand of the Creator in Nature's processes.[14] Indeed, those who insist that certainty about God, and what pertains to God, derives exclusively from Scripture, closing their eyes to philosophy and science, 'must always remain in doubt as to the certitude of these things, for the whole of Revelation can not bring one any further than the possibility there is a God who is the author of everything'.[15] Hence, according to Bredenburg, knowledge of truth which is purely theological, and has no philosophi-cal basis, is limited, uncertain, and harmful since it encourages doubt.

Bredenburg had acquainted himself with various thinkers whom he had read mostly in Dutch but also Latin, including Grotius, Hobbes, whom he refutes at length,[16] Spinoza, and Meyer. But at this stage it was unquestionably Descartes who was the prime influence shaping his thought.[17] For Bredenburg then conceived of man as comprising two 'totally distinct' substances, one 'entirely material' and the other

---

[11] 'Het Licht (dan zegggen wy) is een klare en onderscheidene kennisse van waarheit, in het verstand van een ygelijck mensch, door welk hy zodanich overtuigt is, van het zijn, en hoedanich zijn der zaken, dat het voor hem onmogelijk is, daar aan te konnen twijffelen'; [Balling], *Het Licht*, 4.

[12] Kühler, *Het Socinianisme*, 241–2; Wielema, *Filosofen*, 39–40.

[13] Bredenburg, *Praatje over tafel*, 12–20; Van Bunge, *Johannes Bredenburg*, 51–2.

[14] Bredenburg, *Verhandeling*, 8; Fix, *Prophecy and Reason*, 217–18.

[15] Bredenburg, *Verhandeling*, 6; Wielema, *Filosofen*, 43.   [16] Bredenburg, *Verhandeling*, 19–33.

[17] Wielema, *Filosofen*, 42–3; Van Bunge, *Johannes Bredenburg*, 98, 115.

non-material.[18] While it is, and can only be, philosophical reason which proves that God the Creator, and the realm of the non-material, exist, Revelation remains essential because the incorporeal part of man can not, by definition, be subject to the physical laws of Nature, so that it is directly from God that we must receive the rules governing our conduct. If man is subject only to the laws of nature—as, according to him, Hobbes maintains—then it would be perfectly possible to justify adultery, fornication, theft, and other wrongdoing. Only God's commandments, as revealed to us through Scripture and the Christian religion, reveal to us what is right and wrong.

In 1675 appeared his *Enervatio Tractatus Theologico-Politici* against Spinoza, Bredenburg's only treatise in Latin, a language he read but did not write, and into which it was translated for him from his original Dutch.[19] It was one of the shrewdest early refutations of the *Tractatus* and later acquired international standing, on being singled out for special praise by Bayle, in his article on Spinoza in the *Dictionnaire*,[20] though Poiret suspected Bayle's lauding of Bredenburg was just a convoluted strategem to draw attention to the latter's subsequent defection to Spinozism, implying that he, Bayle, and Bredenburg were the two most perceptive critics of Spinoza when, in reality, neither wrote against him sincerely but were duping the public with the aim of propagating Spinozism.[21] Yet, despite Bredenburg's uncompromising rationalism, and ready acceptance, as a Socinian, of Spinoza's view of Christ as an exceptionally inspired person but not divine, he expressed genuine antipathy to Spinoza's identification of God with Nature, determinism, and rejection of miracles, and resisted all suggestion that Scripture is not a source of truth though, at bottom, the *Enervatio* is indeed less a refutation than a statement of an agonizing predicament.[22]

A key feature of Bredenburg's *Enervatio* is his insistence that the *Tractatus'* disturbing arguments and conclusions stem from an undeclared, hidden philosophy. In 1675 Spinoza's *Ethics* was still unpublished and those works, including the *Tractatus*, which had appeared provided only hints about the core of his system. Those who had some inkling of the overall schema of his philosophy, including Bredenburg, could have derived it, at this juncture, only from reading manuscript versions of the *Ethics* or else the earlier *Korte Verhandeling*, which is probably the source Bredenburg had been able to examine, the text presumably having been made available to him by Jelles or another Collegiant acquaintance.[23] In any case, Bredenburg's knowledge of Spinoza's system clearly demonstrates how the Collegiant colleges served Spinoza and his friends as a useful and accessible forum for disseminating ideas which could not yet be propagated in print. Bredenburg was the first commentator to emphasize that 'Deus sive Natura', the identification of God with Nature, forms the basis of Spinoza's

---

[18] Bredenburg, *Verhandeling*, 32–7.   [19] Meinsma, *Spinoza*, 275.

[20] Charles-Daubert and Moreau, *Pierre Bayle. Écrits*, 23; see also Moréri, *Grand Dictionnaire* ix, 542.

[21] Poiret, *Cogitationes rationales*, 14–15; Kaplan, *From Christianity*, 263–4.

[22] Buddeus, *Theses Theologicae*, 125; Van Bunge, *Johannes Bredenburg*, 137–8; Van Bunge, 'Les origines', 53–5; Wielema, *Filosofen*, 44; Scribano, 'Johannes Bredenburg', 67, 73.

[23] Van Bunge, 'Early Dutch Reception', 229, 234; Van Bunge, 'Johannes Bredenburg and the *Korte Verhandeling*', 322–6.

metaphysics, though earlier critics had hinted at this. The reason the *Tractatus* denies Providence, 'the power of God to act over and beyond the laws of nature', observes Bredenburg, lies in the author's 'identifying Nature with God himself'.[24] Similarly, Bredenburg was the first to explain Spinoza's distinction between *natura naturans* and *natura naturata* in a published work.[25] The doctrine is nowhere explicitly referred to in the *Tractatus*. Bredenburg knows about it from the unpublished material to which he has had access and uses his knowledge to show the *Tractatus* is not based on Biblical exegesis, as its author claims, but on a concealed and 'atheistic' philosophical agenda.

In his *Enervatio*, Bredenburg undertakes the thorny task of attacking a philosophy which he believes underpins the *Tractatus* but which is nowhere disclosed in the text. He feels driven to do so precisely by his awareness of what Spinoza intends and the implications of such an endeavour to 'overturn all religion'. Bredenburg indignantly rejects Spinoza's argument that 'Scripture has no other purpose than to teach and promote obedience,' remarking that if that were so then 'revealed theology is not of the realm of truth' and philosophy would be the only source of fundamental knowledge.[26] But to overpower Spinoza's hidden metaphysics, and uphold Scripture as a source of truth, while simultaneously maintaining his view that only rational proofs drawn from philosophy can verify and justify Revelation, as well as belief in miracles and Providence, Bredenburg has no other recourse than to fall back on Descartes, reaffirming his doctrine of two substances and hence the differentiation of everything into two segregated and differently constituted spheres.[27]

Bredenburg had set himself the problem of reconciling theology with philosophy, beginning with the premise that philosophy must establish the starting-point. However fervent one's Christian faith, he believed 'love of the truth does not permit that love of religion should be based solely on prejudgements.'[28] This meant, if he was to achieve his goal, that he had to demonstrate more conclusively than in his *Enervatio* that Spinoza's system does not, and that Descartes' does, withstand rigorous analytical scrutiny. Thus he began, well before publication of the *Opera Posthuma* in 1678, to examine minutely every step in Spinoza's reasoning, seeking the weak link in the chain which he was convinced must be there. Having stressed in his *Enervatio* the catastrophic consequences of Spinoza's doctrine that all things happen necessarily for religion and morality, he felt it incumbent upon him, for the sake of his community and all humanity, to succeed in this task. Yet, as he worked, throwing himself into this quest with all the passion of his being, he was simply unable to find the vital *non sequitur*. Turning for help to his Collegiant friends and fellow devotees of philosophy, he penned a third treatise 'in geometrical form', setting out the steps of the deterministic argument he needed to demolish. This work, the *Mathematical Demonstration that all Intelligible Occurrence is Necessary (Wiskunstige Demonstratie dat alle verstandelijke*

---

[24] Bredenburg, *Enervatio*, 63–6; Wielema, *Filosofen*, 44.

[25] Van Bunge, 'Johannes Bredenburg and the *Korte Verhandeling*', 324.

[26] Bredenburg, *Enervatio*. 10–11; Scribano, 'Johannes Bredenburg', 68.

[27] Kolakowski, *Chrétiens sans église*, 255–6.   [28] Ibid., 250.

werking noodzaakelijk is) was composed shortly before Spinoza's death, in 1675 or 1676.[29] It sets out a sequence of impeccably consequent propositions yielding the conclusion that 'actions, effects and consequences of a necessary being are, or become, what they are, through an eternal necessity,'[30] the very proposition he sought to overturn. Expounding the proofs, as Bayle expressed it in his article 'Spinoza' in the *Dictionnaire*, showing 'qu'il n'y a point d'autre cause de toutes choses qu'une Nature qui existe nécessairement, et qui agit par une nécessité immuable, inevitable et irrevocable', Bredenburg unwaveringly fought to break the chain. But in vain: 'il tâcha d'en trouver le foible et ne put jamais inventer aucun moien de la détruire, ni même de l'affoiblir.'[31]

By the time he wrote his *Wiskunstige Demonstratie*, Bredenburg had become deeply embroiled in dispute with fellow Collegiants at Rotterdam, who liked neither his concern with philosophy in general, nor his obsession with Spinoza in particular. His chief adversary was Frans Kuyper (1629–91), a former Remonstrant preacher dismissed from that Church for Socinian tendencies in 1653, who approved the use of natural reason in theology but only in the traditional Socinian manner.[32] Like Bredenburg, he accepted neither the divinity of Christ, nor the Trinity, claiming that no genuine Christianity can be based on incomprehensible 'mysteries' upheld by a self-perpetuating priesthood. The sacrament of baptism he deemed nonsensical. Where he parted company with Bredenburg was over whether establishing an authentic Christianity based on reason means that justification for religious faith must finally rest on philosophical foundations.[33] On leaving the Remonstrants, Kuyper had migrated to Amsterdam, where he became the chief publisher of anti-Trinitarian literature and principal editor of the internationally notorious *Bibliotheca Fratrum Polonorum*. Obliged by the magistracy to leave Amsterdam in or around 1669, Kuyper returned to Rotterdam and quickly emerged as a leading figure in Collegiant activity there.

Following a series of encounters with Bredenburg, Kuyper published an entertaining dialogue in three parts entitled *The Philosophizing Boer* (*Den Philosopherenden Boer*), which he had written together with his then ally Barend Joosten Stol (1631–1713), a Schiedam watchmaker who, however, later defected and joined Bredenburg and his supporters. Cast as a discussion between a philosopher (Bredenburg) who in the first two parts is a Cartesian but finally becomes a Spinozist, a misguided Quaker who insists we find God within us by opening ourselves to the 'inner light', and a Socinian farmer who is a paragon of good sense (representing, of course, Kuyper), the text scathingly ridicules the two groups, philosophers and Quakers, Kuyper most despised.[34] While the sensible farmer bases his understanding of God and religion purely on the Bible, insisting that a month reading Scripture provides an infinitely better knowledge of the divinity—as also of angels and demons, in which Kuyper was a

---

[29] Scribano, 'Johannes Bredenburg'. 66.   [30] Bredenburg, *Wiskunstige Demonstratie*, 8.

[31] Charles-Daubert and Moreau, *Pierre Bayle. Écrits*, 57–8; Scribano, 'Johannes Bredenburg', 75.

[32] Kühler, *Het Socinianisme*, 247; Van Slee, *Rijnsburger Collegianten*, 191, 239, 306.

[33] Kühler, *Het Socinianisme*, 246–8; Petry, 'Kuyper's Analysis', 2; Fix, *Prophecy and Reason*, 135, 149, 178.

[34] Petry, 'Kuyper's Analysis', 3; Van Bunge, *Johannes Bredenburg*, 91.

tenacious believer—than 'if I were to spend all my life and time in the school of the philosophers,'[35] the lofty philosopher maintains that religion is unsustainable without philosophy. 'Yes,' he asserts, 'one can say with all justification that philosophy is the "Interpreter of Holy Scripture", the key without which Scripture would be of little use to us.'[36]

The allusion to Meyer's *Philosophia* was a deliberate smear, insinuating that Bredenburg was a disciple of Meyer and Spinoza, and therefore opposed to religion. Only philosophy, Kuyper's 'philosopher' obdurately insists, teaches us what the Bible means when it speaks of 'God and Heaven, and about angels and demons'; indeed, 'one cannot discover any truths except by means of philosophy.'[37] This, holds Kuyper, is a catastrophic error. For construing Holy Writ in the light of philosophy, as his Socinian farmer points out, leads only to scepticism about spirits, angels, and devils, and much else besides. Finally, the farmer triumphs over the abject philosopher who surrenders on all points, admitting that we should not waste our lives idly cultivating philosophy which can only yield meaningless 'sacks full of wind and nonsense' but rather 'fix the anchor of our hope in Heaven with a firm belief and unshakeable faith'.[38]

Recalling the stages of his long feud with Bredenburg years later, in 1687, Kuyper remarked that it was not until 1676, however ruinous his previous notion that all truth must accord with philosophy, that Bredenburg and his brother, Paulus, 'began to sink into atheism' and, in effect, became 'disciples and comrades of Spinoza'.[39] Bredenburg's 'atheism', held Kuyper, stemmed from his acceptance of Spinoza's principle that God is identical with the unalterable laws of nature which inevitably compelled the two brothers, whether they would admit it or not, to deny Revelation, Providence, miracles, Creation, angels, and demons. The vast distance separating Kuyper's Socinian rational theology from Bredenburg's philosophical Christianity became still more apparent from the preface to Kuyper's long treatise proving the existence of spectres, spirits, and demons, published at Rotterdam in 1678. Kuyper, taking up the cudgels against 'atheists and devil-deniers', grants that his adversaries will not easily be dislodged from their ruinous views since, he says, philosophical atheists are the hardest people on earth to persuade, convinced as they are that 'no one is equipped to judge the truth other than themselves', adding resentfully that 'they are great mockers and jeerers' accustomed to deride stories about spirits and ghosts.[40]

During its early stages the quarrel was kept within respectable bounds by the Collegiant leadership in Rotterdam and in particular the elderly Jan Hartigvelt (1616–78), renowned among Collegiants as a saintly pillar of forbearance and goodwill.[41] After his death in 1678, however, all restraint ceased and the Rotterdam Rijnsburgers lapsed into internecine war. Checked in set-piece disputations, Kuyper, after a certain point, gave up trying to convince the Bredenburgs of the folly of their ideas and concen-

---

[35] Kuyper, *Den Philosopherenden Boer*, i, 17. [36] Ibid., 15. [37] Ibid., 50.
[38] Ibid. [39] Kuyper, *Weerlegging*, 94–5.
[40] Kuyper, *Filosophisch en historiael bewijs*, preface and p. 1.
[41] Van Slee, *Rijnsburger Collegianten*, 241–3.

trated instead on trying to isolate and discredit them, openly denouncing them as 'atheists' and 'Spinozists' and exhorting the Collegiant brethren to condemn and expel them. But, to Kuyper's intense frustration, most of the Rotterdam College preferred to follow Hartigvelt's example and accept the Bredenburgs' assurances that they believed in God the Creator and the Christian faith.[42]

Changing tack, Kuyper next sought to outflank his opponents by convincing the Amsterdam Rijnsburgers and turning them against Rotterdam. In particular, he swayed a leading member of the College on the Rokin, Abraham Lemmerman (d.1694), who was soon scarcely less obsessed with the Bredenburgs and Spinoza than Kuyper himself. At a gathering in Amsterdam early in 1681, Lemmerman denounced Bredenburg for maintaining that 'reason teaches there is no God such as the Holy Bible reveals to us,' insisting that 'therefore he can not believe in the God of Scripture.'[43] Bitter acrimony swept the college but Lemmerman could not secure a majority for excluding the Bredenburgs from the symbolic general communion held each year at the movement's birthplace in Rijnsburg. Though he disliked their philosophical preoccupations, and their involvement with Spinozism, Galenus Abrahamsz refused to join those calling for the Bredenburgs' expulsion, deeming their obviously genuine intellectual perplexity less menacing to Collegiant ideals and forbearance than Lemmerman's and Kuyper's relentless campaign of pressure and denunciation.[44]

Anxious to resolve the impasse, the Rotterdam brethren arranged a special gathering in October 1681, at which both sides were given ample opportunity to air their views and elicit communal reaction. When Lemmerman, Kuyper, Bredenburg, and their respective supporters had had their say, both parties were urged to show Christian charity and humility, set aside their differences, and be reconciled. There was much emotion. Lemmerman withdrew his accusations, publicly tearing up his critique of Bredenburg's *Wiskunstige Demonstratie*,[45] and briefly, or so it seemed, the irenical ideals of the movement had, after all, prevailed. But before many weeks had passed, Kuyper and Lemmerman resumed their anti-Bredenburg campaign with redoubled vehemence. In reply, the Bredenburgs, backed by Stol, appeared before the Amsterdam College on 4 December 1681, and solemnly accused Lemmerman of persistent slander and 'spiritual murder of brethren'. Turning into a form of ecclesiastical trial, the proceedings lasted several days in which both parties presented evidence, speaking at immense length, and in which the Bredenburgs comported themselves with noticeably more humility than their antagonists, Lemmerman being especially prone to intemperate outbursts.[46] Finally, the Amsterdam college voted to strip Lemmerman of the right to speak at their assembly until he withdrew his accusations and publicly apologized to the Bredenburgs for the harm and anxiety he had caused. The Rotterdam Rijnsburgers acted similarly against Kuyper.

[42] Ibid., 243–5; Petry, 'Kuyper's Analysis', 2; Fix, *Prophecy and Reason*, 228.
[43] Van Slee, *Rijnsburger Collegianten*, 243.   [44] Fix, *Prophecy and Reason*, 228.
[45] Van Slee, *Rijnsburger Collegianten*, 245.   [46] Ibid., 246; Van Bunge, *Johannes Bredenburg*, 193.

Repulsed, Kuyper and Lemmerman were, however, by no means ready to give up the struggle. On the contrary, the altercation dragged on and became, more than ever, a conflict about the place of philosophy within the Collegiant movement, and the ultimate relationship of theology and philosophy. The wrangling then entered a new stage in 1684, when Kuyper and Lemmerman, without Bredenburg's permission, proceeded to publish his *Wiskunstige Demonstratie* (which hitherto had circulated only in manuscript), together with his earlier *Verhandeling* and their own animadversions on the two texts.[47] The aim, unmistakably, was publicly to label the Bredenburgs as 'Spinozists'. Kuyper remarks that he had over many years fruitlessly argued with Bredenburg, appealing to the 'impartial reader' to note the 'soul-destroying' consequences of his antagonist's claim that 'one can only demonstrate from Nature that there is a God; and that miracles and Revelation can only serve to confirm and explain what is fully proved true from Nature alone.' He explained that from 'Nature' in Bredenburg's terminology means according to 'natural laws' established 'by philosophy, or reason'.[48] Equally, and no less fatal, held Kuyper, Bredenburg contends 'one cannot deduce from the fact there is a God that God created man.'[49] Plainly, he concluded, according to Bredenburg, God lacks the power to modify or act 'contrary in any way to these natural laws'.

Lemmerman followed up this broadside with a pamphlet arguing that if Bredenburg genuinely held his philosophical tenets, then it was impossible for him to believe 'there is such a God as Holy Scripture teaches.' For whoever asserts 'there is no other lord over nature than natural necessity and believes he has proved as much' cannot believe in the God of the Bible.[50] Lemmerman reminds readers that Bredenburg himself had earlier insisted, in his 'book against Spinoza written in Dutch and printed (at his own request and cost) in Latin', that it is 'totally useless and vain' for someone who accepts the absolute necessity of all things to speak of 'religion or miracles',[51] a contention Lemmerman reinforces with quotations from Meyer's *Philosophia*, Spinoza's letters, and Blyenbergh's recent critique of the *Ethics*.

Publication of Bredenburg's *Wiskunstige Demonstratie* meant that the strife within the Collegiant movement, hitherto confined to their assemblies, had now entered the Dutch and the wider European Republic of Letters. This in some degree put the entire Collegiant movement, as well as the Bredenburgs, on trial before the reading public. Bredenburg reacted to the new situation by seeking expert philosophical advice from scholars outside the ranks of the Collegiants, *savants* of standing who, he hoped, would finally help him break Spinoza's chain of reasoning and vindicate his claims for philosophy.[52] In this way the Collegiant crisis could be overcome. Several seasoned outsiders intervened. But in the event this did little either to solve the Collegiants' dilemmas or quell the commotion.

---

[47] Bayle, *Historical and Critical Dictionary*, 297; Leibniz, *Theodicy*, 350; Wielema, *Filosofen*, 40–1; Van Bunge, *Johannes Bredenburg*, 193.

[48] Kuyper, preface to Bredenburg, *Verhandeling*.   [49] Ibid.

[50] Lemmerman, *Eenige Bewijzen*, 7.   [51] Ibid., 7–8.

[52] Bayle, *Historical and Critical Dictionary*, 296–8; Leibniz, *Theodicy*, 350.

Among those to whom Bredenburg appealed, and who now entered the fray, was the Amsterdam Sephardic scholar of Spanish background, Isaac Orobio de Castro, 'a very able Jewish physician', as Leibniz later noted.[53] However, his intervention, as Leibniz also noted, was of little help to Bredenburg. On the contrary, Orobio published a scathing critique of his quasi-Spinozist treatise that same year, in Latin, under the title *Certamen philosophicum . . . Adversus J. B.*, bracketing Bredenburg with Spinoza no less emphatically than Kuyper and Lemmerman had.[54] Praised by Bayle in his *Dictionnaire*, this text was reissued in 1703, and again in Lenglet Dufresnoy's clandestine compilation, *Réfutation des Erreurs de Benoît de Spinosa* of 1731. Orobio explains that he wrote the book partly at the request of a pious and learned person (Bredenburg) who needed philosophical assistance, but also in response to a recent anonymous work by someone falsely purporting to be a Christian (Cuffeler) who claimed that reason proves the universe could not have been created and that there is no providential God.[55] Much of Orobio's text is devoted to disputing a key step in Bredenburg's 'geometric' reasoning, namely the ancient maxim that 'nothing can come from nothing.' This axiom, held Orobio, had been wrongly construed here, as elsewhere, in a way which opens the door wide to 'atheism'. Greatly prized by atheists, who hold there is no God the Creator, and that the universe neither was nor could not have been created, this seemingly sound principle, he remarks, is basic to Spinoza's system. So much so that, if once disproved, 'Spinoza's entire machine of atheism will be utterly overthrown.'[56] Claiming that Bredenburg's 'geometrical' demonstration of the point, far from being cogently argued, actually reveals crass ignorance, Orobio points out that 'nothing' and 'something' are not comparable or logically opposite categories, but rather concepts unlike and non-equivalent. 'Nothing', he explains, can not be defined in an absolute sense but only as the absence of what is created. In logic, he holds, 'nothing positive can be affirmed about not being' since it is requisite in any positive proposition that there be an equivalence or 'identity' between subject and predicate.

Since nothing can be asserted regarding 'not being', it can not be logically ruled out that something can come from nothing in the sense that what is created did not exist before. 'These new philosophers', avers Orobio disdainfully of Spinoza, Cuffeler, and Bredenburg, proclaim principles and doctrines they do not properly understand, nor do they know how to correct the 'fantasies' they call 'demonstrations'.[57] Nor was this the only weak link, in Orobio's opinion, in Bredenburg's chain of Spinozist reasoning. Bredenburg, he remarks, does not analyse Spinoza's concept of 'substance', or his proposition that it is 'impossible there should be more than one substance'. But it is

[53] Leibniz, *Theodicy*, 350.

[54] Orobio seems to have written it himself in Latin, not Spanish; while Bayle says the book appeared also in Dutch, no vernacular version has been located by modern scholarship; Van Bunge, *Johannes Bredenburg*, 273; Kaplan, *From Christianity*, 269.

[55] Orobio de Castro, *Certamen philosophicum*, 389.

[56] Ibid.; [Cuffeler], *Specimen*, i, 65–6; Heidegger, *Exercitationes*, 304–6.

[57] Orobio de Castro, *Certamen philosophicum*, 389.

essential to do so, he holds, 'since this dogma is firmly rooted in the hearts of Spinozists and is the chief foundation of their errors', and especially Spinoza's blasphemous doctrine that God and the totality of being are one.[58] In demolishing Spinoza's doctrine of 'one substance', Orobio says he will invoke no past authorities since 'Spinozists disdain all authority both divine and human,' but rely instead on the irresistible power of logic. His categories Orobio largely derives from his scholastic training in Spain.

A second formidable intervention from outside was that of Noel Aubert de Versé (1645–1714), a deft philosophical theologian who after wavering in his Catholic faith as a student in Paris contrived to defect twice (after a hesitant return) from Catholicism to Calvinism before fleeing France and eventually exchanging Calvinism for Socinianism.[59] In 1679, after a period in England, he migrated to Amsterdam, where he stayed until 1687. An ardent champion of religious toleration much taken with Episcopius, spiritually Aubert evinced considerable sympathy for the Collegiants. Unlike Kuyper and Lemmerman, Aubert had no difficulty at all with the notion that religious faith needs to be justified philosophically. He worried desperately, though, or so he professed, that Bredenburg had cleared a path which leads straight to Spinzosim. In 1684 he produced three writings linked to the Bredenburg imbroglio, two vigorously anti-Bredenburg pamphlets written in Latin and published in a bilingual Latin–Dutch format under the curious pseudonym 'Latinus Serbaltus Sartensis'[60] (which Bayle later disclosed to be Aubert)[61] and a longer work in French entitled *L'Impie convaincu, ou Dissertation contre Spinosa.*

Aubert de Versé classes the Brothers Bredenburg as unapologetic Spinozists who arrived at Spinozism through Cartesianism. He urges, not unlike Poiret some years later, that Cartesianism was the real source of the philosophical contagion now everywhere sapping faith and morality. The Bredenburg disputes, he held, were an occurrence of momentous significance for mankind; and yet the true significance of the furore was being generally missed. In particular, he argues, the broader implications of Spinoza's philosophy were not being fully grasped. Dedicating his *L'Impie convaincu* to the Comte d'Avaux, the then French ambassador in the Netherlands, Aubert proclaims Spinoza 'le plus impie et le plus fameux mais au même temps le plus subtil Athée qu l'enfer ait jamais vomi sur la terre'.[62] But while many discerning minds had fought his blasphemies, they had uniformly failed, the reason being that there can be no true rebuttal of Spinoza without first setting his thought in its proper context, which necessarily involves acknowledging the catastrophic consequences of Cartesianism. Furthermore, negating the 'principes du Cartésianisme qui sont les fondemens du Spinosisme' needs to be accomplished swiftly and as a matter of great

---

[58] Orobio de Castro, 432–3; [Cuffeler], *Specimen*, i, 14–15.   [59] Morman, *Noel Aubert de Versé*, 1–9.

[60] The Latin titles are *Observationes quibus ostenditur J. B. Esse Spinosistam, acque ade Atheus* (n.p., 1684) and *Philosophi Christiani, Vindiciae repititae, pro Divina et Humana Libertate. Contra Bredenburgios fratres* (Amsterdam, 1684): I've not been able to locate either of these; Van Bunge, *Johannes Bredenburg*, 200–1.

[61] Charles-Daubert and Moreau, *Pierre Bayle. Écrits*, 58.

[62] [Aubert de Versé], *L'Impie convaincu*, preface.

urgency for in the Netherlands latterly, claims Aubert, atheism 'y faisoit de furieux ravages par le moyen de Spinosa'. Thus, it was now imperative to 'rebattre la vanité des disciples de cet imposteur' and not least Bredenburg and his allies.[63]

Aubert's originality lies in his being the first European writer, certainly in French, to argue systematically that the foundations of Spinoza's system lay in the 'principales hypothèses du Cartésianisme', and that, consequently, extirpating Spinozism depends on first severing its Cartesian roots.[64] While the 'grande subtilité de ce juif apostat' is not to be denied, the real problem, he proposes, is Descartes' conception of substance, including space, as 'extension' combined with his notion of God as an universal abstract which lacks body but, at the same time, is 'absolument infini'.[65] Here is a tangle of contradiction bound to generate intellectual catastrophe. The misguided Malebranche, for example, by following Descartes here, had landed himself in a philosophical quagmire 'qui n'est éloigné que de deux doigts de celui de l'impie Spinosa'.[66] Yet, at the same time, Aubert has no wish to revert to the scholasticism of the schools. The only way truly to annihilate 'Messieurs les Athées, Cartésiens et Spinosistes', he assures readers, is to advance a new philosophy which safeguards Christian truth within a convincingly rational framework and this, he contends, involves adopting the atomist theory of Gassendi and Boyle. Aubert replaces Descartes' duality of substance with two (again completely distinct) substances which together comprise the totality of what is but, instead of separating 'body' from 'spirit (mind)', separates matter—consisting, in Aubert, of countless indivisible atoms lacking form, force, or life—from the life-giving force, that is, our Creator who, unlike matter, is eternal, intelligent, and providential, albeit not infinite or omnipotent. The life-force, or God, is thus a being with 'extension' but not body, definable as matter or spirit.[67]

It follows from Aubert's system, unlike Kuyper's, that there are no spirits apart from the Creator and hence no Satan, angels, demons, spectres, or ghosts. Evil, he suggests, can be readily accounted for by the limitations of matter, an inherently imperfect and perishable substance.[68] God, according to Aubert, can only shape matter and impart life in the best possible form. Moreover, acknowledging Him to be 'une véritable étendue, mais non pas infinie' is the only way to resolve the problem of substance satisfactorily; for to make Him infinite and omnipotent is assuredly to 'tomber dans le Spinosisme, c'est prendre pour Dieu toute la matière, et l'univers, dont l'étendue corporelle sera le corps de ce Dieu, et la force qui le meut et l'agit sera l'âme et l'esprit.'[69]

Yet there was much in Aubert which seemed, and was, paradoxical and ambivalent, not to say highly heretical. Clearly, there was room in his system neither for separation

---

[63] Ibid.

[64] Vernière, *Spinoza*, 87–8; Charles-Daubert and Moreau, *Pierre Bayle. Écrits*, 174; Hubert, 'Premières réfutations', 20–1; Sauvy, *Livres saisis*, 172.

[65] [Aubert de Versé], *L'Impie convaincu*, 142–3, 152–6.

[66] Ibid., 143; Hubert, 'Premières réfutations', 18, 64–6.

[67] [Aubert de Versé], *L'Impie convaincu*, 190–7; Morman, *Noel Aubert de Versé*, 107–9; Van Bunge, *Johannes Bredenburg*, 202–3; Hubert, 'Premières réfutations', 8–9, 64.

[68] Morman, *Aubert de Versé*, 109.   [69] [Aubert de Versé], *L'Impie convaincu*, 45.

of body and soul in man, nor immortality of the soul. Nor is there any Creation in time, or creation *ex nihilo*.[70] Moreover, God, as the life-giving force, must be inherent in nature and in all living things. Indeed, it was pertinent to ask whether Aubert de Versé was really the uncompromising anti-Spinozist he purported to be. Despite the book's title, Aubert has comparatively little to say specifically against Spinoza.[71] Despite his disparagement of Malebranche, one might legitimately wonder whether his own stance is much more than 'deux doigts' away from Spinoza's distinction between *natura naturans* and *natura naturata*. Indeed Aubert's philosophy could easily be put to work to serve the radical cause and was later employed, in the third quarter of the eighteenth century, by the Baron d'Holbach as an adroit demonstration that discussion of substance leaves only two alternatives: either God is Nature, as Spinoza maintains, or else the motive force of Nature, as Aubert asserts.[72] But are these really very different?

Publications concerning the Bredenburg disputes in Latin and French instantly broadened the scope of the controversy. Bayle briefly reviewed Aubert's *L'Impie convaincu*, remarking that 'la moindre partie du livre est celle qui combat l'hypothèse de Spinosa' in October of that year.[73] Locke, now or later, acquired a copy, doubtless hearing about Bredenburg, as he had of Orobio de Castro, from Limborch and Le Clerc.[74] For his part, Limborch was soon to be a principal participant in the drama. Meanwhile, for the Collegiant brethren the climax of the uproar came in 1685. Relations between the warring factions within the Amsterdam College, irreparably soured by personality clashes as well as the philosophical impasse, deteriorated so far, and the hall hired for their weekly gatherings witnessed scenes of such unruliness, that both parties were expelled from their normal place of worship. Subsequently, they refused any longer to have any dealings with each other.[75] The two factions, Bredenburgers and anti-Bredenburgers, henceforth met separately in different parts of the city, thereby institutionalizing and perpetuating as well as publicizing the schism, which soon extended to Rotterdam and other towns. From 1686 the rival wings of the movement even celebrated their annual reunion and communion at Rijnsburg separately.

Bredenburg's *Wiskunstige demonstratie* holds that all consequences and effects in nature are eternally necessary.[76] Kuyper, Lemmerman, Orobio de Castro, Aubert de Versé, and countless others considered this Spinozistic and redolent of a rigid fatalism incompatible with Revelation and Providence.[77] Deeply shaken by the publication of

[70] Charles-Daubert and Moreau, *Pierre Bayle. Écrits*, 174.

[71] Moréri, *Grand Dictionnaire*, x, 554; Vernière, *Spinoza*, 87.

[72] [D'Holbach], *Système de la nature*, 172.   [73] [Bayle], *Nouvelles*, ii, 313–15; Vernière, *Spinoza*, 86–7.

[74] Harrison and Laslett, *The Library of John Locke*, items 259, 3076; Kaplan, *From Christianity*, 277; Marshall, *John Locke*, 343.

[75] Van Slee, *Rijnsburger Collegianten*, 166–9; Melles, *Joachim Oudaen*, 110–11, 250–1; Fix, *Prophecy and Reason*, 230–5.

[76] Bredenburg, *Wiskunstige Demonstratie*, 6–8.

[77] [Pluquet], *Examen*, ii, 283–4; Kühler, *Het Socinianisme*, 247; Fix, *Prophecy and Reason*, 229; Van Bunge, *Johannes Bredenburg*, 181–2.

a tract composed for private consultation, in order to be shown how to negate the logic of his own demonstration, Bredenburg rushed into print with his *Necessary Reply* (*Noodige Verantwoording*), a hastily written piece which did little to improve his reputation. An emotional outburst, it lambasts Lemmerman for his alleged calumnies and villany, insisting that the charges of 'atheism' were unjustified and malicious.[78] Bredenburg protested, as Leibniz later noted, 'that he was convinced of free will and of religion'.[79] And no doubt he was; but he faced the awesome difficulty of squaring these assurances with his philosophical position. It was to extricate himself from his harsh predicament that Bredenburg here introduced what was possibly his principal contribution to the philosophical debates of the age—his conception of 'double truth', according to which reason and Revelation govern two entirely separate spheres of knowledge and truth. Perceptibly shifting his ground, he now called the propositions expounded in the *Wiskunstige Demonstratie* experimental and provisional and, moreover, only partial truths, albeit complete verities in philosophy. Whenever and wherever philosophy contradicts Revelation, he maintained, Revelation must always have primacy, constituting as it does a higher order of truth.[80] One must simply accept that if philosophy proves the world follows the eternal, necessary, and immutable laws of nature, Revelation confirms that divine Providence and miracles are possible and truly rule the world.[81]

To counter Bredenburg's new position, and capture more of the middle ground, Kuyper likewise modified his former stance, conceding more to reason. Having earlier claimed miracles to be above and beyond reason, he now held that there is no inherent contradiction between reason and belief in miracles, despite Spinoza's and the Bredenburgs' efforts to prove otherwise.[82] Following Orobio, he held that belief in Creation by a providential God does not clash with philosophical reason. If there has eternally existed some simple, unformed matter from which God then made His creatures, then that is unquestionably 'Creation' even if not, in a strict philosophical sense, producing something from nothing. Bredenburg claims that the New Testament miracle in which Christ provides food for several thousands from a few loaves and two or three fishes, leaving more bread and fish at the end than were there at the beginning, contradicts reason. But even granting the questionable assumption that reason teaches 'nothing can come from nothing,' Kuyper demanded how Bredenburg could know that God, or His angels, had not, while Christ dispensed bread and fish, invisibly supplied more bread and fish to the scene of the miracle?

After the sensational split in the Collegiant movement at Amsterdam and Rotterdam came the intellectual high point of the affair, the clash during 1685–6 between Bredenburg and Limborch, known to the erudite as the *Disputatio Limburgico-*

---

[78] Bredenburg, *Noodige Verantwoording*, 8–11, 31; Van Bunge, *Johannes Bredenburg*, 195–8.

[79] Leibniz, *Theodicy*, 350.

[80] Bredenburg, *Noodige Verantwoording*, 10; Van Bunge, *Johannes Bredenburg*, 197; Fix, *Prophecy and Reason*, 232.

[81] Kolakowski, *Chrétiens sans église*, 258–60, 272; Wielema, *Filosofen*, 46–7.

[82] Kuyper, *Bewys*, 3; Van Bunge, *Johannes Bredenburg*, 207–8.

Bredenburgica.[83] To Limborch, Le Clerc, Locke, and their allies, any such teaching as Bredenburg's new doctrine of 'double truth', and the radical disjunction of reason and Revelation it entails, was anathema. Indeed, for Limborch nothing could be clearer than the reasonableness of faith and the impossibility of contradiction between the truths of philosophy and Revelation.[84] The encounter comprised an exchange of letters, first privately and then in print. Bredenburg maintained that if the truths revealed by reason are in fact absolute truths, one has no choice but to surrender to Spinoza and embrace his doctrine that 'reason and philosophy are the sole realm of truth' and that 'everything happens necessarily, that no miracles or revelations can occur.'[85] Anyone who upholds Revelation and religious truth, he claimed, believing miracles have happened and that God is the lord, a prince in his actions, can not extend the scope of reason to encompass all the actions of God or contrive to harmonize these, in their esssence, with reason and the laws of nature.[86] But if one insists, as you do, he assures Limborch, that the 'truths of Nature, reason and rational categories must always accord with all real phenomena, then religion is annihilated; for then there can be no miracles, everything happens necessarily and Nature is not created.'[87] Logical consistency is only possible, affirms Bredenburg who still claimed that no one could dissolve the chain of reasoning in his *Wiskunstige Demonstratie,*[88] 'if one either binds oneself to faith alone, separate from reason, accepting truth as revealed by God or else adheres to reason and the laws of Nature, rejecting all religion, as Spinoza did.'[89] Hence, any thinker who seeks to defend religion, and confirm its doctrines, by bringing reason and faith into harmony is obliged to base his case on contradictions and 'speak confusedly'.

Limborch indignantly rebuffed Bredenburg's summons to cease his endeavours to reconcile philosophy and theology, and establish truth on 'two legs, namely reason and faith.'[90] The Remonstrant professor not only considered Bredenburg's doctrine of 'double-truth' nonsense, he declared it an 'abomination' which will produce only droves of atheists and godless men claiming 'reason teaches there is no God nor any religion.'[91] For those who assert there is no God can then justly claim that their belief 'accords with reason and that they believe rightly.'[92] Furthermore, such a doctrine would make it impossible to punish atheists who deny miracles or, as Locke was to do later, deny them 'to have any right to toleration at all,'[93] since they then believe as

---

[83] Colie, *Light and Enlightenment,* 101; Kolakowski, *Chrétiens sans Église,* 271–3; Van Bunge, *Johannes Bredenburg,* 209–15; Fix, *Prophecy and Reason,* 236–9.

[84] Bredenburg and Van Limborch, *Schryftelycke Onderhandeling,* 62.

[85] Ibid., 63; see also Bredenburg, *Noodige Verantwoording,* 10–12; Scribano, 'Johannes Bredenburg', 75–6.

[86] Bredenburg and Van Limborch, *Schryftelycke Onderhandeling,* 63.

[87] Ibid.   [88] Van Bunge, *Johannes Bredenburg,* 211–12.

[89] Bredenburg and Van Limborch, *Schryftelycke Onderhandeling,* 63; Kolakowski, *Chrétiens sans église,* 272; Wielema, *Filosofen,* 49.

[90] Bredenburg and Limborch, *Schriftelycke Onderhandeling,* 63; Kolakowski, *Chrétiens sans église,* 273; Fix, *Prophecy and Reason,* 237–9.

[91] Bredenburg and Limborch, *Schriftelycke Onderhandeling,* 28.

[92] Ibid., 24.   [93] Locke, *A Third Letter for Toleration,* 236.

reason directs. 'What a wide door,' he admonishes, 'is thereby opened to atheism!'[94] Limborch became increasingly exasperated by Bredenburg's obduracy in sticking to his 'double-truth' theory. Furthermore, in his opinion the *Wiskunstige Demonstratie* was a deplorable text, a statement of pure Spinozism, which Bredenburg, instead of defending, ought categorically to repudiate.[95] Finally, losing patience altogether, Limborch broke off the correspondence, advising Bredenburg, through an intermediary, that he judged his arguments so feeble and conclusions so irrational that he saw no point in continuing.[96]

Undeterred, if shocked at being thus treated by a nephew of his hero Episcopius, Bredenburg published his exchange of letters with Limborch under the title *Korte Aanmerkingen*, vigorously restating his doctrine of separate truths.[97] But he signally failed to deal with Limborch's principal objection, that, consciously or unconsciously, such a stance ineluctably concedes final victory to Spinoza, in which, assuredly, he was right. A noted modern Polish philosopher, Leszek Kolakowski, aptly describes Bredenburg's final position as the capitulation of religion to reason masquerading as the capitulation of reason to religion.[98] Bredenburg chose for his faith. But by segregating the truths of Revelation and philosophy into two totally separate and contradictory realms, he not only powerfully contributed to the growing secularization of philosophy and science so characteristic of the Enlightenment but effectively surrendered to Spinoza's cardinal principle, and that of the whole Radical Enlightenment, that only philosophy yields intelligible truths.

Kuyper's last throw was his attempt to broaden his quarrel with Bredenburg into a general offensive against Spinozism, as a way of undermining the pro-Bredenburg brethren at both Rotterdam and Amsterdam.[99] Contacting Henry More, in Cambridge, whose general position and two refutations of Spinoza he admired—despite the fact that in the earlier of these, the *Ad V. C. Epistola Altera*, More dismisses his own refutation of Spinoza's *Tractatus*, in his *Arcana Atheismi*, as wholly inadequate[100]—he proposed, in July 1686, that, with his assistance, either or both of More's critiques should appear in a Dutch translation. More agreed and his second critique, the *Confutatio* of 1678, with its scathing attack on Spinoza's 'grand title of geometric order', professed, according to More, to impress the unlearned and the common people,[101] was duly translated and, in 1687, published together with Kuyper's own recently completed critique of what he terms Spinoza's 'falsely named' *Ethics*.[102]

After 1687 the controversy persisted, albeit yielding little more of intellectual significance, amid a last flurry of pamphlets assailing personalities, and undiminished

---

[94] Bredenburg and Van Limborch, *Schriftelycke Onderhandeling*, 24.
[95] Van Bunge, *Johannes Bredenburg*, 212.   [96] Ibid., 214.
[97] Bredenburg, *Korte Aanmerkingen*, 199–200; Wielema, *Filosofen*, 48.
[98] Kolakowski, *Chrétiens sans église*, 250, 271–3; Fix, *Prophecy and Reason*, 239.
[99] Wielema, *Filosofen*, 52–5.
[100] More, *Ad V. C. Epistola*, 565, Van Bunge, *Johannes Bredenburg*, 218 19, 234 6.
[101] Jacob, *Henry More's Refutation*, 57.
[102] Ibid., p. xiii; Colie, *Light and Enlightenment*, 74–82; Cristofolini, *Cartesiani e Sociniani*, 126–7.

acrimony, until finally its vehemence abated with Bredenburg's death in August 1691, and Kuyper's soon after.[103] Bredenburg's last text was a reply to Jurieu's *Le Tableau du Socinianisme*, a ringing assault on 'l'impureté et la fausseté des dogmes des Sociniens', among whom he included Aubert de Versé, Limborch, and Episcopius, besides Bredenburg and most of the rest of the Collegiants. Episcopius, who had edged towards Socinianism in his later years, and was venerated by Bredenburg and Limborch alike as chief architect of a universal theologically justified toleration, was abhorred by Jurieu—momentarily forgetting his loathing of Bayle and Spinoza—as 'le plus dangereux ennemi de la religion Chrétienne, et de ses mystères, qui ait paru dans nôtre siècle.'[104] Bredenburg's impassioned defence of Episcopius, toleration, and the Collegiant ideal, as well by implication of his own life's work, against Jurieu lay unpublished, however, until the nineteenth century.

Among the Collegiants, agonized recollection of the Bredenburg disputes lingered for decades. Its bitter legacy ensured that there was no attempt to heal the rift between the two separated Collegiant wings until some years after the deaths of the main participants. Eventually, though, a desire to reunite the movement and end the acrimony led to peace talks, and in 1700 a charter of reconciliation was drawn up and partial reunification of the colleges achieved, though an element of schism continued, including the practice of holding separate annual general gatherings at Rijnsburg, until 1722.[105] A fundamental point for both parties was that there should be no more talk of philosophy or Spinozism. It was otherwise, though, in the Republic of Letters, where the names of Bredenburg, Kuyper, Orobio, and Aubert de Versé continued to reverberate for over half a century.

---

[103] Melles, *Joachim Oudaan*, 111; Van Slee, *Rijnsburger Collegianten*, 261.

[104] [Jurieu], *Tableau du Socinianisme*, 9–10, 154, 188, 336; Van Bunge, *Johannes Bredenburg*, 224.

[105] Kühler, *Het Socinianisme*, 247–8; Van Slee, *Rijnsburger Collegianten*, 265–6.

20 | FONTENELLE AND THE WAR OF THE ORACLES

It was a commonplace dictum of the French High Enlightenment that the *esprit philosophique* 'so widespread today owes its beginnings to Fontenelle'.[1] Bernard Le Bovier de Fontenelle (1657–1757), native of Rouen, nephew of Corneille, and star pupil of the Jesuits, was the first prominent high-society *philosophe* and general commentator on science, and the progress of the new learning, in France. Admired by Voltaire, and Diderot, upon both of whom his influence was considerable,[2] he has invariably been reckoned a key precursor and pioneer of the French Enlightenment and one, moreover, who enjoyed great prestige far beyond the confines of France. He was the *philosophes'* 'prototype', it has been aptly remarked, 'their founder and, finally, their doyen'.[3] It is of some consequence, therefore, to identify the sources and impulses which shaped his philosophical stance.

Broadly, Fontenelle's outlook derives from a blend of Descartes, Bayle, and late seventeenth-century, pre-Newtonian scientific ideas. But there are also less obvious roots which none the less crucially contributed to his ambitious, philosophical reform programme. If he shared Bayle's unremittingly critical-rational attitude to tradition, received ideas, and men's propensity to error and delusion,[4] during the 1680s Fontenelle was also powerfully (if privately) influenced by non-providential deism and Naturalism deriving from illicit sources which, moreover, as we shall see, were not predominantly French.[5] In 1687, soon after the other of his two best-known and most controversial works, the *Entretiens sur la pluralité des mondes* (1686), Fontenelle published his *Histoire des Oracles*. It was a book which attracted great interest and has always been assigned a prominent place among the first stirrings of the Enlightenment, a volume addressed to a broad public, written in an elegant, gentlemanly style with the undisguised intention of 'enlightening' as many people as possible, women included.

Ostensibly, Fontenelle's aim is simply to correct an unfortunate historical mistake, the notion introduced by Eusebius and subsequent Church Fathers, unquestioned over many centuries of Christian tradition, that the long venerated oracles of

---

[1] Marsak, *Bernard de Fontenelle*, 6–7; Gay, *The Enlightenment*, i, 317–18.
[2] Proust, *Diderot*, 179, 205, 239–40, 254.   [3] White, *Anti-Philosophers*, 12.
[4] Hazard, *European Mind*, 198.   [5] Niderst, *Fontenelle*, 533–7.

antiquity possessed magical powers of prognostication and healing imparted by demons and the Devil, who—contriving impressive portents and auguries to deceive the people for their own malevolent ends—wrought all manner of supernatural wonders and prodigies. Against this, Fontenelle held that the divining and healing of the ancient sanctuaries was wrought, not by sorcery and demonic power, but the cunning artifice of priests, intent on promoting their own authority and that of the rich and powerful, their omens and soothsaying being entirely fraudulent. Furthermore, not only did the portents of the oracles stem from the 'finesses des prestres' rather than Satan, but the people's credulous faith in the sacred oracles of Dodona, Delphi, Delos, Didyma, Cumae, and the rest, did not cease, as the Church Fathers assert, with the coming of Christ.[6] On the contrary, he maintained, deception of the masses by self-seeking sanctuary priests, adept at manipulating popular gullibility, ignorance, and superstition, persisted for centuries after, just as before, the advent of the Messiah, Christianity, and the Church.

Adroit socially and intellectually, Fontenelle was a European celebrity and, being one of those later classified during the Revolution as the old régime's 'secte de prudents',[7] never forgot to protect his flanks. Avowing loyalty to the Church and its teaching, Fontenelle claimed that 'reason' as well as 'religion' prove the Devil and lesser demons exist and that these malignant spirits might well have operated the auguries, altars, and shrines of antiquity had the Almighty so wished.[8] However, He evidently did not, and the fact that 'tout le monde tient qu'il y a eu quelque chose de surnaturel dans les oracles' arises from a vast delusion which, without justification, came to be universally adopted in early Christendom.[9] The Church, though, requires no false and credulous notions to underpin its teaching, indeed, it is much better off without them. Accordingly, he concludes, 'j'avance hardiment que les Oracles, de quelque nature qu'ils ayent esté, n'ont point esté rendus par les démons et qu'ils n'ont point cessé à la venue de Jésus-Christ.'[10] On the contrary, he averred, many a pagan oracle had been 'plus magnifique' than ever in the first and second centuries after Christ.

All this contradicted what Bossuet had proclaimed earlier, in his *Discours sur l'histoire universelle*, where rendering impotent the demons who had previously operated the shrines and oracles of ancient Greece and Rome is styled a stupendous miracle engineered by divine Providence.[11] But Fontenelle's critique of the traditional view found ready acceptance, at least in some quarters. In the mid-eighteenth century his thesis regarding the fraudulence of ancient oracular prognostication was deemed indispensable to an 'enlightened' outlook by such leading publicists as Voltaire, Condillac, d'Alembert and Diderot.[12] Condillac takes it for granted that everything

---

[6] Fontenelle, *Histoire des Oracles*, 8; Niderst, *Fontenelle*, 286–7; Phillips, *Church and Culture*, 258–9.

[7] Maréchal, *Dictionnaire*, 94; Wellman, *La Mettrie*, 251.   [8] Fontenelle, *Histoire des Oracles*, 10.

[9] Ibid., 7; Mori, 'Introduction', 131, 332.

[10] Fontenelle, *Histoire des Oracles.*, 226; see also Katz, 'Isaac Vossius', 161, 164.

[11] Bossuet, *Discours*, 302, 307–8; Preati, *L'Arte magica dimostrata*, 75–6, 82–3; Philips, *Church and Culture*, 257.

[12] Condillac, *Traité des systèmes*, 48–54; D'Alembert, *Éloge*, pp. iv–v; Proust, *Diderot*, 274–5.

concerning ancient divination and auguries had been explained 'parfaitement' by Fontenelle.

Outwardly—for Fontenelle was more radical privately than he could disclose publicly—he confirmed the existence of Satan, demons, and magic, acknowledging that both Bible and Church definitely require such belief.[13] But he simultaneously adduced massive evidence from classical literature proving that all divination, necromancy, and other magic in antiquity were bogus and the auguries nothing but imposture and lies. In fact, nothing in the ancient sanctuaries, however much revered by the masses, operated supernaturally. This was bound to erode respect for magic, Devil, and demons, if not prompt questions about their very existence, and subtly implied that popular credulity and ignorance have ruinously detrimental consequences for society and politics, enabling oracle priests to foment superstition and perpetuate an illegitimate authority.[14] His argument suggested that, over many centuries, superstition spread with the support of ruthless and despotic rulers who, avid to oppress the people for their own ends, encouraged credulity and priestly artifice and deception.[15]

The *Histoire des Oracles* is a landmark of the Early Enlightenment, a compelling and important book. Yet it contained not a single new idea and Fontenelle never claimed it did. On the contrary, he declares in the preface, he borrowed everything from the *De Oraculis Ethnicorum* (Amsterdam, 1683) by the Haarlem physician, Anthonie van Dale, confident the precious matter contained therein deserved circulation among a wider audience in a more readable form.[16] Nor subsequently did the *savants* of the eighteenth century forget that Fontenelle's text is no more than a reworking—or, as Radicati puts it, 'translation'—of Van Dale.[17] Few doubted that Fontenelle's rendering improved on Van Dale's ponderous Latin: 'le diamant brut de Van Dale brilla beaucoup,' remarked Voltaire, 'quand il fut taillé par Fontenelle.'[18] Yet Van Dale, while almost forgotten today, was neither a nonentity nor a minor forerunner of the Enlightenment. Indeed, not only was he the real progenitor of the ideas publicized by Fontenelle but, as he himself justly observed in 1686, in the epilogue to the Dutch translation of his book, his own version of his thesis differs from, extends beyond, and has appreciably more radical implications than, Fontenelle's formulation.[19]

Anthonie van Dale (1638–1708) was one of the leading medical men of late seventeenth-century Haarlem, and the first dean of the civic medical college established by the city government in 1692 to regulate medical practice.[20] Raised among the Mennonite community, he was an ardent foe not just of medical quackery, but all types of superstition, and an avid scholar. Disliked by colleagues as arrogant,

---

[13] Fontenelle, *Histoire des Oracles*, 226; [Maffei], *Riflessioni*, 123.

[14] Condillac, *Traité des systèmes*, 52; Hazard, *European Mind*, 195–6.

[15] Condillac, *Traité des systèmes*, 54.

[16] Fontenelle, *Histoire des Oracles*, preface; Katz, 'Isaac Vossius', 161, 164.

[17] Radicati, *Recueil*, 247; [Durand], *Vie et sentiments*, 170; Mylius, *Bibliotheca*, 36; Feijóo, *Ilustración*, 129; Mencke, *Compendiöse Gelehrten Lexicon*, i, 569.

[18] Quoted in Evers, 'Die "Orakel"', 267.

[19] Manuel, *Eighteenth Century*, 48–9; Evers, 'Die "Orakel"', 248.

[20] GA Haarlem Archive Collegium medicum i. res. 15 Dec. 1692 and 2 Feb. 1693.

dogmatic, and self-opinionated, his aversion to popular notions about healing, magic, and witchcraft guided much of his lonely but indefatigable research. In 1674 he translated and published a batch of documents obtained from Denmark, recounting an infamous series of witch trials at Koege, near Copenhagen, which demonstrated, in his view, both the crassness and the tragic consequences of the credulity they reveal.[21] Besides his medical work and scholarly researches, Van Dale, like many Mennonite doctors, also served his congregation as a lay preacher, albeit briefly, being unsuited to this role and tending to exasperate his congregation by dragging too much classical erudition into sermons.[22] Frequenting the Collegiants, Van Dale became friendly with the brothers Bredenburg, whose unremittingly rationalist approach to theological and philosophical issues accorded with his own. By the mid-1680s he found himself accused by such anti-Bredenburg Collegiants as the Rotterdam poet Joachim Oudaen, an old adversary of Van Dale's, of being an 'atheist'.[23] Presumably Van Dale backed the Bredenburgs in their battle with Kuyper and Lemmerman; certainly, he felt some aversion to the prevailing cultural atmosphere in Haarlem, claiming in one letter to be living in 'Arabia Deserta'.[24]

Before Van Dale, the varieties and significance of ancient pagan religion had been most authoritatively studied by the Leiden professor Gerardus Johannes Vossius (1577–1649), in his monumental *De Theologia gentili* (1641). But it was the English writers Edward, Lord Herbert of Cherbury and Charles Blount, both, like Van Dale later, fascinated by Vossius' classifications of ancient pagan beliefs and practices, who first saw the potential of his material for a general critique of popular superstition. Herbert, a friend of Vossius, used his work extensively in his *De religione gentilium* (On the Religion of the Gentiles) posthumously published by Gerardus' son, Isaac Vossius, at Amsterdam in 1663.[25] But it was especially Blount, often too lightly dismissed by modern scholars, as unoriginal and a plagiarist, who first incorporated the theme of ancient paganism into radical thought by highlighting the antagonism between ancient rationalist philosophy and popular superstition, and underlining the political and social implications of priestly fraud.[26] 'Before religions, that is to say sacrifices, rites, ceremonies, pretended revelations and the like, were invented among the Heathens,' contended Blount, in his pamphlet, *Great is Diana of the Ephesians* (1680), 'there was no worship of God but in a rational way, whereof the philosophers pretending to be masters, did to this end, not only teach virtue and piety, but were also themselves great examples of it in their lives and conversations.'[27] In this remote, idyllic age philosophers presided, and, he suggests, it was they 'whom the people chiefly follow'd' until they were 'seduced' by priests 'who, instead of the said virtue and piety, introduced fables and fictions of their own coining, perswading the vulgar that as men could not by any natural abilities of their own know the best manner of serving God, so it was necessary that He should reveal the same to his priests in some extraordinary

---

[21] 'Iets over . . . Antonius van Dale', 14–15. [22] Evers, 'Die "Orakel" ', 226.
[23] Ibid., 226, 240–3.   [24] Ibid., 227.   [25] Popkin, 'Deist Challenge', 204.
[26] Ibid., 205; Champion, *Pillars of Priestcraft*, 139–40, 147; Harrison, *Religion and the Religions*, 73–4.
[27] Blount, *Great is Diana*, 3; Walber, *Charles Blount*, 214–18.

manner, for the better instruction of the people'.[28] Adding a republican twist, Blount remarks that these guardians of divine revelations, 'certainly the wickedest and craftiest of men', seeing 'how serviceable they might be to the Prince, as well as the Prince to them, in a despotick government, soon discover'd their own interest in being contributors to that design'.[29]

But Blount provides little erudition to accompany his thesis. The great merit of Van Dale's enterprise is his massive argumentation, buttressed by innumerable quotations from Greek and Roman texts, proving one by one that the renowned oracles of antiquity were all frauds artfully contrived to foment credulity and herd the superstitious masses in the interest of the few. Of course, Van Dale too had learnt from others and, besides Vossius, acknowledged his debt to Boccalini, the sixteenth-century Englishman Reginald Scot, his Mennonite predecessor Abraham Paling, and the medieval Jewish philosopher Maimonides, whom he repeatedly cites approvingly. Yet he could justly claim to be the first to argue (at least in detail) that all ancient oracles and auguries were bogus and that the Greek oracles did not cease with Christ's coming.[30] Contradicting assertions of the Christian Fathers that the sanctuaries and altars were worked by Satan and his demons, invoked by priests and soothsayers using magical incantations and rituals, he insists that no magic was involved and no spirits participated. The trust of the populace in the auguries and divining powers of the oracles was based on nothing more than cunning craft and the artifice of the sanctuary priests.[31] Indeed, magic, held Van Dale and his vocal apologist, Willem Goeree, does not exist at all and the Devil is powerless to affect the lives of men. Sorcery, divination, necromancy, possession, communication with demons and spirits may have been attested in ancient times by countless pagan and Christian writers, but no single example has ever been demonstrated or proven.[32]

Van Dale, moreover, as an Anabaptist and Collegiant, felt few qualms in suggesting that the frauds of oracle priests demand comparison with the fabrication of bogus miracles and wonders by the main Churches of Christendom. In his eyes, Lutherans, Anglicans, and (one presumes) Calvinists were only marginally less guilty of fomenting credulity than the Catholic clergy, though writing in the Dutch Republic, he naturally felt freer to denigrate the latter with their 'pretended miracles', such as the 'sweating of images and 10,000 other such like idiocies' designed to dupe ordinary folk.[33] Van Dale, like Blount, deems popular credulousness a terrifying force infinitely detrimental to society. Boeotia, he notes, had more sacred oracles than anywhere else in classical antiquity, with the consequence that the Boeotians surpassed all others, as Horace and Strabo remark, for dullness and stupidity.[34]

Fundamental in Van Dale is the impotence of the Devil and the non-reality of divination, demonic power, and sorcery. As part of his drive to eradicate belief in

---

[28] Blount, *Great is Diana*, 3; Sina, *L'Avvento della ragione*, 199.

[29] Blount, *Great is Diana*, 45.   [30] [Durand], *La Vie*, 170.

[31] Van Dale, *Verhandeling*, 150–1; [Bayle], *Nouvelles*, i, 2–3; Le Gendre, *Traité de l'opinion*, ii, 502.

[32] Van Dale, *Verhandeling*, 3v–4, 151; Goeree, *Mosaize Historie*, iii, 126–7, 137–9.

[33] Van Dale, *Verhandeling*, 278   [34] Ibid., 175.

witchcraft, he roundly denies the possibility of 'possession' of humans by spirits whether in an ancient or modern context. Medical scholars, he asserts, had incontrovertibly disproved all recent cases of 'possession' and shown, whatever the clergy may claim, that none of those reported is genuine.[35] Likewise characteristic of Van Dale, as of Blount, is the epic vision of a classical world gripped by unceasing intellectual and ideological strife between enlightened philosophers such as the 'Cynici, Academici en Sceptici, de Epicureen en Aristotelici', on one side, and on the other, priestly guardians of altars and sanctuaries. The former use reason-based philosophy to expose the craft and deceit of the 'Oracle-monks' who, backed by their intellectual allies, the Platonists and Pythagoreans, retaliate by denouncing their opponents as 'atheisten'.[36] Finally, the ancient rationalists were overwhelmed, stifled by the masses who, addicted to superstition, were easily incited against them by artful priests and practitioners of magical power. Still today, most people, urges Van Dale, like most Churches and sects, remain, as they have always been, 'firmly enslaved' to credulous belief in 'magic, witches and witchcraft, prodigies, miracles, soothsaying . . . and also ghosts and the supposedly real supernatural feats of the Devil'.[37]

But if the war was lost in antiquity, it was flaring up afresh in modernity. As a Collegiant and ally of the Bredenburgs, Van Dale could plead all this in the name of 'true Christianity', claiming he was no Spinozist or deist. On the contrary, he professed to want the 'pure light of Gospel' to shine, maintaining that there is no surer way of fomenting 'atheism' than to encourage popular belief in mysteries and inconceivable miracles, such as those with which countless priests who profess to be Christian stuff the heads of gullible parishioners. It was not the advent of Christ or the Church, holds Van Dale—and no less emphatically, Goeree—which ended veneration of the ancient shrines and oracles, but the decrees and penalties of Constantine the Great (ruled 307–37) and his successors, especially Theodosius the Great (ruled AD 346–95).[38] It was through imperial power and edicts that the oracles were dissolved. This proved to Van Dale's satisfaction, as for Blount and, later, Condillac,[39] the intimate ties between credulity and despotism. So formidable is superstition as a device for swaying the masses, and holding them in subjection, that rulers and statesmen have little choice but either to attack credulity or else to become partners and abetters of the priests who foment superstition. As one of his proofs that 'kings and princes sought their own advantage through the craft and artifice of the Oracle-priests, to take advantage of the populace and mock them', Van Dale cites Alexander the Great who, to impress his soldiery as a ruler who is 'religious and given to credulity' kept such soothsayers and interpreters of portents as Aristander and Demophöon always at his side.[40]

Seeing that a French work, professedly based on his own, appearing in separate

---

[35] Van Dale, *Verhandeling*, 200–19; *Bibliothèque Universelle*, VII (1687), 345.

[36] Van Dale, *Verhandeling*, 234, 244, 549.   [37] Ibid., 267.

[38] Ibid., 519, 550; [Bayle], *Nouvelles*, i, 4; Goeree, *Mosaize Historie*, ii, 663–5; see also Le Gendre, *Traité de l'Opinion*, ii, 502.

[39] Condillac, *Traité des systèmes*, 54.   [40] Van Dale, *Verhandeling*, 537.

editions in France and Holland, was creating a stir, Van Dale pronounced himself flat-tered but also protested that Fontenelle's reworking of his material omitted vital ele-ments and significantly altered his basic thesis. In particular, Van Dale points out, Fontenelle does not reject the reality of magic altogether, as he does, or deny that the Devil can affect human thoughts and actions.[41] On the contrary, Fontenelle con-firms satanic power, maintaining that while the Devil did not operate the oracles of antiquity, 'genuine magic' exists and demons do act on men. 'But then we can ask,' objects Van Dale, dismissing Fontenelle's distinction between real magic and fraudu-lent oracle craft, 'how it is possible Satan possesses the power to divine etc., through witches and Devil-adherents, but did not utilize it in the oracle caves and caverns?'[42] Fontenelle, in his opinion, had muddied the water, rendering his thesis logically incoherent. To claim the oracles were counterfeit but simultaneously acknowledge sorcery, and Satan's power, is completely nonsensical, he argues, since magic and oracles belonged to the same belief system in antiquity.[43] The explanation, he sug-gests, for Fontenelle's feeble rigmarole about magic is that he feels obliged to write thus out of fear of Louis XIV and the Catholic Church;[44] and, indeed, it seems highly improbable that Fontenelle was serious in distinguishing between real magic and oracle craft.[45]

Van Dale's foremost adversary was the German scholar Georg Moebius (1616–97), a professor at Leipzig since 1668 and an eminent expert on classical pagan religion. Moebius' own treatise on Greek oracles, of 1657, widely deemed a standard work, affirms the role of Satan and demons in the incantations and prognostications of the ancient oracles. Reacting to Van Dale, Moebius brought out a revised edition in 1685, incorporating new material designed to undercut the Dutchman's arguments.[46] Moebius insists that Van Dale's thesis, even though he stops short of denying the existence of Satan and demons altogether, does deny that any spirits did or could infil-trate the shrines and auguries of the ancients, or intervene supernaturally among men. This is tantamount to denying that Satan and demonic forces operate in the world or influence human life, which, he asserts, is atheistic, anti-Scriptural, and grossly impious. Stung by this attack, Van Dale included some acerbic criticism of Moebius in the 1686 Dutch edition of his book. Unimpressed by Moebius' demon-strations of the reality of magic, soothsaying, and diabolical capability, Van Dale accuses him of deliberately misrepresenting ancient texts in his eagerness to inflate the 'empire' of Satan on earth, predicting that his distortions of Pliny, Livy, and other writers, and generally mediocre scholarship, would sufficiently discredit his book without his help.

Van Dale, meanwhile, did not lacked sympathizers, as was shown by the long and favourable reviews of his work published by Bayle (in the very first article of his

---

[41] Ibid., 'Na-reden'; Bots, 'Fontenelle', 550–1; Evers, 'Die "Orakel" ', 247–8.
[42] Van Dale, *Verhandeling*, 537.   [43] Ibid.; Bots, 'Fontenelle', 551.
[44] Van Dale, *Verhandeling*, 537; Niderst, *Fontenelle*, 287.
[45] D'Argens, *Mémoires secrets*, iv, 185–96; Evers, 'Die "Orakel" ', 248.
[46] *Acta Eruditorum* 1685, p. 375; Evers, 'Die "Orakel" ', 239–40.

Nouvelles de la République des Lettres) and Le Clerc.[47] Discussing the Dutch version in 1687, Le Clerc, recalling Bayle's approval, congratulated Van Dale on his adept renderings of complex Greek and Latin quotations 'en langue vulgaire' and the reorganization of his material to enhance its effectiveness, as well as his adding 'des preuves authentiques de plusieurs fraudes qu'on a découvertes dans ces dernières siècles en de prétendus possedez, sorciers, et magiciens.'[48] He pronounced Van Dale justified in charging Moebius with misquoting texts and contradicting himself by claiming Satan inspired the oracles, but only succeeded in interpreting omens and auguries by guessing, or consulting divine Revelation. The Devil, commented Le Clerc, is clearly ignorant of much that transpires on earth, for when the Pope enlisted all the magicians and diviners of Italy to help locate Luther's place of concealment, when Charles V was searching for him, they proved utterly incapable of revealing his hiding-place.[49] However, like Bayle, Le Clerc was careful to say that he could nevertheless not approve of everything in Van Dale.

Jaquelot too was broadly supportive, if also keenly aware that Van Dale's stance posed a problem for rationalist theologians such as himself, who could hardly champion the fatuous pedantry of Moebius but, on the other hand, could not underwrite the total denial of Satan or magic either.[50] Praising Van Dale's erudition, he reconciled his findings with an authentic Christian viewpoint by claiming that God would not have encouraged idolatry and superstition by allowing demonic forces free rein in the oracle caves and sanctuaries of antiquity. Up to a point, then, Van Dale was justified. Equally, though, God *would* have permitted malign spirits freer rein around the time of Christ's coming 'pour donner matière à la gloire de son fils' and to render mankind's deliverance from evil spirits a wonderful effect of his Messiahship.[51] Other commentators similarly sought an in-between position, synthesizing an 'enlightened' approach with Christian teaching. Thus, Benjamin Binet judged that, while Van Dale rightly contended the ancient oracles frequently entailed deception, and were devoid of supernatural forces, no Christian can 'entièrement exclure les démons des oracles'.[52]

Other commentators, however, rejected both Van Dale and the intermediate stance of Le Clerc, Jaquelot, Binet, and possibly—if his saying he did not necessarily share Van Dale's view in full was sincere[53]—Bayle. A powerfully negative reaction from among Collegiant circles was that of Bredenburg's brother-in-law, the Rotterdam poet Joachim Oudaen (1628–92). Gravely disquieted by the Bredenburg furore, and especially the spread of Socinian and Spinozist tendencies among the Collegiants, Oudaen viewed his former friend, Van Dale's, theories about the ancient oracles with deep misgiving. Furthermore, Van Dale, besides disparaging Moebius, had seen fit, in his new edition, to ridicule Oudaen's classical scholarship and opinions about

---

[47] [Bayle], *Nouvelles*, i, 2–18; *Bibliothèque Universelle*, VII (1687), 345; [Durand], *La Vie*, 170; Cantelli, *Teologia e ateismo*, 35–6, 49.

[48] *Bibliothèque Universelle*, VII (1687), 345.   [49] Ibid., 347.   [50] Jaquelot, *Dissertations*, 654–7.

[51] Ibid., 657, 670.   [52] Binet, *Idée générale*, 125; see also Rambach, *Collegium*, i, 968.

[53] [Bayle], *Nouvelles*, i, 18.

demons.[54] The poet responded by translating Moebius into Dutch and, in 1687, publishing this version in Rotterdam, accompanied by a hard-hitting preface of his own and a polemical poem, denouncing 'philosophical raving', which he had written some years before but which now seemed useful additional ammunition against Van Dale.[55]

Oudaen endeavoured to convince readers there was more to Van Dale's thesis than met the eye, and that the real issue was not the reality of magic but his attempt to promote philosophical reason over Scriptural authority. An ardent foe of Spinozism, which he attacks in several of his poems,[56] Oudaen claims Van Dale totally subverts the authority of the Christian Fathers, mocking successive generations of venerable scholars who had passed on their teachings over the centuries. Worse still, Van Dale had not, he suspected, fully revealed his agenda, his underlying objective being to advance in his typically devious, hypocritical manner, the frightful heresies of the Sadducees, a sect which denied the existence not only of angels, demons, and Satan, but also the immortality of the soul.[57] Van Dale, he grants, does acknowledge that the Devil exists. But this he does only perfunctorily, indeed, urges Oudaen, merely as a ploy, the more easily to seduce readers unfamiliar with the insidious new 'philosophical' attitude.

Van Dale's subtle purpose, held Oudaen, was circuitously to induce people to doubt the reality of angels, Satan, demons, and all supernatural beings. Indeed, Oudaen believed Van Dale was a prime instigator of the philosophical movement which had sprung up Holland in recent years and which was trying to eradicate all belief in the supernatural so as to lessen veneration for Scripture and ultimately undermine religion.[58] Those swayed by Van Dale to be sceptical about spirits and Satan would soon find themselves doubting the immortality of the soul and the resurrection of the dead.[59] Van Dale's ideas, he held, glorify philosophy and degrade Holy Writ, being part of the same wicked sedition which commenced with La Peyrère's *Prae-Adamitae*, gained impetus with the 'utterly licentious, dissipated dictionary of Koerbagh', that 'shameless' book the *Philosophia S. Scripturae Interpres*, and Hobbes' *Leviathan*, and culminated in the *Tractatus Theologico-Politicus* and *Ethics* of Spinoza.[60] These texts, held Oudaen, all belong to the same depraved 'philosophical' project, generating the tide of unbelief and contempt for religion now engulfing society. Their poisonous offspring, he admonished, were the plague of clandestine philosophical manuscripts circulating in Holland, including the text he calls the '*De Tribus Impostoribus*' and the 'writings' of Vanini.[61]

Meanwhile, in France, Fontenelle's reticence, and discreet modifications to Van Dale, proved effective tactics. There was barely a ripple of unease—at least for twenty

---

[54] Van Dale, *Verhandeling*, 20, 24, 62.
[55] Oudaen, *Voor-reden* to [Moebius] *Reden-lievende God-geleerde Verhandeling*; Melles, *Joachim Oudaen*, 109.
[56] Melles, *Joachim Oudaen*, 104–11; Wielema, *Filosofen*, 58; Van Bunge, *Johannes Bredenburg*, 46–7.
[57] Evers, 'Die "Orakel"', 240–1.   [58] Oudaen, *Voor-reden*, 2–4.   [59] Ibid., 4.
[60] Ibid., 6–8; Melles, *Joachim Oudaen*, 109–10.   [61] Oudaen, *Voor-reden*, 5; Siebrand, *Spinoza*, 148.

years.[62] There was no lack of interest in the *Histoire des Oracles*. Fresh editions appeared in Paris in 1698 and Amsterdam in 1701. Many churchmen loathed its contents, but there were no serious complications until, in 1707, the Strasbourg Jesuit Father Jean-François Baltus (1667–1743) launched a vehement attack on Fontenelle's thesis with his *Réponse à l'histoire des Oracles de M. de Fontenelle* (Strasbourg, 1707). With this the clash between 'philosophy' and ecclesiastical authority and tradition became manifest also in France. Baltus, who for some time had distrusted Fontenelle,[63] expressed outrage that he should openly admit borrowing ideas from Van Dale as if that were the most unexceptional thing in the world. For everywhere the Haarlem physician was considered an ultra-heretic, virtually an 'atheist', who himself confesses in the preface to his later treatise *De Origine et Progressu Idolatriae et Superstitione* (Amsterdam, 1696) that he was judged to hold dangerous views even by other Anabaptists.[64]

Baltus failed to raise a major public hue and cry and no formal steps were taken. But behind the scenes there were reverberations, notably at Court. Fontenelle was told to remain silent. The king wanted no public furore. But the situation was delicate, even perhaps dangerous, not just for Fontenelle but the entire Parisian 'philosophic' fringe, which venerated him as their leader. At this point, one of his accolytes, Du Marsais,[65] a key figure of the first generation of the French Radical Enlightenment who in his old age was to be a notable contributor to the *Encyclopédie* and, according to Saint-Simon and others, was an unmitigated 'atheist', resolved to react against Baltus on Fontenelle's behalf. He wrote a forceful counter-critique designed to demolish all Baltus' arguments which, according to D'Alembert's later account of the episode, claimed that the Jesuit had not properly understood the Church Fathers and was guilty of even more errors in classical scholarship than Moebius.[66] Baltus might deplore Fontenelle's borrowings from the Anabaptist, Van Dale, but was no less blameworthy himself for borrowing from an inept Lutheran heretic. Unfortunately for Du Marsais, or perhaps fortunately, given that Louis XIV still reigned—a Jesuit colleague of Baltus noticed his manuscript as it was being prepared for the press. Representations were made at Court. Du Marsais was told he would not be granted a licence to publish. He then requested permission to submit his text to the Sorbonne for formal judgement but was expressly commanded in the name of the king neither to submit it nor try to publish it, in France or abroad.[67]

Thus Du Marsais was relegated to being one of those who, as a late eighteenth-century revolutionary ideologue put it, 'travaillaient dans le silence à émanciper

---

[62] D'Alembert, 'Éloge', p. iv; Landucci, 'Introduzione', 52–3; Evers, 'Die "Orakel" ', 249.

[63] Bots, 'Fontenelle', 551.

[64] Baltus, *Réponse*, 3; Niderst, 'Fontenelle et la littérature clandestine', 162; Pott, *Aufklärung*, 207–8.

[65] César Chesneau, Sieur Dumarsais or Du Marsais (1676–1756), who as a youth studied with the Oratorians in Marseilles, was one of the foremost grammarians and textual critics of eighteenth-century France and the reputed author of several clandestine philosophical manuscripts. According to Naigeon, Dumarsais was 'un des athées les plus fermes et les plus hardis qu'il y ait jamais eu'; Naigeon, *Encyclopédie méthodique*, iii, 172; see also Mori, 'Introduction', 39–44.

[66] D'Alembert, 'Éloge', pp. iv–v.

[67] Ibid., p. v; Krauss,'L'Énigme de Du Marsais', 517; Mori. 'Introduction', 40.

l'esprit humain'.[68] Yet scathing replies to Baltus appeared in French abroad, notably in Le Clerc's *Bibliothèque Choisie*,[69] prompting Baltus to renew his offensive with his 459-page *Suite de la Réponse à l'Histoire des Oracles* (Strasbourg, 1708). Again Baltus chose to be comparatively courteous to Fontenelle who, after all, was the secretary of the Académie des Sciences and possessed influential friends at Court. He professed to accept his assurances that he was a loyal Catholic. Fontenelle was merely at fault, held Baltus, in allowing himself to be misled by the 'vain erudition' of Van-Dale'.[70] But if it was Van Dale who was pernicious, Fontenelle's concurring that the ancient oracles had never been operated by demons, or diabolical power, was 'dangerous' for the Church. 'The ill-digested learning of Mr Van-Dale,' as it is put in the English translation of Baltus of 1709, 'has hinder'd Fontenelle from considering the consequences of his system which tends directly to overthrow the authority of the Fathers and subvert the most constant and grounded traditions: and assuredly, if there be any tradition which is certain and constant 'tis that here in question, since it is maintain'd and attested by all the Fathers and by the ecclesiastical writers of all ages, who have universally own'd the Devil for the author of idolatry in general, and of oracles in particular.'[71] Remarkably, an Inquisition-licensed Portuguese work attacking seditious philosophy, published at Coimbra in 1756, vigorously reaffirms Baltus' charge against Van Dale and Fontenelle, adding that all the chronicles of the Spanish conquest of New Spain confirm that the ancient idols of Aztec Mexico had likewise been operated by the Devil and demons.[72] The only claim of Van Dale with which Baltus could agree was that no one before him had ever argued comprehensively that demons and spirits did not infuse the pagan sanctuaries; not even the 'atheist' Pliny had done that.[73]

Even more subversive than contradicting the Church Fathers, held Baltus, is to imply that whole societies can be so crassly credulous that they can be led to believe unquestioningly what is totally untrue for not just decades or centuries but entire millennia. Is it likely, he demanded, that mankind is so gullible that it can be systematically misled in something so fundamental as religion by a tissue of artifice and lies woven by crafty priests thirsting for power, authority, and pseudo-sacred sex with the prettiest wives of their followers, so that the entire civilized world should have to wait for an Anabaptist physician from Haarlem, appearing sixteen centuries after Christ's coming, to prove 'the famous oracles of antiquity, so much respected through all the heathen world, and so often produc'd by the heathens, as manifest proof of the divinity of their false religion, were nothing but the cheats and gross impostures of idolatrous priests, who abus'd the credulity of the people: and that in all the predictions and surprizing cures, which different authors have related of them, there was nothing of the supernatural, that is, nothing which ought to be ascrib'd to the Devil?'[74]

Baltus, like many others lay and clerical, Lutherans and Anglicans as well as Catholics, held among 'all the miracles that accompanied the establishment of

---

[68] Maréchal, *Dictionnaire*, 73.   [69] Manuel, *Eighteenth Century*, 49; Evers, 'Die "Orakel" ', 251.
[70] Baltus, *Suite à la Réponse*, 9.   [71] Baltus, *An Answer*, 50.
[72] Pina de Sá e Melo, *Triumpho da Religião*, 77.   [73] Baltus, *Réponse*, 362–3.
[74] Baltus, *An Answer*, 14; Baltus, *Suite de la Réponse*, 2.

Christianity upon the ruins of idolatry, there was none more illustrious and more astonishing to the heathens than the silence of their oracles'.[75] Van Dale's perverse notions, asserts Baltus, stem not just from unwarranted Protestant doubt about 'that wonderful power of casting out devils, which the Catholic Church receiv'd from Christ, and has exercised through all the ages in so remarkable a manner' but also the depraved idea that the founding of Christianity was not, after all, accompanied by a 'great number of extraordinary miracles by which God did evidently shew that He was the author of it'.[76] However dazzled by the 'ridiculous fancies of Mr Van-Dale', Fontenelle must surely see the consequences of saying it is 'false that oracles were silenc'd at the birth of our Saviour' and denying that there was 'anything extraordinary in their silence, which ought to be ascrib'd to his power'.[77] Nor could he ignore the risks of Van Dale's pretending that the oracles 'only ceas'd because the temples where they were establish'd, were ruined by those edicts which the Christian emperors publish'd against the pagan religion'.[78] 'The greatest miracle of Christianity, which was it's establishment, ought not to be ascrib'd to the edicts of Christian emperors,' as Fontenelle had dared 'insinuate, but to the divine power of Christ, which was never more illustrious than in this wonderful establishment, and in the destruction of idolatry, that oppos'd all its force against it.'[79] Van Dale, Fontenelle must accept, not only disdains the Church Fathers 'whom he everywhere treats with contempt, but the authority also of Holy Scripture', endeavouring to 'shew, that in the Hebrew text of which alone he allows, there is nothing meant of the Devil, nor of his operations, in all the places where 'tis most evident they are spoken of'.[80]

But if Van Dale was beyond reach, and Baltus failed to humiliate Fontenelle publicly, his campaign was not without some success. Fontenelle and Du Marsais were silenced on the king's orders. During the opening years of the new century, French ecclesiastics redoubled their efforts to buttress belief in supernatural forces and miracles, the reality of angels good and bad, and Satan's rebellion against God, including the power of demons and spirits to influence men.[81] Furthermore, around 1707–8 there was talk at Court of quietly disciplining Fontenelle; and if he remained on amicable terms with Father Tournemine, other Jesuits and dévots believed they could curb the entire 'philosophical' movement in France by dealing with its pre-eminent figure.[82] Fontenelle, Voltaire later recalled, came close to being stripped of his 'pensions, sa place, et sa liberté', for having published, twenty years before, the Traité des Oracles of Van Dale, despite deleting 'tout ce qui pouvait alarmer le fanatisme'.[83] The outlook for Fontenelle's circle became still more ominous after the Jesuit Father Le

---

[75] Baltus, An Answer, 14; Baltus, Religion chrétienne, 217–40; Preati, L'Arte magica dimostrata, 75–6; see also Grew, Cosmologia Sacra, 363.

[76] Baltus, An Answer, 1–2; Mori, 'Introduction', 130.   [77] Baltus, An Answer, 7; Feijóo, Ilustración, 130.

[78] Baltus, An Answer, 7.   [79] Ibid., 208–9; Baltus, Religion Chrétienne, 217 Mori, 'Introduction', 130.

[80] Baltus, An Answer, 80.

[81] Bossuet, Élevations, 142–4; Levasseur, Défense, 44–55; Baltus, Religion chrétienne, 217–20; Briggs, Communities of Belief, 393–4.

[82] Krauss, 'L'Énigme de Dumarsais', 517.

[83] Voltaire, Dictionnaire philosophique portatif (1764), 316.

Tellier became royal confessor in 1709. In 1713, according to Voltaire, Le Tellier accused Fontenelle of 'atheism' before the king, the *philosophe* being saved from ugly consequences only owing to the adroit intervention of the marquis d'Argenson.[84]

Gradually, Fontenelle's argument became a commonplace among 'enlightened' sections of the Republic of Letters, and the public generally. The English translation of his *Histoire* of 1688 reappeared in 1699 and 1718. Yet comment overstepping the guidelines fixed by rationalist theologians like Jaquelot and Binet, that is, unqualified approval of Van Dale's stance, or failure to reiterate Fontenelle's acknowledgement of magic and the Devil, long remained, down to the middle of the century, beyond the pale of decent opinion and was considered a certain sign of adherence to the radical, as against the moderate, Enlightenment. When, for example, Mandeville ridicules the 'vulgar notion that after the coming of Christ, or at least upon the preaching of the Gospel, all the pagan oracles immediately ceased', insisting—without citing any source—that the 'oracles subsisted after the coming of Christ',[85] it may be unclear whether he is echoing Fontenelle or Van Dale but it is certain he is adopting a radical position. Indeed, throughout the first half of the eighteenth century Van Dale continued to be bracketed, everywhere in Europe, with the Naturalists and Spinozists.

In Germany, hostility to Van Dale and Fontenelle was expressed by numerous writers, including Grapius[86] and Loescher, the latter remarking in 1708 that many people now claimed sorcery does not exist, deeming the Biblical story of the feats performed by Pharoah's magicians mere figurative language adapted to the primitive understanding of the common folk of the time. This attitude, he says, stems from Van Dale and, following him, especially Bekker, Lahontan, and Thomasius, the three chief propagators of such ideas in German-speaking lands.[87] According to Loescher, Van Dale is more than just one of the many 'anti-Scriptuarii', as he calls those who disdain Scriptural authority, being someone who maintains that Satan and demonic power play no part in human existence and excludes all possibility of magic and 'possession'. Loescher, consequently, classifies Van Dale with Hobbes, Spinoza, and Koerbagh as one of the worst 'Fanatico-Naturalistici'.

Leibniz, for his part, clearly grasped the connection between Van Dale and Bekker, noting as early as 1691 that Bekker's assault on witchcraft belief and demonic power was rooted intellectually in Van Dale's ideas about ancient oracles.[88] Thomasius, familiar with both Van Dale's main treatises, similarly identifies him as the chief inspirer in German lands of the campaign against belief in sorcery, witches, and witchcraft, culminating in the efforts of Bekker and himself. Consequently, he urged that Van Dale be praised, not condemned, a suggestion deemed scandalous by the Schleswig pastor, Petrus Goldschmidt, who reminded readers that Van Dale was universally considered suspect, an author who, even with Thomasius' approval, failed to persuade any 'upright theologians and philosophers' that his ideas are helpful to the

---

[84] Ibid.; D'Alembert, 'Éloge', pp. iv–v; Maréchal, *Dictionnaire*, 93; Evers, 'Die "Orakel" ', 252.

[85] Mandeville, *Free Thoughts*, 173–6.   [86] Grapius, *Systema*, 96–9.

[87] Loescher, *Praenotiones*, 216, 220.

[88] Leibniz to Meier, Hanover, 4 Dec, 1691 in Leibniz, *Sämtliche Schriften*, 1st ser. vii, 447.

Christian cause. Thomasius was right, he grants, that age-old attitudes about magic and the Devil in Germany were now rapidly changing. But this was not because the old notions were wrong: it was due to false philosophical ideas about spirits and witch-craft, insidiously disseminated by Thomasius and 'Van Dale's wretched follower [i.e. Bekker]'.[89]

Among champions of the mainstream Enlightenment in Germany who continued to disapprove of the full-blown system of Van Dale, as well as Fontenelle unqualified, were Buddeus at Jena, and, at Leipzig, the moderate deist Johann Christoph Gottsched (1700–66), a disciple of Wolff and a declared enemy of Spinozism, who while favouring religious toleration, like Locke firmly excluded 'atheists'.[90] Buddeus held that if Spinoza revived Stoic ideas, those who in recent times 'ont attribué les oracles des gentils aux seules impostures et fourberies des prêtres', without allowing any intervention by demons, are reviving the notions of the Epicureans, adding 'je parle ici d'Antoine van Dale.'[91] Fontenelle had helped spread Van Dale's pernicious influence, he notes, but thankfully the Jesuit Baltus 'les a réfuté tous deux'.[92] The erudite Gottsched, for his part, prepared and annotated the German translation of Fontenelle's *Histoire* in 1730. A moderate to his fingertips, Gottsched ruled deftly that those who, like Buddeus, thought Satan had regularly operated the ancient oracles and those who, like Van Dale, claim Satan had never done so, were both mistaken, the truth lying somewhere in between.[93] But if this sounded judicious, it left a wide gulf between the 'enlightened' outlook of a Gottsched and Van Dale, since a half-way position could only mean, however much priestly fraud and artifice were acknow-ledged, that magic exists and the Devil pervades the lives of men. Gottsched rebuked Van Dale as someone who, even 'among his own sect, is considered a man of evil opinions'.[94]

Similarly in the Netherlands, where Oudaen's translation of Moebius was repub-lished in 1724, and Scandinavia, where the question of spirits and demons was a major topic throughout the Early Enlightenment, the mainstream, moderate position invariably qualified and partially condemned Van Dale. At Lund, Rydelius, whose library contained both Latin treatises of Van Dale but no Fontenelle,[95] held private seminars in the 1730s on the existence of angels and demons and whether spirits in-fluence the lives of men, in which 'Vandelius', as he calls him, emerges as the prime European writer on this subject, but with Bekker and Bayle also being regularly cited.[96] Emulating Buddeus, whose conservative Lutheran style of Enlightenment he admired (despite his Cartesian affiliations), Rydelius harshly condemns the excesses of credulity which had occurred in the past but simultaneously berates Van Dale, affirm-ing the reality of spirits and demons and their power to influence men. Another

---

[89] Goldschmidt, *Verworffener Hexen- und Zauberer Advocat*, 26–7; Pott, *Aufklärung*, 212–13.
[90] Kobuch, *Zensur und Aufklärung*, 63, 72; Otto, *Studien*, 57, 164.
[91] Buddeus, *Traité de l'Athéisme*, 139.   [92] Ibid.
[93] See Gottsched's note to Fontenelle, *Historie der heidnischen Orakel*, 211.
[94] Ibid., 212; Pott, *Aufklärung*, 207.   [95] [Rydelius], *Catalogus*, 16, 54.
[96] UUL MS Rydelius 'Collegium Privatissimum' 1, pp. 532–56; Rosen, *Lunds universitets historia*, ii, 206–10.

prominent personage in the Swedish empire much concerned with questions of magic and witchcraft was Johann Dieckmann (1647–1720) who in 1683 became Lutheran General-Superintendent of the Swedish enclaves of Bremen and Verden. Dieckmann too viewed matters from the perspective of Dutch publications and debates. His copies of Spinoza and Van Dale were in Latin but, while possessing little in French or English, he had most other relevant items, including copies of Reginald Scot, Bayle's article on Spinoza, and pamphlets for and against Bekker, in Dutch.[97]

In Spain too, the typical position of the mainstream moderate Enlightenment, publicized above all by the formidable Feijóo in the 1720s, was that while much (or most) of what went on in the ancient sanctuaries and oracle-caves was bogus, it is impermissible for an enlightened Christian to align with Van Dale. Feijóo argues in the second volume, published in 1727, of his *Teatro Crítico Universal*, the most decisive work of the Spanish Enlightenment, that not only were most of the prognostications of the ancient oracles artfully contrived by priests, but that the oracles did not cease precisely, at any rate, with Christ's coming.[98] Inevitably, he was accused of denying 'the silence of the oracles with the coming of the Redeemer' and being a follower of the heretic 'Antonio Vandale'.[99] Feijóo—who says he has not actually read Van Dale himself but is working from what he has gathered of Van Dale's argumentation from Bayle's *Nouvelles* and other French-language journals[100]—defends himself by demonstrating that Van Dale claims the Devil *never* spoke in the oracles and that 'their replies were *always* fabricated by the priests' whereas he argues the oracles were mostly impostures but that the Devil did speak through them sometimes.[101] As regards the ceasing of the oracles, it was impossible, given the historical evidence, not to concur with Van Dale that the oracles did not cease all at once with Christ's coming, as some Church Fathers wrongly maintain. Nevertheless, unlike Van Dale, he maintains that the ancient oracles ceased little by little as men learnt of the Gospel and its doctrine was received. 'How far the opinion of Antonio Vandale differs from mine,' he concludes, 'is obvious to the whole world.'[102]

In France, Baltus reaffirmed his arguments in his later works, including his general defence of the Christian religion of 1728, claiming that all idolatry was directly linked to the Devil and demonic power and that the Devil had the entire world enslaved to himself until Christ came and liberated it.[103] Even in the France of the mid-eighteenth century, *philosophes* could not publicly declare unqualified approval of the ultra-heretic Van Dale, or even Fontenelle on the subject of the Greek oracles. Nor had the topic lost any of its relevance. Nicolas Fréret,[104] the Parisian savant considered the

---

[97] [Dieckmann], *Catalogus*, 409, 412.

[98] Feijóo, *Teatro Crítico Universal*, ii, 70–91, 94–8; Feijóo, *Ilustración*, 123–5.

[99] Feijóo, *Ilustración*, 125–9.   [100] Ibid., 128.

[101] Ibid.; Feijóo, *Teatro Crítico Universal*, ii, 94–5; Staubach, 'Influence of Pierre Bayle', 84.

[102] Feijóo, *Ilustración*, 130.   [103] Baltus, *Religion Chrétienne*, 217, 239.

[104] Nicolas Féret (1688–1749), from a fervently Jansenist background, was imprisoned for some months in the Bastille in 1714–15; reputed author of one of the principal clandestine manuscripts of the first half of the

country's foremost expert on classical antiquity and ancient religion as well as Chinese philosophy, privately a radical non-providential deist who liked subtly to allude to the parallels between Confucian metaphysics and Spinozism, remarked at the end of his life, in 1749, that it was astonishing that the encounter between Fontenelle and Baltus should still be a question of some delicacy, that 'la question du surnaturel des oracles ait encore besoin d'être traitée sérieusement,' and that the idea the oracles were operated by the Devil still had 'des défenseurs très zélés'.[105] But then 'la superstition,' he adds, 'est une maladie presque incurable de l'esprit humain.'[106]

A few years later, d'Alembert recalled the War of the Oracles, in his *Éloge* to his friend Du Marsais, published as a preface to the seventh volume of the *Encyclopédie* in 1757. He briefly summarized Du Marsais' critique of Baltus—basically that of Fontenelle—found among manuscripts left at his death the previous year. But while restating Du Marsais' conclusion that 'démons n'étoient point les auteurs des oracles' and that the oracles had finally ceased without any supernatural intervention exclusively 'd'une manière naturelle',[107] he nevertheless judged it prudent to add that it is by faith alone that we know that 'il y a des démons' and by faith alone that 'nous pouvons apprendre ce qu'ils sont capables de faire dans l'ordre surnaturel', adding tactfully that it was certainly owing in part to the rise of Christianity, and not only the edicts of the Christian emperors, that finally the oracles ceased to be venerated.[108]

---

eighteenth century, the *Lettre de Thrasibule à Leucippe*, he became a formidable classical historian and philologist. A member of the 'coterie Boulainvilliers' and a friend of the count, he staunchly defended his reputation and achievement after his death. For many years he was one of the principal members of the Académie des Inscriptions et Belles-Lettres in Paris and played a major part in the 1720s in setting a new 'philosophical' standard of historical source criticism; see Grell, *Nicolas Fréret*, 3–23, Pocock, *Barbarism* i, 154–68; Wootton, 'David Hume', 287.

[105] Quoted in Landucci, 'Introduzione', 52; Grell, *Nicolas Fréret*, 46.
[106] Landucci, 'Introduzione', 53.
[107] d'Alembert, 'Éloge', p. v; Mori, 'Introduction', 130–1, 333.
[108] d'Alembert, 'Éloge', pp. v, vii.

21 | THE DEATH OF THE DEVIL

i. From Van Dale to Bekker

During the last third of the seventeenth century, the scene was set for a vast triangular contest in Europe between intellectual conservatives, moderates, and radicals over the status of the supernatural in human life and the reality of the Devil, demons, spirits, and magic. The intellectual battle was heralded by Naudé and Hobbes, the latter, despite being celebrated for his personal timorousness and 'fear of phantoms and demons'—as Bayle and, later, d'Holbach delighted in informing readers—nevertheless injecting a measure of scepticism about diabolical power and the reality of spirits.[1] Then, proceeding several steps further, from the 1660s, the founding fathers of philosophical radicalism initiated their campaign, negating Satan, spirits, and supernatural forces altogether in complete defiance of received ideas.

In the brief chapter 'On devils' of his *Korte Verhandeling* of around 1660, Spinoza rules that Satan and 'devils cannot possibly exist', adding sardonically that if the Devil did exist he would be such a wretched creature, being so opposed to God that 'if prayers could help, we ought to pray for his conversion.'[2] 'The desire men commonly have to narrate things not as they are but as they would like them to be,' he added in 1674, 'can nowhere be better exemplified than in stories about spirits and ghosts,' later remarking, in a teasing letter to a correspondent reluctant to accept that there are no apparitions or spectres, that he was puzzled believers in spirits should waver as to whether only male devils exist, or whether there are also female demons, and that 'those who have seen naked spirits should not have cast their eyes on the genital parts—perhaps they were too afraid, or ignorant of the difference'.[3] Spinoza's remarks were widely (and often indignantly) cited over subsequent decades to demonstrate his unspeakable irreverence and impudence. Not without reason, Bayle pronounced Spinoza the pre-eminent modern adversary of credence in spirits and the supernatural, a claim much reiterated subsequently.[4] But there were, of course,

---

[1] Hobbes, *Leviathan*, 210–19, 331–2, 349–63; Martinich, *Two Gods*, 250–4, 252–5; Clark, *Thinking with Demons*, 303, 310.

[2] *Collected Works of Spinoza*, i, 145.

[3] Spinoza, *Letters*, 262, 268; Falck, *De Daemonologia*, 58–9, 73; Goldschmidt, *Höllischer Morpheus*, 15.

[4] Spinoza, *Letters*, 262–3, 267–9; Masius, *Dissertationes*: section *De Existentia Demonis*, 66; Kortholt, *De Tribus Impostoribus*, 184–5; Kettner, *De Duobus Impostoribus*, B2; Goldschmidt, *Höllischer Morpheus*, 6, 11, 15, 127–8; Labrousse, *Pierre Bayle*, ii, 249–52.

also other resolute opponents of all demonology: the brothers Koerbagh, in their *Bloemhof*, deny Satan, spells, and sorcery, as well as angels, good and bad; and they were followed by the abrasive Knutzen and later Walten, Stosch, Goeree, Collins, Radicati, Edelmann, and others.

After 1650 tension between a thoroughgoing philosophical Naturalism, scorning belief in magic and the demonic, as part of a broader conceptual attack on authority, tradition, and Revelation, and, on the other side, both a moderate and a more fundamentalist, conservative stance, was everywhere evident in western and central Europe. Traditionalists were reinforced by ecclesiastical authority, religious tradition, and folklore, men of the moderate Enlightenment by Cartesian, *Malebranchiste*, empiricist, and Newtonian mechanistic philosophy. For while the Scientific Revolution, the rise of the mechanical world-view, and Lockean empiricism all helped erode the foundations on which older notions about magic, wonder-working, and the supernatural rested,[5] neither Cartesianism with its dichotomy of substances, nor Locke's epistemology, nor any mainstream trend of the Early Enlightenment provided a rationale for total repudiation of belief in spirits and magic. Indeed, leading minds of the mid and late seventeenth century, including Descartes, Boyle, and Malebranche, generally strove to accommodate spirits, magic, and the demonic within the expanding framework of scientific rationality.[6] Locke, admittedly, does not quite do this, postulating instead that 'having of ideas of spirits does not make us know that any such things do exist without us, or that there are any finite spirits, or any other spiritual beings, but the Eternal God.'[7] But equally, his epistemology does nothing to remove the 'ground from Revelation and several other reasons, to believe with assurance that there are such creatures; but our senses not being able to discover them, we want the means to discover their particular existences'.[8] Locke too, in other words, like Bishop Berkeley, leaves ample scope for credence in Satan, demons, magic, and witchcraft to persist.

In England men such as Boyle, Henry More, Ralph Cudworth, and Joseph Glanvill battled to stabilize belief in the existence and operations of apparitions and spirits as part of a wider drive to uphold religion, authority, and tradition.[9] Writing to Glanvill in May 1678, a letter reproduced in Dutch during the Bekker uproar in 1692, More powerfully decried such 'coarse grain'd philosophers as those Hobbians and Spinozians, and the rest of that rabble [who] slight religion and the Scriptures, because there is such express mention of spirits and angels in them, things that their dull souls are so inclinable to conceive to be impossible'.[10] He rejoiced to hear continual reports from every quarter of 'such fresh examples of apparitions and witchcrafts as may rub up and awaken their benumb'd and lethargic mindes into a suspicion at least, if not assur-

---

[5] Thomas, *Religion and the Decline of Magic*, 661–3.

[6] Ibid., 577–8; Clark, *Thinking with Demons*, 175, 299–306, 310–11.   [7] Locke, *Essay*, 393.

[8] Ibid.; see also Berkeley, *Principles*, 139; Clark, *Thinking with Demons*, 305, 608.

[9] Fouke, *Enthusiastical Concerns*, 172–3; Clark, *Thinking with Demons*, 302, 305, 310–11.

[10] Published in Glanvill, *Saducismus Triumphatus*, 16; and in Dutch in Koelman, *Wederlegging*, annex p. 54; see also Thomas, *Religion and the Decline of Magic*, 577, 589; Clark, *Thinking with Demons*, 303.

ance, that there are other intelligent beings besides those clad in heavy earth of clay'; those inclined to scoff at these 'well-attested stories of witches', the 'small philosophick Sir Foplings of this present age', as More styles them, were, he intimated, deep down as 'afraid of the truth of these stories as an ape is of the whip'.[11]

It was exclusively the radicals, then, reviled by contemporaries as Naturalists, *esprits forts*, and 'atheists', who comprehensively spurned traditional notions about magic and the demonic, spirits, divination, possession, and exorcism in the context both of high and popular culture. If there were influential theorists opposed partially to popular notions about sorcery and devils and who were far from being philosophical radicals, only philosophical radicals *stricto sensu* did and could rule out magical power and spirits absolutely. Meanwhile, anyone opposing belief in the Devil's power, even if he stopped short of altogether denying Satan's existence, was apt to be labelled an 'atheistic' thinker, Naturalist, and libertine.

Hence there is some justice in Anthony Collins' challenging remark, in his *Discourse of Free-Thinking*, that mankind was chiefly indebted to 'freethinking' for the recent general decline of belief in the Devil, spirits, and witches, and that it was, consequently, in the Netherlands that the process had gone furthest: 'thus the Devil is intirely banish'd [from] the United Provinces, where Free-Thinking is in the greatest perfection; whereas all round about that commonwealth, he appears in various shapes.'[12] 'This author's idle observation', as William Whiston calls it,[13] provoked outrage in England and was widely decried, chiefly for its presumption regarding freethinking but also the invidious comparison with the Netherlands. 'For England and Holland,' mimicked Jonathan Swift sarcastically, 'were formerly the Christian territories of the Devil.'[14] In so fraught a context, mainstream writers could not permit superstition's receding in Europe to be ascribed primarily to freethinking, or accept that professing Christians had not taken the lead. And certainly, they were right that Collins' claim overlooks the wider consequences of mechanistic ideas and the New Philosophy in questioning and disrupting older notions about spirits and the demonic. It was not 'freethinking which has cured belief in witchcraft', retorted the Newtonian and Boyle Lecturer, Richard Bentley, but rather the general 'growth of philosophy and medicine', adding 'the two strongest books I have read on this subject were both written by priests, the one by Dr Bekker, in Holland, and the other by a Dr of your own, whose name I've forgot.'[15]

It was indeed plainly evident who were the 'strongest' protagonists of the campaign against diabolical power and magic. Besides Spinoza, four reputations particularly stood out. As Luis António Verney, prime spokesman of the Portuguese Enlightenment noted in 1751, the four most prominent and celebrated opponents

---

[11] Glanvill, *Saducismus Triumphatus*, 16–17.

[12] [Collins], *A Discourse of Free-Thinking*, 28; [Swift], *Mr C—ns's Discourse*, 6–7; Van Bunge, 'Einleitung', 1–2.

[13] Whiston, *Reflexions*, 22.   [14] [Swift], *Mr C—ns's Discourse*, 6.

[15] [Bentley], *Remarks*, 32–4; Clark, *Thinking with Demons*, 295–6; see also Harrison, *'Religion' and the Religions*, 78–80.

of belief in satanic power, demons, and magic in mid-eighteenth-century Europe were Anthonie Van Dale, Fontenelle, Christian Thomasius, and, as Bentley noted, Balthasar Bekker.[16] Of the four, moroeover, it was unquestionably Bekker who raised the greatest storm and became the prime focus of controversy.[17] Bekker, moreover, as Bentley assured Collins, was definitely no 'freethinker' but a preacher and true Christian. Yet his tragedy was to write not just an immensely influential book but one which, at the time, could only be construed as a radical assault on authority and tradition. For this he was hounded from his pulpit, declared an agent of Spinozism and 'atheism', and publicly disgraced.

The son of a Westphalian preacher from Bielefeld, Bekker was born in the Frisian village of Metslawier, near Doccum, where his father was minister, in March 1634. After studying theology and philosophy at Groningen in the early 1650s, just when major strife between Cartesians and anti-Cartesians first convulsed the Dutch universities,[18] Bekker started his long and stormy career as a Reformed preacher. Pious, zealous for moral reform, upright if also attention-seeking, what marked him out from the first was his spirit of inquiry, keen interest in science, and aspiration to excel—and to be seen to excel—intellectually.[19] A fervent Cartesian, encountering mounting opposition among colleagues in Friesland, Bekker transferred in 1674 to a rural preaching post in neighbouring Holland. Soon after, he recounts, he visited and had a long discussion with Spinoza, in which the latter acknowledged having written the *Tractatus Theologico-Politicus*.[20] This encounter reflected no liking for Spinoza's philosophy but rather intellectual commitment and a desire to be at the forefront.

Moving to Amsterdam in 1679, he quickly made his mark in the metropolis, combining scholarly zeal with an unfortunate proneness to arouse opposition with his importunate and tactless manner. He began his crusade against the 'empire of Satan' which was to overshadow the rest of his life, by plunging into the 'comets controversy' which agitated the erudite world in the early 1680s, after the sighting of several comets, and a wave of credulous speculation during the winter of 1680–1.[21] Following Graevius, whose *Oratio de cometis*, denouncing popular notions about comets, appeared in 1681, and Bayle, whose powerful *Pensées diverses sur la comète* came out in March 1682, Bekker, burdened with work and late in the field, published only in 1683, but was no less adamant that comets are not supernatural portents.[22]

By the time Bekker began his *magnum opus*, the *Betoverde Weereld* (The World Bewitched) (four volumes, Amsterdam, 1691–3), in the late 1680s, he had developed into a typical representative of the Protestant Early Enlightenment in his eagerness to accommodate to theology the latest findings in philosophy and science. His library of

---

[16] Verney, *De Re Metaphysica*, 16–17.   [17] Trevor-Roper, *European Witch-Craze*, 102.
[18] Thijssen-Schoute, *Nederlands Cartesianisme*, 36, 142–3, 486–7.
[19] Bergsma, 'Balthasar Bekker', 84–5; Van Sluis, 'Human Factor', 101–2.
[20] Fix, 'Bekker and Spinoza', 23–4.
[21] Brink, *Toet-steen*, 92–3; Thomas, *Religion and the Decline of Magic*, 351–2.
[22] Knuttel, *Balthasar Bekker*, 149–56.

over 1,500 volumes projected the broad scientific and philosophical thrust of his concerns. Besides Huygens and Leeuwenhoek, he shelved Overkamp, Blankaart, and other exponents of the new Cartesian medicine, and runs of learned journals, including nineteen volumes of the *Acta Eruditorum* (1682–98) and Le Clerc's *Bibliothèque Universelle*.[23] He possessed works of Descartes, Clauberg, Wittichius, De Raey, Malebranche, and Régis, as well as Richard Simon's critical histories, Tschirnhaus' *Medecina Mentis*, and Petrus van Balen's *Logica* (1691), and a whole array on sorcery and daemonology, including Van Dale's works and the 1609 Leiden edition of Reginald Scot's *Discoverie of Witchcraft* (1584), the appearance of which in 'Low Dutch', according to John Beaumont, had caused 'not a few, from that time, both learned and unlearned . . . to scepticize and turn libertines concerning magick'.[24]

As he absorbed the literature concerning spirits, possession, and witches, his compulsion to speak out grew. In November 1689 he provoked a stir by publicly castigating popular notions about Satan and demons. Soon after he published, in Dutch translation, an account of a witchcraft trial held at Beckington, in Somerset, sent from England, dismissing the alleged 'proofs' as absurd and pronouncing the 'Witch of Somerset' a 'poor old woman probably more devout than most of her accusers'.[25] Colleagues in the consistory began to worry lest his outspokenness create serious difficulties. His announcement, in the Somerset witch pamphlet, that he was preparing a major work to prove conclusively that pacts with the Devil are impossible,[26] prompted appeals to his wife to help dissuade him from publishing it. As he laboured, the text expanded in scope to become the most monumental and comprehensive investigation of Satan, demonology, spirits, apparitions, magic, enchantment, and witchcraft— four volumes broaching the topic from every angle, historical, philosophical, Scriptural, and judicial—ever written so far. It had indeed become Bekker's life 'mission to disenchant the world'.[27]

Bekker was nothing if not thorough. In Book I he reviews the entire history of men's ideas on sorcery and demons, holding that the Jews, early Christians, and Church Fathers had unfortunately not just retained, but further elaborated 'pagan opinions' about magic and spirits which, in fact, have nothing to do with authentic Christian belief.[28] Matters worsened, he claims, under the medieval Church, which deliberately encouraged popular superstition and fear of the Devil's power, and witches.[29] Scorning Aquinas' Aristotelian rigmarole about spirits, he blamed medieval theologians for encouraging absurd speculations about the numbers and activities of angels, good and bad, when Scripture provides barely any data.[30] The Reformation, he held, brought some amelioration but in crucial respects failed to complete the task of purifying Christianity. Consequently, rank 'superstition' persisted still among the Protestant Churches.[31]

---

[23] Van Sluis, *Bekkeriana*, 33, 57–8.   [24] Beaumont, *Treatise of Spirits*, 348.
[25] Bekker, *Engelsche Verhaal*, 3; Simoni, 'Balthasar Bekker', 135–42.
[26] Bekker, *Engelsche Verhaal*, 7–8.   [27] Hazard, *European Mind*, 203.
[28] Bekker, *Betoverde Weereld*, i, 81, 102–4; Fix, 'Angels, Devils and Evil Spirits', 539.
[29] Bekker, *Betoverde Weereld*, i, 105.   [30] Ibid., 107–8.   [31] Ibid., 146.

In subsequent volumes Bekker expounds his philosophical and Scriptural objections to received ideas about magic, Satan, spirits, and witchcraft. He faithfully believes everything stated clearly and distinctly in Scripture, he maintains, and hence acknowledges that Satan and angels exist.[32] Later, he angrily rebuffed claims that he allowed 'there is neither any Hell nor Devil.'[33] What he denied was the near universal conviction that Satan, demons, or any spirits can, through spells, possession, bewitchment, or any magical device, alter the normal workings of nature's laws and influence men's lives. Sticking rigidly to Descartes' dichotomy of 'thought' and 'extension', he claims their being distinct substances precludes all interaction between the two, so that evil spirits, the essence of which is 'thought', can no more influence bodies than bodies can spirits.[34] Contact between disembodied spirits and humans is completely impossible. Nor, he asserts, can there be any contradiction between the truths of philosophy and theology, so that if reason proves bodies and souls distinct, Scripture likewise confirms souls have a separate existence from bodies.[35] 'Rather than question the accuracy or authority of Descartes', remarked the church historian Johann Laurenz Mosheim (1694–1755), Bekker 'thought fit to squeeze the narrations and doctrines of Scripture into a conformity with the principles and definitions of this philosopher'.[36]

Almighty God, holds Bekker, is the only supernatural power capable of changing nature's course and affecting men. God has this power, being neither 'thought' nor 'extension', nor a single substance combining thought and extension 'as Spinoza raves'.[37] Rather God supersedes any substance. Besides God, only good angels act on men since they are tools of the divine will. Even so, nothing about angels is ascertainable through reason, while Scripture reveals so little it is otiose to speculate about their number and capabilities. Much of Book II is dedicated to demonstrating that commonly supposed examples in Scripture of Satan influencing men are really nothing of the kind. Here Bekker stretches Cocceius' exegetical methodology to the limit, or, as the *Acta Eruditorum* preferred, 'perverts the plain meaning of Scripture in innumerable places with great audacity', claiming that apparent interventions of the Devil in the Bible are just poetic, allegorical references to evil inclinations in men.[38] Indeed, Bekker endeavoured to explain every intervention of the Devil and demons in Scripture as purely figurative. Thus, Satan did not really turn himself into a serpent to tempt Eve and contrive the Fall; nor did the Devil tempt Christ—or, for that matter, Job, Paul, or anyone else.[39] Furthermore, he argues, there is no Scriptural basis for belief in possession or exorcism, nor any indication that any prophet could expel evil

---

[32] Bekker, *Betoverde Weereld*, preface to Book II; Mosheim, *Ecclesiastical History*, ii, 515.

[33] Bekker, *Betoverde Weereld*, preface to Book II.

[34] Ibid., ii, 10–17, 36–8; Struve, *Bibliotheca*, 92–3; Loescher, *Praenotiones*, 217–18; Bencini, *Tractatio Historico-Polemica*, 28; Van Bunge, 'Balthasar Bekker's Cartesian Hermeneutics', 61; Van Bunge, 'Einleitung', 21–2.

[35] Bekker, *Betoverde Weereld*, ii, 3–5; Fix, 'Angels, Devils and Evil Spirits', 540–1.

[36] Mosheim, *Ecclesiastical History*, ii, 515.   [37] Bekker, *Betoverde Weereld*, ii, 11–13, 38.

[38] Ibid., ii, 131–43; *Acta Eruditorum* 1692, 27; Van der Waeyen, *Betoverde Weereld*, 14; Scholder, *Birth*, 128–31; Van Bunge, 'Balthasar Bekker's Cartesian Hermeneutics', 72–4.

[39] Bekker, *Betoverde Weereld*, ii, 143–79; Koelman, *Wederlegging* 135–6.

spirits.[40] It is every Christian's duty, he insisted, to deny that the Devil possesses supernatural knowledge or disposes of an empire on earth. For the notion that God allocates part of his power to the Devil, however widespread, is utterly absurd, a form of Manichaeism detracting from God's majesty and the purity of the Christian faith.[41] God accordingly ensures that the Devil remains completely impotent, securely locked up in Hell.

Book III examines the variety of magical processes in which people believe. Applying his Cartesian dualism of bodies and spirits as separate substances which cannot interact, he rules out all possibility of bewitchment or pacts with the Devil—and therefore witchcraft, spells, exorcism, and magic of any type.[42] Even the reality of the supernatural wonders wrought by Pharoah's magicians 'with their enchantments', recounted in Exodus, and accepted by Hobbes, becomes purely figurative in Bekker.[43] Equally, possession and exorcism are pronounced totally impossible and never to have existed.[44] Divination, he maintains, is invariably fraudulent since 'so-called diviners' never disclose anything of the future and cannot do so, lacking supernatural foresight. Nor, no matter how many people believe otherwise, do ghosts, apparitions, and spectres exist, since the laws of nature determined by 'philosophy' preclude any such possibility.[45] Similarly, there are no real curses, haunted houses, bedevilled beings, magical spells, or charms that ward off evil spirits.

Book IV examines a vast catalogue of supposedly attested cases of witchcraft, possession, exorcism, haunted places, soothsaying, and apparitions, showing mankind's inherent proneness to attribute exceptional events for which a natural explanation is lacking to supernatural forces, and the unfortunate consequences of our doing so.[46] Deriding belief in ghosts, and magical folk-tales like the Pied Piper of Hamelin, and deploring the stories parents tell children, and especially the 'unbelievable credulity of the common people in Germany',[47] he reserves his chief indignation for the witch trials about which, for years, he had diligently amassed reports from Germany, Britain, Denmark, and Sweden. He berates the Lutheran and Anglican as well as Catholic clergy, for deliberately encouraging ordinary folk in their morbid credulousness and pressuring magistrates to torment and burn poor wretches charged with witchcraft.[48] To eradicate so much crass ignorance and superstition, cultivated over so many centuries, and negate its pernicious consequences, is a herculean task but also the Christian duty of the Churches, schools, and courts: 'one sees then, clearly, there would be no magic at all if men did not believe magic exists.'[49] Were magistrates to persecute those who bring allegations of witchcraft, to make them produce adequate proofs, with half the zeal with which they torture the

---

[40] Bekker, *Betoverde Weereld*, ii, 191; Bekker, *Ondersoek en Antwoord*, 74–5.

[41] Bekker, *Betoverde Weereld*, ii, 245–6, 260–70; *Acta Eruditorum* 1692, 23; [Walten], *Aardige Duyvelary*, 3.

[42] Bekker, *Betoverde Weereld*, iii, 2–5, 10–11, 130, 172–8; Thomasius, *Kurtze Lehr-Sätze*, 7–13.

[43] Hobbes, *Leviathan*, ch. XXXVII; Loescher, *Praenotiones*, 219–20.

[44] Bekker, *Betoverde Weereld*, iii, 174.   [45] Ibid., iv, 37–8, 138–50.   [46] Ibid., 37.

[47] Ibid., 219; Hazard, *European Mind*, 204.

[48] Bekker, *Betoverde Weereld*, iv, 219, 243.   [49] Ibid., 305.

wretched accused to extract confessions, there would soon be an end, Bekker suggested, to witch-burnings.

ii. The Public Furore

Bekker's 'errors', his campaign to disenchant the world, repudiating the Devil's power and evil spirits, observed Mosheim, 'excited great tumults and divisions, not only in all the United Provinces but also parts of Germany where several doctors of the Lutheran Church were alarmed at its progress and arose to oppose it'.[50] Indeed, measured in terms of publications generated, the Bekker furore was assuredly the biggest intellectual controversy of Early Enlightenment Europe, producing a stupendous 300 publications for and against.[51] But, as we shall see, it had a much wider geographical reach than just the Netherlands and Germany. Bekker's use of Cartesian concepts to combat Satan's power, demonic interference, and magic was triumphantly seized on by conservative theologians as proof that Cartesianism generates scepticism about Satan and angels and, consequently, encourages rejection of Heaven and Hell, and therefore leads ultimately to Spinozism.[52] Voetians for their part deemed Bekker an integral part of the radical intellectual offensive, a writer who wielded philosophy in conjunction with the new Bible criticism with a view finally to subjecting theology to philosophy.[53] Yet Cartesians and Cocceians equally reviled Bekker's arguments, claiming he had overstepped what is warranted by Descartes' or Cocceius' principles.[54]

Thus the furore was in part a new bout of acrimony between Cartesians and anti-Cartesians, each denouncing the other for abetting, or failing to fight, the progress of Spinozism and both vilifying Bekker. But the ramifications extended much further than this. For the controversy over Devil and magic, unprecedented in scale, if not acrimony, rapidly pervaded popular consciousness and the entire public sphere. Numerous reports suggest that the commotion precipitated a fundamental shift in attitude among ordinary folk as well as among the learned.[55] The Middelburg preacher Carolus Tuinman, for instance, expressly ascribes to Bekker, and the commotion surrounding his book, the sliding of the Dutch population away from belief in diabolical power in the 1690s and subsequently, and mounting scepticism in society about the reality of Satan, demons, angels, apparitions, sorcery, and bewitchment.[56] In their petition to the provincial States urging prohibition of Bekker's book, the Holland synods claimed the work had generated more uproar 'both inside and outside the Reformed Church than perhaps any book had ever done' and not only scandalized faithful Christians but vastly encouraged 'atheists and scoffers', providing new pre-

---

[50] Mosheim, *Ecclesiastical History*, ii, 515.   [51] Israel, 'Bekker Controversies', 5–9.
[52] Koelman, *Het Vergift*, 12, 283, 457.   [53] *Bibliothèque Universelle*, xxii (1692), 190.
[54] Bekker, *Brief . . . aan twee eerwaardige Predikanten*, 7–8; Van der Waeyen, *Betooverde Weereld*, 14; [Walten], *Vervolg*, 10; Israel, *Dutch Republic*, 927.
[55] Brink, *Toet-steen*, preface, p. xxi; [Walten], *Beschryvinge*, 9–10; Tuinman, *Johan Kalvijns Onderrichting*, i, 54–5.
[56] Tuinman, *Johan Kalvijns Onderrichting*, i, 55, 59 and ii, 50.

texts for blasphemy and mockery at a time when 'contempt for Scripture, and irreligion, are spreading rapidly.'[57]

The scale of the affair is reflected in the sales of the book. The first two volumes, totalling over 400 pages, appearing in two editions in 1691, in Friesland and Amsterdam, and comprising 5,750 copies, sold out in two months, a staggering performance for the seventeenth century.[58] According to Bekker who, to weed out defective copies, methodically inspected and authenticated them with his signature, over 8,000 had sold by January 1693.[59] By any reckoning *De Betoverde Weereld* was a bestseller. Pamphlets for and (more often) against Bekker streamed from the presses, not solely of Amsterdam and The Hague but also Utrecht, Dordrecht, Enkhuizen, Middelburg, and Franeker. Although numerous professors entered, or were dragged into, the fray, only three refutations—those of Melchior Leydekker, Petrus van Mastricht, and Pierre Poiret—appeared in Latin and the first even of these followed in Dutch.[60] So huge was the public involvement that scholars were obliged to discourse in the vernacular.

But why was there such interest? Most of what is published, remarked one preacher, is ignored. Yet suddenly, countless young folk and their elders are immersed in Bekker's text. This would be inconceivable, he suggests, were it not for the corrosive effect on society of philosophical scepticism and irreligion. Reports reaching him showed that Bekker's work 'especially pleases certain clever minds . . . who habitually make such a fuss about reason and philosophy that they are willing to pit these against the Bible and even—following Spinoza—the Almighty Himself'.[61] Accordingly, if Bekker was the instrument, 'philosophy', the new 'Devil', as some called it, was the real culprit. And what exactly were the intellectual sources of Bekker's principles? Cartesian inspiration was clear, as was that of Van Dale, with whom Bekker admitted being on friendly terms and exchanging ideas and information.[62] Likewise, Bekker acknowledged his debt to the sixteenth-century Englishman, Reginald Scot, and the Huguenot minister, Benjamin Daillon. But most commentators were far more interested in unmasking the undeclared, forbidden well-springs of Bekker's 'system' than in such obvious matter as Descartes and Van Dale.

Bekker, indeed, was continually accused of following Hobbes and Spinoza, and being an adjunct of 'atheistic' philosophy. Hobbes was constantly invoked throughout the Bekker imbroglio. Yet there is no reference or allusion to Hobbes in Bekker's writing and Bekker himself protested he had not read Hobbes' *Leviathan* until after the publication of his first two volumes, when he found himself being labelled a 'Hobbesian' by his enemies.[63] Hobbes, in fact, was only very superficially part of the Bekker

---

[57] Bekker, *Ondersoek en Antwoord*, 93.

[58] Grapius, *Systema*, ii, 80; Kettner, *De Duobus Impostoribus*, B2; Knuttel, *Balthasar Bekker*, 267.

[59] Bekker, *Ondersoek en Antwoord*, 93–4; Israel, 'Bekker Controversies', 2.

[60] Bekker, *Kort Beright*, 60.   [61] [Sylvius], *Consideratien*, 9.

[62] Bekker, *Betoverde Weereld*, i, 132, ii, 82, 203, and iii, 160–2; Koelman, *Wederlegging*, 146–54.

[63] Koelman, *Wederlegging*, 118–28; Leydekker, *Dr Bekkers philosophise Duyvel*, 29–31; Bekker, *Kort Beright*, 62; Kettner, *De Duobus Impostoribus*, B3v; Zobeln, *Declaratio Apologetica*, 2, 6–8.

furore. The real issue, as innumerable writers insisted, was Spinoza. Bekker mentions him several times, albeit (of course) always negatively, and he was plainly crucial to Bekker's thinking, especially his exegetical methodology and account of God which, as Bekker himelf states, is cast directly in opposition to Spinoza's conception.[64] Spinoza's influence, moreover, clearly underlies Bekker's claims that philosophical reason is the only valid criterion when investigating 'natural things', and that Scripture is not intended to teach truth about worldly phenomena, but provide explanations adapted to the understanding of ordinary folk so as to help instil obedience to God's commandments.[65]

Bekker indignantly denied subordinating theology to philosophy like the Spinozists, pronouncing Holy Writ the supreme and only authority in matters of Salvation.[66] But since Scripture seldom explains 'natural things' as they are, 'reason', he also maintained 'must teach how to interpret Scripture in that area according to the circumstances of nature'.[67] Bekker, in effect, contradicted the plain meaning of much of Scripture, and not only Scripture, as Melchior Leydekker and other conservative critics insisted, but also everything Eusebius, Origen, and numerous other Church Fathers had pronounced concerning the oracles and operations of Satan in pagan times, and the ceasing of the oracles and pagan divination with Christ's coming: 'or, si le sentiment de M. Bekker a lieu,' observed Le Clerc, 'il faudra dire que toutes les prétensions de ces anciens Chrétiens étoient fausses, et que tous les raisonnemens de ces grands docteurs de l'Église en faveur de leur religion n'avoient d'autre fondement que cette misérable erreur populaire.'[68] If Bekker was right, then Christ's advent had not, after all, decisively curbed Satan's empire on earth.

Bekker's 'system' for disenchanting the world indubitably involved circumventing the plain meaning of Scripture, and the Church Fathers, and embracing exegetical ideas close to Spinoza's.[69] Furthermore, to render plausible his thesis that seeming references to the Devil in Scripture are actually misconstrued Hebrew expressions designating 'wicked persons', Bekker frequently questions the reliability of passages in the States Bible, implying errors in translation which, critics protested, was bound to prompt the impious to allege grave, even deliberate, deception of the people.[70] 'That an atheist, Spinozist, or freethinker should do this is to be expected,' commented one writer, but it seemed incredible that a minister of the Reformed Church should do so.[71] Jacobus Koelman, a Calvinist fundamentalist theologian, while emphasizing the kinship of Bekker's ideas with those of Hobbes, and especially

---

[64] Bekker, *Betoverde Weereld*, i, 15–16; Fix, 'Bekker and Spinoza', 29–32.
[65] Bekker, *Naakte Uitbeeldinge*, 10; Koelman, *Wederlegging*, 129, 388; *Bibliothèque Universelle*, xxii (1692), 189, 197; *Zweyte Unterredung Oder Gespräche im Reiche der Todten*, 101; Van Scholder, *Birth*, 128–31; Van Bunge, 'Balthasar Bekker's Cartesian Hermeneutics', 71–2.
[66] Bekker, *Naakte Uitbeeldinge*, 11; Fix, 'Bekker and Spinoza', 29.
[67] Bekker, *Naakte Uitbeeldinge*, 10–11; Koelman, *Wederlegging*, 129–35.
[68] *Bibliothèque Universelle*, xxii (1692), 194–5.
[69] *Acta Eruditorum* 1692, 543, 547; Fix, 'Bekker and Spinoza', 28–32; Jaumann, *Critica*, 146.
[70] Bekker, *Betoverde Weereld*, ii, 143–5, 226; Koelman, *Het Vergift*, preface.
[71] *De Gebannen Duyvel*, 35.

Koerbagh, on demonology, magic, and spirits,[72] deemed Bekker's claim to be combating Spinoza a malicious ruse.[73] 'Our famous Bekker,' he admonished readers, 'has known this person and went deliberately—out of curiosity ostensibly—to visit him; what he learnt there we may surmize by comparing his book with Spinoza's.'[74]

Bekker does not, of course, deprive Scripture of all truth content, like Spinoza, but he does maintain that Holy Writ, including Christ's teaching, is adjusted to the ignorant and credulous understanding of the common people of the time. Hence, even those critics who sympathized with his assault on popular superstition and witch trials, repudiated his overall conceptual framework as philosophically and theologically simply too radical. Bayle, while approving Bekker's campaign against superstitious dread of devils and magic, nevertheless objected (whether sincerely or not) that he had overstepped the limits of what was acceptable in a Christian writer.[75] Le Clerc and the *Bibliothèque Universelle* equally felt obliged to distance themselves from his stance.[76] The tragic irony was that Bekker was convinced no one had dealt Spinoza a more devastating blow than himself.[77]

Petrus van Mastricht, at Utrecht, linked Bekker to Spinoza and also the furore over (Meyer's) *Philosophia S. Scripturae Interpres*. The true meaning of the uproar, he urged, was that it proved, despite his disavowal, that 'in matters of Salvation', Bekker places philosophy above Scripture and that theology was being sacrificed to the axiom 'philosophy is the infallible interpreter of Scripture.'[78] Do not Bekker's assertions prove that in everything not directly relating to Salvation he ranks philosophy above theology? Undoubtedly, Mastricht had a point. The battle now under way, he insists, was part of a wider contest between philosophy and theology for supremacy in society: 'will Scripture yield to philosophy, or philosophy to Scripture?'[79] Either Scripture is eternally true and the authentic word of God, held Mastricht, or the world will be overrun by philosophy, scepticism, and atheism.[80]

While most of the hail of anti-Bekker pamphlets were written by Reformed preachers, or other churchmen, Bekker's supporters, those to whom radical minds ascribed 'unhindered reason and understanding', were laymen of a predominantly secular outlook.[81] According to Goeree—and Bekker's most outspoken ally, the radical republican Ericus Walten—many 'philosophically-minded' or 'reason-loving' members of the regent class were disgusted by the tide of anti-Bekker sentiment

---

[72] Koelman, *Wederlegging*, 137.   [73] Koelman, *Het Vergift*, 478, 649; Koelman, *Wederlegging*, 129.

[74] Koelman, *Het Vergift*, 487; Koelman, *Wederlegging*, 129.   [75] Labrousse, *Pierre Bayle*, ii, 12–13.

[76] *Bibliothèque Universelle*, xxi (1691), 122–51; and xxii (1692), 187–210.

[77] Bekker, *Betoverde Weereld*, i, 16; Leydekker, *Dr Bekkers Philosophise Duyvel*, 1; Bergsma, 'Balthasar Bekker', 74, 84.

[78] Bekker, *Betoverde Weereld*, i, 11; Mastricht, *Ad virum clariss. D. Balthasarem Beckerum*, 25; Beckher, *Schediasma*, 25.

[79] Mastricht, *Ad virum clariss. D. Balthasarem Bekkerum*, 25, 36; *Bibliothèque Universelle*, xxii (1692), 187–9; Beckher, *Schediasma*, 36, 52.

[80] Mastricht, *Ad virum clariss. D. Balthasarem Bekkerum*, 52, 73, 76; Beckher, *Schediasma*, 76.

[81] Goeree, *Kerklyke en weereldlyke*, 679.

building on the crass superstition of the unlettered.[82] Bekker himself remarks that, in Amsterdam, his adherents belonged to the more educated lay sectors of society while his hard-line orthodox assailants found support chiefly among the less sophisticated lower strata.[83] At Leiden, reportedly, many students applauded Bekker.[84] Nevertheless, most sympathizers, wary of repression—Walten terms them 'Nicodemites'— kept their heads down, deeming it prudent to remain silent,[85] even though the scale of the commotion and compelling force of the debate simultaneously emboldened a few to emerge publicly, unfurl the banner of 'philosophy', and, for the first time, openly criticize the Reformed Church and its attitudes and proceedings. 'No one in years has done so much,' lamented one pamphleteer, as Bekker with his books to promote the cause of the 'atheists, freethinkers, and mockers of Scripture'.[86]

That Holland's freethinkers and *Spinozisten* should rally behind Bekker and exploit the uproar to promote their ideas was predictable. Indeed, everyone agreed that what adversaries termed the 'atheism of Hobbes and Spinoza', and Walten calls the 'pure light of philosophy', was gaining a major new impetus.[87] A famous coup by the radical philosophical underground was the clandestine production of five triumphal medals celebrating Bekker's 'slaying' of the Devil, embellished with pithy Latin tags, several or all devised by the famous Leiden medallist Johannes Smeltzing.[88] One of these (see Plate 18) depicts Bekker as the 'Frisian Hercules' wielding a powerful club (philosophy) with which he dispatches Satan portrayed as a many-headed dragon.[89] So great an uproar, held Koelman, encouraged the 'New Sadducees', as he and Jacobus Leydekker styled adherents of the new 'religion of philosophy', to 'raise their voices' and advance *en masse*.[90]

Of those intrepid enough to support Bekker's ideas in print, by far the most acerbic was the Orangist political writer—and author of the Latin tags on the Smeltzing medals—Ericus Walten (1663–97). Claiming that the preachers decrying Bekker comported themselves like inquisitors who, if not curbed, would render 'our free Netherlands' worse than 'Spain, Italy, and all other papist lands', labelling all who oppose them 'Spinosisten, Hobbesianen en Socinianen', he himself was publicly denounced as a 'Spinozist' whose purpose was further to inflame the situation.[91] If not exactly a 'Spinozist', Walten was certainly a republican and philosophical radical who held Koerbagh's *Bloemhof* in high esteem and proudly reckoned himself a leader of the philosophical underground; indeed, he boasted of being the chief thorn in the eye of the anti-Bekker party.[92] Not only did he follow Lodewijk Meyer in proclaiming the primacy of philosophy but 'philosophy' in his discourse clearly entails a public campaign

---

[82] Goeree, *Kerklyke en weereldlyke*, 680; [Walten], *Beschryvinge*, 10–11; Bekker, *Ondersoek en Antwoord*, 93.

[83] Bekker, *Nodige Bedenkingen*, 8.   [84] *De Gebannen Duyvel*, 12.

[85] [Walten], *Vervolg*, 3–4, 11.   [86] Ibid., 28; Koelman, *Wederlegging*, 54, 89.

[87] Groenewegen, *Pneumatica*, 52; *Verhandeling van de Mirakelen*, 14; *Philopater*, 49, 65, 140.

[88] Knuttel, 'Ericus Walten', 348.   [89] Van Loon, *Beschrijving*, iv, 225; Knuttel, *Balthasar Bekker*, 268.

[90] Koelman, *Het Vergift*, preface.

[91] [Walten], *Triumpheerenden Duyvel*, 8; 'Leetsosoneus', *Den Swadder*, 12, 20–1; Van Bunge, 'Eric Walten', 42.

[92] Knuttel, 'Ericus Walten', 430–8; Van Bunge, 'Eric Walten', 49–51; Israel, 'Bekker Controversies', 12–13.

to enlighten the people and overcome those, above all ecclesiastics, in whose interest it is to keep the people superstitious and ignorant.[93] While going beyond Bekker in rejecting Satan and demons altogether—the only 'devil' he would acknowledge was that earthly 'devil', Louis XIV—he criticized the Churches' attitude with unprecedented vehemence. The 'people have been kept ignorant and blind long enough,' he maintains in one of his pro-Bekker pamphlets, by those accustomed to abuse the common man as if he were 'Bileam's [i.e. Balaam's] donkey'.[94] 'Since the light of clear philosophy first shone in this century,' he averred, the 'monster of ghosts, sorcery, and fear and terror of the Devil, has been gradually weakened,' until finally the heroic Bekker arose to fight Satan himself, and popular credulousness receded more rapidly so that 'now the gross superstition of the past, fuelled by ignorance and the interests of the clergy, is being destroyed by the power of truth.'[95] Thankfully, he affirms, there were enough 'enlightened' regents to ensure that the synods' efforts to have Bekker's book and ideas prohibited by the States were repulsed.[96]

Carried away by 'philosophical' zeal, Walten recklessly denounced Bekker's assailants as 'seditious, Devil-sick usurpers' avid to rob men of the right to think for themselves, obscurantists who wanted the contest fought in Latin so that the common man should be excluded and remain uncontaminated by 'philosophy'.[97] He even calls his antagonists 'Satan-worshippers' and 'disturbers of the public peace', aspiring to replace the Devil on his throne just as the Jacobites, exuding treason, sought to restore James II to the British thrones.[98] Denounced in November 1692 by the South Holland Synod to the provincial high court of Holland, for blasphemy and slandering the Reformed Church, he was eventually arrested at The Hague in March 1694.[99] With Walten imprisoned, the *procureur-generaal* of the Hof began a lengthy investigation of his papers. Facing charges potentially incurring grave penalties, including allegedly having said the New Testament story of Christ being tempted by the Devil is all 'bagatelles', he was left to meditate on the benefits of philosophy in prison for three years while his case ground on interminably. In despair that William III failed to rescue him, and finding no response to his repeated pleas for his case to be concluded, he was to die in his cell, probably by suicide, universally decried as a godless blasphemer, in 1697.[100]

If linking Bekker to Descartes embarrassed the Cartesio-Cocceians in the Church and universities, connecting him to the 'Cartesian atheist Spinoza' as Koelman styles him, 'after whom nowadays all atheists among us are called *Spinosisten*,'[101] was designed to tar both Bekker and Descartes and maximize the association of the

---

[93] [Walten], *Brief aan den Heer Portland*, 78–80; [Walten], *Triumpheerenden Duyvel*, 10; Van Bunge, 'Eric Walten', 47, 54.

[94] [Walten], *Vervolg*, 5; [Walten], *Triumpheerenden Duyvel*, 10–11.

[95] [Walten], *Vervolg*, 5–6; [Walten], *Triumpheerenden Duyvel*, 12.

[96] [Walten], *Vervolg*, 12.   [97] Ibid., 3, 7, 27.

[98] Knuttel, 'Ericus Walten', 399; Israel, *Dutch Republic*, 929.

[99] Knuttel, 'Ericus Walten', 404–5, 437–8; Van Bunge, 'Eric Walten', 52–5.

[100] Knuttel, 'Ericus Walten', 442, 453.   [101] Koelman, *Het Vergift*, 487.

philosophical, critical spirit in people's minds with Spinoza. It was also hoped that tying Bekker's endeavours to Spinoza would, if not fatally damage, then at least extensively obstruct, the further progress of 'philosophy', putting the critical, 'philosophical' spirit back, as it were, in its cage, by equating the New Philosophy and Bekker with Naturalism and atheism. In this way, traditionalists could conceivably subordinate reason once more to authority and reaffirm theology's hegemony. Answering Cartesian protests that Bekker's ideas are not authentically 'Cartesian' but pervert Descartes' ideas, several writers objected that this was beside the point, because the real issue was Bekker's overriding of the Church's teaching and the untrammelled espousal of philosophy as an instrument for interpreting Man, God, and the universe; and his having done this from within the Reformed Church.[102] 'Philosophy', claimed one, was the real 'Devil' gnawing the intestines of the public Church. How could the faithful rise up as one to combat the *Hobbesianen* and *Spinosisten* whilst the Church was sick unto its very heart with 'philosophy'?[103] Strive as they might, held Koelman, Cartesians and those who embrace mechanistic philosophy could disown neither Bekker nor Spinoza. Spinoza, he argued, drew his fundamental principles from Descartes 'especially the doubting of everything in order to find truth', the notion of the certainty and infallibility of mathematical reason, the technique of interpreting Scripture as a reflection of the imaginings and prejudices of men, the 'dogma' of the movement of the earth round the sun, and finally the 'demonstrating of everything with philosophical reasoning'.[104] From Cartesian ingredients Spinoza had concocted his 'philosophical religion' which was now poised, with Bekker's support, to challenge all established religion, tradition, and authority.

iii. Churches Divided

The convulsion was by no means confined to the Reformed Church. The disputes also involved the Lutherans, Remonstrants, Mennonites, Collegiants, and other Churches, most reaction again being broadly hostile. Effectively, Bekker's *Betoverde Weereld* turned all the Dutch Churches and theological factions against him.[105] Limborch several times mentioned the affair in his letters to Locke, criticizing the excessive zeal of Bekker's opponents and regretting that so devout, scholarly, and fair-minded a man should have imprudently put himself in such a position, but equally, dismissing his doctrines as indefensible. He grants there is too much superstition in the world: but to claim evil spirits never assail men and that Adam and Eve were not led astray by the Devil, to fail 'to ascribe to good angels what the Christian world unanimously believes is ascribed to them in Scripture', and much else which 'contradicts the opinions of the community of Christians', is simply unacceptable.[106] Only among the ultra-liberal Collegiants was there any significant theologically based

---

[102] Leydekker, *Dr Bekkers Philosophise Duyvel*, 31; *Bibliothèque Universelle*, xxii (1692), 187–8, 190.
[103] Leydekker, *Dr Bekkers Philosophise Duyvel*, 115–19, 134–5.
[104] Koelman, *Het Vergift*, 487.   [105] Wielema, 'Met Bekkerianerij besmet', 150–1.
[106] Locke, *Correspondence*, iv, 295–8, 356–9, 559.

support for Bekker, though even here the mainstream condemned his ideas, provoking fierce altercations in the mid-1690s over angels and demons, in which a faction led by Herman Bouman and a certain J. Pel embraced positions resembling, or theologically even more sweeping, than Bekker's.[107] Pel, who remarks that many people, including himself, changed their opinions on spirits and demons as a consequence of reading Bekker,[108] not only insists that the Devil does not operate in the world, or on men, but also denies the very existence of angels and demons.[109]

There was reaction also among dissenting fringe theologians with a private following, such as the influential Willem Deurhoff (1650–1715) who had no formal academic background and knew no Latin, but had immersed himself in the New Philosophy through Glazemaker's translations of Descartes and Spinoza.[110] Detested by the organized Churches as the leader of a popular philosophico-theological tendency in some ways akin to the radicals' universal quasi-religion, Deurhoff, while rejecting Spinoza, from whom he nevertheless borrowed much, proved the appeal of a new type of ordinary man's theology based outside the Churches. Deurhoff agreed with Bekker's maxim that mind and extension cannot interact and therefore that 'neither the human soul, nor angels, nor demons, can work on any body or spirit separate from itself.'[111] But rather than follow Bekker in precluding all action of spirits on men, he adopts Geulincx' 'occasionalist' solution—postulating the absolute synchronization of bodies and minds through divine intervention.[112] The action of human souls on bodies through God's Will is, he held, conceptually exactly the same sort of process as the operations of Satan, demons, angels, and other spirits on bodies. In this way Deurhoff believed he had shown philosophically how the Biblical accounts of spirits acting on men, bedevilment, and even the annihilation of whole Assyrian armies by exterminating angels could be literally true.[113]

But it was the Reformed Church which, from first to last, headed the drive against Bekker, or more precisely, the two rival thrusts of the anti-Bekker campaign, for two opposed solutions to the imbroglio arose within the public Church. The Amsterdam consistory, a relatively liberal body compared with those of Rotterdam, Utrecht, or Middelburg, with a strong Cartesio-Cocceian presence, had long sought to minimize theological friction in the city by carefully balancing, at the burgomasters' bidding, the Voetian and Cocceian blocs among its preachers.[114] Hence while both groups repudiated Bekker's ideas, there emerged two distinct and incompatible responses. The forty-nine members of the assembly first debated the *Betoverde Weereld* on 31 May 1691, after the Frisian, but before the Amsterdam edition had appeared, and before

[107] Knuttel, *Balthasar Bekker*, 236–7; Fix, 'Angels, Devils and Evil Spirits', 545–7; Fix, *Fallen Angels*, 112, 116.
[108] Pel, *Wonderdaden*, dedication.   [109] Ibid.; Fix, *Fallen Angels*, 108–12.
[110] Krop, 'Radical Cartesianism', 55–6.
[111] Blijenbergh and Deurhoff, *Klaare en beknoopte Verhandeling*, 7, 11; Krop, 'Radical Cartesianism', 67.
[112] Fix, 'Willem Deurhoff', 158–61.
[113] Blyenbergh and Deurhoff, *Klaare en beknopte Verhandeling*, 16–17, 40–1, 64.
[114] Koelman, *Het Vergift*, 20; Knuttel, *Balthasar Bekker*, 140, 148.

most members had yet perused the text. The mere recital of its contents, however, caused great consternation, owing to the sensitivity of the subject, since Bekker had ignored both the usual requirement for Reformed preachers to seek approval from their *classis* before publishing and recent admonitions to be prudent.[115] As the weeks passed, disagreement over how to handle the furore gradually intensified.

Initially, the North Holland Synod agreed to let the Amsterdam consistory settle the affair. Bekker was provisionally suspended from his pulpit; and, after key extracts were read out, the consistory formally condemned and 'abominated' his book on 28 June, without a single dissenting vote. However, the comparatively moderate course adopted subsequently, of endeavouring to purge Bekker and his text of unacceptable theses without stripping him of his ministry or asking the civil authorities to suppress the book, reflected the views of the Cartesio-Cocceian faction. To them it was vital, if they were to hold the line against the Voetian offensive, that a work relying on Descartes' principles should not be banned *in toto* but expurgated to remove unacceptable error. A select committee of the consistory, meeting with Bekker, spent months in close scrutiny of texts and exhaustive debate, until ten pages of agreed *Articles of Satisfaction* emerged which Bekker was willing to sign.

He acknowledges, in the preamble, that his book had caused widespread suspicion that he professes opinions akin to those of the 'Sadducees' and 'nonsensical views' of Spinoza.[116] The resulting clarifications were declared necessary in particular to remove 'all suspicion of *Spinosisterie*'. Under the *Articles* Bekker fully accepts the Church's teaching that there are both good and bad angels created by God, that Satan heads the latter, and that good angels, as instruments of the Lord, act—at least indirectly, through Him—on men, carrying out His judgements 'to the benefit of the elect and punishment of the godless'.[117] On the other hand, Bekker was not required to acknowledge that the Devil, or evil angels, similarly act on men. The text of the duly signed *Articles* was approved by both consistory and district *classis*, and published in January 1692.

The Amsterdam *Articles of Satisfaction*, however, served merely to inflame further what was now a national and international disturbance of unprecedented proportions. Rotterdam's predominantly Voetian consistory formally renewed its denunciation of Bekker on 27 February 1692, for his erroneous teaching 'on good and bad angels' and 'shocking method of interpreting Scripture'[118] and, at the same time, roundly rejected the 'so-called Satisfaction' devised in Amsterdam for failing to exact an adequate retraction of 'error', or condemn Bekker's 'distortions' of Scripture, or express the distress and shock caused to the entire Reformed Church in the Netherlands and abroad. Early in March, this body dispatched a circular letter to every *classis* in South Holland and several in North Holland, as well as the consistories of Utrecht, Middelburg, Groningen, Kampen, Leeuwarden, and Nijmegen outside Holland,

[115] *Acten ofte Handelingen*, ii, 2.
[116] *Articulen tot Satisfactie*, preamble.   [117] Ibid., clause v.
[118] GA Rotterdam Acta des Kerckenraedts VII, pp. 361–2. res. 27 Feb. 1692.

highlighting their objections to the Amsterdam proceedings.[119] In their indignant letter of protest to their Amsterdam colleagues, the Rotterdam consistory claimed the continued uproar was causing great harm to the Church and encouraging 'atheists and mockers of Holy Scripture in their godlessness'.[120]

Rotterdam's call for an orchestrated campaign to nullify the Amsterdam *Articles*, condemn Bekker's views categorically, and expel him from the ministry met with a mixed reception. Predominantly Cartesio-Cocceian consistories, such as Delft, wished to see matters left to the Amsterdam consistory to resolve as they thought fit.[121] Voetian consistories supported Rotterdam's hard line. Utrecht intervened particularly strongly, stressing that the commotion was not confined to the Reformed community and that, besides upsetting all pious folk by eroding the Bible's authority, the uproar was serving to 'open the mouths' of the 'freethinkers and mockers', enabling them to spread their gall on all sides.[122] Writing to the Amsterdam consistory, Utrecht reiterated the arguments of Melchior Leydekker and Petrus van Mastricht that Bekker's real offence, however much he disguised his 'novelties' with quotations from Scripture, was to subordinate theology to philosophy, that is, concepts originating in Descartes and also Geulincx—who, in 1666, had arranged disputations with his students at Leiden, in which the Devil was reduced to a mere principle, the evil inclination in man—as well as Hobbes and Spinoza. For if Bekker and Van Dale were right in claiming that the early Christians and Church Fathers, like the Jews, simply borrowed their ideas about Satan and spirits from earlier pagan religions, then it follows that Christ and the Apostles practised a deliberate, conscious 'deception' upon the people, since the Gospel fully subscribes to the people's belief in spirits, magic, and wonders. If so, then Christ's miracles could be said to have 'deceitfully' encouraged and manipulated the common folk in their vulgar delusions.[123]

Another powerful intervention was the missive of the four Zeeland *classes* meeting in emergency session at Middelburg, to the North Holland Synod, written by Carolus Tuinman and dated 20 May 1692. Bekker's 'abominable book', it was reported, was being eagerly lapped up in Zeeland by 'novelty-loving, dissolute, freethinking, persons who like nothing better than to hear the Devil is not so black as he has been painted'; the uproar was encouraging freethinkers in their 'malicious slander' of the province's 'orthodox defenders of the truth' and, worse still, spreading the ideas of 'Hobbes and Spinoza', which, claimed Tuinman, were now gaining such a foothold in Zeeland as to be seriously endangering all authority and religion.[124]

Meanwhile, the struggle within the North Holland Synod mounted towards its acrimonious climax. The Voetians sensed victory. The *classis* of Hoorn headed the

[119] Ibid., p. 365. res. 5 Mar. 1692.

[120] Ibid., pp. 366–7. Rotterdam consistory to Amsterdam consistory, 18 Mar. 1692.

[121] GA Delft Kerkeraaad VII, fos. 207v–210v. res. 9 and 12 Mar. 1692.

[122] GA Utrecht Acta Kerkenraad 11. res. 29 Feb. (old style) 1692.

[123] Ibid.; Knuttel, *Balthasar Bekker*, 238; see also Van der Waeyen, *Betooverde Weereld*, 10, 153; Pel, *Wonderdaden*, 70; *Bibliothèque Universelle*, xxii (1692), 94–5, 187.

[124] *Acten ofte Handelingen*, 47–9.

hard-line anti-Bekker offensive, adamant that the *Articles of Satisfaction* of January 1692 were insufficient, that Bekker's 'pernicious views' must be comprehensively condemned, Bekker dismissed from his pulpit, and his book suppressed. By contrast, the Cartesio-Cocceian bloc, however discomforted by Bekker's ideas, were chiefly fearful lest the Voetians succeed in using the opportunity to overwhelm them in the Church and universities. Several *classes* were deeply split, that of Alkmaar, for instance, only being able to reach a resolution on the Amsterdam *Articles* by putting the issue (unusually) to a formal vote, in which the Articles were rejected by twenty-six hands to seventeen.[125] Bekker, for his part, accused the Voetians of deliberately engineering the interventions of the Utrecht, Middelburg, Groningen, and Leeuwarden consistories, as well as the outcry among the Reformed Churches of Germany, in order to 'vanquish those who follow the teaching of Descartes and Cocceius' in the synods, by tarring them with the brush of Hobbes and Spinoza.[126]

Finally, at a fraught gathering in July 1692, most *classes* of the North Holland Synod voted to repudiate the Amsterdam *Articles*. Bekker's work was duly condemned outright by the synod and he himself declared unfit to be a preacher of the public Church. Bekker, who was present, indignantly protested at what he regarded as the injustice and folly of these resolutions. The outcome left the Amsterdam burgomasters with little choice but to acquiesce in his dismissal, though being anxious not to appear too subservient to ecclesiastical authority, and, given that he had many sympathizers in the city (and city government), they decided to suspend Bekker permanently, without loss of salary, rather than formally eject him from his post.[127] Reporting to the States of Holland, the two Holland synods deplored the huge disturbance precipitated by Bekker's 'damaging ideas', to the encouragement of 'atheists and mockers', and urged the States to ban the publication and sale of Bekker's book in their province and request other provinces to do likewise.[128] The Holland regents, however, mindful that there was public sentiment for, as well as against, Bekker, that the Church was divided, and that the Cartesio-Cocceians had strong reasons for opposing an outright ban, decided not to prohibit it, though the Utrecht city government, disagreeing, did order the book's suppression there.[129] Bekker, for his part, produced a powerful riposte: having withheld publication of the latter two volumes of his work pending the outcome of the Synod's deliberations, he now proceeded with publishing the rest.

iv. The European Diffusion

Bekker's book, as the *Acta Eruditorum* reported in 1692, had a wide impact in the 'orbe literario' (the world of letters).[130] It has been argued by one modern historian that 'by

---

[125] RNH Gereformeerde kerk, Classis Alkmaar, res. 10 June and 16 July 1692; and Classis Edam vol. vi acta 21 July 1692.

[126] Bekker, *Noodige Bedenkingen*, 53–5.   [127] [Tentzel], *Monatliche Unterredungen* 1693, 256–7.

[128] *Acten often Handelingen*, 98–101; Knuttel, *Balthasar Bekker*, 333.

[129] Van de Water, *Groot Placaatboek . . . Utrecht*, iii, 433; Sandberg, *At the Crossroads*, 102–3.

[130] *Acta Eruditorum* 1692, 19; Hazard, *European Mind*, 204.

1706, Bekker seemed forgotten. His work had enjoyed a *succès de scandale* only.'[131] But in reality this was not the case. Outside the Netherlands, awareness of the controversy spread rapidly and remained intense for well over half a century. A German pamphlet published in 1732 proclaimed Bekker incomparably the chief Devil-denier and opponent of magic within German culture.[132] In 1739 another German writer remarked that 'almost everybody' has something to say about Bekker even if they do not have a detailed knowledge of his doctrines.[133] The standard-bearer of the Portuguese Enlightenment, Verney, remarked in 1751 that Bekker was everywhere regarded as the pre-eminent voice denying 'operations of demons' in the contest over demonology, magic, and Satan's power which preoccupied Europe in the early eighteenth century.[134] Admittedly, there was very little interest in the Bekker disputes in Britain. But this was an exception, partly due no doubt to the fact that Cartesianism played a much less central role in establishing the mechanistic world-view there than in continental Europe. Elsewhere, from Portugal to Sweden *Bekkerianismus* was and long remained highly controversial and was generally classified (whatever Bekker's personal Christian convictions) as an integral part of the Radical Enlightenment, a philosophical stance rooted in an illicit variant of Cartesianism and in Spinozism, and hence a grave threat to authority, tradition, and religion.

Those lacking Dutch did not have to wait long to learn what it was all about. Le Clerc, editor of the *Bibliothèque Universelle*, published a 29-page review of Bekker's first two volumes in September 1691. In November Leibniz, then in Hanover and already well-informed, wrote to Magliabecchi in Florence about both Bekker's book and the uproar, explaining that the embattled preacher denied 'omnem Diabolo potestatem' (the Devil has any power).[135] Early in 1692 the *Acta Eruditorum* published its 13-page review, emphasizing Bekker's total denial of magic and diabolical power, as well as his radical Bible exegesis, concluding that Bekker agrees with Spinoza 'in many things' to the point of 'smoothing the path to Spinozism'.[136] As several German authors later noted, the *Acta's* review did much to spread awareness of the Bekker disputes, and the connection with Spinozism, throughout German-speaking lands and beyond.[137] At Wittenberg, the chief citadel of Lutheran orthodoxy, the Bekker disputes were described in 1693 as ringing 'in every ear'.[138] And so it continued for decades: not only did Bekker turn the eyes of all the Dutch upon himself, recalled a German account published at Leipzig in 1719, but his fame spread through neighbouring lands 'until his name was on everyone's lips and in every ear so that everyone wanted to read his book and it circulated, and was read, everywhere'.[139]

---

[131] Trevor-Roper, *European Witch-Craze*, 102.
[132] *Zweyte Unterredung Oder Gespräche Im Reiche der Todten*, 87.
[133] Hauber, *Bibliotheca*, i, 565–6 and ii, 67; Pott, *Aufklärung*, 214–23.
[134] Verney, *De re metaphysica*, 17.
[135] Leibniz to Magliabecchi, Hanover, 8 Nov. 1691 in Leibniz, *Sämtliche Schriften*, vii, 421.
[136] *Acta Eruditorum* 1692, 543, 547.
[137] Zobeln, *Declaratio Apologetica*, 9; Mosheim, *Ecclesiastical History*, ii, 515.
[138] Falck, *De Daemonologia*, 1–3.
[139] Beckher, *Schediasma*, 15; see also Kettner, *De Duobus Impostoribus*, B2; Israel, 'Bekker Controversies', 15.

Although Bekker's book appeared in French and in part in English,[140] as well as German,[141] relatively quickly, and there was talk of translations also into Latin, Italian, and even Spanish,[142] it was in Germany and the Baltic, and later also Italy, that the most powerful impact was felt. In Germany, according to contemporary commentators, the rendering into German being rather poor,[143] the book was widely read also in Dutch and French.[144] In his 1709 survey of the principal intellectual controversies of recent decades, the Baltic scholar, Zacharias Grapius, stresses the centrality of the debates over magic, witchcraft, and the diabolical in this period, citing Van Dale, Bekker, Thomasius, and Daillon as the four principal authors debated, albeit conspicuously allocating more space and emphasis to Bekker than anyone else.[145]

A remarkable instance of diffusion among the wider German public outside academe was the Devil debate in Hamburg in 1694. Johann Winckler, doyen of the city's Pietist clergy, and a churchman deeply disturbed by the recent upsurge of irreligious and atheistic ideas in the city,[146] regularly stressed the power of Satan and magical forces affecting the everyday life of men.[147] In 1694 he delivered a Sunday sermon in one of the principal churches of Hamburg, on the reality of the Temptation of Christ by Satan as related in Matthew 4 expressly 'against Balthasar Bekker'.[148] A veteran foe of 'enlightened' ideas, as well as opera and theatre, Winckler was nevertheless a man of some erudition. His library, later auctioned in Hamburg in 1721, included Hobbes, Spinoza, Craanen, Geulincx, Fontenelle, Malebranche, Locke, Tschirnhaus, Wittichius, De Volder, and numerous works in Dutch, including both parts of *Philopater*. Moreover, besides the *Betoverde Weereld* (in Dutch), he owned numerous Dutch-language pamphlets relating to the Bekker affair.[149]

Anxious to counter 'philosophical' influence, especially Bekker's, on the citizenry's notions about Satan and the satanic, Winckler afterwards expanded his sermon into a 192-page text, in which he warns 'this man's books are in the hands of some among us and, through his poison, our hearts are easily endangered.'[150] Bekker, held Winckler, tries to show that Christians need not fear the Devil, claiming 'there is no Devil among us, on earth, who tempts, seduces or plagues us;'[151] deplorably, he even claims Christ only imagined that Satan tempted him 'which imagining came not from the Devil but from Christ', so that there is no reality to the story of Satan's tempting him.[152] Winckler considered Bekker's ideas intellectually, religiously, and morally catastrophic. Were fear of the Devil to lapse, the world would, in his view, sink inexorably into

---

[140] The English translation of the first volume only, translated from the French, was published in London in 1695; see Clark, *Thinking with Demons*, 690.

[141] The German edition, giving 'Amsterdam' on the title-page, appeared at Hamburg in 1693, the French edition at Amsterdam in 1694; see Van Bunge, 'Einleitung', 56.

[142] *Acten ofte Handelingen*, 101; Kettner, *De Duobus Impostoribus*, B2; Zobeln, *Declaratio Apologetica*, 39.

[143] Lilienthal, *Theologische Bibliothec*, 1106–9; Trevor-Roper, *European Witch-Craze*, 102; Israel, 'Bekker Controversies', 13–14.

[144] Struve, *Bibliotheca philosophica*, 92–3.   [145] Grapius, *Systema*, ii, 90–9.

[146] Winckler, *Schriftmässiges wohlgemeintes Bedencken*, 86, 96–7.   [147] Ibid., 22–3, 37–40.

[148] Geffken, *Johann Winckler*, 395.   [149] [Winckler], *Catalogus Bibliothecae*, 315–17, 349, 356, 758, 783.

[150] Winckler, *Warhafftig vom Teufel erduldete Versuchung*, 6.   [151] Ibid., 5.   [152] Ibid., 103.

1. Benedict de Spinoza (1632–16//). Anonymous portrait. (By courtesy of the Herzog August Bibliothek, Wolfenbüttel)

2. The Ancient Greek philosopher, Epicurus (341–270 BC). Hellenistic marble portrait bust. (By courtesy of the Musée du Louvre, Paris)

3. René Descartes (1596–1650).
Copy of a portrait of Frans Hals.
(By courtesy of the Musée du
Louvre, Paris)

4. Gottfried Wilhelm Leibniz (1646–1716).
Engraved portrait. (By courtesy of the
Herzog August Bibliothek, Wolfenbüttel)

5. Philosophy and the French Catholic Church: Bishop Jacques Bénigne Bossuet (1627–1704). Full-length portrait by Hyacinthe Rigaud (1659–1753). Bishop Bossuet played a leading role in determining the intellectual and censorship policy of the French Crown in the age of Louis XIV (By courtesy of the Musée du Louvre, Paris)

6. Philosophy and the French nobility: Le Grand Condé: Louis II de Bourbon, Prince de Condé, the leading French aristocrat, military commander, and intellectual libertine, who summoned Spinoza to his presence in Utrecht as, in Colerus' words, he 'wanted very much to speak with Spinoza'. Bronze portrait bust by Antoine Coysevox (1640–1720). (By courtesy of the Musée du Louvre, Paris)

7. Miracles made manifest: The miracle at Pentecost (Acts 2): 'Suddenly a sound like the blowing of a violent wind came from Heaven. [The Apostles] saw what seemed like tongues of fire that separated and came to rest on each of them. All of them were filled with the Holy Spirit and began to speak in other langauges as the Spirit enabled them. Even Romans, Cretans and Arabs heard them declaring the wonders of God in their own languages. Some, however, made fun of them and said: "They have had too much wine".' Painting by Jean Restout (1692–1768) (By courtesy of the Musée du Louvre, Paris)

La Princeſs Sophie Palatine

8. Women and philosophy: Sophia of
Braunschweig-Wolfenbüttel, friend of
Leibniz, and mother of the British
King George I. (By courtesy of Phillips
International Auctioneers, London)

9. Philosophy and sexuality: Adriaen
Beverland (1650–1716) with an
emancipated lady friend. Double
portrait by Arie de Vois (1632–80)
painted about 1678. (By courtesy of
the Rijksmuseum, Amsterdam)

10. The 'Universal Library': the celebrated early eighteenth-century Rotunda of the Bibliotheca Augustiniana at Wolfenbüttel. (By courtesy of the Herzog August Bibliothek, Wolfenbüttel)

11. The 'crisis of the universities': a commemorative medal by J. Drappentier to mark the first centenary of the now rapidly shrinking University of Utrecht (1736). Pallas seated, holding Utrecht's coat of arms, receives Hercules, holding the symbol of the Seven Provinces in the Great Hall of the university. (By courtesy of Laurens Schulman B. V., Bussum)

VIVITUR. INGENIO
CÆTERA
MORTIS ERUNT.

NATUS. XVIII. KAL
OCT. CIƆ IƆCCXLI
DENATUS. X. KAL
ECEMB. CIƆ IƆCCXVI

12. The Dutch book auction catalogue: the frontispiece of the sale catalogue of the library of
Gisbertus Cuperus, sold in 1717.

A LA HAYE Chez A. DE ROGISSART.

13. The erudite journals: the frontispiece of the journal *L'Europe Savante* (1718–1720), published at The Hague, featuring a printer's workshop in the background.

14. Monarchy overturned: the frontispiece of the fiercely republican *Aanwysing* (1669), by Pieter de la Court, one of the strongest attacks on monarchy and ecclesiastical power of early modern times. (By courtesy of the Amsterdam University Library)

15. Ehrenfried von Tschirnhaus (1651–1708), philosopher, scientist, mathematician, and friend of Spinoza. Engraved portrait. (By courtesy of the Herzog August Bibliothek, Wolfenbüttel)

16. The scientist and his microscope: Nicolaes Hartsoecker (1656–1725). Portrait of about 1680 by Caspar Netscher (*c.*1635–84). (By courtesy of the Musée du Louvre, Paris)

ABRAHAMUS IOANNES
CUFFELER. I.V.D.
Cedendum Fatis.

r Llas Pinxit   Manaikhuysen Sculp.

17. Abraham Johannes Cuffeler
(c.1637–94), jurist at The Hague,
philosopher, and close friend of
Spinoza. (By courtesy of the
Vereniging Het Spinozahuis)

18. A clandestine medal struck at Leiden by J. Smeltzing (and designed by Ericus Walten about 1692) in celebration of Balthasar Bekker (1634–98). (a) Bekker in profile; (b) Bekker represented as Hercules, with the cudgel of philosophy, overcoming the Devil. (By courtesy of Laurens Schulman B. V., Bussum)

19. John Locke (1632–1704) Copy of a portrait by Godfrey Kneller. (By courtesy of the Governing Body, Christ Church, Oxford)

20. Sir Isaac Newton (1642–1727) in 1718. Portrait by T. Murray. (By courtesy of the Master and Fellows of Trinity College, Cambridge)

21. The Bay of Naples in the mid-eighteenth century. Panorama by Joséphe Vernet (1714–89). By courtesy of the Musée du Louvre, Paris)

22. Denis Diderot (1713–84),
philosophe, encyclopaedist, and
pillar of the Radical Enlightenment.
Portrait by Louis Michel van Loo,
(1707–71). (By courtesy of the
Musée du Louvre, Paris)

23. Engraved portrait of Spinoza some
times found bound into copies of the 1677
edition of the *Opera Posthuma* in both
the Latin and the Dutch versions. (By
courtesy of the Vereniging Het Spinozahuis, Amsterdam)

Natus Amsteled .
MDC.XXXII.
26 Novemb.

Denatus Hage Com.
MDC.LXXVII
21. Febru.

BENEDICTUS DE SPINOZA.

Dit is de fchaduw van SPINOZA's zienlijk beelt,
Daar 't gladde koper geen fieraat meer aan kon geven ;
Maar zijn GEZEGENT brein, zoo rijk hem meêgedeelt,
Doet in zijn SCHRIFTEN hem aanfchouwen naar het leven.
Wie oit BEGEERTE TOT DE WYSHEIT heeft gehad,
Hier was die zuiver en op 't fnedigfte gevat.

boundless iniquity, epicureanism, and atheism. Hamburg's Huguenot editor, Gabriel d'Artis, reviewing Winckler's text in the *Journal de Hambourg*, mischievously suggested that if reports of over a hundred publications so far, for and against Bekker, were correct, the embattled *predikant* had at least given 'grand plaisir aux marchands de papier et aux libraires.'[153]

Winckler's book on the Temptation of Christ 'against Bekker' did not go unnoticed in Amsterdam. A loyal ally, Zacharias Webber (d.1695), a Lutheran portrait painter and amateur theologian who had already assisted Bekker in his earlier feud with Van der Waeyen, worked with Bekker to pen a 'modest but thorough' reply which appeared in both German and Dutch, at Amsterdam in 1695.[154] Winckler received a copy with a covering letter (in Latin) from Bekker, confirming that while Webber wrote it, it accurately reflected his own views. He hoped it would not be a 'declaration of war' but rather a gesture of peace between them.[155] If they disagreed about the Devil, Winckler was unquestionably right, agreed Bekker, that the uproar over Satan, demons, and magic was engulfing the whole of Germany. At the Frankfurt book fair, Bekker had learnt, the controversy had attracted considerable attention, and no less a personage than the Lutheran *General Superintendens* of Lübeck, a former professor of Hebrew and oriental languages at Wittenberg, August Pfeiffer (1640–98), was reported to be preparing a detailed rebuttal. Not without some reason, then, did Webber claim 'all Europe is discussing this business of the Devil' and 'taking sides for and against [Bekker].'[156] His book, published in Sepember 1694 under the pseudonym 'Joan Adolphsz', not only restates Bekker's case adapted to a specifically Lutheran milieu but seemed to some critics to go rather further, effectively denying the existence of the Devil altogether.[157] Webber, Reimann later commented, was 'even more audacious than Bekker asserting the Devil is nothing but the perverse desires of men.'[158]

Pfeiffer's refutation lay unpublished for several years, appearing only after his death at Lübeck in 1700.[159] His analysis closely resembles Winckler's. Recalling that Voetius, himself a Dutchman, had dubbed 'Holland ein Atheisten und Libertiner-Nest', Pfeiffer held that the contagion spreading from there represented a dire threat to Germany. Unless man is restrained by dread of the Devil and divine retribution, the world will lapse ineluctably into iniquity and what we would call today a sexual revolution.[160] For if temptation is natural, and not satanically induced, then in principle extramarital fornication, whoring, and every form of promiscuity is permissible, as are lewd thoughts and words. The Gospel, he insists, expressly affirms the power of the Devil, and the reality of magic and possession, so as to leave no room for doubt.[161] Perhaps the Devil 'has bewitched this man [i.e. Bekker],' he remarked, 'so that he does not see the clear

---

[153] *Journal de Hambourg*, 1 (1694), 273–5.   [154] Beckher, *Schediasma*, 43.
[155] Reimann, *Historia*, 480; Geffken, *Johann Winckler*, 397–8.
[156] [Webber], *Waare Oorspronck*, 2–3; Knuttel, *Balthasar Bekker*, 257–8.
[157] [Webber], *Waare Oorspronck*, 2–3; [Tenzel], *Monatliche Unterredungen* 1698, 835–6; Goldschmidt, *Höllischer Morpheus*, 131, 290; Van Bunge, 'Einleitung', 38.
[158] Reimann, *Historia*, 480.   [159] Jöcher, *Allgemeines Gelehrten Lexicon*, iii, 1492.
[160] Pfeiffer, *Lucta carnis et spiritus*, 294–5.   [161] Ibid., 316, 471.

meaning of Scripture.'[162] Spinoza, he admonishes, denied the Devil, spirits, and 'possession', whether by ghosts or magic, and lurks behind Bekker. 'In short,' concludes Pfeiffer, 'behind this larva is hidden a Sadducee, Spinozist and Atheist.'[163]

It is striking how frequently in the Germany of the 1690s the impact of Bekker was linked to the alleged upsurge of 'atheism' in German society. A work published in Hamburg in 1692 begins by asking whether there was ever a time when 'atheism' showed itself more often and openly 'than today.'[164] Nathaniel Falck, in his widely read *De Daemonologia* of 1694, agrees that Bekker's assault on belief in spirits, sorcery, possession, and bewitchment stemmed from a burgeoning 'Naturalism' rooted in Spinoza, which was rapidly destroying all belief in, and dread of, the supernatural throughout Protestant Germany.[165] Providing a 19-page critique of Bekker's arguments, Falck praises theologians such as Melchior Leydekker, Everard van der Hooght, and Petrus Schaak for their uncompromising attacks on Bekker both in print and from the pulpit.[166] With his *Höllischer Morpheus* (Hamburg, 1698), a work dedicated to the Crown Prince of Denmark-Norway and reissued during the Thomasian furore in 1704, the Schleswig pastor, Petrus Goldschmidt (1662–1713), launched a vitriolic attack on Bekker and his 'armour-bearer', Zacharias Webber, for seeking, in the wake of Spinoza, to minimize Man's fear of the Devil, thereby opening the door yet further to all impiety and godlessness.[167] Goldschmidt concedes that Bekker was not, strictly speaking, an 'atheist' but insisted no one had done more to advance the cause of the present-day 'Naturalisten und Atheisten' and that it was accordingly right to classify him as an 'indirect atheist.'[168]

But in Germany Bekker had defenders, or partial apologists, as well as adversaries. Leibniz, posting a copy of the French edition to the Electress Sophia in September 1694, firmly disapproved of Bekker's claiming the Devil can not influence the minds and actions of men: 'c'est autant que s'il le nioit tout à fait'; but nevertheless deemed *Bekker's* volumes 'excellens pour désabuser le monde des préjugés populaires.'[169] In his *Théodicée* (1710), Leibniz repeats that Bekker was right to prune back the Devil's power but 'pushes his conclusions too far'[170] Also positive, in part, was Christian Thomasius, who headed the German intellectual campaign against witchcraft belief and trials which culminated in the Prussian royal decree of December 1714, requiring magistrates to refer all cases concerning witchcraft to the Crown, a measure which largely brought witch trials in northern Germany to an end.[171] Thomasius fought to disentangle the 'acceptable' face of Bekker from the allegedly dangerous Naturalism pervading his work. Thomasius did not doubt that the two writers who contributed most

[162] Pfeiffer, *Lucta carnis et spiritus*, 316.   [163] Ibid., 315, 317.   [164] Berns, *Altar*, Vorrede.

[165] Falck, *De Daemonologia*, 5–6.   [166] Ibid., 73–92.

[167] Goldschmidt, *Höllischer Morpheus*, ii–iii, 3–4, 22–3, 33–4, 61–2, 58, 290–1.

[168] Ibid., 11, 23, 33; Goldschmidt, *Verworffener Hexen-und-Zauberer-Advocat*, 31–2; Pott, 'Aufklärung und Hexenaberglaube', 194–5; Van Bunge, 'Einleitung', 39.

[169] Leibniz, *Sämtliche Schriften*, 1st ser. x, 68; Van Bunge, 'Quelle extravagance', 114.

[170] Leibniz, *Theodicy*, 221.

[171] The last witch to be legally condemned in Prussia was in 1728; see Pott, *Aufklärung*, 225.

to clearing the path intellectually for discrediting belief in witchcraft, and ending the witch trials in German lands, were Van Dale and Bekker.[172] He believed Germany and enlightened men everywhere owed these two men in particular an immense debt of gratitude. Assuredly, earlier writers, such as Pomponazzi, Scot, and Gabriel Naudé, had begun the work of whittling down Satan's realm on earth, but these made little impact on the overall scene. The decisive breakthrough in applying philosophical reason systematically and comprehensively, the writers who smashed the intellectual foundations of belief in magic and witchcraft, thereby overthrowing Satan's *Reich* in Germany, were, he insisted with every justification, Van Dale and Bekker.

It was vital for Thomasius, accordingly, to rebut Lutheran theologians such as Winckler, Kettner, Pfeiffer, Falck, and Goldschmidt arguing that 'those who, with Bekker, deny the Devil' are necessarily Naturalists and 'atheists.' While adamant that he believed in the existence of the Devil, Thomasius held that there was no justification for labelling men who denied the Devil 'atheists', suggesting jocularly they could more appropriately be called *Adaemonisten*.[173] Even so, Thomasius could no more praise Van Dale, 'whose erudite works about pagan oracles and the origins and advancement of superstition . . . are distributed throughout the learned world and held in no small regard', than he could praise Bekker unreservedly.[174] Like Bayle and Leibniz, Thomasius rebuked Bekker for going too far, bending Scripture to fit his philosophical stance, and denying the Devil has any power on earth; for by so doing, he had, for all practical purposes, denied Satan's existence.[175]

Thomasius took care to distance himself to some extent from Bekker. Yet for venturing to campaign against judicial prosecution of witchcraft in Germany, beginning with his famous lecture *De Crimine Magiae*, delivered at Halle in 1701, followed by publication of the German version of his text, the following year, he became caught up in a bitter controversy which continued for years and led to his frequently being branded a follower of Van Dale and Bekker.[176] His tract in German had a wide impact, powerfully contributing to the waning of the German and Danish witch trials in the early eighteenth century. It reappeared at least half a dozen times between 1703 and 1712 at Halle, Magdeburg, Leipzig, and Frankfurt.[177] Bekker figured from first to last more centrally than any other European intellectual in this specifically German furore, above all because his work provided a uniquely favourable vantage-point for anti-Cartesians to claim that denial of Satan, demons, and witchcraft is implicit in Cartesianism.[178] Though an anti-Cartesian eclectic himself, Thomasius' uncompromising espousal of philosophy as an instrument of social and cultural change, and

---

[172] Thomasius, *Kurtze Lehr-Sätze*, 585; Van Bunge, 'Einleitung', 37.

[173] Thomasius, *Kurtze Lehr-Sätze*, 589; Goldschmidt, *Verworffener Hexen-und-Zauberer-Advocat*, 68.

[174] Thomasius, *Kurtze Lehrsätze*, 585; Trevor-Roper, *European Witch-Craze*, 103.

[175] Thomasius, *Kurtze Lehr-Sätze*, 586; Pott, *Aufklärung*, 225.

[176] Thomasius, *Kurtze Lehr-Sätze*, 13–14; Goldschmidt, *Verworffener Hexen-und-Zauberer-Advocat*, 35–8, 151, 357; Hazard, *European Mind*, 207–8; Pott, 'Aufklärung und Hexenaberglaube', 198.

[177] Van Sluis, *Bekkeriana*, 68–9; Goldschmidt, *Verworffener Hexen-und-Zauberer-Advocat*, 32, 67.

[178] Hoffmann, *Disputatio Inauguralis*, A4, D2; Goldschmidt, *Verworffener Hexen-und-Zauberer-Advocat*, 32, 67; Hauber, *Bibliotheca*, ii, 290.

what his foes called *licentia philosophandi*, allegedly threw everything into doubt, spreading dire confusion among the people. Goldschmidt, one of his foremost adversaries, while detesting Thomasius' espousal of philosophy and campaign against witchcraft prosecutions, entirely concurred that 'reason' and the New Philosophy were changing German society fundamentally,[179] and no less that the two prime architects of the attack on Satan, demons, magic, and witchcraft throughout the German lands and the Baltic were Van Dale and Bekker.[180]

But while granting that Bekker had had a greater impact than anyone else in this sector of German culture, Goldschmidt questioned whether intellectually he really transcended the Haarlem physician. If it seems so superficially, he averred, this is because Van Dale is more insidious: 'what Van Dale did furtively and under cover, Balthasar Bekker, as an outspoken Dutchman, broadcast with mouth wide open and uninhibitedly; where Van Dale entered in felt-soled slippers, Bekker clattered wearing Polish boots so that his stamping could be heard in the streets.'[181] But that is merely a difference of style. In essence, all Bekker's ideas were already worked out in the 'damned books' of Van Dale. Anyhow, he held, Van Dale and Bekker belong to the same dreadful tradition of atheism and 'Sadduceeism' which began reviving in Pomponazzi, Campanella, and Hobbes and culminates in Spinoza.[182]

In Germany, the impact of Bekker was not only deep but also enduring. This, in turn, automatically meant, given the primacy of German and Dutch debates in shaping intellectual and academic culture in the north, that Bekker became central to intellectual activity also in Scandinavia and the Baltic. In Sweden, where witch trials and judicial preoccupation with demonology on the German and Danish model had become firmly established only in the 1660s,[183] and Denmark, where the last witch was burnt in 1693 but popular belief in witchcraft, demons, and magic remained formidably entrenched,[184] the books of Van Dale and Bekker proved highly unsettling over many decades. In his pioneering survey of modern philosophy in Swedish, published in 1718, Rydelius, like his German contemporaries, considers Bekker's *Betoverde Weereld* the foremost of all works denying ghosts, spectres, and apparitions and a favourite handbook of the modern 'Sadducees.'[185] Subsequently, in the early 1730s, Rydelius held seminars on spirits and demonology at the University of Lund, in which noticeably greater prominence was given to the same triumvirate—Van Dale, Bekker, and Thomasius—as dominated the German debate than any other challengers of traditional belief in demonology and magic.[186]

Similarly, other prominent figures of the northern early Enlightenment were

---

[179] Goldschmidt, *Höllischer Morpheus*, 3–4.

[180] Ibid., ii–iii, 23–4, 33–4; Goldschmidt, *Verworffener Hexen-und-Zauberer-Advocat*, 26–7; Pott, *Aufklärung*, 212–13, 222–5.

[181] Goldschmidt, *Verworffener Hexen-und-Zauberer-Advocat*, 30–1; Pott, *Aufklärung*, 214.

[182] Goldschmidt, *loc.cit.*, preface, pp. vii–viii and pp. 20, 30–2.

[183] Hilgers, *Index*, 246; Lindroth, *Svensk lärdomshistoria*, ii, 570.   [184] Henningsen, 'Das Ende', 316.

[185] Rydelius, *Nödiga Fönufftsofningar*, ii, 60–1; see also Holberg, *Epistler*, ii, 51–3.

[186] UUL MS Rydelius, 'Collegium privatissimum', i, 532–56; Hauber, *Bibliotheca*, 513.

keenly interested in the Bekker affair. The Uppsala astronomer Olaf Hiorter, who assisted Celsius in his exploratory observations of the northern lights and, in 1746, became director of the Uppsala observatory, possessed works by Newton, Musschenbroek, Hartsoeker, Nieuwentijt, 's-Gravesande, and Wolff in his library, but also *De Betoverde Weereld* in Dutch, together with a bound volume of Dutch-language pamphlets for and against Bekker, as well as the Latin account of the controversy by the German scholar Beckher.[187] More remarkable still, Lars Roberg, the leading medical reformer in Sweden during the opening decades of the eighteenth century, and a keen supporter of the early Enlightenment, owned no less than three different editions of *De Betoverde Weereld*, at least two in Dutch, besides diverse tracts for and against Bekker and others of his works.[188] In Denmark too there were major connoisseurs of the Bekker controversies, including Gotthilf Weidner, secretary to Queen Charlotte Amalia, whose library, auctioned in Copenghagen in 1704, included an assortment of works by Van Dale and Bekker, among them both Dutch and French versions of the *Betoverde Weereld*.[189]

The fact that the English edition lapsed after the publication of only the first of the four volumes may well be proof there was less interest in Bekker in England than on the continent, but it does not prove there was no significant involvement.[190] In reply to Limborch's several letters about the Bekker affair, in 1691–2, Locke made no comment about the intellectual issues, though he disliked the intolerance of Bekker's foes and asks in two letters how the affair 'of that author of the paradoxes about angels' was going.[191] John Beaumont, in his treatise on 'spirits, apparitions, witchcrafts and other magical practices', published in London in 1705, expressly remarks that English readers were not interested in the Bekker disputes. But he himself *had* read Bekker and explains the Frisian's arguments at considerable length, thereby giving them some additional currency in Britain.[192] There are also indications that interest in Bekker's ideas, as distinct from the Dutch controversies, was not as meagre as has generally been supposed. Collins' remark about the United Provinces being the country 'from which the Devil is intirely banish'd' clearly alludes to the Bekker business, while Bentley's comment that Bekker's was the 'strongest' book against witchcraft he had read shows that in Britain too key intellectual figures appreciated the unparalleled scope and cogency of Bekker's work. Furthermore, an abridged version, published without naming the author, appeared in London in 1700, under the title *The World Turn'd Upside Down*,[193] while several allusions in Tindal, Mandeville, and other writers suggest a pervasive undercurrent of awareness in English culture at that time, albeit indirect and ostensibly stripped of any Dutch context, of the work of both Van Dale and Bekker.

[187] [Hiorter], *Bibliotheca*, 38, 42; Lindroth, *History of Uppsala*, 132.

[188] [Roberg], *Catalogus Bibliothecae*, 87–90.   [189] [Weidner], *Catalogus Librorum*, 120–1, 238, 555.

[190] Trevor-Roper, *European Witch-Craze*, 102; Israel, 'Bekker Controversies', 7, 13.

[191] Locke, *Correspondence*, iv, 329, 400.   [192] Beaumont, *Treatise of Spirits*, 348–66.

[193] The full title is *The World turn'd upside down; or, A plain detection of errors, in the common or vulgar beliefs, relating to spirits, spectres or ghosts, daemons, witches* etc.; see Van Bunge, 'Einleitung', 34.

In any case, lack of explicit reaction in England was untypical of the wider picture, even if in France and southern Europe penetration of Bekker's ideas was slower, and more restricted to scholarly circles than in Germany and the Baltic. The four-volume French translation published at Amsterdam in 1694, under the title *Le Monde enchanté* was of acceptable quality and became a standard work among the Huguenot diaspora, as well as, eventually, in France, Switzerland, Germany and Italy.[194] This was the version discussed by Bayle, who agrees with Bekker that the empire of the Devil needed pruning back, but judged he had been too bold and sweeping: 'c'est une entreprise fort téméraire pour ne rien dire de pis, que de vouloir accorder avec l'Écriture la réjection de tout le pouvoir du Diable.'[195]

More comprehensively, Bekker's tomes were analysed by Benjamin Binet in his *Traité historique des dieux et des démons du paganisme* (Delft, 1696).[196] Partially agreeing with Bekker, Binet, a not untypical champion of the Huguenot moderate Early Enlightenment, nevertheless rebukes him sternly for going too far in discarding received ideas, thereby endangering 'les points fondamenteaux de la religion chrétienne' and implying 'Jésus-Christ et ses Apôtres ayent confirmé les erreurs, en se servant des expressions erronées du vulgaire.'[197] Binet especially regretted the devastating impact of Bekker's ideas on popular belief in angels, demons, and Satan. Credence in angels and the demonic, he admonishes, is not a matter for individual choice or philosophical judgement: 'si le Vieux Testament enseigne l'existence des anges en général, il établit aussi leurs opérations.'[198]

Malebranche could not be expected to take Bekker seriously. He knew of his ideas early on, remarking in a letter of November 1692 that spirits certainly intervene in human affairs, adding 'cependant il y a des gens qui veulent expliquer cela physiquement, et même on a fait en Hollande . . . un livre intitulé *Le Monde Enchanté*, par Bekker ministre, pour prouver qu'il n'y a ny anges ny diables, et cela par l'Écriture Sainte! Quelle extravagance!'[199] Voltaire, who borrowed most of his ideas from Bayle, Fontenelle, Locke, Newton, Collins, and other Early Enlightenment writers, readily granted that it was during the late seventeenth century and the beginning of the eighteenth that superstition in general, and credulous dread of magical forces and demons in particular, first began unmistakably to recede throughout Europe. He was aware that the half-century preceding his own youth was one of the most decisive in the history of the world. Nor did he doubt that the onset of 'philosophy' was the engine, the driving force, of this great revolution in human history: the waning of superstition, he held, was due above all to 'Bayle et les bons esprits qui commençaient à

---

[194] Lilienthal, *Theologische Bibliothec*, 1106–9; Hazard, *European Mind*, 204.

[195] Quoted in Labrousse, *Pierre Bayle*, ii, 12–13, 251.

[196] Binet's book was republished at Amsterdam in 1699 under the title *Idée générale de la théologie payenne servant de réfutation au système de Mr. Bekker*.

[197] Binet, *Idée générale*, 209–10; *Journal de Hambourg*, iii, 147–9.

[198] Binet, *Idée générale*, 211.

[199] Malebranche, *Oeuvres complètes*, xix, 585; Van Bunge, 'Einleitung', 40.

éclairer le monde.'[200] Bekker, he notes, was one of these and had appreciably contributed to the process.

Voltaire, indeed, dedicated a six-page article to Bekker in the full version of his *Dictionnaire philosophique*, though being Voltaire, he could not resist exercising his wit at the long-winded *predikant*'s expense, claiming that nothing would make Bekker desist from attacking the Devil even though his famously ugly face continually reminded everyone of Satan's existence. As for Bekker's text, it was only through pique, he suggests, at the time lost in reading it that it was 'banned', adding 'je suis persuadé que si le Diable lui-même avait été forcé de lire le *Monde Enchanté* de Bekker, il n'aurait jamais pu lui pardonner de l'avoir si prodigieusement ennuyé.'[201] In another piece on Bekker, Voltaire employs a different version of the joke, commenting that even if the Devil had really existed, having to read all of Bekker he would undoubtedly have expired of boredom.[202] For all that, grants Voltaire, Bekker was a 'très-bon homme, grand ennemi de l'Enfer éternel et du Diable.'[203]

In Italy, where Bekker was banned by the Inquisition, copies of the *Betoverde Weereld*, such as the one owned by the Baron von Stosch in Florence, were doubtless exceedingly rare.[204] But it would be wrong to infer from this that Bekker's views failed to penetrate. Italian *savants* may not, in many or most cases, have actually read Bekker but they could, without great difficulty, read about him and his arguments in the *Bibliothèque Universelle*, *Acta Eruditorum*, and other learned journals and lexicons.[205] That they did indeed do so is clearly demonstrated by the great Italian Devil, demon, and witchcraft debate which raged in the 1740s in the Venetian Republic, lasting over a decade. This episode began in 1745 when Girolamo Tartarotti, an admirer of Bacon and English empiricism, and editor of the 1732 Rovereto edition of Valletta's *Lettera* in defence of modern philosophy,[206] one of the architects of the Italian Catholic moderate Enlightenment, and a leading expert on the history and bibliography of witchcraft, wrote a treatise entitled *Congresso Notturno delle Lammie* (Night Congress of the Witches).[207] This was no mere academic exercise for suspected witches were still being investigated, tortured, and burnt in north-eastern Italy at the time, and even in Venice, after a steep fall in such cases since around 1700—following an increase in the number of sorcery trials brought during the seventeenth century—investigations of witchcraft by the Inquisition had still not entirely ceased.[208] Tartarotti's researches had convinced

---

[200] Voltaire, *Dictionnaire philosophique*, i, 560.

[201] Ibid., 562–3; Van Bunge, 'Quelle extravagance', 118.

[202] Voltaire, 'Bekker ou le Monde Enchanté' in *Questions sur l'Encyclopédie*, iii in *Oeuvres Complètes*, xvii, 559–65; Vercruysse, *Voltaire et la Hollande*, 102, 106.

[203] Voltaire, *Dictionnaire philosophique*, i, 559; Vercruysse, *Voltaire et la Hollande*, 102–3; Van Bunge, 'Einleitung', 35.

[204] [Stosch], *Bibliotheca*, ii, 161; Scibilia, 'Balthasar Bekker', 272–3; see also FBM class mark 1 E XII 24.

[205] Giannone, *Opere*, xxiv; Ferrone, *Intellectual Roots*, 14, 61, 66.

[206] Vecchi, *Correnti religiose*, 206, 381; Stone, *Vico's Cultural History*, 58, 299.

[207] Carpanetto and Ricuperati, *Italy*, 131–2; Davidson, 'Toleration', 238, 248.

[208] Georgelin, *Venise*, 1129.

him that most of what commonly passed for evidence of witchcraft, and pacts with the Devil, was credulous nonsense and that, generally, accused and convicted witches were nothing of the sort. He found himself in some difficulty, however, as to how, theoretically, to establish a meaningful, and theologically acceptable, demarcation between superstitious dread of magical power on one side, and what any true Christian must accept is the truth about Satan, demons, possession, and magic on the other.

The Inquisition too found this a baffling and troublesome problem, hesitating for several years before granting Tartarotti permission to publish.[209] His book finally appeared at Rovereto (near Trento) in 1749, but by then he was already immersed in controversy. In 1745 he had sent a manuscript copy to a young professor, a youthful spokesman of enlightened opinion at Padua, Gian Rinaldo Carlì (1720–95), who endorsed his attack on witchcraft belief and trials but heavily queried his prolix but unclear distinction between credulous belief in witchcraft and pious belief in Satan, demons, and sorcery.[210] In his published rejoinder, dated Rovereto 15 June 1746, Tartarotti rejected Carlì's critique, insisting that God no longer permits the Devil as much scope in the world as he had before Christ's coming, so that most of what is commonly believed about demonic inspiration, possession, and witchcraft is crass superstition but, equally, that it is unacceptable and un-Christian to claim, 'like Balthasar Bekker', that Satan has no power to affect men, and that evil spirits cannot operate on bodies, since Scripture unequivocally states otherwise, as does Saint Paul, and because, theologically, the reality of diabolical power, supernatural evil forces, possession, and exorcism cannot be doubted.[211] He admits he has never actually read Bekker but understood that his book 'has become famous more for the extravagance, than cogency, of its arguments.'[212] Bekker hoped to diminish the Devil in men's minds, which would be no bad thing, acknowledged Tatarotti, were Satan really lacking worldly capabilities. But given the unchallengeable truths taught by the Catholic Church, Bekker is to be wholly condemned. For now men are less on their guard than before against demonic temptation and more likely to be seduced by the Devil's wiles. The reality is, held Tartarotti, 'Bekker could not have favoured the Devil's cause more.'[213]

For many years the tentatively liberal Catholic position championed in the Venetian Republic by men like Tartarotti had been besieged by the forces of intellectual reaction or *concinismo*, led by Father Concina, on one side, and, on the other, a bolder, 'philosophical' (albeit, at least nominally, also Catholic) enlightened stance represented by men like Conti and the patrician Scipio Maffei. Much to Tartarotti's alarm, Maffei now weighed in with a controversial treatise on magic entitled *Arte magica dileguata* (Verona, 1749). Maffei declared Tartarotti's commendable and 'necessary' war on popular superstition and witch trials—the so-called *guerra tartarottina*—brave

---

[209] Provenzal, *Polemica diabolica*, 9–10.

[210] Tartarotti, *Congresso Notturno*, 319–50; Carpanetto and Ricuperati, *Italy*, 131.

[211] Tartarotti, *Risposta*, 421; according to Bencini, Bekker 'asserit nec angelos nec daemones operari posse in hominum corpora, vel animos, neque id concipi posse'; Bencini, *Tractatio Historico-Polemica*, 28.

[212] Tartarotti, *Risposta*, 421, 426.   [213] Ibid., 427.

but doomed to humiliating failure unless it was broadened to encompass all super-stitious belief in the demonic and magic.[214] The entire edifice of popular credulity regarding witches, enchantment, and the satanic had to be swept away. Tartarotti was horrified. Maffei and Carlì, he complained to a colleague, effectively denied the Devil's power on earth and, if the Inquisition can license Maffei's work, he could not see 'why they are still unable to license the *Mundus Fascinatus (Betoverde Weereld)* of Bekker himself!'[215]

Yet Maffei too had to avoid being classified with the Naturalists if he was to escape entanglement with the Inquisition and successfully advance his more forthright style of Enlightenment.[216] In campaigning against belief in demonic power while keeping to a moderate path, he showed considerable dexterity in employing Van Dale and Bekker as warning beacons enabling him to separate his position from that of the Radical Enlightenment. When Costatino Grimaldi, at Naples, now in his mid-eight-ies, also intervened in the controversy, in the year before his death (1749–50), he too invoked Bekker, though he was more willing than Maffei to concede the possibility of the Devil's intervention in the world.[217] In his *Dissertazione* on magic and diabolical power, published posthumously at Rome in 1751, Grimaldi reiterated Maffei's claim of a crucial difference between his position and Bekker's: where Bekker and the Natural-ists hold magic to be a 'chimaera' and nonexistent, Maffei contends that magic is a 'chimaera . . . only since the coming of Christ Our Lord' and that the Devil previously exercised wide-ranging power on earth.[218]

In his later interventions, the *Arte magica annichilata* (Verona, 1754) and *Riflessioni sopra l'Arte magica annichilata* (Venice, 1755) Maffei again vigorously rebuts the charge of *Bekkerianismus* and siding with Van Dale and Bekker.[219] Van Dale, he reminded readers, goes beyond Fontenelle in maintaining the Devil never operated through the ancient oracles which, according to him, were invariably fraudulent. Fontenelle, by contrast, while granting that oracles had worked mostly through priestly imposture, unequivocally accepts the reality of magic and demonic power. Thus, theologically, a crucial distinction separates Van Dale and Bekker from the respectable, Christian Enlightenment of the mid-eighteenth century, fighting to end sorcery trials. Maffei could forcefully condemn Bekker while vindicating the supposedly 'Christian' stance of Fontenelle.[220]

The linking of Bekker with Spinoza, from 1691 onwards, in the Netherlands, Germany, and elsewhere, and the prevailing tendency to equate Bekker's 'system' with philosophical Naturalism, obliged spokesmen of the moderate Enlightenment, including Leibniz, Thomasius, and Maffei, to distance themselves in some degree from Bekker, for association with his ideas could only harm their cause.[221] In the Netherlands those who publicly supported Bekker's ideas after 1700 continued to be

---

[214] Maffei, *Arte magica dileguata*, 12–14, 39; Provenzal, *Polemica diabolica*, 32–3.
[215] Ibid., 42.   [216] Ferrone, *Intellectual Roots*, 61, 94, 320.
[217] Stone, *Vico's Cultural History*, 299–300.   [218] [Maffei], *Riflessioni*, 122.
[219] Ibid., 5–6, 35–6, 56, 121–3; [Maffei], *Arte magica annichilata*, 38, 49–51, 190.
[220] [Maffei], *Riflessioni*, 123.   [221] Van Bunge, 'Einleitung', 151, 154.

subjected to ecclesiastical censure and, as the decades passed, few ventured to do so.[222] Conversely, until the 1750s and beyond, explicit support for Bekker, often combined with suggestions that he should have finished the job and denied the existence of Satan and demons altogether,[223] was invariably a sign of adherence to radical thought and perceived as such by its antagonists.

Willem Goeree's remarks in his *Mosaische Oudheden* (Mosaic Antiquities, 1700) and other publications 'in which he not only boldly defends Bekker's ideas but also criticizes the North Holland Synod', 'insolently' suggesting that the synod acted out of vengeful desire to 'kick this good man from his pulpit', so incensed the Holland synods that they requested the Pensionary of Holland, Anthony Heinsius, to goad the States of Utrecht, under whose jurisdiction Goeree lived at Maarssen, to take steps against him.[224] During the early eighteenth century, the Dutch Reformed *classes* regularly confirmed their vigilance against the 'harmful' views of Dr Bekker, not least, as the Alkmaar *classis* noted in July 1718, when examining candidates for the ministry.[225] When a new edition of Bekker's *Betoverde Weereld* came out clandestinely, in four volumes, ostensibly at 'Deventer' in 1739, the Reformed synods reacted with undiminished zeal to curb Bekker's 'harmful' influence. At The Hague, the *classis* reaffirmed its implacable opposition to Bekker's 'condemned opinions', expressing 'sorrow the book of Balthasar Bekker has now again been reprinted with a very mocking frontispiece and loathsome preface.'[226] This was the prevailing view, though efforts at Deventer, Amsterdam, and elsewhere to try to unmask the clandestine publisher seem to have been fruitless.[227] Nor was there any change in the Church's rigid persistence in condemning Bekker's views down to 1750 and beyond. In that year, the *classis* of The Hague, like other *classes* and consistories, once more dutifully recorded its unceasing watchfulness against the 'harmful ideas of Dr Bekker.'[228]

After Goeree, Bekker's most resolute apologist was the German Spinozist Johann Christian Edelmann (see pp. 660–1 below). Edelmann's writings of the 1740s contain several lengthy discussions of the Devil, demonology, witchcraft, possession, apparitions, angels, and magic in which he categorically rejects all this 'Devil superstition', which is nothing, he maintains, but crass credulity and imposture devised by Churches to keep the people permanently sunk in 'Ignoranz und Dummheit.'[229] Every word about angels and demons in the Bible, he insists, is nonsense, the product of 'imagination', dreams, fantasies, dread, and sickness.[230] According to Edelmann's

---

[222] Wielema, 'Met Bekkerianerij besmet', 151, 154.   [223] *Philopater*, 140–1.

[224] ARH OSA 98 South Holland Synod, Acta Gorcum, July 1703, art. 9; Goeree, *Kerklyke en Weereldlyke*, 678–80; Israel, 'Bekker Controversies', 7, 16.

[225] RNH MS Gereformeerde Kerk, Classis Alkmaar, acta 18 July 1718 art. 13; ibid. Classis Haarlem vol. x, acta 18 July 1730, art. 15 and acta 24 July 1731 art. 15.

[226] ARH Classis The Hague vi, p. 12. Acta 29 June 1739, art. 24.

[227] Ibid., vi, p. 46. Acta 27 June 1740, art. 24.

[228] Ibid., vi, p. 289. Acta 22 June 1750, art. 26.

[229] Edelmann, *Moses*, iii, 65; see also iii, 63–70; Edelmann, *Unschuldigen Wahrheiten*, 178–91, 190–1, Edelmann, *Glaubens-Bekentniss*, 286–90; Pratje, *Historische Nachrichten*, 106–9.

[230] Edelmann, *Glaubens-Bekentniss*, 289.

account of mankind's slow and difficult self-emancipation from 'Devil superstition', by far the most heroic, outstanding, and noteworthy writer is Balthasar Bekker,[231] though certainly, he grants, others also deserve praise, especially Knutzen, Stosch, and the 'Dutch lawyer' (Adriaen Koerbagh) who so bravely maintained in his *Bloemhof* that the authentic meaning of the terms 'demon' and 'devil' had been completely obfuscated and misrepresented, having originally signified nothing more than 'accuser' or 'libeller.'[232]

Thus Bekker's system became integrally linked to the Radical Enlightenment and, down to 1750, was everywhere and always considered a vehicle of Naturalism, atheism and Spinozism. Bekker himself would have drawn little comfort from such an outcome. But if his ideas were not respectable, or were judged too radical for Christians to accept, there can be no question as to the unparalleled extent of his influence. If ever there was a writer who was thought by contemporaries to have had an immense impact on attitudes in society at many levels, and across several different countries, then it was Bekker. Hounded and rejected by the churches and by moderate 'enlightened' opinion, he may have been, largely ignored by modern Enlightenment scholars he may be, but in terms of contributing to one of the greatest and most profound shifts in the history of mankind, he was indisputably one of the foremost figures of the European Early Enlightenment.

---

[231] Ibid., 287–9; Edelmann, *Moses*, ii, 63–5.   [232] Edelmann, *Glaubens-Bekentniss*, 288.

22 | Leenhof and the 'Universal Philosophical Religion'

i. Frederik van Leenhof (1647–1712)

In 1710, crossing the Netherlands bound for England, the noted Frankfurt patrician bibliophile, Zacharias Conrad von Uffenbach, stopped off in Zwolle to visit a 63-year-old preacher named Frederik van Leenhof (1647–1712), then about to be expelled from the Dutch Reformed ministry. Uffenbach admired Leenhof's collection of paintings but it was not for that he had interrupted his journey. He was motivated by curiosity to see the man who 'had made himself famous through the great controversy that arose over his book'.[1] He was referring to Leenhof's *Hemel op Aarde* (Heaven on Earth) of 1703, which provoked an uproar about illicit ideas exceeded in scale only by the Bekker affair and unmatched for duration even by that commotion.

Leenhof is almost forgotten today, even in the Netherlands, and historians of the European Enlightenment rarely mention him. Yet there are excellent reasons for rescuing him from oblivion and paying attention to the massive disturbance he provoked. Fifteen years after Uffenbach's visit to Zwolle, Jacob Friedrich Reimann justly remarked that Leenhof generated nearly as much commotion as Bekker and, furthermore, that the outcome of the two episodes was not dissimilar.[2] In fact, there can be no balanced account of the European Radical Enlightenment which does not take careful account of Leenhof and his 'universal philosophical religion'.

A Zeelander by origin, who studied theology in the 1660s, initially at Utrecht under Voetius, and then at Leiden under Cocceius, Leenhof began to be noticed in the Republic of Letters from the early 1680s when, as a still relatively young Reformed preacher at Zwolle, he emerged as a fervent Cartesio-Cocceian in the fight against Voetian fundamentalism.[2] In 1684 he published a tract at Amsterdam, castigating the Frisian Reformed *classis* of Zevenwolden for their sweeping condemnation of

---

[1] Uffenbach, *Merckwürdige Reisen*, ii, 368–70; Schröder, 'Spinozam', 165.
[2] Reimann, *Historia*, 487–8; [Sewel], *Twee-Maandelyke Uyttreksels* 1704, 293; according to Vandenbossche the scandal provoked was almost as great as that caused by the publication of Spinoza's *TTP*; see Vandenbossche, *Frederik van Leenhof*, 4.

Cocceian theology and, not least, their charge that out of Descartes' 'school come atheists and libertines'.[3] The Voetians, complains Leenhof, habitually resort to smear tactics to try to discredit not only Descartes, whom they allege was given to 'unchastity and whoring', but all respectable Cartesio-Cocceian authors by equating their writings with those of 'Averroes, Simplicius, Lucianus, Vaninus, Socinus, Koerbagh, Torrentius, Hobbes, Spinoza, etc.'.[4]

Yet, while Leenhof projected himself publicly as a forthright Cartesio-Cocceian, privately, as a few intimates probably already suspected, he was becoming increasingly immersed in Spinozism.[5] Before taking up his living at Zwolle in 1681, he lodged briefly with Wittichius in Leiden, spending much time discussing Spinoza, as emerges from two remarkable letters he wrote to Wittichius soon afterwards. These letters, in which Leenhof boldly defends Spinoza's stance on substance and Creation, were later published as anonymous pieces together with Wittichius' replies, as an appendix to the latter's *Anti-Spinoza* after his death, by Wittichius' editor without Leenhof's permission.[6] Since Leenhof subsequently admitted having written them, it is certain that he was already an expert on Spinoza's system by 1681, and equally certain that he was sympathetic to some of his key concepts. Unmistakable hints of Spinozism were later spotted also in the 1684 edition of the bulkiest of his early writings, the *Keten der Bybelsche Godgeleerdheit* (Chain of Biblical Learning; two parts, Amsterdam, 1678–82), though few noticed this at the time.[7]

From the outset, however, conservative theologians considered Leenhof more liberal and unconventional theologically than virtually any other leading Cocceian, one critic expressing revulsion in 1691 that Leenhof, a Reformed minister, should actually recommend readers to 'consult Mohammed, Socinus, Spinoza, and all manner of other blasphemous and heretical writers'.[8] In the letters to Wittichius, Leenhof holds that there can be no *creatio ex nihilo* (creation from nothing) and that the very notion involves contradiction since an infinitely perfect Being cannot act otherwise than perfectly.[9] If God's creation is perfect, the universe cannot ever have *not* existed, for God without the universe would be imperfect. The world is thus necessary and eternal and, consequently, inherent in the nature of God, who cannot create something outside and beyond Himself because the concept of a Being generating something outside itself violates the principle of infinite perfection. Similarly, asserts Leenhof, extension must be inherent in God's nature, as it again involves contradiction to suppose a Being consisting of pure spirit can produce another substance characterized by extension which, by definition, has nothing in common with the first. The doctrine

---

[3] *Philopater*, 94; Wielema, 'Ketters en Verlichters', 52.

[4] Leenhof, *Keten*, preface; *Philopater*, 118; Goeree, *Kerklyke en Weereldlyke*, 644.

[5] Reimann, *Historia*, 487; Lilienthal, *Theologische Bibliothec*, 1106; Burmannus, *'t Hoogste Goed*, 27; Israel, 'Spinoza, King Solomon', 30, 309.

[6] Leenof, *Hemel op Aarde Opgehelderd*, 54–5; Burmannus, *'t Hoogste Goed*, 27; Hubbeling, "Frühen Spinozarezeption', 167.

[7] Vandenbossche, *Frederik van Leenhof*, 16; Wielema, *'Ketters en Verlichters'*, 53–4.

[8] Brink, *Toet-steen*, 10, 12.

[9] Wittichius, *Ondersoek*, 564–6: Leenhof to Wittichius, undated [Jan. 1681].

of one substance therefore more logically and convincingly explains the world than Descartes' baffling duality of substances outside of God.[10] Wittichius, staggered that Leenhof should champion Spinoza against Descartes, refused to see any paralogism in the idea of creation out of nothing.[11] On the contrary, he maintained (rather like Rousseau in his *Émile* eighty-one years later),[12] only the doctrine of two substances, and the impossibility of interaction between extension and thought, enables those who seek philosophical truth to circumvent the absurdities of scholasticism on one side, and the fatal trap of Spinoza's 'one substance' on the other.[13]

Although Leenhof published relatively little between 1682 and 1700, his reputation as a leading Cartesio-Cocceian apologist ineluctably dragged him into the morass of the Bekker affair. For the Voetians, the Bekker imbroglio provided a unique opportunity to publicize the dreadful pitfalls of Cartesianism, and Cocceianism, and Leenhof was a perfect target.[14] Henricus Brink, Bekker's chief antagonist in Friesland, published in 1691 his 768-page *Toetsteen der Waarheid* (The Touchstone of Truth), a vitriolic attack on those who embraced 'Cartesian novelties' with, according to him, catastrophic consequences only now becoming apparent. Brink assails Leenhof, alongside Wittichius and Burman, as a chief protagonist of Descartes' 'clear and distinct ideas', and the 'geometric method' of reasoning, as criteria of truth in theology.[15] On scientific questions, Brink disdainfully brackets Leenhof with Bekker as a writer who claims comets are purely natural phenomena, not divine portents, and with Wittichius and Burman, as an advocate of Cartesian heliocentrism.[16]

From the 1680s Leenhof lived and worked in Zwolle, outwardly championing a tolerant, scientifically tinged Calvinism while privately cultivating Spinozism. His radical ideas were philosophical and moral but also extended to social issues, education, sexuality, and politics. It was indeed in the sphere of political ideas that he first revealed his Spinozistic leanings more openly in 1700, publishing two remarkable treatises on the life and views of King Solomon, both ostensibly about the Biblical figure but actually propounding a thinly veiled republican ideology.[17] Leenhof considers monarchy incurably defective, the form of government under which 'human vanity most prevails', noting 'how few worthy kings ruled Israel and Judah and have ruled generally in the world, as well as how little kings trust their subjects whom mostly they oppress rather than protect and therefore must fear.'[18] Monarchy, insists Leenhof, is inherently unstable and corrupt.[19] As the exclusive source of power and favour in their realms, kings are revered almost like 'gods' and abjectly flattered. Since courtiers seek only their own advantage, their hearts are full of guile and, among them, uprightness,

---

[10] Wittichius, 567.   [11] Ibid., 571–5; Goeree, *Kerklyke en Weereldlyke*, 670.

[12] Rousseau, *Émile*, 241–2.

[13] Wittichius, *Ondersoek*, 575–6, Wittichius, *Consensus veritatis*, 148, 392.

[14] Brink, *Toet-steen*, 4, 6, 8, 10.   [15] Ibid., 749–50, 763.

[16] Ibid., 84, 92–3; see also Helvetius, *Adams and graft*, 246, 255–7.

[17] Leenhof, *Prediker*, 132; Jahn, *Verzeichnis*, 1978; Vandenbossche, *Frederik van Leenhof*, 43–4; Israel, 'Spinoza, King Solomon', 310–11; Wielema, 'Ketters en Verlichters', 56.

[18] Leenhof, *Prediker*, 134.   [19] Ibid., 132; Leenhof, *Het Leven*, 44.

sincerity, and respect for the law are despised.[20] Of course, the wise philosopher-king Solomon was an exception but, precisely because he was exceptional, Solomon exposes the baseness of kings and the worthlessness of dynastic values. In Leenhof's politics, as in Spinoza's, there is no political legitimacy based on the hereditary principle, any more than on ecclesiastical sanction or custom.[21] 'Reason', urges Leenhof, is the only measure of legitimacy in government and whatever does not accord with 'reason' is mere 'slavery under pretence of government'.[22] 'Monarchical rule,' he concludes, 'is without doubt the most imperfect.'[23]

Central to Leenhof's republicanism, like Spinoza's, and later that of Diderot and the radical wing of the French Enlightenment, is his definition of true sovereignty as the common good of the community, and its location as being the laws in which that common good is embodied, laws to which everyone must be equally subject. To curb the monarchical impulse and safeguard the 'common good', power within the State must be dispersed and an equilibrium created by means of constitutional checks and balances.[24] The more the royal grip over the military, and the distribution of offices is diminished, the more the interests of the community are upheld. Fatal to the common interest, he argues, very much in the tradition of republican theorists from Machiavelli to Rousseau, are standing armies of hired soldiers. If kings are to be prevented from trampling on the common good, then hired troops must be dispensed with and the State provided with a militia of its own citizens trained to bear arms. Such a militia. he says, is the 'best and securest method to protect life, property and freedom, which indeed comprise all the wages such men could desire'.[25]

A commonwealth is healthiest and 'best adapted to reason and human nature', he asserts, when its decrees apply equally to everyone great and small.[26] 'For reason is everywhere reason and needs no compulsion,' but because human weakness and passions obstruct the common good in every society, it is always necessary to curb crime and unruliness and, to secure this end, impose punishment, including, he says, the death penalty. Laws vary from society to society, but the fundamentals of what is best for the community are both universal and, through reason, knowable. For there is 'only one measure of good and bad', held Leenhof, like Spinoza before, and Diderot (and Rousseau) after him, and only one way of perfecting human nature.[27] Political stability and communal well-being flow from being governed in accord with these principles, instability and corruption from flouting them.

In short, the people will only truly accept and venerate government based on reason. For 'every individual is by nature free and prefers to be governed by noble reason rather than force.'[28] Consequently, the rule of law must be scrupulously upheld

---

[20] Israel, 'Spinoza, King Solomon', 312. [21] Leenhof, *Het Leven*, 51, 81; Leenhof, *Prediker*, 131.
[22] Leenhof, *Het Leven*, 50–1; Leenhof, *Prediker*, 134–6; Israel, 'Spinoza, King Solomon', 312.
[23] Leenhof, *Het Leven*, 132–4. [24] Leenhof, *Het Leven*, 73–4; Leenhof, *Prediker*, 239–44.
[25] Leenhof, *Het Leven*, 51, 74, 81; Leenhof, *Prediker*, 50, 131, 228. [26] Leenhof, *Het Leven*, 50, 228.
[27] Leenhof, *Het Leven*, 81; Leenhof, *Prediker*, 131; [Diderot], Article: 'Droit Naturel' in the *Encyclopédie*, v, 116; Talmon, *Origins*, 25–7; Wokler, *Social Thought*, 57–64.
[28] Leenhof, *Het Leven*, 168.

and institutional safeguards protecting the community from the ambitious must not be diluted or discarded when they no longer suit the interests of powerful or scheming men. Access to high office, moreover, should be open to all on the basis of merit and virtue. Leenhof sees no justification for aristocratic attempts to monopolize political office, or exclude the humbly born from high positions if they possess the right qualities of intellect, 'for history teaches that from the most humble background have come princes, kings and popes who have surpassed their predecessors.'[29] Thus, reverence for, and equality before, the law must be elevated above all other forms of submission and deference, whether to monarchs, rank, tradition, or clergy.

ii. Heaven on Earth

The absence of any hostile response to his texts on Solomon, and harmonious relations between him and his colleagues and congregation at Zwolle, may well have lulled Leenhof into a false sense of security. But his tranquil enjoyment of status and influence was shortly to be rudely shattered. Whether it was hubris, or some other failure of judgement, which induced him to publish a book as challenging to traditional ideas as his *Hemel op Aarde*, he was genuinely astounded by the uproar which greeted its publication. He had for years, he later complained, been quietly propagating the same ideas in sermons, and conversation, encountering nothing but approval. Indeed, it had been with the encouragement of friends that he had ventured to write and publish the work.[30]

The ill-fated text appeared simultaneously in Zwolle and Amsterdam in June 1703 and again the following year. Nowhere does the book refer explicitly to any forbidden philosopher or doctrine. But this was virtually Leenhof's only precaution. Otherwise, it is fairly obvious throughout that he is using familiar theological terms in an unorthodox manner to propagate ideas which had little connection with Christianity as commonly understood. Individually, his unconventional way of putting things and double meanings would have aroused no great concern. But the frequency and variety of such expressions, and their cumulative effect, persuaded almost everyone that he was using coded language to disseminate an undeclared, illicit system of philosophy, morality, and social thought.[31] Not one of his former Cartesio-Cocceian allies sprang to his defence or showed any willingness to interpret his text, or obscure turns of phrase, as essentially Cartesian, Cocceian, or Christian. On the contrary, prominent Cartesio-Cocceians were as persuaded as anyone that Leenhof reveals himself in this work, as one commentator puts it, not just as a false Cartesian and false Cocceian but an 'apostate' from Christianity and an undiluted Spinozist.[32]

Leenhof opens by saying that he writes for every sort of person, in the interest of human well-being generally, and that his aim is to demonstrate the path to heaven on

---

[29] Leenhof, *Prediker*, 243–4.   [30] Leenhof, *Hemel op Aarden*, voorreden.

[31] D'Outrein, *Noodige Aanmerkingen*, 71, 74; 'Eusebius Philomotor', *Brief*, 3–5.

[32] Andala, *Cartesius verus*, 8, 22, 79; D'Outrein, *Noodige Aanmerkingen*, 71; *Twee-Maandelyke Uyttreksels* 1704, 172–5; Mosheim, *Ecclesiastical History*, ii, 577.

earth. No one will deny, he says, that 'true religion must lead the individual to a complete and pure happiness that derives from knowledge and love of God and satisfying
our inborn thirst for the highest good.'[33] But already here the conspicuous absence of
any reference to Christ, Christianity, Revelation, or the Church and the special sense
imparted to the term 'religion', much as Spinoza earlier and Rousseau later deployed
it, inevitably aroused deep misgivings. Furthermore, Leenhof only discusses a
blessedness, salvation, and attainment of heaven in the here and now through pursuit
of a purely worldly 'highest good' (which is equivalent to knowing God) with no role
for Redeemer, Gospel, grace, sacraments, or divine Providence. Assuredly Scripture is
allocated a function in teaching men morality, but plainly not in attaining Salvation.

Leenhof claims Scripture nowhere specifies exactly what or where 'Heaven' is. But
if we examine the passages in which the term occurs, he says, it emerges that Heaven
is not a place distinct from this world but rather a state of mind, or blessedness,
accorded or not accorded to individuals.[34] 'Heaven' he terms the state of stable, enduring happiness gained through acquiring knowledge of God. 'Hell' conversely, he
defines—again analysing the original Hebrew rather than the allegedly misleading
Greek rendering—not as a place distinct from the here and now but a state of mind
inherent in inadequate knowledge of God, in other words, unhappiness and lack of
spiritual repose.[35] Moreover, 'Hell' in Leenhof is not the consequence of sin or divine
retribution, but an inner wretchedness of a sort individuals can and should endeavour
to avoid. Heaven on earth is accessible to all and is what is to be esteemed above all else.

That Leenhof's strategy was a radical one philosophically, theologically, morally,
and politically emerges unmistakably from his astounding pages affirming that knowledge of God, Heaven, and true happiness, instead of being made freely available and
universally cultivated as it should be, is in fact everywhere suppressed and stifled by
malicious 'men who are called learned because they have a good memory and know
. . . languages, history and antiquities', who aspire to power, lack understanding and
judgement, and instead of promoting enlightenment, strive to prevent its spread.[36] It
is due to these usurpers that 'noble truth fails to triumph in the world and ignorance
and superstition prevail. Everywhere one encounters false ideas, such as that comets
are portents of pending doom, that there are ghosts and demons, and that gold can be
obtained through alchemy.'[37] This is why, insists Leenhof, people live in terror of the
'spirits of the night' and poor wretches are burnt as witches in Germany; all this credulous nonsense must be eradicated and in place of our prevailing faith of darkness,
based on fear, the people taught a new 'religion of joy and lightness of heart'.[38]

[33] Leenhof, *Hemel op Aarden*, 3–4.
[34] Ibid., 6–7, 15, 19–20, 33; Jenichen, *Historia*, 174–5; [Pluquet], *Examen* i, 366–7. Vandenbossche, *Frederik van Leenhof*, 39–40; Wielema, 'Ketters en Verlichters', 57–8.
[35] Leenhof, *Hemel op Aarde*, 8–9, 64, 77–9; Burmannus, ''t Hoogste Goed,' 62, 143.
[36] Leenhof, *Hemel op Aarde*, 74.
[37] Ibid., 74–5; Burmannus, ''t Hoogste Goed', 63, 140–3, 147–9; Vandenbossche, *Frederik van Leenhof*, 38–9.
[38] Ibid., 75, 121–2; Raats, *Korte en Grondige Betoginge*, 4; [Goeree], *Philalethes Brieven*, 119–26; Vandenbossche, *Frederik van Leenhof*, 38.

Characteristic of Leenhof, and the whole Radical Enlightenment from Spinoza to Diderot, is the notion that the world is now entering a new age of spiritual and intellectual conflict, of unremitting strife between enlightenment and darkness, to establish what Leenhof designates the 'kingdom of happiness' on earth. An indispensable part of the struggle is the drive to end the credulous belief in spirits, apparitions, and ghosts.[39] Toleration, as with all the radical writers, is deemed one of the most crucial weapons in this cosmic contest, and here Leenhof assigns a critical role to the civic magistracies. For it is in their power to permit greater freedom of thought and expression and thereby assist the common people to emancipate themselves from theological dispute and learn to respect other religions and views.[40] Nothing is more rational, urges Leenhof, than to bend our every effort to foment such a comprehensive toleration.

There was an immediate and huge outcry against the book, but evidently also a few who approved and even openly pronounced it a 'work which contains wonderfully beautiful things'.[41] These, however, were invariably laymen. Among the Republic's preachers and consistories reaction was vehemently negative. The first to denounce Leenhof in print was the Amsterdam *predikant* Florentinus Bomble, a former colleague at Zwolle, who published an open letter in December 1703, reminding readers that whereas Leenhof and his 'Cartesian friends' had always held 'one must not mix philosophy with theology' that was precisely what he had now done, with catastrophic consequences.[42] Bomble was followed by another Cocceian, Taco Hajo van den Honert, who was to emerge as a key figure in the mounting public controversy. Van den Honert berates Leenhof for purveying Spinoza's ideas without saying so, and especially denying the innateness of 'good' and 'evil', precisely, he recalls, as had, seventeen years before, the heterodox Pontiaan van Hattem, a disgraced former Reformed pastor then widely considered a crypto-Spinozist.[43] If one accepted Leenhof's views on the relativity of 'good' and 'evil', he protests, carousing with prostitutes would be no worse than piety and there would be nothing reprehensible about extra-marital sex.[44] Were not Leenhof, Van Hattem, and their like guilty, he asks, of denying the reality of sin and the theological doctrine of the Fall? Since he was giving free licence to whoring, it would have been more appropriate, held Van den Honert, had Leenhof called his book 'Hell on Earth'.[45]

Leenhof replied with a new work—his 107-page *Hemel op Aarden Opgeheldert* (Heaven on Earth Clarified) commonly called the *Opheldering*. Likening his

[39] Leenhof, *Hemel op Aarde*, 122, 146–8; Lilienthal, *Theologische Bibliothec*, 1106.

[40] Leenhof, *Hemel op Aarde*, 115–22; Burmannus, *'t Hoogste Goed*, 62; Jenichen, *Historia*, 63; Israel, 'Locke, Spinoza and the Philosophical Debate', 18–19.

[41] Creighton, *Hemel op Aarde Geopent*, preface; Leenhof, *Hemel op Aarden Opgeheldert*, 1–3; *Acta Eruditorum* 1707, 328–9.

[42] Bomble, *Brief*, 29–30; de Groot, 'De procedure', 285.

[43] Van den Honert, *Briev*, 6–8; Mosheim, *Ecclesiastical History*, ii, 516; Schröder, 'Reception', 159–60; Wielema, 'Ketters en Verlichters', 62.

[44] Van den Honert, *Briev*, 6.   [45] Ibid., 28.

detractors' conduct to Voetius' vilification of Descartes as an 'atheist',[46] he acknowledged having written the now infamous letters sent to Wittichius in 1681, but insisted these were private texts not intended for publication, which, moreover, had been doctored by the editor. He admitted having 'read *that* philosopher attentively' but saw no justification for his critics' reproaches there, since good as well as reprehensible things are found in his writings.[47] Many scholars, he claimed, privately acknowledged that Spinoza had improved on Descartes' account of the passions. From the outset, as Oldenburg's correspondence with him in the *Opera Posthuma* shows, upright God-fearing men had found valuable things in Spinoza.[48]

But this did nothing to placate his antagonists. The Voetian, Melchior Leydekker, answered with a 78-page text, tracing Leenhof's ideas to Spinoza whom, he says, this preacher has the impertinence to call the 'improver' of Descartes, while his views on Satan and Hell, presumably, he derives from Bekker.[49] The dichotomy of worldly happiness and sadness Leenhof advocates, he showed, exactly parallels the duality of *blijschap* (joy) and *droefheyd* (sadness) laid down by Spinoza, and advanced as the fundametnal principle of human 'morality' in the 'godless' second part of *Philopater*, the publisher of which, mercifully, the authorities had put in prison.[50] Others were to follow Leydekker in linking Leenhof to *Philopater*.

But many readers besides theologians took an avid interest in the controversy.[51] A popular dialogue between a farmer and trader conversing on a passenger barge, published at this time, has the latter commenting that even if one has not read the *Hemel op Aarde*, 'it is discussed so much at present there can be hardly anyone to whom it is unknown.'[52] That even quite unsophisticated folk participated is proved, among other evidence, by a number of crude doggerel poems circulating in Overijssel in 1704, in which punning verses pronounce it impossible to obtain grapes or figs from 'Spinoza's thorns' and urge the God-fearing to boycott Leenhof's 'Heaven' which should be left to the 'Spinozists'.[53] That some real Spinozists entered the fray in support of Leenhof is shown by the appearance at this point of an anonymous 64-page counterblast to Van den Honert, entitled *Redenkundige Aanmerkingen*, clandestinely published under the mysterious initials E. D. M.[54] Leenhof himself was accused of writing it but always denied having done so.[55] The Spinozist author, whoever he was, boldly restates Spinoza's Conception of God, Man and the human will and scathingly denounced this 'hateful persecution', arguing that simply because Leenhof agrees on some points with the philosopher of The Hague is no cause for relentlessly hounding him. Had not both Wittichius and Blyenbergh, both adversaries of Spinoza, also borrowed concepts from him?[56] 'Spinozism' is the chorus which all Leenhof's adversaries sing in perfect

[46] Leenhof, *Hemel op aarden Opgeheldert*, 8.   [47] Ibid., 59–61.   [48] Ibid., 60–1.

[49] [Leydekker], *D. Leenhofs Boek*, 5, 10, 15.   [50] Ibid., 16–17, 19; Wielema, 'Ketters en Verlichters', 62.

[51] Israel, 'Controverses pamphlétaires', 255.   [52] Ibid.; 'Philometer', *Discours*, 3.

[53] *Verscheide Gedigten*, 3, 15.

[54] Israel, 'Controverses pamphlétaires', 263; Wielema, 'Ketters en Verlichters', 63.

[55] Van den Honert, *Weder-Antwoord*, 5–7, 69; Leenhof, *Kort Antwoord*, 3–4.

[56] E.D.M., *Redenkundige Aanmerkingen*, 61–2.

unison: Van den Honert who seeks to set up a new Inquisition condemns Leenhof as a 'complete Spinozist' who no longer troubles to conceal himself but 'shows himself everywhere in his nakedness'.[57] But if every writer who draws on 'that thinker' is a 'Spinozist' then 'there must be many Spinozists.'

Van den Honert produced two furious replies to this tract, dated respectively 22 March and 5 April 1704, questioning Leenhof's disavowal and accusing the latter's ally, Barent Hakvoord, the Zwolle bookseller whom he suspected of publishing the *Redenkundige Aanmerkingen*, of spreading scurrilous rumours about Leenhof's opponents among the book trade in Amsterdam.[58] Someone close to Leenhof had written that loathsome tract, he insisted, and the likeliest suspect was Leenhof himself. He reminded Hakvoord, precentor of the Reformed congregation at Zwolle, of the grave consequences of publishing illegal Spinozistic texts.[59] At Amsterdam, a publisher who produces a book without declaring the author's name, he notes, takes responsibility for the contents himself; nor did he believe that in Zwolle the authorities permit anyone to publish with impunity anonymous books which 'remove all the foundations of religion and civil society and have no other consequence than that Church and civil society are disconcerted and shaken, if not entirely overthrown'.[60]

Leenhof answered Van den Honert's argument that the *Hemel op Aarde* and *Redenkundige Aanmerkingen* are Spinozistic and fatally menace society with a 31-page riposte, entitled *Kort Antwoord*, dated 21 April 1704 and published by Hakvoord at Zwolle. What sense is there in stoking up such a commotion? The inevitable result, he predicts, will be to see Spinoza rise again from the grave.[61] Will not everybody now wish to read him? Besides, what manner of refutation is this where it suffices simply to show that something is found in Spinoza to discredit and vilify a writer? For are there not in Spinoza many true and useful things encountered also in other writers?[62] While writing *Hemel op Aarde*, he adds, he had not once used the *Tractatus Theologico-Politicus* and only sparsely consulted the *Ethics*, and while familiar enough with the writings of 'that author', he denied that even a twenty-fifth part of his argument derives from him.[63]

At this juncture Leenhof decided to react also in another fashion.[64] Addressing a gathering of the Zwolle church council on 20 March 1704, summoned at his request and at which he himself took the minutes, he lamented the commotion gripping Zwolle and 'amazing misinterpretations' and 'hateful' calumnies, including despicable verse lampoons, put about by his enemies.[65] For twenty-three years he had laboured conscientiously for the well-being of the community, leading a blameless

---

[57] E.D.M., *Redenkundige Aanmerkingen*, 45.

[58] Van den Honert, *Weder-Antwoord*, 7–8, 16, 20; although the *Redenkundige*'s title-page gives 'Amsterdam', enquiries apparently suggested Zwolle as the place of publication; see Van den Honert, *Briev*, 1–3.

[59] Van den Honert, *Weder-Antwoord*, 40, 42–52.

[60] Ibid., 70.

[61] Leenhof, *Kort Antwoord*, 7; Vandenbossche, *Frederik van Leenhof*, 18.

[62] Leenhof, *Kort Antwoord*, 14.   [63] Ibid.   [64] Vandenbossche, *Frederik van Leenhof*, 4.

[65] GA Zwolle KA 017/6. res. kerkeraad, 20 Mar. 1704.

life. Now he asked his colleagues to stand by him and help stem the agitation being concerted against him and restore his good name. He had fully answered his detractors' accusations in his *Ophelderinge* but this had failed to quell the disturbance. He now proposed that matters be settled by a formal procedure whereby the consistory would accept, and publicly announce, that 'I entirely reject whatever is harmful, directly or indirectly, to our teaching in the writings of Spinoza or others' and endorse his doctrinal orthodoxy.[66]

This was agreed and a committee named to formulate clarifying articles which Leenhof could then consent to, purging the stigma of Spinozism.[67] The opening article affirms that nothing in his *Hemel op Aarde* was intended to 'conflict with Scripture or the teaching of the Reformed Church as expressed in the *Confessio Belgica*, that he acknowledges its doctrines to be the true path to Salvation, disavowing with all his heart everything not in accord with it . . . and especially all the wicked concepts of B. D. Spinoza'.[68] The articles also included an undertaking never to teach or propagate Spinoza's ideas 'by mouth or in writing in public or in private', nor construe Biblical passages in any way other than in which they are understood within the Reformed Church.[69] Expressly repudiating Spinoza's philosophy, Leenhof signed and, on this basis, his submission to the Church's tenets was approved and proclaimed.[70]

By seizing the initiative in this way Leenhof hoped to ensure the business was settled by consistory dominated by laymen from the town where his presence and contacts counted, rather than in the local *classis*, an assembly of preachers, most of whom were from Zwolle's rural hinterland where his position was weaker. However, there was considerable opposition to the Zwolle proceedings in the *classis* and, in May, an open split developed when the former—over six votes mostly from the town—overruled the consistory and tried to take charge of the proceedings, suspending Leenhof from his ministry for two months to allow the district's preachers to study his texts more closely.[71]

The consistory reacted indignantly and, more crucially, so did the burgomasters who refused to permit an external body to decide who could or could not preach in the town or how to resolve a question which deeply agitated the town. The *classis* was told that the city government was amazed they should act so peremptorily as to suspend a preacher in the city without even consulting the magistracy.[72] Here, plainly evident, was that overlapping of theological and jurisdictional issues which was henceforth to bedevil every effort to resolve the affair during the next six years, inflating what otherwise might have been a minor provincial contest into a major national and European philosophico-political encounter. The burgomasters rejected the *classis'* suspension of Leenhof as irregular, disrespectful towards the city, and a source of 'great annoyance and disturbance to the whole community'.[73]

---

[66] Ibid.; De Groot, 'De Procedure', 325, 327.
[67] GA Zwolle Kerkeraad Acta 017/6. res. 25 Mar. 1704, art. 1.   [68] Ibid.
[69] Ibid.   [70] Ibid., res. 7 Apr. 1704, art. 3.   [71] Ibid., res. 23 May 1704, art. 3.
[72] Ibid., res. 24 May 1704; De Groot, 'De Procedure', 340–1.
[73] GA Zwolle Kerkeraad Acta 017/6. 'Extract' res. burgomasters, 24 May 1704.

Deadlock locally meant the business soon reached provincial and then national level. With the Synod of Overijssel, under the jurisdiction of which Zwolle fell, about to convene its annual gathering, the Zwolle burgomasters sought to pre-empt the inevitable outcry against Leenhof with an order from the standing committee of the provincial States, directing the States' commissioners at the synod to prevent discussion of the affair. The manoeuvre worked in the short term. When the synodal delegates met at Steenwijk in May, and the question of 'offensive books' arose, attention instantly focused on Leenhof and the *Redenkundige Aanmerkingen*. But no sooner had the delegates begun denouncing the *Hemel op Aarde* as reeking of the 'principles of fully-fledged Spinozism', than the commissioners stipulated that the States did not wish the matter to be debated or any resolution about it taken.[74] Amazed, the Synod pointed out this would be to ignore the 'uproar provoked by that book in all the congregations of these provinces', reminding the States that everyone's eyes were 'fixed on this Christian Synod expecting appropriate measures to end the commotion and reassure the many agitated by it'.[75] Everyone would consider the States' action 'very strange' and the certain consequence would be yet more commotion. Protesting to the Delegated States, the Synod pronounced Leenhof's *Hemel op Aarde* replete with the 'soul-destroying ideas in the writings of the damned atheist Spinoza which due to their godlessness have been strictly forbidden by the highest authority [i.e. the States General] in these lands'.[76]

Outside Overijssel, the Synod of Friesland had promptly condemned Leenhof's book as 'full of double meanings and offensive phrases taken from the writings of Benedictus de Spinoza tending to . . . licentiousness, the undermining of the Christian religion, and the clandestine promotion of the fatal ideas of the aforementioned Spinoza to the harm of God's Church in our dear Fatherland'.[77] In August, deep concern was expressed by the Synod of Gelderland.[78] But it was especially the two Holland synods, spurred by Van den Honert, which took the lead in concerting efforts to break the impasse. Both synods, and many of the Holland *classes* individually, adopted resolutions condemning the revival of Spinoza's ideas in Leenhof's writings ('Spinozae principia et dogmata in Leenhofii scriptis renovata'), pronouncing Leenhof unfit to be a minister of the Reformed Church unless he unreservedly renounced his Spinozistic views, and indignantly criticizing the Zwolle city government.[79]

At this point the Pensionary of Holland, Heinsius, received a joint delegation from the Holland synods which strongly urged that 'principia Spinozistica' (Spinozistic principles) destroy the foundation of all true religion, and therefore also the State. He was pressed to take up the synods' cause both in Holland's assembly and the States General, to put pressure on Overijssel to cease obstructing resolution of the affair, and

---

[74] ARH Ned. Herv. Kerk OSA 215. Acta May 1704, art. 25.   [75] Ibid.
[76] Ibid., Ned. Herv. Kerk OSA 162, fo. 373.
[77] ARH Ned. Herv. Kerk OSA 292. Acta May 1704, art. 24, res. 23 May 1704.
[78] ARH Ned. Herv. Kerk OSA 85. Acta Zutphen, 20 Aug. 1704 'licentieus boekdrukken'.
[79] ARH Ned. Herv. Kerk OSA 97. Acta Briel 8–18 July 1704, art. 23; RNH Acta classis Edam VII, res. 20 July 1704; RNH Acta classis Haarlem X, res. 22 July 1704.

press for a ban on the further printing and sale of the *Hemel op Aarde*, *Opheldering*, and *Kort Antwoord* in Holland.[80] Both issues were duly raised in the States, but most Holland regents felt that they, and the other provincial governments, should await the outcome of developments in Overijssel before taking any action since, under the Republic's normal procedures, responding to representations from synods and questions of book censorship were properly left in the first instance to the province chiefly concerned.[81]

The Zwolle consistory, having failed in their first attempt to settle matters, but still assured of the burgomasters' backing, now set to work with Leenhof on a more elaborate set of 'Articles of Satisfaction' with a view finally to settling matters. A small committee was formed to collate extracts from Leenhof's texts, compare their wording with Spinoza's, and compile a comprehensive list of apparent points of convergence where clarification was needed.[82] This body met frequently over several months, often with Leenhof present, examining texts and Spinoza's philosophy. Finally, with Leenhof's concurrence, an impressively thorough set of articles was drafted and, on 30 August 1704, presented to the full consistory. After a general review of the 'godless and damaging views of B. D. Spinoza', the consistory approved the articles, recorded Leenhof's abjuration of 'Spinoza's heterodox propositions' and, anxious to keep to proper procedure, investigated the handling of the cases of Bekker and Pontiaan van Hattem.[83]

The Zwolle *Articles of Satisfaction* of 1704 represent a remarkable attempt to fortify religion against radical philosophy by erecting a high wall between the Churches' teaching and Spinozism. Defining 'Spinozism' as a movement or quasi-religion engaged in universal conflict with Christian belief and values, the admirably concise ten articles, submitted to the Zwolle city government on 1 September, represent a remarkable feat of intellectual compression. In particular Article 3 is noteworthy, listing as it does seventeen core Spinozist tenets identified as fundamentally at odds with Christianity. The first five are that there is only one substance which encompasses everything, including God, that there is no God distinct from Nature, that all creatures belong to this single whole, that there is therefore only one infinite order of causes which determines everything that occurs, necessarily, so that Nature is an independent and separate cause of itself which, through a fixed necessity, produces and creates itself.[84] Sixth is the doctrine that body and soul are not separate entities but one and the same thing, and that there are no *anima separata*, that is, spirits separate from bodies, and thus no ghosts, apparitions, angels, or Devil.[85]

Seventh is the doctrine that there is, in the human understanding, no natural innate distinction between good and evil, these notions being human inventions

---

[80] ARH Ned. Herv. Kerk OSA 97. Acta Briel 8–18 July 1704, art. 23; Jenichen, *Historia*, 107–8.

[81] ARH Ned. Herv. Kerk OSA 97. Acta The Hague, 7–17 July 1705, art. 24.

[82] GA Zwolle Kerkeraad Acta 017/6. res. 5 and 30 Aug. 1704; de Groot, 'De Procedure', 342.

[83] GA Zwolle Kerkeraad Acta 017/6. res. 6, 23, and 24 Oct. 1704.

[84] Ibid., res. 30 Aug. 1704, no. 3, propositions i–iv; *Artikelen tot Satisfactie . . . Zwolle*, 11.

[85] *Artikelen tot Satisfactie . . . Zwolle*, 12; Van den Honert, *Nodige Aantekeningen*, 19, 70–3.

designed to 'keep the common, ignorant people in obedience'.[86] Eighth is the concept that everything derives from nature, following an eternally necessary order, so that there is no moral responsibility 'whereby the reasonable creature stands under the Law of God as his true Lord and Lawgiver'.[87] Ninth comes the doctrine that the power of nature, irrespective of the Fall, governs all men under the same play of passions, so that the moral status of mankind is always the same. Next follows Spinoza's teaching that the human will is exclusively determined by natural causes and always determined necessarily—a point heavily emphasized in the *Redenkundige Aanmerkingen*.[88] Eleventh is the doctrine that the 'highest good' is the pure understanding of God's eternal order, leading to 'mastery of the passions and self-conservation in joy and cheerfulness'.[89] That death on earth is the end of the individual with no resurrection of bodies, or Last Judgement, follows next; after which, thirteenth, comes the doctrine that there is 'no divine Revelation and that it is the political authority which institutes all organized religion, Holy Scripture accordingly having no more authority than the writings of Hermes, Plato, Aristotle, Epicurus, Cicero, Seneca, and other such moralists' and being 'written according to the understanding of the common people to inculcate obedience'.[90] Next is the claim that Biblical prophecy and other Biblical books were written on the basis of 'imagination' and confused ideas. Fifteenth is the concept that there is a philosophical 'general religion' (Algemene Gods-dienst), superior to revealed religion, which permits the free expression of all views and which has few or no points of doctrine other than love of God and one's neighbour, the pursuit of salvation without Christ, and obedience to the secular law and the State.[91] Penultimately comes the doctrine that grace is the innate tendency of our nature towards acceptance of God's eternal order;[92] and finally, seventeenth, the claim that it is permissible to tell lies to preserve oneself.

The other articles were largely devoted to combating these seventeen prime forbidden doctrines. Thus Article 5 lays down that reason and Scripture are not two distinct paths, or means to Salvation, and that however much our reason is refined and improved, there is no Salvation through reason alone, reason being innately subordinate to Revelation. This article also expressly denies that the Christian religion was established by political authority, claiming it derives from God alone—though Christian governments are the guardians of God's Church and obliged to maintain and protect it. Article 8 resoundingly affirms God is the one eternal Creator of the universe who has made everything, both spiritual and bodily things 'freely and independently, outside of Himself'—the Spinozist *Redenkundige Aanmerkingen* asserts, on the contrary, that God does not act 'freely' but rather in accordance with

---

[86] *Artikelen tot Satisfactie*, 13; [Leydekker], *D. Leenhofs Boek*, 6, 9–11. [87] *Artikelen tot Satisfactie*, 13.
[88] Ibid.; E.D.M. *Redenkundige Aanmerkingen*, 7–9; Van den Honert, *Nodige Aantekeningen*, 88–92.
[89] *Artikelen tot Satisfactie.*, 14. [90] Ibid.; Van den Honert, *Nodige Aantekeningen*, 29, 130–3.
[91] GA Zwolle Kerkeraad Acta 017/6. res. 30 Aug. 1704, art. 5; *Artikelen tot Satifactie*, 15; Burmannus, *'t Hoogste Goed*, 147–9.
[92] *Artikelen tot Satisfactie*, 15–16; Van den Honert, *Nodige aantekeningen*, 138.

the laws of His being[93]—so that in His being, characteristics, qualities, and actions God differs, and is infinitely distinct, from Nature.[94] Under Article 6, Leenhof was required to acknowledge that in writing his *Hemel op Aarde* he had been 'inadvertent and careless' in his choice of expressions and, regrettably, borrowed many terms and definitions from Spinoza, so that 'grounds are given for him to be suspected of *Spinosisterij* [Spinozism] and concurrence with [Spinoza's] opinions'.[95]

With the articles ratified by both consistory and city government, and Leenhof having signed, it was publicly proclaimed on the first Sunday in November, in Zwolle's three large churches, that 'D. Leenhof has satisfied the consistory and purged himself of heterodoxy and Spinozistic opinions so that the consistory now declares him orthodox and upright.'[96] The vote in the consistory being unanimous, the city government welcomed and endorsed the outcome and pronounced the matter closed. To demonstrate the thoroughness and integrity of the proceedings, the *Articles* were published.[97] But again hopes of settling the commotion, by purging Leenhof of heterodoxy in Zwolle, immediately unravelled. Neither the synods nor the wider public were willing to accept the solution concocted by the Zwolle consistory and burgomasters. On the contrary, as the months passed the uproar intensified, and more and more acerbic publications poured from the press.

A strong impression had been made, by a book published back in May at Enkhuizen, by a preacher there, Franciscus Burmannus, who claimed that Spinozism was spreading rapidly in the Netherlands and that there were now many 'Spinozists, that is wicked God-forsaking atheists in our Fatherland who even hold meetings in some principal cities where . . . under pretext of philosophical debate, the principles of Spinoza and his atheism are inculcated into our silly, undisciplined youth, as everyone knows and is all too true.'[98] Proclaiming Spinoza the 'most godless atheist the world has ever seen', Burmannus warns that the further spread of Spinozism would bring the Republic to the very brink of religious, moral, and social disaster. Among the most pernicious of Leenhof's principles, he claimed, were his political ideas, and not least his Spinozist doctrine of toleration. If the 'highest happiness in so far as it can be derived from reason' means Salvation is of this world then, as Leenhof holds, the laws of the State must be directed solely to enabling citizens to live safely in accordance with reason and the pursuit of this worldly 'highest good'. Such a concept of politics means prizing social peace and stability, avoiding war, and regulating religion so as best to instil reverence for the laws of the State. In such a society, warned Burmannus, all religions would be equally valid. What could be more reprehensible, he asks, than that the secular authorities should permit 'freedom of thought and speech' to

[93] E.D.M., *Redenkundige Aanmerkingen*, 8–10, 34.
[94] GA Zwolle Kerkeraad 017/6. res. 30 Aug. 1704, art. 8; Van den Honert, *Nodige Aantekingen*, 18.
[95] *Artikelen tot Satisfactie*, 17; Van den Honert, *Nodige Aantekeningen*, 3–4, 144–7.
[96] GA Zwolle Kerkeraad Acta 017/6 res. 28 Oct. and 6 Nov. 1704.
[97] Ibid., res. 2 Dec. 1704; Jenichen, *Historia*, 122.
[98] Burmannus, *'t hoogste Goed*, 20.

everyone, including atheists and Spinozists, on the ground that toleration promotes stability and social peace?[99]

Could anything be more pernicious, he asks, than the lapsing of a Reformed minister into Spinozism? Leenhof is steeped in Spinozism, he held, and Spinoza is the distillation of all error and heresy, indeed 'overturns all grounds of truth and certainty, denying there is any God distinct from Nature and abolishing all natural obligation to obey His commandments and true morality'.[100] Spinoza, held Burmannus, introduces the carnal and base doctrines of Epicurus, so that men, 'guided by bodily needs, which he considers the foundation of everything, should seek tranquillity of mind and lasting happiness, making this life (which is followed by no other) the most that is possible for human beings'.[101] On the same basis, he adds, Spinoza dares deny 'ghosts, angels and even the Resurrection, Last Judgment and the reality of eternal life'.[102] Because their ideas contradict all accepted truth and wisdom, Spinoza and his followers evince an 'insufferable arrogance and contempt for everything that can be called divine or worldly wisdom'.[103] Citing the 'conceited Cuffeler', Burmannus deplored their mad presumption in claiming to 'possess all truth' and their conviction that everything else is mere delusion and deception.

The Zwolle magistracy's endeavours suffered a particular setback some weeks later with the publication of Van den Honert's scathing 196-page critique of the *Articles of Satisfaction*, for these adduced cogent grounds for questioning the rectitude and propriety of the settlement arranged in Zwolle. Van den Honert showed not just that the investigating committee failed to uncover all the Spinozistic elements in Leenhof's texts but also that the seventeen inadmissible philosophical tenets, and Leenhof's disavowal of them, had been set out without clearly stating that Leenhof actually advances these views in his books.[104] Indeed, he protests, evasive wording insinuates that the embattled dominie had not really propagated the 'atrocious, godless, Spinozistic teachings' cited but merely been careless enough to leave himself open to suggestions that he might have done, implying that the charges of Spinozism are nothing more than a debatable interpretation of his work, or even a malicious fabrication on the part of his enemies: 'and thus these *Articles* contain a complete, if concealed, accusation against the synods of our Fatherland and all the Heer Van Leenhof's detractors.'[105] Examining every article in turn, Van den Honert plausibly argues that the consistory, or some of its members, had colluded in a web of subterfuge designed to trick the synods and public, save Leenhof, and subtly advance Spinozism. While the *Articles* themselves proclaim God separate and independent from Nature, they fail to point out that in Leenhof's writings no such distinction is to be found. Any reader of the *Hemel op Aarde* or *Opheldering*, he urges, can see that Leenhof uses the terms 'Order van Natuur' and 'God's eeuwige [eternal] Order' interchangeably.[106] If the *Articles*

---

[99] Burmannus; 143, 147–9; Leenhof, *Hemel op Aarde*, 115.   [100] Burmannus, *'t Hoogste Goed*, 3–4.
[101] Ibid., 4.   [102] Ibid.   [103] Ibid., 6.
[104] Van den Honert, *Nodige Aantekeningen*, 3.
[105] Ibid., 6; RNH Ned. Geref. Kerk, Classis Edam VII. res. 20 July 1705.
[106] Van den Honert, *Nodige Aantekeningen*, 18, 22.

loudly proclaim 'soul and body two separate and distinct things', and Leenhof approves the *Articles*, in his books it is nowhere apparent he accepts any such distinction.[107] If the *Articles* declare the 'Christian religion built on the sole foundation of Jesus Christ' the true faith purely taught according to God's Word, and the example of the earliest Christians, only within the Reformed Church, there is no hint in his writings that Leenhof believes any such thing; for not only does he never call Christianity the true religion but he urges that in matters of faith men should leave each other in peace to believe what they wish.[108] In short, the Articles provide no reason to think Leenhof disavows the 'godless principles of B. de Spinoza' in good faith. If he nowhere contends there is only one substance, he could scarcely be expected to affirm anything so blatant, 'for there is no one, even among those who have never read Spinoza, who does not know Spinoza acknowledged only one substance and from that sought to construct his entire moral—or rather immoral and godless—philosophy.'[109] On top of which, he added, Leenhof manifestly does not believe in angels, spirits, or the Devil.[110]

Discontent with the *Articles* surfaced in practically all *classes*, including those of Overijssel. There the synod's standing committee spent several days together with the *classis* of Zwolle in February 1705, minutely scrutinizing the Zwolle *Articles*.[111] Besides the alleged inadequacy of Leenhof's retraction, there was a feeling the consistory had been insufficiently firm in upholding the Church's authority and failed sufficiently to make an example of an erring preacher steeped in heterodox ideas. As part of the purging process, there had earlier been demands that Leenhof be required to write a refutation of Spinoza for publication. Asked why there was nothing about this in the *Articles*, the consistory replied they had not thought it 'necessary' and excused him.[112] Asked whether Leenhof had been made to surrender his unpublished manuscripts, the consistory replied he had, but that these had afterwards been returned to him; when the *classis* then sent to Leenhof for his papers, he said he had undertaken not to divulge them without the consistory's permission and that, anyway, they were no longer in his possession.[113]

Finding the Zwolle *Articles* inadequate, the synod's standing committee, together with the *classis* of Zwolle, drafted a list of supplementary points, for approval by the full synod, which Leenhof would then be asked to accept. These required a categorical assurance that Leenhof believes in a Heaven which is an actual place, the residence of the Saved whither Christ had ascended, and the 'good angels, or spirits created by God without bodies' are, and where 'all the Elect after their death and resurrection shall live eternally with Christ.'[114] Equally, Leenhof had to affirm there is a Hell which is a place of the 'evil, fallen, angels, and the damned, where they will be eternally judged and punished' and that 'this, following Holy Scripture, we must believe.'[115] Thirdly, explicit abjuration was needed of Spinoza's 'universal religion whereby all

---

[107] Ibid., 19.   [108] Ibid., 29–30.   [109] Ibid., 46–7.   [110] Ibid., 73–5.
[111] GA Zwolle Kerkeraad Acta 017/6. res. 24 Feb., 24 Mar., and 2 July 1705; Jenichen, *Historia*, 176–81.
[112] ARH Ned Herv. kerk OSA 162, fo. 380.   [113] Ibid., fo. 380v.
[114] Ibid., fo. 381. Jenichen, *Historia*, 155–6.   [115] Ibid., 156–7.

men, also those who are without Christ, can be saved and, therefore, all views may be freely held and must be tolerated in the [public] Church'.[116] On denying this, Leenhof had to affirm that 'there is one God, one Law, one way to Salvation, in Christ, without which one cannot be saved.'[117] Finally, Leenhof had to undertake in writing never again to advocate the concepts embodied in his *Hemel op Aarde*, verbally or in print.

iii. The Politics of Philosophy

When the provincial synod convened for its annual gathering in June 1705, at Deventer, the supplementary articles having been circulated among the *classes*, the atmosphere was exceedingly fraught. Most delegates favoured adoption of the additional articles as they stood. But the Zwolle representatives refused. A compromise was then devised, incorporating changes to the original ten *Articles* but without adopting all the new clauses.[118] This settled, the synod could finally draw up a text officially condemning Leenhof's three books as irreligious, pernicious, and Spinozistic, and requesting the States of Overijssel to ban their printing, sale, and distribution by public edict. However, to the great surprise of many, this latter step was again deferred for the moment.

Meanwhile the protracted proceedings in Overijssel were causing mounting dismay throughout the Republic. The Frisian Synod, avowing unremitting hostility to 'Spinozistic principles', urged their Overijssel colleagues to act more expeditiously to quash all seeds of that 'abominable' philosophy'.[119] The Synod of Gelderland, gathering at Harderwijk in August, criticized the Zwolle *Articles* and called for stronger action.[120] Still more aggrieved was the North Holland Synod, where anger was expressed in the strongest terms, Haarlem and Amsterdam rejecting the Zwolle *Articles* outright for failing explicitly to condemn Leenhof for propagating the 'godless and damaging opinions of Spinoza'.[121] All this placed the States of Overijssel in a considerable quandary. Never had the politics of philosophy seemed more arduous.

The provincial States and Zwolle burgomasters agreed that their wisest course was to throw their weight behind the compromise reached in the Synod of Overijssel and make it stick. But the amended *Articles* simply failed to win approval outside the province. Furthermore, no sooner had the States begun discussing the Synod's request for a provincial ban on Leenhof's three books than it emerged that the Zwolle burgomasters would consent only to a half-hearted edict provisionally forbidding reprinting, without condemning the texts as 'Spinozist' or prohibiting their continued

---

[116] ARH Ned Herv., 157; Van den Honert, *Nodige Aantekeningen*, 130–1; [Leydekker], *D. Leenhofs Boek*, 16–18.

[117] Jenichen, *Historia*, 157; Lilienthal, *Theologische Bibliothec*, 1105.

[118] ARH Ned. Herv. Kerk OSA 215. Acta Deventer 1705, art. 40.

[119] ARH Ned. Herv. Kerk OSA 292. Acta Sneek, June 1705, art. 25.

[120] ARH Ned. Herv. Kerk OSA 85. Acta Harderwijk, Aug. 1705, art. 4.

[121] RNH Acta Classis Haarlem X res. 3 June and 21 July 1705; GA Amsterdam Acta Kerkeraad XVII, p. 306. res. 30 Apr. 1705.

sale and distribution.[122] Meanwhile the bickering of the Overijssel *classes*, with Deventer and Kampen taking a harder line than the split assemblies of Steenwijk and Zwolle, became increasingly acrimonious. Facing contradictory pressures, the States tried to be resolute, resisting demands for the further stiffening of the Zwolle *Articles*, and insisting the issue was settled and not to be discussed further, either in the *classes* or at the next gathering of the synod but, as events soon proved, to little avail.[123]

Continuing deadlock in Overijssel produced only more anger and revulsion in the other Dutch provinces. All the other synods seethed with indignation. Meeting at Bolsward, the Frisian synod pressed their provincial States, and other synods, to exert every possible pressure on Overijssel to take firmer measures, adamant that Leenhof could not remain a minister of the public Church, having being shown before the 'whole world to approve the godless views of the atheist Spinoza'.[124] This body also demanded that the Overijssel *visitatores*, who had inspected Leenhof's works before publication, should be severely reprimanded for failing to spot their irreligious content, the *visitatores'* plea of insufficient familiarity with Spinoza's thought striking the Frisians as implying an unbelievable degree of obtuseness and negligence.

When the full Synod of Overijssel reconvened in June 1706, the States' commissioners not only refused to permit any revision of the Zwolle *Articles* but any discussion of the Leenhof business whatsoever.[125] Their brusque announcement provoked a furious reaction among the assembly only slightly alleviated by news that the Amsterdam burgomasters had now banned the *Redenkundige Aanmerkingen* as a work 'full of Spinozistic propositions and other bad material'.[126] The States' intervention in the provincial synod provoked still greater outrage among the other Dutch Reformed synods. The Synod of Groningen now categorically condemned Leenhof's three texts as '*intolerabel* and *censurabel*' while at the South Holland Synod's gathering at Woerden in July, bitter criticism was heaped on both the Zwolle magistracy and States of Overijssel.[127] Deputies from both Holland synods again conferred with Heinsius, and a Holland ban on Leenhof's three texts came under active consideration. Meanwhile, the North Holland Synod, spurred on by Van den Honert, dispatched a latter of protest to Zwolle couched in terms of unprecedented vehemence, deploring the 'feebleness and laxness' with which the consistory there had acted, given that no one doubts the *Hemel op Aarde* is based 'partly on the *Ethics* of the renegade Jew and notorious atheist Benedictus de Spinoza, and more especially that cursed book the *Tractatus Theologico-Politicus* forbidden already many years ago by the highest authority in our land'.[128]

---

[122] ARH Provinciale Resolutien 492, fo. 250. res. States of Overijssel, 2 July 1705.

[123] Ibid., fo. 276. res. States of Overijssel, 20 Apr. 1706.

[124] ARH Ned. Herv. Kerk OSA 292. Acta Bolsward, June 1706, art. 16 and 17.

[125] ARH Ned. Herv. Kerk OSA 215. Acta Kampen, June 1706, art. 40 and 41.   [126] Ibid., art. 7.

[127] ARH Ned. Herv. Kerk OSA 97. Acta Woerden, July 1706, art. 18.

[128] RNH Acta Classis Haarlem X. res. 20 July 1706, art. 7; ARH Ned. Herv. Kerk OSA 97 Acta Leerdam, July 1707, art. 18.

Unused to being addressed by another ecclesiastical body in such a tone, the consistory passed the letter straight to the burgomasters, who reacted by setting up a co-ordinating committee to fend off the mounting pressure from outside Overijssel, consisting of themselves, the town's four preachers (other than Leenhof), two elders, and two deacons.[129] Dispensing with normal procedure, the States of Holland on 18 December 1706, dramatically distanced themselves from Overijssel by decreeing (as Monnikhoff noted), a comprehensive ban on Leenhof's last three books as 'Spinozistic'.[130] This precipitated yet greater pressure on Overijssel, where the States found themselves in an increasingly awkward dilemma. In a vote in the States General on 29 December 1706, the other provinces insisted Overijssel proceed immediately to prohibit the three books on the same basis as Holland.[131] Deliberating on how best to protect the dignity of their province, the provincial Delegated States found themselves caught between a tide of recrimination propelling them one way, and their anxiety to defend Overijssel's autonomy the other. Protesting to the other provinces that it was neither usual nor proper for the States General to direct an individual province in an internal matter such as this,[132] they justified their prevarication by explaining that there had been repeated requests from their own synod to prohibit Leenhof's books, but that hitherto they had preferred not to do so 'out of fear this would only provide further encouragement to read them'.[133] They undertook to reconsider though.

A fresh line of attack opened up by Leenhof's adversaries at this juncture was to pursue his ally Barent Hakvoord. Van den Honert was convinced the *Redenkundige Aanmerkingen* had been published in Zwolle by Hakvoord, despite 'Amsterdam' being stated on the title-page;[134] and, in any case, Hakvoord was the declared publisher of Leenhof's two books on King Solomon, both of which had by now been identified as 'Spinozistic'. He was assumed also to have published the 1703 edition of the *Hemel op Aarde*, at the back of which is a list of books then available at his bookshop, including Dutch editions of Hobbes' *De Cive*, Van Dale's work on oracles, and a life of Eugene of Savoy. Furthermore, he had affixed his name as publisher to the title-pages of Leenhof's *Ophelderinge* and *Kort Antwoord*, books now in the curious position of being officially banned in Holland, Friesland, and other provinces, but still freely on sale in Overijssel. In short, Hakvoord had manifestly revealed himself a purveyor of Spinozistic and radical literature.

With the publication at Zwolle in 1706 of a 448-page revised sixth edition, dedicated to the Zwolle burgomasters and city government,[135] of his handbook of the Christian faith, *De Schole van Christus* (The School of Christ), attention inevitably fastened on Hakvoord's own activity as a writer. The work purported to be a common manual of Reformed doctrine expounded in sixty-seven lessons. Scrutiny quickly revealed numerous suspect passages, most of which had already appeared in the third edition

---

[129] GA Zwolle Kerkeraad Acta 017/6. res. 12 Aug. 1706.
[130] KBH MS 128 G 1. Monnikhoff, 'Aantekeningen', fos. 22, 58v.
[131] Jenichen, *Historia*, 224, 228–9.   [132] Ibid.; *Boekzaal der Geleerde Werelt* 1707, i, 184–5.
[133] Jenichen, *Historia*, 229.   [134] Van den Honert, *Briev*, 1–2.
[135] Hakvoord, *Schole van Christus* (1706), title-page.

of 1693, published at Amsterdam when Hakvoord had been in partnership with Aert Wolsgryn. Indeed, when Wolsgryn was arrested by the Amsterdam magistrates in 1698, for producing the second part of *Philopater*, the stock in his shop still included 218 copies of Hakvoord's manual.[136] Denounced at the gathering of the Synod of Overijssel, where two sets of offending extracts from the book were submitted in 1707,[137] Hakvoord's new edition prompted calls for his dismissal as cantor in Zwolle's principal church, and other steps. The *classis* of Steenwijk judged Hakvoord's book to be crammed with 'many false and slanderous propositions taken from the writings of Spinoza', demanding that the work should be banned by public edict, while Deventer accused Hakvoord of purveying 'pure Spinozism' and seeking to weaken the authority of Scripture 'as is the aim of Spinoza'.[138] Particularly brazen, noted the synod, was Hakvoord's remark that 'were we all philosophers able to see things in their original causes . . . there would be no need for divine Revelation.'[139]

Hakvoord was indeed a crypto-Spinozist and had been one since the early 1680s.[140] A variety of passages from the later versions of the *Schole van Christus*, when considered individually, might seem merely odd, such as that 'ignorance is . . . the root of all evil' and that if people are to be 'brought to blessedness one has only to purge them of prejudices and make them aware of God's Word', and 'virtue and blessedness will follow of themselves', which is why, he says, the Devil and the Pope strive so hard to keep the people in ignorance.[141] In another questionable passage, he asks why under Christian governments virtually everyone believes Scripture is God's Word, while under non-Christian rulers practically no one does, answering that this notion is 'taught under a Christian regime, and inculcated, but not under another regime'.[142] In another place, he avers that the only way, in Heaven or on earth, for a man's 'soul to be made happy is through a pure understanding of God and His properties—yes, therein consists the eternal life'.[143] Because most people, he suggests elsewhere, 'are unable to understand God as simple and perfect as He is, He is obliged, so to speak, to reveal Himself through various similes, human ways of speaking and so forth'.[144] But when all these dubious expressions are viewed together, the only conceivable inference is that the Zwolle bookseller was infiltrating a forbidden philosophy lightly veiled as Christianity. Moreover, certain passages unmistakably betray the influence of Spinoza—as well as of Hobbes, Koerbagh, and Bekker—such as Hakvoord's claiming the term 'angel means nothing but a messenger or envoy sent to men on God's part'. No one can know by way of reason, he contends, much less prove, that there are 'angels or other spirits'. What Scripture says of them is mostly unclear 'and no wonder!' he exclaims, given that the Bible's purpose is not to convey truth 'in a scientific manner, explaining things as they are in their nature, but rather as they seem to the senses, according to the notions of the common people'.[145]

---

[136] Maréchal, 'Inleiding', 117.   [137] GA Zwolle Kerkeraad Acta 017/6. res. 24 June 1706.
[138] ARH Ned. Herv. Kerk OSA 216. Acta Zwolle, June 1707, art. 43.   [139] Ibid.
[140] Vandenbossche, *Frederik van Leenhof*, 2.   [141] Hakvoord, *Schole van Christus* (1693), 96.
[142] Ibid., 97.   [143] Ibid., 103.   [144] Ibid., 106.   [145] Ibid., 139–40.

Hakvoord's books—besides the *Schole van Christus* another work, the *Staat der kerke* (The State of the Church) was also denounced—thus in turn became a target of the Reformed *classes* and consistories. The Frisian Synod, convening in June 1707, stigmatized his manual as 'full of godless, Spinozistic opinions and phrases' demanding he be publicly arraigned and stripped of his dignities as a teacher and church cantor in Zwolle.[146] He was similarly denounced by the Synod of Gelderland.[147] Files of 'Spinozistic' passages taken from Hakvoord's text, sent from Deventer and Steenwijk, were read out in Zwolle at the consistory's meeting on 1 September, and Hakvoord himself summoned for interrogation.[148] He began on a defiant note, reminding the assembly that his manual had twice been inspected by Church *visitatores* assigned by the *classis* of Zwolle in 1685 and Kampen in 1689.[149] Since, however, most of the suspect passages had first appeared in the Wolsgryn edition of 1693, this was somewhat beside the point. In a second interrogation, on 3 January 1708, Hakvoord demanded to be shown where all this alleged 'pure Spinozism' was to be located. Where was the proof he was a 'Spinozist'? The Deventer extracts, he pointed out, failed to identify a single direct borrowing. The Steenwijk file, he granted, 'does place several things taken from me and Spinoza side by side but how well or badly I cannot judge since the passages from Spinoza are in Latin which I do not understand'.[150]

The consistory debarred him from the Lord's Supper, and asked the magistracy to strip him of his teaching and Church jobs, which they promptly did.[151] Subsequently, Hakvoord became more contrite, conceding that he had, after all, borrowed 'many phrases' from Spinoza, but he claimed not to have understood how wicked and atheistic they were. Now that he knew better, he abjured Spinoza's 'godless views' unreservedly, promising to eschew them always in the future and undertaking not to sell any more of his books until he had prepared new editions from which all Spinozistic passages had been deleted and obtained fresh approbations from the *classis*.[152] The consistory considered his submission, in May, but ruled that they could not lift the sanctions imposed without the approval of the full Synod of Overijssel, and Hakvoord was provisionally left under censure.

When the Synod of Overijssel reconvened in June 1708, the States' commissioners again forbade any revision of the compromise *Articles* hammered out two years before, despite the deadlock, or indeed any discussion of the Leenhof business.[153] Politically, the imbroglio could now be sorted out only by the States which, indeed, had seemed close to resolving matters the previous April but finally failed to sway the Zwolle magistracy. The States' failure to conclude then, and their refusal now to permit discussion of the affair, not only ensured that the impasse remained unbroken, with Zwolle still blocking the sweeping censure of Leenhof's person, ideas, influence, and books so vociferously demanded by virtually the whole of the Dutch Reformed

---

[146] ARH Ned. Herv. Kerk OSA 292. Acta Franeker, June 1707, art. 17.

[147] ARH Ned. Herv. Kerk OSA 85. Acta Nijmegen, Aug. 1707, art. 6.

[148] GA Zwolle Kerkeraad Acta 017/6. res. 7 July and 1 Sept. 1707.   [149] Ibid., res. 8 Dec. 1707.

[150] Ibid., res. 8 Jan. 1708.   [151] Ibid., res. 25 Mar. 1708.   [152] Ibid., res. 18 May 1708.

[153] ARH Ned. Herv. Kerk OSA 216. Acta Vollenhoven, June 1708, art. 8.

Church, but further heightened the tension between the synod and provincial States. Meanwhile, on their part, the Zwolle burgomasters remained unmoved by the decisions of the North Holland and Frisian synods to boycott for the time being certificates of orthodoxy issued by its consistory for congregants and proponents from there travelling elsewhere, 'since that body had endeavoured to protect Dominie Leenhof as much as possible'.[154] If Reformed opinion elsewhere demanded Leenhof's expulsion from the Church and public disgrace, for the moment, he still enjoyed appreciable support among his congregation and the Zwolle regents.

Nevertheless, the atmosphere at the 1708 gathering of the Synod of Overijssel was so highly charged the States' commissioners were practically compelled to permit not just a vehement debate to let off steam but the formulation of a *praeadvis*, that is, a provisional resolution based on the views of the *classes* which would, however, only take effect when and if approved by the States. The assembly won this ground, adamant that the 'precious souls of the people who daily hear Fredericus van Leenhof preaching on the basis of his imaginary *Heaven on Earth*' were being risked and that, if the States' commissioners did not yield, they and the States would be responsible for subjecting the entire Reformed Church to great and justified 'blame' for retaining in his pulpit, however briefly, 'someone whom the whole world, all Christian synods, including those in lands outside this state, consider infected with the views of the God-forsaker Spinoza'.[155] The *praeadvis* pronounced Leenhof 'guilty of Spinozism, and stubborn adherence to errors in contempt of the Church's admonitions', declaring he 'could not be tolerated as a minister, or member of the Church', and that the Synod of Overijssel 'will no longer recognize him as a preacher or member of the Reformed community'.[156] Simultaneously, the synod pressed the States to ban further production and sale of Hakvoord's manual as being full of 'Spinozistic propositions', instructing every preacher in the province to warn his congregation against that 'damaging book'.[157]

Another feature of the Overijssel Synod's deliberations in 1708 was a more detailed discussion than usual of 'licentious books' in response to the growing pressure in the United Provinces as a whole at this time for tighter control and more safeguards against theologically and philosophically 'dangerous' works. This was a tendency fuelled by the Leenhof uproar and the campaign against Hakvoord, as well as fears of the Hattemists and a more general feeling that the advance of radical ideas in society was having a seriously corrosive effect on faith and attitudes. In 1708 several petitions and representations from the Holland synods reached Heinsius and other key regents, as part of an orchestrated push towards a more comprehensive, systematic banning of philosophically radical books. Thus the meetings of the South Holland Synod in 1707 and 1708 resulted in a formal denunciation of the works of 'Monsieur Bayle' as containing ' many damaging propositions against God's Word and the entire Christian

---

[154] Ibid.; ARH Ned. Herv. Kerk OSA 292. Acta Franeker, June 1707, art. 13.
[155] ARH Ned. Herv. Kerk. OSA 216. Acta Vollenhoven, June 1708, art. 8.   [156] Ibid.
[157] As the States of Friesland had already done, in March; ibid., art. 40.

religion' as well as 'against God's Providence'.[158] Other intellectually seditious works cited by the synods included two by Goeree, the *Mosaische Oudheiden* (Mosaic Antiquities) of 1700, and his *Kerklyke en Weereldlyke Historien* (Church and Worldly Histories) of 1705, both allegedly containing 'offensive' passages in which Bekker's views were defended.[159] Moreover, Goeree comprehensively denied the existence of the Devil and magic.[160]

During 1708 a circular from the standing committee of the synod to the *classes* of North Holland requested lists of 'all books suspected of *Libertinisterey* or other harmful or dangerous views' so that a consolidated file could be compiled, with supporting material proving the danger, for submission to the States. These were to comprise both books 'which are already forbidden and those that should be'.[161] Among publications strongly 'suspected of *Spinosistery*' according to the 'brethren' of the Edam *classis* were Hakvoord's writings and Leenhof's *Prediker*, as well as the last edition of his *Keten*.[162] Additional texts recommended for prohibition at the gathering of the South Holland Synod at Dordrecht in July 1709 included Deurhoff's writings, Hendrik Smeeks' novel *Krinke Kesmes*, and the two latest works of John Toland (then residing in Holland) whose *Adeisdaemon* and *Origines Judicae* had just appeared clandestinely and anonymously, bound together, and provoking an immediate outcry at The Hague.[163]

These efforts were not entirely fruitless. Heinsius was thanked by the South Holland Synod in 1708 not only for helping to secure Holland's edict banning Leenhof's *Hemel op Aarde*, *Opheldering*, and *Kort Antwoord*, but also assistance in broadening the censorship drive.[164] In 1710 the States of Utrecht suppressed Sandvoort's *Zedig Ondersoek* (1709) while the Amsterdam magistracy prohibited Wyermars' text, sentencing him as a 'Spinozist', news widely welcomed in the consistories and *classes*.[165] The republic might have been more tolerant than most other European countries in some respects but was now strenuously demonstrating that, in philosophical matters at least, it was also a resolutely persecuting country. Yet the synods' ultimate objective— for a time shared by Heinsius—of a more far-reaching strategy to suppress radical writings, failed to materialize, though it did result in a draft placard of the States of Holland in 1708.[166] To the evident distress of the synods, many regents, anxious not to strengthen the Church's voice in intellectual censorship at the expense of the town

---

[158] ARH Ned. Herv. Kerk OSA 97. Acta Leerdam, July 1707, art. 18.

[159] Ibid.

[160] Goeree, *Mosaize Historie*, ii, 649–88 and iii, 138–43; Goeree, *Kerklyke en Weereldlyke*, 37, 678–86.

[161] RNH Acta Classis Edam VII, res. 16 Apr., 4 June, and 20 July 1708.

[162] Ibid., res. 16 Apr. 1708.

[163] ARH Ned. Herv. Kerk OSA 97. Acta Dordrecht, July 1709, art. 14; Champion, *Pillars of Priestcraft*, 130–2.

[164] ARH Ned. Herv. Kerk OSA 97. Acta Breda, July 1708, art. 17.

[165] ARH Ned. Herv. Kerk OSA 98. Acta Delft, July 1710, art. 14; ARH Ned. Herv. Kerk OSA 86. Acta Zutphen 1710, art. 8 and 9.

[166] ARH Ned. Herv. Kerk OSA 216. Acta Steenwijk, June 1712, art. 'licentieus boekdrukken'; GA Leiden Kerkeraad ix, p. 341. res. 30 Sept. 1712; ARH Ned. Herv. Kerk OSA 86. Acta Nijmegen, Aug. 1715, art. 17; ARH Ned. Herv. Kerk OSA 98. Acta Den Briel, July, 1715 art. 1713.

governments, in the end preferred not to discard the existing piecemeal system, deeming a comprehensive edict with detailed lists both impracticable and undesirable.

Even so, the drive to ban Leenhof and his books remained pivotal to the wider campaign to target radical literature during these years, and consequently, every conceivable pressure was brought to bear to induce Overijssel to proceed to a comprehensive condemnation. Outside Overijssel, most synods joined North Holland and Friesland in imposing sanctions on the Zwolle consistory during 1708 and, in August, the North Holland Synod ruled further that, not only should Zwolle's certificates of orthodoxy be refused, but neither could preachers from there participate in any meeting or Church gathering in North Holland,[167] an example promptly followed by Gelderland.[168] Nor was refusal of Zwolle's certificates by the synods outside Overijssel merely a symbolic gesture. On the contrary, this boycott produced many curious theologico-philosophical encounters. In April 1711 at The Hague, for instance, a preacher sent to interview a new arrival from Zwolle on the 'essentials of religion', on receiving satisfactory answers to his questions, confirmed that the prospective congregant thoroughly abhorred the 'atrocious ideas of Leenhof'.[169] When a woman named Jannetje Bruynvis reached The Hague, furnished with a certificate from Zwolle, in December 1712, on the other hand, the preacher sent to investigate her beliefs was obliged to explain the 'principles on which Frederik van Leenhof had built his book called the *Hemel op Aarde*', before he could confirm that Leenhof's were ideas 'she declared heartily to detest'.[170]

The impasse in the States of Overijssel was not broken until March 1709. The assembly voted to proceed on the basis of its draft resolution of April 1708, and the *praeadvis* of the synod, signalling a pending general prohibition of Leenhof's three texts and his suspension from his pulpit until he agreed to purge himself entirely of suspicion of Spinozism. Zwolle still resisted, but a majority ruled that 'notwithstanding the dissent of the city of Zwolle, this resolution must be considered a [binding] decision of this assembly.'[171] Zwolle's magistracy had to acquiesce. To avoid ejection from ministry and Church, Leenhof was required to submit to supplementary *Articles of Satisfaction* formulated by the synod. When this body gathered, at Deventer in June 1709, the States' commissioners summoned Leenhof in person, providing his final opportunity to recant unreservedly. At the climax of the human drama the embattled figure appeared—one man confronting an exasperated and extremely hostile assembly. He spoke defiantly, insisting he 'could not agree' to supplement what he had already retracted and that he 'had never taught Spinozism' but only orthodoxy, and would not comprehensively repudiate his three books.[172] That, as far the Synod and States of Overijssel were concerned, was the end of the matter. His books were duly suppressed *in toto*, in Overijssel as in Holland, and the Zwolle magistracy required to

[167] ARH Provinciale Resoluties 493, fo. 51. North Holland Synod to Synod of Overijssel, 6 Aug. 1708.
[168] ARH Ned. Herv. Kerk OSA 86. Acta Arnhem. Aug. 1708, art. 20.
[169] GA The Hague Acta Kerkeraad V, 159. res. 9 Apr. 1711.   [170] Ibid., 198. res. 2 Dec. 1712.
[171] ARH Provincial Resoluties 493, fo. 50. res. States of Overijssel, 7 Mar. 1709.
[172] Ibid., fo. 87. res. States of Overijssel, 5 Mar. 1710.

strip him of his pulpit. This, however, they declined to do and a further period of deadlock ensued.

In April 1710 the States insisted the Zwolle city government must dismiss him, offering a subsidy of 400 guilders yearly 'during the life of the aforesaid Leenhof' so that a replacement could be paid while he continued to receive his salary, without the city incurring added expense.[173] But still nothing happened. Only in December 1710, after the burgomasters informed him he had to resign or they would be obliged to dismiss him, did Leenhof finally yield. But even then, to the anger of synods and *classes* throughout the Republic, the Zwolle burgomasters and consistory persisted in standing by him. Still he received both salary and sacraments, and remained a respected personage in the town, retaining, among other marks of esteem, his seat in the main church on the bench designated for the town's preachers.[174] In his farewell sermon, subsequently published in Amsterdam, Leenhof warmly thanked both burgomasters and people of Zwolle for their long and unwavering support.[175]

The States of Overijssel's refusal to permit further discussion of the Leenhof affair at the gathering of the provincial synod, in Zwolle in June 1711, only strengthened the prevailing feeling there was still unfinished business.[176] The States might insist there was nothing more to discuss, but the Synod fervently disagreed, though it had to be content for the time being with rebuking the now extravagantly contrite Hakvoord instead. Some of the Zwolle consistory felt he had sufficiently purged himself of Spinozism and should have his jobs back; but while the *classis* of Steenwijk agreed, provided he published a formal renunciation of Spinoza, those of Deventer and Kampen persisted in regarding him a 'teacher of pure and complete Spinozism' who should on no account be forgiven his heinous offence.[177]

As the months passed, discontent over Leenhof's still favoured position in Zwolle showed little sign of abating. In the Alkmaar *classis*, as in many *classes* and consistories, there were words of bitter reproach for the Zwolle burgomasters and consistory, and renewed calls for Leenhof's expulsion from the Church and thorough public disgrace.[178] The Synod of Gelderland indignantly protested at the situation in Zwolle in August, insisting that Leenhof be immediately barred from the sacraments.[179] In Holland, Heinsius was pressed to act, though it was not until 1712 that Leenhof's adversaries in the Zwolle consistory finally gained the leverage to force his excommunication and public disgrace. In all, it had taken the Dutch Reformed Church nine long years to resolve what by any reckoning was one of the severest doctrinal controversies in its history. A lonely and estranged figure, Leenhof died in October 1712, no longer participating in any Church. This was not quite the end of the affair, however, since the Zwolle consistory still evinced scant inclination to apologize for its handling of the

---

[173] ARH Provincial Resoluties, fo. 115v. res. States of Overijssel, 24 Apr. 1710.
[174] RNH Acta Classis Haarlem X. res. 21 July 1711; Vandenbossche, *Frederik van Leenhof*, 6.
[175] Leenhof, *Wel-doorwrogte*, 31, 38–9.
[176] ARH Ned. Herv. Kerk OSA 216. Acta Zwolle, June 1711, art. 23.
[177] Ibid., art. 40.   [178] RNH Acta Classis Alkmaar, res. 2 June 1711, art. 3.
[179] ARH Ned. Herv. Kerk OSA 86. Acta Harderwijk, Aug. 1711, art. 16.

case and languished under the censure of various synods for some years.[180] Nor by any means did Leenhof's death curtail the broader cultural impact of the episode.

iv. The Leenhof Controversy in the Netherlands, Germany, and the Baltic

The chief significance of the Leenhof furore was that it demonstrated more clearly than any comparable episode the feasibility of distilling from Spinoza a complete system of social, moral, and political ideas built on philosophical principles totally incompatible with authority, tradition, and revealed religion, which could be effectively popularized and infiltrated into the consciousness of the non-academic reading public, without readers necessarily even realizing they were imbibing Spinozism. In the Netherlands the threat was plainly, and was perceived to be, a real one, not just locally but throughout the United Provinces. What the reverberations of the Leenhof controversy in Germany and the Baltic showed was that the challenge was not confined merely to the United Provinces but was potentially exportable to a wide area.

That Leenhof's writings were never rendered into French or Latin ensured there was little inkling of the uproar in French, British, or southern European intellectual life, though a French-language résumé of the *Hemel op Aarde* appeared in the *Journal des Sçavants* in October 1708, and Leenhof eventually came to be acknowledged in late eighteenth-century France as one of the prime 'Spinosistes' of the early years of the century. Publication in Dutch was no barrier to penetration in Germany and the Baltic, however, and here the furore received considerable attention, notably contributing to the spread of Spinozism and radical thought during the eighteenth century. While historians have long been aware that several Dutch popularizers of Spinozism, or what contemporaries called Spinozism, such as Leenhof, Van Hattem, and the Leiden mystic Jacob Brill, played a major part in popularizing Spinozistic ideas in German-speaking lands,[181] the point has never received sufficient emphasis in broader discussions of the European Early Enlightenment. Also, seemingly, there has been too little awareness of the role of Leenhof in particular, as distinct from other Dutch popularizers. The Hattemist movement had a considerable impact, particularly in Zeeland and States Brabant, and was noticed in Germany, but it can hardly be claimed that Van Hattem's thought, however heterodox theologically, was predominantly Spinozist in character.[182] The same reservation is valid regarding Brill. But with Leenhof the case is different: for while his thought is not always coherent, and possibly some passages can best be described as Epicurean rather than Spinozist,[183] it is predominantly a philosophical, not a theological system, and he comes close to being what contemporaries called a 'complete Spinozist'.

---

[180] ARH Acta Classis The Hague V, fo. 76, res. 29 July 1716; RNH Acta Classis Edam. res. 19 July 1717, art. 14; ARH Ned. Herv. Kerk OSA 216, Acta Zwolle, June 1715, art. 2; [Durand], *La Vie*, 176; Maréchal, *Dictionnaire*, 151.

[181] Baeck, *Spinozas erste Einwirkungen*, 341–2; Schröder, 'Spinozam', 163.

[182] Schröder, 'Spinozam', 163; Wielema, 'Spinoza in Zeeland', 164–6.

[183] Vandenbossche, *Frederik van Leenhof*, 29–32.

In Germany and the Baltic Leenhof's significance sprang from his distinctive role in popularizing Spinozism in the Netherlands itself. In a society where open expression of philosophically radical ideas was forbidden—such as both the Netherlands and Germany—a figure who temporarily succeeded in propagating such concepts in an unadorned style, devoid of academic terminology, in easily understood books which sold very widely, while, in the process, drawing upon himself a torrent of denunciation, inevitably appealed to clandestine opponents of prevailing structures of authority and thought who were themselves obliged to be cautious and guarded. By raising such a storm and so relentlessly pursuing Leenhof as a propagator of *Spinosistery*, the synods themselves helped convert him into a kind of spiritual martyr, a persecuted hero of the European philosophical underground. Thus Goeree, a radical who denied Satan and demons, remarks (in a legally published work) that he preferred to pass over the subject of Leenhof 'with a silent drum' for reasons of prudence, and keep what he thinks about this whole 'assault' to himself.[184] Obviously, he nurtured bitter feelings about Leenhof's persecution. Wyermars several times cites Leenhof approvingly in his banned work of 1710, echoing his praise of Solomon, the philosopher-king who taught that the world is not created but is eternal.[185]

The book which undoubtedly caused the greatest offence to the synods in the closing stages of the Leenhof affair, however, was the clandestinely and anonymously published *Philalethes Brieven* (Letters of Philalethes) which appeared at Amsterdam in 1712. Extracts from *Philalethes* were circulated at the meeting of the South Holland Synod in July 1712. Typically of Goeree, who was probably the author, this text ridicules belief in angels and spirits, questions the divine authorship of Scripture, denies the Trinity, and, following Beverland, reduces the Fall to an allegory of sexual desire.[186] Regarded as exceptionally offensive was the author's contention that because Christ and his Apostles were concerned only to instil obedience, and not to teach the people truth, they made no effort to counter superstitious belief in magic, demons, and the Devil even though such credence is complete nonsense.[187]

Philalethes Brieven are perhaps especially symptomatic of the underground Radical Enlightenment of the early eighteenth century in their fervent belief in the progress of human reason and confidence that, in recent years, philosophy had achieved a crucial breakthrough, building on and completing the humanist philosophy of what we would now call the Renaissance, as well as (as he puts it), 'the Reformation', and utterly demolished the metaphysical foundations of all prejudice and superstitious credulity.[188] Inevitably, for such a writer, the Leenhof episode was emotionally highly charged.[189] When *Philathes* was condemned at the Synod of Gelderland in August 1713, its defiant defence of Leenhof was singled out as one of its most offensive features.[190]

---

[184] Goeree, *Kerklyke en Weereldlyke*, 4, 37.   [185] Wyermars, *Ingebeelde Chaos*, 65, 100, 144.
[186] ARH Ned. Herv. Kerk OSA 98. Acta Schoonhoven, July 1712, art. 13; ARH Ned. Herv. Kerk OSA 86. Acta Nijmegen, Aug. 1712, art. 5.
[187] [Goeree], *Philalethes Brieven*, 119–20, 125.   [188] Ibid., 126–7, 176.
[189] [Goeree], *Philalethes Brieven*, 42–3, 46, 124, 175–6.
[190] ARH Ned. Herv. Kerk OSA 86. Acta Zutphen, Aug. 1713, art. 13.

Indeed, such was the uproar over *Philalethes Brieven* that the Reformed synods felt able to resume their campaign in the States of Holland for tougher and wider intellectual censorship, adamant that 'freedom of the printing press goes too far.' Heinsius did revive the debate over the discarded draft censorship edict of 1708;[191] but again most regents preferred not to adopt a sweeping measure with detailed lists attached, arguing that, among other drawbacks, such a step would provide libertine readers with a complete guide to forbidden philosophical literature.[192]

The public Church was profoundly apprehensive of what Leenhof came to represent. Year after year, at assemblies of the *classes* and synods, it was solemnly recorded that a close watch was being kept against the 'Spinozistic' views of Leenhof. The synods considered Leenhof's legacy a potentially powerful influence in popular culture which needed to be guarded against with unremitting vigilance. The *classis* of The Hague, noting, in June 1739, that the North Holland *classes* were no longer being as stringent as those of South Holland in checking against Leenhovian Spinozism, particularly in examining theology students and proponents, and interviewing prospective preachers for jobs, as well as in setting guidelines for *visitatores* inspecting theological and philosophical manuscripts intended for publication, and re-emphasized the importance of keeping up the Church's guard against Leenhof's legacy.[193] Typically, the *classis* of The Hague was still solemnly recording in its records in June 1750 that it 'condemns the Spinozistic views of Leenhof and will persist in its vigilance against them'.[194]

The German and Baltic reception of Leenhovian popular Spinozism began well before the publication—in 'Amsterdam' according to the title-page—of the German rendering of Leenhof's chief work under the title *Der Himmel auf Erden* in 1706. This was eventually to be the first of two translations, a second appearing nearly half a century later at Leipzig, in 1752 and again in 1758.[195] Before 1706 German interest in the furore was already intense. Indeed, the Leipzig scholar, Gottlob Friedrich Jenichen (1680–1735), whom Buddeus calls 'vir doctissimus', was absorbed in the episode almost from the outset, and it was he who compiled what became the standard account of the early part of the episode, his *Historia Spinozismi Leenhofiani*, published at Leipzig in 1707. While collecting documentation for the book, Jenichen researched in Holland and, among others, visited Colerus at The Hague to discuss Spinoza.[196]

Publication of the German version of Leenhof's embattled work, closely followed by Jenichen's heavily documented account in Latin, and the review of the latter in the *Acta Eruditorum* for 1707,[197] nevertheless rendered the whole episode better known in Germany. That the Dutch, as well as the German text of the *Hemel op Aarde*, and many

---

[191] ARH Ned, Herv, Kerk OSA 86, Acta Nijmegen, Aug. 1715, art. 17.

[192] RNH Acta Classis Edam res. 20 July 1716, art. 8.

[193] ARH Acta Classis The Hague vi, 14. res. 29 June 1739, art. 27; see also RNH Acta Classis Edam viii, res. 18 July 1740 'synodalia' art. 4.

[194] ARH Acta Classis The Hague vi, 290. res. 22 June 1750, art. 29.

[195] Trinius, *Freydenker-Lexicon*, 338; Schröder, *Spinoza*, 143, 338.   [196] Blase, *Johannes Colerus*, 185.

[197] *Acta Eruditorum* 1707, 328–31; Stolle, *Anleitung*, 386.

of the Dutch-language replies it generated, were quite widely disseminated in Germany and the Baltic is shown by early eighteenth-century German library catalogues. Thus Gerhard von Mastricht, syndic of Bremen, had not only the *Hemel op Aarde* in Dutch but Creighton's and several other Dutch-language refutations in his house.[198] Both Uffenbach in Frankfurt and Von Stosch in Florence likewise owned the Dutch version of the book.[199] A remarkably comprehensive collection of *Leenhofiana*, including the *Redenkundige Aanmerkingen*, Leenhof's two works on King Solomon, and the *Opheldering*, as well as the *Hemel op Aarde*, belonging to a theology professor, Johannes Bergius, were auctioned at Frankfurt an der Oder in April 1730.[200]

The review in the *Acta* describes the uproar in the Netherlands and lists some of the published refutations of Leenhof, including those of D'Outrein, Sluiter, Burmannus, Bomble, Van den Honert, and Creighton. This review, together with Jenichen and the German version of Leenhof's *Hemel op Aarde*, also helped spread awareness of the affair in Scandinavia. Many Swedish and Danish scholars had in fact been present at Dutch universities during the long years of the commotion and had personal recollections of it. Sweden's leading philosophical writer of the early eighteenth century, Rydelius, possessed the 1706 German version of Leenhof's chief work in his select library of 2,000 books at Lund.[201] The tiny library of Bishop Barchius, a mere 1,000 books auctioned at Uppsala in 1734, included Jenichen's *Historia*, along with copies of Spinoza, Beverland, Van Dale, Kuyper, and Geulincx.[202]

Aside from Jenichen, most initial German reaction to Leenhof tended to play down the specifically Spinozist character of his thought.[203] Among other examples, a German pamphlet entitled *Eine Sendschrift*, published in 1706 together with *Der Himmel auf Erden*, observes that Leenhof's book was in great demand and that his doctrine of joy and sadness is irreconcilable with Christian orthodoxy, but says nothing about Spinozism.[204] Later, however, as in France, the early disinclination to give Spinoza too much prominence gave way to a massive insistence on his centrality in the rise of incredulity and deism. Especially in the wake of Buddeus' *Theses Theologicae de Atheismo* (1717) which classifies Leenhof's views as 'Spinozistic', explaining that this was chiefly why his books were banned by public authority,[205] it became usual to identify Leenhof as a 'Spinozist'. Poppo, in his *Spinozismus Detectus* (1721), equates Leenhof's 'highest good' with Spinoza's 'summum bonum' as well as that of Geulincx.[206] With the outbreak of the Wolffian controversies in Germany in 1723, the Halle professor, Joachim Lange, who orchestrated the campaign against Wolff, stressed that in no other context since the beginning of the new century had *Spinozismus* arisen more 'speciously and also impudently' than in Leenhof and his book, *Der Himmel auf Erden*.

---

[198] [Mastricht], *Catalogus*, 204–5, 213.
[199] [Uffenbach], *Bibliotheca*, i, 'atheistica', 762, 768; Stosch, *Biblioteca Stoschiana*, ii, 219.
[200] *Catalogus Librorum . . . Bergii*, 13, 20–1.   [201] Rydelius, *Catalogus*, 38.
[202] *Följande salig Herr Biskopens Barchii*, octavos, 110.
[203] Schröder, *Spinoza*, 145; Schröder, 'Reception', 165–6.
[204] Leenhof, *Himmel auf Erden*, appendix *Ein Sendschrift*, pp. 1–2.
[205] Buddeus, *Traité*, 86; Buddeus, *Lehr-Sätze*, 157–8.   [206] Poppo, *Spinozismus Detectus*, 62.

In his writings Lange returns several times to the subject of Leenhof, often linking him with Geulincx and always identifying him as one of the most perfidious propagators of Spinozist fatalism and necessitarianism—the brush with which he strove to tar Wolff. Highlighting the concept of the eternal and necessary order of things, or causes, as a prime component of Leenhof's thought, in his *Modesta Disquisitio* (Halle, 1723) Lange postulates a general parallelism of the systems of Spinoza and Leenhof, which he terms fatalism 'Spinoziano-Leenhofianum'.[207] For them, God is no legislator or Lord of the universe, he contends, while Scripture's account of the Almighty is just a colourful allegory adjusted to the notions of the common people.[208] In another onslaught on Wolffianism, published in German at Halle in 1724, Lange again stresses Leenhof's fatalism, and this-worldly conception of the *summum bonum*, again linking him with both Spinoza and Wolff.[209] Especially pernicious in Leenhof, he argues, is the cunning concealment he had practised until 1703 and his having surreptitiously 'brought [his Spinozism] to the pulpit'.[210] In a text of 1726, Lange, who was aware of the Deistic influences entering Germany from England, as well as the (hitherto stronger) impact of Dutch writing, strikingly equates the 'atheistic systems' of Spinoza, Leenhof, Toland, and Lau.[211]

There was no slackening of interest in Leenhof during the middle years of the eighteenth century in Germany and the Baltic, quite the reverse, as the appearance of two new editions of *Der Himmel auf Erden* in the 1750s shows. Among later writers who mention him, Michael Lilienthal (1686–1750), who was for many years city librarian in Koenigsberg and who, like other savants of East Prussia, had gained part of his academic training in Holland, personally witnessed the closing stages of the Leenhof affair while he was a student there in 1710–11. He remarked many years later that, despite his *Spinosisterey*, Leenhof was a man of learning 'who, however, out of love of novelties, and through Geulincx's writings, absorbed numerous opinions later proved to be Spinozistic'.[212] Remarking on Leenhof's doctrines, he observes that Leenhof did not believe in the existence of Heaven or Hell, or of ghosts and apparitions, which he thought were figments of the imagination.[213] In his dictionary of 'freethinkers' published in 1759, Trinius classifies Leenhof as one of the major radical writers of the first half of the century, noting that during the celebrated controversy in the Netherlands he had had some supporters as well as many antagonists. This Dutchman tried to show men the path to personal happiness, and the truth about Heaven on Earth, he mused, but the only result of his efforts and books, was to build for Leenhof a veritable 'Hell on Earth'.[214]

---

[207] Lange, *Caussa Dei*, 5, 542–3.   [208] Lange, *Bescheidene*, 475–80; Lange, *Modesta Disquisitio*, 44–6.
[209] Ibid.   [210] Lange, *Bescheidene*, 476.   [211] Ibid., 557.
[212] Lange, *Nova Anatome*, 147, 149; Lange, *Caussa Dei*, 123, 135.
[213] Lilienthal, *Theologische Bibliothec*, 1105–7.   [214] Trinius, *Freydenker-Lexicon*, 335–9.

23 | THE 'NATURE OF GOD' CONTROVERSY (1710–1720)

By the early eighteenth century the widening perception of Spinozism as the prime and most absolute antithesis and adversary of received authority, tradition, privilege, and Christianity had generated a psychological tension evident throughout the academic world and 'Republic of Letters', not unlike the intellectual and ideological paranoia regarding Marxism pervading western societies in the early and mid-twentieth century. To label someone a 'Spinozist' or given to Spinozist propensities was effectively to demonize that person and demand his being treated as an outcast, public enemy, and fugitive. Conversely, for an academic, court savant, official, man of letters, publisher, or ecclesiastic to be publicly decried as a 'Spinozist', or privately rumoured to be such, constituted the gravest possible challenge to one's status, prospects, and reputation, as well as standing in the eyes of posterity. Often enough there was only one riposte powerful enough to counter such a threat to one's position and well-being, though it might require some ingenuity to render it plausible: to accuse one's accusers of 'Spinozism'.

Just such an imbroglio erupted at Groningen in 1702. For decades the town's university had been the scene of acrimonious exchanges between Cartesians and anti-Cartesians as well as Cocceians and Voetians.[1] In 1698 a prominent younger member of the teaching faculty, the distinguished Swiss mathematician and scientist from Basel, Johann Bernouilli (1667–1748), visited Burchardus De Volder, the leading scientific thinker at Leiden, to confer about the prevailing state of philosophy and science. Bernouilli taught at Groningen in the years 1695–1705, always placing great emphasis on the central role of mathematical 'reason' in the New Philosophy, but at the same time wavering somewhere between Descartes and Leibniz.[2] Bernouilli and De Volder agreed that Cartesianism was fatally flawed, and could not be revived, and on the importance of finding solutions yielding a robust and enduring general system of philosophy. On this occasion, Bernouilli urged the merits of Leibniz's metaphysics, but De Volder, as the younger man reported to Leibniz by letter, objected that bodies can not conceivably be constructed from infinitely small monads, so far as he could judge, because these must either be extended or not. If extended they are not

---

[1] Steenbakkers, 'Johannes Braun', 203–4.
[2] Sierksma, G. and Sierksma, W., 'Johann Bernouilli', 128, 131–3.

genuinely units of body and spirit any more than the bodies they are intended to explain. If not extended, it is impossible to see how extension can derive from them.[3] Unpersuaded by Leibniz, De Volder, while privately rejecting Descartes, preferred publicly to remain known as a 'Cartesian'.

In May 1699 Bernouilli held a *disputatio medico-physica* at Groningen on the subject of nutrition, maintaining that all parts of the human body are constantly being renewed and changing, so that a human, considered as pure body is not, after approximately three years, the same person as before. From virtually every standpoint, this raised vexing questions about personality, body, and soul, how and why man can be held responsible for his sins, and which of his bodies would ultimately be resurrected. The gap between Christian teaching and scientific reason on this issue Bernouilli resolved with a 'double-truth' strategy reminiscent of Bredenburg, who was still occasionally mentioned in early eighteenth-century debates as a thinker who had formulated one of the ways that Spinoza's arguments could be countered philosophically.[4] A presiding figure of the university, the theologian Paulus Hulsius (1633–1712), declared Bernouilli's proposition heterodox but for the time being elicited no reaction. However, on taking up the rectorate of the university in August 1699, Bernouilli took the opportunity, in his inaugural address, to rebut Hulsius' criticism, albeit discreetly, without mentioning his name. Hulsius too for a time showed admirable restraint. But when Bernouilli held another disputation in which he not only maintained his own orthodoxy but added the corollary that whoever claims the soul acts on the body—he retained the Cartesian dichotomy of mind and extension—renders the soul a body and the body a soul, Hulsius felt compelled to respond. He deemed Bernouilli's argument a pernicious one which needed to be counteracted, and asked his elderly fellow professor of theology, Jean Brun (Johannes Braunius, 1628–1708) to join him in mobilizing their faculty against Bernouilli's corollary. Brun, however, a Cartesio-Cocceian of long standing, unsympathetic to Hulsius, preferred to side with Bernouilli. He told Hulsius he fully approved of the contentious corollary and considered anyone who opposed it to be a 'Spinozist'.[5] He also provided his young Swiss colleague with a signed statement expressly supporting his conclusion.

It was not long before the expected open clash before faculty and students at a crowded disputation materialized. Bernouilli repeated his arguments; Hulsius rose to dispute them, denouncing Bernouilli's propositions as soul-destroying; Bernouilli declared Hulsius' position 'Spinozistic' and fatal and read out Brun's signed statement. In effect, two professors had now publicly condemned Hulsius' reasoning as 'Spinozist' and plunged the entire university into uproar. Hulsius felt obliged to react forcefully, which he did by publishing a 58-page Latin diatribe against Spinozism and Spinozists entitled *Spinozismi Depulsio*.[6] Bernouilli had argued—like Geulincx and

---

[3] Thijssen-Schoute, *Nederlands Cartesianisme*, 57–8.
[4] Klever, *Mannen rond Spinoza*, 244; Klever, 'Spinozisme in het geding', (forthcoming).
[5] Steenbakkers, 'Johannes Braun', 205.   [6] Hulsius, *Spinozismi Depulsio*, 1.

Malebranche—that the soul cannot 'operate on the body' or cause it to move, maintaining that there is neither 'commercium neque nexum' (traffic nor connection) between the two.[7] Moreover, again like Geulincx and Malebranche, he also held that the two function together as a simultaneous unity. This perplexing paradox served as Hulsius' point of atttack. For what in practice, he demanded, is the difference between Descartes' inexplicable union of body and mind and Spinoza's godless conflation of body and soul into a single *substantia intelligens*, unifying extension and mind? In the past, Hulsius had publicly argued 'against Bekker' that the spirit docs operate on the body and that our soul does govern and determine our actions.[8] It may be that we do not know how the mind works on the body. Spinoza laughed at Descartes' fumbling efforts to disprove such interaction. Bekker stubbornly refuses to acknowledge any such possibility. But the truth is any thinker who, like Bernouilli, denies the working of the soul on the body must inevitably slide into either *Bekkerianismus* or Spinozism.[9] Hulsius concludes with a blistering assault on both Bekker and Spinoza, vowing, together with his students, to wage unremitting war on the idea of an extended God of substance that is eternal and can neither be created nor destroyed, against the notion of the infinity of matter, against the Spinozists' laws of motion that flow from the necessity of the divine nature, against the denial of Providence, contempt for Scripture and miracles, against all negation of the divine Word and thus of sin, resurrection, and the Last Judgement.[10]

This onslaught left both Brun and Bernouilli perilously placed. There was room neither to retreat nor remain silent. They had no alternative but to reply resoundingly, as both now did, Bernouilli counter-attacking with his *Spinozismi depulsionis echo* (Groningen, 1702) and Brun with his *Futilis Spinozismi depulsionis . . . Depulsio* (Groningen, 1702). He did not intend, Brun explained, to accuse Hulsius of Spinozism; by declaring the argument the 'body sins' to savour of Spinozism, he meant only that this is a harmful doctrine which can lead to Spinozism.[11] Also unjustifiable in Hulsius' text was his bracketing Descartes and Spinoza together as advocates of the union of body and mind. If both thinkers claim true substances cannot interact, there is much asserted by Cartesians which is also held by Spinoza, without this implying any impiety on the part of the former. Thus Spinoza teaches 'omnia fieri ex dei decreto' (all things happen by the decree of God), something Reformed theologians, as well as Descartes, also profess without this meaning that Reformed preachers are 'Spinozists'.[12] While Descartes' doctrine of substance is sound, to argue, like Hulsius, that the 'body sins' is to claim the mind is nothing but a body and the body a mind. For 'if the body has desires, sense and perception then nothing remains of the distinction between body and mind.'[13] Insisting that neither Bernouilli or himself had lapsed into Spinozism or *Bekkerianismus*, he insisted 'whoever postulates the body sins, postulates the body thinks; and whoever argues the body thinks, proclaims one and not two

---

[7] Hulsius, *Spinozismi Depulsio*, 24; Thijssen-Schoute, *Nederlands Cartesianisme*, 498.
[8] Hulsius, *Spinozismi Depulsio*, 30, 51.   [9] Ibid., 30.   [10] Ibid., 51–3.
[11] Braunius, *Futilis Spinozismi Depulsionis*, 6–7; Thijssen-Schoute, *Nederlands Cartesianisme*, 498.
[12] Braunius, *Futilis Spinozismi Depulsionis*, 8–9.   [13] Ibid., 11.

distinct substances, like Spinoza, and whoever teaches such things teaches, or at least savours, of Spinozism' (Hoc facit Spinoza, ergo qui talia docet, is docet, saltem redolet, Spinozismum).[14]

The furore blew over. Yet the suspicion among the academic fraternity that pre-occupation with the refined mathematical 'Cartesianism' of a De Volder, or the semi-Leibnizian mathematical rationalism of a Bernouilli, might all too readily provide a secure haven, lodged at the heart of academe, for crypto-Spinozism—a suspicion many deemed justified in De Volder's case—remained widespread in the early eighteenth century in the Netherlands, Germany, and the Baltic, lands where Cartesianism remained broadly dominant in the opening two decades of the century. The anxiety and instability resulting from this tension, as well as the innate contradictions within late Cartesianism, erupted again, and with still greater force, during the second decade in an uproar which may appropriately be called the 'Nature of God' controversy.

The central figure in this commotion was Jacob Wittichius (1677–1739), nephew of the older Wittichius, an enthusiastic disciple of De Volder,[15] and later a colleague at Leiden of the eminent Newtonian scientist and philosopher, Willem Jacob 's-Gravesande. A seasoned 'Cartesian', Wittichius had taught uncontroversially for some years at the Prussian university of Duisburg in Cleves, when, in 1710–11, he caused a minor stir with his *Dissertatio philologica de Natura Dei contra Spinozam* (Philological Dissertation on the Nature of God against Spinoza), based on a public disputation designed to refute Spinoza.[16] There was some murmuring at the time, and later even his closest friends conceded it contained 'unusual phrases and curious terms' easily misconstrued, which it would have been wiser to omit, though 'those who have benefited from the Heer De Volder's teaching could explain them in a good sense.'[17]

In this *Dissertatio* Wittichius attempts to define the nature of God, and God's relationship to nature, philosophically, attributing key steps in his argument to De Volder. He begins by maintaining, contrary to prevailing opinion, that Spinoza, strictly speaking, was not an 'atheist' but rather proposes a 'false' system around an erroneous conception of God.[18] A theoretically rigorous account of the 'Nature of God', holds Wittichius—by which he meant one expressed in terms of Cartesian notions of extension and mind—must assert the 'Nature of God, the most perfect being, is either infinite thought [i.e. mind], or infinite extension [i.e. body], or a nature which combines infinite . . . thought and extension' which last, he says, was Spinoza's view 'as is clear from his *Ethics*': 'God, then, Spinoza thinks, is substance infinitely mindful and extended' (Spinoza igitur arbitratur Deum esse substantiam infinite cogitantem et extensam).[19]

The problem of how to proceed any further, declares Wittichius, in defining the 'Nature of God' is one of awesome difficulty. He has researched exhaustively, he

[14] Ibid., 13.   [15] Wittichius, *Oratio Inavgvralis*, 3; Leydekker, *Blyde Spinosist*, 17, 61.
[16] Fabricius, *Delectus argumentorum*, 348; Otto, *Studien*, 80; Mennonöh, *Duisburg*, 229; Schröder, *Spinoza*, 27–8.
[17] Leydekker, *Blyde Spinosist*, 2v.   [18] Wittichius, *Wijsgerige Verhandeling*, 6.
[19] Ibid., 16; Wittichius, *Dispvtatio Philosophica*, 12.

remarks, into the views of natural scientists to see how best we can advance towards a cogent, philosophically workable stance which is 'scientific' in De Volder's specific sense of being consonant with mathematical rationality.[20] The crucial issue, he notes, was highlighted by the unnamed correspondent (Frederik van Leenhof) who embraces Spinoza's view in the correspondence with his uncle, Christopher Wittichius, in the latter's *Anti-Spinoza*, where the writer argues that no final distinction between thought and extension is possible.[21] Rejecting Leenhof's thesis, Wittichius maintains that thought and extension are, both conceptually and actually, totally separate.[22] He then insists that, on both theological and philosophical grounds, we are certain *a priori* that Spinoza's solution *must* be mistaken. For Spinoza, conflating thought and extension into one substance mixes things which must be kept apart, merging God with Nature and effectively denying divine Providence. Accordingly, he contends, 'Spinoza's view concerning God's Nature, combining as it does thought and extension, conflicts with reason' and *must* be invalid.[23] From this it follows necessarily, declares Wittichius (departing significantly from Descartes' ambiguous stance), that 'either God is pure thought, or else pure extension.'[24] He next demonstrates that the 'Nature of the most perfect being can not conceivably consist in extension'.[25] Hence, he concludes, by elimination we can prove 'God's Nature consists solely in infinite thought, that is, in His omniscient understanding and almighty will.'[26]

At Duisburg the disputation generated unease, partly owing to Wittichius' focusing almost entirely on Spinoza as the central issue when enquiring into God's nature, and partly to the less than wholly convincing grounds for rejecting Spinoza's and Leenhof's solution. However, neither Wittichius' Cartesian allegiance nor his Calvinist orthodoxy seemed in doubt, and he continued teaching in Prussia without hindrance. On leaving Duisburg, he had no difficulty obtaining a testimonial confirming his orthodoxy from the consistory.

The controversy proper began in 1717, when Wittichius was considered for a vacant chair in philosophy at Groningen. His candidacy was backed by that university's influential Cartesian contingent but strenuously opposed by Antonius Driessen (1684–1748), a Cocceian theologian but (rather unusually) an anti-Cartesian.[27] The anti-Wittichius campaign which now developed, in both the Netherlands and Calvinist Germany, was organized by the assiduous Driessen, who obtained copies of the 1711 *Dissertatio* and alerted colleagues to its disturbing contents. As a theologian, he was opposed on principle to Wittichius' project of investigating the 'Nature of God' from a pure philsophical standpoint. Philosophically, he was alarmed by the potentially Spinozistic contention (which, however, is also a Cartesian principle) that 'things which have nothing in common with other things can not be their cause' (Quae res nihil inter se habent earum una alterius caussa esse non potest) which to his mind

---

[20] Wittichius, *Wijsgerige Verhandeling*, 15, 25.   [21] Wittichius, *Dispvtatio philosophica*, 14.
[22] Wittichius, *Wijsgerige Verhandeling*, 18–19.   [23] Ibid., 28–9, 34.
[24] Ibid., 34–7.   [25] Ibid., 36–7.
[26] Ibid., 36–7; Wittichius, *Dispvtatio philosophica*, 26; Wittichius, *Abstersio*, 4–5.
[27] Thijssen-Schoute, *Nederlands Cartesianisme*, 495.

cancels Wittichius' ultimate conclusion that God is neither wholly nor in part 'extension'.[28] For the latter would then imply that God is not Creator or prime mover of the physical universe. Driessen's powerful intervention was simultaneously a triple assault on Spinozism, Cartesianism, and philosophical trespassing in theology.

The effort to block Wittichius' candidacy nevertheless failed. In June 1717 the curators of the Academia Groningo-Ommelandica, as the university was officially called, offered him the chair. But this was not the end of the quarrel. Driessen persisted in denouncing the 1711 *Dissertatio* as suspect and full of Spinozistic resonances, calling on the theology faculties at Leiden, Utrecht, and Franeker to put pressure on Groningen. Furthermore, the hitherto purely academic *controversia Driessenio-Wittichiana*, as it was dubbed in the Bremen press, now also entered the wider public sphere with the publication, by an unknown editor, of an unauthorized—and according to Wittichius doctored—Dutch translation of his Latin treatise.[29] This text provoked general uproar in the consistories and synods and was subsequently prohibited as 'pernicieuse ende dangereuse' by the provincial high court of Holland in December 1718, a 300-guilder reward being offered for the name of the editor, printer, or 'disséminateur'.

Driessen's efforts to persuade Professor Van den Honert at Leiden to condemn Wittichius failed. Van den Honert accepted the latter's assurances that he was no 'Spinozist'. Colleagues at Utrecht and Franeker, though, proved more amenable to denouncing Wittichius' views as suspect and harmful.[30] Driessen claimed not to be accusing Wittichius of *Spinozistery* as such but merely adhering stubbornly to 'his very dangerous manner of reasoning', which was apt to encourage Spinozist tendencies and open the door to fully-fledged Spinozism. Driessen particularly deplored his denial of the common notion of Spinoza as an 'atheist' and treatment of Spinoza's definition of God as a proposition to be compared with, and tested against, other definitions of God, including the true conviction of believing Christians, as if these were theoretically of equivalent validity.[31] That Driessen had a point and was not simply hair-splitting or pedantically creating unnecessary difficulties is indicated by Wittichius' admission that it was not clear to him, philosophically, how God, being pure spirit, can have created the physical universe.[32] Nor, it soon emerged, was Wittichius the only target of the rising agitation. Driessen strove to use the furore to emphasize his opponent's links with De Volder and thereby publicly query the soundness of De Volder's intellectual legacy.[33]

In the end Wittichius never came to Groningen, accepting instead, in July 1718, an appointment to a chair in philosophy at Leiden. The news caused consternation in several consistories and *classes*, including Rotterdam and Middelburg, where Carolus Tuinman, the leading adversary of Hattemism and Spinozism in Zeeland, orchestrated the opposition.[34] The Rotterdam consistory meeting to discuss the

---

[28] Driessen, *Aanspraak*, 10, 14–15; Driessen, *Dissertatio*, 22–3; *Bibliotheca Historico-Philologico-Theologica* (Bremen) 1, 362, 552.

[29] Wittichius, *Wijsgerige Verhandeling*, preface.   [30] Driessen, *Aanspraak*, 5.

[31] Ibid., 8.   [32] Ibid., 4; Thijseen-Schoute, *Nederlands Cartesianisme*, 496.

[33] Driessen, *Responsio*, 8–9.   [34] Leydekker, *Blyde Spinosist*, 3.

controversial appointment, on 16 August 1718, was deeply concerned by reports that no less than eight theology professors shared the 'suspicion of his being infected with *Spinozistery*'.[35] The Rotterdam burgomasters were pressed to intervene, which they did. When the Leiden curators, backed by the then strongly republican and pro-Cartesian Leiden city government, vigorously rebuffed their efforts, delegates of the protesting towns were convened with counterparts from Leiden for a special meeting, presided over by Heinsius at The Hague.[36] Leiden, however, obdurately resisted and, on 19 September 1718, a triumphant Wittichius, firmly ensconced in his Leiden chair, even if not altogether free of suspicion of Spinozism in the eyes of the public, delivered his subsequently published Latin inaugural address. He vigorously defended his philosophical stance, thanked the Leiden curators and burgomasters for their support, reminded his audience of the 'appalling calumnies' which his famous uncle had been subjected to, and reaffirmed his reverence for his teacher, De Volder.[37]

The agitation surrounding Wittichius continued, however, for several more years and was stoked up in particular by the arrival, early in 1719, of formal academic judgements, with a covering letter from Buddeus, sent from Thuringia by the University of Jena. These had been requested by Wittichius' enemies as a way of discrediting him and undermining his academic standing. The chief figure in these proceedings was none other than the celebrated Lutheran expert on atheism and Spinozism, Buddeus, who had been activated by correspondents in the Netherlands and who, in turn, mobilized the Jena theology and philosophy faculties against Wittichius. As a philosophical adversary of Cartesianism and Spinozism, a critic of the Leibnizian-Wolffian system, and a sympathizer of Locke and English empiricism, Buddeus gladly seized the opportunity to demonstrate the redundancy, as he saw it, of Cartesian metaphysics (as well as to deliver a knock, by implication, at the Prussian and Calvinist University of Duisburg). The faculty judgements absolved Wittichius of 'Spinozism' in the strict sense, but pronounced his *Dispvtatio* replete with objectionable and suspicious propositions, including principles and corollaries taken from Spinoza's *Ethics*, precisely as Driessen had claimed.[38] Jena's philosophy faculty pointed to several highly questionable steps in Wittichius' argument, showing that his doctrine of motion was not that of Descartes but that of Spinoza and, moreover, that it had induced him to reject proofs demonstrating the existence of God from the phenomenon of motion. Especially disturbing, according to the Jena faculties, was Wittichius' method of philosophizing about the Nature of God on the basis of 'geometric steps', which was essentially Spinoza's approach and leads him to conclusions which are not very different from Spinoza's. Here they cited Proposition VIII of Part II of the *Ethics*, adding that neither does Wittichius' method 'differ much, from that used

---

[35] GA Rotterdam Acta des Kerckenraedt VIII. res. 16 Aug. 1718.
[36] Ibid., VIII. res. 8 and 11 Sept. 1718.
[37] Wittichius, *Oratio Inavgvralis*, 2–3, 15; see also Wittichius, *Wijsgerige Verhandeling*, 15.
[38] *Iudicium . . . Facultatis Ienensis*, 44–7.

by Abraham Joannes Cuffeler, who similarly declares the world to be contained in God'.[39]

The Jena pronouncement that there is no great gap between Wittichius' conception of God and that of Spinoza and Cuffeler served to keep the controversy alive through 1719 and 1720, but failed to topple the resilient Wittichius. Several Reformed consistories, including Rotterdam, continued to complain that a scholar holding such views should not be permitted to teach the youth of Holland and Zeeland because of the grave social threat posed by the 'godless' principles of Spinoza.[40] In May 1719 a leading anti-Wittichius campaigner in Zeeland, Jacobus Leydekker, brought out a general account of the controversy under the title *De blyde Spinosist* (The Joyful Spinozist) once again trumpeting alarm over the progress of Spinozism in Dutch society. There were also complaints from elsewhere in the United Provinces, the Synod of Gelderland, meeting at Arnhem, discussing the question in August 1720, at the prompting of the *classis* of Maastricht, which claimed the disputation 'About the Nature of God' (by Wittichius) could not be deemed 'free from Spinosistery' and posed a danger to society.[41]

Wittichius defended himself with several more publications. Gradually the furore subsided, leaving him in place presiding over the Leiden philosophy faculty through the 1720s and 1730s, the last major Cartesian voice in the Dutch academic context alongside Andala, at Franeker. In a later reply to his detractors, he commended Johannes Bredenburg as someone who had written with 'much discernment and judgement against Spinoza' but who, like himself (some of whose early letters confiding the spiritual doubts of his student days, had later been publicly used against him), had been betrayed by alleged friends, maligned and libelled as a 'Spinozist'.[42] Bredenburg's theory of double truth, however, was pernicious and useless. At Duisburg, as now at Leiden, he had always taught, as Cartesians must, that 'what is philosophically true cannot be theologically false.'[43] Between philosophy and theology no contradiction is conceivable or possible. The disastrous outcome to Bredenburg's project ensued from his failure to grasp that one must not philosophize about the 'mysteries of the faith', not because these are 'contrary to reason', which cannot be, but because they are 'above reason'.[44] This was Bredenburg's ruin and that of the Socinians generally, and invalidates not just the doctrine of double truth but the whole of their theology of rejection of the Holy Trinity. Only Cartesianism, he held, offers a fully convincing and safe path to reconciling faith and reason, accommodating modern science to religion without any contradiction of 'truths' and without opening the flood-gates to Spinozism.

[39] Ibid., 50; Leydekker, *Blyde Spinosist*, 100; *Bibliotheca Historico-Philologico-Theologica* (Bremen), ii, 1099–1100.
[40] GA Rotterdam Acta des Kerckenraedts VIII. res. 19 Apr. 1719.
[41] ARH Ned. Herv. Kerk OSA 86. Acta Arnhem, Aug. 1720, act. 17.
[42] Wittichius, *Zeedig Antwoord*, 24–6.   [43] Ibid., 23.   [44] Ibid., 22, 24.

PART IV | THE INTELLECTUAL
COUNTER-OFFENSIVE

24 | New Theological Strategies

i. Theology and the Revolution in Bible Criticism

No other part of Spinoza's assault on authority, tradition, and faith proved so generally disquieting as his Bible criticism. As the great Swiss theologian and exegete Johann Heinrich Heidegger (1633–98), one of the authors of the strongly Calvinist *Formula Consensus Helveticae* (1675), noted, Hobbes and La Peyrère may have begun the process of eroding confidence in Scripture as divine Revelation in some men's minds, and questioning the Mosaic authorship of the Five Books, 'but no-one struck at the foundations of the entire Pentateuch more shamelessly than Spinoza'.[1] His principles of Bible hermeneutics seemed to threaten the very foundations of theology and religion and, for that very reason, had to be powerfully confronted and refuted.

Admittedly, some key features of the new Bible criticism, such as the search to establish linguistic meanings and usages by a close comparison of passages, and exploring historical context, were in fact pioneered earlier by Grotius, who believed the reconciliation of the Christian Churches could only come about when Scripture is no longer used as an armoury for polemical warfare by one confession against another, but understood as an expression of the thought world of the ancient Israelites and early Christians. During the early Enlightenment, Grotius indeed was not infrequently considered the great exegetical innovator who initiated the process which culminated in Spinoza, Simon, and Le Clerc.[2] Nevertheless, for Grotius too the Bible remained divine Revelation and there is still a considerable gap between his rationalistic methodology, leaving space for Providence, Christ, and the miraculous, and Spinoza's, which does not.

Spinoza begins by dismissing the entire corpus of previous Bible interpretation, whether Christian or Jewish: 'the chief concern of theologians on the whole has been to extort from Holy Scripture their own arbitrarily invented ideas, for which they claim divine authority.'[3] Men being naturally driven by the impulse to self-

---

[1] Heidegger, *Exercitationes*, 304; see also [François], *Preuves de la Religion* i, 452, 508–10.

[2] Faydit, *Remarques*, 106, 110, 140; Van Rooden. 'Spinoza's Bijbeluitleg', 120–1; Schröder, *Ursprünge*, 95–6; Faydit calls Grotius 'l'oracle et le maître de Mr Le Clerc'.

[3] Spinoza, *TTP*, 140; Popkin, 'Spinoza and Bible Scholarship', 396.

preservation and aggrandizement, it is not suprising that there should exist a vast incrustation of misleading, useless, and irrelevant Bible exegesis: 'we see that nearly all men parade their own ideas as God's Word, their chief aim being to compel others to think as they do.'[4] It was all part of the quest for power and authority. The first step towards establishing an objective, truly scholarly, Bible criticism, says Spinoza, is to 'free our minds from the prejudices of theologians and avoid the hasty acceptance of human fabrications as divine teachings', a procedure automatically excluding from the new hermeneutics most of his contemporaries.

Spinoza's maxim that the 'method of interpreting Scripture is no different from the method of interpreting Nature and is, in fact, in complete accord with it' implies that there is only one correct method of studying the Bible, which requires careful research, systematically investigating, sorting, and drawing inferences from Scripture's properties and characteristics, and conversely, that the Bible cannot be understood via theology. There can be no appeal to any criterion or authority external to the usual rules of science governing classification of data and drawing conclusions. Consequently, all valid Bible hermeneutics is primarily 'historical' and 'critical', that is, it approaches Scripture as a collection of historical narratives devoid of any special status or miraculous content, and paying close attention to the 'nature and properties of the language in which the Bible was written and which its authors were accustomed to speak'.[5] Scripture is viewed by Spinoza as a purely human document and entirely secularized, its phraseology, usage patterns, and historical context being the only sources from which we can reconstruct, to an extent, the true and precise meaning of the text. His hermeneutics thus assumes a vastly greater distance between modern man and the mental world of the Bible than even Grotius envisaged.

The only meaningful Bible commentary, then, is 'a historical study of Scripture'. Yet there are formidable difficulties in applying such scholarly criteria. Above all, holds Spinoza, such a method 'requires a thorough knowledge of the Hebrew language' of the Biblical books, and this we have partly or largely lost and can never recover: 'the idiom and modes of speech peculiar to the Israelite nation have almost all been consigned to oblivion by the ravages of time.'[6] This means there are many passages, even leaving aside phrases obscure due to the no longer fully understood intricacies of ancient Hebrew grammar, 'where the sense is very obscure and quite incomprehensible although the component words have a clearly established meaning'.[7] We also face another major obstacle, lacking as we do 'an account of the history of all the biblical books', which means our contextual grasp is at best highly fragmentary. Finally, 'our method of interpretation involves a further difficulty in that we do not possess [parts of the Bible] in the language in which they were first written.'[8] This applies especially to the New Testament and, he thought, the Book of Job. In the case of the

---

[4] Spinoza, *TTP*, 140.

[5] Ibid., p. 142; Klijnsmit, 'Spinoza over taal', 7–8; Roothaan, *Vroomheid, vrede*, 109–10.

[6] Spinoza, *TTP*, 149; along with the original significance of the Scriptural Hebrew accents; Spinoza, *Hebrew Grammar*, 18–19.

[7] Spinoza, *TTP*, 149; Spinoza, *Hebrew Grammar*, 90, 123, 148.   [8] Spinoza, *TTP*, 153.

Gospels, while the text was published in Greek, 'their idiom is Hebraic.'[9] In short, Bible criticism, for Spinoza, is by definition a tentative, conjectural, and very incomplete science: 'these difficulties . . . I consider so grave that I have no hesitation in affirming that in many instances we either do not know the true meaning of Scripture or can do no more than make conjectures.'[10] But what horrified contemporary opinion above all was his contention that Scripture is not written in a manner chosen by, and befitting, an almighty God but in particular and evolving human styles, with different historical contexts becoming mingled during a prolonged process of codification so as to produce a Biblical text that is, in part, incoherent and truncated, and frequently marred by discrepancies and contradictions.[11]

Spinoza thus redefines Bible exegesis as a science, albeit a severely restricted one, and in so doing uncompromisingly absorbs it into general scientific study, that is, in his terms, reduces it to philosophy. As Heidegger and Loescher stress, Spinoza's 'historical study of Scripture' is hence not just a revolution in Bible hermeneutics but simultaneously a revolution in theology and all study.[12] For it is inherent in his exegesis that the 'Creation is impossible', there are no miracles, and the alleged 'miracles' recounted in Scripture are delusions, tricks, and deceptions, that Biblical prophecy is fantasy, that there is no God who is a divine Law-giver, and finally, that Christ is merely a man in whom there is nothing divine or miraculous.[13] In short, divine Providence is shown 'to be nothing other than the order of Nature'.[14]

The key feature of the tradition of Bible interpretation instituted by Spinoza, and elaborated by Meyer, Koerbagh, Isaac Vossius, Goeree, and later Toland, Collins, Wachter, Giannone, and Edelmann, was precisely its strictly philosophical character, its use of philosophy not just to uncover discrepancies in the Biblical text or elucidate perplexing passages in the light of historical context, but to assess its significance, thereby completely detaching our view of Scripture from any theological grounding and ecclesiastical authority. Meyer proclaims philosophy the 'infallible' and sole criterion in the interpretation of Scripture, and this was in effect the clarion call of the entire radical exegetical tradition.

By contrast, the essence of Early Enlightenment, moderate, mainstream Bible hermeneutics was to adapt the critical tools devised by Grotius, Hobbes, La Peyrère, Wittichius, and others, as well as Spinoza and the radicals, to forge an exegesis which is not severed from but still substantially subject to theological concerns and ecclesiastical authority. However, this middle course sometimes (and especially initially) proved scarcely less arduous and risky than that of Spinoza and his disciples, exposing its protagonists to the hostility of traditionalists and radicals alike. The chief exponents of this sort of Bible criticism, the French Oratorian Richard Simon and his great Swiss Protestant counterpart and rival, Jean Le Clerc, from the outset found

[9] Ibid., 143, 153; Klijnsmit, 'Spinoza over taal', 7.

[10] Spinoza, *TTP*, 153; Van Rooden, 'Spinoza's Bijbeluitleg', 130.

[11] Heidegger, *Exercitationes*, 350–5; Loescher, *Praenotiones*, 156–9; Hazard, *European Mind*, 168.

[12] Heidegger, *Exercitationes*, 306–8; Loescher, *Praenotiones*, 26, 35, 48–50, 156–9, 224.

[13] Ibid., 304, 309–25, 331–2, 342–3.   [14] Heidegger, *Exercitationes*, 343.

themselves embroiled in a gruelling two-front war, battling Spinoza, on one side, and the immense corpus of inherited interpretation on the other. Simon's work was banned in France and by the Papacy, and provoked fierce opposition from churchmen everywhere; but his unwavering goal was to anchor the new 'critical' study of Holy Writ in a firmly confessional context, and, not least, to overwhelm the Protestant challenge, elevating the Catholic Church to the role of final judge of Scripture's meaning and significance. The Protestant slogan 'sola Scriptura', he strove to show, is utterly fallacious and untenable because Scripture is full of textual imperfections and difficulties requiring interpretation by a divinely inspired interpreter, which is the Catholic Church with the Papacy at its head: 'la seule et véritable Écriture,' insisted Simon, 'ne se trouve que dans l'Église.'[15] It was a stance which greatly preoccupied Protestant thinkers, not least Le Clerc, Limborch, and John Locke.[16]

Besides Simon and Le Clerc, numerous modernizing theologians employed the new tools afforded by philosophy, science, and philology from the 1650s onwards, to develop a more rigorous textual criticism of Scripture. Wittichius and other Cocceio-Cartesian theologians in the Netherlands refused to accept the Voetian view that 'one cannot theologize from philosophy; for what is true in nature cannot be false in theology, or with God the author of nature.'[17] To Wittichius, building on a Cartesianism infused with liberal Calvinist theology, fell the honour of forging the first genuinely 'critical', scientifically orientated, Protestant Biblical hermeneutics.[18] But his bold position rapidly crumbled. For if no other Protestant theologian claimed so early, or so confidently, that 'Scripture often speaks of natural things according to the view of the people and not in accordance with the exact truth,'[19] it was not long before this stance was pre-empted, and his very maxim captured and radicalized, by Spinoza and his followers.

Rationalizing theological exegetes, such as Grotius, Wittichius, Simon, and Le Clerc, faced a torrent of accusations from more conservative theologians that they were opening the flood-gates to 'atheistic' ideas. Recrimination focused especially on their admitting that the Bible is, in some degree, textually corrupt, containing discrepancies and contradictions, and couched in terms adjusted to the understanding of the common folk of the time rather than absolute truth.[20] On these grounds, Bishop Bossuet, who engineered the suppression of Simon's work in France, deemed it 'plein de principes et de conclusions pernicieuses à la foi'.[21] A leading Lutheran divine, lecturing at Leipzig in 1684, remarked that, while 'Simon may not want to be linked with Spinoza in any way', he nevertheless does no less to weaken the authority of

---

[15] Simon, *Réponse*, 213; Jaumann, *Critica*, 145–7.

[16] Marshall, *John Locke*, 139, 337–8; Champion, 'Père Richard Simon', 40–6; Simonutti, 'Religion, Philosophy', 311–12.

[17] Quoted in Scholder, *Birth*, 10.   [18] Ibid., 114–15, 125, 174–5; Israel, *Dutch Republic*, 890–8.

[19] Quoted in Scholder, *Birth*, 124–5; see also Wittichius, *Consensus veritatis*, 14, 53, 238.

[20] Carpzov, *Historia Critica*, 12; Hazard, *European Mind*, 31, 237; Marshall, *John Locke*, 337–42; Champion, 'Père Richard Simon', 40, 60–1.

[21] Steinmann, *Richard Simon*, 127; Champion, 'Père Richard Simon', 40.

Scripture.[22] Such disparagement compelled Simon, Le Clerc, and their followers to steer directly between the Scylla of radicalism and the Charybdis of tradition, redoubling their attacks on Spinoza while simultaneously defending crucial strands of the Dutch thinker's methodology which they had incorporated into their own. Simon denounces Spinoza's 'ignorance, or rather malice', as his English translator put it, ' in crying down the authority of the Pentateuch by reason of some alterations or additions therein',[23] while simultaneously complaining of being hounded for using the same language 'as the impious Spinoza', and being classed with the 'anti-Scriptuarii' by eminent churchmen who 'vomit forth their most virulent poyson against [him]'. If the 'vile and erroneous part of Spinoza' is abominable, he held, in justification of his methodology, not everything Spinoza 'speaks concerning Sacred Scripture is . . . to be condemn'd, because he agrees in some things with men of conspicuous piety and learning'.[24]

Simon reacted furiously to radical efforts to exploit his mounting difficulties with the Catholic episcopacy and Protestant theologians. Among others, he refused to be trifled with by the Dutch deist and libertine Isaac Vossius (1618–89), a friend of Saint-Evremond and Beverland, opposed, on historical grounds, to the notion that the Biblical Flood had been universal since there is no mention of it in the records of most ancient peoples,[25] who 'out of his malicious spirit against Simon, endeavours to bring an odium upon him, while he equals him to Spinoza the Jew, in those things which he asserts concerning the uncertainty of the Old Testament'.[26] Vossius' base design, declared Simon, was to discredit honest, upright, Bible exegetes such as himself while at the same time insidiously diminishing respect for the ancient Israelites and revealed religion by claiming the 'Jews have mutilated not a few texts of Scripture'.[27] But Simon was never able to escape the crossfire, Collins later eulogizing him mockingly as the scholar 'who has labour'd so much to prove the uncertainty of Scripture'.[28]

Simon employed much the same critical and philological apparatus as Spinoza, learnt much from him, and, like him, concluded that Moses did not compose the Five Books, granting that alterations were made long afterwards not only to the Pentateuch but also 'Joshua, Judges and other Books which Spinoza has endeavour'd to lessen the authority of, pretending that some things have been added'.[29] Not surprisingly, therefore, many a late seventeenth-century observer, including Heidegger at Zürich, viewed Spinoza and Simon as the two greatest Biblical subversives of the

---

[22] Namely Johannes Benedikt Carpzov (1639–99), professor of theology at the university; see Carpzov, *Historia Critica*, 12, 31.

[23] Simon, *A Critical History*, preface, p. ii; Vernière, *Spinoza*, 146.

[24] [Simon], *Critical Enquiries*, 292; Hazard, *European Mind*, 217; Popkin, 'Spinoza and Bible Scholarship', 403–4.

[25] PBM MS 1198/1 'Histoire critique du Christianisme', p. 204; the point was reaffirmed in early eighteenth-century clandestine philosophical literature; see 'Bernard', *Dissertations mêlées*, i, 115–16.

[26] [Simon], *Critical Enquiries*, 292; Steinmann, *Richard Simon*, 182.

[27] Ibid., 71–4.   [28] [Collins], *A Discourse*, 73.

[29] Simon, *A Critical History*, preface, p. v; Heidegger, *Exercitationes*, 269, 279–80; Vernière, *Spinoza*, 140; Steinmann, *Richard Simon*, 100, 214.

age.[30] But, unlike Spinoza and Isaac Vossius, Simon also held that successive generations of Hebrew scribes had conscientiously preserved and propagated the essential
core of what, he insists, is divine Revelation and man's path to Salvation. This impulse
to separate the imperfections of the Biblical text as we have it from its divinely given
core was indeed precisely what Simon, whether he knew it or not, shared with
Le Clerc, Limborch, and Locke.[31]

In fending off the frequently vituperative assaults of conservative divines, leading
modernizers like Wittichius, Simon, and Le Clerc, eager to fortify faith with philosophy and well-grounded textual research, often had the advantage of superior
scholarship. Their glaring weakness was lack of solidarity among themselves. Indeed,
Simon's use of Scripture's imperfections to buttress the Catholic hierarchy's
pretensions infuriated even the most liberal Protestant *savants* and substantially
contributed to the feud between him and Le Clerc. The acutest of Simon's critics from
among the philosophical 'critical' theological camp, Le Clerc, in his *Sentiments de
quelques théologiens de Hollande* (1685), the work which first established his European
reputation, supposes, given the Oratorian's zeal for disclosing imperfections in
Scripture, that readers unaware of his being a Catholic priest would be baffled as to
whether he was a Jew, a muddled Calvinist, or a 'Spinosiste caché', merely pretending
to combat Spinoza while, in reality, cunningly advancing Spinoza's 'sentiments
impies'.[32]

Simon equally denigrated Le Clerc, whose Bible exegesis strenuously defends
Christ's miracles while diluting or eliminating many other Biblical miracles, including
that of the sun standing still in the heavens so that Joshua could finish a battle which
he, like Spinoza, expressly denies.[33] Le Clerc's maxim that God is not lavish with miracles—'non solet Deus sic prodigus esse miraculorum'—was used to turn much of
what traditionally had been thought miraculous in the Bible into nothing more than
the misconstruing of natural effects by primitive and superstitious minds.[34] Le Clerc,
in his *Sentiments*, assails Simon's Bible criticism as crypto-Spinozist while simultaneously outraging traditionalist opinion with his own far-reaching 'critical' conclusions,
in particular (tacitly) agreeing with Spinoza—whose methodology had, by his own
earlier admission to Limborch, deeply impressed him—that serious discrepancies
have crept into the text, including that of the New Testament, and that the Five Books
were not compiled by Moses but by scribes writing many centuries later.[35] Moulded
primarily by Grotius, Spinoza, and (probably) Simon, Le Clerc's Bible exegesis, and
general *ars critica*, was often no less bold than Spinoza's in transcending the traditional

---

[30] Heidegger, *Exercitationes*, 353–89; Popkin, *Third Force*, 17–18; Popkin, *Isaac La Peyrère*, 79, 87–8.

[31] Marshall, *John Locke*, 340–1; Simonutti, 'Religion, Philosophy', 311.

[32] [Le Clerc], *Sentimens*, 93–4.   [33] Ibid., 111–16, 127; Rambach, *Collegium*, ii, 71–3, 76.

[34] Le Clerc, *Opera Philosophica*, ii, 158–9, 166; De Vet, 'Bibliothèque Universelle', 83–5; Pitassi, *Entre croire
et savoir*, 81–2; Hamilton, *Apocryphal Apocalypse*, 243–4.

[35] PBN MS fr. 11075 Boulainvilliers, 'Lectures', fos. 231–3; [Le Clerc], *Sentiments*, 107–16, 125–6; Le Vassor,
De la véritable religion, 164, 175; [Astruc], *Conjectures*, 175, 454; Barnes, *Jean Le Clerc*, 111–12; Pitassi, *Entre croire et
savoir*, 24–5.

philological techniques of Erasmus and Scaliger with new-style historico-critical exegesis designed to elucidate the characteristic ideas and modes of expression of the age in which a given text took shape.[36] But however many contemporaries he enraged, Le Clerc firmly believed his Biblical hermeneutics, unlike Spinoza's and Simon's, uncovered the true meaning of Scripture, removing obfuscating encrustations of allegory, metaphor, superstition, and poetic usage, which hamper comprehension, while leaving the *fundamenta* of Christianity firmly intact.[37]

If Simon discerned broad affinities between Le Clerc's and Spinoza's Bible criticism,[38] he was not alone in doing so. The Abbé Pierre Valentin Faydit (1640–1709), expelled from the Oratorian order in 1671 for his Cartesian fervour, and a zealous exegete himself (though an enemy of both Simon and Le Clerc), denounced Le Clerc along with Grotius and Spinoza, in his meandering volume of Biblical and poetical criticism published in 1705 as one of the three great modern corrupters of Bible hermeneutics.[39] He calls Le Clerc 'notre Arminien-Spinosiste', a 'half-pagan' who denies miracles 'étant Spinosiste et à demi Épicurean'.[40] Boulainvilliers, one of the paramount figures of the Spinozist Early Enlightenment, regularly adduces Le Clerc as well as Spinoza in propounding his own radical Bible criticism, in manuscript, during the years 1700–7.[41] Leading Bible scholars in early eighteenth-century Germany, such as the Giessen professors Johann Jakob Rambach (1693–1735) and his disciple Ernst Friedrich Neubauer (1705–48), did not doubt that Spinoza was 'dux et princeps atheorum nostri temporis' (leader and chief of the atheists of our age) but judged Le Clerc almost as pernicious, his Bible hermeneutics being scarcely less apt to erode belief in miracles and encourage errant minds to regard Scripture as nothing but a 'confusum chaos'.[42]

Tradionalists Catholic, Calvinist, Lutheran, and Anglican strove to answer the radicals and theological modernizers alike with arguments that would prove convincingly that Moses did compose the Pentateuch, Scripture had not been subject to cumulative corruption, and there is no substantial body of textual inconsistencies and discrepancies requiring elucidation by philosophy.[43] A leading adversary of Descartes, Spinoza, and Simon, famed for his erudition—indeed, he heaped so many books into his apartment in Paris that it collapsed—was the French prelate, Pierre-Daniel Huet (1630–1721), renowned in Paris as one of the chief *habitués* of the royal library. Huet devised a remarkable argument which was widely and long deployed to bolster the traditionalist stance in Catholic lands. In his best-known work, the *Demonstratio Evangelica* (1679), Huet, an ally of the Jesuits,[44] tries to outflank Spinoza and restore

---

[36] Le Clerc, *Opera Philosophica*, ii, 166; Jaumann, *Critica*, 176–9.

[37] Pitassi, *Entre croire et savoir*, 14, 24–5, 81–2; Canziani, 'Critica della religione', 62–3.

[38] De Vet, 'Bibliothèque Universelle', 88–9.

[39] Faydit, *Remarques*, 105–6, 140, 247, 583, 592; see also Kors, *Atheism in France*, i, 294–5.

[40] Faydit, *Remarques*, 583, 592.   [41] Brogi, *Cerchio*, 38–48.

[42] Rambach, *Collegium*, i, 428, 508–9, 923 and ii, 339, 535.

[43] Heidegger, *Exercitationes*, 279–80; Lassenius, *Besiegte Atheisterey*, 21–2; Rechenberg, *Fundamenta*, 82–91; Benedetti, *Difesa della terza lettera*, 4–5, 35; Auliseo, *Delle scuole sacre*, i, 95, 162.

[44] Formey, *Histoire abrégée*, 274.

confidence in the incorruptability and antiquity of the Hebrew text by adducing massive contextual research to show that those elements of ancient Egyptian, Babylonian, Persian, Phoenician, Greek, and other pagan religions and traditions worthy of any respect are all derived directly from Moses' example, inspiration, and writings. The impact of this work was widely felt even before it appeared. 'A man of outstanding learning in Hebrew, Aramaic and Greek,' Tschirnhaus reported to Spinoza in May 1676, this famous *érudit*, tutor to the Dauphin no less, was said in Paris to be compiling a complete demolition of 'your *Tractatus Theologico-Politicus*.[45]

To a Spinoza now gravely ill and nearing death, the matter seemed sufficiently challenging to enquire of Tschirnhaus, in his last surviving letter of July 1676, whether Huet's text was out yet and, if so, to send it. He never saw it but, throughout Europe, it found innumerable readers, among them the Prince de Condé, who had long been interested in Spinoza and was, or so he assured Huet, profoundly impressed with his counter-offensive.[46] At Utrecht Graevius, who detested Huet's subsequent anti-Cartesianism, was extremely enthusiastic, assuring Leibniz that the prelate had produced a devastating reply to the Spinozists, leaving the *arx impietatis* (ark of impiety) 'utterly in ruins'.[47] Others, though, were less convinced. Another correspondent of Leibniz, the Huguenot bibliographer Henri Justel, a friend of Simon, then in Paris, in July 1679 unfavourably compared Huet's *magnum opus* with the far briefer refutation, by Henry More, who undermines Spinoza and 'les athées et les libertins', he urged, more cogently than Huet.[48]

The bishop's handsomely produced 725-page treatise, fortified with many ecclesiastical approbations, though aimed against atheists, libertines, and 'anti-Scripturarii' in general, and occasionally citing Hobbes, La Peyrère, and other feared new exegetes, is clearly aimed chiefly against Spinoza. Yet Huet never refers to his principal enemy by name, but always as the 'Adversarius Theologico-Politicus', the 'Theologico-Politicus Philosophicus', or some other such circumlocution. He considers Spinoza the chief exponent of modern exegetical impiety, being the one who conflates all the profanities of Hobbes, La Peyrère, Bodin, Grotius, and other 'atheistic' Bible commentators into a coherent, systematic apparatus of unbelief and scepticism concerning the Bible. Huet's great counter-argument is that the wider historical context is indeed crucial, but what it proves is that the peoples, religions, and civilizations of the Near East drew their founding ideas from Moses and the Five Books, a circumstance establishing beyond question the truth, antiquity, and uniquely powerful influence of the Pentateuch, which is further confirmed by the antique flavour of the Biblical Hebrew. He

---

[45] Spinoza, *Letters*, 351; Huet was appointed by Louis XIV, on Colbert's advice, assistant tutor to the Dauphin, under Bossuet, in 1670 and became a member of the Académie Française in 1674; Henri Justel, a friend of Huet and also close to Colbert, an *érudit* with one of the best libraries in Paris, advised Leibniz of the forthcoming book in February 1677 but expressed some doubt as to its success: 'il faut répondre au *Nizachon* de Lipmannus, au *Tractatus Theologico-Politicus* de Spinosa, et aux objections de Julian l'Apostat, et concilier les passsages'; see Leibniz, *Sämtliche Schriften*, 1st ser. ii, 247.

[46] Huet, *Commentarius*, 273–4; Assoun, 'Spinoza et les libertins', 184–9.

[47] Graevius to Leibniz, Utrecht, 30 May 1679. Leibniz, *Sämtliche Schriften*, 1st ser. ii, 480.

[48] Justel to Leibniz, Paris, 24 July 1679, ibid. 504.

follows this up by rebutting one by one Spinoza's analyses in the *Tractatus* of the books of Joshua, Ezra, Nehemiah, Esther, Isaiah, Jeremiah, and Daniel.[49]

Huet's demonstration that Moses, not Ezra, wrote the Five Books, that the Hebrew text proves, on linguistic grounds, to be uncorrupted and intact, and to have decisively shaped the founding ideas of the ancient Near East, long remained influential in France and appealed to many writers in Italy and Spain. Among other large-scale works, it helped inspire the *Tractatio historico-polemica* (1720) of Domenico Bencini[50] at Rome, and the six-volume *Veritas Religionis Christianae* (Rome, 1735–7) by the powerful Cardinal Vincenzo Lodovico Gotti (1664–1742), a Dominican and a Bologna professor who became an Inquisitor at Milan and a cardinal in 1728, and likewise sought to marshal philology and ancient history to prove the Pentateuch a uniquely influential founding document and that the 'textus hebraicus non est falsatus'.[51] In any case, admonished Gotti, no individual has the right to judge the status or meaning of Scripture for himself: the task of 'knowing the true sense of Scripture lies with the Church and the Roman pontiff, its head'.[52]

Huet, increasingly worried after 1679 by the rapid dissemination of Spinoza's Bible criticism in France, resumed his offensive with his *Alnetanae questiones*, published at Caen in 1690. Spinoza's infamous *Tractatus,* he admonishes, places Christianity 'on the same level as the fables of the Greeks and the teaching of the Koran'.[53] Again he strove to uncover and discredit the intricate artifice and 'cunning' with which Spinoza had feigned to separate reason and faith, claiming to uphold the integrity and dignity of both while really appropriating everything pertaining to truth for philosophy and outrageously reducing faith to 'nihil praeter obedientiam' (nothing except obedience).[54] Against Spinoza's claims that the religious ideas in Scripture must be explained as poetic images, fantasies, and metaphors, philosophically and historically, Huet again upholds the absolute and incontrovertible truth of all these concepts, including the reality of angels, to which he devotes some fifteen pages.

Another influential refutation of radical Bible criticism was the work of a Berlin-based Huguenot pastor, Jacques Abbadie (1658–1727). Originally from Béarn, Abbadie was called to Berlin in 1680 by the Great Elector, who had heard of his eloquence as a preacher. His *Traité de la vérité de la religion Chrétienne*, originally published in Rotterdam in 1684, went through seven recorded editions down to 1729 and was widely admired in France, where there were pirated issues, as well as in Protestant lands.[55] Ludvig Holberg dubbed it a 'book worth its weight in gold', having done more than any other to retrieve him from the clutches of the deists and freethinkers.[56] Abbadie's appeal lay in his ability to combine elements of the conservative armoury developed

[49] Huet, *Demonstratio Evangelica*, 38–42, 136–43; Brucker, *Historia*, 559.

[50] Bencini, *Tractatio*, 25–7, 28–31, 145, 188, 197–8, 258–9, 367; Ferrone, *Intellectual Roots*, 148–9.

[51] Gotti, *Veritas*, ii, 1–2, 86, 156, 166.   [52] Ibid., ii, 238–9, 247.

[53] Huet, *Alnetanae Questiones*, 60.   [54] Ibid., 38, 59–60.

[55] Le Vassor, *De la véritable religion*, preface, p. iv; *L'Europe Savante*, vii (Jan. 1719), 3–31; Labrousse, *Pierre Bayle*, ii, 294; Kors, *Atheism in France*, i, 91; Rosenblatt, *Rousseau and Geneva*, 13, 66–7.

[56] Holberg, *Memoirs*, 152.

by Bossuet and Huet, whom he repeatedly cites, with a willingness to yield some ground to Simon, Le Clerc, and the radicals. His strategy, as his English translator puts it, is to destroy those 'objections raised by Spinoza against the Book of Moses' and out-flank 'our Adversary' (i.e. Spinoza) by shifting emphasis away from the text, close analysis of which produces both proof of authenticity and some discrepancies to the chief elements of Scripture's content.[57] Discarding Huet's sweeping claims about the ancient Near East and anticipating Le Clerc, Limborch, and Locke in stressing the centrality of Christ's miracles, Abbadie relies on just a few crucial empirically 'certain' facts. Above all, he stakes the 'whole demonstration of the truth of the Christian religion' on the absolute certainty that the 'Apostles and Disciples of Christ sincerely believed the Miracles, Resurrection, and Ascension', on the basis of the indisputable evidence before them, so that undeniably they 'could not be imposed upon in his Resurrection'.[58]

ii. Physico-Theology

An increasingly vital bastion—though in itself an old idea—against philosophical radicalism, from the 1670s onwards, was what came to be called the 'argument from design'. Simultaneously a theological and philosophical argument, it was enthusiastically adopted by theologians of every hue as a cogent and widely acceptable basis for reconciling faith in a divine Creator, and Providence, with the advances in science. Indeed, this was to become a vital plank of all the theologico-philosophical systems contending to dominate the middle ground—the mainstream, moderate Enlightenment—and was equally central to Boyle's empiricism, Newtonianism, *Malebranchisme*, and the Leibnizian–Wolffian system.

Boyle, who skirmished with Spinoza, through the mediation of Henry Oldenburg, and heartily despised such 'atheistic' philosophers, firmly denied that a modern philosophy based on natural philosophy and scientific reasoning can cogently yield such conclusions as Spinoza had drawn.[59] 'Speculative atheists' are not 'inclined to irreligion by philosophy,' he argued, 'but having got some smatterings of philosophy, pervert them to countenance those irreligious principles which they brought with them to the study of it'; hence, 'their immorality is the original cause of their infidelity.'[60] Ardently propagating empiricism, Boyle insists on the 'dimness and imperfections of our human understanding'.[61] But no less crucial to his thought is the 'argument from design': 'if we consider the vastness, beauty and regular motions of celestial bodies, the admirable structure of animals and plants, and the multitude of other phenomena of nature, and how these are subservient to mankind, they are sufficient to perswade a rational creature that so vast, beautiful and regular a system, and so admirably con-

---

[57] Abbadie, *Vindication of the Truth*, i, 231–2, 246–9.

[58] Ibid., ii, 162, 199, 230; in 1697 Isaac Jaquelot similarly argued that the miracles performed by Christ and the Apostles are of a different order from other miracles and can not be doubted; Jaquelot, *Dissertations*, 642–51.

[59] Boyle, *Theological Works*, ii, 4–5.   [60] Ibid., ii, 5.   [61] Ibid., ii, 6, 46.

trived a structure as the world, owed its origin to an author supremely powerful, wise and good.'[62]

Not only, maintains Boyle, does this idea convince us that the universe cannot be the 'result of chance and a tumultuous concourse of atoms' but also that divine Providence proves to be God's continual action and that the 'truth of the assertion that God governs the world he hath made, appears from the constancy, regular and rapid motions of celestial bodies'.[63] Furthermore, he asserts, it can justly be inferred from what we see that 'it is not below the dignity and majesty of the Creator to be concerned for the welfare of particular animals,'[64] and that there exists what he terms 'a general design of God for the welfare of man and other creatures'.[65]

Such arguments were heard with growing frequency from the 1670s and proved the strongest single intellectual pillar buttressing the moderate mainstream Enlightenment. In England one of the most avidly read statements of physico-theology was John Ray's *Wisdom of God in the Works of Creation* (1691) a text originally administered as 'morning divinity exercises' in Trinity College Chapel, Cambridge, which went through twelve editions down to 1750.[66] An admirer of Boyle, Ray maintains that eyes are made for seeing and ears for hearing, firmly denying 'bodies of animals can be formed by matter divided and moved by what Laws you will or can imagine, without the immediate presidency, direction and regulation of some intelligent being'.[67] There can be, he says, no more convincing argument that the universe was created by a providential Creator than the 'admirable art and wisdom that discovers itself in the make and constitution, the order and disposition, the ends and uses of all the parts and members of this stately fabrick of Heaven and Earth'.[68]

Newton, for his part, unwaveringly approved Bentley's incorporating his account of the solar system and gravity into an all-encompassing general design argument.[69] In his Boyle Lectures of 1692, Bentley emphasized the distinction between 'common motion which we have already shown to be insufficient for the formation of the world' and 'mutual gravitation or spontaneous attraction' between physical bodies without mutual contact which 'cannot be innate and essential to matter'.[70] Therefore, 'gravity, the great basis of all mechanism is not itself mechanical, but the immediate fiat and Finger of God, and the execution of the divine law.'[71] Hence the 'mechanical atheist', the philosophers Bentley reviles as the 'masters and rabbies of atheism', were no more able to define gravity as 'innate and essential to matter', or account for the motions of the planets without divine Providence, than they could explain the first formation of animals.[72] It seemed a trump card in the war of philosophies.

---

[62] Ibid., 7; Boyle, *A Free Enquiry*, 10–12, 69–75, 101–4.

[63] Boyle, *Theological Works*, ii, 14; McGuire, 'Boyle's Conception', 526.

[64] Boyle, *Theological Works*, ii, 15.   [65] Boyle, *A Free Enquiry*, 73 4, 76.

[66] Cragg, *The Church*, 74–5; Redwood, *Reason, Ridicule and Religion*, 118; Vermij, *Secularisering*, 107–11.

[67] Ray, *Wisdom of God*, 26, 32, 36.   [68] Ibid., 11; Westfall, *Science and Religion*, 45, 127.

[69] Force, 'Newton's God of Dominion', 81.

[70] Bentley, *Folly and Unreasonableness*, Seventh Lecture, 26–7.

[71] Ibid., Fourth Lecture, 6; Harrison, 'Newtonian Science', 537.

[72] Bentley, *Folly and Unreasonableness*, Fifth Lecture, 4 and Seventh Lecture, 28.

In stressing 'design' by an intelligent deity, there were always close affinities between the followers of Boyle and the Newtonians, on the one hand, and the other philosophico-scientific tendencies comprising the moderate mainstream of the early Enlightenment. Hence, both Leibniz and Malebranche held that God, when creating the universe, had chosen one set of general laws in preference to another, knowing those he selected best suited His intentions. In his *Entretiens sur la métaphysique* (1688) Malebranche deploys the design argument in several contexts, including a lengthy discussion of insects. Bees, with the wondrous intricacy of their wings and bodies, one of his interlocutors exclaims, testify not to the 'wisdom and foresight of these small animals, for they have none, but . . . the wisdom and foresight of Him who . . . ordered them so wisely in relation to so many various objects and different ends'.[73] If it seems unlikely God created such a multitude of tiny invertebrates for any reason linked to man, the 'principal design of God in the formation of these small insects,' explains Malebranche, 'was not to do us some good or harm by them, but adorn the universe with works worthy of His wisdom and other attributes.'[74]

The 'argument from design' also served a central function in the French refutations of radical thought which began to proliferate from the 1680s onwards, an early example being the 710-page *De la véritable religion* (Paris, 1688) by the Oratorian priest Michel Le Vassor (d.1718). Here we already encounter that growing conviction, which gradually became more prevalent in Europe during the early eighteenth century, that the age-old struggle between Catholicism and Protestantism, which had dominated theological polemics since the early sixteenth century, was now steadily receding and being replaced, as the central issue in intellectual debate, by the escalating conflict between revealed religion and philosophical irreligion, the war between Christianity and the new heretics—'les athées et les déistes'.[75] So corrupt is the new age, avers Le Vassor, that 'on ne parle que de raison, de bon goût, de force d'esprit,' admiring only those who employ philosophy to elevate themselves above the prejudices of their education and the society in which they are born, with the result 'nos prétendus esprits forts' pride themselves on believing nothing but what reason teaches 'et de traiter les autres de simples et de crédules'.[76] But if the 'esprits forts', intoxicated with philosophy, are irredeemable, they are also a tiny minority. The real war, avers Le Vassor, is for the hearts and minds of those caught in the middle, the many perplexed by the intellectual crosscurrents of the age, those 'qui croient foiblement, parce qu'ils ont toujours entendu dire qu'il falloit croire', who insipidly believe in a providential God and his Revelation 'sans sçavoir pourquoi'.[77]

Father Le Vassor vows to fight impiety unremittingly in the name of an intellectually rejuvenated and modernized theology, a war of ideas and science to be fought to the finish. Nor does he doubt the final triumph of the Church or that the intellectual leaders of the philosophical atheism, deism, and *libertinage* engulfing France will be

---

[73] Malebranche, *Dialogues on Metaphysics*, 194.   [74] Ibid., 211.
[75] Le Vassor, *De la véritable religion*, preface, pp. ii-xii; see also [Mauduit], *Traitté de la religion*, preface.
[76] Le Vassor, *De la véritable religion*, preface, p. vii.   [77] Ibid., p. viii.

overthrown and crushed. Of course, concedes Le Vassor, the leadership and inspiration of such a vast enemy host is diverse. Yet he ignores Vanini and Hobbes and barely mentions Saint-Evremond and the *libertins*. In so crucial a contest, Le Vassor prefers to concentrate all his intellectual force on the principal architect of the incredulity sweeping France, the thinker who provides the new irreligion with its basic cohesion and philosophical backbone. For in his eyes the outcome of the great struggle depends ultimately on defeating the man whom he calls the 'héros des athées', namely Spinoza—'le plus grand athée que l'on ait jamais vû'.[78]

In the France of the 1680s, remarks Le Vassor, there were undeniably a 'grand nombre de gens, qui font profession de suivre les sentimens de Spinosa, et qui ont étudié ses principes'.[79] Yet this intellectual catastrophe cannot be ascribed to real conviction but rather a corrupt predisposition of mind. Despite pretensions to intellectual rigour and apparent cohesion, Spinoza's system, far from being genuinely persuasive, 'c'est la chose du monde la plus incompréhensible.'[80] Thus, ultimately, it is not his arguments but corrosive Bible criticism, and blasphemous dismissal of miracles, which attract impious minds. Far from being rooted in intellectual cogency, the disastrous gains of Spinozism in France flow from an inherent rottenness in society. It is the depraved compulsion not to believe which has caused such unprecedented harm: 'c'est par là que Spinoza s'est fait des adorateurs.'[81] To overthrow Spinoza's philosophy, theologians must learn to turn science to their advantage, mobilize philosophy as well as theology against him, showing how nature corroborates divine craftsmanship. One cannot question the reality of a providential God when one investigates the structure of the universe 'et celle de chaque corps en particulier' or contemplates the intricacy of the tiniest insects under a microscope.

It seemed to Le Vassor just a question of making manifest what everyone knows deep down in their hearts already. For like many theologians of the period, he does not believe there are any confirmed, hardened 'athées de speculation'; he acknowledges only men who, like Spinoza, profess a desperate, unsteady, and ill-founded unbelief out of an insane bravado.[82] Science, and especially the 'argument from design', can and will eventually conquer all such impiety. For when one investigates the structures of the universe, even the most inured freethinkers understand, at least 'intérieurement, que tout cela ne peut être l'effet du hazard, ni d'une nature aveugle'.[83] Favourably reviewed in Holland, Le Vassor's treatise was long esteemed one of the strongest refutations of Spinoza, not least by Bayle, though later it was frowned on in France, following this priest's abandoning his order, and his flight—first to Holland and then England—and defection to Protestantism.[84]

A powerful Huguenot deployment of the design argument was the 705-page *Disertations sur l'existence de Dieu* (1697) by Isaac Jaquelot, preacher in the years 1687–1702 to

---

[78] *Histoire des Ouvrages des Savants*, vi (Mar.–Aug. 1689), 82.
[79] Le Vassor, *De la véritable religion*, 4.   [80] Ibid.   [81] Ibid.
[82] Ibid., p. 3; Kors, *Atheism in France*, i, 36–42.   [83] Le Vassor, *De la véritable religion*, 10–14.
[84] Charles-Daubert and Moreau, *Pierre Bayle. Écrits*, 56; Jöcher, *Allgemeines Gelehrten Lexicon*, iv, 1465.

the Walloon congregation in The Hague, who subsequently joined the French-speaking community in Berlin. For over half a century this work was considered, in France as well as Protestant Europe, one of the ablest defences of Providence and revealed religion of the age. A true child of the Enlightenment, Jaquelot did not doubt his was an era 'savant et éclairé' in which all sciences flourished and which contrasted fundamentally with 'la barbarie des siècles précédents'.[85] Yet mankind was gravely imperilled, he admonishes, precisely by growing familiarity with 'scientific', or rather ostensibly 'scientific', modes of thinking. The problem was that the new philosophical and scientific ideas condition men not to be persuaded by anything except 'certain evidence', a principle essential in science but unfamiliar in religion, a shift consequently generating a dangerous upsurge of scepticism and libertinism. It was therefore of vital importance, held Jaquelot, to counter the new philosophical impiety which claims to be 'scientific', demonstrating that the path of reason leads in fact to faith in a providential God.

Above all, he insists, it is vital to destroy the chief bastion of systematic atheism, namely what he calls the 'système d'Épicure et Spinosa'.[86] Unfortunately, the most depraved strand of ancient philosophy, Epicureanism, had been revived and reworked by Spinoza with no small semblance of cogency, thereby imperilling all humanity. Spinoza's intellectual sway, moreover, was spreading rapidly on all sides. But defeat Spinoza and the peril is over, for no other form of impiety has a remotely comparable intellectual power or cohesion. Indeed for Jaquelot, like Le Vassor, demolishing Spinoza is virtually the same thing as winning the universal war for revealed religion and eradicating philosophical incredulity from the world. For, as it seemed to them, the whole edifice of philosophical impiety collapses if its chief pillar is toppled, hence Spinoza's overthrow will open the way once more for the arts and sciences to flourish in tranquillity.

Jaquelot too, therefore, defends Christianity by focusing attention on just one modern philosopher, the thinker who identifies God with his single substance, forging a *fatalisme* opposed not only to all revealed religion but all forms of traditional morality based on the innateness of virtue and vice.[87] Basic to Jaquelot's counter-offensive is the 'argument from design'. All thinkers who claim matter is eternal, he argues, postulate 'un mouvement dans cette matière'; for if one perversely denies an 'intelligent Créateur du monde' one must assert that all creatures are formed without design.[88] But precisely this, he holds, is the Achilles' heel of the *Spinosistes*. For demonstrating 'design' is a question of scientific observation and analysis. Should scholars be able to prove in the structures of natural bodies a purpose on the part of 'l'auteur de la nature', then fatalism, Naturalism, and all the malign tendencies buttressed by Spinoza immediately disintegrate. The struggle for mankind's redemption will be won by demonstrating that eyes are for seeing and ears for hearing, and that all other

---

[85] Jaquelot, *Dissertations*, preface.   [86] Ibid.; [Pluquet], *Examen*, i, 360–1.
[87] Jaquelot, *Disssertations*, preface; Vernière, *Spinoza*, 64–8.   [88] Jaquelot, *Dissertations*, 319, 333–9.

natural organs are for demonstrably intended purposes.[89] Thus, bodies 'ne sont pas formés sans dessein' and those who refuse to admit this must ridiculously assert that men and animals emerged from the earth through some self-creating natural process, like insects.[90]

Up to a point the 'argument from design' proved an immensely potent weapon for all mainstream, moderate versions of the Early Enlightenment, coalescing admirably with Newtonianism, *Malebranchisme*, Régis' Neo-Cartesianism, Leibnizianism, and so forth. The argument proved vastly popular in France, Germany, Italy, and the Netherlands, besides Britain, the trend gaining added momentum during the early eighteenth century from books such as Fénélon's *Démonstration de l'existence de Dieu par les merveilles de la nature* (1712), William Derham's *Physico-theology* (1713), and Bernard Nieuwentijt's highly influential work, known in English as the *Religious Philosopher*, first published in 1715.[91] However, physico-theology provided a seemingly scientific basis, or criterion, for natural religion, which was soon seen to entail an unforeseen but grave theological disadvantage. For while formidably strengthening belief in Creation by an intelligent deity, and what Malebranche calls 'continuous creation', that is, the ceaseless working of divine providence to conserve the world,[92] it was less clear how the 'argument from design' fortifies belief in the Gospel, Christ, the specifically Christian 'mysteries', and ecclesiastical power. On the contrary, it emerged that physico-theology tended to distract attention from Christ's mission among men, and his unique role as Saviour, thereby encouraging providential deism as much, or more than Christian faith.[93]

Consequently, advocates of the 'argument from design' often coupled it with a philosophical defence of miracles, especially the miracles performed by Christ. Boyle, for instance, believed his doctrine of continuous Providence better accommodates 'what religion teaches us about the extraordinary and supernatural interpositions of divine providence' than doctrines such as Aristotelianism and Cartesianism, which conceive nature as a largely self-sustaining process.[94] The strategy of Boyle, the Newtonians, *Malebranchistes*, and Leibnizians, as well as Nieuwentijt and the Dutch physico-theologians,[95] was to try to narrow the gap between the supernatural and natural as much as possible, virtually denying that there was any great difference, by redefining miracles as events not contrary to the laws of nature, or involving a suspension of those laws, but as divine intervention regulating or deploying the secondary causes of nature to secure some exceptional effect. Thus the Newtonian and ardent anti-Spinozist, Nehemiah Grew, who succeeded Oldenburg, after the latter's death in 1677, as secretary of the Royal Society in London, and who, in his *Cosmologia Sacra* (London, 1701), affirms 'regularity, or the order of things, tho' we see it not

---

[89] Ibid., 337.   [90] Ibid., 336–7.
[91] Bots, *Tussen Descartes en Darwin*, 5–17; Vermij, *Secularisering*, 96–114.
[92] Malebranche, *Dialogues on metaphysics*, 112–13.
[93] Westfall, *Science and Religion*, 124–7.   [94] Boyle, *A Free Enquiry*, 14.
[95] Petry, 'Nieuwentijt's Criticism', 7; Vermij, *Secularisering*, 80–2.

everywhere; yet is it everywhere to be supposed,'[96] simultaneously affirms the truth of the Biblical miracles, explaining wondrous happenings in Scripture, such as the Ten Plagues in Egypt, as unusual deployments, by a providential deity, of 'sundry natural causes'.[97]

The design argument was frequently combined with the argument beginning with Abbadie, Le Vassor, and Le Clerc in the 1680s, and continuing later with Locke, Jaquelot, and Denyse, stressing the empirical basis of belief in the Gospel accounts of Christ's miracles. Abbadie emphasizes the unbroken train of tradition leading back to the Gospel writers in the first century AD and, like all these writers, the trustworthiness of the eyewitness reports of the key Christian miracles such as the Resurrection.[98] Owing to this 'eyewitness' evidence, Le Vassor felt able to assert 'Jésus Christ est incontestablement ressuscité,'[99] while Locke held the 'reasonableness' of accepting the proofs of Christ's miracles and Resurrection to be the principal grounds for allegiance to the Christian faith: 'the evidence of our Saviour's mission from heaven is so great,' he contends, in his *Reasonableness of Christianity* (1695), 'in the multitudes of miracles he did before all sorts of people, that what he delivered cannot but be received as the oracles of God and unquestionable verity.'[100] Furthermore, after the Resurrection, he claims, Christ 'sent his apostles amongst the nations, accompanied with miracles, which were done in all parts so frequently, and before so many witnesses of all sorts in broad daylight that, as I have before observed, the enemies of Christianity have never dared to deny them'.[101]

Jaquelot insisted no less on the empirical nature of the evidence for Christ's miracles and, while admitting that Christ did not show himself to the people after the Resurrection, so that the grounding of that event might seem less robust than it would had he done so, he explains this by saying God wants men to believe on the basis of faith, rather than empirical evidence alone, for there is always someone who might question the latter. Had Christ shown himself to the Pharisees and the people, he asks, why would we have more reason to believe them than we already have for believing the Apostles?[102] The Sorbonne professor Jean Denyse, in his widely acclaimed rebuttal of incredulity, *La Vérité de la religion Chrétienne demonstrée par ordre géometrique* (Paris, 1717), similarly elevates the Apostles' eyewitness accounts of Christ's miracles and Resurrection above all other grounds for belief, the incontrovertible evidence which 'met fin à tous les raisonnements des incrédules et des athées'.[103] Denyse's *Vérité* was ranked by the Berlin *savant* Jean-Henri Samuel Formey (1711–97) as one of the three foremost defences of Christianity of the age—together with Abbadie's *Traité* and Houtteville's *La Religion Chrétienne prouvée par les faits* (Paris, 1722), all three of which principally combat Spinoza, seeing him as the prime author of philosophical incredulity.

[96] Grew, *Cosmologia Sacra*, 87.   [97] Ibid., 194–5, 203; Harrison, 'Newtonian Science', 540.
[98] Abbadie, *Vindication*, i, 231–2, 246–9; Jaquelot, *Dissertations*, 642–51; Denyse, *Verité de la religion*, 340–3; *L'Europe Savante*, ii (Apr. 1718), 257–74.
[99] Le Vassor, *De la véritable religion*, 467–83, 498–511.   [100] Locke, *Reasonableness of Christianity*, 164–5.
[101] Ibid., 169.   [102] Jaquelot, *Dissertations*, 644.   [103] Denyse, *Verité de la religion*, 342.

However, narrowing the gap between miracles and general laws of nature seemed to some less persuasive than the design argument itself.[104] This encouraged a separate trend to deploy the design argument on its own, uncoupled from miracles which, however, tended to bolster a moderate, providential deism rather than Christianity. Thus, for instance, Thomas Morgan (d.1743), a 'poor lad' from Somerset who trained for the Presbyterian ministry but later gravitated to what he calls 'Christian or Gospel deism' or 'true and real' deism, in his *Physico-theology* (1741), on the one hand, vigorously attacks the three great 'monsters' fed by tradition—'superstition, bigotry and school divinity' and, no less strenuously, on the other, 'philosophical, speculative atheism'. Morgan extolled that 'perfect unity, order, wisdom and design' which 'necessarily supposes and implies a universal, designing mind and all-powerful agent, who has contrived, adjusted and disposed the whole into such order, uniformity, concordant beauty and harmony, and who continues to support, govern and direct the whole'.[105] But his is an advocacy of divine Providence from which defence of miracles has lapsed.

In his *Pensees raisonnables* (1749) the Berlin Huguenot pastor Formey, an ardent Wolffian, sums up what by then had come to seem the irreparable defects of the 'argument from design'. Commenting on Diderot's early work, the anonymously published *Pensées philosophiques* (1746), Formey concedes that, at first sight, the most telling blows against philosophical incredulity are not those delivered by philosophers such as Descartes and Malebranche but the findings of natural scientists such as 'Newton, Malpighi, Musschenbroek, Hartsoeker and Nieuwentyt'.[106] A virtuoso of the microscope and telescope, Hartsoeker, who publicly opposed the philosophies of Descartes, Leibniz, Malebranche, and Newton alike, made his mark by revealing new and ever more intricate natural wonders (see Plate 16).[107] Surely it was in the works of these men, held the young and then still deist Diderot, 'qu'on a trouvé des preuves satisfaisantes de l'existence d'un être souverainement intélligent'.[108] But if scientific discoveries had strengthened the sort of deism which accepts and extols a divine Creator, operating a 'machine with wheels, levers and pulleys' as Diderot puts it, at the expense of revealed religion and belief in Scripture,[109] the drawbacks of the 'argument from design', observed Formey, in fact go even beyond this. Ultimately, the problem was that it was not absolutely clear the natural scientists had proved the existence of what Morgan terms 'one supreme, universal, independent, contriver, designer and disposer of all things'.[110] Not just the specifically Christian 'mysteries' but even the proofs of God the Creator and prime mover had, by the 1740s, become unexpectedly vulnerable to philosophical attack, clearing the path once again for non-providential deism and Spinozism.[111] For such revelations of nature's marvels as Hartsoeker's discovery of

---

[104] Vermij, *Secularisering*, 79–80.   [105] Morgan, *Physico-Theology*, 140.

[106] [Formey], *Pensées raisonnables*, 65–6.

[107] Hartsoeker, *Cours de physique*, preface, pp. ix, xi, 9–10; Hartsoeker, *Recueil*, 8–9, 51.

[108] Diderot, *Pensées philosophiques*, 17.   [109] Ibid., 18.   [110] Morgan, *Physico-Theology*, 140.

[111] [Formey], *Pensées raisonnables*, 66–7; La Mettrie, *Machine Man*, 23; Venturi, *Jeunesse de Diderot*, 97–9, 156.

bacteria, which stirred Paris in 1678–9,[112] and Newton's account of gravity in England, no matter how indicative of the intricacy of natural bodies, Formey pointed out, can not finally overthrow the 'système de Spinoza'. In the end, when thoroughly considered, all the scientists had really shown is that 'le mouvement est la cause de tout ce qui arrive dans l'univers,' a principle which favours the Spinozists as much as the Christians and providential deists.[113] If we do not crush Spinoza with philosophical weapons which transcend the bounds of experimental science, warned Formey—and by this he meant adopt the Leibnizian-Wolffian system—he will calmly allow all the Newtons, Malpighis, and Hartsoekers in the world to pile up innumerable examples of nature's beauty and intricacy and then say he marvels no less than we at nature's wonders but concludes that all this stems necessarily from his single universal substance.[114] Apparent 'design', as Diderot was to confirm, could after all be just as convincingly ascribed to Spinoza's unalterable laws of Nature ensuing from motion innate in matter, that is, to Nature's self-formation or evolution, as to the Providence of Newton, Malebranche, and Leibniz.

iii. Le Clerc, Van Limborch, and Locke

The rapid spread of division, controversy, and perplexity within the Churches of the west in the late seventeenth century enabled some of the most capable spokesmen of fringe denominations to emerge from the margins and cut brilliantly across confessional boundaries to achieve a truly European status. The new rifts within the Churches, moreover, ran so deep and proved so enduring that they were bound in some measure to lessen tension between the principal confessional blocs, rendering inter-confessional dialogue easier and, to some extent, more courteous than before 1650;[115] and it was especially spokesmen of the smaller dissenting Churches who benefited from this slackening strife between the main confessions. Indeed, several—most conspicuously Jean Le Clerc, Europe's most tenacious protagonist of rationalist Christian theology—emerged among the pre-eminent theologians of the age.

Having settled in Amsterdam, after finding all doors to a preaching career in Geneva closed to him, and publicly leaving the Reformed for the Remonstrant Church, he loathed the Calvinist bigotry he left behind him in Switzerland and sporadically encountered in the Netherlands.[116] Condemned first in Geneva, with the passage of time he was also denounced in many other quarters. Filled with awareness of the spiritual crisis of his time, Le Clerc urged fundamental reform to rescue Christendom from the perils it faced. In particular, Christians needed, in his view, to purify their faith, by which he meant render it more 'enlightened'. Le Clerc abhorred scepticism, scorning the early seventeenth-century 'fideists', as well as their successors— Bossuet, Huet, and (in matters of faith) Bayle—who demanded of the individual

---

[112] Hartsoeker, *Cours de physique*, 3–8. [113] Ibid., 11–12.
[114] [Formey], *Pensées raisonnables*, 80. [115] Simonutti, *Arminianesimo e tolleranza*, 43.
[116] Pitassi, *Entre croire et savoir*, 5–6.

unqualified faith detached from the dictates of reason, which Le Clerc vehemently dismisses as 'une credulité sans bornes'.[117] In his eyes, reason is the key. More than other Protestants, Le Clerc judged the Catholic doctrine of transubstantiation not just false but disastrous, since it demands a simple, unquestioning credulity which, he believed, plays straight into the hands of the *incrédules*.[118] Le Clerc's 'enlightened' Christianity, by contrast, stemmed from his principle that in religion, as in all spheres, we possess no other tool to help us distinguish truth from falsity except our reason; to which he added, simultaneously opposing Spinoza on one side, and Simon on the other, that Scripture, despite all obscurities and discrepancies, is wholly and self-sufficiently clear 'dans les choses essentielles'.[119]

A key exemplum of the new 'enlightened' method of upholding Christianity, held Le Clerc, was the celebrated encounter of the mid-1680s between his ally, Philip van Limborch (1633–1712), and the Jewish controversialist Isaac (Balthasar) Orobio de Castro. Limborch's English friend John Locke, with whom he too formed a close connection over the winter of 1685–6, also participated. For most of the 1680s Locke, then a political exile, circulated between Dutch towns, colluding with groups of English and Scots plotters against the House of Stuart while simultaneously conferring with learned men on key intellectual issues. One of the houses he frequented belonged to the Amsterdam physician Egbert Veen, a friend of Limborch and colleague of Orobio—to whom Veen had 'much commended Limborch's learning'—and it was there that the 'conference' took place.[120] Orobio had spent most of his life contesting the truth of the Christian religion as a crypto-Jew in Spain and then France, and since the early 1660s as a member of the Portuguese Jewish community in Holland. What evolved into a long and arduous disputation apparently began late in 1684. Orobio, who had a Spanish academic training, as well as years of study of the Jewish sources behind him, was deemed formidable in theological debate, and Veen, Limborch, and Le Clerc all took the encounter with great seriousness. Locke too was drawn in, as we see from his letter to Limborch of February 1685, requesting a second opportunity to study 'those writings of your own and of Don Balthasar which you lent me some time ago'.[121] When Limborch published the disputation, at Gouda in September 1687, he sent a copy to Locke even before Orobio, 'seeing it is through your care this whole discussion appears in a more polished form', Locke having evidently provided additional arguments as well as helping to polish the text.[122]

Locke was enthusiastic, believing their new style of demonstrating the truth of Christianity had indeed 'vanquished the Jew'.[123] Whether their style of proof was quite as novel as Limborch, Locke, and Le Clerc supposed, the dialogue certainly

---

[117] Le Clerc, *De l'Incrédulité*, 230–2, 244; Lomonaco, 'Huguenot Critical Theory', 175–8.

[118] Le Clerc, *De l'Incrédulité*, 246–51.   [119] Ibid., 47, 241; [Le Clerc], *Sentimens*, 61.

[120] Ashcraft, *Revolutionary Politics*, 410–11, 419, 432–3, 469–70; Kaplan, *From Christianity*, 277; Simonutti, 'Religion, Philosophy', 302.

[121] *Correspondance of John Locke*, ii, 690.

[122] Ibid., iii, 258–9; Kaplan, *From Christianity*, 278; Simonutti, 'Religion, Philosophy', 318.

[123] *Correspondence of John Locke*, iii, 260–1.

diverged sharply from traditional patterns of Christian–Jewish disputation, reflecting the wider rationalist and empirical approach favoured by Limborch, Locke, and Le Clerc alike.[124] Discarding the age-old procedure of grounding Christianity on the textual authority of Scripture, maintaining that the Old Testament prefigures the New, which the Jews would then deny, Limborch, Le Clerc, and Locke insisted Christian truth must be proved by reason based on evidence, what Le Clerc called 'd'une manière géométrique', that is, argumentation that permits no possible doubt—the only aspect of Cartesianism Le Clerc admired was its logical rigour[125]—and leaves no difficulty in the minds of those shown the proofs.[126] Christianity must be shown to be true, they held, by virtue of its inherent and incontestable moral perfection, the speed and completeness with which so many lands and peoples had come to venerate Christ, and the irreproachable eyewitness testimonies of Christ's miracles and Resurrection.[127] In this way what Le Clerc calls 'les principes du christianisme' or 'le christianisme en général' could be distilled, truths which transcend confessional barriers and ultimately render them meaningless.

Orobio retorted that the advent of Christ has done nothing to render mankind less sinful or to lessen suffering, that the rise of Christianity, far from being unparalleled, was surpassed by the expansion of Islam, Mohammed having 'propagated his sect in even shorter time and still more regions',[128] and that far from being unchallengeable, Christ's miracles had not been performed publicly, like the miracle at Mount Sinai, but virtually in secret, a circumstance which renders them entirely dubious. These responses and his further claims that the New Testament is unreliable, providing no basis for trust in Christ's miracles, since the text exists only in Greek, a language neither Jesus nor the Apostles had the slightest knowledge of, and that, in any case, Christ's disciples were ignorant, superstitious men of low birth and no standing in the society of their time,[129] made no impact on Limborch, Le Clerc, or Locke, who were convinced of their triumph over Orobio. Nevertheless, Orobio's arguments were fully and objectively reported in the text, and subsequently widely read across Europe, and some of those who read it were not so sure that Orobio was 'vanquished'. Boulainvilliers, who meticulously examined the text, concluded that Limborch's arguments were less securely grounded on reason than he and his allies supposed and that, even without their realizing it, it was Orobio who won the contest, a verdict echoed in other anti-Christian clandestine philosophical literature of the early eighteenth century.[130]

The chief points of Le Clerc's reason-based core Christianity were Creation in time

---

[124] Kaplan, *From Christianity*, 270–85; Van Rooden and Wessselius, 'Early Enlightenment', 140–3.
[125] Lomonaco, 'Huguenot Critical Theory', 174–5, 178.   [126] Le Clerc, *De l'Incrédulité*, 47.
[127] Ibid.; Le Clerc, *Opera Philosophica*, ii, 157–66.
[128] Van Limborch, *De Veritate Religionis Christianae*, 137.
[129] PBN MS fr. 11075, Boulainvilliers, 'Limborgh contra Ozorio (*sic*)', fos. 178–9v; Van Limborch, *De Veritate Religionis Christianae*, 74–6; [Le Clerc], *Bibliothèque Universelle*, vii, 308–9; Witsius, *Meletemata Leidensia*, 354–89.
[130] PBN MS fr. 11075; 193v, 201–2; PBM MS 1198/i 'Histoire critique du Christianisme', 196.

by a providential Creator, Revelation of the divine Word, moral commandments from the divine Law-giver, reward and punishment in the hereafter, Christ's mission as the Saviour of Man, Christ's miracles and Resurrection, and the Last Judgement. Le Clerc, Limborch, and Locke joined forces to stake out a drastically diminished but clear, proven, and (leaving aside Orobio) indisputable sphere of the miraculous, established beyond doubt by means of the new historico-critical method of Bible exegesis, of which Le Clerc especially was an internationally acknowledged master. This wall around a reduced realm of the miraculous fixed both the essential core of religion and philosophy's limits, providing a clear border separating philosophy and theology.[131] In Le Clerc's eyes theology was closely and fruitfully linked to empirical philosophy, and nourished by it but needed, at the same time, to ensure philosophy's confinement to its proper sphere. Needless to add, the whole triumvirate dismissed ecclesiastical authority, as well as tradition and untested dogma, as irrelevant and useless, indeed positively harmful to the Christian cause. Reason alone can prove Christian teaching perfectly compatible with the verities revealed by cogent philosophy.[132]

Since authentic Christianity is purely 'rational', held Le Clerc, it follows, as night follows day, that the pretended rationality of the *incrédules*, Naturalists, *fatalistes*, Epicureans, and sceptics (fideist and non-fideist) is false. In his chief work against irreligion, published at Amsterdam in 1696, Le Clerc wastes no time on varieties of unbelief of marginal, academic, or exotic interest. The pressing danger he confronts is something immediate, all around and specific, an intellectual and spiritual corruption which pretends to be wholly rational and 'geometric'. What this meant, if Christianity was to triumph in the great struggle against philosophical impiety which had now commenced, he urged, was that a purified Christianity of reason and evidence must conquer the most formidable engine of war available to philosophical incredulity which, he says, is the argument that there is only one substance in the universe, a substance composed of both mind and extension which modifies itself, according to unalterable laws of nature, without any 'intelligence suprême, distincte de l'univers même' shaping the process. In short, asserts Le Clerc, tallying here with Huet, Le Vassor, Abbadie, Jaquelot, Tournemine, Grew, and innumerable others, the overriding issue in religion and philosophy is to vanquish philosophical impiety rooted in Spinoza.[133] Limborch who, since reading the *Tractatus Theologico-Politicus* in 1670, considered it, he assured an English correspondent, the 'most pestilential' work he had ever seen, likewise viewed the battle with Spinozism as the crux of the conflict with philosophical unbelief.[134]

Le Clerc, Limborch, and Locke saw their quest to reduce Christian belief to a

[131] Pitassi, *Entre croire et savoir*, 13–15.

[132] Ibid.; Van Limborch and Bredenburg, *Schriftelyke Onderhandeling*, 1, 62–3; Fix, *Prophecy and Reason*, 236–8.

[133] Le Clerc, *De l'Incrédulité*, 46–8, 357–62, 366; Van Limborch and Bredenburg, *Schriftelyke Onderhandeling*, 2, 24.

[134] Van Limborch, *Theologia Christiana*, 94–5, 112–13; Barnouw, *Philippus van Limborch*, 37, 136; De Vet, 'Le Bibliothèque', 84–5.

wholly rational core of *fundamenta*, which they considered empirically grounded and essentially 'reasonable', fencing off a sphere of the miraculous centring around Christ's miracles and the Resurrection, the best defence against philosophical incredulity. Most contemporary churchmen, however, even if many were in some degree influenced by their views, judged their approach risky to the point of recklessness. Many deemed Le Clerc's propensity to explain floods, tempests, and other calamities as happenings issuing not from the particular will of God but rather 'en conséquence des lois générales du mouvement' redolent of Naturalism and his seeming unconcern for the Trinity, and Christ's divinity, of Socinianism.[135] Scarcely less alarming were the consequences of his, and Locke's, insistence on firmly segregating what is demonstrable philosophically from what, in their view, remains uncertain, ruling that philosophy cannot prove the immortality of the soul and therefore a future state of reward or punishment.[136] In England those who most decried Locke's empiricism as 'ruinous', such as the 'nonjuring' High Church clique around George Hickes, were quick to highlight his links with Le Clerc. Hickes and Carroll tried to tar Locke as a 'Spinozist' and, as part of this campaign, pointed out that both Le Clerc and Locke argue that 'we can not tell if mind and body are two substances or one.'[137]

In Carroll's eyes this crucial and deadly admission clinched the matter. The doctrine of only one substance, he asserts, is the 'basis and sum of Spinoza's most absurd, impious and abominable hypothesis', a philosophy which is the 'very quintesssence of folly and atheism . . . such a monstrous mixture of cant, jargon, or nonsense, of frenzy, blasphemy and fury, that the unnatural heats, and unspeakable extravagances of the most disorder'd imagination in Bedlam, cannot advance one jot no not one single point beyond it'.[138] 'In a word,' he held, 'human malice cannot invent a system more injurious to God, or fatal to mankind' and Le Clerc, Carroll agreed with Hickes, was undoubtedly a 'Spinozist', albeit camouflaged and therefore all the more sinister. 'You declare over and over,' he admonished Le Clerc, 'that you are utterly ignorant whether body and mind do subsist in two or in one substance . . . You are the ringleader of our few Spinozists,' he charged, 'and by far the learnedest of 'em.'[139]

In fact, Le Clerc's antipathy to the mainstream Churches could easily induce him to welcome certain radical arguments. His denunciation as a 'Spinozist' in Britain was apparently provoked by his favourable review of Matthew Tindal's scathingly anticlerical *Rights of the Christian Church* (1706) which enraged the High Church party and, according to Carroll, was 'immediately deduc'd from . . . that atheist's [i.e. Spinoza's] hypothesis'.[140] Hickes noted with satisfaction in 1709 that Le Clerc was attracting some

---

[135] Le Clerc, *Opera Philosophica*, ii, 157–68; De Vet, 'Bibliothèque Universelle', 83–5; Sina, *Vico e Le Clerc*, 24–32.

[136] Le Clerc, *Parrhasiana*, 275, 278–9; Taylor, *A Preservative*, 112; Marshall, *John Locke*, 151–3.

[137] Carroll, *Spinoza Reviv'd Part the Second*, 47–8; Le Clerc, *Parrhasiana*, 275–9; De Vet, 'Learned Periodicals', 34.

[138] Carrol, *A Dissertation*, 22.   [139] Carroll, *Spinoza Reviv'd Part the Second*, 75.

[140] Carroll, *Spinoza Reviv'd*, 150, 156, 158; Brown, 'Locke as Secret Spinozist', 220.

highly unfavourable comment in England and that most clergy 'now animadvert upon the loose and dangerous notions of that foreign writer, and what disservice he hath done the Christian Religion, by recommending many other as pernicious books as [Tindal's] in his *Bibliothèque Choisie*'.[141] Vilifying Le Clerc while simultaneously taunting the English deists, Hickes labels him 'their French champion'.[142] Tindal on the other hand reckoned Le Clerc 'as able a divine as this, or perhaps any other age has produc'd' and quotes him approvingly, though twisting his sense to serve deistic ends.[143]

The accusation that Le Clerc and Locke were 'Spinozists' was grotesque. Both were Christians who believed passionately in Revelation, Christ's miracles, and a providential God who sent His son. But there was enough of Spinoza in Le Clerc's Bible hermeneutics, and views on miracles, to leave him vulnerable and acutely sensitive to the charge. An early review of his *Sentiments* which deeply offended him was that of Bayle in the *Nouvelles de la République des Lettres*, where the 'philosopher of Rotterdam' criticized his exegetical methodology, expressly comparing it with Spinoza's. Bayle apologized when Le Clerc remonstrated with him; and for some years the two *érudits* treated each other with some semblance of courtesy. But the tension between the two celebrities gradually escalated until, in 1704, all pretence of mutual regard lapsed and they openly came to blows.[144] Le Clerc, like innumerable others, judged Bayle's protestations of Christian allegiance insincere and believed the chief purpose of his *Dictionnaire* of 1697 was to discredit reason and, with it, his own rational theology. Bayle for his part scorned Le Clerc's ideas, dismissing his quest to establish Christianity securely by means of 'reason' as totally unfeasible. Indeed, he viewed Le Clerc's attempted rational theology as virtually an ally of philosophical deism and atheism.[145] In short, Le Clerc accused Bayle of working to undermine the Christian religion, which is precisely what Bayle accused Le Clerc of doing.[146]

The feud between Bayle and Le Clerc was a clash of personalities by no means unmarked by pettiness. But it also had a wider European significance. While there is much in Bayle's writings, observed Ludvig Holberg in 1743, which gives 'just offence to Christians' and many had striven to refute his less helpful views, Le Clerc had always been his foremost and most important antagonist, especially as regards the crucial question of whether reason can demonstrate God's justice and providence.[147] Holberg acknowledges the greatness of both thinkers, deeming Le Clerc the more learned, and Bayle the more ingenious, and comparing their epic contest to that between 'Pompey' and 'Caesar', of whom the one could bear no equal and the other no superior. He could not refrain from remarking, however, on the irony that two

[141] Hickes, *A Preliminary Discourse*, 56–7.   [142] Ibid., 37.
[143] [Tindal], *Christianity as Old as the Creation*, 39, 127.
[144] Barnes, *Jean Le Clerc*, 232–4; Pitassi, *Entre croire et savoir*, 19–20.
[145] Hartmann, *Anleitung*, 266–7; Labrousse, *Pierre Bayle*, ii, 328–30.
[146] Barnes, *Jean Le Clerc*, 114, 234–5; Cantelli, *Teologia e ateismo*, 343, 346, 368.
[147] Holberg, *Memoirs*, 187–90; Simonsen, *Holbergs livssyn*, 117, 130–1.

such universally acclaimed champions of toleration could be so unmindful of their own maxims as to assail each other with the most intemperate invective.[148]

Le Clerc adhered unwaveringly to his course. His works were comprehensively banned by Louis XIV and the papal Inquisition.[149] In his *Lógica moderna* (1747), Andrés Piquer, a leader of moderate enlightened opinion in mid-eighteenth-century Spain, saw no danger to Spanish Catholics in their reading Descartes, Malebranche, Newton, and Boerhaave, quite the contrary, but warns against Le Clerc, whom he considers a dangerous writer, a 'Socinian heretic' who, without openly saying so, discards the central Christian 'mysteries'.[150] Offering philosophical guidance to Spanish youth in his *Philosophia moral* of 1755, Piquer cited only three thinkers, aside from undisguised atheists and deists like Spinoza and Toland, who should always be avoided—Bayle, Jean Barbeyrac, and Le Clerc.[151] Nevertheless, Le Clerc's writings became known in southern as in northern Europe, not least in Rome where, behind closed doors, theologians carefully pondered his revolutionary theology.[152]

Incurring the disapproval of every major Church—after 1695, even Anglican Latitudinarians such as Bishop Stillingfleet became wary of Locke's 'new way of ideas' and evident Socinian tendencies[153]—Le Clerc, Limborch, and Locke were, in one sense, marginal, being on the extreme fringe of the reformist tendency. Nevertheless, they occupied a central position in the Early Enlightenment, emerging as leading representatives, along with such figures as Malebranche, on the Catholic side, and the two professors Wittichius, Christopher and Jacobus, among the Reformed, of a powerfully modernizing, rational theology claiming to provide the only effective answer to the tide of philosophical incredulity, deism, and rationalistic Judaism *à la* Orobio. Thus, paradoxically, Le Clerc, Limborch, and Locke were simultaneously dreaded innovators, disrupting authority and tradition on one side, and champions of Christianity, leading the fight against the philosophical radicals, on the other.

Their paradoxical position was all the more ironic in that, with the passing decades and growing prestige of their ideas, their intellectual legacy was taken up, and readily exploited, by both sides in the escalating struggle between moderate and radical Enlightenment. By the 1740s Locke and Le Clerc, the former now the more renowned, could be extolled even by Catholic 'enlightened' writers in Italy as among the greatest champions of Providence, miracles, and free will against the *Spinosisti* to be found anywhere in Europe, Protestant or Catholic.[154] Yet while Le Clerc and Limborch had assailed deists and Spinozists as unbelievers purveying a false rationality and meaningless doctrines, radical writers mostly preferred using their writings and ideas as a weapon against more orthodox theology to attacking them. The foremost of the

---

[148] Holberg, *Memoirs*, 189; Bots, *Henri Basnage de Beauval*, ii, 140–2.

[149] Reusch, *Index*, 92–3; Hilgers, *Index*, 435, 440, 443.   [150] Piquer, *Lógica moderna*, 69, 124, 145.

[151] Piquer, *Philosophia moral*, 133.

[152] Among them the Abbot Celestino Galiani (see pp. 113–14 above); Ferrone, *Intellectual Roots*, 66–71, 77–8, 99–104, 156–9.

[153] Aarsleff, 'Locke's Influence', 261–4; Marshall, *John Locke*, 347–8, 419.

[154] Monigilia, *Dissertazione contra i fatalisti*, i, 41–2, 53, 143.

German clandestine philosophic manuscripts circulating during the Early Enlightenment, the *Symbolum Sapientiae*, is strongly Spinozist in tenor but nevertheless frequently cites Le Clerc's powerful critique of traditional theology and ecclesiastical authority.[155] Similarly, Friedrich Wilhelm Stosch, a key radical writer of the 1690s, was chiefly inspired by Spinoza but nevertheless reinforced his assault on Christianity, ecclesiastical power, and traditional demonology with numerous references to Le Clerc.[156] Boulainvilliers, the chief advocate of non-providential deism in early eighteenth-century France, was steeped in Spinoza, but also steeped in Le Clerc, and frequently cites his writings and those of Locke.[157]

iv. From the 'Rationalization' to the 'Irrationalization' of Religion

The ultimate legacy of rationalizing theology was a trend towards a 'Christian deism' typical of the eighteenth century. There were, of course, deists of many diverse hues, only some of whom, those rejecting Providence, the immortality of the soul, and reward and punishment in the hereafter, belong with the Radical Enlightenment. It was the latter who, as early as 1698, inspired an English writer to summon the Christian faithful 'to set all hands on work to countermine the common enemy, who scorn to work any longer under the covert and shelter of the night, but in the open day endeavour to blow up the foundations of our faith'.[158] For the sake of clarity, many early eighteenth-century publicists preferred to reserve the term 'deist' for men such as these who were beyond the pale of respectable opinion. Formey, for instance, classifies the philosophical radicals of his day as 'd'athées, de déistes, d'idéalistes, de matérialistes, etc.'—but had no doubt that those who chiefly define the radical wing and have long and rightly been judged 'les plus dangereux, ce sont les Spinosistes', while those who believe in a providential God he does not classify with this grouping at all.[159] Nevertheless, providential deists are not Christians and the difference generated a tension within the very heart of the moderate mainstream Enlightenment.

Many so-called and self-declared deists, moreover, strongly affirmed their belief in the Creation, divine Providence, the divine origin and absolute validity of morality, the special role of Christ, and the immortality of the soul, and what is more, claimed to be 'Christians'. There was often only a shade of difference between such 'Christian deists', who acknowledged a deity distinct from nature, and other Christians. In some cases, as with the English writer Thomas Woolston,[160] such 'deists' used theological

---

[155] Canzioni, 'Critica della religione', 41, 71.

[156] Ibid., 54–5; Stosch, *Concordia*, 6, 8, 10, 25–6, 28, 37.   [157] Brogi, *Cerchio*, 36–9, 195–202.

[158] Taylor, *A Preservative*, preface, pp. i–ii.   [159] Formey, *Histoire abrégée*, 308.

[160] Thomas Woolston (1670–1733), son of a Northampton currier, studied at Sidney Sussex College, Cambridge, being elected a Fellow there in 1690. An accomplished theologian and preacher, he left the university in 1720, evolving into a fully-fledged 'Christian deist' during the 1720s. By 1725 he was publicly denying the Resurrection and virgin birth of Christ and was first arraigned for 'blasphemy' at that time.

rather than philosophical terminology and were, in their own eyes, genuinely Christian. Woolston has been described as 'addle-brained' and reckless.[161] But actually he was not unlearned; he was an accomplished preacher, and a man of intense religious feeling. He was also no innovator outside theology and assuredly no radical, since he showed little interest in philosophy or overturning existing social, political, or educational structures. He outraged contemporary opinion simply and purely by insisting one should not believe miracles described in the Gospels which, upon examination, turn out to be 'absurdities, improbabilities or incredibilities'.[162] In this he totally disagreed with Locke. 'I am for a spiritual Messiah,' he insisted, repeatedly describing himself as a 'Christian'. If he loathed the Anglican Church and designed its ruin, his positive aims were to 'restore the allegorical interpretation of the Old and New Testament', 'bring out' the true 'spirit of the Scriptures' and ensure that 'Jesus's authority and Messiahship' are not founded on unbelievable miracles. Only in respect to toleration can Woolston perhaps be regarded as a radical, advocating 'an universal and unbounded toleration of religion, without any restrictions or impositions on men's consciences; for which design the clergy will hate and defame me'.[163] Thus Woolston was more of an extreme rationalizing Socinian Christian than a deist in the sense defined by Formey.

Of course, other representatives of the moderate Enlightenment were decidedly more secular in spirit than Woolston. Voltaire, Saint-Hyacinthe, or Hermann Samuel Reimarus,[164] a professor at the Hamburg Gymnasium and privately a deist equally hostile to revealed religion, on the one side, and Spinozism on the other, were not 'Christian' in any meaningful sense, though these all upheld the concept of a providential deity. Reimarus supported the 'argument from design' and rejected the 'Epicureans' concept of natural evolution in an eternal universe which was not 'created' by God.[165] It is also true, as a mid-eighteenth-century English writer remarked, that 'many Deists call themselves Christian Deists but can be suspected to be otherwise.'[166] Both Tindal and Thomas Morgan were widely thought to be trying to have it both ways—publicly styling themselves 'Christians' and members of the Anglican Church, while privately denying miracles and divine Providence—and it became increasingly difficult in practice during the early eighteenth century to draw a clear divide between Christians and moderate deists. The stigma attached to impiety was still strong

---

[161] Harrison, '*Religion' and the Religions*, 87.

[162] Woolston, *A Fifth Discourse*, 1–2; Genovesi, *Elementa Metaphysicae*, ii, 235.

[163] Woolston, *A Fourth Discourse*, 70–1; Woolston, *Mr Woolston's Defence Of his Discourses*, 17–18, 20–1, 70.

[164] Hermann Samuel Reimarus (1694–1768) studied at Jena under Buddeus and taught at Wittenberg in the years 1716–23. He is thought to have become a deist during his visit to Holland and England (1720–1). After some years as rector of the Stadtsschule in Wismar (1723–8), he settled in Hamburg as a professor at the gymnasium in 1728. His famous clandestine manuscript 'Apologie oder Schutzschrift für die vernünftigen Verehrer Gottes' (Apology, or Defence of the reasonable reverers of God) was apparently written in the early 1740s.

[165] Jaynes and Woodward, 'In the Shadow', 8–10.

[166] Leland, *A View*, i, 148–9; Gawlick, 'Deismus', 15–17; Cragg, *The Church*, 77, 159–62; Harrison, '*Religion' and the Religions*, 75–7, 95–7, 62.

enough everywhere to induce many to assume one set of values outwardly and another privately.

Moreover, the impact of Early Enlightenment ideas, and in particular the high prestige of philosophy and toleration, had forced the Churches into a general retreat. By the 1740s traditional confessional thinking and dogmatic theology were everywhere so weakened that the very term *incrédulité* had discernibly changed its meaning, and instead of denoting, as in the past, scepticism about Christianity had come to mean, or often tended to mean, absence of belief in a First Mover, or providential God, in some form or other. The Churches in their debilitated state could not press too hard, let alone persecute or expel discreet 'Christian deists'. Consequently, outright condemnation came to be reserved for non-providential deists alone. Hence, according to Formey, the new *incrédules* strove both 'contre la religion naturelle et contre la religion révélée', with which he tacitly accepted that there was now an alliance between rational Christian theology and advocates of 'natural religion'.[167] As we shall see, this was a development strengthened not only by the advance of Newtonianism on the continent during the second quarter of the century, but also by what had emerged by then as its chief European rival—the Leibnizian–Wolffian philosophy.

Philosophies which infused the world of experimental science and scientific thought with a powerful sense of the dominion of God and His ceaseless providence simultaneously appealed to 'enlightened' Christians and mainstream, moderate deists who accepted the chief points of 'natural religion', and especially an 'intelligent' deity who had created the universe and maintains it, but is distinct from it. Such philosophies narrowed the gap between rationalizing Christianity and providential deism and cemented their alliance against the proponents of radical ideas, whether Naturalists, materialists, non-fideistic sceptics, or Spinozists who denied Providence and the divine origin of moral concepts, as well as Heaven, Hell, Satan, the immortality of the soul, and the God-ordained nature of prevailing social and political structures.[168]

Thus the influence of new philosophical and scientific ideas since the mid-seventeenth century generated a powerful impulse towards the rationalization of religion and even the fusing of science and theology. But if this was the prevailing trend, there was simultaneously a weaker yet not insignificant opposite tendency which has been aptly termed 'l'irrationalisation de la religion' of the late seventeenth century.[169] This was the tendency heralded by Blaise Pascal (1623–62) at the end of his short life, when, in his *Pensées*, left unfinished in 1662, he firmly separated the world of science from religion, claiming that the one, the sphere of reason, is no guide to the other, a realm which we 'know' only through the heart and our emotions. Despising Descartes as 'inutile et incertain',[170] Pascal held that reason and science have their place but only represent one sphere of truth. There is another and higher sphere which reason and

---

[167] Formey, *Histoire abrégée*, 308.   [168] [Mauduit], *Traitté de religion*, 3, 86–7.
[169] Kolakowski, *Chrétiens sans église*, 235–6, 250.   [170] Pascal, *Pensées*, 94.

science cannot penetrate. Our minds, hearts, and will are so constituted, he insisted, that we must 'believe' and must 'love'—if not what is true then, alas, what is false.[171] Pascal was a master of geometrical reasoning but, adopting the opposite stance to Spinoza, passionately denied that reason is the key unlocking the gateway to spiritual and metaphysical truth. Rather, sensing the dangers ahead, Pascal introduced—without resorting to fideistic scepticism—what might be termed an anti-philosophical philosophy: 'se moquer de la philosophie, c'est vraiment philosopher.'[172]

Few could match Pascal's eloquence, but such were the intellectual and psychological pressures of the age that many were driven—not infrequently away from Cartesianism—to follow the same path. Such foes of philosophy in its new sense, and of theological rationalization, included the venerable Pierre Poiret (1646–1719) of Metz, who, first a Catholic and then a Calvinist, subsequently rejected all the main confessions for a private, anti-Enlightenment Christianity of the spirit. After discarding Catholicism and Aristotelianism, he had embraced Cartesianism while studying at Basel, emerging by the 1670s as one of Europe's best-known rationalist theologians. The first edition of his *Cogitationes rationales de Deo, anima et male* (1677), though it annoyed the young (and then Cartesian) Pierre Bayle,[173] was one of the most influential mechanistic philosophico-theological treatises of the decade. But in the 1680s Poiret became a mystical recluse, and recoiled from Cartesianism and all philosophy based on reason and science. Henceforth, while directing much of his effort against Spinozism which he, like so many others, considered the foremost danger posed by modern philosophy, he launched a one-man crusade from his retreat in the Dutch village of Rijnsburg (where, ironically, Spinoza himself had once lived and meditated) against modern philosophy, and the entire Early Enlightenment.[174] Descartes, Spinoza, Locke, Thomasius, and Bayle were all scornfully rejected by Poiret because 'ils vantent la raison humaine corrompue.'[175]

But if few disliked his salvos against Spinoza and 'extravagant scepticks and Pirrhonists', his relentless assault on rational theology was another matter and inevitably provoked broad disapproval. Le Clerc waxed so indignant that he forgot his habitual moderation, remarking, as his English translator puts it, that 'Poiret fancies that the fooleries of mystical men, and all the chimaeras he is pleased to add to them, must pass for oracles; whereas he should be ashamed to make it his business to seduce the simple with his ridiculous spiritual notions'; if Poiret disdains his 'critical learning', Le Clerc advised his unphilosophical antagonist not to 'meddle with what he understands not'.[176] Undeterred, Poiret retorted that to 'understand clearly Mr Le Clerc's censure of my work, you must note that religion and Pelagianism, or Socinianism, are the same thing with him' and that he picks and chooses among the 'bare words of Scripture, out of which our natural faculty of reasoning (as corrupt as it is) assisted

---

[171] The great writer frequently asserts that 'Dieu veut plus disposer la volonté que l'esprit'; Pascal, *Pensées*, 73–5, 94–5, 224–6.

[172] Ibid., 75.   [173] Brucker, *Historia*, 561; Labrousse, *Pierre Bayle*, ii, 150–1.

[174] Walch, *Philosophisches Lexicon*, 132–3; Kolakowski, *Chrétiens sans église*, 685.

[175] Ibid., 686–7; Vernière, *Spinoza*, 49–50.   [176] Le Clerc, *Parrhasiana*, 273.

with grammar, critick and philosophy, without the help of God's internal aid and operation, can raise and find out such ideas, propositions and logical conclusions as please our taste, rejecting and ridiculing whatever else is to be found there however much these may have been valued and esteemed by the holiest of men.'[177]

Another who rejected philosophy late in his career after having originally been, at least privately, favourable to Cartesianism, was Bishop Bossuet.[178] A leading advocate of royal absolutism and the most effective champion of authority, orthodoxy, and tradition in the French Church, he was in many ways an imposing, even magnificent figure (see Plate 5). But his courtly status and outward splendour was, in many respects, just a façade contradicting the deep anxiety of spirit and intellectual uncertainty which lay behind it.[179] The more he investigated the New Philosophy and the implications of science, the more he detected their negative, weakening effect on orthodoxy, spiritual authority, and ecclesiastical power. Bossuet, no less than Huet, Simon, and Le Vassor, became deeply preoccupied with Spinoza, and it is undoubtedly true, as has been claimed, that the latter's shadow hovers over the whole of his spiritual odyssey from the late 1670s onwards, including the evolution and argument of his most famous work, the *Discours sur l'histoire universelle* (1681).[180]

But Bossuet's method of fighting Spinoza, in the *Discours*, diverges markedly from the erudite techniques of Huet and Simon or the modernizing theology of Le Vassor, Le Clerc, or Jaquelot. His strategy was to discard philosophy and rational argument altogether. Without referring once to Spinoza or any philosopher, merely alluding darkly to unspecified 'monstres d'opinion' whose sinister presence pervades his thoughts, Bossuet silently tracks the *Tractatus Theologico-Politicus*, one by one reversing all its contentions, affirming Moses' authorship of the Pentateuch, the integrity of Scripture, the truth of Revelation, the reality of prophecy, the authenticity of miracles, the centrality of Christ in history, the legitimacy of ecclesiastical power and the divinely ordained character of hereditary monarchy, overturning its key planks not with intellectual arguments but his forceful rhetorical appeal to conscience and the imagination.[181] Bossuet fortifies and defends Revelation poetically by conveying a powerful sense of the reality of divine intervention in human history and the interconnectedness of the stages of the Revelation, and of the Old and New Testaments.[182] His forceful demonstration of the *Zusammenhang* of Scripture and history, showing how the successive stages of the world illustrate divine intervention in the shaping of history, constitutes Bossuet's answer to Spinoza and the whole edifice of modern philosophical incredulity, scepticism, deism, and atheism.[183]

---

[177] Poiret, *Divine Oeconomy*, i, preface; Hazard, *European Mind*, 120.

[178] Formey, *Histoire abrégée*, 274; Phillips, *Church and Culture*, 173.

[179] Hazard, *European Mind*, 232–47.   [180] Ibid., 238, 248; Tosel, 'Le Discours', 98–104.

[181] On Moses' authorship, see Bossuet, *Discours*, 54–5, 175–84, 237; on the centrality of divine Providence and the progress of the Church in history, see ibid., 68–75 and Tosel, 'Le Discours', 97–8.

[182] Ibid., 100, 103.

[183] Ibid., 104; Baltus, *Religion Chrétienne*, 220, 279; Monigila, *Dissertazione contra i Fatalisti*, i, 169–71; Hazard, *European Mind*, 247–8.

Where Spinoza denies miracles, Bossuet proclaims miracles the core of history. Where Spinoza denies divine authorization for monarchical or ecclesiastical power, Bossuet shows that political power is, indeed, decreed by God and that the rise and fall of empires belongs to the divine plan, central to which is the advent of Christ and the progress, power, and glory of the Catholic Church, the ultimate sign and confirmation of God's will, the 'miracle des miracles'.[184] Affirming the certainty and coherence of truth while remaining uncertain in his own mind which philosophical underpinning best suited his purpose, and painfully aware of the progressive fragmentation around him, he ultimately rejected modern philosophy and science altogether.

Bossuet's final position in his last years echoed Pascal's downgrading of reason and exaltation of religious emotion. In his last work, the *Élévations sur les mystères* (1704), which remained in manuscript until 1727, Bossuet exalts devotional fervour as the path to truth and Man's salvation, disparaging the human intellect as 'foible . . . ignorante . . . pleine d'erreurs et d'incertitude'. Philosophy (and the *incrédules*) might argue that nothing can be created from nothing, he admonished, but what do the philosophers know![185] Philosophers, he declares, are just the blind leading the blind: 'O Dieu quelle a esté l'ignorance des sages du monde qu'on a appellé philosophes!'[186]

---

[184] Bossuet, *Discours*, 252–7; Du Tertre *Entretiens*, iii, 31, 305–6.
[185] Bossuet, *Élevations*, 77, 121–2.   [186] Ibid., 121.

25 | THE COLLAPSE OF CARTESIANISM

i. Empiricism

A discerning observer of the world of learning, contemplating Europe's war of philosophies in 1700, might well have concluded that Cartesianism and its offshoot, *Malebranchisme*, were most strongly placed to win and, sponsored by governments and Churches, to construct a new general hegemony of ideas in Europe's culture. If scholastic Aristotelianism still officially presided in the colleges of France, Italy, Flanders, Austria, Spain, and Portugal, scholasticism was everywhere in retreat, and patently incapable of fending off Descartes and Malebranche among the intellectual and scientific élite. Meanwhile, in many Protestant lands, including the Netherlands, Sweden, Brandenburg-Prussia, the Palatinate, Switzerland, and Scotland, Cartesianism of various hues enjoyed a broad intellectual ascendancy.[1] If Leibniz presided at Hanover, and most German universities and courts offered an incoherent, fragmented picture, Cartesianism in Germany and throughout central Europe was at any rate as strong as, or stronger than, any other philosophical contender.

Yet of the three rival versions of moderate, mainstream, Early Enlightenment—Neo-Cartesianism, Newtonianism (reinforced with Locke), and Leibnizian–Wolffianism, that which in 1700 appeared most formidable, and enjoyed the widest support amongst Europe's ruling élites, Cartesianism, rapidly proved the most precarious intellectually and was the first to collapse under the strain of escalating philosophical and scientific strife. Many of Europe's acutest minds discarded Cartesianism during the opening years of the new century. Vico came out publicly against Cartesianism, disparaging Descartes' use of the *cogito*, in a public oration before the viceroy of Naples in 1708,[2] and later expanded his critique in a published version, granting Cartesian philosophy had dramatically changed our picture of the world but stressing even more the dangers of teaching men to think in exclusively mechanistic terms, disregarding the whole edifice of received thought and

---

[1] Watson, *Breakdown*, 21; Brockliss, 'Curricula', 585–6; Wood, 'Scientific Revolution in Scotland', 266–9; Stewart, 'Scottish Enlightenment', 275; Israel, *Dutch Republic*, 889–909; Lindroth, *Svensk lärdomshistoria*, ii, 464–5, 577–80.

[2] Vico, *Autobiography*, 146; Croce, *Filosofia*, 11–16; Verene, 'Introduction', 24–5.

education.[3] Bernard Nieuwentijt (1654–1718), a leading Dutch mathematician and theorist of scientific method, having professed but also wrestled with Cartesianism for decades, finally followed Hartsoeker—once a zealous adherent who had long since abandoned that philosophy[4]—and rebelled resoundingly against his Cartesian inheritance. With two major books, the *Religious Philosopher*, as it was known in English, of 1715, and the *Gronden van zekerheid* (Grounds of Certainty) of 1720, Nieuwentijt declared war on Cartesianism (as well as Spinozism), denigrating the former as unhelpful to the progress of 'experimental science', a hypothetical edifice of 'ungrounded guesses' which, he claimed, had been utterly disproved by the microscope and other new instruments of observation;[5] he remained for several decades one of the most widely read scientific authors in Europe.[6]

The leading young French scientist, Dorthous de Mairan, recoiled around 1710 from the Cartesianism and *Malebranchisme* which dominated his early development and, while wrestling privately with Spinoza, publicly edged towards Newton.[7] Meanwhile, in Holland, behind the scenes, such leading intellects as De Volder at Leiden (despite remaining publicly a 'Cartesian' until his death in 1709) increasingly criticized Descartes (as well as Leibniz), making no secret of his preference for experiment over deduction.[8] In an oration on 'certainty in science' delivered at Leiden in 1715, Herman Boerhaave (1668–1738), the most celebrated medical professor of his age, publicly rejected the Cartesianism long dominant at that university, instead embracing Newtonianism.[9]

The increasing trend towards an emphatically experimental stance in science, combined with empiricism in philosophy and (publicly at least) a powerful affirmation of commitment to the truth of revealed religion, reflected in the scientific careers of men like Boyle, Newton, Grew, Hartsoeker, Boerhaave, Nieuwentijt, Willem Jacob 's-Gravesande (1688–1742), and Dorthous de Mairan, drew on a variety of intellectual sources. In the long run Locke's *Essay Concerning Human Understanding* of 1689, arguing that 'there appear not to be any ideas in the mind before the senses have conveyed any in,'[10] and linking Christianity with 'experimental philosophy' by holding that our assent to divine revelation 'can be rationally no higher than the evidence of its being a revelation',[11] proved the most rigorous, systematic, and important. But Locke's *Essay* remained largely unknown on the continent during the first third of the eighteenth century, and while Le Clerc, Locke's principal continental ally, strenuously backed his

---

[3] By trying to elevate the 'geometric method' into the 'authentic voice of nature', held Vico, in his *De nostri tempori studiorum ratione* (1709), Cartesianism had led men to lose sight of what is most precious in education and general culture—a proper grasp of rhetoric, history, law, and the classics, the real grounding of our culture; see Vico, *On the Study Methods*, 19–25, 77; Lilla, *G. B. Vico*, 47–52.

[4] Hartsoeker, *Cours de physique*, 'Éloge de M. Hartsoeker par M. de Fontenelle', p. 3.

[5] Nieuwentijt, *Gronden van zekerheid*, preface by Jacob van Ostade and pp. 1–3; Petry, 'Nieuwentijt's Criticism', 5–7; Vermij, *Secularisering*, 45–7.

[6] Petry, 'Nieuwentijt's Criticism', 2–3; Cook, 'New Philosophy', 140.

[7] Vernière, *Spinoza*, 279–86; Guerlac, *Newton on the Continent*, 65–6, 113–14.

[8] Vermij, *Secularisering*, 45.   [9] Klever,' Herman Boerhaave', 80–1; De Pater, 'In de schaduw', 64–6.

[10] Locke, *Essay*, 97.   [11] Ibid., 414.

empirical philosophy from the start, helping to prepare and publish the *Abrégé*, or French outline, shown to a circle of scholars in the Netherlands—among them Van Leenhof—as early as 1688,[12] it was only several decades later that Locke's philosophy penetrated more widely.

Indeed, the early progress of empiricism as a philosophical antidote to Cartesianism, *Malebranchisme*, and the Radical Enlightenment seems to have had relatively little to do with Locke, springing rather from varied impulses and sources, especially Boyle, Dutch anti-Cartesian academe, Thomasius and the German eclectics, and not least Le Clerc, whose renown was greater than Locke's at that time, a powerful voice for empiricism in his own right, who dedicated his *Logique* in 1692 to his English friend, assuring him 'j'ai infiniment profité de vos lumières, comme vous le verrez.'[13] Advocates of a rigorous empiricism might keep to a consciously modernizing rational theology, like Le Clerc and Locke, but were equally likely to stem from a more traditionalist, 'Voetian', empiricist trend, vying to fill the gap left by the collapse of Aristotelianism while simultaneously battling the new mechanistic systems. Key protagonists of this variety were the Utrecht professor Gerardus de Vries (1648–1705) and his pupil and successor at the head of the Dutch anti-Cartesian academic establishment, Johannes Regius (1656–1738). De Vries, a student of Voetius, figured prominently in the anti-Cartesian backlash at Leiden following the downfall of the De Witt régime in 1672[14] but later, disgusted by Cartesian tenacity there—what he called the 'persecution, affronts and insults of those devoted to the Cartesian philosophy who, with great impudence endeavour to subdue and destroy the old peripatetic philosophy',[15] resigned his chair in 1674, and retreated to the friendlier ambience of Utrecht.

It was at Utrecht, at much the same time Locke's ideas began to evolve in Oxford, that De Vries perfected his 'thorough and powerful' critique of Descartes' 'innate ideas'.[16] While discarding the old Aristotelian terminology and most of its apparatus, he retained the idea of the mind being a *tabula rasa* and sense perception the origin of all human ideas, combining empiricism with residual strands of Aristotelianism. That Locke, who supposes the mind before sensation 'to be, as we say, white paper, void of all characters, without any ideas',[17] was originally often viewed as a Neo-Aristotelian of the De Vries type, is shown by Leibniz's query about whether the mind can be conceived as a *tabula rasa* 'as Aristotle and the author of the *Essay* maintain and everything which is inscribed there comes solely from the senses and experience'.[18] De Vries' chief work, his *Exercitationes rationales de deo, divinisque perfectionibus* (Utrecht, 1685), published when Locke was nearby, strives to annihilate Descartes' 'innate ideas', accusing

---

[12] Le Clerc to Locke, Amsterdam, 19 Apr. 1689 in *Correspondance of John Locke*, ii, 595–6; Simonutti, 'Religion, Philosophy', 312.

[13] Le Clerc to Locke, Amsterdam, 20 Jan. 1692 in *Correspondance of John Locke*, iv, 353–4.

[14] *Philopater*, 191; Thijssen-Schoute, *Nederlands Cartesianisme*, 228–9.

[15] Molhuysen, *Bronnen*, iii, 291.   [16] Nieuwentijt, *Gronden van zekerheid*, preface, 24.

[17] Locke, *Essay*, 89.

[18] Leibniz, *New Essays*, 48; Phemister, 'Locke, Sergeant and Scientific Method', 239; Spruit, *Species Intelligibilis*, ii, 510–12, 519.

him of hampering experimental science, disparaging his (and the sceptics') disdain for perceptions deriving from the senses,[19] and insisting, like Locke and Le Clerc, that sensory experience is the basis of all knowledge.[20] Nor does he fail to use his new empirical apparatus against what he considers the direst threat of the age—namely the irreligious ideas of Spinoza and the *Philosophia* (of Lodewijk Meyer), a work he strenuously attacks.[21]

De Vries' book, recognizably Voetian in its insistence that science must fully accord with Revelation and that Spinozism, the distillation of all that is most pernicious intellectually, is rooted in Cartesianism, was the first major attack on Spinoza and radical thought from an empirical standpoint.[22] Meanwhile, though the Cartesian grip on the Dutch universities perceptibly weakened during the second decade of the new century, it nevertheless remained formidable down to around 1725, as reflected in the younger Wittichius' presiding role at Leiden and Andala's long ascendancy at Franeker.[23] Ruardus Andala (1665–1727), the last of the major Dutch Cartesians, was an academic of humble origins who in time acquired an enviable international reputation, extending across Germany, Sweden, where he was a prime influence on Rydelius, and, more generally, the Baltic and central Europe. His long connection with the numerous Hungarian Calvinist student contingent at Franeker—between 1650 and 1750 no less than 700 Hungarian students studied there—led to his being dubbed the 'good father and protector of the Hungarians'.[24] Compared with most professors of the time, Andala was an indefatigable teacher, presiding at no less than 233 academic disputations, two-thirds philosophical and one-third theological, during his twenty-six years at the university, or over twenty-five times as many as his rival, Regius, in half as many years.[25] Under Andala, Franeker, which in 1710 had 18 professors and around 200 students, was renowned as the most 'Cartesian' of the Dutch universities and most antagonistic to both the new empiricism and the Leibnizian–Wolffian system.[26]

Originally a Reformed preacher, Andala began his scholarly career assisting Van der Wayen's campaign against Bekker, whom he attacked as a false Cartesian, purveying dangerous ideas apt to foment Spinozism.[27] Taking up his chair at Franeker in 1701, Andala for the rest of his life battled equally, on one side, against the rising tide of empiricism championed by Regius, Le Clerc, Boerhaave, Nieuwentijt, 's-Gravesande, and Locke and, on the other, what he deemed the even greater menace posed by radical deism, which to his mind included Bekker. Though firmly opposed also to *philosophia Leibnitio-Wolffiana*,[28] empiricism and Spinozism were always his primary targets. He prided himself on his special aptitude for sniffing out disguised Spinozism, being among those who tarnished De Volder's reputation and put a question

[19] De Vries, *Exercitationes*, 395–6, 410–12.   [20] Ibid., 390–432.
[21] Ibid., 103, 501.   [22] Ibid., 30–1.
[23] Wielema, 'Nikolaus Engelhard', 149; Visser, 'Petrus Camper', 386; Cook, 'New Philosophy', 136–7.
[24] Ridder-Symoens, 'Buitenlandse studenten', 74; De Graaf, 'Zevenburgse en Hongaarse studenten', 97.
[25] Sluis, 'Disputeren in Franeker', 51.   [26] Buddeus, *Compendius*, 494–8.
[27] Thijssen-Schoute, *Nederlands Cartesianisme*, 519–20.
[28] [Strodtmann], *Das Neue Gelehrten Europa*, i (1752), 281; Bouveresse, *Spinoza et Leibniz*, 219.

mark over Boerhaave, as well as the first publicly to denounce Geulincx as a 'Spinozist'.[29]

He expounded his Neo-Cartesianism in such works as his *Exercitationes Academicae* (1708) and *Syntagma Theologico-Physico-Metaphysicum* (1711). Insisting on man's innate knowledge of God, he argues that there is a crucial difference between the purely methodological use of doubt about God's existence, employed in Descartes, and real scepticism about God's existence, which he deems sheer depravity, a perverse form of bravado, not a genuine philosophical stance.[30] He adamantly upheld the Cartesian dichotomy of mind and extension against all critics including Boerhaave, considering the Almighty the only possible author of the otherwise impossible and inexplicable 'union' and 'interaction' of two substances which by definition cannot interact.[31] No less miraculous, and staunchly defended by Andala, are *Creatio ex nihilo* and the freedom of God's will (libertas voluntatis divinae).[32]

Andala ascribes the advance of philosophical empiricism in the first place to De Vries, disparaging his critique of Descartes' 'innate ideas' as an old quarrel stoked up afresh by him in which, latterly, Locke and Le Clerc had mingled their voices. Locke, he remarks, plunges in 'with great energy so that that ancient refrain [concerning innate ideas] should be repeated, boiling up that old cabbage anew with several fresh twists and obscurities, though not without some subtlety'.[33] 'Locke's spit,' he adds contemptuously, 'is licked up by Le Clerc who announces it constantly as if it were a new discovery.'[34] Locke's and Le Clerc's insistence, on empiricist grounds, that we simply have no knowledge about 'any spiritual beings, but the Eternal God' and that it is only from Scripture that we have 'assurance that there are such creatures' evokes only scorn from Andala.[35]

He concedes that Locke goes deeper than Le Clerc, but even he 'is unable to derive all ideas from experience whether from the senses or a reflex of mind, without acknowledging the mind is created by God, so that either ideas take shape within the mind through its own exertions or it receives them from objects through being stimulated', so that the mind 'is simultaneously an active and passive agent'.[36] Andala had a point, since this dualism in Locke did, and does, present difficulties, critics often remarking that Locke fails to distinguish sufficiently clearly between ideas as acts of perception and ideas as logical components of thought.[37] More generally, Locke's and Le Clerc's imposing strict limits on the mind's capacity moved Andala to accuse them of boasting of their ignorance.

Empiricsm might be less ominous than Spinozism, but the two great intellectual challenges of the age, as Andala saw it, were not unconnected. They converge, he argues, in their common assault on belief in spirits and angels and their tendency to

---

[29] Dunin Borkowski, *Spinoza*, iii, 148; Klever, 'Herman Boerhaave', 81.

[30] Andala, *Syntagma*, 14, 16, 22.

[31] Ibid., 30; Thijssen-Schoute, *Nederlands Cartesianisme*, 256, 519–21.

[32] Andala, *Syntagma*, 86–90, 133–5.   [33] Andala, *Dissertationum philosophicarum heptas*, 64.

[34] Ibid.   [35] Ibid.; Locke, *Essay*, 393.

[36] Andala, *Dissertationum philosophicarum heptas*, 78–80, 106–7.

[37] See, for instance, Locke, *Essay*, 92–3; Spruit, *Species Intelligibilis*, ii, 505.

erode the absolute character of 'good' and 'evil', as well as belief in divine Providence and religion generally. Though more tentative, and to that extent less virulent, Locke, Le Clerc, and the empiricists, contended Andala, were nevertheless assisting the further progress of Spinozism. Le Clerc (and presumably also Locke), he claimed, had materially promoted the 'atheists of our time' by demolishing all arguments 'proving the existence of God and the creation of the mind, as well as the conservation of all things and the union of body and mind'.[38]

Implacably opposed to Andala, Johannes Regius (1656–1738), originally also a Reformed preacher, was selected for a chair in theology at Franeker in 1685. He taught at the university for over half a century (1685–1738), disagreeing with his antagonist about practically everything except that the four-cornered philosophical strife between Cartesianism, empiricism, Leibnizian–Wolffianism, and Spinozism was a crisis of ideas in religion, morality, politics, and society, as well as scholarship and science, of unparalleled gravity.[39] In 1714 he emerged in the public sphere as a fervent advocate of the new empiricism, in a work published in the vernacular at Rotterdam. The long and catastrophic ascendancy of Cartesianism in Dutch intellectual life, he complains, had advanced so far that no one who was not a Cartesian was thought to have any merit or ability and those who, like himself, dared to oppose the prevailing tendency were mocked as ignoramuses. Yet if Cartesianism is 'so clear, sure and such a well-lit entrance to truth', he declaimed, 'is it not amazing that thinkers such as Spinoza, Malebranche, Poiret, the writer of the *Betoverde Weereld* [Bekker] and another well known to us [Leenhof], great exponents and advocates of this philosophy, should have lapsed into such vile and grotesque errrors?'[40] He knows, he says, that his claiming the 'principles of Spinoza are implicit in Cartesian thought' will provoke a vitriolic response: 'but I deem it my duty to show those about to sail on the sea of Cartesian philosophy the sunken rocks it conceals so they may guard against becoming shipwrecked,' for 'all those who become full Spinozists had first been Cartesians, like Spinoza himself.'[41] A certain 'astute Cartesian' professor, he added, alluding to De Volder, had notoriously misled 'many a student who later became infected with Spinoza's errors'.

Regius grants that there are substantial differences between Cartesianism and Spinozism, but claims these are less fundamental than many assume. 'We know,' he avers, 'that Spinoza developed his philosophy with greater consistency from his premises and principles than Descartes; for it is easy to improve what another found first and repair its defects.'[42] Spinoza, furthermore, 'is less cautious than Descartes and says straight out, uninhibitedly, what Descartes, owing to circumstances and his desire to pass for a Christian, neither wished, nor dared, to say.'[43] Everyone knows Spinozism

---

[38] Andala, *Dissertationum philosophicarum heptas*, 107; Andala claims that only a providential God can account for the union 'inter mentem et corpus', and considers this union one of the proofs of God's existence; Andala, *Syntagma*, 30, 55.

[39] Walch, *Philosophisches Lexicon*, 2413–14; Thijssen-Schoute, *Nederlands Cartesianisme*, 520; Verbeek, 'From "learned ignorance" ', 44–5.

[40] Regius, *Beginselen*, preface.   [41] Ibid., 92; Buddeus, *Compendium*, 486–7.

[42] Regius, *Beginselen*, 352.   [43] Ibid.

is a vile menace and must be crushed. But to defeat Spinoza one must first demolish his axioms and premises and this the Cartesians are powerless to do.

The battle between Andala and Regius, to the consternation of the entire academic fraternity, had by 1713 degenerated into open strife, adversely affecting every aspect of university life. The climax came in 1718–19 when Regius asserted that only empiricism can save religion, and smash the Spinozist threat, in two hard-hitting Latin treatises, in the title of the first, *De Cartesio Spinozae praelucente* (1718) styling Descartes the precursor and herald of Spinozism. Unshaken by the ensuing storm of protest, he followed this up with his *Cartesius verus Spinozismi Architectus* (Descartes the true Architect of Spinozism, 1719), in which he claims all the most damaging and pernicious intellectual trends of recent decades stemmed from Cartesianism: 'Van Hattem who poisoned much of Zeeland with his venom was a Cartesian; Bekker revered Descartes; and what was Geulincx if not a Cartesian?'[44] 'And what of De Volder? . . . Even if unable wholly to absolve himself of Spinozism,' he publicly paraded as a Cartesian, while Leenhof, undeniably Spinozist, for decades professed Cartesianism. Voetius, Spanheim, Hoornbeek, Mastricht, Leydekker, and his own teacher De Vries, he reminded readers, unanimously 'judged this philosophy a mound of all evil, containing the seeds of every grave error'.[45]

Descartes' freedom of the will, held Regius, is illusory, indeed a negation, implying the same determinism as Spinoza affirms. Cartesians claim their teacher separates God and the universe; but, actually Descartes makes extension the essence of bodies, and extension, being infinite, must in its kind be immutable and infinitely perfect, thus an aspect of God.[46] Likewise, insists Regius, Descartes' notion of substance as 'a se et per se' means that created bodies do not exist absolutely, in and by themselves, and that, therefore, in themselves, bodies do not constitute a substance. Hence, on Descartes' premises, 'Deus solus est substantia' (God alone is substance) for him no less than Spinoza.[47] The true relationship of Descartes and Spinoza, he concludes, is consequently not one of opposition, as the public has been misleadingly assured, but consensus. Nor are those Cartesians who are sufficiently candid, as well as 'perspices et eruditi', to acknowledge the truth unaware of this. Regius illustrates this by describing an encounter with a disciple of De Volder, who acknowledged the latter 'was suspected of Spinozism by many', much to that eminent man's distress.[48] Yet when Regius asked whether it was true De Volder, arguing from Descartes, taught there is really only one substance, his interlocutor reacted angrily but allegedly admitted this too, impudently claiming that no other view of substance makes sense.[49]

Furthermore, held Regius, the blasphemous Spinozistic proposition that God acts only necesssarily, and not out of His free will, is also inherent in Cartesianism. For Descartes affirms God is the First Cause and Prime Mover, and that the world functions only in accordance with *regulas necessarias* (necessary laws).[50] Since these necessary laws derive from the First Cause, and are innate in God's perfection, it follows that

---

[44] Regius, *Cartesius*, preface, fos. 8–8v.   [45] Ibid., 3.
[46] Regius, *Cartesius*, 83–5; Woolhouse, *Descartes, Spinoza, Leibniz*, 85.
[47] Regius, *Cartesius*, 93.   [48] Ibid., 126.   [49] Ibid.   [50] Ibid., 147–51.

when God acts He acts necessarily in accordance with those *regulas* 'because he cannot act contrary to His own nature and perfection'.[51] Nor is Descartes at all safe on the mind–body nexus. He asserts that God is the sole possible author of the mind–body junction yet has endless difficulties with this baffling proposition. Nowhere, for instance, does Descartes explain what exactly this link is and how apparent reactions and interaction between them can arise simultaneously and connectedly. In fact Descartes generates a fog of confusion around the mind–body nexus which, on his premises, can only be resolved by Spinoza's simple but pernicious expedient of reducing mind and body to one and the same substance.[52] The truth is, concludes Regius scornfully, Descartes' rickety system finds its fullest and only consistent realization in Spinoza; and this the Cartesians offer mankind as philosophy 'safe, unique, true, most useful and necessary for the salvation of religion!'[53]

The Cartesian camp had to reply and it was natural that Andala should shoulder the responsibility. He dashed off his 281-page tract *Cartesius verus Spinozismi Eversor* (Descartes the true Destroyer of Spinozism, Franeker, 1719), subjecting Regius to the full blast of his polemical ire. Here his prime concern is to prove Descartes' principles 'are no less different from Spinoza's than is light from darkness';[54] and that not only is Cartesianism comprehensively *contraria* to Spinozism, it is the only effective antidote. Solely by using Descartes' categories can philosophers reliably separate God from Nature, ensuring the independence of 'minded substance', walled round by a firm dichotomy of mind and matter, without which belief in the soul's immortality, as well as angels, demons, ghosts, and Satan, will disintegrate. Hence Regius' calumny that Descartes is 'verus Spinozismi architectus' is not just false, it systematically obfuscates and hinders truth, blighting philosophy, religion, and ultimately, society itself.

Andala needed, in addition, to separate Cartesianism from perversions of Descartes which use his terminology to the detriment of his reputation. Regius rightly condemns the *Philosophia S. Scripturae Interpres* as an atrocious text which impugns the fundamentals of Christianity, denying *Creationem ex nihilo* and *Trinitatem* and even the *Incarnationem* and *Resurrectionem*; but it is also a complete travesty of Cartesian philosophy, its anonymous author being no 'Cartesian' but a treacherous *pseudophilosophus*. Besides the *Philosophia*, he assails Geulincx whom, ever since 1712, he had deemed a crypto-Spinozist, as one of the most insidious of these 'spurious, falsely named Cartesians' and his ideas as 'perverse, crude, Spinozistic dogmata'.[55] De Volder, now also dead, whom earlier he admired as 'very acute' and *subtilissimus*, he now classed with Geulincx and Le Clerc as catastrophic and obvious vehicles of Spinozism.[56] Nothing could be more harmful than the books of Leenhof, Van Hattem, and Deurhoff. But none of these, whatever Regius says, were 'Cartesians: it was from Spinoza's teats that they all sucked.'[57]

---

[51] Regius, *Cartesius*, 93.   [52] Ibid., 201–2.   [53] Ibid., 202.   [54] Ibid., 4.

[55] In company with the Zeelander Cornelis Tuinman, who headed the campaign against Hattemism and crypto-Spinozism in Zeeland in the opening years of the century, see Andala, *Cartesius verus*, preface and pp. 20, 252; Wielema, 'Spinoza in Zeeland', 105.

[56] Andala, *Cartesius verus*, 51, 252.   [57] Ibid., 47–8.

With the new sect of 'deists' spreading and society being increasingly invaded by *scepticismus philosophicus* and atheism, energetic counter-measures were urgently required. The most desirable strategy, urges Andala, would be simultaneously to strengthen Cartesianism and book censorship. Attacks on Cartesianism, he concluded, are an assault on society and also Protestantism. By dividing the philosophical middle ground, the empiricists were despicably weakening the only force capable of defeating Spinoza and buttressing Protestant Christianity. By propagating empiricist ideas Regius was in fact helping the Catholic Church evade the deadly consequences of Cartesianism for their absurd doctrine of transubstantiation, though the Papacy and cardinals had not yet realized (a view shared by Leibniz) that Cartesianism is fundamentally irreconcilable with Catholicism. When the Pope eventually does see how great a service Regius and empiricism perform by demonstrating with a clarity equal to that of the dogmas of the Catholic Church that Descartes is *Spinozismi architectus*, the Holy Father will doubtless with great pleasure, 'add [Regius] to the catalogue of saints'.[58]

ii. Deadlock in France

Ironically, the 1680s, the decade in which Louis XIV and the French court moved to their resplendent new quarters at Versailles and the finishing touches were put to the architectural and decorative backdrop of the most magnificent monarchy in Europe's history, encasing in palaces, décor, and gardens the very essence of divine right, absolute monarchy, hierarchy, and authority, the fraught unity of the French intellectual world began publicly to disintegrate. France possessed outstanding spiritual leaders and philosophers—Bossuet, Fénelon, Huet, Régis, Arnauld, Simon, and Malebranche—but now these all drifted into undisguised public strife, not between two factions but many. Even where an ephemeral alliance formed, as between Bossuet and Fénelon who briefly joined forces to fight Malebranche, it soon dissolved again, leaving behind an ever more splintered and perplexing battleground of competing philosophical, theological, and scientific systems.

Bossuet, the most influential ecclesiastic in France and close to the ear of the king, was eager to give a vigorous lead to safeguard society, education, and the Church, and help fortify royal and ecclesiastical authority. But by the 1680s the philosophical maze in which he and his colleagues were caught had become so complex that he became intellectually immobilized, unsure which way to push, trapped in a philosophical impasse from which he could find no exit.[59] Discarding his earlier sympathy for the New Philosophy, he nevertheless remained unwilling to throw his weight behind the Jesuit campaign to crush Cartesianism in the colleges and universities, though by 1686–7 he was sufficiently disturbed by Malebranche's doctrine of 'general wills', with its troublesome implications for belief in divine Providence, to intervene against him and assist Fénelon with his *Réfutation du système du Père Malebranche*, a work which

---

[58] Ibid.   [59] Hazard, *European Mind*, 248–50; Phillips, *Church and Culture*, 173.

reaffirms the infinite grandeur of God's Providence and its central role in the rise and fall of empires, not forgetting to refer readers to Bossuet's *Discours*.[60] But Malebranche proved a dogged opponent, while the scholastic Aristotelianism of the Jesuits increasingly frayed at the edges. No doubt his predicament would have been less vexing had the Jesuits been more divided than they were and if Aristotelianism simply disintegrated under the impact of Cartesianism. But there was no sign of such a resolution. On the contrary, Jesuits and the Sorbonne battled on tenaciously, rallying the Court and upper echelons of the Church hierarchy behind them while, on the other side, the Cartesians and *Malebranchistes* continued infiltrating the universities, laity, and clergy.

At the same time, disarray within the Cartesian camp became increasingly more obvious. Malebranche's *Traité de la Nature* (1680) appalled not only Bossuet, Fénelon, and the Jesuits but also Arnauld, who likewise judged Malebranche's teaching that God normally acts only by a 'general will'—a system of universal laws which He has previously chosen for their goodness, simplicity, and fitness for His purposes—fatal for popular belief in a world governed by divine Providence.[61] Malebranche held that these laws are only practically and not metaphysically 'necessary', affirming that God's choice of general laws must be consonant with His most perfect wisdom and goodness, a doctrine akin to that of Leibniz, as the great German thinker recognized, except that Malebranche does not claim God could not make the world better than it is, stipulating instead that to make the world more perfect he would need to 'change the simplicity of his ways' and multiply the laws of motion.[62] But Malebranche's idea that 'our world, however imperfect one wishes to imagine it, rests on laws of motion which are so simple and natural that it is perfectly worthy of the infinite wisdom of its author',[63] did little to reassure those worried by its rigidly mechanistic implications.

As Bayle asserts, but Leibniz denies, Malebranche's claiming God's *volontés générales* govern everything that occurs, all relations and effects in the world, effectively imposes a 'metaphysical' necessity on God, notwithstanding his designating these laws a 'general Providence'; this did not, however, prevent the wily Bayle championing Malebranche against Arnauld, or extensively utilizing Malebranche's strategy in his *Pensées diverses* of 1682 and elsewhere.[64] Malebranche's tenet that 'God does not ordinarily distribute His grace except by general laws,'[65] and that it is presumptious and superstitious to suppose that God regularly intervenes in the affairs of men, on the basis of *volontés particulières*, contrary to these rulings, reduces divine Providence, at the very least, to a wholly exceptional suspension of nature's laws.

Malebranche claimed that God governs by 'general laws', not *volontés particulières*,

---

[60] Fénelon, *Oeuvres complètes*, ii, 70–1, 154–5; Riley, 'Introduction', 77–80.
[61] Nadler, *Arnauld*, 181; Sleigh, *Leibniz and Arnauld*, 153–6.
[62] Leibniz, *Theodicy*, 254; Malebranche, *Treatise on Nature*, 116–24.
[63] Malebranche, *Treatise on Nature*, 117; Funkenstein, *Theology*, 291–3.
[64] Riley, 'Introduction', 81–4; Labrousse, *Pierre Bayle*, ii, 204–14.
[65] Malebranche, *Treatise on Nature*, 133.

submitting 'Himself to the laws which He has established because He wills what is good rather than is ruled by an absolute necessity'.[66] Unfavourable reaction compelled the great Oratorian to temporize somewhat so that, from the 1684 edition on, he padded his *Treatise on Nature and Grace* with additional extracts from the Church Fathers and Augustine to heighten the impression of submission to tradition and authority. But he still resolutely stuck to his main points, continually reaffirming his doctrine of 'general providence' and 'general laws', as well as the absolute dichotomy of body and mind, enabling him to mount a sturdy defence of belief in spirits, angels, and demons in his *Entretiens sur la métaphysique et sur la religion* (1688).[67]

Bishop Huet meanwhile intensified his drive against Cartesianism and Spinozism. Despite having, in earlier years, been a zealous Cartesian himself and converted others, including the Caen professor Pierre Cally, to that philosophy,[68] Huet had concluded already, in his *Demonstratio* of 1679, that 'geometrical demonstrations', the mathematical reasoning extolled by Descartes and Spinoza, is assuredly not the only 'clear and distinct' method of argument. On the contrary, he increasingly insisted that proofs based on the evidence of history and Scripture are no less solid and certain than proofs derived from mathematical reasoning.[69] Then, in the late 1680s, he went further, publicly attacking the Cartesians, provoking a storm at Caen, and publishing his *Censura philosophiae Cartesianae* (1689) and *De Concordia Rationis et Fidei* (1690), vehemently anti-Cartesian works which delighted the Jesuits but greatly disturbed Bossuet, denouncing 'geometrical' reason, the reason of Descartes and Spinoza, as entirely illusory, a broken reed.[70] 'Their imagined eternal truths,' he held, 'are really pure abstractions lacking all reality.'[71] What does a line which has no width, or a perfect circle, have to do, he demanded, with the real world? Once himself a Cartesian, Huet had become the leading French philosophical anti-rationalist, sceptic, and fideist.[72]

Huet fought to establish a new relationship between reason and faith, defining true reason as that of philology and 'solid erudition', not the shadowy, empty reason of Descartes. The root cause of the spiritual malaise gripping France, the 'sickness' of the age he calls it, was, according to his diagnosis, the insidious and growing tendency to subordinate Revelation to reason, an impulse deriving from Descartes and culminating in 'Benedictus Spinoza, author of the *Tractatus Theologico-Politicus* . . . that horrible and sacriligious book full of impiety, ignorance and madness'.[73] Cartesian 'reason', he urges, leads directly and inevitably to the triumph of Spinoza and

---

[66] Ibid., 118–19; Leibniz, *Theodicy*, 254.

[67] Malebranche, *Dialogues*, 233–5, 276–9; Labrousse, *Pierre Bayle*, ii, 207–12.

[68] Kors, *Atheism in France*, i, 283–4.   [69] Ibid.; Dupront, *Pierre-Daniel Huet*, 279–84.

[70] [Le Clerc], *Bibliothèque Universelle* XV (1689), pp. 335, 339; Bayle, *Historical and Critical Dictionary*, 393; at Caen, several former friends and colleagues, notably Pierre Cally, broke off all contact with him; in 1686 Cally was obliged to stop teaching and left the university; Huet, *Commentarius*, 338–9, 388–9; Vernière, *Spinoza*, 255; Kors, *Atheism in France*, i, 283.

[71] Tolmer, *Pierre-Daniel Huet*, 436–41.

[72] Popkin, *History of Scepticism*, 212, 214, 290; Popkin, *Third Force*, 236–7, 245.

[73] Huet, *De Concordia*, 76–8; Kors, 'Skepticism', 206–7.

therefore the ruin of everything. For Descartes' methodology of 'clear and distinct' ideas replaces all authority, as well as reason based on 'true erudition', with a mathematical logic which destroys everything accepted in the past, effectively licensing everyone to follow Spinoza's path.

One major cause of the disaster, asserts Huet, is the decline of 'solid erudition', especially knowledge of Hebrew, philology, ancient history, and classical philosophy. Here, as in his *Demonstratio*, he insists on the vital importance of studying ancient peoples and cultures, so as to outflank and discredit the 'geometric reason' of the Cartesians and Spinozists with universal theological truths which, though only realized in their most complete form in Christianity, were rudimentarily adopted and propagated by the pagan philosophers and religions of antiquity.[74] Thus, held Huet, most thinkers of ancient Greece and Rome taught freedom of the will, immortality of the soul, divine Providence, and other essential, timeless, and fundamental doctrines.[75] Yet this, as some contemporaries noted, was a dangerously double-edged argument, apt to encourage the impious to wonder why they needed the Church and its teachings if essentially the same truths were available from ancient Greek authors.[76]

French Cartesians could by no means afford to let the accusation, spread by Huet and the Jesuits, that it was Descartes' principles which 'ont produit le spinosisme', go unanswered. One of those who resolved to blast this calumny was the Benedictine monk Dom François Lamy (1636–1711), accounted by Leibniz 'one of the strongest Cartesians to be found in France'.[77] A nobleman who had abandoned arms for the cloister in 1658, Lamy, long an inmate of the prestigious Congrégation de Saint-Maur, at Saint-Germain-des-Près, became his order's most adept philosopher. Later, while residing in the Benedictine monastery at Maux in the years 1685–7, he conferred with Bossuet and conceived of writing a comprehensive Cartesian refutation of Spinoza *more geometrico*. Initially, Bossuet was encouraging, sharing as he did Lamy's view,[78] also expressed by Le Vassor, that Spinozism was making disconcertingly rapid progress, especially among the upper echelons of French society.

Yet Bossuet, unwilling publicly to exhibit his (gradually diminishing) private sympathies for Cartesianism and mindful of the royal policy on philosophy, rapidly lost his enthusiasm as the task neared completion. When, in 1688, Lamy encountered problems with the censorship authorities and requested his help, Bossuet, who had for a long time equivocated over whether it was best to attack Spinoza explicitly or try to freeze him into oblivion by boycotting all mention of him, declined to assist; meanwhile, Arnauld, having lost his own refutation of the *Tractatus* not only preferred not to refute but, reportedly, refused even to read the *Opera Posthuma*.[79] Malebranche, for his part, politely praised Lamy's method and conclusions but similarly feared lest such a refutation prove counter-productive by further focusing attention on Spinoza. Malebranche considered his own strategy in his *Entretiens* of 1688, countering Spin-

---

[74] Dupront, *Pierre-Daniel Huet*, 55–60, 80–2.   [75] Huet, *De Concordia*, 144–51, 153–65, 166–7.
[76] Hazard, *European Mind*, 64.   [77] Leibniz, *Theodicy*, 359; Leibniz, *New Essays*, 383.
[78] [Lamy], *Nouvel Athéisme renversé*, avertissement, p. v; Vernière, *Spinoza*, 242.
[79] Bossuet, *Correspondence*, iii, 469, 492–3; Arnauld, *Oeuvres* X, p. xvi.

oza's core arguments in general rather than specific terms, and without mentioning the renegade Jew or his books by name, so that only the most learned should recognize to whom he was alluding, a better approach.[80] In any case, the Sorbonne disliked the overtly Cartesian tone of Lamy's text so that approval was withheld and the manuscript left for a nearly a decade to gather dust.[81]

But the policy of silence proved unsustainable. Far from fading, Spinozism seemingly gained ground in the France of the 1690s at many levels of society. If there were still those, observes Lamy in his preface, who prefer to 'dissimuler ces erreurs' rather than confront them openly, the reality was that Spinozism 'a déjà fait trop de bruit chez les libertins et fait tous les jours trop de progrès pour pouvoir prétendre le supprimer par cette dissimulation'.[82] It was essential, he insisted, to disabuse *les Spinosistes* of the notion they might well now have that the French authorities and Church were afraid of them. It was time to show that 'reason' no less than Revelation establishes 'true religion' and can defeat Spinoza's sophisms. Although there was still much hesitation as to whether it was better to keep it back or publish, some powerful figures in the academic and ecclesiastical hierarchy tended to agree, so Lamy's manuscript was dusted down, touched up, primed with approbations, and published.[83]

According to the first approbation, dated 14 June 1696, penned by Monseigneur Fénelon, now Archbishop of Cambrai, in person, the 'erreurs de Spinosa sont si monstrueuses qu'il est étonnant qu'on ait besoin de les réfuter'; yet some people were being misled, Spinoza having given his chimera 'une apparence de grands principes de métaphysique' by employing the geometric method; this semblance 'd'exactitude et de démonstration', lamented Fénelon, had sufficed to induce some 'hommes superficiels et corrompus' to embrace incredulity.[84] The second and third *approbateurs* were, respectively, the Bishop of Soissons and Monsieur Hideux, a prominent figure at the Sorbonne, who deemed Spinoza's philosophy the end of all submission, authority, and faith and 'en matière de religion une indifférence de pensées, de discours et de culte, qu'on ne peut envisager que comme l'impiété même'.[85] The last *approbateur*, the director of the Bibliothèque Mazarine, portrayed the Spinozist threat in even more apocalyptic terms: since it was now evident that Spinozism seduces the unlettered as well as 'tous ceux qui se picquent de bon sens', nothing now mattered more than to overthrow 'tout l'abominable système de ce méchant philosophe, et faire triompher de ses vaines subtilités, la Foi et la morale chrétienne'.[86]

Since the 1680s Spinozism had perceptibly broken through the barriers normally insulating French cultural life from ideas emanating from Protestant lands. How high a hurdle Spinoza's books and ideas had surmounted in becoming widely known in France is reflected in Lamy's comments about what he knew of efforts to combat

---

[80] Malebranche, *Dialogues*, 138, 150; Vernière, *Spinoza*, 248; Spink, *French Free Thought*, 258.
[81] Hubert, 'Premières refutations', 10, 133. [82] [Lamy], *Nouvel Athéisme renversé*, 15.
[83] Ibid.; Charles-Daubert and Moreau, *Pierre Bayle. Écrits*, 154–7.
[84] [Lamy], *Nouvel Athéisme renversé*, 'Approbation de Monseigneur de Fénelon'; Kors, 'Skepticism', 196–7.
[85] [Lamy], *Nouvel Athéisme renversé*, *approbation* dated Paris, 15 May 1696.
[86] Ibid., 'approbation de Monsieur Guland'; Kors, *Atheism in France*, i, 125.

Spinoza in Holland. He has heard, he says, of two Dutch refutations, Kuyper's *Arcana Atheismi* and Aubert de Versé's *L'Impie convaincu*, but had read neither 'c'est à dire point de tout et je n'en ai pas même eu envie,' having gathered from reviews in journals what 'deplorable' sentiments they contain.[87] In consequence, Lamy assaults Spinoza in a 500-page work, on which the very fate of Cartesianism in France was seen by many to depend, working in an intellectual vacuum, knowing virtually nothing of the already huge relevant literature produced outside France.

Lamy, like Huet and Bayle, claims Spinoza's ideas are scarcely original, indeed, that most had long been current and previously attracted nothing but the 'mépris et l'indignation du monde'. They now posed a dire threat both inside and outside France, but not because of their novelty.[88] Spinoza's unequalled malignancy Lamy ascribes (like Bayle) to his ability to weld it all into a 'nouveau système', thereby imparting to old errors 'un tour de nouveauté et un certain air d'enchaînement qui diminue beaucoup l'horreur que la nature même y a attaché'.[89] No one else had successfully integrated the mass of absurd 'extravagances' found in the works of others 'sans ordre, sans méthode, sans suite, et d'une manière disloquée, *tanquam scopiae dissolutae*', into a coherent 'corps de doctrine et un système suivi, comme a fait Spinosa'.[90] Consequently, absurdities which would have had little impact singly radiate a fatal attraction on corrupt, presumptious libertines who 'se picquent de force d'esprit' when seemingly forged into a coherent and cogent whole by Spinoza, cunningly mingled, to lend plausibility, with 'des principes incontestables'.[91]

Lamy's objective is to blast Spinoza but also, and no less important, to rescue Cartesianism from the suspicion of having given birth to Spinozism. Much of his text, accordingly, seeks to prove that Descartes and Spinoza held completely divergent views of God, nature, substance, and also the human soul, on which Lamy was an acknowledged expert, having previously written arguing that no 'cause ordinaire' can explain the interaction of mind and body which can therefore only be attributed 'à la puissance et à la sagesse infinie du Créateur'.[92] Even if Spinoza began as a Cartesian, his systematic perversion of Descartes' key concepts, urges Lamy— reminding readers of Spinoza's letter to Tschirnhaus of May 1676, in his *Opera Posthuma*, in which he disdainfully dismisses Descartes' principles concerning natural things as 'useless' and 'absurd'[93]—should no more be laid at Descartes' door than that of anyone else.[94]

But if Lamy and his *approbateurs* confronted Spinoza they also, in a sense, assisted the cause of radical thought much as Bossuet and Malebranche had feared. Among

---

[87] [Lamy], *Nouvel Athéisme renversé*, 13–14.

[88] Not least in princely courts, he notes, referring to a paper he had written answering Spinoza's 'mockery' of the Incarnation some years before at the request of a diplomat 'qui se trouva engagée dans une cour étrangère, où de jeunes seigneurs devenus, en partie, disciples de Spinosa, dogmatisoient hautement contre la possibilité de l'Incarnation', ibid., 187.

[89] Ibid., 14.   [90] Ibid.   [91] Ibid., 76; Vernière, *Spinoza*, 248.

[92] Charles-Daubert and Moreau, *Pierre Bayle. Écrits*, 154; Kors, *Atheism in France*, i, 335–6.

[93] Spinoza, *Opera*, iv, 332.

[94] [Lamy], *Nouvel Athéisme renversé*, 490–1; Spink, *French Free-Thought*, 259.

previous large-scale French refutations of Spinoza, Huet's had appeared exclusively in Latin and only the now boycotted Le Vassor had debated propositions from the *Ethics* in French. But Lamy went further, justifying his doing so by remarking that it was by no means only hardened libertines who were reading Spinoza in France but also deeply troubled spirits, wrestling silently with 'le spinosisme' and that these readers desired nothing more than to be given convincing arguments with which to repel the Spinozist demon. On these grounds he quoted numerous propositions from the *Ethics*, translating and explaining extensive passages in readily accessible French. It was doubtless owing to this, and the fact that Lamy's book had a wide audience despite his less than convincing counter-arguments, that moved some worried critics to suggest it should itself be assigned 'au nombre des livres dangereux'.[95]

iii. Régis and the Failure of French Cartesianism

Following Lamy's intervention, there was less reticence about Spinoza in French public life and the disturbing reality, now increasingly widely acknowledged, that 'l'athéisme', as Veyssière de la Croze, expressed it in 1711, 'eut fait tant de progrès dans un siècle si éclairé'.[96] At the same time, Lamy failed either to capsize Spinoza or rescue Cartesianism from its deepening double predicament of internal dissension and implication in the origins of radical thought. With Arnauld dead since 1694 and Malebranche refusing to engage Spinoza head on, this left only Pierre-Sylvain Régis among prominent French Cartesians with the weight and reputation to salvage Lamy's faltering counter-offensive. Nor did he evade the challenge. In his 500-page *L'Usage de la raison et de la foi* (1704) Régis sought to provide a sturdier Cartesian refutation of Spinoza, rigorously examining his basic propositions on God, man, and the universe.

After studying at the Sorbonne and becoming a Cartesian in Paris, the young Régis emerged during the 1660s and 1670s as head of a Cartesian coterie in Toulouse and Montpellier. Already a veteran adversary of Aristotelianism and *Malebranchisme*,[97] he figured less prominently in intellectual debate after returning to Paris in 1680 than he would surely otherwise have done, being under pressure not to defy royal policy by propagating Cartesianism too openly. Nevertheless, in 1690 he brought out a three-volume general exposition of his system, firmly differentiating his position from those of Arnauld and Malebranche. He also published a vigorous rebuttal of Huet's *Censura* in 1691, and clashed with Leibniz, in the *Journal des Scavants* for 1697, accusing him of seeking to 'établir sa réputation sur les ruines de celle de M. Descartes'.[98]

In his last major work, *L'Usage* of 1704, Régis proclaims God more emphatically than Descartes 'l'esprit parfait et supersubstantiel' wholly outside the duality of

---

[95] Vernière, *Spinoza*, 250, 258; Charles-Daubert and Moreau, *Pierre Bayle. Écrits*, 76–7, 157–8; Kors, 'Skepticism', 199; Bloch, 'Parité', 205.

[96] Veyssière de la Croze, *Dissertation sur l'athéisme*, 251; Brogi, *Cerchio*, 156.

[97] Walch, *Philosophisches Lexicon*, 143–4; Watson, *Downfall*, 75–81.

[98] Quoted in Vernière, *Spinoza*. 254.

substance constituting the universe.[99] In some respects a more orthodox Cartesian than Malebranche,[100] he affirms the existence of spirits separate from bodies, the immortality of the soul, and the freedom of the will, in typically Cartesian fashion. Nevertheless, Régis diverges markedly from earlier Cartesians not only in designating God 'supersubstantiel' but also in other ways, his rebuttal of Spinoza including strikingly paradoxical elements which presumably disconcerted many a reader and could even be seen as indicative of the pending breakdown of the Cartesian system in the French intellectual world. Indeed, his exposition occasionally lurches perilously close to Spinoza's stance, as in one place, while expounding his disturbingly narrow concept of the 'freedom' of God, he acknowledges himself.[101] Régis, moreover, concedes that death 'détruit l'âme, en détruisant le rapport que l'esprit a au corps avec lequel il est uni', and hence eliminates the soul in its specific individuality, which cannot endure once the union with the body is dissolved.[102] Still more problematic is the startling way Régis combines Cartesian certainty concerning physical reality, or extension, with a thoroughgoing fideism regarding the supernatural and articles of faith, though here too he might be said merely to be following Descartes.[103] Eschewing Malebranche's (and Andala's) majestic integration of nature and grace, Régis proclaims the supremacy of reason in the sphere of the knowable, which he confines to the purely physical domain, while equally urging the total invalidity of reason beyond that sphere. Reason lacks all force, he holds, outside the realm of bodily substance: as regards God, faith, and the soul, the only dependable guide is the Church and its doctrines.

Régis' book is a notable landmark in the French intellectual crisis of Louis XIV's reign, above all because it marks the virtual withdrawal of Cartesianism from the battle to establish the core elements of religion philosophically, by means of reason. It represents a conscious abandonment of the central arena in the face of empiricism, Leibniz, Bayle, and the Spinozists. By firmly limiting reason's applicability to just one of Descartes' substances, Régis effectively concedes, along with Bayle, that reason cannot buttress belief in Scripture, Creation *ex nihilo*, divine Providence, miracles, free will, or ecclesiastical authority and that, conversely, for the philosopher, there is no appeal to Scripture or God when fighting Spinoza's propositions about God, man and the universe. Hence, in the course of his fascinating analysis of Spinoza's theory of religion as a social and political instrument designed to instil obedience, Régis merely remarks that it is useless to appeal to Scripture or the Church when opposing such ideas philosophically.[104] The only intellectual antidote is to expose the contradictions in Spinoza's reasoning.[105] No one can doubt, affirms Régis, that while the faith of Jesus Christ is under threat from many quarters in France at the

---

[99] Régis, *L'Usage de la raison*, 51–5, 77, 79; Vernière, *Spinoza*, 256; Watson, *Breakdown*, 89; Woolhouse, *Descartes, Spinoza, Leibniz*, 23–4; Kors, *Atheism in France*, i, 354–5.

[100] Nadler, *Malebranche and Ideas*, 95, 134, 151.   [101] Régis, *L'Usage de la raison*, 77–9.

[102] Ibid., 79; see also Régis, *Système de philosophie*, i, 265–9.

[103] Régis, *L'Usage de la raison*, 216; Leibniz, *Theodicy*, 305; Vernière, *Spinoza*, 255.

[104] Régis, *L'Usage de la raison*, 284–5.   [105] Ibid., 285.

outset of the new century, the pre-eminent threat comes from Spinoza and the *Spinosistes*.[106] The special potency of Spinozism, Régis, like Bayle, Lamy, Le Vassor, and others, attributes to its supremely integrated, systematic character, its offering a rational and completely connected account of reality. But after dramatically high-lighting the challenge facing philosophers, Régis rather lamely claims there is no philosophical defence, leaving Cartesian opponents of Spinozism without any weaponry based on reason.

In his key chapter 'Comment on peut defendre l'autorité des miracles', Régis first grants that Spinoza denies miracles with a cogency unequalled by previous thinkers and then stipulates that such reasoning can be overthrown only by faith and ecclesiastical authority—not philosophy.[107] Certainly, continues Régis, alluding to Malebranche, some 'modern philosophers' seek to fortify the central Christian mysteries, including the Eucharist, by way of reason. But they are wasting their time, he contends, locked in a self-defeating exercise.[108] Similarly, the other *fundamenta* of Christianity are not defensible philosophically: 'on ne peut démontre,' he insists, 'ni même expliquer le mystère de la Trinité, par la raison naturelle.'[109] Adopting the same stance on the issue of angels and spirits, Régis makes no effort to emulate Malebranche in claiming the 'power of angels over bodies, and consequently over us, derives only from a general law which God has made for Himself, to move bodies at the will of angels.'[110] On the contrary, he admits 'nous ne pouvons concevoir comment les anges opèrent sur les choses extérieures' from which it follows, he says, that everything faith teaches concerning angels 'est inexplicable'; accordingly, here too 'il se faut croire avec soumission à l'autorité divine, sans entreprendre de l'expliquer.'[111]

Most perplexing of all is Régis' 20-page concluding 'réfutation de l'opinion de Spinosa touchant l'existence et la nature de Dieu'.[112] Régis, like Lamy, sets out the basic propositions of Spinoza's *Ethics* but offers no real critique of Spinoza's doctrine of substance. Here again the main defence is fideistic. Thus, when considering Spinoza's axiom 'Id, quod per aliud non potest concipi, per se concipi debet' (What cannot be conceived through something else, must be conceived through itself),[113] Régis grants this is true but only within the domain of what is conceivable. Valid in the realm of reason, this axiom has no applicability, he insists (like Condillac later), with regard to inconceivable things: 'tels sont les mystères de la religion chrétienne, qui ne sont pas proposez pour estre conçus, mais pour estre crus'.[114] At least some readers found this exasperatingly weak.[115]

The disturbing, unsatisfactory results of Régis' project confirmed in not a few minds both the bankruptcy of Cartesianism and the inability of the French

---

[106] Ibid.   [107] Ibid., 288–9.   [108] Ibid., 317–43; see Malebranche, *Dialogues*, 260–2.

[109] Régis, *L'Usage de la raison*, 346.   [110] Malebranche, *Dialogues*, 234.

[111] Régis, *L'Usage de la raison*, 374.   [112] Ibid., 481–500.

[113] Spinoza, *Opera*, ii, 46; *Collected Works of Spinoza*, i, 410; Régis, *L'Usage de la raison*, 488.

[114] Régis, loc.cit.; Condillac, *Traité*, 151–2.

[115] See, for instance, BM Aix-en-Provence MS 818 (774) [Languener (Langenhert?)], 'Apologie de Spinosa contre Régis', 1–3.

intellectual establishment to counter the grave 'conséquences que [Spinoza] tire de ses principes'.[116] If Lamy and Régis had conspicuously failed, where *was* the philosophical antidote to the seeping venom? Several questioning intellects, such as Boulainvilliers and the Dutch philosophy teacher Gaspar Langenhert, a former adherent of Descartes and Geulincx, who had settled in Paris in 1697, evidently considered Régis' fideistic solution completely useless. Langenhert, who had been a teacher in Zwolle (and presumably an acquaintance of Leenhof and Hakvoord), caused a brief stir by opening a private philosophy school in Paris in 1701. Having written a refutation of Spinoza which he dedicated, in July 1698, to the Archbishop of Paris and which remains to this day unpublished (deposited in the Mazarine Library), he gave public lectures outlining what he claimed was a completely new philosophy based on principles of reason and the sciences 'qui renversoient tous les différens systèmes que l'on avoit vu jusqu'alors' and especially those of Descartes and Spinoza.[117] He presented his system in the first issue of a new journal, the *Philosophus Novus*, in October 1701, but, assailed by opponents, and unable to resolve the difficulties which critics pointed out, soon ceased both his journal and lectures.[118]

During the next few years, the French hierarchy redoubled its efforts to check the advance of radical deism. François Lamy's 398-page *L'Incrédule amené à la Religion par la raison* (Paris, 1710) is noteworthy chiefly for its popular tone, being expressly targeted at servants, shopkeepers, and tradesmen with little education. Countering a new kind of popular Spinozism which, according to Lamy, was spreading among the French population, this text broaches the ideas of 'les athées naturalistes ou materialistes' on a somewhat simplistic level, insisting that belief in the Christian mysteries must be a conscious decision based on reason.[119] More substantial and widely noticed was Fénelon's *Démonstration de l'existence de Dieu* (Paris, 1713). Despite its having been written many years earlier, Fénelon decided to publish it at this juncture—two years before his death and that of Louis XIV—owing to the widely perceived need to urge the 'argument from design' more effectively across a broad front of society. But there was still much hesitation as to whether it was tactically better to do so with or without engaging in a direct offensive on Spinoza.

Fénelon, one of the most elegant and effective French prose writers of the age, had, like Bossuet and Malebranche, long felt disinclined needlessly to draw attention to Spinoza's philosophy. However, senior figures in the hierarchy were apprehensive at the prospect of such an important text appearing without any direct engagement with

---

[116] See, for instance, 3–5; Leibniz, *Theodicy*, 305, 330; Boulainvilliers, *Oeuvres philosophiques*, i, 230; Brogi, *Cerchio*, 157.

[117] [Camusat], *Histoire critique*, ii, 130–1; Vernière, *Spinoza*, 235–40; Langenhert published, among other things, an edition of Machiavelli in Amsterdam, in 1699; Vernière does not make the assumpion I have made (previously suggested, among others by Benítez) that Langenhert and the supposed 'M. Languener médecin suisse mort à Paris vers 1740' who wrote the manuscript critiques of Régis and Fénelon defending Spinoza, preserved in Aix-en-Provence, are in fact one and the same; see Vernière, *Spinoza*, 398; Benítez, *Face cachée*, 18, 56, 313.

[118] Kors, *Atheism in France*, i, 284, 376–7; Kors, 'Skepticism', 213–14.

[119] Lamy, *L'Incrédule amené*, 84–5, 104–9.

Spinoza, leaving the bishop vulnerable to the charge that in taking up his pen against France's freethinkers he had unaccountably forgotten (or not dared) to attack 'les Spinosistes'.[120] Consequently, the book appeared furnished with a 50-page preface lambasting Spinoza, apparently unauthorized by Fénelon, by the redoubtable Jesuit, Father René-Josèphe Tournemine, who had been editing the *Mémoires de Trévoux* since 1701. Tournemine's task was to show how Fénelon's arguments against 'atheism' in general apply also specifically to Spinozism, and 'son ouvrage suffit pour destruire toutes les espèces d'athéisme.'[121]

Rejecting Bayle's argument that there exist genuine atheists and Spinozists who really deny the existence of a providential God, Tournemine maintains 'il n'y a point de véritables athées.'[122] He too quotes Spinoza verbatim in translation and, analysing fundamental key propositions from Part I of the *Ethics*, identifies what he considers to be fundamental contradictions in Spinoza's reasoning.[123] The doctrine of one substance is pronounced completely nonsensical given 'l'impossibilité d'une matière pensante'.[124] But such issues, says Tournemine, are secondary to Fénelon's key argument with which he himself was in entire agreement: no one who contemplates the 'structure générale de l'univers', or the marvellously intricate formation of the minute organisms revealed by the miscroscope, can conceivably doubt that our universe was created by a providential, law-giving, omnipotent, and supremely intelligent being.[125] A highly contentious feature of Tournemine's intervention against Spinozism was his claim—evidently 'in the air' at the time—that *Malebranchisme*, which he despised, leads directly to Spinozism. There was a scandal, Malebranche protested in the highest quarters. The king's confessor, the Jesuit Father Le Tellier, ordered Tournemine to apologize which, somewhat grudgingly, he did in his journal.[126]

One of those unimpressed with the efforts of Lamy, Régis, Tournemine, and Malebranche against Spinoza, was the gifted young scientist Dorthous de Mairan. In September 1713 Mairan, possibly prompted by the Tournemine commotion, started a remarkable correspondence with the now elderly and ailing Malebranche. Writing from his home in the southern town of Béziers, Mairan proclaimed himself a zealous student of science and mathematics, strongly influenced by Malebranche's thought, who, however, was encountering grave philosophical difficulties. His Christian faith had been undisturbed until he had begun reading Spinoza. Such was his perplexity since doing so, though, he had felt obliged to reread the *Ethics*, searching for the fallacies which must assuredly be there. Yet while filled with repugnance and moral outrage, and awed by the terrifying social, religious, and political consequences 'qui suivent de ses principes', as well as deep commiseration for mankind should Spinoza

---

[120] Tournemine, 'Préface', 26–8.   [121] Ibid., 54.

[122] Ibid., 13; *L'Europe Savante* viii (1719), pp. 186–8; Kors, *Atheism in France*, i, 42, 179–80; Schröder, *Ursprünge*, 60, 69, 71.

[123] Tournemine, 'Préface', 36–9.   [124] Ibid., 35.

[125] Ibid., 7, 18, 20, 54; Fénelon, *Démonstration*, 225–7; Vernière, *Spinoza*, 230–1.

[126] Kors, *Atheism in France*, i, 378.

prevail, he had been unable to uncover any *non sequitur*. On the contrary, 'plus je le lis, plus je le trouve solide et plein de bon sens.'[127] Though still unknown at the time—he was soon to astound France by winning the Academy of Bordeaux's annual prize three years running (1715–17) with his essays on ice and barometers—he professed himself a scientist sworn to accept only faultless 'geometric' proofs and, while his missive was couched as a plea for help, it was unmistakably also a challenge. In short, he did not know 'par où rompre la chaîne de [Spinoza's] démonstrations'[128] and called on Malebranche, the one philosopher in France, he did not doubt, capable of crushing Spinoza's sophistries, to do so.

Malebranche answered briefly at first, dismissing Spinoza's system as 'fort obscur et plein d'équivoques', as well as contrary to religion.[129] But Mairan refused to be fobbed off with this and wrote again, urging that if, at first sight, Spinoza's propositions seem extravagant paradoxes, on closer examination, it seems that 'au contraire, rien n'étoit plus solide ni mieux lié que ses principes.'[130] Malebranche wrote again at greater length, but still dismissing Spinoza in vague terms which increasingly exasperated the young Mairan. Was one to suppose, he wrote months later in terms barely falling short of impertinence, after vainly trying for nearly a year to be shown the weak link, that Spinoza's principal propositions could not be overthrown? He had repeatedly asked Malebranche to point out 'en rigueur géométrique, le paralogisme d'un système que l'interêt public et particulier vous engagent de détruire' but received no real answer. He had looked up all the relevant arguments in Malebranche's published work, but had no more found Malebranche's reasoning capable of overthrowing Spinoza's 'demonstrations' than he had Lamy's unconvincing 'réfutation, prétendue géometrique, du système dont il s'agit'.[131] Was he to conclude that Spinoza is 'invincible de front, puisque vous ne jugez à propos de le combattre qu'indirectement'.[132] He could not conceive, he answered, how a philosopher of such standing, who had dedicated his entire life to the search for philosophical truth and defending Christianity, could so perfunctorily dismiss the author they were discussing.

Mairan, moreover, not only charged Malebranche with failing to counter Spinoza but holding a view of extension which effectively amounts to Spinozism. Malebranche had sought to outflank Spinoza by distinguishing between 'étendue intelligible' and 'étendue créé', the first 'nécessaire, éternelle, infinie' the second finite and impermanent, the created world before us. But as Mairan observed—and Aubert de Versé and Tournemine had noted earlier[133]—Malebranche's distinction, when carefully examined, scarcely differs from Spinoza's *natura naturans* and *natura naturata* while individual bodies, for Malebranche, relate to his intelligible extension, like Spinoza's to his extended substance, not as parts but as 'modes'.[134] As for Malebranche's

---

[127] Malebranche, *Correspondance*, 102; Radner, 'Malebranche's Refutation', 115–16.
[128] Malebranche, *Correspondance*, 102.   [129] Ibid., 105–6.   [130] Ibid., 109.
[131] Malebranche, *Correspondance*, 125.
[132] Ibid., 123; Moreau, 'Malebranche et le spinozisme', 28, 31, 38.
[133] Hubert, *Premières réfutations*, 18–19.
[134] Malebranche, *Correspondance*, 165, 170; Radner, 'Malebranche's Refutation', 116–17.

crucial but elusive distinction between God and intelligible extension, Mairan ventured to suggest that it was not Spinoza, but he, who was obscure and full of contradictions. Thoroughly exasperated, Malebranche sent a final letter to Mairan in September 1714, saying that he wished to end their correspondence and cease 'de travailler inutilement'.[135]

That Dorthous de Mairan, soon to be a celebrated scientist of the younger generation, firmly renounced both Cartesianism and *Malebranchisme* and could find no paralogism in Spinoza remained, however, an entirely private matter hidden from the Republic of Letters.[136] Outwardly, the deft Mairan kept up a scrupulously neutral philosophical countenance, though in the 1730s, when it became prudent and fashionable to do so, he evinced Newtonian sympathies. According to Montesquieu, Mairan assiduously cultivated his reputation, always striving to present the most favourable profile possible.[137] This gap between inner intellectual development and an outer façade of neutrality and conformity was an integral feature of the early Enlightenment, and perhaps nowhere more so than in France. A barrier had arisen between the private and public intellectual arenas, creating a disconcerting but unavoidable dichotomy of intellectual spheres and levels of debate, from which luminaries of the French Early Enlightenment—Fontenelle, Boulainvilliers, Dorthous de Mairan, Lévesque du Burigny, Saint-Hyacinthe, Montesquieu, Voltaire, and Diderot—could not easily extricate themselves.

Malebranche never produced a major work specifically against the Spinozists, but one of his younger disciples, the Abbé Claude-François Houtteville (1688–1742), did so, publishing his *magnum opus* at Paris in 1722—*La religion Chrétienne prouvée par les faits*, one of the outstanding works against incredulity of the eighteenth century. It was an immediate success in France and eventually acquired a considerable international reputation, appearing in English in 1739, in German in 1745, and also in Italian.[138] Among his admirers was the Neapolitan Genovesi, who warmly praises his eloquence and the force of his arguments.[139] A former secretary to Cardinal Dubois, a connoisseur of forbidden philosophical literature, Houtteville was an *habitué* of the fashionable Paris salons and knew the debates and reading habits of circles around the post-1715 Court. The success of his book is attributable to his lightness of touch, the unobtrusiveness of his *Malebranchisme*, and his judicious and eclectic use of his predecessors' works. As he says, he had greatly benefited from the earlier efforts of such diverse philosophical authors as Fénelon, Huet, Tournemine, Bayle, Jaquelot, and Lamy.[140]

He undertook to write his defence of Christianity by means of philosophical reason and firm evidence, he explains in his preface, after realizing the immense havoc philosophical unbelief had wrought in France. He considers the peril

---

[135] Malebranche, *Corrrespondance* 171; Spink, *French Free Thought*, 261.
[136] Vernière, *Spinoza*, 326, 392.   [137] Montesquieu, *Oeuvres complètes*, 1002.
[138] *Lettre de R. Ismael ben Abraham*, 2; Stolle, *Anleitung*, 750; Schröder, *Ursprünge*, 107, 138–9, 514–15.
[139] Genovesi, *Elementa Metaphysicae*, ii, 137, 176, 233, 257.
[140] Houtteville, *Religion chrétienne*, i, pp. cxci, cc.

even graver than that posed by the Protestant challenge during the sixteenth-century Wars of Religion. Admittedly, in the France of 1720 the clergy were not being openly attacked with swords and cannon, or churches seized by professed enemies. But this, he says, is only because royal power and the simple faith of the common people restrain the audacity of the impious.[141] For those with discerning eyes, it was obvious that forbidden libertine doctrines were permeating large parts of society. This process of corrosion, moreover, was proceeding all the more rapidly in that a hypocritical façade of faith and reverence was generally kept up, an ubiquitous pretence of piety which had lulled the authorities into a 'sorte d'insensibilité sur les pertes de l'Évangile'.[142]

But who were these philosophical foes who had reduced religion, and with it authority and morality in France, to such dire straits? Houtteville has no doubts on this score, answering emphatically and at enormous length—the 'Spinosistes'. In organizing his work, he had numerous impious writers and thinkers in mind, many of whom were not 'Spinozists' in any precise sense and some of whom could not easily be attacked by name. Fontenelle and Boulainvilliers, writers who had eluded public condemnation even in the stricter days of Louis XIV, were now men of some influence, while, of course, in 1722, Voltaire and Diderot had not yet been heard of. Houtteville, it is true, classifies the 'déistes' separately from the 'Spinosistes' but here apparently he meant Bodin and other Renaissance authors rather than contemporary writers.[143] Several English deistic writers, notably Blount and Toland, are mentioned but touched on only in passing, since Houtteville apparently does not regard them as very important, one reason no doubt for Collins' sour judgement of his massive text as 'defective in materials and very ill put together'.[144]

In fact, from first to last, Spinoza and Spinozism are overwhelmingly the main target. Nor is it hard to see why he focuses so heavily on Spinoza, 'qui nous oppose l'immutabilité des loix de la méchanique du monde'. Granting that this thinker had been refuted, and denounced as an enemy of religion and morality often enough, Houtteville insists that those who had entered the lists against him in the past had for various reasons been reluctant to confront his methodology and full range of arguments head on and, by failing to employ adequate analytical tools, played into the hands of the *incrédules*. Only by setting out Spinoza's propositions more systematically and clearly, and refuting them thoroughly with solid arguments, could defenders of authority, tradition, and religion successfully combat the 'grand nom qu'il s'est fait parmi les incrédules de nos jours'.[145]

How had Spinoza achieved his unequalled influence among the *esprits forts* of France? Like Le Vassor, Massillon, Tournemine, La Veyssière, and others, he believed the chief factor was not Spinoza's system as such, but rather the psychological and social appeal of his audacious, unflinching denial of Scripture, Providence, the Creation, miracles, prophecy, and Christ's divinity and Resurrection. Although the air of

---

[141] Houtteville, *Religion chrétienne*, i, p. vi.   [142] Ibid.   [143] Ibid., i, 91–107 and ii, 12–16, 183, 208.

[144] BL Add. MS 4282, fo. 192. Collins to Des Maizeaux, Baddow Hall, 17 Apr. 1722.

[145] Houtteville, *Religion chrétienne*, i, p. clxxiii.

intellectual rigour and inevitability Spinoza conveys in his writings had proved peculiarly seductive in France, and the abbé had personally met 'divers Spinosistes enchantez de la doctrine de leur chef', he was convinced the supposed 'rigour' was more apparent than real.[146] For when asked to explain the essentials of Spinoza's system, not one had managed to do so, from which Houtteville inferred that it was not Spinoza's cogency which accounted for his success but his impudence and unequalled cunning in creating an air of possessing the truth where everyone else remained steeped in confusion, ignorance, and superstition.

To carry off this pretence Spinoza had been deliberately obscure and also resorted to other tricks to captivate his followers, though he was not, in terms of arguments, at all persuasive. Indeed, insists Houtteville, Spinoza's writings are devoid of both lucidity and charm; 'son stile, si pourtant il en a un, est d'une aridité désolante, sans grâce, sans noblesse, sans naturel.'[147] Yet, paradoxically, this had only increased his appeal for 'ces disciples aveugles'. When pressed, asserts Houtteville—in lines later lifted almost verbatim from the article on 'Spinoza' in the *Encyclopédie* of D'Alembert and Diderot—even Spinoza's most sincere admirers confess his philosophy 'leur étoit une énigme perpetuelle' and that if they ranged themselves among his supporters 'c'est qu'il nioit avec intrépidité ce qu'eux mêmes ils avoient un penchant secret à ne pas croire'.[148] Hence Spinoza's special power stems from the psychological link between illicit philosophy and immoral desires, Spinozism providing the *incrédules* of French high society and beyond with a 'débauche d'esprit, où l'homme vain trouve autant ou plus de charmes que dans celle des sens'.[149] This was how Spinoza had been able to 'étonner et de scandaliser l'Europe par une théologie libertine qui n'avoit de fondement que l'autorité de sa parole'.[150]

But if Spinoza's philosophy is 'obscur et confus presque par tout', in Houtteville's view, he is still sworn to rebut him methodically and, in doing so, quotes verbatim lengthy portions from his works, not just in Latin but also, emulating Lamy and Régis, in French, thereby lending them added currency. He will allow no one to say, as they said of Bayle, that he had misrepresented Spinoza or refused to focus on what he actually claims. Thus Houtteville became one of the chief sources for learning about Spinoza in mid-eighteenth-century Europe. Following Malebranche (and Leibniz) Houtteville accepts that the universe operates according to general 'lois de la nature' but does not agree with Spinoza that such general laws 'soient nécessaires, si par ce terme on entend une nécessité de contrainte, une nécessité forcée, une nécessité telle que le contraire implique contradiction, comme Spinosa paroît l'avoir conçu d'après Strato, et avec Hobbes'.[151] The pivot of Houtteville's argument is that miracles are still conceivable as issuing from 'general laws' as adjustments or twists of those general laws of which we are ignorant, that is, 'liez à l'action des loix générales incon-

---

[146] Ibid., p. clxxxviii.   [147] Ibid., ii, 33–4.
[148] Ibid., i, pp. clxxxviii–ix; [D'Alembert and Diderot], *Encyclopédie*, xv (article: 'Spinoza'), 463; Proust, *Diderot*, 121–156–8; on the evident plagiarism and platitudes of the article 'Spinoza' see below p. 712.
[149] Houtteville, *Religion chrétienne*, i, p. clxxxiii.   [150] Ibid., p. clxxxviii.   [151] Ibid., 36.

nues' within an otherwise fully mechanistic universe.[152] Philosophically, Houtteville believed his main accomplishment was to show 'ce raisonnement de Spinosa contre la possibilité générale de tout prodige n'est qu'un vain sophisme.'[153]

Among the passages he quotes in both French and Latin is that in which Spinoza, in private correspondence, affirms 'la résurrection de Jésus-Christ ne fut point réelle et positive, mais seulement spirituelle et mystique' and that it was 'revealed' only to his disciples.[154] Houtteville devotes several pages to his discussion of the Resurrection which, in the context, is indeed a pivotal issue. Houtteville maintains that the Resurrection is a core miracle of the Christian faith, that there is empirical evidence for it, and its truth cannot be contested. But unlike Locke, who claimed no one had ever dared challenge the authenticity of the Apostles' testimony, Houtteville points out that Spinoza does not think this testimony should be read literally but rather as a figurative way of infusing Christ's death with spiritual signficance. Houtteville then inverts Spinoza's argument, claiming it is he, not the Church, who peddles mysteries and secrets and refuses to accept empirical evidence: 'cette explication est une de ces pensées mystérieuses dont Spinosa ne s'ouvroit qu'à ses fidèles disciples.'[155] Based merely on prejudice, Spinoza's lame explanation flies in the face of the facts: 'c'est la raison elle-même qu'on abandonne.'[156]

Houtteville, like Le Clerc, Abbadie, Le Vassor, Jaquelot, Denyse, and Locke, sought to provide a fully 'enlightened' Christianity which is factual and unchallengeable. Though welcomed in many circles, there was an unfavourable response to his book from Jesuit and other conservative quarters, as well as the radical deist underground. Some critics made a point of challenging his overwhelming concentration on Spinoza. A riposte by the Abbé Desfontaines, published at Paris in 1722, grants that one can not within a single book crush all Christ's enemies, and that Houtteville had, albeit briefly, discussed Pomponazzi and Hobbes as well as Spinoza, but nevertheless castigates Houtteville for assigning an excessive and unhealthy prominence to this single philosopher. When one considers the sweep of history there are, after all, other great challengers to Christ: 'Mahomet vaut bien Spinosa; Cardan est aussi considérable que Hobbes.'[157] But the real catastrophe, argues Desfontaines, is that having placed Spinoza centre-stage, Houtteville fails to fight him effectively, particularly on the subject of miracles. If Spinoza denies Christ's miracles then the correct response is to affirm those wonders in all their glory and not temporize by raising difficult philosophical questions about miracles.

Once the possibility of miracles is admitted, Spinoza's system disintegrates. But what Houtteville had done, charged Desfontaines, was to go even further than the ill-advised Malebranche in seeking to accommodate miracles to the laws of nature,

---

[152] Houtteville, *Religion chrétienne*, i, p. xiii; [Desfontaines], *Lettres de M. l'Abbé*, 69–72; Vernière, *Spinoza*, 418–19.

[153] Houtteville, *Religion chrétienne*, i, 50 and ii, 408–12.

[154] Ibid., ii, 411–14; Spinoza, *Letters*, 348; Misrahi, 'Spinoza and Christian Thought', 396–400.

[155] Houtteville, *Religion chrétienne*, ii, 413; Genovesi, *Elementa Metaphysicae*, ii, 233, 237.

[156] Ibid., 415.   [157] [Desfontaines], *Lettres de M. l'Abbé*, 43.

employing dubious arguments which ultimately only further undermine confidence in divine Providence and miracles.[158] Desfontaines even accuses Houtteville and the *Malebranchistes* of assisting, instead of opposing, the *Spinosistes* by seeking to accommodate miracles within the framework of general laws. For the Spinozists can now assert, together with Houtteville, that 'les miracles sont des effets naturels, inconnus et rares.' 'Que votre système, Monsieur, vous fait d'amis nouveaux.'[159] Perhaps it would have been better had Houtteville not published his book at all. Many formidable authors had preceded him in taking on Spinoza, says Desfontaines—naming Huet, Simon, Mauduit, Lamy, Vitasse, Bayle, and Tournemine—and if Bayle is charged with misconstruing Spinoza, Tournemine 'passe pour celui qui a le mieux réussi'.[160]

Houtteville's was the last major refutation of radical thought, deism, and Spinozism from an essentially Neo-Cartesian perspective.[161] *Malebranchisme* was still a force to be reckoned with in the Catholic world, not least in Italy. But by the 1720s the evident difficulties posed by his system, which several of the French clandestine philosophical texts circulating at this time were given to ridiculing, and the Jesuits relentlessly exposed, had stripped the Cartesian-*Malebranchiste* impulse of its prestige and dynamism. By the late 1720s, in France as in the Netherlands—and generally on the European stage, very soon including even Sweden—Neo-Cartesianism of all hues was a spent force. Even Houtteville, in his later work, the 337-page *Essai philosophique sur la Providence* (Paris, 1728), while still insisting on the distinction between absolute necessity, 'necessité métaphysique et géometrique', that is, Spinoza's necessity, and an actual and real 'necessity' which is not metaphysical, deriving from a God 'parfaitement libre dans le choix du meilleur', laws of nature which do not constrain God,[162] now partly detaches his argument from its originally *Malebranchiste* framework, embracing also Leibnizian–Wolffian formulations. Indeed, no modern philosopher had done more than Leibniz, he affirms, to place divine Providence on a secure philosophical footing.[163]

---

[158] Ibid., 70–2.   [159] Ibid., 69.   [160] Ibid., 52.   [161] Vernière, *Spinoza*, 417.
[162] Houtteville, *Essai philosophique*, 226–32, 239, 313–14; Kors, *Atheism in France*, i, 348–9.
[163] Houtteville, *Essai philosophique*, pp. xv, 232.

26 | Leibniz and the Radical Enlightenment

i. Early Encounters

The thinker to whom the early *Aufklärung* was most indebted and, according to Formey, the 'plus grand génie que l'Allemagne ait produit',[1] Leibniz, was, at the same time, unsurpassed as a philosophical critic and observer of his age. He showed consummate discernment in interpreting new intellectual developments wherever in Europe they arose, often, as with his early appreciation of Locke and Newton, preceding most contemporary continental savants by decades. It is therefore of some significance in the history of ideas that Leibniz, more than any other observer of contemporary thought except perhaps Bayle, understood from the outset the wide-ranging implications for all mankind of the new radical philosophical movement. Committed, as he was, to upholding princely authority and religion, and eager to reunite and strengthen the Churches, Leibniz emerged as the foremost and most resolute of all the antagonists of radical thought, as well as the pre-eminent architect of the mainstream, moderate Enlightenment in Germany, Scandinavia, and Russia.

Many besides Leibniz had, by the 1670s, grasped that existing structures of belief, tradition, and control, indeed the entire prevailing religious, moral, and political system, was threatened by the upsurge of philosophical Naturalism, fatalism, and materialism, with Spinozism forming the backbone of the radical challenge. But Leibniz diverged sharply from others, such as Bossuet, Huet, Steno, Mansvelt, Maresius, Wittichius, Le Clerc, Limborch, Jaquelot, Malebranche, Lamy, Régis, and Houtteville, besides innumerable others who shared this view, in that he did not believe any of the existing alternatives could adequately defend authority, religion, and tradition, though he believed all the rival philosophical systems of his time contained grains of truth requiring careful sifting and critical reassessment. Aristotelianism, Cartesianism, *Malebranchisme*, Huet's and Steno's rejectionist fideism, and, later, Locke's empiricism, indeed all available alternatives, were, in his estimation, alike incapable of providing a cogent, viable, and comprehensive new framework.[2]

---

[1] Formey, *Mélanges philosophiques*, ii, 406.
[2] Leibniz, *Philosophical Essays*, 242–5, 255–6, 284–6; Rutherford, *Leibniz*, 238, 252; Ariew, 'G. W. Leibniz', 36–7.

Leibniz first encountered radical thought in connection with Lodewijk Meyer's anonymously published *Philosophia* in 1666. This publication, he later recalled in his *Théodicée* (1710), provoked a great commotion in Holland, scandalizing the public and precipitating bitter clashes between Cartesians and anti-Cartesians over how best to refute the book's unprecedented claims without yielding too much of theology's traditional primacy to the rising power of philosophy.[3] In a letter of December 1669, he notes that 'Serrarius, Wolzogen, Vogelsang, De Labbadie, Andreae and other adversaries' had endeavoured to demolish the *Philosophia* but found to their cost that this was far from easy. He reveals too that he himself was among those who made enquiries about its author.[4]

Leibniz first mentions Spinoza in 1669, in a letter about the Cartesians to his former teacher, Jacob Thomasius, under whom he had studied in Leipzig in 1661–3. Agreeing 'Clauberg is clearer than Descartes,' Leibniz affirms that none of Descartes' chief disciples and expositors, whom he lists as 'Clauberg, De Raey, Spinoza, Clerselier, Heereboord, Tobias Andreae, and Henricus Regius',[5] had added anything of much importance to Descartes' system. While this may not imply that Leibniz had actually read Spinoza's exposition of Descartes—conceivably he merely echoed the prevailing view at the time—his placing Spinoza third in the list does prove that he then considered Spinoza one of the principal 'Cartesians'. This perception was soon to change. The next year the *Tractatus Theologico-Politicus* appeared in both Holland and Germany, provoking a greater uproar even than Meyer's *Philosophia*. Both Thomasius and Leibniz were among those anxious to discover who this relentless challenger of universally accepted truth was. From Graevius, Leibniz learnt in April 1671, that the 'liber pestilentissimus' (most pestilential book) assailing the authority of Scripture, following the 'Hobbesian path' but 'going much further', was the work of a 'Jew called Spinoza expelled from the synagogue some time ago, due to his monstrous opinions'.[6] In a subsequent letter Graevius, likewise an eager observer of the international philosophical scene, reported that Cartesianism was now dominant in the Dutch universities, Aristotelianism 'prostrate', and his colleague Mansvelt labouring on a full refutation of that 'infamous and horrible' book of Spinoza. In his reply Leibniz, who had now closely examined the *Tractatus*, regretted that a learned man such as Spinoza 'appears to be should have sunk so low', ascribing the main influence on his Bible hermeneutics to Hobbes.[7]

It was in October 1671—having tried Hobbes first the previous year but received no answer—that the adept Leibniz sent his first letter to Spinoza. Addressing him with a Baroque flourish as 'Monsieur Spinosa, médecin très célèbre et philosophe très profond', the young savant confined his queries initially to optics, though evidently this was just a pretext to establish contact.[8] He received a courteous answer, requesting

---

[3] Leibniz, *Theodicy*, 82–3.   [4] Bouveresse, *Spinoza et Leibniz*, 220–1.
[5] Ibid., 221; Friedmann, *Leibniz et Spinoza*, 60; Biasutti, 'Reason and Experience', 47.
[6] Leibniz, *Sämtliche Schriften*, 1st ser. i, 142; Graevius to Leibniz, Utrecht, 22 Apr. 1671.
[7] Ibid., 148. Leibniz to Graevius, Frankfurt, 5 May 1671; Bouveresse, *Spinoza et Leibniz*, 221.
[8] Spinoza, *Letters*, 245–6.

that further letters be sent via The Hague rather than Amsterdam and offering a copy of the *Tractatus* should Leibniz not yet have seen it.[9] Leibniz did indeed continue corresponding with Spinoza, and a later letter of his is known to have contained reactions to the *Tractatus* doubtless expressed in relatively complimentary terms, though unfortunately no letters between the two other than the initial exchange have survived.[10] Meanwhile, when discussing Spinoza with other correspondents, such as Antoine Arnauld late in 1671, Leibniz vehemently condemned the *Tractatus* while taking care not to reveal that he himself was in contact with the culprit, or even knew his name, though he makes clear that he ranked him, whoever he was, beside Bacon and Hobbes as among the foremost moderns.[11]

In Germany as in France, Leibniz could not do otherwise than denounce the *Tractatus* as an exceedingly pernicious work. But he made a particular point of insisting it had not thus far been adequately refuted and on the need for this to be done comprehensively and convincingly. Writing to Jakob Thomasius (again omitting all mention of his being in contact with Spinoza), he stressed the powerful intellect and erudition of the anonymous *theologico-politicus*, discounting Thomasius' recent piece on the *Tractatus* with gentle but unmistakable sarcasm, as a 'refutatio brevis, sed elegans'.[12] Leibniz insisted that what was required was a refutation, learned, solid, and incisive rather than vituperative. Among those he encouraged to attack the clandestine writer 'who, they say is a Jew', and who with some learning and 'much poison' strives to overthrow the *antiquitatem*, *genuinitatem*, and *auctoritatem* of Scripture, was the eminent south German Lutheran theologian, Gottlieb Spitzel. In the general interest, urged Leibniz, a renowned scholar steeped in Hebrew and other oriental languages 'such as you, or someone like you', must demolish the book.[13] Spitzel was distinctly unenthusiastic about taking on the task, however, excusing himself by saying he understood the 'very learned Thomasius and his colleague Rappolt, at Leipzig', had already done so.[14] In his next book, published at Augsburg in 1676, Spitzel did no more than denounce Spinoza as a 'Jew . . . and fanatic, estranged from every religion' so 'impious as to repudiate even the truth of the Biblical miracles', referring readers eager to know more to the refutation by Jacobus Batalier, published at Amsterdam.[15]

Leibniz quickly grasped that the issue was not just Spinoza but something considerably larger—Spinoza's circle, an underground, clandestine, philosophical movement which had taken root in the United Provinces. Gradually he collected shreds of information from correspondents about a phenomenon which clearly intrigued and fascinated no less than disturbed him. From the Cartesian Leiden medical professor, Theodore Craanen, he heard indirectly in April 1672, via a German visitor, that one of the clandestine texts about which he had been enquiring, the *De Jure Eclesiasticorum* (see p. 201 above), was there attributed to Van Velthuysen, while the *Philosophia* was

---

[9] Spinoza, *Letters*, 247–8.
[10] Parkinson, 'Leibniz's Paris Writings', 75; Biasutti, 'Reason and Experience', 46.
[11] Friedmann, *Leibniz et Spinoza*, 66–7.   [12] Ibid., 68.
[13] Leibniz, *Sämtliche Schriften*, 1st ser. i, 193. Leibniz to Spitzel, 8 Mar. 1672.
[14] Ibid., 195. Spitzel to Leibniz, 24 Mar. 1672.   [15] Spitzel, *Felix Literatus*, 143–4.

considered the work of 'Jacobus Korbach' (it was clearly Adriaen who was meant) who had died in prison after being locked up for writing 'impious books', while no one doubted that the *Tractatus* was Spinoza's work, as were other texts of similar, or worse, content which would appear only after his death.[16] A subsequent letter to Leibniz, from Craanen personally, reported that the *Philosophia* was not, as many supposed, by Spinoza but 'by some Amsterdam physician'; it also mentions the bitter quarrel between Maresius and the Cartesians, and agrees with Leibniz that there was still no adequate refutation of the *Tractatus*, although Mansvelt was labouring to complete his.[17]

During the years 1672–6 Leibniz lived in Paris. Doubtless the many distractions of that capital, intellectual and otherwise, in some degree diverted him, at least initially, from his previous keen interest in Dutch radical thought.[18] But equally clearly he retained that interest. Early in his stay he visited Van den Enden, now teaching in the French capital, though conceivably he was then unaware of the close connection between Van den Enden, Spinoza, Koerbagh, and the author of the *Philosophia*.[19] Leibniz frequented Huygens, the most eminent mathematician and scientist then in France, and surely learnt more about Spinoza, Meyer, and Van den Enden from him. He also discussed the menace of Spinozism with Arnauld, Justel, and other French scholarly acquaintances. But it was especially from his young compatriot Tschirnhaus, who was deeply impressed by Spinoza's philosophy and personality and had come to be trusted by Spinoza (as Leibniz himself never was) and accepted as one of the clandestine circle, that Leibniz derived additional information.

Leibniz saw a good deal of Tschirnhaus in Paris and the two became friends. So intense was Leibniz's curiosity about Spinoza's ideas, and his desire to see the manuscript copy of the still unpublished *Ethics* which Spinoza had confided to Tschirnhaus before the latter left the Netherlands—but on condition that he revealed it to no one else without the author's express permission—that he prevailed on Tschirnhaus to write to Spinoza's other young German accolyte, Schuller in Amsterdam, requesting Spinoza's assent.[20] 'Our Tschirnhaus', Schuller duly reported to Spinoza, had arrived in Paris, conferred with Huygens, and was discussing Spinoza only with great discretion, even though the *Tractatus* 'is esteemed by many there and there are eager enquiries as to whether more writings of that same author have been published'.[21] Leibniz was reportedly a man of 'remarkable learning, highly skilled in the various sciences and free from the usual theological prejudices'. Tschirnhaus believed that disclosing the *Ethics* to him would benefit both philosophers but undertook to keep his promise, and not reveal it should Spinoza think otherwise. Tschirnhaus also passed on Leibniz's (highly diplomatic) assurances that he greatly esteemed the *Tractatus* about which 'he once wrote you a letter'.[22] Spinoza had not forgotten his correspondence

---

[16] Leibniz, *Sämtliche Schriften*, 1st ser. i, 200. Walter to Leibniz, Leiden, 13 Apr. 1672.
[17] Ibid., 202–4.   [18] Friedmann, *Leibniz et Spinoza*, 71–2.
[19] Ibid., 71.   [20] Ibid.; Meinsma, *Spinoza*, 462–4; Bouveresse, *Spinoza et Leibniz*, 222.
[21] Spinoza, *Letters*, 325.   [22] Stein, *Leibniz und Spinoza*, 41; Gebhardt, *Spinoza. Briefwechsel*, 364.

with Leibniz, but was puzzled that this learned gentleman, earlier holding an honoured position in Frankfurt, should now be in France (with which the Dutch Republic
was then at war), deeming it inadvisable to 'entrust my writings to him so quickly'.[23]
First he wanted to learn what Leibniz was doing in France and Tschirnhaus' opinion
of him, once he knew him better.

But if Leibniz never saw the *Ethics* in manuscript, he certainly had long conferences
with Tschirnhaus about Spinoza's system, jotting down some highly pertinent notes
as to its content. He discerned as its chief points that 'God alone is substance' (Deum
solum esse substantiam), that man is free only to the extent he is determined by no
external things, and the 'mind is the idea of the body' (mentem esse ipsam corporis
ideam).[24] Intensely interested, Leibniz studied the *Tractatus* once more in Paris,
minutely scrutinizng its arguments and transcribing whole pages of excerpts annotated with comments.[25]

Progressing rapidly in mathematics and science, as well as philosophy, Leibniz
remained in Paris until late in 1676. After accepting his new post at Hanover,
he returned to Germany via England, where he stayed a few days, and Holland, where
at that stage he had far more important philosophical and scientific business, spending two months familiarizing himself not just with the respectable world of learning,
visiting Huygens, Hudde, and Van Leeuwenhoek among others, but also the radical
writers.[26] At Amsterdam he cultivated Schuller, who henceforth served as his link
with the world of Dutch Spinozism, and through whom he became acquainted
with Meyer, Bouwmeester, Jelles, and others of Spinoza's circle. He sufficiently
gained their confidence, or at least Schuller's, to procure copies of several of
Spinoza's unpublished letters. After visiting Leiden, where he saw Pieter de la
Court, he proceeded to The Hague to meet Spinoza himself. The importance of
this for Leibniz emerges from a letter to the Abbé Gallois, written some months
later, in which he mentions conferring with Spinoza 'plusieurs fois et fort longue-
ment'.[27] In later years this fact was confided only to those who were particularly
close to Leibniz, such as the Landgrave Ernst of Hessen-Rheinfels, whom he
assured, in March 1684, that he had spoken with Spinoza at great length and
knew 'quelques-uns de ses sectateurs . . . assez familièrement'.[28] Nor indeed was this
encounter just a matter of intellectual fascination and a desire to meet the relevant
personalities. Leibniz's later admission in his *New Essays* that 'I once strayed a little too
far in another direction, and began to incline to the Spinozists' view which allows God
infinite power only, not granting him either perfection or wisdom, and which dismisses the search for final causes and explains everything through brute necessity' is a
clear enough indication that briefly Leibniz was almost sucked into the radical
orbit himself.[29]

[23] Spinoza, *Opera*, iv, 305.   [24] See Beilage ii in Stein, *Leibniz und Spinoza*, 282–3.
[25] Parkinson, 'Leibniz's Paris Writings', 77–9.
[26] Meinsma, *Spinoza*, 466–7; Friedmann, *Leibniz et Spinoza*, 78; Bouveresse, *Spinoza et Leibniz*, 222.
[27] Bouveresse, *Spinoza et Leibniz*, 223.   [28] Rommel, *Leibniz und Landgraf Ernst*, ii, 535.
[29] Leibniz, *New Essays*, 73; Bouveresse, *Spinoza et Leibniz*, 219.

ii. Leibniz, Steno, and the Radical Challenge (1676–1680)

Leibniz quickly settled in and became a trusted counsellor, as well as librarian and resident *philosophe*, at the court of Brunswick-Lüneburg. With his new multiple function at a medium-sized German court, he was a busy man, but neither his zeal for philosophy and science nor his interest in radical ideas slackened. On the contrary, it is clear Spinoza and Spinozism at this juncture became a fashionable, even pressing, topic at the Hanoverian court.[30] The then ruler, Duke Johann Friedrich, cultivated intellectual pursuits while Sophia, the wife of his younger brother, was renowned for her interest in philosophy. In addition, the formidable Danish scientist and now ecclesiastic, Nicholas Steno, having risen to high status in Italy, arrived at Hanover in November 1677 as the Pope's special envoy, or Vicar Apostolic, to Protestant Germany and Scandinavia.[31] Steno resided at Hanover for several years (1677–80) and it was natural that Leibniz should be assigned to escort and assist him. Furthermore, the childless Duke Johann Friedrich, having himself converted to Catholicism and being anxious to co-operate with the Papacy and with Steno in furthering the Catholic cause in Germany, was keen to learn more about Steno's own conversion and that of Spinoza's former disciple, Albert Burgh.

Early in 1677, at the duke's request, Leibniz passed on his copy of Spinoza's as yet unpublished reply to the letter in which Burgh informs Spinoza of his conversion, repudiating Spinoza's philosophy and urging him to humble himself before Christ while there was yet time. This text Leibniz may have obtained from Spinoza himself, though it seems more likely that it issued from one of his circle, presumably Schuller.[32] Commenting, Leibniz says he had not seen Burgh's letter but, judging from Spinoza's reply, gathered its arguments were weak, though he was also dissatisfied with Spinoza's objections.[33] The issues raised, he stresses, are of overriding importance not just for scholars but also for enlightened princes, since a God-ordained order, political legitimacy, and ecclesiastical authority can not be based on the precarious fideistic principles advanced by Burgh while, if Spinoza's arguments against Revelation and divine Providence stand, revealed religion cannot underpin the social, moral, and political order. It was crucial, therefore, that Spinoza's arguments be effectively countered and a philosophical justification for revealed religion achieved.

Leibniz entirely agrees with Spinoza's rejection of fideistic scepticism: 'ce qu'il dit de la certitude de la vraye philosophie et des démonstrations est bon et incontestable.'[34] Sharing Spinoza's impatience with those who demand to know how a philosopher can be sure he is not mistaken when so many have held, and still hold, different views, Leibniz recommends that such sceptics be sent back to study Euclid and Archimedes to learn that geometric certainty is founded, not on diagrams, but abstract ideas of physical realities reflecting certainties in the interaction and

---

[30] Grua, *G. W. Leibniz. Textes*, 157–64.   [31] Scherz, 'Gespräche', 95; Van de Pas, *Niels Stensen*, 37.
[32] Friedmann, *Leibniz et Spinoza*, 95.   [33] Leibniz, *Sämtliche Schriften*, 1st ser. ii, 7.
[34] Beilage v in Stein, *Leibniz und Spinoza*, 302; Garrett, 'Truth, Method', 26–31.

relationships of real things. Leibniz also concurs that 'justice and charity are the true marks of the Holy Spirit'; but it does not follow, he contends, that those who are pious therefore disdain the particular commandments of God or sacraments and rituals of religion. True piety does not concede that 'tout ce que la raison ne dicte pas, doit passer pour superstition.'[35]

Steno, however, proved a far more redoubtable exponent of fideism than Burgh. Given his high standing in Rome, and the Lutheran allegiance of Hanover's citizenry, his mission was bound to attract widespread and hostile attention, placing Leibniz in an extremely delicate position.[36] Ironically, and slightly uncomfortably for them, both men knew Spinoza and his Amsterdam circle personally and both were professionally involved in confronting the Spinozist challenge.[37] But at the same time there was a crucial difference in attitude. For while Leibniz and Steno were equally keenly aware that Spinoza's principal work, the *Ethics*, survived in manuscript somewhere in Holland and that strenuous efforts were under way, on one side to prevent and the other to ensure publication, Steno, representing as he did Pope and Inquisition, sought to ensure suppression, while Leibniz, for all his appreciation of what was at stake, could scarcely contain his impatience to lay eyes on the printed *Ethics*.

The drama of their encounter was heightened by Steno's recent further conversion and virtual abandonment of all scholarly involvement, about which Tschirnhaus had written, warning Leibniz, from Rome.[38] Where Steno deemed the Catholic cause better off detached, free from entanglement with philosophy and science, Leibniz believed only philosophy can demonstrate universal dependence on a First Cause which is omnipotent, omniscient, and infinitely good.[39] Where Steno increasingly scorned reason, insisting that only faith and the Church's authority can bring sinful man to salvation, Leibniz agreed with Spinoza regarding reason's universal scope and ability to ascertain all truths relevant to man.[40] From being what Leibniz later called 'a great physicist', of formidable skill in anatomy and geology, Steno refused any longer to discuss science at all, an attitude Leibniz found incomprehensible and exasperating, not least since he considered him but a 'mediocre theologian'.[41]

Leibniz had prepared for Steno's arrival by examining the text of his open letter, written in 1671 in reaction to the *Tractatus*, and published at Florence in 1675, to the 'Reformer of the New Philosophy'.[42] Although the epistle nowhere mentions Spinoza by name, it was an open secret in Hanover as elsewhere, that the unnamed philosopher Steno denounced in Florence was his former friend, the author of the *Tractatus*. But Steno here repudiates not only Spinoza but the New Philosophy in general, affirming precisely the kind of fideistic scepticism of which Leibniz too disapproved.[43] In his commentary on Steno's epistle, again written for the benefit of his master, Leibniz steers a judicious middle course, rejecting Steno's emotional, unreasoning,

[35] Beilage v in Stein, *Leibniz und Spinoza*, 301.   [36] Scherz, 'Gespräche', 95–6.
[37] Totaro, 'Niels Stensen', 155, 167; Scherz, *Pionier der Wissenschaft*, 33–6.
[38] Grua, *G. W. Leibniz*, 164.   [39] Scherz, 'Gespräche', 86–7; Lagrée, 'Leibniz et Spinoza', 147.
[40] Leibniz, *Theodicy*, 178–9; Rutherford, *Leibniz*, 7–10; Garrett, 'Truth, Method', 25–9.
[41] Leibniz, *Theodicy*, 178.   [42] Scherz, *Pionier der Wissenschaft*, 278.   [43] Ibid., 30–3.

authority-based conception of faith while equally questioning Spinoza's stance. One cannot jettison mathematical reason or science: the way forward, Leibniz urged, was to reform the New Philosophy, correcting Descartes' and Spinoza's errors, and refining the rules of reasoning, while dismissing Steno's notion of 'true philosophy'.[44] If the Pope's representative seemed to have a point in insisting that most of mankind cannot attain philosophical reason and that only the Catholic Church offers eternal happiness to all, whether intelligent or not, learned or ignorant, Spinoza would doubtless have retorted, remarks Leibniz, that 'les promesses sont belles, mais qu'il a fait un voeu de ne rien croire sans preuve.'[45]

Architects of the moderate mainstream Enlightenment, such as Leibniz in Germany and Magliabecchi in Italy, recoiled from Steno's stern Counter-Reformation summons to submission and blind faith, no less (even if more subtly and less conspicuously) than from the radicalism of Spinoza. In Florence as in Hanover, Steno's sweeping rejection of reason prompted a decided, if concealed, reaction in favour of his adversary who, however blasphemous and intolerable his ideas, inevitably emerged in this context as the champion of reason and philosophy.[46] The saintly lifestyle adduced by Steno as 'proof' of the sanctity and veracity of the one true Church is indeed, observes Leibniz, found among various Churches and sects, added to which saintliness is also feigned by hypocrites and the ambitious.[47] Philosophy, he grants, cannot yet explain how body and mind interact or are connected. But there are many 'propositions importantes' philosophy can reliably explain, thereby confirming the efficacy and timeless validity of such 'démonstrations de géometrie et de métaphysique', leaving no question or doubt in the mind that whatever contradicts such solid propositions 'ne seroit asseurement la parole de Dieu'.[48] Doubtless Steno deserves the eulogies of his piety and zeal. But he has not yet grasped the force of 'metaphysical demonstrations', proofs, Leibniz assured his prince, which accord wonderfully with Christianity, and provided him with infinite satisfaction, affording a foretaste of eternal life.[49]

Moreover, Leibniz disliked the relentless authoritarianism which flows directly from Steno's stance, his conviction that the inner harmony of the Christian State, which depends, according to him, on uniformity of doctrine, faith, and sacraments, is attainable only when enforced by the absolutist prince. Of course, Leibniz too served princely absolutism. But he insists that reason, that is, philosophy, not the requirements of the Church, must be its justifying principle. Hence monarchy, he argues, contradicting Steno, is not always and necessarily the best form of government,

[44] We shall never savour 'les véritables principes bien asseurés', asserts Leibniz, until we attain the utmost rigour in our reasoning; Grua, *G. W. Leibniz, Textes*, 159.

[45] Ibid., 160; Steno, *De Vera Philosophia*, 36–8; Spinoza, *Letters*, 314–16.

[46] Totaro, 'Niels Stensen', 165–7.

[47] 'True perfection', argues Leibniz, consists, contrary to what most men believe, not in a saintly lifestyle 'mais dans la perfection de l'entendement et dans l'empire sur les passions', qualities, he notes, 'aussi rares dans l'Église romaine qu'ailleurs'; Grua, *G. W. Leibniz. Textes*, 161.

[48] Ibid., 162.   [49] Ibid.

though assuredly it is 'plus capable de perfection qu'aucun autre'. At this juncture Leibniz was forming the conception of enlightened absolutism which was to inspire his 'Portrait of a Prince' (1679), a text addressed to Johann Friedrich, which stresses, alongside such traditional accoutrements of princely power as the 'divine law which commands peoples to obey their sovereigns', and the hereditary principle sanctioned by God and the Church, the philosophical requirement that the ruler should (with the help of advisers) supersede his subjects in reason and 'virtue', that is, in liberality, clemency, and magnificence. The 'enlightened' prince, avers Leibniz, upholds the common good and, to do so adequately, must cultivate philosophy and practical wisdom, including history, geography, modern languages, and political science, striving for greatness in his 'generous views' and profound insights.[50]

In January 1678, immediately on publication, Leibniz's copies of Spinoza's *Opera Posthuma* arrived in Hanover. Writing a few days later to Justel in Paris, Leibniz pronounced the *Ethics* replete with 'belles pensées conformés aux miennes', affinities, he says, familiar to 'mes amis qui l'ont été aussi de Spinoza', a further allusion to Meyer, Schuller, and doubtless especially Tschirnhaus. But the philosopher of Hanover also found the *Ethics* full of 'paradoxes' which he considered neither true nor plausible.[51] Chief among these were the doctrine of one substance which is God, created things being modes of God, the doctrine that our soul perceives nothing after this life, and that God is consciousness without understanding and will, which acts only from 'naturae necessitate' (the necessity of Nature). He judged the book dangerous, he adds, for those capable of reading it, though doubtless it would have no impact on most people.[52]

In subsequent months Leibniz meditated continuously on Spinoza's *pulchra cogitata* (beautiful thoughts) while condemning his contention that God lacks will and intellect and acts merely from the necessity of His nature, as the essence of a triangle follows ineluctably from its properties. The analogy is mistaken, he held, because thought does not belong to the nature of a triangle but is inherent in God.[53] Only in a limited sense, argues Leibniz, introducing what was to become one of his most characteristic arguments, are those things 'impossible' which God has decided not to do or produce; for in other circumstances He could have done so. This difference was, and was to remain, the pivotal point of encounter between two of the greatest systems of the Baroque era: for Spinoza, the philosopher who grasps the reality of things knows that what exists exists necessarily, and that what does not exist can not exist, whereas for Leibniz what happens could have happened differently, and whatever exists could be otherwise, had God so willed.[54]

---

[50] Leibniz, *Political Writings*, 94; Riley, 'Introduction' (1972), 19–26.

[51] Leibniz, *Sämtliche Schriften*, 1st ser. ii, 317; Stein, *Leibniz und Spinoza*, 307; Bouveresse, *Spinoza et Leibniz*, 217.

[52] Leibniz, *Sämtliche Schriften*, 1st ser. ii, 318; Friedmann, *Leibniz et Spinoza*, 99–100.

[53] Grua, *G. W. Leibniz. Textes*, 79, 277–84; Friedmann, *Leibniz et Spinoza*, 101; Lagrée, 'Leibniz et Spinoza', 142–3; Bouveresse, *Spinoza et Leibniz*, 217.

[54] Uslar, 'Leibniz' Kritik', 80; Parkinson, 'Philosophy and Logic', 202–3; Rutherford, *Leibniz*, 244; Lagrée, 'Leibniz et Spinoza', 145–7.

iii. Leibniz and the 'War of Philosophies'

There was a definite change in Leibniz's philosophical strategy from the end of the 1670s. Hitherto his aim had been to explore and absorb, a universal *érudit* seeking to shield the New Philosophy from detractors and convince Germany's princes and ecclesiastics of its compatibility with the core doctrines and 'mysteries' of Christianity. From around 1680, however, as his own system matured and Europe's war of philosophies intensified, Leibniz became less enquiring and flexible and more combative in his approach to rival systems which, for the time being, chiefly meant Cartesianism and Spinozism,[55] though he was no less resolute later in opposing Bayle, Locke, and Newton. His objective now was to try to shape the outcome.

His increasing hostility to Cartesianism and Spinozism, however, implied no diminution of his earlier antipathy to fideism, scholasticism, and popular credulity and superstition.[56] Rather, from the 1680s Leibniz's philosophical enterprise consistently manifested two distinct reforming impulses: on the one hand, much (though not all) the scholasticism of the past needed to be swept away, while on the other, much of the New Philosophy had to be resisted. If philosophy and science urgently required reform not everything from the past should be discarded, and much of what was new should be opposed. If religion and popular attitudes had to be changed, the Churches had to be gently steered towards the right path. Most of what was objectionable in conventional religion, he wrote to his ally, the Landgrave von Hessen-Rheinfels, in 1684, was really just prejudice and habit masquerading as indispensable doctrine.[57] But the Church has to sharpen its sense of what is essential and what can be dispensed with, and wake up to the dangers of both 'superstition' and Cartesianism.

Cartesianism, held Leibniz, obstructs the forming of an authentic, effective alliance of the Christian Churches with modern philosophy and science such as the English Newtonians and he himself were groping towards. Despite Descartes' assurances, Cartesianism, Leibniz had convinced himself, ultimately negates belief in a providential Creator and cannot protect the central 'mysteries' of Christian teaching or the foundations of Christian morality.[58] 'Descartes' God, or perfect Being, is not a God like the one we imagine or hope for,' he noted in 1679, but rather 'something approaching the God of Spinoza, namely the principle of things and a certain supreme power, or primitive nature, that puts everything into motion.'[59] Consequently, Cartesianism and *Malebranchisme*, in Leibniz's opinion, far from protecting religion and authority, are merely a prelude to Spinozism.[60]

Like Huygens, Newton (and Spinoza), Leibniz firmly rejected Descartes' laws of

---

[55] Friedmann, *Leibniz et Spinoza*, 114–15, 117; Woolhouse, *Descartes, Spinoza and Leibniz*, 54–5; Rutherford, *Leibniz*, 238; Lagrée, 'Leibniz et Spinoza', 141, 153.

[56] Lagrée, 'Leibniz et Spinoza', 149; Garrett, 'Truth, Method', 27–31.

[57] Rommel, *Leibniz und Landgraf Ernst*, ii, 53–4.

[58] Leibniz, *Philosophical Essays*, 237–8; Leibniz, *Theodicy*, 224–5.

[59] Leibniz, *Philosophical Essays*, 242.   [60] Friedmann, *Leibniz et Spinoza*, 129, 145, 154.

motion and furthermore doubted the soundness of his defence of free will. He was also convinced of the incompatibility of Descartes' concept of substance with the Catholic doctrine of transubstantiation, professing not to see how Cartesians could possibly be sincere Catholics in their hearts.[61] Cartesians, moreover, seemed to him as dogmatic as the Aristotelians, men who, believing they knew all the answers already, tended to neglect experimental science. Cartesianism revealed itself to be a halfway house to Spinozism also in its failure to sustain a God-ordained, absolute system of morality. 'To satisfy the hopes of mankind,' held Leibniz, 'we must prove the God who governs all is wise and will allow nothing to be without reward and punishment; these are the great foundations of morality.'[62] Although among the weaker and least convincing parts of his *Théodicée*, Leibniz valiantly endeavoured to provide a defence of the concept of Hell and eternal damnation as integral features of the 'best possible' of all worlds, claiming there is 'no absolute predestination to damnation; and one may say of physical evil that God wills it often as a penalty for guilt, and often also as a means to an end, that is, to prevent greater evils or to obtain greater good.'[63] In any case, as Lessing later noted, whether Leibniz was sincere or not in defending Hell and eternal torment as divine punishment of man, his system demands such belief.[64]

Leibniz first outlined his chief doctrines as a system in his *Discourse of Metaphysics* (1686) and in subsequent writings continually elaborated and refined these key ideas. His system rests especially on four basic notions, all apparently conceived in opposition to Descartes and Spinoza. First, there is his doctrine of an infinite number of substances (later called 'monads' and compounds of monads) and his principle that 'bodies' must be defined as 'extension' with 'motive force', roundly rejecting both Cartesian extension without motion and Spinoza's extension embodying motion; hence, he argued, the scholastics had not been entirely wrong, after all, in deeming bodies to be 'substantial forms' with some inherent relation to souls.[65] Leibniz held that bodies always have 'motive force' but simultaneously denied, against the Spinozists and Epicureans, that bodies are self-moving or that motion is inherent in matter.[66] At the same time, against the scholastics and with Descartes (and not unlike Newton), he claims the 'phenomena of bodies' and interaction between them 'can always be explained mechanically' except for the original cause of the laws of motion.[67]

Leibniz's second primary concept, the idea of the invisible points of energy he later called 'monads', which are in themselves immaterial but which nevertheless, in aggregates, form the constituent components of matter, provides the crucial bridge connecting the mechanistic order of physical cause and effect, governing bodies, with the

---

[61] Rommel, *Leibniz und Landgraf Ernst*, ii, 54.
[62] Leibniz, *Philosophical Essays*, 243; Mates, *Philosophy of Leibniz*, 45–6.
[63] Leibniz, *Theodicy*, 137; Walker, *Decline of Hell*, 207–17. [64] Walker, *Decline of Hell*, 217.
[65] Leibniz, *Philosophical Essays*, 42–4, 139; Woolhouse, *Descartes, Spinoza, Leibniz*, 58–60.
[66] Leibniz, *Philosophical Essays*, 250–2; Leibniz, *Philosophical Writings*, 132, 179.
[67] Leibniz, *Philosophical Essays*, 250.

realm of will, vitality and soul, ingredients or rather building stones of bodies 'which cannot be produced naturally' but emanate from the goodness and Providence of God. With this device, 'simple substances' or 'souls, or, if you prefer a more general term, *monads*', Leibniz sought to share the advantages of Spinoza's demolition of Descartes' duality of substances while simultaneously avoiding the fatal trap of one substance. 'Monads' in effect replaced Spinoza's monism.

A third key concept is Leibniz's vital distinction, rooted in his criticism of Spinoza's *Ethics*,[68] between 'absolute necessity' and 'contingent necessity'. On the one hand there is the absolute necessity of 'eternal truths', such as those of geometry, which are conceptually and eternally unalterable, and, on the other, consequences and effects foreseen by God, and unavoidable but not determined by inherent properties or movements and therefore not 'absolutely necessary'.[69] With this and the closely related distinction between 'absolute necessity' of mechanical cause and effect and the 'moral necessity' of God's choosing always the best of the available possibilities,[70] Leibniz believed he had rescued the free will of God and the human individual, as well as the intelligence of God, from the Spinozists, while simultaneously affirming universal causality and predictability in the sphere of physical things in accord with the mechanistic laws of the new science. Hence his—in his own mind successful—reconciliation of the mechanistic world-view with his famous doctrine that God has created the best of all possible worlds.

The fourth primary idea concerns the origin of motion and how bodies are infused with 'motive force', making them interact. Here he proceeds parallel to Geulincx and Malebranche, maintaining that God conserves and continually produces reality 'by a kind of emanation', with the crucial difference however, that he entirely discards Descartes' fundamental duality of mind and extension.[71] In this way he provides for a divine Providence which constantly intervenes in the world and the affairs of men without disturbing the universal applicability of scientific cause and effect and, supposedly, simultaneously explaining that 'great mystery, the union of the soul and the body'.

With these building-blocks Leibniz proceeded to his crowning concept or vision: the 'universal pre-established harmony of the universe'. Everything is mechanistically caused or decided by God, Providence underlying and conserving the universal laws of mechanics, all according to the 'moral necessity', inducing the Supreme Being to produce the maximum degree of perfection possible. Hence God's Will and Providence, and the prevailing order, are morally and contingently but not 'absolutely' necessary and determined by His goodness. In his *Théodicée*, Leibniz describes the great difference, as he sees it, between his 'predetermined harmony of the universe' and Spinoza's atheistic fatalism, commenting that in Spinoza the 'dominion of God . . . is

---

[68] Mondadori, 'Necessity *ex hypothesi*', 193.

[69] Ibid., 191–6; Leibniz, *Philosophical Essays*, 45–6, 52, 94–8; Garrett, 'Truth. Method', 37, 40.

[70] Rowe, 'Clarke and Leibniz', 66–71.

[71] Leibniz, *Philosophical Essays*, 46–9; Leibniz, *Theodicy*, 156–7; Rutherford, *Leibniz*, 214–15; Moreau, 'Nature et individualité', 447.

nothing but the dominion of necessity, and of a blind necessity (as with Strato) whereby everything emanates from the divine nature, while no choice is left to God and Man's choice does not exempt him from necessity.'[72]

With this Leibniz, reinforced later by Wolff, emerged as one of the strongest contenders for the middle ground in Europe's Early Enlightenment 'war of philosophies'. But had Leibniz really demolished Spinoza's edifice? According to the English Newtonians and especially Samuel Clarke, with these ideas he had by no means extricated himself from the dark and awesome pitfall of mechanistic 'absolute necessity'. For by his definitions, since God exists necessarily and is omnipotent, omniscient, and perfectly good, it is difficult to see how He can be other than 'necessarily' impelled to create or determine the best.[73] 'Hypothetical necessity, and moral necessity,' insists Clarke, 'are only figurative ways of speaking, and in philosophical strictness of truth, are no necessity at all.'[74]

Yet Leibniz's point is precisely that God's decree is not a blind but a knowing, conscious choice. No doubt there is much cogency in Clarke's tightly argued critique of Leibniz, but it is also true that Leibniz advanced as far as any philosopher conceivably could towards sweeping away man's traditional universe of magical forces, superstitious belief, and contingency, while simultaneously preserving divine intelligence, will, and Providence. If one accepts the findings of mathematics and science, then God cannot be omnipotent in an absolute sense. Spinoza, Leibniz remarks in his *Théodicée*, was right to 'oppose an absolute power of determination that is without any grounds; it does not belong even to God'; his mistake was to push this insight to the point of insisting on the universal validity of absolute necessity.[75] The superiority of his own system over those of Descartes, Malebranche, and Bayle, as well as that of Spinoza, and its special aptness for defending religion, morality, and authority both political and ecclesiastical, he believed, lay precisely in his having 'sufficiently proved that neither the foreknowledge nor Providence of God can impair either His justice or goodness, or our freedom'.[76]

---

[72] Leibniz, *Theodicy*, 349; Uslar, 'Leibnizs Kritik', 76, 79–80; Parkinson, 'Philosophy and Logic', 203.

[73] Mondatori, 'Necessity *ex hypothesi*', 191–4; Rowe, 'Clarke and Leibniz', 61, 74; Rutherford, *Leibniz*, 11–12.

[74] *The Leibniz-Clarke Correspondence*, 99.   [75] Leibniz, *Theodicy*, 349.   [76] Ibid., 351–2.

27 | ANGLOMANIA: THE 'TRIUMPH' OF NEWTON AND LOCKE

i. Europe Embraces English Ideas

One of the best known and most striking features of the Early Enlightenment is a cultural and intellectual movement which swept the continent from France to Russia, and Scandinavia to Sicily, in the 1730s and 1740s. This was the so called *anglomanie* of the eighteenth century, a near universal fashion for English ideas, influences, and styles. Suddenly, virtually everything English was in demand in Europe. For the first time, English poetry and plays were widely studied. English grammars and dictionaries, rare in the past, became commonplace. British constitutional monarchy began to be widely admired. Above all, Newton and Locke were almost everywhere eulogized and lionized.

The phenomenon is well known and of crucial importance for the general evolution of western civilization.[1] Yet the particular play of cultural and intellectual forces generating the *anglomanie* of the 1730s and 1740s has not been much considered, or studied. It is certain, in any case, that there are at least two strikingly diverse ways of explaining the phenomenon and relating it to its historical context. Some scholars have been inclined to locate the origins of the Enlightenment itself in precisely those intellectual streams, Newtonianism and Locke's empiricism, which spearheaded, so to speak, Britain's cultural conquest of the west. The notion that the French and other continental *philosophes* 'looked to England as the source of the Enlightenment'[2] and that the 'fashion for deism' in France was a 'daughter of Anglomania'[3] gains plausibility from the incontestable fact that many books proclaiming the mainstream High Enlightenment, published on the continent from the 1730s onwards, clearly professed to be inspired by English ideas. Indeed, it is no exaggeration to say that Voltaire's intellectual, as distinct from rhetorical and literary, contribution to the Enlightenment, consists of little more than introducing Newton and Locke to the continent or, as Paolo Mattia Doria called his *Lettres philosophiques* (1734), mere 'propaganda' for

---

[1] Gay, *The Enlightenment*, ii, 24–5, 58, 230, 454; Feingold, 'Reversal', 234–7, 256–8; Feingold, 'Partnership in Glory', 291–2; Maurer, *Aufklärung und Anglophilie*, 14–16, 32–6.

[2] Harrison, *'Religion' and the Religions*, 3, 176; see also Schouls, *Descartes*, 177; Fitzpatrick, 'Toleration', 25, 43.

[3] Gay, *The Enlightenment*, i, 11–12.

English philosophy.[4] Certainly, Voltaire's *Éléments de la Philosophie de Neuton* (1739) exerted a formidable influence in the expansion of mainstream moderate Enlightenment thought while, intellectually, Voltaire is here nothing more than a forceful and witty mouthpiece for Newtonianism.

Yet there is also another, and arguably a better explanation. Incontrovertibly, from the 1730s there was an international 'cult' of Newton and Locke. The view that while the 'propagandists of the Enlightenment were French . . . its patron saints and pioneers were British: Bacon, Newton and Locke had such splendid reputations on the continent that they quite overshadowed the revolutionary ideas of a Descartes or a Fontenelle' at first glance seems fully supported by d'Alembert's eulogy of these British thinkers in his *Discours préliminaire* to the *Encyclopédie*. If Spinoza dismisses Bacon as a philospher who 'simply makes assertions while proving hardly anything',[5] d'Alembert eulogized Bacon as so great that 'on serait tenté de le regarder comme le plus grand, le plus universel, et le plus éloquent des philosophes'.[6] But the very fact that it is d'Alembert saying this, before going on to praise Newton and Locke to the skies, while largely ignoring other modern thinkers, is a signal that all is not as it seems on the surface.

For apart from the obvious fact that little further use is found for Bacon, D'Alembert was utterly convinced society needs two distinct levels of ideas, one composed of popular philosophy to enlighten the wider but unsophisticated public and, completely different, philosophical truth as cultivated by *philosophes* such as himself and Diderot. While publicly proclaiming them heroes of incomparable wisdom and stature, privately, among his friends and intimates, d'Alembert—and still more, Diderot—was highly critical of much of Locke's philosophy and rejected key elements of Newton.[7] One has to bear in mind that the *Encyclopédie* was produced in a fraught intellectual and ideological atmosphere with the constant threat of suppression emanating especially from the Church and the *parlements*—but at times also sections of the royal Court—hanging over it.[8] Reassuring noises about its doctrinal implications had to be made, above all in its preface, to allay the fears of Church and State, which by no means necessarily matched the views of its compilers. For the crucial point about Newton, Locke, and Bacon is that these thinkers were, from the 1730s, everywhere regarded, even among the most reactionary sections of the French Church, and by the Spanish and Portuguese Inquisition, as intellectually safe writers, innovative perhaps but entirely supportive of revealed religion, Providence, and the political and social order.

Besides Voltaire and Maupertuis, there were undoubtedly other *philosophes* of the mid-century, such as the Abbé Étienne Bonnot de Condillac (1714–80), introduced to English ideas by Voltaire, who were genuine enthusiasts for English empirical philosophy—at least initially. Condillac's *Traité de systèmes* (The Hague, 1749) effectively

---

[4] Hampson, *The Enlightenment*, 78; Niklaus, 'Voltaire et l'empiricisme', 11, 19.

[5] Spinoza, *Letters*, 59, 62.   [6] d'Alembert, *Discours préliminaire*, p. xxiv.

[7] Le Ru, *D'Alembert philosophe*, 98–106, 132–3, 196–7; Hampson, *The Enlightenment*, 90–1.

[8] Hampson, *The Enlightenment*, 86; Proust, *Diderot*, 62–79; Chartier, *Cultural Origins*, 40–2.

completed the discrediting of 'innate ideas' and 'abstract systems', including those of Malebranche, Leibniz, and Spinoza, which Locke and Le Clerc especially (but also de Vries, Hartsoeker, Regius, and others) had begun. But Condillac's advocacy of Locke, insisting that ideas do not allow us to know things as they are but merely as we perceive them, through sense impressions relative to ourselves, soon transcended Locke to reveal certain potentially radical implications which were not lost on contemporaries. Crucial in Locke is the dichotomy of 'sensation' and 'reflection'. If all knowledge comes to us through sense perception, Locke nevertheless still argues for an innate, categorizing, non-material power of the mind which organizes the passive experience of the senses. In his *Traité des sensations* (1754), Condillac eliminates this duality so that mental reflection and analysis too ensue directly from sense impressions.[9] The resulting 'sensationalist psychology' contributed appreciably to the trend towards a purely materialist conception of man evolving in the minds of radical thinkers such as Diderot and Helvétius.

Parodoxically, while Condillac in his Lockean guise did more than any other eighteenth-century thinker to discredit Spinoza's system, at the same time he lent it a new lease of life. Superficially, he seemed right to claim, in his 70-page refutation of Spinoza, to have devised a far more effective way of killing off the demon than Houtteville, Denyse, Jaquelot, Régis, Lamy, and all their predecessors put together: under his rigorous empiricist criteria it is just as much of a waste of time to debate Spinoza's ideas as to propose them in the first place.[10] His system, insists Condillac, 'ne signifie rien'.[11] 'J'ai peine à croire,' he concluded impressively, 'que ses démonstrations renferment rien de plus que des mots.'[12] Condillac gloried in humbling and ridiculing systematic philosphers, 'plus poètes que philosophes' and showing it is men's pride 'qui les empêche d'apercevoir les bornes de leur esprit'.[13] Yet by conflating body and soul, and reducing the mind to pure sense perception, he also powerfully contributed to forming the materialist ideology of a group of mid-century radical thinkers whom Diderot calls the 'nouveaux Spinosistes', the thinkers reviving Spinoza's system in a modernized form precisely by identifying soul with the senses and movement with matter.[14]

But if Condillac's system, and those parts of d'Alembert and Diderot which accorded with him, were derived from Locke and Newton, most essential elements of Diderot's thought, like that of La Mettrie, Helvétius, and d'Holbach, such as their conflation of body and mind, rejection of 'liberty of the will', moral determinism, and materialism, were rooted in late seventeenth-century European radical trends. Fontenelle similarly eschewed Newtonianism and Locke's empiricism, remaining less 'an unregenerate Cartesian', as he has been called, than a systematic mechanicist and

---

[9] Hampson, *The Enlightenment*, 75–6; Jimack, 'French Enlightenment i', 237–43.

[10] Condillac *Traité des systèmes*, 27–8, 66, 139, 145, 210; Hazard, *European Thought*, 329; Vernière, *Spinoza*, 469–75; Le Ru, *D'Alembert philosophe*, 173–4.

[11] Condillac, *Traité des systèmes*, 210   [12] Ibid., 156.   [13] Ibid., 237.

[14] [Diderot], 'Spinosiste' in *Encyclopédie*, xv, 474; Proust, *Diderot*, 121, 124, 289; Jimack. 'French Enlightenment i', 241–7.

materialist who opposed Newtonian insistence on the impossibility of our grasping final causes and the dependence of the material world on divine regulation.[15] This demonstrates beyond doubt not only that there were various intellectual roots to the Enlightenment, but also that in reality there was no fundamental break separating the High Enlightenment of the mid-eighteenth century from the general European philosophical ferment of the late seventeenth.[16] Instead there was a high degree of continuity but with one element (Cartesianism) being eradicated and with a changing balance of internal constituent forces.

Consequently, the Anglomania of the 1730s and 1740s did not so much play a decisive role in generating the Enlightenment as in forming just one particular, albeit major, segment of the moderate mainstream. The craze for English ideas was not a precondition for a general advance towards more modern and more 'scientific' ways of thinking, as is often claimed, but rather a transitory result of a changing balance of philosophical forces of more limited significance. Above all, it is essential to investigate carefully the timing and circumstances of the *anglomanie*. As one does so, one begins to see that the phenomenon flowed from the breakdown of Cartesianism and *Malebranchisme* and the perceived urgent need by the 1720s for more robust defences against the advancing Radical Enlightenment.

The crucial feature of Newtonianism was its ability not just to accommodate theology, but to advance beyond Boyle in integrating experimental science into an absolute framework of mathematical rationality. Indeed, British and international Newtonianism constitutes an entirely new form of triangular partnership between science, philosophy, and theology, while simultaneously discrediting the philosophical quest for final causes. If Newton himself did not necessarily condone everything that disciples such as Bentley, Clarke, and Whiston promulgated in his name in the pulpit or in print, the project of integrating his scientific findings into a broad theologico-philosophical agenda undoubtedly received his unqualified support and blessing, as did his own, and his followers', thrust beyond Boyle's more tentative scientific empiricism.[17] Newton in effect abandoned Boyle's extreme caution regarding proof and the drawing of conclusions in experimental science, and sought to buttress the probabilities demonstrated by experiment into theoretical certainties by means of mathematics and mathematical rationality.

But if Newton laid claim to theoretical certainty based on mathematics as much as experiment, this was only within strictly and empirically delineated limits. His demonstration of forces of attraction or gravitation across empty spaces, for which there was no discernible cause, his insistence on the passivity and inertia of matter, and the evident absence in his system of sufficient foundation for a self-regulating universe, provided a seemingly integral and unbreakable link between science and theology.[18] 'Gravitation', he insisted, was neither innate in matter nor a 'causeless cause'.

---

[15] Hampson, *The Enlightenment*, 75, 77–8.   [16] Cassirer, *Philosophy*, 22.
[17] Jacob, *The Newtonians*, 156–9; Force, 'Break-down', 147–50; Shapin, *Scientific Revolution*, 115–17.
[18] Casini, *L'Universo-macchina*, 206; Westfall, *Life of Newton*, 294–5; Shapin, *Scientific Revolution*, 152.

The 'universal power of gravity', as Whiston put it, 'which is the same in all places, at all times, and to all bodies' is incontrovertibly 'intirely immechanical, or beyond the power of all material agents whatsoever'.[19] Hence, for Newton, gravity is a power emanating directly from God, Providence ceaselessly conserving and regulating the universe.[20] Matter, motion, and the mathematical laws of nature, in so far as we can determine them, consequently originate in the will and power of the Almighty.[21]

The unmistakable conclusion, or so it seemed to Newtonians, was that this 'supreme God, the Creator and Preserver of the world, and the author of the power of gravity, and of all other the immechanical powers of the universe, is a free agent, in no way limited by any necessity or fate, but acting still by choice, and according to his own good pleasure.'[22] Humanity, held Whiston, had every reason to thank Newton for his discoveries, for had the atheistic thinkers with their 'rigid fatality and necessity' been right and the attribute of divine choice been lacking, the 'Supreme Being himself would be below mankind, a meer fatality, and no way worthy of any veneration, or love or gratitude from his creatures'.[23] It seemed that the 'metaphysick subtilties' of 'such strange reasoners as Hobbes and Spinoza' had been totally overthrown by the new Christian philosophy of Newton and the 'plainest experiments, observations and demonstrations from nature'.[24] God had been proven 'an intelligent and omniscient being', the divine architect who had imparted to the world its marvellous design and systematic order.[25]

One of the great strengths of Newtonianism, it transpired, was its unparalleled ability to attract both the Christian theologian and the camp of moderate or providential deists, indeed, its aptness for bridging the gap between the two.[26] For Thomas Morgan, a providential deist, Newton was not just 'a man of the most elevated and uncommon genius' but the scientist who had definitively proved the mechanical laws of nature 'are not esssential to, or the inherent powers and properties of mere passive matter and that consequently, they must arise from some extrinsic, active and intelligent cause, by which matter is continually acted upon'.[27] A second great strength was that it makes God, Providence, and therefore theology central to any proper understanding of science and nature, thereby eliminating not just the pure mechanicism of the Cartesians but all materialistic and mechanistic systems. Cartesianism and Spinozism had threatened to upset everything. 'Ascribing the universal force and energy,' as Morgan puts it, 'by which the whole material world is incessantly acted upon and moved, to the mere passive matter, as the inherent essential powers and properties of

---

[19] Whiston, *Astronomical Principles*, 27, 40, 45; Westfall, *Life of Newton*, 204–5, 238; Wilson, *Leibniz's Metaphysics*, 227–8.

[20] Condillac, *Traité des systèmes*, 228; D'Holbach, *Système*, i, 22 and ii, 143–5; Force, 'Children of the Resurrection', 119–21; Westfall, *Life of Newton*, 290–1.

[21] [Ramsay], *Voyages de Cyrus*, ii, 29; Force, 'Newton's God of Dominion', 84–5.

[22] Whiston, *Astronomical Principles*, 114.   [23] Ibid., 114–15.   [24] Ibid., 114, 242.

[25] Ibid., 116; Force, 'Newtonians and Deism', 48–9.   [26] Feingold, 'Partnership in Glory', 304–5.

[27] Morgan, *Physico-theology*, 23, 29.

the bodies themselves, is in effect to exclude the Deity out of the universe.'[28] But New-tonianism apparently eliminates the threat: since Newton it was virtually impossible, affirmed Morgan, to believe matter and motion 'eternal and necessary, and this with-out any original wisdom, contrivance or design, or without any prior, superior agent or designer, necessarily, or by a mere fortuitous jumble and accidental concourse of atoms, settled into such a universe or system of beings as we now see'.[29]

Yet another great strength of Newtonianism was that Newton's overarching 'dominion of God' and notion of the constantly regulated, divinely supervised order-liness of the world, inevitably imparted a degree of legitimacy to the existing order of things as encountered in society and politics too. If God regulates motion, gravitation, and the continuance of the planetary system, it hardly seems likely He is not also the manager, designer, and regulator of social hierarchy and monarchy. Thus in politics, Newtonianism encouraged, at the very least, a passive attitude, if not one of active veneration, for existing structures of authority and institutions, a message which at least some Newtonians were not slow to underline.[30] Hence the Newtonian Nehemiah Grew, in his *Cosmologia sacra* (1701), dedicated to William III, maintains that monarchy is inherent in the 'natural order and divine government of the world'. Indeed, true republics are an impossibility. For even those that exist in Europe, he observed, were republics only in name and 'do all of them centre upon that which in effect is the regal: as the United Provinces with their Stadholder, and the Venetians, with their Doge'.[31]

No one could dispute Newton's greatness as a scientist, though Huygens deemed the principle of attraction 'absurd' and Hartsoeker (who publicly rejected Cartesian-ism and Leibnizianism, as well as Spinozism) persisted in maintaining 'tout ce que M. Newton avance touchant l'attraction mutuelle des corps, n'est point fondé' and that one can in no way use his concept of gravity to explain the movements of heavenly bodies.[32] Not a few thinkers of the Early and High Enlightenment, however, rejected Newtonianism as a general system, and sought to cut Newton the philosopher and theologian down to size, not just adherents of 'innate ideas', Cartesians, and *Male-branchistes*, but also others who considered Newton's relegation of philosophical reason intellectually, socially, and (sometimes also) politically regressive.

After 1720 Cartesianism and *Malebranchisme* lost their dynamism. But this still left three powerful philosophical blocs vying for hegemony—the Lockean–Newtonian concatenation, the Leibnizian–Wolffian system, and the Radical Enlightenment—and both the latter proved fertile in criticism of Newton. The radicals roundly rejected the wider implications of Newtonianism as a system. Thus Diderot, in his *Intepréta-tion de la nature* (1754), contends that all motion, including gravitation, is inherent in matter, insinuatingly raising the spectre of Spinoza and accusing Newton of 'obscurité'.[33] 'Le sublime Newton' may have been an adept scientist, remarked

---

[28] Morgan, *Physico-theology*, 59–60.   [29] Ibid., 304–5.
[30] Force, 'Newton's God of Dominion', 94–5.   [31] Grew, *Cosmologia sacra*, 90.
[32] Hartsoeker, *Recueil*, 6–9; Westfall, *Life of Newton*, 193.
[33] Diderot, *Oeuvres philosophiques*, 215–16, 225, 229–30; Hampson, *The Enlightenment*, 91.

d'Holbach, but when it comes to philosophy, theology, and politics he was a mere child.[34]

Leibniz, in his *New Essays* (1703–5), was the first continental thinker fully to appreciate the formidable power of the Newton–Locke construct in the contest to dominate the Enlightenment's middle ground. He unreservedly approved Newton's experimental philosophy and mathematical methods. Nevertheless, his objections are of a fundamental kind, prompting him to consider Newtonianism not just intellectually limited but a real threat to society.[35] During the last two years of his life (1715–16) he became embroiled in a laborious dispute with Samuel Clarke, acting on Newton's behalf, in which the German thinker joined the Cartesians, Huygens, and Hartsoeker in rejecting Newton's account of gravity as a bogus explanation, being nothing more than a system of mathematical relationships, elevated into laws, with no cause for the physical phenomenon being offered other than God Himself. This, Leibniz, like Hartsoeker, sees as mere conjecture, tantamount to reintroducing a 'scholastic occult quality' into philosophy for 'whatever cannot be explained by the nature of created things is miraculous.'[36] Nor did he esteem Newton's notion of the unceasing need for divine intervention to 'correct' imbalances and discrepancies arising from the laws of nature: 'I am astonished that M. Newton and his followers believe that God has made his machine so badly that unless he regulates it by some extraordinary means, the watch will very soon cease to function.'[37] He saw little to applaud in (Boyle's and) Newton's insistence that mechanical philosophy has definite limits and cannot explain all the mysteries of nature.

Further differences were the old quarrel about whether or not a vacuum in nature is possible, with the Newtonians affirming and Leibniz (and again Hartsoeker) rejecting the possibility, and a dispute over Newton's (and Boyle's) conception of space and time as something existing absolutely, independently of bodies.[38] Newton's conception of absolute space 'without relation to anything external' was firmly repudiated by Leibniz, who holds that space is nothing in itself but merely the order, or relationship, in which celestial bodies move in respect of each other, so that if God reversed the order of the universe, from left to right, without changing anything else, in his view, all would remain as before, whereas, following Newton's allegedly 'chimerical supposition of the reality of space in itself', everything would be totally the other way about.[39] All this, aggravated by Locke's empiricism, which leaves entirely in doubt whether the soul is material or immaterial, added up, in Leibniz's opinion, to a confused rigmarole, mixing science with philosophical nonsense in a way which signally

[34] D'Holbach, *Système*, ii, 143–5, 147–8.

[35] Hall, *Philosophers at War*, 146–7, 157, 163; Brown, 'Leibniz', 222–3.

[36] d'Alembert, *Discours préliminaire*, p. xxvii; Jolley, *Leibniz and Locke*, 54–7, 64; Garber, 'Leibniz', 333; Rutherford, *Leibniz*, 242.

[37] Leibniz to Conti, Nov. or Dec. 1715 in *The Leibniz-Clarke Correspondence*, 184–5; Shapin, *Scientific Revolution*, 156–7.

[38] *The Leibniz-Clarke Correspondence*, 46, 66–73, 105, 113; McGuire, 'Boyle's Conception of Nature', 531–2; Westfall, *Life of Newton*, 166–7.

[39] Garber, 'Leibniz', 302; Westfall, *Life of Newton*, 294.

departs from Newton's own professed principle of keeping strictly within the bounds of experimental philosophy.

Clarke hit back on Newton's behalf, with some highly pertinent counter-arguments. In particular, he questions whether Leibniz really safeguards, as he claims, divine Providence from the atheists and radicals.[40] Leibniz pronounces the actual world the 'best of all possible worlds' since God is omnipotent, omniscient, and perfectly good, and is consequently led by His own nature to create the best. But how then can God be free in choosing to do so? In his *Théodicée*, Leibniz scrupulously differentiates between 'absolute necessity' and 'moral necessity', claiming it is morally but not 'absolutely necessary' for God to create and conserve the best possible world.[41] But Clarke, like the German anti-Wolffians later, dismisses this as mere trifling with words, a resort to absolute necessitarianism without admitting it.[42] Effectively, Clarke accuses Leibniz of surreptitiously joining the radicals and making God a 'passive being: which is not to be a God, or governor, at all',[43] a charge integrally linked to the dispute about the nature of space and time. For Newton and Clarke the existence of 'extra-mundane space (if the material world be finite in its dimensions) is not imaginary but real'.[44] Since, if space is not independent of bodies, then the material universe cannot be movable or finite and, in that case, 'it follows evidently, that God neither can nor ever could set bounds to matter; and consequently the material universe must be not only boundless, but eternal also' and, therefore, independent of God.[45] This would give the victory to Spinoza.

Always alert to important new developments, Leibniz was the first thinker on the continent to engage seriously with Newton and Locke. Yet it would be a mistake to claim that Leibniz regarded the incipient conflict between his system and Newtonianism, which in any case only broke out in full force in 1711, as the most pressing battle in the European intellectual arena of the time. For the *New Essays* remained unpublished, while in the one published major work of his last years, the *Théodicée* (1710), Leibniz's main priority is not to confront Newton and Locke but to overturn Spinoza and Bayle.[46]

ii. Locke, Newtonianism, and Enlightenment

Both in the modern historiography and the rhetoric of the mainstream High Enlightenment, there is a tradition of impressive claims for Locke's influence on the wider European Enlightenment, which is unquestionably in need of qualification and

---

[40] *The Leibniz-Clarke Correspondence*, 45, 50, 55, 98–9.

[41] Leibniz, *Theodicy*, 387–8; Rutherford, *Leibniz*, 226–32.

[42] 'Necessity, in philosophical questions,' retorted Clarke, 'always signifies absolute necessity. "Hypothetical necessity" and "moral necessity", are only figurative ways of speaking, and in philosophical strictness of truth, are no necessity at all'; see Leibniz, *The Leibniz-Clarke Correspondence*, 99; Rowe, 'Clarke and Leibniz', 61, 63–6, 74.

[43] *Leibniz-Clarke Correspondence*, 98.   [44] Ibid., 46.

[45] Ibid. 108; Westfall, *Life of Newton*, 166, 290.   [46] Leibniz, *Theodicy*, 85–6, 409.

firmer placing in a historical perspective. Locke's influence, it is said, together with Newton's, spread through Enlightenment Europe with such force, and so much capacity to change ideas, that 'men might well feel that they had crossed the threshold into a new age.'[47] Locke has even been called the 'most influential philosopher of modern times'.[48] Certainly, Voltaire in his *Lettres philosophiques* glorifies Locke, as also Newton, as the two titanic figures who laid the intellectual foundations of the new era, but Locke most of all because it was he who had 'ruiné les idées innées'.[49] Just as Newton was the founder of modern physics, holds d'Alembert in his *Discours préliminaire*, so Locke is the creator of modern, 'scientific' philosophy.[50]

Yet until the 1730s the European reception of both Locke and Newton was so hesitant and slow as to constitute a meaningful historical problem on its own.[51] Far from advancing triumphantly, Newtonianism was scarcely known in France before the later 1720s. Beyond Le Clerc's circle in Holland and Leibniz, Locke's empiricism figured only peripherally in continental intellectual debate for some four decades. Of course, one would not expect the English text to abound in continental libraries. But the French translation, prepared in consultation with Locke by the Huguenot Pierre Coste (1668–1747), was published only rather belatedly twelve years after Le Clerc's *Abrégé*, at Amsterdam in 1700. Moreover, even this edition is seldom found in eighteenth-century library catalogues, and while a second edition of the Coste rendering appeared, this was not until nearly a quarter of a century later, in 1723. The Latin version, published at Leipzig in 1709, meanwhile also had little impact. The remarkable disinclination of leading intellectual figures early in the century to engage seriously with Locke's work is also striking. Slow to take offence though he was, even Locke was noticeably irritated by Bayle's studied refusal to comment on his work or take it seriously.[52] Locke's place in the 1702 edition of Bayle's *Dictionnaire* is indeed so peripheral as to be almost insulting, nor is it at all unlikely that Bayle's passing reference to Locke as 'un des plus profonds métaphysiciens du monde' is meant sarcastically.[53]

All the evidence suggests it was the third French edition of 1729 which gave Locke his continental stature. But even then it would be entirely wrong to assume that his profile suddenly became immensely dominant. Locke receives respectable coverage in the largest European encyclopaedia of the mid-eighteenth century, Zedler's *Universal Lexicon*; nevertheless, the space assigned to him was less than one-third of that given to Spinoza and Spinozism.[54] It might, of course, be objected that Germany was an exception with comparatively little interest in Locke there in the eighteenth

---

[47] Hampson, *The Enlightenment*, 39; Feingold, 'Partnership in Glory', 299–303; Fitzpatrick, 'Toleration', 37–43

[48] Aarsleff, 'Locke's Influence', 252.

[49] Voltaire, *Lettres philosophiques*, 63–5, 86–9; Niklaus, 'Voltaire et l'empiricisme', 11, 19.

[50] d'Alembert, *Discours préliminaire*, p. xxvii; Aarsleff, 'Locke's Influence', 255.

[51] Casini, *Introduzione*, i 46–8; Guerlac, *Newton on the Continent*, 43, 64, 73–5; Niklaus, 'Voltaire et l'empiricisme', 11, 19.

[52] Labrousse, *Pierre Bayle*, ii, 155–6, 177–8, 554; Hutchison, *Locke in France*, 15.

[53] Bayle, *Dictionnaire*, iii, 2388, 2609, 3066; Yolton, *Locke and the Way*, 23–4, 136–8, 140.

[54] Zedler, *Grosses Universal Lexicon*, xviii, 107–13 and xxxix, 75–86 and 88–95.

century, while what there was tended to be confined to the Thomasian and the anti-Wolffian camp.[55] But one can actually make exactly the same point about his limited influence, certainly until the 1730s, with regard to Italy, the Netherlands, Scandinavia, and the Baltic. If the Netherlands was the first country on the continent where English ideas came to dominate the Early Enlightenment, this was not until the mid-1720s and even then the role of Locke was rather marginal.[56] Willem Jacob 's-Gravesande, the Leiden professor who did more than anyone else to engineer the triumph of English philosophy and science in the Dutch mainstream Enlightenment in the 1720s, was essentially a Newtonian who turned to Locke only in the 1730s and, even then, never gave much prominence to his ideas.[57]

Meanwhile in Rome, Celestino Galiani, the architect of the Lockean–Newtonian breakthrough in Italy, first read Locke's *Essay* in Coste's translation 'shortly before 1710'.[58] But his own presentation of Locke remained unpublished and, before the 1730s, he made little or no attempt to publicize Locke in his philosophical correspondence. Ludovico Antonio Muratori, librarian of the Duke of Modena and for half a century among the foremost spokesmen of moderate Catholic reformism and enlightenment in Italy, obstinately kept to his early Cartesian outlook, including Descartes' duality of substance, publicly attacking Locke's philosophy in his *La filosofia morale* (1735).[59] For his part, Vico,[60] like Giannone[61] and many other luminaries of the Italian Early Enlightenment, refers to Locke only perfunctorily and what he does say is unfavourable. Paolo Mattia Doria plausibly asserts, in the preface to his *Difesa della metafisica* (Naples, 1732), that it was the 1723 edition of Coste's translation and especially that of 1729 which unleashed the *furore Lockense* in Italy, which he too now undertook to rebuff,[62] a remark which supports the conclusion that the placing of Locke's *Essay* on the papal Index in 1734 reflects Locke's failure to exert a noticeable influence in Italian intellectual life before the 1730s—precisely as in France.

This is not to deny that by the 1740s the *Lochisti*, as Doria terms them, were a potent force in Italian intellectual debate, an impressive fact when one thinks that a mere few decades earlier Locke's ideas had been suspect not only to Catholics and High Church Anglicans but even to such Latitudinarian theologians as Bishop Stillingfleet. Yet Locke continued to face vigorous opposition from the moderate mainstream and traditionalists, especially on the grounds that he leaves the immortality of the soul uncertain and grants the possibility at least of thinking matter.[63] Despite these serious reservations, however, he was eventually powerfully drawn into the Italian arena, as

---

[55] Fischer, 'John Locke', 431–5; Kuehn, 'German *Aufklärung*', 311; Jöcher remarkably gives Locke less space than he does the Calvinist theologian Melchior Leydekker; see Jöcher, *Allgemeines Gelehrten Lexicon*, ii, 1413–15, 2487–8.

[56] Visser, 'Petrus Camper', 386; Wielema, 'Nicolaus Engelhard', 149.

[57] Pater, *Willem Jacob 's-Gravesande*, 32, 35–6.

[58] Rotondò, 'Censura eclesiastica', 1486; Ferrone, *Intellectual Roots*, 127.

[59] Andrade, *Vernei e a cultura*, 91–2; Ferrone, *Intellectual Roots*, 91–2, 103–4, 176–8, 180.

[60] Lilla, *G. B. Vico*, 204, 212; Ricuperati, *L'Esperanza civile*, 426, 471.

[61] Giannone, *Opere*, 620.   [62] Doria, *Difesa metafisica*, preface and pp. 3–4.

[63] Finetti, *De Principiis juris naturae*, 148–9, 154; Rotondò, 'Censura ecclesiastica', 1486–8.

we see, for instance, from the remarkable dissertation 'against the *fatalisti'* published by the Pisan professor of scripture and Church history, Tommaso Moniglia, at Lucca in 1744, because of his usefulness in shoring up authority, tradition, and revealed religion against the Enlightenment's more radical tendencies.[64] Moniglia indignantly rejected the anti-Lockean views of Doria and Muratori.[65] Many people in Italy were worried by the immense influence suddenly accruing to Locke, Newton, and their followers, he grants, but they were wrong to be fearful. For the ideas of Newton and Locke are, in reality, a great blessing, he insists, being not just the best available shield for Revelation and Christian philosophy but an indispensable prop to the social and political order. For public tranquillity, as well as that of the individual, 'absolutely require veneration of God and fidelity to the prince so that there is a very close linkage between these two vital obligations'.[66] The central issue in contemporary philosophical debate, held Moniglia, is the defence of divine Providence, human free will, and an absolute morality of 'good' and 'evil' against the ravages of atheistic fatalism. The inestimable value of Locke's epistemology, he argues, is precisely that it rules out the metaphysical systems of the *fatalisti*.[67] Newton 'whose view regarding both the liberty of Man and God, as expounded by Voltaire, is far more correct than that of Leibniz or Collins' is likewise warmly applauded, as are Le Clerc and Jaquelot for their roles in bolstering divine Providence and free will.[68] Most remarkable of all, at this point Voltaire could still be expressly praised for his services to religion: after all, Moniglia points out, it was his intervention which had crucially advanced Newton's European influence.[69]

But if the formidable advance of Locke and Newton after 1730 heartened many, the battle was not over yet and there was still room for great anxiety. In the first place, the continuing vigour of the *Leibniziani* in Italy was preventing the full triumph of Locke and Newton and dangerously splitting the middle ground. In the second place, noted Moniglia, unremitting strife between the principal rival branches of contemporary Christian thought was enabling the depraved teaching of the *Spinosisti* not just to survive but to prosper and grow, bolstered not least by the insidious Toland and Collins.[70] Though a friend of Locke, Collins, according to Moniglia, is totally opposed to his philosophy as well as all revealed religion and is, in fact, a 'Spinozist'. Indeed, Moniglia, who, unlike Concina, Genovesi, Doria, and Vico, seems to lack first-hand knowledge of Spinoza's works, deploys Collins as his prime surrogate representative of *Spinosismo*. For Collins, like Spinoza, destroys belief in free will and divine Providence.[71] The *Spinosisti*, admonishes Moniglia, 'insolently insult every society, every authority, all principles, Heaven and Earth, ridiculing all laws, all codes of custom and all edicts that sustain them'.[72] Spinozism, he says, entails the abandonment of 'all

---

[64] Ferrone, *Intellectual Roots*, 265–6.   [65] Andrade, *Vernei e a cultura*, 91–2.

[66] Moniglia, *Dissertazione contro i Fatalisti*, i, preface, p. iii verso.

[67] Ibid., preface, p. iii verso, 141–2, 153; Andrade, *Vernei e a cultura*, 92; Ferrone, *Intellectual Roots*, 265–6.

[68] Moniglia, *Dissertazione contro i Fatalisti*, i, 143, 168.

[69] Ibid., 166–8.   [70] Ibid., pp. lxxviii, 135; Ferrone, *Intellectual Roots*, 266.

[71] Moniglia, *Dissertazione contro i Fatalisti*, i, 135–8 and ii, 38, 58–64, 80–3, 140–4.   [72] Ibid., 21.

common happiness for the interests and passions of individuals'.[73] In fact, Spinozism means 'a total revolution in ideas, in language, and in the affairs of the world. Oh Shame! Oh Portent!'[74] A revolution in ideas first and then in everything else. Hence Moniglia, like Concina and Lucchi, deemed it vital not only for defending religion but of 'great importance also for the preservation of States that Spinozism should be better understood than it is'; for 'every people amongst whom it surges up is menaced with immanent destruction and hastens to its ruin with a rapid pace'.[75] Mercifully, Italy's princely governments were actively opposing the spread of Spinoza's influence, tightening censorship and taking tough measures against the *fatalisti*. But assuredly the struggle would be long and hard.

In his later treatise on the philosophical situation in Italy, published at Padua in 1750, Moniglia again extols Newton and Locke, celebrating the spread of their ideas everywhere.[76] Yet despite the universal progress of *Newtonianismo*, a godless materialism rooted in Spinoza was also expanding, and the war of philosophies in Italy growing more embittered and implacable than ever. A particularly worrying feature of the situation, in his view, was the relentless antagonism between adherents of Newton and Locke on one side, and those of Leibniz and Wolff on the other. Each of these philosophico-theologico-scientific blocs was simply too powerful to be eradicated by the other. Under such circumstances to persist in fighting was to weaken both, a dismal prospect when in the last analysis both had the same aim—to vanquish *Spinosismo*.[77]

The ideas of Newton and Locke constituted not just the main element but also much the larger part of the intellectual *anglomanie* of the 1730s and 1740s. If Newton and Locke did eventually possess splendid reputations on the continent, their transmission in French and Latin proved a slow and tentative process which, as a rule, apart from Clarke and Bentley, yielded little renown for the many secondary figures thronging the Newtonian-Lockean camp in Britain. In Europe, it was mostly Italian, German, and especially French and Dutch expositors and commentators who carried the 'triumph' of Locke and Newton to completion, so that the lesser British names remained largely unknown. On the continent, the most celebrated 'Newtonians' of the 1730s and 1740s were frequently names scarcely known in Britain at all. Not untypically, Voltaire, in his *Éléments*, recommends readers interested in deepening their knowledge of Newtonianism to consult four comprehensive guides, two of which were by the Dutch scholars 's-Gravesande and Petrus van Musschenbroek.[78] An arguably still more eminent Newtonian internationally was a third Dutchman—Bernard Nieuwentijt.

The predominance of English thought in the Early Enlightenment, then, was both less evident and less universal than is commonly assumed. Undoubtedly (but also ironically), much the most complete success achieved by English ideas, beginning in

---

[73] Moniglia, *Dissertazione contro i Fatalistis*, ii, 22.   [74] Ibid., 21.   [75] Ibid., 22.

[76] Here Moniglia calls Locke and Newton (together with Bentley) the foremost champions of 'la libertà, la sapienza, la grandezza e la virtù dell' Altissimo'; Moniglia, *Dissertazione contro i Materialisti*, ii, 4, 231.

[77] Ibid., 314–16.   [78] Voltaire, *Éléments*, 12; Hall, *Philosophers at War*, 251–3.

the late 1720s, was in Spain and (eventually) Portugal, lands which, however, were not much admired elsewhere in Europe for intellectual achievement. Newton and Locke did enjoy a vast 'triumph', but only from the 1730s onwards and only within one branch of the moderate, mainstream, 'providential' Enlightenment. Doubtless Voltaire exaggerated when he assured Horace Walpole in 1768 that it was he who initiated the cult of Locke in his country and that, before his *Lettres philosophiques* of 1734, practically no one in France had even heard of him.[79] Yet Voltaire's claim is not without a sizeable kernel of truth: Locke was simply not very important in the Early Enlightenment until the 1730s. To claim that English ideas were the chief inspiration of the European Enlightenment is thus severely to distort the historical record and create a misleading notion of the philosophical balance of forces in the mid-eighteenth century. Admittedly, Neo-Cartesianism and *Malebranchisme* had virtually collapsed by 1730; but this merely reduced a previously quadrangular fight for hegemony to a triangular one. The reality was that except in Britain itself (and Spain and Portugal) the Lockean–Newtonian construct was powerfully resisted by the other two main contenders—the Leibnizian–Wolffian and the Radical Enlightenment and outside Britain rarely achieved anything remotely like the unchallenged general preponderance so often claimed for it. The Wolffian philosophy, far from being confined to Germany, gained the upper hand also in Sweden, Russia, and the Baltic;[80] and it fought Newtonianism to an arduous deadlock in Switzerland and Italy.[81] Even in France, as undercurrents of the *Encyclopédie* reveal,[82] the position in the 1750s was less one of clear superiority for Lockean and Newtonian ideas than a continuing tension in which Wolffianism and Radical thought remained powerful contenders just below the surface. In Paris, the spectacularly unstable intellectual climate was aptly characterized in the late 1730s by d'Argens, who makes one of his Chinese visitors observe that 'les systèmes de philosophie . . . se succèdent ici avec autant de rapidité que les différentes modes des coiffures des femmes, et se détruisent avec autant de facilité.'[83]

---

[79] Voltaire, *Correspondance*, xxxiii, 449; Hutchison, *Locke in France*, 203; Niklaus,'Voltaire et l'empiricisme', 10, 19.

[80] See pp. 556–62 below.   [81] Yolton, *Locke and French Materialism*, 13–24.

[82] Carboncini, 'L'*Encyclopédie* et Christian Wolff', 489–90, 503–4; Proust, *Diderot*, 284–93.

[83] D'Argens, *Lettres chinoises*, i, 129.

28 | The Intellectual Drama in Spain and Portugal

From the 1680s onwards, the spread of Cartesianism, *Malebranchisme*, and other branches of the New Philosophy in Spain and Portugal generated a profound intellectual turmoil followed by a process of sporadic renewal, culminating by around 1750 in the emergence, in essential features, of a characteristically Iberian form of Enlightenment. This tumultuous process transformed not only philosophical debate but the entire fabric of Iberian medicine, science, and higher education, and had major ramifications also in Spanish America and Brazil. Moreover, despite various typically local hallmarks, this Iberian intellectual upheaval was always intimately linked to the wider phenomenon gripping Europe as a whole, indeed it formed an integral part of the five-cornered general contest for supremacy between Aristotelianism, Neo-Cartesianism, Leibnizian–Wolffianism, Newtonianism, and the Radical Enlightenment as it raged everywhere else in Europe with the partial exception of Britain, where the second and third components were missing.

Foreign ideas fed into the Spanish- and Portuguese-speaking world in the early stages primarily from Naples, Rome, and southern France. But the decisive and also unusual feature in both Spain and Portugal was the virtually complete eclipse of the first four strains after around 1730, and the overwhelming triumph of British empiricism to an extent unmatched elsewhere. If there was one part of continental Europe of which it can be justly said that English empiricist ideas almost completely ousted every other competing variety of Enlightenment, that part was the Iberian Peninsula.

In the 1650s and 1660s, when intellectual rebels such as Juan de Prado and Orobio de Castro left Spain, there was as yet no open challenge to authority, faith, or traditional learning. Magalotti, who accompanied Prince Cosimo to Spain on his visit of 1668–9, reported to Florence in November 1668 that Spanish books contained absolutely nothing apart from 'scholastic theology and outdated medicine as found in the works of Galen'.[1] The first stirrings of the Spanish Enlightenment, that is, the initial assault on scholasticism and Galenist medicine, began only in the 1680s and 1690s in Valencia, Seville, and Madrid. According to Matheo Diego Zapata (c.1665–1745)—along with Feijóo and Piquer, one of the three pre-eminent figures of the Spanish Enlighten-

---

[1] Quoted in Kamen, *Spain*, 313.

ment—the most important and earliest forum for new ideas in the Spanish capital were informal 'salons', or gatherings of *érudits* interested in the new learning (among them Alvarez de Toledo,[2] the poet and later Philip V's librarian) which began meeting around 1687 in several noble palaces. In Madrid the chief salons were those of Juan Manuel, marqués de Villena (1650–1725), the royal major-domo and the future founder of the first Spanish royal academy who, according to Zapata, had an excellent grasp of philosophy, and the duque de Montellano, a grandee who served for some years as *presidente* of the Council of Castile.[3] In the town houses of such leading men philosophy became a force at the heart of Spanish culture. In that of Montellano, Zapata remarks, Cartesianism and Gassendism were intensively debated, along with the system of Manuel Maignan, albeit 'always with the closest attention to the purity of our holy faith'.[4]

It was indeed a peculiar feature of the Spanish Early Enlightenment that great prominence was accorded to the philosophy of Maignan, a Minim friar who had taught philosophy for many years at Toulouse, a firm anti-Aristotelian and champion of the New Philosophy who, like Descartes, ridiculed 'substantial forms', and held that the sensible qualities of things change according to movements of material parts, but who was also, in some respects, highly critical of Descartes.[5] His importance in the Spanish context stems from his espousal of the mechanistic world-view without subscribing to Descartes' rigid dichotomy of substances, advocating atomism instead. Also militating in his favour was his unremitting insistence that philosophy is neither hostile to theology nor an alternative path to truth, but an indispensable supplement to theological learning and its outer shield.[6] While Catholic theology alone guides man and teaches the essence of truth, what Maignan terms 'sacred philosophy', with its proofs of the existence of a providential God, and of God's plan for man and Nature, is, he holds, also essential, in particular for disarming unbelievers. Such works as Maignan's *Philosophia sacra* (1661) undoubtedly had a profound effect on Spanish culture, raising the status of philosophy and forging a new partnership of theology and philosophy, but yet, many sensed, one which injected a worrying element of intellectual instability and tension, not least by drawing readers into comparing the respective advantages and disadvantages of Descartes and the atomists, Gassendi and Maignan.[7]

For the wider Spanish reading public, the new era of intellectual crisis was heralded

---

[2] Gabriel Alvarez de Toledo y Pellicer (1659–1714), knight of the order of Alcantara, the first Bourbon royal librarian, came from an Andalusian noble family and was a man of great erudition and refinement who reportedly knew Hebrew, Greek, and Arabic, as well as being versed in the new philosophical learning; he published his chief work, entitled *Historia de la Iglesia y del Mundo*, in 1713; in 1714 he supervised a general reorganization of the royal library; see Mañer, *Anti-Theatro Critico*, 106–7; Díaz, *Hombres y documentos*, i, 240–1.

[3] Zapata, *Censura*, 18–19; Guy, *Historia*, 176–7.   [4] Zapata, *Censura*, 18.

[5] Nájera, *Dialogos*, 130–1; Nájera, *Maignanus Redivivus*, 79–80, 84–94, 121–2; Lessaca, *Colyrio*, 52; Watson, *Breakdown*, 164.

[6] Kors, *Atheism in France*, i, 122–3, 314; Goodman, 'Scientific Revolution', 173.

[7] Palanco, *Cursus philosophicus*, ii, 32–7, 89–95; Nájera, *Dialogos*, 5–19, 130–1; Mindán, 'Corrientes', 474.

in the year 1686 when the Valencian professor of medicine, Juan de Cabriada (c.1665–c.1715), then practising medicine in Madrid, published his epoch-making *Carta filosofica medico-chymica*, dedicated to the conde de Monterrey, president of the royal Council of Flanders, to whom he appeals for help in spreading the 'rays of reason' and dispelling the shadows 'which are so opposed to the light of truth'.[8] The book was prefaced with ecclesiastical approbations declaring Bacon's principles entirely safe with respect to 'our holy faith and good customs'. Cabriada, in this searing attack on the *Galenistas* of Spain, denouncing blood-letting besides much else, rejects the old medicine in its entirety along with its Aristotelian philosophical underpinning, replacing these with a fervent eulogy of 'modern' experimental science and 'libertad filosófica'.[9] Cabriada's chief scientific and philosophical heroes are Boyle, Steno, Francesco Redi, Tommaso Cornelio, Leonardo di Capua, Thomas Willis, Thomas Sydenham, Franciscus van Helmont, and the Leiden professor Dele Boe Sylvius, a list clearly indicating the primacy of Italian (especially Neapolitan), Dutch, and English influences in his intellectual world. Again and again, Cabriada affirms 'reason and experience', and not 'authority', as the keys to scientific and medical progress.[10] Spaniards were shamefully backward in philosophy and the sciences, he laments, so that 'as if we were [American] Indians we have to be the last . . . in all Europe'.[11] This text provoked an acrimonious quarrel between traditionalists and moderns, which spread quickly throughout the land. Zapata himself, prior to his conversion to Cartesianism in the 1690s, attacked Cabriada and the new men as 'seductores' undermining scholastic truth and threatening faith, as well as *medecina galenica*, the medicine 'favoured by the entire Catholic Church'.[12]

Driven by men such as Alvarez de Toledo, Cabriada, and, from the late 1690s, the indefatigable Zapata,[13] the New Philosophy made notable strides in Spain in the years around the turn of the new century. Projected since 1697, in May 1700, despite bitter opposition from the local university, where the *Galenista* medical faculty sent a circular letter of protest 'to all the universities of Spain', the first of Spain's academies of medicine and science was established, 'for the general utility and credit of our nation', in Seville.[14] Founded in the final years of the reign of Carlos II (ruled 1665–1700) with the approval of the Council of Castile, on the initiative of a small pressure-group headed by Zapata and invoking 'Descartes, Gassendi, Helmoncio [i.e. Van Helmont], Le Boe Sylvius, Willis' and other moderns, and backed by powerful courtiers, the new body sought to emulate the academies of 'France, Germany, England, and Italy'.[15] However, the years of the War of the Spanish Succession (1702–14) witnessed severe

---

[8] Cabriada, *Carta philosophica*, dedication.

[9] Ibid., 2–5, 16; López Piñero, *Introducción*, 101–8; López Piñero, *Joan de Cabriada*, 52, 89; Goodman, 'Scientific Revolution', 173; Israel, 'Counter-Reformation', 41, 52.

[10] Cabriada, *Carta philosophica*, 91, 100–2, 108–9.

[11] Ibid., 230–1; Goodman, 'Scientific Revolution', 173.   [12] Zapata, *Verdadera Apologia*, 46, 49, 58, 64.

[13] Mindán, 'Corrientes', 476.

[14] Zapata, *Crisis medica*, preface; Zapata, *Ocaso*, 151–2; Alvarez de Morales, *Ilustración*, 34–5; Goodman, 'Scientific Revolution', 174.

[15] Zapata, *Crisis medica*, preface and p. 42; Caro Baroja, *Judíos*, iii, 84; Vidal and Tomás, 'La Respuesta', 312.

disruption in almost every department of Iberian life. Bitter fighting spread across much of the peninsula, ending only with the fall of Barcelona, after a terrible siege, in September 1714. Seaborne communications with northern Europe and the New World were severely disrupted. For much of the war, sizeable French forces were encamped in the interior of Castile, while Anglo-Dutch expeditionary forces were based in eastern Spain, as well as Gibraltar and Portugal. For years the Inquisition tribunals virtually ceased functioning and many continuities in Spanish life were broken.[16]

With the restoration of peace and the consolidation of the new Bourbon monarchy of Philip V (ruled 1700–46), the emphasis was invariably less on reform, however, than on rebuilding, consolidating, and centralizing royal authority and ecclesiastical power. This included restoring the sway of the Inquisition, for the Bourbons had defeated the Habsburg claimant to the throne, 'Carlos III', in part by successfully labelling the opposition 'heretics' and enemies of the Catholic Church, a strategy which required a show of studiously rejecting all new doctrines, intellectual novelties, and proposals for reducing ecclesiastical influence. Almost immediately, from 1713, a new wave of persecution of crypto-Judaism and crypto-Mohammedanism began. But while repression of traditional forms of heresy could revive smoothly along familiar lines, new philosophical and scientific ideas proved more formidable corrosives.

In the very same year the War of the Spanish Succession ended, philosophical warfare resumed in full force with the publication in Madrid of Alvarez de Toledo's chief work, a history of the Creation which repeatedly appealed to the new mechanistic philosophy and offered a Cartesian defence of belief in angels as beings 'free from all element of matter, purely spiritual and without any physical component which have no parts and are therefore not subject to corruption'.[17] This was followed by the *Dialogus physico-theologicus contra philosophiae novatores* by Fray Francisco Palanco (1657–1720), a leading Aristotelian, foe of Maignan and professor of theology, as well as Minim friar and bishop-elect of Panama.[18] The work was aimed against the *novatores* in Madrid and Seville, especially Alvarez de Toledo, whose predeliction for Maignan and high social status made him an obvious standard-bearer of the new learning. Palanco lambasted Maignan, Descartes, and Gassendi as a heap of dangerous innovation championed by laymen, particularly physicians and officials, but practically never espoused by clergy, a *pseudo-philosophia* apt to damage faith, authority, and the Church. Thus Cartesianism, in his estimation, conjures up profound difficulties for belief in transubstantiation, owing to its unsatisfactory account of the union of body and soul, and rigid duality of substance.[19] He warmly praises Louis XIV for his great wisdom in prohibiting the teaching of Cartesianism in France.[20]

---

[16] Caro Baroja, *Judíos*, iii, 23–6, 91; Israel, *Conflicts of Empires*, 397–410.

[17] Alvarez de Toledo, *Historia*, 6.

[18] Zapata, *Ocaso*, prologo; Mindán, 'Corrientes', 474–5; Guy, *Historia*, 177–8; Vidal and Pardo Tomás, 'La Respuesta', 313–14.

[19] Palanco, *Dialogus physico-theologicus*, 40–2, 57–67, 181–3, 311–23; Mindán, 'Corrientes', 474–5.

[20] Palanco, *Dialogus physico-theologicus*, praefatio, p. ii.

The replies to Palanco reveal a tendency among supporters of the New Philosophy not just to resist the title of *novatores* (innovators) thrust on them by their opponents, since in Spain the term implied what was theologically suspect, but to embrace the New Philosophy from an eclectic or empiricist standpoint rather than one of whole-hearted commitment to the Cartesianism so prevalent elswhere. Thus the *Diálogos filosóficos* (1716) by the Andalusian friar and *Maignanista* Juan de Nájera, who wrote under the pseudonym 'Alexandro de Avendaño', concentrates (like Alvarez de Toledo) on defending the safer Maignan rather than Descartes.[21] Zapata, who wrote a power-ful 146-page preface to Nájera's dialogues, prudently assured readers, 'I am not a Cartesian but a lover of reason and truth,'[22] albeit (while claiming to be a *Maignanista*), he nevertheless robustly defends Descartes against his Spanish detractors: 'no philoso-phy—once a few errors are corrected—conforms more to the Christian religion.'[23] Palanco might despise Descartes, but all over Europe illustrious and pious persons, such as Queen Christina of Sweden, that peerless Catholic heroine, who strove to attract Descartes to her kingdom, held him in the highest esteem.[24] If Palanco's Neapolitan counterpart, the Jesuit Benedetti, tried to crush Cartesianism, has not Grimaldi shattered all his arguments?[25] If the French Bishop Huet polemicizes unremittingly against Descartes, had not Régis nullified his feeble objections?[26] In any case, holds Zapata, all leading thinkers of the age—he lists Descartes, Clauberg, Régis, Boyle, Le Clerc, and Maignan—totally reject scholastic Aristotelianism.[27] Meanwhile, an elderly member of the new Academia in Seville, Miguel Marcelino Boix y Moliner (1636–1722), repeating Cabriada's admonition that foreigners disdained Spanish phi-losophy and science, enthusiastically eulogized Bacon 'to whom all the natural sci-ences owe the growth which they experience today'.[28]

The now elderly Palanco withdrew from the fight, leaving the task of contin-uing the contest to Juan Martín de Lessaca, professor of medicine at Alcalá de Henares, a physician close to the dean and cathedral chapter of Toledo and a declared enemy of Cartesians and especially the suspected crypto-Jew Zapata.[29] But Lessaca's efforts yielded only a new crop of scathing replies, culminating in one of the major works of the Spanish Enlightenment, and a remarkably bold plea for freedom to philosophize, Zapata's *Ocaso de la formas aristotélicas*, written in or before 1724. However, at that point the book was suppressed by the ecclesiastical authorities and, Zapata himself—both of whose parents were of Portuguese New Christian background and had fallen victim to the Holy Office—was arrested by the Inquisition and accused of 'Judaizing'. Although the timing of his arrest suggests that it was some-how linked to the philosophical battle raging in Madrid and Seville, the mid-1720s did mark the climax of a wave of severe repression of suspected crypto-Jews, and his seizure, however timely in the eyes of scholastic reactionaries, may simply have been coincidence.

---

[21] Nájera, *Dialogos*, 5–19.   [22] Zapata, *Censura*, 23.   [23] Ibid., 10; Mindán, 'Corrientes', 476.
[24] Zapata, *Censura*, 16–17.   [25] Ibid., 12, 20.   [26] Ibid., 13, 20.   [27] Ibid., 40.
[28] Boix y Moliner, *Hippocrates acalarado*, 38.
[29] Lessaca, *Colyrio philosophico*, 10; Guy, *Historia*, 177–8; Mindán, 'Corrientes', 477.

In any case, under torture he confessed to having been taught Judaism by his mother at the age of 12, to participating in crypto-Jewish prayer gatherings and practices, embracing the 'Law of Moses' and denying Jesus Christ, not only in his native town of Murcia and later Valencia, but over many years in the Hospital General in Madrid. The 59-year-old bachelor was publicly humiliated at the *auto-da-fé* held at Cuenca on 14 January 1725, when his 'crimes' of apostasy were read out and he was condemned to a year's imprisonement, loss of half his possessions (to the Inquisition), and ten years' banishment from Madrid, besides compulsory instruction 'in the mystery of our holy faith'.[30]

While the *Ocaso* remained unpublished until shortly after his death, in 1745, when it appeared in Madrid, causing a stir as far as Portugal, the text seems to have circulated in manuscript from the mid-1720s and was read, among others, by Lessaca.[31] Zapata, who was known for his adept ridiculing of opponents, suggested that Lessaca desired to justify the insult against the Spanish nation published by the Frenchman Régis, a quarter of a century before, in 1698, in his prologue to the works of Malpighi, where he says Spanish and Portuguese learning, philosophy, and science were now considered so backward by other Europeans that Spaniards are deemed as 'barbarous as the Muscovites'.[32] He also accuses his Aristotelian adversaries of unjustly seeking to discredit modern philosophy by continually insinuating that its procedures are 'suspect, false, erroneous and opposed to the Christian religion'.[33]

Exalting the 'immortal, Catholic philosopher Descartes', the atomism of Maignan, and the 'heroic zeal, great wisdom and most useful doctrine of the famous philospher and theologian Father Malebranche', Zapata strove to convince the public that 'freedom to philosophize' poses no threat to faith and was essential to the welfare and good name of the Spanish nation.[34] Hence, where Descartes safeguards belief in spirits, Aristotle, he points out, denies the existence of angels and demons.[35] Lessaca accused him of slander in speaking of the 'vile slavishness of the Aristotelians' and irreverence towards the Fathers of the Church. But 'in matters purely philosophical,' replies Zapata, 'I will diverge from the opinion of any holy Father of the Church whenever I have some compelling reason to do so.'[36] If in theology, liberty to debate and diversity of opinion is harmful, there is no danger, he maintains, in a typically Cartesian fashion,[37] in liberty to philosophize. 'For what reason is there to consider the Church Fathers infallible in philosophy and the natural sciences which, being useless for our spiritual well-being, we do not have to suppose they are illuminated with a higher knowledge of than is afforded by the natural reason common to infinite numbers of others?'[38] God, he insists, inspired the Church Fathers only in sacred matters so that there is no requirement for 'blind deference' to their views beyond theological issues.

Following Descartes, whom he proclaims the 'enemigo declarado del atheismo'

---

[30] Caro Baroja, *Judíos*, iii, 83–7, 415–18.   [31] Mindán, 'Corrientes', 477.
[32] Zapata, *Ocaso*, 152; Vidal and Pardo Tomás, 'La Respuesta', 303.   [33] Zapata, *Ocaso*, 25.
[34] Ibid., 30–6, 109–10, 133.   [35] Ibid., 47.   [36] Ibid., 369.
[37] Verbeek, 'Spinoza and Cartesianism', 174–5.   [38] Zapata, *Ocaso*, 370–1.

(declared enemy of atheism), Zapata urges the total separation of philosophy from theology. But precisely this was considered an intolerable and improper derogation of theology by many Spanish—as by so many other European—contemporaries. Lessaca published his reply, a 762-page volume entitled *Colyrio Philosophico Aristotelico Thomistico*, in 1724, at Madrid.[39] Accusing Descartes (and Zapata) of undermining, and throwing into turmoil, the entire structure of philosophy, science, and medicine, and threatening to turn all the university teaching in Spain upside down, he denounces 'liberty to philosophize' as in fact something highly dangerous and pernicious.[40] For the certain consequence of Zapata's *libertad philosophica* is that many will espouse Descartes, which means allowing students of philosophy to interpret everything their own way, quite independently of theology and the Church.[41] Worse still, irrespective of whether Descartes was a loyal Catholic or not, Zapata's liberty to philosophize also opens the door to ideas which are completely incompatible with the authority and teaching of the Church. The overriding feature of scholastic Aristotelianism is that it comprehensively subordinates philosophy to theology.[42] Once Descartes (whose doctrine of substance is irreconcilable with belief in the Eucharist)[43] is deemed acceptable, and *libertad philosophica* conceded, the door is open to 'any atheist who denies spirituality and immortality of the soul'.[44] Lessaca insists that once Spaniards swallow the fiction that 'there is no risk in whatever method of philosophizing', it will be impossible to keep radical ideas out of Spain.[45]

With Zapata silenced by the Inquisition, it fell to Benito Jerónimo Feijóo y Montenegro (1676–1764), a Benedictine monk and professor at Oviedo in Galicia, to assume the leadership of the Spanish moderate mainstream Enlightenment. In 1726 he replied to Lessaca and the Aristotelians with the first volume of his monumental series, the *Teatro Crítico Universal*. With skill, discretion, and great energy, step by step, Feijóo promoted a particular version of the Enlightenment first within limited circles, then more widely, and finally beyond the confines of Spain. Within a few years, the scale of his triumph as a resolute and adroit advocate of enlightened ideas was universally apparent and undeniable. José Elizalde, a former rector of the University of Mexico, appointed censor of the sixth volume of the *Teatro Crítico*, in 1734, observed that Feijóo's volumes had fundamentally transformed thinking not only in Spain itself but in the viceroyalties of New Spain and Peru and even as far afield as the distant Philippines.[46]

With the Aristotelians hurled increasingly on the defensive, what Feijóo and his colleagues strove for was an enduring balance between authority and innovation, faith and reason. This implied, particularly in the early stages, working in an eclectic spirit without unequivocally committing himself to any of the main systems of the moderate Enlightenment. Publicly Feijóo, accused of contempt for tradition and commonly held opinions, always maintained that he had resisted the embrace of

---

[39] Mindán, 'Corrientes', 477; Guy, *Historia*, 178.
[40] Lessaca, *Colyrio philosóphico*, preface and pp. 7–11.   [41] Ibid., 10.   [42] Ibid., 7–10.
[43] Ibid., 12–15, 458.   [44] Ibid., 22.
[45] Ibid., 11; see also Verbeek, 'Spinoza and Cartesianism', 175–6.   [46] Ardao, *Filosofía polémica*, 18.

Descartes, Gassendi, and Newton.[47] Descartes and Malebranche, he held, created a system too sweeping and audacious to be broadly acceptable. 'I am ready to follow any new system,' he avowed, 'as long as I consider it based on sound foundations and free of grave difficulties,' making it clear that so far none had met these indispensable criteria.[48] But from his private letters, it is apparent that Feijóo all along considered Boyle, Sydenham, and Newton incomparable geniuses, and English empiricism, with its emphasis on a providential God and the empirically incontestable character of the core Christian miracles, the best and most feasible way to solve the intellectual crisis confronting Spanish culture and society.[49] Initially, the Inquisition was suspicious of British authors because of their Protestant background and their espousal of Copernican astronomy, so Feijóo had to tread carefully. Nevertheless, his strategy was clear, consistent, and finally resoundingly successful.

In the first volume of his *Teatro*, in 1726, he affirms the 'argument from design', tracing it back to Bacon, and disparages Descartes' system as a 'world of glass', vulnerable from every side, pointing out that experiments had clearly disproved several of his laws of motion.[50] In the second volume, of 1727, he laments that Spain was still full of 'semi-scholastics' and continues his critique of Cartesianism, though he grants—in his discussion of Spinoza based on Bayle's article[51]—that the atheism of the former *Cartesiano* 'Benito de Espinosa' (i.e. Spinoza) 'did not come from the philosophy of Descartes'.[52] In the third volume, of 1728, he again rejects the other modern systems in preference for English-style experimental philosophy, asserting that if a completely satisfactory and true philosophy was to emerge from the intellectual turmoil of the times, 'it is most likely to be achieved using the method, and *organon* of Bacon.'[53] By 1732 he was openly praising Newton—while his ally, Fray Martin Sarmiento, heaped praise on Bacon and all *Baconistas*[54]—and in his seventh volume, of 1736, he again spurns other modern systems, insisting that the 'most certain characteristic of the true philosophy is its going hand in hand with religion, and its being a minister and ally to it, and in this respect it is indisputable that the most advantageous is the experimental philosophy [of Bacon, Boyle, and Newton]'.[55]

In effect, by the mid-1730s Feijóo had enthroned *Newtonianismo* as the ruling philosophy in the most rigidly traditionalist and Catholic society in Europe, with the exception only of Portugal. After 1736 his advocacy of Newton and Boyle became more and more emphatic, as did his linking what is best and most valuable in modern thought with the English specifically. He claimed the English had proved themselves profounder and more penetrating in philosophy and science than the French or any other nation.[56] He heaped paeans of praise on Bacon, Boyle, and Newton especially,

---

[47] Feijóo, *Justa Repulsa*, 31–2; Mañer, *Crisol critico*, i, 209 10.
[48] Quoted in Mindán, 'Corrientes', 486.   [49] Guy, *Historia*, 186.
[50] Feijóo, *Teatro Crítico Universal*, i, 263, 268–9, 279–81.
[51] Ibid., ii, 12–14; Domínguez, 'España en Spinoza', 17.
[52] Feijóo, *Teatro Crítico Universal*, ii, 12–14, 17, 20–4.   [53] Ibid., iii, 346.
[54] Sarmiento, *Demostración*, ii, 278–9.   [55] Feijóo, *Teatro Crítico Universal*, vii, 332–3.
[56] Feijóo, *Cartas Eruditas*, iv, 151–2.

assuring his readers that *Newtonianismo* was now being freely taught in Rome, and that only the English had the intellectual equipment to defend belief in miracles and defeat the *filósofos materialistas*. Newton, like most of the English, might be a Protestant, but Feijóo insisted, 'the Holy Office with understanding and prudence permits in Spain the reading of the physical treatises of Boyle and Newton, however heretical they themselves are'.[57] He deftly trumped remaining opponents by repeatedly suggesting that those who claim Boyle and Newton are suspect are calling in question the Catholic zeal of the Holy Office.[58]

Salvos of 'enlightened' works were published in the wake of Feijóo's initial volumes, one of the most notable being Juan Bautista Berní's three-volume *Filosofía racional, metafísica i moral* (Valencia, 1736). A pupil of a renowned Oratorian philosopher and mathematician, Tomás Vicente Tosca (1651–1723), a leader of Valencian Cartesianism, Berní, who considered Bishop Bossuet 'the greatest theologian of our times', discarded Cartesianism for empiricism, writing in plain, non-technical terms, in the 'common language' for the 'public good'. He strove to soften the contrast between scholasticism and the 'moderns', seeking to allay alarm while strongly emphasizing the rationality of the Church's teachings.[59] Science and philosophy were indeed not just beneficial and necessary but should be cultivated by the common man. Spaniards should know about Cartesianism even if one rejects it as defective, and, above all, must learn that English-style experimental philosophy is the true philosophy. Remarkably, though, Berní feels able to combine veneration for [Boyle's] empiricism with insisting that one must accept the Church's ban on Copernican astronomy, that the chronology given in Scripture is incontrovertible, and that any acceptable modern philosophy must confirm the existence of Satan, angels, and demons.[60]

Empiricism and British ideas were indeed the lever which shattered the scholastic stranglehold on Iberian culture and shaped the Iberian and Ibero-American Enlightenment. Marginalizing Malebranche and Leibniz, and warning against Bayle, whose erudition he admired but whose ideas he considered dangerous,[61] Feijóo converted his countrymen into followers of Bacon, Boyle, Locke, Sydenham, and Newton, on the eminently cogent grounds that their thought is the Enlightenment strand which best defends belief in miracles and combines with religion, authority, and tradition, providing reliable defences against the *materialistas*, his term for the radicals and Spinozists.

Similarly in Portugal, the last country in Europe where scholastic Aristotelianism reigned supreme around 1740, Feijóo's critique of Cartesianism and *Malebranchisme*, and his promotion of English empiricism, eventually had a profound impact.[62] The

---

[57] Feijóo, *Cartas Eruditas*, ii, 230.
[58] Ibid., 231; Ardao, *Filosofía polémica*, 28, 40; McClelland, 'Estudio', 10–11, 29.
[59] Berní, *Filosofía racional*, pp. lxx–lxxii; Mindán, 'Corrientes', 485; Guy, *Historia*, 177.
[60] Berní, *Filosofía racional*, ii, 198, 215 and iii, 72, 127–37, 174–86.
[61] Staubach, 'Influence of Pierre Bayle', 80–4, 92.
[62] [Verney], *Verdadeiro metodo*, i, 252 and ii, 20, 38; Andrade, *Vernei e a cultura*, 144, 162.

chief intellectual figure of the Portuguese Enlightenment, Luís António Verney (1713–92), had been born in Lisbon of a French father but imbibed his 'enlightened' ideas as an ecclesiastic in Rome in the late 1730s and early 1740s, at a time when Locke's influence was particularly powerful there. Feijóo's work which, he says he began to read around 1734,[63] was one of the chief influences on him, and it was always his intention to spread Feijóo's influence in Portugal so as to weaken the scholasticism still ensconced in the colleges, restructuring Portuguese intellectual life on the basis of Boyle, Locke, and Newton.

Verney's *Verdadeiro Metodo de Estudar* (Coimbra, 1746), the book which precipitated the decisive breakthrough of the Enlightenment in Portugal and proved influential also in Spain and Spanish America,[64] touched off a lively controversy characterized by a relatively weak Aristotelian response. Verney did not hesitate to declare Spain as much ahead of Portugal in the reception of modern ideas, and furthering the triumph of 'filozofia moderna', as Italy was ahead of Spain.[65] Rebuking the Jesuits, Dominicans, and, by implication, the Inquisition for their age-old suppression of mechanistic philosophy and uncritical adherence to Aristotelianism, he scathingly criticized the backwardness of Portuguese culture, science, and education. With remarkably rapid and far-reaching success, he summoned his compatriots to change the whole basis and structure of their intellectual culture and higher education. But in what direction? For Verney no less than Feijóo, the triumph of the 'Newtonianos' was the triumph of the moderate, mainstream Enlightenment itself.[66]

Aristotelianism was now largely defeated while Neo-Cartesianism and *Malebranchisme*, believed Feijóo and Verney, was a spent force. Neither they, nor the third prime figure of the Spanish Enlightenment, the Aragonese Andrés Piquer y Arrufat (1711–72), a writer inspired by Feijóo and Verney, nor other key reformers such as the erudite Valencian Gregorio Mayáns y Siscar (1699–1781), an ally of Piquer, were either much impressed or disturbed by the Leibnizian–Wolffian system. Piquer calmly dismissed Leibniz's pre-established harmony as 'heretical' and 'purely imaginary'.[67] As the Spanish and Portuguese Enlightenment matured in the 1730s, 1740s, and 1750s, no leading figure contested or doubted that Bacon, Boyle, Locke, and Newton provided the best intellectual basis for a viable moderate Enlightenment. What, however did preoccupy and greatly perturb all these Iberian writers was the growing risk of an upsurge of materialism, fatalism, and Naturalism, in other words, an eruption of radical ideas.

Since the publication of Alvarez de Toledo's *Historia* in 1713, it was clear enough out of what intellectual quarter such a radical outpouring might erupt. Alvarez de Toledo seems to have drawn his knowledge of Spinoza from Basnage's *Histoire des Juifs* rather than directly from that philosopher's works. He nevertheless thought it right to characterize the 'abominable systema' of that 'Jew of Amsterdam' for the benefit of his

---

[63] [Verney], *Verdadeiro metodo*, ii, 20.   [64] Alvarez de Morales, *Ilustración*, 38–40.
[65] [Verney], *Verdadeiro metodo*, i, 252, 277 and ii, 20, 50–7; Hazard, *European Thought*, 102–3, 238.
[66] [Verney]. *Verdadeiro metodo*, ii, 20, 38, 56; Maxwell, 'Pombal', 86, 108, 117.
[67] Verney, *De re metaphysica*, 19–20; Piquer, *Philosophia moral*, 91–7; Piquer, *Discurso*, 90.

countrymen. He embraces Basnages' adoption of Wachter's notion that it was the Jewish Cabbalists, working on the principle that 'nothing can be created from nothing,' who first held 'there is not more than one substance in the universe which is God' and that all bodies and spirits are emanations of that one sole substance.[68] 'This view is the root of *Espinosismo* [Spinozism],' he declared, 'which holds that bodies and spirits are only modifications of the one substance of God.'[69] The basic difference between Spinoza and Cabbala, in his view, is that the former maintains that 'this substance is material and the Cabbalists that it is spiritual so that the opinion of the latter is more reverent than the former but no less absurd'.[70]

Feijóo and Sarmiento likewise seem not to have read Spinoza or to have had any direct knowledge of the writings of Europe's deists and *materialistas*. But they knew Bayle's article on Spinoza and other secondary sources, and did not doubt that Spinoza—and to only a slightly lesser extent, Bayle, whom Feijóo calls 'one of the most acute and erudite enemies of Catholic doctrine'—was a great danger against which society needed to gird itself.[71] Sarmiento claimed in 1732 that the 'impious Espinosa' had spread his 'infamous book' by subterfuge and especially using false titles, first for the *Tractatus Theologico-Politicus* and then others that mislead readers by not corresponding to the reality of their contents.[72]

By contrast, Verney, who lionizes Newton while considering Malebranche suspect and Hobbes an unsavoury subsidiary influence, judges on the basis of a direct knowledge of at least some extracts that the most impious and pernicious system of ethics that exists is that of the 'Dutchman Spinoza who is impious by principle, stripping man of his liberty, confusing man with God, and all this in beautifully sounding expressions, capable of misleading anyone'.[73] Verney, who also knew something of Toland, whom he brackets with Spinoza in his book of 1751, introducing philosophy to Portuguese youth, recommends as the three Catholic authors who have most effectively refuted Spinoza, Huet, Le Vassor, and Lamy.[74] For his part, Piquer, the fourth great figure of the Iberian Enlightenment, claimed that the '*materialistas* and other *sectarios* of our days' were renewing the 'most dreadful errors' of the ancient world, and that the supreme 'impiety of the *materialistas* is to hold Nature for the Divinity Himself', as, he says, 'in our times the impious and blasphemous Spinoza has done'.[75]

One of Piquer's prime goals in all his works is the defence of 'divine Providence'. His *Lógica moderna* (Valencia, 1747), a work addressed not to the scholar or student but to the professional and mercantile stratum of Spanish society, argues that a 'philosophical' attitude, one which detaches theology from philosophy, science, and medicine, is not only permissible but positively desirable, and that members of the

[68] Alvarez de Toledo, *Historia*, 132.   [69] Ibid., 133.   [70] Ibid.

[71] Ardao, *Filosofía polémica*, 118–20; Domínguez, 'España en Spinoza', 17; see also Staubach, 'Influence of Pierre Bayle', 80.

[72] Sarmiento, *Demonstración*, i, 282–3.

[73] [Verney], *Verdaeiro Metodo*, ii, 84; Machado de Abreu, 'Recepción', 110.

[74] Verney, *De Re Metaphysica*, 15–16.   [75] Piquer, *Discurso*, 97–8.

reading public should feel free to explore writers such as Boyle, Locke, and Newton, and sample other safe philosophical systems. At the same time, though, he insists on strong barriers against materialism, fatalism, and Spinozism. The prime criterion for differentiating between the acceptable and unacceptable face of philosophy, he maintains, is the upholding of a providential God and Creator. Nor is such a criterion derived simply from the directives of the Church, for belief in *providencia divina* and the Creation, holds Piquer, is 'rational' and innate in all men, as indeed is belief in the existence of angels, demons, and the power of Satan, while denial of these truths is 'irrational'.[76]

Some may well reply, he says, that 'Benito Spinoza and Pedro Bayle denied the existence of God, employing all their powers of reason'.[77] But this, he contends, is sheer affectation. Such depraved thinkers may claim to argue rationally but in their hearts they know the mendaciousness of their assertions and cannot resist reason's power, so that inwardly they acknowledge what publicly they profess to deny.[78] Hence Spinozism is a form of frenzy, an irrational stance deflecting the light of reason so that 'impious atheists can obscure the idea of God but not extinguish it' even within themselves.[79] The truth that belief in a providential God is innate in man is not changed by the fact that a handful denied it in classical antiquity or that 'there has been found in our times a man so impious, or rather such a monster, as Spinoza': 'for what do those few matter when compared with the universality of the entire human race?'[80]

A remarkable philosophical epic poem entitled *Triumpho da Religião*, by the scholarly courtier Francisco de Pina de Sá e Mello, licensed by three Portuguese Inquisitors in 1754, urged readers to consider all the philosophical systems rationally and take from each what is best and most rational. Much influenced by (the Cartesian) Cardinal Polignac's *Anti-Lucretius*, this 'poema epico-polemico' dismisses Aristotle and gently rebuts the Cartesian tradition, while predictably reserving its greatest praise for Newton and the 'argument from design'.[81] Although it does not overlook heretics and Jews, its main polemical thrust is consistently against the *atheistas*, *deistas*, and *libertinos*, the new orientation of Portuguese culture and pious tradition being neatly combined by emphasizing that the young Spinoza professed the 'Law of Moses', as did his parents who 'for that reason fled from Portugal to Amsterdam' and that Spinoza's rebellion against Scripture began in the synagogue 'seeing the little foundation with which the rabbis explain the text'.[82] Spinoza is placed alongside Epicurus and Lucretius as one of the supreme atheists of human history and the chief representative of modern times.[83] His theory of one substance is explained as the central feature of his thought and repeatedly compared with the doctrines of various ancient thinkers.[84]

By 1750 the Iberian Enlightenment had assumed its characteristic features, and the finishing touches were being put to its triumph not only by writers and educators but

---

[76] Piquer, *Lógica moderna*, 24; Piquer, *Philosophia moral*, 2–3, 55–62.   [77] Piquer, *Lógica moderna*, 24.
[78] Ibid.   [79] Ibid.   [80] Piquer, *Philosophia moral*, 2–3.
[81] Pina de Sá, *Triumpho*, 39, 64, 66–7.   [82] Ibid., 14.   [83] Ibid., 22.
[84] Ibid., 23–4, 83, 96; Machado de Abreu, 'Recepción', 110.

also the royal government and Inquisition. These all endorsed Feijóo's, Verney's, and Piquer's programme, which signified official support for the intellectual hegemony of Bacon, Boyle, Locke, and Newton, coupled with intensifying repression of freethinking, deism, and materialism. On 23 June 1750 the new King of Spain, Ferdinand VI (ruled 1746–59) issued an edict proclaiming that the works of Feijóo, and those containing similar concepts and views, had the full approval of the Crown and that all attacks on them in print were to cease forthwith.[85] Feijóo's Enlightenment had effectively become the official ideology of the State.

[85] Ozanam, 'L'idéal académique', 198; Alvarez de Morales, *Ilustración*, 36.

29 | Germany and the Baltic: the 'War of the Philosophers'

i. Deepening Philosophical Crisis

While the decisive split in the mainstream moderate Enlightenment in Germany and the Baltic occurred only with the banning of Wolff's philosophy by the Prussian Crown in 1723, signs of growing tension were evident well before this. Academic feuding over philosophy spread through the universities, dismaying many by displaying publicly the general loss of intellectual cohesion.[1] Some German universities, such as Duisburg, still broadly adhered to Cartesian, and others, such as Cologne or Heidelberg, preferred scholastic Aristotelian ideas. Halle meanwhile, or at least its philosophy faculty, tended by 1720 towards Wolffian ideas. But most simply languished in a state of chronic disarray. Thomasius' influence was widespread, but while this promoted an enquiring, eclectic outlook, it provided little or no intellectual coherence.[2] The old *philosophia recepta* was disintegrating, but nothing stable or widely acceptable took its place.

The prevailing situation was less a vacuum, however, than a pulsing vortex in which multiple external impulses—the new Biblical criticism, post-Boyle experimental science, Cartesianism and its variants, and latterly Newtonianism and (to a limited extent) Locke—pulsated and clashed with evolving internal spiritual and intellectual forces, especially Pietist fundamentalism and Leibnizian–Wolffian metaphysics. At Halle, by 1720, collisions between Pietists and Wolffians, in some cases marred by student tumult, had created an extremely fraught atmosphere. At Koenigsberg in 1725, according to the Wolffian professor of physics, Christian Gabriel Fischer (c.1690–1751), utter confusion reigned as Pietists and Thomasians fought Cartesian and Wolffian champions of mathematical method and the new science. '*Libertas philosophandi*,' remarked Fischer, 'does not always have beneficial results' but rather often yields only bafflement, strife, and 'pure sophistry'.[3] Many concurred with Leibniz's view that what was required was a new general synthesis accommodating scientific rationality

---

[1] Wessell, *G. E. Lessing's Theology*, 58–68, 78–9; Kuehn, 'German *Aufklärung*'. 310–14.
[2] Ibid., 311–12.   [3] Predeek, 'Verschollener Reorganisationsplan', 76; Wilson, 'Reception', 48–9.

and unhindered philosophical enquiry, while simultaneously giving a firm lead in moral and social affairs and upholding faith, authority, and tradition: the question, though, was how to achieve it?

One pre-eminent professor at Halle, Christian Wolff, believed he possessed the answers. His system, while not identical with that of Leibniz, which it systematizes but also selects from and modifies,[4] combines Leibniz's core doctrines of 'sufficient reason', 'pre-established harmony', the interconnectedness of all being and knowledge, and a variant of his monadology, with an even greater emphasis on the primacy of mathematical rationality in philosophy. Many colleagues, however, and most prominently Thomasius and Buddeus, long averse to Aristotelianism, Cartesianism, and Spinozism, likewise disapproved of Wolffianism. At Jena, Buddeus grew steadily more disconcerted and anxious.[5] Meanwhile, Pietist theologians—who in Prussia had the ear of King Friedrich Wilhelm I (reigned 1713–40)—abhorred both Cartesianism and Wolffianism. Their overriding concern was to ensure the continued subordination of philosophy to theology, and this drew them towards the eclectic, empiricist proclivities of the Thomasians.

Extreme opposition to the claims of mathematical rationality was voiced in particular by Volkmar Conrad Poppo (1691–1763), a theologian-philosopher at Jena who, in 1721, fiercely assailed mechanistic thinking in his *Spinozismus Detectus*. He published it at Weimar, being debarred from doing so at Jena by colleagues worried by his confrontational attitude. Without directly attacking Wolff, whose plea for the 'identity of philosophical and mathematical method' scandalized him,[6] Poppo condemned the 'mathematical method' of reasoning in philosophy championed by Wolffians as spiritual gangrene infesting German society.[7] By equating mathematical rationality with philosophical method, held Poppo, infamous thinkers—among whom he particularly berates Tschirnhaus but includes Wolff by implication—were twisting reality into a uniformly mechanistic structure explicable solely in geometric terms 'from which Spinozism and other impiety will necessarily arise'.[8]

Descartes and Malebranche, grants Poppo, seek to safeguard religion by proclaiming thought and extension totally separate substances; and, mercifully, most Cartesians do affirm their belief in angels, spirits, apparitions, and demons. But having ruled that mind and matter cannot interact, Cartesians are powerless to explain the interplay of spirit and matter, and causal connections between them, perplexity bound to degenerate, he contends, into the naturalistic 'absurdities' Bekker postulates in claiming that Satan and demons exist but cannot influence the doings of men.[9] Cartesianism, he held, despite Malebranche's endeavours, is inherently defective and can only produce *Bekkerianismus* and ultimately Spinozism.

---

[4] Condillac, *Traité des systèmes*, 85; Cassirer, *Philosophy*, 120–3; Wilson, 'Reception', 44–6.
[5] Buddeus, *Lehr-Sätze*, 245–6, 249–50.
[6] Wolff, *Preliminary Discourse*, 77, 109–10; Wilson, 'Reception', 445–6.
[7] Hartmann, *Anleitung*, 842–5; Trinius, *Freydenker-Lexicon*, 439. Otto, *Studien*, 139.
[8] Poppo, *Spinozismus Detectus*, 5; Ludovici, *Ausführlicher Entwurf*, i, 296–7.
[9] Poppo, *Spinozismus Detectus*, 46.

The gravity of the threat, he held, was abundantly illustrated by the furtive publication in Frankfurt four years before of Theodor Ludwig Lau's blasphemous and 'Spinozistic' *Meditationes Philosophicae*.[10]

Without a complete, wholehearted change of course, Germany will soon slide, predicted Poppo, into a moral, religious, and intellectual catastrophe, with the Bible considered a 'book written for ignorant people', miracles dismissed as impossible and reports thereof as 'deception', the Resurrection pronounced 'inconceivable', immortality of the soul denied, and man debased to the level of a 'machine'.[11] The three most heinous ramifications of mechanistic philosophy—which, he says, are Spinozism, *Bekkerianismus*, and Leenhof's popularization of Spinoza—would finally eradicate the Devil from men's minds, transform Heaven into 'tranquillity of mind', and dilute Hell to a troubled conscience.[12] Leenhof's and Geulincx's ethical ideas, recommending that one 'should give oneself over to the Laws of Nature and, on all occasions, whether happy or sad, remain unaffected', would reduce mankind morally and theologically to 'absolute indifference'.[13] To fight the contagion, Poppo summons philosophers and scientists to search for the 'principia vitalia' outside the framework of mechanistic ideas and by adducing 'other principles in nature' uncover the 'divine principles' which will clearly reveal the existence of 'an independent free Spirit who created the world out of nothing' and is 'totally distinct from physical principles'.[14] Only when this is accomplished will Christian learning gain final victory over 'our modern Spinozists and Sadducees . . . who think that they alone see with two eyes and that all other men are either blind or squint-eyed'.[15] If somewhat crude, Poppo's analysis, as history was shortly to demonstrate, reflected the intellectual anxieties and obsessions of an entire generation, fears most eloquently expressed by the Pietists.

Especially prominent among the latter in Prussia was Joachim Lange (1670–1744), professor of theology at Halle since 1709 and a vigorous publicist, who had earlier headed the gymnasium in Berlin and remained in close touch with the Prussian Court.[16] Though doubtful about Cartesianism, particularly Cartesian claims regarding the complete separateness of philosophy from theology, Lange acknowledged that genuine Cartesians were tolerably safe, indeed preferable to most alternatives; and, in particular, he respected the Franeker philosopher Ruard Andala who, like himself, viewed Leibnizians with implacable suspicion.[17] The chief defect of Cartesianism, in Lange's view, was its proneness to produce malignant offspring, 'pseudo-Cartesiani', the most pernicious of whom, he held, were Geulincx, Bekker, De Volder, and Malebranche. Among such hidden *Spinozantes* deemed by him only marginally less reprehensible than undisguised Spinozists, like Cuffeler and Leenhof, he was increasingly inclined to classify his colleague Wolff[18]. Lange, like Buddeus, never doubted that Spinoza was the principal threat to

---

[10] Ibid., 47.   [11] Ibid., 48; see also Wessell, *G. E. Lessing's Theology*, 68.
[12] Poppo, *Spinozismus Detectus*, 48.   [13] Ibid., 62.   [14] Ibid., 66, 75.
[15] Ibid., 76.   [16] Wilson, 'Reception', 450–2.
[17] Altmann, *Moses Mendelssohn*, 52.   [18] Lange, *Causa Dei*, 47–90.

Germany's spiritual well-being, the arch-atheist of modern times as well as the chief reviver of the fatalism and materialism of the ancients and the Naturalism of Pomponazzi, Bruno, and Vanini. Nor was Spinozism, in his view, a menace only to the academic world and the courtly milieu. On the contrary, the Leenhof controversies proved, he maintained, the capacity of popular, simplified Spinozism to infiltrate all levels.[19]

ii. The Wolffian Controversies (1723–1740)

The conflict which began in 1723 developed into one of the most formative cultural encounters of the eighteenth century and was, arguably, the most important of the age of Enlightenment in Central Europe and the Baltic before the French Revolution. While its impact was delayed in Catholic Germany, Bohemia-Moravia, and Austria, the furore was never confined to Protestant Germany. From the mid-1720s onwards, its reverberations were strongly felt northwards as far as Stockholm and Saint Petersburg and to the west and south in the Netherlands, Switzerland, and Italy. The uproar also had some impact in France, particularly during the 1740s. Indeed, only Britain can be held to have remained completely untouched. What this vast confrontation showed was that Europe's official, mainstream Enlightenment was so deeply divided that there was, after all, no possibility of devising a universally acceptable synthesis or ideology of Enlightenment, or any way of uniting the forces of tradition against radical deism and Spinozism. The upheaval also swept away the last lingering vestiges of theological dominance in large stretches of Europe, heralding the undisputed primacy of secular philosophy and science.

For years before 1723 the tension surrounding Wolff at Halle where he taught and, by 1720, had published several widely admired works, was acute.[20] The undercurrent of murmuring became a full-blown campaign against him and such disciples as Georg Bernhard Bilfinger (1693–1750, who, in the late 1720s, was to be his apostle in Russia), following a sensational lecture delivered by Wolff in 1721 on the 'Practical Philosophy of the Chinese'. Imprudently, Wolff, like Leibniz a firm Sinophile, eulogized ancient Chinese philosophy, comparing it with his own in some respects, and claiming that Confucius' moral maxims demonstrate the ability of natural reason to attain moral truth,[21] while simultaneously admitting the atheistic tendencies in Chinese thought.[22] By this time Lange, Wolff's foremost enemy at Halle, had already concluded he was teaching a doctrine of the 'absolute necessity of things', akin to Spinozism (albeit superficially derived from Leibniz) and apt to foment atheism.[23] The affinities between Spinozism and classical Chinese thought had been widely noted in Europe since Bayle's *Dictionnaire* had first drawn attention to them so that Wolff's detractors

---

[19] Lange, *Causa Dei*, 123, 135, 515.   [20] Ludovici, *Ausführlicher Entwurf*, ii, 102–9.

[21] Cassirer, *Philosophy*, 166; Hazard, *European Thought*, 51–2.

[22] Lange, *Kurtzer Abriss*, 10; Saine, 'Who's afraid of Christian Wolff?', 118–19; Kuehn, 'German *Aufklärung*', 310; Wilson, 'Reception', 450–1.

[23] Lange, *Causa Dei*, 9–10, 18, 21; École, 'Critique Wolffienne', 554.

found little difficulty in exploiting the affair to denigrate Wolff in academic and Court circles as a crypto-Spinozist.[24]

Lange mobilized the Halle theology faculty to denounce Wolff's teaching at Court in Berlin where, given Friedrich Wilhelm's rampant bigotry, there was plentiful scope for damaging Wolff's standing. Lange's critique struck home and Wolff's philosophy was peremptorily banned by a royal decree of May 1723 in all the universities and gymnasia under the Prussian crown, hence from Duisburg to Koenigsberg.[25] The philosopher himself was imperiously dismissed from his chair on 8 November 1723, with orders to leave Halle within twenty-four hours, and the Prussian kingdom in forty-eight. Wolff fled to Hesse-Cassel, where influential friends arranged a new chair for him at the University of Marburg and where he was greeted with acclaim, his arrival in Marburg being marked by a public concert given in his honour.[26] Traditionally resistant to the rigid Lutheranism of Saxony, Marburg now became the headquarters of what Bilfinger was the first to dub the 'Leibnizian–Wolffian system'.

Virtually the whole of German academe now slid into bitter wrangling and acrimony.[27] Within two years of Wolff's expulsion from Halle, at least twenty-six argued judgements condemning his thought were submitted in nine different universities, including Wittenberg, Rostock, Koenigsberg and Tübingen, where Bilfinger took up a chair in 1724. Bilfinger was not a man to be cowed by uproar and immediately began eulogizing Leibniz's pre-established harmony and advocating Wolff's philosophy with great zeal, like his mentor stressing the gulf between Wolffianism and Spinoza's immutable 'laws of nature'.[28] But his efforts destabilized the university to such an extent that the Duke of Württemberg felt obliged to intervene, demanding that the theology and philosophy faculties state clearly whether Wolff's philosophy was in fact 'nützlich oder schädlich' (useful or harmful). The answer, after months of vehement bickering, was that it was more 'schädlich' than 'nützlich' and should be suppressed.[29] Although there was no consensus among Tübingen's anti-Wolffians about whether Wolff was a 'Spinozist', a teacher of 'Stoic or Spinozist necessity', a partial ally of atheistic influences, or simply a fomenter of strife and perplexity Württemberg would be better off without, there was sufficient negative pressure for a ban.[30] Accordingly, Württemberg followed Prussia in prohibiting Wolff's philosophy by princely decree.[31]

Bilfinger, provided with an excellent job offer from St Petersburg, prepared to depart. He was to remain in Russia for five years, holding his own and eventually leading the large Wolffian contingent there to victory over both traditionalists and

---

[24] Charles-Daubert and Moreau, *Pierre Bayle. Écrits*, 37–42; Lange, *Nova Anatome*, 83–5; Mañer, *Anti-Theatro Critico*, i, 13.

[25] Lange, *Causa Dei*, preface; Ludovici, *Ausführlicher Entwurf*, i, 102–5, 109.

[26] Zedler, *Grosses Universal Lexicon*, lviii, 584.

[27] Gottsched, *Historische Lobschrift*, 75; Lange, *Nove Anatome*, 140–1.

[28] Bilfinger, *De harmonia animi et corporis*, 11, 113, 150, 176–7; Hartmann, *Anleitung*, 1015.

[29] Ludovici, *Sammlung und Auszüge*, i, 161–70; Gottsched, *Historische Lobschrift*, 75.

[30] Ludovici, *Sammlung und Auszüge*, i, 164.

[31] Hartmann, *Anleitung*, 797–814; École, 'Critique Wolfienne', 554.

Newtonianism. Meanwhile, the intervention of the Court of Hesse-Cassel in support of Wolff and the battle in Württemberg obliged Lange and his allies to expand their campaign throughout Protestant Germany and beyond. Especially pertinent at this point was the attitude of the immensely learned Buddeus, who was widely respected not just as Germany's foremost historian of philosophy but as her prime judge and classifier of philosophical doctrines.

For over a quarter of a century (1705–29) Buddeus was the predominant philosophical voice at Jena, a university which, at the time, enjoyed greater prestige than virtually any other Lutheran academy apart from Halle. An ally of Thomasius, more noticeably influenced by Locke—as Wolff pointed out—than other German savants,[32] Buddeus was no friend of Wolffianism and a vigilant adversary of Spinozism, as his recent intervention in the Dutch-German 'Nature of God' controversy amply showed. He deemed Wolff's system harmful and, up to a point, was ready to work against him behind the scenes. But he shrank from public controversy and had no wish to be dragged into protracted warfare with the numerous Wolffians.[33] At the request of his colleagues and prince, the Duke of Eisenach, as well as Halle University, and assuming his submission would remain confidential, he wrote a detailed judgement of the Wolffian philosophy in January 1724, drawing highly unfavourable conclusions. He expected his intervention would primarily serve to reinforce Halle's stance and assist the local ducal and academic authorities in Jena in drafting their own ban on Wolffianism.[34]

The gist of Buddeus' argument was that Wolff's system erodes belief in Providence, sapping the foundations of Biblically based morality such that 'on the basis of these hypotheses not even any heathen, let alone Christian, religion can be maintained.'[35] Wolff's system, in his opinion, not only precludes freedom of the will but also reward or punishment in the hereafter 'for it would be as senseless were God to punish or reward people who do nothing themselves but merely let happen what the nexus of causes, and the pre-established harmony, bring about, as it would were I to punish a clock or a machine.'[36] The mathematical mode of thought, he contends, is the root of the menace, for Wolff, as a 'mathematician, wishes to explain everything in a mechanistic way'.[37] 'Whether, and how far, this author agrees with Spinoza,' ruled Buddeus, 'is not really the point': for there are different varieties of atheism and just as one can be atheistic 'without being a Spinoza, one can cultivate pernicious doctrines encouraging atheism despite diverging on this or that point from Spinoza'.[38] Nevertheless, it was plain that he detected numerous affinities between Wolff and Spinoza.

Jena too prohibited Wolff's philosophy. But to Buddeus' dismay, and without his permission, colleagues at Halle subsequently published his judgement with its

---

[32] Wolff, *Vernünfftigen Gedancken*, 137; Fischer, 'John Locke', 433–4.

[33] Ludovici, *Ausführlicher Entwurf*, i part ii, p. 111.

[34] Walch, *Bescheidene Antwort*, 79, 94, 105–7; Hartmann, *Anleitung*, 814; Schmidt, *Alma Mater Jenensis*, 120–1.

[35] Buddeus, *Bedencken*, 3.   [36] Ibid., 21.   [37] Ibid.   [38] Ibid., 22.

designation of Wolffianism as 'höchst schädlich und gefährlich' (highly damaging and dangerous) under the title *Bedencken über die Wolffianische Philosophie.*[39] The doughty Wolff instantly produced a devastating reply, which the venerable Buddeus opted not to answer directly, delegating responsibility to his relative and ally Johann Georg Walch (1693–1775), future compiler of the well-known *Philosophisches Lexicon.* Walch did his best to counter Wolff's 'Sophistereyen', reiterating Buddeus' view that the latter's system is unmistakably atheistic, excludes miracles, and leaves no room for Providence. Despite omitting his name from the title-page,[40] he in turn, in August 1724, was treated to a crushing rebuke, in which Wolff resoundingly denied being an 'atheist or Spinozist' and insisted that his philosophy 'puts the securest weapons in our hands with which to combat atheists and other enemies of religion'.[41] Meanwhile, as Brucker later expresssed it, 'almost every German university was inflamed with disputes, about liberty and necessity, and the names Wolffians and anti-Wolffians reverberated everywhere.'[42]

With Buddeus and Walch more than a little daunted, it was left to Lange to intensify the anti-Wolff publicity campaign in both German and Latin. His case was that Leibniz and Wolff conceive our world to be governed by mathematically defined general laws which operate mechanistically, that is, once God has selected his 'pre-established harmony' there is, from then on, an immutable order of cause and effect which, for all practical purposes, does not differ from *necessitas Spinozistica.*[43] Effectively, this rules out miracles, Providence, and free will. By attracting droves of students, trumpeting his 'pre-established harmony', and recruiting supporters, Wolff was polluting all Germany, propagating innumerable *pseudo-philosophi* and atheists, avid to demolish authority, morality, and piety.

Lange and Buddeus accused Wolff not of being a 'Spinozist' *stricto sensu* but, through subterfuge and hypocrisy, knowingly opening the gates to Spinozism. Spinoza, the quintessence of fatalism, Naturalism, deism and atheism, according to Lange, had at any rate openly denied freedom of the will and taught the unalterable necessity of all cause and effect. But since Spinoza's death, disastrously for mankind, contemptible hypocrites, beginning with that 'little flower plucked from Spinoza's garden', Burchardus de Volder, had toiled to convince men there is 'no free choice of the mind, no accident of the body'.[44] Seeing they could win followers only by concealing their real meaning, Spinoza's disciples had devised more and more devious and insinuating ways of fomenting their loathsome views. The only means to defeat them was for Germany's Courts and universities to join together, bending

---

[39] Ibid., 3–4.

[40] Walch, *Bescheidene Antwort,* title-page and pp. 75–8, 94, 105–7; Zedler, *Grosses Universal Lexicon,* lviii, 585; Baumeister, *Institutiones,* 486–91.

[41] Wolff, *Nöthige Zugabe,* vorrede, p. B3.   [42] Brucker, *Historia,* 613.

[43] Lange, *Causa Dei,* 9–10, 18; Lange, *Modesta Disquisitio,* 41–2, 55, 62–3, 79; Lange, *Placidae Vindiciae,* 29, 32–3; Lange, *Nova Anatome,* 83–5; Walch, *Bescheidener Beweis,* 120–3; Hartmann, *Anleitung,* 551–2, 562, 650, 663–4; Altmann, *Moses Mendelssohn,* 50, 52, 187.

[44] Lange, *Causa Dei,* 47, 100.

every effort to suppress not just undisguised atheism and Spinozism but no less the upsurge of 'pseudo-philosophy'—Lange's code for Wolffianism—now everwhere assiduously propagating mechanistic, materialistic, and ultimately Spinozistic concepts of God, man, and the Universe.[45]

Lange grants that Wolff's system differs from Spinoza's in some essential respects and that, in Wolff's thought, God and the universe are separate. Yet the two systems, he held, nevertheless coincide at crucial points. Not only does Wolff, like Spinoza, advocate unrestricted 'freedom to philosophize', equate philosophical and mathematical method, and insist that philosophical knowledge fills the soul with a higher, more enduring pleasure than other things,[46] but he promotes a concept of the highest human good closely resembling 'Leenhof's heaven', that is, he propounds a version of Spinozist ethics cunningly masked with ostensibly Christian vocabulary.[47] Such *philosophia Spinoziano-Leenhofiana*, he argues, is rooted exclusively in what serves the individual's earthly needs and interests, discarding all idea of a God-ordained moral order and absolute good and evil. Leenhof is cited repeatedly as an allegedly key intermediary between Spinoza and Wolffianism.[48]

Wolff claimed to have circumvented the pitfalls into which the Cartesians had sunk, and simultaneously destroyed Spinoza, with his—and Leibniz's—new doctrine of the soul. According to Wolff, the doctrine of *harmonia praestabilita* means 'body and soul are distinct substances' but yet, without actually interacting, function through God's decree in perfect synchrony.[49] Yet according to Lange, all Wolff had accomplished here was to replicate Leibniz's dubious theory of the soul which, on analysis, turns out to be merely Spinoza's conflation of the two into one adeptly camouflaged to trick the public. Circuitously, Wolff is really denying both the separateness and immortality of the soul, making it part of a human being which is like a watch, a mechanism receiving feelings and impressions but lacking freedom to choose.[50] Furthermore, Wolff's mechanistic framework precludes all supernatural intervention of spirits in earthly life. There is no one, avows Lange, who does not know how much scandal and commotion Bekker provoked in Holland with his claims that spirits and demons do not act on men.[51] Wolff's teaching, no less than Bekker's, means spirits detached from bodies cannot act on bodies. *Bekkerianismus*, like Leenhof's teaching, he insists, is a gangrene of the mind, a contagion becoming rampant in Germany as the clandestine publication of the despicable books of Stosch and Lau abundantly demonstrates. Leibniz and Wolff contend that the laws of nature flow from their 'pre-established harmony'. But what, finally, is the difference

---

[45] Lange, *Causa Dei*, 80.   [46] Wolff, *Preliminary Discourse*, 27–9.

[47] Lange, *Causa Dei*, 405.   [48] Ibid., 123, 405, 515, 542–3; Lange, *Modesta disquisitio*, 44–5.

[49] Wolff, *Des Herrn Doct. und Prof. Joachim Langens . . . Anmerckungen*, 67; Wilson, 'Reception', 446–7.

[50] Lange, *Verscheidene und ausfuhrliche Entdeckung*, 199–205; Wolff, *Des Herrn Doct. und Prof. Joachim Langens Anmerckungen*, 48.

[51] Lange, *Modesta Disquisitio*, 122; Lange, *Placidae Vindiciae*, 29; Lange, *Verscheidene und ausführliche Entdeckung*, 60, 110.

between their *praestabilitas* and Spinoza's *praedeterminatio*? Is the first not merely another name for the second?[52]

Though banned in Prussia, Württemberg, and at Jena and inundated with *scripta anti-Wolfiana* everywhere, Wolff, who had friends and loyal former students throughout Germany and beyond, proved an extraordinarily redoubtable opponent. He was, in the first place, staggeringly productive. Besides his scathing replies to Lange, Buddeus, and Walch, from 1723 he produced a series of major works, culminating in the *Theologia Naturalis* (1736) which appeared in a six-volume German edition in 1742, powerfully restating his teaching in a manner designed continually to highlight the differences between the Leibnizian–Wolffian and Spinozist thought.[53] Spinoza, he agrees, denies the possibility of miracles and Providence and his 'unalterable necessity' destroys all religion and morality.[54] But far from disseminating 'fatalism', his own philosophy, he maintains, is much the best available antidote against Spinozist necessitarianism.[55]

First, and fundamentally different from Spinoza, was his absolute dichotomy of body and soul, a true duality akin to that of the Cartesians except that, where the Cartesians lamentably fail to explain the synchronization of the two, Leibniz and he, with their 'pre-established harmony', had resolved this difficulty.[56] Secondly, while granting the Leibnizian–Wolffian system postulates a world functioning in accordance with general laws expressed mathematically, and operating mechanistically, he insisted this does not mean conceding Spinoza's unalterable laws of nature. For, according to Leibniz and Wolff, the universe is not necessarily as it is but could be otherwise in numerous ways, following different rules of nature:[57] 'where I teach many worlds to be possible and God to have chosen freely from among them [plures mundos esse possibiles et ex iis Deum liberrime elegisse] . . . Spinoza acknowledges no other world to be possible other than that which exists' and where 'I affirm many things to be possible which never actually existed, Spinoza denies this.'[58] Wolff held the power of God to extend to countless things that have never existed and never will, but could exist provided they are not in logic inherently impossible.[59]

Where Wolffianism teaches that the laws of motion are not inherent in the nature of bodies but derive from the 'wisdom of God', Spinoza claims these are inherent and immutable.[60] Far from being *fatalistas* sharing in Spinoza's 'absoluta

---

[52] Lange, *Modesta Disquisitio*, 142; Altmann, *Moses Mendelssohn*, 52.

[53] École, 'Critique Wolfienne', 553–8; Buschmann, 'Wolff's "Widerlegung" ', 126–8.

[54] Wolff, *Vernünfftigen Gedancken von Gott*, 402, 433, 625–6.

[55] Wolff, *De Differentia Nexus*, 14–17, 28–31, 68–9.

[56] Ibid., 64, 68–9; Thümmig, *Institutiones philosophicae*, i, 156–9, 192–3, 198–201; Bilfinger, *De harmonia animi et corporis*, 80–2, 176–7.

[57] Wolff, *De Differentia Nexus*, 14, 17; Wolff, *Anmerckungen*, 273–6; Wolff, *Vernünfftigen Gedancken von Gott*, 273–4, 314, 321; Wolff, *Natürliche Gottesgelahrheit* [*Theologia Naturalis*], ii, 30–1; Otto, *Studien*, 143.

[58] Wolff, *De Differentia Nexus*, 30.

[59] Ibid., 31; Wolff, *Natürliche Gottesgelahrheit* [*Theologia Naturalis*], ii, 31, 37.

[60] Ibid.; Wolff, *Vernünfftigen Gedancken von Gott*, 274; Bilfinger, *De harmonia animi et corporis*, 113–14.

et bruta necessitas', Leibnizians and Wolffians are *contingentiarii* (advocates of contingency).[61] Wolff powerfully argued, against Spinoza, that 'God can suspend the Order of Nature when and as often as he wishes'[62] and that his own philosophy fully accommodated Creation of the universe by God 'from nothing'.[63] Strikingly, the core 80-page section against Spinoza in the *Theologia Naturalis*, like his other refutations of Spinoza, is admirably free of the vitriol routinely poured on that philosopher at the time. Wolff does not deny that the *Spinozisten, Naturalisten*, and radicals, being universalists and 'fatalists', are men who 'have no religion'.[64] But his primary concern throughout was not to condemn on any theological ground but to convince readers philosophically that 'Spinoza did not prove the unalterable necessity of all things and nor could he have.'[65]

Meanwhile, those loyal Wolffians who enjoyed less standing internationally than Bilfinger had little choice, especially at Prussian universities, but to keep their heads down and, as far as possible, avoid public entanglement with anti-Wolffians. Thus, the Swiss Niklaus Engelhard (1696–1765), who acquired a chair in Duisburg in 1723, survived five years, keeping his own counsel, before moving on to the freer air of Groningen, where he could openly teach what Wolffians called the 'modern philosophy', becoming the first to challenge the then prevailing disparagement of Leibniz and Wolff in the Dutch academies.[66] Such a survival strategy was scarcely available though to scholars previously already embroiled with Pietists, such as Christian Gabriel Fischer at Königsberg. Fischer, long a vocal critic of the university's conservative establishment, and a known Wolffian, paid a stiff price. Dismissed from his chair for crypto-Spinozism and atheism in November 1725, he was summarily expelled from Prussia. He migrated first to Danzig[67] and later to Holland, Italy, and France but, despite emphatic denials, could never fully shake off the stigma of 'Spinozism'. It was many years before he received permission to return to his home in East Prussia.

In Berlin, meanwhile, there were numerous Wolffian sympathizers, but these too were effectively muzzled. Among their number was the still young and relatively unknown Huguenot savant Charles Étienne Jordan (1700–45), later to attain prominence as an adviser and secretary to Frederick the Great. Eager to make his mark in the Republic of Letters, Jordan ventured to establish contact with Wolff at Marburg in 1727, reporting the latest anti-Wolffian measures in Prussia and expressing the hope these would serve only to stimulate demand for his books.[68] His bravado instantly evaporated, though, when Wolff suggested he might like to assist him by publicly criticizing Lange's crusade against his philosophy. As far as the public sphere was concerned, all Wolff's Prussian adherents remained studiously silent.

---

[61] Wolff, *De Differentia Nexus*, 17, 23; École, 'Critique Wolffienne', 556–7.

[62] Wolff, *Natürliche Gottesgelahrheit* [*Theologia Naturalis*], ii, 37–8; Wolff, *Cosmologia Generalis*, 407, 410.

[63] Wolff, *Natürliche Gottesgelahrheit* [*Theologia Naturalis*], iii, 11–13, 22.

[64] Ibid., vi, 107, 112–13.   [65] Ibid., 107.

[66] [Strodtmann], *Das Neuen Gelehrten Europa* (Wolfenbüttel) 1 (1752), 281–2; Wielema, 'Nicolaus Engelhard', 151–2.

[67] Predeek, 'Verschollener Reorganisationsplan', 65–6.   [68] Häseler, *EinWanderer*, 39.

Two additional royal decrees against Wolffianism were promulgated in Berlin in May of that year, one forbidding bookshops to stock or sell Wolff's books, the other prohibiting reading and discussion of Wolff's 'metaphysical and moral writings' even 'in private' homes, these being banned as 'atheistic in all our universities'.[69] Meanwhile, Lange kept up a relentless barrage of anti-Wolffian theologico-philosophical rhetoric. In a Latin account of the origins of the Wolffian crisis in German academe, he again lauded *genuini Cartesiani* like Andala while stressing what he saw as the deliberate perversion of Cartesianism by *pseudo-Cartesiani*, such as Geulincx and De Volder, whom he considered primarily responsible for laying the intellectual foundations of the mechanistic Naturalism and fatalism endangering German higher education and society.[70] Wolff's system he envisages as a cunning reworking of Spinoza's mechanistic metaphysics, and therefore a vehicle of the host of contemporary *pseudo-philosophi Spinozantes* infesting universities and undermining religion, authority, and the State.[71] Wolff's contention that his system is eminently compatible with Christian truth, Lange likens to the fraudulent pretensions of the anonymous author of the preface to Spinoza's *Opera Posthuma* (Jelles) who has the impudence to claim Spinoza's philosophy is 'Christian' in essence.[72]

But even Lange failed to match the tremendous avalanche of discourse pouring from the pens of Wolff and his lieutenants. Orchestrating his counter-campaign with consummate skill, Wolff built his defence on his sustained, continually reiterated critique of Spinoza. In volumes long and short, concise and prolix, in German and Latin, Wolff unrelentingly asserted the divergences between his doctrine and Spinoza's.[73] By the early 1730s the discerning onlooker might well have concluded that the indefatigable professor had not just survived but basically won his war with Prussia's bureaucracy, reactionary academe and Pietism, indeed, worsted the Prussian state itself. Wolff's intellectual influence and prestige was incontestably on the increase, not only throughout Germany but internationally. In January 1733 the French Court honoured him by making him the sole German foreign associate of the Académie des Sciences in Paris. In 1734 he was fêted at the Swedish Court, where a celebratory medal was issued in his honour.[74] Finally, in Prussia itself, the authorities felt obliged in 1734 to lift the seven-year ban on the sale of his books and on disputing his doctrines in the universities.

But the struggle was not over yet, as further developments proved, and there was still considerable scope, or so it seemed, for derailing the hitherto inexorable progress of Leibnitio–Wolffianism. Lange, meanwhile, strove to deflate the boasts of those who pointed to Wolffian victories abroad. If Wolff was being fêted in Sweden, his thought, retorted Lange, had sown ruinous dissension in the Swedish universities no less than in those of Germany.[75] If Wolff was advancing in Italy, this was unsurprising,

---

[69] Hartmann, *Anleitung*, 819–21. [70] Lange, *Nova Anatome*, 83–5, 91–2.
[71] Ibid. [72] Ibid., 98–9. [73] École, 'Critique Wolfienne', 555.
[74] Hartmann, *Anleitung*, 822. [75] Ibid., 716; Lange, *Kurtzer Abriss*, 13.

he contended, since the Jesuits, always attracted to 'atheism', were bound to flock to his banner.[76]

iii. Wolff and the Rise of German Deism

But if men began to worry less about whether or not Wolffianism opens the door to Spinozism, and whether it combined satisfactorily or not with Christianity, there could be no doubt that Wolffianism, like Newtonianism, did in large part remove spirits and the supernatural from men's ideas about nature, did largely remove theology from science and philosophy, and did encourage a mechanistic, mathematical approach to our understanding of nature.[77] Furthermore, there was another sense in which the Wolffian furore stimulated the growth of deism in Germany and the Baltic. The commotion not only focused the public's attention on Spinozism as the foremost, overriding threat to society but widened the context in which the public viewed the issue. Instead of reiterating traditional and familiar complaints that Spinoza denies miracles and prophecy, subverts the Bible, and overthrows the central Christian 'mysteries', Wolff's increasingly elaborate and detailed, as well as oft repeated, critique raised innumerable complex intellectual questions which spurred readers, including large numbers of university students, to investigate key propositions from Spinoza's writings and related texts, in a deeper and more serious fashion than before. Wolff's writings, in the eyes of many scholars and students, not only vindicated his charge that the theologians had been somewhat inexact in their characterization of his own system but also implied they had only very superficially come to grips with Spinozism. Many were bound to conclude that Wolff's method of sober, objective, detailed investigation of the issues was preferable. But this in turn might well tend to suggest that Spinoza could not be rebuffed theologically, or with decrees, bluster, and denunciation, but only by judicious philosophical argument such as Wolff's.[78]

In short, Lange and the Pietists, as well as Buddeus and his allies, were by no means entirely mistaken in portraying Wolffianism as a conduit for an uncompromisingly philosophical attitude and thus for deism and preoccupation with Spinoza. Moreover, the charge that Wolff was responsible for the troubling growth of deism in German society and culture drew fresh cogency in the mid-1730s from the storm which blew up within the larger Wolffian turbulence over the so-called 'Wertheim Bible', a notorious compilation published by the hitherto little known Johann Lorenz Schmidt (1702–49). 'What kind of fruit grows out of Wolff's philosophy', proclaimed Lange, triumphantly resuming his offensive in 1736, can be readily discerned from the 'Wertheim Bible' with its 'thoroughly Wolffian' preface.[79]

Schmidt, a preacher's son, having learnt Hebrew and studied philosophy and theology at Jena under Buddeus, became an ardent Wolffian, moving in 1725 to Halle,

---

[76] Hartmann, *Anleitung*, 15; Formey, *Histoire abrégée*, 297.
[77] Cassirer, *Philosophy*, 175; Wessell, *G. E. Lessing's Theology*, 68–78.
[78] Ludovici, *Neueste Merckwürdigkeiten*, 73–4.   [79] Lange, *Kurtzer Abriss*, 15.

where he scandalized the university by openly disparaging the professors and praising Wolff.[80] On leaving Prussia, he had obtained an excellent post as tutor to the children of the widowed Countess of Wertheim and began a promising career as resident *philosophe* at that minor Court. His prospects were thoroughly blighted, though, just a few years later, on publishing his German translation of, and commentary on, the Hebrew Pentateuch. Published at Wertheim secretly and anonymously, with the connivance of a local official, his rendering and notes provoked a furious outcry all over Germany. For his text was obviously a systematic attempt to dilute, or explain away, everything miraculous in the Five Books, substituting uncompromisingly naturalistic explanations. Especially offensive, contended Lange, was his deliberate erasing of every (traditionally alleged) Old Testament reference to the future coming of Christ, and dismissal of the doctrine of the Holy Trinity, as unfounded and bogus.[81] The 'Wertheim Bible', with its unmistakably Naturalistic flavour, precipitated a bitter triangular battle fought out in Lutheran, Calvinist, and Catholic Germany alike between the forces of traditionalist reaction, the moderate Enlightenment, and radical thought.[82]

In Prussia, the counter-offensive was orchestrated by Lange, who instantly recognized the affair's potential as a source of ammunition for his war against Wolff. Approximately fifty publications condemning the 'Wertheim Bible' poured from German presses in two years (1735–7), creating a feverish atmosphere in which the linkage of Wolffianism with the widely noted upsurge of radical deism and Spinozism in the country could be continually stressed.[83] But while Schmidt's 'blasphemous arguments' and thesis that in Scripture 'one must not accept anything which cannot be grasped by reason' could in principle be rejected by both moderate Enlightenment and traditionalists, disagreement over the role of reason in Biblical exegesis also exacerbated the rift between these two blocs, the former trying to use Schmidt to pulverize Wolff, while Wolff's adherents endeavoured to thwart their enemies by ditching Schmidt without allowing him to be labelled a 'Wolffian'. The 'Wertheim Bible' was formally condemned by the Lutheran theology faculty at Leipzig in January 1736, and publicly denounced in learned orations at Giessen, Greifswald, Helmstedt, Görlitz, and Heidelberg, as well as Göttingen.

The Emperor and the Imperial Chancery banned the printing, distribution, and sale of the Wertheim Bible by edict of 15 January 1737, as a text which perverts the fundamentals of Christianity, substitutes philosophy for theology, and expunges all reference to Christ from the Mosaic books.[84] At Frankfurt, the Imperial Book Commission searched the stores and bookshops, seizing all copies that could be found. Princely prohibitions of the text poured forth in Mainz, Bavaria, Prussia, Hanover, Hessse-Darmstadt, Electoral Saxony, East Friesland, and Holstein-Gottorp,

---

[80] Kobuch, *Zenzur und Aufklärung*, 69; Goldenbaum, 'Erste deutsche Übersetzung', 109.
[81] Lange, *Kurtzer Abriss*, 15; Kobuch, *Zensur und Aufklärung*, 70.
[82] Zedler, *Grosses Universal Lexicon*, xxv, 1093–9.
[83] Ibid., 1095–8.
[84] Ibid., lv, 614–17; Kobuch, *Zensur und Aufklärung*, 71–2.

Die
göttlichen
Schriften
vor den Zeiten des Messie Jesus
Der erste Theil
worinnen
Die Gesetze der Jisraelen
enthalten sind
nach einer freyen Ubersetzung
welche durch und durch mit
Anmerkungen
erläutert und bestätiget wird

Idem Sapor

Wertheim
Gedruckt durch Johann Georg Nehr, Hof und Cantzley-Buchdrucker
1735

FIGURE 4. The 'Wertheim Bible' of 1735, translated and with a commentary by Johann Lorenz Schmidt, one of the most controversial German publications of the first half of the eighteenth century.

followed, in November 1737, by the book's suppression in Denmark–Norway. Meanwhile the culprit's identity had been discovered, and Schmidt arrested. In July 1737 a special Imperial judicial commission arrived in Wertheim to try him for subverting religion and adherence to *Naturalismus*. To the grave embarrassment of almost everyone, however, local officials released him from custody, enabling him to flee to Holland. Later he returned to Germany, settling in Altona, under Danish jurisdiction.

Schmidt amply acknowledges his debt to Wolff in his preface and notes. Beyond this, experts judged he had been guided chiefly by Le Clerc and Spinoza but also Grotius and the English deists.[85] Ernst Friedrich Neubauer (1705–48), who completed Rambach's monumental commentary on the Old Testament in 1737, added indignant

---

[85] Rambach, *Collegium*, i, 765, 923; Steuber, *Commentatio Epistolica*, 14; Otto, *Studien*, 353–4.

annotations, deploring the 'presumptious insolence' of the Wertheim Bible's 'author' in spurning traditional interpretations of Old Testament Messianic allusions to Christ and his rationalization of the Fall, dismissing the Serpent as mere allegory.[86] He also denounced other 'Naturalistic' touches, such as his denial that Lot's wife really turned into a pillar of salt. A scholar lecturing at Rinteln, in June 1737, expressed horror that the 'Wertheim Interpreter' should blasphemously construe Biblical references to the intervention of the 'Holy Spirit' as merely an unusually 'vehement wind'.[87] The problem for the Wolffians was not just Schmidt's declared admiration for Wolff but the undeniable link between the two. Wolff had backed Schmidt's career hitherto and, reportedly, even seen and approved the text of the 'Wertheim Bible' before publication.[88] Wolff, though, lost no time in disowning Schmidt: 'the translator bases himself on his own interpretation of the Hebrew text, as Grotius and Simon did before him; how can this be the fruit of my philosophy?'[89] But the damage was done. Schmidt stood condemned as a freethinker, Naturalist, blasphemer, and Spinozist but yet, undeniably, had been nurtured by Wolff and Wolff's philosophy.

In Prussia, the change of course in official policy towards Wolffianism, presaged in 1734, was suspended. In June 1736 the king nominated a royal commission of four eminent theologians, not including Lange—two Calvinist and two Lutheran—to re-examine Wolff's philosophy and furnish a definitive judgement of its implications for university teaching, religion, and morality. Its findings were that Wolff's books do contain certain objectionable ideas and passages but not 'les erreurs et les sentiments athées que Lange prétend y avoir trouvées'. With this, Wolff was just a step away from final vindication and rehabilitation.[90] By this stage there was also an increasingly vocal clique in Berlin, notably the Saxon envoy, Count Ernst Christoph von Manteuffel, and Crown Prince Frederick, who were open devotees of Wolff's philosophy.

Wolff and his allies meanwhile worked tirelessly to advance his cause on all sides—in Germany, France, Switzerland, Scandinavia, Italy, and Russia. With growing support from his Huguenot friends in Berlin—Jordan had been friendly with Manteuffel since early 1735[91]—translations of Wolff's texts into French were now becoming available, and this proved crucial not only to the international advancement of his cause but also the promotion of his system within the German Courts, Crown Prince Frederick, for instance, insisting on reading Wolff only in French.[92] With his eye on France, Wolff, in 1737, dedicated the second edition of his *Theologia Naturalis*—a work dubbed by his chief ally at Leipzig, the young professor Carl Günther Ludovici (1707–78), his most devastating assault yet on 'atheism, fatalism, deism, Naturalism, materialism, Spinozism and Epicureanism'—to Louis XV's chief minister, Cardinal Fleury. Fleury replied encouragingly, praising Wolff's philosophy and noting his recent rapid advances internationally, including in France. Fleury professed himself

[86] Rambach, *Collegium*, i, 77, 327, 765, 923.   [87] Steuber, *Commentatio Epistolica*, 11.
[88] Goldenbaum, 'Erste deutsche Übersetzung', 111.   [89] Ibid.
[90] Ludovici, *Recueil*, 6–9.   [91] Häseler, *Ein Wanderer*, 96–7.   [92] Ibid., 98.

honoured by the dedication of a 'livre destiné à combattre les Athées et les sectateurs impies de Spinosa, qui n'ont par malheur que trop de défenseurs'.[93]

Looking back with hindsight, Ludovici considered the years 1736–7 the decisive turning-point in Wolff's conquest of Prussia and all central Europe. After that traditionalist opposition collapsed and the 'Thomasians', as a rival philosophical group, receded into marginality. Meanwhile, Neo-Cartesianism and *Malebranchisme* were manifestly dead. As he and his allies saw it, Wolff's only serious remaining opponent for the mainstream middle ground of the Enlightenment anywhere in Europe was the Newtonianism (or Lockean–Newtonian construct) emanating from Britain and simultaneously making impressive progress, if not in Germany then certainly in France, the Netherlands, Italy, Spain, and soon Portugal.

To the south the crucial arena was the Italian Church. By 1739 Wolff was full of hopes of achieving a decisive breakthrough among the cardinals and theologians of Rome, seeing this as the key to conquering Italy.[94] Interestingly, Wolff ascribed his progress there precisely to the recent gains made by the advocates of Locke and Newton: for this, he claimed, was feeding the growth of *Materialismus* and *Sceptizismus*.[95] In Sweden and Russia, meanwhile, Wolff swept all before him. But most critical of all, as Wolff appreciated, was the battle for Paris. According to his informants in the salons, 'Deismus, Materialismus und Sceptizismus' were now gaining ground at a terrifying rate in France. What was needed, he advised allies in Berlin, was to teach the French that it was his philosophy, and not that of Newton and Locke, which was indispensable if the deist contagion was to be effectively fought.[96] If the salons opted instead for Voltaire's 'Newtonianischen Philosophie', France faced a catastrophe of incalculable proportions.

The intervention of Wolff's principal Huguenot ally, Formey, with his philosophical novel, *La Belle Wolfienne*, in 1746, marked the zenith of the Wolffian offensive in French-speaking Europe. Here again, the crux of Wolffian strategy was to stress the applicability and unique effectiveness of *philosophia Leibnitio–Wolffiana* in combatting 'Spinozism'.[97] According to Formey, the 'Spinosistes' threatened Christendom with utter ruin but had been steadily losing ground since the appearance of Leibniz's *Théodicée*. The war between Wolffianism and Spinozism, contended Formey, hinged on the contradiction between Spinoza's *nécessité* and Leibnizian–Wolffian *raison suffisante*. For Spinoza, 'rien n'est possible, que ce qui est arrivé et ce qui arrivera'; for Wolff 'il y a un grand nombre de choses possibles, qui n'existeroient jamais actuellement, parcequ'il n'y a pas, pour elles en Dieu, une raison suffisante d'exister.'[98] Effectively, Wolff's 'possibles, qui n'existeront jamais' had demolished Spinoza's godless 'impossibles'.

But if Spinozism was crumbling under Wolff's hammer blows, Formey considered Spinoza an antagonist who could never be written off. He drew his power in

---

[93] Ludovici, *Neueste Merckwürdigkeiten*, 66–7.
[94] Wolff to Manteuffel, 7 June 1739 in Ostertag, *Philosophische Gehalt*, 8. [95] Ibid.
[96] Ibid. [97] Formey, *La Belle Wolfienne*, i, 27–30 and ii, 29–33. [98] Ibid., 59–61.

Germany less from the cogency of its arguments than his alleged psychological appeal for resentful, thwarted men. Like Massillon and Houtteville, Formey considered that only rancour could explain how some men 'qui n'ont pas assez d'habilité, pour se faire un nom' stoop to Spinozism, embracing in *fatalisme* a perverse 'preuve de courage et de grandeur d'âme'.[99] But base disgruntlement is widespread and only too liable to fan 'la malignité orgueilleuse d'un grand nombre de personnes'.[100] For his part, Wolff was simultaneously pleased by the novel's wide impact and uneasy at Formey's sometimes rather crude juxtaposition of his system with Spinoza's.[101]

Meanwhile in 1740, Prince Frederick, who considered himself a *philosophe*, and had been on the worst possible terms with his father for years, succeeded to the Prussian throne. One of his first decisions was to recall Wolff from exile, re-install him as the presiding figure at Halle, and show him public favour. In 1743 the now fully rehabilitated philosopher became rector of the university from which he had been expelled twenty years before. Yet, to his chagrin, Wolff soon found that his new sovereign had more appetite for Voltaire than his own writing and, worse still, that by returning to Prussia, he had merely exchanged his former contest with Lange and the Pietists for a new and in some respects even more strenuous philosophical war. For the young monarch was firmly drawn to foreign and mostly French *philosophes*, especially enjoying the company of Voltaire, d'Argens, Algarotti, and later, Maupertuis and La Mettrie. Indeed, the new king displayed freethinking proclivities Wolff could in no way approve of.[102]

Furthermore, the Royal Prussian Academy of Sciences in Berlin, immediately revived by Frederick after his succession, rapidly became, owing to Frederick's predilection for foreign savants, a battleground between German Wolffians and Franco-Swiss Newtonians. Wolff's battle with Newtonian philosophy ceased to be a remote theoretical divergence waged chiefly in foreign salons and journals and became the central issue in Prussian intellectual life itself. The climax of this new strife, indeed the culmination of the long struggle between Newtonianism and Leibnizian–Wolffianism on the continent, was the grippingly tense two-year competition (1745–7), arranged by the Berlin Academy, for the best essay on the subject of Leibniz's monads.[103] By April 1747, a few months after Maupertuis became the Academy's *président perpétuel*, the essays were in and ready to be perused and judged by a commission chaired by the *grand maître* of the Queen of Prussia's household. Yet even before the process of assessing the submissions began, it became apparent that the panel of judges was both irreducibly and rather evenly split between *Wolfiens* and Newtonian–Lockean *Antimonadiers*.

In Berlin, the intellectual arena became fraught as never before. Nothing else could be expected and yet, sighed Formey, leader of the Academy's *Wolfiens*, 'je ne me serois jamais attendu que les choses puissent aller au point de partialité et de puerilité où

[99] Ibid., 30.   [100] Ibid.
[101] Ostertag, *Philosophische Gehalt*, 44.
[102] Blanning, 'Frederick the Great', 274–6; Häseler, *Ein Wanderer*, 131–4.
[103] Calinger,' 'Newtonian-Wolffian Controversy', 322.

elles ont été.'[104] But even without the acrimony and pettiness, the commission found it exceedingly difficult, if not impossible, to apply objective standards to contending essays maintaining irreconcilable positions derived from Locke's empiricism and the metaphysics of monads.[105] In addition, Maupertuis' most prominent ally in the academy, the Swiss Calvinist anti-Wolffian Leonhard Euler (1707–83), powerfully revived the charge that Wolffianism is a covert form of Spinozism.[106] Manteuffel, Formey, and Wolff's other friends countered vigorously. Finally, however, to Wolff's infinite disgust—but no one's great surprise—the prize went to a Newtonian.

But if he lost in Berlin Wolff could draw consolation from the fact that few other German princes shared Frederick's predilections. Elsewhere in Germany, as well as Scandinavia and Russia, he now had the upper hand over the empiricists and Newtonians, while in Italy *philosophia Leibnitio–Wolffiana* had at least emerged as the chief rival to the Lockean–Newtonian edifice. In France and the Netherlands too, Wolffianism, even if appreciably weaker than Newtonianism, was nevertheless a dynamic and pervasive presence, reflected not least in a semi-camouflaged but unmistakable current of Wolffianism detectable in whole batches of articles of the *Encyclopédie*.[107] That great compilation indeed was so far from being ideologically monolithic that behind its façade of Lockean and Newtonian concepts it accommodated a strong dose of Wolff, as well as a sporadically visible underlay of radical thought and Neo-Spinozism.

Thus Wolff remained no less than before locked in combat with fatalism, Naturalism, materialism, and Spinozism. In his opinion, the recipe offered by Voltaire and the English was not really philosophy at all but merely the reduction of philosophy to physics and consequently utterly useless as a prop to authority, morality, and religion and no real bar to atheistic materialism.[108] Perhaps the final irony of the philosophical Battle of Berlin was that barely a year later, in July 1748, Prussia's freethinking king compelled his academicians, Newtonians and Wolffians alike, to nominate La Mettrie—whom they all detested as a materialist and *fataliste*—as a full regular member of the Academy. Wolff seemingly was right after all in his contention that the real winners of the essay competition were not Newton and Locke but Spinoza and the radicals.

iv. Wolffianism versus Newtonianism in the Baltic

Theirs being comparatively remote lands which, in the past, had participated only marginally in Europe's intellectual life, the intellectual élites of Sweden–Finland and Denmark–Norway resented the least suggestion of backwardness in the crucial new areas of philosophy and science. When an editor of the Leipzig *Acta Eruditorum*, failing to restrain his dislike of the Cartesianism still predominant in Sweden, suggested

---

[104] Formey to Manteuffel, Berlin, 3 June 1747 in Ostertag, *Philosophische Gehalt*, 92.
[105] Cassirer, *Philosophy*, 120–1. [106] Calinger, 'Newtonian-Wolffian Controversy', 324.
[107] Carboncini, '*L'Encyclopédie*', 489–90, 503–4. [108] Ostertag, *Philosophische Gehalt*, 101.

that the harsh cold of the Swedish climate was apt to 'freeze' the mind as it does everything else, he was severely taken to task by the editor of the Stockholm *Schwedische Bibliothec* in 1728, in his introduction to a set of documents illustrating the Swedish philosophical conflict of the 1680s.[109] The rebuke was timely, for Sweden was just then being dragged into a new bout of philosophical warfare, strife which this time was not triangular but a four-cornered contest: while Rydelius and the Cartesians fought the invading Wolffians and Newtonians, the latter simultaneously bombarded each other and battled the radicals.

By 1725 the Cartesian ascendancy elsewhere in Europe was over. But in Sweden–Finland it still seemed largely intact. The leading Cartesians in the north included, besides Rydelius, the astronomers Conrad Quensel (1676–1732) at Lund and Olaf Hiorter at Uppsala, and Johan Ihre, an eminent philologist and classical scholar. The principal challenge to their crumbling hegemony, plainly, was not Newtonianism but Wolffianism. In 1729, for example, Ihre concerted a public disputation at Uppsala in which the Cartesian concept of matter, as extension wholly distinct from mind, was vigorously upheld against monadology. The victorious Cartesians denounced *philosophia Leibnitio-Wolffiana* as 'obscure, self-contradictory and dangerous', a philosophy prone to degenerate into 'Spinozismus et materialismus'.[110] None the less, 'dangerous' or not, Wolffianism was conspicuously pervading the Uppsala faculties by the late 1720s.[111]

Theoretically, it was impossible for anti-Cartesians and disillusioned ex-Cartesians, anxious to fortify society against Spinozism and materialism, to incline simultaneously towards two such mutually exclusive systems as Newtonianism and Wolffianism. Yet there was much common ground between the competing systems, as indeed was inevitable, given the aspirations of both to dominate the moderate mainstream in the ideological wars of the time, and this was bound to arouse the enthusiasm of some. After all, Locke and Wolff both stressed the rationality of revealed religion. Wolff himself acknowledged the value of empiricism in experimental science, accepting parts of Locke's epistemology,[112] and like the Newtonians extensively deployed the 'argument from design'. All this encouraged some eminent figures, especially in Denmark, where a more eclectic tradition prevailed than in still solidly Cartesian Sweden–Finland, to try to combine features of both philosophies. Especially Ludvig Holberg, the real initiator of Early Enlightenment philosophical debate in Denmark–Norway, endeavoured to draw on English sources as well as Wolff, and was emulated in this by the twin theological pillars of Denmark's moderate Enlightenment in the 1730s and 1740s—Erik Pontoppidan (1698–1764), professor of theology at Copenhagen in the years 1738–47 and afterwards Bishop of Bergen, and Peder Rosenstand-Goiske (1705–69), who succeeded Pontoppidan in Copenhagen and was no less staunchly averse to deism and freethinking.[113]

---

[109] *Schwedische Bibliothec*, ii (1728), 1–3, 109.   [110] Ibid., iv (1729), 358.

[111] Frängsmyr, *Wolffianismens genombrott*, 66–7, 221–2.   [112] Kuehn, 'German *Aufklärung*', 312–13.

[113] Ellehøj and Grane, *Københavns Universitet*, v, 204–5, 252–7 and x, 28–30; Koch and Kornerup, *Dansk Kirkes Historie*, v, 251–63.

The subtler, more eclectic approach prevailing in Denmark presumably helps to explain why that country avoided the ferocious philosophical battle which now erupted in Sweden, where the monarchy, under strict constitutional limits since the death of Charles XII in 1718, was no longer able to separate the combatants in the way it had in the 1680s. It again intervened, however, since the reigning constitutional monarch, the German-born Frederik I (reigned 1720–51) belonged to the ruling house of Hesse-Cassel which had protected Wolff since 1723, and strongly favoured Wolffianism also in Sweden.[114] Among academics Wolffianism appealed to scholars rumoured to be less than solid in their attachment to Lutheran orthodoxy. Among the leading figures were the astronomer Anders Celsius, a defector from Cartesianism, who headed the Wolffian campaign at Uppsala where, in the late 1720s, he was found to be recruiting energetically for the Wolffian cause, and the prominent mathematician and physicist, Samuel Klingenstierna, who had visited Wolff himself in Marburg in 1727 and was, in turn, recommended by Wolff to the Swedish Court for a chair at Uppsala to which he was appointed in 1731.

Klingenstierna's opening moves served, however, only to arouse the opposition. During the mid-1730s a determined anti-Wolffian reaction made itself felt both at Uppsala and Lund. Thus, in October 1732, pressed by the theologians, the Uppsala chancellor, Count Gustav Cronhielm, addressed the academic senate, firmly condemning the seepage of Wolffianism into teaching.[115] Uppsala theologians, linked to Pietist circles in Germany, publicly denounced Wolff's philosophy as 'heathen' and 'atheistic'. In 1734 the university senate assumed additional powers to vet proposed disputations and theses so as to block further Wolffian infiltration. In 1736, according to reports reaching Germany, the new Uppsala philosophy professor, Petrus Ullén (1700–47), was officially reprimanded for teaching Wolffian ideas.

At Lund meanwhile, Rydelius, an admirer of Buddeus as well as Descartes and Andala,[116] led the anti-Wolffian faction, maintaining that Leibnitio–Wolffian monads undermine a cardinal principal of all Christian thought, namely that motion cannot be innate in matter.[117] Furthermore, Wolff's notion of Providence, he contended, was more a sham than a serious strategy, and his 'freedom of will' utterly unconvincing.[118] In reality, despite its pretensions to solidity, Wolffianism was undermining society's defences against Naturalism, fatalism, and such philosophical atheism as identifies God with the universe.[119] In his philosophical handbook of 1736 for non-academic professionals and students, entitled *Sententiae Philosophicae Fundamentales*, Rydelius unequivocally identifies *philosophia Leibnitio–Wolffiana* as the chief menace to Sweden's intellectual stability, though the empiricism of Locke and 'his follower Le Clerc' is also deemed dangerous as, of course, are Spinozism and

---

[114] *Christian Wolff's eigene Lebensbeschreibung*, 156–7; Gottsched, *Historische Lobschrift*, 86, 90; Frängsmyr, *Wolffianismens genombrott*, 83.

[115] Frängsmyr, *Wolffianismens genombrott*, 88–9, 225.   [116] Almquist, *Andreas Rydelius' etiska*, 187.

[117] Rydelius, *Sententiae philosophicae*, 21–2, 24; Frängsmyr, *Wolffianismens genombrott*, 235.

[118] Rydelius, *Sententiae philosophicae*, 33–6, 77–8.

[119] Ibid., 36, 77; Almquist, *Anders Rydelius' etiska*, 132.

Naturalism.[120] Rydelius persisted in waging war on Wolffians, Lockeans, and Spinozists alike until his death in 1738, after which the Cartesian ascendancy in Sweden–Finland was effectively over.

It was in the late 1730s that the Wolffians gained the upper hand in Sweden–Finland. Wolffianism emerged victorious first at Uppsala, then Åbo,[121] and finally in the mid-1740s at Lund. At the same time Wolffian 'modern philosophy' hardened into a new rigid orthodoxy, fiercely resistant to Newtonianism as well as radical ideas and firmly allied with conservative Lutheran theology.[122] During the 1740s and 1750s, the Swedish Wolffians progressively tightened their grip over higher education and Swedish intellectual culture. In an Uppsala disputation of 1743, Klingenstierna vigorously supported the principle of intellectual censorship, claiming that books and ideas that damage 'religion', 'good morals', and the 'political state' must be effectively suppressed by the authorities.[123] At Uppsala, almost all prominent scientific and intellectual figures of the period, including Ullén, Nils Wallerius, and Linnaeus, adopted a firmly Wolffian stance. This is especially striking in that precisely the middle years of the eighteenth century were also the most creative decades of the Swedish Enlightenment, especially in science. At Uppsala, the botanical gardens under Linnaeus' supervision, a revived version of Roberg's academic hospital, and the university's first chemistry laboratory all evolved at that time.[124] Linnaeus, one of the greatest scientists of the Enlightenment, having begun at Lund as a Cartesian, and then imbibed Newtonianism in the Netherlands during his years there from 1735 to 1738, on returning to Sweden, where he remained pre-eminent at Uppsala over many years, discarded both Cartesianism and Newtonianism, adopting a version of physico-theology powerfully infused with Wolffianism.[125] A declared adversary of the Radical Enlightenment, in the late 1740s he found himself dragged into combat with La Mettrie who, like himself, had been profoundly influenced by Boerhaave's teaching in Leiden and now sought to adapt Linnaeus' botanical theories to his materialist philosophical system.[126]

Meanwhile, the new Russia of Peter the Great emerged as a major philosophical and scientific, as well as naval and military, power in the Baltic. The intellectual culture which developed in early eighteenth-century St Petersburg tended, not unnaturally, to reflect the outlook of the predominantly German savants the Czar recruited to help bring Russia within the European intellectual arena. Almost from the moment Peter founded his new Russian Imperial Academy of Sciences at St Petersburg in 1724, the empire's capital became the scene of some of the continent's most acrimonious philosophical strife.[127] The academy itself was originally the brainchild of Leibniz who, from 1697 onwards, when he first conceived an interest in the future potential of

---

[120] Rydelius, *Sententiae philosophicae*, 24, 35, 54–5, 78; Almquist, *Andreas Rydelius' etiska*, 160–1.

[121] Frängsmyr, *Wolffianismens genombrott*, 235.

[122] Lindroth, *University of Uppsala*, 126, 136; Malmeström, *Carl von Linné's religiösa åskådning*, 34–8; Wessell, *G. E. Lessing's Theology*, 66–7.

[123] Klingenstierna, *Dissertatio academica*, 21–2. [124] Lindroth, *University of Uppsala*, 102, 128.

[125] Malmeström, *Carl von Linné's religiösa åskådning*, 68, 80–9.

[126] La Mettrie, *Machine Man*, 80, 82, 87. [127] Calinger, 'Newtonian–Wolffian Confrontation', 421.

Russia, had been brought into contact with the Czar and enthusiastically praised his schemes to attract foreign scholars and expertise to stimulate his empire's development.[128] In his last years, Leibniz was frequently consulted by Peter and his advisers, and also summoned to confer in person with the Czar during his travels in central Europe, notably at Carlsbad in 1712 and Pyrmont in 1716.

Prodded by Leibniz, the Czar's original plan had been to draw Wolff himself to Russia. On Wolff's expulsion from Prussia, Peter's personal physician, Laurenz Blumentrost, a Moscow-born German who had trained in Holland under Boerhaave and De Volder, and was steeped in Dutch intellectual culture, wrote in December 1723 and again the following month, urging him, on the Czar's behalf, to settle in St Petersburg and preside over the projected new Russian Imperial Academy.[129] Wolff declined, but he did stay in regular contact with the Russian Court, through Blumentrost, who was nominated the first president of the academy instead. It was owing to his recommendations, and Wolff's, that most of the academy's original membership was German or Swiss, with numerous professed Wolffians among them.[130]

Yet there were also German and Swiss anti-Wolffians in St Petersburg, besides a sprinkling of Huguenots who mostly also chose the sole feasible alternative to Wolffian hegemony—Newtonianism laced with Locke. The result, once again, was a bitter conflict. The Newtonian cause was strenuously advocated and gained added momentum from the efforts of German Pietist theologians in the Baltic area to mobilize the Russian Orthodox Church against Wolffianism.[131] Nevertheless, broadly the Wolffians retained the upper hand and were particularly successful during the late 1720s with Bilfinger residing and working in St Petersburg at the Czar's bidding when the outcome of the strife in Germany itself remained entirely uncertain.[132] Moreover, as in Sweden, Wolff's hegemony in Russia, was destined to continue for decades, well beyond 1750.

---

[128] Richter, *Leibniz*, 42–4, 48–52; Vucinich, *Science in Russian Culture*, 46.

[129] Gottsched, *Historische Lobschrift*, 76.

[130] Richter, *Leibniz*, 126–7; Vucinich, *Science in Russian Culture*, 67, 71, 76.   [131] Ibid., 67.

[132] Calinger, 'Newtonian-Wolffian Confrontation', 428–32; Russia's first noteworthy modern scientist, Mikhail Lomonosov (1711–65), received his training in German universities, including in the years 1736–9 a period studying under Wolff himself at Marburg; see Vucinich, *Science in Russian Culture*, 58, 105.

PART V | THE CLANDESTINE PROGRESS OF THE RADICAL ENLIGHTENMENT (1680–1750)

By the 1720s, the endeavours of Malebranche, Bossuet, Huet, Régis, Fénelon, Lamy, and innumerable others to break the vice of philosophical perplexity gripping France while simultaneously fending off scepticism, irreligion, and Naturalism could finally be seen to have failed. Neither Cartesianism nor its offshoot *Malebranchisme*, nor any indigenous French philosophical tradition survived beyond the first quarter of the new century as a serious contender in the fight to conquer the middle ground in what was increasingly an international war of philosophies. The patent contradictions and discrepancies undermining Aristotelianism, and the systems of Descartes and Malebranche, compelled those seeking viable answers to the intellectual issues of the age to turn either to English empiricism, the tradition of Bacon, Boyle, Locke, and Newton, as the young Voltaire and countless others were to do, or the Leibnizian–Wolffian model contending for hegemony in Germany, Scandinavia, and Russia. Alternatively, one might come to terms intellectually and spiritually with the unsettling and revolutionary ideas of the radicals and *Spinosistes*.

Some of the most enquiring minds of the French Early Enlightenment did indeed turn in this direction, including the second founding father—after Fontenelle—of the French Radical Enlightenment, the eminent, if reticent, Norman nobleman, Henri de Boulainvilliers (1658–1722), comte de Saint-Saire. Though it is sometimes claimed the count was at least residually a Catholic and not in any genuine sense a 'Spinosiste', recent research has invalidated this notion, proving he did develop into a fully-fledged Spinozist who rejected not just revealed religion but all notion of a providential God and an absolute morality.[1] He was to exert during his last years, and still more posthumously, a remarkable influence on the dissemination of radical ideas throughout western Europe.

Boulainvilliers was educated at the Oratorian college at Juilly, north-east of Paris, at a time when the college was strongly Cartesian in orientation, among others, during his final year as a teacher there (1673), by Richard Simon.[2] Subsequently, he served for

---

[1] Simon. 'Introduction', p. xii; Simon, *Henry de Boulainviller*, 533, 684; Wade, *Clandestine Organisation*, 123; Torrey, 'Boulainvilliers', 162–9; Vernière, *Spinoza*, 306–22; Schröder, *Ursprünge*, 506; for the two most authoritative recent analyses see Brogi, *Cerchio*, 164–214, and Venturino, *Ragioni*, 143–58.

[2] Venturino, *Ragioni*, 4.

a time (1679–88) in the royal musketeers. A man of delicate health and retiring disposition, after leaving the army he evolved into one of the most adept and discerning connoisseurs of ideas in France. The duc de Saint-Simon judged him a mild, agreeable, and modest nobleman, a delightful conversationalist with an outstanding mind and vast erudition who would indubitably have been more sought after in high society were his researches—and hence also contact with him—not widely considered 'suspect'.[3] His freethinking admirer, Nicolas Lenglet Dufresnoy, accounts him a man 'd'une extrême pénétration', immensely industrious, profound, and erudite.[4] Dogged by family misfortunes, including the early loss of his wife in childbirth and the death of both surviving sons in 1709, the elder killed at Malplaquet, Boulainvilliers abandoned all quest for worldly honours, seeking fulfilment instead in a life of intense, wide-ranging study.[5] But while his philosophical endeavours remained screened from view, he won wide renown as a historian of the French constitution, Crown, and nobility and became, in his quiet way, politically engaged, detesting as he did Louis XIV's rule as 'despotique' and 'odieux' and being close to the duc de Noailles, standard-bearer of the Orléans faction, the closest thing during the closing years of Louis' long reign to a political opposition.[6] His great fault, according to Saint-Simon, was a tendency to undertake too many tasks at the same time and keep interrupting one project to begin another.

Though no democrat, being a champion of noble participation in constitutional life, he was a dedicated enemy of absolutism who ardently hoped for the convening of the States General after Louis' death in 1715. Though disappointed in this, he remained a supporter of the duc d'Orléans, who was himself known to be a freethinker and who likewise held Boulainvilliers in high esteem, as also did the crucially influential marquis d'Argenson, lieutenant-general of police in Paris, who also took a keen interest in Boulainvilliers' philosophical manuscripts, copies of several of which he acquired for his own library.[7] Noailles, Orléans, and d'Argenson sympathized with the philosophical views of the small coterie which gathered around Boulainvilliers in Paris. When Boulainvilliers died in 1722, soldiers were sent on the regent's orders to secure his manuscripts, though whether this was done to prevent their falling into hostile hands or as a measure of control, to prevent their wider circulation, or conceivably both purposes, remains unclear.[8]

Boulainvilliers by his own account was deeply shocked when he first encountered Spinoza's thought; and his original purpose in studying the *Tractatus Theologico-Politicus*, apparently around 1695, was to identify weak points and compose an effective refutation. Though initially intended for publication and written, he remarks, with the encouragement of a 'grand prélat',[9] presumably Fénelon or Bossuet, in the event, like the rest of his writings on Spinoza, Boulainvilliers' critique of the *Tractatus*

---

[3] Saint-Simon, *Mémoires*, lx, 239–40; Simon, *Henry de Boulainviller*, 35.
[4] Sheridan, *Nicolas Lenglet Dufresnoy*, 134.   [5] Vernière, *Spinoza*, 307; Venturino, *Ragioni*, pp. xi–xii.
[6] Boulainvilliers, *Mémoires*, I, 12–13; Ellis, *Boulainvilliers and the French Monarchy*, 77, 110, 145–7.
[7] Sheridan, *Nicolas Lenglet Dufresnoy*, 135; Sheridan, 'Lenglet Dufresnoy', 426–7.
[8] Brogi, *Cerchio*, 14.   [9] Simon, *Henry de Boulainviller*, 460.

failed to appear and long lay burried among his private papers. But even while seeking to overturn Spinoza's principles, Boulainvilliers displayed something of that sensitivity to his arguments which later led to his shifting his ground:[10] 'c'est une entreprise considérable,' he remarks, 'que de vouloir ruiner le système de Spinosa sur les miracles', owing to the cunning and artifice with which he had worked.[11] Though antagonistic, moreover, Boulainvilliers scrupulously avoided misrepresenting the arguments he attacks. Not unlike Régis, De Volder, and Jacob Wittichius, Boulainvilliers at that stage thought it misconceived to label Spinoza an 'atheist'. He also deemed it inappropriate to accuse him of destroying the principles of morality, since, besides living an exemplary life himself, his writings advocate only virtue 'et il explique le nom de vertu par celui de règle, d'ordre, de vie raisonnable et religieuse'.[12]

At this juncture, Boulainvilliers believed the arguments, or rather 'sophismes de cet auteur', were 'infiniment dangereux'. This was because of Spinoza's denial of miracles and divine authorship of Scripture, his view of Christ, and because under the pretext of helping spread the light of natural reason, he in fact casts deep shadows 'dans l'esprit de l'homme', while the advantages he promises amount to nothing more than spreading scepticism about Scripture, generating 'un doute universel'. Typical of Spinoza's artifice, claims Boulainvilliers, is his contentious use of the story of the philosopher-king, Solomon. Spinoza's idealization of a philosopher-king who, through reason and wisdom, rose far above 'idées vulgaires' and even the dictates of Revelation and the laws, is dismissed by Boulainvilliers as 'absurde en toute manière'.[13] Like the Dutch Remonstrant minister, Batalier, who attacked Spinoza's manipulation of the story of Solomon over twenty years earlier, he considered Spinoza's treatment flagrantly un-Biblical and unhistorical, a contemptible ruse to erode respect for other figures in Scripture.[14]

Boulainvilliers' next major project was his *Abrégé d'histoire universelle*, a text composed in the years 1699–1703. Divided into two parts, this consists of a discussion of the Biblical account of the Creation and the beginnings of man down to the Exodus, followed by an account of the early history of the Graeco-Roman world. Despite having himself been taught by Richard Simon, the major influence on Boulainvilliers' Biblical and general textual criticism was Le Clerc, to whom, for a time, he was also in other respects—especially regarding the allegedly perfect accord between reason and Revelation and his insistent uncoupling of the New Testament from the Old—heavily indebted.[15] At the outset, the nobleman expresses his resolve to find 'un juste milieu' between the uncritical servitude of those who cling to the literal meaning of Scripture

---

[10] Cotoni, *L'Exégèse*, 90–1.

[11] Undeniably, he avers, 'il est établi avec beaucoup d'artifice, fort lié dans ses conséquences, et qu'il est appuyé de quelques exemples specieux'; Boulainvilliers, *Oeuvres philosophiques*, i, 77.

[12] Ibid.; Simon, *Henry de Boulainviller*, 489–90.

[13] Boulainvilliers, *Oeuvres philosophiques*, i, 77; Israel, 'Spinoza, King Solomon', 303–7.

[14] Batalier, *Vindiciae*, 36–9, 63; Mannarino, 'Pietro Giannone', 230.

[15] See Boulainvilliers' own notes on Le Clerc's refutation of Richard Simon, PBN MS fr, 11075, fos. 231–45; Brogi, *Cerchio*, 22, 32, 36–9, 100, 102.

on one side, and the licentiousness of the libertines on the other.[16] Religion, he avers, following Le Clerc, can not be built on 'un foy aveugle et le mépris de la raison'. Reason, not Richard Simon's authority of the Church, is proclaimed man's sole secure guide in determining the ultimate meaning of Scripture.

At this juncture, Boulainvilliers is a providential deist avowedly hostile to the doctrines of Lucretius and Spinoza—he never mentions Hobbes[17]—which he dismisses as 'également absurdes' on the subject of Creation.[18] A knowing, providential God, contended Boulainvilliers, created the universe, designed life, and forged man. However, he goes beyond Le Clerc in his distinctly naturalistic account of Biblical events and in allowing no inner, reserved area of undisputed miracles which cannot be challenged, a stance which also put him at odds with Locke.[19] Adopting a position halfway between Le Clerc and Spinoza, he dispenses with the miraculous and Christ the Redeemer but retains Creation and divine Providence. Boulainvilliers' *Abrégé* was never published but nevertheless exerted a noticeable influence on the Early Enlightenment.[20] Copies circulated in manuscript among the count's intimate circle and eventually also reached some outside it, including the unscrupulous Abbé Lenglet Dufresnoy, an admirer of Bayle and one of the most notorious French deists of the 1720s and 1730s, who reproduced hefty chunks plagiarized without acknowledgement from Boulainvillier's text in his *Méthode pour étudier l'histoire* (1729).[21] Lenglet Dufresnoy cheerfully absorbed Boulainvilliers' arguments as his own.

Boulainvilliers entered on a closer dialogue with Spinoza, he recalls, in 1704, after coming by chance across the *Opera Posthuma* while searching for a Hebrew grammar and being directed to Spinoza's short, unfinished, but yet expert treatise on the Hebrew language contained in that volume.[22] No doubt he was stimulated also by the controversial and very mixed reception given to Régis' recently published refutation of Spinoza. The result was his *Exposition du système de Benoît de Spinosa et sa défence contre les objections de Mr Régis*, a text in which Boulainvilliers shows that Régis fails to deliver what he promises and no more succeeds in overthrowing Spinoza's principles than the fumbling Lamy. Like 'Languener' (Caspar Langenhert?), the clandestine author of the (so far as is known) unique manuscript 'Apologie de Spinosa contre Régis' surviving in Aix-en-Provence, Boulainvilliers insists it is Régis, not Spinoza, who is 'obscure', inconsistent, and confused in defining 'substance', 'God', and 'Nature'.[23] Régis, he says, utterly fails to prove the existence of a knowing, providential God.

Indeed, Boulainvilliers now argues, there is little point in seeking to overthrow

[16] BNP MS Fr. 6363: Boulainvilliers, 'Abrégé'. fos. 20–1.   [17] Venturino, *Ragioni*, 65.
[18] BNP MS Fr. 6363: Boulainvilliers, 'Abrégé', fo. 21; Brogi, *Cerchio*, 33; Venturino, *Ragioni*, 146.
[19] Brogi, *Cerchio*, 37–9; Venturino, *Ragioni*, 138–40.   [20] Benítez, *Face cachée*, 22.
[21] Sheridan, *Nicolas Lenglet Dufresnoy*, 99–100.   [22] Boulainvilliers, *Essay*, 154.
[23] BMA MS 818 (774): Languener [Langenhert?], 'Apologie de Spinosa contre Régis', pp. 1–7, 56; Boulainvilliers stresses the 'inexecution de son dessein' and the general failure of scholars to overthrow the 'principes de Spinosa, et qui ne prouvent pas mieux l'existence d'un Dieu'; Boulainvilliers, *Ouevres philosophiques*, i, 229–30; Brogi, *Cerchio*, 157.

Spinoza's proof of the existence of 'God', which should be allowed to stand. It is the ruinous consequences he draws from his definitions which must be vigorously opposed. Nevertheless, Régis rightly denied that Spinoza was an atheist—even if the State religion advocated by Spinoza clearly had an essentially social and political function and 'ne soient rien d'absolu'—since that philosopher had stipulated articles of faith based on acknowledgement of a Supreme Being and the injunction to live a life of justice and charity.[24] The charge of atheism should be avoided when writing about a man who 'en sa manière fait tout en son pouvoir pour prouver l'existence de Dieu'.[25] It is not, he maintains, Spinoza's premises but his 'conséquences' which have to be destroyed and this, he suggests, can best be done by taking refuge in a fideistic scepticism (not unlike that of Bayle, or indeed Régis) holding that there is much philosophers can never know and that, consequently, there is no cogent basis on which Spinoza or any thinker can deny 'les dogmes, les miracles et les mystères de la religion chrétienne'.[26]

The final step in Boulainvilliers' slow conversion to Spinozism, a spiritual odyssey which apparently lasted more than fifteen years, was his *Essay de métaphysique*. It is unknown exactly when he worked on this text, though it must have been between 1704 and 'August 1712', the copyist's date attested in several surviving manuscript copies.[27] The translation of Spinoza's *Ethics* into French, which Boulainvilliers made for his own use and that of his intimate circle, and on which he was working in 1705, demonstrates the intensity of his preoccupation with Spinoza in the period after writing his *Exposition*. Very likely the *Essay* was written soon after he finished his translation, thus rather closer to 1706 than to 1712. Despite the flimsy excuse in the preface, that he is restating Spinoza's system stripped of that 'mathematical dryness' which renders it inaccessible to many so as combat the doctrines contained therein by encouraging 'un plus habile métaphysicien que moy à le refuter', there is little doubt that his real purpose is to reorganize his own thoughts on the basis Spinoza provides, and to defend and propagate the contents of the *Ethics*.[28]

Besides Spinoza and Le Clerc, Bayle is unquestionably the third great influence on the formation of Boulainvilliers' radical outlook. In the preface to his *Essay*, Boulainvilliers begins his task by denying that Bayle, in his article on Spinoza in his *Dictionnaire*, had adequately understood the argument of the *Ethics*, 'le plus dangereux livre qui ait été écrit contre la religion'.[29] The task he sets himself is one of exposition and clarification, and despite occasional laborious entanglements in particular propositions, he generally fares better in conveying Spinoza's sense than those he is criticizing—primarily Bayle, Régis, and Lamy.[30] In contrast to his earlier stance in the *Abrégé*,

---

[24] 'Qu'il y a un Être Suprême qui aime la justice, auquel il faut obéir, et dont le culte consiste dans la charité envers le prochain'; Régis, *L'Usage de la raison*, 284.

[25] Boulainvilliers, *Ouevres philosophiques*, i, 230.   [26] Quoted in Brogi, *Cerchio*, 158–9.

[27] Ibid., 143, 155; Simon, *Henry de Boulainviller*, 460; Sheridan, 'Lenglet Dufresnoy', 427.

[28] Torrey, 'Boulainvilliers', 167; Benítez, 'Spinoza ou Descartes?', 93–4, 104–5; Venturino, *Ragioni*, 21–2.

[29] Boulainvilliers, *Essay*, 154.

[30] Reimann, *Historia universalis*, 550; Brogi, *Cerchio*, 164–77; Benítez, 'Spinoza ou Descartes?', 98–101.

the count now evidently regards the Creation, as traditionally interpreted in Judaeo-Christian culture, as 'un oeuvre impossible et contradictoire'.[31] Boulainvilliers affirms, on the contrary, the non-providential nature—the necessity and absolute interdependence—of all that occurs. He also follows Spinoza in denying that abolition of a knowing, intelligent, personal God means there can be no love of God or any true morality. On the contrary, he holds, the new outlook means that one can attain a higher, more meaningful love of God, through understanding that He is intimately connected to one's own being, that He gives one one's existence and properties 'mais qu'il me les donne libéralement, sans reproche, sans intérêt, sans m'assujétir à autre chose qu'à ma propre nature'.[32] Such an awareness of God, he maintains, dispels all fear, anxiety, defiance, and all the defects of an 'amour vulgaire ou intéressé' such as generally pervades man's religiosity. Nor is there anything reprehensible in expressing love for God in the context of whatever religious cult one happens to have been raised in, provided one is always mindful that its theology is meaningless and strips away those feelings of partiality and hatred which inevitably accompany 'la religion vulgaire', thereby transforming conventional confessional allegiance into a cult worthy of being practised by a rational person ('par un esprit raisonnable').[33]

Boulainvilliers embraces Spinoza's doctrine of one substance and denies that God is separate from the universe, or has will or intelligence. He also accepts that all things are determined and that there is no freedom of the will, human motivation being based on the two primary passions, 'la joye et la tristesse', of which all other passions are but 'modifications'.[34] But the idea of a God who judges human actions, rewarding the good and punishing the evil, which Voltaire and many moderate deists of subsequent decades deemed indispensable to humanity, though radically revised, is not altogether discarded by Boulainvilliers. There is little sense, he urges, in continuing to teach that God directly intervenes in individual lives, dispensing temporary reward and punishment here, and eternal bliss or retribution in the hereafter. But it is still possible, indeed vital, to affirm that those that live virtuously will find happiness in this life and those who live dissolute lives, and are uncharitable to others, will be wretched.[35]

A masterpiece of the Early Enlightenment, Boulainvilliers' *Essay de métaphysique* circulated only in manuscript during the remainder of his life. It was soon destined to become a principal vehicle of Spinozism in France and all Europe, however, as it constituted around half—and much the most impressive part—of the collection clandestinely published by Lenglet Dufresnoy in Amsterdam, under the title *Réfutation des erreurs de Benoît de Spinosa*, with 'Bruxelles' falsely declared as the place of publication on the title-page, in 1731.[36] Despite Lenglet's including Lamy's refutation to make his title look more plausible—as well as, presumably, to enhance the impact of Boulainvil-

---

[31] Torrey, 'Boulainvilliers', 169.   [32] Boulainvilliers, *Oeuvres philosophiques*, i, 103; Brogi, *Cerchio*, 181.
[33] Boulainvilliers, *Oeuvres philosophiques*, i, 103.
[34] PBN MS 12242, Boulainvilliers, 'Essaye' seconde partie, fos. 92v–93.   [35] Brogi, *Cerchio*, 182–3.
[36] Zedler, *Grosses Universal Lexicon*, xxxix, 84; Barbier, *Dictionnaire*, iii, 178; Sheridan, *Nicolas Lenglet Dufresnoy*, 133–4.

liers' text[37]—the publication was immediately identified as 'plus favorable que contraire au Spinosisme' and officially suppressed both in the Low Countries and France, which Lenglet regarded as the prime market.[38] Nevertheless, many copies entered circulation and, according to the *Journal Littéraire* of The Hague, which reviewed the book in 1732, it was already so well known and readily available that the danger involved in failing to denounce its depravity outweighed any risk involved in drawing attention to it.[39] While condemning Lenglet's compilation as a malicious and despicable piece of deception, the *Journal* grudgingly conceded the high quality of Boulainvilliers' argumentation, remarking that his work 'a donné une face en quelque sorte nouvelle au Spinosisme'.[40]

In subsequent years, Lenglet's *Réfutation* figured among the foremost *clandestina* being smuggled into Paris. Thus the large cache of illicit material discovered by the Paris police in 1739, when they arrested Charles Stella, an accomplice of Lenglet and a leading dealer in forbidden books, included thirty-four copies of Lucas' *Vie de Spinosa*, a favourite text of Boulainvilliers, but no less than fifty-eight copies of Lenglet's *Réfutation*.[41] The compilation also became well-known in Germany, where manuscript copies of the French text were also in circulation, replicated from the copy transferred in 1720 to the Imperial Library in Vienna, previously owned by the Baron von Hohendorf.[42] The printed *Réfutation* figured among the forbidden books in the personal collection of the young Frederick the Great in Berlin, alongside his manuscript of Boulainvilliers' *Abrégé* and works of Fontenelle, Tyssot de Patot, and other radical writings in French.[43] There were also various accounts of Boulainvilliers' *oeuvre* in Early Enlightenment German dictionaries and bibliographies, entries which regularly style him 'ein starcker Spinozist' (a strong Spinozist) and a leading commentator on Spinoza's thought.[44]

One of Boulainvilliers' most important works was his last, *La Vie de Mahomed*, a text left unfinished at the time of his death in 1722, and the most striking example of the ideological deployment of Islam, and the life of Mohammed, in the European Early Enlightenment. The book was published in two clandestine editions in 1730 and 1731, probably at Amsterdam albeit with 'Londres' falsely declared on the title-page, and it also appeared in English in 1731, and in German, at Lemgo, in 1747.[45] 'This godless text,'

---

[37] Stolle, *Anleitung*, 705–7; Torrey, 'Boulainvilliers', 171.   [38] Peignot, *Dictionnaire critique*, ii, 132–3.

[39] *Journal Littéraire* 1732, i, 185–98; the unnamed editor's real purpose, concluded the *Journal*, 'étoit d'établir le spinosisme'; Lenglet was also accused of interjecting false interpolations, notably into Colerus' biography of Spinoza, which was also included in the compilation where large sections of Lucas' biography are inserted and the Huguenot publisher, Pierre Gosse (c.1676–1755), at The Hague, is accused of having clandestinely reissued Spinoza's *Opera Posthuma*, decades after the original edition but reproducing the original title-page and date (1677) albeit in a slightly larger quarto format, in order to trick the authorities; ibid., 185; Sheridan, 'Lenglet Dufresnoy', 426, 429.

[40] Ibid., 188.   [41] Weil, 'Diffusion', 207–8.   [42] Sheridan, 'Lenglet Dufresnoy', 428.

[43] Krieger, *Friedrich der Grosse*, 131, 134, 137.

[44] Zedler, *Grosses Univeral Lexicon*, xxxix, 83–4; Lilienthal, *Theologische Bibliothec*, 381–3; [Jahn], *Verzeichnis*, 2194–8.

[45] The German edition appeared under the title *Das Leben des Mahomeds mit historischen Anmerckungen über die Mahometanische Religion*; see [Jahn], *Verzeichnis*, 1714.

a German commentator noted, 'is more a eulogy of Mahomet than a history of his life'.[46] In this work Boulainvilliers takes the opportunity to make some highly unflattering comparisons between historical Christianity and Islam. Ostensibly expounding Mohammed's views, Boulainvilliers, echoing his earlier indictment (following Van Dale) of the ancient Greek and Egyptian priesthoods, depicts the Christian clergy of the sixth and seventh centuries as grasping and corrupt, contemptible seekers after 'domination . . . qui avoient trouvé le secret de persuader aux peuples que l'obéissance aveugle qu'ils en exigeoient est inseparable de celle qui est due à Dieu'.[47] But Boulainvilliers' Mohammed is not just a critic of Christendom but one of the pivotal figures of history, utterly different from the supposedly deceitful impostor portrayed in traditional Christian accounts of Islam, a true prophet and philosopher who, almost single-handedly, brought crashing down the corrupt and rotten empires of the Byzantines and Persians.[48] Above all, Mohammed emerges as a great teacher of man, the power and grandeur of whose thought, characterized by its rationality and freedom from superstition and 'mysteries', is matched only by the grandeur of his exploits. Were it not, remarks Boulainvilliers sardonically, for Revelation, which assures us Christianity is the true faith, no other religious doctrine would seem to conform so completely to the light of reason as that founded by Mohammed.[49] The general absence of theological splits in Islam, compared with Christianity, is adduced as irrefutable proof of its superior rationality and beneficence.

In politics Boulainvilliers remained in the background, but nevertheless, by force of intellect and his subtle presentation of ideas, played a not insignificant role as a promoter of opposition. This is still more true of his activity as a radical Early Enlightenment ideologue. Though he published nothing during his lifetime which directly challenged revealed religion, ecclesiastical authority, or conventional morality, in the quiet of his study he prepared and planned a broad ideological assault, fomenting a culture of philosophical radicalism among his own immediate circle and friends. The purpose of his writings was not just to render more accessible and propagate Spinozism but also, not least in the *Vie de Mahomed*, to make ready siege engines designed to shatter popular belief, deference for ecclesiastical authority, and religious tradition, forcing open a path for an idealized, purely rational, Naturalistic religion, in his last text supposedly the faith of Mohammed but in fact Boulainvilliers' own Spinozistic deism.[50]

The device of portraying Islam as a purer example of natural and rational religion than Christianity—and, as such, closer to true apostolic Christianity than the modern Christianity taught by the Churches—adopted in the years around 1720 by Boulainvilliers in France and Toland, particularly in his *Nazarenus* (1718) in England,[51] was by no

---

[46] [Jahn], *Verzeichnis*, 1713–14.

[47] Quoted in Simon, *Henry de Boulainviller*, 345; see also Venturino, *Ragioni*, 181–6.

[48] Brogi, *Cerchio*, 115–16; Thomson, 'L'utilisation de l'Islam', 253.

[49] Boulainvilliers, *Vie de Mahomed*, 247; Brogi, *Cerchio*, 121.

[50] Boulainvilliers, *Vie de Mahomed*, 249, 255; Venturino, *Ragioni*, 184.

[51] Harrison, 'Religion' and the Religions, 166, 240; Thomson, 'l'Utilisation de l'Islam', 251.

means typical of the Radical Enlightenment as a whole. Overall, the presentation of Islam as a fanatical religion, and its founder as an 'imposter', averred by the *Traité des trois imposteurs* and other clandestine philosophical manuscripts of the late seventeenth century, was and remained more characteristic.[52] Nevertheless, the suggestion that Mohammed was a kind of proto-Spinoza, implicit in Boulainvilliers, much as Toland had depicted Moses as his proto-Spinoza, enhanced the intermittent tendency evident in the first half of the eighteenth century to draw comparisons between Mohammed and Spinoza. The comparison evidently did not seem as far-fetched to contemporaries as it does to us. For just as Mohammed was the foremost enemy of Christendom historically, and in the formidable power of the faith he established, so in the new context of the Early Enlightenment, with the sway of revealed religion receding, Spinoza had emerged as Christendom's chief foe of the new variety.

The Abbé Desfontaines drew the parallel between Mohammed and Spinoza, as antagonists of Christian truth, in his critique of Houtteville (see p. 500 above). It was a parallel also drawn by others. An anonymous Augustinian friar, publishing at Brussels in 1758, held that the union of Epicureanism and Spinozism had produced the frightful progeny which we call 'athées, déistes, incrédules, esprits forts, matérialistes ou Naturalistes, qui forment à présent tous ensemble une secte moderne', tendencies which in his view all shared the same way of comprehending the world, eliminating divine providence and recognizing no other author of nature than Nature itself, and thus really just one sect which adopted as their highest good 'leur propre amour pour les plaisirs sensuels'.[53] The whole gigantic engine of impiety endangering Christendom, he asserted, had been procreated by Spinoza, who had set himself up as a supreme judge of human happiness;[54] and if the immensity of Spinoza's impact amazes and frightens us, so, after all, had that of Mohammed before him. Furthermore, added the Augustinian, expanding the analogy, their respective strategies were by no means dissimilar, for had not both mystified their adherents with their obscure and incomprehensible texts?[55]

But if Boulainvilliers combined unique gifts as a philosophical researcher and propagandist, the subtle power of his ideological legacy was perhaps no less due to the close circle of intimates he drew round him, which met under the protection of the duc de Noailles—according to one report—from 1707 onwards, when a tradition of informal meetings among members of the Parisian Académie des Inscriptions et Belles-Lettres began, which continued after the death of its dominant spirit, Boulainvilliers, in 1722.[56] This was the famous deistic coterie known as the 'Entresol', an élite group, ensconced at the heart of French intellectual and cultural life, which included Nicolas Fréret (1688–1749), author of several atheistic clandestine philosophical texts, a disciple as well as friend of Boulainvilliers, who several times discussed with him the text of his *Essay* and who later cultivated his memory and the spirit of his

---

[52] Gunny, 'L'Image du prophète', 258–9.   [53] J. T. . . . *Le faux heureux detrompé*, pp. xviii, xxi.

[54] Ibid., pp. xxiv, xxviii.

[55] Ibid., pp. xvii–xviii, xxi; Mohammed, he says, had utilized 'un strategèmè à peu pres semblable, en débitant son Alcoran, comme Spinosa a débité le sien'.   [56] Vernière, *Spinoza*, 395.

erudite anti-Christian deism down to the 1740s,[57] besides d'Argenson, Du Marsais, Jean-Baptiste de Mirabaud, Nicolas Boindin, Jean Lévesque de Burigny, and, after 1722, also the philosophical libertine Louis de Bréhant, comte de Plélo (1699–1734), the Chevalier de Ramsay, and other known deists.[58] In this milieu Boulainvilliers' unpublished texts were revered, preserved, copied, and propagated, and helped drive what was in effect a clandestine philosophical counter-culture evolving in Paris from the beginning of the eighteenth century onwards.

[57] Sheridan, 'Lenglet Dufresnoy', 427; Pocock, *Barbarism* i, 167–8; Larrère, 'Fréret', 128–9.
[58] Vernière, *Spinoza*, 392–8; Landucci, 'Introduzione', 42–5; Brogi, *Cerchio*, 22–4.

31 | FRENCH REFUGEE DEISTS IN EXILE

i. The Flight to Holland

Historians have frequently emphasized the importance in European cultural and intellectual history of the exodus of Huguenot *érudits*, pastors, teachers, publishers, booksellers, printers, and lawyers from France following the Revocation of the Edict of Nantes in 1685, and their forming a European diaspora in exile with its intellectual and publishing headquarters in the Netherlands. Much less familiar and discussed but in some ways of comparably profound significance in the history of European culture and thought, is the flight of ex-Catholic monks, priests, teachers, doctors, and *literati* who, estranged from religion and tradition as well as the constraints on theological, philosophical, and literary expression in Bourbon France, sought, like Tyssot de Patot's hero, Father Mésange, greater personal, spiritual, and intellectual freedom abroad. These *émigrés* too formed a close-knit intellectual diaspora from the end of the seventeenth century to the mid-eighteenth, which likewise had its headquarters in Holland while exerting a pervasive impact across Europe.

Those who felt stifled intellectually in pre-1750 France and sought a freer society where they could emancipate themselves intellectually and spiritually, usually derived such aspirations from books and frequenting libraries. Hence, in April 1710, on joining the French-speaking Reformed congregation at The Hague, after fleeing Paris and settling in Holland the previous year, the former Catholic Prosper Marchand, later one of the most eminent journalists of the early eighteenth century, claimed to have perceived the 'errors' of the Roman Church, and inwardly renounced its teachings, owing to reading Scripture and 'plusieurs bons livres'.[1] In particular, he later testified, his eyes were opened by reading philosophy ranging from the 'excellents principes établies si solidement' by Father Malebranche to the strange notions of Bossuet and 'sophismes artificieux' of Arnauld.[2] Given Marchand's subsequent life-long preoccupation with Bayle,[3] the latter too presumably contributed to his prior intellectual formation.

Marchand fled to Holland together with his friend, the engraver and book

---

[1] Jacob, *Radical Enlightenment*, 164–5; Berkvens-Stevelinck, *Prosper Marchand*, 2–4.
[2] Ibid., 3.   [3] Ibid., 66–7, 80.

illustrator Bernard Picart (1673–1733), whom he knew well in Paris before they settled in the Netherlands. Picart too abandoned France and Catholicism primarily as a result of reading. Years later, collaborating with Jean-Fréderic Bernard on the magnificently illustrated eleven-volume *Cérémonies et coutumes religieuses de tous les peuples du monde* (Amsterdam, 1723), a work which treats Judaism, Islam, and fringe Christian Churches with a remarkable degree of objectivity, Picart helped produce one of the enduring Early Enlightenment contributions to religious toleration, a cause to which he became emotionally deeply committed. Of course, such men need not evolve into intellectual radicals. No doubt many became sincere converts to Protestantism or, like Marchand, became providential deists resolutely opposed to more radical strains of deism. Reading philosophy in the manner of Marchand and Picart, however, which meant, in effect, examining one's religious ideas in the light of the New Philosophy, was nevertheless bound to bring such ex-Catholic intellectual refugees settling in the Netherlands into close contact with radical ideas and to draw some towards a radical perspective.

Books and the book trade having generated the process, these subsequently also provided the best prospects for such *émigrés* to earn their living in exile. Aubert de Versé, who defected from the Oratorians and fled France in 1679, two years before Bayle, under threat of being imprisoned (after lapsing for the second time from Catholicism to Protestantism) lived precariously in Holland and later Hamburg, as journalist, proof-reader, and writer, at one stage working on the periodical founded by Saint-Glain and continued by the latter's widow.[4] Through this work he was continually involved with contentious books and ideas. In 1681, for example, after its prohibition in France, he translated into Latin Simon's *Histoire critique du Vieux Testament*. Widely suspected of radical tendencies himself, his *L'Impie convaincu* (1684) ostensibly attacking Spinoza and Bredenburg, was eyed with considerable distrust. His protestations, highlighted by Bayle in the *Nouvelles*,[5] that Malebranche's philosophy, stressing as it does the universality of God's 'general laws', approximates to Spinozism caused a sensation. The real purpose of his book, it seemed clear to Bayle and other commentators, was to undermine both Descartes and Malebranche and promote Spinozism.[6]

Those who discerned in Aubert de Versé a covert advocate of radical ideas were vindicated by his next book, *Le Tombeau du Socinianisme* (1687) which, though purportedly directed against Socinianism, was again a lightly veiled plea for radical ideas and unlimited toleration. This new text provoked outrage among the French-speaking Reformed community in the Netherlands and was condemned by Jurieu as the 'plus détestable de ses ouvrages, et peut-être de tous les livres qui ont jamais été faits'.[7] Jurieu charged Aubert not just with blasphemously abjuring the Trinity and divinity of Christ, but 'feignant être grand ennemi des athées' while surreptitiously spreading

---

[4] Morman, *Noël Aubert de Versé*, 14.   [5] [Bayle], *Nouvelles*, ii (1684), 313–15.
[6] Ibid., 315; Vernière, *Spinoza*, 89; Kirkinen, *Origines*, 42–3; Van Bunge, *Johannes Bredenburg*, 200–3.
[7] [Jurieu], *Factum pour demander justice*, 21; Knetsch, *Pierre Jurieu*, 259.

Naturalist conceptions. While feigning to oppose Spinoza in fact, insisted Jurieu, Aubert rejected the omnipotence and infinite presence of God as well as belief in the Creation, and rendered matter eternal.[8] To escape this new uproar, Aubert fled in 1687 to Hamburg.[9] On being expelled from there, he sought refuge in Danzig and then England before finally returning, at some point after 1690, to France, where he reverted to Catholicism for the third time.

If conversion to any faith for the third time smacks of insincerity, former French Catholics who became Protestants seem not infrequently to have become disillusioned to some extent with the Protestant confessions in their places of refuge. The case of Aubert suggests that this might well impel them towards radical ideas or a cynical charlatanism, or even a mixture of both. A somewhat disreputable outcast with radical inclinations who provoked exasperation everywhere was the former Benedictine monk claiming descent from a Piedmontese noble family, Jean Aymon (1661–1734?). Having fled France and converted to Calvinism in Geneva, Aymon too migrated to Holland where, though now an ordained Reformed minister, he supported himself and his family with a pension from the States General and by teaching mathematics. According to Marchand, he later colluded with Rousset de Missy in touching up *L'Esprit de Spinosa* prior to its clandestine publication by Charles Levier at The Hague in 1719.[10] But by that time he had been unsuccessfully attempting for years to make a name for himself in the Republic of Letters. Early in the War of the Spanish Succession, either feigning or genuinely professing a wish to reconvert to Catholicism, and offering valuable information about the Huguenot diaspora in Holland, Aymon was allowed to return to Paris. But then, in 1706, after months of intensive research in the Bibliothèque du Roy, he betrayed the librarian, Nicolas Clément, who had sponsored his return, and fled for the second time to Holland, bringing in his bags stolen Greek manuscripts of great rarity concerning early Church schisms and disputes over the Eucharist.[11] However, his striving to become an expert on early Church controversy, and a Protestant hero through having 'rescued' vital evidence from the clutches of the Roman Church, alike failed woefully. Despite the war, Clément's letters to key Huguenot *érudits* and publishers thoroughly discredited him in the Republic of Letters, and, in 1709, the States of Holland pronounced him guilty of theft. He was obliged to return what he had filched to the French. Subsequently sinking into obscurity, he remained a peripheral figure among The Hague *Spinosistes*, in contact with Levier and Toland among others. Marchand scorned him as a man without religion, scruples, or intellectual ability.[12]

An intellectually more substantial ex-Benedictine refugee from Louis XIV's France was the exotic figure of Yves de Vallone (*c*.1666–1705), who in 1681, as a youth of 15, had been sent by relatives to a monastery in Paris. After a decade of philosophy and, as

---

[8] [Jurieu], *Factum pour demander justice*, 20–1; Hubert, *Premières réfutations*, 108–9; Howe, *The Living Temple*, ii, pp. xiii, 45; Reimann, *Historia*, 492; Kirkinen, *Origines*, 43–4.

[9] Knetsch, *Pierre Jurieu*, 261.   [10] Marchand, *Dictionnaire* i, 324–5.

[11] Goldgar, *Impolite Learning*, 175–6.

[12] Berti, 'First Edition', 195; Laursen, 'Impostors', 79–80; Champion, 'Introduction', 64.

with Marchand later, immersion in Malebranche, growing restlessness of spirit and weakening faith, prompted Vallone to discard his monk's habit and flee France.[13] Embarking on a life of personal liberty, he wandered first in Switzerland and then Germany, publicly abjuring Catholicism and converting to Calvinism in March 1697, in a ceremony at Schwabach. He arrived in the United Provinces in 1700, settling first in Zwolle at a time when Leenhof was at the height of his influence.[14]

Not inconceivably, it was at Zwolle and through Leenhof (who knew Paris and spoke French fluently) that Vallone first encountered the philosophy which predominantly shaped the remainder of his short life, namely Spinozism. There is no evidence for this, although, given Zwolle's small size and the fewness of its French-speakers, he presumably at least knew Leenhof. In any case, he left Zwolle a few months later, transferring to The Hague, where there were better prospects of work in a French-speaking milieu. He found employment as a teacher and assistant preacher in the community there but, in 1703, became embroiled in an acrimonious quarrel with Jacques Bernard, whom he publicly denounced as a Socinian, Spinozist, and mocker of Scripture. The *consistoire* at The Hague, anxious to quell the disturbance, and deeming Vallone chiefly at fault, obliged him to retract publicly, a humiliating experience which seems to have exacerbated his already considerable feelings of estrangement from the Reformed faith.

Around this time Vallone began writing the clandestine manuscript which constitutes his chief claim to fame—*La Religion du Chrétien conduit par la raison éternelle.*[15] As he explains in the 'avertissment', he composed the text for his own edification rather than publication, intending to burn the manuscript before his death. Should he be prevented from doing so, though, he entreats whoever might come upon it not to condemn him out of hand but, laying aside all prejudice, carefully ponder his arguments.[16] The work did survive, though at his early death, in 1705, it lay unfinished. Subsequently, it came into the possession of Prince Eugene, who probably acquired it during his stay at The Hague in 1707, and subsequently found its way to Vienna, where it survives today.[17]

Unlike other unpublished deistic philosophical texts of the early eighteenth century, *La Religion du Chrétien* seems never to have circulated. The only other two known surviving copies, also in Vienna,[18] belonged to the Prince's trusted aide, Hohendorf. Vallone's writing had no discernible influence, was never cited or quoted, and—with the possible exception of Giannone, who spent years working in the Viennese Court library—remained unread by all other important writers of the Radical Enlightenment. Yet despite its obscurity, it is still noteworthy, being arguably the most vigorous reworking of Spinoza's critique of revealed religion of the age. Precisely because it was not intended for publication, Vallone makes no effort to dilute his radical stance with circumlocutions or evasion. His rejection of Revelation and the divine authorship of Scripture is absolute and categorical.

---

[13] O'Higgins, *Yves de Vallone*, 18.   [14] Ibid., 36.   [15] Ibid., 60–1.   [16] Ibid., 68.
[17] Ibid., 63; Benítez, 'Du bon usage', 82–3.   [18] Benítez, *Face cachée*, 48.

His own allegiance was to a form of deism acknowledging a universal intelligence which animates matter and regulates the world, a kind of *mélange* of Spinoza, Aubert, and Malebranche.[19] Besides the *Tractatus Theologico-Politicus*, he uses Bayle, Simon, Malebranche, and Orobio de Castro's *Certamen*, but apparently does not know the *Ethics*. What he chiefly owes to Spinoza are the principles and techniques of his Bible hermeneutics. His aim is not simply to restate Spinoza but rather to reorganize his arguments in a different order and style, with an eye in particular to other recent commentators whom he seeks to refute. Above all, his object is to demolish Simon's claim that Scripture *is* divine Revelation, and invalidate his entire critique of Spinoza, insisting that anyone with any grasp of the issues could see that the former Oratorian had borrowed Spinoza's methodology but tried to deflect its impact by modifying his principles.[20] Vallone, by contrast, leans in quite the opposite direction. Thus, while endorsing Spinoza's notion of the Biblical prophets as men of exceptional 'imagination', but not divinely inspired, he makes no attempt to follow Spinoza in emphasizing their piety and good morals.[21] Similarly, he depicts Christ as just an exceptionally eloquent prophet without maintaining, like Spinoza, that Christ, while not divine, was the 'mouthpiece of God' who 'perceived things truly and adequately'.[22] Vallone, however, did not consider he was departing from or distorting Spinoza's views, but rather presenting his argument in a purer form, stripped of the artifice Spinoza was obliged to enter into for the purposes of publication.

ii. Gueudeville and Lahontan

Another remarkable member of the contingent of defrocked monks who joined the diaspora of French refugee authors and editors in Holland in the early eighteenth century was Nicolas Gueudeville (1652–c.1721). Born and raised in Rouen, Gueudeville joined the Benedictines as a youth at their famous Norman abbey of Jumièges. By the 1680s, though, largely through reading, Gueudeville lost his faith and lapsed into a deep spiritual crisis.[23] In August 1688 he fled from his monastery near Alençon, by climbing down the walls, and escaped to Holland where, in July 1689, he was accepted into the French-speaking Reformed community in Rotterdam. There, over the next decade, he earned his bread by teaching Latin while establishing himself on the fringes of the Huguenot literary *monde*, becoming acquainted, among others, with Bayle and Jacques Basnage.[24]

The Reformed faith failed to satisfy his spiritual yearnings either, however, and slowly he drifted away from the path of Calvinist propriety, impelled by unsatisfied inclinations for freethinking, drink, and more personal freedom, especially as regards women. In May 1699 he moved to The Hague, where he edited a monthly political review, *L'Esprit des Cours de l'Europe*, the chief aim of which was to pour vituperation

---

[19] Ibid., 433; O'Higgins, *Yves de Vallone*, 90–1; Mori, 'Introduction', 5.

[20] O'Higgins, *Yves de Vallone*, 68, 74.   [21] Ibid., 158–65; Benítez, 'Du bon usage', 437–8.

[22] Spinoza, *TTP*, 107, 114; Benítez, 'Du bon usage', 438.

[23] Rosenberg, *Nicolas Gueudeville*, 1–5.   [24] Ibid., 5–6.

upon Louis XIV. He was also noted in the literary world for the instalments, published in 1700–2, of his 'critique générale' of one of the most celebrated literary texts of the age, Fénelon's *Télémaque*.[25] In later years, he spent much time working on translations of Erasmus.

A tireless champion of toleration, Gueudeville never seems to have lost his enthusiasm for his adopted land. 'Je suis tout Hollandois d'inclination,' he once remarked 'je fais gloire de la déclarer.'[26] His radicalism consisted of a strongly anti-monarchical republican attitude combined with implacable hostility to ecclesiastical power and revealed religion.[27] As a writer, his foremost contribution proved to be his extensively revised and expanded version of Lahontan's *Nouveaux Voyages* of 1702. Louis-Armand de Lom d'Arce, baron de Lahontan (1666–1715), was a member of the impoverished nobility of the Basses-Pyrénées who, having little to detain him in France after inheriting an estate heavily burdened with debts and litigation, and with his family effectively ruined, served approximately a decade (1683–93) as an officer in the French army in Canada. A born critic and rebel, in 1693 he became involved in some imbroglio in Newfoundland and was obliged to flee to Europe to elude arrest.[28] Having deserted France, New France, and the French army, he spent the rest of his life wandering in Holland, Germany, England, and Denmark, dying shortly before Leibniz, in Hanover. His *Nouveaux Voyages*, and especially his account of the Canadian Indians, constitute his prime claim to fame and, both in the original version and that doctored by Gueudeville, were indeed the most widely read descriptions of native Americans of the first half of the eighteenth century.

As originally published in two volumes at The Hague by the firm of L'Honoré, in the middle of 1702 (albeit with '1703' on the title-page), and reviewed in the *Histoire des Ouvrages des Savans* in August, Lahontan claimed the Indians 'se moquent des Chrétiens, qui sont escalaves les uns des autres, et qui ne peuvent vivre en société sans renoncer à leur liberté naturelle'[29] and derided the credulity of Europeans concerning the miracles recounted in the Old and New Testaments.[30] Another provocative feature of his text was its indirect disparagement, through the mouths of the Indians, of the Catholic missionaries and the Church of New France for their pride, corruption, and the 'empire despotique qu'ils exercent en ce païs là'.[31] If Lahontan's biting criticism of royal policy in French America, and especially the subordination, as he claims, of the secular to the ecclesiastical arm, and the policy of excluding the Huguenots with their aptitude for trade and manufacture from settling there, guaranteed a frosty reception from the French authorities,[32] what chiefly antagonized mainstream opinion in Europe generally was his use of what he claimed were the Indians' beliefs mercilessly to expose and disparage the basic institutions of European society and culture.

There were indeed two prongs to the Lahontan–Gueudeville critique—rejection of

---

[25] Jaumann, *Critica*, 212–13, 238, 250.   [26] Quoted in Rosenberg, *Nicolas Gueudeville*, 83.

[27] Ibid., 125, 138.   [28] Hazard, *European Mind*, 28; Rosenberg, *Nicolas Gueudeville*, 123.

[29] *Histoire des Ouvrages des Savants* 1702, 346.   [30] Ibid., 349.

[31] Lahontan, *Noueaux Voyages*, ii, 72–4; *Histoire des Ouvrages des Savants* 1702, 350.

[32] Lahontan, *Nouveaux Voyages*, ii, 72, 83.

the European social system and a harsh assessment of European religion. Claiming that the Indians knew no 'mine' and 'yours', rejected money, and found it strange that among Europeans some possessed more than others and that those who possess most 'sont estimez davantage que ceux qu'en ont le moins', Lahontan has these natives hurl back the title of 'sauvages' with which Europeans designate them, implying it better fits the Europeans, with their ridiculous social hierarchy and system of rank, honours, and titles. Lahontan idealized Indian society as one where equality prevails, life is in accord with Nature, and 'au reste, ils ne se querellent, ni se battent, ni ne se volent, et ne médisent jamais les uns les autres.'[33] His noble savages, like Rousseau's later, 'se moquent des sciences et des arts, ils se raillent de la grande subordination qu'ils remarquent parmi nous'.[34] Because we quarrel and fight incessantly and willingly subject ourselves to kings and other superiors, reports Lahontan, they call us 'slaves'. They argue, he says, that men are created equal by Nature and that therefore, 'il ne doit point y avoir de distinction ni de subordination entre eux.'[35] To this, he adds, they hold 'leur contentement d'esprit surpasse de beaucoup nos richesses' and that all our sciences are worth less than their knowledge of how to experience life 'dans une tranquilité parfaite'.[36]

The opprobrium provoked by Lahontan's account of the Indians' views on the Christian religion, though he dubs these 'impertinentes', was both vehement and enduring. The Iroquois insist, contends Lahontan, that the existence of God 'étant inséparablement unie avec son essence, il contient tout, il paroît en tout, il agit en tout, et il donne le mouvement à toutes choses'.[37] In effect, God, in their eyes, is identical to Nature; and if the jealous, providential God of the Christians is misconceived, the innumerable divisions and sects among them sufficiently prove that the Christian religion is not a God-given faith.[38] Nowhere, however, did it appear less likely that Lahontan faithfully recounted what he had heard from the Indians, rather than fabricating a radical philosophical construction of his own making, than where he claimed they maintain that mankind should never discard the advantages of 'reason' when discussing religion, since it is the most noble faculty which God has given us.[39]

In his catalogue of early eighteenth-century forms of impiety in Germany, Loescher classifies Lahontan as not just one of the prime perpetrators of a Spinozistic conception of God, an unbeliever who expressly elevates reason above Revelation,[40] but also, together with Van Dale and Bekker, among the foremost deniers of magical power and the existence of spirits and Satan.[41] Indeed, Lahontan emphatically rejects the prevailing notion, found in many books, that the Canadian Indians fervently acknowledged the existence of the Devil. He says he has read numerous absurdities 'sur ce sujet écrites par des gens d'Église', claiming the Indians confer with Satan and

---

[33] Ibid., 97; Hazard, *European Thought*, 390.

[34] Lahontan, *Nouveaux Voyages*, ii, 97; Hazard, *European Mind*, 28–9, 503; Kors, *Atheism in France*, i, 150.

[35] Lahontan, *Nouveaux Voyages*, ii, 98.　　[36] Ibid., 99; Hazard, *European Thought*, 390.

[37] Lahontan, *Nouveaux Voyages*, ii, 113; [Lévesque de Burigny], *Histoire*, i, 64.

[38] Lahontan, *Nouveaux Voyages*, ii, 119–20.　　[39] Ibid., 117.

[40] Loescher, *Praenotiones*, 58, 146.　　[41] Ibid., 220–1.

render him homage. In fact, he says, all such accounts are absurd, native Americans possessing in reality no knowledge or awareness of the Devil whatsoever.[42]

The original version was sufficiently successful, as well as controversial, to encourage the publishers, Jonas and François L'Honoré, to contemplate an enlarged second edition. Lahontan himself being unavailable, Gueudeville was activated to revise the text and, in particular, expand the sections in which the religious and philosophical views of the Indians are recounted. When this new version was published in June 1705, there was a furious outcry. Gueudeville was publicly accused by Le Clerc and by Jean-Frédéric Bernard of having outrageously manipulated Lahontan's text, converting it into an unmistakable vehicle of Spinozism permeated with hostility to revealed religion and the Churches.[43] In subsequent decades the work retained an undiminished notoriety throughout Europe. The general view was that the work was partly bogus, but did also bear some relation to Lahontan's real experiences among the Indians.[44] In the Parisian salons Lahontan was read and quoted, among others, by Fontenelle and Lévesque de Burigny.[45] In Italy the work was deemed entirely unsuitable for Catholic readers and banned by the papal Inquisition in 1712.[46] Radical socially, politically, and in sexual matters (see p. 89 above) as well as theology, Lahontan—without and, still more, with Gueudeville's supplementary material—stood out as the foremost champion in the era between Spinoza and Rousseau of 'natural man' as a tool of criticism of existing social and cultural realities.

iii. Antagonist of Voltaire: Saint-Hyacinthe (1684–1746)

Among the most assiduous philosophical adventurers of the early eighteenth century was Thémiseul de Saint-Hyacinthe (1684–1746), a long-standing foe of Voltaire. The son of an impoverished French army officer, Saint-Hyacinthe studied as a youth with the Oratorians at Troyes, after which he himself served briefly in the French army. He first experienced the Netherlands as a prisoner of war, after being captured at the battle of Blenheim in 1704. Imprisonment and his subsequent voluntary sojourn in Holland turned the young man into a voracious reader and an aspiring *philosophe*. He returned to France in 1706 but, in 1711, with the war still raging, and seeing few openings for his talent in France, he returned to seek his fortune as a writer at The Hague. There he lived for the next five years, until 1716, collaborating from 1713 with Marchand, 's-Gravesande, Van Effen, and Sallengre in editing and compiling the reviews for the *Journal Littéraire*.[47] Saint-Hyacinthe specialized in religious and philosophical topics.

In Saint-Hyacinthe's mind philosophy was closely tied to literature, and his first success as a writer came in 1714, with the publication of his satirical novel, the *Chef d'oeu-*

---

[42] Lahontan, *Nouveaux Voyages*, ii, 126–7; Betts, *Early Deism*, 129.

[43] Rosenberg, *Nicolas Gueudeville*, 124–5.

[44] Loescher, *Praenotiones*, 146; Lilienthal, *Theologische Bibliothec*, 379–80.

[45] [Lévesque de Burigny], *Histoire*, i, 64; Niderst, 'Fontenelle', 167.   [46] Reusch, *Index*, 867.

[47] Berkvens-Stevelinck, *Prosper Marchand*, 110–11.

vre d'un inconnu. Although the book remained popular well beyond his death (what were called the 'eighth' and 'ninth' editions—there were probably more—appearing at Lausanne in 1754 and 1758)[48] and while he was widely known to be the author (despite Voltaire's attempts to cast doubt on this), the anonymous status of the publication brought him less public recognition than a comparable work under his own name would have done. At this time his reputation was that of an *esprit fort*, who conforms in public but in private makes no secret of radical deist views and rejection of Christianity. Encouraged by Louis XIV's keenly awaited death, and the advent of the duc d'Orléans as regent in France, he again returned to his native land in 1716, and for several years moved in an elevated Parisian milieu close to the ruling group around Orléans, of whose family his father had been a client and whose freethinking opinions were evidently much to his taste.[49] It was in this connection, in 1718, that Saint-Hyacinthe wrote a political work in support of the duke's foreign policy, denouncing the Spanish Bourbons for supporting the 'despicable' absolutists of the British house of Stuart.

This text was published at The Hague in 1719, and is remarkable for its rejection of the principle of dynastic legitimacy as well as 'divine right'. Strongly infused with republican undertones, it endorses the right of the English people through their Parliament to dispossess the Stuarts of the British thrones and allocate them instead to the House of Hanover. Saint-Hyacinthe proclaimed as his supreme political maxim: 'agir tousjours pour le plus grand bien.'[50] Excellent on the subject of government, in his opinion, were the writings of the executed English republican Algernon Sidney, styled by Saint-Hyacinthe 'aussi célèbre par son zèle pour la liberté, que par ses malheurs'.[51] Invoking Grotius, Pufendorf, Locke, and Noodt, Saint-Hyacinthe insists on the right of popular resistance to tyrannical rule, however legitimate it may be dynastically, declaring the needs of the people the sole true source of political legitimacy.[52]

During this period Saint-Hyacinthe remained in contact with various correspondents in the Netherlands and especially the Spinozist publisher Charles Levier, who produced his unsuccessful *Mémoires littéraires* of 1716, a rambling rag-bag containing, besides much else, fierce attacks on Louis XIV and the Jesuits, a eulogy of Confucius and Chinese philosophy, enthusiastic praise for the Koran along with implied disparagement of Christianity, and passionate anti-monarchism.[53] For some unexplained reason—the pretext given was that he needed to nurse his health—Saint-Hyacinthe, departed from Paris early in 1720, returning to The Hague, where he remained until the end of 1722, by which time he had spent altogether over ten years in Holland. He then moved to England, where he resided for nine years, initially at Worcester and later in London, albeit with appreciable interludes, including the whole first half of 1724, in Holland. Like the rest of his life, his English period is in several respects highly

---

[48] Corsini, 'Quand Amsterdam', 110–11. [49] Carayol, *Thémiseul de Saint-Hyacinthe*, 57–9.
[50] [Saint-Hyacinthe], *Entretiens*, 135. [51] Ibid., 159–60.
[52] Ibid., 153–4, 188–90; Carayol, *Thémiseul de Saint Hyacinthe*, 60.
[53] Carayol, *Thémiseul de Saint Hyacinthe*, ii, 22.

perplexing. He was not uninterested in English ideas and made some effort to cultivate links with English *savants* and the Royal Society. But these endeavours bore little
fruit, and with time he became increasingly at odds philosophically with the English
philosophical mainstream. Apparently his only close associate, then as later, in England, was the Huguenot *savant* Des Maizeaux.

During these years, without relinquishing his republicanism or his deism, Saint-
Hyacinthe drifted away from the more radical stance characteristic of his earlier phase
and such comrades as Lévesque de Burigny, Sallengre, and Levier.[54] In the late 1720s his
deism assumed an almost mystical quality and he became intellectually entrenched
somewhere between the Radical and moderate Enlightenment, embracing the doctrine of the immortality of the soul, and reward and punishment in the hereafter,
believing that without such credence man would have no reason to avoid wrongdoing
and the moral order would disintegrate. In an intensely personal letter to Lévesque,
written in September 1727, he urged his closest friend to abandon his 'prejudices' and
join him in acknowledging an omnipotent 'Supreme Being'.[55] It was shortly after this,
in London, that his subsequently interminable feud with Voltaire began, Voltaire's
stay in London (1726–8) overlapping with Saint-Hyacinthe's sojourn from early 1728 to
1731 by a few months. The quarrel seems to have originated in pique at what Voltaire
considered the older man's lukewarm praise and support. For decades afterwards
the two *philosophes* regularly traded insults. But while there was a gulf between the
two philosophically, with Saint-Hyacinthe indifferent to, if not actively opposing,
Voltaire's ardent advocacy of Locke and Newton, there never seems have been any
declared issue of substance behind their ceaseless mutual animosity.

Another French literary *émigré* Saint-Hyacinthe encountered in London was the
future author of the famous novel *Manon Lescaut*, the Abbé Antoine-François Prévost
(1697–1763), a figure in many respects typical of this brilliant if unpredictable, refugee
intellectual diaspora. After escaping from the abbey of Saint Germain-des-Près in
November 1728, Prévost discarded his monk's habit and fled France to escape a *lettre de
cachet* issued for his arrest. Following a spell in London, from late 1728 to September
1730, he moved on to Holland where he reported, among other things, that Saint-
Hyacinthe was now reduced to desperate financial straits.[56] He stayed there for several
years. What Prévost wanted was freedom and he took full advantage of the freer air
intellectually, socially, and sexually. This in turn gave him that capacity to compare
society and attitudes in France with those he found and eulogized in Holland, which
fed the critical and satirical impulse so characteristic of the entire ex-Catholic refugee
mentality. On returning to France in 1733, Prévost became a familiar figure of Paris
café society and editor of a journal, *Le Pour et le Contre*, offering 'critical examination'
of both reality and literature.[57]

Saint-Hyacinthe's most successful years were the decade 1731–40, which he spent
back in Paris as a familar figure of the French capital's *grands salons* and fashionable

---

[54] Carayol, *Thémiseul de Saint Hyacinthe*, 186.   [55] Ibid., 111–14.
[56] Ibid., 123.   [57] Ibid., 146–7; Chartier, *Cultural Origins*, 158.

cafés. In continual creative contact with Lévesque and the latter's brothers, as well as André Michel Ramsay, Maupertuis, and others, and clashing intermittently with Voltaire, he seemed securely established as a leading critic, *philosophe*, and man of letters, at the forefront of French intellectual debate. He remained personally committed to his deist beliefs and also eager to broaden his awareness of radical philosophical literature. In October 1737, he contacted Des Maizeaux in London, requesting the latest edition of Newton's *Principia* and works by Mandeville, Tindal, and Rochester.[58]

Saint-Hyacinthe's Parisian success was rudely shattered, however, in August 1741, while he was abroad in the Netherlands. His daughter, Suzanne, born at Worcester and raised in a deistic milieu but increasingly disturbed by the severe strictures against deism she continually encountered in France, having confided her worries to a curate and a noble lady, was persuaded to join in a pious plot against her father. Suddenly she was 'taken into care' under a *lettre de cachet* and installed in a special convent in Paris for 'nouvelles catholiques'.[59] Her defection from a publicly named 'deist' endangered Saint-Hyacinthe and prejudiced the prospect of the rest of his children being left under his roof. Realizing that he could not safely return to France, he sent word to his wife to leave at once with the other children and join him in the Netherlands. He spent—first near Sluis and later near Breda—the remaining five years of his life once again in Dutch exile, troubled by mounting financial and personal difficulties.

His most substantial philosophical work is his 514-page *Recherches philosophiques*, a work undertaken to combat scepticism and uncertainty about man, God, and the world, and the first of his writings openly disclosing his deism and rejection of Christianity, a work published simultaneously at The Hague and London in 1743. There was a considerable outcry and the work was promptly banned in France, causing him much difficulty in getting copies through to his principal friends and allies—Lévesque de Burigny, Lévesque de Pouilly, Ramsay, and Dorthous de Mairan.[60] A colleague of Marchand's in Brussels, who had been expecting something less radical, lamented that Saint-Hyacinthe should end up 'à côté des Voltaires et des Spinosa'.[61]

Philosophically, the *Recherches philosophiques* represents a curious blend of elements. Remarkably, despite his long sojourn in England, Locke's empiricism is cavalierly dismissed in a few pages, and innate ideas—in defiance of Spinoza as well as Locke—are retained.[62] Saint-Hyacinthe's criterion of certainty in philosophy is essentially the restricted 'geometric method' of Descartes and Malebranche.[63] He constructs a basic duality of substances, body and soul, with the latter immortal, which parallels Descartes and Malebranche but nevertheless radicalizes the conception within a deist format. His principal objective is to rebut the 'matérialistes, les Naturalistes et les Panthéistes' who blasphemously identify God with Nature, by irrefutably

[58] BL Add. MS 4284, fo. 161v. Saint-Hyacinthe to Des Maizeaux, Paris, 23 Oct. 1737.
[59] Carayol, *Thémiseul de Saint-Hyacinthe*, 160–2.   [60] Ibid., 174.
[61] Berkvens-Stevelinck and Vercruysse, *Métier*, 51.
[62] Saint-Hyacinthe, *Recherches philosophiques*, 503–9.
[63] Ibid., 10–12, 20–42, 175; Carayol, *Thémiseul de Saint-Hyacinthe*, 176–8.

advancing a providential deism, proclaiming the existence of a God who is real, who acts, and who judges. Saint-Hyacinthe never doubts that everything hinges on successfully demolishing Spinoza. Anxious to avoid the charge incurred by Bayle of not having understood Spinoza correctly, he assures readers he has read the *Opera Posthuma* through three times and the 'other works of Spinoza' twice and also carefully studied the *Specimen Artis Ratiocinandi* (of Cuffeler), which he considers the 'best' commentary on Spinoza.

Man's happiness and welfare depend on his establishing the truth of his own nature and that of the universe through reason, philosophy, and science. Christianity is superstition and prejudice. The truth lies in a deism firmly segregated from the nonprovidential deism of the Spinozists. The problem is that the entire deist project is threatened with catastrophe by the tremendous force of 'le spinosisme' which, however, derives from purely psychological factors and not any intellectual cogency.[64] What is most pernicious in Spinoza is his fatalism—his claim that man is not 'un agent libre' and that 'l'Être éternel infini et tout-puissant soit un agent nécessité et non un agent libre.'[65] For these doctrines erode man's veneration for the providential Supreme Being and destroy the basis of human morality. Of course, Spinoza is not the only modern philosophical *fataliste*. Saint-Hyacinthe knows the *Pantheisticon* and *Letters to Serena* of Toland and also refers to Mandeville. But in so far as Toland is a Pantheist and non-providential deist who rejects the notion of God as a 'agent libre', Saint-Hyacinthe not unreasonably regards him as merely a pendant to Spinoza. All non-providential deism collapses, and the curious cross between radical and mainstream thought constructed by Saint-Hyacinthe stands firm once Spinoza's system is smashed and man acknowledges the Supreme Being, who is a free and active agent 'dont la puissance nécessaire n'est pas necessité'.[66] In Saint-Hyacinthe's mental world Locke and Toland also figure, but are clearly deemed marginal. As for Voltaire, Saint-Hyacinthe may have thought him the most impudent and exasperating of men, but he also considered his philosophical views too derivative and superficial to merit serious discussion.

iv. The Marquis d'Argens (1703–1771)

One of the most widely read radical deist writers of Early Enlightenment Europe, an author steeped in Bayle and Spinoza, a born rebel, and unrelentingly hostile to the European *status quo*, if not politically then certainly in everything concerning thought and belief,[67] was the remarkable Jean-Baptiste de Boyer, Marquis d'Argens (1703–71). Born into a mixed *parlementaire* and military family at Aix-en-Provence, he was destined to spend most of his life outside France. After travelling widely as a young man, among other places to Rome and Constantinople, and a brief military career which ended in 1734, after suffering injury falling from his horse during a siege on the Rhine,

---

[64] Saint-Hyacinthe, *Recherches philosophiques*, 58.   [65] Ibid., 59–62, 328–31, 355.
[66] Ibid., 355, 357–99.   [67] Concina, *Della religione revelata*, ii, 390; Vernière, *Spinoza*, 407.

he settled in the United Provinces without resources, cut off from his family and resolved to live by his pen. Most of his books date from the mid- and late 1730s. A philosophical writer, it was not for scholars that he wrote but, like Fontenelle, for cavaliers and the 'beau sexe'.[68]

He lived in various places in the United Provinces, including Amsterdam, The Hague, and Maastricht, remaining on friendly terms for some years with several of the French *émigré* intellectual community, notably Marchand, until he quarrelled with him in August 1739.[69] Later he rose in society and, somewhat to the pique of his former literary comrades, graduated from the world of books and publishing. Becoming a polished courtier after moving to Germany at the end of the decade, he distinguished himself first in Stuttgart, where he became chamberlain of the Duchess of Württemberg and, from July 1742, in Berlin at the newly enlivened court of the young King of Prussia, Frederick the Great, whose friend he became and where he joined Voltaire and Algarotti to form a philosophical coterie later reinforced by Maupertuis and La Mettrie. Reckoned one of the best conversationalists in Berlin, as well as a noted libertine notorious for his many mistresses, he retained his place and pension there despite causing general disgust—shared by his ex-friends in Holland—in 1747 when he married an opera *comédienne*, a lady of humble background and presumed easy virtue, named Barbe Cochois.[70]

D'Argens' philosophical odyssey, according to his *Mémoires*, began in 1727 in Constantinople, where he lived for some time and was converted to a philosophical cast of mind by a sophisticated Sephardic Jew and a formidable Armenian who had lived in Amsterdam where he had become a 'grand Spinosiste'.[71] The latter lent him a copy of an aggressively radical clandestine philosophical manuscript, one of the most important of the genre, entitled *Doutes ou Examen de la religion dont on cherche l'éclaircissement de bonne foi*, which made a considerable impression on him, though he says he subsequently lost this text while travelling in Italy. This work, later published clandestinely in Holland in 1745, attributed (whether sincerely or playfully) to 'Saint-Evremond',[72] firmly rules out the possibility of miracles, denies the reality of the Christian 'mysteries', and sharpens Spinoza's strictures about the Hebrew text of Scripture into the slogan: 'l'original hebreu est plein d'équivoques.'[73]

Though his works were banned in France and Italy, d'Argens was a fashionable author writing to sell his books, in particular to an upper-class readership in the Netherlands, Germany, and (clandestinely) in France, and could not therefore flaunt his philosophical radicalism too openly. Consequently, he regularly resorts to artifice,[74] implying that he is a follower of Locke[75] and, while clearly revering Bayle and discussing Spinoza more than any other philosopher in his voluminous writings,

---

[68] Johnston, *Marquis d'Argens*, 47. [69] Berkvens-Stevelinck and Vercruysse, *Métier*, 39–40.
[70] Ibid., 100–1; Häseler, *Wanderer*, 102, 123.
[71] D'Argens, *Mémoires*, 115; Vernière, *Spinoza*, 408; Mori, 'Introduction', 26, 35–6.
[72] Schwarzbach and Fairburn, 'The *Examen*', 110–11. [73] [Du Marsais], *Examen*, 161, 315.
[74] Pigeard de Gurbert, 'La philosophie', 368.
[75] D'Argens, *Philosophie du Bon-Sens*, i, 13; D'Argens, *Lettres juives*, iv, 180–2.

covers himself by assuring readers that the more one examines the latter's system, the more 'on le trouve rempli d'absurdités.'[76] But there are several unmistakable ploys which d'Argens adopts to convey indirectly and covertly the realities of his message. One method, reminiscent of Aubert, was to stress the parallels between Spinoza and Malebranche, whose influence in France, Spain, and Italy was then still considerable, thereby damaging the *Malebranchistes* by classifying Malebranche's philosophy as 'une espèce de Spinozisme spirituel' by which he renders all immaterial substances simple modifications 'd'une substance spirituelle, unique et infinie'.[77] Following Bayle and Lévesque de Burigny, he also stresses that Spinoza was the prime modern restorer of the ancient systems of atheism of Strato, Anaximenes, Democritus, and so forth, systems which 'avoit bien des partisans chez les Romains'.[78] Another favourite technique was to express Spinozisic views without mentioning their source and then highlight Spinoza's role in spreading similar ideas spiced with extravagantly—but in the context illogically—hostile references to him. Thus, when discussing the hindrances philosophers encounter in trying to spread their ideas, he wryly laments that Locke won only a few disciples despite his great insights while, by contrast, 'Spinoza trouva le secret de faire goûter son absurde et criminel système à beaucoup de gens.'[79] He then demands 'Quel mal ses opinions n'ont-elles pas causé en Europe?' painting an overdramatic picture of a Europe half overrun by Spinoza's atheistic 'monstrueux système' which, mercifully, is now being redeemed and won back, thanks to several English 'personages illustres tels que Boyle, Bentley, Kidder, Williams, Gastrell, etc.'[80]

Another favourite ploy was to stress the parallels between Spinoza and Confucius, classical Chinese philosophy having, ever since Isaac Vossius, been eulogized by Temple, Bayle, Saint-Hyacinthe, Lévesque de Burigny, Wolff, and others as an entirely 'natural' philosophy based solely on reason and steeped in moral and metaphysical truth.[81] In his *Lettres chinoises*, one of his longest works, d'Argens' Chinese observer reports home from Paris that there are many Europeans who follow a system of philosophy which closely resembles that of the classical Chinese thinkers: 'Spinoza, savant hollandois, en a été l'inventeur, ou plûtôt le restaurateur, car l'on prétend que ses sentimens, à quelque chose près, ont été ceux de plusieurs philosophes anciens.'[82] He then takes the opportunity to explain several passages from the *Ethics* in French, including the infamous Proposition XIV of Part I: 'quidquid est, in Deo est, et nihil sine Deo esse, neque concipi potest,'[83] and then elaborates in the space of more than seventy pages his close identification of the ideas of 'les Européens Spinosistes' with those of the 'commentateurs modernes chinois'.[84] Naturally, remarks d'Argens, Christian missionaries working in China never tell the Chinese about Spinoza and

[76] D'Argens, *Philosophie du Bon-Sens*, i, 346–7.   [77] Ibid., 363–6, 378; Northeast, *Parisian Jesuits*, 64.
[78] D'Argens, *Philosophie du Bon-Sens*, i, 330–4.
[79] D'Argens, *Lettres cabalistiques*, vi, 194–5; Vernière, *Spinoza*, 411.
[80] D'Argens, *Lettres cabalistiques*, vi, 195.   [81] Johnston, *Marquis d'Argens*, 53.
[82] D'Argens, *Lettres chinoises*, i, 106.   [83] Ibid., 106–7.   [84] Ibid., 50–127.

carefully avoid mentioning the 'grand nombre de partisans' that Spinoza has 'en France, en Allemagne, en Angleterre, en Hollande, et surtout en Italie'.[85]

But most revealing of all is the insinuating, suggestive manner in which he promotes his own recipe for human happiness and welfare, what he calls 'la bonne philosophie'. In the first place nothing is made more obvious than the fact that this was not what then prevailed in France. According to his Sephardic traveller in Paris, intellectual life there is dominated by theological dispute, and 'la bonne philosophie' is unfortunately rarely to be found. Even someone who is privately a 'Spinosiste', we are told, cannot avoid being dragged into the ceaseless (and senseless) theological bickering and, in particular, must take sides for or against Jansenism and Molinism.[86] Nevertheless, love of philosophy had made impressive strides in Paris since Descartes, and now even many of the nobility, amid their usual intrigues and pleasurable pursuits, customarily spend a few moments each day immersed in philosophy.[87] Indeed, philosophical deism in the 1730s was so prevalent among the upper classes in Paris, according to d'Argens, that he has his Sephardic interlocutor comically report to his rabbinic correspondent in Constantinople that he has discovered in Paris 'un nombre infini de Juifs qui le sont, sans croire l'être, et sans en rien savoir .[88] D'Argens nurtured a strongly philo-Semitic attitude, at least regarding such emancipated and culturally sophisticated Sephardic Jews as he had met in Venice and Holland, and deliberately deploys the term 'Jew' polemically to designate individuals who have escaped bondage to theological ways of thinking. In Paris, according to his Sephardic observer, there are innumerable *esprits forts*, often courtiers and officials, and many fine ladies known as *femmes du monde*, who remain Christians solely 'dans l'extérieur'. They believe there is a God but are divided between those who, like the ancient Sadducees, believe the soul mortal like the body and those who proclaim it immortal. The latter, suggests d'Argens, the providential deists as we would call them, can hardly be denied 'le titre de Juifs'.[89]

In d'Argens' view, Europe is now in the midst of a vast spiritual conflict. He detests superstition and bigotry and delights in the progress of intellectual freedom and deism. But the cosmic struggle of which he feels himself part is in fact only just starting, for thus far it is predominantly what he calls 'les gens de lettres' who are emancipated from the yoke of superstition.[90] For him, as for the entire European Radical Enlightenment, the overriding difficulty is that the great majority remain as sunk as ever 'dans son aveuglement'. Echoing Van Dale and Fontenelle, he reminds readers how the priests of ancient times cunningly fomented, over millennia, the most abject popular credulity and dread, in order to bolster their authority and, in the same way, 'les prêtres . . . trompent aujourd'hui les gens crédules comme on séduisit autrefois les Egyptiens, les Persans, les Grecs et les Romains', all hopelessly duped by those who

---

[85] Ibid., 108.   [86] D'Argens, *Lettres juives*, ii, 179–80.   [87] Ibid., 412.
[88] Ibid., iv, 34.   [89] Ibid., ii, 412.
[90] D'Argens, *Lettres cabalistiques*, v, 56–7; D'Argens, *Lettres juives*, i, 24–5, 107, 111, 275.

promised to teach them the commandments and mysteries of the Divinity.[91] The Christian Fathers, he alleges, borrowed the techniques of spreading credulousness and belief in magic from the pagans, with a shrewd eye as to how to conquer and triumph over them, thereby acquiring unsurpassed power and influence themselves.[92]

D'Argens' recipe for a better Europe is that society must become more like what it is in Holland, 'la patrie des philosophes', as he calls it,[93] and England. He is full of praise for the liberty found in Holland where, he says, 'l'air inspire de l'amour pour la philosophie';[94] and he also praises England for its great progress in philosophy and science, the fruit, he says, of the intellectual freedom which increasingly prevails there. In one respect, though, the English are definitely not to be emulated by others—their habitual disdain for the rest of mankind, 'aiant en général le grand défaut de s'estimer infiniment plus que les autres hommes'.[95] For the struggle in hand has nothing to do with nationhood, location, or climate. The Flemish, the near neighbours of the Dutch, are of all European peoples the most sunk in superstition; all Italy and Spain, he says, contain fewer 'puérilités religieuses' than just the cathedral of Ghent.[96] If Italians know how to think as well as any nation, they remain too repressed to write, while in Spain, where the Inquisition, the mortal enemy of 'la bonne philosophie', persecutes whoever tries to enlighten men, 'la bonne philosophie est entièrement inconnue.'[97] The position is worse still in Portugal and in no way better in the Islamic world.[98] But if the freedom found in Holland, 'le païs du bon sens et de la liberté', and in England can be generally propagated, all Europe will share the inestimable blessings of both liberty and the philosophy of 'bon sens', these two inestimable treasures in his view being not just closely but 'nécessairement' linked together.[99]

---

[91] D'Argens, *Lettres cabalistiques*, v, 57.   [92] Ibid., 55, 57.

[93] D'Argens, *Mémoires*, 308.   [94] D'Argens, *Lettres juives*, iii, 212.

[95] Ibid., iv, 117; d'Argens notes that he is being charged by some with showing 'autant d'amitié et de passion pour les Hollandois, qu'Arouet de Voltaire pour les Anglois'; ibid., ii, preface.

[96] Ibid., i, 330.   [97] Ibid., iii, 353.   [98] Thomson, *Barbary and Enlightenment*, 21–4.

[99] D'Argens, *Mémoires*, 308.

32 | THE SPINOZISTIC NOVEL IN FRENCH

The interchange between the Netherlands and France which played so large a part in the formation of Early Enlightenment radical thought was a two-way transmission, not only of works of philosophy and Bible criticism, of scientific theories, theology, and political thought, but also of an entirely new phenomenon, thoroughly characteristic of the new era—the philosophical or deistic travel novel. If the Spinozistic novel in Dutch begins with *Philopater* in the 1690s, and assumes the guise of a travel romance with Smeeks' *Krinke Kesmes* (1708), the radical philosophical novel in French began in the late 1670s with two utopian travel stories set in the remote South Pacific, Gabriel de Foigny's *La Terre australe connue* (1676) and, more especially, the 'dainty', widely read, and notorious *Histoire des Sévarambes* (1677) by Denis Vairesse d'Alais.[1]

Vairesse, a Protestant lawyer from Alès and a minor official who played a part in concerting the Anglo-French attack on the United Provinces in 1672, lived for some years (1665–74) in London, knew such eminent Englishmen as Locke and Lord Arlington, and spoke English fluently. His utopian novel depicts a gullible people inhabiting the South Seas who are imbued with a revealed religion, invented by the 'Impostor' Omigas, a parody of Moses and Christ, who 'par diverses ruses et plusieurs faux miracles', including the 'curing' of several persons whom he pays to feign blindness and other infirmities, gains total mastery over this society, based on revelation.[2] Indeed, the people were so credulous and completely under the spell of this 'imposteur' that he has no difficulty in convincing them that the Sun—to whom he has taught them to sacrifice—is displeased with his political opponents. Of course, they unhesitatingly banish the latter from their own country for ever.[3] However, this devout society, based on unquestioning authority, is starkly contrasted with another Pacific society, that of the Sévarambes, which is based on deism. The latter have no cult and no clergy and believe in an infinite and eternal God who prefers to be adored without prayer, priestly intercession, rituals, and sacrifices, purely through the mind.[4] Here the people are not shamelessly abused by false prophets.

---

[1] Weber, *Beurtheilung*, 133–4; Morhof, *Polyhistor*, 75; Rosenberg, 'Introduction', 20.
[2] [Vairasse], *Histoire des Sévarambes*, ii, 134–7.
[3] Ibid., 140–2.   [4] Vernière, *Spinoza*, 216–17; Funke, *Studien*, i, 17.

Vairasse's novel was reprinted several times, mostly in the Netherlands, and became one of the most widely known of the clandestine novels of the late seventeenth century. It was also clearly a prime source of inspiration for a still more daring text, apparently written in the years 1680–2, entitled *l'Histoire des Ajaoiens*. The strange name is a parody of Huet's construing the term 'Jao', in his *Demonstratio Evangelica*, as an abbreviation for 'Jehovah'. 'Ajaoiens' therefore signifies non-believers in Jehovah.[5] Philosophically, the most audacious of the French Spinozist novels of the Early Enlightenment, the *Ajaoiens* remained unpublished until it was clandestinely printed in Holland in 1768, and apparently never circulated in manuscript form. But if it was infinitely less influential during the early Enlightenment than the *Histoire des Sévarambes*, it is nevertheless of considerable interest, reflecting as it does the early and forceful emergence of radical ideas in France during the 1680s.

When finally published in the late eighteenth century, the novel, renamed *La République des philosophes, ou l'Histoire des Ajaoiens*, was attributed by its editors to Fontenelle, and while this attribution is not wholly certain, it has ever since been generally regarded as at least highly probable.[6] The book purports to have been translated from Dutch and, like Smeeks' novel, concerns a Dutchman (M. van Doelvelt) voyaging in the East Indies. Having sailed from Batavia and undergone various adventures, Van Doelvelt finds himself marooned among a remote island people, the Ajaoiens, who inhabit a republic where there is no public religion or sacred book, and no written laws. Being 'plus soumis que nous aux claires lumières d'une raison saine et sans préjugé', they dwell peacefully in accordance with a few basic principles 'émanés du sein de la raison', notably that one should treat others as one wishes to be treated oneself and that 'ce qui n'est point ne peut donner l'existence à quelque chose'[7]. Trusting more in reason than Europeans, Ajaoiens know the notion of creation out of nothing is absurd and have not thought to invent any mythical epoch in which the first creatures were created, from nothing, by 'un Être incompréhensible' and invisible.[8] Indeed, remarkably, their God is identical to Nature: 'les Ajaoiens se croient donc fondés en raison, pour mettre la Nature à la place de ce que nous nommons Dieu.'[9] They regard this 'Nature' as a kind of universal mother, 'la mère commune de toutes les créatures qui, par un admirable circulation, sortent continuellement de son sein et y retournent de même'.[10]

Consequently, the Ajaoiens are blessed with no priests, altars, cult, temples, or public religious ceremonies, and firmly believe not in the immortality but the mortality of the soul.[11] In fact, they have absolutely no 'cérémonies propres à nourrir la supersti-

---

[5] Funke, 'Manuscrit retrouvé', 196–7.

[6] Ibid., 198–200; Niderst, *Fontenelle à la recherche*, 22–3, 229–38; McKenna, 'Reflexions', 358–60, 361–5; Funke, *Studien*, i, 21, 28; Niderst, 'Fontenelle', 165–7.

[7] [Fontenelle], *Histoire des Ajaoiens*, 37.   [8] Ibid., 38, 40–1.

[9] Ibid., 38, 42, 45; Funke, *Studien*, i, 238–54; Funke, 'Manuscrit retrouvé', 201.

[10] [Fontenelle], *Histoire des Ajaoiens*, 39.

[11] '. . . ainsi tout ce qui les Européens disent de l'immortalité de leur âme, n'est qu'une chimère inventée par d'habiles politiques, leurs législateurs, pour les tenir dans une crainte continuelle d'un prétendu avenir'; ibid., 49; Funke, 'Manuscrit retrouvé', 201.

tion des peuples, à les endormir, et à faire réussir les desseins des politiques'.[12] As for their view of Nature, its laws are unalterable: 'ses révolutions se font toujours avec le même ordre, et rien ne peut la détourner le moins du monde de son cours ordinaire.'[13] Needless to say, in this philosophical utopia no kings or aristocrats are tolerated, the republic being governed by a senate consisting of elected members with fixed terms of office, which upholds the common good and promotes virtue.[14] The land belongs to the State which then distributes its produce according to need, a system designed to reinforce feelings of equality and fraternity.[15] Finally, to prevent nubile girls being exploited like pieces of property, and to enable them to choose their own partners, females are not permitted to marry before the age of 18.[16]

Unpublished and unknown, *l'Histoire des Ajaoiens* had no known impact during the Early Enlightenment. Aside from the probably semi-fictional philosophical *Voyages* of the Baron de Lahontan, of 1702, there was evidently no further French attempt to develop the fictional innovation introduced by Foigny and Vairesse, despite the continuing notoriety internationally of the *Histoire des Sévarambes*. However, the genre was spectacularly revived some three decades after the writing of *l'Histoire des Ajaoiens* in the Netherlands, by Tyssot de Patot, in part in conscious emulation of Vairesse and, possibly, Smeeks.[17]

Simon Tyssot de Patot (1655–1738), the most important exponent of the Spinozistic novel in French, was a Huguenot *philosophe* who wrote only in that language but whose upbringing and intellectual formation, after his family moved from Normandy to Delft in 1662, when he was 7, evolved exclusively in the Netherlands.[18] Tyssot spent most of his adult life in Deventer, not far from Zwolle, home of Hendrik Smeeks as well as of Leenhof, whose writings he knew but who, according to Tyssot himself, he never met.[19] However, he does seem to have known Bekker, for whom he had considerable sympathy.[20] For no less than forty-seven years, he earned a humble living teaching first as a schoolmaster among the Deventer Walloon congregation and, from 1699, as professor of mathematics at the town's higher education college (Illustre School). He remained, not out of any particular affection for Deventer, but uninterrupted failure to find a more prestigious post elsewhere. A competent mathematician and linguist, and an adept conversationalist, he was evidently only a mediocre teacher. Neither did he gain the reputation for erudition in the Republic of Letters of the kind he believed he deserved. Burdened from an early age with both young and elderly dependents, he battled for decades with lack of both money and recognition, the twin torments which shaped his increasingly fraught career.

Since the early eighteenth century, Tyssot has been generally recognized as the author of what became the best-known of all the radical philosophical novels of the Early Enlightenment—the anonymously and clandestinely published *Voyages et*

---

[12] [Fontenelle], *Histoire des Ajaoiens*, 44.   [13] Ibid., 45.
[14] Ibid., 68–9; Funke, *Studien*, i, 413–15.   [15] [Fontenelle], *Histoire des Ajaoiens*, 70.
[16] Ibid., 110; Funke, 'Manuscrit retrouvé', 194.   [17] Rosenberg, 'Introduction', 20–1.
[18] Ibid., 7–12; Trousson, 'Simon Tyssot de Patot', p. viii.
[19] Tyssot de Patot, *Lettres choisies*, ii, 212.   [20] Trousson, 'Simon Tyssot de Patot', p. xvi.

avantures de Jaques Massé, a work which, according to its title-page, appeared in 'Bordeaux' in '1710', but in fact appeared at The Hague, probably in 1714.[21] Publicly, our Deventer schoolmaster felt obliged to deny rumours that he had written this 'mauvais ouvrage', as Prosper Marchand called it, though Tyssot readily agreed with a correspondent that it was a 'brilliant' book. But while Marchand—and at least one modern scholar—have questioned his authorship,[22] Tyssot himself claimed in 1720 to have written it, in a letter to his son, who was then in Ceylon, and modern scholarly opinion, on the whole, supports the attribution.[23] Besides *Jaques Massé*, Tyssot was also the author of another substantial Spinozistic novel, *La Vie, les aventures et le voyage de Groenland du Révérend Père Cordelier Pierre de Mésange* (two volumes, Amsterdam, 1720) which likewise provoked a stir. However, since both were and remained anonymous works, neither earned him the status of an internationally known writer and scholar that he craved.

After 1720 Tyssot became gradually more prone to take imprudent risks. In 1722 he boldly published under his own name, in the *Journal Littéraire* of The Hague, a 35-page treatise on Biblical chronology in which he claims the Creation as recounted in Genesis requires two different levels of comprehension—a literal understanding adjusted to the ignorant minds of the majority and an entirely different non-literal reading for the sophisticated.[24] In effect, he urges, scholars should emulate Moses who, appreciating the credulousness of the common people 's'accommode à leurs foiblesses, et parle à peu près leur langage, comme cela est assez ordinaire dans l'Écriture'.[25] Outside the popular context, however, virtually nothing in Scripture should be construed literally by minds emancipated from vulgar notions and, in particular, Biblical chronology should be deemed little more than a 'fable'.[26] Tyssot was careful, though, to acknowledge a providential God and prime mover of the universe, expressly repudiating Epicurus and Spinoza, who claim all movement is internal to and inherent in matter.[27] Yet despite its provocative thrust, and unmistakable echoes of Spinoza's hermeneutics, instead of precipitating the sort of lively controversy Tyssot anticipated, this foray yielded nothing more than a disapproving murmur.

Thwarted ambition led him next, in 1726, to take the disastrous step of publishing under his own name the still more audacious *Lettres choisies*, more than 1,000 pages of text on a range of scholarly topics containing a plethora of observations and remarks almost bound to provoke outrage. With calculated indiscretion, he broaches the Leenhof furore, denying that there are seeds of 'atheism' in the *Hemel op Aarde* and styling its author 'un homme poli, bien tourné, fort savant, et qui mène une vie beau-

---

[21] Lilienthal, *Theologische Bibliothec*, 348–51; Barbier, *Dictionnaire* iii, 321; Betts, *Early Deism*, 186; Rosenberg, 'Introduction', 23–5; Rosenberg, 'Tyssot de Patot', 209.

[22] Vermij, 'English Deists', 250.

[23] Rosenberg. 'Introduction', 11; Rosenberg, 'Tyssot de Patot', 206–7; Delon, 'Tyssot de Patot', 708–9; Schröder, *Ursprünge*, 68.

[24] Tyssot de Patot, 'Discours', 154–89; Rosenberg, 'Tyssot de Patot', 208.

[25] Tyssot de Patot, 'Discours', 160; Valkoff, 'Wonderbaarlijke reizen', 243.

[26] Tyssot de Patot, 'Discours', 189.   [27] Ibid., 165.

coup plus édifiante que ne font bien de tartufes, qui le décrient'.[28] Spinoza's works, he urges, echoing Leenhof, contain wholesome as well as reprehensible things and it was chiefly from the former that Leenhof drew inspiration.[29] Bekker is warmly championed, Biblical prophets disparaged, and the metaphysical aspects of Descartes dismissed as a 'chimaera',[30] his argument for the immortality of the soul being rejected in a manner which plainly implies there is no such immortality.[31] While the *Lettres choisies* contain no explicit denial of miracles, Tyssot maintains 'la Nature est uniforme dans toutes ses operations' and that God does not depart from the ordinary laws of Nature in order to intervene in the lives of individuals.[32]

The predictable outcry was immediate. Denounced before the Deventer Walloon consistory which, in turn, urged the town government to take steps against him, Tyssot was first denied Holy Communion, publicly disgraced, and ostracized from the Reformed community, and then declared guilty by the magistrates of blasphemy, atheism, writing obscenities, and Spinozism, stripped of his post, and expelled from the city.[33] Stunned by the speed of his downfall, the unfortunate *érudit* then spent the remainder of his life subsisting precariously with his family mainly in IJsselsteen, near Utrecht, pathetically endeavouring to repair his blighted reputation. In the preface to the first volume of his *Oeuvres poétiques* (1727), he vigorously rejected the accusation of Spinozism, demonstrating 'd'une manière claire et concise' God's existence and the immortality of the soul 'afin qu'l'on aprenne à juger par là, de mes véritables sentiments'.[34] But in vain. The sole surviving autograph letter of Tyssot, written to a friend in January 1737, a few months before his death, shows that at the end of his life he still suffered acutely from his 'exile' from Deventer 'd'où mes ennemis m'ont cruellement chassé', and the loss of his status and salary. Wretchedly, he reminded everyone who would listen of the exemplary moral example he had always striven to set as a teacher, never having been accused of a dissolute or disorderly lifestyle.

Yet if Tyssot de Patot never won the honoured place in the Republic of Letters of which he dreamt, his *Jacques Massé* surpassed practically every other work of philosophical fiction of the age for notoriety. Lenglet Dufresnoy referred to it in 1734 as a novel 'contre la religion . . . que l'on a même proscrit en Hollande'.[35] Its French Catholic hero, having studied to become a ship's surgeon in Paris in the 1640s, and afterwards participated in the Cartesian circle around Mersenne, leaves France in search of new opportunity. Shipwrecked *en route* to the East Indies, a thousand leagues from Saint Helena, he finds himself stranded with a sole companion on a remote shore from which, stumbling on, they eventually reach a terrestrial paradise, where they are welcomed by hospitable folk with whom they communicate by means of

---

[28] Tyssot de Patot, *Lettres choisies*, ii, 221.   [29] Ibid., 223.

[30] Mori, 'L'ateismo "malebranchiano" ', 124.

[31] Tyssot de Patot, *Lettres choisies*, ii, 225–6, 283–5, 357–8; [Jahn], *Verzeichnis*, 2165–7.

[32] Tyssot de Patot, *Lettres choisies*, ii, 176–7; Valkoff, 'Wonderbaarlijke reizen', 249.

[33] Trousson, 'Simon Tyssot de Patot', p. ix; Rosenberg. 'Introduction', 11–14; Mijnhardt, 'Dutch Enlightenment', 204.

[34] Quoted in Rosenberg, 'Introduction', 12.   [35] Ibid., 29.

gestures. Remaining among them for the next five years, Jacques and his companion, impressed by the harmony and peace which characterized their society and politics, learn everything about their manners, religion, government, and language. Eventually, Jacques judges the moment opportune to explain the Christian religion to them. But his talk of Creation, miracles, prophets, a Messiah who is the Son of God, Original Sin, and Redemption is greeted with derision and deemed completely absurd. The local wise men conclude that Christianity is a fantastic concoction of 'fictions fort mal concertées'.[36] Moreover, the doctrine of a God who creates, and then eternally damns, wrongdoers was deemed outrageously unjust, since there is no such thing as innate 'goodness' or 'evil' and only laws proclaimed by society can render conduct 'good' or 'bad'.[37] Scorning the doctrines of the soul's immortality and resurrection of the dead, they spoke so disrespectfully of Christ's person, and his mother's virginity, that Jacques subsequently dared not repeat what they said.[38]

After leaving this utopia, Jaques undergoes numerous further experiences until, in 1663, he finds himself in Goa, where he lodges, amicably at first, with a Dominican. However, unable to refrain from commenting on the gross credulity he encounters, he is hauled before the Inquisition, which he soon learns to consider the most terrible and unjust tribunal extant in the world. Sentenced by the Holy Office to serve on the galleys of Portugal, he is put on a ship for Lisbon which was intercepted by Algerian corsairs *en route* and brought to Algiers. Here Jaques encounters a young Gascon who has converted to Mohammedanism even though he no more believes in Islam than Christianity or Judaism, being the most resolute 'atheist or deist' Jacques has ever met. The Gascon's opinions about religion and the Church are unutterably shocking; and yet Jaques can not deny that everyone who knows him considers him a paragon of virtue, who invariably behaves with 'beaucoup de douceur et de bonté'.[39]

The novel culminates in a parable recounted by this Spinoza-like figure which he claims to have heard from an Arab philosopher. This 'Fable of the Bees'—the idea possibly owed something to Mandeville's book published not long before—was later reported by the Marquis d'Argenson to be the part of the novel most excitedly read in Paris.[40] The parable tells of an absolute monarch of an island paradise, who greatly loved his bees but nevertheless damned them to eternal destruction for disobeying his commandment not to suck from certain prohibited blooms which he had specified. The ban had not been for any comprehensible reason but merely to test his authority and the bees' obedience. However, their natural disposition caused them to suck from these very flowers. Unwilling to destroy them all, the king sent his infinitely beloved son among them, metamorphosed into a bee, in order to save those of them who believed and repented sufficiently.[41] Appearing among them as a bee, the king's son laboured among them, urging them to strive harder to obey his omnipotent father's commandments. But the bees mocked and killed him. Resurrected, he then returned

---

[36] [Tyssot de Patot], *Voyages et avantures*, 94–6. [37] Ibid., 98; Du Marsais, *Examen*, 327.

[38] [Tyssot de Patot], *Voyages et avantures.*, 92. [39] Ibid., 184–7.

[40] Rosenberg, 'Introduction', 28. [41] [Tyssot de Patot], *Voyages et avantures*, 189–93.

to his father's side, where he interceded for those for whom he had died so that those who believed in him, and only those, should be saved. In fact, most bees did believe in one or other of the different versions of this story; but unfortunately, the adherents of the different accounts pitilessly attacked and massacred each other. Furthermore, a few bees did not believe the story at all and these were ferociously assailed, slaughtered, or driven from their hives 'comme dangereuses et séditieuses'.[42]

The bees who taught the other bees the various versions of this parable were so venerated that they were excused all labour and allowed to live at their ease off the efforts of the rest, whom they easily kept subservient by encouraging their hopes of being saved. Like *Sévarambes*, the *Histoire des Ajaoiens*, Lahontan's *Voyages*, and Smeeks' novel, *Jaques Massé* seeks to persuade readers of the irrationality of European religion, politics, morality, and society by describing in detail an exotic and remote atheistic society, where peace and harmony reign, and virtue is better cultivated than among Europeans. The specificity of these atheistic societies served to detract from the so-called universal consensus of peoples, the widely upheld alleged proof of a providential God, the immortality of the soul, and so forth on the basis of universal consent, by concretely illustrating Bayle's proposition that a society of atheists based on moral principles is perfectly feasible.[43] Though banned in Holland as well as France, *Jaques Massé* was surreptitiously published in two Dutch editions in the years 1714–17 while a third, again bearing the date '1710' on the title-page, appeared at Rouen around 1734.[44] A fourth French edition, also possibly produced at Rouen, was published around 1742 and an English translation came out in 1732, with further printings in 1743 and 1760, and a German version in 1737, followed by a second printing in 1751.[45]

Tyssot de Patot's other major philosophical novel, the *Voyage de Groenland* is likewise decidedly Spinozistic. Its hero is an ex-monk, the Reverend Pierre Mésange, who discards his habit for a life of freedom, and flees France initially for Holland and then Hamburg, where he teaches French. Hungry for adventure, he signs on with a whaling vessel which, however, is blown off course, far to the north of Greenland by a storm and hopelessly trapped in ice. Mésange and some others escape and meet some natives who conduct them through a crevice in the ice to the subterranean kingdom of Rufsal. Obliged to hunt in summer for enough food to last them through the dark months, these amiable troglodytes spend the entire winter underground, discussing philosophy, science, and religion, Mésange stays several years and becomes a favourite of the king. The State philosophy (and religion) of Rufsal turns out to be Spinozism.[46] God, according to the Rufsalians, is identical to Nature: in their eyes He is 'par tout, il remplit tout, il est en tout; hors de luy, et sans luy, il n'y a absolument rien qui existe'.[47] Through a gradual process of enlightenment from hearing parables and long debates, Mésange learns many fundamental truths he had previously had no inkling of. He

---

[42] Ibid., 190–1.   [43] Schröder, *Ursprünge*, 68–9.   [44] Rosenberg, 'Introduction', 28–9.
[45] Ibid.   [46] Delon,' Tyssot de Patot', 712; Trousson. 'Simon Tyssot de Patot', p. xv.
[47] Tyssot de Patot, *La Vie, les aventures*, i, 63.

discovers there is no magic, and no satanic power, and that the best way to be rid of sorcerers and accusations of witchcraft is not to persecute or execute alleged witches but depict their accusers 'pour des fous'.[48]

Equally, there is no justifiable basis for monarchy, nobility, or hierarchy, all of which predominate in Europe only because of the people's ignorance, credulousness, and proneness to systematic deception.[49] In reality, humbly born men are no less capable of leadership than those nobly born, and various exemples are given, including that of Masaniello who, as everyone knows, 'devint de simple pêcheur qu'il étoit, vice-roi de Naples'.[50] The novel also contains a remarkable discussion of relations between the sexes. As part of his becoming enlightened, Mésange discovers that women are absolutely equal to men and that there is no reason why men alone should exercise political power and responsibility. He grasps that in Europe over the centuries, women have been shamefully tyrannized over and, unfortunately, have generally contributed to, or willingly acquiesced in, their own enslavement through ignorance, weakness, and gullibility.[51] This has led them abjectly to submit to male arrogance and despotism instead of working towards their own emancipation.

Like all the novels in the radical tradition, the *Voyage de Groenland* not only elevates philosophy above theology but extols philosophy as the instrument of liberation by which individuals and whole societies can be emancipated, changed, and improved. Philosophers, for their part, are deemed exceptionally deserving of our esteem because they bring enlightenment into the world and spread understanding among the people. Returning to the Netherlands at the end of the novel, Mésange passes through Deventer, where he completes his philosophical odyssey by attending a course in geometry given by a certain brilliant professor, a veritable 'homme d'esprit', capable of reasoning cogently on every subject who, of course, is the (unnamed) Tyssot de Patot himself. This novel, like its predecessor, is fiercely anticlerical and anti-Christian. But the ultimate goal is not just to sweep aside revealed religion and ecclesiastical power but, in the realm of fantasy at least, construct an entirely new society from which monarchy, nobility, and hierarchy are excluded, along with institutionalized inequality of the sexes, and in which the well-being of man comes to be based instead on philosophy, enlightenment, equality, virtue, and justice.

[48] Tyssot de Patot, *La Vie, les aventures*, 131; Trousson, 'Simon Tyssot de Patot', p. xvi.
[49] Tyssot de Patot, *La Vie, les aventures*, i, 234–5.   [50] Ibid., 235.   [51] Ibid., 207–17.

33 | ENGLISH DEISM AND EUROPE

i. The Deist Challenge

It has perhaps never been sufficiently emphasized that in England and Ireland, where intellectual debate unfolded within a predominantly national context sometimes tinged with xenophobia, and with very few foreign writers being regularly cited, a pervasive, even at times obsessive, preoccupation with Spinoza persisted from the mid-1670s throughout the rest of the early Enlightenment. Spinoza and his books were indeed discussed by an extraordinarily large number of British and Irish writers, including—leaving aside the deists—key scientists, such as Boyle and Nehemiah Grew, university dons such as Henry More, Ralph Cudworth, and Richard Bentley, and churchmen of many hues, ranging from High Church non-jurors such as George Hickes, William Carroll, and Matthias Earbery, via a host of middling and liberal Anglicans, including Bishops Stillingfleet, Kidder, and Berkeley, as well as Thomas Browne, Samuel Clarke, Francis Gastrell, John Harris, and Brampton Gurdon, to dissenting ministers such as Richard Baxter, John Wilson, and John Howe.

Admittedly, only two of these, Henry More and Samuel Clarke, showed much appetite for grappling with Spinoza's philosophy as such. Henry More (1614–87), ensconced at Christ's College, Cambridge, since 1631, and head of the so-called 'Cambridge Platonists', endeavoured to refute Spinoza twice in the late 1670s, first in his *Epistola altera*, against the *Tractatus* (1677), and, in 1678, following the appearance of Spinoza's *Opera Posthuma*, in his *Confutatio*, seeking to overturn two fundamental propositions from the *Ethics* which he termed 'two columns of atheism'.[1] More tries to reconcile the claims of revealed religion with a philosophy of reason by postulating the existence of two basic substances in the universe, classifying these, not altogether unlike Descartes, as 'spirit' and 'matter'. These substances, he contends, have 'diverse, even contrary, attributes'.[2] Where matter is 'discerptible and impenetrable', and devoid of motion, spirit as substance is 'indiscerptible and penetrable' and endowed with self-motion.[3] Hence reality is a dualism of fundamentally separate spheres of being and occurrence, one mechanistic, the other spiritual. Scornfully repudiating

---

[1] Colie, *Light and Enlightenment*, 74–82; Colie, 'Spinoza in England', 186; Jacob, *Henry More's Refutation*, p. ix; Simonutti, 'Premières réactions anglaises', 131–2.

[2] More, *Confutatio*, 64.

[3] Ibid.; Colie, *Light and Enlightenment*, 84–93; Jacob, *Henry More's Refutation*, pp. xviii, xxi.

Spinoza's 'grand title of geometric order',[4] together with his doctrine of one substance, More attacks him for denying God the Creator, mixing 'Heaven and earth', and preferring 'his crass, false and absurd philosophy to the peace and salvation of the universal human species'.[5] Appalled by Spinoza's letter to Burgh, in which belief in future reward and punishment, and the Devil's power to suborn men, is openly derided, More rhetorically flails Spinoza: 'Oh you most impudent impostor and hypocrite with your crass and fatuous philosophy' (crassa tua ac fatua philosophia)![6]

Clarke unequivocally cites Spinoza, above all other philosophers, as his prime adversary in his most important work, *A Demonstration of the Being and Attributes of God* (1705). But he is no less convinced than More that Spinoza's is a 'foolish and destructive opinion' and that it chiefly rests on 'that absurd definition of substance, that it is something the idea of which does not depend on or presuppose the idea of any other thing from which it might proceed but includes in itself necessary existence'.[7] He tries to overthrow it not with a rival theory of substance but his Newtonian doctrine 'contradictory to Spinoza's assertion' that 'there is not the least appearance of an absolute necessity of nature (so as that any variation would imply a contradiction)'. 'Motion itself,' he argues, 'and all its quantities and directions with the laws of gravitation are entirely arbitrary, and might possibly have been altogether different from what they now are.'[8] Invoking the latest discoveries in astronomy, Clarke holds that these prove that the 'number and motion of the heavenly bodies have no manner of necessity in the nature of the things themselves' and that 'the number of planets might have been greater or less.'[9] The planetary movements and comets, he adds, prove 'these things are solely the effect of wisdom and choice' and that 'everything upon earth is still more evidently arbitrary and plainly the product not of necessity, but will'.[10]

Clarke's chief weapon, though, for exposing the 'vanity, folly and weakness of Spinoza' is his powerful rendering of the 'argument from design'. Spinoza's holding the universe governed by 'a blind and unintelligent necessity', instantly collapses, Clarke asserts, when we concede, as we must, that almost everything in nature when closely examined 'upholds undeniable arguments to prove that the world and all things therein are the effects of an intelligent and knowing cause'. 'Who without blushing dare affirm that neither the form, nor order, nor any of the minutest circumstance or mode of existence' of the many species of the world's animals and plants 'could possibly have been in the least diversified by the supreme cause?'[11]

English preoccupation with Spinoza in the Early Enlightenment, however, was not primarily philosophical or scientific, but rooted chiefly in the conviction that he had transcended Hobbes, and all other intellectual malefactors, in undermining belief in the divine authorship of Scripture and, beyond this, had become the chief inspiration and resource of the deists. Several of Spinoza's English adversaries, such as Kidder and Wilson, were indeed almost entirely concerned with the erosion of respect for the

---

[4] More, *Confutatio*, 57.   [5] Ibid., 103, 106; Cristofolini, *Cartesiani e Sociniani*, 126–7.
[6] More, *Confutatio*., 103.   [7] Clarke, *A Demonstration*, 37.   [8] Ibid., 49.
[9] Ibid.   [10] Ibid., 50; [d'Holbach], *Système de la nature* i, 89–137; Colie, 'Spinoza in England', 207–8.
[11] Clarke, *A Demonstration*, 50.

Bible: 'it hath been the business and study of some men, of late years,' complained Kidder, 'to disparage the Holy Scriptures, and all revealed religion.'[12] 'Those who set up for wit,' he noted, 'have openly avowed their disbelief of the Scriptures,' the three writers whom he holds principally responsible for this growing disrespect being Hobbes, the 'author of the *Praeadamitae*' [i.e. La Peyrère], and Spinoza,[13] the last of whom he rebuts in detail. But most critics looked beyond the assault on Scripture, deploring what they saw as a much wider affront to the stability and legitimacy of the social order, law, and morality, as well as theology and Scripture, the 'character of a Spinozist being so very odious, and that atheist's hypothesis so infinitely prejudicial to all the societies and concerns of mankind'.[14] The perceived threat sprang from Spinoza's function as a source of ideas, methodology, phrases, and even whole chunks of text, for deist publicists and indeed the entire freethinking and libertine fraternity.

It is true that radical deism in the English Enlightenment is generally considered in modern historiography an essentially home-grown product,[15] rooted in Hobbes and Herbert of Cherbury, as well as the religious and social radicalism of the Civil War and Cromwellian commonwealth, which, not unfrequently, as with Gerard Winstanley, had been tinged with pantheism.[16] Even in the late seventeenth century, there were claims that English philosophical incredulity was essentially different from the continental variety, and its intellectual roots were to be found far more in Hobbes than Spinoza: 'there may be some Spinosists, or immaterial fatalists, beyond seas,' commented Bentley in a letter in 1692, 'but not one English infidel in a hundred is any other than a Hobbist, which I know to be rank atheism in the private study and select conversation of these men.'[17]

But there are cogent reasons for urging a different view. First, the pantheism of a Winstanley had a theological, strongly poetic, even magical quality,[18] and altogether lacked the pretensions to philosophical rigour characteristic of Spinoza, the Dutch Spinozists, and the British deists of the Early Enlightenment. Second, if some contemporary English and Irish authors persisted in seeing Hobbes as the chief inspiration of philosophical incredulity in Britain, others no less emphatically declare Spinoza to be, as Bishop Berkeley put it, in 1732, 'the great leader of our modern infidels, in whom are to be found many schemes and notions much admired and followed of late years'.[19] Third, and most important, several leading English deists, and not least the prime figure of the first generation of radical English deists, Charles Blount (1654–93), 'the one who really launched Deism in England',[20] and with whose writings

---

[12] Kidder, *A Commentary*, i, preface, p. i.   [13] Ibid., preface, p. xiv.

[14] [Carroll], *Spinoza Reviv'd*, 157.

[15] Hill, *World Turned Upside Down*, 313–19; Brown, 'Theological Politics', 181–3, 187; Sullivan, *John Toland*, 194; Jacob, *The Radical Enlightenment*, 2–3, 48–53; Brown, 'Locke as secret "Spinozist"', 232.

[16] Winstanley, *Law of Freedom*, 170–1, 347; Brailsford, *The Levellers*, 666; Hill, *World Turned Upside Down*, 113–14, 145, 179, 219, 266–8, 346; Brown, 'Theological Politics', 182.

[17] Quoted in Berman, *History of Atheism*, 50.   [18] Hill, *World Turned Upside Down*, 179, 317–19.

[19] Berkeley, *Alciphron*, 155–6.   [20] Harrison, *'Religion' and the Religions*, 73.

'we have the beginnings of the Deist canon', a writer who, not without reason, has been called Spinoza's 'English disciple',[21] manifestly did not derive their ideas from a purely indigenous context but, on the contrary, incontrovertibly betray extensive borrowing from continental and especially Dutch thought.

There are also other reasons for discarding the traditional insistence on British deism being an essentially insular phenomenon. Hobbes was always a powerful factor in the genesis of radical thought: 'notwithstanding his several false opinions and his High-Church Politicks', observed Anthony Collins, Hobbes was a 'great influence of learning, virtue and free-thinking'.[22] But in the final analysis, Hobbes could not serve as the philosophical underpinning of a broad-based philosophical radicalism opposed to all existing structures of authority and tradition, ecclesiastical power, and the existing social hierarchy, as well as divine-right monarchy, precisely because of his anti-libertarian politics, High Church sympathies, and support for rigorous political and intellectual censorship. Hobbes was an absolutist in politics and a pessimist about human nature, on top of which he admitted (however half-heartedly) miracles and Revelation, and temporized on the immortality of the soul.[23]

Hence precisely the same factors which prevented Hobbes serving as a major stimulus to radical thought on the continent, in the end subordinated him to Spinoza as a formative influence on British deism as well. In his *Praenotiones*, Loescher frequently mentions Hobbes as a factor in the advent of philosophical incredulity in Germany, but when it came to denial of miracles, repudiation of prophecy, and rejection of magical power and the Devil, cites Spinoza alone, without Hobbes, as the primary inspirer.[24] Diderot, the chief philosophical strategist of the French *Encyclopédie*, and author of the article 'Hobbisme' which features in that compilation, lacked neither interest in, nor, to some degree, sympathy for Hobbes' thought. Nevertheless, he was also repelled by Hobbes in several respects. In particular, he abhors Hobbes' claim that there is no difference between subject and citizen, that the citizen is obligated to an unconditional obedience to the state, and that the sovereign has the right to deny freedom of thought and expression to its citizens.[25]

Admittedly, in Britain Hobbes and Spinoza were also regularly cobbled together in many minds, jointly forming the basis of what one author called 'Mr Blount's commonwealth of learning',[26] frequently perceived as joint instigators and inspirers of what one adversary of Blount, in 1698, called the 'common enemy'.[27] However, those who routinely coupled 'Hobbes and Spinoza' as the twin inspirers of English incredulity invariably did so opposing what Whiston called 'a rigid fatality and necessity' with Newtonian and physico-theological notions of 'an intelligent and omniscient being' governing the universe. Thus Whiston says, 'such strange reasoners as Hobbs and Spinoza, etc., pretend by metaphysick arguments to demonstrate this fatality and necessity,' and are proved wrong by the 'plainest experiments, observa-

---

[21] Redwood, *Reason, Ridicule and Religion*, 99.   [22] Collins, *Discourse of Free-Thinking*, 152.

[23] Ibid.; Colie, 'Spinoza and the Early English Deists', 30–1.   [24] Loescher, *Praenotiones*, 220–4.

[25] Glaziou, *Hobbes en France*, 142, 147–9; Proust, *Diderot*, 343—4, 427–30.

[26] King, *Mr Blount's* Oracles, 33.   [27] Taylor, *A Preservative against Deism*, preface, p. ii.

tions, and demonstrations from nature'.[28] But this very emphasis on the antithesis between fatality and divine will inevitably focused attention increasingly on Spinoza at the expense of Hobbes, for Spinoza was far more consistently and cogently 'necessitarian' than the English thinker. Hence Samuel Clarke could, within the British context, reasonably style Spinoza—in a phrase echoed subsequently by William Carroll—'the most celebrated patron of Atheism in our time',[29] while there is abundant logic in the remark of a German *savant* visiting London in 1709, who reported home to his brother that 'le Spinosisme s'est répandu extrêmement ici aussi bien qu'en Hollande.'[30]

Spinoza, then, to a considerable extent came to displace Hobbes as the chief intellectual bogeyman and symbolic head of philosophical deism and atheism in Britain and Ireland, as well as on the continent, even if modern British historiography does not acknowledge this. The idea that Spinoza had little impact on the Early Enlightenment in England may be firmly entrenched, but it has relatively little basis in fact. As one of the Boyle Lecturers, Brampton Gurdon, declared in 1722, 'Spinoza is the only person among the modern atheists that has pretended to give us a regular scheme of atheism; and therefore I cannot act unfairly in making him the representative of their party, and in proving the weakness and absurdities of the atheistick scheme, by shewing the faults of his.'[31]

In England worries about the growth of atheistic, deistic, and pantheist attitudes had been in the air since the 1650s.[32] But, as we have seen, fear of philosophical deism and atheism gained added intensity in the mid-1670s with the arrival in Britain of batches of Spinoza's *Tractatus*. A decidedly new note was sounded in June 1675, when the Latitudinarian bishop, Edward Stillingfleet, wrote *A Letter to a Deist*, owning to being deeply troubled by a 'late author mightily in vogue among many who cry up anything on the atheistical side, though never so weak and trifling'.[33] Though, in his published tract, he purposely refrains from naming either author or book, the context clearly shows he is alluding to Spinoza and the *Tractatus Theologico-Politicus*.[34] Stillingfleet thought it easy enough to 'lay open the false reasonings and inconsistent hypotheses' of the unnamed philosopher posing this severe threat which, he declares, had 'been sufficiently done already' in Latin. What disturbed him was the prospect of this thinker's ideas ramifying in England in the vernacular: 'if for the advancement of irreligion among us, that book be, as it is talked, translated into our tongue, there will not, I hope, want those who will be as ready to defend religion and morality, as others are to decry and despise them.'[35]

---

[28] Whiston, *Astronomical Principles*, 114–16.

[29] Clarke, *A Demonstration*, 20; [Carroll], *Remarks on Mr Clarke's Sermons*, 3.

[30] Quoted in Bohrmann, *Spinozas Stellung*, 76.

[31] Gurdon, *Pretended Difficulties*, 86, Bohrmann, *Spinozas Stellung*, 78; Colie, 'Spinoza in England', 209.

[32] Colie, 'Spinoza and the early English Deists', 30; Hill, *World Turned Upside Down*, 313–19.

[33] [Stillingfleet], *A Letter to a Deist*, preface.

[34] Bamberger, 'Early Editions', 4; Simonutti, 'Premières réactions anglaises', 130.

[35] [Stillingfleet], *A Letter to a Deist*, preface; Sina, *L'Avvento della ragione*, 205–6.

Stillingfleet's encounter with Spinoza and Spinozism was to prove long and deep.[36] But it began simultaneously with that of several prominent scholars who reacted no less anxiously and indignantly, including, as we have seen, Henry Jenkes of Gonville and Caius College, Ralph Cudworth (1617–88), Master of Christ's College, and Henry More. More, as he himself noted, writing to Boyle in December 1676, was not only disturbed by the *Tractatus Theologico-Politicus*, but had been 'informed out of Holland, from a learned hand there, that a considerable company of men appeared there, mere scoffers at religion and atheistical, that professed themselves Cartesians', a report which reinforced his suspicion that Cartesianism 'may naturally have such an influence as this'; he added he had lately learnt that 'Spinosa, a Jew first, after a Cartesian, and now an atheist, is supposed the author of the *Theologico-Politicus*.'[37]

English philosophical incredulity effectively began with Blount, who, though often disparaged as unoriginal and a plagiarist, was nevertheless a crucial figure in the rise of English radicalism.[38] His first clearly deistic work, the *Anima Mundi*, appeared in 1678. Already here, and in his works of the early 1680s, Blount, deploying Herbert's conception of a true natural religion which requires no priests or formal theology, discards the theological systems of the revealed religions as fraud and trickery contrived by cunning impostors for their own advantage, linking this analysis to radical republicanism by showing that, generally in history, despots encourage such priestly manipulation to strengthen their own sway while, equally, priests sanctify tyranny the better to nurture their own status and authority. Similarly, he dismisses all religious prophecy, precisely like Spinoza, as the result of exceptional 'imagination': 'to set up for a Prophet, the chief thing necessary is a lively strong fancy and imagination.'[39] But this self-proclaimed disciple of Herbert, who clearly borrowed much from Hobbes, also drew extensively not just on Spinoza but other Dutch sources, including the elder Vossius[40] and his son Isaac Vossius (1618–89), the *savant* and former acquaintance of Spinoza of whom Charles II quipped that 'he believed everything except what was in the Bible'—a confirmed libertine who, after a short period in Sweden, settled in England.[41] It was seemingly Isaac Vossius who inspired Blount's claims that the Biblical Flood occurred only in Palestine and that Chinese history is older than that of the Jews.[42]

It was Blount, moreover, who, in 1683, anonymously published the first text of Spinoza—the notorious chapter from the *Tractatus* denying miracles—to appear in

[36] Hutton, 'Edward Stillingfleet', 260–74; Simonutti, 'Premières réactions anglaises', 131–4; at his death, Stillingfleet's personal library included all Spinoza's works, Meyer's *Philosophia*, Kuyper, *Arcana*, Wittichius, *Anti-Spinoza*, Bredenburg's *Enervatio*, Aubert de Versé's *L'Impie* and Yvon's *L'Impieté convaincu*. See Hutton, 'Edward Stillingfleet'.

[37] *Works of the Honourable Robert Boyle*, v, 514; Colie, *Light and Enlightenment*, 73; Cristofolini, *Cartesiani e Sociniani*, 118–19.

[38] Popkin, 'Deist Challenge', 205–10; Champion, *Pillars of Priestcraft*, 142–7; Harrison, *'Religion' and the Religions*, 73–4, 162–3.

[39] Quoted in Walber, *Charles Blount*, 207.   [40] Popkin, *Deist Challenge*, 196–210.

[41] Katz, 'Isaaac Vossius', 142.   [42] King, *Mr Blount's Oracles*, 21, 24, 179.

English.[43] Probably it was again Blount who anonymously brought out the first complete English translation of the *Tractatus* in 1689, presumably hoping to use its vigorous advocacy of freedom of thought to influence the toleration debate then under way in England.[44] The anonymous translator's preface loudly echoes Blount's customary scorn for clergy and lawyers, challenging both the 'crape gown' and the 'long robe' to prove there are any tenets in (Spinoza's) 'treatise half so dangerous or destructive to the peace and welfare of human society, as those doctrines and maxims are, which have of late years been broached by time-serving church-men and mercenary lawyers, for which they justly deserve the hatred and contempt of all mankind'.[45]

Thomas Browne in his *Miracles Works Above and Contrary to Nature* (1683), replying to Blount's *Miracles no Violation of the Laws of Nature* (1683), was the first to identify the latter as a collage partly lifted from the sixth chapter of the *Tractatus Theologico-Politicus* 'written by Spinoza . . . to instill the principles of Deism and Atheisme into the minds of his readers'.[46] Browne sees this undeclared smuggling of Spinoza by Blount and his accomplices as insidious 'subversion' of both 'religion' and 'civil authority', since 'asserting that there is no such thing as a miracle, i.e. a work above nature undermines the foundations of both law and Gospel.'[47] Decrying Blount's blatant manipulation and plagiarism, Browne demonstrates that his book is a concoction from three authors—Hobbes, Spinoza, and Thomas Burnet—but also shows that the deployment of Hobbes and Burnet is peripheral to the author's purpose and, strictly speaking, irrelevant. For Hobbes does not altogether deny the possibility of miracles, though he questions the veracity of particular miracles, indeed 'he admits and supposes miracles in that very sense, wherein he is produced to deny them here.'[48] Hobbes, stresses Browne, 'defines a miracle to be, a work of God beside his operation by the way of nature ordained in the Creation which is flatly contradictory to that assertion [of Blount's] that nothing can fall out but according to the order of nature.'[49]

If Hobbes and Spinoza are both destructive of faith, holds Browne, 'they differ notwithstanding very widely in the way of compassing it, as far as the opposite parts of a contradiction can set them at odds, the one asserting that there are works above nature, the other denying it,' so that the anonymous contriver of the work was mistaken to 'think they would cotton so well together'.[50] Consequently, Blount's denial of miracles rests not on 'his own great reach in natural philosophy, whereby he could undertake to solve mechanically all the effects related in Scripture for miraculous; but from arguments purely metaphysical proving in his opinion the impossibility of any such thing as a work above nature.'[51] Browne then demonstrates the close convergence of the anonymous writers' ideas with Spinoza's system, citing both the

[43] Ibid., 206; Boucher, *Spinoza in English*, 32; Brown, 'Theological Politics', 185–6.
[44] Popkin, 'Deist Challenge', 207; Boucher, *Spinoza in English*, 5.
[45] [Spinoza], *A Treatise partly Theological*, translator's preface.   [46] Browne, *Miracles*, 2.
[47] Ibid., 1; Walber, *Charles Blount*, 249; Brown, 'Theological Politics', 186.
[48] Browne, *Miracles*, 3; Colie, 'Spinoza and the early English Deists', 38.
[49] Browne, *Miracles*, 3.   [50] Ibid., 4.   [51] Ibid., 19; Sina, *L'Avvento della ragione*, 200–1.

Tractatus and the *Opera Posthuma*, and especially Part I of the *Ethics*, where Spinoza contends 'there is but one substance in the world and that is God.'[52]

Unlike Blount, Sir William Temple (1628–99), a far less abrasive deist but likewise a key figure in the emergence of English deism, seems to borrow little or nothing directly from Spinoza. Yet Temple was a widely read man who, as we know from his own writings, was familiar with Fontenelle and greatly admired Machiavelli, Sarpi, Montaigne, and Saint-Evremond.[53] Like Blount, he too learnt from Isaac Vossius, a deist, Epicurean, and Sinophile from whom he chiefly derived his enthusiasm for Confucianism.[54] Furthermore, it seems that his partiality for republican ideas—despite being a servant of the royal house of Stuart—and religious and intellectual toleration, both strongly reflected in his *Observations upon the United Provinces of the Netherlands* (1673), were stimulated by his long residence as English ambassador in Holland and personal friendship for De Witt. The two most distinctive features of Temple's thought, his Epicureanism and admiration of Confucius, the 'most, learned, wise and virtuous of all the Chineses' may not demonstrate, any more than his residence in The Hague at a time Spinoza lived there, that he knew the latter's philosophy. But they do show close affinities between Temple and the views of Vossius and Saint-Evremond, both of whom knew Spinoza personally, and that it was primarily the continental context which shaped his thought.

One might add that Temple's contention that 'every man ought to study and endeavour the improving and perfecting of his own natural reason to the greatest height he is capable, so as he may never (or as seldom as can be) err and swerve from the law of nature in the course and conduct of his life' reflects, at the very least, a marked parallelism between his thought and Spinoza's,[55] as does his analysis of theological zeal as driven by desire for power over others: 'pretending to sovereignty, instead of liberty, in opinion, is indeed pretending the same in authority too, which consists chiefly in opinion; and what man, or party soever, can gain the common and firm belief, of being most immediately inspired, instructed and favoured of God, will easily obtain the prerogative of being most honour'd and obey'd by men.'[56]

Doubtless there is much paranoid fantasy and sensless bluster in Carroll's High Church conspiracy theory, encouraged by George Hickes (if no one else),[57] detecting a vast percolation of Spinozism into England camouflaged with 'such shifts, tricks, stratagems and equivocations to conceal themselves and to set off his doctrine under . . . a variety of disguises and abuse of words' that it was not easy to recognize 'that atheist's dreams and folly' in the works of Locke, Le Clerc, Samuel Clarke, and other

---

[52] Browne, *Miracles*, 37–8; Redwood, *Reason, Ridicule and Religion*, 23, 99; Curley, 'Spinoza on Miracles', 423; on the differences between Spinoza's views on miracles and those of Hobbes and Hume, see also Martinich, *Two Gods of Leviathan*, 236–46; Champion, *Pillars of Priestcraft*, 134–7; Gaskin, *Hume's Philosophy of Religion*, 160–5.

[53] Temple, *Five Miscellaneous Essays*, pp. xix, xxii, xxv, 65. [54] Craven, *Jonathan Swift*, 139–40.

[55] Temple, *Five Miscellaneous Essays*, 113–14; Bayle, *Historical and Critical Dictionary*, 288–93.

[56] Temple, *Observations*, 126. [57] Brown, 'Locke as Secret "Spinozist"', 217–24.

improbable guises.[58] But such feverish talk shows that at least some contemporaries judged Spinoza's reputation in Britain sufficiently awesome to offer a real prospect of fatally wounding opponents whom one could successfully tar with his name. Whatever else divided them, High-Flyers and Latitudinarians could readily agree that Spinoza's system surpassed all others in depravity and as a general intellectual threat.[59] Carroll penned half a dozen texts in as many years (1705–11) claiming 'this atheistical shopkeeper [i.e. Spinoza] is the first that ever reduced atheism into a system, and Mr Locke is the second; with this difference that the latter has only copied the former as to the main.'[60]

More plausibly, he also denounced Tindal and Collins as 'Spinozists'. To lend substance to his accusations, Carroll urged that the English, being a solid, decent Christian nation, would have nothing to do with Spinoza's philosophy when expounded 'in plain, precise and determined terms' but that Locke, by divesting words of their usual connotations, had sought to smuggle in the Jew's 'most absurd, impious and abominable hypothesis . . . covertly',[61] arguing that had Locke 'defin'd his names as Spinoza did, I mean his chief terms . . . he would have quite ruin'd his design, especially in these nations . . . hence it is, that he declin'd Spinoza's method.'[62] Furthermore, if Carroll was an intellectual lightweight, his mentor and ally, George Hickes (1642–1715), was a respected scholar who, as Dean of Worcester Cathedral, had been a leading Anglican voice before 1688.[63] The day after William III's landing in Devon, in November 1688, Hickes preached against sedition, revolution, and the invading Dutch in Worcester Cathedral. After the Glorious Revolution he emerged as a leading ideologue of the Jacobite 'non-jurors' and one not without a certain following in High Church circles, at any rate in Oxford.[64]

In 1709 Hickes published a long preface to Carroll's diatribe *Spinoza Reviv'd* in which he excoriates the notorious Dutch republican tract *De Jure Ecclesiasticorum* (see above p. 201) which certainly derived from the radical circle around Spinoza (and probably the pen of Meyer) but which at the time was often wrongly attributed to Spinoza himself. Recognizing the tract for a devastating assault on ecclesiastical authority, Hickes accounts it a cunning prelude to the broader onslaught of the *Tractatus Theologico-Politicus*, after which Spinoza 'handed his atheism into the world in plain terms unmask'd and bare-fac'd in his Posthumous Works'.[65] What Hickes above all deplores in *De Jure Ecclesiasticorum*, is the claim—basic to Spinozism, he contends—that 'all power and authority is originally in, and immediately from the people,' from which Spinozists infer that the magistrate's power derives from the people and then finally

---

[58] Ibid., 215; [Carroll], *Spinoza Reviv'd*, 157–8; Brown, 'Theological Politics', 187, 193–5; see also De Vet, 'Learned Periodicals', 34; Yolton, *Locke and the Way of Ideas*, 144–7.

[59] Carroll, *A Dissertation*, 22.   [60] [Carroll], *Remarks upon Mr Clarke's Sermons*, 9.

[61] Carroll, *A Dissertation*, 2, 15, 22; [Carroll], *Remarks upon Mr Clarke's Sermons*, 9–16; [Carroll], *A Letter to the Reverend*, 16, 24.

[62] Ibid., 24.   [63] Brown, 'Locke as Secret "Spinozist" ', 223.

[64] Beddard, 'Tory Oxford', 886–7.

[65] Hickes, 'Preface' to Carroll, *Spinoza Reviv'd*, 15; Yolton, *Locke and the Way of Ideas*, 179.

that 'all the privileges, power and authority of the clergy is from the magistrate' and thus ultimately also from the people.[66] 'Spinoza,' held Hickes, 'gives the people a natural, inalienable inherent right to rebel against their lawful sovereign wherever or whenever he abridges them of their liberty.'[67]

Another probable Jacobite who insisted on the centrality of Spinoza in the forming of British deism was the Kent schoolmaster, Matthias Earbery the elder (1658–1730?), whose *Deism examin'd and confuted* appeared in 1697. Where Hobbes, according to Earbery, is merely 'trifling' with Scripture and 'wresting some particular places to his odd opinions', Spinoza 'begins at the very root and foundation by taking away all divine authority from prophecy, miracles or inspiration, and making all the sacred pen-men, to be no other than either mad-men or impostors'.[68] 'The perfect Deist', he remarks sarcastically, is so inordinately fond of Spinoza that 'every summer he carried him into the fields with him in his hands, and each winter he wore him in his muff'.[69] The 'perfect deist', moreover, delights in comparing Hobbes with Spinoza but, while venerating the former, he nevertheless concludes that the anonymous author of the *Tractatus* 'deserves rather to be esteemed his tutor than his scholar; he has such a knack of exposing all the defects of those books you call the Scriptures, with that strength of reason and solidity of judgment, that apparently shews it to be the work of the incomparable Spinoza.'[70] On these grounds Earbery designates the notorious young deists who frequent London's coffee-shops Spinoza's 'little disciples of the town' and terms the *Tractatus* the single most flagrant manifestation of a philosophical incredulity rapidly producing in England a 'general corruption of manners, contempt of the clergy', and advancement of irreligious ideas.[71]

A writer of a very different vintage, but who yet likewise assigns a pre-eminent role to Spinoza in the genesis of English radical thought, was Nehemiah Grew (1641–1712), Oldenburg's successor as secretary of the Royal Society and one of the foremost scientific minds in the kingdom. Having graduated from Leiden in 1671, he also had a detailed knowledge of the Dutch intellectual scene and presumably knew Dutch. A Newtonian and advocate of the 'argument from design', Grew claims there is a 'vital substance in nature' distinct from matter and bodies, a 'vital substance' which, like Newton's gravity, emanates directly from the divine will. In 1701 he published a large work, his 372-page *Cosmologia Sacra*, dedicated to William III, in which he seeks to reconcile science with revealed religion, motivated, he says, by the 'many lewd opinions, especially those of Anti-Scripturalists, which have been published of late years, by Spinoza and some others, in Latin, Dutch and English'.[72] Grew was an alarmist, convinced the prevailing conjuncture in England, with the rise of radical deism, was one of the direst menace and peril. His book was not intended for scholars or clergy but the general public, and especially, he says, the citizens of London who 'grown of late more bookish, are very dangerously infected'.[73] His aim is to assist the 'antidoting of

---

[66] Hickes, 'Preface' to Carroll, *Spinoza Reviv'd*, 16.
[67] Ibid., 19; Redwood, *Reason, Ridicule and Religion*, 23.   [68] Earbery, *Deism Examin'd*, preface, p. v.
[69] Ibid., 3.   [70] Ibid., 4–5.   [71] Brown, 'Theological Politics', 189–90.
[72] Grew, *Cosmologia Sacra*, preface, 1.   [73] Ibid.; Westfall, *Science and Religion*, 99, 109, 131.

this city and kingdom, against a contagion so dismal in itself, and the consequences of it'.[74] But if the situation was catastrophic, the only modern thinker held responsible, indeed the only modern philosophical malefactor mentioned by name, is Spinoza, Grew considering his philosophy and Bible criticism the primary cause of England's malaise.[75]

If Grew is no less alarmist than Earbery, Hickes, and Carroll, a far more influential and cogent Newtonian, Samuel Clarke, similarly identifies 'Spinoza and his followers' as the intellectual leaders of the radical campaign to prove that the 'material world is God' and deny 'the supreme cause to be properly an intelligent and active being'.[76] Furthermore, Clarke's focusing on Spinoza when combating radical deism was regularly emulated over subsequent decades, not least in the philosophical dialogue, the *Alciphron* (1732), by the leading luminary of Trinity College, Dublin, George Berkeley (1685–1753). Fascination not just with the dangers but also the philosophical allure and power of Spinoza is reflected in Berkeley's philosophical jottings as early as 1708;[77] and while in his early philosophical dialogues against incredulity, of 1713, he does not differentiate between the three most 'strenuous' advocates of atheism— those wild imaginations of Vanini, Hobbes and Spinoza', establishing no hierarchy between them,[78] in the *Alciphron*, a work conceived against the freethinkers and libertines of contemporary English society, Berkeley unambiguously proclaims Spinoza the chief inspirer of the 'incredulous,'[79] 'a man of close argument and demonstration' who goes further than any other in attempting to construct a rational system of atheism. It was Spinoza, he insists, who leads in 'persuading men that miracles are to be understood only in a spiritual and allegorical sense', that it is 'not necessary to believe in Christ, according to the flesh', and that 'men are mere machines impelled by fatal necessity.'[80]

ii. John Toland (1670–1722)

One of the 'infidels' whom Earbery, Gurdon, and Berkeley had in mind was the foremost of 'British' deists—in fact he too was Irish—and one of those most frequently called a 'Spinozist', John Toland (1670–1722). Toland was regularly classified a 'Spinozist' in the early eighteenth century, particularly (but by no means only) by continental authors. Buddeus, Germany's prime authority on atheism, considered Toland 'a zealous disciple of Spinoza'.[81] Listing Europe's chief 'Spinozists' in 1744, Zedler's universal dictionary includes only one British name and that was Toland's.[82] Similarly, there are also some modern scholars for whom Toland gravitated 'to pan-

---

[74] Grew, *Cosmologia Sacra*, preface, 1–2.
[75] Ibid., pp. 142–3, 164–5, 179–81, 194–5, 200–3; Harrison, 'Newtonian Science', 540; Westfall notes 'Spinoza more than Hobbes was Grew's bête noire'; Westfall, *Science and Religion*, 131.
[76] Ibid., 46–7.   [77] Brykman, 'Berkeley lecteur de Spinoza', 88–9.
[78] Berkeley, *Three Dialogues*, 199.   [79] Berkeley, *Alciphron*, ii, 207–8.
[80] Ibid., i, 120, 244 and ii, 208.   [81] Buddeus, *Traité*, 128.
[82] Zedler, *Grosses Universal Lexicon*, xxxix, 86.

theism and to becoming a devout disciple of Spinoza'.[83] Yet there is a far stronger historiographical tradition which insists that Toland was a product of indigenous British influences, stemming from the republicanism of Harrington and Milton, as well as the religious and social radicalism of the English Revolution.[84] 'The attempt to interpret Toland as a disciple of Spinoza', it is frequently claimed, 'stumbles' on the objection that several earlier English writers 'held views virtually indistinguishable from those which connected Toland with Spinoza'.[85]

But does it stumble? While the religious and social radicalism of the English Revolution manifests a pantheistic strain, it is pantheism of a type far removed from Spinoza's.[86] Furthermore, even were it more plainly evident than it is that Toland and other deists of the era derived their inspiration originally from an older tradition of English religious radicalism, this could still mean that major segments of British deism evinced close conceptual affinities with Spinozism, justifying the proneness of continental writers such as Buddeus, Zedler, Lilienthal, and Thorschmid to class them together for analytical purposes since—following Bayle (and like Brampton Gurdon)—they did not mean to say Spinoza invented the patterns of thought to which Toland adhered but rather that Spinoza was the chief representative and main exponent of a tendency which had allegedly existed since the remotest beginnings of philosophy, and of which Toland too was a major representative. Nor were contemporary English writers unaware of these affinities. Thus John Leland remarked that Toland, especially in his *Pantheisticon* (1720) has shown himself a favourer and admirer of the Pantheistic philosophy, i.e. that of Spinoza which 'acknowledgeth no other God but the universe'.[87]

In any case, there was undeniably a pervasive and powerful continental influence in the forming of Toland's deism. Crucial to his development as a thinker were his long sojourns in the Netherlands and Germany, starting with his stay in Leiden in 1692–3. Still more pivotally formative were the years 1699–1702, when he spent much time, in part as a diplomatic messenger, in both those countries, familiarizing himself with erudite and publishing circles in Hanover and Berlin as well as Amsterdam and The Hague. He encountered numerous scholars and absorbed diverse influences, being greatly impressed, among others, by the studies of Van Dale.[88] Among *savants* he met were Leibniz, who was friendly initially, and the 'Queen of Prussia', the Electress Sophia of Hanover's daughter, Sophie Charlotte, who was reportedly captivated by his bold and irreverent conversation.[89] By 1702, he was pontificating about the innateness of motion in matter, albeit according to the rapidly disillusioned Leibniz simply reiterating what was in Lucretius and other ancient sources.[90] The Electress Sophia,

---

[83] Redwood, *Reason, Ridicule and Religion*, 143.
[84] Sullivan, *John Toland*, 193; Jacob, *Radical Enlightenment*, 22–49, 83–4; Jacob, 'Crisis of the European Mind', 253; Lurbe, 'Le Spinozisme de John Toland', 44; Brown, 'Theological Politics', 189.
[85] Sullivan, *John Toland*, 193.
[86] Winstanley, *Law of Freedom*, 166, 347; Hill, *World Turned Upside Down*, 112, 176, 318–19.
[87] Leland, *A View*, i, 62.   [88] Torrey, *Voltaire*, 18–19.
[89] Klopp, *Correspondance de Leibniz*, ii, 276, 333.   [90] Ibid., 362, 364–5.

for her part, by 1702 agreed with Leibniz that Toland's was a facile, unoriginal mind, lacking in genuine ability as well as zeal for philosophy.[91] Leibniz disliked Toland's exhibitionism and shying away from serious discussion with true *savants*. Toland, he commented, 'veut seulement se distinguer par la nouveauté et par la singularité' being interested only in uttering paradoxes and contradicting whatever is commonly thought and believed.[92] By October 1702, reportedly, Toland had rendered himself thoroughly detested by everyone at Court in both Hanover and Berlin.[93]

Likewise of great importance in his formation was his prolonged sojourn in Holland in the years 1708–11, when he frequented the deistic circle of Eugene of Savoy, 'who gave him several marks of his generosity', and the Baron Hohendorf.[94] Two of his most radical tracts, the *Adeisdaemon* and *Origines Judaicae*, were written at The Hague and anonymously published there, bound together, in 1709, provoking a considerable scandal on account of their seditious content. The *Adeisdaemon* ostensibly concerns Roman religion, and follows Van Dale whom he warmly praises—and from whom he also extensively borrows—as well as the 'ingenious Bayle' and the 'acute and learned Le Clerc', in convicting the ancient Roman priesthood of systematic deceit, manipulation, and fraud in misleading the common people.[95] More obviously irreligious was the *Origines Judaicae*, the work in which Toland first publicly labelled his own philosophy 'Pantheist' and maintains—fiercely attacking Huet's *Demonstratio*[96]—that not only did Moses not write the Five Books but that their account of his role is a travesty. The real Moses, he claims, was a republican legislator and philosopher who decreed a religion very different from that subsequently fabricated by the ancient Jewish priesthood. A key classical source which, according to Toland, Huet had totally misconstrued, 'Strabo, unequivocally proclaims Moses to be a Pantheist or as we in these modern times would style him, a Spinozist, and he introduces him as maintaining that no divinity exists separate from the universal frame of nature, and that the universe is the supreme and only God.'[97]

Toland's thesis that Moses was a pantheist and 'nowhere makes any mention of the immortality of the soul or of a future state of rewards and punishments', was indeed a kind of ancient Spinoza, and the early worship of Jehovah a primitive form of Spinozism, provoked fury, not least in the Reformed *classis* of The Hague, which fulsomely condemned the book at the gathering of the South Holland Synod in July 1709. Full-length refutations of the anonymous author's contentions followed in the shape of a 251-page critique by Jacob de la Faye, published at Utrecht in 1709, which stressed

[91] Ibid., 365, 371.   [92] Ibid., 372.   [93] Ibid., 380–1, 384.

[94] [Des Maizeaux], *A Collection*, i, p. lxv; Zedler, *Grosses Universal Lexicon*, xliv, 1091; Champion, *Pillars of Priestcraft*, 125; Vermij, 'English Deists', 248.

[95] JRL MS 3 f 38 Toland, 'Adeisdaemon'. fo. 50; Klopp, *Correspondance de Leibniz*, iii, 306–7; Benoist, *Mélange*, 3, 88–9.

[96] JRL MS 3 f 38 Toland, 'Origines Judicae', fos. 14–15, 26v, 51v; Mosheim, *Vindicae*, preface C; Toland first coined the term, apparently, in a pamphlet of 1705 but uses it there in a philosophically non-specific sense; see Champion, 'Politics of Pantheism', 270–1.

[97] Ibid., fo. 15; De la Faye, *Defensio Religionis*, 201, 249–50; Nicéron, *Mémoires*, i, 256; Naigeon, *Philosophie ancienne et moderne*, iii, 657; Walber, *Charles Blount*, 252; Assmann, *Moses*, 8, 92–5; Berti, 'At the Roots', 566.

Toland's debt to Bayle and Van Dale, as well as Spinoza and Lucretius,[98] and a 374-page reply by the Huguenot pastor Elie Benoist, published at Delft in 1712.

That Toland was in the habit of using the term 'Pantheist' interchangeably with 'Spinozist'[99] and in general was much in Spinoza's debt,[100] is indeed obvious. Yet, at the same time, he evinced a distinctly ambivalent attitude towards the great thinker.[101] In the *Letters to Serena*, a work written in the Netherlands or possibly Germany, in or around 1702, Toland agrees that Spinoza's enemies had 'gain'd nothing on his disciples by the contumelious and vilifying epithets they bestow on his person for the sake of his opinions'.[102] But he also styles Spinoza 'a man of admirable natural endowments, though his share of learning (except in some parts of the mathematicks and in the understanding of the rabbins) seems to have bin very moderate' and declares himself 'persuaded the whole system of Spinoza is not only false, but also precarious and without any sort of foundation'.[103] Yet this apparent dismissal can scarcely be taken at face value, as William Wotton observed in his retort entitled *A Letter to Eusebia* (1704). For in his subsequent remarks Toland, far from substantiating objections to Spinoza's system, merely restates one of the latter's key doctrines, namely that motion is inherent in matter. 'What Mr Toland therefore superadds to Spinoza's scheme,' remarks Wotton, 'is that he makes motion to be essential to matter i.e. he makes matter to be self-moving, whereby we may suppose that he intends to supply all the defects of Spinoza's hypothesis: i.e. make the world without a God.'[104]

Since Toland grants there is just one substance in the universe and 'finds fault with Spinoza' only because he does not assert matter is 'self-moving', Toland, in Wotton's view, was clearly a Spinozist. His disparagement of Spinoza arguably reflects not disagreement but more likely something of the envy which was a noted feature of Toland's less than prepossessing personality. 'I am inclin'd to suspect,' remarked Toland of Spinoza, 'that his chiefest weakness was an immoderate passion to become the head of a sect, to have disciples and a new system of philosophy honor'd with his name, the example being fresh and inviting from the good fortune of his master Cartesius.'[105] The charge is not without foundation but, as has been pointed out, in fact applies even more to Toland himself than to Spinoza.[106] Thus it seems that in the *Letters to Serena*, Toland pretends to refute but in reality defends Spinozism,

---

[98] De la Faye, *Defensio religionis*, 75–6, 111, 201.

[99] JRL MS 3 f 38 Toland, 'Origines Judicae', fos. 45v, 71v; Sullivan, *John Toland*, 193; for a different view, see Champion, 'Politics of Pantheism', 271–3.

[100] Naigeon, *Philosophie ancienne et moderne*, iii, 652, 657; Champion, 'Introduction', 75, 89; Brogi, *Cerchio*, 139.

[101] Brown, 'Theological Politics', 189.   [102] Toland, *Letters to Serena*, 134.

[103] Ibid., 133, 135; Naigeon, *Philosophie ancienne et moderne*, iii, 700; Lurbe, 'Spinozisme de John Toland', 35.

[104] Wotton, *Letter to Eusebia*, 47–8, 53; Gurdon, *The Pretended Difficulties*, 153–4, 156–61, 167; the same point is made by Moniglia, *Dissertazione contra i materialisti*, ii, 48–55; see also Colie, 'Spinoza and the early English Deists', 44–5; Mori, 'L'ateismo', 128.

[105] Toland, *Letters to Serena*, 135–6.

[106] Pocock, *Virtue, Commerce*, 233; Vermij, 'The English Deists', 248–9; Vermij, 'Matter and Motion', 287–8.

while simultaneously insinuating that he himself was a truer 'Spinozist' than Spinoza and has a better right to be acknowledged the head of the growing Spinozist underground.[107]

The *Pantheisticon* (1720), a tract proclaiming a 'Pantheist' (i.e. Spinozist) universal philosophical religion, somewhat along the lines of Leenhof's, circulated in both Latin and French manuscript versions as well as in printed form.[108] It is, as has been remarked, a piece of only minor significance.[109] D'Holbach's atheistic ally, Naigeon, who thought it an 'ouvrage médiocre', commented sourly that, in this case, as in that of his *Christianity not Mysterious*, 'on fit beaucoup de bruit pour bien peu de choses.'[110] But the text does illustrate Toland's yearning to set up and lead an underground quasi-religious philosophical sect. By that date, though, it must have been clear even to Toland that his aspiration to preside over such a Tolandist clandestine movement, given his conspicuous lack of close friends and adherents, was sheer fantasy. In March 1728, the Huguenot savant, Veyssière de la Croze (d.1739), writing from Berlin, assured Toland's biographer, Collins' friend Des Maizeaux, in London, that he considered it highly improbable such a man, whom he had known and entertained, could found a sect, since any followers would need exceptionally compliant minds, Toland being in general not very persuasive.[111] Still more unflattering was the later assessment of Naigeon, who austerely pronounces Toland a *Spinosiste* who adds scarcely anything to Spinozism, remarking that nothing could be more ridiculous, or indeed more useless, than to stand on the shoulders of a giant 'pour ne pas voir plus loin que lui'.[112]

But Naigeon's perception, if broadly correct, goes too far. In reality, Toland was not so facile and unoriginal as many detractors alleged. Indeed, his more significant writings, such as his *Letters to Serena*, *Adeisdaemon*, *Origines Judicae*, and his astounding quasi-theological project, the *Nazarenus* (1718), in which he seeks to dechristianize Christianity and remodel it as a republican civic religion designed only to teach the common people morality, demonstrate his original, creative side and some depth.[113] Moreover, he had an exceptionally strong consciousness of the public sphere and the need, on republican grounds, not just for an 'entire liberty of conscience' but a robustly constructed civic religion based on a 'purefied Christianity' (i.e. dechristianized civic religion) which would provide political society with 'rules for virtue and religion'.[114] His contribution to the development of the Radical Enlightenment was in fact rather substantial. Yet if, due to personal shortcomings, he could never shake off an unenviable reputation for superficiality, unreliability, and charlatanism, which

---

[107] Nicéron, *Mémoires*, i, 249; Lurbe, 'Spinozisme de John Toland', 44; Iofrida, 'Matérialisme', 39, 42; Champion, 'Politics of Pantheism', 271–2; Vermij, 'Matter and Motion', 287–8.

[108] PBN MS NA 21799 Toland 'Pantheisticon is dated 1720 whilst another copy in Paris, PBM MS 4496 is dated 'à Cosmopoli 1725'; see also Benítez, *Face cachée*, 44.

[109] Harrison, *'Religion' and the Religions*, 88.   [110] Naigeon, *Philosophie ancienne et moderne*, iii, 660–1.

[111] BL Add. MS 4283, fo. 170,. Veyssière de la Croze to Des Maizeaux, Berlin, 7 Mar. 1728.

[112] Naigeon, *Philosophie ancienne et moderne*, iii, 662.

[113] Champion, *Pillars of Priestcraft*, 125–9, 234; Harrison, *'Religion' and the Religions*, 164–6.

[114] Champion, 'Politics of Pantheism', 276–8; Champion, 'Making Authority', 190.

dogged him until the end of his days,[115] what his more cogent texts demonstrate is that he was a creative 'Spinozist' in the sense generally understood in the Early Enlightenment. Tolandism, as the Neapolitan philosopher Antonio Genovesi remarked in 1743, represents a new kind of political and religious outlook and yet is simultaneously just an appendix to Spinoza and Spinozism.[116]

iii. Anthony Collins (1676–1729)

A key figure and one who, at first sight, seems to exemplify the often postulated separate line of British development and, simultaneously, the powerful influence of English ideas on the emerging continental Enlightenment, was the self-proclaimed apostle of 'freethinking', Locke's amiable friend—Anthony Collins (1676–1729). While in public he denied being an 'infidel' or 'irreligious', and some modern scholars have supposed he believed in divine providence and 'a future life',[117] others firmly classify him as a radical deist who rejected Revelation, miracles, and the immortality of the soul, as well as a providential God and any form of afterlife. Either way, he possessed a more congenial personality than Toland and, as one of the chosen guardians of Locke's legacy, had special credentials affirming the distinctively insular pedigree of his ideas. Belonging to the affluent gentry class, educated at Eton and King's College, Cambridge, a refined wit and polished host who loved conviviality, fine food, and was especially fond of Tuscan wines, Collins was acceptable in the most select circles— until the publication of *A Discourse of Freethinking* (London, 1713)—and was 'visited several times by Queen Anne' as well as 'noblemen and ladies of quality who took delight in walking in his fine gardens'.[118] Later, while his books and ideas were boycotted, he largely retained his social status.

Voltaire, who considered Collins 'un des plus terribles ennemies de la religion chrétienne', thought he represented the best of English deism, a noble-minded blend of Hobbes' Naturalism and Locke's empiricism.[119] Others appraised Collins' contribution very differently. Indeed, on the continent there developed a strong tradition of viewing Collins essentially as a 'Spinozist'. The Pisan professor Moniglia, for example, considers Collins a leading 'Spinozist', indeed virtually a surrogate Spinoza, because, correctly understood, he rules out Providence and is a thoroughgoing determinist,[120] precisely that kind of 'immaterial fatalist' in fact which Bentley deemed rare in Britain. Similarly, various German *savants*, including Urban Gottlob Thorschmid who, in 1755, published the first full-length biography of Collins, and considered him the foremost of the English deists,[121] claimed that Collins acquired his radical ideas chiefly among freethinking, deistic, and Spinozistic circles in the Netherlands during his two

---

[115] Cragg, *Church*, 78; Sullivan, *John Toland*, 21, 28.   [116] Genovesi, *Elementa Metaphysicae*, i, 105.

[117] O'Higgins, *Anthony Collins*, 77, 239–45; Berman, 'Determinism', 251–2.

[118] BL Add. MS 4282, fo. 240. Dighton to Des Maizeaux, Great Baddow, 14 Mar. 1730.

[119] Torrey, *Voltaire*, 25.   [120] See p. 525 above.

[121] 'Der erste und grösste Freydenker in Engelland', Thorschmid, *Critische Lebensgeschichte*, Vorrede.

sojourns there in 1710 and 1713.[122] In fact, much of Collins' system clearly evolved before 1710. Nevertheless, Thorschmid's thesis regarding the origins of Collins' ideas, as we shall see, by no means deserves to be disregarded.

Collins possessed a plentifully stocked library and, besides much else, a comprehensive array of Spinozana and Spinozistic novels. Together with the *Opera Posthuma* and *Tractatus*, he owned Spinoza on Descartes' principles, Tyssot de Patot's *Jacques Massé*, *Voyages de Groenland*, and *Lettres choisies*, and diverse clandestine manuscripts, including the unpublished treatises of Orobio de Castro and *La Vie et l'Esprit de Mr Benoît de Spinosa*.[123] Collins' familiarity with Orobio de Castro and other Dutch Sephardic writers whose work appealed to radical deists in the eighteenth century— such as Saul Levi Morteira and Juan de Prado—does seem to date specifically from his book- and manuscript-buying expeditions to Amsterdam and The Hague in 1710 and 1713.[124] But in itself, this only confirms that Collins' visits to Holland enhanced his stock of freethinking and radical literature. The visits also provided opportunities to meet and, in some cases, become friends with sundry Huguenot men of books, notably Sallengre,[125] Marchand, Le Clerc, Levier, and Jean-Louis Lorme, a publisher who took a keen interest in Collins' Huguenot ally in London, Des Maizeaux, especially his editing of Bayle's unpublished papers.[126]

There was little warmth, though, between Collins and Le Clerc, and in 1716, the former wrote disparagingly about the latter to 'l'aimable et savant Mr Des Maizeaux, que tous ceux qui font profession de la littérature connoissent',[127] his friend for some twenty years,[128] professing to owe it to Locke's memory 'to think of some plan of vindication of him from the treatment of Mr Le Clerc and Mr Coste, who both servilely flattered him during his life, and made panegyricks upon him immediately after his death', but now exploited his legacy in ways of which Collins disapproved.[129] By contrast, Collins cherished gratitude towards the gifted young deist Sallengre 'for a great deal of civility shown me in Holland'.[130] Presumably, he also encountered the young journalist Rousset de Missy, who rendered his *Discourse* into French prior to its clandestine publication under the title *Discours sur la liberté de penser* at The Hague (with 'Londres' falsely declared on the title-page) in 1714. Reportedly, he also 'paid the duke

---

[122] Thorschmid, *Critische Lebensgeschichte*, 76–7, 102, 123–4; O'Higgins, *Anthony Collins*, 77.

[123] O'Higgins, *Anthony Collins*, 36–8; Berman, 'Determinism', 252.

[124] Collins stressed the rarity of Orobio's *Provenciones Divinas* and Morteira's *Providencia Divina*, saying of the latter that 'no copies are to be procured of it but by the greatest accidents'; Collins, *A Discourse of the Grounds*, 82; Des Maizeaux later noted that Collins nevertheless 'found means to get them when he was in Holland, but paid dear for them'; see Des Maizeaux's notes on Orobio, BL Add. MS 4254, fo. 10.

[125] Albert-Henri de Sallengre (1694–1723), a *savant* of distinctly radical tendencies born at The Hague of Huguenot parents, was, together with Marchand and Saint-Hyacinthe, one of the editors of the *Journal Littéraire*; he later quarrelled with Marchand; see Nicéron, *Mémoires*, i, 119–24; Anderson, 'Sallengre, La Monnoye', 258–64, 270.

[126] Thorschmid, *Critische Lebensgeschichte*, 76–7, 102, 123–4; O'Higgins, *Anthony Collins*, 77.

[127] *Histoire d'un voyage*, 148.   [128] Almagor, *Pierre des Maizeaux*, 4–5.

[129] BL Add. MS 4282, fo. 125. Collins to Des Maizeaux, Hatfield Peverel, 28 Feb. 1716.

[130] Ibid., fo. 224.

of Marlborough several visits at The Hague and was several times in conversation with Prince Eugene there'.[131]

What is implausible in Thorschmid's analysis is not that Collins was basically a 'Spinozist' powerfully influenced by Dutch radical, Huguenot, and Sephardic ideas, but rather his claim that it was in the *Discourse* of 1713 that he first 'showed himself to be a true Spinozist'.[132] For Collins' 'doctrine of necessity', as he calls it, was already preponderant in his mind at a much earlier stage. Thus, at 31, in 1707–8, a confident young Collins clashed with the venerable Samuel Clarke over the nature of the mind and the immortality of the soul, and it is especially in his *Answer to Mr Clarke's Third Defence of His Letter to Mr Dodwell* (London, 1708) that he expounds his concept of necessity.[133] Invoking Locke and Newton, Clarke claimed there are precise limits to what we can know about substance but that it is certain matter does not think and that, consequently, thought must reside in an immaterial being (the soul), that the soul is immortal, and that there is a 'future state of rewards and punishments'. When Collins retorted, implying that mind is inherent in matter, Clarke answered that 'if the mind of man were nothing but a system of matter, and thinking nothing but a certain mode of motion in that system, it would follow that since every determination of motion depends necessarily upon the impulse that causes it, therefore every thought in a man's mind must be necessary and depending wholly upon external causes; and there could be no such thing as liberty or a power of self-determination.'[134]

In his reply, Collins first feigned to deny he was proposing mind is matter and then asks what if he had 'affirm'd the mind of men to be nothing but a certain system of matter, and that thinking is a mode of motion in that system, how does it follow that my notion is destructive of religion?' 'Whenever . . . the doing or forbearing any action, according to the determination of my will is in my power, I am then always free and at liberty, that is free from any agents hindering me from acting as I will, but not free from necessity. For when I will, or prefer, going abroad to staying at home, that act of volition or preference as much determines me to act according to that preference, if it is in my power to go abroad, as locks and bars will hinder one from acting according to that preference. The only difference is that in one case I am necessitated to act as I will, and in the other case to act contrary to my will. This seems to me,' concludes Collins, 'to contain the whole idea of human liberty.'[135]

This argument, as has been pointed out, is not just totally at variance with Locke's empiricism and the arguments of Pascal, Arnauld, and Nicole, with which Collins was then already familiar, but closely shadows Propositions XXXII and XXXIII of Spinoza's *Ethics*.[136] Spinoza, and to some degree also Hobbes, are the seventeenth-century philosophers who reject the possibility of free will and who 'pretend by metaphysick arguments to demonstrate fatality and necessity',[137] that is, they hold every human

[131] BL Add. MS 4282, fo. 242v.   [132] Thorschmid, *Critische Lebensgeschichte*, 77.

[133] Walber, *Charles Blount*, 253; Berman, 'Determinism', 251–4; Berman, *History of Atheism*, 80.

[134] [Collins], *An Answer*, 53–5.

[135] Ibid., 56–7; Naigeon, *Philosophie ancienne et moderne*, i, 751–2; Proust, *Diderot*, 312–13.

[136] Berman, 'Determinism', 252.   [137] Whiston, *Astronomical Principles*, 114–15.

volition to be a 'necessary and compelled one' and related to the laws of nature just 'as motion and rest are and as are absolutely all natural things'.[138] Moreover, it is clear Collins takes his cue from Spinoza specifically since he maintains that Clarke, given his Lockean premises, can not show that there is more than one substance, dropping an obvious hint that, in his own view, there *is* only one. Deploying Locke tactically, he then holds, since we can have 'no idea of substance and substance is something distinct from what are conventionally called properties, it is impossible for any Spinozist or materialist to prove there is no other substance in the universe but material substance.'[139] This, of course, is an inverted way of saying it is impossible, within Locke's framework, to show there is more than one substance, or, in other words, to prove Spinoza wrong. He then cavalierly discards Locke: 'all this talk of the essences of things being unknown is a perfect mistake; and nothing seems clearer to me, than that the essence or substance of matter consists in solidity and that the essence of substance or being distinct from matter, must consist in want of extension, and is truly defin'd as an unextended being.'[140]

Collins again seems to be drawing on Spinoza (and the 'acute and penetrating Mr Bayle'),[141] not Hobbes, as he expounds his doctrine of human freedom and necessity within the confines of one substance. 'As far as I can judge of the opinions of Strato, Xenophanes and some other ancient atheists from a few sentences of theirs that yet remain, and of that sect call'd the *Literati* in China,' he holds, 'they seem all to me to agree with Spinoza (who in his *Opera Posthuma* has endeavour'd to reduce atheism into a system) that there is no other substance in the universe but matter, which Spinoza calls God, and Strato Nature.'[142] Collins then presses his onslaught on Clarke—having dismissed his Newtonian contention that 'material impulse cannot be the cause of gravitation'[143]—by sarcastically embracing his view that much the best way to destroy Spinoza's atheistic reasoning is to 'prove the Creation of matter *ex nihilo* or which is all one, that matter is not a self-existant being'.[144] Locke, assuredly, has shown us how to proceed. By following Locke, he observes, 'we may be able to aim at some dim and seeming conception, how matter might at first be made, by the power of the External First Being.'[145] Unfortunately, Locke himself had abandoned the task 'as he thought this would lead him too far from the notions on which the philosophy now in the world is built and that it would not be pardonable to deviate so far from them'.[146] And if Locke would or could not prove that matter is not a 'self-existant thing', it is surely pardonable for Collins 'who own myself to be infinitely below him in abilities' to dispense with the labour of 'shewing the falsehood of so many receiv'd prejudices and opinions as is necessary to give an idea of Creation *ex nihilo*'.[147] With a final sardonic flourish, he proposes it would be best to leave 'so useful a design . . .

---

[138] *Collected Works of Spinoza*, i, 435; Tuck, *Hobbes*, 46–7; Deleuze, *Spinoza*, 69–70.

[139] [Collins], *An Answer*, 77–8, 81.   [140] Ibid., 83.

[141] Collins, *A Philosophical Enquiry*, 27; Miller, 'Freethinking', 605.

[142] [Collins], *An Answer*, 89.   [143] Ibid., 83–5.

[144] Ibid., 90; Berman, *History of Atheism*, 80.   [145] [Collins], *An Answer*, 92.

[146] Ibid.   [147] Ibid.

entirely to some of those gentlemen that are appointed annually to preach at the Lecture founded by the Honourable Robert Boyle'.[148]

Collins' paradoxical argument that the 'doctrine of necessity is too generally suppos'd to be irreligious and atheistical' and that in reality it is the sole viable solution to the problem of the human will and the sole truly 'religious' view,[149] recurs in his later work *A Philosophical Inquiry Concerning Liberty* (1717). Here he notes the 'great Episcopius' acknowledged the 'asserters of necessity have seeming experience on their side' and that 'other asserters of liberty seem driven into it on account of suppos'd inconveniences attending the doctrine of necessity'.[150] However, the latter are utterly mistaken. For fundamentally, it is belief in 'liberty . . . or a power to act or not to act, to do this or another thing under the same circumstances' which is 'an impossibility and atheistical'.[151] To grasp his thesis that liberty 'can only be grounded on the absurd principles of Epicurean atheism', or what he terms the 'Epicurean system of chance', one only has to glance back, he says, at the history of ancient thought. For the 'Epicurean atheists who were the most popular and most numerous sect of atheists of antiquity, were the great asserters of liberty, as on the other side, the Stoicks, who were the most popular and most numerous sect among the religionaries of antiquity were the great asserters of fate and necessity'.[152] Hence, to postulate 'freedom of the will', he insisted, is 'atheistical'.

From 1707 Collins was continually assailed by numerous English and Anglo-Irish writers, Jonathan Swift, Clarke, and Berkeley among them. In Britain and Ireland he became a figure of considerable notoriety. In the longer run, though, perhaps even as early as the 1740s, his impact seems to have been greater in France than in England, and he became an appreciable force also in Germany and Italy, albeit one routinely classified as a 'Spinozist'.[153] Indeed Collins apparently exerted a stronger influence on Voltaire and mid-eighteenth century French thought generally than Toland, little of whose work was available in French.[154] Commenting on the Clarke–Collins exchange towards the end of the century, Naigeon noted that Collins had forcefully upheld the doctrine of necessity, pointing out the irony that, while the writings of Clarke, whom he considered 'plus théologien que philosophe', embedded in the dust of libraries, would soon be wholly forgotten, those of Collins, whom he rates among the 'bons esprits du dix-huitième siècle' would long continue to be read with profit.[155]

Collins was a philosophical necessitarian and radical Bible critic who firmly believed great benefits would accrue to society from the new freedom to philosophize. The rapid receding of belief in magic and satanic power of the Early Enlightenment he attributes specifically to the advance of freethinking. Likewise the progress of scholarship and science: 'thus before the restoration of learning, when men were

---

[148] [Collins], *An Answer*, 92.   [149] Ibid., 58.   [150] Collins, *A Philosophical Inquiry*, 22–3.
[151] Ibid., 59; Miller, 'Freethinking', 602–4.
[152] Collins, *A Philosophical Inquiry*, 59–60; Berman, *History of Atheism*, 81.
[153] O'Higgins, *Anthony Collins*, 201.
[154] Ibid.; Torrey, *Voltaire*, 15, 25–9; Vernière, *Spinoza*, 359; Spink, *French Free-Thought*, 272.
[155] Naigeon, *Philosophie ancienne et moderne*, i, 749–51.

subject to the impositions of priests, a prodigious ignorance prevail'd.'[156] No less great a blessing was the wresting 'out of the priests' hands the power of taking away so many innocent people's lives and reputations'.[157] But was all this freedom and intellectual progress worth the disillusionment and disruption? When asked of what use his freethinking was if man has no 'freedom of will' and all his actions are determined, he retorted that demonstrating the truth benefits mankind by assisting us in 'establishing laws and morality, rewards and punishments, in society'.[158]

iv. Matthew Tindal (*c.*1657–1733)

An age of intellectual ferment though it was, many universities seemed hopelessly immured in obscurantist lethargy. Oxford and Cambridge, in the judgement of 'most ingenious men', held Bishop Berkeley, were little better than 'nurseries of prejudice, corruption, barbarism and pedantry'.[159] Even so, enlightened and even radical opinions were also to be found there and, at Oxford, no reputedly godless spirit provoked more indignation, among High-Flyers and Latitudinarians alike, than Matthew Tindal, Fellow of All Souls, that 'grand apostate and corrupter', as one of his countless detractors styled him, 'of the principles and morals of the youth of the present age'.[160] Tindal's style was to propagate radical ideas among a small coterie, in college and in anonymous publications, while sufficiently deferring to the Anglican faith 'in outward shew' to retain his fellowship. For it was observed that he 'was not so angry with the universities neither, notwithstanding the many scandalous and abusive things which he hath said of them, as to throw [his fellowship] up, but continued to eat the [All Souls] founder's bread to the last moment of his life'.[161]

A don who antagonized all Oxford other than his handful of converts, one of whom was Sedgwick Harrison, professor of history, 'this gentleman', noted one supporter, was 'embroiled in a continual warfare in the Republic of Letters for the space of above forty years'.[162] Ironically, on first arriving at the university in 1672, Tindal had been a pupil, at Lincoln College, of none other than his future antagonist George Hickes, who had been an Oxford Fellow until 1680 when he embarked on his career in the Church. Associated originally with the High Church party and—with consummate irony—elected to his All Souls fellowship, in 1678, with Hickes' backing, Tindal converted to Catholicism after James II's accession, hoping for the wardenship of All Souls from the king, in which ambition, however, he was thwarted. Later, discarding first Catholicism, and then divine-right principles, he greeted the Glorious Revolution by re-entering the Anglican Church as a Latitudinarian and college politics as a Whig. But he did not cease his trimming in 1688. In the 1690s he emerged as a (privately) professed deist. Jonas Proast, the foremost critic of Locke's views on toleration and a leading adversary of the deists, told Hickes in 1708 of a conversation he had had with

---

[156] [Collins], *A Discourse*, 5; *An Answer to the Discourse*, 7–8.   [157] [Collins], *A Discourse*, 24–5.
[158] Quoted in Torrey, *Voltaire*, 35.   [159] Berkeley, *Alciphron*, i, 313.
[160] *The Religious, Rational and Moral Conduct*, 1.   [161] Ibid., 19.
[162] *Memoirs of the Life and Writings*, 1.

Tindal in All Souls' quadrangle around 1696, in which the latter had unashamedly retorted there is 'no such thing as Revelation'. Proast, who approved Hickes' campaign to capsize Locke as a 'Spinozist', urged his ally to use this disclosure about Tindal in any way he could 'against the underminers of our most Holy Faith'.[163]

Tindal, a notorious glutton, was resilient as well as provocative, and despite being rumoured by critics to have been 'distinguished' at the time of his election to All Souls 'by nothing but the insatiableness of his belly',[164] his studied moderation in wine afforded 'no small advantage' in encounters at high table. In 1706 he caused a sensation with his *Rights of the Christian Church Asserted*, an onslaught on Church authority, favourably reviewed by Le Clerc in Holland, which produced bitter recrimination from 'most of the ecclesiastical bellows in the kingdom'.[165] Yet despite being an Oxford don and a veteran controversialist, it continued to be alleged that his erudition was limited, indeed that his 'whole stock of learning was no more than a few modern books and a great many pamphlets'.[166] His critics denounced his *Rights* as a 'farrago' of borrowed extracts, his own contribution having been merely to 'work up the materials which this terrible piece was to consist of', the intellectual substance being furnished by 'others in Oxford and London and even Holland'.[167]

Tindal, though one of the three most famous English deists, along with Toland and Collins, was, unlike them, not much of a thinker and practically devoid of originality. But he was nevertheless influential, his publications having some impact both in Britain and later, in translation, in Germany. Jonathan Swift deemed him a dangerous adversary, one of the foremost of England's 'atheistical writers'.[168] His *Christianity as Old as Creation* (1730), a reworking of Blount's thesis that natural religion was the original religion which was then perverted by self-seeking priests, and that the Law of Nature given by God is perfect and can not be improved on by any other kind of Revelation, provoking as it did some thirty replies, can with some justification be considered the climax of the deist controversies in Britain.[169]

Tindal's significance for the Early Enlightenment, then, lies not in his intellectual contribution but his effectiveness in transmitting the ideas of others. But precisely what did he propagate? Hickes for one claimed it was among Tindal's 'fraudulent practices to write after, and out of, other books', his *Rights*, according to Hickes and Carroll, being essentially 'borrowed from Spinoza's book *De Jure Ecclesiasticorum*', his text and its model both being 'grounded upon downright atheism', Tindal and his associates having taken their 'execrable principles with their consequences' from 'that and [Spinoza's] other works'.[170] For Tindal's arguments, according to Hickes, were

---

[163] *Memoirs of the Life and Writings*, 50–2.   [164] *The Religious, Rational and Moral Conduct*, 13.

[165] *Memoirs of the Life and Writings*, 12.   [166] *The Religious, Rational and Moral Conduct*, 14.

[167] Ibid., 31; according to Harrison, 'Tindal is possibly the most overrated of the British freethinkers'; see Harrison, 'Religion' and the Religions, 167.

[168] Craven, *Jonathan Swift*, 68.

[169] Cassirer, *Philosophy*, 173–4; Hazard, *European Thought*, 74, 396; Cragg, *Church*, 159–61; Harrison, 'Religion' and the Religions, 167–8.

[170] Hickes, *A Preliminary Discourse*, 1; Carroll, *A Dissertation*, 276–80; *Memoirs of the Life and Writings*, 50; Champion, *Pillars of Priestcraft*, 136.

also partly 'stollen from Spinoza's *Theological-Political Treatise*', one illustration of this being the notion that the ancient 'Jews were not bound by any Law of God til they receded from their natural right in the Horeb-contract', that is, received their basic laws from Moses at Mount Sinai.[171] Spinoza was undoubtedly one of Tindal's sources, at least in a general way, and especially for his claim there are innumerable textual imperfections and discrepancies in the Biblical text.[172] 'And is not "spirit",' asks Tindal, citing Spinoza's *Tractatus*, 'nay the "spirit of God" taken, at least, in twenty different senses in the Scripture?'[173] But he also several times cites, and praises, Le Clerc,[174] and borrowed extensively also from Bayle, Fontenelle, and Toland. A Sephardic free-thinker whom Tindal applauds is Uriel da Costa, whose deist admonitions for warring theologians he approvingly upholds, quoting his remark that 'when men depart ever so little from natural religion, it is the occasion of great strifes and divisions; but if they recede much from it, who can declare the calamities which ensue!'[175]

Hickes believed his former pupil's reasoning gave English readers 'just reason to presume that as Dr Tindal wrote his Book of the *Rights* upon the plan of Spinoza's *De Jure Ecclesiasticorum* which was written by the atheist against the divine institution and authority of the Christian priesthood; so in another, that he will follow his subtil method in his *Tractatus Theologico-Politicus*, to destroy as much as in the Devil and him lies, the authority of the Scriptures and divine Revelation'.[176] Furthermore, admonished Hickes, when Tindal 'hath done this with impunity, I doubt not but he will proceed to the apostate's Posthumous Works, and from thence, in more plain terms, bring atheism into the world bare-fac'd, without any sort of masks or disguises which he hath used in his Book of *Rights*.' 'Spinoza and his followers,' held Hickes, might be 'loose and trifling arguers, whose writings will not endure the test of true logick and sound reason' but they, and especially 'the captain of his school, Dr Tindal' were plainly wreaking great havoc. Tindal, like Spinoza, averred Carroll, maintains that 'no sort of privileges of divine institution can be found in the Holy Scriptures of the Old and New Testaments which can rightly and truly be ascribed to the clergy.'[177] As for the deists' pernicious plea for 'a universal, impartial, inviolable toleration in matters of religion', Carroll judged that 'all this is bottom'd upon those men's favourite principle, to wit, that as to matters of conscience or religion, mankind is actually in their state of nature, wherein every man has a natural, inalienable, inherent right, to believe, or not to believe, whatever he pleases.'[178] Worst of all was Tindal's deistic conception of 'God' which, according to Carroll, is the same as Spinoza's and entirely rests on the latter's doctrine of one substance.[179]

---

[171] Hickes, *A Preliminary Discourse*, 6; De Vaux, *Ancient Israel*, 147, 281.

[172] [Tindal], *Christianity as Old as Creation*, 296–7.

[173] Ibid., 309: 'in short the words of Scripture on which things of the greatest consequence depend, are, as is show by a learned Author [i.e. Spinoza], sometimes taken, not only in a different, but a contrary sense.'

[174] Ibid., 39, 127, 203, 207.

[175] [Tindal], *Christianity as Old as Creation*, 147; Da Costa, *Examination*, 562.

[176] Hickes, *Preliminary Discourse*, 7–8.   [177] [Carroll], *Spinoza Reviv'd*, 9.

[178] Ibid., 72.   [179] Ibid., 103–4, 112, 120.

Tindal's deist ethics, based on what Carroll terms 'our author's, and his master's [i.e. Spinoza's] darling state of nature',[180] is indeed a typically Spinozist construct. Asserting that 'God has endow'd Man with such a nature as makes him necessarily desire his own good', and 'endeavouring to subsist as conveniently as his nature permits',[181] he claims it is impossible to establish any meaningful system of morality except on the principle that we should do everything possible to preserve ourselves, maintaining the 'health of the body and the vigour of the mind' and avoiding all 'excess of sensual delights' and 'immoderate desires': 'we cant but know we ought to use great moderation with relation to our passions, or in other words, govern all our actions by reason, that and our true interest being inseparable.'[182] It was regarded as one of his chief (and most objectionable) tenets that 'the perfection and happiness of all rational beings, supreme, as well as subordinate, consists in living up to the dictates of their nature' and that consequently 'God requires nothing for His own sake, no, not the worship we are to render Him, nor the faith we are to have in Him.'[183]

Another typical theme is Tindal's constant denunciation of superstition which, he claims, echoing Bayle, is worse than atheism.[184] 'The more superstition the people have,' he asserts, 'the easier they may be impos'd on by designing ecclesiastics.'[185] Fortunately, enlightened attitudes are now spreading in some northern lands, but 'whoever knows anything of France and Italy, not to mention other countries, can't but know that the better sort are sensible of the prevailing absurdities, but, over-aw'd by the priests and mob, are forced to submit.'[186]

Though he exerted little influence abroad during his lifetime, Tindal's work became a significant factor, particularly in Germany, during the 1740s.[187] In broad terms, he was indeed a 'Spinozist', as his detractors claimed, and these would have dearly loved to have made an example of him, but how? Though condemned in Oxford as a 'noted debauchee' and deist who rejected divine Providence, removal of an unwanted Fellow at All Souls, then as now, entailed procedures of such baffling complexity as the gluttonous don 'knew how to make crafty use of to preserve himself from expulsion'.[188] Though his conversation and opinions were deemed 'generally of the lowest and most trifling sort', he had to be put up with, a seemingly indestructible embarrassment to academe. All that could be done was to pulverize his reputation, in conversation and print, where he was continually lambasted for his impiety, and his Bible hermeneutics for their lack of solidity, originality, and 'acquaintance with the oriental languages', his mediocre scholarship leaving him even in the 'common criticks and commentators' completely 'feeble and his artillery contemptible'.[189]

---

[180] [Carroll], *Spinoza Reviv'd*, 92, 150, 157. [181] [Tindal], *Rights of the Christian Church*, 10.
[182] [Tindal], *Christianity as Old as Creation*, 14. [183] *Memoirs of the Life and Writings*, 44–5.
[184] [Tindal], *Christianity as Old as Creation*, 87–8. [185] Ibid., 152. [186] Ibid.
[187] Geissler, 'Littérature clandestine', 484; Schröder, *Ursprünge*, 469, 473.
[188] *The Religious, Rational and Moral Conduct*, 19, 54. [189] Ibid., 57.

v. Bernard Mandeville (1670–1733)

If Blount, Toland, Collins, and in a different way Shaftesbury[190]—a more restrained but one of the most creative and influential of the English deists—all had crucial connections with the United Provinces and the shuttered world of Dutch radical thought, the Dutch dimension impinges still more strongly in the case of Bernard Mandeville (1670–1733). He was himself Dutch by origin and education and had already become an active radical—he was one of the chief instigators of a serious riot in Rotterdam in 1691—and a trained thinker before leaving Holland and starting out on the travels preceding his settling in London in 1693.

Mandeville, who grew up in Rotterdam within a family linked to the anti-Orangist States' party, had been a pupil at the civic high school there, and consequently had been taught by Jurieu and, more important, Bayle, who profoundly influenced his subsequent intellectual development.[191] Perhaps still more significant, during his years at Leiden, Mandeville studied under Burchardus de Volder,[192] which means he gained not only a thorough training in De Volder's scientifically orientated Cartesianism but was almost certainly introduced at an early stage to Spinoza. Mandeville's first publication, his *Disputatio philosophica* (Leiden, 1689), written under De Volder's supervision, ends with the ringing Cartesian contention that 'except for mind and extension there is no other substance' (praeter cognitationem et extensionem nulla datur substantia).[193]

Despite his Dutch background, Mandeville, it is usually assumed, developed intellectually within an essentially insular and, particularly, a Hobbesian, intellectual tradition.[194] So it is worth emphasizing that Mandeville's involvement with the Dutch intellectual scene by no means ceased with his settling in London.[195] On the contrary, he continued his reading in Dutch, as well as French and Latin, while practising medicine in London, as is shown by footnotes citing Aitzema, Bayle, Van Dale, Saint-Evremond, and Leti, and often looked to the Dutch context for exempla. He does not think it easy, for example, 'to name a great city better govern'd than that of Amsterdam', while he considers Hamburg, in glaring contrast, the most 'deplorable instance'

---

[190] Anthony Ashley Cooper, third Earl of Shaftesbury (1671–1713), one year Mandeville's junior, presents a most interesting foil to the evolution of Mandeville's thought; an aristocrat and Whig parliamentarian, he thoroughly approved of Dutch republicanism and toleration and spent long periods in the Netherlands in 1698 and 1703–4; in his widely read *Characteristics of Men, Manners, Opinions, Times* (1711) he presented a relatively discreet form of deism and system of ethics; Shaftesbury was frequently critical of both Spinoza and his own deist contemporaries and showed considerable originality in the formulation of his thought; McNaughton, 'British Moralists', 203–10.

[191] Wielema, *Filosofen*, 69–70; Redwood, *Reason, Ridicule and Religion*, 88, 91; Cook, 'Bernard Mandeville', 117.

[192] Mandeville, *Disputatio philosophica*, 1.   [193] Ibid., 4.

[194] See, for example, Pocock, *Machiavellian Moment*, 467; Pocock, *Virtue, Commerce and History*, 122–3; Hundert, *The Enlightenment's Fable*, 25.

[195] Cook, 'Bernard Mandeville', 111–19.

of a great city, one which 'at this day labours still under the misery of civil discord which [is] altogether owing to, and never had any other cause than, the unbridled zeal of furious preachers'.[196] In his *Fable of the Bees*, that 'flagitious and detestable book', one of its innumerable detractors called it, Mandeville warmly praises the 'fortitude and resolution' of the Dutch Revolt and Dutch economic success.[197] Similarly, on the question of women, whose enslavement to men Mandeville habitually condemns, he contrasts the polished but contrived 'respect and tenderness' shown to women in England, which, he says, is mere 'outward show', unfavourably—despite the fact the English fondly imagine 'those Butter-boxes dont know how to treat ladies'—with the greater involvement of women in economic life typical of Holland.[198]

Holland is also Mandeville's measure when airing his republican preference for greater equality. If most European contemporaries disliked Dutch society because social hierarchy and aristocratic values were there in decay, Dutch egalitarianism wins Mandeville's full approval: 'France,' he declares, 'is the reverse of Holland' because 'the difference between the degrees of people which I spoke of before is every way less in commonwealths than it is in kingdoms, and yet not so great in limited monarchies as it is in those that are arbitrary.'[199] Hence there was more equality in Britain than France, he believed, but more still in the United Provinces. This difference he deemed partly an economic issue but also a question of mentality, attitude, and the inherent characteristics of a republic. Thus, he says, the Dutch poor were less destitute than those of Britain and France, while the 'notion they have of liberty makes 'em so proud, that the ordinary man thinks himself as good as the best in the land; and knowing that all are subject to the same laws naturally scorns to pay any homage to men that by their birth have no prerogative over him.'[200]

Mandeville's radical activism in Rotterdam in 1690–1 may be regarded as political, social, and philosophical. It is scarcely surprising that such a man should reflect the influence of Johan and Pieter de la Court, as has been emphasized by several recent commentators.[201] But what has been less noticed but is arguably still more important is the close affinity of his political and moral philosophy to that of Spinoza, with whose work, though he never cites it, there is every reason to infer he was intimately acquainted. Mandeville's guiding ethical principle is that 'there is nothing more sincere in any creature than his will, wishes and endeavours to preserve himself,' this being in his eyes a 'law of nature by which no creature is endowed with any appetite or passion but what either directly or indirectly tends to the preservation either of himself or his species'.[202] Furthermore, like Spinoza (but unlike Hobbes), Mandeville assigns no role to organized religion in curbing men's appetites, other than the quasi-political function of instilling obedience. It is the State and law which must shoulder the burden of imposing order and security: 'the only useful passion then that man is

---

[196] Mandeville, *Free Thoughts*, 356–7.   [197] Ibid., 164, 168.

[198] Mandeville, *The Virgin Unmask'd*, 127–8.   [199] Ibid., 164–5; Mandeville, *Fable of the Bees*, 168.

[200] Mandeville, *The Virgin Unmask'd*, 164.

[201] Hundert, *Enlightenment's Fable*, 24–9; Cook, 'Bernard Mandeville', 113–16.

[202] Mandeville, *Fable of the Bees*, 182; Hundert, *The Enlightenment's Fable*, 51–5.

possess'd of toward the peace and quiet of a society, is his fear, and the more you work upon it the more orderly and governable he'll be.'[203] The challenge is to 'civilize men and establish them in a body politick' and this, for Mandeville, requires being 'thoroughly acquainted with all the passions and appetites, strengths and weaknesses of their frame'.[204]

In Mandeville, unlike Hobbes, no contract is involved and no government or Church has, or can expect, any automatic right to obedience or loyalty. Rather, as in Machiavelli, Johan de la Court, and Spinoza, governments maintain themselves only through their power to conserve themselves and not owing to any obligation or formal submission. 'Good government', in Mandeville, means using strong penalties and punishments to curb unruly passions. Thus 'when various laws to restrain [Man] from using force are strictly executed, self-preservation must teach him to be peaceable; and as it is every body's business to be as little disturb'd as possible, his fears will be continually augmented and enlarg'd as he advances in experience, understanding and foresight.'[205] Mandeville's republicanism, deism, and libertinism are thus all parts of a larger philosophical vision of man as driven by egotistical impulses, always seeking his own individual preservation and advancement, but gradually becoming accustomed, through a protracted civilizing process, to management by law-makers and statesmen whose chief expertise lies in their ability to regulate and restrain self-seeking drives by playing on Man's insecurity and fear.[206]

Mandeville was one of the most widely denounced of early eighteenth-century radical writers. What especially appalled contemporaries was his elimination of all Bible-based and religion-based morality and his redefinition of man not just 'as an animal having like other animals nothing to do but to follow his appetites',[207] but as an entirely determined being lacking free will: 'a compound of various passions, that all of them as they are provok'd and come uppermost govern him by turns whether he will or no'.[208] Mandeville's principle that 'there is nothing more sincere in any creature than his will, wishes and endeavours to preserve himself' buttresses both a Spinozist ethics and a Spinozist system of republican and egalitarian political thought. Shaftesbury, whose deist philosophy has some parallels with Spinozism, but also exhibits a declared and conscious antagonism,[209] was attacked by Mandeville precisely for trying to construct, outside revealed religion and on a philosophical basis, a new absolute criterion for moral qualities and judgements.

In his *Characteristics of Men, Manners, Opinions, Times* (1711), Shaftesbury accepts the 'naturalist' starting-point, common to Hobbes, Spinoza, and later Mandeville, that every individual creature seeks its own conservation and 'private good', but also

---

[203] Mandeville, *Fable of the Bees*, 191; Hundert, *The Enlightenment's Fable*, 66–70.

[204] Mandeville, *Fable of the Bees*, 194.   [205] Ibid., 191.

[206] Hundert, *The Enlightenment's Fable*, 76–7.

[207] Law, *Remarks*, 2; Law was tutor to Edward Gibbon's father and one of Mandeville's 'most astute critics'; see Hundert, *The Enlightenment's Fable*, 19.

[208] Quoted in Law, *Remarks*, 4; Rosenblatt, *Rousseau and Geneva*, 53, 65–6.

[209] Gurdon, *The Pretended Difficulties*, 104, 268.

insists our power to reflect, our conscience and emotions, by revealing the 'private good' of others, and the common good, generates, both intellectually and emotionally, an innate sense of 'right' and 'wrong' which constitutes a moral absolute.[210] In Shaftesbury, moral goodness pertains to a person induced by his or her character and temperament 'primarily and immediately, and not secondarily and accidentally, to good and, against ill'.[211] Such conscious seeking after good in humans is what Shaftesbury means by 'virtue', a quality which, in his opinion, serves a crucial function in human and all existence. He classifies the philosophical moralists of ancient and modern times in two broad categories, the Stoic and Epicurean, the first, to which he assigns himself, being rooted in the 'common good', virtue, and public spiritedness, and the latter egotistical, hedonistic, and dismissive of 'virtue', in the 'Stoic' sense, as mere delusion.[212] His private notes suggest that Shaftesbury viewed Spinoza and Descartes as the foremost of the modern Epicureans whom he repudiates.[213]

Mandeville rejects Shaftesbury's conception of an innate morality and system of 'virtue', arguing that in polite society, men simply learn their notions of 'virtue' as a superficial veneer from the rules of courtesy and sociability.[214] Insisting on the force of law and requirements of social interaction as the true source of ideas of virtue, Mandeville maintains the 'nearer we search into human nature, the more we shall be convinc'd that the moral virtues are the political offspring which flattery begot upon pride'.[215] Likewise, revealed religion plays only a secondary role.[216] 'Once for all,' Mandeville sums up his position on Revelation, 'the Gospel teaches us obedience to superiors and charity to all men'—a strikingly Spinozistic sentiment.[217] Like most writers in English of the late seventeenth and early eighteenth century, and like Tindal and the other English deists,[218] Mandeville had only a slight impact on the continent before the 1720s but began, during the second quarter of the century, to exert a growing influence internationally. While there was no translation of the *Fable of the Bees* available until 1740,[219] Mandeville first emerged as an leading advocate of an egotistical, individualistic morality 'indifferentistisch und naturalistisch',[220] and of an extreme Spinozist 'freedom of thought', relatively soon after the publication of his *Free Thoughts on Religion* in 1720. A French version of this work, translated by Van Effen, appeared at Amsterdam in 1722[221] while a German rendering, omitting Mandeville's name from the title-page and translated from Van Effen's French, not directly,[222] came out four years later at Leipzig. German interest in Mandeville

---

[210] Mortensen, 'Shaftesbury', 631–2, 648–9; McNaughton, 'British Moralists', 205–6, 210; Klein, *Shaftesbury*, 60–6, 68, 80, 157; Craven, *Jonathan Swift*, 89–91.

[211] Quoted in McNaughton, 'British Moralists', 204–5; see also Berkeley, *Alciphron*, 73–4.

[212] McNaughton, 'British Moralists', 203–4; Klein, *Shaftesbury*, 60–9.

[213] Klein, *Shaftesbury*, 61.   [214] Hundert, *The Enlightenment's Fable*, 181.

[215] [Mandeville], *Fable of the Bees*, 34.   [216] Ibid., 32–4.

[217] [Mandeville], *Free Thoughts on Religion*, 246.   [218] Schröder, *Ursprünge*, 473.

[219] Hundert, *The Enlightenment's Fable*, 102–3.   [220] Trinius, *Freydenker-Lexicon*, 345.

[221] Fabian, 'Reception', 695; Fabian dates the French edition to 1722, Hundert, however, states 1724; see Hundert, *The Enlightenment's Fable*, 102–3.

[222] Fabian, 'Reception', 695.

received added impetus from a pamphlet published in 1724 by the Dresden *super-intendens*, Loescher, denouncing his *Free Thoughts* as a 'satanic work' distilled from Bayle and Hobbes and designed to enthrone an unrestricted toleration of ideas everywhere.

Appraised as a group, how then can one best characterize the place of the English deists in the rise of the Radical Enlightenment? In view of historiographical traditions about the origins of the Enlightenment, perhaps what needs most to be stressed is that their thought shows a certain unity but is much more derivative, and linked to the wider continental context, than is usually supposed. Conversely, the links with Hobbes, Locke, and Newton are less fundamental than is habitually claimed. Furthermore, while this group played little part in establishing or formulating the main themes of the Radical Enlightenment, and also had relatively little influence within the wider context of the European Radical Enlightenment before the 1720s, from that point on they assumed real importance in international intellectual debate, essentially as skilful publicists and popularizers of a *fataliste*, Naturalist, and ultimately Spinozist revolutionary impulse which was social, sexual, and political as well as philosophical and religious.

34 | GERMANY: THE RADICAL *AUFKLÄRUNG*

i. Initial Reaction

As in France and England, it was specifically in the 1670s that academics, theologians, and philosophers in Germany first became seriously alarmed by what was perceived as a sudden, powerful upsurge of philosophical sedition against authority, tradition, and revealed religion. This intellectual rebellion powered by philosophy was diversely classified as 'Naturalismus', 'Deisterey' (deism), 'Freydenkerey' (freethinking) and 'Indifferentisterey', but these names all refer to the same disturbing phenomenon. Various books and writers were denounced but, invariably, much the fiercest outcry was in reaction to the *Tractatus Theologico-Politicus*, copies of which arrived in Leipzig, the chief book distribution centre of northern Germany, immediately following the work's clandestine publication in Amsterdam, early in 1670.

The first noted figure to respond to Spinoza's perceived onslaught on Revelation and revelation-based authority was Leibniz's teacher, Jacob Thomasius (1622–84), professor of moral philosophy at Leipzig and father of Christian Thomasius. He denounced the book in a lecture on 8 May 1670 as inimical to religion and society, deploring especially its advocacy of unrestricted 'freedom of thought and speech'.[1] The same month his Leipzig colleague, Friedrich Rappolt (1615–76), who was similarly unaware of the anonymous writer's identity, but equally appalled by his ideas, likewise fulminated against this attempt to redefine 'religion' as nothing other than 'justice' and 'charity' (cultum Dei in sola justitia et charitate consistere) rather than truth revealed to man through God's Providence. Rappolt especially abhorred its subversive call to every individual to interpret Scripture for himself, according to his own judgement.[2] This detestable rebellion against God's Word, he declared, claims true, genuine religion is nothing other than the 'faith' taught by reason, that is, 'natural religion', thereby contradicting Scripture and ecclesiastical authority.

In his *Oratio contra Naturalistas*, delivered a month later, Rappolt again trumpeted

---

[1] Subsequently published under the title *Adversus anonymum de libertate philosophandi* (1670); see Walther, 'Machina Civilis', 187–90.

[2] Rappolt, *Opera Theologica*, 2162–3; Walther, 'Machina Civilis', 190; Otto, *Studien*, 16, 26.

the alarm over the advent of *Naturalismus* in German culture, proclaiming the *Tractatus* its most virulent manifestation by far. 'Naturalism', he declared, may be an ancient evil, stretching back in time to the ancient Greeks but it had long been quiescent, submerged in darkness until quietly revived, a few decades before, by the English 'Naturalist' Herbert of Cherbury.[3] Herbert, though, was merely a herald of something far worse. The contagion now revealing itself in all its malignancy in German lands originated, held Rappolt, in the new fashion for philosophy, the modern 'idol', he calls it contemptuously, an alluring but fatal distraction from genuine piety and religion. This philosophical form of corruption is devastating, literally 'soul-destroying', because neither the new philosophies, nor any philosophy, he held, can lead mankind to salvation—only Christ and Revelation can do that.[4]

The furore at Leipzig quickly spilled over to other academic centres. In June 1670 the Heidelberg professor, Friedrich Ludwig Mieg, son of the electoral chancellor, alerted his Calvinist colleague Samuel Andreae, professor at the Calvinist academy at Herborn, that the author of the abominable work causing such uproar in Holland and Germany was the same as the one who expounded Descartes 'by geometric method', namely 'Spinoza, a former Jew'.[5] Beyond academe, the alarm was sounded first in Hamburg by the Lutheran pastor Johannes Müller,[6] in his *Atheismus Devictus* (1672), and then, in 1673, in a furious counterblast to Naturalism and atheism by the Pomeranian pastor Johannes Lassenius (1636–92). Müller and Lassenius both discerned a powerful new upsurge of Naturalism and atheism among sections of urban and aristocratic society. According to Müller, the malaise had started in the 1660s, nurtured in part by foreign travel, especially to France, England, and Holland, lands where harmful intellectual 'novelties' were rife, and in part by the growing influx of pernicious philosophical books.[7] Lassenius' diagnosis was identical, except that he adds Italy, the age-old home of 'atheism', and Poland, home of Socinianism, to the stock of contagious countries. The notorious books denounced by these two writers were unpublishable in Germany, but incessantly coming in from the Netherlands. 'Who can give account,' complains Müller, 'of all the pernicious books which arrive here from Holland in which heaps of atheistic, Epicurean, and blasphemous teachings are found?'[8] Such unwholesome material was being avidly consumed in Hamburg and other cities, he contended, and it was to counter its ill effects that he had taken up his own pen.

The worst of these pestilential books, holds Müller, were the *Praeadamitae* (by Isaac La Peyrère), a work prized, he remarks scornfully, by Hamburg's 'mockers and atheists' and overflowing with 'atheistic ideas'; 'Friedrich Warmund's *Blumenhoff*'—

---

[3] Rappolt, *Opera Theologica*, 1404–5; Stolle, *Anleitung*, 713.

[4] Rappolt, *Opera Theoligica*, 1390–1.

[5] Freudenthal, *Lebensgeschichte*, 193.

[6] This is the same Müller who in an earlier work, his *Judaismus oder Judenthumb* (Hamburg, 1644) first reported the suicide, in 1640, of Uriel da Costa; see Salomon and Sassoon, 'Introduction', 23.

[7] Müller, *Atheismus Devictus*, preface and pp. 28–30, 35–9; Lassenius, *Besiegte Atheisterey*, 889–93.

[8] Müller, *Atheismus Devictus*, 30; Israel, 'Publishing of Forbidden Philosophical Works', (forthcoming).

that is, the *Bloemhof* (1668) of Adriaen Koerbagh, who employed the pseudonym 'Frederik Warmond' and which, he explains, denies Moses wrote the Pentateuch; and worst of all, the *Tractatus Theologico-Politicus*, written, he declares, by an 'ex-Jew, blasphemer and formal atheist' impudently declaring 'Hamburg' its place of publication though, like the rest, it was produced in Amsterdam. Its anonymous author deserved, he says, to be thrown with his book into the flames.[9] Keen to link whatever is corrupt and dangerous with the Jews, Müller predicted—not altogether mistakenly as it turned out—that one consequence of the new ferment in ideas would be that older Jewish texts such as Uriel da Costa's *Examen* and Isaac of Troki's *Chizzuk Emuna* (1593), refuting Christian interpretations of Scripture and traditionally shunned by Christians, would now be looked at afresh, gaining a new lease of life in German society.[10]

A practical reminder of the shattering impact of radical ideas on German culture was a sensational occurrence at Jena in 1674. Manuscript copies of three brief but unprecedentedly radical philosophical tracts were found strewn on the professors' pews of the main church.[11] These designated Scripture nothing but 'a Fable' full of obscurity and contradictions, proclaiming 'reason' 'another and much better Bible', insisting only 'Nature is truth'.[12] The existence of a providential God, Satan, Heaven, and Hell were all rejected: 'there is only one life after which there is neither reward nor punishment' (unicam esse vitam, post quam nec praemium nec poena).[13] Organized religion is declared an instrument to cheat and manipulate the people, and the secular authorities were denounced along with the town 'magistrates', whom 'we utterly despise'.[14] Marriage is pronounced meaningless and married intimacy no different from extramarital sex.[15] Sympathy is expressed for the 'poor working men and peasants' who were allegedly ruthlessly taken advantage of by magistrates and priests alike. The people are summoned to adopt a new creed, namely to believe nothing except what reason teaches and live according to a simple morality of conscience, living honestly and hurting no man.[16] A sect of Naturalists cultivating this universal natural faith reportedly already existed and had assumed the name *Conscientiarii*, or 'men of conscience'. According to the author of the tracts, his movement already boasted over 700 adherents in Jena alone and had followers not only in Paris, London,

---

[9] Müller, *Atheismus Devictus*, preface.

[10] Ibid.; extremely rare and long lost to modern scholars, a copy of Uriel da Costa's *Examen das tradicões phariseas* (Examination of Pharisaic Traditions), denying among other things the immortality of the soul, was found in Copenhagen, and the work has now been published in a modern edition (1993) edited by H. P. Salomon; on Isaac of Troki in the early Enlightenment, see Popkin, 'Image of the Jew', 22–4.

[11] Musaeus, *Ableinung*, 1–2; Grossmann, *Johann Christian Edelmann*, 120–1.

[12] Knutzen, 'Schriften', 38, 48, 53; Pfeiffer, *Thesaurus hermeneuticus*, 115; Veyssière, *Dissertation sur l'athéisme*, 402–15. Schröder, *Ursprünge*, 420–1.

[13] Knutzen, 'Schriften', 36–7; Musaeus, *Ableinung*, 2, 13; Pfeiffer, *Thesaurus hermeneuticus*, 115, 119–20.

[14] Knutzen, 'Schriften', 38; Wagner, *Johann Christian Edemanns verblendete Anblicke*, ii, 101–6, 216–20.

[15] Knutzen, 'Schriften', 54; Grossmann, *Johann Christian Edelmann*, 147.

[16] Knutzen, 'Schriften', 38, 72, 75; Buddeus, *Traité*, 95–6; Otto, *Studien*, 77–8; Wild, 'Freidenker', 93–5; Schröder, *Ursprünge*, 165, 420–1.

Amsterdam, and Hamburg, but as far afield as Koenigsberg, Copenhagen, Stockholm and even Rome.[17]

Stunned, the ducal government nominated a commission of inquiry. Little more was discovered, though, than had already been revealed in the tracts. Their author was Matthias Knutzen (1646–?), an organist's son from Holstein, who had frequented various universities before Jena, notably Koenigsberg and Copenhagen.[18] Studying theology, with a view to an ecclesiastical career, he had become estranged from the Lutheran Church, and then Christianity generally, owing to Scripture's discrepancies and a rebuff from the *General-Superintendent* of the Danish Church or 'Danish Pope' as he calls him. Expelled from Denmark, Knutzen had migrated to Jena. Though an expression of personal frustration and social resentment, his tracts were also clearly products of intensive scholarly endeavour.[19] Knutzen had read widely and been influenced by various forbidden books. He himself mentions in particular the writings of the sixteenth-century Dutch Spiritualist David Joris and La Peyrère's *Praeadamitae*.[20] There are also distinct echoes of Koerbagh's *Bloemhof* in his texts, though nothing else directly links him with Spinoza.[21] What worried the ducal court was the unambiguous evidence provided by his tracts that the new Bible criticism and radical philosophy could easily be welded to a sweeping revolutionary agenda.[22]

But in Jena, no less than Leipzig or Heidelberg,[23] no one doubted that the chief intellectual challenge, and the single most dangerous text, was the *Tractatus Theologico-Politicus*. One of the Jena professors appointed to investigate the Knutzen affair, and the author of an account of it, Johannes Musaeus (1613–81), in the same year, 1674, penned a 96-page rebuttal of the *Tractatus* dedicated to the Court of Brunswick, at Wolfenbüttel. Long judged one of the most acute of Spinoza's early adversaries,[24] Musaeus agreed with those who thought Germany was confronting a new and deadly peril, an insurrection of philosophical 'fanatics', sworn to enthrone *Naturalismus* in place of the sacred faith of Christ. Both community and State were gravely imperilled by the 'great siege engine of irreligious philosophy' introduced by the *Tractatus*, a form of sedition which attacks faith, undermines social stability, perverts law into licentiousness, and subverts the State by means of 'freedom of thought'.[25]

---

[17] Knutzen, 'Schriften', 37–8; Zedler, *Grosses Universal Lexicon*, xv, 1174.

[18] Buddeus, *Traité*, 95–6; Grossmann, *Johann Christian Edelmann*, 120.

[19] Knutzen, 'Schriften', 51, 72; Musaeus, *Ableinung*, 4–5, 11, 15–16; Trinius, *Freydenker-Lexicon*, 329–31; Schröder, *Ursprünge*, 396.

[20] Knutzen, 'Schriften', 50, 73–4.   [21] Schröder, 'Spinozam tota armenta', 159.

[22] La Veyssière, *Dissertation sur l'athéisme*, 400–16.

[23] Two south German Lutheran scholars who sounded the alarm in the mid-1670s were Gottlieb Spitzel at Augsburg, a correspondent of Leibniz, and the Altdorf professor Johann Christoph Sturm; according to Sturm, who blames Cartesianism for the intellectual crisis besetting Germany, the contagion attacking religion and authority originated in Holland and its single worst manifestation was the *TTP*; see Spitzel, *Felix Literatus*, 143–5; Sturm, *De Cartesianis*, 213–15.

[24] Colerus, *Vie de B. de Spinosa*, 139–41; Struve, *Bibliotheca Philosophica*, 118; Buddeus, *Lehr-Sätze*, 152; Walther, 'Machina Civilis', 194–201.

[25] Musaeus, *Tractatus*, preface; Rambach, *Christliche Sitten-Lehre*, 175.

Musaeus grants that the ranks of the incredulous, and varieties of irreligion, are many. But who, he asks, has wrought greater havoc in Church and State than this 'impostor', the anonymous *Theologico-Politicus*? His name, he declares, is 'Benedictus Spinosa, a Jew by nation' but in truth enemy to 'all religion'.[26] Quoting liberally from the reviled text—and in the process lending it added currency—Musaeus shows how Spinoza tries to undermine belief in the prophecies and 'supernatural happenings' of Scripture, accounting miracles mere *opera naturalia*, the causes of which eluded the unlettered minds of the ancient Israelites and others who witnessed them.[27] As for Spinoza's plea for unrestricted freedom of thought, nothing could be more disastrous, for it implies that Socinians and other anti-Trinitarians, and those believing no matter what, should all be tolerated.[28] Spinoza affirms the 'power of Nature to be the power of God itself', a thesis, observes Musaeus, not just theologically but also politically catastrophic. For the very basis of princely power, the upholding of religion and its sanction, the Church, was at stake.[29] The supreme function of government, declares Musaeus, is not, as Spinoza maintains, to enforce justice and deter wrongdoing, thereby inducing men to live peaceably with, and charitably towards, one another, but rather to inculcate reverence for religion, virtue, and authority and in that way uphold the social order.[30] The king of kings, he avers, installs princes to direct the State and defend the Church, for it is ecclesiastical authority which interprets what God decrees, partly through our reason and partly through Revelation, stipulating what is true and virtuous. It is no individual's right to decide for himself what truth is and how to lead his life. Nothing could be more disruptive of society and morality than Spinoza's 'libertas philosophandi'.

Nor did the torrent of denunciation of Spinoza diminish during the 1680s and 1690s. On the contrary, it intensified. A treatise deploring the growth of incredulity regarding demons, satanic power, and witchcraft, published at Wittenberg in 1694, vehemently denounced the philosophical premises of the new *Naturalisten*. Its author, Nathanael Falck, located the origins of the 'new atheism' in the Italian 'atheists' of the Renaissance, particularly Vanini, and Bodin (despite Bodin's firm belief in witchcraft).[31] Their blasphemous teaching, he held, began the 'confounding' of God with the 'order of secondary causes' of nature which, in more recent times, Hobbes and Spinoza developed and amplified. But it was especially the latter, he insists, citing passages from the *Ethics*, who supplied arguments enabling Germany's Naturalists to advance a seemingly rational scheme for 'confounding' God with Nature.[32] Fundamental to this malignant Naturalism, he holds, are Spinoza's 'monstrous opinions' concerning Satan, demons, and the supernatural, and his perverse denial of the existence of spirits, ghosts, spectres, and apparitions.[33] The damage is incalculable, he affirms, for it was from Spinoza that Bekker learnt his ruinous ideas about satanic and demonic power, while, in turn, it was Bekker who was chiefly responsible in Germany

---

[26] Musaeus, *Tractatus*, 1–2. [27] Ibid., 2–4, 54–5. [28] Ibid., 5–6.

[29] Ibid., 21–7, 84–92; Colerus, *Vie de B. de Spinosa*, 140.

[30] Musaeus, *Tractatus*, 87; Walther, 'Machina civilis', 197–8. [31] Falck, *De Daemonologia*, 2–5.

[32] Ibid., 5–6. [33] Ibid., 58–9.

for propagating the now increasingly fashionable scepticism about Satan and witchcraft.[34]

The first attempts to compile a more comprehensive record of the rise of radical ideas in Early Enlightenment Germany appeared in the opening decade of the new century. In his *Systema novissarum controversarium* (1709), the Rostock professor Zacharius Grapius (1671–1713), deplores the crumbling of belief in Providence, Creation, miracles, Christ's divinity, and the Resurrrection, as well as Satan and Original Sin, seeing the disaster as a cumulative process in which Spinoza primarily, but secondarily also Hobbes, Wittichius, Burman, Bayle, La Peyrère, Limborch, Kuyper, Van Dale, Bekker, Beverland, and Toland had all contributed.[35] Since Spinoza's death, his teachings had been broadcast especially by Stosch, Wachter, and Leenhof,[36] while, at the same time, in Germany, Van Dale and Bekker were the publicists primarily responsible for ruining the people's belief in the Devil's power, demons, magic, and witchcraft.[37] Even more insistent on Spinoza's centrality in the rise of modern incredulity was the prominent Dresden scholar and bibliophile, Valentin Ernst Loescher. Loescher was well-placed to investigate and assess the intellectual origins of the phenomenon which so troubled him, possessing as he did a library of over 30,000 titles.[38] In his *Praenotiones Theologicae* (Wittenberg, 1708) subsequently re-issued four times down to 1752, he declares war on the entire host of Naturalists, atheists, deists, Spinozists, 'anti-Scriptuarii', and 'indifferentistas' infesting Germany. Those who had chiefly shaped the new incredulity, he says, were Vanini, Bayle, Spinoza, Lahontan, Stosch, Locke, Toland, Velthuysen, Wolzogen, Van Dale, Bekker, Hobbes, Herbert of Cherbury, and Wachter.[39] But if the list was long, Spinoza is singled out as playing a surpassing role, having a significance in this process which no other thinker, not even Hobbes or Bayle, could match.

Spinoza's unique responsibility derived, in Loescher's eyes, partly from his formative influence on more recent subversives, such as the Berliner Friedrich Wilhelm Stosch, whom he calls a 'discipulus' of Spinoza, Bekker, who, he says, follows Spinoza in making philosophy the sole judge of Scripture, and Lahontan, whose *Nouveaux Voyages* (1702) were widely influential in Germany and unashamedly Spinozist.[40] But, beyond this, Loescher judges Spinoza uniquely harmful and disruptive because he alone among modern writers provides an ostensibly coherent, philosophical framework for amalgamating body and soul and identifying matter with spirit, daring to call Nature 'God', thereby assembling in an integrated system elements found in the rest only incoherently and fragmentarily.[41] Interestingly, Loescher carefully distinguishes between 'Pantheism' which he accounts a form of religious 'fanaticism' which does not rule out divine Providence, or a divine being in some sense distinct from the

---

[34] Ibid., 73–6.   [35] Grapius, *Systema*, ii, 14, 34–9, 56–63.
[36] Ibid., ii, 52–5.   [37] Ibid., ii, 64–9.
[38] Raabe, 'Gelehrtenbibliotheken', 113; Jöcher, *Allgemeines Gelehrten Lexicon*, ii, 1497–9.
[39] Loescher, *Praenotiones*, 58, 146, 151, 217–18, 220.   [40] Ibid., 26–36, 48–54, 146–50, 182, 211, 224–30.
[41] Ibid., 222; Philipps, *Dissertatio*, 132.

universe, and Spinoza's identification of God and the universe, which is a strictly philosophical position and inherently 'atheistic'.[42]

However, the fullest German account of the advent of radical thought was compiled by the great Jena scholar, and opponent of the Leibnizian–Wolffian system, Johann Franz Budde, or Buddeus (1667–1729). Buddeus' *De Atheismo et Superstitione* (Jena, 1717), published several times in Latin and 'widely read' in France as well as Germany,[43] and eventually issued also in German (Jena, 1723) and later French, under the title *Traité de l'athéisme et de la superstition* (Amsterdam, 1740), is imposing in both analysis and scope. Massively erudite, Buddeus' historical approach, also sketched out in several of his earlier writings, in turn pervaded various other interpretations of the rise of irreligious philosophy in early eighteenth-century Europe, such as Giambattista Capasso's history of philosophy, dedicated to the Portuguese king and published at Naples in 1728.[44] Buddeus too considers the intellectual situation in Germany and all Europe to be critical, the old *philosophia recepta*, scholastic Aristotelianism, having now largely disintegrated, at least in Protestant lands, while it was proving excruciatingly difficult to devise a generally acceptable and stable new consensus reconciling religion with the New Philosophy and science which, at the same time, adequately protected authority, tradition, and the primacy of theology. Consequently, atheism, deism, Naturalism, 'fatalism', and 'materialism' were everywhere rampant, not least in Germany's Courts, academic life, and professional élites.

Spinoza, afffirms Buddeus, 'est estimé avec raison le chef et le maître des athées de notre siècle'; he unequivocally places him centre-stage, styling him Christendom's chief enemy.[45] This is because only Spinoza, unlike Hobbes and the many others driving the pernicious intellectual tendencies undermining authority and religion, deploys philosophy in an ostensibly systematic manner to deny Providence, miracles, Christ's divinity, the Resurrection, and other fundamental 'mysteries'.[46] Where Buddeus, influenced here by Bayle, goes beyond Loescher and Grapius is in historically connecting the various trends and atheistic thinkers, demonstrating Spinoza's role as the prime integrating force in the evolution of modern philosophical incredulity. Spinoza, for Buddeus, is not just an individual thinker but the universal and timeless link, the crucial intellectual intersection, embodying, relating, and linking ancient Greek materialism, Chinese Confucianism, the anti-Christian strand of Italian Renaissance thought, Bayle's noxious Pyrrhonism, and modern Naturalism, welding them all into one gigantic engine of impiety, profanity, and insurrection.[47]

Buddeus acknowledges that Spinoza had been more often, insistently, and comprehensively refuted than any other modern thinker. Even the most rudimentary list of his adversaries must include, he says, Musaeus, Mansvelt, Velthuysen, Blyenbergh,

---

[42] Otto, *Studien*, 122.   [43] Kors, *Atheism in France*, i, 46.

[44] Capasso, *Historiae Philosophiae Synopsis*, 342–3, 396–7.

[45] Buddeus, *Traité*, 78–9; or also 'atheorum princeps', Buddeus, *De Atheismo*, 120–1, 447; Buddeus, *Lehr-Sätze*, 144; Philipps likewise calls Spinoza 'princeps atheorum'; see Philipps, *Dissertatio*, 128.

[46] Buddeus, *De Atheismo*, 214, 218–22; Walch, *Philosophisches Lexicon*, 2411–13.

[47] Buddeus, *Traité*, pp. vi, 27–32, 108, 112, 128; Walther, 'Spinozissimus', 196.

Kuyper, Bredenburg, Van Til, Wittichius, Jaquelot, Bayle, Jensius, Petrus van Mas-tricht, Aubert de Versé, Melchior Leydekker, Henry More, Colerus, La Mothe, Jenichen, Rappolt, Huet, Le Vassor, Lamy, Yvonne, Poiret, Jacob Thomasius, and Christian Thomasius; but besides these principal combatants there were innumerable others.[48] Yet, despite their efforts, not only were Spinoza's ideas percolating every-where, but society was increasingly infested by an underground intellectual move-ment of both declared and undeclared adherents of Spinozism. If Koerbagh, Cuffeler, and Leenhof were the three most impudent, more or less undisguised agents of Spinozism in European letters,[49] a still greater menace was posed by such insidious writers as Bayle and Geulincx, who hypocritically claim to be loyal Christians, pretending to fight atheism, but in fact subtly advocate irreligion and Spinozism.[50] Like all the German commentators, Buddeus sees Bekker as the most potent voice undermining belief in spirits, ghosts, angels, witchcraft, and Satan, and believes that, by doing so, Bekker too is opening the flood-gates to Spinozism.[51]

It might be objected that the prominence given by Buddeus, Loescher, and Grapius, not only to Spinoza but to Bekker, Van Dale, Koerbagh, Cuffeler, and Dutch influ-ences more generally, in generating the radical Enlightenment in Germany is scarcely reflected in modern German historiography, which often strongly asserts the influ-ence of English ideas in the early eighteenth century. This is true but, like many deeply rooted historiographical *idées fixes*, seems to be based more on a tradition of later cultural preferences than solid contemporary evidence. The frequent insistence on British influence claimed in nineteenth- and twentieth-century German books can doubtless mainly be explained by the enormous impact of the *Anglophilie* which con-quered German culture, as it did all Europe, in the 1730s and 1740s, reinforced perhaps by the feeling that it is more fitting for a great and powerful nation to have been deci-sively influenced at such a crucial juncture by another great and powerful nation rather than a traditionally disdained (being republican and Calvinist) as well as small, neighbouring country such as the Netherlands.

In any case, examination of early eighteenth-century academic disputations dealing with the upsurge of deism and incredulity leaves little room for doubt that the German academic consciousness of the Early Enlightenment overwhelmingly reflected the same emphases that we see in Buddeus, Loescher, and Grapius. Before 1720 English deists were rarely debated in German academic treatises and disputa-tions, and the chief concern was predominantly if not invariably with the Spinozist origins of radical thought. Besides several set-piece disputations against Spinoza and Spinozism at Wittenberg and Jena, such encounters occurred, among other places, at Marburg (1696), Greifswald (1707), Koenigsberg (1707), Rostock (1709), and Tübingen (1710),[52] the last presided over by Johann Wolfgang Jaeger (1647–1720), Lutheran *General-Superintendens* of Württemberg and chancellor of Tübingen

---

[48] Buddeus, *Lehr-Sätze*, 152–3; Buddeus, *De Atheismo*, 125–6; Capasso, *Historiae Philosophiae Synopsis*, 397.
[49] Buddeus, *Traité*, 84–6.   [50] Ibid., 36, 72–7, 116, 132–3, 173, 236–7.
[51] Ibid., 135–9, 277; Buddeus, *Compendium Historiae Philosophicae*, 487–9.
[52] Otto, *Studien*, 28; Walther, 'Spinozissimus', 196.

University. Nothing is worse, he held, than the 'plague' of atheism 'which overthrows all divine and human things' and no other 'architect' of incredulity had gone so far in systematizing atheism, or had been so widely influential, as Spinoza. Jaeger depicts *Spinocismus* as the ultimate distillation of all that most fatally threatens Christian society.[53] Accounting the *Tractatus Theologico-Politicus* 'famosissimus', Tübingen's chancellor identifies as its core contention the view that 'God cannot act against the Laws of Nature, because he cannot act against His own nature'.[54] Hence, argues Spinoza, there never have been, and never could be, any miracles, Biblical prophecy arises from overactive imaginations, and theology is not the path to truth but useful only to instil 'piety'.[55] Philosophy is proclaimed the sole path to 'truth' and 'salvation' and there is accordingly an overriding need for 'libertas philosophandi' (liberty to philosophize).[56]

Spinoza's philosophy was generally reviled, but also perceived to have spread widely in Courts, universities, and among the scholarly; and what was equally frightening, Paul Theodor Carpow noted in 1740, was that it also attracted some of the unlearned.[57] Furthermore, beginning with Gottfried Arnold[58] who published his 'impartial' ecclesiastical and 'heresy' history in 1700, there was a tendency in some quarters, to adopt a less stridently hostile, more respectful, and 'nuanced' approach to Spinoza, which had the effect of encouraging many people to read and seek to come to grips with his writings.[59] Admittedly, as the Early Enlightenment unfolded, new influences appeared on the German scene and, from the late 1720s, British deism increasingly became an active force in German culture. By the 1740s, moreover, the impact of French *philosophes* such as Voltaire, La Mettrie, and Diderot began to be felt. Nevertheless, not only is it impossible, as we have seen, to overlook the ties between these new waves of radical thought and the original 'Dutch' wave, but preoccupation with the earlier sources of radical thought remained, and even as late as the 1750s, it was entirely normal in Germany and the Baltic to insist, as a Greifswald professor expressed it in 1752, that in the contemporary world 'Spinoza atheorum facile princeps' (Spinoza is by far the chief of atheists).[60]

[53] Jaeger, *Spinocismus*, preface, p. A2.   [54] Ibid., 7–11.   [55] Ibid., 10, 14–15.

[56] Ibid., 15; several key propositions from the *Ethics* were also disputed and note taken of Spinoza's political ideas; ibid., 18–19, 27–9; the refutations of Spinoza recommended by Jaeger are 'Kortholtus, Museaus, Buddeus, Wittichius, Henry More, Velthuysen, Mansfelt, Jaquelot, Poiret, Abbadie, Yvonne, Aubert de Versé, Le Vassor, Blyenbergh, Bredenburg and Kuyper'; ibid., 32.

[57] Carpow, *Animadversiones*, 37–9.

[58] Gottfried Arnold (1666–1714) was a leading liberal Lutheran theologian won over to Pietism by Spener at Dresden in 1689. Briefly he was a professor of history at Giessen University but, repelled by the rigid theology he encountered there, resigned his chair in 1698. As an opponent of Lutheran orthodoxy he was especially eager to downgrade the importance of confessional conformity. His *Unpartheyische Kirchen- und Ketzer-Historie* (2 vols., 1699–1700) outraged most Lutheran clergy by severely questioning the concept of orthodoxy and 'heresy' and vindicating the Christian validity in large part of a wide variety of 'heretics', including Spinoza. His comparatively positive assessment of Spinoza has long been acknowledged to be a turning-point in Spinoza's reception in Germany; Jöcher, *Allgemeines Gelehrten Lexicon*, i, 560–2; Hazard, *European Mind*, 472–3; Walther, 'Machina civilis', 213–14.

[59] Otto, *Studien*, 115, 129–31; Walther, 'Spinozissimus', 197–8.

[60] Herslov, *De Vera Notione Miraculi*, 9.

ii. Ehrenfried Walther von Tschirnhaus (1651–1708)

Though no other German thinker before the rise of Wolffianism enjoyed the stature of Leibniz, nevertheless Tschirnhaus, together with Christian Thomasius and, a little later, Buddeus, figures among the major founding thinkers of the German Enlightenment. He was also, to a greater extent than any other prominent German intellectual celebrity of the day, intimately connected with intellectual, and especially radical intellectual, circles in Holland.

Tschirnhaus arrived in the Netherlands in 1668, as a 17-year-old, eager to study law and medicine at Leiden. He stayed seven years and while, subsequently, his visits to London, Paris, and then Italy (in the years 1676–9), also left their imprint, the Netherlands apparently remained his true intellectual and spiritual home. After leaving Holland he met Boyle and Oldenburg in London, and then Malebranche, Gallois, Borelli, and other French and Italian savants. But it was his friendship with Spinoza, acquaintance with Christian Huygens, and his links with Spinoza's circle in Amsterdam and The Hague which evidently formed his most fruitful and enduring foreign connections. The friendships cemented in Holland during his first long stay he renewed periodically over the years, returning for short periods, mainly to Amsterdam, in 1679, 1682, 1685, and 1701.

Introduced to Spinoza through Van Gent and Schuller in the autumn of 1674, Tschirnhaus quickly won his trust and, early in 1675, the young savant was assigned a manuscript copy of the *Ethics*.[61] The discussions between Tschirnhaus and Spinoza on free will, human motivation, Descartes' laws of motion, and other questions were clearly among the most stimulating of the last phase of Spinoza's life.[62] The powerful effect of these on Tschirnhaus is plainly apparent from his conduct during his subsequent travels. Crossing to England in May 1675, he spent the summer in London conferring with Fellows of the Royal Society and becoming known in England, in particular, as a 'great algebraist'.[63] At the same time he remained in contact with his Dutch friends, by corresponding with Schuller in Amsterdam, through whom he forwarded several more penetrating questions to Spinoza, notably about his doctrine of attributes. He also broached Spinoza and his philosophy, his letters show, with Oldenburg and Boyle who, he reported back to Holland, 'had formed a strange conception of [Spinoza's] person' which he was confident he had corrected, substituting instead 'reasons which induced them not only to consider you again in a most worthy and favourable manner, but also to value your *Tractatus Theologico-Politicus*'.[64] In reality both Oldenburg, formerly friendly but now cool towards Spinoza, and Boyle, who loathed his ideas, were appalled by the *Tractatus*. But the aristocratic Tschirnhaus was apparently so insistent in defending Spinoza that even Boyle felt obliged to humour

---

[61] Wurtz, 'Tschirnhaus', 62.
[62] Spinoza, *Letters*, 280–9, 301–2, 351–6; Klever, *Mannen rond Spinoza*, 210–12.
[63] Oldenburg, *Correspondence*, xi, 324 and xiii, 14.
[64] Spinoza, *Letters*, 297; Pätzold, 'ist Tschirnhaus' *Medicina Mentis?*', 340.

him somewhat on this point. The young noble savant, in other words, remained sufficiently loyal to Spinoza to risk prejudicing his own reputation in the Republic of Letters.

In Paris he again stayed in touch through Schuller. Becoming acquainted with Huygens, as Spinoza and Schuller had urged, he assured him of Spinoza's high esteem for his scientific endeavours. 'This greatly pleased him,' Schuller reported to Spinoza, 'and [Huygens] replied that he likewise respects you greatly and had lately received from you the *Tractatus Theologico-Politicus*.'[65] Tschirnhaus, this and other evidence indicates, discussed Spinoza with prominent men in Paris, just as he had in London and doubtless continued to do after leaving Paris in November 1676, and embarking on his Italian journey. In Rome and Florence he met such leading scholars as Steno and Magliabecchi, who had already engaged profoundly with Spinoza's thought and needed no reminding of its potentially wide impact. Magliabecchi had had a letter from Graevius in Utrecht in July 1675, reporting rumours that a new book by Spinoza, on 'God and the mind' was pending and that, in the Netherlands, unfortunately, 'many young men had become imbued with his pestilential views', news Magliabecchi promptly passed on to others.[66] Doubtless Tschirnhaus was one of those Graevius and Magliabecchi had in mind, and it is clear that Steno bent every effort to coax Tschirnhaus, as he had others, out of his veneration for mechanistic philosophy in general, and Spinoza in particular, and embrace Catholicism. Tschirnhaus, though impressed with the power of his personality, was not attracted to Steno's arguments.

Returning to Holland in 1679, Tschirnhaus revived his ties with Spinoza's friends. On subsequent visits to Amsterdam, in 1682 and 1685, he was occupied in preparing for the press his chief work, the *Medicina Mentis et Corporis*, which he had begun in Italy. Although he planned to publish it initially in both Latin and Dutch, and spoke as well as read these languages, he had written the work in German and lacked proficiency in writing Latin. For help he turned to Pieter van Gent, one of his Amsterdam friends, a mathematician who had known Spinoza, and had been one of the editorial team which prepared the *Opera Posthuma* for the press. He was an accomplished Latinist who was also a convinced Spinozist.[67] The book was published in Latin at Amsterdam by Jan Rieuwertsz the Younger in 1686, with Tschirnhaus' name indicated only by initials after the dedication. A Dutch version was prepared by another friend, Ameldonk Block and brought out again by the younger Rieuwertsz the following year.[68] The German version, under the title *Die Curiöse Medecin*, appeared at Leipzig in 1688, and again at Lüneburg in 1708. Further Latin editions appeared in 1695 and 1733.

Although Tschirnhaus was not uninfluenced by Huygens and Boyle, he presents himself in his *Medicina Mentis* as a passionate follower of the 'incomparable'

---

[65] Spinoza, *Letters*, 325.   [66] Quoted in Totaro, 'Niels Stensen', 168.

[67] Winter, 'Der Bahnbrecher', 17, 23; Klever, *Mannen rond Spinoza*, 165–6; Steenbakkers, *Spinoza's Ethica*, 35–40; Schröder, *Spinoza*, 24–5.

[68] Under the title *Geneesmiddel der Ziele*; Winter, 'Der Bahnbrecher', 56–7; Steenbakkers, *Spinoza's Ethica*, 36.

Descartes, whom he praises lavishly.[69] Sometimes Tschirnhaus' claim to be a Cartesian is taken by modern historians of philosophy largely at face value.[70] But if he apparently defends freedom of the will, and rejects the doctrine of one substance, neither stance can be deemed entirely sincere. It is clear that from the time of his first letter to Spinoza, Tschirnhaus had diverged from him somewhat on the first point, claiming that 'both he who argues for [free will] and he who argues against seem to me to speak the truth, according to how one conceives freedom'.[71] He nevertheless expressly states in that letter that 'I agree with you [i.e. Spinoza] that in all things we are determined to something by a definite cause, and that thus we have no free will,' yet in his book, presumably out of prudence, he expresses the point essentially in accordance with Descartes' formulation.[72]

Furthermore, on other questions Tschirnhaus criticizes, or diverges from, Descartes and here it is often manifest that he is in effect advancing Spinoza's position. Thus, his theory of knowledge echoes Spinoza's contention that 'as the light makes both itself and the darkness plain, so truth is the standard both of itself and what is false,' meaning that what is mathematically correct, or geometrically symmetrical must be true, and what is a *non sequitur* in terms of mathematical logic must be false.[73] Likewise, Tschirnhaus' ethical theory parallels Spinoza's. For Tschirnhaus, as for Spinoza, philosophy is more than just a quest for knowledge and wisdom; it is a path above all to serenity and self-liberation, what Spinoza termed 'salvation'.[74] Moreover, Tschirnhaus' concept of 'good' and 'bad' exactly parallels Spinoza's contention in his *Ethics* IV, Proposition XVIII, that 'good' is what conserves and enhances my being and 'bad' is what, on the contrary, damages or reduces my being, so that virtue is then defined as the power in man to conserve his being according to the dictates of reason or, as Tschirnhaus expresses this, 'virtus est potentia in homine ex legibus sanae rationis suam naturam conservandi' (virtue is the power in man to conserve his nature according to the laws of right reason).[75] Living virtuously, which derives from living according to reason, and mastering the passions, generates a joy which Tschirnhaus, like Spinoza, considers 'much greater' than that afforded by 'sensual pleasures'.[76] Tschirnhaus defines ethics in typically Spinozist style as pursuit of the health of the mind in parallel to that of health of the body. Finally, Tschirnhaus unambiguously rejects Descartes' notion of motion, contending, like Spinoza and later Toland, that motion is innate in matter.[77]

When his book appeared, Tschirnhaus was living quietly on his family estate of Kieslingswalde in Oberlausitz (Upper Lusatia), near Görlitz, in eastern Saxony,

---

[69] [Tschirnhaus], *Medicina Mentis*, 50–1.   [70] Verweyen, *Ehrenfried Walther von Tschirnhaus*, 123–4.
[71] Spinoza, *Letters*, 281.   [72] Ibid.; Wurtz, 'L'éthique', 233.
[73] [Tschirnhaus], *Medicina mentis*, 47; *Collected Works of Spinoza*, 1, 479; Verweyen, *Tschirnhaus*, 60, 123; Winter, 'Der Bahnbrecher', 96; Wurtz, 'Théorie de la connaissance', 123–6.
[74] Wurtz, 'Théorie de la connaissance', 135–6; Wurtz, 'L'Éthique', 232–4.
[75] [Tschirnhaus], *Medicina Mentis*, 52; Pätzold, 'ist Tschirnhaus' *Medicina Mentis*?', 358.
[76] 'Est autem delectatia haec multa major delectationibus sensualibus'; ibid., 6.
[77] Klever, *Mannen rond Spinoza*, 175–6.

enjoying a growing reputation locally and throughout Germany as a mathematician, a regular contributor to the *Acta Eruditorum*, and an expert in chemical processes and experiments with furnaces, mirrors, and lenses. However, his tranquillity was soon rudely shattered. In 1688 Christian Thomasius launched his groundbreaking new journal in German, the *Monatgespräche*, using it to familiarize the non-Latin-reading public with recent developments in the world of learning. In this connection, and in part to deflect conservative disapproval from himself and his projects,[78] in the March issue he vehemently denounced the growing Spinozist presence in German culture, introducing for the first time the term 'Spinozismus' into the German language. The first target of his campaign was the *Medicina Mentis*, which he firmly attributed to Tschirnhaus and declares a vehicle of disguised Spinozism and materialism, masquerading as a Cartesian and Christian work. In particular, Thomasius unhesitatingly classifies Tschirnhaus' epistemological and ethical theories, and his conception of 'God', as Spinozist,[79] and draws attention to the letters to and from Tschirnhaus in Spinoza's *Opera Posthuma*, revealing him to have been a friend of Spinoza.

For a prominent Saxon noble to be publicly labelled a Spinozist, Epicurean, and materialist was as injurious as it was for anyone else. Tschirnhaus had little choice but to counterattack energetically, writing a robust defence which he then circulated in manuscript among key contributors to the *Acta Eruditorum*. He did not deny having been influenced in some points by 'that philosopher', but insisted that the crucial question was whether he had adopted anything incompatible with revealed religion, lambasting his assailant as an 'author obscurisissimus et confusissimus' driven to propagate calumny by sheer malice.[80] Having obtained a copy, Thomasius promptly published the text in his journal and retaliated by repeating his allegations.[81] The parallels with Spinoza's ethical and epistemological theories were, in fact, incontestable. But in this battle much depended on whether Thomasius could substantiate his charge regarding Tschirnhaus' conception of God. Tschirnhaus had scrupulously avoided espousing Spinoza's doctrine of substance and the identification of God with Nature in his book. But there were grounds for doubting the sincerity of his disavowal and inferring (as he himself practically admitted to Leibniz in a letter of April 1677) that in reality he accepted Spinoza's assimilation of God into a single substance embracing all reality.[82]

Tschirnhaus' social status and high standing at the Saxon Court, in Dresden, helped rescue him from a potentially ugly situation. The public quarrel displeased the electoral authorities and, before long, Thomasius was ordered to cease his attacks on his enemy and apologize. This he could not avoid, and some tepid words of

---

[78] Winter, 'Der Bahnbrecher', 29–30; Walther, 'Spinozissimus', 194.

[79] Thomasius, *Monatsgespräche* 1688, i, 354–62, 386–442; Wurtz, 'Tschirnhaus', 61; Wollgast, 'Spinoza', 168–9; Klever, *Mannen rond Spinoza*, 167–8.

[80] Thomasius, *Monatsgespräche* 1688, i, 779–80; Verweyen, *Ehrenfried Walther von Tschirnhaus*, 125; Winter, 'Der Bahnbrecher', 30; Otto, *Studien*, 84–6.

[81] Wurtz, 'Tschirnhaus. 63; Wollgast, 'Spinoza', 170.   [82] Wurtz, 'Tschirnhaus', 235.

reconciliation duly appeared in the *Monatgespräche* in January 1689. But relations between the two *érudits* had been irredeemably ruptured, and the charge of 'Spinozism' continued to cast a shadow over the rest of Tschirnhaus' life and career. No doubt the clash with Thomasius rendered him more cautious than he had been previously. Nevertheless, it seems clear that he continued, in his last years, to revere Spinoza and defended both his legacy and his memory, as he had done ever since 1674. A poignant experience in the early development of Christian Wolff was a long meeting with Tschirnhaus in 1705. Wolff later recalled that, when they discussed Spinoza, Tschirnhaus maintained that Spinoza had not in fact equated God with Nature in the way most people supposed and had in reality defended God more cogently than Descartes.[83]

iii. Friedrich Wilhelm Stosch (1648–1704)

A slightly older man than Tschirnhaus, but one considerably tardier in entering the public sphere, was Friedrich Wilhelm Stosch, author of the foremost Naturalistic clandestine publication produced in Germany before 1700, and the first to use expressly Spinozistic terms and concepts positively.[84] A son of the Berlin Court preacher Bartholomeus Stosch—a figure noted for his advocacy of toleration and especially reconciliation between Calvinists and Lutherans (and suspected by some of Socinian sympathies),[85] Stosch was raised in a liberal Calvinist and Court milieu. After studying at Frankfurt an der Oder, he embarked on a study tour abroad in the United Provinces, France, and Italy. Subsequently he entered the service of the Great Elector as a Court secretary in Berlin, but abandoned his career, owing to poor health, after only a decade, in 1686, henceforth devoting himself to scholarship. Besides his considerable erudition and competence in Latin, the only other relevant detail known about his life prior to the uproar which erupted in 1692 are his links with Socinian circles, and especially the anti-Trinitarian writer Johann Preuss.[86]

His solitary book, the *Concordia Rationis et Fidei*, appeared clandestinely in 1692, with 'Amsterdam' on the title-page, but was later found, from its typography, to have been printed in fact, like several Socinian writings, in the Brandenburg town of Guben an der Neisse, near Frankfurt an der Oder.[87] Although, both then and later, there have been attempts to classify him as a basically Socinian and indigenous product, Stosch's radicalism is essentially philosophical and non-local. Referring to the *Ethics* as well as the *Tractatus Theologico-Politicus*, Stosch firmly identifies God with Nature, maintaining that 'Deus est unica et sola substantia' (God is the one and only substance).[88] He never relies on the Bible and categorically rejects the immortality of the soul—points which clearly distinguish him from the Socinians. He rejects Descartes' duality of

---

[83] Wurtz, 'L'Éthique', 235, 237.   [84] Walther, 'Machina Civilis', 210.

[85] Ibid.; Schröder, *Spinoza*, 32.   [86] Ibid.

[87] Mylius, *Bibliotheca*, 205; Küster, *Marchiae Litteratae Specimen*, 4; Schröder, 'Einleitung' (1992), 9.

[88] Stosch, *Concordia*, 35–6, 81; Grapius, *Systema*, i, 52; Loescher, *Praenotiones*, 147; Hazard, *European Mind*, 176; Schröder, *Ursprünge*, 333, 467.

'mind' and 'extension' as 'absurd and useless' and denies that the soul is separable from the body.[89]

Citing Bekker and Geulincx, he proclaims the Devil nothing other than life-diminishing or harmful conduct while, like Spinoza (and the unmentioned Tschirn-haus) he proclaims 'good' and 'bad' purely relative terms designating what is life-enhancing and conserving: 'nihil enim absolute et per se bonum vel malum est, sed respective quatenus res alteri utilis vel noxia est' (nothing is absolutely good or bad in itself, but only respectively in so far as it is useful or damaging to another thing).[90] Angels and demons are figments of the imagination.[91] Equally abhorrent to contemporary opinion, Stosch repudiates the concepts of Hell and divine retribution for wrongdoing. Truths drawn from reason, the 'light of nature', and Revelation 'can never contradict each other', he maintains, adding that since Revelation is frequently obscure, it has to be interpreted in the light of reason, referring the reader to Spinoza, Le Clerc, Malebranche, La Peyrère, and Hobbes.[92] Adam was not the first man, he affirms, echoing La Peyrère, while the 'history of the Creation as told in the Book of Genesis is full of obscurity and contradictions'.[93]

It has recently been argued, once again, that the fact that Stosch knows and cites Spinoza does not mean his inspiration and motivation were not basically Socinian and local.[94] Yet aside from one or two phrases, the tone of Stosch's writing is predominantly non-theological and plainly his approach to Scripture, the soul, and the role of Christ clashes with any authentically Socinian view. Admittedly, Stosch denies outright the divinity of Christ and the doctrine of the Trinity, claiming he was just a man like any other; and, in itself this could be a Socinian stance. But he also asserts that Christ taught nothing that does not conform to the dictates of natural reason because this 'prophet' wanted men 'by means of laws to be just and happy', offering as authority for this Jarig Jelles' preface to Spinoza's *Opera Posthuma*, surely evidence here of Spinozism not Socinianism.[95] Philosophy not theology reveals the path to 'salvation', proclaims Stosch, and the 'goal of philosophy is a life of happiness' (finis philosophiae est vita beata), a strikingly Spinozistic sentiment when linked to Stosch's contention that the human soul 'begins and ends, and grows and declines, together with the body'.[96] His conception of the human body is strictly mechanistic and shaped chiefly by the views of the Dutch-German Cartesian Theodore Craanen.[97] The virtuous man, for Stosch, is one who is 'led by reason'; the sinful life is that which is swayed by the passions 'without reason or contrary to reason', sin being in essence 'ignorance' about God, society, and natural things.[98]

---

[89] Stosch, *Concordia*, 77–8, 82–3, 117; Schröder, *Ursprünge*, 288.   [90] Stosch, *Concordia*, 7–8, 38, 41.

[91] 'Quae de angelis et daemonibus tam in S. Scriptura quam historia humana traduntur, sunt partim somnia, partim visiones, sive apparitiones, partim phantasmata, partim morbi, partim figmenta et illusiones'; ibid., 8.

[92] Ibid., 97–8.   [93] Ibid., 104–5.

[94] Schröder, *Spinoza*, 35–7, 41–3; Wollgast, 'Spinoza', 171–2; Schröder, *Ursprünge*, 465–7.

[95] Stosch, *Concordia*, 110–11.   [96] Ibid., 83–4.   [97] Ibid., 64–5.

[98] 'virtus in genere, est Dei, Sui, Societatis, et rerum naturalium cognitio tanta quantam quisque assequi potest, et cultus divinus, cultura sui, et custodia societatis'; ibid., 39–41.

This incisive 156-page text was printed in only 100 copies and, according to his subsequent testimony, never intended for general circulation or sale.[99] Nevertheless, against Stosch's wishes, copies surfaced in the bookshops of Frankfurt an der Oder late in 1693, provoking an immediate outcry.[100] The electoral Court reacted vigorously, seizing the copies and launching an official inquiry which ramified from the Oder towns to Amsterdam. It was soon realized, though, that the publication originated not in Holland but Brandenburg.[101] The printer was caught; Stosch was traced, arrested, and imprisoned. On 9 January 1694 the book was condemned in the Elector's name from all church pulpits in Berlin and the immediate surrender of copies already in circulation decreed under threat of severe penalties.[102] Most copies were apparently seized, or handed in, and subsequently burnt.[103]

With Stosch incarcerated, the Elector nominated a mixed commission of Calvinist and Lutheran jurists and theologians, including Samuel Pufendorf and Philipp Jacob Spener, to examine the affair.[104] The prisoner's testimony was recorded, together with extensive other evidence, including a detailed refutation furnished by the Frankfurt an der Oder theology faculty. Both the investigating tribunal and the faculty chiefly targeted Stosch's alleged theological errors, with an eye to linking him with the undercurrent of suppressed Socinian influence evident in Brandenburg. It is true that no attempt was made to associate Stosch with Spinozism or any other philosophical stream.[105] The defendant was accused of six heretical doctrines: the first five being his denials of Christ's divinity and the Trinity, the divine authorship of Scripture, the Last Judgement and Hell, and the existence of angels and demons, as well as Original Sin; the sixth stemmed from his identifying God with Nature.[106]

The official trial records are primarily concerned with theological heresies and make scant reference to philosophy, despite the fact that Pufendorf and other members of the tribunal were unquestionably already familiar then with Spinoza's thought. Similarly, Stosch's formal retraction of his heterodox views, published in Berlin on 17 March 1694, refers only to theological offences.[107] These facts have been adduced to support the argument that Spinozism as such was not perceived to be a major problem in northern Germany at the time.[108] But, arguably, this rigidly theological approach was adopted not because the electoral authorities were untroubled by new trends in philosophy—on the contrary, such a conclusion would fly in the face of much contextual evidence—but because tried and tested legal and ecclesiastical procedures for suppressing Socinianism were readily at hand, and it was easier and

---

[99] *Acta Stoschiana*, 640, 664.
[100] Reimann, *Historia*, 512; Schröder, *Spinoza*, 34–5; Schröder, 'Einleitung' (1992), 10.
[101] Küster, *Marchiae Litteratae Specimen*, 319.   [102] [Tentzel], *Monatliche Unterredungen* 1694, 355.
[103] Wild, 'Freidenker', 96; Schröder, *Spinoza*, 34.
[104] *Acta Stoschiana*, 245–54; [Tentzel], *Monatliche Unterredungen* 1694, 356.
[105] Schröder, *Spinoza*, 36–7; Otto, *Studien*, 94; Walther, 'Machina Civilis', 210.
[106] *Acta Stoschiana*, 641, 649–50; [Tentzel] *Monatliche Unterredungen* 1694, p. 356; Lange, *Caussa Dei*, 137; Otto, *Studien*, 92.
[107] *Acta Stoschiana*, 699–700.
[108] Schröder, *Spinoza*, 35–6; Otto, *Studien*, 93–4; Walther, 'Spinozissimus', 193.

more pertinent to indict Stosch in this way than as a Spinozist. If correct, this implies that the strongly theological, anti-Socinian bias of the trial records is more indicative of prevailing methods of suppression in Brandenburg in that period than the character of Stosch's thought. A hint that this was a conscious strategy is the curious distinction introduced by the Frankfurt theology faculty—to circumvent the awkward fact that Stosch was not in any authentic sense a Socinian—between 'old' and 'new' Socinians.[109] The reality of the situation was aptly expressed by his former Socinian friend, Johann Preuss, when he was asked to comment on Stosch's text. Preuss firmly denied there was anything 'Socinianisch' about the book at all. Despite his professed purpose of reconciling reason and faith, in reality Stosch abolishes faith and replaces it exclusively with philosophical reason, identifying philosophy as the true and sole path to 'salvation'. If Stosch employs terms from Scripture and theology, urged Preuss, this was only to mislead true Christians, precisely 'as in Spinoza and his progenitors and disciples'.[110]

In any case, if the official proceedings ignored Stosch's Spinozism, subsequent commentators on the inception of radical thought in Germany obviously did not. Beginning with Staalkopf and Loescher in the next decade, it became usual to designate Stosch as a 'discipulus' of Spinoza, who represented a radical strain of thought emanating from Holland.[111] Buddeus rightly insists that the central feature of Stosch's book is its Spinozism, as is evident from his defining God as the only 'substance', with its inevitable concomitant that God has no freedom but acts only out of necessity.[112]

One might deduce, given the paucity of copies printed, the destruction of most of these, and the screening out of his philosophical stance from the official proceedings, that Stosch's ideas were effectively neutralized and made little contribution to the spread of radical thought in Germany. But while the book itself was never reprinted and remained virtually unobtainable, it did not lapse into oblivion. On the contrary, remarkably enough Stosch and his ideas became a favourite topic in German erudite circles, while the book's extreme rarity and notoriety helped to make it one of the best-known, and most sought-after, bibliographical curiosities of the new century.[113] Tentzel's German-language *Monatliche Unterredungen* discussed the scandal of the 'new atheistic book which the secretary at Berlin Stoschius had printed' in the spring of 1694, noting that every *érudit* of any standing had something to say about it. Connoisseurs of clandestine literature went to extraordinary lengths to obtain a copy, Prince Eugene of Savoy reportedly offering unheard-of sums.[114] To fill a glaring gap in the otherwise unrivalled collection of Burgomaster von Uffenbach of Frankfurt, the

---

[109] *Acta Stoschiana*, 686.   [110] Ibid., 695–6.

[111] Loescher, *Praenotiones*, 146–7; Lange, *Bescheidene und ausführliche Entdeckung*, 234; Otto, *Studien*, 95; Walther, 'Machina Civilis', 212.

[112] Buddeus, *Analecta Historiae Philosophicae*, 113–22, 316.

[113] Reimann, *Historia*, 512–14; Lilienthal, *Theologische Bibliothec*, 259–61; Küster, *Marchiae Litteratae Specimen*, 7.

[114] Vogt, *Catalogus historico-criticus*, i, 208.

latter was offered a manuscript copy, in May 1725, but refused, being adamant that he must have an authentic copy of the 1692 edition.[115] He eventually succeeded, obtaining his precious copy from a relative of the deceased author via the efforts of the Berlin-based Huguenot savant, Charles Étienne Jordan. For less discriminating or wealthy collectors, however, manuscript versions filled the gap, circulating not infrequently also outside the confines of Germany. The Baron Thott, in Copenhagen, for instance, acquired no less than three manuscript copies.[116] The manuscript copy in the Biblioteca Palatina, at Parma, bears an inscription showing that the librarian, Paciaudi, who rebuilt the collections there in the mid-eighteenth century, purchased it in person while visiting Leipzig.[117]

Furthermore, outlines of Stosch's system, sometimes quoting key propositions from his text verbatim, were offered by sundry early eighteenth-century German bibliographers, lexicographers, and historians of philosophy, including Staalkopf, Loescher, Grapius, Buddeus, Lange, Reimann, Trinius, Zedler, Lilienthal, and Brucker. It even became feasible in the freer intellectual atmosphere prevailing in Prussia after the accession of Frederick the Great in 1740, to give public lectures on the Stosch affair. Thus the rector of the Berlin Gymnasium, Georg Gottfried Küster, delivered an oration on Stosch and his book on 21 January 1743, and while he refrained from expounding Stosch's stance in any detail, in the subsequently printed version of his text, he helpfully provided readers with precise references to those books which did discuss his ideas.[118]

iv. Spinoza and Cabbala: Wachter and Spaeth

A curious feature of the early penetration of Spinozism in Germany was its linkage to a discussion of traditional Jewish mysticism, or cabbala, in particular owing to the activities of a remarkable deist, Johann Georg Wachter (1673–1757). Born in Memmingen, where his father was the civic physician, Wachter descended from a long line of Lutheran preachers and began his scholarly career at 16 in 1689, studying theology at Tübingen under Jaeger.[119] After further study at Leipzig, Halle, Berlin, and Frankfurt an der Oder, he embarked on what proved the most formative cultural encounter of his life, his Dutch study tour of 1698–9.[120]

In Amsterdam Wachter discovered, and began exploring, the traditions of Jewish mysticism while simultaneously entering into a fraught, convoluted dialogue with a strange compatriot by the name of Johann Peter Spaeth (alias Moses Germanus, c.1644–1701), an Austrian or Swabian Catholic who, having first converted to Lutheranism and then reverted to Catholicism, later veered to the Socinians and then the Quakers. After this he contemplated submission to Catholicism for the third time,

---

[115] Häseler, *Wanderer zwischen den Welten*, 42.   [116] Benítez, *Face cachée*, 27.
[117] See MS note by Paciaudi in PBP MS Parmense 232.
[118] Küster, *Marchiae Litteratae Specimen*, 7–14.   [119] Schröder, *Freidenker*, part i, vol. ii, 162–3.
[120] Schoeps, *Barocke Juden*, 83–91; Popkin, 'Spinoza, Neoplatonic Kabbalist?', 394–5; Walther, 'Machina Civilis', 202–3.

but was dissuaded at Frankfurt by the Pietist leader, Spener.[121] Spener decisively deflected him from Rome but found, to his consternation, that instead of reverting to Lutheranism, Spaeth abandoned Christianity altogether. Shortly before Wachter appeared on the scene in 1697, he migrated to Amsterdam and converted to Judaism, entering the congregation of Portuguese Jews from which Spinoza had been expelled in 1656, assuming the name 'Moses Germanus'.

Both in conversation and a recently published Latin tract, Spaeth abjured both the New Testament, which he calls a 'figmentum und pigmentum', and the path of philosophy, expressly repudiating Spinoza.[122] As their dialogue unfolded, however, Wachter became convinced that Spaeth actually supported strands of cabbala which, in his opinion, closely resembled core Spinozism. After several conferences with Spaeth in which the latter restated his objections to Christianity and Spinozism, Wachter worked up their encounter into a book which he published under the title *Der Spinozismus im Jüdenthumb* (Amsterdam, 1699). Wachter's aim was to demolish Spaeth, and his advocacy of Judaism, by equating the latter with cabbala and cabbala with Spinozism, thereby showing Judaism itself to be Spinozistic and consequently atheistic.

Wachter's book proved remarkably influential and permanently fixed in many minds an image of Spaeth as the perverse antagonist of Christianity who equates Christ's Incarnation and Resurrection with Ovid's fables and revealed himself to be a fervent cabbalist and Spinozist.[123] Leibniz, in his *Théodicée*, repeats Wachter's contention that Spaeth 'having adopted the dogmas of Spinoza, believed Spinoza had revived the ancient cabbala of the Hebrews',[124] adding that Wachter effectively refuted Spaeth while agreeing with him that Spinoza's core tenets are those of the cabbala.[125] Also beyond Germany, Wachter's thesis was taken up with no small zest. Basnage in his highly influential *Histoire des Juifs* (1706), reiterated Wachter's thesis while, in 1713, Alvarez de Toledo, in what was possibly the first printed discussion of Spinozism in Spain, echoing Basnage, similarly asserted the 'broad parallel between this cabalistic view and *Espinosismo*'.[126]

Most readers interpreted Wachter's *Spinozismus* as a vigorous assault on Spaeth, Judaism, cabbala, and Spinozism and warmly applauded. But even then some detected a distinctly disturbing element in Wachter's convoluted argument. For Wachter claims that mankind's discovery of God originated not with the Jews but, following the 'light of reason', the gentiles, and in many different contexts, the concept of God being wholly rational and innate in human nature. It emerged subsequently that Wachter was actually arguing from a deistic and Naturalistic stance and was implicitly rendering Revelation redundant. Moreover, where traditional Christian anti-Jewish polemics scorn rabbinic literature and Talmud but not the Old

---

[121] Schröder, 'Einleitung' (1994), 14–15.

[122] Wachter, *Spinozismus*, i, 30–1, 72; Lilienthal, *Theologische Bibliothec*, 1127–8; Israel, *European Jewry*, 187, 193; Walther, 'Machina Civilis', 202.

[123] Buddeus, *Introdvctio*, 320–32.   [124] Leibniz, *Theodicy*, 79.

[125] Ibid.; Altmann, *Moses Mendelssohn*, 687.   [126] Alvarez de Toledo, *Historia*, 133.

Testament (which is part of the Christian Bible), Wachter also disparages Moses and the Hebrew Bible, even suggesting the greater part of 'your Torah is a heathen Egyptian codex.'[127]

Wachter denies the Jews were a people chosen by God to receive His Revelation. 'The universal grace of God,' he asserts, 'does not confine itself to one branch of humanity.'[128] It is indeed 'entirely false', he claims, that 'God revealed Himself only to the Jews and that one cannot know God through the light of reason'.[129] It is reason, he insists, which 'has from the beginning of the world called men to God and which calls them to Him still'.[130] Extolling the power of 'natural religion', Wachter holds 'Jewish theology is no older than Moses while pagan theology [of one God] is as ancient as human reason.'[131] Not unlike Toland a few years later in his *Origines Judicae*, Wachter derides Huet's *Demonstratio Evangelica*, a work intended to combat incredulity, Naturalism, and Spinozism by demonstrating the centrality of Moses, ancient Judaism, and the Biblical narrative in Man's spiritual evolution. It is only the Jews, sneers Wachter, who have any reason to thank Bishop Huet.[132] In reality, it was not the gentiles who followed the Jews in adopting a true understanding of God but the Jews who with their cabbala perverted what reason and natural religion teach all men, cobbling together the 'errors' of Plato, Plotinus, Pythagorus, Parmenides, and 'many others', until they eventually arrived at the infamous blasphemy 'that the world is God'.[133]

Spaeth, argues Wachter, had simply restated and elaborated what Jewish cabbalistic writers such as Isaac Luria and the Sephardic wanderer, Abraham Cohen Herrera (*c.*1570–1635), in his principal work, the *Puerta del Cielo* (Gate of Heaven), had done decades before, namely dress the Lurianic cabbala in the terminology of western philosophy, and especially Neoplatonism.[134] Perverting Greek ideas, says Wachter, the Jews built their depraved cabbalistic notion of God around their identification of God and the world, precisely the conception central to Spinoza's philosophy. Spaeth indeed had gone beyond Herrera by claiming that God and the universe constitute one and the same substance, albeit without going as far as Spinoza, who retains only the foundations, stripping away the entire upper edifice of cabbalistic categories and vocabulary, and reworking cabbala into an ostensibly cogent but in reality incoherent philosophy.[135] By contrast, reason, holds Wachter, demonstrates a God independent of, and above, the visible world.[136]

Wachter furnishes extensive quotations from the *Ethics* in both Latin and German, thereby making available propositions hitherto never publicly formulated in the vernacular. Though deemed a denunciation of Spinoza,[137] the 77-page third part of

---

[127] Wachter, *Spinozismus*, i, 65. [128] Schröder, 'Einleitung' (1995), 26–7.

[129] Wachter, *Spinozismus*, i, 57. [130] Ibid.

[131] Ibid.; Lilienthal, *Theologische Bibliothec*, 1128. [132] Wachter, *Spinozismus*, i, 63–4.

[133] Ibid., 69.

[134] Ibid., 22–3, 69, 71, 81, 89–97, 117–19; Scholem, 'Wachtersche Kontroverse', 17–18; Israel, *European Jewry*, 66, 189.

[135] Wachter, *Spinozismus*, i, 14–15, 22–3, 117–19; Leibniz, *Animadversiones*, 12–13, 26–7.

[136] Ibid., 15. [137] Schröder, *Spinoza*, 65.

Wachter's *Spinozismus* was, at the same time, one of the fullest and most vigorous expositions of Spinoza's philosophy of God, man, and substance available in German and one bound to further its propagation. Wachter concludes by reaffirming that Spinoza's *Natura Naturans* and *Natura Naturata* are one substance under different guises, and that precisely here lies the *Spinozismus* in Judaism generally and Spaeth in particular.[138] The cabbalistic–Spinozist vision of God means there is no religion or morality in the conventionally accepted sense and that sin is meaningless. It implies that God is the author of evil, that wars are conflicts which God incites against Himself, and that the baseness, anger, and aggression of men is all hatred of God of Himself.[139]

Most readers welcomed Wachter's powerful denunciation of Judaism, cabbala, Spinozism, and Spaeth as pernicious and atheistic. Yet his discarding Revelation for reason, denigration of the Old Testament, and linkage of Spinoza with Luria, Cohen Herrera, and Spaeth, all of whom allegedly adhere to proto-Spinozism, aroused in some quarters not just unease but suspicion concerning Wachter's real intentions.[140] No doubt later comments in eighteenth-century German philosophical literature are coloured by the knowledge that Wachter subsequently performed an astounding volte-face and proclaimed himself a Spinozist.[141] But it was impossible to doubt that the seeds of Wachter's subsequent Spinozism were already discernible in 1699. Reimann later remarked sardonically that Wachter's *Spinozismus* should have been entitled *Der Spinozismus in Moses Germani Judenthum und J. G. Wachteri Christenthum*.[142]

Furthermore, in the immediate wake of Wachter's book, a few orthodox Lutheran scholars were sufficiently troubled to intervene in defence not just of the Biblical Hebrews but of traditional cabbala, stressing the considerable difference between mainstream cabbala and the innovations of Luria and Cohen Herrera. Buddeus, then still at Halle, disputed Wachter's claims in his *Defensio Cabalae Ebraeorum* (1700) and *Introductio ad Historiam Philosophiae Ebraeorum* (1702), insisting that Cohen Herrera's concept of the emanation of all things from God, as the sole source of being, was a strictly spiritual process, quite distinct from what he calls the crass, atheistic materialism of Spinoza.[143]

To the amazement of Leibniz, who followed all this with close attention, reports began to circulate during 1701 that Wachter was now veering towards Spaeth's views on religion, Spinozism, and cabbala.[144] Buoyed by the success of his book and backed initially by one of the Elector's chief advisers, Paul von Fuchs, Wachter had entered as a candidate for a vacant chair in philosophy at the Prussian (and still predominantly

---

[138] Wachter, *Spinozismus*, iii, 60.   [139] Ibid., 61–2.

[140] Lilienthal, *Theologische Bibliothec*, 1127–8; Schröder, 'Einleitung' (1994), 16.

[141] Grapius, *Systema*, i, 54, 58–9; Leibniz, *Animadversiones*, 1–3; Altmann, *Moses Mendelssohn*, 687–8; Schröder, *Spinoza*, 65.

[142] Lilienthal, *Theologische Bibliothec*, 1127.

[143] Buddeus, *Introductio*, 398–9, 320–32; Buddeus, *Traité*, 6–7; Staalkopf, *De Atheismo*, 7.

[144] Grapius, *Systema*, i, 54; Leibniz, *Animadversiones*, 3.

Cartesian) university of Duisburg. By 1702, however, rumours that he was privately championing Spaeth, Lurianic cabbala, and Spinozism had effectively blighted both his Duisburg candidacy and his scholarly reputation. Deprived of all prospect of an academic career, Wachter settled in Berlin and henceforth spent his time ensconced in the 'excellent library' maintained by the Prussian king.[145] He eked out a living as a salaried researcher and Latinist attached to the library.

Even so, Wachter refused to be deflected from his intellectual course. Recasting his ideas on cabbala, Spinozism, and revealed religion, he wrote a short work entitled *Elucidarius Cabalisticus* in 1702, which was later published in 1706. To prepare the ground for this re-evaluation of cabbala and Spinozism, he first published a less provocative work, his 44-page *Origines Juris Naturalis* (Berlin, 1704), on the motivation of man, the origins of the State, and the nature of political power, which largely rests, though silently and inconspicuously, on the less contentious parts of Spinoza's analysis of man and society. This tract contains numerous unacknowledged verbatim quotations from both the *Ethics* and especially the then little studied *Tractatus Politicus*.[146]

The *Elucidarius Cabalisticus*, which appeared with Wachter's name on the title-page, provoked a general outcry. From 1706, Reimann later observed, Germany possessed no more open advocate of Spinoza than 'Wachter who, in both his published and unpublished works, openly Spinozises'.[147] Having denounced cabbala, Judaism, and Spinozism in 1699, Wachter now boldly reversed the very thesis he had so energetically propounded, extolling the cabbala as a venerable and ancient tradition worthy of the highest respect but nevertheless one still to be equated with Spinozism which, he now claimed, contrary to common supposition, is not 'atheistic'.[148] How Wachter could simultaneously concede that Spinoza denies Christ's Resurrection and nevertheless claim that Spinoza acknowledges Christianity to be a divinely revealed religion, Leibniz confessed, was beyond him.[149]

Wachter holds 'natural religion' and philosophical truth to be virtually identical and to reach back in man's consciousness to the remotest times. However, owing to historical circumstances, both had been cultivated largely in secret, concealed from the general view. This was because natural religion and philosophical truth surpass the understanding of most men so that 'priests and prophets' found they could only bring the common people to awareness of God and morality by exploiting their credulity and gullibility, filling their minds with wild imaginings, 'revelations', and fabricated miracles. The early Christians, he contends, borrowed their knowledge of truth from the Jews, whose scholars had embedded the teachings of natural religion in their cabbala which, however, had had to be hidden under an obfuscating veneer of priestly dogma and official religion.

---

[145] Schröder, *Freidenker*, part i, vol. ii, 165. [146] Schröder, 'Einleitung' (1995), 25.

[147] Reimann, *Historia*, 514–22.

[148] Grapius, *Systema*, i, 58–9; Buddeus, *Lehr-Sätze*, 147; Herwech, *Dissertatio critico-philosophica*, para. 25; Scholem, 'Wachtersche Kontroverse', 22.

[149] Leibniz, *Animadversiones*, 3.

Centuries later Christian cabbalists, such as Pico della Mirandola and Reuchlin, had begun unravelling the truth contained in cabbala. This process of retrieving the truth culminates in Spinoza who, according to Wachter, merely uncovers, purifies, and restates in all its philosophical majesty the fundamental tenets of cabbala and natural religion, acknowledging 'Christ's divinity and the verity of the universal Christian religion'.[150] Previously, Wachter grants, with a bow to Buddeus, he had erred in condemning cabbala as 'atheistic' and antagonistic to Christianity.[151] During his conferences with Spaeth he was still blinded by the power of 'popular prejudice', but nevertheless had been right to stress the basic affinities between cabbala and Spinozism.[152] In his new work, Wachter quotes verbatim and expands on over twenty propositions and demonstrations from Spinoza's *Ethics* and correspondence. Affirming, for example, that *substantia cogitans* (thought substance) and *substantia extensa* (extended substance) 'are one and the same thing', he refers to the *Ethics*, Part II, Proposition VII: 'the order and connection of ideas is the same as the order and connection of things,' noting Spinoza's explanation that this truth 'seems to have been glimpsed as if through a cloud by some among the Hebrews who definitely considered God, the intellect of God [i.e. thought], and the things understood by Him, to be one and the same'.[153]

Finally, Wachter notes that the 'wise and prudent' Elector Karl Ludwig of the Palatinate invited Spinoza to teach at Heidelberg, promising unrestricted 'freedom to philosophize' which was scarcely conceivable had Spinoza really been an atheist and opposed Christianity.[154] Here again, Wachter vigorously differentiates between genuine 'truth' which is unavoidably recondite, lofty, and scorned by ordinary folk and Churches, and the vast mass of false doctrine deemed true by people, Church, and State. By projecting back to ancient times the painful dilemma in which he and fellow advocates of radical thought found themselves, their needing to hide their true views from society's guardians of doctrine and morality, Wachter had hit upon a clever means of equating Spinozism with 'true religion'—that is, true Christianity and 'true Judaism' (which are fundamentally the same thing)—thereby building a common front encompassing all who clandestinely search for truth throughout the millennia in the face of the overpowering hegemony of what is commonly believed, which is as intolerant and unforgiving as it is fallacious and false.

Such was the outcry against the *Elucidarius* that it was made clear to Wachter that he was risking his job and security. Consequently, for the rest of his career he scrupulously refrained from publishing anything of the sort again. But he continued researching indefatigably into the 'true' nature of Christianity, Judaism, and Spinozism, leaving unpublished a remarkable manuscript, written in 1703 but

---

[150] Wachter, *Elucidarius Cabalisticus*, 7.　　　[151] Ibid., 8, 13, 39; Schröder, 'Einleitung' (1995), 22.

[152] Wachter, *Elucidarius Cabalisticus*, 13.

[153] 'Hoc quidam Hebraeorum', quotes Wachter, 'quasi per nebulam vidisse videntur, qui scilicet statuunt, Deum, Dei intellectum resque ab ipso intellectas unum et idem esse'; Wachter, *Elucidarius Cabalisticus*, 47; Spinoza, *Opera*, ii, 90; Leibniz, *Animadversiones*, 32.

[154] Wachter, *Elucidarius Cabalisticus*, 77–8; Staalkopf, *De Atheismo*, 14–15.

extensively revised in 1716–17,[155] described by its modern editor as his 'most original contribution to the critical study of religion'.[156] Wachter seems indeed to have been the first to advance the idea which began to circulate with his manuscipt[157] and was later taken up by Voltaire and others, that Christianity originated in the Jewish sect of the Essenes and that Jesus, who 'often reprehended the Pharisees and Sadducees but never the Essenes',[158] was actually an Essene, a theory resurrected in the twentieth century with the discovery of the Dead Sea Scrolls. The Essenes, however, according to Wachter, were merely a link in the chain, their core teachings proclaiming love of God, of virtue, and of men,[159] reaching back to the early Greek thinkers, who first glimpsed the truths of 'natural religion' and passed on this priceless treasure camouflaged under diverse theological and philosophical terminologies until it could be more effectively spread through the esoteric, cabbalistic techniques of the Jews and finally reach its fullest and most majestic expression in Spinoza.

Early eighteenth-century deists who privately repudiated Christian claims regarding miracles, Christ's divinity, and Revelation, believing the historical Jesus to have been an important teacher of the people rather than the son of God, required a viable historical explanation for the impressive rise of Christianity and the immense support for its teachings and veneration for the Church. By claiming Jesus was a Jewish sectary, an Essene, and a teacher of 'natural religion',[160] Wachter provided just such a historically cogent account of the origins of Christianity, while simultaneously reducing Judaism and Christianity to historical offshoots of what were only ostensibly distinct and antagonistic spiritual traditions, termed 'Christianity' and 'Judaism', but in reality a single—albeit hidden—tradition of truth reaching back across the ages to the early Greeks. Among those persuaded by Wachter's Essene thesis was Frederick the Great, who wrote to d'Alembert in October 1770, insisting the historical Jesus was undoubtedly an Essene, that Essene views contained much of the teaching of Zeno, and that the Christian religion as commonly understood is a mere tissue of fiction.[161]

For years Wachter retained his modest post in Berlin despite public attacks on him, such as the disputation, presided over by Staalkopf at Greifswald in 1706. Despite his contriving to pose as a Christian, concluded Staalkopf, Wachter was nothing but a devious and pernicious advocate of Spinozism.[162] But it was not his Spinozism which finally eradicated Wachter from the electoral library. What eventually drove him from the Prussian capital in 1722 was the resolution of the new monarch, Friedrich Wilhelm I—a philistine who loathed scholars and libraries—to divert funds his predecessor had lavished on the electoral library to his beloved regiments of guards. The king stopped

---

[155] Wachter, *De Primordiis*, 114.   [156] Schröder, 'Einleitung' (1995), 12.
[157] Among those in possession of a copy was Bekker's opponent in Hamburg, Johan Winckler; see Winckler, *Catalogus*, no. 2177.
[158] Wachter, *De Primordiis*, 74.   [159] Ibid., 80.   [160] Ibid., 74, 80–1, 83.
[161] 'Jesus était proprement un Essenien', wrote Frederick, 'il était imbu de la morale des Esseniens, qui tient beaucoup de celle de Zenon. Sa religion était un pur déisme, et voyez comme nous l'avons brodée'; quoted in Schröder, 'Einleitung' (1995), 13.
[162] Staalkopf, *De Atheismo*, 4–5, 16.

the pay and suppressed the jobs of the library staff. Wachter, dogged as ever, found another post though, this time in Saxony, at the civic library of Leipzig, where he eked out the remainder of his life in relative tranquillity.

v. Theodor Ludwig Lau (1670–1740)

In the wake of Knutzen, Tschirnhaus, Stosch, and Wachter, the next radical thinker to provoke outrage in Germany was Theodor Ludwig Lau.[163] Born and raised in East Prussia, Lau's father had been a senior official in the Prussian bureaucracy who, as a young man, had studied at Leiden, as was then common among the German-speaking civic and noble élites of the eastern Baltic. Lau's elder brother, Karl Friedrich, also studied in Holland before embarking in turn on an administrative career. Lau himself studied in Koenigsberg, Halle—where he was taught by both Buddeus and Christian Thomasius—and finally Holland, where he spent three years (1695–8) at Leiden and The Hague, after which he also visited England and France.[164]

Having completed his studies, Lau returned to the eastern Baltic and likewise embarked on a career in administration, entering the employ of Duke Friedrich Wilhelm of Courland. Intelligent, personable, and skilled in French and Latin, as well as German and Dutch, his worldly prospects seemed excellent. In 1710 he was sent to Saint Petersburg in connection with the proposed marriage of his prince with a Russian princess. Unfortunately, his master died prematurely in 1711, and Lau, for some reason, failed to secure comparable employment elsewhere. Searching for a suitable position befitting his quality and abilities, he turned into a kind of aristocratic vagrant, wandering from Court to Court across Germany.

Seeking solace in study and writing, in 1717, at the age of 47 while lodging at Frankfurt am Main, he published anonymously a brief Latin tract entitled *Meditationes Philosophicae de Deo, Mundo, Homine* (Philosophical Meditations about God, the World and Man). Crammed with what were deemed impious doctrines incompatible with revealed religion, the text caused uproar in the city.[165] The Lutheran pastors protested to the burgomasters, who seized the stocks of copies from the bookshops and had these publicly burned.[166] Enquiries led to Lau, who was briefly imprisoned, after which he was declared an 'atheist' and undesirable influence and banished from the city.

His reputation ruined, Lau decided to contest the legality of his expulsion and, in the hope of obtaining a favourable judgement from the law faculty, appealed to his former university at Halle.[167] He protested his innocence, claiming to have purposely donned the mask of a 'philosophical and freethinking pagan' the better and more forcefully to demonstrate the truth of Christianity. He appealed also to the most eminent of his teachers, Thomasius, whose renown as a champion of toler-

---

[163] Trinius, *Freydenker-Lexicon*, 333–5; Lilienthal, *Theologische Bibliothec*, 261–8.

[164] Schröder, *Spinoza*, 124.   [165] Pontoppidan, *Sandhed's kraft*, 120.

[166] See MS additional note to PBP Parmense MS 3, Lau 'Meditationes', fo. 84v.

[167] Pott, 'Einleitung', 21–2.

ation was second to none in Early Enlightenment Germany, and who had often enough shown he was not afraid to court the wrath of the clergy in his drive against bigotry and superstition and his quest for a new German culture based on enlightened values. But unhappily for Lau, Thomasius also detested radical ideas, and especially Spinozism, and, on examining his text, firmly concluded that Lau's views originated in discussion with 'atheists' and reading the 'writings of the infamous Spinoza'.[168]

Answering Thomasius' unfavourable judgement, and the criticism of the Halle law faculty, in a tract dated 20 October 1717, Lau again claimed his *Meditationes* were purely a philosophical exercise in no way designed to attack Christianity. Recalling that Thomasius had once condemned the trial and execution of Vanini in Toulouse as the 'greatest injustice in the world', he demanded to know whether he had now changed his opinions, abandoned the noble cause of toleration, and was planning a new 'Vaninische Tragödie' with Lau in the chief role.[169] Paranoid and prone to view himself as a tragic philosophical hero, a hounded modern Socrates, locked in a life and death struggle to free mankind from loathsome bigotry and the 'realm of darkness', Lau retaliated by circulating manuscript versions of his book and preparing a second instalment of *Meditationes*. This new text was intended partly to justify the first and partly to strengthen his plea for toleration, by demonstrating that the 'confiscation and burning of books' for theological or philosophical reasons can only lead to despotism and the triumph of zealotry and superstition.[170]

This extremely radical 34-page tract was published anonymously in Frankfurt in 1719.[171] There was a second furore; again the burgomasters seized the stock of copies and destroyed them. Thomasius publicly backed this suppression, pronouncing the new tract even more despicably irreligious than the first. Driven from Frankfurt, the now totally discredited Lau wandered from place to place, seeking a niche where he could continue his one-man crusade for a real Enlightenment. For a decade, he managed to earn a precarious living through translating, journalism, and librarianship. When eventually he reached his native city of Koenigsberg, he found that his reputation as an 'atheist', and an author of forbidden books, had preceded him and blocked every path to his re-establishing himself. Desperate over his now wretched predicament, and mounting a show of contrition, he submitted to a public ceremony of reconciliation with the Lutheran Church in October 1729, abjuring his 'errors' and 'indifferentism' in religion. But even this last resort failed and he was still generally shunned.[172] After departing, never to return, he apparently passed his last years in Hamburg, continually fearful of being unmasked again as an 'atheist' and public enemy, living under the assumed name of 'Lenz' in impecunious obscurity, broken in body and spirit.

The ideas Lau conveys in his uncomplicated Latin represent an uninhibited

---

[168] Thomasius, *Elender Zustand*, 241, 256, 259; Pott, 'Einleitung', 21.
[169] Thomasius, *Elender Zustand*, 278, 288.   [170] Lau, *Meditationes, Theses, Dubia*, 1–2.
[171] Schröder, *Spinoza*, 129; Otto, *Studien*, 102.
[172] Lau, 'Original-Rede', 19–21; Pontoppidan, *Sanheds kraft*, 121–3.

Naturalism and materialism. God and Nature are proclaimed one and the same, their oneness qualified only by the distinction, borrowed from Spinoza, between *Natura Naturans* and *Natura Naturata*.[173] 'Divine Revelation' consists in His works and their operations, a 'Revelation' we see, hear, feel, and taste all around us and which Lau maintains is 'certain, mathematical and infallible'.[174] Nature and its study, the different branches of science and their findings Lau terms his Bible, prophets, apostles and priests. By contrast, the 'Revelation' of Scripture he belittles as man-made, historical, fallible, and 'subject to many defects'.[175] The core Christian 'mysteries' must be set aside as vulgar superstition and a form of polytheism: 'to multiply God is to destroy the Deity.' Just as 'true religion' in Lau's eyes is 'natural' or 'rational' religion, so revealed religion is merely a fraud and a political tool.

Organized religion is thus nothing but an instrument of social control, an immensely powerful mechanism fuelled by the 'pious frauds' concocted by Moses, Mohammed, and Confucius, no less than Christ, Luther, and Calvin, the people being regimented in mind and body by a vast host of prophets, apostles, disciples, saints, and venerable teachers wielding their alleged 'holy books'.[176] 'Reason' Lau proclaims the sole authentic measure of truth, thereby effectively reducing theology to philosophy and science. Neither Providence nor miracles are possible. The universe exists eternally, and man is not a duality, as Descartes imagined, but rather body and soul are one, a single human 'machine', the soul consisting of fine matter. The soul is not immortal and there is no life in the hereafter, and hence no Heaven or Hell. Death is just the reunion of the body (and mind) 'with God and the world'.[177] There is no absolute 'good' or 'evil'.

According to Thomasius, Lau borrowed his 'dangerous and atheistic principles' principally from Spinoza and expressed them 'much more impudently and shamelessly in these few pages than Spinoza had done in his extensive writings'.[178] Indeed, Lau at times expresses his radicalism with an incisiveness recalling Knutzen.[179] But if Spinoza was the prime influence, Lau did not lack erudition and liked juxtaposing and reworking perceptions drawn from diverse sources. A veritable *philosophus eclecticus*, he professed to have read 'Aristotle, Plato, Pythagoras, Epicurus, Descartes, Herbert of Cherbury, Hobbes, Machiavelli, Spinoza, Beverland, La Peyrère, Boccalini, Lucretius, Le Clerc, Montaigne, La Mothe–le-Vayer, Blount, Bayle, Huygens, Toland, Bruno, etc. etc.'[180] If Spinoza far outweighs the rest in the shaping of Lau's thought, this is not because he adopted Spinoza's system in all its particulars or had an especially thorough grasp of his insights, but rather because, once again, it served as the organizing principle, providing a viable framework enabling him to order his thoughts on philosophy, theology, and science into a meaningful whole.

---

[173] Lau, *Meditationes*, 9; Otto, *Studien*, 104; Schröder, *Ursprünge*, 330–1.
[174] Lau, *Meditationes*, 10.   [175] Ibid.   [176] Ibid., 42–5.
[177] Ibid., 19, 28–9; of the working of the world Lau says 'quo rationaliter, eo verior' and of its eternality 'est ergo mundus ab aeterno'; see also Pontoppidan, *Sanheds kraft*, 118–19; Schröder. *Ursprünge*, 287.
[178] Thomasius, *Elender Zustand*, 264.   [179] Schröder, *Spinoza*, 128–9.
[180] Thomasius, *Elender Zustand*, 273.

vi. Schmidt and the Maturing of German Spinozism

In Wolff's opinion the triumph of Newton and Locke in Britain and France was an unmitigated disaster, opening a breach through which was bound to flow what Formey terms 'les détestables principes des Spinosistes'. In reality, however, Wolffianism proved a scarcely less serviceable conduit by which the Radical Enlightenment irresistibly seeped into the mainstream of European culture. For Wolff's system indubitably helped spread deistic ideas, and raise the prestige of philosophy and science at theology's expense; and if Lange and his allies lost their fight to keep Prussia on a traditionalist course, it cannot be said they, or Buddeus, were altogether mistaken in designating Wolff's philosophy a species of backdoor Spinozism.

During the 1730s and 1740s, and to a considerable degree as a consequence of the Wolffian uproar, deism in Germany spread and, for the first time, became integrally linked to, even a direct participant in, mainstream philosophical debate. The progress of deism and radical thought, and the public's increasing familiarity with deistic concepts, were everywhere apparent. Reverberations from the culminating furore in England, over Tindal's *Christianity as Old as the Creation* (1730), were more marked in Germany than in the case of any previous foreign freethinking controversy. In 1734 a Leipzig university inaugural lecture was devoted expressly to refuting Tindal's 'errors';[181] and by the time Zedler's encyclopaedia published its entries on Tindal and Toland in 1745, noticeably more space was assigned to discussing their doctrines, and especially Tindal's, than had been allotted to Collins back in 1733.[182] If in the years 1736–7 the Wertheim Bible was everywhere prohibited by the authorities in central Europe, there were patently some who applauded and even who dared to review it half favourably, notably Wolf Balthasar Adolf von Steinwehr (1704–71) who, back in 1727, had delivered a dissertation at Wittenberg on the subject of the Creation from nothing, against Spinoza, but was now severely reprimanded by the Saxon Court for comments that could be construed as supportive of Schmidt.[183] If La Mettrie was detested by the rest of the Berlin Academy, he was nevertheless, at the wish of the Prussian monarch, made a full member. If Edelmann was eventually silenced by a chorus of denunciation, he was not crushed, and it was obvious he had supporters and sympathizers in many places.

Especially remarkable was the post-Wertheim career of Johann Lorenz Schmidt. Driven from respectable society, he fought doggedly on as a translator and advocate of the Radical Enlightenment, subsisting in obscurity under Danish jurisdiction in tolerant Altona, illustrating Formey's thesis that philosophical radicalism is the psychological and social consequence of thwarted ambition and resentment.[184] His initial riposte to ostracization was to champion the growing German reception

---

[181] Jöcher, *Allgemeines Gelehrten Lexicon*, iv, 1216; Zedler, *Grosses Universal Lexicon*, xliv, 354.
[182] Zedler, *Grosses Universal Lexicon*, xliv, 351–7 and 1089–94.
[183] Kobuch, *Zensur und Aufklärung*, 76–7; Otto, *Studien*, 167.
[184] Thorschmid, *Critische Lebensgeschichte*, 44; Gawlick, 'Deismus', 16–17.

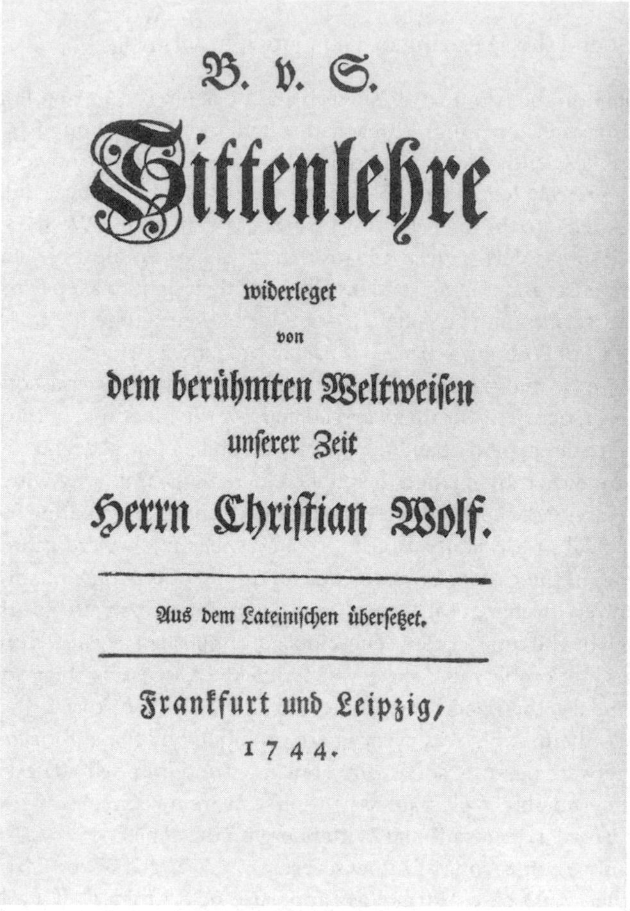

FIGURE 5. Title-page of the German rendering of Spinoza's *Ethics*,
translated and edited by Johann Lorenz Schmidt, and published in
1744.

of Tindal. In 1741 he boldly published his translation of *Christianity as Old as Creation*
into German, together with a perfunctory refutation, serving as a pretext for publishing it. His account of the freethinker's life not only reinforced the trend making
Tindal the best-known of all British deists in the Germany of the 1740s, but was
prefaced by a 130-page treatise advocating full liberty of thought and freedom to
publish.[185]

Schmidt's chief venture subsequent to the Wertheim Bible, however, was his
sensational translation of Spinoza's *Ethics* into German, a rendering published at

---

[185] Jöcher, *Allgemeines Gelehrten Lexicon*, iv, 1217; Hazard, *European Thought*, 75; Gawlick, 'Deismus', 17;
Mori, 'Postface', 344–5; Schröder, *Ursprünge*, 469.

Frankfurt in 1744, together with his German version of Wolff's latest refutation of Spinoza drawn from his *Theologia Naturalis*. This crucial publication appeared under the title *B. v. S. Sittenlehre widerleget von dem berühmten Weltweisen unserer Zeit Herrn Christian Wolff* (B. v. S. *Ethics* refuted by the famous philosopher of our time Herr Christian Wolff) and represents both the first of Spinoza's writings to appear in German and, simultaneously, the first printed vernacular rendering of the *Ethics* in any language other than Dutch. Considerable care was taken in preparing the translation, which is of excellent quality and helpfully provided with a comprehensive 60-page index designed to assist with cross-referencing between Wolff's refutation and the original.[186]

There was some question at the time, and has been ever since, whether Schmidt was actually a Spinozist or simply a Wolffian deist advocating open-minded, impartial consideration of Spinoza. He unquestionably considered close study of Wolff's confrontation with the Dutch philosopher an overriding priority for anyone seriously engaged in philosophy.[187] As he himself explains in his preface, his aim was to make Spinoza's principal work more accessible to the public and bring Spinoza out of the closet so that he would no longer be universally condemned as a frightful spectre but become instead a familiar author readily available for study.[188] Following Wolff, he held that Spinoza should first be understood and then countered with solid arguments, not shouted down with empty bluster and vituperation. Schmidt's decision to include the text of Jelles' preface to the *Opera Posthuma*, with its contention that Spinoza's philosophy is essentially Christian, no doubt reflects his desire to create a bridge between Spinoza's philosophy and what was generally acceptable to help justify his claiming that Spinoza deserves serious discussion.

Such a publication had become feasible in a Germany which by the 1740s was perceptibly changing and where, since Frederick the Great's accession, there had been a definite easing of philosophical and theological, if not political, censorship. The changed atmosphere was indeed particularly obvious in Berlin where, in the early and mid-1740s, with the revival of the Royal Academy of Sciences, intellectual debate became exceptionally open and where, next to the conflict between Wolffianism and Newtonianism, the key philosophical question was precisely the unresolved problem of Spinoza. Between 1743 and 1746 an almost constant debate in which such Huguenot members of the Academy as Jordan, Formey, and the jurist Philippe Josèphe de Jariges (1706–70) were prominently involved, re-examined Spinoza from every angle, and with Wolffian thoroughness, even if the conclusion was still that Spinoza's system comprises 'monstrous contradictions'.[189] Bayle's article on Spinoza was declared a travesty and meticulous study of Spinoza's system indispensable.[190]

Further signs that the appearance of Spinoza's *Ethics* in an excellent German version was symptomatic of a wider cultural shift were discernible in the strangely

---

[186] Goldenbaum, 'Erste deutsche Übersetzung', 115–16. [187] Ibid., 113; [Schmidt], *Vorrede*, 1–4.
[188] [Schmidt], '*Vorrede*', 5; Walther, 'Spinozissimus ille Spinoza', 199–200.
[189] Häseler, *Ein Wanderer*, 40, 130–2; Otto, *Studien*, 168. [190] Altmann, *Moses Mendelssohn*, 35–6.

Janus-headed reaction to Schmidt's compilation. If there was still plentiful denunciation of Spinoza as the 'most frightful' of all Christianity's enemies, and of his anonymous translator as a monstrous hypocrite covertly introducing Spinoza under the pretext of promoting Wolff's refutation, other reviewers guardedly accepted his good faith, granting that Spinoza's *Ethics* needed to be studied impartially and with meticulous care.[191] That some of the most creative intellects of the younger generation were now doing precisely that emerges from the case of Karl August Gebhardt and the early development of such leaders of the German High Enlightenment as Lessing and the Jewish philosopher, Moses Mendelssohn (1729–86). Gebhardt was a long-standing follower of the Leibnizian–Wolffian system in Saxony, also immersed in Spinoza, Bekker, Mandeville, and Tindal, who formed a connection with Edelmann and who, in 1743, published two audacious, semi-deistic works on the supernatural which verged on propagating natural religion, and denying the existence of the Devil. The books were printed in Berlin by the house of Johann Andreas Rüdiger (d.1751), with 'Amsterdam' falsely stated on the title-pages.[192] Both were banned and seized from the bookshops in Leipzig and Dresden.

Mendelssohn never gravitated as close to Spinozism as Lessing, and indeed, given his loyalty to revealed religion and Judaism, could not do so. But he was unquestionably fascinated by, and deeply preoccupied with, the figure of Spinoza from the start of his philosophical venture in the early 1750s, well before he met and became friends with Lessing in 1754.[193] The early philosophical discussions of Lessing and Mendelssohn revolved, in large part, around Spinoza, as is reflected in Mendelssohn's first published work, his *Philosophische Gespräche*, anonymously published in Berlin in 1755, in which Spinozism is a central issue. Mendelssohn's purpose was to come to terms with Spinoza in his own mind and, following Arnold and Wolff, to some extent rehabilitate him, freeing him from the stigma of being an out and out 'atheist', while reserving his primary philosophical loyalty for Leibniz and Wolff. To achieve this, Mendelssohn depicts Spinoza as the strategic precursor of Leibniz and Wolff, the real inventor of key concepts vital to the Leibnizian–Wolffian system, which he then considered the definitive answer to both British empiricism and French freethinking and the supreme manifestation of German depth and genius in philosophy.[194]

Mendelssohn argues that Spinoza, not Leibniz, was the true originator of the 'pre-established harmony', the basic idea being already found in Spinoza's proposition (*Ethics* II, Prop. VII) that 'the order and connection of ideas is the same as the order and connection of things'.[195] Leibniz could not, however, publicly acknowledge 'that he borrowed the essential part of his harmony from Spinoza', held Mendelssohn, for this would then have served as the chief ground for attacking his philosophy. Leibniz, he remarks, with presumably unconscious irony, 'was not merely the greatest, but

---

[191] Goldenbaum, 'Erste deutsche Übersetzung', 119–21.

[192] Entitled *Cogitationes Rationales* and *Vernünftmässige Betrachtung derer übernatürlichen Begebenheiten*; see Kobuch, *Zensur und Aufklärung*, 80–2; Otto, *Studien*, 356.

[193] Altmann, *Moses Mendelssohn*, 31–5.   [194] Mendelssohn, *Philosophical Writings*, 7, 106.

[195] Ibid., 103; *Collected Works of Spinoza*, i, 451; Altmann, *Moses Mendelssohn*, 51.

also the most cautious philosopher'.[196] Spinoza then, in Mendelssohn's eyes, was the vital bridge between Cartesianism and Wolffianism. Certainly he perpetrated dreadful errors; but he did so as part of a heroic philosophical achievement. He judges his fate a tragic one greatly to be pitied: 'he was a sacrifice for the human intellect, but one which deserves to be decorated with flowers' since without him, 'philosophy would never have been able to extend its borders so far'.[197]

Furthermore, contends Mendelssohn, by misconstruing, oversimplifying, and vilifying Spinoza whole generations of philosophers and theologians had merely encouraged the very godlessness and disdain for Revelation they had striven so hard to combat. Unbelievers had simply become more stubborn, seeing the injustice of the calumnies to which Spinoza was subjected. 'Impartial minds regard him as the insulted party and magnanimously take his side'.[198] 'Of all Spinoza's adversaries,' he held, 'only Wolff is not subject to this reproach'.[199] In order to refute Spinoza, Wolff had dared to reveal his philosophy in its proper light, demonstrating his strengths as well as weaknesses, with the result that only he had identified his weaknesses correctly and accurately. In effect, the Leibnizian–Wolffian system is the only viable answer to Spinoza: 'anyone who has read [Wolff's] refutation attentively,' declared Mendelssohn, 'will certainly never again be tempted to agree with Spinoza'.[200]

vii. Johann Christian Edelmann (1698–1767)

The most notable spokesman of German radical thought of the generation following that of Stosch and Lau, and conceivably the most important intellectually of all the German 'Spinozists' of the Early Enlightenment, Johann Christian Edelmann (1698–1767) was, remarkably enough, like Knutzen, the son of an organist. His father had a good position at the Court of the Saxon Duke of Sachsen-Weissenfels, not far from the university town of Jena, where the young Edelmann studied, supported the anti-Wolffian camp among the students, and was strongly influenced by the scholar he later called 'my former dear teacher Buddeus'.[201] Edelmann groped his way only slowly towards radical ideas and was never to show any great originality. Indeed, one of his innumerable later detractors, the Lutheran *Generalsuperintendent* of Bremen, called him a third-rate mind in the 'Reich' of the freethinkers, a writer who borrowed practically everything from his 'hero' Spinoza and others.[202] But he showed a resourcefulness, tenacity, and ingenuity as a publicist which enabled him partially to overcome the censorship and make an impact, throughout Germany and even beyond, particularly in Scandinavia,[203] which exceeded that of any German predecessor. He was also the first radical writer in a vernacular language other than Dutch openly to champion Spinoza's doctrines and books.[204]

---

[196] Mendelssohn, *Philosophical Writings*, 104. [197] Ibid., 106.
[198] Ibid., 107.   [199] Ibid.   [200] Ibid.
[201] Edelmann, *Unschuldigen Wahrheiten*, 426.   [202] Pratje *Historische Nachrichten*, 138, 140.
[203] Rosenstand-Goiske, *Billige Frie-Tanker*, i, 91–104, 15–22, 163–4, 251, 318.
[204] Grossmann, *Johann Christian Edelmann*, 111; Schröder, *Spinoza*, 25–7; Otto, *Studien*, 105.

Edelmann—at least from around 1740—was, like Lau, a radical eclectic devising a concoction, as one learned critic disparagingly put it, drawn from 'Spinozismo, Naturalismo, Pythagorismo, Sadduccismo, Fanaticismo, Scepticismo und Indifferentismo'.[205] His work undoubtedly represents a *mélange* of disparate strains of thought.[206] But he was not seeking to exhibit great intellectual power but rather to change society by reforming men's notions about life, education, liberty, politics, sex, and, above all, religion. When arguing later that revealed religion ineluctably divides and disrupts mankind, and only a deism of pure reason can heal the wounds and reunite humanity, he buttressed his argument by invoking and citing Koerbagh, Knutzen, Stosch, Bekker, Van Hattem, Toland, and Collins, besides Spinoza.[207]

After completing his studies at Jena, Edelmann spent some years in Austria, including Vienna, employed as a tutor to the sons of one of the few remaining Austrian Protestant noble families. On leaving Austria in 1731, he became a trainee Lutheran pastor but owing to his increasingly heterodox tendencies, and inner theological turmoil, ultimately failed to secure a career within the public Church. He settled in the mid-1730s in the tiny, but exceptionally liberal, State ruled by Count Casimir of Sayn-Wittgenstein-Berleburg (1687–1741), one of the most tolerant princes of the age, where he formed ties with an intensely pious and mystical Spiritualist group.[208] The decisive occurrence in his intellectual development began shortly before or in 1740, when he embarked on an exhaustive study of Spinoza's *Tractatus Theologico-Politicus*, the text which finally extricated him from the irresolvable theological perplexities within which he felt trapped.

The *Tractatus* convinced Edelmann that the Bible is not a divinely revealed book and transformed almost every aspect of his life,[209] inspiring him to publish his discoveries in a sensational three-volume work entitled *The Revealed Face of Moses* (*Moses mit aufgedeckten Angesichte*), published clandestinely, probably at nearby Frankfurt, late in 1740. Long influenced by Arnold, he now possessed a completely new *Weltanschauung*, viewing Scripture as merely a human book promulgating commandments of purely worldly origin. He became a tireless champion of full 'freedom of thought' and expression, in this connection also drawing on the work of Toland.[210] Rejecting the notion of Original Sin, and indeed of sin in any sense, he became convinced of the legitimacy of sexual freedom, holding that there is no need for the institution, much less the sacrament, of marriage to sanction sexual intercourse between man and woman.[211]

Besides Spinoza's, Edelmann especially came to esteem the writings of Knutzen.

---

[205] Pratje, *Historische Nachrichten*, 127.

[206] Wagner, *Johann Christian Edelmanns verblendete Anblicke*, i, vorrede.

[207] Edelmann, *Göttlichkeit der Vernunft*, 578–9.   [208] Grossmann, *Johann Christian Edelmann*, 88–9.

[209] Ibid., 111–15; Kobuch, *Zensur und Aufklärung*, 85; Otto, 'Johann Christian Edelmann's Criticism', 172.

[210] Edelmann, *Glaubens-Bekentniss*, 171–81.

[211] Edelmann, *Moses*, ii, 54, 60; Wagner, *Johann Christian Edelmanns verblendete Anblicke*, ii, 195; besides Spinoza, he was clearly influenced on the subject of sin also by Van Hattem.

Deriding those 'fools' who prize whatever is rare and expensive, he remarks that it was precisely the wealthy bibliophiles and connoisseurs of German Court society who had preserved the manuscripts of his proscribed predecessor, saving them for posterity, like 'dry seeds' that would one day sprout forth and deliver their oppressors a double harvest of 'bitter fruit' equal to their shame and disgrace.[212] Having somehow borrowed a manuscript of Knutzen's writings, Edelmann saw it as part of his mission in life to rescue him and his legacy from the oblivion to which they had been consigned by princely and ecclesiastical authority. Though he disapproves of Knutzen's anarchistic rejection of the State, believing that, given man's natural characteristics, government is indispensable to maintain order.[213] He wholeheartedly approves the rest of Knutzen's programme, and especially his denying Providence, Satan, Heaven, and Hell.[214] Edelmann resurrected Knutzen as a force in German culture by boldly publishing all three of his surviving tracts, one in Latin and two in German, within the huge text of his *Moses*.

The appearance of Edelmann's *Moses*, replete with Knutzen's salvos, provoked a general outcry in Germany and Denmark. Around twenty-four published refutations appeared, including one which found it necessary—albeit with a great show of hesitation—to reproduce Knutzen's three texts in their entirety,[215] thereby lending them added currency, as part of its efforts to rebut Edelmann. Henceforth, in German intellectual invective, Edelmann and Knutzen became names virtually as infamous as Tindal's.[216] In his *Moses*, Edelmann not only rejects divine Providence but repudiates all 'Bible faith', echoing Tindal and Collins (and beyond them, Meyer) in contending that the discrepancies and contradictions in Scripture can be ironed out only by philosophical 'reason'.[217] Ecclesiastical authority is negated together with the Christian 'mysteries', and Christ held to be a man like any other. God is declared identical to Nature, Edelmann noting that, in Germany, this idea of God as the totality of what exists was universally considered the 'most dangerous *Atheisterey* in the world'.[218] 'Not only the clergy,' he says, 'but also the common people—who affect to understand more than they do—grimace with disgust if someone should by chance mention Spinoza's name.'[219] This, he suggests, only demonstrates the overriding need to teach the people the truth regarding Spinoza and Spinozism.

Following Wachter and Toland (in his *Origines Judicae* of 1709), Edelmann restates Spinoza's contention that Christ's teaching, and early Christianity, differ totally from what he regards as the degenerate, completely bogus teaching of the modern Churches. Indeed, he goes so far as to assure readers the early Christians were really

---

[212] Edelmann, *Moses*, ii, 34.   [213] Ibid., ii, 60–1; Grossmann, *Johann Christian Edelmann*, 125.

[214] Pratje, *Historische Nachrichten*, 96, 106, 109.

[215] Wagner, *Johann Christian Edelmanns verblendete Anblicke*, ii, 96–8, 101–6, 146–56, 233–42; Schröder, *Ursprünge*, 420.

[216] Grossmann, *Johann Christian Edelmann*, 111.

[217] Edelmann, *Moses*, i, 131 and ii, 118–62; Otto, 'Johann Christian Edelmann's Criticism', 180–1.

[218] Edelmann, *Moses*, i, 131 and iii, 6–7; Edelmann, *Göttlichkeit der Vernunfft*, 279, 360–1, 562; Rosenstand-Goiske, *Billige Fric-Tanker*, i, 115–22; Otto, *Studien*, 107–8; Schröder, *Ursprünge*, 333.

[219] Edelmann, *Moses*, ii, 118.

'gute Spinozisten' (good Spinozists).[220] But his radicalism was by no means confined to religion and philosophy. Though no political theorist, his animosity towards the political absolutism overwhelmingly dominant in Germany at the time, and his republican sympathies, emerge clearly enough. He concludes with some scornful remarks about Voltaire's recent poetic eulogy on Frederick the Great's accession to the Prussian throne, which he considers a thoroughly despicable piece of sycophancy.[221]

The book was widely banned in German-speaking lands. Even in easy-going Berleburg, the count and his officials felt impelled to act: the work was formally condemned and the count's secretary sent to impound the author's stock of copies. After his death, in 1741, the count's successor also withdrew the State's protection, obliging Edelmann to depart. After a period of wandering insecurely from place to place, he eventually found temporary refuge in another tiny and exceptionally liberal principality, Neuwied, on the Rhine below Coblenz.[222] Here a general toleration of religions had been proclaimed in 1680 by Count Friedrich III (1618–98), a Calvinist prince who countenanced not only Catholics, Lutherans, and Jews, but even Mennonites, a policy inspired in part by mercantilist designs to stimulate commerce and the crafts. Nevertheless, the Reformed consistory in Neuwied stirred up a vigorous local campaign against Edelmann, which intensified in 1746, after he published another hefty and openly Spinozistic work, his soon notorious *Glaubens-Bekentniss* or confession of faith. Although the title-page bore neither a real nor a fictitious place of publication, the book was discovered to have been clandestinely produced at Neuwied. Already banned at Hamburg and some other places in 1747, the following year the Imperial Book Commission at Frankfurt initiated a full-scale investigation into this publication and Edelmann's output generally. In contrast to his *Moses* which, the commission learnt, had appeared in two editions totalling 1,000 copies, only around 300 copies of the no less shocking *Glaubens-Bekentniss* were reportedly in circulation.[223] Compelled to flee Neuwied, Edelmann found to his dismay that he now had no other recourse but to throw himself on the mercy of the despised and detested Frederick the Great, who, however much of a tyrant, was at least a freethinker.

During an earlier stay in Berlin in 1747, Edelmann had faced a public campaign for his expulsion from Prussia, fomented by Calvinist and Lutheran clergy and, in particular, a certain Johann Peter Süssmilch, who, in 1748, published a vitriolic 150-page denunciation accusing the outcast, and his followers, of regarding as 'fools those who believe in any other God than Edelmann derives from Spinoza'.[224] No doubt Edelmann's reappearance on the scene, and pleas for shelter, appealed to Frederick's somewhat perverse sense of humour, affording an opportunity to display his

---

[220] Edelmann, *Moses*, 120–1; Wagner, *Johann Christian Edelmanns verblendete Anblicke*, ii, 414.

[221] Edelmann, *Moses*, iii, 160–1; Grossmann, *Johann Christian Edelmann*, 137–8.

[222] Pratje, *Historische Nachrichten*, 2; Grossmann, *Johann Christian Edelmann*, 147–9; Whaley, 'A tolerant Society?', 186.

[223] Grossmann, *Johann Christian Edelmann*, 165; copies of Edelmann's *Moses* were reportedly especially common in his native Saxony; see Otto, *Studien*, 109.

[224] Süssmilch, *Unvernunft und Bosheit*, 32.

contempt for all parties simultaneously. Since the Prussian capital, he reportedly remarked, already contained a great many fools, he could not see why Edelmann should not be admitted too. He stipulated though that while he might stay indefinitely at the royal pleasure in Prussia, this was conditional on his publishing nothing more and remaining completely silent. Frederick carefully cultivated his reputation for toleration and enlightenment, and personally had no objection to Edelmann's ideas on philosophy, religion, and sex, at least outside the public and educational spheres. What he was unwilling to permit was not just anti-monarchical tendencies but the propagation of radical philosophy generally among the common people: 'le vulgaire,' as he characteristically put it, 'ne mérite pas d'être éclairé'.[225]

Thus Edelmann was allowed to live in Berlin. Nevertheless, condemnation of his writings was practically universal throughout the German states. At Frankfurt, the Imperial Book Commission capped his general suppression by persuading the burgomasters to stage a high-profile, public burning of his works. On 9 May 1750, seventy guards and eight drummers formed up around a prepared square pile of birchwood. As the entire magistracy and city government looked on, the Commission's condemnation of Edelmann's publications and radical doctrines was read out to the assembled crowd. The writing and publication of godless and blasphemous books was strictly forbidden, the people were reminded, and the present spectacle was intended to serve as an example to others. After a fanfare, the bonfire was lit and nearly 1,000 confiscated copies of various of his writings consigned to the flames.[226]

Yet, to some extent, the Frankfurt book-burning was also a kind of victory for the radical intellectual underground, and not least for Edelmann. A ceremonial book-burning dedicated to just one author is, after all, a form of public recognition and, at Frankfurt, presided over by the Imperial Book Commission, expressly a national rather than a local event. Even so, silenced and effectively cowed, Edelmann played no further part in German intellectual life. Years later, Moses Mendelssohn recalled meeting the fugitive in Berlin 'who had to live here under a false name', remarking that there was 'no more miserable figure than his as he timidly sneaked into the room for fear of being recognized'.[227] Yet Edelmann had not been entirely defeated. He had, after all, stirred up a wider, more sustained commotion than Knutzen, Stosch, Wachter, or Lau, and proclaimed Spinoza's name and doctrines with a tenacity and impact which irreversibly penetrated the public consciousness, materially contributing to the broad shift towards deism in the 1740s, a process which could never subsequently be reversed.

[225] Grossmann, *Johann Christian Edelmann*, 138.
[226] Ibid., 149, 165; Kobuch, *Zensur und Aufklärung*, 85.   [227] Altmann, *Moses Mendelssohn*, 565.

35 | THE RADICAL IMPACT IN ITALY

i. Giambattista Vico (1668–1744)

Vico and Doria are often characterized as 'anti-moderns' and it is not hard to see why. Cartesianism initiated the assault on received ideas and tradition in Italy in the last two decades of the seventeenth century. But having first espoused Descartes' ideas, like the rest of the Neapolitan philosophical coterie at that time, both philosophers subsequently abjured Cartesianism—Vico during the first decade of the new century, Doria rather later. In his *On the Most Ancient Wisdom of the Italians* (1710) Vico roundly rejects Descartes' ideas on substance, mind, matter, and motion.[1] Later, in the 1730s, as Locke's ideas penetrated Italy, Doria became the leading opponent of the new empirical philosophy in Italy, while his learned colleague, if less outspoken in this regard, at any rate has nothing positive to say about Locke or the *Lochisti*.[2] Vico moreover was a vigorous advocate of absolute monarchy. Not only does he claim that 'monarchy is the form of government best adapted to human nature when reason is fully developed,' he apparently frowns on the Glorious Revolution, deeming early eighteenth-century England an arrested, or retarded, monarchy, like Poland, countries which, however, 'if the natural course of human civil institutions is not impeded . . . will become perfect monarchies'.[3]

Yet spurning the systems of Descartes, Locke, and Newton is by no means necessarily a sign of anti-modernity in the Early Enlightenment. Superficially, Vico may sometimes sound like a traditionalist, with his acerbic comments on Machiavelli, Hobbes, Spinoza, and Bayle.[4] But, as has been shown, there is much that is paradoxical in his rebuttals of these writers from whom, in reality, he derives a great deal.[5] Like Doria, Vico knows them all thoroughly, as he does Bacon, Grotius, and Le Clerc, a form of intellectual engagement which is in itself, whatever else one says about Vico, an entirely modern one.[6] Indeed, there are grounds for regarding Vico's whole enterprise, his quest to uncover the true nature of morality, law, institutions, and politics, as these evolved through the ages, as not just a profoundly modern but also, though today—in contrast to the later eighteenth century—this is usually denied,[7] essentially

---

[1] Vico, *On the Most Ancient Wisdom*, 74–5, 79–82.   [2] Croce, *Filosofia*, 129, 222.
[3] Vico, *The New Science*, 379, 413.   [4] Lilla, *G. B. Vico*, 61–6.
[5] Morrison, 'Vico and Spinoza', 48–50; Remaud, 'Conflits', 35, 56–60.
[6] Vico, *Autobiography*, 139, 146, 154–5, 158–9, 164–5; Sina, *Vico e Le Clerc*, 10–14.
[7] See, for instance, Stone, *Vico's Cultural History*, 243.

a radical response to the philosophical and spiritual dilemmas confronting the Italian *literati* of his age.

The case for classifying Vico as an 'anti-modern', or traditionalist, rests primarily on his alleged theological concerns, particularly the 'Fall of Man', man's inherent weakness and limited capabilities, and especially his continual affirmation of 'divine Providence' as the prime shaping force in history.[8] If one believes Vico employs these terms in a traditional Christian sense, then the later eighteenth-century attacks on Vico, by Finetti and others, as a godless radical and 'atheist' who sought to disguise his atheistic ideas and pervert the Christian doctrine of Providence, introducing a revolutionary new concept of the natural workings of history without the intervention of God, Christ, or the Christian Church,[9] indeed without any supernatural intervention, are not just groundless but misconceived. Vico's preoccupation with the patterns and stages of history can then be viewed as a robust championing of authority, law, and tradition, as well as absolute monarchy, against the corrosive consequences of Descartes, Spinoza, Locke, Bayle, and other 'moderns'.

But there is another and more cogent reading of Vico's *magnum opus*, the *Scienza Nuova*, the first edition of which appeared in 1725, and the definitive third edition of which was published shortly after his death, in 1744: namely as an attempt to argue that peoples, communities, and individuals mould their identities, and assert their own goals unconsciously, laws and institutions being shaped by the irrational impulses in man guided by a 'divine Providence' which, in reality, has neither Christian nor any supernatural connotations. The key elements in any community or commonwealth—religion, marriage, property, and government—are, on this reading, not rationally conceived or established, but evolve 'strictly ordered by God's Providence which arranges the course of history identically for every nation' with no theological event, or new gospel, altering or affecting the basic pattern of human development.[10]

The claim that Vico is a conservative thinker who supports the efforts of Church and princes against modern ideas and, most of all, philosophical radicalism, depends crucially on construing Vico's 'divine Providence' in a Christian sense for which it is hard to find convincing evidence. Of course, there is an element of intentional obscurity in his argumentation. Vico belonged to a philosophical coterie in Naples which was eyed with deep suspicion by the Church and Inquisition, and eventually also the secular government, a coterie acutely conscious of the need to present their ideas in a certain light. Thus, when discussing a hostile review of his *Scienza Nuova* in the Leipzig *Acta Eruditorum*, for 1727, Vico says his work is being disparaged for being adapted to the taste of the Catholic Church 'as if the conception of a divine Providence were not basic to the Christian religion in all its forms, or indeed to all religions'; 'thus,' he adds, 'the reviewer proves himself an Epicurean or Spinozist and

---

[8] Pompa, *Vico*, 51–3, 197–201; Lilla, *G. B. Vico*, 8–13, 144–54, 240, 243–4.   [9] Croce, *Filosofia*, 286.
[10] Pompa, *Vico*, 51–2, 60; Lilla, *G. B. Vico*, 11–12.

instead of the rebuke intended, pays the author the highest compliment, that of being pious.'[11] Publicly, Vico had no choice but to denounce Spinoza's metaphysics as apt to lead 'fragile minds ... to atheism' and his geometric method as fundamentally flawed; at the same time he was genuinely seeking a way round Spinoza's absolute and eternal necessity.[12] But (as with regard to Machiavelli) such apparently disparaging judgements simply cannot be taken at face value.

Spinoza, of course, also speaks of 'God's Providence', but outraged contemporary readers by imparting a special meaning to the term, linked to his insistence that God's decrees are unalterable and follow a fixed order, and that 'God' has no freedom or power to contradict Himself by intervening to change the natural order of things. Thus 'Providence' in Spinoza means the impossibility of any miraculous or super-natural intervention 'contrary to Nature'.[13] But it is hard to see that Vico's usage, even if more discreetly formulated, is fundamentally different except that Vico clearly refuses to allow that man as an individual is fully determined in his actions. Rather, in his thought man is conditioned by social conditions and circumstances. Vico's chief claim to greatness as a thinker lies precisely in his profoundly novel vision of history as a sequence of stages in the development of peoples, a process in which they evolve through a series of functionally related but not identical phases of culture, institutions, and politics in a fixed order. What is providential about Vico's vision of the historical process is that it is universal and, within a natural framework, immutable. Nothing could be further from Bossuet's demonstration of the play of Providence in history.

Furthermore, in Vico the distinction between sacred and profane history, between Christian and non-Christian history, totally disappears and a fundamental similarity, comparability, and moral validity is assigned to all societies and all stages of human development. Hence, despite some occasional rhetoric to the contrary, Christ the Redeemer, the rise of the Christian Church, and ecclesiastical authority are in fact stripped of functional significance in the workings of human history. A prime instance, almost *the* supreme example, of Vico's 'divine Providence' in action is the unparalleled stability and durability over many centuries of the Roman Empire. What is so impressive about ancient Rome, holds Vico, is her success in synthesizing laws and institutions of 'divine origin' with a rational conception of justice based on a universal right 'observed equally among all the nations'.[14] But this unrivalled Roman greatness, based, claims Vico, on 'divine Providence', was providential not in any theological sense but merely in the sense that men understood Rome's institutions to be infused by divine will. Thus, Vico asserts, neither the Epicureans who consider God to be exclusively material, 'nor the Stoics who, in this respect were the Spinozists of their day, and make God an infinite mind, subject to fate, in an infinite body', were capable of properly conceiving, let alone upholding, law, institutions, and politics. Spinoza, claims Vico, 'speaks of the commonwealth as if it were a society of traders',

[11] Vico, *Autobiography*, 187–8.   [12] Chaix-Ruy, *J. B. Vico*, 77–8; Pompa, *Vico*, 54–6, 78, 158.
[13] Reusch, *Systema metaphysicum*, 743–59; 836–48, 886, 1032, 1042–4.   [14] Lilla, *G. B. Vico*, 110.

failing to grasp the irrational drives, fears, ideals, and so forth which shape so much of human conduct.[15]

It is a remarkable allegation since it is primarily Spinoza who seeks to explain founding institutions, and especially organized religion, as deriving from irrational drives, fears, and ideals. Vico compliments Cicero for refusing to discuss laws with any Epicurean 'unless he first granted the existence of divine Providence'. But he then concludes that both Epicureanism and Stoicism, which he aligns closely with Spinozism, were entirely incompatible with the essence of 'Roman jurisprudence which takes divine Providence for its first principle'.[16] What Vico is surely saying here is that commonwealths are most stable and endure longest where the State's laws and institutions are believed to be authorized and governed by 'divine Providence'. The implication must be that this is a 'divine Providence' accommodated to the beliefs and notions of the common people, in this case the pagan Romans, and hence not a Providence infused with any Christian significance or inspired by religious ideals which any modern thinker could advocate.

In another revealing passage, discussing Hobbes, Vico claims the latter failed to grasp the principle that religion is the only powerful means whereby a savage and primitive people 'can be brought from their outlaw state to humanity'.[17] He then asserts 'this axiom establishes that divine Providence initiated the process by which the fierce and violent' first received laws and institutions in a settled society, being 'reduced' to obedience 'through the terror of this imagined divinity'. This clearly shadows Spinoza's doctrine of the origin of revealed religion, even if Vico is not consciously alluding to Spinoza (as I assume he is) when he adds that what the Christian religion 'commands is not merely justice but charity toward all mankind'.[18] Here again, Vico's rhetoric of 'divine Providence' reveals that what is really entailed is a radical secularization of history, designating organized religion as, if not quite the deliberate instrument of political and social management envisaged by Machiavelli and Spinoza, then certainly as a felt, unconscious guiding force which buttresses laws and institutions.[19]

At the close of his *Scienza Nuova* Vico once again rebukes Machiavelli, Hobbes, and Spinoza, insisting (like Doria) that for a truer and wiser philosophy we must turn to the 'divine Plato who shows that Providence directs human institutions'.[20] Again he applauds Cicero who—despite being a firm atheist and sceptic himself—refused to discuss laws with Epicureans who deny that 'Providence' governs human institutions. Family, property, and law, contends Vico, can not be based on anything but religion since in our modern times, the age of monarchies, 'religion must be the shield of princes: if religion is lost among the peoples, they have nothing left to enable them to live in society, no shield of defence nor means of counsel nor basis of support, nor even form by which they may exist in the world at all'.[21] In the context, this can only be

---

[15] Vico, *The New Science*, 98; Croce, *Filosofia*, 78; Pompa, *Vico*, 17–18, 22–3, 51–5.
[16] Vico, *The New Science*, 98.   [17] Ibid., 70.   [18] Ibid.
[19] Morrison, 'Vico and Spinoza', 52–3.   [20] Vico, *The New Science*, 425.   [21] Ibid., 426.

read as signifying that the religion the people believe in, whether Christianity or some other religion, upholds the 'divine Providence' which, in the minds of the common people, performs vital political and social functions.

According to Vico, Bayle's scepticism is utterly useless and the 'reasoned maxims of the philosophers concerning virtue' of only limited use. He reproaches the 'princes' of natural law theory—Grotius, Selden, and Pufendorf—who 'all err together' in relying too much on 'men enlightened by fully developed natural reason, from which philosophers emerged and rose to meditation of a perfect idea of justice'. But Vico is neither attacking the truth claims of 'fully developed natural reason', nor the general tendency of modern thought; he is simply warning against its inappropriate application in the sphere of law and institutions, where reason cannot be one-sidedly imposed without due regard for tradition, beliefs, and 'divine Providence'. Ultimately, Vico's *Scienza Nuova* is a statement about human reality and the human dilemma which, far from being basically 'theological' in character, irrevocably severs the link between theology and history as well as politics. On this reading, Vico intends to supply a corrective to Spinoza, many of whose ideas about human nature, the common good, the origin of society, and organized religion he accepts, supplementing his austere view of man, God, and truth by demonstrating that the truth of the philosophers can never be the truth of the people and must remain segregated, excluded from the sphere of commonly held and publicly approved notions which underpin institutions, laws, and government.

Even those modern commentators who insist that Vico was a philosophical opponent of Naturalism and Spinozism are obliged to concede that Spinoza exerted a significant influence on many of Vico's key formulations, on his critical philological method (also considerably influenced by Le Clerc), on his ethical philosophy, and finally, especially on his approach to the interaction of religion and society.[22] For the evidence for this is unanswerable. The allusions and parallels are simply too numerous to be denied. The parallel between Spinoza's claim that the Pentateuch is not divine revelation but was written many centuries after Moses, employing allegory, fables, and reports of miracles, adjusted to the credulity of the people, to teach obedience to law and authority, and Vico's argument, expounded at great length, that Homer's epics are an accumulation of collective primitive poetic wisdom, a fund of ideas expressed in the form of myth, intended to underpin the basic institutions of society, has often been noted.[23] Vico's treatment of the origins of modern reason, and the formation of human concepts more generally, is indeed one of the key elements of his philosophy. Especially noteworthy is his perception of human ideas as arising in a natural order determined by the needs and impulses of the human body and condition. In the archaic and heroic stages of development, man needs and has the same basic concepts as he has later but expresses them in terms of poetic wisdom, fable,

---

[22] Vico, *The New Science*, 73–6; Morrison, 'Vico and Spinoza', 49–50; Stone, *Vico's Cultural History*, 302–4.

[23] Morrison, 'Vico and Spinoza', 55; Stone, *Vico's Cultural History*, 303–4.

myth, and revelations.[24] Only subsequently do these ideas emerge in a more orderly fashion in the light of pure reason. Thus, in Vico no less than Spinoza, intellect derives from primitive sense, yielding the doctrine that the archaic poets 'were the sense and the philosophers the intellect of human reason'.[25]

For readers who are philosophically literate, Vico discreetly renders his debt to Spinoza explicit without mentioning Spinoza's name by paraphrasing, in a section emphasizing the close interaction of mind and body, Proposition VII of Part II of the *Ethics* where Spinoza holds 'The order and connection of ideas is the same as the order and connection of things.' Vico's formulation originally read 'the order of human ideas must proceed according to the order of human things,' but in the third edition this is amended to 'the order of ideas must proceed according to the order of things.'[26] Moreover, Vico not only embraces Spinoza's epistemology along with the methodology of his Bible criticism and views on the origin and social functions of religion, but he is clearly a radical thinker. For while he was neither a republican nor democrat, Vico's advocacy of 'enlightened' monarchy is unquestionably linked to a vigorous social egalitarianism. Indeed, within the entire corpus of Early Enlightenment radical thought no other thinker produced so devastating a critique of nobility as did Vico.

Vico's Providence is in fact nothing other than the historical process which gradually shepherds mankind, as he describes it, from barbarism to a more settled, orderly state, and a society based upon reason. People act from selfish motives, but this does not inhibit the wider historical process. Thus, for example, 'the reigning orders of nobles mean to abuse their lordly freedom over the plebeians' but in time, precisely through trying to exploit them, they themselves 'are obliged to submit to the laws which establish popular liberty'.[27] Nobility in Vico's schema arises during the heroic age and entails domination of society and property through sheer violence and exploitation. But with time 'and the far greater development of human minds, the common people finally grow distrustful of the claims of heroism and begin to conceive themselves to be of equal human nature with the nobles'.[28] With this the principle of equality begins and Providence, as Vico puts it, 'permitted' a struggle in which the people emerged as sovereign. Moreover, once the power of the nobles declines it cannot be revived. 'For the plebeians, once they know themselves to be of equal nature with the nobles, naturally will not submit to remaining their inferiors in civil rights; and they achieve equality either in free commonwealths or under monarchies.'[29] But Providence, insists Vico, ensures that popular régimes, with their inherent weaknesses, rapidly degenerate into 'anarchy or the unchecked liberty of free peoples which is the worst of all tyrannies'. Thus great monarchies, according to Vico, spring from liberty itself, that is, 'Providence ordains that the very form of

---

[24] Vico, *The New Science*, 76–9; Sina, *Vico e le Le Clerc*, 71.

[25] Vico, *The New Science* 297; Stone. *Vico's Cultural History*, 304.

[26] Vico, *The New science.*, 78; Spinoza, *Opera*, ii, 89; Stone, *Vico's Cultural History*, 306.

[27] Vico, *The New Science*, 425.   [28] Ibid., 422.   [29] Ibid., 412.

the monarchic state shall confine the will of monarchs, in spite of their unlimited sovereignty.' 'For without this universal satisfaction and content of the peoples,' contends Vico, not unlike Spinoza in the *Tractatus Politicus*, 'monarchic states are neither lasting nor secure.'[30] By their nature monarchies 'seek to make their subjects all equal', and 'humble the powerful and thus keep the masses safe and free from their oppressions'.[31]

A drastic inequality in distribution of land and wealth prevails during the heroic age, which is based partly on violence but equally, or more, on credulity and ignorance. For both nobles and serfs believe their social system is ordained by the gods.[32] The fact that for Vico 'monarchy is the form of government best adapted to human nature when reason is fully developed,'[33] implies that the progress of human reason involves a related process of social and political struggle. Hence social violence, including revolution, is neither good nor bad in itself, but just the inevitable accompaniment of historical development.[34] Before making judgements about popular tumults one must first determine what they are about. For if its purpose is to overthrow the tyranny and pretensions of aristocracy, Vico seems clearly to infer that revolution is good. Hence, Vico's 'divine Providence' furnishes what has aptly been termed a 'natural right to insurrection' arising from man's inevitable eventual quest for self-liberation from oppression and exploitation.[35]

ii. Paolo Mattia Doria (1662–1746)

If Vico was indeed not an 'anti-modern' but a radical, the same appears to be true of his ally and friend, Paolo Mattia Doria. Doria's antipathy to Descartes, Locke, and Newton, his partiality for Plato, and his contention that the political and social virtues attained a higher level in classical Greece than eighteenth-century Europe have led to his being considered an eccentric out of tune with his own time. Yet one only need consider his pleas for social, political, and cultural reform, advocacy of women's right to participate in intellectual life, contempt for princes, and detailed grasp of the philosophies vying for hegemony in early eighteenth-century Italy, to appreciate his relevance to the budding Enlightenment and his rightful claim to the title of *philosophe*.

A central figure among the Neapolitan *letterati* during the opening three decades of the century, and for the first two still a Cartesian and *Malebranchiste*,[36] from around 1730 Doria found himself increasingly marginalized owing to his unremitting antagonism to Descartes, Malebranche, and Locke, the last of whom he denounced as a demi-Epicurean and herald of Spinozism.[37] He was also highly critical of Muratori, Conti, and Maffei. As his opponents multiplied, rumour implicating him in heterodoxy became rife. He himself describes how reports spread among

---

[30] Vico, *The New Science*, 423.   [31] Ibid., 379.   [32] Lilla, *G. B. Vico*, 182.
[33] Vico, *The New Science*, 379.   [34] Remaud, 'Conflits', 54.
[35] Ibid., 55–6; see also Pompa, *Vico*, 187–90.   [36] Zambelli, 'Il rogo postumo', 152–4.
[37] Doria, *Filosofia*, ii, 305–6; Conti, *Paolo Mattia Doria*, 61.

people 'who are incapable of grasping even the easiest part of the Platonic doctrine and consequently confuse Plato with the impious Benedetto Spinoza and claim that my philosophy is similar to that of Spinoza'.[38] Thus, he says, implying that his enemies would dearly like to see him suffer just such a fate, he is decried by the ignorant masses of Naples as a 'Spinozist', precisely as in ancient Athens Democritus branded Socrates a Sophist. These endeavours to persuade Neapolitans that 'the teaching of Plato, a follower of Socrates and Spinoza's are one and the same thing' hinged on the fact both Plato and Spinoza hold that there is 'only one substance'. 'But what the plebs fail, or pretend not, to understand,' maintains Doria, 'is that Spinoza acknowledges only one infinite material substance exactly as Democritus taught and that this is why Spinoza deprives God of intelligence, Providence, and all attributes of perfection just as Democritus and Epicurus denied Him the same attributes.'[39] Plato by contrast 'acknowledges an infinite substance purely spiritual and immaterial which creates through its love, goodness, and intelligence and conserves the universe through its eternal and infinite Providence'. In short, where 'Spinoza is the author of the sect of the *deisti*' who proclaim an infinite substance which they call God, while in no way differing from the *Epicurei* and atheists since they deprive God of His intelligence and Providence, Plato 'institutes a religion rather like our holy Christian religion'.[40]

One of Doria's chief antagonists was Caloprese's disciple, Francesco Maria Spinelli, Prince of Scalea, who in the 1730s was at the forefront of what, in Italy, was still a potent Cartesian bloc. In his *Riflessioni* (Naples, 1733) Spinelli not only vehemently rebuts Doria's 'calumny' that Cartesianism is inherently prone to evolve into Spinozism, but repeats in print the allegations that Doria himself was a crypto-Spinozist, who impugns others to deflect suspicion from himself, circulating in Naples by then for over a decade.[41] Not only is Descartes innocent of Doria's charges, contends Spinelli, but he alone among thinkers furnishes the necessary armament 'against that malignant snake' as we see from the fact that only Cartesians had seriously and effectively battled Spinoza, among them Lamy, Régis, Wittichius, and, above all, 'my master Gregorio Caloprese who . . . dealt with that author in such a way, uncovering his infinite contradictions, that he left him not a stone to stand on'.[42] Moreover, since Descartes, Cartesians 'have taken up arms not only against Spinoza but all Deism'.[43] Spinelli's challenge and the ensuing *scandalosa disputa* rendered Doria vulnerable, obliging him to defend himself publicly with regard to Cartesianism, Spinozism, and Platonism, not least since, as a young thinker before 1709, he had penned some undeniably Spinozistic dialogues in manuscript, a copy of which had been in Caloprese's possession and had latterly been passed to Spinelli. Doria acknowledged writing these but insisted they were youthful indiscretions, which he now disowned, and into which he had briefly lapsed through reading Descartes.[44] He agreed there were numerous

---

[38] Doria, *Difesa della metafisica*, 30.   [39] Ibid., 30–1; Doria, *Risposte*, 16.

[40] Doria, *Difesa della metafisica*, 31; Doria, *Lettere e ragionamenti*, i, 290–300; see also Pompa, *Vico*, 79.

[41] Doria, *Discorsi Critici filosofici*, 24–5.   [42] Spinelli, *Riflessioni*, 2.

[43] Ibid., 5.   [44] Zambelli, 'Il rogo postumo', 154–5.

upright and God-fearing Cartesians and that Cartesianism is by no means equivalent to Spinozism. His point was that there are inevitable dangers in Descartes' system apt to lead some to Spinozism, and that Cartesianism was the route by which Spinoza himself had arrived at his execrable heresies.[45]

Spinelli proclaimed Descartes' doctrine of two substances to be fundamentally at odds with Spinoza's one-substance metaphysics: thus 'what Spinoza lays down as the basis of his sect, Renato entirely rejects as a chimaera.'[46] Doria countered by emphasizing the weakness of Descartes' conception of the Creation in time and space in the Sixth Meditation and elsewhere.[47] While Descartes was doubtless a loyal Catholic, his account of the Creation is so incoherent that 'following Renato's doctrine we ought not to believe in the Creation in time, and from nothing, because he urges us to consider nothing true if we lack a clear and distinct idea of it'.[48] Worse still, Descartes' account of Creation, like his muddled concept of substance, invites the Spinozist endeavour which feeds on the defects of Cartesianism to 'demonstrate that Creation in time, and from nothing, by God is impossible'.[49]

The two antagonists agreed that the central question in early eighteenth-century philosophy was how to defeat the *Epicurei* and *Spinosisti*.[50] Deriding Spinelli's two-substance doctrine, Doria offers his Neoplatonic philosophy underpinned with arguments which, however, were bound to strengthen suspicions of disturbing affinities between his Neoplatonism and Spinozism. If Doria is a loyal Catholic who believes Christ's coming is the decisive event in history, why continually claim that in most of the virtues and general culture Europe had lamentably retrogressed since classical Greece?[51] Doria claimed to have rescued the Providence, intelligence, and Will of God from the *Spinosisti*, but it was far from evident that Plato's and Doria's God was distinct from the totality of the universe. When Doria (and for that matter Vico) affirms that the 'Providenza di Dio' is the same as the infinitely perfect order of things, one could hardly fail to suspect that both thinkers were subsuming Providence into the unalterable laws of Nature.[52] How miracles are safeguarded and the *Spinosisti* thwarted by equating the 'Will of God' with the Intelligence and Compassion of God, and proclaiming God a perfect being whose will is 'eterna ed immutabile', was far from clear.

Spinelli was less than altogether fair in claiming that, in ethics like metaphysics, the *Spinosisti* would wholeheartedly embrace Doria's teaching. For there were some solid differences between Doria and Spinoza, notably in his emphatic Neoplatonic insistence on the soul's immortality and the scope this affords, as he says, for reward and punishment in the hereafter, and his related dismissal of Spinoza's moral

---

[45] Doria, *Discorsi critici filosofici*, 41, 51, 53; Doria, *Risposte* 5, 76, 88, 116; Doria, *Filosofia*, ii, 303–4.
[46] Spinelli, *Riflessioni*, 130, 150, 400–1.
[47] Doria, *Risposte*, 88; on this weakness, see Cottingham, *A Descartes Dictionary*, 43–4.
[48] Doria, *Risposte*, 88.   [49] Doria, *Filosofia*, i, 185.
[50] Ibid., 146–7, 172, 184–8; Doria, *Lettere e ragionamenti*, i, 41–4, 398–40; Doria, *Discorse critici filosofici*, 222–4.
[51] Doria, *Filosofia*, ii, 122–7.
[52] Ibid., i, 237–9, 242; Spinelli, *Riflessioni*, 115–17; Zambelli, 'Il rogo postumo', 156.

determinism.[53] Doria claimed that Epicurean and Spinozist ethics undermines virtue and public-spiritedness in the republic, and discourages military valour and love of glory, inducing men to prize only their own particular concerns and pleasures.[54] But objections to Spinoza on such grounds as these patently failed to reassure the reading public about Doria.

In his late work, the three-volume *Lettere e ragionamenti* (1741), Doria reiterates his Neoplatonism against Descartes, Spinoza, and Locke, and now also adds Voltaire to his list of *bêtes noires*. Voltaire, he says, is vastly overrated.[55] His *Lettres philosophiques* may have made an impact on the world, but Doria refuses to grant that his Newton-ianism, and advocacy of Locke, in any way help to defend Providence, the Christian mysteries, or the immortality of the soul against Spinoza who, here again, is identified as the founder of modern deism and what, according to Doria, is effectively the same thing, the new philosophical atheism.[56] Given his own previous strictures on the topic, it is curious to find him censuring Voltaire for defending belief in the soul's immortal-ity on the grounds that society needs this if it is to regulate men's conduct, claiming such an argument reduces religion to politics and lowers Voltaire virtually to the loathsome level of Spinoza, Hobbes, and Machiavelli.[57] Plato, he asserts, is totally opposed to such a weak attitude and, once more, it is still Plato, he urges, who offers the best armaments against Spinoza. Cartesianism, mercifully, was now in full decline but alas, he laments, 'our Italians have become in everything servile imitators of for-eign nations.'[58] The Italians had at last discarded Descartes but were now slavishly adopting Newton and Locke instead.[59]

During 1741 Doria also drafted his last major work, his *Idea for a Perfect Republic*, which seems to have been a challenging blend of politics and philosophy. Increas-ingly under question, and aware this book was apt to provoke greater opposition than ever, Doria decided not to publish it during his lifetime. Shortly before his death, in 1746, he announced he was leaving his unpublished manuscripts, including this new text, in the library of San Angelo at Nido, where interested readers could consult them. Most remained unpublished until the twentieth century. But he left some money in his will specifically to fund publication of his *Idea*. However, in 1753, as the text was being prepared for the press, the printer was arrested and the manu-script copies seized by the police. Rumours were circulating about the work's allegedly godless content, which alarmed the secular, as well as the ecclesiastical authorities.

Doria had never hidden his preference for republics over monarchies. As a young man, a foe of Louis XIV and an admirer of the Dutch Republic, he had published *La Vita Civile* (1706), a work of political thought based on the Hobbesian–Spinozist prin-ciple that human conduct is always motivated by the impulse to 'conservazione di si stesso' (conservation of the self). Like Vico, Doria disapproved of democracy as

---

[53] Doria, *Discorsi critici filosofici*, 178–9, 182–4. [54] Ibid., 184.
[55] Doria, *Lettere e ragionamenti*, ii, 8–18, 119–20, 376; Conti, *Paolo Mattia Doria*, 71–2.
[56] Doria, *Lettere e ragionamenti*, i, 41, 132. [57] Ibid., ii, 121.
[58] Doria, *Discorsi critici filosofici*, 160. [59] Doria, *Lettere e ragionamenti*, ii, 371.

inherently unstable and prone to lead directly to dictatorship and tyranny.[60] Ancient Athens, being democratic, was fatally tainted in Doria's eyes. Rather he extolled the 'perfection of the Spartan republic', that is, an aristocratic republic which cultivates valour and public service.[61] In his new work, Doria developed further his thesis that monarchy is fundamentally defective and fails to encourage genuine virtue. In his view, it also degenerates naturally into tyranny. In addition, he plainly revealed his antipathy to ecclesiastical authority, and the educational influence of the Jesuits, and restated his Neoplatonism in a way which was bound to re-awaken suspicions of Spinozism.

The Bourbon government's public censor (*revisore*) of books particularly objected, it seems, to Doria's dismissal of the Church's doctrine of the eternal damnation of those who are not saved,[62] and judged the book apt to undermine marriage by insinuating that extramarital intercourse is not sinful. He also ruled unacceptable its critical observations about priestly celibacy and attitudes to education. The regime decided the work should be suppressed *in toto*. It was duly condemned in a public ceremony on 13 March 1753, and consigned to the flames by the public executioner. Doria's image as a radical, an enemy of the Church and of monarchy, and a crypto-Spinozist was thereby given the imprimatur of high authority.

iii. Pietro Giannone (1676–1748)

In exile in Vienna, Giannone had enjoyed privileged access to the bibliographical splendours of Prince Eugene's library and steeped himself in the literature of radical thought from Spinoza to Toland's latest productions.[63] By 1726 the exiled historian is known to have embarked on a close study of Spinoza, making notes on both the *Ethics* and the *Tractatus Theologico-Politicus*, as well as the *Letters*, which continued over the years and profoundly influenced his subsequent development as an Early Enlightenment spokesman.[64] Initially, he anticipated that his exile in Austria would be brief. But the increasingly reactionary stance of the régime in Naples in the late 1720s and early 1730s gradually undermined his hopes and, from 1731, Giannone threw himself into the intensive studies which prepared the way for his major work of Bible criticism, his *Triregno*.[65] Besides radical literature and such authors as Le Clerc and Vico, he carefully studied the Biblical books and Homer.[66]

Meanwhile, from the comparative safety of Vienna, Giannone also continued his one-man feud, markedly intensified since the accession of Pope Benedict XIII (in office 1724–30), with the Papacy and Inquisition over his *Civil History of Naples*. The publication in Rome (with 'Cologne' falsely declared on the title-page), late in 1728, of a defamatory tract openly declaring Giannone a rebel against the Pope and the

---

[60] Doria, *La Vita Civile*, 77, 94–5; Zambelli, 'Il rogo postumo', 162.
[61] Doria, *La Vita Civile*, 95–6. [62] Zambelli, 'Il rogo postumo', 188–9, 195.
[63] Ricuperati, 'Giannone', 62–3.
[64] Ricuperati, 'Libertinismo', 637, 654–7; Berti, 'At the Roots', 564.
[65] Venturi, 'Gli anni' 30, 11; Giannone, *Opere*, 203. [66] Giannone, *Opere*, 214–221.

Church and excoriating his 'impious', 'seditious', 'heretical', and 'scandalous' propositions was answered with a brusque reply, the caustic, almost Voltairean, tone of which, not least in its attack on papal supremacy, only aggravated matters. The Roman Inquisition, having heard late in 1731 that Giannone was planning to republish his *Civil History* in Holland, instructed the papal nuncio in Brussels to contact the Dutch Catholic authorities with a view to attempting by every means to 'prevent the printing of the work there'.[67]

Though it remained unpublished at the time, and indeed until 1895,[68] the *Triregno*, largely written between 1731 and 1734, was indubitably Giannone's most important book and has been styled 'one of the most significant works of European culture of the first half of the eighteenth century'.[69] It is a wide-ranging philosophical and theological odyssey of the mind, reflecting the breadth of reading Giannone had acquired in Vienna. Like Doria, Giannone devastatingly assails Descartes and Malebranche, lambasting their doctrine of two substances and account of the human soul, and the feebleness of Descartes' theory of Creation.[70] If one thinks through Descartes' propositions logically, he insists, extension and thought become mere modifications of substance and hence one arrives at the impossibility of separating general substance from 'divine substance' and must acknowledge that 'God himself is substance, the nature and essence of all things,' a doctrine which is not only the thesis of Spinoza but, in tendency, also that of Malebranche.[71] This, Strabo and other classical sources report, was also Moses' view and this is the reason, he says, alluding to Toland's *Origines Judicae* (1709), that some maintain, contradicting our theologians, that Moses was really a *panteista* or *Spinosista*.[72]

In Part I Giannone also effectively rejects divine authorship of the *Pentateuch*. In his lengthy critical examination of the Biblical books, referring to Hobbes and La Peyrère occasionally, but relying principally on Spinoza and Toland,[73] Giannone accepts neither that Moses wrote the Five Books nor the argument that the moral content of Scripture proves their divine inspiration. Spinoza, he remarks, while demonstrating that the *divinità* of the Five Books can not be proved from the miracles they recount, or the prophecies they contain, 'says the only proof is that in them true virtue is taught'.[74] But no one can take this seriously as confirmation of the divine origin of the *Pentateuch*, comments Giannone, since the Egyptians, Greeks, Romans, and others say as much about the texts of their philosophers.

Crucial to Giannone's radicalism is his stance on the soul's immortality. Toland claimed that the notion of the soul's immortality was originally unknown to the Hebrews and derives from gentile societies, especially the Egyptians.[75] This idea is readily embraced by Giannone, who finds that the doctrine of the soul's immortality,

---

[67] Marini, 'Documenti', 713–14. [68] Giannone, *Opere*, 593.
[69] See Giuseppe Ricuperati's remarks in Giannone, *Opere*, 581. [70] Giannone, *Opere*, 624–48.
[71] Ibid., 638. [72] See Giannone, *Opere*, 640 and p. 611 above.
[73] Mannarino, 'Pietro Giannone', 227–41; Ricuperati, 'Libertinismo', 657, 670, 687.
[74] Giannone, *Il Triregno* (full version), i, 21; Spinoza, *TTP*, 211–12; Bertelli, *Giannoniana*, 176–7.
[75] Champion, *Pillars of Priestcraft*, 148–9.

upheld by the Pharisees but dismissed by the Sadducees—who, in this respect as in others, were closer to early Israelite and Biblical tradition—has no Biblical basis or other legitimacy.[76] He dismisses the doctrine as a false and vulgar notion wholeheart-edly adopted only in comparatively recent centuries.[77] This established, he proceeds in rapid steps to demolish the Church's teaching on Purgatory, Heaven, and Hell.

No less radical is Giannone's attempt to undermine, and discredit, the Catholic Church's claims to supremacy. Marked by a general tone of hostility towards the Papacy, ecclesiastical authority, and the Church Fathers, as well as the Biblical prophets, Giannone contends that political circumstances, especially the conversion of Constantine the Great, and the enforcement of Christianity as the imperial religion in the fourth century, rendered the Church politically but not spiritually supreme in matters of faith and belief. The bishops and the Church hierarchy received not only privileges, power, and wealth, but magnificent vestments and adornments so that they should be 'rendered more august and respected by the people'.[78] Hence, the 'Church began to assume another form from that in which Christ and his apostles had left it'.[79] Other later bogus accretions, dismissed as worthless by Giannone, include the cult of images and relics, and doctrines such as the Eucharist, confession, penitence, and Purgatory.

All this and other uninhibitedly radical positions, such as his libertine attitude towards sexual relations, echoing Doria in claiming that extramarital intercourse is not sinful,[80] suggest the book was never intended for publication but solely for private use or clandestine circulation in manuscript. For Giannone had by no means yet lost all hope of rehabilitation and recovering his former status and influence in Naples. The Spanish reconquest of the viceroyalty in 1734 simultaneously reawakened his hopes and precluded remaining at the Viennese Court, now the prime enemy of the reigning prince in Naples.[81] He departed, migrating in September 1734 to Venice which, since the eclipse of Naples, was emerging as the liveliest centre of intellectual debate in Italy and where friends urged him to produce the long-awaited new edition of his *Civil History*. But despite the much freer atmosphere prevailing there since the beginning of the new century, Venice proved a bold, even perhaps a reckless choice. Lodging near Saint Mark's, a notorious figure abhorred by numerous and powerful elements in Italian society, he promptly fell under the surveillance of Inquisitors and Jesuits, acting on orders from Rome. During 1735, 'whenever I came into Saint Mark's Square,' he later recalled, 'they had persons there who noted all my utterances and movements.'[82] However, he was strenuously urged to stay by allies such as Antonio Conti, and greatly enjoyed the company of the erudite and enlightened men he met, particularly in Conti's circle.[83] Meanwhile, his approach, through the Spanish ambas-sador, to the new Neapolitan régime yielded only the dispiriting news that there was no prospect of his ever returning to Naples.[84]

[76] Giannone, *Il Triregno*, ii, 165–6, 171–5, 195–250; Carpanetto and Ricuperati, *Italy*, 110–11.
[77] Giannone, *Il Triregno*, ii, 250; Bertelli, *Giannoniana*, 175.   [78] Giannone, *Opere*, 656–7.
[79] Ibid., 659.   [80] Bertelli, *Giannoniana*, 176.   [81] Giannone, *Opere*, 261.
[82] Ibid., 279, 282.   [83] Ibid., 267, 280.   [84] Ibid., 288.

The efforts of the Inquisition's spies were in fact signs of a pending counter-stroke in Venice against the Radical Enlightenment more generally. As part of this, Giannone was arrested by the Venetian 'Inquisitors of State' in September 1735, at the Papacy's request, the papal authorities, among other things, being anxious to prevent a new edition of the *Civil History*. Giannone was declared an undesirable influence by the Venetian authorities and summarily deported by boat. He was unceremoniously deposited with his books and possessions near Ferrara, on the papal side of the river marking the boundary with the Papal States. But luck had not deserted him yet. The communication from the nuncio in Venice alerting the Ferrarese Inquisitors arrived too late for them to catch him before he reached the fleeting safety of Modena, while the Inquisitors there were likewise too slow to intercept his rapid flight northwards. Seeking a safe haven close to Italy, he settled in Geneva. But that was the end of his good fortune. Early in 1736, while making a clandestine visit across the border, he was betrayed to soldiers of the Savoyard monarch and imprisoned at Turin.[85] The new king, Carlo Emmanuele (ruled 1730–73), detesting everything Giannone stood for, wished neither to release him nor to send him for trial to Rome. Giannone's tragic fate was to languish in prison in Turin for the rest of his life. Permitted books, pens, and paper, his only solace was scholarly research and writing.

The result, directed in some degree perhaps at procuring a pardon, or conditional release, through a show of contrition and abjuring his former principles, was a substantial retreat from his former radicalism to a respectful attitude towards revealed religion and the Church, and what has been called a 'Catholic deism'. He wrote several further critical, historical, and theological works, all exuding quiet deference to the authorities. It made no difference to his wretched fate. After more than twelve years of incarceration in the citadel of Turin by one of the most reactionary and despotic regimes of the day, a bastion of opposition to deism and irreligious philosophy, Giannone died in his cell at the age of 72 on 17 March 1748, a lonely martyr, like Koerbagh and Walten, to radical ideas.

iv. Radical Thought in Venice

The expulsion of Giannone and Grimaldi from Naples, and suppression of their works there, combined with the conservative crack-down in Rome and Savoy, and the slow recovery in Tuscany from the severities of Cosimo III's reign, created a situation in which Venice and its satellite university town of Padua emerged as the chief focus of radical debate and ideas in Italy from the late 1720s onwards. But here too there was repression. That there was a close connection between the deportation of Giannone and the subsequent crack-down in Venice on those who held radical views was evidently assumed by everyone at the time, as we see from a letter written by the Venetian savant Apostolo Zeno, in September 1735, in which he describes Giannone's arrest, remarking that the 'party of his admirers and partisans being bewildered and

[85] Ibid., 326–8.

dejected . . . all the decent folk here are exulting'; furthermore, noted Zeno, 'with this event, rumours are circulating about other persons who profess modern opinions and new philosophies.'[86] Indeed, investigation into the opinions of several suspect figures, including Antonio Conti, the leader of the Venetian radical philosophical coterie, had already started.

Antonio Conti (1667–1749) who had frequently been in Giannone's company during the latter's stay in Venice, had spent many years abroad in northern Europe, and made an extensive study of contemporary European philosophy, science, and scientific theory. He is in fact one of the most impressive figures of the Italian Early Enlightenment. A member of the Venetian nobility who became a priest as a young man and a member of the Oratory, he left the Oratorians in 1708, deciding to devote himself henceforth to the study of philosophy. At Padua he became a disciple of Fardella, and for some years was an ardent Cartesian and adherent of Malebranche. In 1713, out of 'love for philosophy', he moved to Paris to continue his studies and meet the venerable Malebranche himself; but after several meetings with the great thinker he found that his difficulties with the latter's 'volontés générales' remained unresolved.[87] He turned next to Leibniz, with whom he began corresponding, and even more, Newton. In April 1715 he crossed the Channel to confer with Newton in person and other *érudits* in London, and eight months later, on Newton's recommendation, was elected an associate of the Royal Society.[88] Punctuated by visits to Holland and Germany in 1716, he stayed three years in England and, besides discussions with Newton and Clarke, met 's-Gravesande and became friendly with Des Maizeaux.

Yet Conti was no more convinced by Newton and Clarke than by Malebranche or Leibniz and, in March 1718, returned to Paris where he stayed until late 1726, becoming a familiar figure of the Parisian salons on close terms with Fontenelle, Dorthous de Mairan, and Fréret. He also became friendly with Montesquieu, whom he later showed round Venice during his stay there in 1728.[89] After returning to Italy in 1726, he was widely recognized as 'un gran filosofo' but one with highly suspect opinions.[90] In December 1726, he reported to his closest ally in Venice, the biologist and one of the editors of the Venetian *Giornale*, Antonio Vallisnieri, that in both England and France most of the savants were now deists highly sceptical about Scripture.[91]

Deeply influenced by Galileo, Conti, like Vallisnieri, was an extreme mechanist who had come to reject all the strains of the mainstream moderate Enlightenment. He was as intrigued by Leibniz's pre-established harmony as he was by Newton's concept of a universally diffused divine force constantly in operation, but could find no conclusive philosophical basis for preferring one to the other or assuming that the force intrinsic in all bodies is not a motion innate in matter, the 'system of plastic natures in the sense of Strato and Spinoza' as he calls it.[92] Throughout his career his abiding preoccupation was the question of the motive force in bodies and genera-

---

[86] Giannone, *Opere*, 510.   [87] Gronda, 'Antonio Conti', 353; Badaloni, *Antonio Conti*, 27, 50.
[88] Ibid., 185.   [89] Montesquieu, *Oeuvres complètes*, 225, 229, 232, 402.
[90] Ibid., 189.   [91] Badaloni, *Antonio Conti*, 189.
[92] Conti, *Risposta*, 120–3, 126; Badaloni, *Antonio Conti*, 34–5, 95; Ferrone, *Intellectual Roots*, 101.

tion of living things. By 1728 at the latest, Conti had come to recognize the origin of life in the motion innate in all matter and the capacity of a single substance to evolve and recreate itself.[93] Another enduring theme was the origin of Man's ideas. He carefully examined Locke's philosophy but firmly rejected this too, believing Locke had fallen into the error of confusing primitive with 'simple' ideas, arguing that original sensations of the primary qualities of things such as size, texture, shape, temperature, and so forth, are quite a different thing from the simple abstractions inferred by the mind through an intellectual process of reflection.[94] Meanwhile, the same refusal to accept a divine Providence outside Nature as an organizing principle in philosophy, which led to his rejection of Newton rendered him, after his return to Italy, an enthusiastic admirer of Vico's new way of contemplating Providence and interpreting history.[95]

In the privacy of their inner circle Conti and Vallisnieri developed a philosophy and scientific outlook in conscious opposition to Newtonian providentialism and the 'argument from design'.[96] Scorning Descartes' soulless machines, in a letter to Conti in 1727, Vallisnieri averred that 'all organic bodies, that are born, that grow . . . have a soul, as we do, and it would not be such a mortal sin in philosophy to believe that all plants have one.'[97] But in the fraught atmosphere of the 1730s it was also inevitable that Conti should be identified as the leader of a philosophical undercurrent eyed by many with intense suspicion. Shortly before Giannone's deportation, and his own encounter with the Inquisition in September 1735, Giannone and Conti engaged in a series of long philosophical discussions, until deep into the night, a principal theme being the soul's mortality or immortality.[98] On 11 August 1735, a month before Giannone's expulsion, Conti was secretly denounced to the Inquisition by two Venetian priests, one the confessor of the nuns of San Rocco, who could testify to his uttering impieties in conversation.[99] His indiscretions included saying that Scripture consists of 'fatuous fables' and is a 'secular history' which one should read as one does 'Cicero or Livy', dismissing the Christian mysteries, 'freedom of the will', and immortality of the soul, and claiming the universe is eternal and motion is innate in matter.[100] Thanks to the intervention of friends among the Venetian nobility, no formal trial for 'atheism' occurred and Conti was let off with a stern rebuke.

The deportation of Giannone and the denunciation of Conti sufficed to cast a pall of fear and threw the entire circle of Venetian *spiriti forti* into disarray. These events also lent added urgency to the question of Spinoza and Spinozism in the minds of the entire Venetian intellectual establishment, conservative, moderate, and radical.[101] Back in the 1690s, Fardella had proclaimed the indispensability of the New Philosophy

---

[93] Vernière, *Spinoza*, 390; Badaloni, *Antonio Conti*, 103; Ferrone, *Intellectual Roots*, 104–5.

[94] Badaloni, *Antonio Conti*, 118, 137–9.   [95] Ibid., 112–13, 149–50.

[96] Ferrone, *Intellectual Roots*, 106–7.   [97] Ibid., 110–11.

[98] Ibid., 260; Giannone, *Opere*, 520–2, 530.

[99] Giannone, *Opere*, 530; Gronda, 'Antonio Conti', 358; Ferrone, *Intellectual Roots*, 106, 414.

[100] Giannone, *Opere*, 991; Badaloni, *Antonio Conti*, 190–2; Gronda, 'Antonio Conti', 358.

[101] Ferrone, *Intellectual Roots*, 106.

as the intellectual armour of Church and faith in the struggle against the 'followers of Epicurus' and, not least, as the chief safeguard of belief in the 'immortality of the soul'.[102] By the mid-1730s, however, nothing could be plainer than that Venice's radical philosophical coterie scorned Descartes, rejected the soul's immortality, and embraced the innateness of motion in matter and the self-generation of bodies. The future progress, the very survival, of the moderate mainstream Enlightenment in the Venetian Republic, as well as the respectability of studying the new philosophies and scientific discoveries emanating from Protestant lands such as England, Germany, and the Netherlands, depended, as Maffei later stressed, on a much more combative and vigorous segregation of the radical tendency from moderate thought.[103]

A striking manifestation of this post-1735 enhanced relevance of the Spinozist challenge within Venetian culture, and of efforts to bring it into the light of day and shatter it philosophically, was a public oration on Spinoza, delivered at Padua in 1737, and published the following year, by the professor of metaphysics, Bonaventura Lucchi. Lucchi provides a detailed account of Spinoza's life and works, mentioning a number of refutations of his ideas, including the article in Bayle's *Dictionnaire*, and lavishes attention on several key propositions from the *Ethics*, quoting verbatim, among others, Proposition XV of Book I: 'quicquid est, in Deo est, et nihil sine Deo esse, neque concipi potest' (Whatever is, is in God and nothing can exist, or be conceived, apart from God).[104] Significantly, given the subsequent controversy in the Veneto in the 1740s over magic and spirits, in which Maffei played a leading role, Lucchi also denounces (while simultaneously highlighting) Spinoza's sweeping denial of Satan, demons, ghosts, spectres, and all supernatural powers.[105]

The drama of September 1735 passed. But the feeling that Venice was besieged by a new atheism did not. In his magisterial *Theologia Christiana Dogmatico-Moralis* in twelve volumes (Rome, 1749–51), in terms of robustness and bulk one of the most imposing works by a Venetian scholar of the age, Concina singles out Spinoza as the chief inspiration of the *spiritus fortes* (*esprits forts*), citing Huet, Le Vassor, Buddeus, and Nieuwentijt for their powerful refutations of his thought.[106] Concina subsequently again highlighted Spinoza, this time more extensively, in his imposing defence of revealed religion in two volumes, published at Venice in 1754. This indeed is a most revealing work for understanding Venetian, and all European, culture in the mid-eighteenth century. A Dominican friar of great austerity and pro-Jansenist sympathies, detested by the Jesuits, and a declared enemy of Maffei, though not of modern philosophy more generally, Concina enjoyed a formidable reputation as a leading Catholic apologist in Venice, Rome, and all Italy.[107] He wrote the work, he explains in

---

[102] Fardella, *Filosofia Cartesiana Impugnata*, 1st Letter, 18; Fardella, *Animae Humanae Incorporea*, 388–90, 251–3, 276–7.
[103] Maffei, *Arte magica dileguata*, 46–7.
[104] Lucchi, *Spinozismi Syntagma*, 38; Spinoza, *Opera*, ii, 56; Ferrone, *Intellectual Roots*, 106.
[105] Lucchi, *Spinozismi Syntagma*, 46–7.
[106] Concina, *Theologia Christiana*, i, 34, 41.
[107] Vecchi, *Correnti religiose*, 343–5; Ferrone, *Intellectual Roots*, 226–7.

the preface, at the prompting of Pope Benedict XIV (in office 1740–58) whose policy it was to broaden and intensify the Church's counter-offensive against *incredulità* in Italy and all Europe.

Especially noteworthy is Concina's assessment of the spiritual state of Europe at this juncture, when the Early Enlightenment was evolving into the High Enlightenment. A key point is that in the earlier history of the Church down to the new century, the chief concern of the ecclesiastical authorities had been to combat Mohammedans, Jews, and Idolators. But now all that belonged to the past having given way to a new age of the Church in which the chief enemy was entirely novel and, in some respects, more dangerous than any predecessor.[108] 'The deists and *spiriti forti* of our days,' he wrote, 'are incomparably more blind, more obstinate, and more malign, that the Jews themselves.'[109]

Concina, inflexibly Catholic though he is, entirely agrees with the fringe Protestant theologian, Jean Le Clerc, whose book on incredulity he warmly praises,[110] that *incredulità* was now the central issue in European intellectual debate: 'not only is it possible but it is an undeniable, factual truth that there exist not one, not ten, not a hundred, but innumerable men who call themselves atheists, deists, materialists, Naturalists, and *Indifferenti*' and who believe men are just 'material machines which function according to the laws of *mechanismo*' and that all 'their actions and sensual motions of anger, avarice, pride, and ambition are without evil' and that men act 'with equal innocence when they pray and when they commit adultery when they give alms and when they commit murder'.[111] Such 'monstrous errors' not only destroy the souls of those that espouse them but threaten society generally with destruction.

Consequently, throughout Europe, the splendour and truth of revealed religion is everywhere locked in a total, universal, and unremitting struggle with atheists, deists, and materialists who with their 'malign sarcasm', and with sacrilegious books against the sacred Christian mysteries, seek to overturn faith and propagate their venomous impiety everywhere.[112] As the weapons of this new war are philosophical more than theological, Concina praises Locke for defending miracles and applauds Moniglia for harnessing Lockean empiricism to the defence of authority and faith.[113] Locke's *Reasonableness of Christianity*, indeed, plays a pivotal part in Concina's defensive strategy: the truth of the Resurrection cannot be denied and the 'miracles performed publicly by Jesus Christ demonstrate evidently his divinity and the truth of his revealed religion'.[114] Eyewitness proof is decisive here and all the more so in that the Apostles were all Jews who then abandoned their Judaism for the new faith.[115]

'*Incredulità* in our time,' proclaims Concina,' is not some phantasm of the mind but a real pestilence' evident to a greater or lesser degree 'in many places'.[116] Paris was obviously one and he cites the general order of Archbishop Monseigneur Christophe de Beaumont, published on 29 January 1752, condemning the 'dreadful progress made

---

[108] Concina, *Della religione rivelata*, i, pp. ix–xiii.   [109] Ibid., 229.   [110] Ibid., p. xiv.
[111] Ibid., 2–3.   [112] Ibid., 7.   [113] Ibid., 34, 51.
[114] Ibid., 144–5, 159–62.   [115] Ibid., 162.   [116] Ibid., 8.

every day by that proud and bold philosophy'.[117] Yet it is not France but England and Holland which are the prime sources of *incredulità* and not France but England, Holland, and Protestant Germany where most impious books are printed.[118] Nothing could be more real, more clear, or more important than this sea-change that has come about in European life. But who or what is responsible for this plague of *incredulità*? Perhaps the most striking feature of Concina's two-volume analysis of this Europe-wide phenomenon is that, while the French *philosophes* of his day such as Voltaire, Diderot, and La Mettrie do figure, La Mettrie and Diderot appear only in passing,[119] while Voltaire is only slightly less marginal.[120] Without any doubt, contemporary French *philosophes* are in every way subsidiary within Concina's conception of the great theologico-philosophical drama of his time. As it seemed to him, writing in the early 1750s, they are simply not a central factor in the intellectual war he is describing. Bayle, by contrast, is a key culprit, having applied himself, now openly, now in a masked manner, 'to expand and amplify the number of atheists in many places in his pestilential books and especially in his book called *Pensées diverses*'.[121] Another agent of radicalism fairly extensively denounced is the marquis d'Argens. Others who have contributed to denying human liberty and turning us into amoral machines are Saint-Evremond, Toland, Collins, and Mandeville. Indeed, he refers to the *Evremondisti* and *Tolandisti* as a not insignificant element in the equation.[122]

Yet even these are clearly subsidiary. The backbone of the *incredulità* overrunning Europe, according to our Dominican, is the philosophy of one particular thinker who overwhelmingly dominates both the analysis and content of Concina's book. Indeed, here once again, as in so many other instances, Spinoza is the strategic pivot around which the entire battle rages. It may be true, remarks Concina, that of 'every thousand *spiriti forti* scarcely five have read the dark works of either Spinoza, or Hobbes or the others [i.e. Toland, Collins etc.]',[123] but the pestilence percolates from these few to the rest. If miracles are the 'first pillar' of revealed religion, it is Spinoza who launches the gravest attack on miracles by claiming that 'natural laws are the necessary decrees of God' and that 'these decrees are immutable because God is immutable' and, consequently 'miracles are impossible.'[124] This monstruous *Divinità Spinosiana*, avers Concina, is a revival of the ancient pantheistic philosophy of Epictetus and Strato.[125] Prophecy is another pillar of revealed religion and, again, it is Spinoza with his new Bible criticism who advances furthest towards undermining belief in prophecy with his argument that Biblical prophecy is merely 'imagination'.[126]

As for Spinoza's thesis that Moses is not the true author of the Pentateuch, and that the text was compiled by Ezra, this shows, declares Concina, that this 'unbeliever was not ashamed to vend the most putrid and ridiculous lies'.[127] Moses, he insists, did write the Pentateuch. If modern deists claim the Resurrection did not happen, it is

---

[117] Concina, *Della religione rivelata*, 20–1.   [118] Ibid., 239, 243.   [119] Ibid., 180.
[120] Ibid., ii, 286–7, 288, 299–302.   [121] Ibid., i, 23–4.   [122] Ibid., 336–7.
[123] Ibid., ii, 151.   [124] Ibid., i, 62–4 and ii, 226–7; Concina, *Theologia Christiana*, i, 34.
[125] Concina, *Della religione rivelata*, i, 64.   [126] Ibid., 77–81.   [127] Ibid., 80.

the Jew Spinoza, writing to Oldenburg, who primarily denies its possibility, blasphemously claiming 'this resurrection was spiritual or mystical, not real.'[128] Besides religion, morality is essential to society, but here again, Spinoza is the *maestro* of the *spiriti forti*, the philosopher who teaches them that there is no absolute 'good' or 'evil'. If modern deists deny human liberty, arguing that man's actions are determined, it was Spinoza and Saint-Evremond who attempted to turn men not into so many animals but 'machines driven by internal movement'.[129] Finally, if Spinoza urges the impious to face death with tranquillity of heart, this is vile pretence, a charade which a desperately agitated Spinoza himself could not achieve.[130] Finally, Spinoza will be vanquished and the tide of modern atheism and deism irresistibly rolled back. Modern man wants to decide what is true on the basis of facts. Well then, 'the conversion of the world to the faith of Jesus Christ confirms his divinity, the prophecies and the miracles.'[131]

Spinoza offers mankind philosophy, but what do his doctrines amount to? His is not a new system—in that respect Bayle was right—but just the rehashed doctrines of sundry ancient philosophers.[132] In the second volume, Concina attacks the foundations of Spinoza's system, like Lucchi, quoting verbatim several key propositions,[133] including the now notorious and frequently repeated Proposition XIV from Part I: 'praeter Deum nulla dari, neque concipi potest substantia' and Proposition XXXIII about the order of ideas and things being the same.[134] Demonstrating what he believes are fatal contradictions in Spinoza's system, Concina argues that 'the confusion, obscurity, aridity, and in a word, blind stupidity of Spinoza' are undeniable.[135] Furthermore, besides the errors in Spinoza's reasoning, the modern thinker has additional proofs at hand. Thus, it is irrational to deny the soul's immortality, since not only the Christian Churches but also the Mohammedans, Jews, pagans and Japanese assert it, together with 'future punishments prepared for the impious and rewards destined for the virtuous'.[136] Yet if potentially modern philosophy can completely, if not easily, overthrow Spinoza, Concina entertains considerable doubts about all the available versions of the moderate mainstream Enlightenment. Malebranche is now too discredited to be useful. The 'celebrated philosopher' Locke is marvellously helpful on miracles and Resurrection, but his epistemology can lead to unwanted consequences. Concina is fairly positive, as so many in Venice were, towards Leibniz and Wolff but here again sees insurmountable difficulties.[137] But this too serves his purpose. For ultimately it is not in philosophy but faith that man finds salvation.

---

[128] Ibid., 174–9.   [129] Ibid., 336–7.   [130] Ibid., ii, 213; Concina, *Theologia Christiana*, i, 34.
[131] Concina, *Della religione rivelata*, i, 193.   [132] Ibid., ii, 229–34.   [133] Ibid., 212–29, 363–77.
[134] See pp. 231–2 above; ibid., 226.   [135] Ibid., ii, 229; Concina, *Theologia Christiana*, i, 41.
[136] Concina, *Della religione rivelata*, ii, 430.   [137] Ibid., ii, 295–8.

i. Categories

The diffusion of forbidden philosophical literature in manuscript, for the most part in French, immeasurably furthered the spread of radical thought in late seventeenth- and early eighteenth-century Europe. Clandestine philosophy circulating in manuscript was not, of course, in itself new. As a European cultural phenomenon, it reaches back at least to the era of Bodin and Giordano Bruno, and possibly earlier. Yet there was a decisive broadening and intensification of such activity from around 1680, after which it fulfilled a crucial function in the advance of forbidden ideas for over half a century, until the easing of the censorship regarding theological and philosophical topics, especially in Prussia and (less conspicuously) France, but also Switzerland, Denmark, and other states from around 1740, rendered the propagation of this kind of manuscript less relevant, if not yet obsolete, by expanding opportunities for the dissemination of clandestine printed versions.

While the most widely known of the clandestine manuscripts, the *Traité des Trois Imposteurs* (or *La Vie et l'Esprit de Mr. Benoît de Spinosa*), was secretly printed at The Hague in 1719, this first edition could be sold only surreptitiously, in tiny numbers, and evidently remained rarer than the manuscript versions. In 1731 Lenglet Dufresnoy, an expert in everything concerning clandestine literature, furtively published at 'Bruxelles' (Amsterdam) a collection of Spinozistic texts including Boulainvilliers' *Essay* together with several refutations. But it was not until 1743 that there appeared, without disguise or any attempt to feign rebuttal, the first printed collection of clandestine philosophical texts previously circulating in manuscript. This publication, a landmark in the history of the Enlightenment, though produced anonymously and announcing its place of publication as 'Amsterdam', actually appeared in Paris, edited seemingly by Du Marsais.[1] Entitled *Nouvelles Libertés de penser*, it comprises five texts including Fontenelle's *Traité de la Liberté*, which dates from the 1680s and is known to have been circulating in Paris by 1700, when copies were publicly condemned and burnt by order of the Parlement,[2] and Du Marsais' own scathing rejection of traditional philosophiz-

[1] PBA MS 2858, fo. 278.
[2] On this important publication, see Benítez, *Face cachée*, 83, 86, 88, 91; Landucci, 'Introduction', 7; Mori, 'Du Marsais philosophe clandestin', 178, 189.

ing in his *Le Philosophe*, written in the early 1720s.[3] After 1750 published *clandestina* became more frequent and gradually drove out the clandestine manuscript. Hence, what might be termed the classic era of the clandestine philosophical manuscript, the age in which it surpassed the printed clandestine literature as a force in European culture, extended from the 1680s to around 1750. During this period, forbidden manuscripts constituted the chief method of propagating radical thought in Europe, laying the intellectual foundations, and opening the way psychologically and culturally, for the printed onslaught of such radical *philosophes* as La Mettrie, Diderot, Helvétius, and D'Holbach.

Appreciable numbers of clandestine philosophical manuscripts produced and copied in the decades between 1680 and 1750 survive in archives and libraries all over Europe, especially France, the Netherlands, and Germany but also Scandinavia, Britain, east-central Europe, and Italy. Not only was this output generated by many different authors, professing divergent philosophies in disparate styles, there was also a marked tendency to concoct collages, interpolating, borrowing, and mixing ingredients from diverse authors and traditions in a single text. Thus, *l'Ame matérielle*, apparently a coherent denial of immortality of the soul written shortly after 1724, albeit a rarity known in only one surviving copy, is a *mélange* of extracts from—among others—Bayle, Moréri, Malebranche, Le Clerc, and Lahontan.[4] Incontrovertibly, the post-1680 proliferation of such writings was, as one scholar has expressed it, 'un phenomène d'une extraordinaire complexité'.[5] Yet these revolutionary texts assailing authority, religion, tradition, and despotism can be grouped into families, broadly classified according to sources and approaches and it is, moreover, essential to do so if a tolerably coherent picture of the character and provenance of the intellectual impulses feeding the Radical Enlightenment is to emerge.

Those who bought, read, and discussed this underground literature were nobles—especially courtiers, army officers, diplomats, or officials—mixed with a sprinkling of medical men and other highly literate persons of middling status, and a few professional writers and publishers. Besides rich aristocratic collectors, there were connoisseurs of relatively modest means who amassed impressively comprehensive collections, such as that of the minor Provençal nobleman, Benoît de Maillet (1656–1738), a low-level diplomat of the French Crown who not only collected clandestine texts but, encouraged by Fontenelle, doyen of the French clandestine philosophical world, wrote the *Telliamed*, expounding a rudimentary theory of evolution, arguing for the formation of life in and from the sea, which circulated in manuscript from the early 1730s until it was published at Amsterdam in 1748, though the printed version lacks some of the more daring passages of the original. This text reveals Maillet to have been an adherent of Fontenelle's clandestine Spinozistic philosophy and a pantheistic Naturalist.[6] Similarly, a prime connoisseur in early eighteenth-century

---

[3] See PBA MS 2239 'L'Ame matérielle', pp. 1–174; Benítez, *Face Cachée*, 23, 217n,; McKenna, 'Recherches', 1.

[4] McKenna, 'Recherches', 10.   [5] Benítez, *Face cachée*, 1–8.   [6] Ibid., 223–4, 230–2, 290.

Germany, Peter Friedrich Arpe (1682–1740), who assiduously gathered forbidden texts in Hamburg, Kiel, and Copenhagen and, while in attendance at the Utrecht peace congress in 1713 in Holland, served as a minor official in Danish service.

Socially more elevated connoisseurs included, of course, Prince Eugene in Vienna, and his aide-de camp, the Baron Hohendorf who, besides the *Traité des Trois Imposteurs* acquired copies of the *Symbolum Sapientiae*, foremost of the German clandestine writings and Boulainvilliers' *Essay de métaphysique*.[7] The most indefatigable aristocratic collector in northern Europe, beginning in the 1720s, however, was probably Count Otto Thott, at Copenhagen. Prominent among Thott's astounding cache of *clandestina*, probably unsurpassed anywhere in Europe, were multiple copies of both the *Traité* and Lau's *Meditationes philosophicae*.[8] In Dresden, Johann August Ponickau, a scion of one of the six or so leading families of the Saxon electorate, amassed a famous library in the 1740s and 1750s, including numerous forbidden manuscripts, among them copies of the *Traité* and the *Symbolum sapientiae*, which remain today in the Halle University library.[9] Most eminently of all, Frederick the Great acquired a taste for such literature as a youth, many years before ascending the Prussian throne.[10]

Being rare, costly, and illegal such manuscripts were kept securely out of sight. They circulated furtively, not infrequently passing from one land to another concealed in diplomatic bags. In capital cities and great commercial centres, such as Amsterdam and Hamburg, they changed hands under the counter, circulating especially among small groups of initiates who knew and trusted each other. Occasionally, titles (known only to connoisseurs) could be discreetly advertised, as in 1743 when the Amsterdam Huguenot publisher Pierre Mortier (1704–54) produced a catalogue of books for sale in his shop, including several manuscripts, among them Du Marsais's *Examen* and Lévesque de Burigny's *De l'Examen de la religion*.[11] Motives for writing, as distinct from trafficking in, such texts might encompass thirst for renown within these rarefied cosmopolitan circles but can scarcely have included a desire for profit. Such writings originated in a new kind of zeal, or spiritual militancy, consciously aiming at undermining prevailing structures of faith, authority, and tradition, which were deemed to fetter the human spirit. As the fullest dictionary of 'atheists' published during the French Revolution remarked of Du Marsais, he was one of those who for fifty years 'travaillaient dans le silence à emanciper l'esprit humain'.[12]

The foremost writers of clandestine philosophical texts were mostly men whose commitment to illicit philosophy remained hidden from the authorities and wider public, though they enjoyed appreciable reputations as scholars in other fields. This was true of Fontenelle and Boulainvilliers and also of Du Marsais, who was recorded in Paris police files in 1749 as a 'grand grammairien', a well-known scholar, and 'un athée', but not the author of forbidden texts.[13] Similarly, Lévesque de Burigny was

---

[7] *Bibliotheca Hohendorfiana*, iii, 261.   [8] Benítez, *Face cachée*, 41, 51.

[9] HUB MS Misc. Oct. 2 'Symbolum Sapientiae' and HUB MS Misc. quart. 25.

[10] Krieger, *Friedrich der Grosse*, 37, 134, 175.   [11] Landucci, 'Introduction', 7.

[12] Maréchal, *Dictionnaire*, 73.   [13] Mori, 'Du Marsais philosophe clandestin', 169.

widely known as an *habitué* of the salons and an eminent classical scholar while Nicolas Fréret, a friend of the Venetian radical Conti, was an internationally renowned classicist. Another leading practitioner of the craft, Jean-Baptiste de Mirabaud (1675–1760), a former army officer turned savant, belonged to the circle around the duc de Noailles and Boulainvilliers and, in 1742, succeeded Houtteville as secretary to the Académie Française.[14] The two most important coteries involved in this activity behind the scenes were based in Paris and Holland, but there were also more isolated contributors elsewhere.

This illicit philosophical reading-matter easily penetrated opposition-minded, high-society court cliques, select diplomatic circles, the Paris salons, and the like. Nor did the infiltration of such material go unnoticed among courtiers and ecclesiastics resolved to defend authority, tradition, and piety. In 1734 the Abbé Jean-Baptiste Molinier, a leading French preacher, publicly denounced the growing seepage of forbidden philosophical manuscripts, naming *De l'Examen de la religion*, attributed by modern scholarship to Lévesque de Burigny, such writings in his opinion being not only more scandalous, but also more dangerous, than anonymously published works such as Voltaire's *Lettres philosophiques*. For being intended to circulate illicitly only in manuscript, they made no effort to veil or moderate their attacks on morality and religion.[15] The Abbé Houtteville noted in 1740 the penetration of such flagrantly anti-Christian texts as Bodin's *Colloque Heptoplomères* and the tracts of Orobio de Castro into the most fashionable 'cabinets' of Paris.[16]

The Paris police, though aware that Du Marsais was a philosophical atheist, apparently failed to connect him with the diffusion of clandestine manuscripts. Nevertheless, by the 1730s and 1740s, if not earlier, the police were increasingly worried by the spread of this new form of sedition. Several copyists of, and traffickers in, forbidden manuscripts were arrested and imprisoned, including a certain Jacques Guillier, sent to the Bastille in 1747 for vending 'manuscrits contraires à la religion et aux bonnes moeurs'.[17] A former nobleman's valet, Guillier purveyed both philosophical and pornographic material, and confessed under interrogation to selling Du Marsais' *Examen de la religion*, the *Traité des Trois Imposteurs* and Mirabaud's *Opinions des Anciens sur la nature de l'Ame*, besides the obscene *Jean Foutre puni*, though he denied trafficking in the likewise scandalous *Paris foutant*.[18] Asked where he had procured the originals from which he prepared his copies, Guillier named a retired minor army officer, a deceased friend, formerly residing in Les Invalides.

Guillier had been vending copies of the *Traité* expensively at six *livres* apiece.[19] To peddle such literature one needed to be fashionably dressed, highly literate, and to have access to noble residences—or indeed be a nobleman oneself. Normally self-respecting nobles would disdain any kind of small-scale trading but might well be tempted if financially hard pressed. Thus a young noble, the Sieur Dupré de

[14] Maréchal, *Dictionnaire*, 180; Schröder, *Ursprünge*, 407, 495, 508.
[15] Mori, 'Note', in *La Lettre Clandestine*, i, p. 9.   [16] Houtteville, *La religion Chrétienne*, i, p. ccxxxviii.
[17] PBA MS 11616, fos. 572–6; Benítez, *Face cachée*, 178.
[18] PBA MS 11616, fos. 578–81; Schwarzbach, 'Critique Biblique', 73.   [19] PBA MS 11616, fo. 579.

Richemont, reported for making copies of a manuscript 'contre la religion', was raided by the Paris police in June 1749. The police found the young gentleman 'in bed with a girl' and under his mattress a 'prodigious quantity' of manuscript notes in his own hand, frequently extracts from the dictionaries of Bayle and Moréri, both prime sources of the clandestine *philosophes*. Though the particular manuscript in question remained undiscovered, the police unearthed sufficient evidence of contacts with dealers of prohibited books in Paris and Rouen to justify sending Richemont to the Bastille for a few months, considering it necessary to combat these 'demi-auteurs et arrêter la license des brochures anonymes qui inondent le public'.[20]

Four categories of *clandestina* can be classified as essentially marginal to the philosophical core of the Radical Enlightenment, if not to its progress in the broadest sense. These obviously include the not unimportant group of much older Renaissance texts and sources, such as Pomponazzi, Bodin, Bruno, and Vanini, dating from the late sixteenth and early seventeenth century, which were doubtless being more widely circulated, and avidly collected and read, in this period than ever before, but can not be said to have significantly shaped the radical philosophical outlook of the time, their archaic tone, obsolete philosophy, and sometimes superstitious ways of looking at the world being significantly different from those of the post-1680 era. Secondly, there was a group of at least seven or eight originally Jewish manuscripts, in particular, writings of Orobio de Castro, translated into French and adapted (in several instances by Lévesque de Burigny and Saint-Hyacinthe), shorn of their specifically Jewish features and, beginning in the 1720s and 1730s, likewise put to work to sap confidence in tradition, authority, and Christianity.[21] Thirdly, also at the fringe of the Radical Enlightenment, if not outside it altogether, were several treatises, such as the *Difficultés sur la religion proposées au P. Malebranche* (thought to be by Robert Challe), which affirm divine Providence as a supernatural force, enjoining divine worship and separation of body and soul as well as freedom of the will.[22] Challe, while rejecting Christianity, is equally resolute in assailing the Spinozists as 'esprits forts fols et opiniâtres, esclaves de la vanité de paroître spirituels et subtils', who, instead of acknowledging a providential First Mover, admit only 'une force mouvante, qui met toute la matière en train du quel train toute la machine du monde s'est formée'.[23]

Fourthly and finally, among the lesser categories marginal to the philosophical geneaology of the Radical Enlightenment were the score or so manuscripts deriving from the English deists. Admittedly, these were much more in accord with the tone and mental climate of contemporary continental radical thought than the *clandestina* of the late Renaissance or the Jewish manuscripts. But the remarkably small number

---

[20] *Archives de la Bastille*, xi, 311–12.

[21] Benítez, 'Orobio de Castro', 219–26; Popkin, 'Jewish Anti-Christian Arguments', 171–4; McKenna, 'Sur l'hérésie', 301–4.

[22] This manuscript in some cases has the alternative title 'Système de Religion purement naturelle adressé au P. Malebranche', PBM MS 1192 'Système', 250–1, 287, 292, 324; as regards freedom of the will 'si on ne sentoit pas les autres libres, on se fâcheroit contre un horloge comme contre un homme'; ibid., 290.

[23] Ibid., 243.

of such texts rendered into French before 1740, and the striking paucity of surviving copies from the period before 1750, is important proof that English sources and ideas were not, as has been so often claimed, one of the prime impulses shaping and for-mulating the clandestine radical philosophy which so decisively and powerfully per-vaded Europe before Voltaire.

Perusal of the main body of philosophical texts written between 1680 and 1750 proves beyond any question that the intellectual core of the Radical Enlightenment possessed a high degree of intellectual coherence and was predominantly French, Dutch, and German in origin. The extent and interconnectedness of the two largest and most crucial categories are irrefutable proof of this. First and foremost are the writings which are either expressly Spinozistic, such as the ubiquitous *Traité des Trois Imposteurs* (or *L'Esprit de Spinosa*) and Boulainvilliers' two main clandestine tracts, his *Essay* and *Abrégé*, supplemented by a number of much rarer openly Spinozistic writ-ings such as the *Exposition du système de Benoit Spinosa contre les objections de Régis*,[24] and a group of French translations of Spinoza's *Ethics* circulating in part or in whole in manuscript,[25] or else which lean heavily on direct borrowing from Spinoza, as with the *Symbolum Sapientiae*,[26] the *Opinions des Anciens sur la nature de l'âme* of Mirabaud,[27] and *La Religion Chrétienne analysée*, often attributed to Du Marsais but probably in fact not by him.[28]

The *La Religion Chrétienne analysée*, one of the half dozen or so most widespread and infamous of the clandestine philosophical texts composed after 1680 (see Table 2) can neither be attributed firmly to any author nor dated with any precision. Nor is there anything to indicate whether the work was composed in France or Holland. All that can be said for certain is that it was written soon after 1722, one of its concerns being to combat Houtteville's *magnum opus* of 1722,[29] and that Spinoza is referred to repeatedly as a prime source of inspiration. The reader is assured his *Tractatus*, rec-ommended under its French title, *Des Cérémonies superstitieuses des juifs*, is the best tool for learning the art of Biblical hermeneutics.[30] Scripture is pronounced full of contra-dictions and the authority of the New Testament no more real or certain than the Old.[31] Like Spinoza, this writer deems Christian morality politically and socially use-ful, but nullifies the spiritual authority of all Churches and Church Fathers, contend-ing that Christ nowhere teaches the almost universally believed but totally bogus Christian 'mysteries'—and that neither Christ's divinity nor the Incarnation, Trinity, Immaculate Conception, or Resurrection have any basis in Scripture or reason.[32] The tract concludes with a discussion of the ancient oracles and evidence about the extent

---

[24] Benítez, *Face cachée*, 35.   [25] Ibid., 35.

[26] Marchand remarks on the kinship of the *Symbolum Sapientiae* to the *Traité des Trois Imposteurs*, Marc-hand, *Dictionnaire*, i, 325; Canziani, 'Critica della religione', 52–6.

[27] [Mirabaud], *Sentimens*, 90–7; the author of several clandestine manuscripts, Jean-Baptiste de Mirabaud (1675–1760), was a former soldier who fought at the battle of Steinkerk; see Maréchal, *Dictionnaire*, 180; Vernière, *Spinoza*, 372–3; Benítez, *Face cachée*, 43, 49.

[28] Mori, 'Du Marsais philosophe clandestin', 179–83

[29] ABM MS 63 (580), p. 118; Benítez, *Face cachée*, 144–5.   [30] MBM MS 338, pp. 21–38.

[31] Ibid., pp. 41–3, 80.   [32] Ibid., 8–9, 80, 144; Mori, 'Du Marsais philosophe clandestin', 182.

TABLE 2. The Major Clandestine Philosophical Manuscripts of the Early Enlightenment (1680–1750).

Title	Presumed author	Approximate date	Catalogued copies
1 Traité des Trois Imposteurs (L'Esprit de Spinosa)	Lucas (Vroesen ?), Revised by Levier, Aymon and Rousset de Missy	1690	*c.*200
2 Colloque Heptoplomères	Bodin	1580	105
3 Examen de la Religion	Du Marsais	1705	53
4 Mémoire des Pensées et Sentiments	Meslier		35
5 Opinions des Anciens sur la Nature de l'âme	Mirabaud	1730	32
6 Meditationes Philosophicae	Lau	1717	31
7 La religion Chrétienne analysée	?	1723	28
8 Essay de Métaphysique	Boulainvilliers	1705	24
9 Traité des Préventions divines (Prevenciones divinas)	Orobio de Castro	1665	24
10 Pantheisticon.	Toland	1720?	24
11 Lettre de Thrasybule à Leucippe	Fréret	1725	22
12 Symbolum Sapientiae	Wachter?	1700?	18
13 Examen Critique du Nouveau Testament	Mirabaud	1708	18
14 Abrégé de l'histoire universelle	Boulainvilliers	1700–7	15
15 Telliamed	Maillet	1730	15
16 Concordia Rationis et Fidei	Stosch	1692	14
17 Lettre d'Hippocrate à Damagète	Boulainvilliers	1695	14
18 Spaccio della Bestia Trionfante	Bruno	1584	11
19 La Divinité de Jésus-Christ détruite	Orobio de Castro	1675	11
20 Doutes sur la religion proposés à MM. les Docteurs de Sorbonne	?	1710	10
21 De l'Examen de la religion	Lévesque de Burigny	1730	8
22 Examen critique des apologistes de la religion Chrétienne	Lévesque de Burigny	1735	8

Sources: Benítez, 'Matériaux', 501–31; Benítez, *Face cachée*, 22–54; Landucci, 'Introduction', 9, 11, 14, 23; Schwarzbach, 'Critique Biblique', 69–86; Cotoni, *L'Exégèse*, 91–2, 97; Brogi, *Il Cerchio dell'Universo*, 14, 16, 105–6; McKenna, 'Recherches', 3–14; Mori, 'Du Marsais philosophe clandestin', 172–89; Schröder, *Ursprünge*, 404–526.

and nature of popular credulity and priestly artifice in the ancient world, referring to both Van Dale and Fontenelle.[33] The *Traité* too, and several others of this first and principal category of texts which can be broadly classified as 'Spinozistic', devote consid-

---

[33] MBM MS 338, pp. 119–20.

erable space to discussing the ancient oracles and condemning belief in demons, spirits, sorcery, divination, and the Devil, invoking Van Dale and Fontenelle.

The *Symbolum Sapientiae*—also known as the *Cymbalum Mundi* (not to be confused,
however, with the sixteenth-century text by Bonaventure des Periers which has the
same title)—was never published but circulated in Latin manuscript fairly widely,
especially in Germany and Scandinavia.[34] A German-language manuscript version is
known to have existed but no known copy survives. On internal evidence, its author
was clearly German and it dates from the 1680s or 1690s and is likely to have been at
least touched up, if not originally written, by Wachter.[35] The manuscript copies are
dated 'Eleutheropoli, 1678' (or sometimes '1668' or '1688') though all surviving copies
were apparently made during the eighteenth century. The work features frequent
direct borrowings from the *Tractatus Theologico-Politicus*, besides references to Le
Clerc, the latter presumed to have been added after the original redaction of the text.
It ascribes everything evil in human life to priests and kings, proclaiming revealed religion and 'superstition' one and the same thing. The *Symbolum* insists that a 'wise man
cannot be religious because religion is the mother and procurator of error'.[36] The Biblical text is full of disparities. Miracles are impossible. The style of the New Testament
is 'dreadful' (vitiosissimus). Organized religion is portrayed as exclusively an instrument of social and political control, its purpose being to instil 'obedience'.[37]

A second major category, of which Du Marsais' widely diffused *Examen de la
religion*, the same author's *Le Philosophe*, and Lévesque de Burigny's *De l'Examen de
la religion* are prime examples, is characterized by its strong philosophical affinities
with the first group, rejecting Revelation and prophecy, claiming man to be an exclusively 'natural' phenomenon[38] and 'good' and 'evil' to be not absolute but relative
concepts, defining God (particularly in Du Marsais) as incapable of deeds, creativity,
or effects 'qui soient formellement contraires à sa nature et à ses attributs',[39] and
finally, denying that theology has any place in, or connection with, philosophy. These
texts likewise contend that theology is not and can never be the path to salvation,
but is just a social and political tool perennially used to blind and enslave the people.
As in Spinoza, miracles are pronounced impossible, those which are alleged being
invariably ascribable to priestly fraud or physical cause and effect. The Biblical text
itself is denigrated, in particular as 'plein de contradictions'.[40] Furthermore, the
civil law, adjusted to uphold the common interest, is the only legitimate and
genuine authority.[41] In short, they too insist that 'true religion' can not be based on
'mysteries', or what *De l'Examen* calls 'l'abus de la raison, en croyant sans motifs

---

[34] Dunin Borkowski, *Spinoza*, i, 488–9, 602; Schröder, *Ursprünge*, 415.
[35] Schröder, 'Das *Symbolum Sapientiae*', 229; Canziani, 'Cymbalum Mundi', 38; Schröder, *Ursprünge*, 412–14.
[36] HUB MS Misc. Oct. 2 'Symbolum Sapientiae'. fo. 33v.
[37] Ibid., fos. 32–3; Schröder, 'Das *Symbolum sapientiae*', 231; Canziani, 'Cymbalum Mundi', 45.
[38] BL MS Lansdowne 414 [Du Marsais], 'Examen', p. 82.
[39] Ibid , p. 111; 'l'immutabilité du conseil de Dieu est une suite nécessaire de sa sagesse'; ibid , p. 112.
[40] Ibid., p. 33.
[41] BL MS Lansdowne 414 [Du Marsais] 'Examen'. 98–9; [Du Marsais], *Le Philosophe*, 188, 192–5.

raisonables',[42] but must, on the contrary, be based on reason; 'la raison pure nous donne un idée bien plus digne de Dieu que la Religion Chrétienne'.[43]

However, this group, while plainly rooted in Fontenelle, Bayle, Boulainvilliers, and a highly critical reading of Malebranche, contains no direct borrowings from Spinoza, does not invoke Spinoza, and makes no explicit use of the doctrine of one substance. Hence the texts are not strictly Spinozistic in the same sense as the first main category. Yet it must be admitted this closely allied group, the second main category of early Enlightenment radical *clandestina*, encapsulates almost the same corpus of doctrine as the first, this very high degree of intellectual convergence deriving above all from the ubiquitous influence of Fontenelle, Boulainvilliers, Du Marsais, Fréret, and Lévesque du Burigny. Lévesque's *De l'Examen* has been decribed as 'hyper-cartésien' and one might indeed wish to categorize the whole of this latter group as 'radical Cartesian' rather than specifically Spinozist, though such terminology, while differentiating the second from the first main category, and stressing its primarily French provenance, tends to mislead by overstating by implication at least the influence of the scorned Malebranche, as well as a Descartes lambasted by Du Marsais, for example, for proposing to believe only what he could see himself while wilfully but unwarrantably shutting his eyes in metaphysics, theology, and religion.[44] Accordingly, since these writings contain no trace of Descartes' duality of spirit and matter but stress rather the oneness of body and mind, it seems best to avoid classifying them as in any sense 'Cartesian'.

In this connection, a striking feature, in particular of Du Marsais' writing, is his deployment of Locke's empiricism within a rationalistic, anti-religious materialism, insisting 'que toutes nos connoissances nous viennent des sens', and that the true philosopher only bases his principles 'sur l'uniformité des impressions sensibles', but at the same time categorically equating 'thought' with the 'senses' as part of the same 'substance'[45] and thenceforth proceeding chiefly on the basis of 'la raison pure', confidently denying 'freedom of the will' and much else in blithe disregard of both Locke's epistemology and efforts to rationalize Christianity.[46] A similar procedure is followed in *l'Ame matérielle*, likewise a product of the 1720s, a collage in which Descartes' dichotomy of substances, separating mind and body, is ridiculed and Locke invoked for the sole purpose of helping to undermine the age-old orthodoxy, or 'superstition' as it is termed here, 'que la matière ne peut sentir'.[47] Plainly, the sole purpose of introducing Locke in this context is in fact Spinozistic—namely to reinforce the contention that thought and matter are the same substance.[48]

---

[42] [Lévesque de Burigny], *De l'Examen*, 59.

[43] BL MS Lansdowne 414,[Du Marsais],'Examen', p. 19.

[44] Ibid., p. 18.   [45] [Du Marsais], *Le Philosophe*, 180–1.

[46] Ibid., 177–80; BL MS Lansdowne 414 [Du Marsais] 'Examen', 98; see also Fairbairn, *'L'Idée d'un philosophe'*, 76; Mori,'Du Marsais philosophe clandestin', 181.

[47] PBA MS. 2239, pp. 16, 30–2, 35–8, 164–5.

[48] Ibid., pp. 164–5; PBM MS 1189/3 'L'Âme mortelle', 38, 40, 63, 66, 72.

The arguments of Du Marsais' *Examen*, a text composed around 1705,[49] can be broadly aligned with a Spinozistic standpoint, but totally discard Spinoza's dignified, philosophical calm, adopting instead, like so many of these texts, a vitriolic, pugnacious rhetoric. Thus the Biblical text is disparaged as full of imperfections and 'fautes des copistes qui ont bouleversé le sens de plusieurs passages'.[50] The Hebrew of Scripture is scorned as 'plein d'équivoques'.[51] Likewise, Biblical prophecy is styled the fruit of 'vivid imagination' but more acerbically than in Spinoza. 'L'imagination vive', contends Du Marsais, is more prevalent in Asia and Africa than Europe, which explains, he intimates, why Jerusalem inspires such a prodigious number of prophets. There is no notion, he concludes, however bizarre, that an overheated imagination cannot produce.[52] In one respect, moreover, Du Marsais' unyielding reductionism produces a concrete difference: where *La Religion Chrétienne analysée*, for example, follows Spinoza, in acknowledging the political and social usefulness of revealed religion and its role in instilling 'obedience', Du Marsais claims Christianity 'n'est pas nécessaire pour la société civile', that it restrains bad conduct in fewer people than is supposed, hampers progress of human knowledge and the sciences, and by disparaging worldly riches 'détruit entièrement le commerce qui est l'âme de la société'.[53]

Bibliophiles and *érudits* who themselves condemned and detested radical ideas, or professed to do so, nevertheless often engaged in the absorbing game of trying to identify and locate illicit texts and their shadowy authors and sources. Teasing their audience, when such writings were copied, or illegally printed, they were often playfully furnished with false dates and fictitious attributions to authors and places. Du Marsais' *Examen de la Religion*, written whilst Louis XIV still reigned, was first secretly printed in Amsterdam in 1745 ascribed to 'Saint-Evremond' and supposedly published at the French Jesuit headquarters of 'Trévoux'. Discussing this scandalous publication, a Leipzig journal conjectured that it was a new edition of a suppressed work, the *Découverte de la vérité et le monde détrompé à l'égard de la philosophie et de la religion* by 'Veridicus Nassaviensis', published at The Hague in 1745. The latter, a fierce assault on revealed religion and the Bible, which denounces Moses as an impostor and Descartes, Newton, and Clarke as confused, was vigorously suppressed by the States of Holland, nearly all 950 copies of the edition being publicly burnt.[54] The States successfully obliterated the *Examen* too. But then a second clandestine edition appeared, in 1747, according to Rousset de Missy, at Potsdam.[55] Very likely it was this edition which was read by La Mettrie, then at Berlin, and strengthened him in his conviction

---

[49] Thomson, 'L'Examen', 355; Mori, 'Du Marsais philosophe clandestin', 173.

[50] [Du Marsais] 'Saint-Evremond', *Examen*, 46; BL MS Lansdowne 414 [Du Marsais], 'Examen', 30–3.

[51] [Du Marsais], 'Saint-Evremond', *Examen*, 134–5.

[52] BL MS Lansdowne 414 [Du Marsais] 'Examen', pp. 30, 40, 54.

[53] Ibid., 98–9, 106; [Du Marsais], *Le Philosophe*, 191–2, where Du Marsais says the threat of divine chastisement has no real effect: 'malgré les vives peintures des peines et recompenses éternelles . . . le peuple est toujours le même. La nature est plus forte que les chimères'; see also Mori, 'Du Marsais philosophe clandestin', 182.

[54] Schwarzbach and Fairbairn, 'The *Examen*', 112–13.   [55] Ibid., 121.

that 'good' and 'evil' are not absolute, bad conscience, or remorse, deriving purely from upbringing and conditioning.[56] In Holland, France, and Germany, *cognoscenti* attributed the *Examen* variously to Fontenelle, Boulainvilliers, Mirabaud, Lévesque de Burigny, d'Argens, and Voltaire, besides Du Marsais, though no one apparently took the attribution to 'Saint-Evremond' seriously.[57] When the Hamburg press repeated rumours claiming the real author was a thoroughly disreputable Huguenot named La Serre, formerly a copyist working for Rousset de Missy and executed in the fortress at Maastricht for spying for the French, the incorrigible Edelmann published an indignant open letter protesting that these reports were just a despicable ploy to discredit freethinking.[58]

Even before Frederick the Great ascended the Prussian throne in 1740, Berlin and Potsdam had joined The Hague, Amsterdam, Paris, and Rouen as a principal centre of production of clandestine philosophical literature. One of the leading Berlin *cognoscenti* was the former Huguenot pastor and now deist (or at least professed Socinian) Charles Étienne Jordan (1700–45), who in 1736 became the Crown Prince's literary secretary. A savant immersed in Bayle and deistic literature, though claiming to be a moderate who upheld the Creation, 'argument from design', and divine Providence, in 1725 Jordan began corresponding with Burgomaster Zacharias von Uffenbach of Frankfurt-am-Main, in his capacity as a leading collector of *libri prohibiti*, offering to help locate and procure rare items missing from the burgomaster's celebrated collection in return for duplicates superfluous to Uffenbach's needs. In this way, Jordan obtained from Frankfurt manuscript copies of Lau's *Meditationes* and Bodin's *Colloque*, as well as Beverland's *État de l'homme*.[59] But while Jordan proudly exhibited his expertise in this field behind closed doors, not least in the Crown Prince's company, outwardly he still adhered firmly to faith in a providential deity. When justifying himself to Von Uffenbach, Jordan insisted that his purpose in collecting philosophical *clandestina* was neither to propagate them or the ideas they embodied, nor to endeavour to refute them. It was, he stated, sheer intellectual curiosity rather than anything else which spurred him on.[60]

ii. *L'Esprit de Spinosa*

Analysis of Europe's clandestine philosophical literature fully supports what all the other evidence indicates regarding the intellectual origins and sources of the Radical Enlightenment. While Italian, Jewish, British, and what might be termed French indigenous sources played a substantial part around the edges, the central thrust, the main bloc of radical ideas, stems predominantly from the Dutch radical milieu, the world of Spinoza and Spinozism. There is, moreover, no better illustration of this fundamental historical reality than the most widely diffused of all the illicit manuscripts,

---

[56] Thomson, 'Introduction', p. xxiii. [57] Mori, 'Du Marsais philosophe clandestin', 172.
[58] See Anne Thomson's note in Bloch and McKenna, *La Lettre clandestine*, iv, 161–3.
[59] Häseler, 'Réfugiés français', 378–9. [60] Ibid., 379.

the *Traité des Trois Imposteurs* or, as it came to be alternatively named *L'Esprit de Spinosa*. Philosophically, the text is of little significance and less originality, being little more than a crude vulgarization of Spinoza supplemented with a collage of additional matter drawn from several writers. But none of this detracts from its appreciable historical significance as a propaganda tool of the Radical Enlightenment, the most ubiquitous and influential of the clandestine philosophical manuscripts throughout Europe as far afield as Stockholm, St Petersburg, Poland, and Hungary.[61] Vehement in tone, it constitutes a veritable declaration of war on the entire existing structure of authority, faith, and tradition, proving that by the 1680s there was already a European intellectual fringe fired with a zealotry which was unabashedly revolutionary, dogmatic, and intolerant. However, while its vitriolic, bellicose tone evidently appealed to some, it doubtless shocked vastly more. As the German scholar Mosheim remarked, the *Traité* 'surpasses infinitely in atheistical profanity even those works of Spinoza which are regarded as the most pernicious'.[62]

The fullest published catalogue of surviving copies lists 172 in French (though, in fact, more have been traced) besides a small number of contemporary translations into Latin, German, English, and Italian.[63] Accordingly, the *Traité* survives to around four times the extent of the next most widely disseminated illicit philosophical text written between 1650 and 1750, namely Du Marsais' *Examen* (see Table 2). Its only real rival in popularity was Bodin's *Colloque Heptoplomères*, a work percolating much more widely after around 1700 than in the past but which was nevertheless written over a century before and is replete with what the *esprits forts* of 1700 must have regarded as thoroughly antiquated and absurd indications of belief in supernatural forces such as demons and witches.[64] Moreover, and again like Bodin's *Colloque*, the *Traité* spread geographically much more widely than most other *clandestina*.

Dating the *Traité* has long posed a thorny problem. The opening chapters lean heavily on the French translation of the *Tractatus Theologico-Politicus* published in 1678 and also the *Ethics* (1678). So it cannot antedate that year, though much confusion was caused in the eighteenth century, and since, due to the fact a Latin work, likewise entitled *De Tribus Impostoribus* but quite different in content, had been known much earlier.[65] Several references to a *Traité des Trois Imposteurs*, presumed to be *L'Esprit de Spinosa*, date from the decade 1700–1709 and the reference in Oudaen's attack on Van Dale (see p. 367 above) may be a hint that the text was known in Holland already in the 1680s. But while it is possible tentatively to suggest a date as early as 1680, it is unlikely to have been written any later than 1690.[66] Nevertheless, it is certain that the *Traité* remained rare and made only a very limited impact before 1711–12. Some surviving

---

[61] Benítez, *Face cachée*, 51–2; Skrzypek, 'Libertinisme polonais', 514–15,.

[62] Mosheim, *Ecclesiastical History*, ii, 319.

[63] Benítez, 'Histoire interminable', 54; this article supplements the list of 160 given in Benítez, *Face cachée*, 51–2.

[64] Schröder, 'Jean Bodin's Colloquium', 122.   [65] Ibid., 29–30.

[66] Schwarzbach and Fairbairn, 'History and Structure', 92–3, 95, 98, 101–6, 128; Charles-Daubert, '*L'Esprit de Spinosa*', 135–6.

copies are dated or can be dated precisely. Virtually all belong to the first half of the eighteenth century, but none carries a date earlier than 1706.

The principal author of the text, according to Prosper Marchand and Peter Friedrich Arpe, both great connoisseurs (as well as at least one leading modern authority), was Johan Vroesen (d.1725), a diplomat and official from a strongly anti-Orangist Rotterdam regent family who had served in France and had excellent French.[67] Other scholars remain sceptical about this attribution, however, deeming it more likely to have been written by a Huguenot Spinozist resident in Holland, such as the personage Levier himself claims wrote it, namely the author of *La Vie de Spinosa*, Jean-Maximilien Lucas.[68] The likelihood that it was in fact Lucas who composed both *La Vie* and *L'Esprit* of Spinoza, possibly as early as around 1680, is marginally further strengthened by the fact that Lucas is cited as author on some surviving copies of *L'Esprit*.[69] The evidence for the subsequent editing and diffusion of the text shows it to have been reworked by a radical Huguenot coterie in The Hague, revolving around the figure of Charles Levier (d.1734),[70] an active publisher and a central figure in the irreverent philosophical dining club entitled the order of the *Chevaliers de la Jubiliation*, which existed in The Hague in 1710, and in which he was the club's 'arlequin et boufon', the engraver Bernard Picart being its 'enlumineur' and Marchand its secretary.[71] According to the brother of the publisher Caspar Fritsch who, in 1737, imparted this information to Marchand, Levier borrowed a manuscript copy of the *Traité* from Locke's friend, the erudite English Quaker, Benjamin Furly, in Rotterdam in 1711, from which he made copies which he subsequently further revised and elaborated.

It was at this point, presumably, that Jean-Maximilien Lucas' *Vie de Spinosa* was annexed as a preface while Levier himself prepared the catalogue of Spinoza's works, listing besides published writings the *Apologie*, in which Spinoza 'justifies his departure from the synagogue', and his treatise on the rainbow 'which he threw on the fire', a bibliography appearing in the printed version Levier clandestinely published at The Hague in 1719. According to Marchand, it was also Levier and his accomplices who inserted the passages borrowed from Charron and Naudé, as well as a short new chapter on the first Roman king, Numa Pompilius. In this process of expanding, touching up, and then clandestinely propagating Lucas' text, Levier was reportedly assisted by

---

[67] Marchand, *Dictionnaire*, i, 324–5; Berti. 'First Edition', 205–8; Berti, '*L'Esprit de Spinosa*', 26–31.

[68] Charles-Daubert, '*L'Esprit de Spinosa*', 152–3; Schwarzbach and Fairbairn, 'History and Structure', 97–8.

[69] One of the surviving copies at Halle is entitled '*L'Esprit de Mr Spinoza par Mr Lucas médecin à La Haye*', HUB MS Yg 4 27, title-page.

[70] Marchand, *Dictionnaire*, i, 325; Jacob, *Radical Enlightenment*, 161; Berti, 'First Edition', 194–7; Berti, '*L'Esprit de Spinosa*', 26–31.

[71] BL MS 4295, fos. 18–18v; Margaret Jacob claims it was a clandestine Masonic lodge in which Toland played a central role, but there is no evidence that Toland had much to do with it or that it amounted to anything more than a joke; if it had a serious purpose this was the underground propagation of clandestine philosophical literature; Jacob, *The Radical Enlightenment*, 157–70; Harrrison, '*Religion' and the Religions*, 89; Vermij, 'English Deists', 245–7.

the unscrupulous Jean Aymon and Jean Rousset de Missy (1686–1762), a Huguenot raised in the Netherlands, who translated Collins' *Discourse of Freethinking* into French in 1713–14, and later Locke's political treatises, an *habitué* of the world of Dutch publishing and journalism and a friend of Marchand.[72]

The *Traité* in its final form is a collage drawn from Spinoza, Hobbes, Charron, Naudé, La Mothe le Vayer, and Vanini, skilfully woven by Levier, Rousset, and Aymon into a coherent, dynamic unity. The opening two chapters, setting the scene and laying down the basic philosophical principles on which the work is based, are borrowed directly from Spinoza. The first chapter, entitled, like the first part of the *Ethics*, 'De Dieu', echoes the *Tractatus* in maintaining that God's nature can only be known philosophically and not from Revelation or prophecy, that the Biblical prophets had no more access to divine truth than other men, only more 'imagination', having, in reality, encountered God only in their dreams and visions, obsessions which have no validity for others.[73] But the common people, sunk in ignorance and superstition, understood nothing of this and allowed themselves to be systematically deceived and exploited by crafty theologians and priests. 'Were men but able,' as the English version of the *Traité* expresses it, to 'comprehend what a dreadful abyss their want of knowledge has thrown them, they, undoubtedly, would soon shake off the yoke put upon them by these venal tyrants, and were they but ever so little to follow the light of reason, they could not possibly miss a speedy discovery of the truth.'[74]

The second chapter considers the reasons inducing men to imagine an invisible supreme being 'qu'on nomme communément Dieu' who created the universe. Based on the appendix to Part I of the *Ethics*, it explains man's propensity to believe in supernatural beings and forces in terms of his fears and hopes and especially his anxiety about whether there is a higher power or powers which can harm or help him.[75] Hence, man's notions of vengeful or magnanimous gods, spirits, and demons are literally phantoms, figments of his imagination invoked in adversity to explain suffering, disappointment, and hardship and, in prosperity, experiencing good fortune.[76] Following Spinoza (and the rest of what was to become the main body of clandestine philosophical texts), the *Traité* proceeds to dismantle ideas of divinely given laws, the absolute nature of 'good' and 'evil', and freedom of the will.[77]

Once the philosophical framework is established in the opening chapters, however, the *Traité* no longer draws directly on Spinoza. Subsequently, material is taken from writers representing quite different philosophical traditions,[78] a circumstance which has led to the frequently repeated thesis that the *Traité* is really eclectic rather than representative of a particular philosophical outlook. But the borrowings from Hobbes, Naudé, and others are actually used only to illustrate Spinozistic arguments and do not substantially influence the systematically mechanistic, deterministic, materialist,

---

[72] Marchand, *Dictionnaire*, i, 325; Berti, 'First edition', 203–4; Benítez, 'Histoire interminable', 60–1.
[73] *La Vie et l'Esprit*, 66–77; Berti, 'L'Esprit de Spinosa', 30, 34–5.   [74] See BL MS Stowe 47, fo. 14.
[75] Berti, 'L'Esprit de Spinosa', 35; Schwarzbach and Fairbairn, 'History and Structure', 117.
[76] *La Vie et l'Esprit*, 78.   [77] Ibid., 86.
[78] Charles-Daubert, 'L'Image de Spinoza', 64–5; Charles-Daubert, 'L'Esprit de Spinosa', 144–6.

and non-providential principles on which the work is uncompromisingly based. Hobbes, for instance, is deployed among other things to support the concluding onslaught on belief in spirits and demons. But the *Traité*'s claims that there is no Devil and that all the spirits and demons which have awed mankind over the millennia were nothing but 'phantômes, qui n'existoient que dans l'imagination', transcend anything contended by Hobbes or indeed any other source utilized apart from Van Dale and Spinoza.[79] The fundamental aim of the *Traité* is nothing less than to convince readers 'there are no such things in Nature as either God or Devil or Soul or Heaven or Hell, after the fashion as they are described' and that the 'theologians, that is to say, these men who exhibit and spread about ridiculous *Fables* for sacred truths divinely revealed are all of them except some few ignorant dunces . . . people of villaneous principles, who maliciously abuse and impose on the credulous populace.'[80] This was not remotely Hobbes' message (even if he agreed with parts of it privately) and still less was it the battle cry of intellectual libertines like Charron or Naudé. Nor were any of the latter intending to destroy the presumption of the theologians that 'all that far greatest part of mankind, whom they audaciously term the lay vulgar, were only capable of chimera or that they ought not to be nourished with any other food than this insipid truth of theirs, wherein is to be found nothing but folly, emptinesse and nonsense, without a single grain of the salt of truth and wisdom.'[81] The Spinozists alone entertained this design. It was evidently in the years 1711–12, when Levier and Rousset de Missy finalized the text, that the *Traité*'s alternative name, *L'Esprit de Spinosa*, was adopted, a change which, together with Levier's catalogue of Spinoza's works and Lucas' biography, was presumably designed to tighten the association between Spinoza and the *Traité*'s militant deism.[82]

Presumably there was also some connection between the new phase in the life of the *Traité*, from 1712, and the European diplomatic gathering at Utrecht held to negotiate an end to the War of the Spanish Succession (1702–13). Prince Eugene and his aide-de-camp, the Baron Hohendorf, participated in the talks, as did another leading connoisseur of clandestine literature, Peter Friedrich Arpe, who spent the years 1712–14 in the entourage of the Danish envoy in Holland. Arpe is thought not to have possessed a copy of the *Traité*, or even known about it, before 1712, and to have obtained his copy around that time, which was also the moment he formed a connection with the publishing house of Fritsch and Böhm, publishers that same year of his *Apologia pro Vanino* at 'Cosmopolis' (i.e. Rotterdam).[83] Baron Hohendorf, then using The Hague as his base for secret diplomatic missions to Paris and London, married into a Dutch noble family, and acquired a country seat near Bergen-op-Zoom where he concentrated much of his library. A substantial batch of copies of the *Traité* were evidently prepared in Holland in 1712, sometimes bound together with copies of

---

[79] Hobbes, *Leviathan*, ch. xlv; Martinich, *Two Gods of Leviathan*, 244–55.
[80] BL MS Stowe 47, fos. 68–68v.   [81] Ibid., fo. 68v.
[82] Schwarzbach and Fairbairn, 'History and Structure', 96, 99, 107–8.
[83] *Bibliotheca Lvbecensis*, v, 145–64; Mulsow, 'Freethinking', 222–32.

Boulainvilliers' *Essay*.[84] Another batch were copied after the Peace of Utrecht, with Hohendorf's permission, from a version belonging to Prince Eugene, but in his care. These are inscribed 'permittente Dno. Barone de Hohendorf descripsi hunc codicem ex autographo bibliothecae Serenissimi Principis Eugenii a Sabaudia, Anno . . .' (By permission of the lord Baron de Hohendorf I copied this manuscript from the original belonging to the library of the most serene Prince Eugene of Savoy, in the year . . .).[85] Sometimes, including in the case of the translation 'faithfully Englished' in the British Library,[86] no date is supplied. Elsewhere a date is given but, evidently, always within the narrow frame 1716–18.[87] Marchand attests to having personally seen three manuscript copies of the *Traité*, one of which carried this caption dated 1717.

In 1712 the *Traité* was still a relatively unknown, marginal phenomenon. In 1716, however, a clever publicity stunt gave it universal notoriety in one fell swoop. In that year, someone active in Levier's Spinozist circle at The Hague published under the mysterious initials J. L. R. a 21-page reply to a dissertation on the treatise of the 'Three Impostors' by the French *érudit* La Monnoye.[88] The latter categorically, but as events were soon to prove, prematurely, dismissed all the rumours of the existence of such a treatise as the *Traité*. La Monnoye's piece appeared in 1712, in a four-volume miscellaneous collection entitled *Menagiana*, illustrating the erudition of an older French scholar, Gilles Ménage (1613–92).[89] La Monnoye pointed out that for centuries tales of the existence of a treatise denouncing Moses, Jesus, and Mohammed as impostors had been circulating in Europe. But such a work had been seen by no living member of the Republic of Letters and was nowhere discussed, refuted, or banned. Consequently, there was no adequate reason to believe it was anything more than a fable.[90]

The anonymous *Réponse* to La Monnoye electrified the international literary scene by roundly contradicting these claims, its anonymous author (possibly Rousset de Missy or Levier himself) claiming not only to have laid eyes on the manuscript in question but to have it open, in front of him, in his study as he wrote. Providing a completely fictitious account of how, supposedly in 1706, he had acquired what he termed a French translation of an ancient Latin text, from a German officer in Frankfurt, he described the contents of the manuscript with some concrete detail, assuring readers it advances 'une idée assez conformé au système des Panthéistes', that is, the

---

[84] BL Add. MS 12064, fo. 68; Schwarzbach and Fairbairn, 'History and Structure', 107; Charles-Daubert, *'L'Esprit de Spinosa'*, 140.

[85] Mulsow, 'Freethinking', 218.   [86] BL MS Stowe 47, title-page, fo. 3.

[87] HHL MS Fr. 1, p. 282; Dunin Borkowski, *Spinoza*, i, 601; Schwarzbach and Fairbairn, 'History and Structure', 97; Charles-Daubert, *'L'Esprit de Spinosa'*, 138.

[88] The *Réponse* has been attributed to Jean Rousset de Missy by Margaret Jacob, but there is apparently no real evidence of his authorship; Jacob, *Radical Enlightenment*, 219, 278; Anderson, 'Sallengre, La Monnoye', 255–7; Charles-Daubert, *Le 'Traité'*, 62–3.

[89] [Sallengre], *Mémoires de littérature*, i, 382–4; Berti, 'First Edition', 197; Benítez, 'Histoire interminable', 60.

[90] Barbier, *Dictionnaire*, iii, 211; Schwarzbach and Fairbairn, 'History and Structure', 99–100; Charles-Daubert, *Le 'Traité*, 36–41.

Spinozists, maintaining that God is extended substance 'et par conséquent éternelle et infinie'.[91] This ultimate Spinozist attack on revealed religion did then exist. The consternation the article produced was heightened further by the anonymous writer's deliberately teasing, concluding remark that the text was now ready for publication although, for various reasons, it might not in the end appear.

Among those astounded by this news was Leibniz who, in March 1716, wrote to Veyssière de la Croze, an expert on deism, Spinozism, and atheism in Berlin, passing on reports that the mysterious respondent to La Monnoye was none other than Peter Friedrich Arpe who, however, it emerged later, could not have been J. L. R. as he was unable to write French.[92] In the spring of 1717 there was panic in Dresden and Leipzig, following rumours that copies of this Spinozist 'Three Impostors' were illicitly circulating there. The censorship authorities thoroughly searched the bookshops.[93] Further dismay was caused by the ill-advised reprinting in French of the reply to La Monnoye, the same year, in a Leipzig journal edited by the Silesian librarian and historian Johann Gottlieb Krause (1684–1736), one of the leading savants in Saxony and yet another noted connoisseur of clandestine literature, who had indeed himself gone to some lengths to unearth a copy of the *Traité*. For his pains, Krause not only had the main stock, 538 copies, of his journal seized by the now distinctly nervous Saxon authorities, but was subjected to official investigation and considerable damage to his reputation and academic hopes.[94]

It was in 1719 that Levier and a fellow publisher at The Hague, Thomas Johnson, 'remplis d'irreligion', as Marchand puts it, printed (rather than published) *La Vie et l'Esprit* as a small octavo volume of 208 pages, without mentioning either a publisher's name or place of publication.[95] In their *avertissement* the publishers claimed only a few copies had been produced so that the work would be scarcely less rare than if it had stayed in manuscript, a tactic chiefly intended presumably to avoid endangering the publishers.[96] Levier added the sardonic—and according to Marchand—vile pretext that the work was being published for the benefit of such acute scholars as could refute it, since the gross impiety of this 'écrit monstrueux' would undoubtedly provoke powerful replies and the 'renversement total du système de Spinosa, sur lequel sont fondez les sophismes de son disciple'.[97] By 'disciple', Levier meant Jean-Maximilien Lucas.[98] Marchand later confirmed that Levier sold very few copies and that on his deathbed, in 1734, he instructed relatives to destroy what remained of his carefully hidden stock.[99] Three hundred copies were duly delivered to his former friend and associate Marchand and burnt.

---

[91] [Rousset de Missy?], *Réponse*; Anderson, 'Sallengre, La Monnoye', 270; Anderson, *The Treatise*, 59, 76, 79.

[92] Mulsow, 'Freethinking', 194–5.   [93] Kobuch, *Zensur und Aufklärung*, 58–9.

[94] Ibid., 60–3; Schröder, *Ursprünge*, 457–8; Mulsow, 'Freethinking', 199–200; Charles-Daubert, *Le Traité*, 105.

[95] Berti, 'First Edition', 196–9.   [96] Ibid., 199; Berti, 'L'Esprit de Spinosa', 13.

[97] Marchand, *Dictionnaire*, i, 324.   [98] Ibid.; Berti, 'L'Esprit de Spinosa', 24.

[99] Marchand, *Dictionnaire*, i, 325.

iii. Despotism, Islam, and the Politicization of 'Superstition'

A notable feature of the *Traité des Trois Imposteurs*, the *Symbolum Sapientiae*, and other radical clandestine texts from the two main groups is the denunciation of political oppression and despotism as the universal ally and concomitant of revealed religion and 'superstition'. The *Traité*, like the *Symbolum Sapientiae*, is indeed a highly political as well as a philosophical work. Likewise, other clandestine texts stress the link between superstitious faith and tyranny and the need to oppose despotism if men are to be free.

The short new chapter Levier inserted into the text of the *Traité* (chapter VI in the edition of 1719) undertakes to consider how the legendary Numa Pompilius managed, by stealth and craft, to establish the principle of monarchy among the Romans when they began to tire of consultative rule by the senate. Numa grasped that the most effective way to establish absolute authority over 'hommes igno-rans, grossiers et superstitieux', such as Rome's early inhabitants, was to inspire in them 'la plus grande crainte des dieux' as is possible.[100] To succeed, however, Numa perceived that some gross fiction or 'miracle' was needed in order completely to overawe the ignorant and credulous Roman mind. It proved easy work to convince a people already irredeemably addicted to divination and oracles that the tyrannical laws and institutions to which he obliged them to submit had been dictated to him from 'Heaven'. As the centuries passed, adds Levier, Roman credulity increased more and more, hand in hand with the growth of political oppression, until finally their minds were so shrouded by credulous superstition that the notion of a virgin birth encompassed 'rien d'incroyable pour des gens qui admettoient, comme des veritez divinement réveleés, une infinité de choses plus absurdes et plus contradictoires'.[101]

This inserted chapter exemplifies the technique also regularly used in other clandestine texts, of illustrating radical philosophical ideas, with vivid historical exempla. The idea that revealed religion is essentially a political device goes back to Machiavelli and is elaborated by Spinoza. The argument that the ancient oracles were essentially a web of priestly fraud reached back to Van Dale and Fontenelle. But the story of Numa Pompilius dramatizes the message embedded in such ideas, showing how rev-elations and miracles could be used by a ruler, in alliance with a priestly class, to crush human liberty. 'Révélation et prophéties' had been constantly employed over the ages, holds the *Traité*, alternately to astonish, terrify, and elate the people and by this means manipulate them for hidden political purposes.

The inevitable result is oppression and despotism. Nor can one achieve political lib-erty without resolving to 'combattre la superstition' and champion 'la pure vérité', philosophy being an indispensable accoutrement of emancipation, without which one can not be an 'esprit libre'.[102] Here, as in other respects, the *Symbolum Sapientiae*

---

[100] *La Vie et l'Esprit*, 116.   [101] Ibid., 118.   [102] Ibid., 188, 212.

approaches the *Traité* in militancy.[103] With equally relentless zeal the *Symbolum* insists that 'religion and superstition indeed are by nature entirely apt for forcing the common people under the yoke and keeping them in labour, subjection, and obedience'.[104] The more oppressive a system of government, argues this text, the more men are corrupted and depraved by error and superstition.[105] Indeed, political dominance and usurpation is the sole and unique source of all error and superstition.

Several texts stress the allegedly Asiatic character and origins of revealed religion and its prophets, seeking to tighten the association in western minds of Asia with despotism. 'Qu'est-ce donc que Jésus-Christ,' asks a mid-eighteenth-century text rhetorically, 'un oriental, un asiatique, un Juif c'est à dire une imagination chaude.'[106] A culminating statement of this view is found in a manuscript of Nicolas-Antoine Boulanger (d.1759), probably written around 1750 and later published, at Geneva in 1761, entitled 'Recherches sur l'origine du despotisme oriental'.[107] This text argues that human violence and aggression, however malignant, are by themselves inadequate to sustain the general hegemony of tyranny and absolute power everywhere evident in the world. The explanation as to how and why oppression is so widespread must lie in its being mentally, rather than physically, rooted in human society, its most essential foundations being ignorance, credulity, and superstition: 'le despotisme est une erreur et une suite des erreurs du genre humain; ce n'est donc point dans la physique ni dans aucun système philosophique qu'il faut en chercher la source.'[108] Boulanger refuses to attribute what he considers the essential difference in the political history of Europe and Asia primarily to physical causes such as climate. Whereas history shows us 'l'Europe toujours brave et toujours jalouse de sa liberté', she also displays 'au contraire l'Asie esclave et effeminée dans tous les tems'.[109] But this is the consequence of idolatry, superstition, wretched education, and cultural conditioning.

The Radical Enlightenment, as has been noted, entertained a curiously schizoid view of Islam and Mohammed. On the one hand, from the late seventeenth century and culminating in Boulainvilliers' *Vie de Mahomed* ('Londres', 1730), a work widely diffused though Europe—and republished in English (London, 1731) and Italian (Venice, 1744)—Islam is viewed positively, even enthusiastically, as a purified form of revealed religion, stripped of the many imperfections of Judaism and Christianity and hence ressuringly akin to deism.[110] On the other, Islam is more often regarded with hostility and contempt as a primitive, grossly superstitious religion like Judaism and Christian-

---

[103] Schröder, 'Das "Symbolum Sapientiae"', 231–2; the author of this text holds 'Nam fons superstitionum, servitutis, ignorantiae, errorum ac praeiudiciorum omnium indeque pullulantium miseriarum et malorum quibus genus humanum vexatur, solus ac unicus est imperium'; HUB MS Misc. 8 oct. 2 'Symbolum Sapientiae', fo. 32.

[104] HUB Misc. 8. oct. 2 'Symbolum Sapientiae', fos. 32–32v; Dunin Borkowski *Spinoza*, i, 488.

[105] 'Hinc quo strictius est imperium, eo lactior errorum seges apparet, hominesque tyrannide et superstitione corrumpuntur et depravantur'; ibid., fo. 32.

[106] ABM MS 62 (585),'Doutes sur la Religion', p. 127.   [107] In 206 pages, see PBM MS 1198/3.

[108] PBM MS 1198/3, p. 10.   [109] Ibid., p. 8.

[110] Brogi, *Cerchio*, 119–36; Harrison, *'Religion' and the Religions*, 111, 163; Thomson, 'L'Utilisation', 248, 251–3.

ity and one no less, or still more, adapted to promoting despotism. For his part, d'Argens, in his various works, seems alternately to reflect both attitudes.[111]

However, the main (i.e. Spinozistic) bloc of clandestine manuscript philosophical literature, despite Boulainvilliers' considerable influence, clearly shares the latter attitude.[112] Spinoza himself, in his letters, accounts Mohammed a 'deceiver' and Islam even better equipped than the Roman Catholic Church to 'mislead the common people and keep men's minds in its grip', and consequently the most unified and coherent of all revealed religions.[113] D'Argens, in his *Lettres juives*, describing the alleged cultural desolation and ignorance prevailing in Algiers and Tunis, compares the government of the Barbary states to that of Rome under Caligula, Nero, and Diocletian[114] and speaks of the prejudice that the Muslims 'avaient portés aux sciences et aux beaux-arts'.[115] It is this contemptuous attitude to Islam, invariably linking superstition with despotism and the enslaving of the human spirit, that is chiefly echoed in the clandestine manuscripts. The *Symbolum Sapientiae* unhesitatingly dismisses the Koran as no less absurd and contradictory than the Old and New Testaments.[116] According to the *Traité*, Mohammed was in no way less adroit in fabricating revelations, visions, and miracles, and manipulating the passions of the people, than Moses or Jesus.[117]

Yet neither the *Traité* nor the other clandestine manuscripts go much beyond drawing a general equation between despotism and superstition. The Radical Enlightenment sought to demolish the foundations of Revelation, authority, and tradition, while at the same time consciously undermining the legitimacy of monarchy and aristocracy. The ultimate goal of its endeavours, its very *raison d'être*, was to emancipate society and the individual from bogus bonds of authority and by doing so reinstate human liberty. This 'liberty' was deemed political as well as intellectual, moral, and sexual, and on occasion the writers of the clandestine texts, for example, Boulanger,[118] reveal powerful republican sympathies and tendencies. Spinoza's 'philosophy', notes Boulainvilliers, means that monarchy rests not on any rightful basis but purely on fear 'ou la superstition', and it is especially the latter on which the founders of monarchies rely.[119] Yet while the illicit philosophical literature unremittingly highlights, elaborates, and intensifies the consequences of Spinozism for religion and morality, it signally fails to do so to a comparable extent with regard to political life.

---

[111] Thomson, 'L'Utilisation', 251–2; Thomson, *Barbary and Enlightenment*, 45, 51, 55, 59.

[112] Thomson, 'L'Utilisation', 250–1; Gunny, 'L'Image du prophète', 257–9.

[113] Spinoza, *Briefwisseling*, 413; Spinoza, *Letters*, 343.   [114] Thomson, *Barbary and Enlightenment*, 55.

[115] D'Argens, *Lettres juives*, v, 99; Thomson, *Barbary and Enlightenment*, 21.

[116] HUB MS Misc. 8 oct. 2 'Symbolum sapientiae', fo. 38; this author's maxim; 'apparet igitur sapientiam et religionem esse opposita' clearly applies to Islam as much as Judaism and Christianity; ibid., 33; Schröder, 'Das "Symbolum Sapientiae"', 231.

[117] *La Vie et l'Esprit*, 148–50; Gunny, 'L'Image du prophète', 258–62.; Charles-Daubert, *Le 'Traité'*, 143–4, 511–13.

[118] PBM MS 1198/3 [Boulanger], 'Recherches', pp. 192–5.

[119] PBN MS Fr NA 11074 'Extraits des lectures de M. le Comte de Boulainvilliers', 179.

| # From La Mettrie to Diderot

i. Materialism

The two authors who most effectively summed up the radical thought of the early Enlightenment era in the middle of the eighteenth century were both Frenchmen— La Mettrie and the famous chief editor of the *Encyclopédie*, Diderot. In their published writings a tradition of thought stretching back a century to the 1650s was powerfully restated and rendered into one of the central planks of the European Enlightenment as a whole. Both writers, and especially Diderot, also added some original touches of their own. But the essential ideas making up their radicalism were those of a late seventeenth- and early eighteenth-century tradition which culminated in their work.

No one more forcefully proclaimed the uncoupling of individual salvation from religion, and the relocation of personal redemption in this world, than Julien Offray de la Mettrie (1709–51). A physician from a middle-class background, born and raised in Brittany, his starting-point in the world of scholarship was the study of medicine. It was to further his studies in that discipline that he travelled to Holland as a young man, at the age of 24, and his experience of studying under Boerhaave, the most famous medical man of the age in Europe, which shaped the initial phase of his career as a writer and *philosophe*.[1] After two years (1733–4) studying at Leiden, La Mettrie returned to France and began translating and editing Boerhaave's writings, starting with his treatise on venereal disease, which appeared under the title *Système de M. H. Boerhaave sur les maladies vénériennes* (Paris, 1735). Among the several other editions of Boerhaave's works he produced over the next fifteen years were an abridgement of the latter's handbook of chemistry and a full rendering of his *Institutiones medicae* (1708) under the title *Institutions de médicine de M. Herman Boerhaave* (Paris, 1743–50).

Whether La Mettrie acquired his taste for philosophy in Holland, as so many others had before him, remains uncertain. But there are clear indications that his philosophical enterprise began with his pondering the comments on the human soul of another of Boerhaave's disciples, Albrecht von Haller, a Calvinist—and later a pillar of the mainstream moderate Enlightenment in Switzerland—who edited an important collection of annotations on the master's *Institutiones*.[2] Boerhaave had, since the first

---

[1] Gay, *The Enlightenment*, i, 15, 136.   [2] Thomson, 'Introduction', p. xiv.

decade of the century, been an anti-Cartesian and emphatic empiricist, but he was also a pupil, and warm admirer, of De Volder, from whom, seemingly, he had imbibed more than a trace of the latter's crypto-Spinozism.[3] Boerhaave's renown rested on the double basis of his inspired teaching and his medical-chemical-botanical system—the most consistently mechanistic philosophy of illness, the human body, and medicine yet seen, which included a conception of man's mental states as being intimately related to his physical condition. Haller, by contrast, withdrew into a strictly orthodox conception of the duality of body and soul. Boerhaave, publicly accused more than once of being a 'Spinozist', avoided discussing such matters in print. But La Mettrie undoubtedly had some justification for claiming that Haller's interpretation of Boer-haave's view of the relationship of body and soul was a distortion. It was to counter Haller that he presented his radical, materialist conception of the soul in his first substantial philosophical work, the *Histoire naturelle de l'âme* which he had published at The Hague in 1745.[4] Large sections of this are lifted directly from Boerhaave and Haller, but La Mettrie makes the materialist tendency implicit in Boerhaave's thought more explicit, suggesting that Spinoza had rightly claimed man resembles a 'watch', or a 'ship without a pilot' which, owing to its construction, can negotiate the waves but is propelled indiscriminately this way and that by external motion, waves and currents.[5] In this work Boerhaave is once again praised to the skies while Spinoza is conventionally denounced as 'un monstre d'incrédulité'.[6] 'Le grand Boerhaave fut le plus éclairée, le plus sage des Déistes,' insists La Mettrie, and no one was ever 'moins Spinosiste' than he since he recognized God's hand in everything.[7]

Despite its espousal of physico-theology and disparagement of Spinoza, the work provoked an outcry in France, its materialist implications and implied determinism being easily discerned. In Paris copies were seized from the bookshops by the police and, in the wake of the scandal, La Mettrie himself was stripped of his post as physician to a crack regiment and compelled to flee France. He withdrew to the Netherlands, first Middelburg and then Leiden, where he wrote his most notorious work, *l'Homme machine*, published anonymously at Leiden in 1747. Here La Mettrie attempts to explain man's nature and his behaviour in purely materialist terms, claiming that medical experience proves the different states of the soul are always linked to those of the body. His materialist system is rooted in the radical argument that matter is both self-moving and sensitive and that its sensitivity is the origin of thought.[8] 'Given the slightest principle of movement,' argues La Mettrie, 'animate bodies will have everything they need to move, feel, think, repent, and, in a word, behave in the physical sphere and in the moral sphere which depends on it.'[9]

In his *Histoire naturelle de l'âme*, La Mettrie observes that 'aujourd'hui . . . le système cartesien n'est plus qu'un roman philosophique; le monde entier devient

---

[3] Klever, 'Herman Boerhaave', 78–87.

[4] Vartanian, *La Mettrie's* l'Homme machine, 47–8; Thomson, 'Introduction', p. xvi.

[5] La Mettrie, *Histoire naturelle*, 150–1.   [6] Ibid., 247.   [7] Ibid., 248.

[8] Thomson, 'Introduction', pp. xviii–xix; Wellman, *La Mettrie*, 192–4.

[9] La Mettrie, *Machine Man*, 26.

Newtonien' but then remarks (echoing d'Argens) that philosophers come and go like words, or opinions, and that he expected Newton too to be eclipsed before long—if he had not been already.[10] In *l'Homme machine*, La Mettrie comments further on the great philosophical battle in progress in Europe. Disparaging Descartes and his Oratorian disciple, Malebranche, as outmoded and untenable, he dismisses Leibniz's monads as an 'hypothèse inintelligible'[11] and, more controversially, rejects physico-theology, Newtonianism, and the 'argument from design', styling the 'works of Fénelon, Nieuwentijd, Abbadie, Derham, Ray and so on' boring verbiage by devout but unconvincing publicists more apt to foment than rebut atheism.[12] An accumulation of examples demonstrating that animate bodies have a marvellous intricacy perfectly adapted for bodily functions is no proof, when logically considered, of a divine maker. The work culminates in La Mettrie's uncompromising call to acknowledge that man is a machine and that there is only one substance: 'et qu'il n'y a dans tout qu'une seule substance diversement modifiée'.[13] With this La Mettrie firmly pinned his colours to Spinoza's monism of body and mind.

The furore which greeted *l'Homme machine*, and its formal suppression by the States, obliged both author and publisher to flee from Holland. La Mettrie sought refuge at the court of the freethinking Prussian king, Frederick the Great, where he spent the remaining three years of his short life elaborating his anti-Newtonian, anti-Lockean, and anti-Leibnizian theories, basking in the Prussian monarch's favour. In Berlin, despite being a publicly denounced and detested figure and a notorious glutton and hedonist, he became a figure of some standing and rubbed shoulders with Voltaire, d'Argens, and Maupertuis. Much to the chagrin of almost the entire Prussian Royal Academy, Frederick who personally wrote the *éloge* his secretary read out on that occasion, required them in July 1748 to adopt La Mettrie as a full member of their body.[14] His books, though clandestinely or semi-clandestinely produced, sold well and won him a European reputation.[15] His last writings, *l'Homme-plante* (1748), *Système d'Epicure* (1750), and *Anti-Senèque, ou le souverain bien* (1750), besides his collected *Oeuvres philosophiques*, the last declaring 'à Londres' on the title-page, were all in fact published in Berlin or nearby Potsdam. In November 1751 he died suddenly, to his enemies' amusement, reportedly from overeating and food poisoning caused by a spoiled game pie.

His final philosophical stance was expressed in the 78-page *Discours préliminaire* written in 1750 as a preface to his *Oeuvres philosophiques*. Here he admits that philosophy, as he understands it, is in theory diametrically opposed to what is conventionally considered religion and morality. Contrary to what is commonly believed, radical thought is not, however, in practice detrimental to either, rather it 'ne peut que . . . les

---

[10] La Mettrie, *Histoire naturelle de l'âme*, 205.
[11] La Mettrie, *Machine Man*, 3–4.
[12] Ibid., 3, 23; Vartanian, *La Mettrie's* l'Homme machine, 48, 62–3.
[13] La Mettrie, *Machine Man*, 39; Comte-Sponville, 'La Mettrie', 138.
[14] Maréchal, *Dictionnaire*, 96; Winter, *Die Registres*, 48; Berkvens-Stevelinck and Vercruysse, *Métier*, 139.
[15] Berkvens-Stevelinck, *Prosper Marchand*, 158.

fortifier de plus en plus'.[16] This is because morality, like the laws, originates, according to la Mettrie, exclusively in the political sphere, having no divinely decreed or supernatural basis, so that legislation, and not belief, constitutes the true basis of morality and the social order.[17] It is therefore impossible, he urges—echoing Voltaire—that philosophy should harm society or any individual. Answering, if also modifying, Bayle's question as to whether a society of atheists is conceivable, he affirms that not only does he think that 'une société d'athées philosophes se soutiendroit très bien, mais je crois qu'elle se soutiendroit plus facilement qu'une société de dévôts'.[18] The public should not imagine that he, La Mettrie, is an enemy of morality just because he writes 'librement ce que je pense': 'je ne suis plus Spinosiste,' he maintains, 'pour avoir fait *l'Homme Machine* et exposé le système d'Épicure' than wicked for having written satirically against the charlatanism of his French medical colleagues.[19]

Although on several occasions La Mettrie hints at being a 'Spinosiste',[20] elsewhere he expressly disavows this title. His view of Spinoza, it has been suggested, grew more positive as he became more radical after 1745, and as his opinion of Locke became less favourable.[21] Yet while he never took much interest in Hobbes' philosophy,[22] his references to Spinoza were always highly charged and purposely ambivalent, even teasing, and must be seen as part of a dialogue with his innumerable critics, some of whom routinely denounced him as a 'Spinozist'.[23] Nevertheless, for all his referring to Spinoza and Spinozism at crucial junctures, he does so apparently only for rhetorical effect, and it is far from clear that he ever studied Spinoza seriously or made more use of his writings than he does of Hobbes. He never quotes Spinoza directly and all his references to him are very general or exceedingly vague, as when he remarks 'suivant Spinosa . . . l'homme est un véritable automate'.[24] The comparison of man to a 'watch', or a ship without a pilot, is actually borrowed from Saint-Hyacinthe's critique of Spinoza.[25] La Mettrie's observation that Malebranche is a 'Spinosiste sans le savoir', and other such allusions, also derive from Saint-Hyacinthe and other deist predecessors.[26] Odd though it seems, La Mettrie apparently had no direct knowledge of Spinoza at all, and thus the spectre of Spinoza he conjures up is not the real Spinoza, or his writings, but the public 'Spinoza' which had become so profound a fixation of the society in which he lived.

It is sometimes claimed that La Mettrie was the most extreme radical and

---

[16] La Mettrie, *Discours préliminaire*, 1.

[17] Ibid.; La Mettrie, *Anti-Seneca*, 129; Wellman, *La Mettrie*, 213–31.

[18] La Mettrie, *Discours préliminaire*, 39.   [19] Ibid., 48.

[20] La Mettrie, *Oeuvres philosophiques*, 238; Comte-Sponville, 'La Mettrie', 133; Thomson. 'La Mettrie', 241; Thomson, 'Introduction', p. xiii.

[21] Vartanian, *La Mettrie's* L'Homme machine, 47–9.

[22] Glaziou, *Hobbes en France*, 198–200.

[23] Vernière, *Spinoza*, 385; Vartanian, *La Mettrie's* l'Homme machine, 62–3, 110; Thomson, 'Introduction', p. xiii.

[24] La Mettrie, *Oeuvres philosophiques*, 236; Comte-Sponville, 'La Mettrie', 133–4, Thomson, 'La Mettrie', 537.

[25] See Verbeek's comment in Comte-Sponville, 'La Mettrie', 144.   [26] Ibid., 134, 144–5.

materialist of the eighteenth century.[27] In a sense this is right; and yet it is equally true to say that, to an even greater extent than Voltaire, he is a borrower, copyist, and plagiarist, regurgitating past work and ideas, the great summarizer of the previous half-century, except that he builds on a different, and more radical, strand of the Early Enlightenment. La Mettrie, one might almost say, was the Voltaire of the Radical tradition. Seven key organizing ideas can be identified as fundamental to his thought, all largely deriving from the corpus of simplified, debased 'Spinozism' which increasingly pervaded the Netherlands and France. First, La Mettrie shares with Spinoza, Boulainvilliers, and all radical thinkers who espoused the doctrine of one substance, the idea that the universe operates under only one set of rules, governed by 'Nature', and that there is no second or reserved sphere of cause and effect beyond the realm of mathematical rationality, and therefore no separate spiritual dimension, as Descartes, Leibniz, Newton, and Locke all in their different ways maintain.[28] From this it follows that the origin of thought lies in sense and sensibility and is, therefore, innate in matter.[29] Third, rejection of the 'argument from design', and divine Providence, in turn entails a theory of spontaneous generation of life from the motion innate in matter.[30]

Fourth, as in Spinoza, Boulainvilliers, Collins, and Conti, 'Nature' in La Mettrie is conceived as a single infinite chain of mechanistically determined and inevitable consequences, man being merely another link in the chain. Consequently, everything that happens, happens according to the unalterable laws of 'Nature'. Free will, consequently, is impossible and everyone is determined to act as they do, 'machinalement portés à notre bien' as La Mettrie expresses it, governed by Nature like a 'pendulum in the hands of a watchmaker'.[31] Fifth, La Mettrie shares with Spinoza and the Spinozist tradition the idea that there is neither an original nor any absolute 'good' or 'evil'. Nothing is absolutely good or bad, just or unjust; only society, through laws and education, can generate virtue and justice and does so for the benefit of its members.[32] No doubt Spinoza would have disliked La Mettrie's vulgarization of his ethical theory, and the strain of voluptuousness he imparted to it; nevertheless, the basic idea that everyone inevitably acts to conserve and advance themselves and that only political intervention, legislation, and policing can create right and wrong and institute a pattern of disciplined conduct in society, in the interest of all, is essentially the same.

Sixth, there is the idea, stemming from Machiavelli but first systematized by Spinoza, that organized religion is nothing other than a political and social device

---

[27] Hazard, *European Thought*, 137–8; Thomson, 'Introduction', pp. xxiv, xxvi; Audi, *Cambridge Dictionary of Philosophy*, 416.

[28] Comte-Sponville, 'La Mettrie', 138; Thomson, 'Introduction', pp. xiii–xv.

[29] La Mettrie, *Machine Man*, 35; La Mettrie, *System of Epicurus* (in *Machine Man*), 97.

[30] Ibid., 35–8; Hazard, *European Thought*, 138; Wellman, *La Mettrie*, 204–7.

[31] La Mettrie, *Discours préliminaire*, 1–18; La Mettrie, *System of Epicurus*, 103; La Mettrie, *Anti-Seneca* (in *Machine Man*), 141; Hampson, *The Enlightenment*, 114; Comte-Sponville, 'La Mettrie' 138–9.

[32] La Mettrie, *Machine Man*, 39; La Mettrie, *Anti-Seneca*, 129, 131–4, 141–2; La Mettrie, *Discours préliminaire*, 8.

instituted to serve the well-being of men, and that its true nature and functions have to be understood particularly by statesmen and philosophers. To a greater degree per- haps than some other radicals, such as Van den Enden, Koerbagh, Knutzen, and Edel- mann, and even perhaps than Spinoza, La Mettrie seems to have concluded that most people will always be ignorant, superstitious, and barbaric and therefore inwardly guided by the irrational. Accordingly, he too attributes to organized religion a contin- uing usefulness—especially for teaching 'obedience'.[33] Seventh, and last, to safeguard the lives, activities, and writings of philosophers, thinking statesmen, and others amenable to reason, it is of paramount importance that society should uphold com- plete and unimpaired freedom of thought and toleration, a toleration based less on permitting varieties of belief and religious practice than freedom to express and debate intellectual arguments and points of view, in other words, Spinoza's 'libertas philosophandi'.

ii. Diderot

La Mettrie distilled the essence from the radical tradition and restated it so auda- ciously as to marginalize himself almost entirely. Outside Frederick the Great's Berlin, he was beyond the pale of respectability and his writings could not be respectably adduced, or his name mentioned, except for purposes of outright denunciation. Indeed, he made himself hated not only by fellow doctors, theologians, and the mod- erate mainstream Enlightenment, but even to some extent by non-providential deists and *fatalistes* who believed such uninhibited outspokenness could only damage the cause of man's 'enlightenment'. For most of the *philosophes* believed that emancipa- tion of society and the self was attainable only by means of a gradual, philosophically and educationally flexible approach.[34] Among those who distanced himself from La Mettrie's audacity and extremism was the young Denis Diderot (1713–84).

Diderot read and absorbed a great many late seventeenth- and early eighteenth- century philosophers and scientists, as well as translating and editing Shaftesbury, and in the first stage of his philosophical odyssey emerged, or at least projected himself, in the wake of Voltaire and others, as a professed deist, advocating divine Providence and the immortality of the soul.[35] The early Shaftesbury of the *Inquiry concerning Virtue* (1699), the work Diderot brought out in French in 1745, had tried to construct a deism which would effectively counter fatalism and Naturalism, and bolster belief in divine Providence and the immortality of the soul. Diderot's own stance, in his first original work, the *Pensées philosophiques*, published in June 1746, was intentionally ambiguous but designed to be read as expressly deist. He agrees with Bayle that 'la superstition est plus injurieuse à Dieu que l'athéisme'[36] but seemingly affirms the existence of a

---

[33] Comte-Sponville, 'La Mettrie', 139, 143.

[34] Proust, *Diderot*, 327–8; Thomson, 'Introduction', p. xxvi; Gay speaks even of Diderot's 'detestation of La Mettrie's *Anti-Sénèque*'; Gay, *The Enlightenment*, ii, 194.

[35] Venturi, *Jeunesse de Diderot*, 74–9; Vernière, *Spinoza*, 563; Bourdin, *Diderot*, 26.

[36] Diderot, *Pensées philosophiques*, 14.

Supreme Being, God, who designs and creates Nature, and decrees the immortality of the soul. It was clearly an anti-Christian work, leaving no legitimate role for the Church and, consequently, was condemned by the *Parlement* and publicly burnt in Paris on 7 July. But this work also appears to insist that providential deism has the full force of physico-theology and the 'argument from design' behind it and thereby triumphs not only over the superstition of the past, and the teaching of the Churches, but also over atheism: 'le déiste seule peut faire tête à l'athée'.[37]

Without necessarily claiming the title 'atheist', for he was not, any more than Spinoza, a professed atheist in the strict sense, La Mettrie with his radical non-providential deism felt affronted by Diderot's claims that natural science backs the 'argument from design' and expressly attacks him, on this issue, in his *L'Homme machine*. Where Diderot here insists that it is experimental science and the works of Newton, Musschenbroek, Hartsoeker, and Nieuwentijt which provide 'des preuves satisfaisantes de l'existence d'un être souverainement intelligent', La Mettrie retorts that the evidence of the miscroscope and telescope, properly considered, proves nothing of the sort.[38]

But the later Shaftesbury shifted to a more radical position and within a year or two, influenced among others by La Mettrie, Diderot altered his stance too. He read and meditated voraciously during these years, as well as, together with d'Alembert, planned the great project of the *Encyclopédie*, the first license for which was promulgated early in 1746. By 1748 Diderot had become a non-providential, radical deist, and the first fruit of his new outlook was his famous *Lettre sur les aveugles*. This powerful essay, for which La Mettrie expressed warm appreciation in 1751,[39] revolves around a remarkable deathbed scene in which a dying blind philosopher, Saunderson, rejects the arguments of a deist clergyman who endeavours to win him round to belief in a providential God during his last hours. Saunderson's arguments are those of a neo-Spinozist Naturalist and fatalist, using a sophisticated notion of the self-generation and natural evolution of species without Creation or supernatural intervention. The notion of 'thinking matter' is upheld and the 'argument from design' discarded (following La Mettrie) as hollow and unconvincing. The work appeared anonymously in Paris in June 1749, and was vigorously suppressed by the authorities. Diderot, who had been under police surveillance since 1747, was swiftly identified as the author, had his manuscripts confiscated, and was imprisoned for some months, under a *lettre de cachet*, on the outskirts of Paris, in the dungeons at Vincennes where he was visited almost daily by Rousseau, at the time his closest and most assiduous ally.[40]

Diderot was released from Vincennes on 3 November, after signing a letter of submission undertaking not to write or edit irreligious works again, under threat of severe penalty should he disobey. It was a lesson this 'second La Mettrie', as Rousset de Missy dubbed him in 1752,[41] did not forget and which fundamentally influenced the

[37] Diderot, *Pensées philosophiques*, 14.
[38] Ibid., 17; La Mettrie, *Machine Man*, 23–4; Venturi, *Jeunesse de Diderot*, 156; Bourdin, *Diderot*, 28, 36.
[39] La Mettrie, *Machine Man*, 171; Venturi, *Jeunesse de Diderot*, 154–5.
[40] Wokler, *Social Thought*, 52.   [41] Berkvens-Stevelinck and Vercruysse, *Métier*, 137–8.

future course of his work.[42] His subsequent major works directly exploring the great philosophical issues of man, God, Creation and the universe, including the famous dialogue, the *Rêve d'Alembert* (1769), with its forthright declaration of Naturalism, fatalism, and Neo-Spinozism, reducing the human soul to 'matière et sensibilité', and indeed all material things to an interaction of body and sensitivity, one of the culminating philosophical works of the High Enlightenment, remained unpublished until as late as 1830.

But Diderot did not cease his efforts to promote radical philosophical deism in France. Rather, in his capacity as chief editor of the *Encyclopédie*, and a well-known publicist on a variety of topical issues, he found enough subterfuges to enable him to propagate his Naturalist message. An eloquent example is his critique of Maupertuis' treatise on the origin of life and the propagation of species. Maupertuis, admitting that neither Cartesian 'extension' nor the Newtonian principle of gravitation helps to explain the generation of life, came close to amalgamating matter and consciousness, but without actually saying so.[43] Diderot responded by publishing his *Pensées sur l'interpretation de la nature* (1753), calling attention to this feature of Maupertuis' work, pretending to condemn it for its Spinozist implications and 'terribles conséquences', but in fact seizing the opportunity to embarrass the president of the Berlin Academy and uncover the contradictions within Newtonianism, while reworking the concept of 'thinking matter' with its ultimate implication that 'le monde peut être Dieu.'[44] Maupertuis retorted sarcastically that if one did not know Diderot to be a man of religion one would suspect that his real purpose was not to oppose the argument in question but rather advocate the 'terribles conséquences'.[45] A degree of artifice and circumlocution was unavoidable, but discerning readers were left in no doubt either then or subsequently that Diderot's 'God', as Sylvain Maréchal later expressed it, 'diffère peu de celui de Spinosa'.[46]

The *Encyclopédie*, the most famous and one of the greatest projects of the European Enlightenment, from the time that it was tentatively licensed in 1746 was continually under threat, on the verge of being suppressed by the French Crown or the *Parlement*. It evolved precariously, remarked Maréchal after the Revolution, 'sous le règne d'une double Inquisition, politique et religieuse'.[47] The predominant tone and ideology of the vast enterprise had to correspond ostensibly to the guidelines of the moderate mainstream Enlightenment. There was no alternative. Hence, in the preliminary discourse, d'Alembert praises Bacon, Locke, and Newton to the skies, assuring readers 'rien ne nous est donc plus nécessaire qu'une religion révelée'.[48] But within the mainstream there was plentiful scope for an intermittently glimpsed undercurrent in which Diderot could deftly insinuate his own philosophy. This was revealed in several

---

[42] Vernière, *Spinoza*, 558.   [43] Vartanian, 'Diderot and Maupertuis', 49–51.

[44] Diderot, *Oeuvres philosophiques*, 228–9; Vernière, *Spinoza*, 596; Proust, *Diderot*, 121; Cassirer, *Philosophy*, 86–90.

[45] Diderot, *Oeuvres philosophiques*, 228–9.

[46] Maréchal, *Dictionnaire*, 121; Vartanian, 'Diderot and Maupertuis', 52–5.

[47] Diderot, *Oeuvres philosophiques*, 81.   [48] D'Alembert, *Discours préliminaire*, p. viii.

articles he wrote himself or closely edited, such as the article 'animal' in the first volume, where he asserts that the power to think is an extension of the capacity to feel and diminishes by stages as one descends towards lower and simpler forms down the chain of animate and inanimate beings.[49] The editors, remarked Maréchal later, employed all their art to say what they really intended 'sans trop se compremettre' but often they were also prevented from doing so.[50]

Two intriguing articles, one very long, the other extremely short, which by their contrast vividly exemplify the tension between mainstream and undercurrent in the *Encyclopédie*, are two adjoining pieces in the fifteenth volume, entitled respectively 'Spinosa' and 'Spinosistes'. There was never any question that the main article dealing with Spinoza in the *Encyclopédie* would need to be, or at least appear to be, unremittingly negative, and it is. But the peculiar manner in which it denounces Spinozism— its vast length, being five times as long as the article on Locke, combined with the absurdity of its prolix borrowing—in places repeating almost verbatim, without acknowledging the fact, entire passages not only from Bayle's article but from Houtteville—sources outdated, widely known, and heavily criticized—seems to have been intended as a nod to discerning readers that its pompous argumentation was not meant to be taken seriously, and, furthermore, was ripe for ridicule. For example, having previously declared Bayle the most effective of 'tous ceux qui ont réfuté le spinozisme', the article lets slip that not only Spinoza's 'plus grand admirateurs . . . prétendent qu'on ne l'a pas entendu',[51] but according to not a few critics Bayle himself had 'nullement compris la doctrine de Spinoza'.[52] This and the earlier remarks that 'il n'est pas vrai que ses sectateurs soient en grand nombre,' that of those who are suspected of being Spinozists 'il y en a peu qui l'ayent étudié,'[53] and that it is surprising that Spinoza 'respectant si peu la raison et l'evidence, ait eu des partisans et des sectateurs de son système',[54] were bound to make readers wonder why on earth so much attention was being lavished on a thinker whose doctrines are absurd and irrational but whom hardly any critics, including Bayle, understand or read correctly.

Ostensibly Spinoza's philosophy is condemned as 'ce système monstrueux' and its doctrines dismissed as grotesque. Yet precisely the Spinozist teachings seemingly derided in the main article were, at this very time, being explored with great seriousness, and increasingly embraced, by Diderot himself. For example, it is proclaimed 'la dernière des absurdités de croire et de dire que l'oeil n'a pas été fait pour voir, ni l'oreille pour entendre',[55] and no less absurd to think the first men emerged from the earth, yet these were the very contentions La Mettrie and Diderot had been recently advancing. The discrepancy between surface and reality becomes all the more striking in the light of the very short next article 'Spinosiste' which, unlike the long article, is known to have been written by Diderot personally.[56] Here the main point is that we should not confuse 'les Spinosistes anciens' with 'les Spinosistes modernes'. The

---

[49] Proust, *Diderot*, 137, 260, 263; Bourdin, *Diderot*, 7, 66.   [50] Maréchal, *Dictionnaire*, 81.

[51] *Encyclopédie*, xv, 466.   [52] Ibid., xv, 468.   [53] Ibid., xv, 463.

[54] Article 'Spinosa', *Encyclopédie*, xv, 469.   [55] Ibid., 473.

[56] Vernière, *Spinoza*, 596–7; Proust, *Diderot*, 121, 124, 138, 289.

'principe général' of the latter 'c'est que la matière est sensible' and that animate bodies can evolve from inert bodies. From this, we are told, the modern Spinozists conclude 'qu'il n'y a que de la matière, et qu'elle suffit pour tout expliquer'.[57] For the rest, 'ils suivent l'ancien Spinosisme dans toutes ses conséquences'—in other words, modern and traditional Spinozists are the same except that the former are more emphatically materialist and committed to the principle of evolution.[58]

[57] Article 'Spinosiste', *Encyclopédie*, xv, 474.
[58] Ibid.; Vernière, *Spinoza*, 596; Vartanian, 'Diderot and Maupertuis', 55–8.

38 | Epilogue: Rousseau, Radicalism, Revolution

The French Revolution was, by any reckoning, one of the great defining episodes in the history of modernity. Whether one sympathizes with or reviles the aspirations, endeavours, and consequences of the Revolution, no one can doubt the immensity of the changes it wrought. Above all, the Revolution overtly challenged the three principal pillars of medieval and early modern society—monarchy, aristocracy, and the Church—going some way to overturning all three. Inevitably in the context, ideology—and linked to ideology, radical philosophy and political thought—were prime factors in the complex of pressures and impulses which shaped the Revolution. To question whether ideas and books can in fact cause revolutions and dislodge kings, a favourite historiographical pastime of recent years, may sound astute momentarily but on a closer view seems as shallow as the notion that great events in history may well have small, short-term, accidental, and unnecessary causes. Matching cause and effect is the essence of scientific logic. It is surely also the essence of meaningful historical interpretation.

A revolution of fact which demolishes a monarchical courtly world embedded in tradition, faith, and a social order which had over many centuries determined the distribution of land, wealth, office, and status seems impossible, or exceedingly implausible, without a prior revolution in ideas—a revolution of the mind—that had matured and seeped its way through large sections of society over a long period before the onset of the revolution in actuality. Claims that just such an upheaval of the mind had indeed paved the way were common in the years preceding the Revolution—as well as during the revolutionary years and the succeeding period through to the early nineteenth century. There is much room for debate about the precise nature of this revolution in ideas. One might, for instance, argue that only after 1750 did the *philosophes* change the mental map of Europe. One might quarrel with the diagnosis of a Rotterdam *predikant* who, the year before the outbreak of the Revolution, described his century as one in which authority, tradition, and faith had already largely been swept away by 'philosophy' propounded by 'a whole host of Spinozisten, Deurhofisten, Hattemisten, Leenhofisten, Naturalisten, Materialisten, Deisten, Atheisten, Vrijgeesten [freethinkers] and Sociniaanen with which weeds not only England, France and Germany but also our republic are strewn' and his identifying Spinoza as the chief author of the disaster.[1] One might prefer to think it was the French *philosophes* who set the pace from the 1740s onwards, or that the latter took their inspiration from the English. One might postulate that there was not one Enlightenment but several, each with a different national basis. Or one might argue, as in this book, that there was just one highly integrated European Enlightenment encapsulating a four-way conflict between Newtonians, neo-Cartesians, Leibnitio–Wolffians, and radicals. But whichever view of the philosophical ferment one adopts, there is no scope for ignoring the universal conviction during the revolutionary age, beginning in the early 1780s, that it was 'philosophy' which had demolished the *ancien régime*, and in particular the ideas, beliefs, and loyalties on which it rested, and that it had accomplished this feat long before the first shots were fired at the Bastille.

Radical ideas, then, undeniably helped to make the Revolution. But it is certainly also true that the Revolution in an important sense reinterpreted, codified, and recast in new terminology the thought of the Enlightenment[2]. The revolutionaries assigned a 'radically critical function to philosophy', thereby constructing a conceptual if to some extent an unhistorical 'continuity that was primarily a process of justification and a search for paternity'.[3] In the perceptions of the revolutionaries themselves there was no need to look beyond France and little need to look further back than the middle of the eighteenth century. Furthermore, they showed a distinct propensity to lionize, and to some extent radicalize, certain key philosophical heroes, of whom Voltaire and Rousseau were much the most celebrated.

The decision of the Constituent Assembly of April 1791 to create in Paris a Panthéon, a sort of French 'Westminster Abbey' to elevate the great men of the new France into enduring monuments for all mankind, was prompted by a widely felt desire to commemorate a key radical leader and publicist of the early stages of the Revolution—the lately deceased Comte Honoré-Gabriel de Mirabeau (1749–91). The resolution may have been symptomatic of a growing craving for political leaders and heroes, as a psychological prop amid the turmoil of revolution,[4] but certainly it also reflected a powerful impulse to embody monumentally the abstract principles generally perceived as the basis of the Revolution.

The case of Mirabeau himself reflects this. A veteran of the American War and notorious for his erotic escapades, he had been a vocal opponent of royal absolutism since the late 1770s and was also a man of both wide reading and experience of the world. He was not an outright republican like Lafayette but rather a constitutional monarchist. A key figure in the Constituent Assembly, he was a very effective propagandist and man of action, but also saw himself as a *philosophe*, dedicated above all to the abolition of absolutism, aristocracy, and privilege. This he proved through his rhetoric and still more a stream of pre-revolutionary publications chiefly attacking despotic government and privilege, but also, as with his pornographic *Erotika Biblion* (à Rome, de l'Imprimerie du Vatican, 1783) showing a keen interest in other forms of

---

[1] Pieter Kaas, 'Verhandeling over de waarheit' in Wielema, *Filosofen*, 257.
[2] Chartier, *Cultural Origins*, 5.   [3] Ibid.   [4] Schama, *Citizens*, 546.

emancipation.[5] Besides America, he had stayed for periods in Holland (1776), England, and Germany (1785–7), and spent over three years (1777–80) in the dungeons of Vincennes, after gravely offending the French Court. Among other works published by him before 1789 in the name of liberty was a tract entitled *Sur Moses Mendelssohn, sur la réforme politique des juifs* (1787), arguing that the degradation of the Jews was due to the squalid conditions in which they were being compelled to live. It was chiefly based on what he had seen in Germany where, among other developments, he witnessed part of the *Pantheismusstreit*, the public controversy over Lessing's Spinozism which erupted in the 1780s and in which Mirabeau firmly took the side of the deceased Lessing and the *Spinozistes*.[6] A year before the Revolution, the count addressed his *Aux Bataves sur le Stadhouderat* (1788) to the Dutch people, eulogizing De Witt and seventeenth-century Dutch republicanism. Most of his library of over 3,000 books consisted of historical and political works; but it is striking that a high proportion of his handful of books on speculative philosophy consisted of radical works by Spinoza, Toland, and d'Holbach. Of Spinoza, he had three different versions of the *Tractatus* besides the *Opera Posthuma* of 1677.[7]

Mirabeau's public funeral, escorted by the National Guard and a large crowd, and burial amid the austerely classical architecture of what was henceforth called the Panthéon, marked the advent of a remarkable cultural phenomenon. Already in the crypt were the remains of Descartes, a great thinker who was in some respects a progenitor of the Enlightenment deemed sufficiently appropriate by many, if only because his philosophical legacy had been partially suppressed by Louis XIV. A few months later, in July, Voltaire's remains were transferred there, the occasion once again being marked by public festivities and evident enthusiasm, the general view being that the Revolution was partly the fruit of his writings.[8] Other *philosophes* and revolutionary statesmen followed, much the most important being Rousseau, who was disinterred from his tomb at his rural retreat and relocated there in October 1793 amid general acclaim. But there were also removals, Mirabeau's remains later being taken away on Robespierre's initiative, when it became known that during his last months he had been in secret league with the Court.

Admittedly, the total of *grands hommes* glorified in the Panthéon down to 1794, whether *philosophes* or not, was very few. But there were numerous revolutionary events and contexts in which other *philosophes* were honoured and their influence in preparing the ground for, and shaping the conceptual course of, the Revolution acknowledged. While no other *philosophes* were so often invoked as Voltaire and Rousseau, the egalitarian and radical contributions of Fontenelle, Diderot, Helvétius, Morellet, Raynal, and Mably—the last a major influence on Robespierre's Jacobin subordinate Saint-Just—were widely and fulsomely acknowledged.[9] Especially among the intellectual and artistic leadership of Revolutionary France, the conviction that

---

[5] Chartier, *Cultural Origins*, 63, 77, 79.   [6] Vernière, *Spinoza*, 681–2.
[7] Ibid., 682.   [8] Schama, *Citizens*, 561–4; Chartier, *Cultural Origins*, 88.
[9] Talmon, *Origins*, 23–4, 34–7, 64–5; Chartier, *Cultural Origins*, 83–9.

egalitarianism, republicanism, and morality without Revelation were the fruits of a long process, engineered by an army of thinkers and writers stretching back for over a century, became deeply rooted. Replying to the conservative allegation that the revolutionaries were attacking religion and morality, Sylvain Maréchal admits the former but firmly denies the latter, invoking 'studieux Bayle! Vertueux Spinosa! Sage Fréret! Modeste Du Marsais! Honnête Helvétius! Sensible d'Holbach!' all of whom he describes as *athées* who openly reject the God of the Christians, and as wise philosophical writers, asking how anyone can conceivably charge such men with having 'démoralisé le monde'.[10]

If, on the other hand, few took much interest in the origins and sources of the radical philosophical tradition—and while many recent *philosophes* were thought to have influenced the course of the Revolution, including a handful of genuinely learned savants, who actively participated and eventually became its victims, such as the Girondin marquis de Condorcet, 'last of the *philosophes*'—no other Enlightenment thinker had anything like as many professed disciples as Rousseau. The overriding political concept in Robespierre's mind and rhetoric was that the shortcomings and defects of individual men (who, however, are all politically equal) must be counterbalanced by asserting the 'common good' which he thought of as the will of the people considered collectively, that is, 'l'intérêt général'. This notion, the guiding thread of principled politics in his estimation, he derived from Rousseau's 'general will'. Robespierre and Saint-Just, before and during the Terror, considered themselves highly principled egalitarian republicans, charged with stripping away what was superfluous and corrupt, inspired above all by Rousseau. Robespierre's overriding difficulty was the disconcerting gap between what the people, or bafflingly large elements of the people, actually wanted and his austere Rousseauist 'general will' based on the 'common good'. The essential challenge facing the Revolution, as Robespierre expressed it in November 1792, was practically identical to that identified by the radical *Spinosistes* of the early eighteenth century: 'le secret de la liberté est d'éclairer les hommes, comme celui de la tyrannie est de les retenir dans l'ignorance.'[11]

Ceremonial and symbolic occurrences of the more radical phases of the Revolution invoked Rousseau and his core ideas. Thus the ceremony held on the site of the demolished Bastille, organized by the foremost artistic director of the Revolution, Jacques-Louis David, in August 1793 to mark the inauguration of the new republican constitution, an event coming shortly after the final abolition of all forms of feudal privilege, featured a cantata based on Rousseau's democratic pantheistic deism as expounded in the celebrated *Profession de Foi d'un vicaire savoyard* expounded in Book 4 of *Émile*.[12] When in May 1794 Robespierre officially launched the cult of the Supreme Being, as part of his counter-move against the Jacobin 'dechristianizers' among his opponents, whom he saw as being under the pernicious sway of such atheistic

---

[10] Maréchal, *Dictionnaire*, p. xix.   [11] Cobban, 'Fundamental Ideas', 140–3, 150.
[12] Schama, *Citizens*, 745–8.

philosophes as Diderot, Helvétius, and d'Holbach, he emphasized the need for a public cult, insisting on its republican functions and expressly citing Rousseau as the architect of the new civic religion.[13]

Yet if Rousseau's philosophy proved vastly more attractive and influential, and was deeper and more original than that of most other *philosophes* invoked by the Revolution, it is no more true of him than of such derivative (and, in some cases, hack) utopians, proto-socialists, and atheistic materialists as Morellet, Mably, Mirabeau, d'Holbach, Naigeon, Maréchal, Saint-Just, and Babeuf that the core radical ideas arose, or were principally shaped in the later eighteenth century. Nor, any more than Voltaire or the others, does Rousseau represent a basically new set of concepts and approaches. On the contrary, any proper appreciation of Rousseau's role and greatness has to concede that his thought springs from a long, and almost obsessive dialogue with the radical ideas of the past—in many cases as filtered through the mind of his former comrade Diderot.[14] The highly productive period of creativity which Rousseau enjoyed at his rural retreat away from Paris in the years 1756–62, during which he wrote his three masterpieces—the *Nouvelle Héloise* (1761), the *Contrat social* (1762), and *Émile* (1762)—began shortly after his break with his former inseparable ally, Diderot, and ended with the public furore provoked by *Émile*, and its resounding *profession de foi*. This was a work widely denounced as irreligious and seditious and formally banned. A warrant was issued for Rousseau's arrest, and he was obliged to flee into temporary exile near Bern. Written at the same time as the *Contrat social*, *Émile* forms, together with that work, the fullest, most mature statement of Rousseau's thought, constituting the cornerstone of a potent new radicalism which is at once philosophical, political, and moral.

As with Diderot—and Spinoza, whose work he undoubtedly knew—Rousseau's starting-point is that man must live according to Nature. The upbringing and formation of the individual, to his mind, mirrors the wider evolution of mankind, with the more primitive abilities and faculties developing first and the use of reason, which he viewed as a compound of all the other faculties, emerging last and with the greatest difficulty. Émile grows into a youth who represents Rousseau's social ideal of the 'natural man' whose life is based on the authentic needs and aspirations of men and who lacks the frivolity, vices, empty courtesy, addiction to fashion, and desire to flatter usual in society. He is a model of honesty, plain dealing, and self-reliance. The culminating phase of Émile's education, that is, his learning to live according to Nature, rejection of conventional ideas and culture, and self-reliance for ideas, is his induction to the ideas of the Savoyard *vicaire*.

The chief ingredients of Rousseau's outlook, as expressed in the *Profession de foi*, are a sweeping rejection of tradition, Revelation, and all institutionalized authority, denial of scepticism as only theoretically but not actually possible—since man's mind is so organized that he has to believe something,[15] and the principle that the universe is 'in motion and its movements ordered, uniform and subject to fixed laws', but yet that the

---

[13] Doyle, *Oxford History of the French Revolution*; Touchefeu, 'Vicaire', 236–8, 276.
[14] Talmon, *Origins*, 40–2; Wokler, *Social Thought*, 51, 54–7.   [15] Rousseau, *Émile*, 230, 232.

'first causes of motion are not to be found in matter;[16] for matter receives and transmits motion but does not produce it.'[17] From this Rousseau deduced that 'there is a will which sets the universe in motion and gives life to nature,' rejecting outright the systematic atheism of d'Holbach, Helvétius and, above all, his discarded ally Diderot. 'Matter in motion according to fixed laws,' affirmed Rousseau, 'points me to an intelligence' and also 'some common end which I cannot perceive': 'I believe therefore that the world is governed by a wise and powerful will.'[18] Regarding man's place in the universe, Rousseau stresses the paradox that 'Nature showed me a scene of harmony and proportion' while the 'human race shows men nothing but confusion and disorder.'[19]

There is a great deal in society, according to Rousseau, which is misplaced or superfluous and needs to be stripped away, but the starting-point has to be a philosophically meaningful appraisal of man. The key, he argues, is to acknowledge that there is a basic duality, two divergent principles in man, one raising him to the pursuit of eternal truths, the other dragging him downwards within himself, rendering him a slave to his passions. He grants Diderot and other radical predecessors that to put oneself first, motivation rooted in the drive to self-preservation, is 'an inclination natural to man'. But he insists that the 'first sentiment of justice' is likewise innate in man and essential to his sensibility; 'let those who say man is a simple creature'—clearly an allusion to Spinoza as well as Diderot—'remove these contradictions and I will grant that there is but one substance.'[20] He agrees, continuing his dialogue with both old and new *Spinosistes*, that we should indeed have to 'acknowledge one substance' if all the elementary qualities known to us, whether within or outside man, can be united in one and the same being. 'But if there are qualities which are mutually exclusive, then there are as many different substances as there are such exclusions.'

The dialogue with the *Spinosistes* continues into the latter stages of the *Confession*. 'No doubt I am not free not to desire my own welfare,' concedes Rousseau, attacking the doctrine of necessity laid down by Spinoza, Collins, and his former friend, 'but does it follow that I am not my own master because I cannot be other than myself?'[21] 'It is not the word freedom that is meaningless,' he concludes, 'but the word necessity. From this Rousseau arrives at one of his most basic contentions—and points of divergence from the Spinozist tradition—that 'man is animated by an immaterial substance.' By propounding a doctrine of 'two substances' in man, Rousseau believes he has found the key to human nature and, from this, also to politics. Like Descartes, Rousseau argues that one of the substances in man is indissoluble and immortal, namely the soul. From this he was also able to argue for a form of reward and punishment in the hereafter and the absolute quality of good and evil.[22]

His confident belief that he had circumvented Diderot and Spinoza only sharpened Rousseau's sense of grievance during his exile in Switzerland. Commenting in July 1762 on the *horreur* with which he was regarded by the local Reformed preachers, he

---

[16] Ibid., 235. [17] Ibid., 239. [18] Ibid., 241. [19] Ibid.
[20] Ibid. [21] Ibid., 243. [22] Ibid., 246.

averred that 'Spinoza, Diderot, Voltaire, Helvétius, sont des saints auprès de moi.'[23] He complained a few months later in a letter to the Archibshop of Paris that 'l'athée Spinoza' had been permitted to live and propagate his doctrine in tranquillity whilst he, Rousseau, 'le défenseur de la cause de Dieu', had been shamefully hounded from France.[24]

To his deistic metaphysics and doctrine of substance and morality, Rousseau added his political philosophy based on the idea of the 'general will'. Here again the great thinker was elaborating in close dialogue with predecessors rather than introducing something broadly new. Rousseau's personality and passionate temperament being what they were, the fervour with which he subsequently rejected elements of the new *Spinosisme* of Diderot and Helvétius has its counterpart, evidently, in a strong propensity prior to the mid-1750s to accept and rely heavily on Diderot's formulations.[25] Originally, the term 'volonté générale' had been Diderot's and was employed, for example, in the latter's article 'Droit naturel' in the *Encyclopédie* to denote the collective, common good in any group or society, a good which, according to Diderot, is the absolute and only higher good enabling us to define what is 'just' or 'unjust', 'good' or 'bad', since the individual is always driven to seek only his own welfare so that inevitably 'les volontés particulières sont suspectes.' Whereas the individual will might be either good or bad, 'la volonté générale est toujours bonne: elle n'a jamais trompé, elle ne trompera jamais.'[26] This is what Spinoza meant by the *dictamen* of the 'common good' and constitutes the foremost of all affinities linking Spinoza, Diderot, and Rousseau. Admittedly, Rousseau's 'general will' is not the same as Diderot's or Spinoza's 'common good'. It is a far more developed conception which, unlike the former, can only be realized in the context of civil society, under the State, not in the state of nature. But this does not alter the fact that it emerged in conscious opposition to Diderot's system and is still a variant of what, right from the outset in Spinoza and Van den Enden, is the only possible criterion for judging 'good' and 'bad' once Revelation and ecclesiastical authority are discarded, namely the common good defined as what best serves the interests of society as a whole.

What is especially remarkable about Rousseau's thought is its Janus-headed mixing of elements from both the radical and mainstream Enlightenment. In its stress on the existence of a Creator and First Mover, on two substances, on the immortality of the soul, and the absolute quality of 'good' and 'evil' in ethics, it is aligned with the mainstream moderate Enlightenment and rejects the radical tradition of Spinoza and Diderot. Yet in its sweeping rejection of tradition and authority, its delegitimizing of the social and political structures of the day, its egalitarianism, underlying pantheism and, above all, in the doctrine of the 'general will', it is aligned unmistakably with a radical philosophical tradition reaching back to the mid-seventeenth century. Spinoza, Diderot, Rousseau: all three ground their conception of individual liberty in man's obligation to subject himself to the sovereignty of the common good.

---

[23] Vernière, *Spinoza*, 479.   [24] Ibid.

[25] Talmon, *Origins*, 40–1; Wokler, *Social Thought*, 55–7, 61, 65.

[26] [Diderot], *Encyclopédie*, v, 116.

Bibliography

Published Primary Sources

Pseudonyms and false attributions to authors are given within inverted commas, as are fictitious and presumed false places of publication. In the case of rare works and editions the location of the copy used is indicated by the relevant abbreviation.

AALSTIUS, JOHANNES, *Inleiding tot de Zeden-leer* (Dordrecht, 1705). BL

ABBADIE, JAQUES, *A Vindication of the Truth of the Christian Religion against the Objections of all modern Opposers* (2 vols.; London, 1694). BL

An Account of the Life and Writings of Spinoza to which is added an Abstract of His Theological Political Treatise (London, 1720). UCLA

Acta Eruditorum (*Acta Lipsiensia*), ed. Otto Mencke (periodical 50 vols.; Leipzig, 1682–1731). DL

Acta Stoschiana (1694, Leipzig, 1749) in W. Schröder (ed.), Stosch, *Concordia*, 239–312

Acten ofte handelingen van de Noord-Hollandsche Synodus gehouden binnen Edam en Alcmaer Anno 1691 en 1692 rakende Dr Balthasar Bekker (Enkhuizen, 1692). UCLA

Advisen van sommige theologanten van Utrecht . . . over het boek van Lodovicus Wolzogen (Utrecht, 1669). Kn. 9797 AUB

D'ALEMBERT, J. LE ROND, *Discours préliminaire* in vol. I (1751) of the *Encyclopédie* pp. i–xlv

——'Éloge de M. du Marsais', in *Encyclopédie* vol. VII (1757) pp. i–xiv

Allgemeines Historisches Lexicon (6 vols.; Leipzig, 1730).

ALLINGA, PETRUS, *Cartesianismi gangraena insanabilis* (Utrecht, 1680). BL

ALVAREZ DE TOLEDO, GABRIEL, *Historia de la Iglesia, y del Mundo* (Madrid, 1713). SBU

ANDALA, RUARD, *Cartesius verus Spinozismi eversor et physicae experimentalis architectus* (Franeker, 1719). BL

——*Dissertationum philosophicarum heptas* (Franeker, 1711). BL

——*Dissertationum Philosophicarum in quibus praemissa introductione sententiae quaedam paradoxae ex Ethica Cl. Geulingii examinantur* (Franeker, 1715). AUB

——*Exercitationes academicae in philosophiam primam et naturalem* (Franeker, 1708). BL

——*Syntagma theologico-physico-metaphysicum* (Franeker, 1711). BL

'ANDLO, DANIEL', *Ad clarissimi theologi Samuelis Maresij* (Amsterdam, 1673). UCLA

'ANDLO, PETRUS VAN', [Mansvelt, Renier van], *Specimen Confutationis Dissertationis quam Samuel Maresius edidit* (Leiden, 1670). UCLA

——*Animadversiones ad vindicias dissertationes qvam Samuel Maresius edidit De Abusu Philosophiae Cartesianae* (Leiden, 1671). UCLA

Annales Literari Mecklenburgenses, Oder Jahr-Register von denen Geschäften der Gelehrten in Mecklenburg, vol. 1 (Rostock, 1721). BL

An Answer to the Discourse of Free-Thinking . . . by a Gentleman of Cambridge (London, 1717). BL

Archives de la Bastille. Documents inédits, ed. F. Ravaisson (19 vols.; Paris, 1866–1904).

D'ARGENS, JEAN-BAPTISTE DE BOYER, MARQUIS, *Lettres Cabalistiques, ou correspondance philosophique, historique et critique* (1737–40; 2nd edn., 7 vols.; The Hague, 1759). UCLA

—— *Lettres chinoises ou correspondance philosophique, historique et critique* (5 vols.; The Hague, 1739). UCLA

—— *Lettres juives, ou correspondance philosophique, historique et critique* (1738; 2nd edn. 6 vols.; The Hague, 1742). UCLA

—— *Mémoires de Monsieur le Marquis d'Argens* (2nd edn., 'Londres', 1737). UCLA

—— *Mémoires secrets de la République des Lettres* (7 vols.; Amsterdam, 1744). ABM

—— *La Philosophie du Bon-Sens ou réflexions philosophiques sur l'incertitude connoissances humaines* (2 vols.; new edn., The Hague, 1747). UCLA

[D'ARGENS], *Thérèse Philosophe ou Mémoires pour servir a l'histoire du P. Dirrag et de Mlle Eradice*, ed. G. Pigeaud de Gurbert (Avignon, 1993).

ARNAULD, ANTOINE, *Oeuvres* (50 vols.; Paris, 1775–83). BL

ARND, CARL, 'Eine akademische Ferienreise von Rostock bis Königsberg im Jahre 1694', *Baltische Studien* (Stettin), ix (1905), 1–54.

ARNOLD, GOTTFRIED, *Unpartheyische Kirchen- und Ketzerhistorie* (2 vols.; Leipzig, 1699–1700). UCLA

ARPE, PETER FRIEDRICH, *Theatrum fati sive notitia scriptorum de providentia fortuna et fato*, (Rotterdam, 1712). WHA

[ARPE, PETER FRIEDRICH], *Apologia pro Jul. Caesare Vanino Neapolitano* ('Cosmopoli' [Rotterdam], 1712).

Articulen Tot Satisfactie van de eerw. Classis van Amsterdam van D. Balthasar Bekker Overgeleverd den 22 January 1692 (Amsterdam, 1692). UCLA

Artikelen tot satisfactie van de . . . kerkenraad van Zwolle aan D. Frederik van Leenhof (Zwolle, 1704). LUB

[ASTRUC, JEAN], *Conjectures sur les mémoires originaux dont il paroît que Moyse s'est servi pour composer le livre de la Genèse* ('Bruxelles', [Paris] 1753). BL

AUBERT DE VERSÉ, NOEL, *L'impie convaincu ou dissertation contre Spinoza* (Amsterdam, 1685) UCLA

—— *Le Tombeau du Socinianisme* ('Francfort' [Amsterdam] 1687). BL

AULISEO, DOMENICO, *Delle scuole sacre* (2 vols.; Naples, 1723). FBN

BALEN, PETRUS VAN, *De verbetering der gedachten* (1684), ed. M. J. van den Hoven (Baarn, 1988).

BALLING, PIETER, *Het Licht op den kandelaar* (Amsterdam, 1662). AUB

BALTUS, JEAN-FRANÇOIS, S. J., *An Answer to M. de Fontenelle's History of Oracles* (London, 1709). UCLA-Cl

—— *Jugement des SS. Pères sur le morale de la philosophie payenne* (Strasbourg, 1719). PBM

—— *La Religion Chrétienne prouvée par l'accomplissement des propheties de l'Ancien et du Nouveau Testament* (Paris, 1728). PBM

—— *Réponse à l'Histoire des Oracles de M. de Fontenelle* (2 vols.; Strasbourg, 1707). BL

—— *Suite de la Réponse à l'Histoire des Oracles* (Strasbourg, 1708).

BARBAPICCOLA, GIUSEPPA-ELEONORA, 'La Traduttrice a Lettori', preface to *I Principi della filosofia di Renato Des-Cartes* ('Torino' [Naples], 1722). NBN

BARRIOS, DANIEL LEVI DE (MIGUEL) DE, *Triumpho del govierno popular en la casa de Jacob* (Amsterdam, 1683). BL

BASNAGE, JAQUES, *Histoire des juifs depuis Jésus-Christ jusqu'à présent* (12 vols.; The Hague, 1716). BL

BASNAGE DE BEAUVAL, HENRI, *Tolérance des religions* (Rotterdam, 1684; repr. New York, 1970).

BATALIER, JACOB, *Vindiciae miraculorum . . . adversus auctorem Tractatus Theologico- Politici* (Amsterdam, 1673). AUB

BAUMEISTER, FRIEDRICH CHRISTIAN, *Institutiones Metaphysicae* (Wittenberg, 1738; repr. Hildesheim, 1988).

BAUMGARTEN, SIEGMUND JACOB, *Nachrichten von einer Hallischen Bibliothek* (Halle, 1750). BL

BAYLE, PIERRE, *Commentaire philosophique sur les paroles de Jésus-Christ, 'Contrains-les d'entrer'*, ed. Jean-Michel Gros (1686; n.p. [Paris?], 1992).

——*Dictionnaire historique et critique* (3 vols.; Rotterdam, 1702).

——*Écrits sur Spinoza*, ed. Françoise Charles-Daubert and Pierre-François Moreau (Paris, 1983).

——*Lettres* (3 vols.; Amsterdam, 1729). BL

——*Oeuvres diverses* (4 vols.; The Hague, 1737). BL

——*Pensées diverses sur la comète* (1683), ed. A. Prat (Paris, 1994).

——*Recueil de quelques pièces curieuses concernant la philosophie de Monsieur Descartes* (Amsterdam, 1684). BL

——*Historical and Critical Dictionary: Selections*, trans. and ed. R. H. Popkin (Indianapolis, Indiana, 1991).

[BAYLE, PIERRE], *Nouvelles de la République des lettres* (4 vols.; Amsterdam, 1684–7). BL

BEAUMONT, JOHN, *An historical, physiological and theological Treatise of Spirits, Apparitions, Witchcrafts and other magical Practices* (London, 1705). BL

—— *Historisch Physiologisch-und Theologischer Tractat von Geistern*, with 'Vorrede' by Christian Thomasius (Halle, 1721). BL

BECKHER, WILHELM HEINRICH, *Schediasma critico-litterarium de controversiis praecipiis Balthasari Bekkero . . . quondam motis* (1719; Königsberg, 1721). BL

BEELDTHOUWER, JAN PIETERSZ, *Antwoordt op het Boeck genaemt, De Philosophie d'Uytleghster* (Amsterdam, 1667). AUB

BEKKER, BALTHASAR, *De Betoverde Weereld* (1691–4; new edn. 4 vols.; Deventer, 1739). BL

——*Engelsch verhaal van ontdekte tovery wederleid* (Amsterdam, 1689). BL

——*Kort Begryp der algemeine kerkelijke Historien* (Amsterdam, 1686). BL

——*Kort bericht . . . aangaande alle de schriften* (Franeker, 1692). GrUB

——*Naakte Uitbeeldinge van alle de vier boeken der B. W.* (Amsterdam, 1693).

——*Nodige bedenkingen op de nieuwe bewegingen . . . tegen den auteur van 't boek De Betoverde Weereld* (Amsterdam, 1692). BL

——*Brief . . . Aan twee eerwaardige Predikanten D. Joannes Aalstius . . . ende D Paulus Steenwinckel* (Amsterdam, 1693). UCLA.

——*Ondersoek en Antwoord . . . op 't request in den herfst des jaars 1691 ingegeven aan de Ed. Gr. Mog. Heeren Staten van Holland* (Amsterdam, 1693). AUB

——*De Philosophia Cartesiana* (Wesel, 1668). BL

BENCINI, FRANCESO DOMENICO, *Tractatio historico-polemica chronologicis tabulis* (Turin, n.d. [1720]). FBN

BENEDETTI, GIOVANNI BATTISTA S. J., *Difesa della scolastica teologia* (Rome, 1703). FBN

——*Difesa della terza lettera apologetica di Benedetto Aletino* (Rome, 1705). FBN

——*Lettere apologetiche in defesa della teologia scolastica* (Naples, 1694). NBN

BENOIST, ELIE, *Mélange de remarques critiques, historiques, philosophiques, théologiques sur les deux dissertations de M. Toland* (Delft, 1712). BL

BENTLEY, RICHARD, *The Folly and Unreasonableness of Atheism* (London, 1693–4). BL

——*Remarks upon a late Discourse of Free-Thinking* (London, 1713). BL

BERKELEY, GEORGE, *Alciphron: or, the minute philosopher in seven Dialogues*, ed. David Berman (London and New York, 1993).

—— *Three Dialogues between Hylas and Philonous in Opposition to Sceptics and Atheists*, ed. R. M. Adams (Indianapolis, 1979).

BERNI, JUAN BAUTISTA, *Filosofia racional, natural, metafisica i moral* (3 vols.; Valencia, 1736). MBN

BERNS, MICHAEL, *Altar Der Atheisten, der Heyden und der Christen* (Hamburg, 1692). BL

[BERNS, MICHAEL], *Gründliche und völlige Wiederlegung der Bezauberten Welt Balthasar Beckers* (Hamburg, 1708). BL

BEVERLAND, ADRIAEN, *De Peccato Originali* (Leiden, 1679). BL

[BEVERLAND, ADRIAEN] *État de l'homme dans le péché originel* (n.p. [Amsterdam?], 1714). BL

BIANCHINI, FRANCESCO, *La historia universale provata con monumenti e figurata con simboli degl'antichi* (Rome, 1747). NBN

Bibliothèque ancienne et moderne, ed. Jean Le Clerc (periodical; Amsterdam, 1714–26). BL

Bibliotheca Historico-Philologico-Theologica, ed. T. Hase and F. A. Lampe (periodical; Bremen, 1718–20). BL

Bibliothèque Choisie, ed. Jean Le Clerc (periodical; Amsterdam, 1703–13). BL

Bibliothèque Universelle et Historique, ed. Jean Le Clerc (periodical; Amsterdam, 1686–93). BL

BILFINGER (also BÜLFINGER) GEORG BERNHARD, *Dilucidationes philosophicae de Deo, anima humana, mundo et generalibus rerum affectionibus* (Tübingen, 1725). UCLA

—— *De Harmonia animi et corporis humani maxime praestabilita* (1723; 3rd edn. Tübingen, 1741; repr. Hildesheim, 1984).

BINET, BENJAMIN, *Traité historique des dieux et des démons du paganisme* (1696; 2nd edn. Amsterdam, 1699). BL

BLIJENBERGH, WILLEM, *Wederlegging van de Ethica of Zede-kunst van Benedictus de Spinoza* (Dordrecht, 1682). AUB

BLIJENBERGH, WILLEM VAN, and DEURHOFF, WILLEM, *Klaare en beknopte verhandeling van de natuur en de werkinge der menschelijke zielen, engelen en duivelen, vervat in gewisselde brieven* (Amsterdam, 1692). AUB

[BLOUNT, CHARLES], *Anima Mundi: Or, An Historical Narration of the Opinions of the Ancients Concerning Man's Soul* ('Amsterdam' [London], n.d.). HHL

—— *Great is Diana of the Ephesians* (London, 1680). HHL

—— *Miracles No Violations of the Laws of Nature* (London, 1683).

—— *The Oracles of Reason* (London, 1693). CUL

De Boekzaal van Europe, ed. Pieter Rabus (periodical; Rotterdam, 1692–1702). BL

De Boekzaal der Geleerde Weereld, ed. W. Sewel (periodical; Amsterdam, 1705–7). BL

BOIX Y MOLINER, MARCELINO, *Hippocrates aclarado y sistema de Galeno impugnado* (Madrid, 1716). CBU

BOLKIUS, BARTHOLOMEUS, *Animadversiones philosophicae in decantam Spinozae propositionem, quae res nihil commune inter se habent, earum una alterius caussa esse non potest* (Amsterdam, 1719). AUB

BOMBLE, FLORENTINUS, *Brief aan den Heer Fredericus van Leenhof . . . behelsende noodige aanmerkingen over desselfs Hemel op Aarden* (Amsterdam, 1703). Kn. 15059 LUB

BONTEKOE, CORNELIS, *Apologie van den Autheur tegens sijne Lasteraars*, printed as an Annex to the same author's *Tractaat van het Excellenste Kruyd THEE* (The Hague, 1679). BL

BOSSUET, JAQUES-BÉNIGNE, BISHOP, *Correspondance*, ed. Ch. Urbain and E. Levesque (15 vols.; Paris, 1909–25).

——*Discours sur l'histoire universelle*, ed. J. Truchet (Paris, 1966).

——*Élévations sur les Mystères*, ed. M. Dreane (Paris, 1962).

BOULAINVILLIERS, HENRI DE, *Essai de Metaphysique* in Lenglet-Dufresnoy, *Réfutation* ('Bruxelles', 1731). BL

——*Mémoires présentés à Monseigneur le Duc de d'Orléans* (The Hague and Amsterdam, 1727). BL

——*Oeuvres philosophiques*, ed. Renée Simon (2 vols.; The Hague, 1973).

——*La Vie de Mahomed* ('Londres', 1730). BL

BOUREAU-DESLANDES, ANDRÉ-FRANÇOIS, *Histoire critique de la philosophie* (3 vols.; Amsterdam, 1737). BL

BOYLE, ROBERT, *A Free Enquiry into the vulgarly received Notion of Nature*, ed. E. B. Davis and M. Hunter (Cambridge, 1996).

——'Letter on Miracles (Mr Boyle's Answer to Spinosa)' and other Boyle papers in Colie, 'Spinoza in England', appendix, pp. 211–19.

——*The Theological Works* (3 vols.; London, 1715). BL

——*The Works of the Honourable Robert Boyle*, ed. Thomas Birch (6 vols.; London, 1772). BL

BOYS, J. DU, *Schadelickheyt van de Cartesiaansche philosophie* (Utrecht, 1656). BL

BRAUNIUS, JOHANNES (BRUN, JEAN), *La Véritable religion des Hollandois* (2 vols.; Amsterdam, 1675). BL

——*Futilis Spinozismi depulsionis nominatim circa corporis peccata et poenas Pauli Hulsii . . . depulsio necessaria* (Groningen, 1702). LUB

BREDENBURG, JOHANNES, *Enervatio Tractatus Theologico-Politicus* (Rotterdam, 1675). BL

——*Noodige Verantwoording op de ongegronde beschuldiging van Abrah. Lemmerman* (Rotterdam, 1684). AUB

——*Verhandelinge van de oorsprong van de kennisse Gods* (Amsterdam, 1684). AUB

——*J. B., Wiskundige demonstratie, dat alle verstandelijke werking noodzaakelijk is* (Amsterdam, 1684). AUB

——*Korte aanmerkingen op de brieven van . . . Philippus van Limborch* (Rotterdam, 1686). AUB

BREDENBURG, JOHANNES, and LIMBORCH, PHILIPPUS VAN, *Schriftelyke onderhandeling . . . rakende 't gebruyk der reden in de religie* (Rotterdam, 1686). Kn 12544 BL

BREITHAUPT, CHRISTIAN, *Zufällige Gedancken über die Methode, wie ein Atheist von . . . der Wahrheit . . . zu überzeugen* (Helmstedt, 1732). BPK

Briefwechsel der Herzogin Sophie von Hannover mit ihrem Bruder dem Kurfürsten Karl Ludwig von der Pfalz (ed.), E. Bodemann (Leipzig, 1885).

BRING, SVEN (ed.), *Samling af åtskilliga Handlingar och Påminnelser*, ii (Lund, 1754). SRL

BRINK, HENRICUS, *Toet-steen der waarheid en der meyningen* (Utrecht, 1691). GrUB

[BROWNE, THOMAS], *Miracles Works above and contrary to Nature or, an Answer to a late Translation out of Spinoza's Tractatus Theologico-Politicus* (London, 1683). CUL

BRUCKER, JACOB, *Historia critica philosophiae*, trans. William Enfield as *The History of Philosophy from the earliest Periods* (London, 1837).

BRUN, JEAN *see* Braunius.

BUDDEUS, FRANZ, *Analecta historiae philosophicae* (2nd edn., Halle, 1724). BL

——*Bedencken über die Wolffianische Philosophie* ('Freyburg' [Halle], 1724). BL

——*Compendium historiae philosophicae* (Halle, 1731). BL

——*Introductio ad historiam philosophiae Ebraeorum* (Halle, 1702). UCLA

——*Lehr-Sätze von der Atheisterey und dem Aberglauben* (Jena, 1723). BL

——*Theses theologicae de atheismo et superstitione* (1717; Utrecht, 1737). UCLA

——*Traité de l'athéisme et de la superstition* (Amsterdam, 1740). UCLA

BURCKHARD, JOHANN HEINRICH, *Bibliothecae Bvrckhardianae publica avctione Wolffenbvtteli in beate defvncti aedibus* (3 vols.; Helmstedt, 1743). BPK

BURMANNUS, FRANCISCUS, *Burmannorum pietas* (Utrecht, 1700). BL

—— *'t Hoogste Goed der Spinozisten vergeleken met den Hemel op Aarden* (Enkhuizen, 1704). AUB

CABRIADA, JUAN DE, *Carta philosophica medica chymica* (n.p., 1686). CBU

[CAMUSAT, DENYS FRANÇOIS], *Histoire critique des Journaux* (2 vols.; Amsterdam, 1734). BL

CAPASSO, GIAMBATTISTA, *Historiae philosophiae synopsis* (Naples, 1728). NBN

CAPASSO, NICCOLO, *Institutiones theologicae dogmaticae* (2 vols.; Naples, 1754). NBN

CAPOA, LEONARDO DI, *Del Parere di Signor Leonardo di Capoa divisato in otto ragionamenti* ('Colonia' [Naples?], 1714). NBN

CARPOV, PAUL THEODOR, *Animadversiones philologico-critico-sacrae* (Leipzig, 1740). BL

CARPZOV, JOHANN BENEDICT, *Historia Critica Veteris Testamenti auctore Richardo Simoni oratione inavgvrali discussa* (Leipzig, 1684). BL

CARROLL, WILLIAM, *A Dissertation upon the tenth Chapter of the fourth Book of Mr Locke's Essay* (London, 1706). LDrW

—— *A Letter to the Reverend Dr Benjamin Prat* (London, 1707). LDrW

—— *Remarks upon Mr Clarke's Sermons preached at St Paul's against Hobbs, Spinoza and other Atheists* (London, 1705). LDrW

—— *Spinoza Reviv'd or, A Treatise proving the book entitled the Rights of the Christian Church . . . to be the same with Spinoza's Rights of the Christian Clergy* (London, 1709). BL

—— *Spinoza Reviv'd, Part the Second, Or, a Letter to Monsieur Le Clerc* (London, 1711). LDrW

CASTRIES, HENRI DE (ed.), *Les Sources inédites de l'histoire du Maroc de 1530 à 1845* 2nd ser. (6 vols.; Paris and The Hague, 1906–23).

Catalogue des Livres Imprimez de la Bibliothèque du Roy. Théologie (3 vols.; Paris, 1742). BL

CHALLE, ROBERT, *Difficultés sur la religion proposées au Père Malebranche* (Oxford, 1982).

CHAUFEPIÉ, JACQUES-GEORGE DE, *Nouveau Dictionnaire historique et critique* (4 vols.; Amsterdam and The Hague, 1750).

CHEVREAU, URBAIN, *Chevraeana, ou diverses pensées d'histoire, de critique, d'érudition et de morale* (Amsterdam, 1700). BL

CLARKE, SAMUEL, *A Demonstration of the Being and Attributes of God: more particularly in Answer to Mr Hobbs, Spinoza and their Followers*, ed. E. Vailati (1705; Cambridge, 1998).

CLARMUND, ADOLPH, *Das Leben und die Schriften des sehr berümten Mannes Wilhelm Ernst Tentzels* (Dresden, 1708). HUB

COLERUS, JOHANNES, *La Vie de B. de Spinoza* (The Hague, 1706). UCLA

[COLLINS, ANTHONY], *An Answer To Mr Clark's Third Defence Of his Letter to Mr. Dodwell* (London, 1708). BL

—— *A Discourse of Free-Thinking* (London, 1713). BL

—— *Discourse of the Grounds and Reasons of the Christian Religion* (London, 1724). BL

—— *A Philosophical Inquiry Concerning Human Liberty* (2nd edn., London, 1717). BL

CONCINA, DANIELE, *Della storia del Probabilismo, e del Rigorismo* (2 vols.; Luccha, 1743). VBM

—— *Theologia Christiana dogmatico-moralis* (12 vols.; Rome, 1749–51). VBM

—— *Della religione rivelata contra gli ateisti, deisti, materialisti, indifferentisti che negano la verità de' Misteri* (2 vols.; Venice, 1754). FBM

CONDILLAC, ÉTIENNE BONNOT DE, *Traité de sistèmes* (1749; Paris, 1991).

CONTI, ANTONIO, *Risposta Del Signor Abate Conte Antonio Conti, Nobile Veneziano, Alla Difesa del Libro delle Considerazioni intorno alla Generazione de' Viventi* (Venice, 1716). BL

CORNELIO, TOMMASO, *Progymnasmata physica* (Naples, 1688). NBN

COSTA, URIEL DA, *Examination of Pharisaic Traditions*, ed. H. P. Salomon and I. S. D. Sassoon (Leiden, 1993).

——[*Exemplar Humanae Vitae*] *Uriel da Costa's Own Account of his Life Englished by John Whiston* (1740) in Da Costa, *Examination*, 556–64.

CREYGHTON, JOHANNES, *De Hemel op aarde, Geopent voor alle waare Christenen uyt Godts heylig woordt* (Amsterdam, 1704). BL

CROUSAZ, JEAN-PIERRE DE, *Examen du Pyrrhonisme ancien et moderne* (The Hague, 1733). UCLA

CUDWORTH, RALPH, *A Treatise concerning Eternal and Immutable Morality*, ed. Sarah Hutton (Cambridge, 1996).

CUFFELER, ABRAHAM, *Specimen artis ratiocinandi* (3 vols.; 'Hamburg' [Amsterdam], 1684). BL

CUNHA, D. LUÍS DA, *Testamento Político ou Carta escrita pelo grande D. Luiz da Cunha ao senhor rei D. José 1 antes do seu governo* ed. N. Leonzo (São Paulo, 1976).

DALE, ANTHONIE VAN, *Dissertationes de origine ac progressu idololatriae* (Amsterdam, 1696). UCLA

—— *De oraculis veterum ethnicorum* (1683; 2nd edn. Amsterdam, 1700). BL

—— *Verhandeling van de oude orakelen der heydenen* (1687; new edn., Amsterdam, 1718). HHL

Daneschiold in Samsoe, Count Christian of, *Bibliotheca Daneschioldiana* (Copenhagen, 1732). CRL

Dänische Bibliothec oder Sammlung von alten und neuen gelehrten Sachen aus Dännemark, vol. 1 (Copenhagen and Leipzig, 1738). BL

DENYOD, JEAN, *La nature expliquée par le raisonnement et par l'expérience* (Paris, 1719). BL

—— *La Vérité de la religion chrétienne démontrée par ordre géometrique* (Paris, 1719). BL

DERHAM, WILLIAM, *Dimostrazione della essenza, ed attributi d'Iddio del' opere della sua Creazione* (Florence, 1719). VBM

[DESFONTAINES, ABBÉ], *Lettres . . . à Monsieur l'Abbé Houtteville au sujet du livre de la Religion chrétienne prouvée par les faits* (Paris, 1722). MBM

DES MAIZEAUX, PIERRE, *La Vie de Monsieur de Saint Evremond*, in vol. 1 of *Oeuvres de Monsieur de Saint-Evremond*, ed. P. Des Maizeaux (5 vols.; Amsterdam, 1726). BL

DEURHOFF, WILLEM, *Voorleeringen van de H. Godgeleerdheid steunende op de beginzelen van waarheid en deuchd* (Amsterdam, 1687). AUB

DIDEROT, DENIS, *Pensées philosophiques* (1746) in Diderot, *Oeuvres philosophiques*, pp. 9–72.

—— *Lettre sur les aveugles* (1749) in Diderot, *Oeuvres philosophiques*, pp. 81–164.

—— *Oeuvres philosophiques*, ed. P. Vernière (Paris, 1990).

—— *Oeuvres romanesques*, ed. H. Bénac (Paris, 1962).

Dissertations mêlées sur divers sujets importans et curieux, ed. 'J. F. Bernard' (2 vols.; 'Amsterdam', 1740).

DORIA, PAOLO MATTIA, *Il Capitano filosofo* (2 vols.; Naples, 1739). NBN

—— *Difesa della metafisica degli antichi filosofi contro il Signor Giovanni Locke, ed alcuni altri moderni autori* (2 vols.; Venice, 1732). BL

—— *Discorsi critici filosofici intorno alla filosofia degl' antichi, e degli moderni* (Venice, 1724). VBM

—— *Filosofia di Paolo Mattia Doria con la quale si schiarisce quella di Platone* (2 vols.; Amsterdam, 1728). VBM

—— *Lettere e ragionamenti vari dedicati alli celebri e sapientissimi signori dell' Accademia Etrusca* (3 vols.; 'Perugia', 1741). PBP

—— *Ragionamenti . . . ne' quali si dimostra la donna in quasi che tutte le virtù più grandi, non essere all' uomo inferiore* ('Francfort' [Naples], 1726). VBM

Doria, Paolo Mattia, *Risposte di Paolo Mattia Doria ad un libro stampato in Napoli . . . col titolo Riflessioni di Francesco-Maria Spinelli* (Naples, 1733). VBM

—— *La Vita Civile* (Naples, 1729). FBN

Dortous de Mairan, Jean-Jacques, *Éloge de M. le Cardinal de Polignac* (Paris, 1742). BL

Doutes sur la religion suivies de l'analyse du Traité Theologi-politique de Spinoza 'par le Comte de Boulainvilliers' ('Londres', 1767).

D'Outrein, Johannes, *Noodige aanmerkingen . . . benevens een Na-reden tegen Fredericus van Leenhof* (Dordrecht, 1704). LUB

Driessen, Anthonie, *Aanspraak van Antonius Driessen . . . aan de Kerk van Nederland* (n.p., n.d.). HKB

—— *Dissertatio cl. J. Wittichii disputationis De Natura Dei opposita* (Groningen, 1718). GrUB

Du Marsais, César Chesneau, *Examen de la religion ou Doutes sur la religion dont on cherche l'éclaircissement de bonne foi*, ed. Gianluca Mori (Oxford, 1998).

[Du Marsais] *Le Philosophe* in [Du Marsais], *Nouvelles libertés*, pp. 173–204.

[Du Marsais, ed.?] *Le Monde, son origine, son antiquité* ('Londres' [Paris], 1751). BL

[Du Marsais, ed.?] *Nouvelles libertés de penser* ('Amsterdam' [Paris], '1743' [1743]). BL

[Durand, David], *La Vie et les sentiments de Lucilio Vanini* (Rotterdam, 1717). BL

Earbery, Matthias, *Deism examin'd and confuted in an Answer to a book intitled Tractatus Theologico-Politicus* (London, 1697). CUL

Edelmann, Johann Christian, *Abgenöthigtes jedoch andern nicht wieder aufgenöthigtes Glaubens-Bekentniss* (n.p. [Neuwied?], 1746). BL

—— *Die Göttlichkeit der Vernunfft* (n.p., n.d.). BL

—— *Moses mit aufgedeckten Angesichte* (3 vols.; 'Freyburg' [Berleburg], 1740). BL

—— *Unschuldigen Wahrheiten* (1743), vols. 5–6 in J. C. Edelmann, *Sämtliche Schriften in Einzelausgaben*, ed. Walter Grossmann (6 vols.; Stuttgart, 1970).

[E. D. M.], *Redenkundige aanmerkingen tot wederlegging van den Brief van den Heer Tako Hajo van den Honert geschreven tegen den Hemel op Aarden* (Amsterdam, 1704). LUB

Elert N. (ed.), *Catalogi Bibliothecae Thottianae* (13 vols.; Copenhagen, 1788–95). BL

Encyclopédie ou Dictionnaire raisonné des sciences des arts et des métiers, eds. D. Diderot and J. L. d'Alembert (17 vols.; Paris, Geneva, and Neufchâtel, 1751–72).

Enden, Franciscus van den, *Philedonius*, ed. Marc Bedjaï (Paris, 1994).

—— *Vrije politijke stellingen* (1665; Amsterdam, 1992).

L'Europe Savante (periodical; The Hague, 1718–20). BL

Examen critique des apologistes de la religion chrétienne [attrib. 'N. Fréret'] (n.p., 1767). BL

Examen de la religion dont on cherche l'éclaircissement de bonne foy [by Du Marsais] ('Trévoux', [Paris?] 1745). UCLA

Fabricius, Johann Albrecht, *Delectus argumentorum et syllabus scriptorum . . . adversus atheos, epicureos, deistas seu naturalistas* (Hamburg, 1725). UCLA

Falck, Nathanael, *De Daemonologia novatorum autorum falsa* (2nd edn., Wittenberg, 1694). BL

Fardella, Michelangelo, *Animae humanae incorporea et immortalis substantia Adversus Epicurum, ejusque sectatores* (Venice, 1724). PBP

—— *La Filosofia Cartesiana Impugnata* (Venice, 1698). VBM

—— *Utraque dialectica, rationalis et mathematica* (2 vols.; Amsterdam, 1695). PBP

Faydit, Pierre-Valentin, Abbé, *Remarques sur Virgile et sur Homer, et sur le style Poétique de l'Écriture Sainte, où l'on réfute . . . Spinosa, Grotius et Mr Le Clerc* (Paris, 1705). UCLA

Faye, Jacob De la, *Defensio religionis . . . contra duas dissertationes Joh. Tolandi* (Utrecht, 1709). BL

FEIJÓO Y MONTENEGRO, BENITO JERÓNIMO, *Cartas Eruditas, y Curiosas* (new edn., 5 vols.; Madrid, 1774). BL

——— *Ilustración apologética al primero y segundo tomo del* Teatro Crítico (6th edn., Madrid, 1751). BL

——— *Justa Repulsa De Iniquas Acusaciones* (Madrid, 1749). SBU

——— *Teatro Crítico Universal* (1726–36; 8 vols.; Madrid, 1773). BL

FÉNELON, FRANÇOIS DE SALIGNAC DE LA MOTHE, *Démonstration de l'existence de Dieu* (2nd edn., Paris, 1713). BL

——— *Oeuvres complètes de Fénelon, Archevêque de Cambrai* (10 vols.; Paris, 1831–2).

FINETTI, GIOVANNI FRANCESCO, *De principiis juris naturae et gentium adversus Hobbesium, Pufendorfium, Thomasium, Wolfium et alios* (Venice, 1764). NBN

FOERTSTIUS, MICHAEL, *Selectorum theologeorum breviarium, id est discussio principalium punctorum theologicorum nostro tempore maxime controversorum* (Jena, 1708). UCLA

FONTENELLE, BERNARD LE BOVIER DE, *Entretiens sur la pluralité des mondes* (Amsterdam, 1687). BL

——— *Histoire des Oracles* (1686; new edn., Paris, 1698). BL

——— *Historie Der Heijdnischen Orakel . . . vemehret von Joh. Christoph Gottsched* (Leipzig, 1730). BL

——— *De l'Origine des Fables* (1724), ed. J. R. Carré (Paris, 1932).

——— *Traité de la Liberté* in [Du Marsais] *Nouvelles Libertés*, pp. 112–51. BL

[FONTENELLE, BERNARD LE BOVIER DE], *La République des philosophes, ou Histoire des Ajaoiens* (Geneva, 1768).

FORMEY, JEAN LOUIS SAMUEL, *La belle Wolfienne* (6 vols.; The Hague, 1741–53). BL

——— *Conseils pour former une bibliothèque peu nombreuse mais choisie* (3rd edn., Berlin, 1755). BL

——— *Histoire abrégée de la philosophie* (Amsterdam, 1760). BL

——— *Mélanges philosophiques* (2 vols.; Leiden, 1754). BL

[FORMEY], *Pensées raisonnables opposées aux pensées philosophiques* (Berlin, 1749). BL

FRANCO MENDES, DAVID, *Memorias do estabelecimento e progresso dos judeus portuguezes e espanhôes nesta famosa citade de Amsterdam* in *Stud. Ros.* vol. 9 (Amsterdam, 1975).

[FRANÇOIS, LAURENT], *Preuves de la religion de Jésus-Christ contre les Spinosistes et les déistes* (3 vols.; Paris, 1751). UCLA

Free Thoughts On Mr Woolston And His Writings In a Letter to a Gentleman at Leyden (2nd edn., London, 1730). BL

[FRÉRET, NICOLAS], *Lettre de Thrasybule à Leucippe*, ed. S. Landucci (Florence, 1986).

FREUDENTHAL, J. (ed.), *Die Lebensgeschichte Spinozas in Quellenschriften, Urkunden und nichtamtlichen Nachrichten* (Leipzig, 1899).

GALIANI, CELESTINO, and GUIDO GRANDI, *Carteggio (1714–1729)*, ed. F. Palladino and Luisa Simonutti (Florence, 1989).

[GAULTIER, ABBÉ JEAN-BAPTISTE], *Les Lettres persanes convaincues d'impiété* (n.p., 1752). BL

GAUKES, YVONIS, *Innocentia Cartesii Defensa contra cl. A Driessenium* (Groningen, 1735). HKB

Genees-Middelen voor Hollands Qualen vertoonende de quade Regeeringe der Loevesteynse Factie ('Antwerp', 1672). Kn. 10378 HKB

GENOVESI, ANTONIO, *Discorso sopra il vero fine delle lettere e delle scienze* (1753). in Franco Venturi (ed.), *Illuminati Italiani*, vol. 5 (Milan, 1965), pp. 84–131.

——— *Elementa metaphysicae* (4th edn., 5 vols.; Naples, 1760). BL

——— *Elementorum artis logicocriticae libri V* (1745; 4th edn., Naples, 1758). BL

——— *Lettere filosofiche ad un amico provinciale* (2 vols.; Naples, 1759). VBM

GEULINCX, ARNOLD, *Compendium physicae* (Franeker, 1688). AUB

GIANNONE, PIETRO, *Anecdotes ecclesiastiques contenant la police et la discipline de l'Église . . . tirées de l'histoire du royaume de Naples de Giannone* (Amsterdam, 1738).

GIANNONE, PIETRO, *Opere postume di Pietro Giannone in difesa della sua storia civile del regno di Napoli* ('Palmyra', 1755). BL

——— *Giannoniana: autografi, manoscritti e documenti*, ed. Sergio Bertelli (Milan, 1968).

——— *Opere*, ed. Sergio Bertelli and G. Ricuperati (Milan and Naples, 1971).

Giornale de'Letterati (periodical; Rome, 1668–81). BL

Giornale de'Letterati d'Italia (periodical; Venice, 1710–40). BL

GLANVILL, JOSEPH, *Saducismus Triumphatus* (London, 1681). BL

GOEREE, WILLEM, *De Kerklyke en weereldlyke historien* (new edn., Leiden, 1729). UCLA

——— [*Mosaische Oudheden*] *Mosaize Historie Der Hebreeuwse Kerke* (4 vols.; Amsterdam, 1700). AUB

[GOEREE, WILLEM], [*Philalethes Brieven*]. *Verzameling van uitgelezene keurstoffen* (Amsterdam, 1713). AUB

GOLDSCHMIDT, PETRUS, *Höllischer Morpheus* (Hamburg, 1698). BL

——— *Verworffener Hexen- und Zauberer-Advocat* (Hamburg, 1705). BL

GOTTI, VINCENZIO LODOVICO, *Veritas religionis Christianae . . . contra atheos, polytheos, idolatros, Mahometanos et Judaeos demonstrata* (6 vols.; Rome, 1735–7). BL

GOTTSCHED, JOHANN CHRISTOPH, *Historische Lobschrift des . . . Freyherrn von Wolff* (Halle, 1755). BL

[GÖTZE, JOHANN CHRISTIAN], *Die Merckwürdigkeiten der königlichen Bibliothek zu Dresden ausführlich beschrieben* (3 vols.; Dresden, 1743). HSUB

GRAEVIUS, JOHANN GEORG, *Catalogus bibliothecae luculentissimae* (Utrecht, n.d.). WHA

GRAPIUS, ZACHARIAS, *Systema novissimarum controversiarum seu theologia recens controversa* (1709; 3 vols.; Rostock, 1719). WHA

GRAVINA, GIANVINCENZO, *Orationes* (1699), ed. F. Lomonaco (Naples, 1997).

GREW, NEHEMIAH, *Cosmologia Sacra: Or A Discourse of the Universe* (London, 1701). LDrW

GRIMALDI, COSTATINO, *Discussioni istoriche, teologiche e filosofiche* (3 vols.; 'Lucca' [Naples?], 1703). NBN

——— *Memorie di un anticurlialista del settecento*, ed. V. I. Comparato (Florence, 1964).

——— *Risposta alla Lettera Apologetica in difesa della Teologia Scolastica di Benedetto Aletino* ('Colonia' [Geneva], 1699). FBN

——— *Risposta alla Terza Lettera Apologetica contro il Cartesio . . . di Benedetto Aletino* ('Colonia' [Naples], 1703). FBN

GROENEWEGEN, HENRICUS, *Pneumatica ofte leere van de geesten* (Enkhuizen, 1692). AUB

Groot Placaet-Boeck vervattende de placaten . . . van de Staten generael der Vereenigde Nederlanden (9 vols.; The Hague, 1658–1796).

GRUA, GASTON (ed.), *G. W. Leibniz. Textes inédits* (Paris, 1948).

GURDON, BRAMPTON, *The Pretended Difficulties in Natural or Reveal'd religion no Excuse for Infidelity* (London, 1723). LDrW

HAKVOORT, BARENT, *De Schole van Christus* (new edn., Zwolle, 1706). BL

HALMA, FRANÇOIS VAN, *Aanmerkingen op't Vervolg van Philopater* (Utrecht, 1698). BL

HARTMAN, NICOLAAS, *De bedrieglyke philosooph ontdekt* (Zwolle, 1724). AUB

HARTMANN, GEORG VOLCKMAR, *Anleitung zur Historie der Leibnizisch-Wolffischen Philosophie* (Frankfurt and Leipzig, 1737; repr. Hildesheim, 1973).

HARTSOEKER, NICHOLAS, *Cours de Physique* (The Hague, 1730). BL

——— *Recueil de plusieurs pièces de physique où l'on fait principalement voir l'invalidité du système de Mr Newton* (Utrecht, 1722). BL

HATTEM, PONTIAAN VAN, *Den Val van 's Wereldts Af-God*, ed. Jacob Roggeveen (3 vols.; The Hague, 1718–27). LUB

HAUBER, EVERHARD DAVID, *Biblioteca, acta et scripta magica* (3 vols.; Lemgo, 1739). BL

HEIDEGGER, JOHANN HEINRICH, *Exercitationes Biblicae Capelli, Simonis, Spinozae et aliorum . . . oppositae* (Zurich, 1700). BL

HELVETIUS, JOHAN FREDERIK, *Adams oud graft, opgevult met jonge Coccei Cartesiaenschen* (The Hague, 1687). BL

[HERING, J. G.] *Compendieuses Kirchen- und Ketzer- Lexicon* (Schneeberg, 1731). UCLA

HERSLOV, GEORG PETER (pres.) *De vera notione miraculi* (Greifswald, 1752). UUL

HERWECH, GUSTAV, *Dissertatio critico-philosophica* (Rostock, 1709). UUL

HICKES, GEORGE, *A Preliminary Discourse* to William Carroll's *Spinoza Reviv'd* (London, 1709). BL

HIORTER, OLAUS, *Bibliotheca selecta b. def. Dn. Olavi Hiorter* (Arosia, 1752). UUL

Histoire des Ouvrages des Savants, ed. H. Basnage de Beauval (periodical; Rotterdam, 1687–1709). BL

HOBBES, THOMAS, *Leviathan*, ed. A. D. Lindsay (1914; repr. London, 1962).

HOHENDORF, BARON GEORG WILHELM VON, *Bibliotheca Hohendorfiana* (3 vols.; The Hague, 1720). BL

HOLBACH, PAUL HENRI DIETRICH, BARON d', *Lettres à Eugenie ou préservatif contre les préjugés* ('Londres', 1768). BL

—— *Système de la nature* (2 vols.; 'Londres', 1770). BL

HOLBERG, LUDVIG, *Epistler*, ed. F. J. Billeskov Jansen (8 vols.; Copenhagen, 1944–54).

—— *Memoirs*, ed. S. E. Fraser (Leiden, 1970).

HONERT, TAKO HAJO VAN DEN, *Briev aan den Heer Fredericus van Leenhof* (2nd edn. Amsterdam, 1704). AUB

—— *Noodige aantekeningen op de Artikelen tot Satisfactie van de eerw. Kerken-Raad tot Zwolle* (Amsterdam, 1705). UCLA

—— *Weder-Antwoord op het Korte Antwoord van den Heer Fredericus van Leenhof* (Amsterdam, 1704). AUB

HOUTTEVILLE, CLAUDE-FRANÇOIS, ABBÉ, *Essai philosophique sur la Providence* (Paris, 1728). BL

—— *La Religion Chrétienne prouvée par les faits* (1722; 2nd edn., 2 vols.; Paris, 1740). UCLA

HOWE, JOHN, *The Living Temple* (2 vols.; London, 1702). BL

HUET, PIERRE-DANIEL, *Alnetanae quaestiones de concordia rationis et fidei* (Caen, 1690). BL

—— *Censura philosophiae Cartesianae* (Helmstedt, 1690). BL

—— *Demonstratio evangelica* (Paris, 1679). UCLA

—— *Huetiana*, ed. l'abbé d'Olivet (Paris, 1722). BL

HULSIUS, PAULUS, *Spinozismi depulsio, circa corporum peccata et poenas* (Groningen, 1714). CRL

HUME, DAVID, *An Enquiry Concerning Human Understanding* (1748), ed. E. Steinberg (2nd edn., Indianapolis, 1993).

—— *Treatise of Human Nature* (1739–40; Buffalo, NY, 1992).

HUYGENS, CHRISTIAN, *Oeuvres complètes* (12 vols.; The Hague, 1888–1910).

Hydra of Monster-Dier, Dat tzedert den Jare 1650 in de Vereenigde Nederlanden Gewoed heeft (Rotterdam, 1672). Kn. 10601 HKB

Iudicium theoligicae et philosophiae facultatis Ienensis (1719) in Wittichius, *Disputatio philosophica*, pp. 41–52.

JÄGER, JOHANN WOLFGANG, *Spinocismus sive Benedicti Spinosae famosi atheistae vita et doctrinalia* (Tübingen, 1710). JUB

731

[JAHN, JOHANN CHRISTIAN GOTTFRIED], *Verzeichnis der Bücher so gesamlet Johann Christian Gottfried Jahn* (Frankfurt and Leipzig, 1755–7). BL

JAQUELOT, ISAAC, *Conformité de la foi et de la raison* (Amsterdam, 1705). BL

——*Dissertations sur l'existence de Dieu, où l'on démontre cette verité . . . par la réfutation du système d'Épicure et de Spinoza* (The Hague, 1697). BL

JELLES, JARIG, *Belydenisse des algemeenen en Christelycken geloofs* (Amsterdam, 1684). AUB

——'Voorreeden' to Spinoza's Posthumous Works of 1677 in *LIAS*, vol. 6 (1979), pp. 110–52.

JENICHEN, GOTTLOB FRIEDRICH, *Historia Spinozismi Leenhofiani* (Leipzig, 1707). BL

JENS, PETRUS, *Examen philosophicum sextae definitionis part. 1 Eth. Benedicti de Spinoza* (Dordrecht, 1697). BL

JÖCHER, CHRISTIAN GOTTLIEB, *Allgemeines Gelehrten Lexicon* (4 vols.; Leipzig, 1750).

JORTIN, JOHN, *Remarks on ecclesiastical History* (2 vols.; London, 1767). UCLA

Journal de Hambourg ed. Gabriel d'Artis (periodical; Hamburg, 1694–6). BL

Journal Littéraire (periodical; The Hague, 1713–37).

[J. T.], *Le faux heureux détrompé, où l'impie fortuné devenu malheureux* ('Brussels', 1758). ABM

[JURIEU, PIERRE], *Factum pour demander justice aux puissances contre le nommé Noel Aubert . . . convaincu des crimes d'impureté, d'impiété, et de blasphème* (n.p., n.d. [1688?]). LUB

——*Le Philosophe de Rotterdam accusé, atteint et convaincu* (Amsterdam, 1706). BL

KETTNER, FRIEDRICH ERNST, *De duobus impostoribus, Benedicto Spinosa et Balthasare Bekkero, dissertatio historica* (Leipzig, 1694). BL

KIDDER, RICHARD, *A Commentary on the Five Books of Moses* (London, 1694). BL

KIELMANNS-EGGE, Count Johannes Adolphus von, *Bibliotheca Kielmans-Eggiana* (3 vols.; Hamburg, 1718). CRL

KING, JOSIAH, *Mr Blount's* Oracles of Reason *Examined and Answered* (Exeter, 1698). LDrW

KLINGENSTIERNA, SAMUEL, *Dissertatio academica de Censura Librorum* (Stockholm, 1743). BL

KLOPP, O. (ed.), *Correspondance de Leibniz avec l'electrice Sophie de Brunswick-Lunebourg* (2 vols.; Hanover, 1874).

KNUTTEL, W. P. C. (ed.), *Acta der particuliere Synoden van Zuid-Holland, 1621–1700* (6 vols.; The Hague, 1908–16).

KNUTZEN, MATTHIAS, 'Schriften', repr. in vol. ii of J. Ch. Edelmann, *Moses* ('Freyburg' [Berleburg], 1740).

KOELMAN, JACOBUS, *Den Duyvel van Tedworth* (Amsterdam, 1692). BL

——*Het Vergift van de Cartesiaansche Philosophie grondig ontdekt* (Amsterdam, 1692). UBA

——*Wederlegging van B. Bekkers Betoverde Wereldt* (Amsterdam, 1692). BL

KOENIGSMANN, ANDREAS LUDWIG, *Catalogus Bibliothecae b. m. Andr. Ludov. Konigsmanni* (Copenhagen, 1729). CRL

——*De persuasione Prophetarum per signa contra Bened. de Spinoza* (Kiel, 1711). CRL

[KOERBAGH, ADRIAEN], *'t Samen-spraeck tusschen een gereformeerden Hollander en een Zeeuw* (Middelburg, 1664). Kn. 8923 HKB

[KOERBAGH, ADRIAEN and KOERBAGH, JOHAN] *Een Bloemhof van allerley lieflijkheyd sonder verdriet* (Amsterdam, 1668). HKB

——*Een Ligt schijnende in duystere plaatsen*, ed. H. Vandenbosche (1668; Brussels, 1974).

KORTHOLT, SEBASTIAN, *Praefatio* to Christian Kortholt's *De tribus Impostoribus magnis* (Hamburg, 1700). UCLA

KÜSTER, GEORG FRIEDRICH, *Marchiae litteratae specimen tertium* (Berlin, 1743).

KUYPER (CUPERUS), FRANS, *Arcana Atheismi revelata philosophice et pardoxe refutata* (Rotterdam, 1676). BL

——*Bewys dat noch de Schepping van de Natuur, noch de Mirakelen die de H. Schrift verhaalt . . . teegen de natuurlijke reeden strijdig zij* (Amsterdam, 1685). AUB

——*De diepten des Satans of geheymenissen der Atheisterey ontdekt* (Rotterdam, 1677). Kn. 11547 HKB

——*Filosofisch en Historiaal Bewijs dat er Duyvelen zijn . . . Tweede Deel* (Rotterdam, 1678).

——*Korte verhandeling van de duyvelen* (Rotterdam, 1676). Kn. 11484 HKB

——*Den Philosopherenden boer* (n.p., 1676). Kn. 11474 AUB

——*Weerlegging van de voornaamste gronden van de valselijk genaamde Zeedekunst van B. D. Spinosa* (n.p., 1687). HKB

LAHONTAN, BARON DE, *Nouveaux voyages de Mr le Baron de Lahontan dans l'Amérique septentrionale* (2 vols.; The Hague, 1703). BL

LAMBERT, ANNE THÉRÈSE DE MARGUENAT MARQUISE DE, *Réflexions nouvelles sur les femmes* (Amsterdam, 1732). BL

LA METTRIE, JULIEN OFFRAY DE, *Histoire naturelle de l'ame* (The Hague, 1745). BL

——*Machine Man and other Writings*, ed. Ann Thomson (Cambridge, 1996).

——*Oeuvres philosophiques* (1751; Amsterdam, 1753). BL

——*Preliminary Discourse* in Thomson ed. La Mettrie, *Machine Man*.

LAMY, DOM FRANÇOIS, *L'Incrédule amené à la religion par la raison* (Paris, 1710). BL

——*Le Nouvel athéisme renversé ou Réfutation du sistème de Spinosa* (Paris, 1696). UCLA

LANGE, JOACHIM, *Anmerckungen über des Herrn Hoff Raths und Professor Christian Wolffens Metaphysicum* (Cassel, 1724). BL

——*Caussa Dei et religionis naturalis adversus atheismum* (1723; 2nd edn., Halle, 1727; repr. Hildesheim, 1984).

——*Kurtzer Abriss derjenigen Lehr-Sätze welche in der Wolffischen Philosophie der natürlichen und geoffenbahrten Religion nachtheilig sind* (n.p., 1736). BL

——*Medicina mentis, qua . . . genuina philosophandi ac litterarum studia tractandi methodus . . . ostenditur* (Halle, 1718). UCLA

——*Modesta disquisitio novi philosophiae systematis de Deo, Mundo et homine* (Halle, 1723). UCLA

——*Nova anatome, seu idea analytica systematis metaphysici Wolfiani* (Halle, 1726; repr. Hildesheim, 1990).

——*Placidae vindiciae modestae disquisitionis de systemate philosophiae novo* (Halle, 1723).

——*Bescheidene und ausführliche Entdeckung der falschen und schädlichen Philosophie in dem Wolffianischen systemate metaphysico* (Halle, 1724). BL

LANGE, SAMUEL GOTTHOLD ('Veramander'), *Partheyischer und der Wahrheit nachtheiliger Historicus* (Leipzig and Halle, 1737). BL

LASSENIUS, JOHANNES, *Besiegte Atheisterey* (Copenhagen, 1693). JUB

LAU, THEODOR LUDWIG, *Medidationes philosophicae de Deo, mundo, homine* (n.p. [Frankfurt], 1717; repr. Stuttgart, 1992).

——*Meditationes theses. Dubia philosophico-theologica* ('Freistadt' [Frankfurt], 1719). BL

——*Die Original-Rede . . . an das klare Sonnen-Licht gestellet* (Altona, 1736; repr. Stuttgart, 1992).

LAW, WILLIAM, *Remarks Upon A Late Book Entitled* The Fable of the Bees (1724; 2nd edn., London, 1725). LDrW

LE CLERC, JEAN, *De l'Incrédulité* (Amsterdam, 1696). UCLA-Cl

——*Monsieur le Clerc's Observations upon Mr Addison's Travels through Italy* (London, 1715). BL

——*Opera philosophica* (4 vols.; Amsterdam, 1694). NBN

——*Parrhasiana, Or Thoughts upon several Subjects as, Criticism, History, Morality and Politics* (London, 1700). BL

[LE CLERC, JEAN], *Sentiments de quelques théologiens de Hollande sur L'Histoire Critique du Vieux Testament* (Amsterdam, 1685). BL

LEENHOF, FREDERIK VAN, *Den Hemel op Aarden; of een waare en klaare beschrijvinge van de waare en stantvastige blydschap* (2nd edn., Amsterdam, 1704). AUB

—— *Den Hemel op Aarden opgeheldert* (Zwolle, 1704). LUB

—— *Der Himmel auff Erden* (Amsterdam, 1706). BL

—— *De keten der Bybelsche Godgeleerdheyt* (2 vols.; 3rd edn., Amsterdam, 1684). BL

—— *Kort Antwoord op de Brief van den Heer T.H. van den Honert wegens de Redenkundige Aanmerkingen* (Zwolle, 1704). Kn. 15300 LUB

—— *Het Leven van den wijzen en magtigen konink Salomon leerzaamelijk voorgedragen* (Zwolle, 1700). LUB

—— *De prediker van den wijzen en magtigen konink Salomon* (Zwolle, 1700). LUB

—— *Wel-doorwrogte en aanmerkelyke Affscheids-Predikatie* (Amsterdam, 1712). AUB

—— *Zedig en Christelijk Verandwoordschrift van het bewaarde classis van Seven-Wolden* (Amsterdam, 1684). BL

[LEETSOSONEUS, IRITIEL], *Den Swadder, die E.W. op Cartesianen en Coccejanen geworpen heeft in sijn twee deelen van aardige Duyvelarye* (Amsterdam, 1692). WHA

LE GENDRE, GILBERT-CHARLES, marquis de S. Aubin-sur-Loire, *Traité de l'opinion, ou mémoires pour servir à l'histoire de l'esprit humain* (6 vols.; Paris, 1733). UCLA

LEIBNIZ, GOTTFRIED WILHELM, *Animadversiones ad Joh. Georg Wachteri librum*, ed. A. Foucher de Careil, published as *Réfutation inédite de Spinoza par Leibniz* (Paris, 1854).

—— *The Leibniz-Clarke Correspondence*, ed. H. G. Alexander (Manchester, 1956; repr. 1998).

—— *New Essays on Human Understanding*, ed. P. Remnant (Cambridge, 1996).

—— *Philosophical Essays*, ed. R. Ariew and D. Garber (Indianapolis, 1989).

—— *Philosophical Writings*, ed. G. H. R. Parkinson (new edn., 1973; repr. 1990).

—— *Political Writings*, ed. P. Riley (Cambridge, 1972; repr. 1989).

—— *Sämtliche Schriften und Briefe* (Darmstadt and Leipzig, 1923–).

—— *Theodicy*, ed. A Farrer (London, 1951; repr. Peru, Ill., 1993).

LELAND, JOHN, *A View of the Principal Deistical Writers that have appeared in England* (3 vols.; London, 1754–5). BL

LEMMERMAN, ABRAHAM, *Eenige bewijzen dat Johannes Bredenburg staande zijn stellingen, geenszins kan geloven dat er een God is als de H. Schrift leert* (Amsterdam, 1684). Kn. 12260 HKB

LENGLET DUFRESNOY, NICOLAS, ABBÉ, *Recueil de dissertations anciennes et nouvelles sur les apparitions, les visions et les songes* (2 vols.; Avignon, 1751–2). MoBM

—— (ed.), *Réfutation des erreurs de Benoit de Spinoza* ('Bruxelles' [Amsterdam], 1731). BL

LESSACA, JUAN MARTÍN DE, *Colyrio philosóphico aritotélico thomístico* (Madrid, 1724). MBN

'Letters to and from Neercassel about Spinoza and Rieuwertsz', ed. Wim Klever in *St. Spin.*, iv (1988), pp. 329–38.

Lettre de R. Ismael ben Abraham, Juif converti à M. l'Abbé Houtteville (Paris, 1722). BL

Lettres critiques sur divers écrits de nos jours contraires à la religion et aux moeurs (2 vols.; 'Londres', 1751). UCLA

Lettres sur la vie et sur la mort de Monsieur Louis de Wolzogue pasteur de l'Église Wallone d'Amsterdam (Amsterdam, 1692). BL

LEVASSEUR, MICHEL, *Défense de la religion Catholique contre tous ses ennemis* (1705; 2nd edn., Paris, 1721). BL

LE VASSOR, MICHEL, *De la véritable religion* (1688; 2nd edn., Paris, 1689). BL

Het Leeven van Hai Ebn Yokdhan, trans. from the Latin of Edward Pocock by S. D. B. [Johannes Bouwmeester] (new edn., Amsterdam, 1701). UCLA

LÉVESQUE DE BURIGNY, JEAN, *Histoire de la philosophie payenne ou sentimens des philosophes et des peuples payens* (2 vols.; The Hague, 1724). BL

—— *Théologie payenne* (2 vols.; Paris, 1754). UCLA

[LEVIER, CHARLES], 'Catalogue des ouvrages de Mr. de Spinosa', in *La Vie et l'Esprit* (ed.), Berti, pp. 60–3.

[LEVIER, CHARLES], *Histoire de l'admirable Dom Inigo de Guipuscoa, chevalier de la Vierge et fondateur de la monarchie des Inighistes* (2nd edn., 2 vols.; The Hague, 1758). BL

LEWIS, THOMAS, *The History of Hypatia, A most impudent School-Mistress of Alexandria* (London, 1721). BL

LEYDEKKER, JACOB, *Dr Bekkers philosophise Duyvel* (Dordrecht, 1692). BL

—— *De blyde Spinosist en de bedroefde Christen leeraar* (Rotterdam, 1719).

LEYDEKKER, MELCHIOR, *D. Leenhofs boek genaamt den Hemel op Aarde strijdende tegen het Christendom . . . ontdekt* (Utrecht, 1704). LUB

—— *Verder Vervolg van de kerklyke historie van de Heer Hornius beginnende met het jaar 1666 tot het jaar 1687* (Amsterdam, 1696). UCLA

LILIENTHAL, MICHAEL, *Selecta Historica et Literaria* (2 vols.; Königsberg, 1715–19).

—— *Theologische Bibliothec* (Königsberg, 1741). BL

LIMBORCH, PHILIPPUS VAN, *Theologia Christiana* (1686) (new edn., Amsterdam, 1730). NBN

—— *De Veritate religionis Christianae. Amica collatio con erudito Judaeo* (Gouda, 1687). BL

LOCKE, JOHN, *The Correspondence of John Locke*, ed. E. S. de Beer (8 vols.; Oxford 1976–89).

—— *An Essay concerning Human Understanding*, abridged and ed. A. D. Woozley (London, 1964).

—— 'Passages from [the] Journal for 1684' in C. D. van Strien, *British Travellers in Holland during the Stuart Period* (Leiden, 1993), pp. 306–28.

—— *Political Writings*, ed. David Wootton (London, 1993).

—— *The Reasonableness of Christianity* (1965), ed. G. W. Ewing (Washington, DC, 1965; repr. 1989).

—— *A Third Letter for Toleration* (London, 1692). LDrW

LOESCHER, VALENTIN ERNST, *Praenotiones theologicae contra naturalistarum et fanaticorum omne genus, atheos, deistas, indifferentistas, antiscriptuarios*, etc. (Wittenberg, 1708). BL

LOON, G. VAN, *Beschryving der Nederlandsche Historipenningen* (4 vols.; The Hague, 1726–31). LIHR

LUCCHI, BONAVENTURA, *Spinozismi Syntagma in Gymnasio Patovino* (Padua, 1738). PBP

LUDOVICI, CARL GÜNTHER, *Ausführlicher Entwurff einer vollständigen Historie der Leibnitzischen Philosophie* (3 vols.; Leipzig, 1735–8; repr. Hildesheim, 1976).

—— *Neueste Merckwürdigkeiten der Leibniz-Wolffischen Weltweisheit* (Frankfurt, 1738; repr. Hildesheim, 1973).

—— *Sammlung und Auszüge der sämmtlichen Streitschriften wegen der Wolffischen Philosophie* (2 vols.; Leipzig, 1737; repr. Hildesheim, 1976).

Maandelyke Uitreksels of Boekzaal Der Geleerde Werelt (periodical; Amsterdam, 1715–32). BL

MAFFEI, SCIPIO, MARCHESE, *Arte magica annichilata libri tre* (Verona, 1754). NBN

—— *Arte magica dileguata* (2nd edn., Verona, 1750). PBP

—— *Dell' Impiego del danaro* (Verona, 1744). NBN

[MAFFEI, SCIPIO?], *Riflessioni sopra l'Arte magica annichilata* (Venice, 1755). NBN

MALEBRANCHE, NICOLAS, *Correspondance avec J. J. Dorthous de Mairan*, ed. Joseph Moreau (Paris, 1947).

MALEBRANCHE, NICOLAS, *Dialogues on Metaphysics and on Religion*, ed. N. Jolley (Cambridge, 1997).

—— *Oeuvres complètes*, ed. H. Goutier and A. Robinet (20 vols., Paris, 1958–84).

—— *Treatise on Nature and Grace*, trans. and ed. P. Riley (1680; Oxford, 1992).

MANDEVILLE, BERNARD DE, *Disputatio philosophica de Brutorum operationibus . . . sub praesidio B. de Volder* (Leiden, 1689). BL

—— *An Enquiry into the origin of Honour and the Usefulness of Christianity in War* (2nd edn., London, 1732). BL

—— *The Fable of the Bees, Or, private Vices, publick Benefits* (London, 1714). BL

—— *Free Thoughts on Religion, the Church and National Happiness* (London, 1720). BL

[MANDEVILLE, BERNARD DE], *The Virgin Unmask'd* (London, 1709). BL

—— *The Mysteries of Virginity* (London, 1714). BL

MAÑER, SALVADOR JOSEPH, *Anti-theatro Critico sobre el primero y segundo tomo del* Teatro Critico Universal (3 vols.; Madrid, 1729–31). SBU

—— *Crisol Critico* (2 vols.; Madrid, 1734). SBU

MANSVELT, REINIER VAN [see also 'Andlo, Petrus van'], *Adversus anonymum Theologico-Politicum* (Amsterdam, 1674). BL

MARCHAND, PROSPER, *Dictionnaire historique ou Mémoires critiques et littéraires* (2 vols.; The Hague, 1758). BL

MARÉCHAL, SYLVAIN, *Dictionnaire des athées anciens et modernes* [Paris an VIII] (new edn., Brussels, 1833). BL

MARESIUS (DES MARETS), Samuel, *De Abusu philosophiae Cartesianae* (Groningen, 1670). BL

—— *Catalogus variorum et insignium librorum . . . D. Samuelis Maresii* (The Hague, 1673). UCLA-Cl

—— *Clypeus Orthodoxiae* (Groningen, 1671). UCLA

—— *Dissertatio theologica de abusu philosophiae Cartesianae* (Groningen, 1670). BL

—— *Vindiciae dissertationis suae nuperae* De Abusu philosophiae Cartesianae (Groningen, 1670). UCLA

MARINI, L. (ed.), 'Documenti dell' opposizione curiale a Pietro Giannone (1723–1735)', *RSI* lxxix (1967), 696–731.

MASIUS, HECTOR GOTTFRIED, *Dissertationes academicae* (2 vols.; Hamburg, 1719). BPK

MASSILLON, J. B., *Pensées sur différens sujets de morale et de piété* (Paris, 1762). BL

MASTRICHT, GERHARD VON, *Catalogus Bibliothecae Gerh. von Mastricht* (Bremen, 1719). SRL

MASTRICHT, PETRUS VAN, *Novitatum Cartesianarum gangraena* (Amsterdam, 1677). WHA

—— *Ad Virum Clariss. D. Balthasarem Beckerum* (Utrecht, 1692). BL

[MAUDUIT, MICHEL], *Traitté de religion contre les athées, les déistes et les Nouveaux Pyrrhoniens* (Paris, 1697). MBM

J. M. V. D. M. [MELCHIOR, JOHANNES], *Epistola ad amicum continens censuram libri, cui titulus:* Tractatus Theologico-Politicus (Utrecht, 1671). HSUB

Mémoire historique sur la Bibliothèque du Roy (1742) in *Catalogue des Livres Imprimez. Théologie* vol. 1, pp. 1–82.

Memoirs of the Life and Writings of Matthew Tindal, LL.D. with a History of the Controversies wherein he was engaged (London, 1733). BL

MÉNAGE, GILLES, *Menagiana* (3rd edn., Paris, 1695). UCLA

MENCKE, JOHANN BURKHARD, *Compendiöses Gelehrten-Lexicon* (2 vols.; Leipzig, 1715). BL

MENDELSSOHN, MOSES, *Philosophical Writings*, ed. D. O. Dahlstrom (Cambridge, 1997).

[MEYER, LODEWIJK], *Philosophia S. Scripturae Interpres* ('Eleutheropolis' [Amsterdam], 1666). BL

—— *La Philosophie interprète de l'Écriture Sainte* trans. and ed. J. Lagrée and P. F. Moreau (Paris, 1988).

—— *De philosophie d'uytleghster der H. Schrifture* ('Vrystadt' [Amsterdam], 1667). HKB

—— *Woordenschat* (6th edn., Amsterdam, 1688). BL

[MEYER, LODEWŸK], *De Jure Ecclesiasticorum* (Amsterdam, 1665).

[MIRABAUD, JEAN-BAPTISTE DE?], *Sentimens des philosophes sur la nature de l'âme* in [Du Marsais], *Nouvelles libertés*, pp. 63–110.

MOEBIUS, GEORG, *Reden-lievende God-geleerde verhandeling . . . in der heydensche Orakelen* (Rotterdam, 1687). BL

Monatliche Unterrredungen einiger guten Freunde von allerhand Büchern und andern annemlichen Geschichten, ed. Wilhelm Ernst Tentzel (periodical; 10 vols.; Leipzig, 1689–98). BL

MONIGLIA, TOMMASO VINCENZIO, *Dissertazione contro i Fatalisti* (2 vols.; Lucca, 1744). PBP

—— *Dissertazione contra i materialisti e altri increduli* (2 vols.; Padua, 1750). PBP

MONNIKHOFF, JOHANNES, 'Beschrijving van Spinozas leeven', *Chronicum Spinozanum*, iv (1926), 201–19.

MONTAIGNE, MICHEL DE, *The Complete Essays*, ed. M. A. Screech (London, 1993).

MONTESQUIEU, CHARLES DE SECONDAT, BARON DE, *Oeuvres complètes*, ed. D. Oster (Paris, 1964).

MORE, HENRY, *A Brief and firm Confutation of the . . . two Propositions in Spinoza which are the chief Columns of Atheism*, in A. Jacob, *Henry More's Refutation of Spinoza* (Hildeshcim, 1991), pp. 55–119.

—— *Ad V. C. Epistola altera, Quae brevem* Tractatus Theologico-Politici *confutationem complectitum* (London, 1679) in More, *Opera Omnia* (3 vols.; London, 1675–9), ii, 563–614.

    Korte en Bondige Wederlegging van het wiskunstig bewijs van B. D. Spinosa, trans. F. Kuyper (n.p., 1687). HKB

MORÉRI, LOUIS, *Le Grand Dictionnaire historique* (10 vols.; Paris, 1759).

MORGAN, THOMAS, *Physico-Theology, or a Philosophico-moral Disquisition* (London, 1741). LDrW

MORHOF, DANIEL GEORG, *Polyhistor, literarius, philosophicus et practicus* (4th edn., 2 vols.; Lübeck, 1747). UCLA

MOSHEIM, JOHANN LORENZ, *An Ecclesiastical History ancient and modern* (2 vols.; n.p. 1765).

—— *Vindiciae antiquae Christianorum Disciplinae* (Kiel, 1720). BL

MÜLLER, JOHANN, *Atheismus devictus* (Hamburg, 1672). WHA

MÜLLER, JOHANN HEINRICH, *Dissertatio inavgvralis philosophica de miraculis* (Altdorf, 1714). JUB

MUSAEUS, JOHANNES, *Ableinung der ausgesprengten abscheulichen Verleumbdung* (Jena, 1674). WHA

—— *Theologico-Politicus . . . examinatus Tractatus* (Jena, 1674). CRL

MYLIUS, JOHANN CHRISTOPH, *Bibliotheca Anonymorum et Pseudonymorum detectorum* (2 vols.; Hamburg, 1740). UCLA

NAIGEON, JACQUES-ANDRÉ, *Encyclopédie méthodique. Philosophie ancienne et moderne* (3 vols.; Paris, 1791).

NÁJERA, JUAN DE ['ALEXANDRO DE AVENDAÑO], *Diálogos philosophicos en defensa del Atomismo* (Madrid, 1716). MBN

—— *Maignanus Redivus* ('Tolosa', 1720). CBU

NAUDÉ, GABRIEL, *Advis pour dresser une bibliothèque présenté à Monseigneur le Président de Mesme* (2nd edn., 1644; Paris, 1876).

NAUDÉ, PHIL., *Examen De deux Traittez nouvellement mis au jour par Mr La Placette* (2 vols.; Amsterdam, 1713). BL

NICÉRON, J. P., *Mémoires pour servir à l'histoire des hommes illustres dans la République des Lettres* (43 vols.; Paris, 1727–45).

NIEUHOFF, BERNARD, *Over Spinozisme* (Harderwijk, 1799). UCLA

Nieuwentyt, Bernard, *L'existence de Dieu démontrée par les merveilles de la nature* (Amsterdam, 1727). BL

—— *Gronden van zekerheid . . . ter wederlegging van Spinosaas denkbeeldig samenstel* (Amsterdam, 1720). BL

Nouvelles de la Republique des Lettres, ed. Jacques Bernard (periodical; Amsterdam, 1699–1718).

Nouvelles Littéraires, vol. 1 (The Hague, 1715). BL

Nova Literaria Helvetica, ed. Johannes Jacob Scheuchzer (periodical; Zurich, 1702–4). BL

Nova Literaria Maris Balthici et Septentrionis (periodical; Lübeck and Rostock, 1698–1708).

Oldenburg, Henry, *The Correspondence of Henry Oldenburg*, ed. A. R. and M. B. Hall (13 vols.; Madison, Wis., and London, 1963–86).

Ordeel van eenige theologanten tot Deventer over het boeck Ludovici Wolzogen van den Uyt-Legger der H. Schrifture (Middelburg, 1669). Kn. 9798 HKB

Orobio de Castro, Isaac (Balthasar) *Certamen philosophicum propugnata veritatis divinae et naturalis adversus Joh. Bredenburg* (2nd edn., Amsterdam, 1703). BL

Ostertag, H. (ed.), *Der philosophische Gehalt des Wolff-Manteuffelschen Briefwechsels* (Leipzig, 1910).

Oudaen, Joachim, *Voor-reden* to Moebius, *Reden-lievende God-geleerde Verhandeling* (Rotterdam, 1687), pp. 1–22. BL

Palanco, Francisco, *Dialogus physico-theologicus contra philosophiae novatores* (Madrid, 1714). MBN

Pascal, Blaise, *Pensées*, ed. Ch.M. des Granges (Paris, 1961).

Pel, J., *De wonderdaden der Alderhoogsten* (Amsterdam, 1693). AUB

Pfeiffer, August, *Lucta carnis et spiritus Oder Streit des Geistes und Fleisches* (Lübeck, 1700). HUB

—— *Thesaurus hermeneuticus, sive de legitima Scripturae Sacrae interpretatione* (Leipzig, 1724). JUB

Philipps, J. Th., *Dissertatio historico-philosophica de Atheismo* (London, 1716). UCLA

[Philolethes, Theotimus], *A Dissertation on the Unreasonableness, Folly, and Danger of Infidelity* (London, 1725). LDrW

'Philometer, Eusebius', *Discours ofte schuyt-praetje tusschen een koopman en een boer over den Heer Fredericus van Leenhofs Hemel op Aarden* (Amsterdam, 1704). AUB

—— *Brief aan den Heer Fredericus van Leenhof* (Amsterdam, 1704). AUB

'Philopater' [attrib. Johannes Duijkerius], *Het Leven van Philopater* (1691) and *Vervolg van 't Leven van Philopater* (1697), ed. G. Maréchal (Amsterdam, 1991).

Piquer, Andrés, *Disurso sobre la aplicacion de philosophia a los assuntos de religion para la juventud española* (Madrid, 1757). MBN

—— *Lógica moderna o arte de hallar la verdad* (Valencia, 1747). MBN

—— *Philosophia moral para la juventud española* (Madrid, 1755). MBN

—— *Obras Póstumas* (Madrid, 1785). BL

Pina de Sà e Melo, Francisco de, *Triumpho da Religião. Poema epico-polemica* (Coimbra, 1756). BL

Plockhoy, Pieter Cornelisz., (Peter Cornelis van Zurik-zee), *A Way propounded to make the Poor in these and other Nations happy* (London, (1659). BL

[Pluquet, François, Abbé], *Examen du fatalisme* (3 vols.; Paris, 1757). UCLA

Poiret, Pierre, *Cogitationum rationalium de Deo, anima, et malo libri quattuor* (1685; 3rd edn., Amsterdam, 1715). UCLA

—— *The Divine Oeconomy: or, An universal System of the Works and Purposes of God towards Men demonstrated* (6 vols.; London, 1713). UCLA-Cl

—— *De Eruditione Solida, Superficiaria, et falsa* (new edn., Frankfurt and Leipzig, 1694). UCLA

POLIGNAC, MELCHIOR, CARDINAL DE, *L'Anti-Lucrèce, Poème sur la religion naturelle* (2 vols.; Paris, 1750). UCLA

PONTOPPIDAN, ERIK, *Sanheds kraft til at overwinde den atheistiske og naturalistiske vantroe* (Copenhagen, 1768). CRL

POPPO, VOLCKERTSZ CONRAD, *Spinozismus detectus* (Weimar, 1721). HUB

POST, JACOBUS, *Het masker der Hattemisten afgeligt* (Amsterdam, 1734). HKB

POULAIN DE LA BARRE, FRANÇOIS, *The Equality of the sexes*, trans. and ed. D. M. Clarke (Manchester, 1990).

PRATJE, JOHANN, *Historische Nachrichten von Joh. Chr. Edelmann, eines beruchtigen Religionspötters Leben, Schriften und Lehrbegrif* (Hamburg, 1755). BL

PREATI, BARTHOLOMEO, *L'Arte magica dimostrata. Dissertazione . . . contro l'opinione del signor marchese Maffei* (Venice, 1751). BPK

PROAST, JONAS, *A Third letter concerning Toleration in Defence of the Argument of the Letter concerning Toleration* (Oxford, 1691). LDrW

RAATS, JOHANNES, ADRIANUS, *Korte en grondige betoginge . . . tegen de valsche gronden en stellingen van Spinoza* (The Hague, 1743). AUB

RADICATI, ALBERTO, *Recueil de pièces curieuses sur les Matières les plus intéressantes* (Rotterdam, 1736). BL

——*A Philosophical Dissertation upon Death composed for the Consolation of the Unhappy* (London, 1732). BL

—— *Twelve Discourses concerning Religion and Government, inscribed to all Lovers of Truth and liberty* (2nd edn., London, 1734). BL

RAMBACH, JOHANN JACOB, *Christliche Sitten-Lehre* (Halberstadt and Leipzig, 1736). HUL

——*Collegium historiae ecclesiasticae Veteris Testamenti*, with 'Vorrede' and notes by Ernst Friedrich Neubauer (Frankfurt and Leipzig, n.d [1736]). BL

[RAMSAY, MICHAEL DE, CHEVALIER], *Les Voyages de Cyrus* (1727) (2nd edn., 'Londres', 1730). ABM

RAPPOLT, FRIEDRICH, *Opera theologica* (Leipzig, 1693). HUB

RAY, JOHN, *The Wisdom of God manifested in the Works of Creation* (London, 1691). BL

RECHENBERG, ADAM, *Fundamenta verae religionis . . . adversus Atheos, deistas et profanos homines* (Leipzig, 1708). BPK

Récit véritable de ce qui s'est passé au Synode des Églises Walonnes des Pays Bas assemblé à Dordrecht (Leiden, 1669). BL

RÉGIS, PIERRE SYLVAIN, *Système de philosophie contenant la logique, la métaphysique, la physique et la morale* (3 vols.; Paris, 1690). BL

——*L'Usage de la raison et de la foy* (Paris, 1704). BL

REGIUS, JOHANNES, *De beginselen der beschouwende filozofy* (Rotterdam, 1714). BL

——*Cartesius verus Spinozismi architectus* (Franeker, 1719). BL

REIMANN, JACOB FRIEDRICH, *Historia universalis atheismi et atheorum* (1718; 2nd edn., Hildesheim, 1725). UCLA

REINBOTH, FRIEDRICH ADOLPH, *Pars Bibliothecae viri quondam perillustris celeberrimi . . . Friderici Adolphi Reinbothi* (Altona, 1751).

The Religious, Rational and Moral Conduct of Matthew Tindal, LL.D. late Fellow of All Souls College in Oxford (London, 1735). BL

Rencontre de Bayle, et de Spinosa dans l'autre monde (1711; 2nd edn., 'Cologne' 1713). UCLA

La République des philosophes ou l'histoire des Ajaoiens [by Fontenelle?] (Geneva, 1768). PBA

Resolutien van de Heeren Staten van Holland en West-Vriesland (276 vols.; The Hague, c.1750–98).

REUSCH, JOHANN PETER, *Systema metaphysicum antiquiorum atque recentiorum* (Jena, 1735).

ROBERG, LARS, *Catalogus Bibliothecae b. def. D. Laurentii Roberg dum viveret med. doct. et profess. Upsal. celeberrimi* (Uppsala, 1742). UUL

ROJAS, BERNARDO DE, *De formarum generatione contra Atomistas* (Naples, 1694). FBM

ROMMEL, CHR. VON (ed.), *Leibniz und Landgraf Ernst von Hessen-Rheinfels. Ein ungedruckter Briefwechsel* (2 vols.; Frankfurt, 1847).

'ROODENPOORT, J.' [unidentified pseudonym], *'t verleidend levens-bedrijf van Kakotegnus* (Amsterdam, 1700). HKB

ROSENSTAND GOISKE, PEDER, *Billige Frie-tanker over ubillig frie-taenkerie* (Copenhagen, 1753). CRL

ROSENKRANTZ, JANUS, *Bibliotheca Rosenkrantziana* (Copenhagen, 1696). WHA

ROSTGAARD, FREDERIK, *Bibliotheca Rostgardiana* (Copenhagen, 1726). WHA

ROUSSEAU, JEAN-JACQUES, *The Social Contract and Discourses*, trans. G. D. H. Cole (new edn., 1973; 5th repr. London, 1983).

[ROUSSET DE MISSY, JEAN?], *j.l.r. Réponse à la dissertation de M. de La Monnoye sur le 'Traité des Trois Imposteurs'* (Rotterdam, 1716).

RUYTER, JOHAN, *Funus philosophico theologicum* ('Groningen', 1708). UCLA

RYDELIUS, ANDREAS, *Catalogus librorum reverendissimi Dni D. And. Rydelii* (n.p., 1739). UUL

—— *Nödiga fönufftsöfninga för all slags studerande ungdom* (Linköping, 1718). SRL

—— *Sententiae philosophicae fundamentales* (Uppsala, 1736). BL

RYSSENIUS, LEONARDUS, *De oude rechtsinnige waerheyt verdonckert . . . door Des Cartes, Coccejus, Wittich, Burman, Wolzogen, Perizon, Groenewegen Allinga etc.* (Middelburg, n.d. [1674]). AUB

—— *Justa defensio sceleratissimi libelli Adriani Beverlandi . . . De Pecccato Originali* (Gorkum, 1680). BL

SAINT-HYACINTHE, THÉMISEUL DE, *Recherches philosophiques sur la nécessité de s'assurer par soi-même de la vérité* (Rotterdam and The Hague, 1743). BL

[SAINT-HYACINTHE, THÉMISEUL DE], *Entretiens dans lesquels on traite Des Entreprises de l'Espagne, Des Prétensions . . .* (The Hague, 1719). BL

SAINT-SIMON, LOUIS, DUC DE, *Mémoires de Saint Simon*, ed. A. de Boislisle (41 vols.; Paris, 1923–8).

[SALLENGRE, ALBERT HENRI DE], *Mémoires de Littérature*, vol. 1, pt 1 (The Hague, 1715). BL

[SANDVOORT, DIRK], D. S. J., *De oorsaak van de Beweeging en de beginselen der vaste lichamen* (Utrecht, 1703). AUB

[SANDVOORT, DIRK], D. S., *Zedig Ondersoek Of de Geleertheid en Wetenschap Meerder en de Zeden of quade Manieren der Menschen erger zijn dan in voorgaande tijden* (Utrecht, 1709). AUB

SARMIENTO, FRAY MARTÍN, *Demonstracion Critico-apologetica de el* Theatro Critico Universal (1732; 3rd edn., Madrid, 1751). SBU

[SCHMIDT, JOHANN LORENZ], *Vorrede*, Preface to Spinoza, *B. v. S. Sittenlehre widerleget*. HHL

SCHRÖDER, WINFRIED (ed.), *Freidenker der europäischen Aufklärung*, part 1, vol. 2 (Stuttgart, 1995).

[SCHROEDTER, GUSTAV], *Catalogus Bibliothecae Gustavi Schroedteri* (Hamburg, 1724). WHA

Schwedische Bibliothec (4 vols.; Stockholm, 1728–9). BL

SECKENDORFF, VEIT LUDWIG VON, *Christen-Staat* (2 vols.; Leipzig, 1693). BL

SERRARIUS, PETRUS, *Responsio ad Exercitationem Paradoxam anonymi cujusdam Cartesianae sectae discipuli* (Amsterdam, 1667). UCLA

SHAFTESBURY, ANTHONY ASHLEY COOPER, THIRD EARL, *Characteristicks of Men, Manners, Opinions, Times* (4 vols.; London, 1758).

SIMON, RICHARD, *Critical Enquiries into various Editions of the Bible* (London, 1684). BL

—— *A Critical History of the Old Testament* (London, 1682). BL

—— *Lettres choisies* (Amsterdam, 1700). BL

—— *Réponse au livre intitulé Sentimens de quelques théologiens de Hollande* (Rotterdam, 1686). BL

Sleutel ontsluytende de boecke-kas van de Witte bibliotheek (The Hague, 1672). Kn. 10442 HKB

SMEEKS, HENDRIK, *Beschryvinge van het magtig koningryk Krinke Kesmes* (Amsterdam, 1708). LUB

SORIA, GIOVANNI ALBERTO DE, *Della esistenza e degli attributi di Dio* (2nd edn., Lucca, 1746). VBM

—— *Raccolta di opere inedite* (2 vols.; Livorno, 1773). BL

—— *Raccolta di opusculi filosofici et filologici* (3 vols.; Pisa, 1766). VBM

SPANDAW, WILLEM, *De bedekte Spinosist ontdekt in de persoon van Pontiaan van Hattem* (Goes, 1700). HKB

[SPIDBERG, LAURENTIUS], *Catalogus librorum selectorum beati Laurentii Spidberg* (Christiania, 1735). CRL

SPINELLI, FRANCESCO MARIA, *De origine mali dissertatio* (Naples, 1750). PBP

—— *Riflessioni . . . su le principali materie della prima filsofia* (Naples, 1733). NBN

SPINOZA, BENEDICT DE (BARUCH), *Briefwisseling*, ed. A. Akkerman, H. G. Hubbeling, and A. G. Westerbrink (Amsterdam, 1992).

—— *The Collected Works*, ed. Edwin Curley (1 vol. so far, Princeton, NJ, 1985).

—— *Correspondence*, ed. and trans. A. Wolf (London, 1966).

—— *Korte Geschriften*, ed. F. Akkerman, H. G. Hubbeling, F. Mignini, M. J. Petry, and N. and G. van Suchtelen (Amsterdam, 1982).

—— *Hebrew Grammar*, ed. M. J. Bloom (London, 1962).

—— *The Letters*, trans. S. Shirley (Indianapolis, 1995).

—— *De Nagelate Schriften van B. D. S* (n.p. [Amsterdam], 1677). AUB

—— *Opera*, ed. Carl Gebhardt (4 vols.; Heidelberg, 1925).

—— *B. v. S. Sittenlehre widerleget von dem berühmten Weltweisen unserer Zeit Herrn Christian Wolff* (Frankfurt, 1744). HHL

—— *Tractatus Theologico-Politicus* (Gebhardt edition 1925) trans. S. Shirley (Leiden, 1989).

—— *Tractatus Politicus* in A. G. Wernham (ed.), Spinoza, *The Political Works* (Oxford, 1958).

—— *A Treatise partly theological and partly political* [ed. Charles Blount?] (London, 1689). BL

—— *The Way to Wisdom* (*Treatise on the Emendation of the Intellect*), ed. Herman De Dijn (West Lafayette, Ind., 1996).

SPITZEL, GOTTLIEB, *Felix literatus ex infelicium periculis et casibus* (Nuremberg, 1676). UCLA

STAALKOPFF, JAKOB, *Benedictum de Spinoza atheismi convictum, contra autorem praefationis in opera eius posthuma* (Greifswald, 1707). CRL

—— *De Atheismo Benedicti de Spinoza . . . adversus Io. Georgium Wachtervm* (1707) in Schröder (ed.), *Freidenker*, part i, vol. 2, pp. 291–308.

STENO, NICHOLAS, *Epistolae et epistolae ad eum datae* (2 vols.; Freiburg, 1952).

—— *Ad novae philosophiae reformatorem de vera philosophia epistolu* (Florence, 1675). BL

—— *Ad virum eruditum . . . novae philosophiae reformatorem* (Florence, 1675). BL

STEUBER, JOHANN ENGELHARD, *Commentatio Epistolica ad Oratores Sacros* (Rinteln, n.d. [1737]).

STIEBRITZ, JOHANN FRIEDRICH, *Erläuterung der vernüftigen Gedancken von den Kräfften des menschlichen Verstandes Wolffs* (Halle, 1741; repr. Hildesheim, 1977).

[STILLINGFLEET, EDWARD], *A Letter to a Deist* (London, 1677). BL

STOLLE, GOTTLIEB, *Anleitung zur Historie der theologischen Gelehrheit* (Jena, 1739). BL

—— 'Notes manuscrites', trans. J. P. Osier in Meinsma, *Spinoza*, pp. 513–15.

STOSCH, FRIEDRICH WILHELM, *Concordia rationis et fidei* (1692), ed. W. Schröder (Stuttgart, 1992).

[STOSCH, PHILIPP VON], *Bibliotheca Stoschiana* (2 vols.; Florence, 1759). BL

STOUPPE, JEAN-BAPTISTE, *La Religion des Hollandois* ('Cologne', 1673). BL

[STRODTMANN, J. C.], *Das neue gelehrte Europa* (21 vols.; Wolfenbüttel, 1752–81). BL

STRUVE, BURCHARDUS GOTTHELF, *Bibliotheca philosophica in suas classes distributa* (Jena, 1704). UCLA

STURM, JOHANN CHRISTOPH, *De Cartesianis et Cartesianismo* (Altdorf, 1677). BL

[SWIFT, JONATHAN], *Mr. C—ns's Discourse of free-Thinking, Put into plain English* (London, 1713).

S[YLVIUS], J., *Consideratien over het boek van der Heer Doctor Balthasar Bekker genaamt* De Betoverde Weereld (Amsterdam, n.d. [1692]). UCLA

Den Swadder die E[ricus] W[alten] op Cartesianen en Coccejanen geworpen heeft (Amsterdam, 1692). WHA

TARTAROTTI, GIROLAMO, *Del Congresso notterno delle lammie libri tre* (Roverato, 1749). BL

——*Risposta . . . alla Lettera, intorno all' origine e falsità delle dottrine de' maghi*, separately paginated annex to Tartarotti, *Del Congresso*.

TAYLOR, NATHANIEL, *A Preservative against Deism shewing the great Advantage of Revelation above Reason* (London, 1698). LDrW

TEMPLE, SIR WILLIAM, *Five Miscellaneous Essays*, ed. S. H. Monk (Ann Arbor, Mich., 1963).

——*Observations upon the United Provinces of the Netherlands* (Cambridge, 1932).

TEPELIUS, JOHANNES, *Historia Philosophiae Cartesianae* (Nuremberg, 1674). BL

TERTRE, RODOLPHE DU, *Entretiens sur la religion où l'on établit les fondemens de la religion revelée contre les athées et les déistes* (3 vols.; Paris, 1743). MBN

Theophrastus Redivivus, ed. G. Canziani and G. Paganini (2 vols.; Florence, 1981).

THOMASIUS, CHRISTIAN, [*Monats-Gespräche*]. *Freymüthige lustige und ernsthaffte iedoch vernunfft- und gesetz-mässige Gedancken Oder Monats-Gespräche über allerhand, fürnehmlich aber neue Bücher* (7 vols.; Halle, 1690). AUB

——*Dreyfache Rettung des Rechts evangelischer Fürsten in Kirchen-Sachen* (Frankfurt, 1701). HUB

——*Elender Zustand eines in die Atheisterey verfallenen Gelehrten*, in Lau, *Meditationes*, ed. Pott, pp. 189–316.

——*Von der Kunst vernüftig und tugendhaft zu lieben* (Halle, 1726). HSUB

——*Kurtze Lehr-Sätze von dem Laster der Zauberey* (1703; Halle, 1704). UCLA

——*Theses Inavgvrales de crimine magiae* (Halle, 1701). JUB.

THORSCHMID, URBAN GOTTLOB, *Critische Lebensgeschichte Anton Collins des ersten Freydenkers in Engelland* (Dresden, 1755). BL

THÜMMIG, LUDWIG PHILIPP, *Institutiones philosophiae Wolfianae* (1725; repr. Hildesheim, 1982).

TIL, SALOMON VAN, *Het Voor-Hof der heydenen voor alle ongeloovigen geopent* (Dordrecht, 1694). BL

——*Theologiae utriusque compendium cum naturalis tum revelatae* (Leiden, 1704). UCLA

[TINDAL, MATTHEW], *Christianity as old as the Creation* (London, 1731). BL

——*A Defence of the Rights of the Christian Church* (1709). BL

——*The Rights of the Christian Church Asserted* (London, 1706). BL

TOLAND, JOHN, *Adeisdaemon sive Titius Livius a superstitione vindicatus* (The Hague, 1709). BL

——*Anglia Libera* (London, 1701). BL

——*Christianity not Mysterious* (London, 1696). BL

——*A Collection of Several Pieces of Mr John Toland now first publish'd from his original manuscripts*, ed. P. Des Maizeaux (2 vols.; London, 1726). BL

——*Hodegeus, or the Pillar of Cloud and Fire* (London, 1720). BL

——*Letters to Serena* (London, 1704). BL

—— *Origines Judicae* (The Hague, 1709). BL

—— *Nazarenus or, Jewish, Gentile and Mahometan Christianity* (London, 1718).

—— *Tetradymus* (London, 1720). BL

Tournemine, René-Joseph, S. J., 'Préface' to Fénélon's *Démonstration* (Paris, 1713). BL

[Triewald, Samuel], *Viri Illustri D. Samuelis a Triewald . . . Biblioteca* (Stockholm, 1746). UUL

Trinius, Johan Anton, *Freydenker-Lexicon* (Leipzig, 1759). BL

Tschirnhaus, E. W. von, *Médecine de l'esprit ou préceptes généraux de l'art de découvrir*, (ed.), Jean-Paul Wurtz (Paris, 1980).

—— *Medicina mentis* (Amsterdam, 1687). BL

Tuinman, Carolus, *Johan Kalvijns onderrichting tegen . . . de secte vrygeesten die zich Geestelijke noemen* (Middelburg, 1712). AUB

—— *Korte afschetzing der ijsselijkheden, welke van de Spinozistische vrijgeesten uitdrukkelijk worden geleert* (Rotterdam, 1719). AUB

—— *De liegende en bedriegende vrygeest ontmaskert* (Middelburg, 1715). AUB

Twee-Maandelyke Uyttreksels van alle eerst uytkomende boeken, ed. P. Rabus (periodical; Rotterdam, 1701–4). BL

Tyssot de Patot, Simon, 'Discours de M. Simon Tyssot', *Journal Littéraire* xii (1722), 154–89.

—— *Lettres choisies* (2 vols.; The Hague, 1727). LUB

—— *La Vie, les aventures et le voyage de Groenland du Reverend Père Cordelier Pierre de Mésange* (2 vols.; Amsterdam, 1720; repr. Geneva, 1979).

[Tyssot de Patot, Simon], *Voyages et avantures de Jaques Massé*, ed. A. Rosenberg (Paris and Oxford, 1993).

Uffenbach, Zacharias von, *Bibliotheca Uffenbachiana universalis* (4 vols.; Frankfurt, 1729–31). BL

—— *Merkwürdige Reisen durch Nieder-Sachsen, Holland und Engelland* (3 vols.; Ulm, 1753). BL

Undereyck, Theodor, *Der närrische Atheist entdeckt und seiner Thorheit überzeuget* (Bremen, 1689). BPK

[Vairasse, Denis], *Histoire des Sévarambes* (1677; 2 vols.; Amsterdam, 1702). BL

Valckenier, Petrus, *'t Verwerd Europa* (1667; 2 vols.; Amsterdam, 1742). LIHR

Valletta, Giuseppe, *Lettera in difesa della moderna filosofia* (Rovereto, 1732). BL

—— *Opere filosofiche*, ed. M. Rak (Florence, 1975).

Vauvenargues, Luc de Clapiers, marquis, de, *Oeuvres*, ed. P. Varillon (3 vols.; Paris, 1929).

—— *Oeuvres posthumes et oeuvres inédites*, ed. D. L. Gilbert (2 vols.; Paris, 1857).

Velthuysen, Lambert van, *Tractatus de cultu naturali . . . oppositus* Tractatui Theologico-politico *et Operi Posthumo B.D.S.* in Velthuysen *Opera Omnia* (2 vols.; Rotterdam, 1680). CUL

Venus dans le cloître ou la Religieuse en chemise (c.1682; 'à Londres' [Paris?], 1737). PBA

Verney, Luis António, *De re metaphysica ad usum lusitanorum adolescentium* (1751; 2nd edn., Lisbon, 1765). BL

—— *Verdadeiro metodo de estudar por ser util a republica, e a igreja* (2 vols.; Valensa, 1746). BL

Verscheide gedigten soo voor als tegen den Hemel op Aarde gefatsoenert van D. F. van Leenhof naar de gronden van B.D.S. (2nd edn., Amsterdam, 1704). LUB

[Verwer, Adriaen], *'t Momaensicht der Atheisterey afgerukt* (Amsterdam, 1683). AUB

Veyssière de la Croze, Mathurin, *Dissertation sur l'athéisme et sur les athées* in vol. 2 of Veyssière de la Croze, *Entretiens sur divers sujets d'histoire et de religion* (London, 1770). BL

Vico, Giambattista, *The Autobiography*, trans. M. H. Fisch and Th. Bergin (1944; 4th repr., Ithaca, NY, 1990).

—— *On Humanistic Education* (Six Inaugural Orations, 1699–1707) (Ithaca, NY, 1993).

—— *The New Science*, trans. Th. Bergin and M. H. Fisch (1948; 5th repr. Ithaca, NY, 1994).

VICO, GIAMBATTISTA, *On the Study Methods of our Time*, ed. E. Gianturco (Ithaca, NY, 1990).
—— *On the Most Ancient Wisdom of the Italians*, trans. and ed. L. M. Palmer (Ithaca, NY, 1988).
La Vie et l'Esprit de Mr Benoit de Spinosa, ed. Charles Levier (n.p, [The Hague], 1719). UCLA
La Vie et l'Esprit de Mr. Benoit de Spinosa (1719) ed. Silvia Berti (Turin, 1994).
VOGELSANG, REINIER, *Contra libellum cui titulus* Philosophia S. Scripturae Interpres . . . *indignatio justa* (Utrecht, 1669). HKB
VOGT, JOHANNES, *Catalogvs historico-criticus librorum rariorum* (2 vols; Hamburg, 1747). BL
VOLDER, BURCHARDUS DE, *Disputationes philosophicae omnes contra atheos* (Middelburg, 1685). WHA
—— *Bibliotheca Volderina* (Leiden, 1709). WHA
VOLTAIRE, FRANÇOIS-MARIE AROUET DE, *Dictionnaire philosophique* (supplemented version, 4 vols.; Paris, 1878).
—— *Dictionnaire philosophique portatif* (1764), ed. R. Pomeau (Paris, 1964).
—— *Elémens de la philosophie de Neuton* ('Londres', 1738). BL
—— *Elementi della filosofia del Neuton* (Venice, 1741). BL
—— *Lettres philosophiques ou Lettres anglaises*, ed. R. Naves (Paris, 1988).
—— *Oeuvres complètes* (52 vols.; Paris, 1877–83).
—— *Traité sur la Tolérance*, ed. R. Pomeau (Paris, 1989).
VRIES, GERARDUS DE *Exercitationes rationales de Deo, divinisque perfectionibus* (Utrecht, 1695). UCLA
WACHTER, JOHANN GEORG, *Elucidarius Cabalisticus* (1706) in Schröder (ed.), *Freidenker*, part i, vol. 2, pp. 115–97.
—— *Origines Juris Naturalis* (1704) in Schröder ed. *Freidenker* part i, vol. 2, pp. 199–276.
—— *De Primordiis Christianae religionis* (1703) in Schröder ed. *Freidenker* part i, vol. 2, pp. 33–114.
—— *Der Spinozismus im Jüdenthumb* (1699), ed. W. Schröder (Stuttgart, 1994).
WAEYEN, JOHANNES VAN DER, *De Betooverde Wereld ondersoght en weederlegt* (Franeker, 1693) BL
WAGNER, GEORG THOMAS, *Johann Christian Edelmanns verblendete Anblicke des Moses mit aufgedeckten Angesicht* (3 vols.; Frankfurt, 1747). BL
WALCH, JOHANN GEORG, *Bescheidene Antwort auf Herrn Christian Wolffens Anmerckungen über des Buddeische Bedencken dessen Philosophie betreffendt* (Jena, 1724). UCLA
—— *Bescheidener Beweis dass das Buddeische Bedencken noch fest stehe wieder Herrn Christian Wolffens Nöthige Zugabe aufgesetzet* (Jena, 1725). UCLA
—— *Philosophisches Lexicon* (1726; Leipzig, 1740). BL
[WALTEN, ERICUS], *Aardige Duyvelary* (n.p., n.d. [Rotterdam, 1691]). WHA
—— *De Regtsinnige Policey* (The Hague, 1689). BL
—— *Den triumpheerende Duyvel spookende omtrent den berg van Parnassus* (Middelburg, 1692). WHA
—— *Vervolg van de Aardige Duyvelary* (Rotterdam, 1691). WHA
—— *Beschryvinge van een vreemd Nagt-Gezigte* (n.p., n.d. [Rotterdam, 1692]). UCLA
—— *Brief aan sijn excellentie de heer Graaf van Portland* (n.p., 1692). BL
WATER, J. VAN DE, *Groot Placaat-Boeck vervattende alle placaaten . . . der Staten 's Lands van Utrecht* (3 vols.; Utrecht, 1729). LIHR
WEBBER, ZACHARIAS [under the pseudonym 'Joan Adolphsz.']. *De waare oorspronk voort-en ondergank des satans* (3rd edn., Amsterdam, 1716). WHA
WEBER, IMMANUEL, *Beurtheilung der atheisterey wie auch derer mehresten deshalben berüchtigsten Schrifften* (Frankfurt, 1697). HUL

[WEIDNER, GOTTHILF], *Catalogus librorum Dni Gotthilf Flaminii Weidneri* (Copenhagen, 1704). CRL

WHISTON, WILLIAM, *Reflexions on an anonymous Pamphlet entitled a Discourse of Freethinking* (London, 1713). BL

——*Astronomical Principles of Religion Natural and Reveal'd* (1717; new edn, London, 1725). LDrW

WILSON, JOHN, *The Scriptures genuine Interpreter asserted: or, a Discourse concerning the right Interpretation of Scripture* (London, 1678). CUL

WINCKLER, JOHANNES, *Catalogus Bibliothecae Wincklerianae* (Hamburg, 1721). HSUB

——*Die warhafftig vom Teuffel erduldete Versuchung Christi . . . wider Balthasar Beckern* (n.p., n.d. [Hamburg, 1694]). WHA

——*Schriftmässiges wohlgemeintes Bedencken über . . . die Frage Ob Gott . . . nicht mehr heutiges Tages durch göttliche Erscheinung den Menschen-kindern sich offenbahren wolle?* (Hamburg, 1692). WSB

WINSTANLEY, GERRARD, *The Laws of Freedom and Other Writings*, ed. Christopher Hill (1973; repr. Cambridge, 1983).

WITSIUS, HERMAN, *Melemata Leidensia* (Leiden, 1703). BL

WITTICHIUS, CHRISOPHER, *Anti-Spinoza* (Amsterdam, 1690). BL

——*Consensus veritatis in Scriptura divina et infallibile cum veritate philosophica* (2nd edn., Leiden, 1682). AUB

——*Ondersoek van de Zede-konst van Benedictus de Spinoza* (Amsterdam, 1695). UCLA

WITTICHIUS, JACOB, *Abstersio Calumniarum, quibus ejus Disputatio De Natovra Dei ante aliquot jam annos habita* (Leiden, 1718). CRL

——*Oratio Inavgvralis de evidentia et certitudine* (Leiden, 1718). BL

——*Dispvtatio philosophica De Natvra Dei* (The Hague, 1720). CRL

——*Wijsgerige verhandeling van de Natuure Gods* (Leiden, 1719). Kn. 16454 AUB

——*Zeedig Antwoord . . . op het Laster-Schrift tegen hem gemaekt door Johannes Alexand. Röell* (Leiden, 1723). Kn. 16603 HKB

WOERGER, FRANCISCO, *Psychologia Salomonis . . . adversus Spinozae aliorumque Atheorum inanes cavillationes* (Hamburg, 1686). CUL

WOLF, JOHANN CHRISTOPH, *Bibliotheca Hebraea* (4 vols.; Hamburg and Leipzig, 1715–33). BL

WOLFF, CHRISTIAN, *Cosmologia Generalis* (Frankfurt and Leipzig, 1731). BL

——*Christian Wolffs eigene Lebensbeschreibung*, ed. Heinrich Wuttke (Leipzig, 1841).

——*De Differentia Nexus rerum sapientis et fatalis necessitatis nec non systematis Harmoniae Praestabilitae et hypotheseum Spinosae* (Halle, 1724). BL

——*Des Herrn Doct. und Prof. Joachim Langens Anmerckungen über . . . Christian Wolfens Metaphysicam* (Cassel, 1724). BL

——*Natürliche Gottesgelahrheit nach beweisender Lehrart*, trans. Gottlieb Friedrich Hagen (6 vols. in two parts; Halle, 1742). BL

——*Nöthige Zugabe zu den Anmerckungen über Herrn D. Buddens Bedencken von der Wolffischen Philosophie* (Frankfurt, 1724). BL

——*Preliminary Discourse on Philosophy in General (Discursus praeliminaris de philosophia in genere,* 1728), ed. and trans. R. J. Blackwell (Indianapolis and New York, 1963).

——*Der vernünfftigen Gedancken von Gott, der Welt und der Seele des Menschen auch allen Dingen überhaupt* (1724; repr. Frankfurt, 1733). UCLA

WOLZOGEN, LOUIS, *Catalogus instructissimae bibliothecae viri. D. Ludovici Wolzogen* (Amsterdam, 1691). WHA

WOLZOGEN, LOUIS, *De Scripturarum Interprete* (Utrecht, 1668). BL

WOOLSTON, THOMAS, *A Fourth Discourse on the Miracles of our Saviour* (London, 1728). LDrW

——*Mr Woolston's Defense of his Discourses on the Miracles of our Saviour* (London, 1729). LDrW

WORM, CHRISTIAN, *Catalogus librorum beati D. Christiani Wormii episcopi* (Copenhagen, 1738). CRL

[WOTTON, WILLIAM], *A Letter to Eusebia* (London, 1704). BL

WYERMARS, HENDRIK, *Den Ingebeelde Chaos* (Amsterdam, 1710). AUB

YVON, PIERRE, *L'Impiété Convaincue* (Amsterdam, 1681). AUB

ZACCARIA, FRANCESCANTONIO, *Storia polemica delle proibizioni de' libri* (Rome, 1777). BL

ZAPATA, DIEGO MATHEO, *Censura del Doctor D. Diego Matheo Zapata, fundador y presidente de la Regia Sociedad Medica de Sevilla* (1716) published as preface to Nájera, *Dialogos philosophicos*. MBN

——*Crisis medica sobre el antimono y carta responsoria a la regia Sociedad medica de Sevilla* (n.p. [Madrid?], 1701). MBN

——*Ocaso de las formas aristotelicas* (Madrid, 1745). MBN

——*Verdadera apologia de defensa de la medecina racional philosophica* (Madrid, 1690). MBN

ZEDLER, JOHANN HEINRICH, *Grosses vollständiges Universal Lexicon* (64 vols.; Leipzig and Halle, 1732–50). BL

ZOBELN, ENOCH, *Declaratio Apologetica . . . wider Herrn Balthasar Bekkers . . . Die bezauberte Welt* (Leipzig, 1695). BL

Secondary Literature

AARSLEFF, HANS, 'Locke's Influence', in V. Chappell (ed.), *The Cambridge Companion to Locke* (Cambridge, 1994), 252–89.

ÅKERMAN, SUSANNA, *Queen Christina of Sweden and her Circle* (Leiden 1991).

AKKERMAN, FOKKE, *Studies in the Posthumous Works of Spinoza* (Meppel, 1980).

——'J. H. GLAZEMAKER, an Early Translator of Spinoza' in Deugd (ed.), *Spinoza's Political and Theological Thought*, 23–9.

——'Inleiding' to F. Akkerman (ed.), Spinoza, *Theologisch-Politiek Traktaat* (Amsterdam, 1997), 9–29.

AKKERMAN, FOKKE, and HUBBELING, H. G., 'The Preface to Spinoza's Posthumous Works and its Author Jarig Jelles (c.1619–1683)', *LIAS* vi (1979), 103–73.

ALBERTI, ALBERTO, *Alberto Radicati di Passerano* (Turin, 1931).

ALBIAC, GABRIEL, *La sinagoga vacía: Un estudio de las fuentes marranas del Espinosismo* (Madrid, 1987).

ALLARD, E., 'Die Angriffe gegen Descartes und Malebranche im *Journal de Trévoux*, 1701–1715', *Abhandlungen zur Philosophie und ihrer Geschichte* (Halle) xliii (1914), 1–58.

ALLISON, H. E., *Benedict de Spinoza: An Introduction* (rev. edn., New Haven, 1987).

ALMAGOR, JOSEPH, *Pierre des Maizeaux (1673–1745)* (Amsterdam, 1989).

ALMQUIST, K. G., *Andreas Rydelius' Etiska Åskådning* (Lund, 1955).

ALTMANN, ALEXANDER, *Moses Mendelssohn: A Biographical Study* (London, 1973).

ALVAREZ DE MORALES, ANTONIO, *La Ilustración y la reforma de la universidad en la España del siglo XVIII* (1971; 3rd edn., Madrid, 1985).

ANDERSON, A. (BROM), 'Sallengre, La Monnoye, and the *Traité des Trois Imposteurs*', in Berti *et al.* (eds.), *Heterodoxy*, pp. 255–71.

—— *The Treatise of The Three Impostors and the Problem of Enlightenment* (Lanham, Ma., and Oxford, 1997).

ANDRADE, ANTÓNIO ALBERTO, *Vernei e a cultura do seu tempo* (Coimbra, 1965).

ANDRIESSE, C. D., 'The Melancholic Genius', *De Zeventiende Eeuw* xii (1996), 3–13.

ANNERSTEDT, CLAES, *Uppsala universitets historia* (3 vols.; Uppsala, 1877–1913).

ARDAO, ARTURO, *La filosofia polémica de Feijóo* (Buenos Aires, 1962).

ARIEW, R., 'G. W. Leibniz, Life and Works', in N. Jolley (ed.), *Cambridge Companion to Leibniz*, 18–42.

ARNOLD, W., and VODOSEK, P., *Bibliotheken und Aufklärung.* (Wiesbaden, 1988).

ASHCRAFT, R., *Revolutionary Politics and Locke's* Two Treatises of Government (Princeton, NJ, 1986).

ASSMANN, JAN, *Moses the Egyptian* (Harvard, 1997).

ASSOUN, PAUL-LAURENT, 'Spinoza, les libertins français et la politique (1665–1725)', *Cahiers Spinoza*, iii (1980), 171–207.

AUDI, ROBERT, *The Cambridge Dictionary of Philosophy* (Cambridge, 1995).

AZEVEDO, J. LÚCIO DE, *História dos Cristãos Novos Portugueses* (1921; 2nd edn., Lisbon, 1975).

BADALONI, N., *Antonio Conti: Un abate libero pensatore tra Newton e Voltaire* (Milan, 1968).

BAECK, L., *Spinozas erste Einwirkungen auf Deutschland* (Berlin, 1895).

BALIBAR, ETIENNE, 'Jus, Pactum, Lex: sur la constitution du sujet dans le *Traité Théologico-Politique*', *St. Spin.*, i (1985), 105–42.

—— *Spinoza and Politics* (1985; London and New York, 1998).

—— 'Le politique, la politique: de Rousseau à Marx, de Marx à Spinoza', *St. Spin.* ix (1993), 203–15.

BAMBERGER, FRITZ, 'The Early Editions of Spinoza's *Tractatus Theologico-Politicus*, a Bibliohistorical Re-examination', *Studies in Bibliography and Booklore* v (1961), pp. 9–33.

BARBIER, M., *Dictionnaire des ouvrages anonymes et pseudonymes* (4 vols.; Paris, 1822–7).

BARNOUW, P. J., *Philippus van Limborch* (The Hague, 1963).

BARNES, A., *Jean Le Clerc (1657–1736) et la République des Lettres* (Paris, 1938).

BEALES, DEREK, 'Christians and *philosophes*: the Case of the Austrian Enlightenment', in D. Beales and G. Best (eds.), *History, Society and the Churches* (Cambridge, 1985), 169–94.

BEDDARD, ROBERT, 'Tory Oxford' in Tyacke (ed.), *Seventeenth-century Oxford*, 863–905.

BEDJAÏ, MARC, 'Metaphysique, éthique et politique dans l'oeuvre du docteur Franciscus van den Enden', *St. Spin.* vi (1990), 291–301.

—— 'Franciscus van den Enden, maître spirituel de Spinoza', *Revue de l'histoire des Religions* ccvii (1990), 289–311.

—— 'Le Docteur Franciscus van den Enden, son cercle et l'alchimie dans les Provinces-Unies du XVIIème siècle', *NRL* (1991), 19–50.

—— 'Libertins et politiques', *Revue de la Bibliothèque Nationale*, xliv (1992), 29–33.

—— 'Horizons philosophiques: le théâtre de Van den Enden et Spinoza', *Revue de la Bibliothèque Nationale* xlix (1993), 35–7.

—— 'Les Circonstances de la publication du *Philedonius* (1657)', in Marc Bedjaï (ed.), Franciscus van den Enden, *Philedonius* (Paris, 1994), 9–55.

BELL, DAVID, *Spinoza in Germany from 1670 to the Age of Goethe* (London, 1984).

BENÍTEZ, MIGUEL, 'Du bon usage du *Tractatus Theologico-Politicus*', in Bloch (ed.), *Spinoza au XVIIIᵉ siècle*, pp. 75–83.

—— 'Matériaux pour un inventaire des manuscrits philosophiques clandestins des XVIIᵉ et XVIIIᵉ siècles', *Rivista di Storia della Filosofia*, iii (1988), 501–31.

BENÍTEZ, MIGUEL, 'Spinoza ou Descartes? Le point de départ de l'éthique selon Boulainvilliers', *St. Spin.* x (1994), 93–108.

——*La Face cachée des Lumières* (Paris and Oxford, 1996).

——'Une histoire interminable: origines et développement du *Traité des Trois Imposteurs*' in Berti *et al.* (eds.), *Heterodoxy*, pp. 53–74.

BENNETT, JONATHAN, *A Study of Spinoza's* Ethics (Indianapolis, 1984).

——'Spinoza's Metaphysics' in Garrett, *The Cambridge Companion to Spinoza*, 61–88.

BERENGO, MARINO (ed.), *Giornali veneziani del settecento* (Milan, 1962).

BERGSMA, W., 'Balthasar Bekker als predikant, dienaar en doctor', *It Beaken: Tydskrift fan de Fryske Akademy* lviii (1996), 73–91.

BERKEL, K. VAN, 'De wetenschappelijke revolutie: een nieuwe kans voor een versleten metafoor?' *Tijdschrift voor Geschiedenis* cviii (1995), 483–98.

BERKVENS-STEVELINCK, CH., *Prosper Marchand. La Vie et l'oeuvre (1678–1756)* (Leiden, 1987).

BERKVENS-STEVELINCK, CH., BOTS, H., HOFTIJZER, P. G., and LANKHORST, O. S. (eds.), *Le Magasin de l'Univers: The Dutch Republic as the Centre of the European Book Trade* (Leiden, 1992).

BERKEVENS-STEVELINCK, CH., and VERCRUYSSE, JEROOM, *Le Métier de journaliste au dix-huitième siècle* (Oxford, 1993).

BERKVENS-STEVELINCK, CH., ISRAEL, J. I., and POSTHUMUS MEYJES, G. H. M. (eds.), *The Emergence of Tolerance in the Dutch Republic* (Leiden, 1997).

BERMAN, DAVID, 'Determinism and Freewill: Anthony Collins' *A Philosophical Inquiry*', *Studies: An Irish Quarterly Review* (1977), 251–4.

——'Enlightenment and Counter-Enlightenment in Irish Philosophy', *AGPh* lxiv (1982), 148–65.

——*A History of Atheism in Britain from Hobbes to Russell* (London, 1988).

——'Disclaimers as Offence Mechanisms in Charles Blount and John Toland', in Hunter and Wootton, *Atheism*, pp. 255–72.

——'George Berkeley' in Brown (ed.), *British Philosophy*, pp. 123–49.

——(ed.), *George Berkeley. Alciphron in Focus* (London and New York, 1993).

BERTI, SILVIA, 'Radicati in Olanda'. *RSI* xcvi (1984), 510–22.

——'Jan Vroesen, autore del *Traité des Trois Imposteurs*', *RSI* ciii (1991), 528–43.

——'Scepticism and the *Traité des Trois Imposteurs*', in Popkin and Vanderjagt (eds.), *Scepticism and Irreligion* (1993), pp. 216–29.

——'The First Edition of the *Traité des Trois Imposteurs* and its Debt to Spinoza's *Ethics*', in Hunter and Wootton, *Atheism*, pp. 182–220.

——'Introduzione' to Berti (ed.), *La Vie et l'Esprit de Mr. Benoit de Spinosa* (Turin, 1994), pp. xv–lxxviii.

——'At the Roots of Unbelief', *JHI* lvi (1995), 555–75.

——'*L'Esprit de Spinosa*: ses origines et sa première édition dans leur contexte spinozien', in Berti *et al.* (eds.), *Heterodoxy, Spinozism and Free Thought*, pp. 3–51.

——'Unmasking the Truth: the Theme of Imposture in Early Modern European Culture, 1660–1730', in Force and Katz, *Everything Connects*, pp. 19–36.

BERTI, SILVIA, CHARLES-DAUBERT, FRANÇOISE, and POPKIN, RICHARD H. (eds.), *Heterodoxy, Spinozism, and Free Thought in Early Eighteenth-Century Europe. Studies on the* Traité des Trois Imposteurs (Dordrecht, 1996).

BETTS, C. J., *Early Deism in France* (The Hague, 1984).

BIAGIOLI, MARIO, 'Scientific Revolution, Social Bricolage, and Etiquette' in Porter and Teich (eds.), *Scientific Revolution*, 11–54.

Biasutti, Franco, 'Reason and Experience in Spinoza and Leibniz', *St. Spin.* vi (1990), 45–71.

Blanning, T. C. W., 'Frederick the Great and Enlightened Absolutism', in H. M. Scott (ed.), *Enlightened Absolutism* (Basingstoke, 1990), pp. 265–88.

——'Frederick the Great and German Culture', in R. Oresko, G. C. Gibbs and H. M. Scott (eds.), *Royal and Republican Sovereignty in early modern Europe* (Cambridge, 1997), pp. 527–50.

Blase, J. E. B., *Johannes Colerus en de groote twisten in de Nederlandsche Luthersche kerk zijner dagen* (Amsterdam, 1920).

Blechet, Françoise, 'Quelques acquisitions hollandaises de la Bibliothèque du Roi (1668–1735)', in Berkevens-Stevelinck, *Le Magasin de l'Univers*, pp. 33–47.

Bloch, Olivier (ed.), *Le Matérialisme du XVIIIe siècle et la littérature clandestine* (Paris, 1982).

——*Spinoza au XVIIIᵉ siècle* (Paris, 1990).

——'Parité de la vie et de la mort', in Canzioni (ed.), *Filosofia e religione*, pp. 175–208.

Bloch, O., and McKenna, A. (eds.), *La Lettre clandestine. Bulletin d'information sur la littérature philosophique clandestine de l'âge classique* (8 vols. so far, Saint Étienne, 1992–).

Blom, Hans, *Morality and Causality in Politics* (Utrecht, 1995).

——'The Moral and Political philosophy of Spinoza' in G. H. R. Parkinson (ed.), *The Renaissance and Seventeenth-Century Rationalism. The Routledge History of Philosophy*, vol IV (London, 1993), pp. 313–48.

Bodemann, E., 'Herzogin Sophie von Hannover', *Historisches Taschenbuch* vi (Leipzig, 1888), 27–86.

Boer, T. J. de, 'Spinoza en England', *Tijdschrift voor Wijsbegeerte* x (1916), 331–6.

Bohrmann, Georg, *Spinozas Stellung zur Religion* (Giessen, 1914).

Bordoli, Roberto, 'Account of a Curious Traveller', *St. Spin.* x (1994), 175–82.

——*Ragione e Scrittura tra Descartes e Spinoza* (Milan, 1997).

Borroni Salvadori, F., 'Tra la fine del Granducato et la reggenza: Filippo Stosch a Firenze', *Annali della Scuola Normale Superiore di Pisa*, 3rd ser. viii (1978), 565–614.

Bossy, John, 'English Catholics after 1688' in Grell, Israel, and Tyacke (eds.), *From Persecution to Toleration*, 369–87.

Bots, Hans, 'Fontenelle et la Hollande' in Niderst (ed.), *Fontenelle*, pp. 545–56.

——'Le rôle des périodiques Néerlandais pour la diffusion du livre (1684–1747)', in Berkvens-Stevelinck, *Magasin du l'Univers*, pp. 47–70.

——'Le Refuge et les 'Nouvelles de la République des Lettres' de Pierre Bayle', in H. Bots and G. H. M. Posthumus Meyjes (eds.), *La Revocation de l'Édit de Nantes et les Provinces Unies* (Amsterdam, 1986), pp. 85–96.

Bots, Hans (ed.), *Pieter Rabus en de Boekzaal van Europe, 1692–1702* (Amsterdam, 1974).

——*Henri Basnage de Beauval en de Histoire des Ouvrages des Savans, 1687–1709* (2 vols.; Amsterdam, 1976).

Bots, Hans et al. (eds.), *De 'Bibliothèque Universelle et Historique' (1686–1693)*, (Amsterdam, 1981).

Bots, Hans, and Van de Schoor, R., 'La tolérance à travers les dictionnaires', in Berkvens-Stevelinck, Israel, and Posthumus Meyjes (eds.), *Emergence of Tolerance*, 141–53.

Bots, J., *Tussen Descartes en Darwin* (Assen, 1972).

Boucher, W. I., *Spinoza in English: A Bibliography* (Leiden, 1991).

Bourdin, Jean-Claude, *Diderot: Le matérialisme* (Paris, 1998).

Bouveresse, Renée, *Spinoza et Leibniz* (Paris, 1992).

——(ed.), *Spinoza, Science et Religion*. Actes du Colloque du Centre Culturel International de Cerisy-la-Salle (1982) (Paris, 1988).

Bove, Laurent, 'Puissance d'agir et vertu; le spinozisme de Vauvenargues', in Bloch, *Spinoza*, pp. 185–201.

—— 'La politique et l'histoire: le spinozisme de Vauvenargues', in Van Bunge and Klever (eds.), *Disguised and overt Spinozism*, pp. 333–51.

—— *La stratégie du* conatus (Paris, 1996).

Bowden, D. K., *Leibniz as a Librarian and Eighteenth-Century Libraries in Germany*, Occcasional Publication no. 15 of the School of Library Studies (University College London, 1969).

Bracken, H. M., 'Bayle's Attack on Natural Theology: The Case of Christian Pyrrhonism', in Popkin and Vanderjagt (eds.), *Scepticism and Irreligion*, 254–66.

Brailsford, N. N., *The Levellers and the English Revolution* (London, 1961).

Bräuning-Oktavio, H., 'Die Bibliothek der grossen Landgräfin Caroline von Hessen', AGB vi (1964), 682–875.

Brechka, F. T., *Gerard van Swieten and his World (1700–1772)* (The Hague, 1970).

Briggs, Robin, *Communities of Belief* (1989; repr. Oxford, 1995).

Brockliss, L. W. B., 'The Scientific Revolution in France', in Porter and Teich (eds.), *Scientific Revolution*, pp. 55–89.

—— 'Curricula', in Ridder-Symoens (ed.), *History of the University*, 565–620.

Brogi, Stefano, *Il Cerchio dell' universo. Libertinismo, Spinozismo e filosofia della natura in Boulainvilliers* (Florence, 1993).

Brown, Stuart, 'Theological Politics and the Reception of Spinoza in the Early English Enlightenment', *Stud. Spin.* ix (1993), 181–200.

—— 'Leibniz: Modern, Scholastic, or Renaissance Philosopher?' in Sorell (ed.), *Rise of Modern Philosophy*, pp. 213–30.

—— 'Locke as Secret 'Spinozist': the Perspective of William Carroll', in Van Bunge and Klever (eds.), *Disguised and Overt Spinozism*, pp. 213–34.

—— (ed.), *British Philosophy and the Age of Enlightenment. Routledge History of Philosophy*, vol. V (London and New York, 1996).

Brykman, Geneviève, *La judéité de Spinoza* (Paris, 1972).

—— *Berkeley. Philosophie et apologétique* (2 vols.; Lille, 1984).

—— 'Berkeley lecteur de Spinoza', in Pierre-François Moreau (ed.), *Architectures de la raison. Mélanges offerts à Alexandre Matheron* (Paris, 1996), pp. 87–102.

Bullough, V. L., 'Prostitution and Reform in Eighteenth-Century England', in R. P. Maccubbin (ed.), *Unauthorized Sexual Behaviour during the Enlightenment*, special issue of *Eighteenth-Century Life* ix (1985), 61–74.

Bunge, Wiep (Louis) van, 'Johannes Bredeburg and the *Korte Verhandeling*', St. Spin. iv (1988), 321–8.

—— 'On the early Dutch Reception of the *Tractatus Theologico-Politicus*', St. Spin. v (1989), 225–51.

—— *Johannes Bredenburg (1643–1691), Een Rotterdamse Collegiant in de ban van Spinoza* (Rotterdam, 1990).

—— 'Balthasar Bekker's Cartesian Hermeneutics and the Challenge of Spinozism', BJHP 1 (1993), 55–79.

—— 'Spinozas atheisme', in E. Kuypers (ed.), *Sporen van Spinoza* (Leuven and Apeldoorn, 1993).

—— 'Einleitung' to W. van Bunge (ed.), Balthasar Bekker, *Die bezauberte Welt* (1693) (Stuttgart, 1996), pp. 7–61.

—— 'Eric Walten (1663–1697): An Early Enlightenment Radical in the Dutch Republic', in Van Bunge and Klever (eds.), *Disguised and Overt Spinozism*, pp. 41–54.

—— 'Les origines et la signification de la traduction française de la prétendue démonstration mathématique par Jean Bredenbourg', in McKenna and Mothu (eds.), *Philosophie clandestine*, 49–64.

—— 'Quelle extravagance: Balthasar Bekker (1634–1698) in Germany and France', *De Achttiende Eeuw* xxx (1998), 113–24.

BUNGE, WIEP VAN, and KLEVER, WIM (eds.), *Disguised and Overt Spinozism around 1700* (Leiden, 1996).

BURBAGE, F., and CHOUCHAN, N., 'À propos du rapport Diderot-Spinoza' in Bloch, *Spinoza*, 169–82.

BURR LITCHFIELD, R., *The Emergence of Bureaucracy: The Florentine Patricians, 1530–1790* (Princeton, NJ, 1986).

BUSCHMANN, C., 'Wolffs "Widerlegung" der *Ethik* Spinozas', in Delf, *Spinoza*, pp. 126–41.

BUZON, FRÉDERIC DE, 'Religion naturelle et religion civile chez Rousseau', *Les Études Philosophiques* lxviii (1993), 331–43.

CALINGER, R. S., 'The Newtonian-Wolffian Confrontation in the St Petersburg Academy of Science (*c*.1725–46)', in *Cahiers d'histoire mondiale* xi (1968 / 9), 417–33.

—— 'The Newtonian-Wolffian Controversy (1740–59)', *JHI* xxx (1969), 319–30.

CANTELLI, G., *Teologia e ateismo. Saggio sul pensiero filosofico e religioso di Pierre Bayle* (Florence, 1969).

CANZIANI, GUIDO (ed.), *Filosofia e religione nella letteratura clandestina* (Milan, 1994).

'Critica della religione e fonti moderne nel *Cymbalum Mundi* o *Symbolum Sapientiae*', in Canziani (ed.), *Filosofia*, pp. 35–81.

CARAYOL, E., *Thémiseul de Saint Hyacinthe* (Paris and Oxford, 1984).

CARBONCINI, SONIA, 'L'*Encyclopédie* et Christian Wolff', *Les Études Philosophiques* lxii (1987), 489–504.

CARO BAROJA, JULIO, *Los judíos en la España moderna y contemporánea* (3 vols.; 2nd edn., Madrid, 1978).

CARPANETTO, D., and RICUPERATI, G., *Italy in the Age of Reason, 1685–1789* (London, 1987).

CARRANZA, N., *Monsignor Gaspare Cerati provveditore dell' Università di Pisa nel Settecento delle Riforme* (Pisa, 1974).

CARVAJAL, JULIÁN, 'Resonancias de Gracián en Spinoza' in Domínguez (ed.), *Spinoza y España*, pp. 201–14.

CASINI, PAOLO, *L'Universo-macchina: Origini della filosofia newtoniana* (Bari, 1969).

—— *Introduzione all' illuminismo da Newton a Rousseau* (1973; new edn., 2 vols.; Bari, 1980).

CASSIRER, ERNST, *The Philosophy of the Enlightenment* (1951, repr., Princeton, NJ, 1979).

CHAIX-RUY, J., *J. B. Vico et l'Illuminisme athée* (Paris, 1968).

CHAMPION, JUSTIN, *The Pillars of Priestcraft Shaken* (Cambridge, 1992).

—— 'John Toland: the Politics of Pantheism', *Revue de Synthèse* iv (1995), 259–80.

—— 'Introduction' to John Toland, *Nazarenus* (ed.), Justin Champion (Paris and Oxford, 1997).

—— 'Père Richard Simon and English Biblical Criticism, 1680–1700', in Force and Katz, *Everything Connects*, pp. 37–6.

—— 'Making Authority: Belief, Conviction and Reason in the Public Sphere in Late Seventeenth-Century England' in *Libertinage et Philosophie* iii (Saint-Étienne, 1995), 143–90.

CHARLES-DAUBERT, FRANÇOISE, 'L'Image de Spinoza dans la littérature clandestine et l'*Esprit de Spinosa*', in Bloch (ed.), *Spinoza au XVIIIe siècle*, 51–74.

—— 'L'*Esprit de Spinosa* et les *Traités des Trois Imposteurs*', in Berti, Charles-Daubert, and Popkin (eds.), *Heterodoxy*, 131–89.

751

CHARLES-DAUBERT, FRANÇOISE, *Le 'Traité des Trois Imposteurs' et 'L'Esprit de Spinosa': Philosophie clandestine entre 1678 et 1768* (Oxford, 1999).

CHARTIER, ROGER, 'Espace social et imaginaire social: les intellectuels frustrés au XVIIe siècle', *Annales* xxxvii (1982), 389–99.

—— *The Cultural Origins of the French Revolution*, trans. L. G. Cochrane (Durham, NC, 1991; 4th repr. 1995).

CLARK, RONALD W., *Einstein: The Life and Times* (1971; repr. New York, 1994).

CLARK, STUART, *Thinking with Demons. The Idea of Witchcraft in Early Modern Europe* (Oxford, 1997).

COBBAN, ALFRED, 'The Fundamental Ideas of Robespierre', in A. Cobban, *Aspects of the French Revolution* (London, 1971), pp. 137–58.

COCHRANE, ERIC, *Florence in the Forgotten Centuries, 1527–1800* (Chicago, 1973).

COHEN, GUSTAVE, *Le séjour de Saint-Evremond en Hollande et l'entrée de Spinoza dans le champ de la pensée française* (Paris, 1926).

COLIE, R. L., *Light and Enlightenment: A Study of the Cambridge Platonists and the Dutch Arminians* (Cambridge, 1957).

—— 'Spinoza and the Early English Deists', *JHI* xx (1959), 23–46.

—— 'Spinoza in England, 1665–1730', *Proceedings of the American Philosophical Society* cvii (1963), 183–219.

COMPARATO, V. I., *Giuseppe Valletta. Un intellectuale Napolitano delle fine del seicento* (Naples, 1970).

COMTE-SPONVILLE, ANDRÉ, 'La Mettrie et le 'système d'Épicure', *Dix-Huitième Siècle* xxiv (1992), 105–15.

—— 'La Mettrie: un Spinoza moderne?' in Bloch, *Spinoza*, pp. 133–50.

CONTI, V., *Paolo Mattia Doria* (Florence, 1978).

COOK, H. J., 'The New Philosophy in the Low Countries', in Porter and Teich (eds.), *Scientific Revolution*, 115–49.

—— 'Bernard Mandeville and the Therapy of the "Clever Politician"', *JHI* (1999), 101–24.

CORSINI, S., 'Quand Amsterdam rime avec Lausanne', in Berkvens-Stevelinck *et al.* (eds.), *Magasin de l'Univers*, pp. 95–119.

COTONI, MARIE-HÉLÈNE, *L'Exégèse du Nouveau Testament dans la philosophie française du dix-huitième siècle* (Oxford, 1984).

COTTINGHAM, JOHN, *A Descartes Dictionary* (Oxford, 1993).

COULET, HENRI, 'Réflexions sur les *Meditationes* de Lau', in Bloch, *Le Matérialisme*, pp. 31–44.

CRAGG, J. R., *The Church and the Age of Reason, 1648–1789* (1960; Harmondsworth, 1970).

CRAMER, J. A., *Abraham Heidanus en zijn Cartesianisme* (Utrecht, 1889).

CRAVEN, K., *Jonathan Swift and the Millennium of Madness* (Leiden, 1992).

CRISTOFOLINI, PAOLO (ed.), *The Spinozistic Heresy: The Debate on the* Tractatus-Theologico-Politicus, *1670–1677* (Amsterdam, 1995).

—— *Cartesiani e Sociniani. Studio su Henry More* (Urbino, 1974).

CROCE, BENEDETTO, *La filosofia di Giambattista Vico* (1911; Bari, 1965).

CURLEY, E., 'Spinoza on Miracles' in Giancotti (ed.), *Spinoza*, pp. 421–38.

—— *Behind the Geometrical Method: A Reading of Spinoza's Ethics* (Princeton, NJ, 1988).

—— 'Notes on a Neglected Masterpiece', in J. A. Cover and M. Kulstad (eds.), *Central Themes in Early Modern Philosophy: Essays Presented to Jonathan Bennett* (Indianapolis, 1990), 109–59.

—— 'Kissinger, Spinoza and Genghis Khan' in Garrett (ed.), *Cambridge Companion to Spinoza*, 315–42.

752

CURLEY E., and MOREAU, PIERRE-FRANÇOIS (eds.), *Spinoza. Issues and Directions* (Leiden, 1990).

DAGEN, JEAN, 'Fontenelle et Spinoza' in Niderst (ed.), *Fontenelle*, pp. 379–95.

DANN, OTTO, 'Vom *Journal des Scavants* zur wissentschaftlichen Zeitschrift', in Fabian and Raabe (eds.), *Gelehrte Bücher*, pp. 63–80.

DARNTON, ROBERT, *The Literary Underground of the Old Regime* (Cambridge, Mass., 1982).

—— *Forbidden Best-Sellers of Pre-revolutionary France* (London, 1996).

DAVIDSON, NICHOLAS, 'Unbelief and Atheism in Italy, 1500–1700', in Hunter and Wootton (eds.), *Atheism*, pp. 55–85.

—— 'Toleration in Enlightenment Italy', in Grell and Porter (eds.), *Toleration*, pp. 230–49.

DAVIS, E. B., and HUNTER, MICHAEL (eds.), 'Introduction' to Robert Boyle, *A Free Enquiry*, pp. ix–xxv.

DEKKER, RUDOLF, 'Private Vices, Public Virtues Revisited: The Dutch Background of Bernard Mandeville', *History of European Ideas* xiv (1992), 481–98.

DELEUZE, GILLES, *Spinoza: Practical Philosophy* (San Francisco, 1988).

—— *Expressionism in Philosophy: Spinoza*, trans. M. Joughin (New York, 1990).

DELF, HANNA *et al.* (eds.), *Spinoza in der europäischen Geistesgeschichte* (Berlin, 1994).

DELLA ROCCA, M., *Representation and the Mind–Body Problem in Spinoza* (New York, 1996).

DELON, MICHEL, 'Tyssot de Patot et le recours à la fiction', *Revue d'Histoire Littéraire de la France* lxxx (1980), 707–19.

DEUGD, C. DE (ed.), *Spinoza's Political and Theological Thought* (Amsterdam, 1984).

DÍAZ DÍAZ, GONZALO, *Hombres y documentos de la filosofía española* (5 vols. so far, Madrid, 1980–   ).

DIJKSTERHUIS, E. J., *The Mechanization of the World Picture* (1959; Princeton, N.J., 1986).

DIJN, HERMAN DE, 'Wisdom and Theoretical Knowledge in Spinoza', in Curley and Moreau, *Spinoza: Issues and Directions*, pp. 147–56.

—— 'Einstein and Spinoza'. *MvSp* lxiv (1991).

—— 'Knowledge, Anthropocentrism and Salvation', *St. Spin.* ix (1993), 247–62.

—— 'Spinoza and Revealed Religion', *St. Spin.* ll (1995), 39–52.

—— 'Introduction' to *Spinoza. The Way to Wisdom* (West Lafayette, Ind. 1996).

DINTLER, ÅKE, *Lars Roberg, akademiska sjukhusets grundare* (Uppsala, 1959).

DOMÍMGUEZ, ATILANO, 'España en Spinoza y Spinoza en España', in A. Domínguez (ed.), *Spinoza y España* (Murcia, 1994), pp. 9–25.

DONAGAN, ALAN, 'Spinoza's Theology', in Garrett, *Cambridge Companion to Spinoza*, pp. 343–82.

DOOLEY, B., *Science, Politics and Society in Eighteenth-Century Italy: The* Giornale de' Letterati d'Italia *and its World* (New York and London, 1991).

DOWNIE, JOHN, *Peter Cornelius Plockhoy: Pioneer of the First Co-operative Commonwealth*, 1659 (Manchester, 1934).

DOYLE, WILLIAM, *The Oxford History of the French Revolution* (Oxford, 1989).

DÜLMEN, R. VAN, *The Society of the Enlightenment* (Cambridge, 1992).

DUNIN BORKOWSKI S. VON, S. J., *Spinoza* (4 vols, Münster, 1933–6).

DUNN, JOHN, 'The Claim to Freedom of Conscience', in Grell, Israel and Tyacke (eds.), *From Persecution to Toleration*, 97–128.

DUPRONT, A., *Pierre-Daniel Huet et l'exégèse comparatiste au xviie siècle* (Paris, 1930).

EBERT, FRIEDRICH ADOLF, *Geschichte und Beschreibung der königlichen öffentlichen Bibliothek zu Dresden* (Leipzig, 1822).

ÉCOLE, JEAN, 'La Critique Wolfienne du Spinozisme', *Archives de Philosophie* xlvi (1983), 553–67.

EEGHEN, I. A. VAN, *De Amsterdamse boekhandel 1680–1725* (5 vols.; Amsterdam, 1963–78).

ELIAS, WILLEM, 'Het Spinozistisch Erotisme van Adriaan Beverland', *TvSV* ii (1974), 283–320.

ELLEHØJ, S., and GRANE, L. (eds.), *Københavns Universitet, 1479–1979* (14 vols.; Copenhagen, 1991).

ELLIS, H. A., *Boulainvilliers and the French Monarchy* (Ithaca, NY, 1988).

ENDERLE, W., 'Die Jesuitenbibliothek im 17. Jahrhundert', *AGB* xli (1994), 147–213.

EVENHUIS, R. B., *Ook dat was Amsterdam. De Kerk der hervorming in de Gouden Eeuw* (3 vols.; Amsterdam, 1965–71).

EVERS, MEINDERT, 'Die "Orakel" von Antonius van Dale (1638–1708): eine Streitschrift', *LIAS* viii (1981), 225–67.

FABIAN, BERNHARD, 'Göttingen als Forschungsbibliothek im achtzehnten Jahrhundert', in Raabe (ed.), *Öffentliche und Private Bibliotheken*, 209–39.

—— 'The Reception of Bernard Mandeville in Eighteenth-Century Germany', in T. Besterman (ed.), *Transactions of the Fourth International Congress of the Enlightenment* (Oxford, 1976), pp. 693–722.

—— and Paul Raabe (eds.), *Gelehrte Bücher vom Humanismus bis zur Gegenwart* (Wiesbaden, 1983).

FAIRBAIRN, ANDREW, 'L'*Idée d'un philosophe*, le texte et son auteur', in McKenna and Mothu (eds.), *La philosophie clandestine*.

FAUCETT, D., 'Introduction' to Henrik Smeeks, *The Mighty Kingdom of Krinke Kesmes* (1708) (Amsterdam, 1995).

FEINGOLD, MORDECHAI, 'Partnership in Glory: Newton and Locke through the Enlightenment and beyond', in P. B. Scheurer and G. Debrock (eds.), *Newton's Scientific and Philosophical Legacy* (Dordrecht, 1988), pp. 291–308.

—— 'Huygens and the Royal Society', *De Zeventiende Eeuw* xii (1996), 22–36.

—— 'Reversal of Fortunes: The Displacement of Cultural Hegemony from the Netherlands to England', in D. Hoak and M. Feingold (eds.), *The World of William and Mary* (Stanford, Cal., 1996), pp. 234–61.

FERRONE, VINCENZO, *The Intellectual Roots of the Italian Enlightenment* (Atlantic Highlands, NJ, 1995).

FISCHER, CAROLINE, 'Les aspects philosophiques de la littérature érotique' in McKenna and Mothu (eds.), *La philosophie clandestine*, 405–12.

FISCHER, K. P., 'John Locke in the German Enlightenment', *JHI* xxxvi (1975), 431–46.

FITZPATRICK, M., 'Toleration and the Enlightenment Movement', in Grell and Porter (eds.), *Toleration*, 23–68.

FIX, ANDREW, 'Angels, Devils and Evil Spirits in Seventeenth-Century Thought: Balthasar Bekker and the Collegiants', *JHI* l (1989), 527–47.

—— 'Willem Deurhoff (1650–1717): Merchant and Philosopher' *GWN* l (1990), 53–64.

—— *Prophecy and Reason The Dutch Collegiants in the Early Enlightenment* (Princeton, NJ, 1991).

—— 'Balthasar Bekker and the Crisis of Cartesianism', *History of European Ideas* xvii (1993), 575–88.

—— 'Hoe cartesiaans was Balthasar Bekker?' in Van Sluis (ed.), *Balthasar Bekker*, pp. 118–37.

—— 'Bekker and Spinoza', in Van Bunge and Klever (eds.), *Disguised and Overt Spinozism*, pp. 23–40.

—— *Fallen Angels, Balthasar Bekker, Spirit Belief, and Confessionalism in the Seventeenth-Century Dutch Republic* (Dordrecht, 1999).

FONTENAY, ÉLISABETH DE, *Diderot ou le matérialisme enchanté* (Paris, 1981).

FORCE, J. E., 'The Newtonians and Deism' in Force and Popkin (eds.), *Essays*, pp. 43–73.

754

—— 'The Break-down of the Newtonian Synthesis of Science and Religion: Hume, Newton and the Royal Society' in Force and Popkin (eds.), *Essays*, pp. 143–63.

—— 'Children of the Resurrection' and 'Children of the Dust': Confronting Mortality and Immortality with Newton and Hume', in Force and Katz, *Everything Connects*, pp. 115–42.

FORCE, J. E., and KATZ, D. S., *Everything Connects: In Conference with Richard H. Popkin* (Leiden, 1999).

FORCE, J. E., and POPKIN, RICHARD, *Essays on the Context, Nature and Influence of Isaac Newton's Theology* (Dordrecht, 1990).

FOUKE, DANIEL, *The Enthusiastical Concerns of Dr Henry More* (Leiden, 1997).

FRANCES, M., 'Un gazetier français en Hollande: Gabriel de Saint Glain, traducteur de Spinoza', *Revue des Sciences Humaines* lxxix (1955), 407–20.

FRÄNGSMYR, TORE, *Wolffianismens genombrott i Uppsala* (Uppsala, 1972).

FREITAS, JORDÃO DO, *O marquêz de Pombal e o Santo Oficio da Inquisição* (Lisbon, 1916).

FREUDENTHAL, JACOB, *Spinoza, Leben und Lehre* (2 vols.; Heidelberg, 1927).

FRIEDMANN, GEORGES, *Leibniz et Spinoza* (1946; 2nd edn., Paris, 1962).

FRIJHOFF, WILLEM, 'Patterns' in Rydder-Symons (ed.), *Universities*, pp. 43–110.

—— 'Graduation and Careers', in Rydder-Symons (ed.), *Universities*, pp. 355–415.

FRÜHSORGE, G, 'Zur Rolle der Universitätsbibliotheken im Zeitalter der Aufklärung', in Arnold and Vodosek, *Bibliotheken*, pp. 61–81.

FUNKE, HANS-GÜNTER, *Studien zur Reiseutopie der Frühaufklärung: Fontenelles 'Histoire des Ajaoiens'* (2 vols.; Heidelberg, 1982).

FUNKENSTEIN, AMOS, *Theology and the Scientific Imagination from the Middle Ages to the Seventeenth Century* (Princeton, NJ, 1986).

GABBEY, ALAN, 'Spinoza's Natural Science and Methodology', in Garrett (ed.), *Cambridge Companion to Spinoza*, pp. 142–91.

GAIFFE, FELIX, *L'Envers du Grand Siècle* (Paris, 1924).

GARBER, DANIEL, *Descartes' Metaphysical Physics* (Chicago, 1992).

—— 'Leibniz: Physics and Philosophy' in Jolley (ed.), *Cambridge Companion to Leibniz*, 270–352.

GARDAIR, JEAN-MICHEL, *Le 'Giornale de' Letterati' de Rome (1668–1681)* (Florence, 1984).

GARRETT, DON, 'Truth, Method, and Correspondence in Spinoza and Leibniz', in *St. Spin.* vi (1990), 130–43.

—— 'A free Man always acts honestly not deceptively' in Curley and Moreau (eds.), *Spinoza*, pp. 221–38.

—— 'Spinoza's Ethical Theory', in Garrett (ed.), *Cambridge Companion*, pp. 267–314.

—— (ed.), *The Cambridge Companion to Spinoza* (Cambridge, 1996).

GASKIN, J. C. A., *Hume's Philosophy of Religion* (1978; 2nd edn., Basingstoke, 1988).

—— 'Hume on Religion' in Norton (ed.), *The Cambridge Companion to Hume* (Cambridge, 1993), 313–44.

GAWLICK, GÜNTER, 'Der Deismus als Grundzug der Religionsphilosophie der Aufklärung', in *Herman Samuel Reimarus (1694–1768)* no editor (Göttingen, 1973) pp. 15–43.

GAY, PETER, *The Enlightenment. An Interpretation* (2 vols.; new edn. New York, 1977).

GEBHARDT, CARL, 'Einleitung' and 'Anmerckungen' to Spinoza, *Briefwechsel* (ed.), Carl Gebhardt (Leipzig, 1914).

—— *Die Schriften des Uriel da Costa* (Amsterdam and Heidelberg, 1922).

—— 'Juan de Prado', *Chronicum Spinozanum* iii (1923), 269–91.

—— 'Pieter Ballings Het Licht op den Kandelaar', *Chronicon Spinozanum* iv (1926), 187–93.

—— *Supplementa* to Spinoza, *Opera*, published as vol. 5 (1938; repr. Heidelberg, 1987).

GEFFKEN, JOHANNES, *Johann Winckler und die hamburgische Kirche seiner Zeit* (Hamburg, 1861).

GEIGER, MAX, *Die Basler Kirche und Theologie im Zeitalter der Hochorthodoxie* (Biel, 1952).

GEISMANN, GEORG, 'Spinoza—beyond Hobbes and Rousseau', *JHI* lii (1991), 35–53.

GELDER, H. A. ENNO VAN, *Getemperde Vrijheid* (Groningen, 1972).

GELDERBLOM, ARIE-JAN, 'The Publisher of Hobbes' Dutch Leviathan' in S. Roach (ed.), *Across the Narrow Seas* (London, 1991), 162–6.

GENERALI, DARIO, 'Il "Giornale de' Letterati d'Italia" e la cultura veneta del primo setttecento', *Rivista di Storia della Filosofia* xxxix (1984), 243–81.

GEORGELIN, JEAN, *Venise au siècle des lumières* (Paris, 1978).

GEYER-KORDESCH, JOHANNA, 'Comparative Difficulties: Scottish Medical Education in the European Context (*c.*1690–1830)', in V. Nutton and Roy Porter (eds.), *The History of Medical Education in Britain* (Amsterdam, 1995), pp. 94–115.

GIANCOTTI BOSCHERINI, E., 'Réalisme et utopie', in Deugd (ed.), *Spinoza's Political and Theological Thought*, pp. 37–43.

—— 'La teoria del'assolutismo in Hobbes e Spinoza', *St. Spin.* 1 (1985), 231–58.

—— 'Notes sur la diffusion de la philosophie de Spinoza en Italie' in Cristofolini (ed.), *l'Hérésie Spinoziste*, 229–52.

—— (ed.), *Spinoza nel 350° anniversario della nascità* (Naples, 1985).

GLAZIOU, YVES, *Hobbes en France au XVIIIe siècle* (Paris, 1993).

GOLDENBAUM, U., 'Die erste deutsche Übersetzung der Spinozaschen "Ethik"', in Delf (ed.), *Spinoza*, pp. 107–25.

GOLDFRIEDRICH, JOHANN, *Geschichte des deutschen Buchhandels von Westfälischen Frieden bis zum Beginn der klassischen Literaturperiode (1648–1740)* (Leipzig, 1908).

GOLDGAR, ANNE, *Impolite Learning* (New Haven and London, 1995).

GOLDIE, MARK, 'The Theory of Religious Intolerance in Restoration England', in Grell, Israel, and Tyacke (eds.), *From Persecution to Toleration*, pp. 331–68.

GOODMAN, DAVID, 'The Scientific Revolution in Spain and Portugal', in Porter and Teich (eds.), *Scientific Revolution*, pp. 158–77.

GOODMAN, DENA, *The Republic of Letters: A Cultural History of the French Enlightenment* (New York, 1994).

GOUDRIAAN, A., *Philosophische Gotteserkenntnis bei Suárez und Descartes* (Leiden, 1999).

GRAESSE J. G. TH., *Trésor des livres rares et précieux ou Nouveaux Dictionnaire bibliographique* (8 vols.; Dresden, 1858–69).

GRAF, ARTURO, *L'Anglomania e l'influsso inglese in Italia nel secolo XVIII* (Turin, 1911).

GREGORY, TULLIO, 'Pierre Charron's "Scandalous Book"', in Hunter and Wootton (eds.), *Atheism*, pp. 87–109.

—— '"Libertinisme érudit" in Seventeenth-Century France and Italy: The Critique of Ethics and Religion', *BJHP* vi (1998), 323–49.

GRELL, CHANTAL, 'Nicolas Fréret. La Critique et l'histoire ancienne', in Grell, Chantal and Volpilhac-Auger, C. (eds.), *Nicolas Fréret, légende et vérité* (Paris and Oxford, 1994), pp. 51–71.

GRELL, O. P., and PORTER, ROY (eds.), *Toleration in Enlightenment Europe* (Cambridge, 2000).

GRONDA, D., 'Antonio Conti', in *Dizionario Biografico degli Italiani* xxviii (1983), 352–9.

GROOT, D. J., 'De procedure tegen Frederik van Leenhof', *Gereformeerd Theologisch Tijdschrift* xxxvii (1936), 274–94, 325–50, 365–87, 487–502, 545–63.

GROSSMANN, W., *Johann Christian Edelmann. From Orthodoxy to Enlightenment* (The Hague and Paris, 1976).

GRÜNDER, K., and SCHMIDT-BIGGEMANN, W. (eds.), *Spinoza in der Frühzeit seiner religiösen Wirkung*. Wolfenbütteler Studien zur Aufklärung xii (1984).

GUERLAC, HENRY, *Newton on the Continent* (Ithaca, NY, 1981).

GUGGISBERG, KURT, *Bernische Kirchengeschichte* (Bern, 1958).

GULLAN-WHUR, M., *Within Reason: A Life of Spinoza* (London, 1998).

GUNNY, AHMAD, 'L'Image du prophète de l'Islam dans quelques textes clandestins', in McKenna and Mothu (eds.), *La Philosophie clandestine*, pp. 257–65.

GUY, ALAIN, *Historia de la filosofía española* (1983; Spanish edn., Barcelona, 1985).

HABERMAS, JÜRGEN, *The Structural Transformation of the Public Sphere* (Cambridge, Mass., 1996).

HALL, A. R., *Philosophers at War: The Quarrel between Newton and Leibniz* (Cambridge, 1980).

HAMILTON, ALASTAIR, *The Apocryphal Apocalypse* (Oxford, 1999).

HAMPSHIRE, STUART, *Spinoza* (new edn., Harmondsworth, 1976).

HAMPSON, NORMAN, *The Enlightenment* (Harmondsworth, 1968).

HARRIS, E. E. *Spinoza's Philosophy: An Outline* (Atlantic Highlands, NJ, 1992).

HARRIS, IAN, *The Mind of John Locke* (Cambridge, 1994).

HARRISON, J., and LASLETT, P., *The Library of John Locke* (Oxford, 1971).

HARRISON, PETER, *'Religion' and the Religions in the English Enlightenment* (Cambridge, 1990).

—— 'Newtonian Science, Miracles and the Laws of Nature', *JHI* lvi (1995), 531–53.

HASELER, JENS, *Ein Wanderer zwischen den Welten: Charles Étienne Jordan (1700–45)* (Sigmarungen, 1993).

—— ' "Liberté de pensée". Eléments d'histoire et rayonnement d'un concept', in McKenna and Mothu (eds.), *La Philosophie clandestine*, 495–507.

—— 'Refugiés français à Berlin lecteurs de manuscrits clandestins', in Canziani (ed.), *Filosofia e religione*, pp. 373–85.

HAUTZ, JOHANN FRIEDRICH, *Geschichte der Universität Heidelberg* (2 vols.; Mannheim, 1862–4; repr. Hildesheim, 1980).

HAZARD, PAUL, *The European Mind 1680–1715*, trans. J. May (1935; Harmondsworth, 1964).

—— *European Thought in the Eighteenth Century*, trans. J. May (1946; repr. Harmondsworth, 1965).

HEILINGSETZER, GEORG, 'Wissenschaftspflege und Aufklärung in Klöstern der Augustiner Chorherren und Benediktiner im bayerisch-österreichischen Raum' in Arnold and Vodosek (eds.), *Bibliotheken*, 83–101.

HENNINGSEN, GUSTAV, 'Das Ende der Hexenprozesse und die Fortsetzung der populären Hexenverfolgung', in S. Lorenz and D. R. Bauer (eds.), *Das Ende der Hexenverfolgung* (Stuttgart, 1995), 183–202.

HESSEL ALFRED, *Leibniz und die Anfänge der Göttinger Bibliothek* (Göttingen, 1924).

HEYD, MICHAEL, *Between Orthodoxy and Enlightenment: Jean-Robert Chouet and the Introduction of Cartesian Science in the Academy of Geneva* (The Hague, 1982).

—— *'Be Sober and Reasonable': The Critique of Enthusiasm in the Seventeenth and Early Eighteenth Centuries* (Leiden, 1995).

—— 'The Limits of Toleration in the early 18th Century', in Berkvens-Stevelinck et al. (eds.), *The Emergence of Tolerance*, pp. 155–76.

HILGERS, JOSEPH, *Der Index der verbotenen Bücher* (Freiburg im Breisgau, 1904).

HILL, CHRISTOPHER, *The World Turned upside Down* (1972; Harmondsworth, 1975).

—— *The English Bible and the Seventeenth-Century Revolution* (London, 1994).

HOININGEN-HUENE, CH. F., *Beiträge zur Geschichte der Beziehungen zwischen der Schweiz und Holland im XVII Jahrhundert* (Berlin, 1899).

757

HOVEN, J. VAN DEN, 'Inleiding' to J. van den Hoven (ed.), Petrus van Balen, *De Verbetering der gedachten* (Baarn, 1988), pp. 11–47.

HUBBELING, H. G., *Spinoza* (Baarn, 1966).

—— 'Zur frühen Spinozarezeption in den Niederlanden' in Gründer and Schmidt-Biggemann (eds.), *Spinoza* (Heidelberg, 1984), pp. 149–80.

—— 'Aperçu général de la reception de la philosophie de Spinoza en Hollande au XVIIe siècle', *Cahiers Spinoza* (1985), 167–85.

—— 'Leven en werk van Spinoza' in Spinoza. *Briefwisseling* (ed.), F. Akkermann, H. G. Hubbeling, and A. G. Westerbrink (Amsterdam, 1992), pp. 29–48.

—— 'Philopater. A Dutch Materialistic Interpretation of Spinoza in the Seventeenth Century', in Giancotti, *Spinoza*, pp. 489–514.

HUBERT, CHR., *Les premières réfutations de Spinoza: Aubert de Versé, Wittich, Lamy* (Paris, 1994).

HULSHOFF POL, E., 'The Library' in Th. H. Lansingh Scheurleer and G. H. M. Posthumus Meyjes (eds.), *Leiden University in the Seventeenth Century* (Leiden, 1975), pp. 395–459.

HUNDERT, E. J., *The Enlightenment's Fable: Bernard Mandeville and the Discovery of Society* (Cambridge, 1994).

HUTCHISON, ROSS, *Locke in France, 1688–1734* (Oxford, 1991).

HUTTON, SARAH, 'Henry Oldenburg and Spinoza' in Cristofolini (ed.), *The Spinozistic Heresy*, 106–19.

—— 'Edward Stillingfleet and Spinoza' in Van Bunge and Klever (eds.), *Disguised and Overt Spinozism*, pp. 261–74.

—— 'Introduction' to Ralph Cudworth, *A Treatise Concerning Eternal and Immutable Morality* (Cambridge, 1996), pp. ix–xxx.

—— 'Lord Herbert of Cherbury and the Cambridge Platonists' in Brown (ed.), *British Philosophy*, 20–42.

'Iets over het leven en de schriften van Antonius van Dale' (no author) in *Vruchten ingezameld door de Aloude Rederijkkamer De Wijngaardranken* (no editor) (Haarlem, 1833), 1–15.

IOFRIDA, M., 'Matérialisme et hétérogénéité dans la philosophie de Toland', *Dix-Huitième Siècle* xxiv (1992), pp. 39–52.

—— 'Linguaggio e verità in Lodewijk Meyer (1629–81)', in P. Cristofolini (ed.), *L'Hérésie Spinoziste* (1995), 25–35.

ISRAEL, JONATHAN I., 'Toleration in Seventeenth-Century Dutch and English Thought' in S. Groenveld and M. Wintle (eds.), *Britain and the Netherlands* xi (1994), 13–30.

—— 'Spinoza, King Solomon and Frederik van Leenhof's Spinozistic republicanism', *St. Spin.* xi (1995), 303–17.

—— *Dutch Primacy in World Trade, 1584–1740* (Oxford, 1989).

—— *The Dutch Republic: Its Rise, Greatness and Fall, 1477–1806* (Oxford, 1995).

—— 'The Banning of Spinoza's Works in the Dutch Republic (1670–1678)', in Bunge and Klever (eds.), *Disguised and Overt Spinozism* (1996), pp. 3–14.

—— 'The Bekker Controversies as a Turning-Point', *Dutch Crossing* xx (1996), 5–21.

—— 'The Intellectual Debate about Toleration in the Dutch Republic' in Berkvens-Stevelinck *et al.* (eds.), *The Emergence of Tolerance* (1997), 3–36.

—— 'Spinoza, Locke and the Enlightenment Battle for Toleration', in Grell and Porter (eds.), *Toleration* (2000), 102–13.

—— (ed.), *The Anglo-Dutch Moment: Essays on the Glorious Revolution and its World Impact* (Cambridge, 1991).

—— *European Jewry in the Age of Mercantilism, 1550–1750* (3rd edn., London, 1998).

—— 'Locke, Spinoza and the Philosophical Debate concerning Toleration in the Early Enlightenment (c.1670–c.1750)', *Mededelingen van de Afdeling Letterkunde*, Royal Netherlands Academy of Sciences, new ser. no. 62 (1999), 5–19.

—— 'The Publishing of Forbidden Philosophical Works in the Dutch Republic and their European Distribution', in Lotte Hellinga *et al.* (eds.), *The Bookshop of the World* (Leiden, 2001), 233–43.

—— 'Philosophy, Commerce and the Synagogue: Spinoza's Expulsion from the Amsterdam Portuguese Jewish Community in 1656', in J. I. Israel and R. Salverda (eds.), *Dutch Jewry: its History and Secular Culture* (Leiden, 2002).

JACOB, ALEXANDER, *Henry More's Refutation of Spinoza* (Hildesheim, 1991).

JACOB, MARGARET, *The Newtonians and the English Revolution* (Ithaca, NY, 1976).

—— *The Radical Enlightenment* (London, 1981).

—— 'The Crisis of the European Mind: Hazard Revisited' in P. Mack and M. C. Jacob (eds.), *Politics and Culture in Early Modern Europe* (Cambridge, 1987), 251–71.

—— *Living the Enlightenment. Freemasonry and Politics in Eighteenth-Century Europe* (New York and Oxford, 1991).

—— 'Radicalism in the Dutch Enlightenment' in Margaret Jacob and W. W. Mijnhardt (eds.), *The Dutch in the Eighteenth Century* (Ithaca, NY, 1992), pp. 224–40.

JAPIKSE, N., 'Spinoza en De Witt' in *Bijdragen voor vaderlandsche geschiedenis en oudheidkunde*, 6th ser. vi (1928), 1–16.

JAUMANN, HERBERT, *Critica: Untersuchungen zur Geschichte der Litereraturkritik zwischen Quintilian und Thomasius* (Leiden, 1995).

JAYNES, JULIAN, and WOODWARD, WILLIAM, 'In the Shadow of the Enlightenment: Reimarus against the Epicureans', *Journal of the History of the Behavioral Sciences* x (1974), 3–15 and 144–59.

JENSEN, LOTTE, 'Johannes Monnikhoff: Bewonderaar en bestrijder van Spinoza', *GWN* v (1994), 27–34.

JENSMA, G. TH. *et al.* (eds.), *Universiteit te Franeker, 1585–1811* (Leeuwarden, 1985).

JIMACK, PETER, 'The French Enlightenment: Science, Materialism and Determinism', in Brown (ed.), *British Philosophy*, pp. 228–50.

—— 'The French Enlightenment: Deism, Morality and Politics', in Brown (ed.), *British Philosophy*, pp. 251–73.

JOHNSTON, E., *Le Marquis d'Argens: Sa vie et ses oeuvres* (Paris, 1928).

JOLLEY, NICHOLAS, *Leibniz and Locke: A Study of the* New Essays on Human Understanding (Oxford, 1984).

—— (ed.), *The Cambridge Companion to Leibniz* (Cambridge, 1995).

JONES, HOWARD, *The Epicurean Tradition* (1989; repr. London, 1992).

JONGENEELEN, G. H., 'An Unknown Pamphlet of Adriaen Koerbagh' *St. Spin.* iii (1987), 405–15.

—— 'La philosophie politique d'Adrien Koerbagh', *Cahiers Spinoza* vi (1991), 247–67.

—— 'Adriaen Koerbagh: een voorlooper van de Verlichting?' *GWN* viii (1997), 27–34.

—— 'Disguised Spinozism in Adriaen Verwer's *Momaensicht*' in Van Bunge and Klever (eds.), *Disguised and Overt Spinozism*, 15–21.

KAMEN, HENRY, *Spain in the Late Seventeenth Century, 1665–1700* (London, 1980).

KANNEGIETER, J., *Geschiedenis van de vroegere Quakergemeenschap te Amsterdam* (Amsterdam, 1971).

KAPLAN, YOSEF, *From Christianity to Judaism. The Story of Isaac Orobio de Castro* (Oxford, 1989).

—— 'The Intellectual Ferment in the Spanish-Portuguese Community of Seventeenth-Century Amsterdam', in H. Beinart (ed.), *Moreshet Sepharad: The Sephardi Legacy*, vol. ii (Jerusalem, 1992), pp. 288–314.

KAPLAN, YOSEF, *Judíos Nuevos en Amsterdam* (Barcelona, 1996).

KASHER, A., and BIDERMAN, SH., 'Why was Baruch de Spinoza excommunicated?' in D. S. Katz and J. I. Israel (eds.) *Sceptics, Millenarians and Jews* (Leiden, 1990), pp. 98–141.

KATZ, DAVID, 'Isaac Vossius and the English Bible Critics, 1670–1689' in Popkin and Vanderjagt (eds.), *Scepticism and Irreligion*, pp. 142–84.

KEESING, ELISABETH, 'Les frères Huygens et Spinoza', *Cahiers Spinoza* v (1985), 109–28.

KENNEDY, M. L., *The Jacobin Clubs in the French Revolution. The Middle Years* (Princeton, NJ, 1988).

KEOHANE, N. O., *Philosophy and the State in France. The Renaissance to the Enlightenment* (Princeton, NJ, 1980).

KEULS, E. C., *The Reign of the Phallus* (Berkeley and Los Angeles, 1985).

KINGMA, J., and OFFENBERG, A. K., 'Bibliography of Spinoza's Works upto 1800', *Studia Rosenthaliana* II (1977), 1–32.

KIRKINEN, HEIKKI, *Les origines de la conception moderne de l'homme machine* (Helsinki, 1960).

KLEIN, L. G., *Shaftesbury and the Culture of Politeness* (Cambridge, 1994).

KILCULLEN, J., *Sincerity and Truth. Essays on Arnauld, Bayle and Toleration* (Oxford, 1988).

KLEVER, WIM, 'Burchardus de Volder (1643–1709): A Crypto-Spinozist on a Leiden Cathedra', *LIAS* xv (1988), 191–241.

—— 'Moles in Motu: Principles of Spinoza's Physics', *St. Spin.* iv (1988), 165–94.

—— 'Spinoza and Van den Enden in Borch's Diary in 1661 and 1662', *St. Spin.* v (1989), 311–25.

—— 'Anti-falsificationalism: Spinoza's Theory of Experience and Experiments', in Curley and Moreau (eds.), *Spinoza*, pp. 124–35.

—— 'Insignis Opticus. Spinoza in de geschiedenis van de optica', *De Zeventiende Eeuw* vi (1990), 47–63.

—— 'Proto-Spinoza Franciscus van den Enden', *St. Spin.* vi (1990), 281–9.

—— 'Steno's Statements on Spinoza and Spinozism', *St. Spin.* vi (1990), 303–13.

—— 'La clé d'un nom: Petrus van Gent et Schuller à partir d'une correspondance', *Cahiers Spinoza* vi (1991), 169–202.

—— 'Lodewijk Meyer's Ethics', *St. Spin.* vii (1991), 241–60.

—— 'Inleiding' to Franciscus Van den Enden, *Vrije Politieke Stellingen* (Amsterdam, 1992), pp. 13–119.

—— 'The Motion of a Projectile: Elucidation of Spinoza's Physics', *St. Spin.* ix (1993), 335–40.

—— 'A New Document on De Witt's Attitude to Spinoza', *St. Spin.* ix (1993), 379–88.

—— 'Herman Boerhaave (1668–1738) oder Spinozismus als rein mechanische Wissenschaft des Menschen', in Delf (ed.), *Spinoza*, pp. 75–93.

—— *Omtrent Spinoza*, Openbaar College gehouden op 15 November 1995 (Rotterdam, 1995).

—— 'Spinoza's Life and Works' in Garrett (ed.), *The Cambridge Companion to Spinoza*, pp. 30–60.

—— *Ethicom. Spinozas Ethica vertolkt in tekst en commentaar* (Delft, 1996).

—— *Mannen rond Spinoza (1650–1700)* (Hilversum, 1997).

—— 'Gravität bei Spinoza und seinen Nachfolgers', in W. Klever (ed.), *Die Schwere der Luft in der Diskussion des 17. Jahrhunderts* (Wiesbaden, 1997), pp. 89–103.

—— 'Spinoza en Huygens', *Gewina* xx (1997), 14–31.

KLIJNSMIT, A. J., 'Spinoza over taal', *Studia Rosenthaliana* xix (1985), 1–38.

KLINGENSTEIN, GRETE, 'Van Swieten und die Zensur' in E. Lesky and A. Wandruszka (eds.), *Gerard van Swieten und seine Zeit* (Vienna, 1973), pp. 93–106.

KNETSCH, F. R. J., *Pierre Jurieu. Theoloog en politicus der Refuge* (Kampen, 1967).

KNOCHE, MICHAEL, 'Universitätsbibliotheken' in W. Arnold, W. Dietrich, and B. Zeller (eds.), *Die Erforschung der Buch- und Bibliotheksgeschichte in Deutschland* (Wiesbaden, 1987), pp. 420–4.

KNOOP, MATHILDE, *Kurfürstin Sophie von Hannover* (Hildesheim, 1964).

KNUTTEL, W. P. C., *Balthasar Bekker de bestrijder van het bijgeloof* (1906; repr. Groningen, 1979).

——*Verboden boeken in de Republiek der Verenigde Nederlanden* (The Hague, 1914).

KOBUCH, AGATHA, *Zensur und Aufklärung in Kursachsen* (Weimar, 1988).

KOCH, H., and B. KORNERUP, *Den danske kirkes historie* (8 vols.; Copenhagen, 1950–66).

KOCH, H. W., *A History of Prussia* (Harlow, 1978).

KOLAKOWSKI, LESZEK, *Chrétiens sans église: la conscience religieuse et le lien confessionel au XVIIe siècle* (Paris, 1969).

KOPANEV, N. A., 'Nederlandse uitgevers en boekhandelaren en de zaak van Peter de Grote', in R. Kistemaker *et al.*, *Peter de Grote en Holland* (Bussum, 1996), pp. 94–102.

KORS, ALAN CHARLES, *D'Holbach's Coterie. An Enlightenment in Paris* (Princeton, NJ, 1976).

——'Scepticism and the Problem of Atheism in Early Modern France' in Popkin and Vanderjagt (eds.), *Scepticism and Irreligion*, pp. 185–215.

——*Atheism in France, 1650–1729*, vol. 1 (no more so far; Princeton, NJ, 1990).

KORS, ALAN, and KORSHIN, P. J. (eds.), *Anticipations of the Enlightenment in England, France and Germany* (Philadelphia, 1987).

KOSSMANN, E. F., *De boekhandel te 's-Gravenhage tot het einde van de 18de eeuw* (The Hague, 1937).

KRAUSS, W., 'L'Énigme de Du Marsais', *Revue d'Histoire Littéraire* lxii (1962), 514–22.

KRIEGER, B, *Friedrich der Grosse und seine Bücher* (Berlin, 1914).

KROOK, D., *John Sergeant and his Circle: A Study of Three Seventeenth-Century English Aristotelians* (Leiden, 1993).

KROP, HENRI, 'Radical Cartesianism in Holland: Spinoza and Deurhoff', in Bunge and Klever (eds.), *Disguised and Overt Spinozism*, pp. 55–81.

KROP, HENRI, VAN RULER, J. A., and VANDERJAGT, A. J. (eds.) *Zeer Kundige Professoren. Beoefening van de filosofie in Groningen (1614–1996)* (Hilversum, 1997).

KUEHN, MANFRED, 'The German Aufklärung and British Philosophy', in Brown (ed.), *British Philosophy*, pp. 309–31.

KÜHLER, W. J., *Het Socinianisme in Nederland* (1912; repr. Leeuwarden, 1980).

LABROUSSE, ELISABETH, *Pierre Bayle* (2 vols.; The Hague, 1963–4; repr. Paris, 1996).

——'Reading Pierre Bayle in Paris' in Kors and Korschin, *Anticipations*, pp. 7–16.

LACHTERMAN, D. R., 'Laying down the Law: the theological-political Matrix of Spinoza's Physics' in A. Udoff (ed.), *Leo Strauss's Thought: Towards a Critical Engagement* (Boulder, Col., 1991), pp. 123–54.

LAEVEN, A. H., *De Acta Eruditorum onder redactie van Otto Mencke* (Amsterdam, 1986).

——'The Frankfurt and Leipzig Book Fairs and the History of the Dutch Book Trade' in Berkvens-Stevelinck *et al.* (eds.), *Le Magasin de l'Univers*, pp. 185–97.

LAGRÉE, JACQUELINE, 'Sens et verité: philosophie et théologie chez L. Meyer et Spinoza', *St. Spin.* iv (1988), 31–43.

——'Une traduction française du Traité théologico-politique de Spinoza au XVIIIe siècle' in *GRSTD* i (Paris, 1989), 109–7.

——'Le thème des deux livres de la Nature et de l'Écriture' in *GRSTD* iv (1992), 9–40.

——'Christian Kortholt (1633–1694) et son *De tribus Impostoribus Magnis*', in Cristofolini (ed.), *L'Hérésie Spinoziste*, pp. 169–83.

——'Leibniz et Spinoza' in Van Bunge and Klever (eds.), *Disguised and Overt Spinozism*, pp. 137–56.

——'La Querelle du paganisme' in Force and Katz, *Everything Connects*, pp. 243–61.

LAGRÉE, JACQUELINE, and MACHEREY, PIERRE, 'Condillac et Spinoza: une lecture biaisée' in Bloch, *Spinoza*, pp. 241–54.

LAGRÉE, JACQUELINE, and MOREAU, PIERRE-FRANÇOIS, 'Introduction' to Louis Meyer, *La Philosophie Interprète de l'Écriture* (Paris, 1988), pp. 1–17.

LAMM, M., *Swedenborg: Eine Studie über seine Entwicklung zum Mystiker* (Leipzig, 1922).

LANDUCCI, SERGIO, 'Introduzione' to S. Landucci (ed.), Nicolas Fréret, *Lettre de Thrasybule à Leucippe* (Florence, 1986).

—— 'Introduction' and appendices to *'De l'Examen de la religion'* attribuable à Jean Lévesque de Burigny (Paris and Oxford, 1996), pp. 7–25, 63–139.

LANDWEHR, H., *Die Kirchenpolitik Friedrich Wilhelms, des Grossen Kurfürsten* (Berlin, 1894).

LANKHORST, O. S., 'Les ventes aux enchères des livres à La Haye dans la première moitié du 18ᵉ siècle', in Berkvens-Stevelinck, *Magasin de l'Univers*, 199–210.

LARKIN, S., *Correspondence entre Prosper Marchand et le marquis d'Argens* (Oxford, 1984).

LARRÈRE, C., 'Fréret et la Chine', in Grell and Volpilhac-Augur, *Nicolas Fréret, Légende et vérité* (Oxford, 1994), pp. 109–29.

LAURSEN, JOHN CHRISTIAN, 'Impostors and Liars: Clandestine Manuscripts and the Limits of Freedom of the Press in the Huguenot Netherlands', in J. Ch. Laursen (ed.), *New Essays on the Political Thought of the Huguenots of the Refuge* (Leiden, 1995), pp. 73–100.

LÉCRIVAIN, ANDRÉ, 'Spinoza et la physique cartésienne', *Cahiers Spinoza* i, 235–65.

LEMAY, E. H., 'La part d'*Émile* dans la 'régénération' de 1789', in R. Thiery (ed.), *Rousseau, l'Émile et la Révolution* (Paris, 1992), 375–83.

LEMMERICH, JOST, 'Die künstleriche Ausstattung der Barockbibliotheken in Deutschland' in Raabe (ed.), *Öffentliche und Private Bibliotheken*, 317–44.

LENNON, TH. M., 'Bayle, Locke and the Metaphysics of Toleration', in M. A. Stewart (ed.), *Studies in Seventeenth-Century European Philosophy* (Oxford, 1997) pp. 177–95.

LE RU, VÉRONIQUE, *D'Alembert philosophe* (Paris, 1994).

LEVINE, J. M., 'Giambattista Vico and the Quarrel between the Ancients and the Moderns', *JHI* lii (1991), pp. 55–79.

LILLA, MARK, *G. B. Vico. The Making of an Anti-Modern* (Harvard, 1993).

LINDBORG, ROLF, *Descartes i Uppsala* (Uppsala, 1965).

LINDEBOOM, G. A. (ed.), *Bibliographia Boerhaaviana* (Leiden, 1959).

LINDEBOOM, J., *Stiefkinderen van het Christendom* (The Hague, 1929).

LINDROTH, STEN, *Svensk lärdomshistoria* (4 vols, Stockholm, 1975–81).

—— *A History of Uppsala University, 1477–1977* (Stockholm, 1976).

LOMONACO, FABRIZIO, 'Huguenot Critical Theory and "Ius Maiestatis" in Huber and Althusius', in J. Ch. Laursen (ed.), *New Essays on the Political Thought of the Huguenots of the Refuge* (Leiden, 1995), 171–92.

LÓPEZ PIÑERO, JOSÉ M., *La introducción de la ciencia moderna en España* (Barcelona, 1969).

—— *Joan de Cabriada i la introducció de la ciencia mèdica moderna a Espanya* (Valencia, 1994).

LOSMAN, ARNE, LUNDSTRÖM, A., and REVERA M. (eds.), *The New Age of Sweden* (Stockholm, 1988).

LURBE, PIERRE, 'Le Spinozisme de Toland', in Bloch, *Spinoza*, pp. 33–47.

MACHADO DE ABREU, LUIS, 'La Recepción de Spinoza en Portugal' in Domínguez, *Spinoza y España*, pp. 107–19.

MACHEREY, PIERRE, *Introduction à l'Éthique de Spinoza* (Paris, 1994).

—— 'Spinoza lecteur et critique de Boyle', *Revue du Nord* lxxvii (1995), pp. 733–74.

—— 'Spinoza et l'origine des jugements de valeur' in Pierre-François Moreau (ed.), *Architectures de la raison* (Paris, 1996), pp. 205–12.

MANEN, W. C., 'De procedure tegen Pontiaan van Hattem', *Archief voor Nederlandse kerkgeschiedenis* (1885), 273–348.

MANNARINO, L., 'Pietro Giannone e la letteratura "empia"', *Annali dell' Istituto de Filosofia, Università di Firenze* ii (1980), 301–40.

MANUEL, FRANK, *The Eighteenth Century confronts the Gods* (Cambridge, Mass., 1959).

—— *The Religion of Isaac Newton* (Oxford, 1974).

MANZONI, CLAUDIO, *Il 'Catholicesimo illuminato' in Italia. Tra Cartesianismo, Leibnizianismo e Newtonianismo nel primo settecento (1700–1750)* (Trieste, 1992).

MARÉCHAL, GERALDINE, 'Inleiding' to G. Maréchal (ed.), Johannes Duijkerius, *Het Leven van Philopater* (Amsterdam, 1991).

MARION, MICHEL, *Recherches sur les bibliothèques privées à Paris au milieu du XVIIIe siècle (1750–59)* (Paris, 1978).

MÄRKER, A., *Geschichte der Universität Erfurt* (Weimar, 1993).

MARQUES, MARIA ADELAIDE SALVADOR, 'A Real Mesa Censória e a cultura nacional', *Boletim da Biblioteca da Universidade de Coimbra* xxvi (1964), 1–206.

MARSAK, L. M., 'Bernard de Fontenelle: the Idea of Science in the French Enlightenment', *Transactions of the American Philosophical Society*, new ser. xlix (1959), part 7, pp. 3–64.

MARSHALL, JOHN, *John Locke. Resistance, Religion and Responsibility* (Cambridge, 1994).

MARTIN, JULIAN, 'Francis Bacon, Authority and the Moderns' in Sorell (ed.), *Rise of Modern Philosophy*, pp. 71–88.

MARTÍNEZ VIDAL, ALVARO and PARDO TOMÁS, JOSÉ, 'La respuesta de los novatores españoles a la invectiva de Pierre Régis' in *Dynamis. Acta Hispanica ad Medicinae Scientiarumque Historiam Illustrandam* (Granada) xv (1995), 301–40.

MARTINICH, A. P., *The Two Gods of the Leviathan* (Cambridge, 1992).

MASON, R., *The God of Spinoza* (Cambridge, 1997).

MASTELLONE, SALVO, *Pensiero Politico e vita culturale a Napoli nella seconda metà del seicento* (Florence, 1965).

—— *Francesco d'Andrea, politico e giurista (1648–1698)* (Florence, 1969).

—— 'Holland as a Political Model in Italy in the Seventeenth Century', *BMGN* 98 (1983), 568–82.

MATHERON, ALEXANDRE, *Individu et communauté chez Spinoza* (1969; new edn., Paris, 1988).

—— *Le Christ et le salut des ignorants chez Spinoza* (Paris, 1971).

—— 'Spinoza et la sexualité', *GCFI* 1977, 436–57.

—— 'Femmes et serviteurs dans la démocratie Spinoziste' in S. Hessing (ed.), *Speculum Spinozanum 1677–1977* (London, 1977), pp. 368–86.

—— 'La fonction théorique de la démocratie chez Spinoza', *St. Spin.* i (1985), 259–73.

—— 'Le problème de l'évolution de Spinoza du *Traité Théologico-Politique* au *Traité Politique*', in Curley and Moreau (eds.), *Spinoza*, pp. 258–70.

—— 'Physique et ontologie chez Spinoza: l'énigmatique réponse à Tschirnhaus', *Cahiers Spinoza* vi (1991), 83–109.

MAULL, N., 'Spinoza in the Century of Science' in Grene and Nails (eds.), *Spinoza and the Sciences*, pp. 3–13.

MAURER, M., *Aufklärung und Anglophilie in Deutschland* (Göttingen, 1987).

MAXWELL, K., 'Pombal: the Paradox of Enlightenment and Despotism' in Scott (ed.), *Enlightened Absolutism*, pp. 75–118.

MAYER, M., 'Spinozas Berufung an die Hochschule zu Heidelberg', *Chronicum Spinozanum* iii (1923), 20–44.

McClelland, Ch. E., *State, Society and University in Germany, 1700–1914* (Cambridge, 1980).

McClelland, I. L., 'Estudio preliminar' in McClelland (ed.), Benito Jerónimo Feijóo, *Obras (selección)* (Madrid, 1985), pp. 7–39.

McGuire, J. E., 'Boyle's Conception of Nature', *JHI* xxxiii (1972), 523–42.

McKenna, Anthony, 'Sur l'hérésie dans la littérature clandestine', *Dix-Huitième Siècle* xxii (1990), 301–13.

——— 'Spinoza et les "Athées Vertueux" dans un manuscrit clandestin du XVIIIe siècle' in Bloch (ed.), *Spinoza*, pp. 85–92.

——— 'Spinoza in clandestine Manuscripts' in Van Bunge and Klever (eds.), *Disguised and Overt Spinozism*, pp. 305–20.

——— 'L'Éclaircissement sur les Pyrrhoniens, 1702', in *Le Dictionnaire de Pierre Bayle* (Actes du Colloque de Nimègue, 24–27 Oct. 1996) (Amsterdam, 1997), pp. 297–320.

——— 'Pierre Bayle et la superstition', in B. Dompnier (ed.), *La Superstition à l'âge des Lumières* (Paris, 1998), pp. 49–65.

——— 'Recherches sur la philosophie clandestine à l'Age classique', in McKenna and Mothu (eds.), *La Philosophie clandestine*, pp. 3–14.

——— 'Rationalisme moral et fidéisme' in Hubert Bost and Ph. de Robert (eds.), *Pierre Bayle, Citoyen du Monde* (Paris, 1999), pp. 257–74.

——— 'Sur l'*Esprit de M. Arnauld* de Pierre Jurieu', *Chroniques de Port-Royal* (1999), 179–238.

——— 'Le marquis d'Argens et les manuscrits clandestins', in Jean-Louis Vissière (ed.), *Le Marquis d'Argens: Colloque international du Centre Aixois d'Études et Recherches sur le XVIIIe siècle* (Aix-en-Provence, 1990), pp. 113–40.

——— 'Recherches sur la philosophie clandestine à l'Âge classique', in McKenna and Mothu (eds.), *La Philosophie clandestine*, pp. 1–14.

——— and Mothu, A. (eds.), *La philosophie clandestine à l'age classique* (Paris and Oxford, 1997).

McNaughton, D., 'British Moralists of the Eighteenth Century' in Brown (ed.), *British Philosophy*, pp. 203–27.

Méchoulan, Henri, 'Le *herem* à Amsterdam et l'excommunication de Spinoza', *Cahiers Spinoza* iii (1980), 117–34.

Meihuizen, H. W., *Galenus Abrahamsz 1622–1706* (Haarlem, 1954).

Meijer, Willem, 'Spinozas demokratische Gesinnung und sein Verhältnis zum Christentum', *AGPh* xvi (1903), 455–85.

——— 'Drie ambtleijke stukken betrekking hebbende op Spinozas levensgeschiedenis', *Chronicum Spinozanum* i (1921), 20–30.

——— 'De Joanne Caseario', *Chronicum Spinozanum* iii (1923), 232–52.

Meininger, J. V., and Guido van Suchtelen, *Liever met wercken, als met woorden. De levensreis van Doctor Franciscus van den Enden* (Weesp, 1980).

Meinsma, K. O., *Spinoza et son circle* (1896; expanded French edn., Paris, 1983).

Melles, J., *Joachim Oudaen* (Utrecht, 1958).

Mellot, Jean-Dominique, 'Relations ambiguës des libraires Rouennais et hollandais à la fin du XVIIe siècle', in Berkvens-Stevelinck et al. (eds.), *Magasin de l'univers*, 211–22.

Mennonöh, P. J., *Duisburg in der Geschichte des niederrheinischen Buchdrucks und Buchhandels* (Duisburg, 1970).

Mercer, Christia, 'The Vitality and Importance of Early Modern Aristotelianism', in Sorell (ed.), *Rise of Modern Philosophy*, pp. 33–67.

Mercier, Roger, *La réhabilitation de la Nature humaine (1700–1750)* (Villemomble, 1960).

MERTENS, F., 'Franciscus van den Enden: tijd voor een herziening van diens role in het ontstaan van het Spinozisme?', *Tijdschrift voor filosofie* lvi (1994), 717–37.

MIGNINI, FILIPPO, 'Inleiding' to Spinoza's *Korte Verhandeling* in F. Akkerman et al. (eds.), *Spinoza. Korte Geschriften* (Amsterdam, 1982), pp. 223–41.

—— 'Sur la genèse du Court Traité', *Cahiers Spinoza* v (1985), pp. 147–65.

—— 'Nuovi contributi per la datazione e l'interpretazione del *Tractatus de Intellectus Emendatione*' in Giancotti (ed.), *Spinoza*, pp. 515–25.

—— 'Spinoza's Theory on the Active and Passive Nature of Knowledge', *Studia Spinozana* ii (1986), pp. 27–58.

—— 'La dottrina spinozana della religione razionale', *St. Spin.* xi (1995), 53–80.

—— *L'Etica di Spinoza: Introduzione alla lettura* (Rome, 1995).

MIJNHARDT, W. W., 'De Nederlandse Verlichting. Een terreinverkenning', *Kleio* xix (1978), 245–63.

—— 'The Dutch Enlightenment: Humanism, Nationalism and Decline' in Jacob and Mijnhardt (eds.), *The Dutch Republic in the Eighteenth Century*, pp. 197–223.

MILLER, PETER N., ' "Freethinking" and "Freedom of Thought" in Eighteenth-Century Britain', *Historical Journal* xxxvi (1993), 599–617.

MINDÁN, MANUEL, 'Las corrientes filosóficas en la España del siglo XVIII', *Revista de Filosofía* xviii (1959), 471–86.

MISRAHI, ROBERT, 'Spinoza and Christian Thought: A Challenge' in S. Hessing (ed.), *Speculum Spinozanum 1677–1977* (London, 1977), 387–417.

MONDADORI, FABRIZIO, 'Necessity *ex Hypothesi*' in *The Leibniz Renaissance* (Florence, 1989), pp. 191–222.

MÖNNICH, C. W., 'De verhouding van theologie en wijsbegeerte in het *Tractatus Theologico-Politicus*', *MvSp* xv (1958).

MONTAG, W., and STOLZE, T., *The New Spinoza* (Minneapolis, 1997).

MOREAU, JOSEPH, 'Nature et individualité chez Spinoza et Leibniz', *Revue philosophique de Louvain* lxxvi (1978), pp. 447–55.

MOREAU, PIERRE-FRANÇOIS, 'Spinoza et le *Jus circa sacra*', *St. Spin.* i (1985), 35–44.

—— 'Les principes de la lecture de l'Écriture Sainte dans le T. T. P.' in *GRSTD* iv (1992), 119–31.

—— 'Rezeption und Transformation des Spinozismus in der französischen Aufklärung' in Delf (ed.), *Spinoza*, pp. 96–106.

—— 'Spinoza's Reception and Influence' in Garrett (ed.), *The Cambridge Companion to Spinoza*, pp. 408–33.

MORI, GIANLUCCA, 'La philosophie téméraire d'André-Robert Perrelle (1695–1735)' *LIAS* xix (1992), 119–57.

—— 'Du Marsais philosophe clandestin: textes et attributions' in Mckenna and Mothu (eds.), *La philosophie clandestine*, pp. 169–92.

—— *Bayle philosophe* (Paris, 1999).

—— 'Introduction' to Du Marsais, *Examen de la Religion*, pp. 3–139.

—— 'Postface: l'*Examen de la Religion* au XVIIIe siècle', in Du Marsais, *Examen*, pp. 337–59.

—— 'L'ateismo "malebranchiano" de Meslier', in Canziani (ed.), *Filosofia*, pp. 123–60.

MORMAN, P. J., *Nöel Aubert de Versé* (Lewiston, NY, 1987).

MORRISON, J. C., 'Vico and Spinoza', *JHI* xli (1980), 49–68.

MORTENSEN, FREBEN, 'Shaftesbury and the Morality of Art Appreciation', *JHI* lv (1994), 631–50.

MOUTAUX, JACQUES, 'D'Holbach et Spinoza' in Bloch (ed.), *Spinoza*, 151–68.

MOWBRAY, MALCOLM DE, 'Libertas philosophandi: Wijsbegeerte in Groningen rond 1650', in Krop, Van Ruler, and Vanderjagt (eds.), *Zeer kundige professoren*, 33–46.

MÜHLPFORDT, GÜNTER, 'Die Oder-Universität, 1506–1811' in *Die Oder-Universität Frankfurt Beiträge zu ihrer Geschichte* (Weimar, 1983), pp. 19–72.

MULSOW, MARTIN, 'Freethinking in Early Eighteenth-Century Protestant Germany: Peter Friedrich Arpe' in Berti, Charles-Daubert and Popkin (eds.), *Heterodoxy*, pp. 93–239.

MUNCK, THOMAS, 'The Danish Reformers' in Scott (ed.), *Enlightened Absolutism*, pp. 245–63.

NADLER, STEVEN, *Arnauld and the Cartesian Philosophy of Ideas* (Manchester, 1989).

—— *Malebranche and Ideas* (New York, 1992).

—— 'Occasionalism and the Mind-Body Problem', in Stewart (ed.), *Studies*, pp. 75–95.

—— *Spinoza. A Life* (Cambridge, 1999).

NAUTA, D., *Samuel Maresius* (Amsterdam, 1935).

NAUTA, L., and VANDERJAGT, A. (eds.), *Between Demonstration and Imagination Essays in the History of Science and Philosophy Presented to John D. North* (Leiden, 1999).

NETO, JOSÉ R. MAIA, 'Bayle's Academic Scepticism', in Force and Katz, *Everything Connects*, pp. 264–78.

NIDERST, ALAIN, *Fontenelle à la recherche de lui-même (1657–1702)* (Paris, 1972).

—— 'Fontenelle et la littérature clandestine' in Canzioni (ed.), *Filosofia*, pp. 161–73.

—— (ed.), *Fontenelle* (Actes du Colloque tenu à Rouen, octobre 1987) (Paris, 1989).

NIETZSCHE, FRIEDRICH, *The Gay Science*, trans. Walter Kaufmann (New York, 1974).

NIFTRIK, G. C. VAN, 'Spinoza en de sectariërs van zijn tijd', *MvSp* XVIII (Leiden, 1962).

NIJENHUIS, I. J. A., *Een Joodse Philosophe. Isaac de Pinto (1717–1787)* (Amsterdam, 1992).

NIKLAUS, ROBERT, 'Voltaire et l'empiricisme anglais', *Revue Internationale de Philosophie* xlviii (1984), 9–24.

NORTHEAST, C. M., *The Parisian Jesuits and the Enlightenment (1700–1762)* (Oxford, 1991).

OFFENBERG, A. K., 'Spinoza's Library: The Story of a Reconstruction', *Quaerendo* iii (1973), 309–21.

O'HIGGINS, JAMES, *Yves de Vallone: the Making of an* Esprit-Fort (The Hague, 1982).

OKENFUSS, M. J., *The Rise and Fall of Latin Humanism in Early Modern Russia* (Leiden, 1995).

ORCIBAL, JEAN, 'Les Jansénistes face à Spinoza', *Revue de Littérature Comparée* xxiii (1949), 441–68.

OSBAT, LUCIANO, *L'Inquisizione a Napoli: Il proceso agli Ateisti, 1688–1697* (Rome, 1974).

OTTO, RÜDIGER, *Studien zur Spinozarezeption in Deutschland im 18. Jahrhundert* (Frankfurt, 1994).

—— 'Johann Christian Edelmanns's Criticism of the Bible and its Relation to Spinoza' in Van Bunge and Klever (eds.), *Disguised and Overt Spinozism*, pp. 171–88.

OZANAM, D., 'L'idéal académique d'un poète éclairé: Luzán et son projet d'Académie Royale des Sciences (1750–1)', *Bulletin Hispanique* lxiv bis (1962), 188–208.

PAGANINI, GIAN, *Analisi delle fede e critica della ragione nella filosofia di Pierre Bayle* (Florence, 1980).

PALMER, L. M., 'Introduction' to Vico, *On the Most Ancient Wisdom of the Italians*, pp. 1–40.

PARKINSON, G. H. R., 'Leibniz's Paris Writings in Relation to Spinoza', *Studia Leibnitiana. Supplementa* xviii (1978), pp. 73–89.

—— 'Philosophy and Logic', in Jolley (ed.), *Cambridge Companion to Leibniz*.

PARROCHIA, DANIEL, 'Physique et politique chez Spinoza', *Kairos. Revue de la Faculté de Philosophie de l'Université de Toulouse* 11 (1998), 59–95.

PAS, W. VAN DE, *Niels Stensen: Een apostel der diaspora* ('s-Hertogenbosch, 1955).

PATER, C. DE, 'In de schaduw van Newton', *De Zeventiende Eeuw* xii (1996), 64–73.

—— *Willem Jacob 's Gravesande. Welzijn, wijsbegeerte en wetenschap* (Baarn, 1988).

PATY, M., 'Einstein et Spinoza', in Bouveresse *Spinoza, Science*, pp. 183–207.

PÄTZOLD, DETLEV, 'Ist Tschirnhaus' *Medicina Mentis* ein Ableger von Spinozas Methodologie?' in Nauta and Vanderjagt (eds.), *Between Demonstration*, pp. 339–64.

PAUNEL, EUGEN, *Die Straatsbibliothek zu Berlin* (Berlin, 1965).

PAUTHE, L., *Massillon: Sa prédication sous Louis XIV et Louis XV* (Paris, 1908).

PAYNE, H. C., *The* Philosophes *and the People* (New Haven, 1976).

PEDERSEN, OLAF, 'Tradition and Innovation' in Rydder-Symons (ed.), *Universities*, 452–88.

PEIGNOT, G., *Dictionnaire critique littéraire et bibliographique des principaux livres condamnés au feu, supprimés et censurés* (2 vols, Paris, 1806).

PERROT, M., 'Spinoza, Rousseau et la notion de *dictamen*', *Les Études Philosophiques* i (1972), 399–410.

PETRY, M. J., 'Nieuwentijt's Criticism of Spinoza' *MvSp* xl (1979).

—— 'Kuyper's analysis of Spinoza's axiomatic method', in K. Cramer, W. G. Jacobs and W. Schmidt-Biggemann (eds.), *Spinozas Ethik und ihre frühe Wirkung* (Wolfenbüttel, 1981), pp. 231–41.

—— 'Hobbes and the Early Dutch Spinozists' in Deugd (ed.), *Spinoza's Political and Theological Thought*, pp. 150–70.

—— 'Inleiding en aantekeningen' to 'Stelkonstige reeckening van den regenboog' in F. Akkerman, H. G. Hubbeling *et al.* (eds.), Spinoza. *Korte Geschriften* (Amsterdam, 1982), pp. 497–511.

PHILIP, I. G., and Morgan, P., 'Libraries, Books and Printing', in Tyacke (ed.), *Seventeenth-Century Oxford*, pp. 659–85.

PHILIPS, HENRY, *Church and Culture in Seventeenth-Century France* (Cambridge, 1997).

PIGEARD DE GURBERT, GUILLAUME, 'Thérèse, ou la face cachée du philosophe', in d'Argens, *Thérèse Philosophe*, pp. 151–71.

—— 'La philosophie du bon sens de Boyer d'Argens', in McKenna and Mothu (eds.), *La Philosophie clandestine*, pp. 367–74.

PITASSI, M. C., *Entre croire et savoir: Le problème de la méthode critique chez Jean Le Clerc* (Leiden, 1987).

PLETICHA, EVA, *Adel und Buch* (Neustadt a.d. Aisch, 1983).

POCOCK, J. G. A., *The Machiavellian Moment* (Princeton, NJ, 1975).

—— *Virtue, Commerce and History* (Cambridge, 1985).

—— *Barbarism and Religion* (2 vols.; Cambridge, 1999).

POMPA, LEON, *Vico. A Study of the 'New Science'* (1975; 2nd edn., Cambridge, 1990).

POPKIN, R. H., *The History of Scepticism from Erasmus to Spinoza* (Berkeley and Los Angeles, 1979).

—— *Isaac La Peyrère (1596–1676). His Life, Work and Influence* (Leiden, 1987).

—— 'Spinoza's earliest philosophical years, 1655–61', *St. Spin.* iv (1988), 37–55.

—— 'Spinoza and the *Three Impostors*' in Curley and Moreau (eds.), *Spinoza. Issues and Directions*, pp. 347–58.

—— 'The Deist Challenge' in O. P. Grell, J. I. Israel, and N. Tyacke (eds.), *From Persecution to Toleration* (Oxford, 1991), pp. 195–215.

—— 'Introduction', to Bayle, *Historical and Critical Dictionary: Selections*, pp. 8–29.

—— 'Jewish Anti-Christian Arguments as a Source of Irreligion from the Seventeenth to the early Nineteenth Century', in Hunter and Wootton (eds.), *Atheism*, pp. 159–81.

—— *The Third Force in Seventeenth-century Thought* (Leiden, 1992).

—— 'Spinoza and Bible Scholarship', in J. E. Force and R. H. Popkin (eds.), *The Books of Nature and Scripture* (Dordrecht, 1994), pp. 1–20.

POPKIN, R. H., 'The First Published Reaction to Spinoza's *Tractatus*' in Cristofolini (ed.), *l'Hérésie Spinoziste*, pp. 6–12.

——and Arjo Vanderjagt (eds.), *Scepticism and Irreligion in the Seventeenth and Eighteenth Centuries* (Leiden, 1993).

PORTER, ROY, 'The Scientific Revolution and Universities' in Ridder-Symoens (ed.), *Universities*, pp. 531–62.

——, and TEICH, M., (eds.), *The Scientific Revolution in National Context* (Cambridge, 1992).

PORTER, S., 'University and Society', in Tyacke (ed.), *Seventeenth-Century Oxford*, pp. 25–101.

POTT, MARTIN, *Aufklärung und Aberglaube. Die deutsche Aufklärung im Spiegel ihrer Aberglaubenskritik* (Tübingen, 1992).

——'Einleitung' to M. Pott (ed.), Th. L. Lau, *Meditationes philosophicae* (Stuttgart, 1992).

——'Aufklärung und Hexenaberglaube' in S. Lorenz and D. R. Bauer (eds.), *Das Ende der Hexenverfolgung* (Stuttgart, 1995), pp. 183–202.

PRAT, A., 'Introduction' to Prat (ed.), Bayle, *Pensées diverses*, pp. v–xxxii.

PREDEEK, H., 'Ein verschollener Reorganisationsplan für die Universität Königsberg aus dem Jahre 1725', *Altpreussische Forschungen* iv (1927), 65–107.

PROIETTI, Omero, 'Le "Philedonius" de Franciscus van den Enden et la formation rhétorico-littéraire de Spinoza (1656–1658)', *Cahiers Spinoza* vi (1991), 9–82.

——'Il "Satyricon" di Petronio e la datazione della Grammatica Ebraica Spinoziana', *St. Spin.* v (1989), 253–72.

PROUST, JACQUES, *Diderot et l'Encyclopédie* (1962; new edn., Paris, 1995).

PROVENZAL, DINO, *Una polemica diabolica nel secolo xviii* (Rocca S. Casciano, 1901).

QUONDAM, AMADEO, *Cultura e ideologia di Gianvincenzo Gravina* (Milan, 1968).

RAABE, PAUL, 'Gelehrte Nachschlagwerke im 18. Jahrhundert in, Deutschland', in Fabian and Raabe (eds.), *Gelehrte Bücher*, 97–117.

——(ed.), *Öffentliche und Private Bibliotheken im 17. und 18. Jarhundert* (Bremen, 1977).

——'Gelehrtenbibliotheken im Zeitalter der Aufklärung' in Arnold and Vodosek (eds.), *Bibliotheken*, pp. 103–22.

——'Die Niederländische Büchererwerbungen in der fürstlichen Bibliothek Wolfenbüttel im 17. und frühen 18. Jahrhundert', in Berkvens-Stevelinck *et al.* (eds.), *Le Magasin de l'Univers*, pp. 223–35.

RADNER, D., 'Malebranche's Refutation of Spinoza', in R. W. Shahan and J. I. Biro (eds.), *Spinoza: New Perspectives* (Norman; Okla., 1978), pp. 113–28.

RAMELOW, T., *Gott, Freiheit, Weltenwahl: Die Metaphysik der Willensfreiheit zwischen A. Perez S. J. (1599–1649) und G. W. Leibniz (1646–1716)* (Leiden, 1997).

REDWOOD, JOHN, *Reason, Ridicule and Religion: The Age of Enlightenment in England, 1660–1750* (London, 1976).

REMAUD, OLIVIER, 'Conflits, lois et mémoire. Vico et Machiavel', *Revue Philosophique de la France et de l'Étranger* cxxiv (1999), 35–60.

REESINK, H. J., *L'Angleterre et la littérature anglaise dans les trois plus anciens périodiques français de Hollande de 1654 à 1709* (Paris, 1931).

REIN, TH., *Åbo Universitets lärdomshistoria*, vol. x. *Filosofien* (Helsinfors, 1908).

RÉTAT, PIERRE, *Le Dictionnaire de Bayle et la lutte philosophique au XVIIIe siècle* (Paris, 1971).

REUSCH, HEINRICH, *Der Index der verbotenen Bücher* (2 vols.; Bonn, 1883).

RÉVAH, I. S., *Spinoza et le Dr Juan de Prado* (Paris and The Hague, 1959).

——*Des Marranes à Spinoza* (Paris, 1995).

RIBEIRO CORREIA, MARIA ALCINA, *Sebastião José de Carvalho e Mello na Corte de Viena de Austria* (Lisbon, 1965).

RICCI, S., 'Bruno "Spinozista", Bruno "martire luteraro". La polemica tra Lacroze e Heumann', *GCFI* lxv (1986), 42–61.

RICHTER, L., *Leibniz und sein Russlandbild* (Berlin, 1946).

RICUPERATI, Giuseppe, 'Giannone e i suoi contemporanei: Lenglet du Fresnoy, Matteo Egirno e Gregorio Grimaldi', in *Miscellanea Walter Maturi* (Turin, 1966), 55–87.

—— 'Libertinismo e deismo a Vienna: Spinoza, Toland e il *Triregno*' *RSI* lxxix (1967), 628–95.

—— *L'Esperienza civile e religiosa di Pietro Giannone* (Milan, 1970).

—— 'Studi recenti sul primo 700 italiano—Gian Vicenzo Gravina e Antonio Conti', *RSI* lxxxii. (1970), 611–44.

RIDDER-SYMOENS, HILDE DE, 'Buitenlandse studenten aan de Franeker universiteit, 1585–1811', in Jensma *et al.* (eds.), *Universiteit te Franeker*, pp. 73–89.

—— (ed.), *Universities in Early Modern Europe (1500–1800)*, vol. ii of A *History of the University in Europe* (general editor, W. Rüegg) (Cambridge, 1996).

RILEY, P., 'Introduction', in *Malebranche, Treatise on Nature and Grace*, ed. Riley.

RING, WALTER, *Geschichte der Universität Duisburg* (Duisburg, 1920).

ROBINET, ANDRÉ, *G. W. Leibniz. Iter Italicum* (Florence, 1988).

ROCHE, DANIEL, *Les républicains des Lettres* (Paris, 1988).

RODEN, GÜNTER, *Die Universität Duisburg* (Duisburg, 1968).

ROGERS, G. A. J., 'Science and British Philosophy: Boyle and Newton' in Brown (ed.), *British Philosophy*, pp. 43–68.

ROODEN, P. T. VAN, 'Spinozas Bijbeluitleg', *Studia Rosenthaliana* xviii (1984), 120–5.

——, and WESSELIUS, J. W, 'The Early Enlightenment and Judaism: The 'Civil Dispute' between Philippus van Limborch and Isaac Orobio de Castro (1687)', *Studia Rosenthaliana* xxi (1987), 140–5.

ROOTHAAN, A., *Vroomheid, vrede, vrijheid. Een interpretatie van Spinoza's* Tractatus Theologico-Politicus (Assen, 1996).

ROSÉN, J., *Lunds Universitets historia* (4 vols.; Lund, 1968).

ROSENBERG, AUBREY, *Nicolas Gueudeville and his Work (1652–1720?)* (The Hague, 1982).

—— 'Introduction' to A. Rosenberg (ed.), Simon Tyssot de Patot, *Voyages et aventures de Jaques Massé* (Paris and Oxford, 1993), pp. 5–30.

—— 'Tyssot de Patot et *Jaques Massé*: un problème d'attribution?' in McKenna and Mothu (eds.), *La Philosophie clandestine*, pp. 205–11.

ROSENBLATT, H., *Rousseau and Geneva* (Cambridge, 1997).

ROSKOFF, GUSTAV, *Geschichte des Teufels* (2 vols.; Leipzig, 1869).

ROTHER, WOLFGANG, 'The Teaching of Philosophy at Seventeenth-Century Zürich', in L. Brockliss (ed.), *History of Universities*, vol. xi (1992), pp. 59–74.

ROTONDÒ, ANTONIO, 'La censura ecclesiastica e la cultura' in Giulio Einaudi (ed.), *Storia de Italia* section v. *I Documenti* vol. ii, pp. 1399–1492.

—— 'Europe et Pays-Bas: évolution, réélaboration et diffusion de la tolérance aux XVIIe et XVIIIe siècles', *NRL* (1993), 7–33.

ROUSSET, BERNARD, 'La réflexion Spinoziste sur l'immortalité', *St. Spin.* II (1995), 111–35.

ROWE, W. L., 'Clarke and Leibniz on Divine Perfection and Freedom' in *Enlightenment and Dissent* xvi (1997), 60–82.

ROWEN, H. H., *John de Witt. Grand Pensionary of Holland 1625–1672* (Princeton, NJ, 1978).

RULER, J. A., VAN, *The Crisis of Causality* (Leiden, 1995).

RULER, J. A., VAN, ' "Something, I know not what". The Concept of substance in Early Modern thought', in Nauta and Vanderjagt (eds.), *Between Demonstration*, pp. 365–91.

RUTHERFORD, D., *Leibniz and the Rational Order of Nature* (Cambridge, 1995).

SACCENTI, MARIO, *Lucrezio in Toscana* (Florence, 1966).

SAINE, TH. P., 'Who's afraid of Christian Wolff?' in Kors and Korschin (eds.), *Anticipations*, pp. 102–33.

SALOMON, H. P., 'La vraie excommunication de Spinoza' in H. Bots and M. Kerkhof (eds.), *Forum Litterarium. Miscelânea de estudos literários, linguísticos e históricos oferecida a J. J. van den Besselaer* (Amsterdam, 1984), pp. 181–99.

SALOMON, H. P., and SASSOON, I. S. D., 'Introduction' to Uriel da Costa, *Examination*, pp. 1–50.

SANDBERG, K. C., *At the Crossroads of Faith and Reason* (Tucson, Ariz., 1966).

SANDBLAD, HENRIK, 'The Reception of the Copernican System in Sweden', *Colloquia Copernica* 1 (Wroclaw, 1972), 241–70.

SANTINELLI, CRISTINA, *Spinoza in Italia* (Urbino, 1983).

SANTSCHI, C., *La Censure à Genève au XVIIe siècle* (Geneva, 1978).

SAPERSTEIN, MARC, 'Saul Levi Morteira's Treatise on the Immortality of the Soul', *Studia Rosenthaliana* xxv (1991), 131–48.

SASSEN, F., *Het wijsgerig onderwijs aan de Illustre School te 's-Hertogenbosch (1636–1810)* (Amsterdam, 1963).

SAUVY, A., *Livres saisis à Paris entre 1678 et 1701* (The Hague, 1972).

SAVAN, DAVID, 'Spinoza: Scientist and Theorist of Scientific Method', in M. Grene and D. Nails (eds.), *Spinoza and the Sciences* (Dordrecht, 1986), pp. 95–123.

SBIGOLI, FERDINANDO, *Tommaso Crudeli e i primi Framassoni in Firenze* (Milan, 1884).

SCHAMA, SIMON, *Citizens* (London, 1989).

SCHERZ, GUSTAV, *Pionier der Wissenschaff. Niels Stensen in Seinen Schriften* (Copenhagen, 1963).

—— 'Gespräche zwischen Leibniz und Stensen', *Studia Leibnitiana Supplementa* v (1971), 81–104.

SCHMIDT, S., *Alma Mater Jaenensis. Geschichte der Universität Jena* (Weimar, 1983).

SCHMIDT-BIGGEMANN, W., 'Spinoza dans le Cartésianisme', in *GRSTD* iv (Paris, 1992), 71–89.

—— 'New Structures of Knowledge' in Ridder-Symoens (ed.), *Universities*, pp. 489–530.

SCHMITT, CHARLES, B., 'The Rise of the Philosophical Textbook', in Ch. Schmitt and Quentin Skinner (eds.), *The Cambridge History of Renaissance Philosophy* (1988; repr. Cambridge, 1992), pp. 792–804.

SCHNEPPEN, H., *Niederländische Universitäten und deutsches Geistesleben* (Münster, 1960).

SCHOEPS, HANS-JOACHIM, *Barocke Juden, Christen, Judenchristen* (Bern, 1965).

SCHOLDER, KLAUS, *The Birth of Modern Critical Theology* (1966; London, 1990).

SCHOLEM, GERSHON, 'Die Wachtersche Kontroverse über den Spinozismus und ihre Folgen', in Gründer and Schmidt-Biggemann, *Spinoza*, pp. 15–26.

SCHOULS, P. A., *Descartes and the Enlightenment* (Edinburgh, 1989).

SCHRÖDER, WINFRIED, *Spinoza in der deutschen Frühaufklärung* (Würzburg, 1987).

—— 'Das "Symbolum Sapientiae / Cymbalum Mundi" und der *Tractatus Theologico-Politicus*' *St. Spin.* vii (1991), 227–39.

—— 'Spinozas Einfluss auf die praktische Philosophie der französischen Aufklärung', *St. Spin.*, ix (1993), 133–62.

—— 'Einleitung' to W. Schröder (ed.), Johann Georg Wachter, *Der Spinozismus* (Stuttgart, 1994), pp. 7–35.

—— 'Spinoza im Untergrund', in Delf, *Spinoza*, pp. 142–61.

—— 'The Reception of the Early Dutch Spinozists in Germany' in Van Bunge and Klever (eds.), *Disguised and Overt Spinozism*, pp. 157–70.

—— 'Jean Bodins Colloquium Heptaplomères in der deutschen Aufklärung', *Wolfenbütteler Forschungen* lxvii (1996), 121–37.

—— *Ursprünge des Atheismus* (Stuttgart, 1998).

SCHRÖPFER, HORST, 'Die Polemik zwischen Christian Wolff und Johann Franz Buddeus' in H. M. Gerlach, *et al.* (eds.), *Christian Wolff als Philosoph der Aufklärung in Deutschland* (Halle, 1980), pp. 93–100.

SCHWARZBACH, B. E., 'La critique biblique dans les *Examens de la Bible* et dans certains autres traités clandestins' in Bloch and McKenna (eds.), *La Lettre clandestine* iv (1995), 69–86.

——, and FAIRBURN, A. W., 'The *Examen de la Religion*' in *SVEC* 249 (1987), 91–156.

—— 'History and Structure of our *Traité des Trois Imposteurs*', in Silvia Berti *et al.* (eds.), *Heterodoxy*, pp. 75–129.

SCOTT, H. M. (ed.), *Enlightened Absolutism* (Basingstoke, 1990).

SCOTT, JONATHAN, *Algernon Sidney and the Restoration Crisis, 1677–83* (Cambridge, 1991).

SCRIBANO, EMANUELA, 'Johannes Bredenburg (1643–1691) confutatore di Spinoza?', in Cristofolini (ed.), *L'Hérésie Spinoziste*, pp. 66–76.

SCRUTON, ROGER, *Spinoza* (Oxford, 1986).

SÉGUY, JEAN, *Utopie coopérative et oecuménisme: Pieter Cornelisz Plockhoy van Zurik-zee (1620–1700)* (Paris, 1968).

SERVAAS VAN ROYEN, A. J., *Inventaire des livres formant la bibliothèque de Bénédict Spinoza* (Paris and The Hague, 1888).

SETH, IVAR, *Universitetet i Greifswald och des ställning i svensk kulturpolitik 1637–1815* (Uppsala, 1952).

SHAPIN, STEVEN, *The Scientific Revolution* (Chicago, 1996).

SHERIDAN, GERALDINE, *Nicolas Lenglet Dufresnoy and the Literary Underworld of the ancien régime* (Oxford, 1989).

—— 'Lenglet Dufresnoy, La *Refutation de Spinosa* (1731) et la tradition clandestine', in McKenna and Mothu (eds.), *La Philosophie clandestine*, pp. 425–32.

SIEBRAND, H. J., *Spinoza and the Netherlanders* (Assen, 1988).

SIMON, R., *Henry de Boulainviller: Historien, politique, philosophe, astrologue, 1658–1722* (Paris, n.d.).

SIMONE, MARIA ROSA DI, 'Admission' in Ridder-Symoens (ed.), *Universities*, pp. 285–325.

SIMONI, ANNA, 'Balthasar Bekker and the Beckington Witch', *Quaerendo* ix (1979), 135–42.

SIMONSEN, ANDREAS, *Holbergs Livssyn* (Copenhagen, 1981).

SIMONUTTI, LUISA, *Arminianesimo e tolleranza nel seicento olandese* (Florence, 1984).

—— 'Premières réactions anglaises au *Traité théologico-politique*' in Cristofolini (ed.), *L'Hérésie Spinoziste*, pp. 123–37.

—— 'Spinoza and the English Thinkers', in Van Bunge and Klever (eds.), *Disguised and Overt Spinozism*, 191–211.

—— 'Religion, Philosophy and Science: John Locke and Limborch's Circle in Amsterdam', in Force and Katz, *Everything Connects*, pp. 293–324.

SINA, MARIO, *L'avvento della ragione* (Milan, 1976).

—— *Vico e Le Clerc: tra filosofia & filologia* (Naples, 1978).

SKINNER, QUENTIN, 'The Idea of Negative Liberty' in R. Rorty, J. B. Schneewind, and Quentin Skinner (eds.), *Philosophy in History* (Cambridge, 1984), pp. 193–221.

—— 'The Republican Ideal of Political Liberty' in G. Bock, Quentin Skinner, and M. Viroli (eds.), *Machiavelli and Republicanism* (Cambridge, 1990), pp. 293–309.

SKINNER, QUENTIN, *Liberty before Liberalism* (Cambridge, 1998).

SKRZYPEK, MARIAN, 'Le libertinisme polonais et la littérature clandestine', in McKenna and Mothu (eds.), *La philosophie clandestine*, pp. 509–20.

SLEE, J. C. VAN, *De Rijnsburger Collegianten* (1895; repr. Utrecht, 1980).

SLEIGH, R. C., *Leibniz and Arnauld* (New Haven, Conn., 1990).

SLUIS, JACOB VAN (ed.), *Bekkeriana. Balthasar Bekker biografisch en bibliografisch* (Leeuwarden,1994).

SLUIS, JACOB VAN, BERGSMA, W. and JANSMA, L. G., *Balthasar Bekker (1634–1698)*. in *It beaken. Tydskrift fan de Fryske Akademy* lviii (1996), 71–160.

SMET, RUDOLF DE, 'The Realm of Venus: Hadriani Barlandi [H. Beverland] *De Prostibulis Veterum*', *Quaerendo* xvii (1987), 45–59.

—— *Hadrianus Beverlandus (1650–1716): Studie over het leven en werk van Hadriaan Beverland* (Brussels, 1988).

—— 'Traces of Hadriaan Beverland (1650–1716) in the Zeeuws Documentatiecentrum at Middelburg', *LIAS* xix (1992), 73–91.

SMITH, G. L., *Religion and Trade in New Netherland* (London, 1973).

SMITH, S. B. *Spinoza, Liberalism and the Question of Jewish Identity* (New Haven, 1997).

SORELL, TOM (ed.), *The Rise of Modern Philosophy* (Oxford, 1993).

SPECK, W. A., *Reluctant Revolutionaries: Englishmen and the Revolution of 1688* (Oxford, 1988).

SPINK, J. S., *French Free-thought from Gassendi to Voltaire* (London, 1960).

SPISANI, FRANCO, 'The Influence of Leibniz on Italian Philosophy between the Seventeenth and Eighteenth Centuries', *Studia Leibnitiana* xii (1973), 293–304.

SPRUIT, LEEN, *Species Intelligibilis: From Perception to Knowledge*, vol. ii (Leiden, 1995).

STAUBACH, CH. N., 'The Influence of Pierre Bayle on Feijóo', *Hispania* xxii (1939), 79–92.

STEENBAKKERS, PIET, 'De meetkundige betoogtrant: schil of kern?' in E. Kuypers (ed.), *Sporen van Spinoza* (Louvain, 1993), pp. 59–88.

—— *Spinoza's* Ethica *from Manuscript to Print* (Assen, 1994).

—— 'Johannes Braun (1628–1708), Cartesiaan in Groningen', *Nederlands Archief voor Kerkgeschiedenis* lxxvii (1997), 198–210.

STEIN, ANNEGRET, 'Leibniz und der Buchhandel' in *WSGB* xlvi (1980), 78–87.

STEIN, LUDWIG, *Leibniz und Spinoza* (Berlin, 1890).

STEIN-KARNBACH, A., 'G. W. Leibniz und der Buchhandel', *AGB* xiii (1982), 1190–1418.

STEINMANN, J., *Richard Simon et les origines de l'exégèse biblique* (Bruges, 1960).

STONE, H. S., *Vico's Cultural History: The Production and Transmission of Ideas in Naples, 1685–1750* (Leiden, 1997).

STROMBERG, R. N., *Religious Liberalism in Eighteenth-century England* (Oxford, 1954).

STUART, MATTHEW, 'Locke on Superaddition and Mechanism', *BJHP* vi (1998), 351–79.

SUCHTELEN, GUIDO VAN, *Spinoza's sterfhuis aan de Pavilioensgracht* (The Hague, 1977).

—— '*Nil Volentibus arduum*: les amis de Spinoza au travail', *St. Spin.* iii (1987), 391–404.

SULLIVAN, R. G., *John Toland and the Deist Controversy* (Cambridge, Mass., 1982).

SUPPA, SILVIO, *L'Accademia di Medinacoeli* (Naples, 1971).

SUTCLIFFE, ADAM, 'Reason, Religion, Toleration: Judaism and the European Early Enlightenment *c*.1665–*c*.1730' (unpublished Ph.D. thesis, University of London, 1998).

—— 'Sephardi Amsterdam and the European Radical Enlightenment', in J. Targarona Borrás and A. Sáenz-Badillos (eds.), *Jewish Studies at the Turn of the Twentieth Century, Volume 2: Judaism from the Renaissance to Modern Times* (Leiden, 1999), 399–405.

SYMCOX, GEOFFREY, *Victor Amadeus II: Absolutism in the Savoyard State (1675–1730)* (Berkeley and Los Angeles, 1983).

SzABO, FRANZ, *Kaunitz and Enlightened Absolutism 1753–1780* (Cambridge, 1994).

TAK, W. G. VAN DER, 'Spinoza's Payments to the Portuguese Israelitic Community and the Language in which he was Raised', *Studia Rosenthaliana* xvi (1982), 190–5.

—— 'The Firm of Bento and Gabriel de Spinoza' *Studia Rosenthaliana* xvi (1982), 178–89.

TALMON, J. L., *The Origins of Totalitarian Democracy* (1952; London, 1970).

TERPSTRA, M., *De wending naar de Politiek* (Nijmegen, 1990).

THIJSSEN-SCHOUTE, C. L., *Nederlands Cartesianisme* (1954; repr. Utrecht, 1989).

—— 'Lodewijk Meyer en diens verhouding tot Descartes en Spinoza', *MvSp* xi (1954).

—— *Uit de Republiek der Letteren* (The Hague, 1967).

THOMAS, KEITH, *Religion and the Decline of Magic* (1971; new edn., New York, 1997).

THOMSON, ANN, *Barbary and Enlightenment* (Leiden, 1987).

—— 'L'Examen de la Religion' in Canzioni, *Filosofia*, pp. 355–72.

—— 'Introduction' to La Mettrie, *Machine Man*, pp. ix–xxx.

—— 'L'Utilisation de l'Islam dans la littérature clandestine', in McKenna and Mothu (eds.), *La Philosophie clandestine*, pp. 247–56.

TOLMER, L., *Pierre-Daniel Huet (1630–1721)* (Bayeux, 1949).

TORREY, N. L., 'Boulainvilliers; the Man and the Mask', *SVEC* I (1955), 159–73.

—— *Voltaire and the English Deists* (New Haven, 1930).

TOSEL, ANDRÉ, 'Théorie de la pratique et la fonction de l'opinion politique dans la philosophie politique de Spinoza' *St. Spin.* i (1985), 183–208.

—— 'Le *Discours sur l'histoire universelle* de Bossuet' in Cristofolini (ed.), *L'Hérésie Spinoziste*, pp. 97–105.

—— 'Que faire avec le *Traité Théologico-Politique?*', *St. Spin*, xi (1995), 165–88.

TOTARO, GIUSEPPINA, 'Nota su due manoscritti delle *Adnotationes al Tractatus Theologico Politicus* di Spinoza', *NRL* (1990), 107–15.

—— 'Antonio Magliabechi e i libri' in E. Canone (ed.), *Bibliothecae Selectae da Cusano a Leopardi* (Florence, 1993), pp. 549–70.

—— 'Da Antonio Magliabechi a Philip von Stosch', in E. Canone (ed.), *Bibliothecae Selectae da Cusano a Leopardi* (Florence, 1993), pp, 377–417.

—— 'Niels Stensen (1638–1686) e la prima diffusione della filosofia di Spinoza nella Firenze di Cosimo III', in Cristofolini (ed.), *L'Hérésie Spinoziste*, pp. 147–68.

—— 'La Congrégation de l'Index et la censure des oeuvres de Spinoza' in Van Bunge and Klever (eds.), *Disguised and overt Spinozism*, pp. 353–76.

TOUCHEFEU, YVES, 'Le Vicaire savoyard et la Révolution', in R. Thiéry (ed.), *Rousseau, l'Émile et la Révolution*. Actes du Colloque international de Montmorency 27 septembre–4 octobre 1989 (Paris, 1992), 227–42.

TREVOR-ROPER, H. R., *The European Witch-Craze of the 16th and 17th Centuries* (Harmondsworth, 1969).

TROUSSON, R., 'Simon Tyssot de Patot. *Le Voyage de Groenland*', in Tyssot de Patot, *La Vie, les avantures*, pp. vii–xxii.

TUCK, RICHARD, *Hobbes* (Oxford, 1989).

TURNER, J. G., 'The Properties of Libertinism' in R. P. Maccubbin (ed.), *Unauthorized Sexual Behaviour*, Special issue of *Eighteenth-Century Life* ix (1985), 75–87.

TYACKE, NICHOLAS (ed.), *The History of the University of Oxford iv: Seventeenth-Century Oxford* (Oxford, 1997).

USLAR, D. VON, 'Leibniz Kritik an Spinoza', *Studia Leibnitiana Supplementa* v (1971), 72–80.

VALKHOFF, P., 'De wonderbaarlijke reizen van Simon Tyssot de Patot'. *De Gids* xcv (1931), 239–60.

VANDENBOSSCHE, HUBERT, *Spinozism en kritiek bij Koerbagh* (Brussels, n.d.).

——'Henrik Wyermars' *Ingebeelde Chaos* (1710)', *TvSV* ii (1974), 321–69.

——*Frederik van Leenhof* (Brussels, 1974).

——'Adriaan Koerbagh en Spinoza'. *MvSp* xxix (Leiden, 1978).

VARRENTRAPP, C., *Der Grosse Kurfürst und die Universitäten* (Strasbourg, 1894).

VARTANIAN, Aram, *La Mettrie's* L'Homme Machine. *A Study in the Origins of an Idea* (Princeton, NJ, 1960).

——'Diderot and Maupertuis', *Revue Internationale de Philosophie* xxxviii (1984), 46–66.

VAUX, ROLAND DE, *Ancient Israel* (2nd edn., London, 1965).

VAZ DIAS, A. M., *Uriel da Costa. Nieuwe bijdragen tot diens levensgeschiedenis* (Leiden, 1936).

——, and VAN DER TAK, W. G., 'Spinoza Merchant and Autodidact', *Studia Rosenthaliana* xvi (1982), 109–71.

VECCHI, ALBERTO, *Correnti religiose nel sei-settecento veneto* (Venice and Rome, 1962).

VENN, JOHN, *Alumni Cantabrigienses* 1st ser., iv (Cambridge, 1927).

VENTURI, FRANCO, *Jeunesse de Diderot (1713–1753)* (Paris, 1939).

——*Saggi sull' Europa illuminista i. Alberto Radicati di Passerano* (Milan, 1954).

——'Gli anni' 30 del settecento' in *Miscellanea Walter Maturi* (Turin, 1966), pp. 91–153.

VENTURI, FRANCO (ed.), *Illuminati Italiani*, vol. 5: *Riformatori Napolitani* (Milan and Naples, 1962).

VENTURINO, DIEGO, *Le ragioni della traditione: Nobiltà e mondo moderno in Boulainvilliers (1658–1722)* (Turin, 1993).

VERBEEK, THEO, *Descartes and the Dutch* (Carbondale, Ill., 1992).

——'Tradition and Novelty: Descartes and Some Cartesians' in Sorell (ed.), *Rise of Modern Philosophy*, pp. 167–96.

——'From "Learned ignorance" to Scepticism: Descartes and Calvinist Orthodoxy', in Popkin and Vanderjagt (eds.) *Scepticism and Irreligion*, pp. 31–45.

——*De vrijheid van de filosofie: Reflecties over een Cartesiaans thema* (Utrecht, 1994).

——'Spinoza on Theocracy and Democracy', in Force and Katz, *Everything Connects*, pp. 325–38.

——'Spinoza and Cartesianism' in A. P. Coudert, S. Hutton, and R. H. Popkin (eds.), *Judaeo-Christian Intellectual Culture in the Seventeenth Century* (Dordrecht, 1999), pp. 173–84.

VERCRUYSSE, JEROOM, *Voltaire et la Hollande* (Geneva, 1966).

VERENE, D. PH., 'Introduction' to Giambattista Vico, *On Humanistic Education* (Ithaca, NY, 1993).

VERMIJ, RIENK, *Secularisering en Natuurwetenschap in de zeventiende en achttiende eeuw: Bernard Nieuwentijt* (Amsterdam, 1991).

——'Le Spinozisme en Hollande: le cercle de Tschirnhaus', *Cahiers Spinoza* vi (1991), 145–68.

——'Het Copernicanisme in de Republiek', *Tijdschrift voor Geschiedenis* cvi (1993), 349–67.

——'The English Deists and the *Traité*', in Silvia Berti *et al.* (eds.), *Heterodoxy*, pp. 241–54.

——'Matter and Motion: Toland and Spinoza', in Van Bunge and Klever (eds.), *Disguised and Overt Spinozism*, pp. 275–88.

VERNIÈRE, PAUL, *Spinoza et la pensée française avant la Révolution* (1954; 2nd edn., Paris, 1982).

VERWEYEN, JOHANNES, *Ehrenfried Walther von Tschirnhaus als Philosoph* (Bonn, 1905).

VET, J. J. V. M. DE, *Pieter Rabus (1660–1702)* (Amsterdam, 1980).

——'Learned Periodicals from the Dutch Republic and the Early Debate on Spinoza in England', in *Miscellanea Anglo-Belgica*, no editor (Leiden, 1987), pp. 27–39.

——'La *"Bibliothèque Universelle et Historique"'*, *LIAS* xvi (1989), 81–110.

——'On Account of the Sacrosanctity of the Scriptures', *LIAS* xviii (1991), 229–61.

—— 'In Search of Spinoza in the *Histoire des Ouvrages des Savans*', in Van Bunge and Klever (eds.), *Disguised and Overt Spinozism*, pp. 83–101.

VIROLI, MAURIZIO, *Jean-Jacques Rousseau and the 'Well-Ordered Society'*, trans. D. Hanson (Cambridge, 1988).

VISSER, R. P. W., 'Petrus Camper en het empiricisme in de geneeskunde', in Jensma *et al.* (eds.), *Universiteit te Franeker*, pp. 386–94.

VRIES, PH. DE, 'Christiaan Huygens entre Descartes et le siècle des lumières', *Theoretische Geschiedenis* vi (1979), 3–19.

VUCINICH, ALEXANDER, *Science in Russian Culture: A History to 1860* (2 vols., London, 1963).

VUILLEMIN, JULES, 'Physique panthéiste et déterminisme', *St. Spin.*, vi (1990) 231–50.

WADE, I. O., *The Clandestine Organisation and Diffusion of Philosophic Ideas in France from 1700 to 1750* (Princeton, NJ, 1938).

WALBER, KARL JOSEF, *Charles Blount (1654–1693). Frühaufklärer: Leben und Werk* (Frankfurt, 1988).

WALKER, D. P., *The Decline of Hell* (London, 1964).

WALL, ERNESTINE VAN DER, 'Petrus Serrarius (1600–1669) et l'interprétation de l'Écriture', *Cahiers Spinoza* v (1985), 187–217.

—— *De Mystieke Chiliast Petrus Serrarius (1600–1669) en zijn wereld* (Leiden, 1987).

—— 'Orthodoxy and Scepticism in the early Dutch Enlightenment' in Popkin and Vanderjagt (eds.), *Scepticism and Irreligion*, pp. 121–41

—— 'The *Tractatus Theologico-Politicus* and Dutch Calvinism, 1670–1700', *St. Spin.* xi (1995), 201–26.

WALTHER, MANFRED, 'Die Transformation des Naturrechts in der Rechtsphilosophie Spinozas', *St. Spin.* i (1985), 73–104.

—— 'Philosophy and Politics in Spinoza'. *St. Spin.*, ix (1993), 49–57.

—— 'Biblische Hermeneutik und historische Erklärung' *St. Spin.* xi (1995), 227–300.

—— 'Machina Civilis oder Von deutscher Freiheit' in Cristofolini, *l'Hérésie Spinoziste*, pp. 184–221.

—— 'Spinozissimus ille Spinoza oder Wie Spinoza zum 'Klassiker' wurde', in H. Reinalter (ed.), *Beobachter und Lebenswelt. Studien zur Natur-, Geistes- und Sozialwissenschaft* (Vienna, 1996), pp. 183–238.

WANGERMANN, ERNST, *The Austrian Achievement, 1700–1800* (London, 1973).

WAQUET, FRANÇOISE, *Le modèle français et l'Italie savante (1660–1750)* (Rome, 1989).

WATSON, R. A., *The Downfall of Cartesianism, 1673–1712* (The Hague, 1966).

—— *The Breakdown of Cartesian Metaphysics* (Atlantic Highlands, NJ, 1987).

WEEKHOUT, I., *Boekencensuur in de Noordelijke Nederlanden* (The Hague, 1998).

WEIL, FRANÇOISE, 'La Diffusion en France avant 1750 d'éditions de textes dits clandestins' in Bloch (ed.), *Le Matérialisme*, pp. 207–12.

—— 'Le Rôle des libraires hollandais dans la diffusion des livres interdits en France dans la première moitié du XVIIIe siècle', in Berkvens-Stevelinck *et al.* (eds.), *Le Magasin de l'Univers*, pp. 281–8.

WELLMAN, KATHLEEN, *La Mettrie, Philosophy, and Enlightenment* (Durham, NC. 1992).

WERNHAM, A. G. 'Introduction and Notes' to *Spinoza: The Political Works* (Oxford, 1958).

WESSEL, L. P., *G. E. Lessing's Theology. A Reinterpretation* (The Hague, 1977).

WESSELIUS, J. W., 'De Ban van Spinoza. Oude en nieuwe inzichten', *GWN* I (1990), 193–203.

WESTFALL, R. S., *Science and Religion in Seventeenth-century England* (New Haven, 1958).

—— *The Life of Isaac Newton* (1993; Cambridge, 1994).

WHALEY, JOACHIM, *Religious Toleration and Social Change in Hamburg 1529–1819* (Cambridge, 1985).
—— 'A tolerant Society? Religious Toleration in the Holy Roman Empire, 1648–1806', in Grell and Porter (eds.), *Toleration*, pp. 175–95.

WHELAN, RUTH, 'The Wisdom of Simonides: Bayle and la Mothe Le Vayer', in Popkin and Vanderjagt (eds.), *Scepticism and Irreligion*, pp. 230–53.

WHITE, R. J., *The Anti-Philosophers: A Study of the Philosophes in Eighteenth-Century France* (London, 1970).

WIDMALM, S., 'Instituting Science in Sweden' in Porter and Teich (eds.), *Scientific Revolution*, pp. 240–62.

WIELEMA, MICHIEL, *Filosofen aan de Maas* (Baarn, 1991).
—— 'Spinoza in Zeeland: the Growth and Suppression of "Popular Spinozism" (c.1700–1720)' in Van Bunge and Klever (eds.), *Disguised and Overt Spinozism* (1996), pp. 103–15.
—— 'Een onbekende aanhanger van Spinoza. Antony van Dalen', *GWN* iv (1993), 21–40.
—— 'Met Bekkerianerij besmet', in Van Sluis *et al.* (eds.), *Balthasar Bekker*, pp. 150–9.
—— 'Nicolaus Engelhard (1696–1765). De Leibniz-Wolffiaanse metafysica in Groningen', in Krop (ed.), van Ruler, and Vanderjagt (eds.), *Zeer kundige professoren*, pp. 149–61.
—— 'Ketters and Verlichters. De Invloed van het Spinozisme en Wolffianisme op de Verlichting in Gereformeerd Nederland' (doctoral thesis of the Free University of Amsterdam, 1999).
—— Frederik van Leenhof en zijn 'Hemel op Aarden' (1703). Spinozisme en Spinoza-kritiek in de vroege Verlichting (forthcoming).

WILD, REINER, 'Freidenker in Deutschland', in *Il Libertinismo in Europa* (no editor) (Milan and Naples, 1980), pp. 81–116.

WILDENBERG, IVO, W., *Johan en Pieter de la Court (1622 1660 cn 1618–1685)* (Amsterdam, 1986).

WILLEY, BASIL. *The Eighteenth-Century Background* (Harmondsworth, 1962).

WILLIAMS, BERNARD, *Descartes: The Project of Pure Enquiry* (1978; repr. Harmondsworth, 1986).

WILSON, CATHERINE, *Leibniz's Metaphysics* (Manchester, 1989).
—— 'The Reception of Leibniz in the Eighteenth Century', in Jolley (ed.), *Cambridge Companion to Leibniz*, pp. 442–74.

WILSON, M. D., 'Spinoza's Theory of Knowledge', in Garrett (ed.), *Cambridge Companion to Spinoza*, pp. 89–141.

WINTER, E., *Die Registres der Berliner Akademie der Wissenschaften, 1746–1766* (Berlin, 1957).
—— 'Der Bahnbrecher der deutschen Frühaufklärung' in Winter, E. (ed.), *E. W. von Tschirnhaus und die Frühaufklärung in Mittel-und Osteuropa* (Berlin, 1960), pp. 1–82.

WOKLER, ROBERT, *Social Thought of J. J. Rousseau* (New York, 1987).
—— 'Multiculturalism and Ethnic Cleansing in the Enlightenment', in Grell and Porter (eds.), *Toleration*, pp. 69–85.

WOLFSON, H. A., *The Philosophy of Spinoza* (new edn., 2 vols., Cambridge, Mass., 1983).

WOLLGAST, SIEGFRIED, 'Spinoza und die deutsche Frühaufklärung', *St. Spin.* ix (1963), 163–79.

WOLTERSTORFF, N., 'Locke's Philosophy of Religion' in V. Chappell (ed.), *The Cambridge Companion to Locke* (1994), pp. 172–9.

WOOD, PAUL, 'The Scientific Revolution in Scotland', in Porter and Teich (eds.), *The Scientific Revolution*.

WOOLHOUSE, R. S., *Descartes, Spinoza, Leibniz: The Concept of Substance in Seventeenth-Century Metaphysics* (London and New York, 1993).
—— 'Locke's theory of knowledge', in Chappell (ed.), *Cambridge Companion to Locke*, pp. 146–71.

WOOTTON, DAVID, 'New Histories of Atheism' in Hunter and Wootton (eds.), *Atheism*, 13–53.

—— 'Introduction' to John Locke, *Political Writings* (Harmondsworth, 1993).

—— 'David Hume, "the Historian"', in D. F. Norton (ed.), *The Cambridge Companion to Hume* (Cambridge, 1993), pp. 281–312.

—— 'Pierre Bayle, libertine?' in Stewart (ed.), *Studies*, 197–226.

WOJCIK, JAN, '"The Due Degree of Blindness": Boyle, Hume, and the Limits of Reason', in Force and Katz (eds.), *Everything Connects*, pp. 361–78.

WRANGEL, E., *De betrekkingen tusschen Zweden en de Nederlanden op het gebied van letteren en wetenschap* (Leiden, 1901).

WURTZ, J. P., 'Tschirnhaus und die Spinozismusbeschuldigung: die Polemik mit Christian Thomasius', *Studia Leibnitiana*, xiii (1981), 61–75.

—— 'L'Éthique et le concept de Dieu chez Tschirnhaus: l'influence de Spinoza', in De Deugd (ed.), *Spinoza's Political and Theological Thought*, pp. 230–42.

—— 'La théorie de la connaissance de Tschirnhaus', in Bouveresse (ed.), *Spinoza. Science et religion*, pp. 123–39.

—— 'Un disciple hérétique de Spinoza: Ehrenfried Walther von Tschirnhaus', *Cahiers Spinoza* vi (1991), 111–43.

YAKIRA, ELKANAN, 'What is a mathematical truth?' in *St. Spin.* vi (1990), 73–101.

YATES, FRANCES, *Giordano Bruno and the Hermetic Tradition* (1964; repr. Chicago, 1991).

YOLTON, J. W., *Locke and French Materialism* (Oxford, 1991).

—— *Locke and the Way of Ideas* (1956; repr. Bristol, 1996).

YOVEL, Y., *Spinoza and other Heretics: The Marrano of Reason* (Princeton, NJ, 1989).

ZAMBELLI, P., 'Il rogo postumo di Paolo Mattia Doria' in P. Zambelli (ed.), *Ricerche sulla cultura dell' Italia moderna* (Rome and Bari, 1973), pp. 149–98.

ZILVERBERG, S. B. J., 'Jan Pieterszoon Beelthouwer (c.1603–c.1669) en de Joden', *Studia Rosenthaliana* iii (1969), pp. 156–67.

Index

Aalstius, Johannes (1660–1712), Dutch Reformed preacher 5, 295–6

Abbadie, Jacques (1658–1727), Huguenot theologian 63, 102, 126, 455–6, 462, 467, 500, 636 n., 706

Åbo (Turku) University (Finland) 37–8, 561

'above Nature' 220–1, 325, 461–2

Abrahamsz, Galenus (1622–1706), Dutch Mennonite preacher 343, 349

absolutism, *see* monarchy

Acta Eruditorum (Leipzig) 142, 150, 379–80, 392–3, 401, 433–4, 558–9, 640, 665

Adam and Eve 50, 88, 168 n., 380, 388, 642

Africa 180, 693

   Barbary states 703

Aitzema, Lieuwe van (1600–69), Dutch historian 125, 623

Aix-en-Provence 61, 69, 494 n.

alchemists and alchemy 15, 170, 288 n., 308, 411

d'Alembert, Jean le Rond (1717–83), French *philosophe* 117, 516–17, 711

   and Locke 13, 516, 523, 711

   oracles 360, 374

   Discours préliminaire à l' Encyclopédie (1751) 13, 516, 523, 711

   Éloge de M. du Marsais (1757) 360, 368, 374

Alexander the Great (356–323 BC) 364

Alkmaar, Reformed *classis* 392, 404

Altdorf University, *see* Nuremberg

Algarotti, Conte Francesco (1712–64), Venetian *philosophe* 557, 587

Althann, Cardinal, Austrian viceroy of Naples (1722–8) 111–12

Alting, Jacobus (1618–79), Dutch Reformed theologian 276

Altona (Hamburg) 554, 655

Alvarez de Toledo y Pellicer, Don Gabriel (1659–1714), Spanish royal librarian 529, 531–2

   Historia de la Iglesia y del Mundo (1713) 529 n., 531, 537–8, 646

American colonies, of England 72–3, 138, 151

Amsterdam:

   book shops 146, 170, 186, 190

   book censorship 315–19, 325–6, 413, 423, 425

city government 190, 192, 194–6, 315, 318, 324, 326, 385, 392, 423, 623

clandestine publishing 186, 190, 200, 202, 275–94, 303–4, 312, 315–19

Collegiants, *see* Collegiants

consistory (Reformed) 188–90, 190, 193, 276, 316, 318, 389–92

'enlightened' civic administration 146, 385–6, 392

freethinkers (post-1680) 386, 307–11, 315–20, 323–6

Portuguese Jewish Synagogue 165, 171–2, 286

Rasphuis (prison) 195–6, 219, 319, 326, 413

scientific research 248

Spinoza's and Van den Enden's circle 164 n., 168–71, 186, 193, 195, 197–8, 208, 286–90, 309, 637

Spinozists 307–11, 315–19, 322, 324

Anabaptism 23, 310, 361–2, 388, 662

Anaxagoras of Clazomenae (500–428 BC), pre-Socratic Greek philosopher 118, 136, 340

Anaximander of Miletus (c.610–546 BC), pre-Socratic Greek philosopher 118

Anaximenes of Miletus (6th cent. BC), pre-Socratic Greek philosopher 118

Andala, Ruardus (1665–1727), Dutch Cartesian 38, 443, 480–5, 492, 543, 560

   Cartesius verus Spinozismi Eversor (1719) 484–5

'Andlo, Petrus van', *see* Mansvelt

d'Andrea, Francesco (1625–98), Neapolitan Cartesian 49, 51

Andreae, Tobias (1604–76), Dutch Cartesian 32, 503

angels, in philosophical debate 54, 191, 219, 244, 255, 347–8, 353, 367, 370, 376, 379, 382, 388–90, 400, 404, 417, 420–1, 425, 455, 481, 484, 533, 536, 539, 642

Anglican Church 19, 73, 97, 369, 381, 468–70, 472–3, 606–8

   see also Latitudinarians; Non-Jurors

Anglo-Dutch Wars, impact on ideas and the book trade:

   First (1652–4) 166–7

   Second (1664–67) 179, 249–50

   Third (1672–4) 283–4